SPECIAL EDITION

USING

Mac® OS X, v10.4 Tiger

Brad Miser

800 East 96th Street
Indianapolis, Indiana 46240

Contents at a Glance

SPECIAL EDITION USING MAC® OS X, V10.4 TIGER

Copyright © 2006 by Que Publishing

International Standard Book Number: 0-7897-3391-9

Library of Congress Catalog Card Number: 2005922648

Printed in the United States of America

First Printing: July 2005

08   07   06   05   4   3   2   1

Trademarks

All terms mentioned in this book that are known to be trademarks or service marks have been appropriately capitalized. Que Publishing cannot attest to the accuracy of this information. Use of a term in this book should not be regarded as affecting the validity of any trademark or service mark.

Mac OS X is a registered trademark of Apple Computer, Inc.

Warning and Disclaimer

Bulk Sales

Que Publishing offers excellent discounts on this book when ordered in quantity for bulk purchases or special sales. For more information, please contact

U.S. Corporate and Government Sales
1-800-382-3419
corpsales@pearsontechgroup.com

For sales outside the United States, please contact

International Sales
international@pearsoned.com

Associate Publisher
Greg Wiegand

Acquisitions Editor
Laura Norman

Development Editor
Laura Norman

Managing Editor
Charlotte Clapp

Project Editor
Tonya Simpson

Production Editor
Megan Wade

Indexer
Chris Barrick

Proofreader
Carla Lewis

Technical Editor
Brian Hubbard

Publishing Coordinator
Sharry Lee Gregory

Designer
Anne Jones

Page Layout
Michelle Mitchell
Julie Parks

CONTENTS

V Mac OS X: Expanding Your System

ABOUT THE AUTHOR

Brad Miser has written extensively about all things Macintosh, with his favorite topics being OS X and the amazing "i" applications that empower Mac OS X users to unleash their digital creativity. In addition to *Special Edition Using Mac OS X, v10.4 Tiger*, Brad has written many other books, including *Special Edition Using Mac OS X, v10.3 Panther*; *Absolute Beginner's Guide to iPod and iTunes*; *Absolute Beginner's Guide to Homeschooling*; *Mac OS X and iLife: Using iTunes, iPhoto, iMovie, and iDVD*; *iDVD 3 Fast & Easy*; *Special Edition Using Mac OS X v10.2*; and *Using Mac OS 8.5*. He has also been an author, development editor, or technical editor on more than 50 other titles. He has been a featured speaker on various Macintosh-related topics at Macworld Expo, at user group meetings, and in other venues.

Brad is the senior technical communicator for an Indianapolis-based software development company. Brad is responsible for all product documentation, training materials, online help, and other communication materials. He also manages the customer support operations for the company and provides training and account management services to its customers. Previously, he was the lead engineering proposal specialist for an aircraft engine manufacturer, a development editor for a computer book publisher, and a civilian aviation test officer/engineer for the U.S. Army. Brad holds a Bachelor of Science degree in mechanical engineering from California Polytechnic State University at San Luis Obispo (1986) and has received advanced education in maintainability engineering, business, and other topics.

In addition to his passion for Macintosh computers, Brad likes to ride his motorcycle, run, and play racquetball; playing with home theater technology is also a favorite pastime.

Once a native of California, Brad now lives in Brownsburg, Indiana with his wife Amy; their three daughters, Jill, Emily, and Grace; and their guinea pig, Buddy.

Brad would love to hear about your experiences with this book (the good, the bad, and the ugly). You can write to him at bradmacosx@mac.com.

DEDICATION

To those who have given the last full measure of devotion so that the rest of us can be free.

ACKNOWLEDGMENTS

To the following people on the *Special Edition Using Mac OS X, v10.4 Tiger* project team, my sincere appreciation for your hard work on this book:

Laura Norman, my acquisitions and development editor, who helped me get the focus of the first edition of this book on track when I had gone astray and kept me in line the rest of the way. She also made sure that I kept the text flowing when we revised this tome for Mac OS X version 10.4. Laura, getting through such a big book with me as the author four times should earn you a medal of some kind!

Marta Justak of Justak Literary Services, my agent, for getting me signed up for this project. Marta was also a constant source of support for me during the process and was always ready to lend an ear to listen to whatever I needed to say. Marta, many times I needed to bounce an idea or complaint off someone—thanks for being there for me!

Brian Hubbard, my technical editor, who did a great job to ensure that the information in this book is both accurate and useful. Brian, I tried my best to sneak mistakes past you, but you caught me every time—thanks for a job well done!

Megan Wade, my copy editor, who corrected my many misspellings, poor grammar, and other problems. Megan, you made the text appear to have been written by someone who actually knows how to write. Thanks!

Tonya Simpson, my project editor, who skillfully managed the hundreds of files that it took to make this book. Tonya, thanks for keeping everything current and making sure that things got where they needed to be when they needed to be there.

Anne Jones, for the interior design and cover of the book. You made this book a pleasure to look at! Also, a thanks for developing the book's cover. It is too bad that you can't judge a book by its cover because, if you could, everyone would believe that this book is top-notch—thanks!

Que's production and sales team for printing the book and getting it into your hands. Thanks, everybody!

And now for a few people who weren't on the project team, but who were essential to me personally:

Amy Miser, for supporting me while I took on this mammoth project for the fourth time and for being understanding about my need to do it yet one more time; living with an author isn't always lots of fun, especially with a big, complex book like this one. Amy, I promise, no more big books—until the next one! ;-)

Jill, Emily, and Grace Miser, for helping me remember that there is a lot more to life than pounding the keys—even though sometimes it seemed as if that was all I was doing. Girls, you brought lots of smiles to my face in stressful times. Thanks for reminding me of what is really important. And, a special thanks to Buddy the guinea pig for his early-morning visits to cheer me up while I was working!

Rick Ehrhardt for being such a good friend to me; I especially appreciate the occasional evening out—La Hacienda and Best Buy anyone?

WE WANT TO HEAR FROM YOU!

As the reader of this book, *you* are our most important critic and commentator. We value your opinion and want to know what we're doing right, what we could do better, what areas you'd like to see us publish in, and any other words of wisdom you're willing to pass our way.

As an associate publisher for Que, I welcome your comments. You can email or write me directly to let me know what you did or didn't like about this book—as well as what we can do to make our books better.

Please note that I cannot help you with technical problems related to the topic of this book. We do have a User Services group, however, where I will forward specific technical questions related to the book.

When you write, please be sure to include this book's title and author as well as your name, email address, and phone number. I will carefully review your comments and share them with the author and editors who worked on the book.

Email: feedback@quepublishing.com

Mail: Greg Wiegand
            Associate Publisher
            Que Publishing
            800 East 96th Street
            Indianapolis, IN 46240 USA

For more information about this book or another Que title, visit our website at www.quepublishing.com. Type the ISBN (excluding hyphens) or the title of a book in the Search field to find the page you're looking for.

INTRODUCTION

In this introduction

WELCOME TO MAC OS X

Now in its fourth major release (version 10.4), Mac OS X has been called many things, from revolutionary to evolutionary to being so innovative that it threatened the very existence of the Mac as we had come to know and love it. And all of those descriptions were appropriate.

The first release of Mac OS X was a giant leap forward for the Mac platform. Its innovations in basic architecture, the way it works, and even its user interface made Mac OS X the most significant event for Mac users since the first Mac was introduced back in the Jurassic period, circa 1984. Mac OS X was more stable, more powerful, and even more beautiful than any previous version. However, the first version of Mac OS X had some rough spots, not surprising at all because it was the first release of a brand-new OS (despite the version number implying it was the successor to Mac OS 9).

About a year later, version 10.2 was released. This release smoothed many of the rough edges left over from version 10.1 and added many new features. Due to some fundamental improvements in the core operating system, version 10.2 caused some ripples in the Mac universe because many applications had to be updated to run under that version.

Version 10.3 began to show the maturity of Mac OS X's more than two years of life. Version 10.3 continued the process of refining the OS along with adding some excellent new features, such as a totally redesigned Finder, Expose, improved applications, and so on. It also continued to improve the stability and performance of the OS. Much of the foundation work for the OS was accomplished by the previous two releases; version 10.3 was less disruptive than the previous releases while continuing to make major improvements in functionality, reliability, and performance.

Version 10.4 is less of a change than previous releases of Mac OS X were. This is good news because it means that the core OS functionality has stabilized, and transitions to each subsequent version will have lots of benefits with less pain. In version 10.4, new features abound, such as the totally new Dashboard and widgets, which provide instant access to accessory applications; the Spotlight, which enables you to quickly search your Mac for information of all kinds at the same time; and others, but your transition from previous versions of OS X will be smooth (unlike some of the previous transitions). Of course, if you are new to the Mac or have never used Mac OS X before, all the previous versions don't matter. You get to enjoy the results of Mac OS X's evolution without having been through the growth process.

Mac OS X is a very powerful and feature-rich OS. Although many of the features of the OS are intuitive, some might not be obvious to you. And because of the amazing number of powerful applications that are part of the standard Mac OS X installation, such as Safari, iTunes, and many others, using Mac OS X effectively is much more than just manipulating the Finder and using the Dock. That is where this book comes in.

Introduction to *Special Edition Using Mac OS X, v10.4 Tiger*

This book has two fundamental purposes:

- To help you make the jump to Mac OS X as efficiently as possible
- To provide a reference for you to use as you continue to grow in your Mac OS X use

To accomplish the first purpose, this book is written in a straightforward style; you won't find any fluff here. The book is designed to help you *use* Mac OS X as efficiently and effectively as possible. Everything about the book is an attempt to make specific information accessible and applicable to your daily Mac life. You will find only the background information you need to understand how to apply specific techniques and technologies; the focus is on the information you need to apply what you learn to your own Mac.

To accomplish the second purpose, this book covers an extremely broad range of topics. In addition to coverage of the core functionality of the desktop, you will find extensive coverage of topics to enable you to accomplish productive work with your Mac, such as creating digital movies, surfing the Net, and creating and hosting a website. This book also contains substantial amounts of information to help you add devices to expand your system so you can accomplish even more. Because Mac OS X has been designed to be networked, you will learn how to use its capabilities in this area to connect with other Macs, as well as to Windows networks. You'll learn how to both prevent and solve OS X problems along the way.

How This Book Is Organized

This book consists of several parts, each of which contains at least two chapters. The following list provides an overview of this book's contents:

- **Part I, "Mac OS X: Exploring the Core"**—This part gets you started on the right foot. You'll learn the core operations of the OS, from getting started with Mac OS X to working with the Finder, the Dock, the Dashboard, and more.

- **Part II, "Mac OS X: Mastering the System"**—After Part I, you'll be ready to take your Mac use further. This part starts with information you need to get the most of your applications. Then you'll explore Mac OS X in depth, such as customizing it. You'll also find out how to automate tasks using the Automator (which gets my vote for best new feature in 10.4) and learn to use Unix on your Mac. If you use a mobile Mac, you'll want to read the last chapter in this part, which shows you Mac OS X on one of these cool machines.

- **Part III, "Mac OS X: Connecting to the World"**—Mac OS X has been designed to facilitate your interaction with the Internet. This part of the book explains how to configure Mac OS X for the Internet and how to use the tools it provides after you are connected.

- **Part IV, "Mac OS X: Living the Digital Life"**—The Mac has always been preeminent in creative activities, such as graphics, video, and imaging. Mac OS X continues this tradition and provides digital media tools that are unmatched by any other platform. From creating and editing digital images to making movies with iMovie to watching DVDs you create, this part of the book shows you how.

- **Part V, "Mac OS X: Expanding Your System"**—No Mac is an island; this part of the book helps you understand the input and output technologies supported by Mac OS X to enable you to select and add the peripheral devices you need.

- **Part VI, "Mac OS X: Living in a Networked World"**—From the Internet to a local network, your Mac is most likely connected to one or more other computers. In this part of the book, you will learn how to establish, maintain, and use a network.

- **Part VII, "Mac OS X: Protecting, Maintaining, and, Repairing Your Mac"**—As great as Mac OS X is, you still need to know how to minimize problems and be able to effectively solve any problems you do experience.

- **Part VIII, "Mac OS X: Appendix"**—Appendix A will help you install and maintain the OS.

SPECIAL FEATURES

This book includes the following special features:

- **Chapter roadmaps**—At the beginning of each chapter, you will find a list of the top-level topics addressed in that chapter. This list will enable you to quickly see the type of information the chapter contains.

- **Troubleshooting**—Many chapters in the book have a section dedicated to troubleshooting specific problems related to the chapter's topic. Cross-references to the solutions to these problems are placed in the context of relevant text in the chapter as Troubleshooting Notes to make them easy to locate.

- **Mac OS X to the Max**—Some chapters end with a "Mac OS X to the Max" section. These sections contain extra information that will help you make the most of Mac OS X. For example, tables of keyboard shortcuts are included to help you work more efficiently. Other sections include summaries of information that is outside the scope of the book, but which you should be aware of.

- **Notes**—Notes provide additional commentary or explanation that doesn't fit neatly into the surrounding text. You will find detailed explanations of how something works, alternative ways of performing a task, and comparisons between Mac OS X and previous versions of the OS.

- **On the Web notes**—These notes provide you with URLs you can visit to get more information or other resources relating to the topic being discussed.

- **Tips**—Tips help you work more efficiently by providing shortcuts or hints about alternative and faster ways of accomplishing a task.

- **Cautions**—These sidebars provide a warning to you about situations that involve possible danger to your Mac or its data.

- **The new version icon**—This icon indicates a significant change from versions of Mac OS prior to version 10.4. This icon will be meaningful to you if you have used a previous version of Mac OS X because it points out significant new features or major changes made for version 10.4.

- **Cross-references**—Many topics are connected to other topics in various ways. Cross-references help you link related information together, no matter where that information appears in the book. When another section is related to one you are reading, a cross-reference will direct you to a specific page in the book on which you will find the related information.

CONVENTIONS

To make things as clear as possible, this book doesn't use many special conventions or formatting techniques to identify specific kinds of information. However, there are a few things you need to be aware of:

- Menu commands are referred to by starting with the menu name and moving down to the specific command while separating each layer with a comma. For example, rather than writing, "Open the Terminal menu, then select the Services command, then select the Mail command, and then select Mail Text," I use a shorthand technique. In this example, I would write, "Select Terminal, Services, Mail, Mail Text." This shorthand makes the command structure more clear and cuts back on the number of words you have to read.

- When you are working in the Terminal, the commands you enter and the output you see are in a `monospace font like this`.

- Variables that stand for text that is specific to you are usually in *italics*. For example, if I need to refer to your username in a specific location, I write, "Users/*username*, where *username* is your username," to indicate that you should look for your own information in place of the italicized phrase.

WHO SHOULD USE THIS BOOK

In this book, I've made certain assumptions about your specific experience with the Mac OS and your general comfort level with technology. The biggest assumption is that you are quite comfortable with the fundamentals of using the Mac OS. For example, you won't find any explanations of how to use a mouse, how to copy and move files, the basics of drag and drop, and so on. When there are significant differences in these basic tasks under Mac OS X as compared to the previous versions of the OS, you will find those differences explained, but probably not in enough detail to teach you how to do them if you have never done them before.

If you are completely new to computers, you will still find this book very useful, but you will also need a companion book that explains the fundamentals of using a Mac in more detail than is provided in this book, such as *Easy Mac OS X Tiger* (0-7897-3313-7).

If you have used previous versions of the Mac OS, such as Mac OS 9 or earlier versions of Mac OS X, and are comfortable with basic tasks, this book will help you make the jump to Mac OS X version 10.4 in a short time. It also will serve as a comprehensive reference for you as you explore this amazing operating system.

PART I

MAC OS X: EXPLORING THE CORE

Mac OS X: Foundations

In this chapter

1

MAC OS X: THE FUTURE IS NOW

When the Mac OS was first introduced in 1984, it was a completely radical way of interacting with a computer. Rather than having to type long strings of arcane commands, a user could manipulate the system, files, documents, and data by simply pointing to icons and clicking. The success of the Mac OS drove the other PC-oriented operating systems to also adopt a graphical user interface (GUI).

NOTE

> Just to give credit where credit is due, the user interface made mainstream by the Mac was based on work done at Xerox. I guess that just goes to show that the inventor of something doesn't always get the most out of it.

Since that time, the Mac OS has undergone many improvements as it moved from early versions up to versions 8, 9, and finally 9.2 to carry it into the year 2001. These versions successfully made the transition from 68K processors to PowerPCs. They included Internet features early in the life of the Internet and then integrated the Net into the OS under 9. Each of the versions further refined the OS and added features (some of which were useful and survived, while others went by the wayside). Mac OS 9.2 was an excellent computer operating system.

However, as the saying goes, all good things must come to an end.

Even as powerful and capable as Mac OS 9.2 was, by the end, it was showing the core architecture's age. It lacked modern, fundamental design features that are needed to support the demands of today's user in terms of speed, reliability, and stability. It didn't provide all the tools that today's power-hungry Mac users need. The time had definitely come for something new.

Mac OS X was all that and more. Although it was called version ten, a more appropriate name might have been Mac OS: The Next Generation. Although Mac OS X shared some interface commonality with previous versions, that is where the similarities stopped—at the surface. Mac OS X was a completely new operating system. From its Unix core to the desktop's Dock, Mac OS X was and still is the future of the Mac platform—and it's a very bright future indeed.

Now in version 10.4, also called Tiger, Mac OS X continues to evolve with amazing new features and improved existing ones. From the Dashboard (new to 10.4) to the Dock (part of OS X since version 10.0), version 10.4 is the best Mac operating system yet—and that is saying something!

MAC OS X BENEFITS

Listing all of Mac OS X's advantages and benefits could consume this entire chapter; however, following are some of the highlights as to why Mac OS X is a very good thing:

- **Stability and reliability**—Because the operating system has been designed using modern architectural principles, it is very stable. When an application does crash or hang, only that application is affected. The system manages its resources much more effectively than previous versions of the OS did. The result is that Mac OS X keeps working without those annoying crashes that were far too common with previous versions. Mac OS X is as stable as a rock.

- **Speed**—The OS is optimized for maximum performance on Mac hardware, such as dual-processor G5 Macs and G4 PowerBooks. It also takes advantage of other modern Mac hardware features such as faster memory, modern data buses, and so on. All operations under Mac OS X are much faster than under previous versions; these improvements in speed have continued in version 10.4. Mac OS X flies.

- **Beauty**—Although it might seem odd to list beauty as a benefit of an operating system, if you have seen Mac OS X before, you probably understand why I listed this. Because of the advanced graphics subsystem, the images, fonts, icons, and other graphic elements of the operating system are very pleasing to look at. The new interface design uses color and other graphic effects in a visually stunning way. Mac OS X looks very, very good.

- **Multiple user support**—Mac OS X is designed to facilitate many people using the same machine. This support is native to the OS rather than being an add-on. Mac OS X is meant to be shared.

- **Organization**—Mac OS X features a logical organization that is user friendly—things are where you expect them to be. Mac OS X is your digital housekeeper.

- **Security**—Mac OS X has many security features you can employ to protect your machine and its data from other people who use it, from those who share the same network as you, and even from Internet attacks. Mac OS X makes your digital life more secure.

- **Compatibility**—Because Mac OS X is based on Unix, it is compatible with many Unix applications. This brings hundreds of sophisticated applications to the Mac that were previously unavailable. With its Classic environment, Mac OS X can use most applications that are written for earlier versions of the Mac OS. This means that from the day Mac OS X was introduced, there were thousands of Mac OS X–compatible applications. And, support for Windows networking is built-in to the operating system so that Macs and Windows computers can peacefully and productively co-exist. Mac OS X definitely plays well with others.

- **Power**—Mac OS X is a very powerful OS. Its multiple layers provide this power in many areas, such as graphics, the Internet, and so on. Its standards-based networking architecture enables you to connect to any system, anywhere. And you have much greater, direct access to system processes than ever before. You can access this power at many levels, from the GUI to using Unix text commands. Mac OS X has all the power you need.

- **Network-readiness**—Mac OS X provides support for all sorts of networks, from those containing all Macintosh computers to those composed of Windows PCs. Mac OS X's networking system is powerful, flexible, and relatively easy to configure. With its Bonjour technology, Mac OS X Macs can automatically seek out and configure other Bonjour devices with which they can communicate. From LANs to WANs, Mac OS X has been built to connect.

- **High-technology support**—Mac OS X supports many advanced technologies, such as Bluetooth, that enable the OS to interact with wireless devices, such as cell phones and PDAs. Built-in AirPort support means that you can connect to networks, including the Internet, without being tied down by wires. The Ink system provides Mac OS X with handwriting recognition so that you can provide input with graphics tablets and other devices in all your Mac OS X applications. FireWire 800 support means you can access the fastest hard drives and other peripherals. When it comes to high-tech, Mac OS X is all you need.

- **Ease of use**—Although power and ease of use are usually conflicting terms, Mac OS X provides both. Its interface features the tools and techniques that have made the Mac OS the most intuitive and easiest-to-use operating system there is. You don't have to be a rocket scientist to use Mac OS X (although it is a great OS for rocket scientists, too).

- **Customizability**—It wouldn't be a Mac if you couldn't tweak the interface to suit your preferences. Mac OS X is fully customizable, and you can adjust and tweak it to your heart's content. After all, what good is an OS if you can't make it your own?

MAC OS X ARCHITECTURE AND TERMINOLOGY

Understanding the architecture and terminology of Mac OS X is important to be able to use it effectively.

Functionally, the Mac OS X architecture consists of several *layers* that are often shown graphically as in Figure 1.1. The base level of the operating system is its Unix core, which is called Darwin. Moving "up" through the layers, the next layer is the graphics subsystem, which consists of three parts: Quartz Extreme, OpenGL, and QuickTime. Then comes the application layer, which has four components, those being Classic, Carbon, Cocoa, and Java. Finally, the top layer is the user interface, which is called Aqua.

THE CORE OS: DARWIN

Mac OS X is built on a Unix core; the Darwin core is based on the Berkeley Software Distribution (BSD) version of Unix. The heart of the Darwin core is called Mach. This part of the operating system performs the fundamental tasks, such as data flow into and from the CPU, memory use, and so on. Mach's major features include the following:

Figure 1.1
You can think of Mac OS X being composed of four layers; the bottom layer provides the core OS services, whereas each layer toward the top provides services that are "closer" to the user.

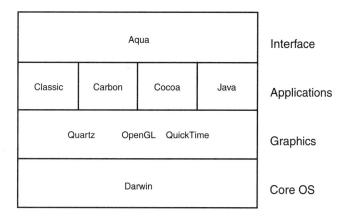

- **Protected memory**—Mach provides a separate memory area in which each application can run. It ensures that each application remains in its own memory space and so does not affect other applications. Therefore, if a running application crashes or hangs, other applications aren't affected. You can safely shut down the hung application and continue working in the others.

   In contrast, previous versions of the Mac OS did not have protected memory. When one application crashed, it usually took down others and often the OS itself, which resulted in your losing unsaved data in all the applications. Under Mac OS X, only the data in the crashing application is at risk.

- **Automatic memory management**—Mac OS X manages RAM for you; it automatically allocates RAM to applications that need it. Under Mac OS X, you don't need to think about how RAM is being used; the OS takes care of it for you (if you have ever struggled to manually allocate RAM under OS 9 and earlier, you know why not having to do this is a very good thing).

- **Preemptive multitasking**—Under Mac OS X (or, more specifically, Mach), the operating system controls the processes that the processor is performing to ensure that all applications and system services have the resources they need and that the processors are used efficiently. This ensures both stability and maximum performance for both foreground and background processes.

   This is in contrast to the cooperative multitasking in previous versions of the Mac OS. Under that scheme, applications had to fight among themselves for the resources they needed. This resulted in instability when applications couldn't get the resources they needed and poor performance for those applications that were not able to "grab" the system resources they needed (this is why some processes stopped when you moved them to the background).

- **Advanced virtual memory**—The Mach core uses a virtual memory system that is always on. It manages the virtual memory use efficiently so that virtual memory is used only as necessary to ensure maximum performance.

Under previous versions of the Mac OS, you had to control how virtual memory was used manually. Because the virtual memory system was not very efficient, you had to be careful about when you had it turned on because it would cause the performance of some applications to slow to a crawl, even if you had plenty of RAM.

NOTE

> Darwin is open source. This means that the code of which Darwin is composed is freely available to anyone who wants to use it. A programmer can download the Darwin code and modify it. Thus, it is possible to provide alternative versions of the Darwin core to change and enhance Mac OS X. The Darwin code and documentation can be found at developer.apple.com/darwin/.

Darwin also provides the input/output services for Mac OS X and easily supports three key characteristics of modern devices: plug-and-play, hot-swapping, and power management.

Darwin, through its Virtual File System (VFS) design, supports several file systems under Mac OS X, including the following:

- **Mac OS Extended (Case-sensitive) Format**—Also known as Hierarchical File System Plus (HFS+), this file system efficiently supports large hard drives by minimizing the smallest size used to store a single file. This format also makes filenames and folder names case-sensitive (for example, `filename.file` is not the same as `FileName.File`).

- **Mac OS Extended (Journaled)**—OS X also supports the Mac OS Extended Journaled format. This enables the OS to track changes while they are being made so the process of recovering from errors is much more reliable.

- **Mac OS Extended (Case-sensitive, Journaled) Format**—This file format uses the journaling feature and makes filenames and folder names case-sensitive.

NOTE

> Unix is a case-sensitive operating system. The ability for Mac OS X to support case-sensitive file systems makes Unix on the Mac purer.

- **Mac OS Extended Format**—This file system efficiently supports large hard drives by minimizing the smallest size used to store a single file. It does not use journaling or case-sensitivity.
- **Unix File System**—The standard file system for Unix systems.
- **UDF**—The Universal Disk Format, it's used for DVD volumes.
- **ISO 9660**—A standard for CD-ROMs.

Darwin supports many major network file protocols. It supports Apple File Protocol (AFP) over IP client, which is the file-sharing protocol for Macs running Mac OS 8 and Mac OS 9. Network File System (NFS) client, which is the dominant file-sharing protocol on

Unix platforms, is also supported. Mac OS X also provides support for Windows-based network protocols, meaning you can interact with Windows machines as easily as you can with other Macs.

Because of Darwin, Mac OS X supports bundles; a *bundle* is a directory containing a set of files that provide services. A bundle contains executable files and all the resources associated with those executables; when they are a file package, a bundle can appear as a single file. The three types of bundles under Mac OS X are as follows:

- **Applications**—Under Mac OS X, applications are provided in bundles. Frequently, these bundles are designed as file packages so the user sees only the files with which he needs to work, such as the file to launch the application. The rest of the application resources might be hidden from the user. This makes installing such applications simple.

- **Framework**—A framework bundle is similar to an application bundle except that a framework provides services that are shared across the OS; *frameworks* are system resources. A framework contains a dynamic shared library, meaning different areas of the OS as well as applications can access the services provided by that framework. Frameworks are always available to the applications and services running in the system. For example, under Mac OS X, QuickTime is a framework; applications can access QuickTime services by accessing the QuickTime framework. Frameworks are not provided as file packages, so the user sees the individual files that make up that framework.

- **Loadable bundle**—*Loadable bundles* are executable code (just like applications) available to other applications and the system (similar to frameworks) but must be loaded into an application to provide their services. The two main types of loadable bundles are plugins (such as those used in web browsers) and palettes (which are used in building application interfaces). Loadable bundles can also be presented as a package so the user sees and works with only one file.

NOTE

Because of its Unix architecture, you will see many more filename extensions under Mac OS X than there were under previous versions of the OS. Most of the extensions for files you will deal with directly are easily understood (for example, .app is used for applications), but others the system uses are not as intuitive.

THE GRAPHICS SUBSYSTEM

Mac OS X includes an advanced graphics subsystem, which has three main components: Quartz Extreme, OpenGL, and QuickTime.

Quartz Extreme is the name of the part of the graphics subsystem that handles 2D graphics. Quartz Extreme provides the interface graphics, fonts, and other 2D elements of the system, as well as on-the-fly rendering and antialiasing of images. Under Mac OS X, the Portable Document Format (PDF) is native to the OS. This means you can create PDF versions of any document without using a third-party application, such as Adobe Acrobat (to

1

get special features in PDF documents, such as navigation features, you still need to use an application that provides those features). You can quickly create a PDF version of any document with which you work; that document can be viewed with Acrobat Reader or Mac OS X's own Preview application. Quartz Extreme also supports TrueType, Type 1, and OpenType fonts and blends 3D and QuickTime content with the 2D content it provides directly.

Because of Quartz Extreme, you don't need to install a font-smoothing utility, such as Adobe Type Manager, to be able to view and use all sizes of PostScript fonts, as you had to do under Mac OS 9 and earlier.

The OpenGL component of the graphics subsystem provides 3D graphics support for 3D graphics applications and games. OpenGL is an industry standard that is also used on Windows and Unix systems. Because of this, it is easier to create 3D applications for the Mac from those that were designed to run on those other operating systems. The Mac OS X implementation of OpenGL provides many 3D graphics functions, such as texture mapping, transparency, antialiasing, atmospheric effects, other special effects, and more.

> **NOTE**
> *Antialiasing* reduces the pixelated appearance of a graphic to provide smooth edges instead of jagged ones.

QuickTime provides support for many types of digital media, such as digital video and audio, and is the primary enabler of video and audio streaming under Mac OS X. QuickTime enables both viewing applications, such as the QuickTime Player, and creative applications, such as iMovie, iTunes, and many more. QuickTime is also an industry standard, and QuickTime files can be used on Windows and other computer platforms.

THE APPLICATION SUBSYSTEM

Mac OS X includes four different application environments (Cocoa, Java, Carbon, and Classic) that enable you to run a wide variety of applications, which, after all, is the primary reason you have a computer.

The Cocoa environment offers developers a state-of-the-art, object-oriented application development environment. Cocoa applications are designed for Mac OS X from the ground up and take the most advantage of Mac OS X services and benefits. Most major applications, and lots of minor ones, have been created using Cocoa, which is good news for all Mac users.

The Java 2 application environment enables you to run Java applications, including pure Java applications and Java applets. Java applications are widely used on the Web because they enable the same set of code to be executed on various platforms. You can also develop Java applications under Mac OS X.

The other two application environments are primarily provided as bridges to older versions of applications that were created for previous Mac OS releases.

The Classic environment enables Mac OS X to run applications that were written for previous versions of the OS (Mac OS 9.2 and earlier) without modification. Classic applications run as they did under previous versions of the Mac OS; in other words, they do not benefit from the advanced features of Mac OS X such as protected memory (Classic applications can be affected by other Classic applications, and the Classic environment itself can be affected when a Classic application has problems).

NOTE

> Because Mac OS X has been around for a number of years now, it isn't likely that you will need to run any Classic applications. However, it is nice to know that you can should you ever need to.

The Carbon environment enables developers to port existing applications to use Carbon application program interfaces (APIs); the process of porting a Classic application into the Carbon environment is called *Carbonizing* it. The Carbon environment offers the benefits of Darwin for Carbonized applications, such as protected memory and preemptive multitasking. Carbonizing an application is significantly less work than creating a new application from scratch, which enabled many applications to be delivered near the release of Mac OS X. Like Classic, Carbon was really intended as a means to make as many applications available under Mac OS X as possible. It is a transition environment rather than a permanent one (like Cocoa).

THE USER INTERFACE

The Mac OS X user interface, called Aqua, provides Mac OS X's great visual experience as well as the tools you use to interact with and customize the interface to suit your preferences. From the drop shadows on open windows to the extensive use of color and texture to the extremely detailed icons, Aqua provides a user experience that is both pleasant and efficient.

MAC OS X COSTS: HARDWARE REQUIREMENTS

Mac OS X is a good thing, but as with all good things, it does come with a price. You must have a modern Mac to be able to use it.

Apple states that you must have a Mac with a G3, G4, or G5 processor, such as a Power Mac G5, Power Mac G4, or PowerBook G4. Apple also says your Mac must have at least 256MB of RAM, a DVD drive, and built-in FireWire. Also, your Mac needs to have a built-in display or one that is connected to an Apple-supplied video card. Finally, you need at least 2GB of disk space.

That's what Apple says and you probably can run OS X with a Mac that meets these minimum requirements. However, if you want to have a good experience with Mac OS X, I'd suggest the following two changes to Apple's minimum requirements:

■ **A Mac with a G4 or G5 processor**—Macs with G3 processors just don't perform that well with Mac OS X. Fortunately, unless your Mac is more than a couple years old, it likely has one or more G4 processors or better (G5).

■ **At least 512MB of RAM**—You can get by with only 256MB of RAM, but you will have better performance with more RAM. I recommend adding as much RAM as your Mac supports. For example, Power Mac G4s and G5s support multiple gigabytes of RAM. RAM is relatively inexpensive and easy to add, so maxing out your RAM is a good idea.

→ For help moving to Mac OS X version 10.4 from previous Mac OS X versions, **see** Appendix A, "Installing and Maintaining Mac OS X," **p. 1079**.

NOTE

> Apple does not support Mac OS X running on older hardware, although you might be able to get it to run on a machine not on the support list. However, I don't recommend that because you'll miss out on the performance and features that modern Macs provide. You might also be able to get Mac OS X to run on a machine that has an upgrade card installed in it; however, support for specific upgrade cards is a hit-or-miss proposition.

As with any tool as sophisticated and powerful as Mac OS X, learning how to use it effectively can take some time. This learning curve can also be considered one of Mac OS X's costs. This cost is one that this book can lower for you. As you read through the rest of this book, you will quickly become comfortable with all aspects of Mac OS X. And as you explore more of the OS, you can always come back to specific parts of the book to guide you on your way.

CHAPTER 2

GETTING STARTED WITH MAC OS X

In this chapter

2

WELCOME TO MAC OS X

After reading Chapter 1, "Mac OS X: Foundations," you should understand a bit about Mac OS X, such as its features, architecture, and so on. Now it's time to start using it! The functions you'll explore in this chapter are fundamental to your use of Mac OS X.

If you have not yet installed Mac OS X, before you go any further in this chapter, read Appendix A, "Installing and Maintaining Mac OS X," to get help installing the OS and setting up an administrator user account. When you have worked through the tasks in that appendix, come back here.

If you have already installed Mac OS X, you have probably already started using it; you have created at least one user account whether you realize it or not because that is part of installing the OS. This chapter will help you gain a better understanding of and set up more user accounts, start and stop your Mac efficiently, and learn how to customize the startup process.

STARTING UP MAC OS X

As you read in Chapter 1, Mac OS X is truly a multiuser operating system. This offers many benefits to you, but it also means that when you use the OS, you have to log in as a particular user. When you do so, what you can see and do depends on the settings for the user account you use to log in to the system. Understanding and managing the user accounts on your Mac is critical to getting the most from your computer.

NOTE

> When you first start up Mac OS X after installing it, you didn't need to select a user account to log in. That's because by default Mac OS X uses the automatic login mode, which means that a designated user account is selected by your Mac automatically when it starts up. Because your Mac does it for you, you might not even realize that you have logged in. After your Mac starts up, the desktop appears just like when you log in to a user account manually. However, your Mac has gone through the login process—it just entered all the required information for you automatically.

UNDERSTANDING USER ACCOUNTS

Each user account on your Mac has its own set of preferences and resources that are specific to that user account.

Many preferences are stored individually for each user account, so how the OS looks and works is mostly unique to each user. A simple example of user account customization is the desktop picture, which is stored as a preference within each user account; this means that for each account, the user's desktop can look different. Most other customizable aspects of Mac OS X, such as the Dock, are also specific to each user account. Many applications can also store preferences specific to each user account so that those applications can be tailored to each person who uses your Mac.

TIP

To disable automatic login without creating additional user accounts, open the System Preferences application, select the Accounts icon, click the Login Options button, and uncheck the "Automatically log in as" check box.

Equally important is that under Mac OS X, user accounts also define a user's ability to perform specific actions that are either allowed or denied by the account's security privileges. Actions controlled by a user's account security privileges include whether the user can view or change specific files, change certain system preferences, and so on. For example, a user account must have administrator privileges to modify a Mac's network settings. You'll learn much more about Mac OS X security features later in this book.

User account's also come with a set of resources to which only the user has access. Most of these are contained in the user's Home folder.

Directory Versus Folder
Under Mac OS X, the terms *directory* and *folder* are basically synonymous. Typically, non-GUI operating systems use the term *directory*, whereas GUI operating systems, such as Mac OS X, use the term *folder*. Because Mac OS X has Unix as its foundation and the term *directory* is used under Unix, you will see folders referred to as *directories* in many places. The reason for this is that you can access the Unix command line; when you access your Mac's files using the command line, the concept of folder doesn't really apply (because there is no graphical element to the user interface). Practically speaking, however, the terms are equivalent and are interchangeable. You will see that I use both throughout this book.

UNDERSTANDING THE HOME FOLDER

Each user account on your Mac has a Home folder. This folder contains folders that are used to store private files, public files, and system resources (such as preferences and keychains) for that user account. With two exceptions (the Public and Site folders), only someone logged in under a user account can access the folders in that user account's Home folder.

NOTE

The exception to the general rule about accessing the folders in another user's Home folder is the *root* account. The root user account can access everything on your Mac and is outside the normal security provided by user accounts. You should use the root account only in special situations, and you really need to understand it before you use it.

→ To learn about the root account, **see** "Logging In As Root," **p. 253**.
→ To learn more about Mac OS X directories, **see** "Understanding Mac OS X Directories," **p. 109**.

By default, a user's Home folder contains the folders shown in Figure 2.1. However, you can create additional folders within your Home folder if you'd like to. And, of course, you can create additional folders within the default folders contained in your Home folder as well.

Figure 2.1
Every user account on your Mac has a Home folder; this folder contains folders that only that user can access (except for the Public and Sites folders).

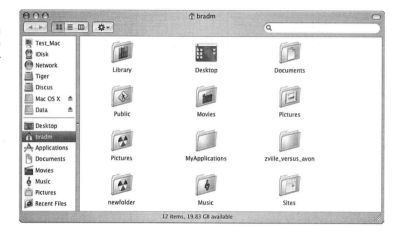

Most of these folders are easy to understand because they are used to organize a user's files. For example, the Documents folder is the default location in which the user stores documents he creates. The Desktop folder contains items that are stored on that user's desktop (which, by the way, means that each user account has a unique desktop), and so on.

Some applications will automatically select a folder when storing files. For example, when you add music files to your iTunes Library, they are stored in the Music folder. Likewise, when you create movies with iMovie, they are stored in the Movies folder.

TIP

You can quickly tell which user account is active by looking at the Home directory icon in the Finder window's Places sidebar, which is always located at the left side of Finder windows. It looks like a house for the current user's Home folder; the other Home directory icons are plain folders. The short name for a user account appears in the title bar of that user's Home folder (in Figure 2.1, the currently logged in account is called bradm).

Only someone logged in under a user account can access the contents of the folders in that user's Home folder—except for the Public and Sites folders that can be accessed by anyone using your Mac. Locked folders have an icon that includes a red circle with a minus sign (see Figure 2.2). If someone other than those who have permission attempts to open one of these protected folders, they only see a warning message and not any of the contents of the protected folder. Accessible folders in another user's directory have the plain folder icon, which means their contents are available to that user. Unlocked default folders in the current user's Home directory have the decorative Mac OS X icons (refer back to Figure 2.1). (Folders you create will have the generic folder icon but will be protected in the same way as the default folders.)

NOTE

Notice in Figure 2.2 that the title of the window shown is "kidsaccount." This is the name of another user account; you can tell that it isn't the one currently logged in because it doesn't appear in the Places sidebar nor does its icon look like a house.

Locked folders

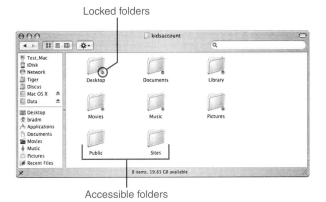

Figure 2.2
When you view another user's Home directory, the protected folders are marked with the minus icon to indicate that their contents are inaccessible to you.

Accessible folders

There are three folders in each Home folder that don't behave like the others; those are the Public, Sites, and Library folders.

WORKING IN THE PUBLIC FOLDER

A user's Public folder is accessible by users logged in under any account (see Figure 2.3). Its purpose is to enable users to share files that are stored within different user accounts on the same computer. To share your files with other users, simply store them in your Public folder. Other users can then open your Public folder to get to those files. Likewise, to access files other users have shared with you, you can open their Public folder.

Figure 2.3
In this example, I've opened another user's Public folder; I can work with any files it contains (as can other users) or I can place files in the Drop Box folder.

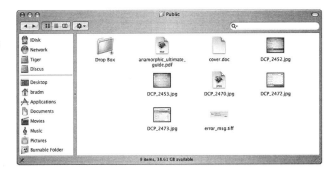

As you can see in Figure 2.3, the Public folder also contains a Drop Box folder. This folder can be seen by other users and they can place files in it, but it can't be opened by anyone except the owner of the user account under which that drop box is stored. This is useful when you want other users to be able to transfer files to you, but you want those files to be hidden from other users.

WORKING THE SITES FOLDER

The Sites folder contains files for each user's Web site. Part of each user account's resources is a wbsite that can be accessed over a local network, from another user's account, or from the Internet (depending on how the Mac's Internet access is configured). You place the files for a user's account's website in the Sites folder to publish that site.

WORKING IN THE LIBRARY FOLDER

The Library folder is the only one in the Home directory that is not intended for document storage. It contains items related to the configuration of the user account and all the system-related files for that account. For example, user preferences are stored here, as are font collections, addresses, keychains, and so on. Basically, any file that affects how the system works or looks that is specific to a user account is stored in the Library directory. You won't usually access this folder unless you are troubleshooting problems; you will learn more about the Library folder later in this book.

UNDERSTANDING THE ADMINISTRATOR ACCOUNT

When you installed Mac OS X, you created the first user account. The account you created was actually an administrator account. Administrator accounts are special because they provide wide access to the system and are one of only two accounts that can control virtually every aspect of Mac OS X (the other being the root account). A user who logs in as an administrator for your Mac can do the following:

- **Create other user accounts**—An administrator for your Mac can create additional user accounts. By default, these user accounts have more limited access to the Mac than does an administrator account, but you can allow other accounts to administer your Mac as well (you can create multiple administrator accounts).

- **Change global system preferences**—The administrator can change global system settings for your Mac; other user accounts can't. For example, to change the network settings on your Mac, you must be logged in as the administrator (or you must authenticate yourself as an administrator).

- **Configure access to files and folders**—An administrator can configure the security settings of files and folders to determine who can access those items and which type of access is permitted.

- **Install applications**—Applications you install under Mac OS X require that you be logged in as an administrator or that you authenticate yourself as one.

When you attempt to perform an action that requires an administrator, such as updating your software via the Software Update tool, you will see an Authentication dialog box. To authenticate yourself, you enter a valid administrator account username and password and click OK (if you are currently logged in as an administrator, the username is filled in automatically). After you have been authenticated, you can perform that action.

In areas where you need to be authenticated to perform an action, you will see the Lock icon. When the Lock is "open," you are authenticated (see Figure 2.4). When the Lock is "closed," you can click it to open the Authentication dialog box.

Figure 2.4
The Lock icon, here shown in the System Preferences application, indicates whether you are currently authenticated as an administrator.

An open lock means that changes can be made.

You should control who has access to the administrator accounts for your machine. If someone who doesn't understand Mac OS X—or who wants to cause you trouble—logs in with your administrator account, you might be in for all kinds of problems. You also need to ensure either that you can remember the username and password for an administrator account you set up or that you write them down. If you forget this vital information, you could have trouble later.

NOTE

Administrator accounts are a fundamentally different concept for some Mac users. Traditionally, all areas of the operating system (such as control panels) were easily accessed by anyone who used the Mac. Although you can use the automatic login mode so that you don't have to log in to your Mac, the fact remains that Mac OS X is a multi-user system. To get the most out of it, you need to get comfortable with user accounts because whether you have to log in or not, you will always be utilizing user accounts under Mac OS X at some level.

UNDERSTANDING PARENTAL CONTROLS

In Mac OS X version 10.4, user accounts also include the parental controls feature. This feature enables you to tighten the security of a user account in specific situations, such as for email, web browsing, and so on. For example, you can set the specific people with whom the user can exchange email.

NOTE

The ability to limit a user account's access to specific applications has been part of Mac OS X since version 10.0. This function is under the Finder & System part of the Parental Controls option under version 10.4.

While this feature is primarily intended to be used for younger people, it can be useful for any user account that you want to set some limits on.

CREATING AND CONFIGURING USER ACCOUNTS

If you share your Mac with other people, you should create a user account for each person who will be using your machine. As you read previously, user accounts provide specific folders for each user that are used to store information (such as application preferences) and documents and other files that are specific to them. Each user account can be customized in many ways; for example, you can have a different set of applications start up for each user and each can have her own Dock and desktop configuration.

Rather than creating a single user account for each person, you can create a user account that several people share. This can be useful if there are people who use your Mac but don't necessarily need private directories or individual customization. For example, if you share your Mac with children, you might want to create a single user account for them to use.

TIP

> Whether you share your Mac, you should create at least two administrator accounts. Use one for your normal activities, such as configuring the machine, installing applications, and so on. Save the other account for use during troubleshooting. Sometimes, preferences associated with specific user accounts can become corrupted and other problems related to a specific user account can develop. As part of the troubleshooting process, you can log in under the "clean" administrator account to recover from problems and troubleshoot and solve them. This step often tells you whether a problem is related to a specific user account or your Mac OS X installation, applications, or hardware.

CREATING USER ACCOUNTS

The System Preferences application is used to create additional user accounts. Follow these steps:

1. Open the System Preferences application by clicking its icon on the Dock or by selecting Apple menu, System Preferences. When the System Preferences window opens, you will see that it is organized in sections that relate to the areas of the OS for which you can set system preferences (those being Personal, Hardware, Internet & Network, and System). Within each section are the icons for each area of the OS that you can configure (see Figure 2.5).

NOTE

> When you install some software (especially that associated with hardware, such as a third-party keyboard), additional preferences tools are installed. When you do this, a section called "Other" is added at the bottom of the System Preferences application and the buttons related to the additional software's preferences appear there. You'll see examples of this later in this book, such as when you install a third-party keyboard that includes additional software.

Figure 2.5
The System Preferences application enables you to configure many aspects of Mac OS X.

When you click an icon, the lower pane of the window is replaced by the controls for the area to which the icon is related.

2. Click the Accounts icon in the System area to open the Accounts pane of the System Preferences application (see Figure 2.6).

Along the left side of this pane is the list of user accounts currently configured on the Mac. At the top of this list in the My Account section, the user account under which you are logged in is shown. Under the Other Accounts heading are the other user accounts that exist on the machine. Under each username, you will see the type of account it is, such as Admin, Managed, and so on. At the bottom of the user list is the Login Options button, and just below that are the Add User (+) and Delete User buttons (-). The right part of the pane shows the tools you use to configure a user account.

Figure 2.6
You create user accounts with the Accounts pane of the System Preferences application.

Only an administrator can create new user accounts. If you aren't logged in as an administrator for your Mac, you have to authenticate yourself as being an administrator before you can create an account. To do so, click the Lock icon located in the lower-left corner of the System Preferences window, enter the username and password for an administrator account, and click OK. This identifies you as an administrator temporarily so that you can make changes, such as adding a user account.

NOTE

> Notice in Figure 2.6 that the lock icon in the lower-left corner of the window is open indicating that I am currently authenticated as an administrator for this machine.

3. Click the New User button, which is the plus sign located under the list of users. A sheet appears in which you enter basic information for the user account you are creating.

4. Enter the name for the user account in the Name box. The name is the "full" name for the user account; it doesn't have to be a real full name—the name can be pretty much whatever you want it to be.

5. Press Tab to move to the Short Name box. When you do, Mac OS X creates a short name for the user account. The short name is used for specific areas under that user account (such as the name of the user's Home folder) and for access to services provided under that account (such as the account's FTP site). The short name can be used instead of the name to cut down on the number of characters you have to type in specific situations, such as when you log in to the account (in which case the short name and name are interchangeable). However, the Home directory is always identified by the short name only.

Mac OS X automatically creates a short name for the account; it just places all the letters in the name together with no spaces. You can choose to use this one, or you can change it to something else.

TIP

> The short name is used in several places, such as in the website address for the user account. Because of this, you should choose a meaningful short name, preferably some variation of the person's name, such as his first initial and last name.

6. Edit the short name as needed, such as by replacing it if you don't like the one Mac OS X created for you automatically.

The short name can be as few as one character and can't contain any spaces, dashes, or other special characters (Mac OS X won't let you enter any characters that are unacceptable). Underscores are acceptable. You should adopt a general rule about the short name for an account, such as using the first initial of the first name and the complete last name. Keeping the short name consistent will help you deal with other user accounts more easily.

After it's created, you can't change the short name for a user account, so be deliberate when you create it.

TIP

> You can use a user account for any purpose you want. For example, because each user account has its own website, you might want to create a user account simply to create another website on your machine. For example, you might want to create a user called "Group Site" to serve a web page to a workgroup of which you are a member.

7. Create the password that the user will enter to log in under the user account. For better security, use a password that is eight characters long and contains both letters and numbers (this makes the password harder to crack). Passwords are case sensitive; for example, mypassword is not the same as MyPassword. If you want help creating a password, move to step 9 without typing a password. If you want to type it in without help, do so and skip to step 15.

   If you leave the Password field empty, a password will not be required to log in to the account. When you choose to do this, you will see a warning dialog box when you attempt to save the account. If you ignore this warning, the account is created without a password. When the user logs in to the account, he can select it on the list of user accounts and log in without entering a password. Obviously, this is not a secure thing to do, but it can be useful nonetheless. For example, you might choose to create an account for children whom you don't want to have to use a password. When you create such "unprotected" accounts, you should use the Parental Controls tools to limit access to your Mac, such as by using the Simple Finder option.

   TIP

   > You can remove a password from an existing account even though the system tells you this can't be done. Just remove the password, save the account changes, click Ignore in the warning dialog box, and then click OK in the dialog box that tells you this change won't be accepted. It is actually accepted and the account no longer requires a password.

   → To learn how to configure an account's capabilities, **see** "Configuring a User Account," **p. 32**.

 8. Mac OS X can help you create a password if you want it to. Click the Key button to the right of the Password field. The Password Assistant will open.

9. Select the type of password you want to create on the Type pop-up menu (see Figure 2.7). There are several options:

   - **Manual**—Enables you to type a password manually. Memorable creates a password that your Mac thinks that users will be able to remember.

   - **Numbers Only**—Creates a password consisting of only numbers.

- **Random**—Creates a random password. FIPS-181 compliant creates a password that is compliant with the federal requirements for automatic password generation.

Figure 2.7
Under Mac OS X version 10.4, your Mac can help you create passwords.

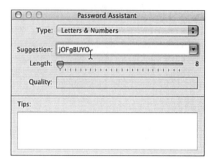

10. Select the length of the password you want to create using the Length slider. The minimum number of characters is 8. The maximum is 31, but I suspect your users won't be happy with a password that long!

    After you select a type and length, your Mac will generate a password for you and it will appear in the Suggestion box.

    If you chose the Manual option (step 9), you need to type the password yourself.

11. If you don't like the suggested password shown, use the Suggestion pop-up menu to select another option.

    As you select passwords, the Quality gauge shows you a relative measure of the quality of the password you are choosing. The more of the bar that is filled, the more secure the password will be. Of course, this is from the security perspective, which isn't necessarily the same as the user's preferences!

12. When you find a password you like, copy it by pressing ⌘+C.

13. Close the Password Assistant.

14. Paste the password into the Password field.

15. Press Tab and retype or paste the password in the Verify box.

16. Press Tab and enter a hint to remind the user what the password is. This reminder is optional; if a user fails to log in successfully after three attempts, this hint can appear to help him remember him password.

17. If you want the new account to be an administrator account, check the "Allow user to administer this computer" check box.

NOTE

> If you have not turned off the Automatic Login mode and you create a new user account, you will see a dialog box asking whether you want that mode to be turned off. The account that is logged in automatically is also shown in this dialog box. (If you have disabled the Automatic Login mode already, you won't see this dialog box.)

18. Review the information you have entered and update it as needed; when you are ready to create the account, click Create Account (see Figure 2.8). (If you didn't enter a password, you'll be warned in a dialog box, click OK if you are sure you want to create a user account without a password.)

Figure 2.8
When you complete the information on this sheet, you are ready to create a new user account.

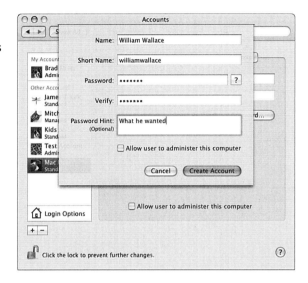

You'll return to the Accounts pane and the user account you created will be shown at the bottom of the Other Accounts list (see Figure 2.9). Under the account, you'll see the type of account it is. *Standard* means that the account can't administer the Mac and it doesn't include parental controls. *Admin* means that the account can administer the Mac. *Managed* means that Parental Controls have been used to limit the account's access to the Mac in some way.

Figure 2.9
The account called "William Wallace" has been created and is ready to configure.

CONFIGURING A USER ACCOUNT

After you have created a user account, you can configure it to determine the kind of access that account has to your Mac and to customize certain aspects of it.

When you select one of the accounts shown in the Other Accounts section, along the top of the Accounts pane you'll see three buttons that enable you to access specific aspects of the user account, those being Password, Picture, and Parental Controls.

When you select the account under which you are currently logged in (the one shown in the My Account area), the Login Items button also appears. You use this to set the items that open automatically when you log in.

The following sections explain how to configure each of these areas.

 If you unable to select a user account to modify it, see "I Can't Change a User Account" in the "Troubleshooting" section at the end of this chapter.

CONFIGURING A USER ACCOUNT'S PASSWORD

You can use the somewhat mislabeled Password pane to configure the full name for a user account and to reset the user's password (this is handy if a user forgets his password):

1. Open the Accounts pane of the System Preferences application and select the user whose account you want to update.
2. Click the Password button if it isn't selected already.
3. To change the user's full name, edit the name shown in the Name box.

> **NOTE**
>
> As mentioned previously, you can't change a user's short name.

4. To reset a user's password, click Reset Password. The Password sheet will appear.

> **TIP**
>
> When you select the currently logged-in user account, the Reset Password button becomes the Change Password button, but it does the same thing.

5. Configure the new password using the same steps that you use when you create a password for a new user account (see steps 7–15 in the "Creating User Accounts" section).

→ For detailed information about creating passwords, **see** "Creating User Accounts," **p. 26**.

6. Click Reset Password. The user's password will be reset to the new value and you'll return to the Password pane.
7. To enable the user to administer your Mac, click the "Allow user to administer this computer" check box. To prevent the user from administering your Mac, uncheck this check box.

CONFIGURING A USER ACCOUNT'S PICTURE

You can associate a picture with a user account. This picture will show up in a number of places, such as next to the user's account in the Login window, in the user's Address Book card, in their iChats, and so on. There are two sources of images that you can use. One is the default images that are part of Mac OS X. The other is any other image that you create or that you download from the Internet. To configure a user's image, perform the following steps:

1. Open the Accounts pane of the System Preferences application and select the user whose picture you want to set.

2. Click the Picture button. The Picture pane will appear. At the top of the window, you will see the image currently associated with the account; unless you have changed it, Mac OS X selected an image for you when you created the account from the Mac OS X default images.

3. To choose a different image from those included with Mac OS X, click the Apple Pictures collection. The images it contains appear in the right pane of the window. You can browse the images using the scroll bar. To select an image, click it. It will be shown in the Image well at the top of the pane and will be associated with the user account (see Figure 2.10).

Figure 2.10
This bolt of lightening represents William Wallace better than a flower, but still isn't quite right.

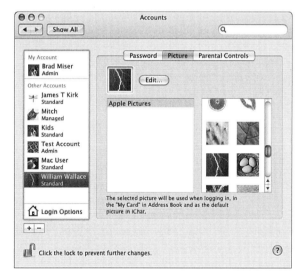

4. If you want to use a custom image for the account, click the Edit button. The Images dialog box appears (see Figure 2.11).

5. To place an image in the dialog box, drag an image onto the image well in the center of the box, click Choose and move to and select an image, or click Take Video Snapshot to capture an image from a video camera (such as an iSight camera) attached to your Mac.

   The image you use as the login picture can be a JPEG or TIFF. However, you can't use a GIF as a login picture.

Figure 2.11
You can use the Images dialog box to select an image for a user account.

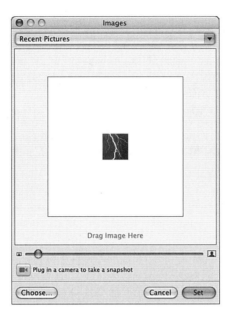

6. When the image is shown in the image well, use the slider to crop the image to the part you want to use.

> **TIP**
>
> If you have worked with other images recently, click the Recent Pictures pop-up menu at the top of the Images dialog box and select the image you want to use.

7. Drag the image around in the image well to select the portion of it to be used as the account's picture (see Figure 2.12).

8. When the picture is what you want it to be, click Set. The image is shown in the image well on the Picture tab and is used for that user account (see Figure 2.13).

> **TIP**
>
> The default login pictures (those shown on the scrolling list) are stored in the directory *Mac OS X*/Library/User Pictures, where *Mac OS X* is the name of your Mac OS X startup volume. You can install additional images in this directory to make them available as part of the Apple Pictures collection.

LIMITING ACCESS OF A USER ACCOUNT USING PARENTAL CONTROLS

You might want to limit the access a user has to your Mac. For example, if the user is a child, you might not want that child to be able to use certain applications or to burn CDs or DVDs. You can use the Parental Controls to set these kind of limits on a user account. Follow these steps:

Figure 2.12
This looks better than the lightning.

Figure 2.13
This image seems a much better fit for William's user account as I am sure you will agree.

1. Open the Accounts pane of the System Preferences application and select the user whose access you want to limit.

2. Click the Parental Controls button. The Parental Controls pane will appear. In this pane, you will see the various areas on which you can set limits.

3. Select Finder & System and then click its Configure button. The Configure sheet will appear (see Figure 2.14).

Figure 2.14
You can control a user's access using Parental Controls (of course, you don't have to be a parent to use them).

There are two basic options:

- **Some Limits**—Enables you to customize the user's access.
- **Simple Finder**—Presents very limited Finder functionality to the user.

To configure some limits on the user account, perform the following steps:

1. Click the Some Limits radio button.
2. Choose among the following options by clicking the appropriate check boxes:
   - **Open all System Preferences**—If this option is allowed, the user will be able to view all system preferences. The requirement to be an administrator to change some of these preferences remains in effect. If the user is not an administrator, she will only be able to view current settings.
   - **Modify the Dock**—If this is enabled, the user can configure his Dock.
   - **Administer printers**—This control allows or prevents a user from being able to configure printers.
   - **Change password**—This option is active only if "Open all System Preferences" feature is enabled. If enabled, the user can change passwords for other users.
   - **Burn CDs and DVDs**—This one is easy to figure out; if enabled, the user can burn discs. If not, the user won't be able to write to CD or DVD.
   - **Allow supporting programs**—This enables the user to access programs that support those to which direct access is granted.
   - **This user can only use these applications**—When this option is enabled, the lower part of the pane enables you to select specific applications that the user can access. To allow all the applications stored in a specific area, such as in the

Applications folder, check the box for that area. To limit a user to specific applications within an area, click the area's Expansion triangle, which causes a list of the applications in that area to be shown. Check the box next to each application you want the user to be able to use; uncheck the box for those applications you don't want the user to be able to use.

3. Click OK to set the limits you have configured on the user account.

The Simple Finder provides the most basic level of access. As you might expect from its name, the Simple Finder provides a less complex interface for a user and greatly restricts what that user can do. When a user is logged in with the Simple Finder, the Dock contains only five icons: Finder, My Applications, Documents, Shared, and Trash. These are the only areas the user can access. For example, under the Simple Finder, a user can store documents only in his Documents folder and can't open other folders. The only Finder commands the user can access are Sleep, Log Out, About Finder, the Hide/Show Finder commands, and Close Window. The Simple Finder makes your machine more secure because it limits the actions of a user so severely. Using the Simple Finder can be a good choice if the user for whom you are creating an account has minimal computer skills, such as for very young children or someone who is totally new to the Mac.

To activate Simple Finder for a user, perform the following steps:

1. Click the Simple Finder radio button.
2. Configure the applications that you want the user to be able to use. To allow all the applications stored in a specific area, such as in the Applications folder, check the box for that area. To limit a user to specific applications within an area, click the area's Expansion triangle, which causes a list of the applications in that area to be shown. Check the box next to each application you want the user to be able to use; uncheck the box for those applications you don't want the user to be able to use.
3. Click OK to make the Simple Finder active for the user (see Figure 2.15).

Following are a few more important points to note about setting a user account's capabilities:

- Some settings are dependent on others. For example, if you uncheck the "Open all System Preferences" check box, the "Change password" check box becomes disabled. This is because, if the user can't access the System Preferences utility, she won't be able to access the Accounts pane that contains the tools needed to change the password.
- You can use the Check All or Uncheck All button to select or deselect all applications at the same time.
- The Locate button enables you to select applications that don't appear on the list of applications by default. When you click this button, an Open dialog box appears. You can use this dialog box to move to and select an application.

Figure 2.15
He might have caused trouble for England, but the Simple Finder will keep William from causing trouble on your Mac.

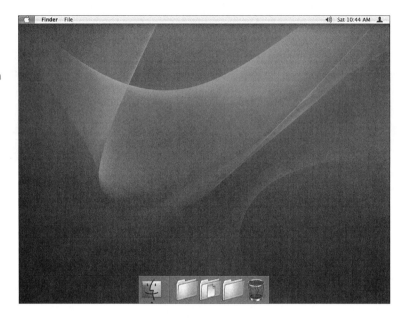

- The last entry on the list of application folders is Others. If your machine can access applications that aren't stored in one of the standard Mac OS X application folders, they appear under the Others category.

TIP

Under Mac OS X, the default button in a dialog box is indicated by the pulsing (also called *throbbing*) action. As under previous versions of Mac OS X, you can activate the default button by pressing the Return or Enter key (as with the OK button in the Configure sheet).

When you use Parental Controls for any user, the word "Managed" appears under that user's account on the account's list. This indicates that the user's account has additional restrictions on it.

→ To learn how to user Parental Controls to limit Internet access to and from a user account, **see** "Defending Users from Online Attacks," **p. 1038**.

CONFIGURING YOUR ADDRESS BOOK CARD

In the Address Book application, each user has a card that provides his contact information. When viewing the user account pane for the currently logged in account (the one listed in the My Account section), the Address Book Card Open button will appear. If you click this button, the Address Book application will open and you will move to your Address Book card. You can then edit your card as needed.

→ To learn more about using the Address Book application, **see** "Setting Up and Using an Address Book," **p. 400**.

LOGGING IN, LOGGING OUT, RESTARTING, AND SHUTTING DOWN MAC OS X

Basic tasks like logging in, logging out, restarting, and shutting down Mac OS X are performed frequently as you and others use your Mac. The sections that follow briefly outline these processes.

LOGGING IN TO A USER ACCOUNT

As you learned previously, you must log in to be able to use a Mac OS X–powered Mac. To log in, you simply select or enter the name of the user account, enter the password, and press Return. You then move to the desktop for that user account.

LOGGING OUT OF A USER ACCOUNT

Under older versions of the Mac OS, when you were done working with the computer and wanted to "turn it off," you shut it down using the Shut Down command. Under Mac OS X, you can still do this, but most of the time you will log out instead. When you log out, all the processes currently running are stopped and the user account is "closed." To log out of the current user account, select the Apple menu, and then select Log Out (or press Shift-⌘-Q). In the resulting confirmation dialog box, press Return or click Log Out (if you don't do this within 2 minutes, the system logs you out automatically). The processes that are currently running are stopped (you are first prompted to save any open documents that have unsaved changes), and you return to the Login dialog box.

If you have enabled Fast User Switching, you can also select the Login Window command on the User Switching menu to protect access to your account while keeping it logged in.

TIP

> Logging out and then logging back in is a lot faster than stopping and starting your machine. In fact, there aren't many reasons to shut down your machine, and if you use it to serve web pages, you shouldn't shut it down at all. To secure your Mac when you aren't using it, just log out.

RESTARTING YOUR MAC

Although Mac OS X is very stable, there might be occasions when you need to restart your Mac to correct some problem that is occurring. Also, occasionally, you will need to restart your Mac after making system changes or installing new software.

NOTE

Some Mac-compatible keyboards (not produced by Apple) and some older Apple keyboards have a Power key, which you can use to start the machine when it is off or to bring up a dialog box that enables you to shut down, restart, or put your Mac to sleep. Newer Apple keyboards don't have this key, and some Macs running Mac OS X don't support it even if the keyboard has the Power key. If your keyboard has the Power key, press it and see whether anything happens. If the dialog box appears, you can use its controls to shut down, restart, or put your Mac to sleep. If nothing happens, you know that you never need to press the Power key again.

Restarting Mac OS X is simple. You can restart Mac OS X in a couple of ways:

- Click Restart in the Login window.
- Select the Apple menu, Restart.

TIP

If you click the Power button on a PowerBook or iBook, you will see a dialog box that enables you to shut down, restart, or put your PowerBook or iBook to sleep.

If Fast User Switching is enabled and other user accounts are logged in, you will see a warning dialog box when you attempt to restart your Mac. To be able to restart, you need to input an administrator user name and password and then click the Restart button.

SHUTTING DOWN YOUR MAC

Because today's machines use very little energy, there isn't really much reason to shut them off. Most of the time, when you are done working with your computer, you should simply log out. This stops all the processes that are running and puts your Mac in a safe condition. Logging in is much faster because you don't have to wait for your computer to start up. Even better, select Login Window on the Fast User Switching menu to keep your account logged in and protected.

Still, if you are leaving your Mac for a long time, you might want to shut it down. You can do so in the following ways:

- Select Apple menu, Shut Down.
- Press Shift-⌘-Q to log out, confirm the logout, and then click Shut Down in the Login window.

You can perform a hard shutdown by pressing the Power key and holding it down until the Mac turns off. You won't have a chance to save any open files so you should use this method only when all other options have failed and your Mac is locked up.

NOTE

> To turn on most modern Macs, you need to press the Power key located on the CPU.
>
> If you use an Apple Studio or Cinema Display, you can also turn on the Mac by pressing the Power button located on the display. If you press the Power button on the display while your Mac is on, it goes to sleep. If you press and hold down the Power button for a few seconds, your Mac is powered off without going through the shutdown process (use this only when the machine is totally locked up).
>
> Also, with certain Apple displays, you will see the Options tab on the Displays pane of the System Preferences utility. You can use this tab to configure what happens when you press the Power button on these displays. Your options are to have it control the display's power only or to control the computer's power too. This tab isn't available for newer Apple displays.

CONFIGURING THE LOGIN PROCESS

You can configure the Login window and process in a number of ways:

- Enable/disable the Automatic Login mode.
- Control how user accounts appear in the Login Window.
- Show/hide the Sleep, Restart, and Shut Down buttons.
- Show/hide the Input menu in the Login Window.
- Have the contents of the Login Window read to you.
- Show/hide the password hints.
- Enable fast user switching.

The following sections explain these options in detail.

CONFIGURING AUTOMATIC LOGIN

When you started Mac OS X for the first time, you were in the Automatic Login mode. In this mode, you don't have to enter login information; Mac OS X does it for you. This means that you don't have to enter a username and password each time you start or restart your machine; by default, the first user account (created during the Mac OS X installation process) is used.

CAUTION

> You should enable Automatic Login mode only if you are the only person who uses your Mac. If you enable Automatic Login mode with the administrator's account, you provide access to many of your system's resources, which is an unsecure way to operate. However, if you have a Mac in a secure location and are the only person who uses it, the Automatic Login mode eliminates the need to log in every time you start or restart the machine.

TIP

> If you are going to enable Automatic Login mode, create a non-administrator account to use. That way, even if someone does get access to your Mac, he won't be able to use the administrator account. Of course, you might have to log out and then log back in as the administrator to perform certain tasks, but this strategy provides a good compromise between security and convenience.

To configure the Automatic Login mode, use the following steps:

1. Open the Accounts pane of the System Preferences application.

2. Click the Login Options button. You'll see the Login Options pane (see Figure 2.16).

Figure 2.16
Use the Login Options pane to configure how you log in to your Mac.

3. To enable automatic login mode, check the "Automatically log in as" check box and select the user account that should automatically be logged in on the pop-up menu. The password prompt sheet will appear, and the user account you selected on the pop-up menu is selected in the sheet.

4. Enter the password for the account that you selected in step 3.

5. Click OK.

The next time you start or restart your Mac, the account you specified is automatically logged in and you move directly to the desktop for that account.

This setting affects only the start or restart sequence. When you log out instead of shutting down or restarting, you still see the Login window again and have to log in to resume using the Mac.

To disable automatic login, uncheck the "Automatically log in as" check box.

CONTROLLING HOW USER ACCOUNTS APPEAR IN THE LOGIN WINDOW

You can configure several aspects of how user accounts appear in the Login window:

1. Log in under an administrator account and open the Accounts pane of the System Preferences application.
2. Click the Login Options button.
3. To display empty Name and Password fields in the Login window instead of a list of the user accounts you have configured, click the "Name and password" radio button. When this button is selected, you have to type the name or the short name and password for an account to log in to it. To display the list of user accounts, click the "List of users" radio button instead. With this option, each account (and its image) appears onscreen. To log in, the user clicks her account, enters her password, and clicks the Login button.

> **NOTE**
>
> As you will learn later, most of the changes you make using the System Preferences application are implemented immediately so you don't need to save them. In fact, you can leave the application open and make changes as needed. These are reflected in your Mac's operation immediately.

HIDING THE SLEEP, RESTART, AND SHUT DOWN BUTTONS

If you enable Automatic Login mode, you might run into trouble if you leave the Restart and Shut Down buttons in the Login Window enabled. Here's how that could happen. Say you are using your Mac and decide that you want to take a break for a while, but there are people in your area whom you don't want to be able to use the machine while you step away. You log out, and your machine is protected, right? Not necessarily. If the Restart and Shut Down buttons are enabled, someone can restart the Mac from the Login window and then it would start up in the automatic account, giving the person access to the machine. Disabling these buttons prevents someone from using them to access an account that is automatically logged into.

The previous scenario might make you pause to ask a question before you enable Automatic Login mode. If you do disable the Restart and Shut Down buttons and then log out, can someone simply press the hardware Restart or Reset button on the CPU to start up the Mac to automatically log in to the automatic login account? This would bypass the protection offered by disabling the buttons, right? Nope; when the Mac is not shut down properly (by using the Shut Down command), the automatic login feature is disabled when the machine is started or restarted the next time. So, if you have to use one of those buttons, you must log in the next time you start or restart the machine.

To disable the Sleep, Restart, and Shut Down buttons, do the following:

1. Open the System Preferences application and then the Accounts pane, and then click the Login Options button.
2. Uncheck the "Show the Restart, Sleep, and Shut Down buttons" check box.

When the Login window appears, these buttons are hidden and the only way to use the Mac is to log in under a valid account. If you want these buttons to appear in the Login Window again, simply check the check box. When these buttons do appear in the Login Window, the related actions can be performed without being logged into a user account.

SHOWING THE INPUT MENU IN THE LOGIN WINDOW

You can use a variety of languages with Mac OS X. The specific language you use at any point in time determines the keyboard layout you should be using. This is controlled on the Input menu from which you can select the keyboard configuration you want to use. To show this menu on the Login Window, check the "Show Input menu in login window" radio button on the Login Options pane of the Accounts pane of the System Preferences application. When the Login Window appears, the keyboard layout can be selected on the Input menu. When it isn't shown, the layout associated with the currently selected language is used.

→ To learn about working with languages, **see** "Configuring Your Keyboard's Language Settings and the Input Menu," **p. 840**.

HAVING THE CONTENTS OF THE LOGIN WINDOW READ TO YOU

Mac OS X's VoiceOver feature enables your Mac to read the contents of windows to you. If you want the contents of the Login Window to be read, select the "Use VoiceOver at login window" radio button. With this enabled, your Mac will read the contents of the Login Window when it appears on the screen.

→ To learn more about VoiceOver, **see** "Understanding and Using VoiceOver," **p. 263**.

SHOWING PASSWORD HINTS

You learned earlier that you can configure password hints that are displayed to help a user remember her password. If you check the "Show password hints" radio button, the Forgot Password button is displayed on the Login Window. When a user clicks this button, the password hint appears.

If the user tries to log in, but is unsuccessful in three attempts, the password hint appears even if he doesn't click the Forgot Password button.

NOTE

If the user clicks the Forgot Password button, it becomes the Password Reset button. If this button is clicked, the steps to reset a password by using the installation disc are shown. This is usually a last resort. It is better to reset a user's password via the Account tools.

ENABLING AND USING FAST USER SWITCHING

When a user logs out of his account, all documents are closed and all applications and processes are quit. When a user logs in again, any of these must be restarted to get back to where the user was when he logged out. Prior to Mac OS X version 10.3, this process had to be suffered every time users changed. As of the release of Mac OS X 10.3 and later, you can take advantage of *fast user switching*. What this means is that you can log in to another user account without logging out of the accounts that are currently logged in. This is very nice because you can leave applications and documents open in an account and log out to prevent someone from using those items. And, another user can log in and work with his account. When he is done, you can log back in to your account and everything will be as it was when you left it. This saves a lot of time and hassle reopening items, and processes you are running can continue to run while another user is logged in to the machine.

NOTE

> If your Mac has limited RAM, you might not want to enable Fast User Switching because applications running under other user accounts will consume resources even if your user account is the active one. This means performance might be slower for you because the applications under other user accounts are using RAM and so it isn't available to your applications.

To enable this feature, do the following steps:

1. Open the Accounts pane of the System Preferences application and click the Login Options button.

2. Check the "Enable fast user switching" check box. A new menu appears in the upper-right corner of the screen that enables other users to log in.

3. Use the "View as" pop-up menu to determine how the Fast User Switching menu appears on the Finder toolbar. Your options are

   - **Icon**—A silhouette appears at the top of the menu.

   - **Short name**—The short name of the user account currently logged in appears at the top of the menu.

   - **Name**—The full name of the user account currently logged into appears at the top of the menu.

Then, logging in and out of accounts can be done fast and easily with the Fast User Switching menu (see Figure 2.17).

To log in under another account, select it on the menu. You will see the Login window with the account you selected (see Figure 2.18). Enter the password for the account and click the Log In button or press Return. After a cool, 3D spinning effect, that user is logged in and his desktop appears.

NOTE

> Sadly, not all hardware can handle the spinning 3-D effect. If you use an older Mac, you might not get to enjoy this cool effect.

Figure 2.17
The Fast User Switching menu enables you to log in to other accounts without logging out of the current one.

Figure 2.18
Perhaps William needs to use his Mac to plan his next move.

TIP

> If you create a user account without a password and enable the Fast User Switching feature, you can log in to the account without a password immediately by selecting it on the Fast User Switching menu. You will bypass the Login Window altogether.

To temporarily block access to the current user account without logging out, open the Fast User Switching menu and select Login Window. The Login window will appear. You can leave the machine without worries that someone will be able to access your account. When you are ready to log in—or when anyone else is, for that matter—select the user account, enter a password, and click Login (you get to see the cool 3D spin again, too).

NOTE

> On the Fast User Switching menu and in the Login window, users who are currently logged in have the circle with a check mark icon next to them.

If another user account is logged in and you attempt to restart or shut down the machine, a warning dialog box appears that explains that other users are logged in and the action you are taking could cause them to lose data. If you enter an administrator username and password and click Shut Down or Restart, the other users are logged out and the action you want is performed. Be careful about doing this though since the other users can lose unsaved data.

TIP

> You can jump quickly to the Accounts pane of the System Preferences application by selecting Account Preferences on the Fast User Switching menu.

TESTING AND CHANGING USER ACCOUNTS

After you have created user accounts, you should log in under those accounts to test and configure them (some configuration can be done only while logged in under an account).

TESTING USER ACCOUNTS

After you create a new user account, you should test it by logging in under that account to make sure it works:

1. Select Apple menu, Log Out (or press Shift-⌘-Q).

TIP

> If you have enabled fast user switching, you can use the Fast User Switching menu instead. It really is faster and easier.

2. When the logout confirmation dialog box appears, press Return (or click the Log Out button). You will return to the Mac OS X login window. At the top of the Login window, you see the computer name. If you have configured the window to show a list of users, in the center part of the window, you see the login picture and name of each user account on the machine. If several user accounts appear, this will be a scrolling pane. At the bottom of the window are the Sleep, Restart, and Shut Down buttons (unless they are hidden).

NOTE

> The system automatically logs you out 2 minutes after you select the Log Out command, even if you don't click the Log Out button.

3. If the Log In window shows the user accounts on the machine, click the User account under which you want to log in. The dialog box will contract and you see the selected user account and an empty Password box. If the User Name and Password fields appear instead, enter the username (name or short name) for the account you want to log in to.

NOTE

> If the user account does not have a password, you are logged in as soon as you select that account's icon.

You can return to the full login window by clicking the Back button.

4. Enter the password for the user account and click Log In (or press Return or Enter).

If the user account information is not valid, the login dialog box "shudders" to indicate that the information you entered is invalid (remember that this information is case sensitive). After three unsuccessful attempts, the password hint appears if one has been entered for the user account and that feature is enabled.

When you enter correct information for the user account, the login process is completed and you see the desktop for that user account, which might look quite different from the administrator's desktop.

5. After you have logged in to the new account, you can make any changes to the configuration of the user account that you want; for example, create a startup configuration by adding items to the Login Items pane or customize the Dock.

→ To learn about customizing the Dock, **see** Chapter 5, "Using and Customizing the Dock," **p. 143**.

6. Make sure that the security of the account is correct. For example, if you meant to block access to some applications, check to ensure that you can't access those applications.

7. From the desktop, press Shift-⌘-Q and then press Return to log out of the account.

 If you are unable to log in to a user account you have created, see "I Can't Log In on a User Account" in the "Troubleshooting" section at the end of this chapter.

Setting Applications and Documents to Open Automatically at Login

To make your Mac even more efficient, you can have applications automatically start or documents open when a user logs in to an account. And you can have a different set of applications start up for each user account; this lets you customize each user's startup experience.

To configure the startup items for a user account, perform the following steps:

NOTE

In order to be able to configure login items, a user account must have access to the System Preferences application. If not, the user won't be able to access the Accounts tools.

1. Log in to the account for which you want to set the login items (you don't have to be logged in as an administrator to configure login items as you do to create user accounts or configure the Login window).

2. Open the System Preferences application.

3. Click the Accounts tab and then click the Login Items tab. The Login Items pane will appear (see Figure 2.19). You place any items you want to open in the list window to have them opened when the user account logs in. The order in which they are listed in the window determines the order in which they open (the topmost item opens first).

Figure 2.19
When you add applications or documents to the Login Items list, they automatically open when you log in.

4. Click the Add button, which is the plus sign (+) at the bottom of the pane.

5. Use the Add sheet to move to the item you want to be opened at login, select it, and click Add. When the Open dialog box appears, the Applications directory is selected automatically and you can select the applications that are installed there. If you want to add documents to the login items window, use the Add sheet to move to the files you want to be opened, select them, and click Add.

→ To learn more about Mac OS X directories, **see** "Understanding Mac OS X Directories," **p. 109**.

→ To learn more about working with the Open dialog box, **see** "Opening Documents in Mac OS X," **p. 198**.

TIP

You can also drag application or document icons directly onto the Login Items window instead of using the Add button.

When you place an item in the window (by using the Add button or dragging it there), an alias to that item is created.

6. If you want the item to be automatically hidden when it is opened, check the Hide check box. This is useful for applications that you don't need to see right away but still want to open. For example, you might want to open your email application but leave it hidden until you receive new email.

7. When you have all the items in the window, drag them up to make them open earlier in the process or down to have them open later in the sequence.

NOTE

Some applications might rely on others to function. In that case, you want the dependent application to open after the application on which it depends, so it should be lower on the list.

8. To remove an application or document from the list (so that it doesn't open on startup), select it and click the Remove button, which is the minus sign (–) at the bottom of the pane. This doesn't affect the item at all—it only removes it from the Startup Items list.

9. Continue adding, removing, and rearranging items until all the startup items are listed in the window in the order in which you want them to open (see Figure 2.20).

Figure 2.20
When William logs in, these applications will open automatically.

10. When you are done, quit System Preferences.

The next time the user logs in, the login items will open automatically, in the order you specified.

TIP

> Login items are a great way to customize your Mac for other users. Simply log in to the other accounts and create a different set of login items for those users.

EDITING USER ACCOUNTS

You can make changes to an existing user account. To do so, use the following steps:

NOTE

> If a user account is logged in, you won't be able to change it. Log out of that account before trying to edit it.

1. Open the Accounts pane of the System Preferences application.
2. Select the user account you want to edit. That user's information appears in the right part of the window.
3. Make changes to the user's information (such as changing the Picture or Parental Controls) as needed. If you aren't logged in as an administrator, you can change only a few items, such as the picture and login items.

TIP

> Remember that, even if you aren't logged in under an administrator account, you can authenticate yourself as an administrator so that all the account editing tools become available to you. To do this, click the closed lock icon in the lower-left corner of the System Preferences application window, enter an administrator username and password, and click OK. The lock icon opens and you can do all the actions that are allowed while logged in as an administrator.

NOTE

> Because it is used as the Home directory name for the account as well as for other items (such as in the website address for the user account), you can't make any changes to the short name. Once created, the short name can never be changed.

4. Use the controls on each tab to make changes to the account. These work just like they do when you create a user account.

→ To learn how to create a user account, **see** "Creating User Accounts," **p. 26**.

NOTE

> Even if you are logged in as an administrator and are changing your own name, password, or password hint, you have to confirm your password by entering it at the prompt before you can make those changes.
>
> If the current user account has permission to change the password, it can be changed by selecting the current password and trying to change it. When this is done, a sheet prompts the user for the current password. If the user enters the current password successfully, the Name, Password, Verify, and Password Hint fields become editable and the user can change the data in these fields as needed (the short name still can't be changed).

5. Test the account to make sure it works with the changes you have made.

 If you are unable to use the buttons in the Accounts pane of the System Preferences utility, see "The Buttons in the Accounts Pane Are Inactive" in the "Troubleshooting" section at the end of this chapter.

NOTE

> After you have entered a password, you won't be able to see it, even when you edit the user account. The only way to recover from someone forgetting his password is to reset it to a new one by editing the user account.

After you have tested and verified users accounts, provide the names and passwords for the user accounts you created to the people who need them. You should explain the limitations of the accounts to the users as well.

DELETING USER ACCOUNTS

You can also delete user accounts that you no longer need by doing the following:

1. Open the Accounts pane of the System Preferences application.
2. Select the account you want to delete.
3. Click the Delete User button, which is the minus sign at the bottom of the user list. You will see the delete user confirmation dialog box.

    When you delete a user, you have two options for the contents of that user's Home folder: You can choose to save the user's Home folder so the files it contains can be accessed, or you can choose to delete the folder immediately.

4. If you choose to save the user's Home folder, click the OK button. The deleted user account's Home directory will be moved to the Deleted Users folder. Within this folder, you will see a disk image for the deleted user's Home folder. You can open this disk image to work with its contents.

5. If you want to delete the user's Home folder immediately, click the Delete Immediately button. The account and all of the files associated with it will be deleted from your Mac.

After you delete it, the user account you deleted is no longer available in the Login Window and can no longer be used.

If you elected to preserve the user's Home folder, the Home directory for that account is converted into a disk image file that is stored in the location `Mac OS X/Users/Deleted Users`, where `Mac OS X` is the name of your Mac OS X volume.

The name of the disk image is `shortusername.dmg`, where `shortusername` is the short user-name of the account that was deleted. To access the files that were in the account's Home directory, open its disk image file. The Home directory for that account will then be a mounted volume on your machine, which you can use just like another volume you mount.

The Deleted Users folder is accessible only to those accounts that have administrative privileges on your Mac. If you want other users to be able to access files that were in the deleted account's Home directory, you must change the permissions associated with the disk image.

→ To learn how to configure permissions, **see** "Understanding and Setting Permissions," **p. 959**.

TROUBLESHOOTING

I CAN'T CHANGE A USER ACCOUNT

When I try to select a user account in the Other Accounts list, it is grayed out and I am unable to work with it.

The most likely cause of this error is fast user switching is turned on the user account is currently logged in. You can't modify a user account that is currently active. To see if this is the problem, look closely at the user account's icon in the account list. If there is a checkmark in a circle in it, the user account is logged in. Switch to that user account and log out. Then you will be able to modify its settings.

I CAN'T LOG IN ON A USER ACCOUNT

When I try to log in under a particular user account, the login window shudders and I can't log in.

The most likely cause of this error is that you are entering the user account information incorrectly. If you are selecting a user account from the list, you must be entering the password incorrectly. If you are entering both the account name and password, you have to ensure that you use the correct combination. Try entering the information again. Remember that both name and password are case sensitive.

If you are logging in using the short name, try using the full name instead.

If you are still not able to log in under that account, log in as the administrator and open the Users pane of the System Preferences utility to check the account or edit it. You can also delete the account and start over.

If you can't log in to an administrator account because you have forgotten the password, do the following steps:

1. Restart the Mac using the Mac OS X Install disc.

2. When the installer opens, select Utilities, Reset Password.

3. Follow the onscreen instructions to reset the administrator password.

THE BUTTONS IN THE ACCOUNTS PANE ARE INACTIVE

When I open the Accounts pane of the System Preferences utility, the buttons are all inactive.

The Lock icon in the lower-left corner of the window enables you to lock or unlock the ability to make global system changes. If this icon is in the "locked" mode, you need to authenticate yourself as the administrator (even if you are logged in under that account). Click the Lock icon, enter the Administrator User Name and Password in the Authentication dialog box, and press Return. If you enter valid information, the buttons become active and you are able to make changes to the account configurations.

CHAPTER **3**

VIEWING AND NAVIGATING MAC OS X FINDER WINDOWS

In this chapter

THE MAC OS X FINDER

The basic purpose of the Finder under Mac OS X version 10.4 is the same as it has always been; the Finder is the Mac application that provides the desktop, enables you to work with folders and files, and provides the basic interface for interacting with the system. The Finder does look a bit different than it did under previous versions of the OS, and it offers many more features, but most of the basic tasks work in the same or very similar ways. These tasks include those that you use to view and navigate Finder windows. In addition to its new appearance, the Mac OS X version 10.4 Finder also offers better views, more customization options, and more tools.

WORKING WITH FINDER WINDOWS

Mac OS X version 10.4 Finder windows provide the same function that Finder windows always have; that is, just like windows in your car, Finder windows enable you to see things. Of course, in the case of Mac OS X, you won't be looking for on-coming traffic, but rather you'll be looking for disks, discs, folders, and files with which you want to work. In addition to their nice appearance, Finder windows offer lots of functionality, some of which is more obvious than others (see Figure 3.1). In this section, you'll learn everything you need know to master using Finder windows.

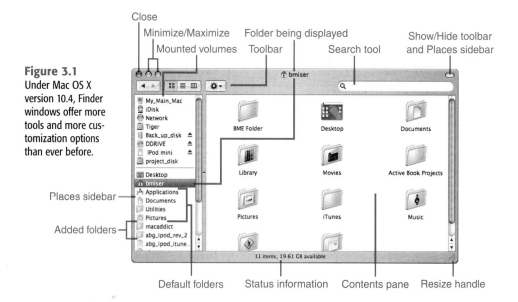

Figure 3.1
Under Mac OS X version 10.4, Finder windows offer more tools and more customization options than ever before.

OPENING FINDER WINDOWS

You can open Finder windows in several ways. If you click the Finder icon on the Dock (which is the Mac OS icon), one of two things can happen. If no Finder windows are currently open, a new Finder window appears showing the contents of the default location you select (initially, this is your Home folder, but you can select any folder you'd like). If at least one Finder window is already open, you will move to the Finder window in which you most recently worked.

TIP

> If you hold down the Control key while you click the Finder icon, click it and linger a moment, or right-click the icon on the Dock, a menu showing all open Finder windows appears. Select a window to jump into it. (To right-click something, you need to use a mouse with at least two buttons. If you haven't done so already, I highly recommend you replace Apple's mouse with a third-party mouse with at least two buttons. Throughout this book, whenever I refer to Control-clicking something, you can also right-click it with a two-button mouse.)

You can also open a new Finder window by selecting File, New Finder Window (⌘-N). When you open a new Finder window, the result is always the same: The contents of your default location are displayed (this is initially set to be your Home folder).

The Mac OS X Finder uses a web-like model in that each new Finder window you open starts a "chain" of windows (thus, the Back and Forward buttons in the Finder window toolbar). The first window in every new chain you start by using the New Finder Window command is always the directory you define as the default. You can have many window chains open at the same time, which is another similarity to web windows. (You can quickly jump into specific folders using the toolbar, the Places sidebar, the Go menu, and keyboard shortcuts.)

→ To learn how to navigate Finder windows, **see** "Navigating Finder Windows," **p. 69**.

By default, when you open an item (such as a folder), its contents replace the contents of the previous item that appeared in the Finder window you were viewing. (You can change this behavior globally with a preference setting.) You can also override this behavior so the new Finder window is separate from the first one by holding down the ⌘ key while you double-click an icon. This opens a new chain of Finder windows, with the contents of the item you opened displayed in the first window.

TIP

> This default behavior assumes that the toolbar and Places sidebar are shown in a Finder window. If not, opening a folder always opens a new, separate chain of Finder windows.

After you have one Finder window open, you can open other Finder windows (either in the same chain of windows or by starting a new chain) to view the contents of a different folder, volume, disc, and so on. To view the contents of a folder, volume, or disc shown in the current Finder window, double-click the icon for the item you want to open, or select an item and select File, Open. The Open keyboard shortcut works, too—just select an item and press ⌘-O to open it. You can also open an item's contextual menu by right-clicking it or by holding the Ctrl key down and selecting Open. If those aren't enough options for you, here is one more: Select an item and choose Open on the Action menu. The contents of the item you opened replace the window's current contents and the name shown at the top of the window becomes the name of the item you opened.

As you probably know, you can choose different views for Finder windows. When you open a new Finder window, it always assumes the view you selected the last time you viewed that item in a Finder window. You'll learn more about Mac OS X Finder window views later in this chapter.

NOTE

If you select an item while a Finder window is in the Column view, its contents are displayed in a new column.

To reiterate this sometimes confusing behavior of Mac OS X windows, the view in which a new window opens is determined by the view you used for that window the last time you viewed it. In other words, windows retain their view settings, even if the window from which you opened a separate Finder window is different. For example, if you viewed the Applications directory in List view, it appears in List view whenever you open it in a new Finder window until you change the view in which it appears.

Along the left edge of every Finder window is the Places sidebar. This handy tool consists of two panes. In the upper pane are all the volumes mounted on your Mac, including hard disk volumes, the Network volume, disk image volumes, your iDisk, CDs, DVDs, and so on. In the lower pane are some of the folders in your Home folder, the Burn folder, and the Applications folder. You can add any folders, applications, documents, or other files to or remove them from this area to completely customize it. The purpose of the Places sidebar is to enable you to quickly open a Finder window that displays the contents of any item it contains.

When you select a volume or folder in the Places sidebar, its contents appear in the Finder window. The currently selected item is highlighted so you can easily tell what is selected. (The name of the currently selected item appears at the top of the window as well.) If you select a document or application, that item opens just like when you double-click it.

TIP

If you hold down the ⌘ key while you click an item in the Places sidebar, that item opens in a new Finder window chain. If you hold down the Option key when you click an item in the Places sidebar, that item opens in a new Finder window and the previous window closes.

CONFIGURING HOW NEW FINDER WINDOWS OPEN

To configure how Finder windows open, perform the following steps:

1. Select Finder, Preferences or press ⌘-,; when the Finder Preferences window opens, click the General tab if it isn't selected already (see Figure 3.2).

Figure 3.2
Use the General pane of the Finder Preferences window to configure how new Finder windows open.

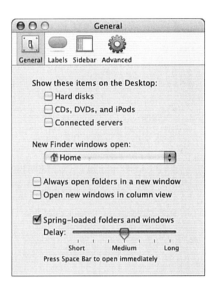

2. On the "New Finder windows open" pop-up menu, select the location where you want new Finder window chains you open to start.

   On the pop-up menu, you will see each volume mounted on your Mac along with your Home and Documents folders. To choose one of these as the starting location for new Finder window chains, simply select it on the menu.

   To select a location not shown on the pop-up menu, choose Other. Then use the "Choose a Folder" dialog box to move to and choose the folder that you want to be your starting place. Navigating such dialog boxes is very much like navigating in a Finder window in the Column view.

→ To learn how to navigate in Finder windows using the Column view, **see** "Navigating Finder Windows," **p. 69**.

NOTE

One of the nice features of Mac OS X is that most preference changes are made in real time—you don't have to close the Preferences window to see the results of your changes. For example, when you make the change in the previous steps, the window-opening behavior becomes active as soon as you make a selection on the pop-up menu. A good habit is to leave preference windows open as you make changes and close the windows only when you are happy with all the changes you have made.

3. If you prefer that when you open an item, the item's contents always appear in a new Finder window chain, check the "Always open folders in a new window" check box. However, because this option can lead to a proliferation of Finder windows, I recommend that you leave this option off. (Remember that you can always open a new Finder window chain by holding down the ⌘ key when you double-click an item.) A better way to view content is to use the Column view, which enables you to quickly move to any location, as you will see later in this chapter.

4. If you want all new windows to open in the Column view, check "Open new windows in column view." I recommend that you select this option because the Column view is the most efficient view for moving among the items on your Mac.

5. Close the Finder Preferences window.

→ To learn more about Mac OS X directories, **see** "Understanding Mac OS X Directories," **p. 109**.

> **NOTE**
>
> As you can see, you can choose a number of options for working with new Finder windows. Because my preferences are to have my Home folder open, open new items in the current Finder window, and always have new windows open in the Column view, that is what this chapter assumes. I point out differences along the way if you choose other preferences.

WORKING WITH SPRING-LOADED FOLDERS

Mac OS X Finder windows can be *spring-loaded* (this feature is turned on by default), meaning that they pop open when you drag an item onto a closed folder. This enables you to quickly place an item within nested folders without having to open each folder individually. Simply drag an item onto a closed folder so the folder is highlighted and "springs" open. After the delay time (which you can set) has passed, the highlighted folder opens in a separate Finder window chain (unless you are viewing the window in Column view, in which case a new column appears for the item onto which you are dragging the item). You can then drag the item onto the next folder and continue the process until you have placed it in its final destination. When you release the mouse button, what happens depends on the Finder preference you have selected. If new folders open in the same Finder window, you remain in the location in which you placed the item. If new folders always open in a new Finder window, you return to the window in which you started (however, the destination folder will remain open in its Finder window).

> **TIP**
>
> You can cause a folder to spring open immediately by pressing the spacebar when you drag an item onto a closed folder.

You can configure your Mac's spring loaded behavior by following these steps:

1. Click the General tab in the Finder Preferences dialog box.

2. Check the "Spring-loaded folders and windows" check box to turn this feature back on if you have turned it off (it is on by default).

3. Use the Delay slider to set the amount of delay time (the time between when you drag an item onto a folder and when that folder springs open).

4. Experiment to see whether the delay time is set correctly for you; if not, change it.

5. Close the Finder Preferences window when you have set the delay time to your liking.

SCROLLING FINDER WINDOWS

When the contents of a Finder window can't be shown in the amount of space the window currently has, you use the scrollbars to view contents that are out of sight. By default, the scrollbars are Mac OS X blue; you can change this to graphite with the Appearance pane of the System Preferences application. You can set the scroll arrows to both be located in the lower-right corner of Finder windows, or have an arrow located at each end of the scrollbars.

Mac OS X scrolling controls work as you expect them to. You have the following options:

■ Drag the scrollbars.

NOTE

> As with previous versions of the OS, the length of the scrollbar is proportional to the amount of the window you can see in the view. For example, if most of the scrollbar is filled in with color, you can view most of the window's contents. If the colored portion is relatively small, you can't view very much of the window's content.

■ Click above or below or to the left or right of the bar to scroll one screen's worth at a time.

■ Click the scroll arrows.

■ Press the Page Up and Page Down keys to scroll vertically.

■ Press the Home key to jump to the top of the window or the End key to jump to the bottom.

■ Use the arrow keys or Tab (and Shift-Tab) to move among the items in the window (which also scrolls the window when you move outside the current view).

■ When using the Icon or List views, hold down the ⌘ and Option keys and drag (when you can drag to scroll, the pointer changes to the gloved hand icon).

You can modify several aspects of scrolling behavior. You can change the location of the scroll arrows. And, rather than moving an entire page each time you click above, below, to the left, or to the right of a scrollbar, you can set the scrolling such that you move to the relative location you click instead. You can also turn on smooth scrolling, which smoothes out the appearance of a window when you scroll in it. Follow these steps to modify these scrolling features:

1. Open the System Preferences application.

2. In the Personal section, click Appearance.

3. To change the locations of the scroll arrows, click the Together radio button to have the scroll arrows in the lower-right corner of windows or the "At top and bottom" radio button to place an arrow at each end of the scrollbars (see Figure 3.3).

Figure 3.3
The Appearance pane of the System Preferences utility enables you to modify the behavior of window scrolling.

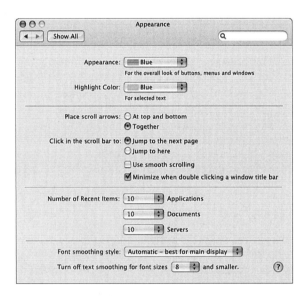

4. To change how scrolling works when you click in the scrollbar, click the "Jump to the next page" radio button to scroll a screen at a time or the "Jump to here" radio button to move to a position in the window that is relative to where you click in the scrollbar.

5. Check the "Use smooth scrolling" check box to turn on smooth scrolling.

TIP

This is a good chance to practice Mac OS X preference setting techniques. Make your changes to the Appearance pane, but leave the System Preferences application open. Click in a Finder window; your changes immediately become active. If you are satisfied, jump back to the System Preferences application and quit it. If not, jump back into the Appearance pane and continue making changes until you are satisfied.

RESIZING WINDOWS

Resizing windows also works as you might expect. To change the size of a window, drag its resizing handle until the window is the size you want it to be.

You can also use the Maximize button to make a window large enough to display all the items it contains or until it fills the screen, whichever comes first. Click the button and the window jumps to the size it needs to be to show all the items it contains or until it fills the available screen space. Click the button again to return it to its previous size.

You can also use this button to quickly swap between two sizes for a window. Make the window a size you like. When you click the Maximize button, it expands to its maximum size. Click the button again and it returns to the previous size. Each time you click the Maximize button, the window returns to the size it was previously (either the maximum size or the size you set).

If you are like me and have lots of Finder windows open on the Desktop, you can use this resizing behavior to make working between multiple windows more convenient. Select an open window and make it the size you want it to be so it is out of the way and you can store many windows of this size on your desktop; make it just large enough so you can see the window's title. You can click the Maximize button to open the window to work in it. Then, click the Maximize button again to return the window to its small size. Use the button to toggle between the two sizes. When you need to work in the window, make it large by clicking the Maximize button. When you are done, click the button again to make it small. You might find this even more convenient than minimizing windows (which you'll learn about shortly).

RESIZING THE PANES OF FINDER WINDOWS

As you learned earlier, Finder windows have two panes. The left pane is the Places sidebar, whereas the right pane is the Contents pane that displays the contents of the item you are viewing in the Finder window. You can change the relative size of the Places sidebar by dragging the resize handle that is located in the center of the border between the two panes (the handle is the familiar "dot"). Drag this to the left and the Places sidebar takes up less room in the window. Drag it to the right and the Places sidebar takes up more window space.

When you resize the Places sidebar, the text and icons within the sidebar become smaller so you can still see as much of them as possible within the allocated space. When the pane becomes too narrow to display all of an item's name, the first part of the name appears, followed by an ellipsis.

You can collapse the sidebar so that just the icons show. You can also collapse it all the way so that it doesn't show at all by dragging its Resize handle all the way to the left. To reveal it again, drag the resize handle to the right.

> **TIP**
>
> You can also collapse or expand it by double-clicking its resize handle.

The Places sidebar retains your settings as long as you work within the same Finder window chain. When you open a new chain, the Places sidebar becomes its default size. That is, unless you have collapsed the sidebar all the way, in which case it remains collapsed when you start a new Finder window chain.

CLOSING, MINIMIZING, AND MAXIMIZING FINDER WINDOWS

Among the most distinctive features of Mac OS X are the three stoplight-type controls located in the upper-left corner of windows (refer to Figure 3.1). The red button (on the far left) closes the window. The gold button (in the middle) minimizes the window, which shrinks it and moves it to the right side of the Dock. The green button maximizes the window, which makes it as large as it needs to be to display all the items in the window until that window fills the screen (and returns it to the previous size, as you learned in the previous section).

→ To learn how to use the Dock, **see** Chapter 5, "Using and Customizing the Dock," **p. 143**.

By default, you can also minimize a window (thus moving it onto the Dock) by double-clicking its title bar.

> **TIP**
>
> If for some reason you don't want to be able to minimize a window by double-clicking in its title bar, open the Appearance pane of the System Preferences application and uncheck the "Minimize when double clicking a window title bar" check box.

The Close, Minimize, and Maximize buttons work even if the window on which they appear is not active. For example, you can close a window that is in the background by clicking its Close button without making the window active first. (When you point to a button on an inactive window, the button becomes colored so that you know it is active, even though the window itself is not.)

> **TIP**
>
> As under previous versions of the Mac OS, you can close all open Finder windows by holding down the Option key while you click the Close button in one of the windows.

MOVING FINDER WINDOWS

You can move a Finder window around the desktop by dragging its title bar or its left, right, or bottom borders.

> **NOTE**
>
> If the Places sidebar is collapsed, you can't move the window by dragging its left border. That's because this is actually the Places sidebar's Resize handle.

USING THE ICON, LIST, OR COLUMN VIEWS FOR A FINDER WINDOW

You can view Finder windows in three different views: Icon, List, and Column.

VIEWING A FINDER WINDOW IN ICON VIEW

You can easily argue that icons made the Mac. Using friendly pictures to represent files and folders made the computer much friendlier and more approachable than any command line could ever hope to be. Mac OS X version 10.4 continues the use of icons to represent objects, and with their improved appearance under OS X, icons have never looked so good.

You can view Finder windows in the Icon view by opening a window and then selecting View, As Icons; by pressing ⌘-1; or by clicking the Icon view button in the toolbar (see Figure 3.4). The objects in the window become icons, and if you have never seen OS X icons before, prepare to be impressed.

Icon view button

Figure 3.4
Other operating systems might have copied the Mac's icons, but none can compare to the snazzy look of Mac OS X.

→ You can customize the Icon view for Finder windows. **See** "Customizing Finder Windows," **p. 77**.

If you find that a window in the Icon view is messy, you can use the Clean Up command (View, Clean Up) to straighten up the window for you. This command neatly arranges icons so they line up in an orderly fashion.

TIP

If you select one or more icons and open the View menu, you'll see that the command is now Clean Up Selection. This places the selected items back in an orderly location.

To arrange icons by a specific criterion, select View, Arrange By, and then select the criterion by which you want the window's icons ordered. Your options are the following: Name, Date Modified, Date Created, Size, Kind, or Label.

Although the Icon view is clearly the most pleasing view to look at, it is one of the least useful in terms of the information you see.

VIEWING A FINDER WINDOW IN LIST VIEW

The List view presents more information than does the Icon view (see Figure 3.5). To switch to the List view, click the List view button; select View, as List; or press ⌘-2.

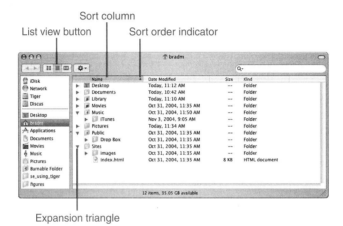

Sort column
List view button | Sort order indicator

Figure 3.5
At the top of the window are the same controls that are visible in the Icon view. However, the lower part of the window contains more information than is available in the Icon view.

Expansion triangle

The information in the List view is organized into columns, with a header at the top of the column indicating the information in it. The information in the List view is always sorted—you can select the column that is used to sort the contents of the window. You can also determine the order in which the columns appear, change the width of columns, and expand or collapse the contents of folders. The information for each item you see in the default List view is the following:

- **Name**—This is the filename for files, the folder name for folders, the volume name for volumes, and so on.

- **Date Modified**—The most recent date on which the object was changed. If the date is the current date, the time at which the object was changed is shown.

- **Size**—The size of the item, in kilobytes (KB), megabytes (MB), or gigabytes (GB). By default, the size of folders is not calculated (you can set Mac OS X to calculate folder sizes if that information is important to you).

- **Kind**—The type of object it is, such as folder, document, application, volume, and so on.

→ You can customize the List view for a single window or for all windows. **See** "Customizing Finder Windows," **p. 77**.

The column by which the window is sorted is highlighted with the highlight color (blue or graphite). To change the sort column, click the Column heading of the column by which you want the list to be sorted. That heading is highlighted and the list is re-sorted by that criterion. At the right edge of the column heading for the column by which the window is sorted, you see the Sort order indicator. This shows you in which direction the list is sorted. For example, if the list is sorted by the Name column, an up arrow indicates that the list is sorted alphabetically and a down arrow indicates that the list is sorted in reverse alphabetical order. To change the direction of the sort, click the Column heading—the list is sorted in the opposite order (from ascending to descending or from descending to ascending).

You can resize a column by moving the pointer to the right edge of the column heading. When you do, the cursor changes from the pointer to a vertical line with outward-facing arrows on each side of it. When you see this cursor, drag the column border to resize the column.

You can change the order in which columns appear by dragging the column heading of the column you want to move and dropping it in the new location. The columns reshuffle and then appear in the order you have indicated.

NOTE

> You can't change the location of the Name column; it is always the first column in a window in List view.

One of the other benefits of the List view is that you can expand the contents of a folder so you can view them without having to open the folder's window first. To do this, click the right-facing Expansion triangle next to the folder's name. The folder expands, and its contents are listed in the window. Click the triangle again to collapse the folder down to its icon.

TIP

> When you Option-click the Expansion triangle for a collapsed folder, the folder and all the folders it contains are expanded. When you Option-click the Expansion triangle for an expanded folder, the folder and all its contents are collapsed again.

VIEWING A FINDER WINDOW IN COLUMN VIEW

The Column view was introduced for Mac OS X, and its benefit is that you can use it to quickly see and navigate levels of the hierarchy (see Figure 3.6). To switch to the Column view, click the Column view button on the toolbar; press ⌘-3; or select View, as Columns.

NOTE

> One reason the Column view is so important is that you use this view to navigate within Open, Save, and other dialog boxes. When you are using the Column view in dialog boxes, it works just as it does in Finder windows.

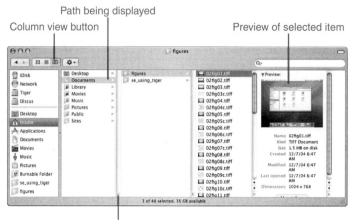

Path being displayed

Column view button

Preview of selected item

Figure 3.6
The Column view is a great way to see the hierarchical organization of directories and folders.

Column resize handle

As you might suspect, in the Column view, the window is organized into columns, with each column representing a level of the file organization hierarchy. The leftmost column shows the highest level you can see, each column to its right shows the next level down the structure, and the column on the far right shows the lowest level you can see. When you select a file, the rightmost column shows a preview of the selected file. The "path" at which you are looking is indicated by the highlighted items in each column.

Folder icons have a right-facing arrow at the right edge of the column in which they appear, to indicate that when you select them, their contents appear in the column to the immediate right.

For example, put a Finder window in the Column view and click your Home folder on the Places sidebar to see its contents. The Home folder's contents are shown in the first column in the window (refer to Figure 3.6). If you click one of the folders in your Home folder, it becomes highlighted and its contents appear in one of the middle columns. As you select folders within folders, their contents appear in the column to their right. This continues all the way down into a folder until it contains no more folders.

You can move down into the hierarchy by clicking the item about which you want more detail. The column to the right of the item on which you click shows the contents of what you click. If you click something in the right column and the window is not large enough to display the contents of all the columns, the view shifts and the columns appear to move to the left. You can use this approach to quickly see the contents of any folder on your Mac, no matter how far down in the hierarchy it is stored.

TIP

One of the best reasons to use the Column view is that you can move inside a window with the arrow keys on the keyboard. This is the fastest way to move among the folders and files on your Mac.

When there are more columns than can be displayed in the window, you can use the scrollbars to view all the columns. Scrolling to the left moves up the hierarchy, whereas scrolling to the right moves down the hierarchy. You can also make the window larger to view more columns at the same time.

You can resize the width of the columns in a window by dragging the resize handle located in the lower-right corner of each column. Each column in a window can have a different width.

When you click a file to select it, the far-right column shows a large icon or a preview of the file and information about that file is displayed (refer to Figure 3.6).

If you click document files for which Mac OS X can create a preview, you see the preview in the column. If the file you select has dynamic content, you can play that content in the preview that you see in the Column view. For example, if you select a QuickTime movie, you can use the QuickTime Player controls to watch the movie without opening the file. Certain types of text files are also displayed so you can read them (scrollbars appear in the column to enable you to read the entire document). You can also see large thumbnail views of graphics stored in certain formats. For those items that Mac OS X cannot create previews of (an application is one example), you see a large icon instead of a preview.

NOTE

> If you switch from the Column view to one of the other views, the contents of the folder you most recently selected are shown in the window.

If you prefer not to see the preview, there are two ways to hide it. You can hide it in individual windows or you can hide it by using the View Options.

To hide the preview in specific windows, click the Expansion triangle next to the word `Preview` that appears just above the preview of a selected file in the Preview pane. This hides all previews for the current window and shows detailed information about the item that is selected, along with the More info button (which opens the Info window that you will learn about later).

→ To learn about the Column view's View Options, **see** "Customizing the Column View," **p. 87**.

NAVIGATING FINDER WINDOWS

Mac OS X includes many features that enable you to navigate Finder windows. The two basic navigation tasks you do are moving around inside Finder windows (to select items, for example) and changing the contents of Finder windows to view other volumes or folders.

USING THE KEYBOARD TO SELECT ITEMS IN A FINDER WINDOW

Although you can use the mouse to point to and click items to select them (or double-click to open them), moving to items and selecting them using the keyboard can be faster. There are two basic ways to navigate inside a window using the keyboard.

You can type an item's name to move to and select it. The OS matches item names as you type, so most of the time you don't need to type the item's whole name to move to it (for example, typing "mp3" moves you to the first item whose name begins with mp3). The more of the name you type, the more specific your movement becomes.

You can also move among items using the Tab and arrow keys. How this works depends on the view you are using for the windows.

USING THE KEYBOARD TO SELECT ITEMS IN THE ICON VIEW

When you are in the Icon view, pressing the Tab key selects the next item according to alphabetical order. Holding down the Shift key while you press Tab moves you among the items in reverse alphabetical order.

You can also use the arrow keys to move to and select items. The keys work just as you might expect. The up-arrow key moves you up the window, the right-arrow key moves you right, and so on.

The window will scroll automatically to keep the items you select in view.

USING THE KEYBOARD TO SELECT ITEMS IN THE LIST VIEW

When a window is shown in List view, you can use the up- and down-arrow keys to move up and down the list of items in the window.

When you select an item, you can use the right-arrow key to expand it and the left-arrow key to collapse it.

TIP

> The Option key works with the arrow keys as well. If you hold down the Option key and press the right-arrow key, all the folders within the selected folder are expanded as well.

USING THE KEYBOARD TO SELECT ITEMS IN THE COLUMN VIEW

In the Column view, the right-arrow key moves you down the hierarchy, whereas the left-arrow key moves you up the hierarchy. The up- and down-arrow keys enable you to move up and down within a selected folder (which appears in a column).

Using these keys, you can move around your directories rapidly. As you move through the structure using these keys, the window scrolls so that you always see the currently selected item. It maintains your view at all times so you can quickly jump into different areas without scrolling manually.

When you get used to it, using the keyboard in combination with the Column view is the fastest way to navigate Mac OS X Finder windows.

TIP

After you have selected an item, press ⌘-Down arrow to open it. For example, you when you select an application and press these keys, the application will launch.

USING THE FINDER WINDOW'S SEARCH TOOL TO SELECT ITEMS

Under version 10.4, the Finder window toolbar's Search tool transforms a folder into a Smart folder. You can set the criterion used and the smart folder will find all folders and files that meet this criterion and display them in the folder's Finder window. To search for files or folders, perform the following steps:

1. Open a Finder window.

2. Type the text or numbers for which you want to search in the Finder window Search box. As you type, the Finder starts finding folders and files that meet your search criterion and displays them for you (see Figure 3.7). The items listed can be displayed by choosing the location in which you are interested. These are shown at the top of the window. From left to right they are the folder currently selected, your Home folder, or your Computer. The status of the search is shown in the lower-right corner of the window; when the "moving circle" is displayed, the search is underway.

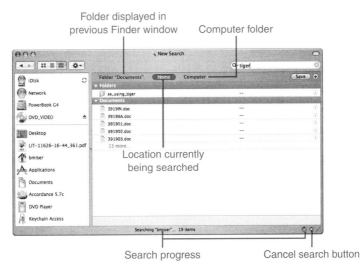

Folder displayed in previous Finder window   Computer folder

Figure 3.7
A smart folder gets its name for good reason; as you type something in the Search tool, files and folders that match what you type are displayed in the Finder window.

Location currently being searched

Search progress   Cancel search button

3. Select the location in which you want to see items that match your search. For example, to find items anywhere on your computer, click Computer. The window will be refreshed and you will see items that match your search criterion that are located in the location you selected.

4. When you find an item in which you are interested, click in the Contents pane and use the up- and down-arrow keys to select the item in the upper pane. Its location will appear in the lower pane of the window (see Figure 3.8).

Figure 3.8
You can use the Finder window Search tool to search various areas of your Mac for files and folders that include specific text in their names.

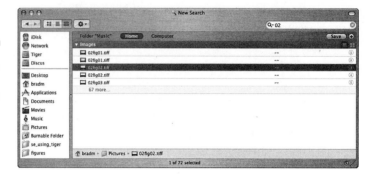

5. If you want to clear the search and return to the previous Finder window, click the Clear Search button, which is the "x" located in the right end of the Search tool.

→ To learn more about Smart folders, **see** "Searching Your Mac with Smart Folders," **p. 123**.

NAVIGATING UP AND DOWN THE DIRECTORY STRUCTURE

There are several ways to move up and down the directory structure within Finder windows. You can use the keyboard as discussed in the previous section. You can also use the icons in the Places sidebar as well as the Path pop-up menu. The Go menu enables you to jump to specific directories quickly.

CHANGING DIRECTORIES WITH THE PLACES SIDEBAR

The Finder's Places sidebar is a fast way to change the directory displayed in the current Finder window. The sidebar contains icons that take you to specific directories. As you read earlier, the sidebar contains two panes. The upper pane shows all the mounted volumes, including your hard disks, network drives, iDisk, CDs, DVDs, and so on. The lower pane shows your Home folder, some of the folders it contains (such as the Desktop and Documents folders), the Applications folder; and any folders, documents, or applications you have added manually. You can customize the items that appear on the sidebar to suit your preferences.

→ To learn how to customize the sidebar, **see** "Customizing the Places Sidebar," **p. 77**.

To view the contents of an item shown in the sidebar, simply click its icon. The right pane of the Finder window shows the contents of the item you select. For example, if you click your Home folder (the icon with your user account short name as its name), you'll see the contents of your Home folder in the Contents pane of the Finder window.

USING THE BACK AND FORWARD BUTTONS TO MOVE AMONG FINDER WINDOWS

Click the Back button on the toolbar to move back to the previous Finder window in the current Finder window chain. You can continue to click the Back button as many times as you want until you reach the first window you viewed using the current Finder window chain; at that point, the Back button is grayed out. Similarly, the Forward button moves you forward in a chain of Finder windows. You can also use the Go, Back and the Go, Forward commands to move back in the chain or forward in the chain, respectively.

TIP

> You can press ⌘-[to move back and ⌘-] to move forward.

→ To learn how to customize the toolbar, **see** "Customizing the Toolbar," **p. 79**.

If you open a new Finder window, the Back and Forward buttons are grayed out because there is no window to move back or forward to. Opening a new Finder window starts a new chain of windows, so both buttons are disabled. As soon as you open a second window within the same Finder window chain, the Back button becomes active. If you move back along that chain of windows, the Forward button becomes active.

CHANGING DIRECTORIES WITH THE PATH POP-UP MENU

The Path pop-up menu enables you to quickly move up and down the directory structure of your Mac. To change directories, hold down the ⌘ key and click the window name in the title bar of a Finder window. When you do so, you see all the directories from the one currently displayed in the window up to the Computer directory (which is the highest level on your Mac). Select a directory from the menu and the Finder window displays the directory you chose.

You can add the Path button to your toolbar so you can select a directory without using the ⌘ key.

→ To learn how to add buttons to the toolbar, **see** "Customizing the Toolbar," **p. 79**.

TIP

> You can also move up the directory structure by pressing ⌘-Up arrow, which is the keyboard shortcut for the Enclosing Folder command that moves to the folder enclosing the item you are currently viewing.

CHANGING DIRECTORIES WITH THE GO MENU

The Finder's Go menu enables you to move into many areas of your Mac. The menu is divided into several areas that contain various kinds of options (see Figure 3.9).

Figure 3.9
The Go menu provides quick access to various folders on your Mac.

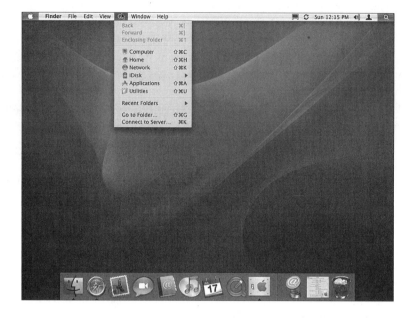

At the top of the menu are the Back and Forward commands, which do the same thing as the Back and Forward buttons on the toolbar.

Just under these commands is the Enclosing Folder command. When you are displaying an item in a Finder window and press ⌘-up arrow or select Go, Enclosing Folder, the folder that contains the currently selected item is shown in the Finder window.

You can also use the Finder's Go menu to open specific directories. To do so, open the Go menu and select the directory you want to view. Its contents replace those shown in the active Finder window (if no Finder windows are active, the directory's contents appear in a new Finder window). For example, to display your Home folder, select Go, Home.

> **TIP**
>
> Keyboard shortcuts are available for the specific directories on the Go menu. See the "Mac OS X to the Max" section at the end of this chapter for a list of these shortcuts.

If you select Go, Recent Folders, you can quickly move back to one of the folders you have recently viewed (you can set the number of recent folders on this list using the Appearance pane of the System Preferences application).

> **TIP**
>
> To clear the list of recent folders, choose Go, Recent Folder, Clear Menu.

You can also move to a folder using the Go to Folder command. Select Go, Go to Folder to see the Go to Folder dialog box (see Figure 3.10). You can type a pathname in this dialog box and click Go to open a Finder window for that directory. Following are some tips on how to type pathnames:

- Pathnames are case sensitive.
- A slash (/) separates each level in the path.
- Almost all paths should begin and end with the slash (/).
- The exception to the previous rule is when you want to move to a specific user's Home directory, in which case you can just type ~*username*/, where *username* is the short name for the user's account.
- If the path begins with the directory on which Mac OS X is stored, you can skip that directory name and start the path beginning with the next level. If it is on another volume, you can include that volume's name at the beginning of the path.

Figure 3.10
This Go to Folder directory shows the path to the Movies folder within my Home folder.

Although you should be careful to use the proper case in pathnames, sometimes it doesn't make a difference. For example, the path to the Mac OS X System directory can be /SYSTEM/, /system/, or /System/. Sometimes, however, the case of the path you type must match exactly, so it is good practice to always match the case of the directory names you type.

Table 3.1 provides some examples of paths you would enter in the Go to Folder dialog box to move to specific directories.

TABLE 3.1   PATHS TO SPECIFIC DIRECTORIES

Location	Path
Directory called Documents on a volume named Mac OS 9	`/Mac OS 9/Documents/`
The Documents folder in the Home directory for the user account with the short name `bmiser`	`~bmiser/Documents/`
The Mac OS X System Folder	`/System/`
A folder called `Ch_02_figs` located in the Documents directory in the user bmiser's Home folder	`~bmiser/Documents/Ch_02_figs`

Following are some additional tips for the Go to Folder command:

- You can open the Go to Folder dialog box by pressing ⌘-Shift-G. Type the path and press Return to move there.

- If you are patient when you type, Mac OS X will try to match the path you are typing and complete it for you. This usually takes more time than typing it yourself, but if the path is filled in for you, press Return to accept that path entered for you to move there.

- The most recent path you have typed remains in the Go to Folder dialog box; you can modify this path to move to a different directory.

TIP

> Although pathnames should end in /, you don't really have to type the last /. If it is needed, Mac OS X adds it for you. If not, the path works without it.

NOTE

> You can use the Connect to Server command to move to directories located on your network.

→ To learn how to connect to servers, **see** "Accessing Shared Files from a Mac OS X Computer," **p. 948**.

CHANGING DIRECTORIES WITH THE KEYBOARD

One of the cool navigation features of Mac OS X is the capability to move up and down the directory structure using only the keyboard. Use the previous tips to select an item, and then press ⌘-down arrow to move into the item, such as a folder, an application, a document, and so on. For example, if you use the Tab key to select an application icon and then press ⌘-down arrow, that application opens. Similarly, if you press this key combination when you have a folder selected, the contents of that folder are shown in its previous view state.

This technique also works in the Column view to open applications or documents. When you are viewing folders and volumes, you don't need to hold down the ⌘ key because, in the Column view, the contents of a folder or volume are displayed when you select it.

To move up the directory structure, press ⌘-up arrow.

CUSTOMIZING FINDER WINDOWS

Mac OS X enables you to customize many aspects of Finder windows, including the Places sidebar, the toolbar, the status bar, and the views you use.

CUSTOMIZING THE PLACES SIDEBAR

The Places sidebar provides a convenient way to access the mounted volumes on your Mac along with specific folders, documents, and applications (see Figure 3.11). As you read earlier, the upper pane of the sidebar shows all the mounted volumes on your Mac and the lower pane shows folders, documents, and applications. By default, you will see several of the folders within your Home folder, the Applications folder, and a Burn folder, but you can add or remove folders, documents, or applications to this area to customize it.

Figure 3.11
The Places sidebar makes getting into any mounted volume on your Mac or into specific folders easy.

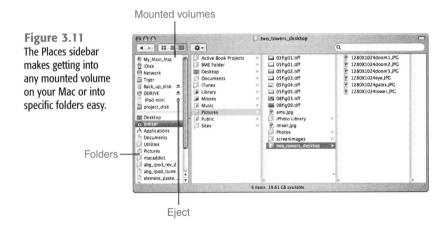

Mounted volumes

Folders

Eject

You can also store files in the lower pane of the Places sidebar.

To view the contents of a volume or folder, click it; its contents will appear in the Contents pane of the Finder window. For volumes, a button enables you to perform an action. For example, when you have an ejectable volume, such as a disk image or DVD, you can click an

Eject button. When you have inserted a blank CD or DVD, you can click the Burn button that appears to burn the disc.

Determining the Default Items in the Places Sidebar

Finder preferences determine which items appear in the Places sidebar. To set them, follow these steps:

1. Select Finder, Preferences or press ⌘-,.
2. Click the Sidebar tab (see Figure 3.12).

Figure 3.12
Use the Sidebar pane of the Finder Preferences window to configure the default items in the Places sidebar.

3. Check the check box next to each item you want to appear in the Places sidebar.
4. Uncheck the box next to each item you don't want to appear in the sidebar.

The next time you view a Finder window, its sidebar will contain the items you specified.

Organizing Your Places Sidebar

You can further organize the Places sidebar by doing the following tasks:

- You can add any folder or file to the Places sidebar by dragging it onto the lower pane of the sidebar.
- You can also add a folder or file to the sidebar by selecting it and selecting File, Add To Sidebar or pressing ⌘-T.
- You can remove folders from the sidebar by dragging them out of the sidebar. When you do, they disappear in a puff of smoke. Of course, the original item isn't affected.

NOTE

> If you remove an item whose check box is checked on the Sidebar pane of the Finder Preferences window, that folder is removed and its check box becomes unchecked in the Preferences window.

- Resize the sidebar to make it fill up more or less of the Finder window (your change lasts only as long as the current Finder window chain).
- You can also collapse it by double-clicking its Resize handle.
- Drag icons up and down within the lower pane of the sidebar to reorganize them.

As you add, remove, or reorganize the sidebar, it is resized automatically. As the Finder window in which it appears is resized, the Places sidebar is also resized so that you can see as much of it as possible.

CUSTOMIZING THE TOOLBAR

Along the top of Finder windows, you see the toolbar. This toolbar contains the Back and Forward buttons, the View buttons, the Action menu (covered in a later section), and the Search tool. As with the sidebar, you can customize many aspects of this toolbar. You can show or hide it and customize the tools it contains.

NOTE

> Many applications, especially those that come with Mac OS X, also provide a Mac OS X toolbar in their windows. You can use these same techniques to work with those toolbars.

SHOWING OR HIDING THE TOOLBAR

You can hide or show the toolbar in a Finder window in any of the following ways:

- Click the Show/Hide Toolbar button in the upper-right corner of the Finder window.
- Select View, Hide Toolbar or View, Show Toolbar.
- Press Option-⌘-T.

The state of the toolbar controls how new Finder windows open when they are viewed in the Icon or List view. If the toolbar is displayed, new Finder windows open according to the preferences you set using the Finder Preferences dialog box. If the toolbar is hidden, new Finder windows always open in a separate window.

When you open a new Finder window from a window in which the toolbar is hidden (for example, by holding down the Option key when you open a new Finder window), the toolbar is hidden in the new window. When you open a Finder window from a window in which the toolbar is shown, the toolbar is shown in the new window as well.

The toolbar state in currently open Finder windows is independent. For example, you can show the toolbar in one Finder window while it is hidden in another. In fact, if you have two Finder windows for the same directory open at the same time, you can hide the toolbar in one window while it is shown in the other.

CHANGING THE TOOLS ON THE TOOLBAR

The default toolbar contains various useful buttons, but you can customize its content by adding tools to it or removing tools from it:

1. Open a Finder window.

2. Select View, Customize Toolbar. The contents of the Finder window are replaced by the Toolbar customization window (see Figure 3.13).

Figure 3.13
You can add buttons to or remove them from the toolbar using the Customize Toolbar command.

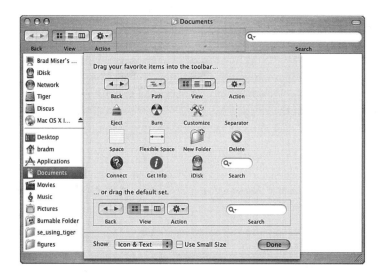

3. To add a button to the toolbar, drag it from the window to the toolbar, placing it in the location where you want it. (Table 3.2 lists the available buttons and what they do.)

   When you move a button between two current buttons on the toolbar, existing buttons slide apart to make room for the new button.

   NOTE

   If you place more buttons on the toolbar than can be shown in the current window's width, a set of double arrows appears at the right edge of the toolbar. Click this to pop up a menu showing the additional buttons.

4. Remove a button from the toolbar by dragging it off the toolbar.

5. Change the location of the icons by dragging them. You can move buttons and menus that you add as well as those that are installed by default.

6. Use the Show pop-up menu to determine whether the buttons have text and an icon, text only, or an icon only.

7. To use the small icon size, check the Use Small Size check box.

8. Click Done.

The toolbar now reflects the changes you made (see Figure 3.14).

Figure 3.14
Now I am using a customized toolbar.

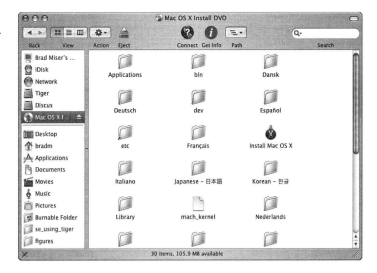

TABLE 3.2   USEFUL TOOLBAR BUTTONS

Button Name	What It Does
Back/Forward	Moves you back or forward in a chain of Finder windows.
Path	Pops up a menu that shows the path to the current directory. You can select a directory on the pop-up menu to move there.
View	Changes the view for the current window.

continues

TABLE 3.2 CONTINUED

Button Name	What It Does
Action	Provides a pop-up menu with access to various context-sensitive commands.
Eject	Enables you to eject items, such as mounted volumes, CD-ROM discs, and so on, from the desktop.
Burn	Enables you to burn a CD-R, CD-RW, or DVD-R.
Customize	Enables you to open the Customize Toolbar window.
Separator	A graphic element you can use to organize your toolbar.
Space	Adds a block of space to the toolbar.
Flexible Space	Adds a block of flexible space to the toolbar.
New Folder	Creates a new folder.
Delete	Deletes the selected item.
Connect	Opens the Connect to Server dialog box.
Find	Opens the Finder's Find tool.
Get Info	Opens the Get Info window for a selected item.
iDisk	Accesses your iDisk.
Search	Enables you to search Finder windows.

TIP

If you add more buttons than can be displayed and then want to remove some of the buttons you can't see (you see the double arrows instead), you have to make the window wider so that you can see the button on the toolbar to remove it; you can't remove a button from the pop-up menu. You can also temporarily remove other buttons until you can see the one you want to remove.

CUSTOMIZING THE STATUS BAR

The status bar provides status information for the current directory, volume, or whatever else is being displayed in the Finder window. Mostly, the status bar provides information about the number of items in the window and the amount of free space on the current volume.

Where the status bar is displayed depends on whether the toolbar is shown.

If the toolbar is shown, the status bar information is displayed at the bottom of the window. For example, if you are viewing a folder, the number of items it contains and the amount of space available on the drive on which it is stored will be shown.

If the toolbar is hidden, the status bar appears immediately under the title bar (see Figure 3.15). As with the toolbar, you can hide or show the status bar using the View menu. Unlike the toolbar, however, you can't change the contents of the status bar.

Figure 3.15
When the toolbar is hidden, the status bar appears immediately under the title bar. (Finder windows look a bit pitiful without the toolbar and Places sidebar, don't they?)

CUSTOMIZING FINDER WINDOW VIEWS

For each view type of Finder window view, you can set Global view preferences that affect all windows you open using that view type. You can then set Window options for individual windows to override the global settings for that view type for that specific window. For example, one of the customization options for the List view is the data you see in the window. You can choose to display the Comments column for a window in List view. If you set this as a Global preference, each time you open a new window in List view, you see the Comments column. If there is a window in which you don't want to see the Comments column, you can change the Window preferences for that window so the Comments column is not displayed.

When you change a Global preference, which is called the "All windows" option, it affects all windows shown in that view. When you change a window's preference, called "This window only," it affects only the current window.

CUSTOMIZING THE ICON VIEW

The Icon view has the following view options:

- **Icon size**—You can set the relative size of the icons you see.
- **Text size**—You can set the size of text displayed next to the icons you see.
- **Label position**—You can set the location of the text next to icons. Your choices are on the bottom or to the right of the icon.
- **Snap to grid**—With this option enabled, icons align themselves to an invisible grid.

- **Show item info**—With this option enabled, you see information for the items in a window. The information you see depends on the items being displayed. For example, when the window shows volumes, you see the total space on the volume and the free space on each volume. When you view folders, you see the number of items in that folder. When you see files, information about the file is shown, such as the sizes of image files.

- **Show icon preview**—By default, graphic file icons contain a preview of the file's content within the icon. Some types of files don't include this icon information and their icon doesn't contain a preview. If you turn this preference on, Mac OS X creates a preview of the file in the file's icon even if the file type doesn't include one by default.

- **Keep arranged by**—You can choose to keep icons grouped by a criterion you select, including Name, Date Modified, Date Created, Size, Kind, and Label.

- **Background**—You can choose the background used for a Finder window. Your choices are White, a color of your choice, or a picture of your choice. If you select Color or Picture, tools appear to enable you to select the color or picture you want to use.

Set your Global preferences for the Icon view using the following steps:

1. Open a Finder window so you can preview the preferences you will set.

2. Select View, Show View Options or press ⌘-J. The View Options window appears (see Figure 3.16). You use this window to set both global and window settings. At the top of the window is the name of the folder you are currently viewing.

Figure 3.16
The View Options window enables you to customize Finder window views.

3. Click the "All windows" radio button.

4. Use the Icon size slider to set the relative size of the icons you see. As you move the slider, the icons in the open window reflect the size you set. When you are happy with the size of the icons, release the slider.

5. Use the "Text size" pop-up menu to set the size of the icon labels.

6. Use the radio buttons in the "Label position" area to select the location of icon labels.

7. Use the four check boxes to enable or disable the options described in the previous bulleted list.

8. If you enabled "Keep arranged by," select the criterion by which you want icons grouped using the pop-up menu (Name is selected by default).

9. Select the folder background option by selecting one of the radio buttons under Background.

10. If you chose Color, use the Color button to open the Color Picker to select the background color you want to use.

11. If you chose Picture, click the Select button, and then use the Select a Picture dialog box to select a background image.

> **NOTE**
>
> Supported image formats include PICT, TIFF, and JPEG. The background image you choose appears in folders you view using the Global icon settings. This does not affect any image you are using as a background image on your desktop.

After you have made these settings, any window you view in Icon view will be displayed using your global preferences unless you override the Global settings by setting a window's preference.

To change the preferences for an individual window, do the following:

1. Open the window you want to view and put it in the Icon view.

2. Open the View Options window by selecting View, Show View Options (or press ⌘-J).

3. Click the "This window only" radio button.

4. Use the controls to set the Icon view preferences for the window you opened in step 1 (see the previous steps for help).

This window uses the preferences you set for it until you change them.

> **TIP**
>
> You can also modify the view of the desktop, which is always in Icon view. Click anywhere on the desktop and open the View Options window. You can then set the icon size, text size, and other options just like a folder window (except for the folder background that is set using the Desktop pane of the System Preferences Utility).

You can reapply the global preferences to a window at any time by returning to the View Options dialog box and clicking the "All windows" radio button. The window returns to your global view settings. Click "This window only" to return the window to its previous set of view options.

3

> **TIP**
>
> You can leave the View Options window open while you select other windows. If you do so, the name shown at the top of the dialog box changes, as do the controls you see if the window you select is in a view different from the current one.

CUSTOMIZING THE LIST VIEW

Customizing List view works pretty much the same way as Icon view, except that you have different options.

Set your global List view preferences using the following steps:

1. Open a Finder window in List view.
2. Open the View Options window (⌘-J).
3. Click the "All windows" radio button.
4. Check the radio button for the icon size you want to use.
5. Select the text size on the "Text size" pop-up menu.
6. Check the boxes next to the data columns you want to be displayed in List view. The default data are Date Modified, Size, and Kind. The other data available are Date Created, Version, Comments, and Label. Data for which you check the boxes is displayed in columns in the List view.
7. Check the "Use relative dates" check box if you want to use relative dates. When you use the relative dates option, you see relative date information (such as yesterday) for some dates rather than the full date for all dates.
8. Check the "Calculate all sizes" check box if you want the size of folders to be displayed in the Size column. This option uses extra computing power, especially for those folders that contain many folders and files. You should usually leave this box unchecked unless folder size information is critical to you.

Every window you see in List view uses these options, unless you override the Global settings for a particular window.

Overriding the Global options for a specific window is analogous to what you do for the Icon view. Open the window, open the View Options window, click the "This window only" radio button, and use the controls to set the view options for the current window.

To reapply the global List view preferences to a window, click the "All windows" radio button in the View Options window.

> **TIP**
>
> The Window settings for a window are retained (although not used) even after you reapply the global settings to it. You can easily switch back to them by clicking the "This window only" radio button again. The window returns to the most recent window settings you applied to it.

CUSTOMIZING THE COLUMN VIEW

The Column view has fewer customization options than the other views. The Column view preferences you set apply to all windows in the Column view. Do the following:

1. Open a Finder window in Column view.
2. Open the View Options window (⌘-J).
3. Uncheck the "Show icons" check box to hide the icons in the window.
4. Uncheck the "Show preview column" check box if you prefer not to see the preview of a file you have selected in the window.

NOTE

As far as I can tell, there isn't a way to select the List view or the Icon view for every window you open (you can set the Column view for every new window you open by using Finder Preferences). The Finder remembers the view you used the last time you opened a specific window and maintains that view each time you open that window—until you change that window's view. Unfortunately, you can't set the view to be List or Icon on a systemwide basis.

Similarly, you can't tell the Finder to apply the global view preferences to all windows at the same time. If you have changed the view preferences for individual windows, you have to reapply the global view preferences to that window if you want to use them (by using the View Options window).

3

WORKING WITH THE FINDER WINDOW'S ACTION POP-UP MENU

One of the default tools on the Finder window toolbar is the Action pop-up menu (see Figure 3.17). This menu provides access to context-sensitive commands, which means that commands on the menu depend on the item you have selected on the desktop. For example, when you select a folder and open the menu, you see commands including New Folder, New Burn folder, Open, Get Info, Move to Trash, Make Alias, Create Archive, Copy, Paste, Show View Options, and Color Label. If you select a file and open the menu, you see New Folder, New Burn folder, Open, Open With, Print, Get Info, Move to Trash, Duplicate, Create Alias, Create Archive, Copy, and Color Label.

NOTE

As you probably suspect, the commands on the Action pop-up menu are similar to the commands on an item's contextual menu, which you can open by pointing to an item, holding down the Control key, and clicking the item (or right-clicking the item if you use a two-button mouse). If you do this, you'll see a couple more options on the contextual menu that you will learn about later in this book.

To use a command on the menu, select the item on which you want to use the command, open the menu, and select the command you want to use.

Figure 3.17
The commands on the Action pop-up menu change depending on the items you have selected.

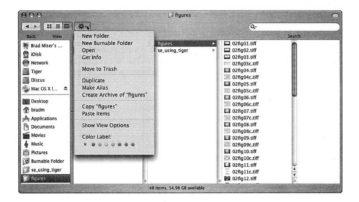

WORKING WITH LABELS

Labels enable you to color code and text code files and folders as a means of identifying and organizing them. For example, you can assign all the folders for a specific project using the same label. In addition to making the relationship between these folders clearer, you can choose to group items within a window by label, which keeps them near one another as well. You can also use Smart Folders to automatically gather files and folders that have the same label.

SETTING UP LABELS

You can assign text to the color labels by following these steps:

1. Open the Finder Preferences window.

2. Click the Labels button to open the Labels pane, which contains the seven label colors. Next to each color is its text label, which by default is the name of the color.

3. Edit the text labels for each color to match your label needs. For example, you can replace the color with the name of a project.

APPLYING LABELS

You can apply labels to a folder or file by following these steps:

1. Select the items to which you want to apply a label.

2. Open the Action pop-up menu or the contextual menu.

3. Select the label you want to apply to the selected labels.

When an item has a label applied to it and you view the enclosing folder in Icon view, its name is highlighted in the label's color. When you view a window in the Columns or List view, a large dot filled with the label color appears next to the item you have labeled. If you view a window in the List view and select to show the Label column, the label text appears in the Label column for the item.

TIP

> If you view a window in Icon view, you can choose to keep items grouped by label. This keeps all the files with which you have associated a specific location together in the window.

MAC OS X TO THE MAX: FINDER WINDOW KEYBOARD SHORTCUTS

Table 3.3 lists keyboard shortcuts for working with Finder windows.

TABLE 3.3   KEYBOARD SHORTCUTS FOR FINDER WINDOWS

Menu	Action	Keyboard Shortcut
None	Opens an item on the Places sidebar and closes the current window	Option-click
None	Opens an item on the Places sidebar in a new Finder window	⌘-click
None	Closes all open Finder windows	Option-click the Close button
None	Opens an item in a new Finder window	⌘-double-click a folder
Finder	Preferences	⌘-,
File	New Finder Window	⌘-N
File	New Folder	Shift-⌘-N
File	New Smart Folder	Option-⌘-N
File	Open	⌘-O
File	Close Window	⌘-W
File	Get Info	⌘-I
File	Show Original	⌘-R
File	Add to Sidebar	⌘-T
View	as Icons	⌘-1
View	as List	⌘-2
View	as Columns	⌘-3
View	Show/Hide Toolbar	Option-⌘-T
View	Show/Hide View Options	⌘-J
Go	Back	⌘-[
Go	Back	⌘-]
Go	Enclosing Folder	⌘-up arrow

continues

3

TABLE 3.3 CONTINUED

Menu	Action	Keyboard Shortcut
Go	Computer	Shift-⌘-C
Go	Home	Shift-⌘-H
Go	Network	Shift-⌘-K
Go	iDisk, My iDisk	Shift-⌘-I
Go	Applications	Shift-⌘-A
Go	Utilities	Shift-⌘-U
Go	Go to Folder	Shift-⌘-G
Go	Connect to Server	⌘-K
Window	Minimize Window	⌘-M
Window	Cycle Through Windows	⌘-`

3

CHAPTER **4**

WORKING ON THE MAC OS X DESKTOP

In this chapter

THE MAC OS X DESKTOP

The Mac's desktop has always been the place from which you work with files, folders, system configuration, and so on (see Figure 4.1). The desktop enables you to manipulate the files and folders on your Mac. You also can access commands that appear nowhere else and can control many aspects of how your system performs. And, of course, you can use the Finder to find folders and files stored on your machine.

Figure 4.1
The most obvious aspects of the Mac OS X's desktop are the beautiful appearance of its icons, the controls provided in Finder windows, and the Dock.

→ For information on viewing and using Finder windows, **see** Chapter 3, "Viewing and Navigating Mac OS X Finder Windows," **p. 55**.

→ Because the Dock is such an important part of Mac OS X, it has a chapter dedicated to it; **see** Chapter 5, "Using and Customizing the Dock," **p. 143**.

WORKING WITH MAC OS X MENUS

One of the strengths of the Mac OS is that it has always featured certain menus that are very similar in all applications.

THE MAC OS X APPLE MENU

The Apple menu has long been one of the staples of the Mac desktop. Its main purpose has always been to provide continuous access to specific commands whether you are working on the desktop or within an application. The Mac OS X Apple menu contains the commands listed in Table 4.1.

TABLE 4.1   COMMANDS ON THE MAC OS X APPLE MENU

Command	What It Does
About This Mac	Opens a window showing the version of Mac OS X installed, the physical RAM installed, the number and type of processors, and the startup disk. You can also open Software Update to get the latest versions of Apple software and the System Profiler from this window to get more information about your Mac.
Software Update	Opens the Software Update tool, which you can use to get the latest versions of the Apple software installed on your Mac.
Mac OS X Software	Opens the default web browser and moves to the Mac OS X software downloads web page.
System Preferences	Opens the System Preferences application.
Dock	Provides control over the Dock's magnification, hiding, and position settings and enables you to open the Dock Preferences pane of the System Preferences application.
Location	Enables you to select a location for your Mac, which changes the network settings you are using.
Recent Items	Provides a menu of applications, documents, and servers that you have recently accessed; you can select an item to move back to it. The menu is organized into separate sections for each type of item. It also has the Clear Menu command, which clears the menu.
Force Quit	Opens the Force Quit Applications window that enables you to kill open applications (for example, when they are hung).
Sleep	Puts the Mac to sleep.
Restart	Restarts the Mac.
Shut Down	Shuts down the Mac.
Log Out *username*	Logs the current user (whose account name is *username*) off the Mac and opens the Login window.

→ To learn more about working with locations, **see** "Configuring and Using Locations," **p. 330**.

→ To learn more about Mac OS X's Force Quit command, **see** "Controlling Open Applications," **p. 241**.

TIP

> If you use an Apple Cinema Display, you can put your Mac to sleep by pressing the Power button on the display. If you are using a PowerBook or iBook, you can put it to sleep by closing its lid.

MAC OS X APPLICATION MENUS

Under Mac OS X, every application has its own Application menu. The Application menu provides the commands you use to control the application in which you are working. A standard set of commands is consistent among all Mac OS X applications, however, specific applications can have additional commands on their Application menu (but they must support at least the standard commands on that menu). The name of the Application menu is the name of the application itself. For example, the desktop's Application menu is the Finder menu (because Finder is the name of the application that controls the desktop).

NOTE

> If you used Mac OS 9 or earlier versions, don't confuse the Application menu in those versions with Application menus under Mac OS X. In versions previous to Mac OS X, the Application menu was a single menu that showed you all the applications running on the computer; this menu was always located in the upper-right corner of the desktop. You used the Application menu to hide or show applications as well as switch between running applications. Under Mac OS X, this functionality is provided by the Dock and the Application menus. You still see the Mac OS 9 Application menu when you use the Classic environment.

The following commands appear on all Application menus:

- **About *Application***—The About *Application* command, where *Application* is the name of the active application, displays version information about the application. Some About windows also provide links to support sites, the publisher's website, and so on. The About Finder command displays the version of the Finder you are using.

- **Preferences**—You use the Preferences command to set the preferences for an application. For example, you can use Finder's Preferences command to control specific properties of the desktop.

→ To learn about Finder Preferences, see "Changing the Desktop's Appearance," **p. 136**.

TIP

> The keyboard shortcut for the Preferences command has been standardized (for all Apple applications and most of those from other sources) to be ⌘-,. This enables you to open the Preferences dialog box for any application with the same keys. This is a good thing.

- **Hide and Show commands**—The Hide and Show commands enable you to control which running applications are visible. There are three of these commands on the Application menu. The Hide *CurrentApplication* command (where *CurrentApplication* is the name of the running application) hides the current application. The Hide Others command hides all the running applications except the current one, and the Show All command shows all open applications.

NOTE

Hiding an application causes all its windows and its menu bar to disappear. The application continues to run and any processes that are underway continue. You can also minimize application windows, which places the window on the Dock; the application's menu bar continues to appear while the application is active, even if its windows are minimized.

All Application menus, except the Finder menu, also contain the following commands:

- **Quit**—The Quit command does the same thing as it always has—it stops the running application.

- **Services**—The Services command provides commands to enable you to work with other applications from within the current application. For example, if you are using the TextEdit word processing application, you see the Grab command on its Services menu. Selecting this command activates the Grab application that enables you to capture something on the screen. After you capture the image, it is automatically pasted into the current TextEdit document. Many other commands appear on this menu; the commands available depend on the applications installed on your Mac and how those applications support the Services menu.

→ To learn more about using the Services command with Mac OS X applications, **see** "Working with Mac OS X Application Menus," **p. 184**.

TIP

The keyboard shortcut for the Quit command hasn't changed. It is still ⌘-Q. When you are working on the desktop, ⌘-Q doesn't do anything because you can't quit the Finder. However, you can relaunch the Finder using the Force Quit command.

4

The Finder's Application menu (the Finder menu) also has the Empty Trash and Secure Empty Trash commands, which are unique to its Application menu. The Empty Trash command does what it always has, which is to delete any files located in the Trash. The Secure Empty Trash deletes files located in the Trash and overwrites the disk space on which those files were stored so they can't be recovered. Because the Secure Empty Trash command overwrites the disk space on which the files where written, it takes much longer to execute than does the Empty Trash command (of course, because it works in the background, that shouldn't slow down your work any).

MAC OS X FILE MENUS

The Mac has always had a File menu; under Mac OS X, this menu is purer than it was in previous versions of the OS. For example, in previous versions, the File menu contained commands for working with files as well as controlling the application. Under Mac OS X, the File menu contains only commands for working with files or folders.

The specific commands you see on an application's File menu depend on the application. Most applications' File menus have the New, Open, Save, Save As, Print, and Page Setup commands. Many other commands might appear on the File menu as well.

The Finder's File menu contains the commands listed in Table 4.2.

TABLE 4.2 COMMANDS ON THE FINDER'S FILE MENU

Command	What It Does
New Finder Window	Opens a new Finder window
New Folder	Creates a new folder
New Smart Folder	Creates a new smart folder
New Burn Folder	Creates a new folder intended to be burned onto a disc
Open	Opens the selected item
Open With	Enables you to open a selected file with a specific application
Print	Enables you to print a selected file
Close Window	Closes the active window
Get Info	Opens the Info window
Duplicate	Creates a duplicate of the selected item
Make Alias	Creates an alias of the selected item
Show Original	Exposes the original item for which an alias was created
Add to Sidebar	Adds an alias of the selected item to the Places Sidebar
Create Archive	Compresses the selected folders and files into a Zip file
Move to Trash	Moves the selected item to the Trash
Eject	Ejects the selected item (disc, disk image, server volume, and so on)
Burn Disc	Burns the selected CD or DVD
Find	Opens the Finder's Find tool so you can locate files and folders
Color Label	Applies the label you choose to the selected items

NOTE

The Mac OS X Archive command is one of the most useful Finder commands. This command enables you to create compressed files from any folders and files on your Mac. Even better, Mac OS X now supports the ZIP compression format, which is the standard, native compression format on Windows computers. You no longer need a separate application to compress files. You can also expand any Zip file from the desktop by simply opening it.

MAC OS X EDIT MENUS

Under Mac OS X, the Edit menu is much as it has always been. The Edit menu contains commands for editing data. When you are working with most applications other than the Finder, the commands that appear on the Edit menu are Cut, Copy, and Paste. Applications can provide many more commands on this menu, such as Undo, Redo, Select All, and so on.

The Finder's Edit menu is somewhat different than this menu under most applications because you don't use the Finder to edit documents. Its commands apply to files and folders instead. For example, when you select a file and choose Edit, Copy, the file is copied. You can move to a different location and choose Edit, Paste to place a copy of the selected item in the new location. The Finder's Edit menu also has the Select All command, which selects everything in the active window; the Show Clipboard command, which shows what has been copied to the Clipboard; and the Special Characters command, which opens the Character palette.

THE FINDER VIEW MENU

The Finder's View menu contains the commands you use to view Finder windows.

→ To learn about using the Finder's View commands, **see** Chapter 3, "Viewing and Navigating Mac OS X Finder Windows," **p. 55**.

THE FINDER GO MENU

The Finder's Go menu, as you might guess from its name, contains commands you use to go places. The Go menu enables you to move to the following locations:

- **Back or Forward**—You can move among the windows in a chain of open Finder windows by using the Back and Forward commands.

- **Enclosing Folder**—You can move into the folder that contains the currently selected item by choosing this command.

- **Directories**—You can move to any of the directories listed on the Go menu by selecting the directory into which you want to move.

- **Recent Folders**—This command lists the most recent folders you have used; select a folder to return to it. You can clear the Recent Folders menu by selecting Clear Menu.

- **Folders**—Use the Go To Folder command to enter the path to a specific folder to open it.

- **Servers**—Use the Connect To Server command to open a server on your network.

→ To learn how to use the Go menu to navigate directories, **see** "Changing Directories with the Go Menu," **p. 73**.

→ To learn how to connect to servers, **see** "Accessing Shared Files from a Mac OS X Computer," **p. 948**.

MAC OS X WINDOW MENUS

Another standard Mac OS X menu is the Window menu. This menu provides commands you use to work with windows that are currently open. Common choices on the Window menu include the following:

4

- **Minimize**—This does the same thing as clicking the Minimize button in a window—it moves a window onto the Dock.

- **Zoom**—This does the same thing as the Maximize button: It makes the active window as large as it needs to be to display all the window's contents or to fill the desktop, whichever comes first. Choosing it again toggles the window back to its previous size.

- **Cycle Through Open Windows**—This moves you among the open windows, one at a time.

- **Bring All to Front**—This command brings all open windows to the front. For example, if you have a lot of open Finder windows and then switch to an application and then back to the Finder, you might not see all your open Finder windows. If you use this command, they all come to the foreground so you can see them.

- **List of Open Windows**—The Window menu always displays a list of the windows open for the application providing that menu. You can switch to an open window by selecting it on the menu.

- **Close Window**—This closes the active window. (You won't see this command on the Finder's Window menu.)

> **TIP**
>
> A great way to manage all open windows (not just those open in the current application) is by using the Exposé feature. More on that later in this chapter.

On the Window menu, the active window in the application you are currently using is marked with some sort of icon. The active Finder window is marked with a check mark; other applications might use a different indicator (for example, a diamond). Be aware that a window can be both active and minimized, in which case the active icon on the Window menu can help you identify the active window even if you can't see that window (because it is on the Dock).

If you hold the Option key down while you open the Window menu, you'll see two additional commands that replace default commands. Minimize becomes Minimize All, which causes all open windows in the application, such as the Finder, to be minimized and moved to the Dock. The "Bring All to Front" command becomes the Arrange in Front command, which causes all open windows in the current application to be brought to the front and arranged neatly on the desktop.

You might see more or fewer commands on the Window menu when you are working in specific applications.

MAC OS X HELP MENUS

Most applications provide a Help menu that enables you to open their help system. Most applications provide help through the standard Mac OS X Help application.

The Finder's Help menu contains one command—Mac Help. This command opens the Mac Help application, which provides extensive help for many areas of the OS (see

Figure 4.2). Even better, many applications you install integrate their help systems into the OS help system. This enables you to access plenty of help using the same tool.

Figure 4.2
You can get a lot of
Mac OS help by using
the Help application.

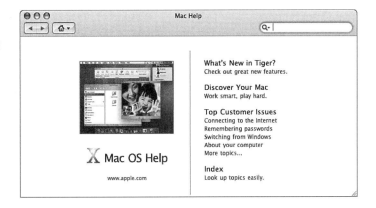

The Help application is based on HTML, so it works the same way web pages do. You can search for help and click links and buttons to access information and move around. Fortunately, the Help engine works much more quickly in Mac OS X version 10.4 than it did under previous versions.

The Home button in the Help Center's toolbar takes you back to the current help's home page. If you click the Home button, you will see a list of all areas in which you can access help, such as AirPort Help, Mail Help, and so on. You can also view and choose these areas on the Help application's Library command.

> **TIP**
>
> When you search for help, you frequently see the Tell Me More link. This link opens other pages that contain topics related to the one for which you searched.

You can search the Help application using the Search tool located in the toolbar. This tool works just like the Search tool in other areas. Select the help area you want to search (either Mac Help, which limits your search to the Mac's help data, or all help, which searches all help modules) using the Magnifying Glass icon and then type the text for which you want to search. Press Return to perform the search; the results appear in the Search Results window (see Figure 4.3).

> **TIP**
>
> You can also browse most help systems from their home pages. This is often an even better way to find a specific topic because you don't have to be concerned about using specific words as you do when you search for help.

Figure 4.3
You can search the
Help application to
find specific topics.

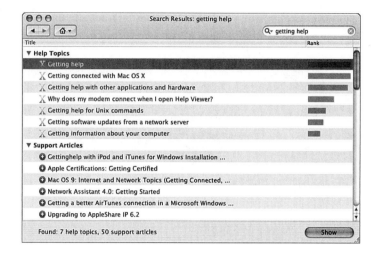

The results window is organized into two areas: Help Topics and Support Articles.

Help Topics lists each help topic within the Help system that matches your search. By default, this area is sorted by the Relevance column, which is the Help system's judgment of how well a topic addresses your search criterion. You can open a topic by double-clicking it or selecting it and clicking Show. The topic appears in the window for viewing. If you select a topic by single-clicking it, a summary of the topic appears in the bottom pane of the Help window.

In the Support Articles section, you will see articles on the Web that the Help application has found for you—of course, your Mac must be able to connect to the Internet to be able to search for information. Just like topics, you can access an article by double-clicking it or by selecting it and clicking Show. The article will be downloaded from the Web and will appear within the Help window.

> **NOTE**
>
> Articles on the Web are marked with the plus icon (+) while topics within the Help system are marked with the application's icon. For example, Mac OS X help topics are marked with the OS X icon (the "X").

The Help Viewer's Go menu tracks the recent topics you have visited; you can return to a topic by selecting it on the menu. You can use the Library menu to view a list of all help resources served through the Mac OS X Help application; to move into another help resource such as iMovie Help, click it in the list.

> **NOTE**
>
> Need help with Help? Select Help, Help Viewer Help. (Try to use the word *help* more times in the same sentence than that!)

Some help topics assist you in performing the action about which you are asking by providing hyperlinks that open the related application or resource.

THE SPOTLIGHT MENU

The Spotlight menu, which is always located at the far right end of the menu bar, enables you to search for information on your Mac.

→ To learn how to use the Spotlight, **see** "Searching Your Mac with Spotlight," **p. 118**.

OPTIONAL FINDER MENUS

As you work with various parts of the system, you can add menus to the Mac OS X menu bar to make those tools available at all times. For example, you can add the Displays menu, which has a display as its icon, to the menu bar so that you can jump immediately to the Displays pane of the System Preferences application. There are many possibilities as you will learn throughout this book.

MAC OS X CONTEXTUAL MENUS

Mac OS X supports contextual menus. *Contextual menus* are pop-up menus that appear in various locations and contain commands specifically related to the context in which you are working. You can access contextual menus by pointing to an object that provides a contextual menu, holding down the Control key, and clicking the mouse button. The contextual menu appears and you can select a command on it.

> TIP
>
> Mac OS X supports a two-button mouse by default. You can open an item's contextual menu by right-clicking it. You can also program most multibutton input devices to perform a right-click. This is one area where Windows has been ahead of the Mac for some time; all Windows mouse devices have at least two buttons. I strongly recommend that you use a mouse or trackball that has at least two buttons, if for no other reason than the convenience of opening contextual menus with one hand.

The desktop and Finder provide contextual menus, as do many applications, including those not provided by Apple. For example, the Microsoft Office application provides excellent support for contextual menus.

A summary of some of the more useful Finder contextual menu commands is provided in Table 4.3.

TABLE 4.3 USEFUL FINDER CONTEXTUAL MENU COMMANDS

Object	Command	What It Does
All	Automator	Opens the Automator so you can create a workflow.
Desktop	Change Desktop Background	Opens the Desktop & Screen Saver pane of the System Preferences application.

continues

TABLE 4.3   CONTINUED

Object	Command	What It Does
Desktop, Finder window	New Burn Folder	Creates a new burn folder on the desktop or within the current folder. (You'll learn more about these folders later in this chapter.)
Desktop, Finder window	New Folder	Creates a new folder.
Desktop, Finder window, folder, file	Folder Actions commands	Folder actions are AppleScripts you can attach to folders so those actions are performed automatically. You use the Enable Folder Actions command to select the actions associated with the selected item. You use the Configure Folder Actions command to configure how actions for an item work. You use the Disable Folder Actions command to disable an item's folder actions.
Desktop, Finder window, folder, file, mounted volume	Automator	Enables you to create a workflow with the selected items or to create a new workflow. You can also choose workflows that you have already created to work with them. (You'll learn all about the Automator in Chapter 10.)
Desktop, Finder window, folder, file, volume	Get Info	Opens the Info window (this is covered in more detail later in this chapter).
Desktop, folder with not items selected	Show View Options	Opens the View options window for the desktop or the current folder.
File	Open With	Enables you to choose the application to use to open the selected file.
File	Print	Prints the selected files.
Folder	Paste item	Pastes the previously created copy of files or folders in the current location.
Folder, file	Color Label	Applies a label to the selected items.
Folder, file	Copy	Copies selected items.
Folder, file	Create Archive	Creates a Zip file containing the selected items.
Folder, file	Duplicate	Duplicates the selected items.
Folder, file	Make Alias	Creates an alias of the selected items.
Folder, file	Move to Trash	Moves the selected items to the Trash.
Folder, file	Open	Opens the selected item.

Object	Command	What It Does
Mac OS X window toolbars	Customize Toolbar	Enables you to customize the current toolbar.
Mac OS X window toolbars	Toolbar Format commands	Use these to change the format of the toolbar, such as Text Only to hide the icons and display only text.
Mounted volume	Open Enclosing Folder	Opens the folder in which the selected item is stored.
Mounted volume	Rename	Enables you to rename the selected volume.
Sidebar item	Remove From Sidebar	Removes the selected item from the Places sidebar.
Sidebar items	Rename	Enables you to rename the select Sidebar item.

THE FINDER ACTION POP-UP MENU

The Action pop-up menu, represented by a gear located on all Finder windows' toolbar by default. This pop-up menu provides contextual commands that work similarly to those on contextual menus. When you select an item or view a folder, commands appropriate to that object appear on the menu (see Figure 4.4).

Figure 4.4
The Action pop-up menu provides contextual commands, this case, the commands are for the selected folder.

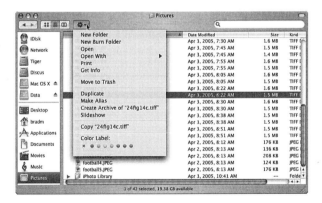

The commands that appear on this menu are the same as those that appear on contextual menus (refer to Table 4.3).

NOTE

> Some applications, especially Apple applications, also provide an Action menu that is marked with the same gear icon.

WORKING WITH THE SYSTEM PREFERENCES APPLICATION

The System Preferences application enables you to set preferences for many areas of Mac OS X and some third-party applications and peripheral devices. If you read through the previous chapters, you already have some experience with this application. However, because you will use the System Preferences application so frequently, it is worthy of a more detailed look.

You can open the System Preferences utility in various ways, including the following:

- Select Apple, System Preferences.
- Click the System Preferences icon on the Dock.
- Open the Applications folder and then open System Preferences using its icon.

NOTE

Because the System Preferences application is used so frequently, Apple should have provided a keyboard shortcut to open it but didn't. If you use a macro utility, such as QuicKeys, you should set and use a keyboard shortcut to open this application.

The System Preferences application provides a window with a toolbar at the top and a series of icons or buttons in the bottom part (see Figure 4.5). To access the controls for a specific area, you click its icon. The System Preferences window will change to show a pane containing controls for that area (see Figure 4.6).

Figure 4.5
The System Preferences application enables you to configure and customize Mac OS X to suit your needs and personal preferences.

The default panes contained in the System Preferences utility (listed in alphabetical order) are the following:

- .Mac
- Accounts
- Appearance

- CDs & DVDs
- Classic
- DashBoard & Exposé
- Date & Time
- Desktop & Screen Saver
- Displays
- Dock
- Energy Saver
- International
- Keyboard & Mouse
- Network
- Print & Fax
- QuickTime
- Security
- Sharing
- Software Update
- Sound
- Speech
- Spotlight
- Startup Disk
- Universal Access

Figure 4.6
The Sound pane of the System Preferences application enables you to change your system's sound settings.

By default, these buttons are organized into the following categories: Personal, Hardware, Internet & Network, and System. The Personal panes configure aspects of the user account that is currently logged in. The panes in the other three categories make system wide changes (and so require that you are logged in under or authenticate yourself as an administrator account).

You can choose to list the icons in alphabetical order if you prefer. Just select View, Organize Alphabetically. The categories disappear and the icons are listed in alphabetical order (from left to right, top to bottom).

If you prefer to use a menu to open a pane, select the pane you want to open on the View menu.

After you have opened a pane, you can show all the panes of the window again by clicking the Show All button or by selecting View, Show All Preferences (⌘-L).

NOTE

> Specific panes are covered in the parts of this book that explain the features they are related to. For example, the Accounts pane is explained in the section "Creating User Accounts," in Chapter 2, "Getting Started with Mac OS X."

When you add hardware or software to your system, additional panes can appear to enable you to configure the device or software you added. Common examples of this are the Bluetooth pane, which appears when your Mac supports Bluetooth, or Ink, which appears when you attach a handwriting recognition device (such as a tablet) to your Mac.

Panes added by Apple-produced tools, such as the Bluetooth pane, appear within the related categories, such as Hardware. Panes added by third-party tools, such as keyboard customization panes, are contained in the Other category (see Figure 4.7).

Figure 4.7
Compare this figure to Figure 4.5 and you will see that a new category, called "Other," has been added to the System Preferences application; it contains preference panes for peripheral devices.

MANAGING OPEN WINDOWS WITH EXPOSÉ

Because it is so useful to have multiple applications and multiple documents within each application open at the same time, you might have dozens of windows open simultaneously with those windows layered one on another. Getting to the specific window in which you are interested can be difficult. That is where Exposé comes in. It is designed to help you quickly manage all the open windows on your desktop.

TIP

You can customize the controls used to activate Exposé functions, as you will learn in the next section.

USING EXPOSÉ

Exposé offers a number of useful functions, which are the following:

- **See all open windows at the same time**—If you press the F9 key, all open windows will be reduced in size and tiled such that they can all be displayed on the desktop at the same time (see Figure 4.8). When you point to a window, its title will appear so you can definitely identify it if you couldn't already do so just by its appearance (in Figure 4.8, I am pointing to the Mail application). You can click a window to move into that window; the other windows return to their previous sizes and locations. You can also move into a window in which the cursor is located by pressing F9 again.

Figure 4.8
Using Exposé, you can show all open windows on your desktop at the same time.

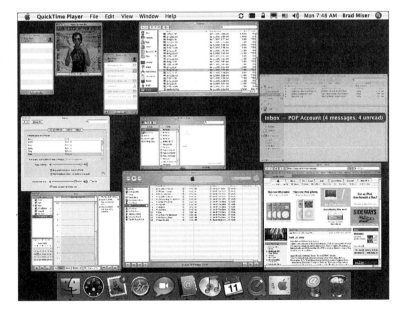

4

NOTE

If you use multiple monitors and activate Exposé, the windows on all monitors shrink and remain on the monitor they were on.

- **See all the windows in the current application at the same time**—If you press the F10 key, all the windows in the current application will be shown. Just like the previous command, you can point to a window to see its title, click it to move into it, and so on.

TIP

> If you hold down the Shift key while you activate Exposé, you see its effects in slow motion.

- **Hide all open windows and show the desktop**—If you press F11, all open windows will be hidden and you will see your desktop. This is useful if you have a bad case of desktop clutter and want to work on the desktop without closing or moving the current windows. You can return all windows to their previous locations by pressing F11 again. You can also open an item on the desktop by double-clicking it; when you do, the other windows return to their previous locations. Another option is to click one of the window borders that will be visible along the edges of your screen to return windows to their previous states.

- **Cycle through the Open windows in each application**—If you activate Exposé by pressing F9 or F10, you can cycle through the set of open windows in each application by pressing the Tab or Shift-Tab keys (to move in the opposite direction). Each time you do, the next application becomes active and you see all its open windows. Windows open in other applications remain at their current sizes and are unselectable. When the window in which you want to work is exposed, click in it to deactivate Exposé and start working.

CONFIGURING EXPOSÉ

You can customize the following aspects of Exposé using the Dashboard & Exposé pane of the System Preferences application (see Figure 4.9):

Figure 4.9
The Dashboard & Exposé pane of the System Preferences application enables you to customize various aspects of Exposé.

- **Active Screen Corners**—Use the pop-up menu located at each corner of the preview monitor to set an action that happens when you move the cursor to that corner. The actions you can set are All Windows (the default F9 key), Application Windows(the default F10 key), Desktop (the default F11 key), Start Screen Saver, Disable Screen Saver, and No Action (-). To set an action for a corner, select the action on the related pop-up menu. When you point to that corner of the screen, that action will occur.

■ **Keyboard**—Use the Keyboard pop-up menus to set the keys to activate each Exposé action. In addition to the keys on the menus, you can see other combinations by scrolling down the pop-up menu. If you hold down a modifier key (such as the ⌘ key), you can add that modifier to the shortcut.

■ **Mouse**—If you use an input device with more than one button, such as a two-button mouse, the Mouse pop-up menus will appear. Use the Mouse pop-up menus to set Exposé actions for specific buttons on the device you use, such as the right button on a two-button mouse.

NOTE

> You also use the Dashboard & Exposé pane to configure the Dashboard.

→ To learn about the Dashboard, **see** Chapter 6, "Working with the Dashboard and Widgets," **p. 159**.

UNDERSTANDING MAC OS X DIRECTORIES

Mac OS X includes many standard folders, often called *directories* in Mac OS X lingo. You have seen several of these as you learned about using the Go menu, working with Finder windows, and so on.

Some directories, such as the Mac OS X System directory, are critical to your Mac's operation, whereas others are merely organizational devices, such as the Documents directory within each user's Home directory.

There are two general groups of directories you will work with: those for the system and those for users.

MAC OS X SYSTEM DIRECTORIES

Two main directories provide access to Mac OS X system-level files and folders.

THE COMPUTER DIRECTORY

The Computer directory is the highest-level folder on your Mac. It shows the volumes mounted on your machine, including hard drives, drive partitions, disk images, DVDs, CD-ROMs, and so on (see Figure 4.10). The name of the Computer directory is the name of your Mac.

Figure 4.10
The Mac OS X
Computer directory
represents all the con-
tents of your machine
as well as the network
resources you can
access.

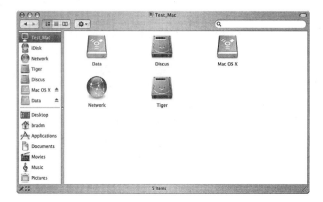

Most of the contents of the Computer directory should be familiar to you, such as volumes, CD-ROMs, and so on.

One exception to this is the Network folder, which contains the resources you can access via a network.

→ To learn more about the Network volume, **see** Chapter 33, "Building and Using a Network," **p. 935**.

THE MAC OS X STARTUP VOLUME

One of the directories in the Computer directory is the one on which you installed Mac OS X. The name of this directory depends on what you named the volume (for example, I called mine Tiger).

By default, your startup volume directory contains the following four directories that are part of the Mac OS X installation:

- **Applications**—Under Mac OS X, all Carbon and Cocoa applications are stored in this directory.

→ To learn how to install applications, **see** Chapter 7, "Installing and Using Mac OS X Applications," **p. 175**.

- **Library**—The Library folder contains many subfolders that provide resources to support applications, hardware devices, and other items you add to your Mac. This library directory contains the system folders that can be modified.

- **System**—This folder contains the Library folder that provides the core operating system software for Mac OS X. The items in this folder can't be modified except by installation applications, system updaters, or using the root account.

→ To learn more about the Library and System directories, **see** "Mac OS X to the Max: Exploring Mac OS X System Folders," **p. 256**.

- **Users**—The Users directory contains the Home directory for each user for whom an account has been created. The Home directory of the user currently logged in has the Home icon; the Home directories for the rest of the users have plain folder icons. If you have deleted user accounts, it also contains folder called "Deleted Users" that contains a disk image for each deleted user account (if you elected to keep the user's resources when you deleted his folder).

The Users directory also contains the Shared folder. Items placed in this folder can be accessed by any user who logs in to the Mac.

NOTE

> If you installed Mac OS X version 10.4 using the Archive and Install option, the startup volume also includes the Previous Systems folder, which contains the folders from the previous Mac OS X installations.

MAC OS X USER DIRECTORIES

As you learned in Chapter 2, each user account includes a Home folder. By default, this folder contains eight directories in which the logged-in user can store folders and files.

→ To learn about the specific directories in a user's Home directory, **see** "Understanding the Home Folder," **p. 21**.

Although the Home folder contains the eight default directories, you can add directories within these folders as well as create new folders within the Home folder itself.

The benefit to using the standard directories is that they are integrated into the OS so you can access them quickly and in many ways. For example, you can select the Documents directory in Mac OS X Save and Open dialog boxes. This makes keeping your documents organized easier than if you create your own directories outside your Home folder.

TIP

> You can add any folder to the Places sidebar, which is visible in all Open and Save dialog boxes along with Finder windows (when the sidebar is displayed). Adding a folder to the sidebar makes that folder accessible from many locations.

Another benefit of using the standard Mac OS X directories is that they take advantage of the default security settings that go with the user account. When you use directories outside a user account's Home folder, you should check and set the security of the folders you are using if you want to limit the access to those resources by other people who use your Mac.

→ To learn how to configure an item's security, **see** "Understanding and Setting Permissions," **p. 959**.

Most of the user directories are self-explanatory, such as Documents, Movies, and Music. A few of them are worthy of more detailed attention, though.

THE DESKTOP DIRECTORY

The user's Desktop folder contains the items the user has placed on his desktop. Each user can have as much or as little on his desktop as he likes. When another user logs in, she sees only the contents of her desktop folder on the desktop.

THE LIBRARY DIRECTORY

In the Library directory are system files specifically related to the user account. The Library directory includes a number of subdirectories (see Figure 4.11).

Figure 4.11
Each user has a
Library directory in
which files that relate
to that user's system
resources, such as
preferences, are
stored.

The particular folders you see depend on the applications you have used and what you have done. For instance, if you have installed iMovie, iPhoto, and iTunes, you'll find folders and files related to each of these applications. In the Fonts folder are fonts that only you can access. Your Internet plug-ins are stored in the Internet Plug-Ins folder, and the Preferences directory is where applications store your personal preferences.

THE PUBLIC DIRECTORY

A user's Public directory is available to all users who log in to a particular Mac. This directory lets users conveniently share or transfer files because placing files or folders within the Public directory makes them available to all the other users on a particular machine.

To access the files and folders in another user's Public folder, perform the following steps:

1. Open the Users folder (select your startup volume to see it).
2. Open the Home folder for the user who has a file you want to share.
3. Open the Public folder and use the files contained within it.

> **TIP**
>
> You can open a file or folder within another user's Public folder, or you can drag the file to your own folder to make a copy of it.

Within the Public folder, you will also see a Drop Box folder. Other users can place items into this folder, but no one else can open it. This is useful when you want others to transfer items to you but don't want all the other users to be able to see what has been shared.

THE SITES DIRECTORY

The Sites directory contains the files and folders that make up the website for each user account.

→ For more information on sharing a website under Mac OS X, **see** "Mac OS X to the Max: Using Mac OS X to Serve Web Pages," **p. 514**.

WORKING WITH FILES AND FOLDERS

Working with files and folders under Mac OS X version 10.4 is straightforward.

Under Mac OS X, you can move and copy files and folders as in previous versions of the OS. Just drag the folders or files to where you want them to reside.

To place a copy of an item in a different folder, hold down the Option key while you drag the item. To duplicate an item (make a copy of it in its current location), select it and select File, Duplicate (or press ⌘-D).

NOTE

> The Column view is one of the more useful for moving files and folders around because it gives you a good view of the entire hierarchy of the volume you are working with.

You can also create copies of files and folders using the contextual menu commands and the commands on the Edit menu. You can place a copy of the items in a new location by selecting them, choosing the Copy command, and then pasting them in a new location.

When you move an object over a folder, it becomes highlighted so you can easily see in which folder the item you are moving will be placed. This is especially useful when you are viewing Finder windows in the Column view. Similarly, when you drag something over a folder on the Places sidebar, the folder will be highlighted so it is clear which folder the object will be moved into when you release the mouse button.

CREATING AND NAMING FOLDERS

The purpose of folders under Mac OS X version 10.4 is to enable you to organize files. You can create a new folder by using the New Folder command (such as File, New Folder, or ⌘-Shift-N). The new folder will be created in your current location. Immediately after you create it, its name will be editable so you can simply type the name of the new folder.

Naming a folder is mostly a matter of personal preference; the maximum number of characters that you can use in a folder name is 256. Of course, you aren't likely to ever use a folder name that long because it would be very difficult to read, but at least you have lots of flexibility with folder names.

To name a folder or edit its current name, select the folder and press Return. The folder's name becomes highlighted and you can create a new name.

NAMING FILES

Naming files is very similar to naming folders, with one exception. The underlying architecture of the Mac OS X uses *filename extensions*— for example, .doc at the end of a Word document filename.

File extensions are a code that helps identify a file's type and thus the application used to view or edit that file. Many Mac OS X applications also use filename extensions; the OS uses these extensions to launch the appropriate application for that document when you open the file.

→ To understand more about filename extensions under Mac OS X, **see** "Saving Documents in Mac OS X," **p. 206**.

When you name a document from within an application that uses filename extensions, the correct extension is appended automatically to the filename you enter. However, when you rename files on the desktop or in a Finder window, you need to be aware of a filename's extension if it has one (not all applications use an extension).

A complication in this is that you can choose to show or hide filename extensions on a file-by-file basis or at the system level. However, filename extensions are almost always in use, whether you can see them or not. Hiding them simply hides them from your view.

I wrote "almost always in use" because all Mac OS X applications add filename extensions to files with which they work. And most Classic applications do not use filename extensions. Fortunately, you can use the Info tool to associate applications with specific files so the lack of a proper filename extension is not a significant problem.

→ To learn how to associate files with specific applications, **see** "Opening Documents in Mac OS X," **p. 198**.

If you want to rename a file that has an extension, you should leave the extension as it is. If you change or remove the extension, the application you use to open the file might not be launched automatically when you try to open the file.

The filename extensions you see under Mac OS X include some of the three- or four-letter filename extensions with which you are no doubt familiar, such as .doc, .xls, .html, .jpg, .tiff, and so on. However, there are many, many more filename extensions you will encounter. Some are relatively short, whereas others (particularly those in the system) can be quite long. There isn't really any apparent rhyme or reason to these filename extensions so you just have to learn them as you go. Because you will mostly deal with filename extensions that are appended by an application when you save a document, this isn't a critical task. However, as you delve deeper into the system, you will become more familiar with many of the sometimes bizarre-looking filename extensions Mac OS X uses.

NOTE

> Depending on the file type, some files open properly even if you do remove or change the file's extension. But it is better to be safe than sorry, so you should usually leave the file extension as you find it.

You can choose to hide or show filename extensions globally or on an item-by-item basis. To configure filename extensions globally, use the following steps:

1. Select Finder, Preferences to open the Finder Preferences window.
2. Click the Advanced icon.
3. To globally show filename extensions, check the "Show all file extensions" check box.

4. To allow filename extensions to be shown or hidden for specific items, uncheck the "Show all file extensions" check box.

→ To learn how to show or hide filename extensions for specific items, **see** "Working with Name and Extension Information," **p. 132**.

CREATING AND USING ALIASES

As with previous versions of the Mac OS, an alias is a pointer to a file, folder, or volume. Open an alias and the original item opens. The benefit of aliases is that you can place them anywhere on your Mac because they are very small in file size, so you can use them with little storage penalty.

There are several ways to create an alias, including

- Select an item and select File, Make Alias.
- Select an item and press ⌘-L.
- Hold down the Option and ⌘ keys while you drag an item.
- Open the Action menu for an item and select Make Alias.
- Open the contextual menu for an item and select Make Alias.

After you have created an alias, you can work with it much like you can the original. For example, you can open it or move it to a new location.

Occasionally, you might need to find the original from which an alias was created. For example, if you create an alias to an application, you might want to be able to move to that application in the Finder. Do the following:

1. Select the alias.
2. Select File, Show Original (or press ⌘-R). A Finder window containing the original item will open.

Occasionally, an alias *breaks*, meaning your Mac loses track of the original to which the alias points. The most common situation is that you have deleted the original, but it can happen for other reasons as well. When you attempt to open a broken alias, you will see a warning dialog box that provides the following three options:

- **Delete Alias**—If you click this button, the alias is deleted.
- **Fix Alias**—If you click this one, you can use the Fix Alias dialog box to select another file to which you want the alias to point.
- **OK**—If you click OK, the dialog box disappears and no changes are made to the alias.

TRASHING FILES AND FOLDERS

Since its inception, the Mac's Trash can has been the place where you move files and folders that you no longer want so that you can delete them from your computer. Under Mac OS X, the Trash is located at the right end of the Dock.

To move something to the Trash, use one of the following methods:

- Drag the item to the Trash on the Dock. When you are over the Trash icon, it will become highlighted so you know you are in the right place.

- Select an item, open its contextual menu, and select Move to Trash.

- Select an item and choose File, Move to Trash.

- Select an item and press ⌘-Delete.

After you have placed an item in the Trash, you can access it again by clicking the Trash icon on the Dock. A Finder window displaying the Trash directory opens, and you can work with the items it contains.

When you want to delete the items in the Trash, do so in one of the following ways:

- Select Finder, Empty Trash. In the confirmation dialog box, click either OK (or press Return) to empty the Trash or Cancel to stop the process. You can skip the confirmation dialog box by holding down the Option key while you select Empty Trash.

- Open the Trash's Dock contextual menu and select Empty Trash on the resulting pop-up.

- Press Shift-⌘-Delete. In the confirmation dialog box, click either OK (or press Return) to empty the Trash or Cancel to stop the process. You can skip the confirmation dialog box by pressing Option-Shift-⌘-Delete instead.

To permanently disable the warning dialog box when you empty the Trash, perform the following steps:

1. Select Finder, Preferences to open the Finder Preferences window.
2. Click the Advanced icon.
3. Uncheck the "Show warning before emptying the Trash" check box. The warning will no longer appear, no matter how you empty the Trash.

Under Mac OS X version 10.4, you can securely delete items from the Trash. When you do this, the data that makes up those items is overwritten so it can't be recovered. To perform a secure delete, place items in the Trash and select Finder, Secure Empty Trash.

CREATING AND USING BURN FOLDERS

Burn folders are a special type of folder that are designed to help you move files and folders onto CD or DVD more easily. One of the differences between a regular folder and a burn folder is that everything you move into a burn folder becomes an alias. This means you can build a CD or DVD without disturbing the location of the items that you want to put on disc. Simply create a burn folder and place items into it. When you are ready to burn a disc, you can do so quite easily.

TIP

> You can use burn folders as back-up mechanism. For example, suppose you want to back up your iPhoto Library to DVD. Simply create a burn folder and place your Pictures folder in it. To create a fresh back up of your library, just burn the folder. (You don't need to move the files into it again because the aliases are updated automatically.)

To create a burn folder, use one of the following options:

- Choose File, New Burn Folder.
- Open the Action menu and choose New Burn Folder.
- Open the contextual menu and choose New Burn Folder.

When the new folder appears, you will see it has the radioactive icon and the name "Burn Folder." The name will be highlighted so you can rename it immediately. Do so and press Return to save the new name.

After you have created a burn folder, move the files and folders that you want to place on a disc into it. As you move files and folders into it, aliases to the original items will be created inside the burn folder. Continue placing items inside the folder until you have moved all files you want to place on disc into it (see Figure 4.12).

Figure 4.12
A burn folder contains aliases to items you place in it along with the black bar containing the folder name and Burn button shown at the top of its window.

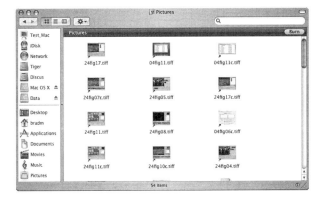

For quick access, add a burn folder to the Places sidebar so you can get into it easily to add more files to it.

TIP

You can organize files and folders within a burn folder just like other folders with which you work. For example, you can create new "regular" folders within the burn folder and place items within those folders.

NOTE

> Unfortunately, using a Burn folder supports burning to a disc in a single session. After you burn a folder to a disc, that disc will be closed and can't be burned to again (unless it is an erasable disc, in which case you can erase its contents). Hopefully, someday the Finder will allow multisession burns so you can add files to a disc you have burned.

When you are ready to burn a disc from the burn folder, view the folder and click its Burn button. You will be prompted to insert a disc; in this prompt, you'll see the amount of space needed to burn the files on a disc. When your Mac mounts a disc that is ready to burn, you'll see the Burn prompt. Enter the name of the disc (it will default to the name of the Burn folder), choose the burn speed on the Burn Speed pop-up menu, and click Burn. A progress window will appear and the disc will be burned.

You can quickly burn the contents of a burn folder at any time by repeating these steps; such as when you want to refresh your backups of important files.

NOTE

> You might wonder why it is better to create and use a burn folder than it is just to place files and folders directly on a disc. If you are only going to burn a disc once, there isn't a lot of benefit to creating a burn folder because it is just as easy to insert a blank disc into your burner and add files and folders to it. Burn folders become valuable when you want to re-create a disc, such as to refresh a back up or to make multiple copies of the same disc. Or, you might want to use them to organize files you are going to burn later in the order they will be on the disc.

SEARCHING YOUR MAC WITH SPOTLIGHT

One of the problems that we computers users have always faced is that of finding information, including documents, files, email messages, and other data, we need. Mac OS X version 10.4 introduces an amazingly easy way to find things on your Mac, regardless of what kind of "thing" it is.

This new feature is called Spotlight and it enables you to search your entire Mac quickly and easily.

Spotlight works so amazingly well because it searches metadata. *Metadata* is information that is associated with every file on your computer. Metadata includes obvious information such as the file name, creation date, modification date, and so on, but it also includes file type, content information, and much more. Because Spotlight searches metadata, it can search the entire contents of your computer without limiting you to searching for specific data (such as a folder or file name). A Spotlight search will return all files, folders, email, bookmarks, contact information, and so on that relate to your search.

CONFIGURING SPOTLIGHT

Before you start searching your Mac, you need to configure Spotlight so it works as you intend. Do so with the following steps:

1. Open the Spotlight pane of the System Preferences application. By default, the Search Results tab will be selected (see Figure 4.13).

Figure 4.13
Use the Spotlight pane to configure the items for which Spotlight will search.

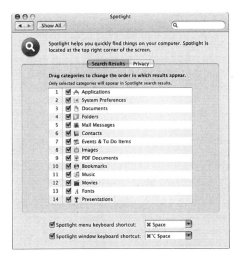

2. Check the check boxes next to the items you want to be included in Spotlight searches, such as Applications, Folders, and so on. Uncheck the check boxes for items that you don't want to be searched.

3. Set the keyboard shortcut you will use to launch Spotlight using the "Spotlight menu keyboard shortcut" check box and pop-up menu. The default is ⌘-spacebar, but you can change this to be a function key if you prefer. If you don't want to be able to activate Spotlight with a key for some reason, uncheck the check box.

4. Use the "Spotlight window keyboard shortcut" check box and pop-up menu to configure the keys you will use to move into the Spotlight search results window. The default is ⌘-Option-spacebar, but you can use the pop-up menu to choose a function key instead. If you don't want to use any keyboard shortcut, uncheck the check box.

5. Click the Privacy tab. You use this pane to select areas on your computer you don't want Spotlight to search. For example, if you keep sensitive documents in a folder within your Documents folder, you might want to block that folder from Spotlight searches.

6. Click the Add Folder button (+) at the bottom of the pane. The choose folder sheet will appear.

7. Move to the folder you want to shield, select it, and click Choose. That folder will be added to the list and won't be included in Spotlight searches.

8. Repeat steps 6 and 7 until you have protected all your sensitive folders.

4

SEARCHING WITH SPOTLIGHT

To use Spotlight to search your Mac from the desktop, perform the following steps:

1. Click the Spotlight icon (the magnifying glass) in the upper right corner of your desktop or press the Spotlight menu keyboard shortcut (⌘-spacebar by default). The Spotlight search bar will appear (see Figure 4.14).

Figure 4.14
You can enter any text or numbers in the Spotlight search bar to perform a search.

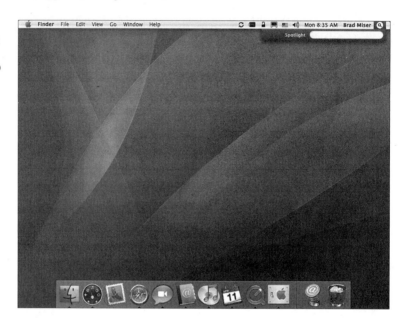

2. Type your search criterion in the search bar. As you type, Spotlight will immediately begin searching your Mac and will start presenting results in the Spotlight results window (see Figure 4.15). Within this window, you will see that results are organized for you by type. At the top of the window is the Show All selection, which you'll learn about in the next step. Just under that is the Top Hit, which is the item that Spotlight believes best matched your search criterion. Under that, the remaining results are organized by group, including Applications, System Preferences, Documents, Folders, Mail Messages, and so on.

> **NOTE**
>
> If you used the Spotlight preference pane to prevent a type from being included in Spotlight searches, that category won't appear in the results window.

3. To open an item on the results list, select it. The item will open. For example, if you select a document, it will open. If you select a folder, you will be able to view its contents. If you select an application, it will launch.

Figure 4.15
This search has found many items that are associated with the "itunes" criterion, including applications, preferences, documents, mail messages, and so on.

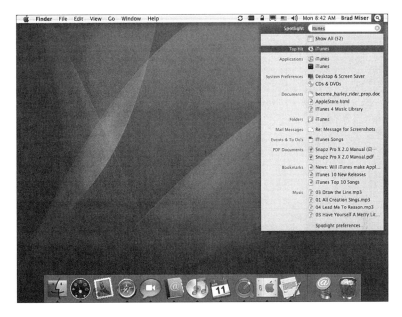

4. To return to the search results, click the Spotlight icon again. Your previous search results will appear because Spotlight remembers your search until you indicate that you are done with it.

   The results shown in the initial Spotlight window might be limited if there are a large number of them; as mentioned previously, the first item on the results list in the Show All option. This choice will present every item that meets your search criterion.

5. To show all the results of a search, click Show All. The Spotlight window will appear (see Figure 4.16).

The Spotlight window has many features, including the following:

- Use the expansion triangles to expand or collapse groups.

> **TIP**
>
> Just like the Finder, if you hold the Option key down when you click an expansion triangle, all sections will be expanded or collapsed.

- Click "more" link to display all of the results in a group.
- Click one of the "Group by" options to change how the results are grouped. The default grouping option is by Kind. Click Date to group results by date, People to group them by the people with whom they are associated (such as document creators), or Flat List to present them in an ungrouped list.

Click "more" links to display all items in a group

Use these options to change how results are grouped and sorted

Figure 4.16
You can use the Spotlight window to display all of your search results and to change how they are listed.

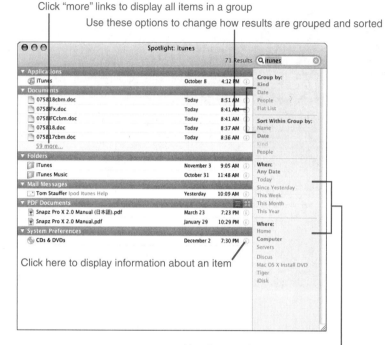

Click here to display information about an item

Use these options to change the timeframe and location of the results

- Use the "Sort Within Group by" options to change how results are ordered within a group. The options are Name, Date, Kind, or People. Only the available options will be active. For example, you can't choose Kind if the results are already grouped by Kind.

- Use the "When" options to choose the dates associated with the items in the results window. For example, if you click Today, only items with today's date as the creation or modification date will be displayed. The other relative date options work similarly.

- Use the "Where" options to choose the locations of the results that you want to view. You will see all mounted volumes in this area, such as your startup volume, your iDisk, and so on. Select an area, and only items stored in that location will be shown in the results list.

- Click the information button (the "i") to display more information about items(see Figure 4.17). Click the button again to collapse the information displayed. You can use the information area to preview some items. For example, you can listen to audio files, watch movies, and so on.

- For some types of items, you'll see the Icon and List view buttons. Click the button for the view in which you want to see the items in that group.

- To open an item on the list, double-click it. The appropriate application or Finder window will open. You can return to the Spotlight window by moving back to the desktop.

Figure 4.17
Here, the information button has been selected to display additional information about a couple of items on the results list.

> **TIP**
>
> You can move back to the Spotlight window or open it any time using the keyboard shortcut, which is Option-⌘-spacebar by default. You can also configure a search using the Search box in the Spotlight window just like you do using the Spotlight bar.

■ Minimize the Spotlight window to move it out of your way while you look at an item you found. You can jump back to the results by clicking the Spotlight menu button or using the keyboard shortcuts for the menu or window.

> **TIP**
>
> Take advantage of Exposé as you work with Spotlight results because that feature makes it easy to manage multiple open windows.

To clear a Spotlight search, click the "x" in the Spotlight search tool or close the Spotlight window.

SEARCHING YOUR MAC WITH SMART FOLDERS

Under Mac OS X version 10.4, the Finder's search tools have been replaced by smart folders. A smart folder displays its contents based on search criteria that you define as opposed to a "regular" folder that displays items that have been manually placed within it. Even better, you can save smart folders so that you can repeat searches simply by refreshing the smart folders you create.

Just like Spotlight, smart folders search metadata so that there are many kinds of criteria you can use to search your Mac. Because of this, you can search by many different kinds of information, including the content of files and many attributes that aren't even displayed in the Finder.

Smart Folder Versus Spotlight

Spotlight and smart folders enabled you to do a similar task—searching for files and folders on your Mac. However, these tools work differently, and which one you should use for a specific search depends on what you want to do with that search.

If you want to save a search so you can run it again, a smart folder is your best bet.

If you are performing a one-time search, which tool you use depends on how narrow you want the results to be. Although you can select general types of objects to search using the Spotlight pane of the System Preferences application, you can't focus the search all that tightly and are limited to only one search criterion at a time. Using smart folders, you can make your search as specific as you want and include multiple search criteria in a single search.

Generally, use Spotlight for quick searches when you don't mind having to scan a large number of hits. Otherwise, a smart folder is probably the way to go.

NOTE

If you choose the Finder's File, Find command or press ⌘-F, you'll see a New Search window. Except for the slightly different name ("New Search" versus "New Smart Folder"), these two search tools work very similarly. When you save a search you started with the Find command, you actually create a new smart folder so both tools end up with the same result.

CREATING AND SAVING A SMART FOLDER

To search your Mac using a smart folder, perform the following steps:

1. Choose File, New Smart Folder or press Option-⌘-N. A smart folder with the title "New Search" will appear (see Figure 4.18).

2. Choose the location in which you want to search by clicking the appropriate Search location button. To search your entire Mac, click the Computer button. To limit the search to your Home folder, click Home. To limit the search to specific volumes, click Others and then choose the volumes you want to search using the resulting sheet. To search servers to which you are connected over a network, click Servers.

   Next, you need to build the specific criteria that you want to use for the search.

3. Click the first Search Criteria button, which shows Kind by default. When you do, you'll see a pop-up menu that lists a large number of options including Kind, Last Opened, Last Modified, Created, Keywords, Color Label, Name, Contents, Size, and Other.

   Choose the first criterion by which you want to limit your search. For example, to limit the search by the date something was last changed, choose Last Modified.

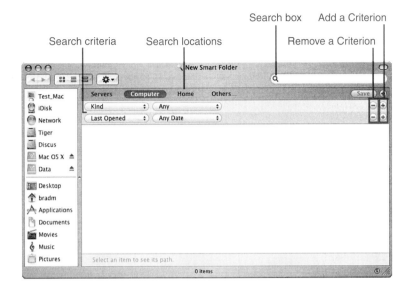

Figure 4.18
Don't let its simple looking appearance fool you; a smart folder lives up to its name.

If you choose the Other option, you'll see a sheet that enables you to select from a very large number of options (see Figure 4.19). You can browse this list to see all of the criteria that are possible. A brief description is provided in the sheet for these options.

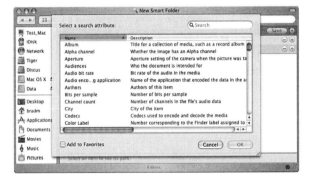

Figure 4.19
When you choose Other on a Search Criteria pop-up menu, you can choose from any of the possible search criteria.

To choose a criterion on this list, select it and click OK.

TIP

You can search for a criterion by typing text in the Search box at the top of the Other sheet. As you type, the criteria shown in the sheet will be limited to those that match your search. To add a criterion to the Search Criteria pop-up menu, select it and check the "Add to Favorites" check box.

After you have selected a criterion, controls appropriate for that criterion will appear. For example, when you choose a text criterion, a text box will appear. When you select a date criterion, a pop-up menu of options appears. If you choose Kind, a list of kinds of files appears as a pop-up menu.

4. Configure the criterion you selected by entering text, making a choice from the pop-up menu, and so on.

   In some cases, making a choice will result in additional tools you can use to configure the criterion. For example, if you choose Before for a date criterion, a date box will appear so that you can enter a date.

5. If an additional tool has appeared, such as a date box, complete the data for the criterion.

   As you define criteria, the location you selected will be searched and items that meet the current search criteria will be shown in the Results section of the folder.

6. Click the "Add a Criterion" button, which is the "+" at the end of each criterion's row, to add another criterion to the search; two criteria appear by default so you only need to do this if you want to include more than two criteria.

> **TIP**
>
> You can also add criteria to a smart folder by clicking the + that appears next to the Save button at the top of the folder.

7. Configure the next criterion with the same steps you did to configure the first one (steps 3–6).

8. To remove a criterion from the search, click the "Remove a Criterion" button, which is the "-" at the end of each criterion's row. That criterion will be removed from the smart folder and will no longer impact the search.

9. Continue adding, configuring, or removing criteria until you have fully defined your search (see Figure 4.20).

10. When the search is configured, click the Save button. You'll see a Save sheet.

11. Name your search, choose a location in which to save it, and determine if it will be added to the Places sidebar by checking or unchecking the "Add To Sidebar" check box, and then click Save (see Figure 4.21).

    You'll return to the smart folder, which will now be named with the name you entered. If you opted to have the search added to the Places sidebar, you will see it there as well.

Following are some points to ponder when you are working with smart folders:

- If you don't want to limit your search, don't configure any search criteria and instead just type the text or numbers for which you want to search in the Search box at the top of the smart folder's window. This can be literally anything from text contained in documents, resolution of images, dates associated with documents, people's names, and so on. As you start to type, your Mac will begin its search and documents, folders, bookmarks, and anything else that meets your search text will appear in the results section of the folder.

Icon view

List view

Play slideshow

Results   Selected item

Figure 4.20
This search will find all items created by "Miser," last opened before 12/22/2004, that include the word "Dock," and that are less than 50MB in size.

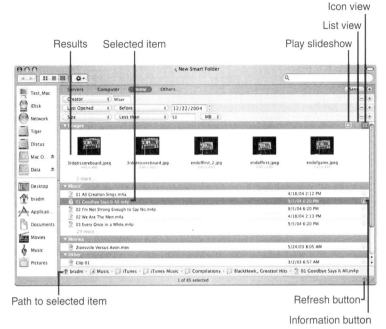

Path to selected item

Refresh button

Information button

4

Figure 4.21
You can name and save the smart folders that you create so that you can repeat searches easily.

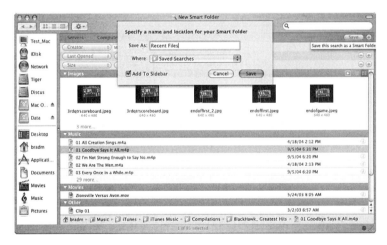

- Like other areas, you can collapse or expand the sections in the results area by clicking the expansion triangle next to a group heading.

- You can open any item found by double-clicking on it. You can use any action or contextual commands on items as well, just as you can in a regular folder.

- For some groups, such as Images, the Icon and List view buttons will appear. Click the button for the view in which you want to see that section.

- If a group contains images, you can click the Play button to view the images in a slideshow.

- If you click the information button (the "i") associated with an item, you'll see a preview of it in the window. Click the collapse button (a upward facing arrow inside a circle) to hide the preview again.

- If a group includes the "more" link, click it to see all of the items in that group.

- When you select an item in the results area, the path to its location will be shown at the bottom of the window. You can double-click on any part of the path shown to open that part. For example, if the Pictures folder is part of the path shown, double-click on the Pictures icon to open that folder.

- If you close a smart folder without first saving it, you'll be prompted to do so.

- After you have saved a smart folder and then opened it again, the search tools will be replaced by the text smart folder and you'll see the Edit button. Click the Edit button to change the criteria used for that smart folder.

- You can renew a search by clicking the Refresh button located in the lower-right corner of a smart folder's window.

- The default save location for smart folder searches is the Saved Searches folder within the Library folder that is within your Home folder. If you want to remove searches, open this folder and delete any smart folder files you want to remove from your computer. If you also added the smart folder to your Places sidebar, you'll need to remove its icon by dragging it off the sidebar.

TIP

> Want to find all the documents on your Mac that have changed recently so you can back them up? Create and save a smart folder with search criteria of Last Modified Since Yesterday and Kind Documents. The results will display all documents that have changed since yesterday.

USING SMART FOLDERS

After you have created a smart folder, you can perform the search again by opening the smart folder. If you choose to add it to your Places sidebar, click its icon. You'll see the current results of the search.

Click the Refresh button to ensure that a smart folder's window shows the most current results of a search.

NOTE

> When you save a smart folder, you save the search criteria, not the results. This means that each time you use the smart folder, the search is repeated. If something has changed such that an item now meets the search criteria, it will appear in the smart folder.

There are several ways to search with a saved smart folder:

■ Place it on the Places sidebar and click its icon.

■ Drag the smart folder from its saved location onto the Dock. You can run the search by clicking the icon on the Dock.

■ Select a smart folder's icon and choose File, Open or press ⌘-O.

■ Double-click the smart folder's icon.

TIP

> For immediate access to all your smart folders without cluttering up your Places sidebar, add the Saved Searches folder to the sidebar instead of each individual smart folder. Then you can click that folder's icon to view all your smart folders and then double-click a smart folder to perform the search.

CHANGING SMART FOLDERS

You can change an existing smart folder, such as to change one or more of its search criteria.

1. Open the smart folder you want to change. Notice that the Save button has been replaced by the Edit button.

2. Click Edit. The search criteria tools will appear again.

3. Reconfigure the search by changing existing criteria, adding new ones, or removing them. You can also change the search location.

4. Click Save. The smart folder will now contain the revised search criteria.

GETTING INFORMATION ON ITEMS

The Info window is a tool you use to learn about various items on your desktop and in Finder windows. For some items, you can also control specific aspects of how those items work and how they can be used.

You can access all the tools in the Info window from a single pane by using its expansion triangles. The window is organized into sections; you expose a section by clicking its expansion triangle. You can have multiple information windows open at the same time (which is helpful when you want to compare items).

The Info window has slightly different features and information for each of the following groups:

■ Folders and volumes

■ Applications

■ Documents

The sections you see for each type of item are described in Table 4.4.

TABLE 4.4 SECTIONS OF THE GET INFO WINDOW

Section	Applicable Items	Information/Tools It Provides
Spotlight Comments	Folders and volumes; applications; documents	Enables you to enter comments that will be searched when you use Spotlight or choose this as a criterion for a smart folder search.
General	Folders and volumes; applications; documents	Provides identification information about the item, such as its name, type, and significant dates.
More Info	Folders and volumes; applications; documents	Provides additional information about an item such as the date on which it was last opened, resolution information (for images), and so on.
Name & Extension	Folders and volumes; applications; documents	Gives the full item name, including its filename extension if applicable.
Preview	Folders and volumes; applications; documents	Shows the icon of everything except documents. For documents, a preview of the document's content is provided (this is the same preview the Column view provides).
Languages	Applications	Displays and enables you to choose the languages that should be available in the application.
Plug-ins	Applications	Enables you to configure plug-ins for the application. You can enable or disable plug-ins and can add or remove them.
Open with	Documents	Enables you to select an application with which to open a document. You can also set the application used for all documents of the same type.
Ownership & Permissions	Folders and volumes; applications; documents	Enables you to configure the access permissions for an item.

Examples of how to use each of these parts of the Info Window are provided in the following sections.

WORKING WITH THE SPOTLIGHT COMMENTS INFORMATION

The Spotlight Comments section enables you to add comments to the selected item:

1. Open the Info window for the item in which you are interested.
2. Expand the Spotlight Comments section.

3. Enter your comments in the field. The comments you enter remain with the item, and you can read them by either expanding the Comments section or adding the Comments column to the List view and viewing a Finder window in that view.

> **TIP**
>
> You can use the Comments field as a search criterion for a smart folder. This can be useful to create and easily gather a group of related items together in a smart folder.

WORKING WITH GENERAL INFORMATION

The General section of the Info window is used mostly to provide detailed information about an item. However, for specific items, you can also use the controls it provides:

1. Select the item you are interested in and choose File, Get Info or press ⌘-I. The Info window will appear.

> **TIP**
>
> You can also use the Actions pop-up menu or contextual menu to open the Info window.

2. Expand the General section if it isn't expanded by default.
3. View the information provided at the top of the window.
4. Use any tools that appear to configure the item.

Depending on the item you select, you have the following choices:

- You can select the Locked check box that appears when the selected item is a document, a folder, or an application to prevent the item from being changed.
- You can use the Stationery Pad check box to convert a selected document into a template.
- If the selected item is an alias, you can associate it with a different file by using the Select New Original button and then choosing the file you want it to point to.
- You can apply a color label by clicking the color you want to apply to the item. Click the "x" button to remove a label from the item.

WORKING WITH MORE INFO INFORMATION

The More Info section provides a variety of data that depends on the kind of item about which you are viewing information. For example, when you have selected an image file, this section displays resolution information. For most items, you will see the date on which the item was last opened. In some cases, Mac OS X can't generate any more information for an item in which case you'll see No Info in this section. To view more info for an item, do the following:

1. Select the item and press ⌘-I. The Info window will open.

2. Expand the More Info section.

WORKING WITH NAME AND EXTENSION INFORMATION

The Name & Extension section enables you to view and change the name of the selected item:

1. Select the item you are interested in and press ⌘-I. The Info window will appear.

2. Expand the Name & Extension section.

3. Edit the item name in the Name & Extension field that appears. Remember to add or edit filename extensions as appropriate (volumes and folders don't have filename extensions).

NOTE

Applications have the filename extension `.app`.

When you are displaying Name & Extension information for a document, the "Hide extension" check box will be enabled. When this is checked, the filename extension for the file is hidden in Finder windows. This check box is overridden by the Finder's file extension preference. If the "Show all file extensions" check box in the Finder Preferences window is checked, filename extensions are shown regardless of the "Hide extension" check box for an individual file. The Finder preference must be unchecked for this box to hide or show a file's filename extension.

WORKING WITH PREVIEW INFORMATION

The Preview section provides a preview of the selected item. For everything except documents, this preview is simply the item's icon. However, when you use this feature on a document, you get a preview of the item's content, just as you do when you view a Finder window in Column view. If the content is dynamic, such as a QuickTime movie, you can view or hear that content from the Preview section:

1. Select the item you are interested in and press ⌘-I to open the Info window.

2. Expand the Preview section.

3. Use the Preview section to preview the item's content. For example, use the controls to view the item if it is a QuickTime movie. If you selected an image, you can view a preview of the image.

For documents for which Mac OS X can't generate a preview, you see the appropriate icon instead.

WORKING WITH LANGUAGES INFORMATION

Mac OS X applications can support various languages. The Languages section of the Information window enables you to choose the languages you want to be available in an application. Do the following steps:

1. Select the application you are interested in and press ⌘-I.
2. Expand the Languages section.
3. Remove the check box next to any language you want to disable for that application.
4. Check the check box next to any language you want to enable in the application.
5. To remove a language from the application, select the language and click Remove. After you confirm what you are doing, that language's support files are removed from the application's files and are no longer available.
6. To add language support to the application, click the Add button and select the language file you want to add.

TIP

> You can have more than one section of the Info window expanded at the same time. In fact, you can have as few as none expanded, or you can have all of them expanded.

WORKING WITH PLUG-IN INFORMATION

Mac OS X applications can use plug-ins to provide additional capabilities and functionality. You can enable or disable plug-ins for an application and remove or add plug-ins using the following steps:

1. Select the application for which you want to configure plug-ins and press ⌘-I.
2. Expand the Plug-ins section.
3. Uncheck the box next to any plug-in you want to disable for that application.
4. Check the box next to any plug-in you want to enable in the application.
5. To remove a plug-in from the application, select the plug-in and click Remove. After you confirm what you are doing, that plug-in is removed from the application and is no longer available.
6. To add a plug-in to the application, click the Add button and select the plug-in file you want to add.

WORKING WITH OPEN WITH INFORMATION

You can use the "Open with" section to determine which application is used to open a file:

1. Select the document you are interested in and press ⌘-I.
2. Expand the "Open with" section.

3. Select the application with which you want the file to be opened on the pop-up menu; the application currently associated with the document is shown in the pop-up menu. The "suggested" applications appear on the menu by default. If you want to select an application that is not shown on the pop-up menu, click Other and select the application you want to be used.

4. If you want all files of the same type to be opened with the application you selected, click the Change All button.

WORKING WITH OWNERSHIP AND PERMISSIONS INFORMATION

The Ownership & Permissions section is used to configure access to the item (see Figure 4.22). This area enables you to control who has access to an item, as well as defining the type of access provided.

Figure 4.22
The Ownership & Permissions section of the Information window is an important security tool whether you share your Mac directly or across a network.

→ To learn how to configure access to an item, **see** "Understanding and Setting Permissions," **p. 959**.

WORKING WITH THE INSPECTOR

When you work with the Info window, each item has its own window. This is nice because you can display the Info window for multiple items at the same time. However, it can get tedious when you don't want to do this because you have to select each item, open its Info window, and then close the Info window when you are done.

You can use the Inspector to see information about the *currently selected* item rather than the one that was selected when you opened the Info window. This is handy because you can leave the Inspector open and as you select items, their information will be displayed. You don't clutter up your desktop with lots of Info windows and you don't have to keep opening the Info window for items.

To open the Inspector, hold the Option key down and choose File, Show Inspector or press ⌘-I. The Inspector window will appear. It looks just like the Info window except it has square corners instead of rounded ones. As you select items on the desktop, the information in the Inspector will change to reflect the currently selected item.

CUSTOMIZING THE MAC OS X DESKTOP

Although the default Mac OS X desktop is very nice to look at, you will probably want to customize it to suit your preferences. You can customize the appearance of your desktop in many ways, including the following:

- Change the clock
- Change the mounted disk behavior
- Change the desktop icon size
- Change the desktop icon arrangement
- Set desktop pictures

NOTE

> You can also change the menu bar by adding icons to it, such as the Displays icon, the Volume icon, the AirPort icon, and others. These icons are discussed in the related sections of this book. For example, you will learn about the Displays menu bar icon in the section on configuring monitors using the Displays pane of the System Preferences application.

4

CHANGING THE CLOCK DISPLAY

By default, Mac OS X provides a clock in the upper-right corner of the desktop. You can also configure the clock to be shown in a window that floats on the desktop if you prefer. You can control the appearance of the clock by using the System Preferences application:

1. Open the System Preferences application.
2. Click the Date & Time icon.
3. In the Date & Time pane, click the Clock tab (see Figure 4.23).
4. To hide the clock, uncheck the "Show the date and time" check box. The clock is removed and all the clock options are disabled.
5. If you want the clock to be displayed on the right end of the menu bar, click the Menu Bar radio button. If you want the clock to appear in a floating window, click the Window radio button.
6. If you prefer the time to be displayed in digital format, click the Digital radio button; to see it as an analog clock, click the Analog radio button.
7. If you chose the menu bar clock, check the "Display the time with seconds" check box to include the seconds in the display.

Figure 4.23
The Clock tab of the Date & Time pane of the System Preferences application enables you to customize the clock on the desktop.

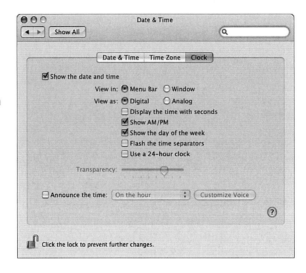

8. If you want the AM/PM indicator to be shown, check the Show AM/PM check box.

9. If you have selected the digital menu bar clock, click the "Show the day of the week" check box to include the day in the clock display.

10. If you want the colon between the hour and minutes to be displayed, check the "Flash the time separators" check box.

11. If you want to use a 24-hour clock, check the "Use a 24-hour clock" check box.

12. If you chose the window display, use the Transparency slider to set the transparency of the window. Because the window floats on top of all the others, making it less transparent can block the view of underlying windows.

13. If you want the time to be announced, check the "Announce the time" check box. Then select the time interval on the pop-up menu. Finally, click the Customize Voice button to select the voice used to announce the time.

TIP

> You can click the menu bar clock to briefly display the full date. The menu on which the date appears also enables you to change the view option (analog or digital) and open the Date & Time pane of the System Preferences application.

CHANGING THE DESKTOP'S APPEARANCE

You can customize other aspects of the appearance of the desktop using the following steps:

1. Select Finder, Preferences or press ⌘-, to open the Finder Preferences window.

2. Click the General tab.

3. Check the check boxes for the mounted items you want to appear on the desktop. Your choices are "Hard disks," "CDs, DVDs, and iPods," and "Connected servers." If you uncheck the check boxes, you don't see the items on your desktop; you can access these items through the Computer folder or within any Finder window. If you check the check boxes, the items appear on the desktop.

4. Close the Finder Preferences window.

5. Click on the desktop.

6. Press ⌘-J to open the View Options window for the desktop.

7. Use the View Options controls to configure how icons on the desktop appear, such as size and grouping.

→ To learn about the details of these options, **see** "Customizing Finder Window Views," **p. 83**.

8. Close the View Options window.

9. Open the Desktop & Screen Saver pane of the System Preferences application. This pane has two tabs. The Desktop tab enables you to set your desktop picture, whereas the Screen Saver tab enables you to configure the screen saver.

10. Click the Desktop tab (see Figure 4.24). The Image well shows the desktop picture currently being used. In the left pane of the window, the Source pane shows the available image collections. The right pane shows the images contained in the selected source.

Figure 4.24
While writing a book, I use the ever-exciting Aqua Blue desktop picture.

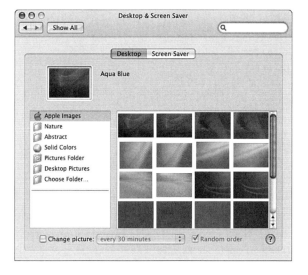

4

TIP

If you just want to replace the current image with another one, drag the image you want to use onto the well. It replaces the image currently shown there and appears on the desktop immediately.

11. Select the source containing the image you want to apply to the desktop. You have the following options:

    - By default, Mac OS X includes three image collections (Apple Images, Nature, and Abstract); these appear at the top of the Source pane.

    - You can select the Solid Colors source to apply a solid color to the desktop.

    - The Pictures folder is the Pictures folder in your Home directory.

    - Desktop Pictures is the Desktop Pictures folder included in the Library folder (basically, all the default Apple background images, but you can add images to this folder to be able to select them).

    - Choose Folder enables you to select any other folder to use as a source of images.

    - The lower part of the pane contains iPhoto collections if you have iPhoto installed on your Mac. You can select your Photo Library to choose any image in your iPhoto Library or select any photo album to use its images.

    - Except for the Choose Folder option, when you select an option, the images contained in the location appear in the preview pane in the right part of the window.

      If you select the Choose Folder option, you can use the resulting sheet to move to and select a folder. When you do so, the images contained in that folder are shown in the preview pane.

    - When you select a folder, including the predefined ones, only the images at the root level of that folder are available on the preview pane. For example, if you select your Pictures folder, only the images that are loose in that folder are available. Any images contained within folders that are inside the Pictures folder are not available.

12. Apply the image to the desktop by clicking it on the preview pane. It appears in the Image well and on your desktop.

13. If you want to change desktop pictures automatically, check the "Change picture" check box. The image in the well becomes the "recycle" icon to show that you have selected to have the system change images periodically. The images contained in the source selected in the Source pane will be applied to the desktop based on the criteria you configure.

14. Use the pop-up menu to select the time at which you want the images to be changed. The options include "when logging in," "when waking from sleep," and a time interval from every 5 seconds to once per day.

15. To have the images selected at random, check the "Random order" check box. If you uncheck this, the images appear in the same order as they appear in the selected source (for example, alphabetically).

You can use just about any graphic file as a desktop image, such as JPEG, TIFF, and PICT files.

If you want to install images in the Mac OS X Desktop Pictures folder so they appear by default, just place them in the location `macosx/Library/Desktop Pictures/`, where `macosx` is the name of your Mac OS X startup volume.

This folder contains the collections of images that appear on the Collection pane. You can add your images to the default folders, and they will appear in those collections. Unfortunately, you can't add collections to the menu by creating folders within the Desktop Pictures folder.

NOTE

> If you use more than one monitor, each monitor has its own desktop picture. A Desktop Picture pane appears on each desktop. You use that pane to configure the desktop images on each monitor.

TIP

> If you want to change the image that is shown when the login window is displayed, name an image file "Aqua Blue.jpg" and copy it to the following location `Mac OS X/Library/Desktop Pictures/` where `Mac OS X` is the name of your startup volume. You will be prompted to replace the existing file. Do so. The next time the background image is displayed, such as when you log out, the new image will be shown. (If you will want to use the default image again, save a copy of the file before you replace it.)

4

MAC OS X TO THE MAX: DESKTOP KEYBOARD SHORTCUTS

Table 4.5 lists keyboard shortcuts for working with the Finder.

TABLE 4.5   KEYBOARD SHORTCUTS FOR THE FINDER

Action	Keyboard Shortcut
Add to Sidebar	⌘-T
Close All	Option-⌘-W
Close Window	⌘-W
Connect to Server	⌘-K
Copy item	⌘-C
Cut item	⌘-X
Duplicate	⌘-D
Eject	⌘-E

continues

TABLE 4.5   CONTINUED

Action	Keyboard Shortcut
Empty Trash	Shift-⌘-Delete
Find	⌘-F
Force Quit	Option-⌘-Esc
Get Info	⌘-I
Go Back	⌘-[
Go Forward	⌘-]
Go to Applications Folder	Shift-⌘-A
Go to Computer Folder	Shift-⌘-C
Go to Enclosing Folder	⌘-up arrow
Go to Folder	Shift-⌘-G
Go to Home Folder	Shift-⌘-H
Go to iDisk Folder	Shift-⌘-I
Go to Network Folder	Shift-⌘-K
Go to Utilities Folder	Shift-⌘-U
Hide Finder	⌘-H
Hide Toolbar	Option-⌘-T
Log Out	Shift-⌘-Q
Mac Help	⌘-?
Make Alias	⌘-L
Minimize Window	⌘-M
Minimize All	Option-⌘-M
Move to Trash	⌘-Delete
New Finder Window	⌘-N
New Folder	Shift-⌘-N
New Smart Folder	Option-⌘-N
Open	⌘-O
Paste item	⌘-V
Preferences	⌘-,
Select All	⌘-A
Show Original	⌘-R

Action	Keyboard Shortcut
Show View Options	⌘-J
View as Columns	⌘-3
View as Icons	⌘-1
View as List	⌘-2

4

CHAPTER **5**

Using and Customizing the Dock

In this chapter

UNDERSTANDING THE DOCK

The Dock was one of the most revolutionary parts of the original Mac OS X desktop, and it remains one of the most noticeable aspects of the OS under version 10.4. If you want to master Mac OS X, you should learn to take full advantage of the Dock's capabilities.

The Dock provides you with information about, control over, and customization of Mac OS X and the applications and documents with which you work (see Figure 5.1). By default, the Dock appears at the bottom of the desktop, but you can control many aspects of its appearance and where it is located. You can also control how it works, to a great degree.

Figure 5.1
The Dock is an essential part of Mac OS X.

Running application markers

Application separation line

The Dock is organized into two general sections; the application/document separation line, as shown in Figure 5.1, divides them. On the left side of this line, you see application icons. On the right side of the line, you see icons for documents, folders, minimized Finder or application windows, and the Trash/Eject icon.

NOTE

In addition to applications or documents and folders, you might encounter another type of Dock icon. This type is called a *dockling*. Docklings are modules you can use to control applications or provide additional functionality on the Dock. Many docklings are available; some applications include docklings, whereas other applications consist entirely of a dockling. Docklings can be placed on either side of the Dock's dividing line.

The Dock performs the following functions:

- **Shows running applications**—Whenever an application is running, you see its icon on the Dock. A small triangle is located at the bottom of every running application's icon (refer to Figure 5.1). The Dock also provides information about what is happening in open applications. For example, when you receive email, the Mail application's icon changes to indicate the number of messages you have received since you last read messages.

- **Enables you to open applications, folders, minimized windows, and documents quickly**—You can open any item on the Dock by clicking its icon.

- **Enables you to quickly switch among open applications and windows**—You can click an application's or window's icon on the Dock to move into it. You can also use the ⌘-Tab key and ⌘-Shift-Tab keyboard shortcuts to move among open applications.

- **Enables you to control an application and switch to any windows open in an application**—When you hold down the Control key and click (or right-click a two-button mouse) the icon of an open application, a pop-up menu appears. This menu lists commands as well as all the open windows related to that application; you can choose an item by selecting it from this menu.

- **Enables you to customize its appearance and function**—You can store the icon for any item (applications, folders, and documents) on the Dock. You can also control how the Dock looks, including its size, whether it is always visible, where it is located, and so on.

TIP

> When you open an application whose icon is not installed on the Dock, its Dock menu includes the Keep in Dock command. If you choose this, the icon is added to the Dock.

5

When the Trash Is Not the Trash
Here is a question for you, "When is the Trash not the Trash?" If you have worked with Mac OS X before, you know the answer to this one! When you select an ejectable item, such as a CD or a mounted network volume, the Trash icon located on the right (or bottom if you use a vertical Dock) on the Dock becomes the Eject icon. When you drag an ejectable item onto this icon, it is ejected from your Mac. This makes more sense than dragging something onto the Trash to eject it.

USING ITEMS ON THE DOCK

By default, the Dock is preconfigured with various icons you can begin using immediately. When you point to an item on the Dock, a ToolTip appears above the icon that provides the name of the item (you will probably recognize many of the items on the Dock by their icons).

The default items on the Dock can include the following:

- **Finder**—The Finder icon opens a new Finder window that shows your default new Finder window location (which can be to your Computer, Home folder, Documents folder, or just about any other location you choose) if no Finder windows are visible on the desktop. If at least one Finder window is open on the desktop, clicking the Finder icon while another application is frontmost takes you back to the Finder window that was most recently active. If you hold down the Control key while you click this icon (or right-click on it), you will see a list of all Finder windows that are open; choose a window from the list to move into it.

→ To learn how to set your default new Finder window location, **see** "Configuring How New Finder Windows Open," **p. 59**.

> **TIP**
>
> There are at least two other ways to open a Dock icon's menu. One is to just click the Dock icon and hold down the mouse button. After a second or two, the Dock item's menu appears. Even better, if you use a two-button mouse (which I strongly recommend), you can right-click a Dock item to open its menu.

→ To learn about two-button mice, **see** "Finding, Installing, and Configuring a Mouse," **p. 842**.

- **Dashboard**—This application provides access to widgets, which are mini-applications that pop up when you press the Dashboard's default key.
- **Safari**—This is Mac OS X's excellent web browser. Safari offers many great features as you will learn later in this book. When you open the Safari Dock icon's menu, you can quickly jump to any web page that is open, among other things.
- **Mail**—Mail is Mac OS X's email application. When you receive email, an attention icon showing how many new messages you have received appears. If you open Mail's Dock icon menu, you can choose from several commands, such as Get New Mail and Compose New Message.
- **iChat**—This is Apple's instant messaging application, which you can use to communicate with others on your local network or over the Internet (it is compatible with AOL Instant Messenger) via text chats or audio/video conferencing.
- **Address Book**—Address Book is Mac OS X's contact manager application. You can store all sorts of information for everyone with whom you communicate, such as email addresses and phone numbers.
- **iTunes**—iTunes is the Mac's excellent digital music application. Its Dock menu offers selections you can use to control music playback.
- **iCal**—You can use iCal to manage your calendar; it offers other cool features such as the ability to publish your calendar to the Web so other people can access it.
- **QuickTime Player**—The QuickTime Player application enables you to view all sorts of dynamic content, such as video, that is stored on local discs or disks or on the Internet.

- **System Preferences**—The System Preferences application enables you to configure and customize various aspects of Mac OS X. You will be using it frequently, which is why its icon is included on the Dock by default.
- **Apple - Mac OS X**—Clicking this icon takes you to Apple's Mac OS X web page.
- **Trash/Eject**—Some things never change; under Mac OS X, the Trash does what it always has. It is always located on the right end of the Dock (or the bottom if you use a vertical Dock). When you select an ejectable item, the Trash icon changes to the Eject symbol. When the Trash contains files or folders, its icon includes crumpled paper so that you know the Trash is "full."

TIP

> Another way to have an application open automatically when you log in is to open its Dock menu and choose "Open at Login."

Using items on the Dock is easy: Simply click an icon to open whatever the item is. If the icon is for an application, that application opens (or moves to the front if it is already open). If the item is a document, the document opens, and if the item is a folder, the folder opens in a new Finder window. If the item is a dockling, a pop-up menu containing commands appears, and if the icon is a minimized Finder window, that window becomes active and moves onto the desktop. I'm sure you get the idea.

NOTE

> When you click a non-running application's icon, you might notice that it "bounces" as the application opens. This provides feedback to you that your selection was registered with the OS and it is working on opening your application. You can turn off this feature, as you will learn later in this chapter.

Unless the application is permanently installed on the Dock (in which case the icon remains in the same position), the icon for each application you open appears on the right edge of the application area of the Dock. As you open more applications, the existing application icons shift to the left and each icon becomes slightly smaller.

NOTE

> The Dock is very insistent about getting your attention, even when it is hidden. If the Dock is hidden and an application needs to present information to you, such as an error dialog box, its icon appears to bounce up out of nowhere and continues to bounce up and down until you switch to that application to see what it has to say.

To move among the open applications you see on the Dock, you can press ⌘-Tab. As long as you hold down the ⌘ key, a menu appears across the center of the screen (see Figure 5.2). On this menu, you will see the icon for each open application (which, by no mere coincidence, are the icons that have the open application marker under them on the Dock).

5

The icons are listed in the order in which you have most recently used the applications, with the current application being on the left side of the menu. Each time you press ⌘-Tab, the icon for the open application you are selecting becomes highlighted and you see the application's name below its icon. When you release the ⌘-Tab keys, the application you select becomes active (and visible, if it is hidden). You can move backward through the open applications on the menu by continuing to hold down the ⌘ key and pressing Shift-Tab.

Figure 5.2
This list of open applications appears when you hold down the ⌘ key and press the Tab key.

If you don't hold down the ⌘ key and instead just press ⌘-Tab, the menu won't appear; instead you will move immediately into the next application on the list of open applications. Again, this list is organized according to the applications you have most recently used. For example, suppose you checked your email in Mail and then began working in Word. If you pressed ⌘-Tab once, you would jump back into Mail. If you pressed ⌘-Tab again, you would move back to Word because that was the application you were most recently using. Likewise, if you pressed ⌘-Tab twice in a row, you would move back to the application you were using before the most recent one. Although this might be a bit hard for me to describe, this technique enables you to easily switch among open applications by using only the keyboard.

NOTE

> If an application is open but the window in which you want to work is minimized, when you select that application with the ⌘-Tab shortcut, you will move into the application but any windows that are minimized will not appear on the desktop because they are minimized. You have to click a minimized window's icon on the Dock for it to move back onto the desktop.

Unlike open applications, open documents don't automatically appear on the Dock. Document icons appear on the Dock only when you add them to the Dock manually or when you have minimized the document's window. Remember that, when you open an application's menu in the Dock, you will see a list of all the windows open in that application. You can then choose a listed window (such as a document window) to move into it.

NOTE

Just like all icons on the Dock, the names of folders, minimized windows, and documents are shown above their icons when you point to them.

When you minimize a window, by default, the window moves into the Dock using the Genie Effect, during which it is pulled down into the Dock and becomes an icon that is a thumbnail view of the window. The icon for a minimized window behaves just like icons for other items do. To open (or maximize) a minimized window, click its icon on the Dock and it is pulled back onto the desktop. You can change this so that the Scale Effect is used instead. This looks like the window is being quickly scaled down while it is placed on the Dock. Functionally, these effects do the same thing, but the Scale Effect is a bit faster, although not as impressive looking.

Minimized windows are marked with the related application's icon in the lower-right corner of the Dock icon so you can easily tell from which application the windows come. For example, minimized Finder windows have the Finder icon in the lower-right corner, minimized Safari icons have the Safari icon, and so on.

TIP

You can quickly minimize an open window by pressing ⌘-M.

When you minimize an application window, it is moved onto the Dock, just like any other window. However, when you hide an application, its windows do not appear on the Dock. The hidden application's icon continues to be marked with the arrow so you know that the application is running. You can open a hidden application's Dock menu to jump into one of its open windows.

As you add items to the Dock and as icons are added when you open applications, the icons on the Dock continue to get smaller and the Dock expands so it shows all open items as well as the icons that are permanently installed on the Dock (see Figure 5.3).

Just as with an application's icon, if you point to a folder, an application, or a dockling icon on the Dock and press the Control key while you click, a pop-up menu appears. What is on this menu depends on what you click.

5

Figure 5.3
The items on the Dock shrink and the Dock expands so you can have as many items on it as you'd like (compare this figure to Figure 5.1).

5

TIP

> Remember that if you don't want to press the Control key while you click, just click an icon and hold down the mouse button. The menu will appear after a second or two. Or, right-click a Dock icon if you use a two-button mouse.

When you use Dock icon menus, the following outcomes are possible:

- If you open the menu for the Finder Dock icon, the pop-up menu shows a list of all the open Finder windows, whether the windows are minimized or are on the desktop. Select a window on the menu to make it active. If you are working in another application, you can also select Hide to hide all open Finder windows.

- If you open the Dock menu for a closed application, folder, or document, you will see the Show In Finder command, which opens a Finder window containing the item on which you clicked; the item is selected when the Finder window containing it appears. This can be a quick way to find out where something is located.

- If you open the Dock menu for a folder, a hierarchical menu showing the contents of that folder will appear. You can jump to an item within the folder by selecting it on the menu. This is a great way to make access to items within specific folders fast and easy (see Figure 5.4). Any folders within a folder on the Dock also become hierarchical menus so that you can also quickly access nested folders.

Figure 5.4
Adding the Utilities folder to the Dock enables you to choose any of Mac OS X's utility applications from the Dock.

- If you open the Dock menu for a dockling, the commands provided by that dockling appear.

- If you point to a URL reference or other item (such as a minimized document window) on the Dock, identification text appears above the icon to explain what the item is. If the icon is for a document, you can open the document by selecting Open on its Dock menu.

- If you open the Dock menu for an open application, you will see some basic commands, including Quit. You will also see a list of open windows; you can quickly jump to an open window by selecting it. Some applications also enable you to control what is happening from the Dock menu. For example, when iTunes is open, you can control music playback by using its Dock menu.

When you quit an open application, its icon disappears from the Dock—unless you have added that application to the Dock so that it always appears there. Minimized windows disappear from the Dock when you maximize them or when you close the application from which the document window comes.

TIP

If you fill the Dock with many open applications, documents, and folders, it can be a nuisance to switch to each item and close it. Instead, log out (either select Apple menu, Log Out, or press Shift-⌘-Q). When you log out, all open applications are shut down, all documents are closed, and all minimized folder windows are removed from the Dock. When you log back in, the Dock is back to normal. All Finder windows that were on the Dock are gone from there, but they remain open on the desktop. Hold down the Option key and click the Close box of one of the open windows to close them all.

5

ORGANIZING THE DOCK

The default Dock is powerful, but it gets even more useful when you include the items in it that you use often and organize the Dock to suit your preferences. You can move icons around the Dock, add more applications to it, remove applications that are currently on it, and add your own folders and documents to it so they are easily accessible.

MOVING ICONS ON THE DOCK

You can change the location of any installed item on the Dock by dragging it. When you move one icon between two others, they slide apart to make room for the icon you are moving. However, you can't move most icons across the dividing line; for example, you can't move an application icon to the right side of the Dock.

NOTE

> You can't move most icons across the dividing line on the dock; however, exceptions to this are dockling icons, which can be placed on either side of the line.

If you move the icon of an open application that isn't installed on the Dock, that icon moves to the location to which you drag it and becomes installed on the Dock.

The Dock has two icons you can't move at all: Finder and Trash/Eject. The Finder icon always appears on the left end of the Dock (or top if you use a vertical Dock), and the Trash is always on the right end (or bottom if you use a vertical Dock). Other than these two end points, you can change all the other icons on the Dock as much as you like.

ADDING ICONS TO THE DOCK

You can add applications, folders, and files to the Dock so it contains the items you want. Drag the item you want to add down to the Dock and drop it where you want it to be installed. Application icons must be placed on the left side of the dividing line, and all others (folders and files) are placed on the right side (the exception is docklings, which can be placed on either side). Just as when you move icons on the Dock, when you add items between other icons already installed on it, the other icons slide apart to make room for them. When you add an item to the Dock, an alias to that item is created and you see its icon on the Dock.

TIP

> You can add multiple items to the Dock at the same time by holding down the ⌘ key while you select each item you want to add to the Dock and then drag them there.

REMOVING ITEMS FROM THE DOCK

You can remove an icon from the Dock by dragging it up onto the desktop. When you do this, the icon disappears in a puff of digital smoke and no longer appears on the Dock. Because the icons on the Dock are aliases, removing them doesn't affect the applications or files that those aliases represent.

If you drag a minimized window from the Dock, it snaps back to the Dock when you release the mouse button. You remove minimized windows from the Dock by maximizing or closing them.

ADDING FOLDERS TO THE DOCK

You can also add any folder to the Dock; when you click a folder's Dock icon, the folder opens in a Finder window.

When you place a folder on the Dock, you can open its Dock menu that will list the contents of that folder (refer to Figure 5.4). All the subfolders also appear in hierarchical menus.

This feature is one of the most useful that the Dock offers. You can use it to create custom menus containing anything on your Mac (literally). The uses for this feature are almost unlimited. Some ideas include the following:

- Add your Home directory to the Dock so you can easily move to an item within it.
- Add your project folders to the Dock so you can easily get to the files you need for the project on which you are working.
- Add smart folders to the Dock so you can search your Mac by clicking a smart folder's icon.
- Add the Applications folder to the Dock. This gives you quick access to all the applications on your Mac that are installed in the default Applications folder.

> **NOTE**
>
> Although adding folders to the Dock is useful, it can be easier and just as useful to add folders to the Places sidebar in Finder windows. The benefit to adding folders to the Dock is that you can access them without bringing the Finder to the front.

You might find that adding folders to the Dock is even more useful than adding application or file icons to it. Remember that you can make more room on the Dock by removing items that you don't use from it. For example, you might choose to remove most or all of the application icons from the Dock and instead add the Applications folder to it.

5

CUSTOMIZING THE APPEARANCE AND BEHAVIOR OF THE DOCK

The Dock offers several behaviors you can change to suit your preferences. You can also change various aspects of its appearance, as follows:

- **Size**—You can change the default or current size of the Dock.

- **Magnification**—The magnification effect causes items on the Dock to be magnified when you point to them. This can make identifying items easier, especially when many items are on the Dock or when it is small (see Figure 5.5). You can set the amount of magnification that is used.

Figure 5.5
The magnification effect makes identifying items easier, although the magnification level of this particular Dock would be a bit much for most Mac users.

- **Hide/Show**—The Dock does consume some screen space. Because it is always topmost, it can get in the way when you are working near its location on the screen. You can set the Dock so that it is hidden except when you point to it. When this behavior is enabled and you point to the Dock's location, it pops onto the desktop and you can use it. When you move off the Dock, it is hidden again.

  If the Dock is hidden, you need to hover a moment in the area of the screen in which it is located before it will appear. This prevents the Dock from popping up when you are working in a document near the edge of the screen and pass the mouse over the Dock's location.

- **Dock location**—The Dock can appear at its default location on the bottom of the screen, or you can move it to the left or right side of the desktop.

- **Minimize Effect**—You can choose either the Genie Effect or the Scale Effect.
- **Icon animation**—You already know about this one because it is on by default. When you click an application's icon to open that application, the icon bounces to show you that the application is opening.

NOTE

> The amount of magnification is not relative to the size of the Dock. For example, the magnified icons are the same size whether the Dock is large or small. Of course, because the Dock size is different, the magnified icons do make more contrast with a smaller Dock, but that is only because of the comparison your eye makes.

You can control these settings using the Dock pane of the System Preferences utility. Do the following:

1. Open the System Preferences application by clicking its icon on the Dock.
2. Click Dock to open the Dock pane of the utility (see Figure 5.6).

Figure 5.6
Use the Dock pane of the System Preferences utility to configure the appearance and behavior of the Dock.

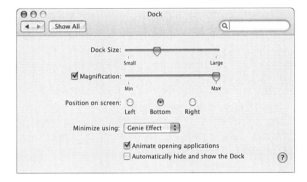

TIP

> You can also open the Dock preferences pane by selecting Apple menu, Dock, Dock Preferences. The Dock command on the Apple menu also enables you to quickly turn Dock magnification and hiding on or off; you can also change its location by selecting the location in which you want it to be.

3. Use the Dock Size slider to set the default size of the Dock.

   Using the Dock Size slider changes the size of the Dock as well as the items on it. The best practice is to configure the Dock with the items you will want it to contain. Then, use this slider to set its size when it contains those items. As you add items to it, it gets wider or taller until it fills the screen. After the Dock has expanded to the width of the screen, the items on it get smaller as you add more items to the Dock.

TIP

You can also change the size of the Dock by pointing to the line that divides the application side of the Dock from the document and folder side. When you do so, the cursor becomes a horizontal line with vertical arrows pointing from the top and bottom sides. Drag this cursor up to make the Dock larger or down to make it smaller.

4. Check the Magnification check box to have the Dock use that behavior, and then use the slider to set the amount of magnification.

NOTE

Changes you make in the Dock pane of the System Preferences application are live, and you see their effects on the Dock immediately. Of course, to see the magnification effect, you must point to an item on the Dock.

5. Click the Left, Bottom, or Right radio button to set the Dock's location on the desktop.

6. Use the "Minimize using" pop-up menu to choose the minimize/maximize effect; the options are Genie Effect or Scale Effect.

7. If you prefer that application icons not bounce when the application opens, uncheck the "Animate opening applications" check box.

8. Check the "Automatically hide and show the Dock" check box if you want the Dock to be visible only when you linger at its location on the screen.

TIP

You can also configure the Dock by using its pop-up menu. Point to the application/folder dividing line. When you see the size-change pointer (the horizontal line with vertical arrows coming from it), hold down the Control key and click. You will see a pop-up menu that enables you to control the magnification, hiding, position, and minimization effects.

All Dock settings are specific to each user account, meaning that each user can have her own items installed on her Dock, configure the Dock to be hidden, and so on. One user's Dock settings do not affect any other user's Dock.

NOTE

There are applications that are designed to be used only from the Dock; these are called Docklings. For example, you can add a calendar dockling to your Dock so that the current calendar is always displayed there. Docklings never have taken off even though the Dock has been part of OS X since its inception. In version 10.4, similar but better, functionality is provided by the Dashboard and its widgets.

→ To learn about widgets, **see** Chapter 6, "Working with the Dashboard and Widgets," **p. 159**.

MAC OS X TO THE MAX: USING DOCK KEYBOARD SHORTCUTS

Dock-related keyboard shortcuts are listed in Table 5.1.

TABLE 5.1   KEYBOARD SHORTCUTS FOR THE DOCK

Action	Keyboard Shortcut
Turn hiding off or on	Option-⌘-D
Move to the next open application	⌘-Tab
Move to the previous open application	Shift-⌘-Tab
Minimize a window	⌘-M
Highlight/unhighlight the Dock	Control-F3
Move among Dock items when it is highlighted	Left/Right arrow keys

NOTE

If you are using a mobile Mac, you might need to press the Function key (fn) to cause its function keys to act like true function keys. For example, on some mobile Macs, the F3 key controls volume unless you press the fn key, in which case it acts like the F3 key.

5

CHAPTER 6

WORKING WITH THE DASHBOARD AND WIDGETS

In this chapter

USING THE DASHBOARD AND WIDGETS

Mac OS X's Dashboard is a way to quickly access and use mini-applications, called *widgets*. Some widgets are separate applications, while others enable you to access other, full-blown Mac OS X applications.

By default, the Dashboard application is always running so that its widgets are always available to you. Unless you remove it from the Dock, the Dashboard's icon is located to the immediate right of the Finder icon on the Dock (or below the Finder icon if you use a vertical Dock).

To use the Dashboard, you activate it. When you do so, the widgets that you have configured to appear will open on your desktop in the foreground and all other windows will move into the background. After you have used the widgets you want to use, you deactivate the Dashboard again and the widgets become hidden and open windows come to the foreground again in the same condition as when you activated the Dashboard.

ACTIVATING AND DEACTIVATING THE DASHBOARD

By default, you can activate the Dashboard in the following ways:

- Press F12 on the keyboard for desktop Macs.

> **TIP**
>
> If you use a mobile Mac, such as a PowerBook or iBook, open the Dashboard & Expose pane of the System Preferences application and look at the key listed on the Dashboard pop-up menu to determine what the default Dashboard activation key is on your Mac.

- Click the Dashboard icon on the Dock.
- Open the Dashboard Dock icon menu and choose Show Dashboard.
- Double-click the Dashboard's icon in the Applications folder.
- Double-click a widget's icon.

When you activate the Dashboard, the widgets that are configured to open when it is activated will appear (see Figure 6.1). You can then use those widgets or see the information they provide.

When you are done using widgets, you can deactivate the Dashboard again by pressing the default hot key, which is F12, or by clicking on the desktop outside of any open widget. All the widgets will disappear and you will return to your Mac's desktop.

CONFIGURING THE WIDGETS THAT OPEN WHEN YOU ACTIVATE THE DASHBOARD

You can configure the widgets that open when you activate the Dashboard by performing the following steps:

1. Press F12 to activate the Dashboard. The widgets currently configured to open will appear along with the Open Widget Bar button (shown in Figure 6.1).

Figure 6.1
When you activate the Dashboard, you'll be able access the widgets that are configured to open with it.

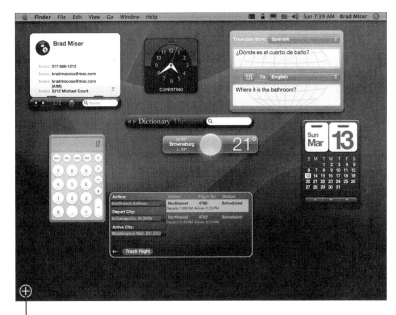

Open Widget Bar

2. Click the Open Widget Bar button. The Widget Bar will open and you will see all of the widgets that are currently installed on your Mac (see Figure 6.2). Widgets are shown in alphabetical order from left to right.

Figure 6.2
The Widget Bar shows all of the widgets that are currently installed on your Mac.

Close button

Browse arrows

3. Scroll through the installed widgets using the Browse arrows. At the bottom of each widget's icon, you'll see the widget's name.

4. To have a widget open when you activate the Dashboard, click its icon on the Widget Bar. The widget will appear on the screen (see Figure 6.3).

Figure 6.3
If you compare this figure to the previous one, you'll notice that the iTunes widget is now open.

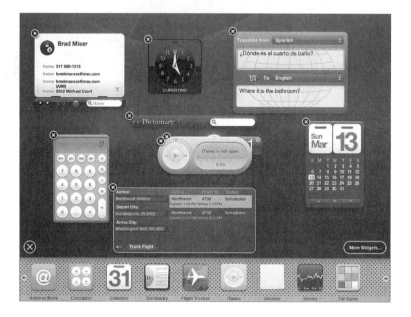

TIP

You can open multiple instances of the same widget at the same time by continuing to click its icon. Each time you do so, a new version of that widget will appear. This is useful for some widgets such as the Weather widget if you are interested in information about the weather in more than one area.

5. Drag the open widget to the location on the screen at which you want it to appear when you activate the Dashboard.

6. Close any widgets that you don't want to open when you activate the Dashboard by clicking the Close button, which is the "X" located in the upper-left corner of each widget's window.

7. Continue opening and placing widgets that you do want to use and closing those that you don't want to use until the Dashboard is configured to suit your preferences.

8. Close the Widget Bar by clicking the Close button, which is the X located just above the Widget Bar. The next time you activate the Dashboard, you will see and can use the widgets as you configured them.

TIP

You don't need to close the Widget Bar. When you deactivate the Dashboard, the Widget Bar is closed automatically. The next time you activate the Dashboard, the Widget Bar will remain closed.

USING AND CUSTOMIZING USEFUL WIDGETS

Mac OS X includes a number of useful widgets along with some that aren't so useful. In this section, you'll find a mini-review of some of the default widgets I think are worth using.

→ To learn how to remove widgets that you don't use, **see** "Removing Widgets from the Dashboard," 170 **p. 170**.

→ To learn how to install widgets in the Dashboard, **see** "Mac OS X to the Max: Finding and Installing More Widgets," **p. 171**.

USING THE ADDRESS BOOK WIDGET

The Address Book widget enables you to access information in your Address Book more quickly than by using the Address Book application itself. The Address Book widget provides a number of useful tools as you can see in Figure 6.4 and in the following list:

- View a contact's information in the Address Book widget's window. If not all of a contact's information will fit in the window, use the scroll arrows that will appear to move up and down in the contact's information.

- Browse contact information by clicking the Previous or Next buttons

- Search for a contact by typing the name of the contact in the Search tool. As you type, the contacts in the window will be reduced to include only those that meet your search text. You can only search by name.

- To view information at a larger size, click it. It will be magnified on the screen. This works only for unlinked information, such as telephone numbers.

- Use the linked information for a contact to perform an action. Click an email address to send an email to the contact (when you do this, Mail will open and a message to the recipient will be created). If you click on an address, your web browser will open and the address will be shown on a Mapquest map.

Figure 6.4
The Address Book widget is a useful way to use your Address Book.

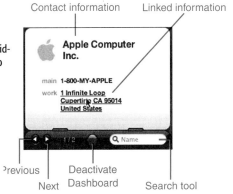

Contact information   Linked information

Apple Computer Inc.

main 1-800-MY-APPLE
work 1 Infinite Loop
      Cupertino CA 95014
      United States

1 / 2   Q Name

Previous   Deactivate
      Next   Dashboard   Search tool

6

→ To learn how to configure contact information in your Address Book, **see** "Setting Up and Using an Address Book," **p. 400**.

TIP

You can remove a widget from the Dashboard anytime the Dashboard is active by holding the Option key down while you point to the widget. When you do so, the Close button will appear; click the button to close the widget.

USING THE CALCULATOR WIDGET

The Calculator widget is simple, but useful. When it appears on the screen, you can use it to perform basic calculations (see Figure 6.5). You can "press" the Calculator's keys using the mouse or the keyboard.

Figure 6.5
It isn't much to look at, by the Calculator widget might be one of the more useful ones.

USING THE ICAL WIDGET

The iCal widget isn't the most aptly named one. From its name, you might think you can access your iCal calendar information from it. However, that isn't the case. This widget presents an on-screen calendar that you can use to view dates, such as today's date or any date in the past or future (see Figure 6.6).

Figure 6.6
Too bad you can't view your iCal events by clicking on a date in the iCal widget.

Previous month ————   ———— Next month

Today

Following are some iCal widget pointers:

- Click in the month and date area at the top of the widget to collapse it so that the daily calendar disappears. Click it again to open the full widget.
- Move ahead or back by a month in the calendar using the Next or Previous buttons.
- View today's day and date by clicking the Today button.

USING THE DICTIONARY WIDGET

This is a very handy widget that you can use to access the Mac OS X Dictionary application. You can use the widget both for its dictionary and thesaurus functions. To use this widget, perform the following steps:

1. Activate the Dashboard and click Dictionary to use the dictionary mode or Thesaurus to use that mode (this assumes you have configured the Dictionary widget to be part of the Dashboard of course).

2. Start typing the word in which you are interested in the Search tool and press Return. The widget will find words that match your search text (see Figure 6.7).

Figure 6.7
If you can spell as well as I, you'll find the Dictionary widget very helpful.

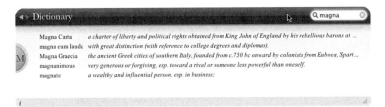

3. Continue typing until the word you are interested in appears in the widget's window.

> **TIP**
>
> The Dictionary widget is one of the few whose window you can resize by dragging its Resize handle.

4. If a list of words appears, click the word in which you are interested. It's definition will appear in the widget's window (see Figure 6.8). It will also be moved into the Search tool.

> **TIP**
>
> You can clear your current search by clicking the Clear button that appears in the Search tool.

5. To move back to the list of words, click the Back button. Your original search term will appear in the Search box again.

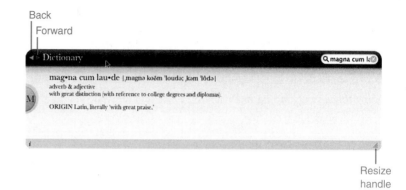

Figure 6.8
Ever had this term applied to you?

Back

Forward

Resize handle

6. If the Scroll bar appears instead, use it to move up and down the window to view the entries that meet your search.

TIP

> To see which dictionary is being used, click the Info button, which is the "i" that appears in the lower left corner of the widget.

USING THE ITUNES WIDGET

You can use the iTunes widget to view and control music playback via iTunes. To use it, open iTunes. When iTunes is running, you can use the iTunes widget to select and play music (see Figure 6.9).

Figure 6.9
Use the iTunes widget to take control of your music.

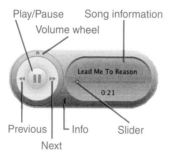

Play/Pause   Song information
Volume wheel

Previous   Info   Slider
Next

To use the iTunes widget, take heed of the following notes:

- To choose a playlist, click the Info button. The Select Playlist pop-up menu will appear. Use this to choose the playlist you want to hear. Click Done to move to the widget's controls.

- Use the straightforward Play/Pause, Previous, and Next buttons to control the music.

- View the song currently playing in the Song information area.
- Adjust the volume by dragging the Volume wheel clockwise to increase it or counter-clockwise to decrease it.
- Drag the slider to fast forward or rewind in a song.

USING THE UNIT CONVERTER WIDGET

If you ever need to convert from the English system to the Metric or vice versa or perform other such unit conversions, such as among different currencies, the Unit Converter widget can take all the work out of the process for you. To use this handy widget, perform the following steps:

1. Access the Unit Converter widget.
2. Choose the type of unit you want to convert on the Convert pop-up menu. There are many options from which you can choose, including Area, Currency, Energy, Time, and so on.
3. Use the lower-left pop-up menu to choose the specific unit you want to convert. The options you see will depend on what you selected on the Convert pop-up menu. For example, if you choose Temperature, the options on this menu will be various units of temperature, including Fahrenheit, Celsius, and so on.
4. Use the lower-right pop-up menu to choose the unit into which you want to convert the measurement.
5. Type the data you want to convert in the lower left box. The converted measurement will be shown in the lower right box (see Figure 6.10).

TIP

> If you choose a conversion for which data is provided by a third-party, such as Currency, click the Info button to see who is providing the data.

USING THE WEATHER WIDGET

The Weather widget displays current weather conditions and temperature forecasts for an area that you select. To use it, perform the following steps:

NOTE

> Many widgets, such as the Weather and World Clock widgets, require an Internet connection to work. Others, such as the Calculator, don't.

6

Figure 6.10
Ever wondered when the temperature in Fahrenheit is the same as it is in Celsius?

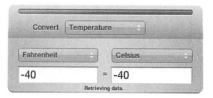

1. Open the Weather widget.

2. Move the pointer over the widget. When you do, the Info button will appear.

3. Click the Info button located in the lower-right corner of the widget's window. You'll see the configuration tools.

4. Enter the city or ZIP Code for which you want to see weather information in the box. The simplest approach is to just enter the ZIP Code, but you can enter the city and state if you don't know the ZIP Code.

5. Choose the unit of temperature you want to be displayed on the Degrees pop-up menu. The options are Fahrenheit and Celsius.

6. If you want lows to be included in the 6-day forecast, check the "Include lows in 6-day forecast" check box.

7. Click Done. You'll return to the widget. You'll see the city you selected and an icon representing the current weather conditions in that area. Also displayed will be the current temperature and the current day's temperature forecast (see Figure 6.11).

Figure 6.11
Ah, another lovely day in Brownsburg, Indiana.

Following are a few tips to help you make the most of the Weather widget:

- To see a 6-day forecast, click the widget's window. It will expand and you'll see the latest predictions for the current day plus five days into the future. To collapse the widget again, click its window.

- You can track the weather in multiple areas at the same time by opening a Weather widget and configuring it for each area in which you are interested. When you activate the Dashboard, you'll see the weather in all your favorite spots (see Figure 6.12).

- Click the city shown in the Weather widget window. Your default web browser will open and you'll move to the AccuWeather.com web page for that city. Here, you can get into the details of the weather, present and future.

Figure 6.12
Where would you like to be?

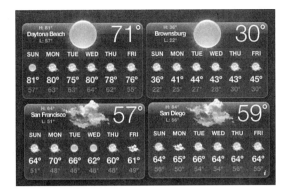

USING THE WORLD CLOCK WIDGET

This simple widget displays the current time in a city of your choice.

1. Open the widget and click the Info button.
2. Choose the continent in which you are interested on the Continent pop-up menu.
3. Choose the city on the City pop-up menu.
4. Click Done. When you return to the widget, you'll see the current time in the city you selected (see Figure 6.13).

Figure 6.13
Use the Work Clock widget to keep track of the time your favorite cities.

NOTE

As you explore other widgets, keep an eye out for the Info button. Some widgets have this and some don't. If a widget has it, make sure you open it to see where it leads. In many cases, this button will enable you to configure options for a widget.

CONFIGURING THE DASHBOARD

There are a couple of things you can do to configure the Dashboard itself. You can change its hot key and active screen corner and you can remove any widgets you never use.

SETTING THE DASHBOARD'S HOT KEY AND ACTIVE SCREEN CORNER

You can change the default hot key for the Dashboard by opening the Dashboard & Exposé pane of the System Preferences application. Choose the new hot key on the Dashboard pop-up menu.

You can also configure the Dashboard to open when you move the pointer to a corner of the screen by choosing Dashboard on the pop-up menu located at the corner you want to use. When you move the pointer to this corner, the Dashboard will activate just like it does when you press the hot key.

REMOVING WIDGETS FROM THE DASHBOARD

Some of the widgets that come with Mac OS X probably won't be useful to you (my least favorite is the Tile Game widget). You can remove any widgets you won't use by performing the following steps:

NOTE

You have to authenticate yourself as an administrator to be able to remove widgets. And if you remove them, no one who uses your Mac will be able to use the widgets you remove.

1. Open the Widgets folder that is located in Library folder of your startup drive (see Figure 6.14).

Figure 6.14
The Widgets in this folder will be on the Widget Bar when you activate the Dashboard.

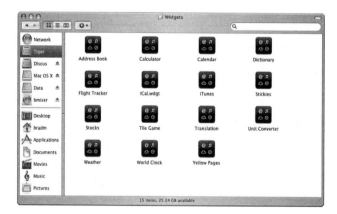

2. Drag the widget you don't want to use out of the Widgets folder. If you might want to install it again sometime, save the widget file. If not, you can delete it.
3. Restart your Mac. The undesirable widget will no longer be part of the Dashboard.

→ To learn how to install widgets in the Dashboard, **see** "Mac OS X to the Max: Finding and Installing More Widgets," **p. 171**.

TIP

> Unlike other applications, the Dashboard's icon on the Dock doesn't serve much of a purpose. The Dashboard is always running, whether its icon appears on the Dock or not. To get rid of the Dashboard's Dock icon, open its menu and choose Remove from Dock. If you want it to be displayed there again, drag it from the Applications folder onto the Dock.

Mac OS X to the Max: Finding and Installing More Widgets

As the Dashboard becomes widely used, you can expect that lots of people and companies will get into the widget production game. You have to install new widgets on your Dashboard to be able to use them.

Finding and Downloading Cool Widgets

The Dashboard can be expanded with new widgets that you download from the Internet.

1. Activate the Dashboard and open the Widget Bar.
2. Click the More Widgets button. Your default web browser will open and take you to the widgets web page.
3. Browse or search until you find a widget you want to try.
4. Download the widget.

→ To learn how to download and prepare files, **see** "Downloading and Preparing Files," **p. 481**.

Installing Widgets Not Included with Mac OS X

There are two ways widgets can be installed. One is to use an installer if one was provided with the widget. Otherwise, just place the widget file in the Widgets folder that is in the Library folder on your startup disk; restart your Mac and then use the Widget Bar to open and use the new widget.

6

MAC OS X: MASTERING THE SYSTEM

CHAPTER **7**

INSTALLING AND USING MAC OS X APPLICATIONS

In this chapter

UNDERSTANDING APPLICATIONS YOU CAN RUN UNDER MAC OS X

You can run the following types of applications under Mac OS X:

- **Classic applications**—Classic applications are those designed to run under previous versions of the Mac OS; however, because of Mac OS X's Classic environment, you can also run these applications under Mac OS X. Because Mac OS X has been around for a while, there are Mac OS X versions of almost all Mac applications. You should use Classic applications only when there isn't a Mac OS X version available to you.

- **Unix applications**—Because Mac OS X is based on Unix, you can run many Unix applications on your Mac. Some of these applications have to be recompiled to run on the Mac, but most will work as they are. Of course, you will need to run them from the command line (unless you find and install a graphical user interface for the Unix subsystem). Because Unix is such a prevalent OS, thousands of Unix applications are available for you to use.

> **NOTE**
>
> The X11 environment that you can choose to install when you install Mac OS X provides a graphical interface for Unix applications. If you run Unix applications regularly, you should install and use this environment.

- **Java applications**—You can run applications written in the Java and Java 2 programming languages. Because Java is a platform-independent programming language, the same applications work on Windows, Macintosh, and other platforms. You mostly encounter Java applications on the Web, but you will find some standalone Java applications as well.

- **Carbon applications**—These applications are written using the Carbon programming environment, which is designed to take advantage of the Mac OS X architecture. Many are Classic applications that have been ported over to Mac OS X—in Mac OS X-lingo, they have been *carbonized*. Because carbonizing an application requires considerably fewer resources than does creating a Cocoa application, most Mac OS X applications were carbonized Mac OS 9 applications early in Mac OS X's life. As Mac OS X has continued to mature, most applications have been written or rewritten specifically for Mac OS X (using Carbon or Cocoa).

- **Cocoa applications**—These applications are written using the Cocoa programming architecture, which means they take full advantage of all the advanced features Mac OS X provides. Cocoa applications have to be written from the ground up in the new environment rather than being ported over as carbonized applications can be. Most new Mac OS X applications are based on Cocoa and many applications written for previous versions of the Mac OS have been rewritten in Cocoa.

→ To learn about installing and using Classic applications, **see** "Working with Mac OS 9, the Classic Environment, and Classic Applications," **p. 218**.

INSTALLING MAC OS X APPLICATIONS

Although carbonized and Cocoa applications behave somewhat differently, their similarities are at least as great as their differences. This is especially true when it comes to installing them.

Under Mac OS X, the two basic strategies by which applications are installed are the following:

- **Drag and drop**—Under this method, you simply drag the application files (usually just one file or folder) from one location to the location in which you want to install the application (usually the Applications folder).

- **Installer**—Some applications use an installation program to install the application and related files for you. Most applications use the standard Mac OS X Installation application as their installation mechanism. These applications are provided as package files, which have the file extension .pkg.

Because Mac OS X is designed as a multiuser OS, where you install Mac OS X applications is an important consideration. The two locations in which you should install Mac OS X applications are

- **The Applications folder**—If you want the application to be accessible to everyone who uses your Mac, you should install it in the Applications folder. To do this, you must be logged in as an administrator. Most applications that use an installer are installed in the Applications folder, and you usually don't have the option to install them elsewhere.

TIP

> Remember that you can use the Accounts pane of the System Preferences application to limit a user's access to specific applications.

- **The Home folder**—You can sometimes install applications in a user's Home directory (primarily applications that have drag-and-drop installation). You should install applications in a user's Home directory only if you don't want everyone who uses your Mac to be able to use that application. Because users can access only areas to which they have been granted permission through their security settings, you need to ensure that everyone who needs to use the application can access the location in which it is stored.

These installation locations are appropriate only for Mac OS X (carbonized or Cocoa) applications. You install Classic or Unix applications in locations that are appropriate for those types of applications.

7

CAUTION

> If you have trouble installing an application, make sure you are logged in as an administrator. Many application installations can be done only while using an administrator account.

INSTALLING MAC OS X APPLICATIONS WITH DRAG AND DROP

Under Mac OS X, applications can be provided as *bundles*. A bundle is a collection of the executable files and other resources required for an application. An application bundle can be presented to you as a single icon, which makes the drag-and-drop installation technique possible. Instead of having to deal with an installer application or a bunch of individual files, you can easily act on an entire application bundle by acting on its single icon.

Installing applications that use the drag-and-drop method is especially simple. Most of these applications are provided as self-mounting image (.smi) or disk image (.dmg) files. This means that the file behaves just as if it were a volume you mount on your desktop.

Many Mac OS X applications use this method, making installation of these applications almost trivially easy.

NOTE

> The only difference between the behavior of .smi and .dmg files is that .smi files auto-matically mount on your desktop when you launch them. Disk image files use Apple's Disk Utility software to mount—because this application is installed on your Mac by default, these files behave quite similarly and you probably won't notice any difference between them. However, you could use a .smi file even if Disk Utility wasn't installed on your machine, whereas you can't use a .dmg file without the Disk Utility application.

The general process to install an application provided in a .smi or .dmg file is the following:

1. Download and uncompress the .smi or .dmg file.
2. If the file isn't mounted on your Mac automatically, double-click the file (which is likely a .dmg file). Its volume is mounted on your desktop, just like any other volumes, such as a CD, DVD, or volume on a hard drive.
3. Open the resulting volume and drag the application's folder or file to the appropriate directory on your Mac.
4. Unmount the mounted volume by selecting it and pressing ⌘-E (or select File, Eject).
5. Discard the .smi or .dmg files if you won't need to install the application again. However, in most cases, I recommend that you keep the original file in the event you need to reinstall the application (for example, you can copy it to a CD or DVD).

→ To learn how to download files from the Web and prepare them for use, **see** "Downloading and Preparing Files," **p. 481**.

NOTE

> Some applications don't even provide a .smi or .dmg file. After you download and uncompress the file, you will have the application's folder immediately. Drag this folder to where you want the application to be installed.

Many Mac OS X applications that you can download from the Web are provided in the .dmg format. As an example, download and install Netflix Freak, which is a great application if you use the Netflix DVD rental service like I do:

NOTE

You can get information about and download Netflix Freak at www.thelittleappfactory.com.

1. Log in as an administrator for your Mac.

2. Go to http://www.thelittleappfactory.com/, click the Our Software icon, and then click the Netflix Freak icon.

TIP

Netflix Freak enables you to manage you Netflix account much more easily than using a web browser to access it. You can do all the functions you can from the Netflix website from within the Netflix Freak application, and these tasks are easier and faster. I find this application very useful and hardly ever visit the Netflix website anymore.

3. Download Netflix Freak. After the file is downloaded, it is uncompressed and decoded automatically. When the process is complete, you see the netflixfreak.dmg file. The disk image is the Netflix Freak volume on your desktop; its folder is opened for you automatically.

→ To learn how to download files from the Web and prepare them for use, **see** "Downloading and Preparing Files," **p. 481**.

4. Open another Finder window and display the Applications folder.

TIP

The fastest way to open the Applications folder is to press Shift-⌘-A.

5. Drag the Netflix Freak icon into the Applications directory to copy it there (see Figure 7.1).

6. Eject the Netflix Freak volume and store the original .dmg file in a safe location.

7. Launch Netflix Freak to start using it.

TIP

If you want to save a little disk space, save the original .sit or .zip files that you download instead of the .dmg files. When you want to access the .dmg files again, you can uncompress the .sit or .zip files. You don't need to save both versions. The .dmg file is slightly more convenient than the .sit or .zip file, but it also requires slightly more disk space.

7

Figure 7.1
Installing the excellent Netflix Freak is a simple matter of drag and drop.

CAUTION

Some companies remove the installers for one version from their website when the next version is released. In such cases, you might not be able to download and install the application again without paying an upgrade fee to get the new version. Although this is not a very good practice in my opinion, some companies do have this policy. The only way to ensure that you will be able to reinstall the same version of an application you downloaded and licensed is to keep the original installer files. You should also keep any updates you download and install for that version.

If you aren't able to place the application in the appropriate directory, see "I Can't Install an Application Because I Don't Have Sufficient Privileges" in the "Troubleshooting" section at the end of this chapter.

INSTALLING MAC OS X APPLICATIONS USING AN INSTALLER

All Mac OS X applications that use the standard Mac OS X installer application install in a similar fashion; however, minor variations can exist.

Under Mac OS X, applications that use the Installer application come in package files, which have the extension .pkg. For example, when you installed Mac OS X on your machine, you used this installer.

NOTE

When you download an application that comes in a .pkg file, it often is included in a .dmg or .smi file. This usually is done when there are files outside the application to be installed that the developer wants to include with the application but that should not be installed as part of it (readme files, for example).

The general process to install and use .pkg files is the following:

1. Download and prepare the file containing the application you want to install.
2. Mount the disk image and open it.
3. Double-click the .pkg file.
4. Work through the steps in the installer application.

An example of an application that uses this technique is the excellent Snapz Pro X screen capture utility:

1. Log in as an administrator for your Mac.
2. Go to www.ambrosiasw.com, move to the Utilities page, and click the Snapz Pro X icon.
3. Download Snapz Pro X. The .dmg file is opened automatically; then the volume containing the software is mounted and appears on the desktop.
4. Look at the contents of the volume and read any readme files you see.

NOTE

> Some installer packages also come with an uninstaller application; you should definitely keep the original files so you can run the uninstaller to easily remove the application later should you need to. This is especially important for those applications that install resources in the system, such as software that supports peripheral devices.

5. Open the package file, which has the .pkg file extension, such as Snapz Pro X.pkg. You will see the Installer window (see Figure 7.2). Just as when you installed Mac OS X, the left pane shows you the steps you will work through using the installer. The right pane provides information about each step. You use the Continue and Go Back buttons to move through the installation process.

Figure 7.2
Running the installer for most applications is a simple of matter of following onscreen instructions.

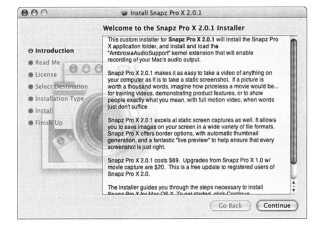

7

6. If prompted, verify that you are an administrator by entering your administrator password (and username if you aren't logged in under an administrator account).

NOTE

Some installations require that you authenticate yourself as an administrator before you can begin the installation—even if you are already logged in as the administrator.

7. Continue working through the steps in the installer until you get to the screen that tells you that the software was successfully installed.

8. Quit the Installer application.

TIP

To unmount a disk image, click the Eject button next to it in the Places sidebar; select it and select File, Eject; or select it and press ⌘-E.

 If Classic launches when you run an application's installer application but the installer has problems, see "I Can't Install an Application Because I Am Having Problems with Classic" in the "Troubleshooting" section at the end of this chapter.

LAUNCHING MAC OS X APPLICATIONS

There are many ways to launch Mac OS X applications, including the following:

- Select the application in a Finder window and select the Finder's Open command (⌘-O).
- Double-click the application's icon.
- Single-click an application's icon on the Dock or Places sidebar.
- Open an alias to the application, such as one stored in your Favorites directory.
- Open a document of the file type that the application is set to open.
- Drag and drop a document onto an application's icon (or an alias's icon).
- Select an application's icon or alias and press ⌘-down arrow.
- Launch the application from within another application. (For example, you can launch a web browser by clicking a URL in an email program.)
- Add the application to the Login Items window so it is launched automatically when you log in.
- Launch the application from a script created by the Automator, AppleScript, or another scripting utility.

If you have used a Mac before, you have probably used many of these methods to open applications. Most of them are very straightforward and require no discussion. A couple of them, though less often used, can be effective techniques for quickly opening an application.

NOTE

> The first time you launch an application under Mac OS X, you will see a dialog box that explains you are opening the application for this first time. In this dialog box, you'll see the name of the application that is trying to open, along with tools you can use to control it. The primary purpose of this is to warn you when an application first opens so you can confirm it is a legitimate application and not some Trojan horse or other application that is trying to launch without your knowledge. If you want to proceed with opening the application, click Open. If you aren't sure about the application, stop the process and check it out before opening it again.

One of the most powerful methods— although it's underused by many Mac users—is to launch an application by drag and drop. Macintosh drag and drop is a function of the OS whereby you move information from one location to another by simply selecting it, dragging it to where you want it to go, and then dropping it.

The drag-and-drop approach is especially efficient when you want to open a document with an application that wasn't used to create it initially. For example, if you receive a plain-text file and double-click it, it opens in TextEdit. If you want to open it in Word instead, you can simply drag and drop the document onto Word's icon and Word is used to open the file. Otherwise, you would have to first open Word, use the Open command, maneuver to the text file, and then open it. (You could also use the Open With command by opening the document's contextual menu.)

If the file type is compatible with the application on which you drag it, the application icon becomes highlighted to indicate that it is a compatible file.

TIP

> You can force an application to attempt to open a document with which it is not compatible by holding down the Option and ⌘ keys while you drag the document onto the application's icon. If the application is capable of opening files of that type, the file is opened. If not, either the application still launches but no document window appears or the document window appears and is filled with garbage.

You can also use drag and drop to open documents using applications installed on the Dock. Simply drag the file you want to open onto the icon on the Dock for the application you want to use to open it. If the application is capable of opening the document, its icon becomes highlighted. When you release the mouse button, the application launches and the document is opened.

If the drag-and-drop technique doesn't work, see "I Can't Drag a Document on an Icon to Open It" in the "Troubleshooting" section at the end of this chapter.

If a file opens, but its contents are "munged," see "When I Open an Application, What I See Is Incomprehensible" in the "Troubleshooting" section at the end of this chapter.

7

UNDERSTANDING AND USING STANDARD MAC OS X APPLICATION MENUS

Just like under all versions of the Mac OS, Mac OS X applications designed to work on the Mac follow certain conventions when it comes to the menus they provide. Although applications can provide more menus than the core set of standard menus, they are not supposed to provide fewer.

CAUTION

The information in this section is based on standard Mac OS X menus for Cocoa applications. Classic applications provide Mac OS 9 menus, whereas carbonized applications provide a mixture of the two sets of menus. For example, all carbonized applications provide an Application menu, but not all provide Cocoa's Format menu.

WORKING WITH MAC OS X APPLICATION MENUS

All Mac OS X applications have an application menu, which provides the commands you use to control the application itself as well as to interact with the OS (see Figure 7.3).

Figure 7.3
This TextEdit menu is typical of the application menu provided by Mac OS X applications.

Typical commands on an application's application menu are the following:

- About
- Preferences
- Services
- Hide/Show
- Quit

One of the more interesting commands on the application menu is the Mac OS X Services command. This command enables you to access functions provided by other applications to add information or perform functions while you are using the current application. Although it is not supported in all applications, when it is supported, it can be quite useful.

NOTE

Game applications are the most likely to not provide standard menus, and that is okay. After all, who needs a Format menu when you are shooting bad guys?

There are various uses for the Services command, but as an example, suppose you are having trouble understanding an error message you are getting in a certain application and you want to send an email to the technical support organization to get some help. That email might be a lot more meaningful if you can include an image of the actual error dialog box that you see with your explanation. Using the Services commands from within the Mail email application, you can do just that:

1. Move to the dialog box you want to capture; perhaps it is an error message that suddenly pops up on your screen.

2. Without doing anything in the dialog box (for example, don't click its OK button), launch the Mail application by clicking its icon on the Dock.

3. Create a new email message and move into its body.

4. From the Mail menu, select Services, Grab, Timed Selection.

5. Bring the dialog box you want to capture to the front by clicking its window.

6. Wait for Grab's timer to go off.

7. Move back into the Mail application. The screen that Grab captured is pasted into the new email message.

8. Finish your message and send it.

The specific services offered on the Services menu depend on the application you are using and the data with which you are working. You should explore Services options that you have with the applications you use most often. Most Apple applications do provide some services, but even with those, support for Services can be spotty. The only way to know is to explore the Services menu for the applications you use.

Even though Apple's basic Mac OS X text editing application, TextEdit, isn't all that great for word processing, it does provide a great example of how many Services commands can be supported. For a list of some of the Services commands available in TextEdit and what they do, see Table 7.1.

TABLE 7.1   COMMANDS ON THE TEXTEDIT SERVICES MENU

Services Command	What It Does
Finder	Activates various Finder commands, such as Open, Reveal, and Show Info, on the selected item
Grab	Enables you to capture screen shots and paste them into the current document
Import Image	Enables you to import images from an imaging device, such as a digital camera, connected to your Mac
Mail	Emails selected text or the entire document via the Mail application

7

continues

Table 7.1   Continued

Services Command	What It Does
Make New Sticky Note	Creates a new sticky note from the selected text
Open URL	Opens a selected URL in the default web browser
Script Editor	Enables you to work with AppleScript, such as creating a new AppleScript or running an existing one
Search with Google	Searches for the selected text on www.google.com
Send File To Bluetooth Device	Sends a file to a Bluetooth device, such as a PDA
Speech	Enables you to have your Mac speak selected text
Summarize	Launches Mac OS X's Summary Service application that creates a summary of selected text
TextEdit	Opens a selected file in TextEdit or creates a new TextEdit file from selected text

NOTE

Some third-party applications can add their own commands to the Services menu. For example, QuicKeys, which enables you to create and run macros, adds a command to the Services menu that enables you to create a macro from within any application.

Working with Mac OS X File Menus

The Mac OS X File menu provides the commands you use to work with files. Most of these are fairly obvious, such as New, Open, Save, Save As, and so on.

Working with Mac OS X Edit Menus

Although all applications should provide an Edit menu, the commands on this menu can vary widely from application to application. At the least, the Cut, Copy, and Paste commands will appear on this menu. There might be others as well, such as Find, Spelling, Speech, and so on. As with the File menu, these commands should be familiar to you unless you are new to using a Mac.

Working with Mac OS X Format Menus

As you might expect from its name, the Format menu provides commands that enable you to format the file with which you are working. The specific commands on the Format menu depend on the particular application you are using.

NOTE

The Mac OS X Format menu, including the Fonts panel, is available only in Cocoa applications that are designed to use it. Many Mac OS X applications provide format and font commands that are specific to those applications.

One of the most useful commands on most applications' Format menus is the Font command. This command enables you to work with the fonts you use in a document (see Figure 7.4). In addition to the commands you expect to see, such as Bold, Italic, and so on, you also will see the Show Fonts command, which opens the Font panel.

Figure 7.4
TextEdit's Font command is typical of this command on many applications' Format menus.

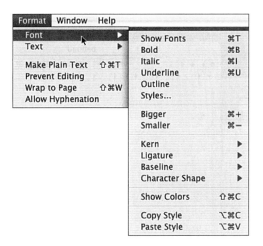

The Mac OS X Font panel enables you to choose and work with the fonts installed on your Mac. The Font panel provides control over the particular font used in your documents as well as enables you to manage the fonts installed on your Mac (see Figure 7.5).

Figure 7.5
The Mac OS X Font panel provides complete control over your fonts.

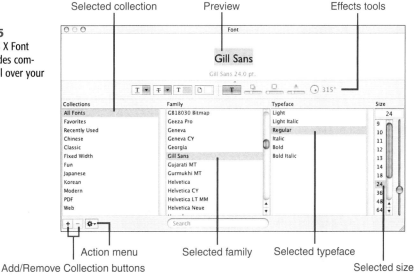

7

TIP

In most applications, you can open or close the Font panel by pressing ⌘-T.

CAUTION

Not all applications support Mac OS X's Font system. If an application doesn't use this system, it provides its own set of formatting tools that you use to format a document. For example, Microsoft Word X for Mac, service release 1 does not support Mac OS X's font system so you can't access the Font panel from within the application. If an application doesn't support the Mac OS X Font panel, you have to use its own font tools instead.

The Font panel has a number of panes, and you can choose to display some panes while others are always visible. The various panes of the Font panel are the following:

- **Collections (always displayed)**—Under Mac OS X, the ability to group fonts together in collections is built in to the operating system and into the Font panel. Font collections make selecting fonts easier because you can group fonts into collections, so you can select a set of fonts by choosing the collection in which those fonts are contained. You can use the default font collections and you can create your own; you use the Collections pane to select the collection with which you want to work. The collections you see in the Collections pane of the Font panel include all those fonts and collections that are installed and enabled via the Font Book application. Applications can also provide distinct collections. For example, in TextEdit, you see the Favorites collection, which contains a set of fonts, typefaces, and sizes you have added via the Add to Favorites action, and the Recently Used collection, which contains the fonts, typefaces, and sizes of text formatting you have recently applied in the current document.

→ To learn about installing and maintaining fonts on your Mac using the Font Book application, **see** "Installing and Using Mac OS X Fonts," **p. 247**.

- **Family (always displayed)**—The Family pane lists all the font families that are part of the selected collection. You select the family you want to work with on the list of available families in the selected collection.

- **Typeface (displayed except when working with the Favorites and Recently Used collection)**—In the Typeface pane, you choose the typeface for the selected font family, such as Regular, Bold, and so on.

- **Size (always displayed)**—You choose the size of the font you are applying in the Size pane.

- **Preview (displayed when you select Show Preview on the Action menu)**—This pane, which appears at the top of the Font panel, provides a preview of the font you have configured.

- **Effects (displayed when you select Show Effects on the Action menu)**—This pane provides buttons you use to configure underline, strikethrough, text color, background color, and text shadow effects.

A couple of the default collections are worth some additional detail. The PDF collection contains font families that are suited to the creation of PDF documents (PDF is a native file format under Mac OS X). The Favorites collection is empty by default and is a collection designed for you to be able to create a customized set of your favorite font families, type-faces, and sizes so you can reapply specific text formats by selecting the Favorites collection and clicking the text formatting you want to apply. The Recently Used collection automatically gathers the families, typefaces, and sizes you have recently used so you can reapply them easily. The web collection contains fonts that are designed to be used on the Web.

The Action menu at the bottom-left corner of the panel provides access to the following commands:

- **Add to Favorites**—This command adds the current font, typeface, and size to the Favorites collection.
- **Show/Hide Preview**—This choice opens or hides the Preview pane.
- **Show/Hide Effects**—This command opens or hides the Effects pane.
- **Color**—Choosing this causes the Color Picker to open.
- **Characters**—This command opens the Characters palette.
- **Typography**—This command opens the Typography panel that you can use to choose ligatures, adjust the space before and after characters, and shift the text baseline.
- **Edit Sizes**—Using this command, you can customize the sizes that appear in the Size pane.
- **Manage Fonts**—This command opens the Font Book that enables you to manage the fonts installed on your Mac.

PREVIEWING FONTS

If you select Show Preview on the Action menu, a new pane appears at the top of the panel. This pane provides a preview of the currently selected family, typeface, and size. You can use this preview to help you make better selections more quickly. To hide the Preview pane, select Hide Preview on the Action menu.

USING FONT FAVORITES

When you select a font family, typeface, and size and then use the Add to Favorites command on the Action menu, that font is added to your Favorites collection. When you select the Favorites collection in the Font panel, you can quickly choose one of your favorite fonts to use; this saves you a couple of steps (see Figure 7.6).

NOTE

The capability to save specific combinations of family, typeface, and size as a favorite makes using specific fonts easy. This is much like the styles feature offered in Word and other text applications. By designating a combination as a favorite, you can reapply it quickly and easily. Unfortunately, you can't make changes to the favorite and have those changes be made wherever that favorite is used as you can with styles.

7

Figure 7.6
When you add a font, typeface, and size to your Favorites collection, you can easily apply that formatting to selected text in a document.

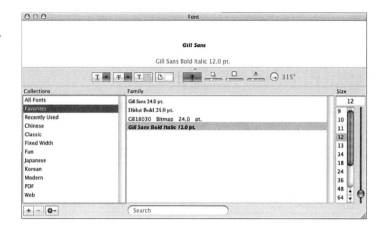

CREATING OR REMOVING FONT COLLECTIONS

You can add or remove font collections from the Font panel. When you do so, the font collection is also added or removed to the Collections available in the Font Book application (which contains all the fonts installed on your Mac).

→ To learn about the Font Book application, **see** "Installing and Using Mac OS X Fonts," **p. 247**.

From the Font panel, you can make the following changes to the collections shown in the Collections list:

- Add new font collections.
- Remove font collections.
- Add fonts to collections.

Although you can manage font collections from within the Font panel, you should generally use the Font Book application. This is because font collections are really a system-level resource, so it is better practice to manage them using a system tool—that being the Font Book.

→ To learn about the Font Book application, **see** "Installing and Using Mac OS X Fonts," **p. 247**.

CAUTION

If you select a collection and click the – button to delete it, the collection is removed from the Font Book, which means the included fonts are deleted from your Mac. Using the Font Book, you can disable both font collections and individual fonts from within collections. This is the best technique because you can prevent collections and fonts from being available within an application but maintain those collections and fonts on your Mac.

7

APPLYING EFFECTS TO FONTS

Using the Effects tools, you can apply the following effects to selected text:

- Apply underline effects
- Apply strikethrough effects
- Apply color to text

NOTE

You can also apply color effects by selecting Color on the Action menu.

- Apply color to a document's background
- Apply text shadow effects

To apply effects to text, do the following steps:

1. Select the text to which you want to apply the effects.
2. Open the Font panel.
3. Open the action menu and select Show Effects. The Effects pane appears (see Figure 7.7).

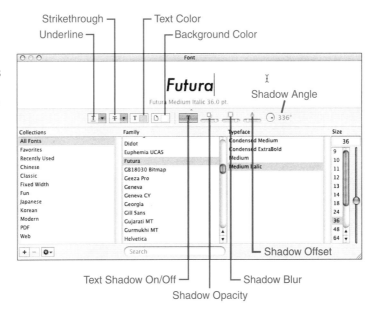

Figure 7.7
You can use the Effects pane to apply various effects to selected text.

4. Select from the underline effects on the Underline pop-up menu. The options are None, Single, Double, or Color. If you select Color, use the Color Picker to choose the color of the underline.

→ To learn how to use the Color Picker, **see** "Choosing Colors," **p. 192**.

5. Select the strikethrough effects on the Strikethrough pop-up menu. The options are None, Single, Double, or Color. If you select Color, use the Color Picker to choose the color of the strikethrough.

6. Click the Text Color button and use the Color Picker to choose the text color.

7. Click the Background Color button and use the Color Picker to select the background color of the document on which you are working.

8. To apply a shadow to the text, click the Text Shadow button; when a shadow is applied, the button is blue.

9. Use the Shadow Opacity, Show Blur, and Shadow Offset sliders to configure those properties of the shadow.

10. Use the Shadow Angle wheel to set the angle of the shadow.

NOTE

> Unfortunately, you won't see the text effects you apply in the Preview pane of the Font panel. You need to be able to see the document on which you are working to see the results of the text effects you apply.

CHOOSING COLORS

When you choose to apply color from the Font panel, you use the Color Picker (see Figure 7.8). You use the Color Picker to define and choose the color to apply to specific items—in this case, text effects.

Figure 7.8
You can control the color applied to fonts using the text effects tools using the Color Picker.

TIP

> You can open or close the Color Picker directly by pressing Shift-⌘-C or by selecting Format, Font, Show/Hide Colors. You don't need to have the Font panel open to use the Color Picker.

7

As an example of how the Color Picker works, the following steps show you how to use the Color Picker to choose the color of underline:

1. Select the item to which you want to apply color (such as text).

2. Open the Color Picker by clicking the Text Color button or selecting Color on the Underline pop-up menu.

3. At the top of the Color Picker window, select the color tools with which you want to work. For example, click the Color Wheel to use the standard color wheel as shown in Figure 7.8.

4. Use the color tools to select the color you want to apply. The color you select is applied to the selected item.

> **TIP**
>
> You can drag the color you select to the palette at the bottom of the Color Picker so you can easily apply it again later. This palette serves as a place in which you can store your favorite colors so you can apply them again easily.

EDITING THE SIZES AVAILABLE ON THE SIZE PANE

If you select Edit Sizes on the Action menu on the Fonts panel, you will see the Font Size sheet, which you can use to change the sizes that appear in the Size pane of the Font panel (see Figure 7.9).

Figure 7.9
You can control the specific sizes of font that appear in the Fonts panel using the Font Size sheet.

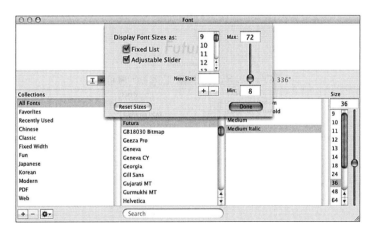

Using the Font Size sheet, you can perform the following tasks:

- To add a size to the Size pane, enter the size you want to add in the New Size box and click + (the plus sign).

- To remove a size from the Size pane, select it on the size list and click – (the minus sign).

- To remove the list of fixed sizes from the Size pane, uncheck the Fixed List check box. Check that box again to display the list of fixed sizes again.

7

- To add a size slider to the Size pane, check the Adjustable Slider check box. Then, enter the minimum font size and maximum size to be included on the slider in the Min Size and Max Size text boxes.

- To reset the sizes to the default values, click the Reset Sizes button.

Save your changes by clicking the Done button. The sheet disappears and the changes you made are reflected in the Size pane.

APPLYING TYPOGRAPHY EFFECTS TO FONTS

The Font panel enables you to apply some basic typography effects to text. To do so, use the following steps:

1. Select Action, Typography. The Typography window appears (see Figure 7.10).

Figure 7.10
You can use the Typography tools to apply typography effects to text (in this case, the Hoefler Text font family has been selected in the Font panel).

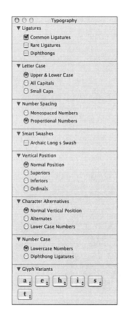

NOTE

> The specific Typography effects you see in the Typography window depend on the font family currently selected. Try selecting various families with the Typography window open to see the options that become available.

2. Use the resulting tools to apply a variety of typographical effects to the selected text.

WORKING WITH THE CHARACTER PALETTE

Special characters can be a pain to enter because remembering which font family the character you need is part of is often difficult. The Character Palette is designed to help you find special characters in various languages and quickly apply those characters to your documents. You can also add characters you use frequently for even easier access.

NOTE

> If you are a longtime Mac user, you probably remember the Key Caps application you could use to locate and use special characters. The Mac OS X Character Palette is like that application, but it is much more powerful.

You can open the Character Palette from within applications that use the Mac OS X Font panel, or you can install the Character Palette menu on the Mac OS X menu bar.

To open the Character Palette from the Mac OS X Font panel, select Characters on the Action menu. The Character Palette will open (see Figure 7.11).

Figure 7.11
The Mac OS X Character Palette enables you to efficiently work with special characters.

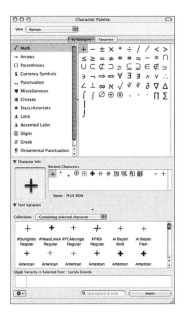

INSTALLING THE CHARACTER PALETTE

You can also install the Character Palette on the Input menu on the Mac OS X menu bar so it is available in all applications, whether they use the Mac OS X Font panel or not. To install the palette, perform the following steps:

1. Open the System Preferences application.

2. Click the International icon. The International pane opens. Click the Input Menu tab.

3. Check the box next to Character Palette.

4. Check the boxes next to any languages you want to install on the Input menu.

7

5. Check the "Show input menu in menu bar" check box. This enables the Input menu that will appear on the right end of any application's menu bar, including the Finder (see Figure 7.12).

Figure 7.12
The Input menu enables you to access the Character Palette from any application.

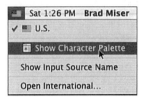

After you have installed the Character Palette on the Input menu, you can open it by selecting Input menu, Show Character Palette.

USING THE CHARACTER PALETTE

The Character Palette has two tabs. The "by Category" tab enables you to select and insert characters you need. When you find a character you use regularly, you can add it to the other tab, which is the Favorites tab, so you can grab it easily and quickly.

To find and use a character, carry out the following steps:

1. Open the Character Palette (either through the Font panel or from the Input menu).
2. On the Character Palette, select the language sets you want to view on the View pop-up menu. For example, to see Roman characters, select Roman.
3. Click the "by Category" tab and choose the category of character you want to view in the left pane. For example, select Math to view mathematical symbols.
4. Select the character with which you want to work by clicking it.
5. Expand the Character Info section. You will see a large version of the selected character along with its name. You'll also see characters to which the selected one is related. You can choose to work with one of the related characters by clicking it. The one you click will become selected, even if it is not in the currently selected category.
6. To apply different fonts to the character, click the Expansion triangle next to the Font Variation tab. Select the font collection you want to use on the Collections pop-up menu. Then, click the font you want to apply to the character you selected. When you expand the Font Variation section, a preview pane will appear; this shows a preview of the character you have selected along with its name. You can see a version of the character in each font family in the collection selected on the Collections pop-up menu.

7

TIP

> To limit the fonts shown in the Font Variation pane to only those that contain the character you are working with, select "Containing selected character" on the Collections pop-up menu. The character is shown with the fonts that contain it.

7. Continue adjusting the character until it is the way you want it.

8. Click Insert with Font. The character is pasted into the active document at the insertion point.

NOTE

If you don't apply a font to the character, the Insert with Font button is just the Insert button.

 If the symbol you selected doesn't appear correctly in the document you inserted it in, see "The Special Character I Inserted Doesn't Look Correct" in the "Troubleshooting" section at the end of this chapter.

TIP

You can search for special characters by description or code using the Search tool that appears at the bottom of the Character Palette window.

SETTING UP CHARACTER FAVORITES

You can create a set of favorite characters on the Character Palette to let you quickly choose a character to insert into a document. This is especially useful when you have applied specific fonts to a character.

To create favorite characters, take the following steps:

1. Open the Character Palette.

2. Create the character just as you would to insert it into a document.

3. Open the Action menu and select Add to Favorites. This copies the character onto the Favorites tab (see Figure 7.13).

Figure 7.13
The characters shown on the Favorites tab can be inserted into a document quickly and easily.

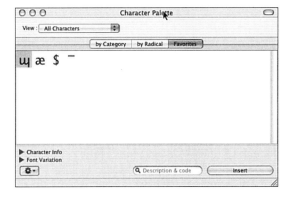

To insert a favorite character from the Favorites tab into a document, perform the following steps:

1. Open the Character Palette.
2. Click the Favorites tab.
3. Select the character you want to insert.
4. Click Insert.

You can remove a character from the Favorites tab by selecting it and selecting Remove from Favorites on the Action menu.

WORKING WITH MAC OS X APPLICATION WINDOW MENUS

When applications can have more than one window open at the same time, you can use the Window menu to manage those open windows. You can also manage any existing windows on the desktop. Using the commands on the Window menu, you can do the following:

- Zoom the current window.
- Minimize the current window.
- Bring all open application windows to the front.
- Choose a window to bring it to the front.

Using the Window menu is simple. To bring an open window to the front, select it on the menu. To use one of the Window commands, select it.

NOTE

> Some applications mark the frontmost window with a check mark or diamond symbol; however, this behavior is not consistent. In many cases, the frontmost window is marked with some sort of character.
>
> Windows that are open and minimized also appear on the Window menu. If you use the Bring All to Front command, minimized windows remain on the Dock (windows on the Dock are always at the front).

The commands on the Window menu can vary from application to application, and many applications include additional commands on this menu. For example, in Safari, commands on the Window menu take you to the Downloads and Activity windows.

OPENING DOCUMENTS IN MAC OS X

Using most applications involves opening documents; Mac OS X offers several features that applications can use to make opening documents fast and easy.

There are several ways in which you can open documents:

- Select the document's icon in a Finder window and select the Finder's Open command (press ⌘-O).
- Double-click a document's icon in the Finder.

- Single-click a document's icon on the Dock or Places sidebar.
- Drag a document icon or alias onto an application's icon or alias (on the desktop, in a Finder window, or on the Dock).
- Select the document's icon or alias and press ⌘-down arrow.
- Open the document using an Automator application, AppleScript, or other macro.
- Open a compatible application and use its Open command to open a document.

NOTE

> If you see the document's icon on the Dock, an alias to that document has been placed there. If you see a thumbnail of the document's window on the Dock, that document is open and its window has been minimized. In either case, single-clicking the icon causes the document to open so you can work on it.

Most of these techniques are simple. The Mac OS X Open dialog box is a good model of all the file selection dialog boxes you will encounter, so you should get very familiar with the way in which it works. Also, you need to understand how you can associate documents with specific applications so you can determine which application opens when you open a document.

Using the Mac OS X Open Dialog Box

Under Mac OS X version 10.4, Open dialog boxes are harmonized with Finder windows so behavior of these windows, which serve a similar purpose (that being to enable you to access files and folders), is similar.

As under previous versions of Mac OS X, different applications can add features to the Open dialog box for specific purposes, but most Open dialog boxes offer a similar set of features.

NOTE

> Many dialog boxes, although not called Open, are actually the Open dialog box with the name modified to suit the specific purpose at hand. These dialog boxes have names such as Choose a Picture, Choose a File, and so on. However, they all work in basically the same way and offer similar features as the Open dialog box.

A typical Open dialog box is shown in Figure 7.14.

If you read through earlier chapters in this book, you are quite knowledgeable of Finder windows, and Open dialog boxes work like Finder windows in many ways. For example, the Places sidebar enables you to choose the location from which you want to open a file. When you select a place, its contents appear in the center pane of the window. You can choose to view this pane in the List view or the Columns view; again, these views are the same as when you are viewing Finder windows. You can use the List View or Columns view button

7

to change the view used in the dialog box. You can use the Forward and Back buttons to move back to locations you viewed previously.

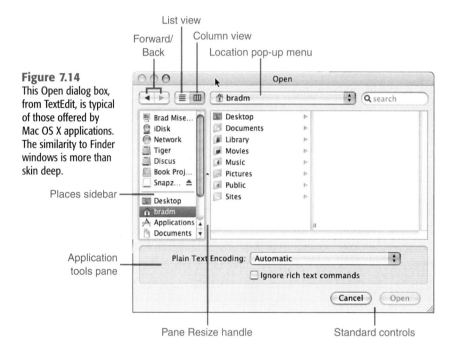

Figure 7.14
This Open dialog box, from TextEdit, is typical of those offered by Mac OS X applications. The similarity to Finder windows is more than skin deep.

→ To learn how to work with Finder windows, **see** Chapter 3, "Viewing and Navigating Mac OS X Finder Windows," **p. 55**.

The location shown in the Location pop-up menu is the currently selected folder whose contents are displayed in the pane. For example, if Documents is shown in the Location pop-up menu, the Documents folder is selected and its contents are displayed. If you have selected the Columns view, the contents of the location selection on the Location pop-up menu appears in the leftmost column.

You can also use the Location pop-up menu to quickly access many areas of your Mac, from your current location up to the volume on which Mac OS X is installed (see Figure 7.15).

If you use the List view, to open a file or folder, simply move to it, select it, and click Open or double-click the file or folder you want to open. If you use the Columns view and select a folder, that folder becomes selected and you see its contents in the pane to the right of the folder. You can then select a folder or document it contains. In either view, you can select a document and double-click it or click Open.

You can change the Open dialog box in several ways, including the following:

- Use the Pane Resize handle to make the Places sidebar wider or narrower.
- Use the resize handle to make the dialog box larger or smaller.
- Click the Maximize button to make the dialog box its maximum size, such as to fill up the screen.

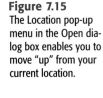

Figure 7.15
The Location pop-up menu in the Open dialog box enables you to move "up" from your current location.

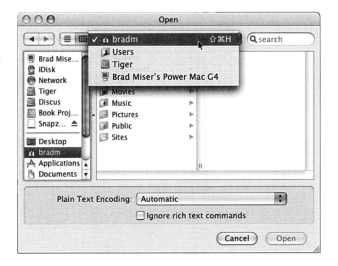

NOTE

The Maximize button is not included in the Open dialog box under all applications—typically, only Cocoa applications include this feature.

■ Drag the dialog box around the screen. Because the Open dialog box is an independent window, you can move it around on the screen.

The Open dialog box might contain application-specific controls. For example, in Figure 7.15, you saw the Plain Text Encoding pop-up menu that lets you choose the type of encoding you want to use. In the Application Tools pane, you will also see different tools depending on the application in which you are working. As you locate and open files or documents, you should be aware of these additional options and apply them as needed.

DETERMINING THE APPLICATION THAT OPENS WHEN YOU OPEN A DOCUMENT

When you open a document, the system determines which application should be used to open that file (other than when you open a document from within an application using its Open command, of course). Typically, the document's creator opens if it is installed on your Mac, such as Microsoft Word opening a .doc file.

When opening a file from outside an application, several factors determine which application opens when you open a document, including the document's file type and creator information, as well as the file's filename extension. Mac OS X does a good job evaluating these properties to ensure that the correct application opens.

However, there might be situations in which you want to use a different application than the one the system selects, or you might not have the application that was used to create the document. In such cases, you can choose the application in which a document opens.

7

You can also change the association for all files of a specific type to determine which application opens when you open any file of that type.

There are two ways to associate document types with the applications used to open them. One is by using the Get Info window; the other is by using a document's contextual menu.

USING THE GET INFO WINDOW TO ASSOCIATE DOCUMENTS WITH AN APPLICATION

You can use the Open with section of the Info window to determine which application is used to open a file:

1. Select the document you are interested in and press ⌘-I. The Info window appears.

2. Expand the Open with section. The application with which the document is currently associated is shown on the pop-up menu. The associated application is called the default application—the text (default) appears after the application name when you open the pop-up menu.

3. Open the pop-up menu. You will see all the applications the system recognizes as being able to open the document, along with the Other selection (see Figure 7.16).

Figure 7.16
This menu lists all the applications Mac OS X thinks you can use on the document.

4. If one of the listed applications is the one you want to associate with the document, choose it on the menu. The document is opened with that application the next time you open it.

5. If you want to select an application that is not shown on the pop-up menu, select Other. You will see the Choose Other Application dialog box (see Figure 7.17).

   The Choose Other Application dialog box moves to the Applications directory automatically, and by default, it shows you only the recommended applications, which are those that Mac OS X recognizes as being compatible with the document. This set of applications might or might not be the same as you saw on the pop-up menu in the Info window. Mac OS X recognizes that some applications that can open files of that type might not really be intended to work with files of that type and so doesn't show them in the pop-up menu. However, they might be active in the Choose Other Application dialog box. Applications Mac OS X doesn't think can be used at all are grayed out.

Figure 7.17
You can use the
Choose Other
Application dialog box
to select applications
to open a document,
even if Mac OS X
doesn't recommend
them.

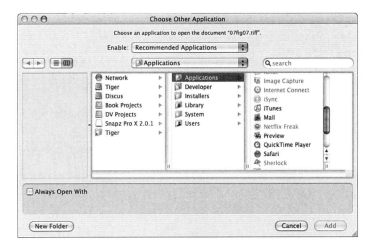

6. To make all applications active, select All Applications from the Enable pop-up menu.

7. Use the dialog box's controls to move to the application you want to select, select it, and click Add. After you click Add, you return to the Info window and the application you selected appears in the window. That application is used the next time you open the file.

TIP

> If you want to permanently change the application used to open the document, check the "Always Open With" box.

CAUTION

> Just because you told Mac OS X to use a specific application, even if it is the one that Mac OS X recommended, that doesn't mean you will actually be able to open the document with the application you select. If you try to open the document and generate error messages, you need to go back and select an application that can handle the type of file you are working with.

If you choose an application that Mac OS X isn't sure can open files of the selected type, you see a warning saying so in the dialog box after you select the application. You can proceed even when you see the warning, but you might get unexpected results.

TIP

> Even though Mac OS X tries to recommend applications that are appropriate for the selected document, it doesn't always do a great job. For example, it doesn't usually list a Classic application even when that application is the best choice for the selected document. In those situations, use the All Applications command on the Enable pop-up menu to add the application you want to use for the document.

7

You can also use the Info window to associate all files of a specific type with an application. Here's how:

1. Use the previous steps to associate a file of the type you want to associate with an application. After you have changed the application association, the Change All button becomes active.

2. Click the Change All button. You will see a warning dialog box that explains what you are about to do; for example, it lists the document types you are changing and the application with which you will associate documents of that type (see Figure 7.18).

Figure 7.18
This warning dialog box provides the information you need to ensure that the file association you are creating is the correct one.

3. If you are sure that you want to make the change, click Continue. All files of the selected type become associated with the application you selected. The application you selected becomes the default application for all documents of that type.

USING A CONTEXTUAL MENU TO OPEN A DOCUMENT WITH A SPECIFIC APPLICATION

You can also use a file's contextual menu to determine which application is used to open it by doing the following:

1. Select a document that you want to open with a specific application.

2. Hold down the Control key and click the file to open its contextual menu.

3. Select Open With. Another menu appears that lists all the applications the system recognizes as being compatible with the document you are trying to open. The application currently associated with the document is marked as the default (see Figure 7.19).

4. Select the application with which you want to open the document from the list. If you want to use an application that is not on the list, select Other and use the Choose Other Application dialog box to move to and select the application you want to use. (See the preceding section for detailed information on how this dialog box works.) The document opens in the application you selected.

When you use this technique, the document is associated with the application only if you save the document from within that application. If you simply open it and view it, the previous application continues to be associated with the document.

If you want the file to always be opened with a different application, even if you don't make any changes to it, open the contextual menu and then press the Option key. The Open With command becomes the Always Open With command. After you choose an application, the file is associated with that application and always opens in it.

Figure 7.19
This menu provides the same controls as the Open with section of a document's Info window.

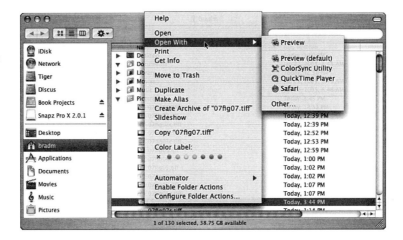

Note that setting an application for all files with a specific type and creator combination does not override any documents for which you have set a specific application. For example, suppose you set the application to use for a specific document. Then, using another document, you change the application used for documents of that type and creator to be a different application. The first document would still open with the specific application you selected previously.

You can also access the same Open, Open With, and Always Open With commands on the Action pop-up menu in the Finder window's toolbar.

USING FILENAME EXTENSIONS TO ASSOCIATE DOCUMENTS WITH APPLICATIONS

You can also try to change the application associated with a specific document by changing the document's filename extension. For example, to associate QuickTime Player with a document, you would change its extension to .mov. When you do so, the file's icon might change to reflect that extension and the document opens with the application that extension is associated with. But this doesn't always happen. Do the following:

1. Edit the filename extension of the file you want to associate with an application so the extension is unique to that application. For example, you can change .rtf to .doc to associate a file with Microsoft Word.

    The filename extension you use must be specific to an application for this to work. For example, some filename extensions, such as .tiff, can be associated with many applications. You must use the Info window or contextual menu to change the association for such files.

    A warning dialog box appears (see Figure 7.20). In this dialog box, you see two buttons: One keeps the file's current filename extension, and other causes the new one to be used.

7

Figure 7.20
When you change a filename extension, you have to confirm the change by clicking the Use button in a dialog box like this one.

2. Click the Use button; the filename extension is changed. The file is associated with the application currently associated with files that have the filename extension you chose to use. (If you click the Keep button, nothing is changed.)

Changing the filename extension does not override a selection you have made with the Info window. If you associate an application with a document by using the Info window tools and then subsequently change the filename extension, the choice you made with the Info window overrides the filename extension and determines the application used to open that document.

SAVING DOCUMENTS IN MAC OS X

When you use applications, you will also be saving documents frequently. Fortunately, Save sheets under Mac OS X are also similar to Finder windows, just like Open dialog boxes.

The specific Save sheet or dialog box you see depends on the application you are using. Cocoa and some carbonized applications use the Save sheet that is described in this section. Some carbonized and all Classic applications use the older Save dialog boxes from Mac OS 9.

A typical Mac OS X Save sheet is shown in Figure 7.21.

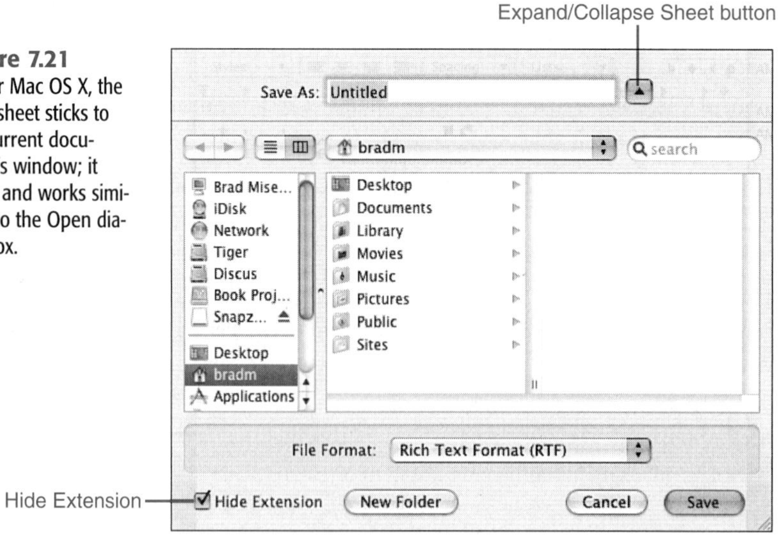

Expand/Collapse Sheet button

Figure 7.21
Under Mac OS X, the Save sheet sticks to the current document's window; it looks and works similarly to the Open dialog box.

Hide Extension

Mac OS X Save sheets are a good example of the dialog type called *sheets*. A sheet drops down from the top of the document window you are saving. Unlike the Open dialog box, the Save dialog box is attached to the top of the window and therefore moves when you move the document window.

NOTE

> The size of a sheet is fixed, but you can still resize the document to which it is attached. In fact, you can make the document so small that it is completely hidden behind the sheet, but I wouldn't recommend it.

The sheet contains the Save As text box in which you enter the filename. If you click the Expand/Collapse button, the sheet expands so you see a window that is very similar to the Open dialog box you learned about in the previous section. If you click this button again, you see the collapsed version of the sheet.

NOTE

> One of the benefits of a sheet is that an open sheet will not prevent you from working with other documents, even within the same application. The sheet stays with the document to which it is attached. You can open, work with, and save other documents without closing the sheet.

Save sheets and Open dialog boxes look and work very similarly, but a couple of items on Save sheets aren't on Open dialog boxes so you need to pay attention to them.

One is the Format pop-up menu, which is sometimes called File Format depending on the application in which you are working. You use this pop-up menu to choose the format of the file you are saving.

The other is the Hide Extension check box. If you check this box, the filename extension is hidden. If you uncheck this box, which I recommend that you do, the filename extension is shown in the Save As box. Because filename extensions are important clues about how a document will open, you should generally choose to display them.

Some applications work in an opposite way: Instead of the Hide Extension check box, their Save sheets include the "Append file extension" check box. When this box is checked, the filename extension is added to the file's name.

TIP

> Creating a new folder (using the New Folder button) in the Save As sheet can be a bit confusing. The new folder is created in the currently selected directory, which is shown in the Location pop-up menu. Because viewing multiple levels of the hierarchy using the Columns view controls is easy, you might be creating a new folder in a location you didn't realize you had selected. Before using that command, double-check the Location pop-up menu to ensure that you have selected the correct location in which to create the new folder.

7

In some applications' Save As sheet, you will see additional controls, such as an Options button that enables you to configure options for the file format you have selected.

UNDERSTANDING FILENAMES AND FILENAME EXTENSIONS

An important aspect of saving documents under Mac OS X is that it uses filename extensions. Filename extensions consist of a period and three or more characters that are added to the end of the filename. When you save a document, most Cocoa and carbonized applications automatically append the correct filename extension for the type of file you are saving. Mac OS X uses the filename extension to associate the file with a particular application.

The addition of filename extensions to Mac filenames can be confusing because one of the Mac's strengths has traditionally been the lack of such extensions. However, because most applications tack the appropriate filename extension onto the filename you enter automatically, you generally don't have to worry about them.

NOTE

> In fact, if an extension is left off a filename, the Mac still uses the file creator and type information to open the file in a compatible application. However, you should include filename extensions for all documents you save.

Most Mac OS X files have a filename extension, including documents, system resources, and so on. In fact, a bewildering number of filename extensions exist under Mac OS X, and because it is based on the Unix operating system, Mac filename extensions are not limited to a certain number of characters. However, most document filename extensions consist of three or four characters. Some examples are shown in Table 7.2.

TABLE 7.2   EXAMPLES OF MAC DOCUMENT FILENAME EXTENSIONS

Filename Extension	What It Stands For	Application Associated with It Default
.mov	Movie	QuickTime Player
.tiff	Tagged Interchange File Format	Preview
.rtfd	Rich Text Formatted Document	TextEdit
.rtf	Rich Text Format	TextEdit
.jpg or .jpeg	Joint Photographic Experts Group	Preview
.pdf	Portable Document Format	Preview
.html	Hypertext Markup Language	Default web browser (such as Safari)
.doc	Microsoft Word Document	Word
.xls	Microsoft Excel Spreadsheet	Excel
.mp3	Motion Picture Experts Group, Audio Layer 3	iTunes

System Filename Extensions

Although dealing with document filename extensions is fairly straightforward, dealing with system filename extensions can get really ugly. Some are straightforward, such as .app for applications and .dock for docklings, but many seem to be gibberish. Usually, you can just take system filename extensions as they are (because you can't change them), and sometimes you can even figure out what they stand for. For example, the .kext filename extension stands for kernel extension, which is an extension to the operating system software.

One system filename extension that is useful to know is .plist. It indicates a preference file, as in loginwindow.plist, which is the preferences for the Login window.

At the top of the Save sheet, you enter the filename you want to use. Under Mac OS X, you can use long filenames—up to 255 characters, including the filename extension and the period between the filename extension and the filename itself (so be sure to allow room for the filename extension when you enter a filename). When you save a document in many applications, the appropriate filename extension is added to the filename automatically (you won't see it if the Hide Extension check box is checked). As mentioned previously, in some applications, you have to check a box to add the filename extension to the filename.

If you intend to share your files with people who use Mac OS 9.1 or earlier, you need to keep the name under 31 characters, including the filename extension the application will add to the name you enter.

If you want to share your files with Windows computer users, you need to ensure that the filename extension used is comprehensible to Windows PCs.

NOTE

> Some applications provide a File Format pop-up menu in the Save As sheet that you can use to choose the file format in which you want to save the document. Sometimes, the options on it are disabled. In such cases, look for the Save To command. This command enables you to save one file type to another type. The Save To dialog box looks and works exactly as the Save As sheet does, except that the options on the File Format pop-up menu are enabled.

VIEWING OR HIDING FILENAME EXTENSIONS

Under Mac OS X, you have the option to view or hide filename extensions. However, filename extensions are usually used whether you can see them or not. Generally, I recommend that you always view them because they provide valuable information.

You can choose to hide filename extensions for specific files, or you can set the Finder to always display filename extensions for all files (regardless of the filename extension setting for a specific file).

You can show or hide the filename extensions for specific files by using the following steps:

1. In a Finder window, select the file for which you want to hide the filename extension.

2. Open the Info window.

3. Expand the Name & Extension section.

4. Check the "Hide extension" check box. (To show the extension for a file, uncheck this box.)

5. Close the Info window.

> **TIP**
>
> You can edit a file's name and filename extension in the box in the Name & Extension pane of the Info window.

To override the filename extension display setting for every file, use the following steps:

1. Open the Finder Preferences window.

2. Click the Advanced button to make the Advanced pane appear.

3. Check the "Show all file extensions" check box.

4. Close the Finder Preferences window.

Filename extensions will always be shown, regardless of the "Hide extension" check box in the Info window.

Under most applications, the filename extension status (hidden or not) for specific files is saved, even when you use the Finder preferences to always display filename extensions. If you turn off "Show all file extensions" again, the filename extensions for any files you have hidden become hidden again.

Some applications, especially carbonized applications, don't automatically add filename extensions unless the appropriate check box is checked in the Save sheet.

SAVING DOCUMENTS AS PDFS

One of the many benefits of Mac OS X is that the Portable Document Format (PDF) is a native format. This means you can create a PDF from *any* application without using Adobe's Acrobat or Distiller (although those tools offer some special features that are not available to Mac OS X natively).

PDF documents are useful for two primary reasons. First, they retain their appearance regardless of the fonts and applications installed on the viewing computer. Second, PDF documents can be viewed natively in Mac OS X (using the Preview application) or by Adobe's free Reader application (which is available for all platforms). These reasons make PDF the ideal format for distributing and viewing documents electronically.

PDFs also retain their formatting when they are printed. This makes PDF a good way to distribute documents that you know the recipient will want in hard copy. You can email a PDF and the receiver can print it. Unlike faxing, in which the document format degrades significantly, when the recipient prints the PDF, it will look as good as it does when you send it.

7

An additional benefit to PDFs is that they can't be easily modified. When you send a PDF to someone, he will have a difficult time changing it (it can't be changed at all without special tools). So, PDFs are also a good way to secure documents you provide to others.

→ To learn more about working with PDFs, **see** "Working with PDFs," **p. 888**.

To create a PDF version of a document, you use the Print command to "print" the document to a PDF file:

1. Create your document using the appropriate application.
2. Save the document.
3. Select File, Print to open the Print sheet.

> **NOTE**
>
> You probably noticed that the Print dialog box is also a sheet. This means you can leave it open and work with other documents in the same or different applications.

4. Open the PDF drop-down menu and select Save as PDF.
5. Use the Save to File sheet to name the file and choose a location.
6. Click Save.

A PDF file is created in the location you specify. This document can be viewed using the Preview application or with Adobe Reader.

→ To learn more about printing documents, **see** "Finding, Installing, and Using Printers," **p. 874**.

> **NOTE**
>
> You can also choose to print documents in the PostScript file format. To do this, select "Save PDF as PostScript" on the PDF drop-down menu on the Print sheet. Then use the Save to File sheet to choose a location and save the document.

Faxing Documents

Under Mac OS X, you can fax documents from within the application you use to edit those documents:

1. Prepare the document you want to fax.
2. Select File, Print to open the Print sheet.
3. Open the PDF drop-down menu and select Fax PDF. The Fax sheet will appear (see Figure 7.22).
4. Enter the fax number in the To box or click the Address Book button to choose a fax number from your Address Book.

7

Figure 7.22
Using the Fax sheet, you can fax any document you can open.

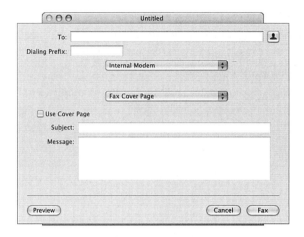

→ To learn how to use the Address Book, **see** "Setting Up and Using an Address Book," **p. 400**.

5. If you need to dial a prefix to connect to the fax number you entered in step 2, enter it in the Dialing Prefix box.

6. Choose the modem by which you want to send the fax on the Modem pop-up menu. In most cases, you will use the Internal Modem option, but you can use any dial-up modem that is configured on your Mac.

7. With Fax Cover Page selected on the lower pop-up menu, check the "Use Cover Page" check box if you want to include a cover page on the fax.

8. Type the subject in the Subject box.

9. If you elected to use a cover page, enter its text in the Message box.

10. Use the other choices on the Options pop-up menu as needed. For example, to configure the modem, select Modem.

11. To preview your fax, click the Preview button. The fax will open in the Preview application.

12. Click Fax to fax the document to the recipients you selected.

TROUBLESHOOTING

I CAN'T INSTALL AN APPLICATION BECAUSE I DON'T HAVE SUFFICIENT PRIVILEGES

When I try to install an application, I see an error message stating that I do not have sufficient privileges.

To install an application in the Applications folder, you must be logged in as an administrator. If you can't log in as an administrator, try installing the application in your Home folder instead.

If this doesn't work, you might have to log in as root to install the application.

→ To get additional help, **see** "Logging In As Root," **p. 253**.

I CAN'T INSTALL AN APPLICATION BECAUSE I AM HAVING PROBLEMS WITH CLASSIC

When I try to run an application's installer, Classic starts up but is unable to install the application.

If a Classic application won't install under Mac OS X, reboot in OS 9.2 and run the installer from there. If you use a Mac that can't boot under Mac OS 9, you are pretty much out of luck. You will have to get an OS X version of the application.

I CAN'T DRAG A DOCUMENT ON AN ICON TO OPEN IT

When I try to open a document by dragging its icon on top of an application's icon, the icon doesn't highlight so that it will open.

This happens when you try to open a document for which the application is not recommended. You can force it to open by holding down the Option-⌘ keys while you drag the document's icon onto the application's icon.

You can also associate an application with a document using the document's Info window.

WHEN I OPEN AN APPLICATION, WHAT I SEE IS INCOMPREHENSIBLE

I opened a document, but what appears onscreen is a bunch of gobbledy-gook.

This happens when you open a file that contains data the application can't interpret. Use the Info window for the document to associate a different application with the document; using an application that Mac OS X lists as a recommended application makes it more likely to open successfully. You can also try opening the document from within an application rather than from the Finder.

THE SPECIAL CHARACTER I INSERTED DOESN'T LOOK CORRECT

I inserted a special character from the Character Palette into a document, but the character that appeared wasn't the one I selected.

This can happen if the application you are working with does not support the Mac OS X font and formatting tools. The most likely case is that the format information you associated with the character, such as the font, was not translated into the application properly.

To solve the problem, use the application's formatting tools to apply the same font to the character as is selected in the Character Palette. The symbol should then appear just as it does in the Character Palette.

MAC OS X TO THE MAX: TAKING APPLICATIONS FURTHER

While using Mac OS X is fun, the real reason you use any OS is to run applications. In this section, you'll learn about the applications that are included as part of the standard OS install. You'll also get a quick glimpse into the past with the Classic environment.

USING APPLICATIONS THAT SHIP WITH MAC OS X

Mac OS X includes many applications you can use to both customize and work with the operating system itself and to do work you need to do. Table 7.3 lists many of the applications that are part of the Applications directory of the standard Mac OS X installation. For the applications that are discussed elsewhere in this book, you will see a cross-reference to where information about that application is provided. If the application isn't covered elsewhere in the book, you will see a brief summary of the application's purpose.

NOTE

> Many other applications are installed as part of Mac OS X. However, because these are used by the system to perform various tasks and you aren't likely to use them directly, they are not listed in Table 7.3.

TABLE 7.3 APPLICATIONS THAT SHIP WITH MAC OS X

Application	Default Directory	What It Does	Cross-Reference or Overview
Address Book	Applications	Stores contact information	"Setting Up and Using an Address Book," p. 400.
Activity Monitor	Applications/ Utilities	Monitors your Mac's performance	Chapter 36, "Solving Mac Problems," p. 1045.
AirPort Admin Utility	Applications/ Utilities	Enables you to configure an AirPort network	Chapter 14, "Using an AirPort Network to Connect to the Internet," p. 371.
AirPort Setup Assistant	Applications/ Utilities	Guides you through the configuration of an AirPort network	Chapter 14, "Using an AirPort Network to Connect to the Internet," p. 371.

7

Application	Default Directory	What It Does	Cross-Reference or Overview
AppleScript (several applications	Applications/ AppleScript	Writes and runs scripts	You can create and run AppleScripts to automate various tasks that you perform. AppleScript is widely used to make cumbersome and complex processes more efficient. AppleScript's scripting language uses English-like com mands, and you can create very complicated scripts. The Script Editor application enables you to create and edit AppleScripts. You can also run scripts that other people create either as standalone applications or using Script Runner.
Automator	Applications	Create macros/scripts	Chapter 10, "Using the Automator to Make Your Mac Work for You," p. 279.
Audio MIDI Setup	Applications/ Utilities	Configures and manages MIDI devices	You can use this application to configure and manage MIDI devices.
Bluetooth File Exchange	Applications/ Utilities	Transfers files via Bluetooth	This application is used when you exchange files with Bluetooth-compatible devices.
Bluetooth Setup Assistant	Applications/ Utilities	Configures Bluetooth on your Mac	You use this application to configure Bluetooth devices on your Mac.
Calculator	Applications	Calculates	Does just what you think; it provides an onscreen calculator.
Chess	Applications	Game	Enables you to play chess against the computer or against another person.
ColorSync Utility	Applications/ Utilities	Repairs ColorSync Profiles	"Synchronizing Color Among Devices," p. 890.
Console	Applications/ Utilities	Provides information on system activity	"Using the Console to View Logs," p. 1063.
Dashboard	Applications	Provides access to widgets	Chapter 6, "Working with the Dashboard and Widgets," p. 159.
Dictionary	Applications	Provides a dictionary	Provides a basic dictionary and thesaurus.

continues

7

TABLE 7.3   CONTINUED

Application	Default Directory	What It Does	Cross-Reference or Overview
Digital Color Meter	Applications/ Utilities	Analyzes the makeup of colors	Enables you to choose a color being displayed on your monitor to determine the RGB values and other properties of which that color consists. You can also copy colors so that you can replicate them.
Directory Access	Applications/ Utilities	Provides directory information for a network	Provides directory information for Mac OS X and applications that use directory information to provide services. You aren't likely to use this application unless you are setting up these services for a large network.
Disk Utility	Applications/ Utilities	Provides many disk and volume functions, such as formatting, burning, and so on	"Maintaining Your Disk Drives," p. 1000.
DVD Player	Applications	Plays DVD movies	Chapter 25, "Watching DVD Movies with DVD Player," p. 741.
Font Book	Applications	Manages your Mac's fonts	"Installing and Using Mac OS X Fonts," p. 247.
Grab	Applications/ Utilities	Captures screen shots	"Capturing Screen Images with Grab," p. 677.
iCal	Applications	Keeps your calendar	"Using iCal," p. 790.
iChat	Applications	Chat via text, audio, or video	"Communicating with iChat," p. 803.
Image Capture	Applications	Downloads images from a digital camera	"Working with Image Capture," p. 667.
Internet Connect	Applications	Connects to the Internet via a phone modem	"Connecting to the Net with a Dial-up Account," p. 352. "Connecting to an AirPort Network with Mac OS X," p. 888.
iSync	Applications	Enables you to synchronize Macs	"Synchronizing with iSync," p. 801.
iTunes	Applications	Digital music manager	Chapter 18, "Listening to and Managing Your Music with iTunes," p. 521.

Application	Default Directory	What It Does	Cross-Reference or Overview
Keychain Access	Applications/ Utilities	Manages your keychains	"Securing Your Mac with Keychains," p. 1024.
Mail	Applications	Email client	Chapter 15, "Using Email," p. 399.
NetInfo Manager	Applications/ Utilities	Administers network	"Using the NetInfo Manager to Administer Your Network," p. 963.
Network Utility	Applications/ Utilities	Provides information and utilities for network	"Using the Network Utility to Assess Your Network," p. 957.
ODBC Administrator	Applications/ Utilities	Configures and manages ODBC databases	Enables you to configure and administer ODBC databases on your Mac.
Preview	Applications	Views images and PDFs	"Working with Preview," p. 658.
Printer Setup Utility	Applications/ Utilities	Installs and manages printers	"Finding, Installing, and Using Printers," p. 874.
QuickTime Player	Applications	Plays and edits QuickTime movies	Chapter 23, "Viewing QuickTime Movies," p. 681.
Safari	Applications	Web browser	"Browsing the Web with Safari," p. 460.
Sherlock	Applications	Finds things	"Using Sherlock to Search the Web," p. 490.
Stickies	Applications	Simulates sticky notes	Enables you to create and view electronic "sticky notes" and "paste" them to your monitor.
System Preferences	Applications	Configures Mac OS X	Provides various panes you use to configure various aspects of Mac OS X.
System Profiler	Applications/ Utilities	Reports on the configuration of your system	"Using System Profiler to Create a System Profile," p. 1050.
Terminal	Applications/ Utilities	Provides a terminal window for working in Unix window	Chapter 11, "Unix: Working with the Command Line," p. 299.
TextEdit	Applications	Basic text	Enables you to create text documents.

7

NOTE

If you have purchased a Mac recently, you will also have the iLife applications (iMovie, iPhoto, iDVD, and GarageBand) installed on it by default. However, these are not part of the standard Max OS X installation. Because these are so important to making good use of Mac OS X, you'll find complete coverage of those applications in Part III, "Mac OS X: Connecting to the World."

WORKING WITH MAC OS 9, THE CLASSIC ENVIRONMENT, AND CLASSIC APPLICATIONS

In rare cases, you might need to run an application that hasn't been moved into the Mac OS X world (perhaps there is a Mac OS 9 application whose publisher went out of business). You can use Mac OS X's Classic environment to run applications that were designed to work under Mac OS 9. Here's a quick summary of the steps you need to follow:

1. Install Mac OS 9 on your system, preferably on its own volume.

2. Open the Classic pane of the System Preferences application (see Figure 7.23).

Figure 7.23
Use the Classic pane of the System Preferences application to configure your Mac to run Mac OS 9 applications.

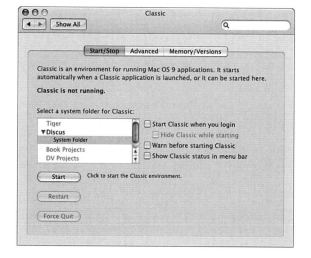

TIP

You don't need to manually start the Classic environment. It will start up automatically when you open a Mac OS 9 application.

3. Select the Mac OS 9 system folder and click Start. The Classic environment will begin to run and you will see the "Classic is starting" progress window.

4. After Classic has completed the startup process, launch the Mac OS 9 application. It will work just like it did on a Mac OS 9 system.

Because Mac OS X offers so many benefits over Mac OS 9, you really should get Mac OS X versions of any applications on which you rely. However, if you do need to use Mac OS 9 applications, take some time to explore the Classic pane of the System Preferences application to fine-tune your Classic environment.

7

CHAPTER 8

CONFIGURING, CUSTOMIZING, AND EXPLORING MAC OS X

In this chapter

8

SETTING YOUR PREFERENCES

The System Preferences application is an important tool you use to control how your Mac OS X system works and looks. If you have read through other chapters this book, you have already used some of the panes it contains to work with various parts of the system. Table 8.1 provides a summary of each pane and tells you where in this book you can learn more about it.

TABLE 8.1   SYSTEM PREFERENCES APPLICATION PANES

Category	Pane	What It Does	Where You Can Learn More About It
Personal	Appearance	Sets interface colors, scrollbar behavior, the number of recent items, and font smoothing	"Setting Appearance Preferences," p. 226.
Personal	Desktop & Screen Saver	Sets the background image of the desktop and configures the screensaver you use	"Customizing the Mac OS X Desktop," p. 135. "Using the Mac OS X Screen Saver," p. 230.
Personal	Dock	Controls how the Dock looks and works	"Customizing the Appearance and Behavior of the Dock," p. 154.
Personal	Dashboard & Exposé	Configures the hot keys and active screen corners for the Dashboard and Exposé	"Managing Open Windows with Exposé," p. 106. "Configuring the Dashboard," p. 169.
Personal	International	Controls the language and formats used depending on the language you are working with	"Setting International Preferences," p. 227.
Personal	Security	Configures FileVault and other security settings	"Securing Your Mac with the Security Pane," p. 1020.
Personal	Spotlight	Configures how Spotlight searches your Mac	"Searching Your Mac with Spotlight," p. 118.

Category	Pane	What It Does	Where You Can Learn More About It
Hardware	Bluetooth (appears only if your Mac can work with Bluetooth devices)	Configures Bluetooth services on your Mac	"Finding, Installing, and Using Bluetooth Devices," p. 847.
Hardware	CDs & DVDs	Configures the actions that occur when you insert CDs or DVDs	Chapter 31, "Understanding and Using Data Storage Devices," p. 893. "Using Disks and Discs," p. 243.
Hardware	Displays	Controls the display properties you use	"Finding, Installing, and Using a Monitor," p. 858.
Hardware	Energy Saver	Controls when your Mac sleeps	"Managing Your Mobile Mac's Power," p. 329.
Hardware	Ink (appears only when a tablet device is connected to your Mac)	Configures handwriting recognition	Use this pane to configure how your Mac recognizes your handwriting as input if you use a tablet input device.
Hardware	Keyboard & Mouse	Sets keyboard and mouse preferences	"Finding, Installing, and Configuring a Keyboard," p. 836. "Finding, Installing, and Configuring a Mouse," p. 842. "Using and Configuring the Trackpad," p. 329.
Hardware	Print & Fax	Configures printer settings and fax services	"Finding, Installing, and Using Printers," p. 874. "Working with Mac OS X's Built-in Fax Capability," p. 886.

8

continues

8

TABLE 8.1   CONTINUED

Category	Pane	What It Does	Where You Can Learn More About It
Hardware	Sound	Manages your system sound and alert sounds	"Controlling Your System's Sound," p. 234.
Internet & Network	.Mac	Configures your .Mac account and enables you to work with your iDisk	Chapter 17, "Using .Mac to Integrate Your Mac onto the Internet," p. 493.
Internet & Network	Network	Configures your network settings for both Internet access and your LAN	Chapter 13, "Connecting Your Mac to the Internet," p. 337. Chapter 33, "Building and Using a Network," p. 935.
Internet & Network	QuickTime	Enables you to configure QuickTime for your Mac	"Configuring QuickTime," p. 684.
Internet & Network	Sharing	Controls access to your computer's services from the network and the Internet and enables you to configure Mac OS X's built-in firewall and set up Internet account sharing	"Mac OS X to the Max: Using Mac OS X to Serve Web Pages," p. 514. Chapter 33, "Building and Using a Network," p. 935. "Using a Mac Running OS X to Share an Internet Account," p. 976. "Defending Your Mac Against Net Hackers," p. 1032.
System	Accounts	Creates, configures, and manages user accounts	"Creating User Accounts," p. 26.
System	Classic (appears only when you have a Mac OS 9 startup volume available)	Controls your Classic environment	"Working with Mac OS 9, the Classic Environment, and Classic Applications," p. 218.
System	Date & Time	Manages the time and date settings and the clock for your system	"Changing the Clock Display," p. 135. "Configuring Your Mac's Date and Time," p. 238.

Category	Pane	What It Does	Where You Can Learn More About It
System	Software Update	Maintains your system software	"Using Software Update to Maintain Your Software," p. 996.
System	Speech	Manages speech recognition and Text-to-Speech	"Mac OS X to the Max: Configuring and Using Speech Recognition," p. 272.
System	Startup Disk	Selects the startup volume that is used the next time you start your Mac	"Choosing a Startup Volume with System Preferences," p. 244.
System	Universal Access	Controls options to improve access for physically or mentally challenged users	Chapter 9, "Making Your Mac Accessible to Everyone," p. 261.
Other	Panes to configure third-party hardware or software	If you install third-party hardware devices, such as keyboards hardware or or PCI cards, they will often have panes installed in the System Preferences application that you use to configure those devices. Some applications also include a System Preference pane.	See the documentation that came with the software.

> **NOTE**
>
> You might see more or fewer panes in the System Preferences application than are listed in Table 8.1 depending on the hardware and software you have installed. For example, if your Mac doesn't support Bluetooth hardware, you won't see the Bluetooth pane.

Following are some tips to work with the System Preferences application:

- You can open a pane by selecting it on the View menu.
- To see all the panes again, select View, Show All Preferences; press ⌘-L; or click the Show All button on the System Preferences application's toolbar.
- You can search for a pane by typing text in the System Preferences application's Search tool. (You can move into the tool by clicking in it; selecting View, Search; or pressing ⌘-F.) As you type, the panes that meet your search will become "spotlighted" and the rest of the panes will be darkened.

- If you prefer that the panes be listed alphabetically rather than by category, select View, Organize Alphabetically. The System Preferences application will be reorganized and the panes will appear alphabetically from the upper left to the bottom right.
- Use the toolbar's Back and Forward buttons to move among panes you have opened.

SETTING APPEARANCE PREFERENCES

Use the Appearance pane of the System Preferences application to control several basic settings for your system. This pane is organized in four sections. From top to bottom, they control basic appearance settings, scroll behavior, the number of recent items tracked, and font smoothing.

Use the Appearance pop-up menu to select Blue if you want color in the buttons, menus, and windows. Select Graphite if you want to mute the color so the color elements are gray instead. Use the Highlight Color pop-up menu to select the highlight color.

Use the "Place scroll arrows" radio buttons to set scrolling behavior. You can place the scroll arrows together (the Together radio button) or choose to have a scroll arrow placed at each end of the scrollbar (the "At top and bottom" radio button). You can select "Jump to here" to cause a window to jump to the relative position in the scrollbar on which you click or "Jump to the next page" to scroll a page at a time when you click above or below the scroll box. If you want scrolling to be smooth (instead of jumping when you scroll, your Mac kind of strolls to the new location), check the "Use smooth scrolling" check box. Uncheck the "Minimize when double-clicking a window title bar" check box if you don't want to be able to minimize a window by double-clicking its title bar for some reason.

Set the number of recent items tracked on the Apple menu for applications, documents, and servers using the Number of Recent Items pop-up menus. You can track as few as none or as many as 50 recent items.

The bottom section of the pane provides the controls you use to configure how font smoothing is enabled on your Mac. *Font smoothing* (known as antialiasing for graphics) reduces the jaggies that occur when you view certain fonts onscreen; this is most noticeable when you use larger sizes or thick fonts or when you apply bold or other formatting. Font smoothing is always turned on, but you can configure it specifically for your system:

1. Open the Appearance pane of the System Preferences application.
2. Using the "Font smoothing style" pop-up menu, select the smoothing style you want your Mac to use. Your options are: "Automatic — best for main display," "Standard — Best for CRT," Light, "Medium — best for Flat Panel," or Strong. You will probably be satisfied with the option appropriate for the display type you use, but you can experiment with the other options to see whether one of them matches your needs better.
3. Select the font size at or below which text smoothing is disabled on the "Turn off text smoothing for font sizes" pop-up menu. Because the effect of smoothing is less noticeable at small font sizes, your system can save some wasted processing power by not smoothing fonts displayed at small sizes. The default value is 8 points, but you might not even notice if you increase this value slightly.

SETTING INTERNATIONAL PREFERENCES

Mac OS X includes support for a large number of languages; language behaviors; and date, time, and number formats. You control these properties through the International pane of the System Preferences application (see Figure 8.1).

Figure 8.1
You can use the International pane of the System Preferences application to control various language and format properties based on a language and the conventions of particular nations.

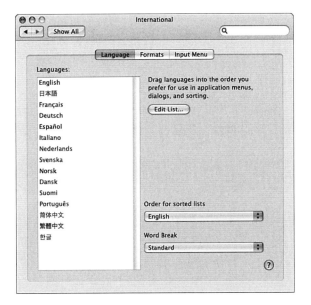

Use the Language tab to configure the languages you want to use. The Languages list shows the languages that are currently active. You can drag these languages up and down in the list to set the preferred order in which you want to use them on menus and in dialog boxes. If you click the Edit List button, a sheet will appear on which you can choose the languages that appear in the Languages list by unchecking the Show check boxes for the languages you don't want to use. After you click OK, the languages whose check boxes you unchecked will no longer appear on the language list. Use the "Order for sorted lists" pop-up menu to choose the language by which lists will be sorted. Use the Word Break pop-up menu to choose how you want word breaks to occur.

NOTE

Changes you make to languages will become active in the Finder the next time you log in.

Use the Formats tab to configure the format of the dates, times, and numbers used on your Mac. When you open this tab, you see a section for each of these areas along with the Region pop-up menu (see Figure 8.2).

Figure 8.2

Use the Formats tab of the International pane to set the format of dates, times, and numbers for your system.

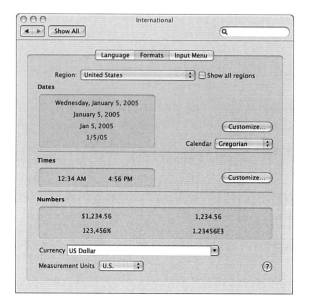

Select the region setting for your Mac on the Region pop-up menu. By default, you see region choices that relate to the languages you have installed. If you want to see all possible region options, check the "Show all regions" check box. When you make a selection, default formats for the region you selected are applied to each setting area (dates, times, and numbers).

After you have set general format preferences via the Region pop-up menu, you can customize the format in each area.

NOTE

> The options described in the following paragraphs are for the United States region. If you choose a different region, different options might be available to you, but they can be set using similar steps.

In the Dates section, click the Customize button. The Customize Dates sheet will appear. Use the controls on this sheet to set the date formats displayed in Finder windows and other locations. There are four general date formats: Short, Medium, Long, and Full. Use the pop-up menus, check boxes, and text fields to set the format for each type of date. Choose the date format you want to configure on the Show pop-up menu. The default format will be shown in the box below the pop-up menu. Click each element, such as the month, to customize it. For example, you can customize the month format by selecting the abbreviated form. Drag the elements around to change the order in which they appear. If you want to add more elements to the default format you selected, drag them from the Date Elements section of the sheet to the location in which you want the elements to appear. Repeat these steps to configure each of the date format options (such as for the Short format). Click OK to save your settings and close the sheet.

TIP

> To remove an element from the date or time customization, select it and press the Delete key.

In the Times section, click the Customize button. The Customize Times sheet will appear. Choose the time format you want to configure on the Show pop-up menu. The default format will be shown in the box below the pop-up menu. Click each element, such as the minute, to customize it. For example, you can customize the minute display by choosing to show the leading 0 or not. Drag the elements around to change the order in which they appear. If you want to add more elements to the default format you selected, drag them from the Time Elements section of the sheet to the location in which you want the elements to appear. Repeat these steps to configure each of the time format options (such as for the Short format). To determine the modifier that is displayed when the time is before or after noon, enter the modifier in the Before Noon and After Noon boxes. Click OK to save your settings and close the sheet.

NOTE

> The settings you make in the Dates and Times sheets affect the format of these values in the Finder and other locations. They do not affect the clock display; you control the format of the clock using the Time & Date pane.

NOTE

> Is time really important to you? With Mac OS X version 10.4, you can choose to display milliseconds by adding the Milliseconds element to one of the standard time formats.

You can see the format of numbers using the region you have selected in the Numbers section. You can't change the number format except with the following two controls.

Use the Currency pop-up menu to choose the currency format you want to use.

Use the Measurement Units pop-up menu to select the default measurement units used (U.S. [aka English] or Metric).

NOTE

> When you make changes to a standard format, the selection on the Region pop-up menu becomes Custom to indicate that you have customized your settings.

Use the Input Menu tab to control and configure the Input menu that appears on the menu bar.

→ To learn how to configure the Character Palette, **see** "Working with the Character Palette," **p. 194**.
→ To learn how to configure a keyboard for different languages, **see** "Configuring a Keyboard," **p. 837**.

USING THE MAC OS X SCREEN SAVER

Mac OS X was the first version of the Mac OS that included a built-in screen saver. Many Mac users enjoy having a screen saver, and Mac OS X's version provides the features you would expect. However, the quality and style with which the screen saver displays images are quite nice. It can be especially nice when you use your own images.

Display Sleep Time

If you really want to protect your screen, use the Energy Saver pane to set a display sleep time. Display sleep actually turns off the display mechanism, which saves the screen. Of course, a blank screen isn't nearly as interesting as the screen saver.

Using a screen saver with modern CRT displays isn't really necessary because they do not suffer the screen burn-in that earlier generations of such displays did.

Although flat-panel monitors haven't been around long enough to be sure, some theorize that using display sleep is very important to maximize the working life of such displays. To be safe rather than sorry, you should keep the display sleep setting at a relatively short amount of time if you use a flat-panel display so it sleeps when you aren't actively using your Mac.

You use the Screen Saver tab of the Desktop & Screen Saver pane of the System Preferences application to configure a screen saver for your computer (see Figure 8.3).

Figure 8.3
You can use one of Mac OS X's built-in screen saver modules, create your own screen saver, or add a screen saver that someone else created (such as by using one that has been posted to a user's .Mac account).

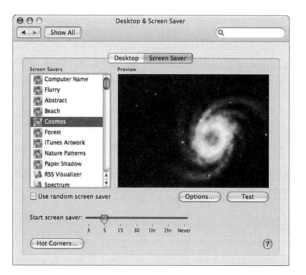

You have four general choices: Use one of Mac OS X's default modules, use a module from images you have created or downloaded, use a module that someone else has created and published via his .Mac account, or use the Apple Hot News module (if it appears on your Mac).

USING A BUILT-IN SCREEN SAVER MODULE

Using one of Mac OS X's built-in modules is straightforward. The general steps are the following:

1. Open the Screen Saver tab of the Desktop & Screen Saver pane.

2. If you want your Mac to randomly select and use a screen saver, check the "Use random screen saver" check box and skip to step 6.

3. Select the screen saver module you want to use from the Screen Savers list; you see a preview in the Preview window.

4. Use the Options button to set various parameters for the screen saver you select, such as whether a cross-fade is used between slides and whether slides are kept centered on the screen (not all modules have configuration options). The available display options are the following:

   - **Cross-fade between slides**—When enabled, one image fades into the next. If disabled, one image disappears before the next image appears.

   - **Zoom back and forth**—When enabled, the screen saver zooms in and out of each image.

   - **Crop slides to fit screen**—When enabled, images are sized so they fit onto the display by cropping the parts that don't fit.

   - **Keep slides centered**—When enabled, images are always centered on the screen.

   - **Present slides in random order**—When enabled, images appear in a random order rather than the order in which they are listed in the folder that contains them.

   N O T E

   > Most of the default Mac OS screen saver modules use standard images Apple has pro-vided. One of them—the iTunes Artwork module—is more interesting, however. It creates a screen saver using the artwork associated with albums in your iTunes Music Library. When you select this module, the artwork is gathered from iTunes automatically and the album covers appear in a large square consisting of subsquares, each of which rotates through various album covers.

   → To learn how to work with iTunes artwork, **see** "Working with Album Artwork," **p. 567**.

5. Test the screen saver by clicking the Test button. The images that are part of the screen saver are rendered and displayed with the configuration options you selected.

   N O T E

   > If you use multiple displays, a different image from the selected screen saver module is shown on each display.

8

6. Use the "Start screen saver" slider to set the idle time that must pass before the screen saver is activated.

7. Click the Hot Corners button.

8. On the resulting sheet, select the corners to which you can move the mouse to manually start or disable the screen saver by selecting the action you want to occur on the pop-up menu located at the corner you want to configure. For example, if you select Start Screen Saver on the pop-up menu located in the upper-left corner of the sheet, you can start the screen saver by moving the cursor to the upper-left corner of the display. The default is to have no action occur at any corner.

9. Click OK

NOTE

> If the display sleep time set on the Energy Saver pane is less than the time you set in step 6, you will never see the screen saver because the display will sleep before the screen saver is activated. If this is the case, a warning appears on the Energy Saver pane and a button enables you to jump to the Screen Saver tab. However, you don't see any warning on the Screen Saver tab. If you want to see a screen saver, check the display sleep setting on the Energy Saver pane to ensure that the display sleep time is greater than the screen saver activation time.

CREATING A CUSTOM SCREEN SAVER MODULE

Some of the built-in modules are pretty cool (I especially like iTunes Artwork), but you can have even more fun by creating or using a custom module. There are several ways to do this:

- Gather the images you want to use for a screen saver in a folder and use the Choose Folder module to select that folder.
- Create a screen saver from a collection of your own images by creating a photo album for that purpose in iPhoto. You can access any images in your iPhoto Photo Library as well as any of its photo albums on the Screen Savers list.
- Use a screen saver that someone has made available through .Mac.
- Use a screen saver you download from the Internet.

To create a screen saver from your own images, use the following steps:

1. Create a folder containing the images you want to use. The images can be in the standard image formats, such as JPG or TIFF.

2. Open the Screen Saver tab and select the Choose Folder module.

3. Use the Choose Folder sheet to move to and select the folder containing the images you want to use; then click Choose.

4. Use the other controls on the tab to configure the screen saver. You have the same display options as for the built-in screen saver modules.

You can choose to use the images within your Pictures folder by selecting it on the list of Screen Savers. Only the images located in the root folder (not within folders that are inside the Pictures folder) are used. You configure the screen saver using the same steps you use for other options.

If you have installed and use iPhoto, you can choose any images in your iPhoto Photo Library as a screen saver by selecting Photo Library, which is located under the Choose Folder module. You can also select any photo album you have created in iPhoto as a screen saver by selecting it on the list that appears under the Photo Library on the screen saver list.

→ To learn how use iPhoto, **see** Chapter 21, "Creating, Editing, and Organizing Digital Images Using iPhoto," **p. 623**.

USING .MAC SCREEN SAVER MODULES

Using the .Mac service, people can make their screen savers available to you and you can make your screen savers available to other people.

→ To learn how to use .Mac services, **see** Chapter 17, "Using .Mac to Integrate Your Mac onto the Internet," **p. 493**.

To use a module available via .Mac, perform the following steps:

1. Open the Screen Saver tab and select the .Mac module. (A default .Mac module provided by Apple is available and is selected automatically.)

2. Click Options to see the Configuration sheet. The top of the sheet contains a list of .Mac screen savers to which you are subscribed. If the Selected check box is checked, the images in the screen saver are used. If not, they aren't used. You can see that you are already subscribed to the .Mac public slideshow.

3. Enter the .Mac member name of someone whose slideshow you would like to use as your screen saver in the .Mac Membership name field. The person whose .Mac name you entered will appear on the list of slideshows to which you are subscribed.

4. Use the Display Options check boxes to configure the slideshow. (The same display options apply to all the .Mac screensaver modules you use.)

5. Check the Selected check box for each slideshow you want to use in your screen saver. If the check box is unchecked, the slideshow is still available to you but isn't displayed. Because the .Mac screen saver displays all the images to which you are subscribed in the same screensaver, uncheck any screensavers whose images you don't want to be included.

6. Click OK.

TIP

> To unsubscribe from a public slideshow, select the slideshow and press Delete. Of course, you can always just uncheck the box to prevent the images in that screen saver from being included. The difference is that if you unsubscribe, the images will no longer be downloaded to your Mac.

7. Configure and test the screen saver just like one of Mac OS X's built-in screen savers.

TIP

If you have people who are interested in you (such as relatives), you can create a .Mac public slideshow and inform those people who are interested that it is available. As you update your slideshow, people who subscribe to and use it see the images you add to the collection.

→ To learn how to publish a .Mac screen saver, **see** "Creating a .Mac Slideshow," **p. 652**.

USING SCREEN SAVERS ACQUIRED FROM THE INTERNET AND OTHER SOURCES

You can also download and use other screen savers from the Internet or other sources. Screen saver modules have the `.saver` filename extension. To do this, follow these steps:

1. Download the screen saver you want to use and prepare it for use.

→ For help with downloading and preparing files, **see** "Downloading and Preparing Files," **p. 481**.

2. Place the `.saver` file in the directory `Mac OS X`/Library/Screen Savers, where `Mac OS X` is the name of the startup volume.

3. Use the Screen Saver tab to choose and configure the screen saver you added.

USING THE APPLE HOT NEWS SCREEN SAVER

The Apple Hot News screen saver presents a feed of Apple news to your screen. To use this module, select Apple Hot News on the list of screen savers. You'll see a preview in the Preview pane. Set the activation time using the "Start screen saver" slider and then test it. (There are no display options with this module.)

CONTROLLING YOUR SYSTEM'S SOUND

You use the Sound pane of the System Preferences application to control the volume, sound effects, and input sources for your system (see Figure 8.4). The Sound pane has three tabs: Sound Effects, Output, and Input. You use the Sound Effects tab to configure your system alert sounds and various audio feedback. You use the Output tab to control the sound output of your Mac and use the Input tab to configure sound input devices attached to your Mac, such as USB microphones.

You can control your system's volume using the "Output volume" slider at the bottom of the pane. Use the Mute check box to mute all system sound. Check the "Show volume in menu bar" check box to show the Volume menu in the menu bar. You can control your main system volume by clicking this icon and using the pop-up slider to set the volume level.

8

Figure 8.4
You use the sliders, list, pop-up menu, and check boxes on the Sound pane of the System Preferences application to control various sound properties of your system.

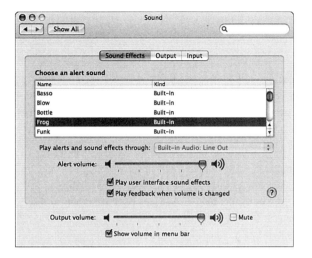

To configure your system alert sound, carry out the following steps:

1. Open the Sound pane of the System Preferences application.

2. Click the Sound Effects tab.

3. Select the alert sound you want to use on the list—you will hear a preview of the sound you select.

4. Select the output device through which you want the alert sound to be played on the "Play alerts and sound effects" pop-up menu. If you have USB speakers installed, such as SoundSticks, or an audio card connected to speakers, you can choose to play alerts through those devices, or if you want to use your Mac's internal speaker, select Internal speakers.

5. Use the "Alert volume" slider to control the relative volume level of the alert sound compared to the general system volume level set on the "Output volume" slider.

TIP

> If you have external USB speakers or speakers connected to a PCI audio card, it is usually a good idea to play the alert sound through the Mac's built-in speakers, especially if you like to listen to music or watch movies with high sound volume. This prevents the alert sound from knocking you out of your chair (if this has ever happened to you, you know exactly what I mean). If you set things this way, you probably need to set the alert volume high because the Mac's built-in speaker will be overwhelmed by your external speakers.
>
> If you have analog speakers plugged in to the Mac's speaker jack, you won't be able to do this because the Mac's built-in audio controller controls the output to those speakers. You must be using USB speakers or those connected to another interface such as the digital audio port on a Power Mac G5 or a PCI audio card.

Mac OS X can play various sound effects when you perform specific actions or when something specific happens (such as when you send an item to the Trash). This feature is enabled by default. To disable it, uncheck the "Play user interface sound effects" check box.

To configure the sound output for your system, use the following steps:

1. Open the Sound pane and click the Output tab. A list of all sound output devices attached to your machine appears; at the least, you see the Internal speakers option, which is your Mac built-in speaker or speakers, depending on which type of Mac you use.

2. Select the output device you want to configure. If output options are available for the selected output device, controls appear just under the list of available devices (see Figure 8.5).

Figure 8.5
You can configure the attached audio output device by selecting it on the list and using the controls that appear. In this case, only one audio device is available and the balance can be configured using the Balance slider.

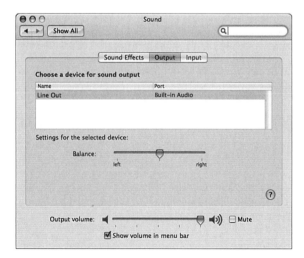

3. Use the controls to configure the selected output sound source. For example, if you use a two-speaker system, use the Balance slider to set the relative volume balance between the speakers. Other sound output devices might have other options. For example, if you use a PowerMac G5's digital audio output, you can configure the output using the additional controls that appear.

To configure sound input devices attached to your Mac, perform the following steps:

1. Attach the sound device you want to use. For example, to use a USB headset microphone, attach it to an available USB port.

2. Open the Sound pane of the System Preferences application and click the Input tab. You see a list of all input devices your Mac recognizes.

3. Select the device you want to configure.

4. Use the "Input volume" slider to configure the device's sensitivity. Dragging the slider to the right increases the level of sound through the device.

5. Test the device by speaking into it or making some other noise. The relative sound level appears on the "Input level" indicator.

6. Continue adjusting the device until you achieve the proper level of input.

Although these sound options satisfy most Mac users, there are more sound options you can choose to implement.

INSTALLING ADDITIONAL ALERT SOUNDS

Under Mac OS X, system alert sounds are in the Audio Interchange File Format (AIFF). This is a good thing because you can use many sounds as your alert sound, and using iTunes, you can convert almost any sound into the AIFF format.

→ To learn how to convert audio files into the AIFF format, **see** "Using iTunes to Convert Files into Various Audio Formats," **p. 581**.

> **NOTE**
>
> Under Mac OS X, AIFF files have the `.aiff` filename extension. By default, iTunes appends the `.aif` filename extension to files when you convert them to the AIFF format. Be sure to add the second *f* to the filename extension for the sound you want to add as an alert sound. If you don't, the file will not be recognized as a valid alert sound.

There are two basic ways in which you can add alert sounds. You can add them to specific user accounts or to the system so they are accessible to everyone who uses your Mac.

To add an alert sound to a specific user account, perform the following steps:

1. Create or download the AIFF files you want to add to your available alert sounds.

2. Log in to the user account under which you want to make the alert sounds available.

3. Drag the new alert sounds to the following directory: /shortusername/Library/Sounds. The new alert sound is available to that user account on the Alert Sounds list in the Sound pane of the System Preferences application.

> **NOTE**
>
> If the System Preferences application is open when you install a new alert sound, you must quit and restart it to see the new sound on the list.
>
> When you install your own system alert sounds in the alert sound list, the type for the sounds you add is Custom instead of Built-in. Built-in sounds are stored in the Sound folder in the System Library folder instead of the user's Library folder.

You can also add alert sounds to the system so they are available to all the user accounts on your machine. However, to do this, you must log in under the root account.

> **CAUTION**
>
> You can't modify files or directories that are within the Mac OS X system directory without being logged in under the root account. Be careful when you are logged in under the root account because you can change anything on your system, including changing vital system files in such a way that your Mac fails to work. You can also delete any files on the machine while you are logged in as root.

→ To learn how to enable and log in under the root account, **see** "Logging In As Root," **p. 253**.

To add alert sounds to your system, do these steps:

1. Create or download the AIFF files you want to add to your alert sounds.
2. Log in under the root account.
3. Drag the AIFF file into the directory Mac OS X/System/Library/Sounds, where Mac OS X is the name of your Mac OS X startup volume.
4. Log out of the root account and then log back in under another account. The new sounds are available on the Alert Sounds list on the Sound pane of the System Preferences application.

> **NOTE**
>
> The kind of alert sounds you add to the system are Built-in, just as the alert sounds that are installed with Mac OS X.

CONFIGURING YOUR MAC'S DATE AND TIME

The Date & Time pane of the System Preferences application enables you to set and maintain your system's time and date (see Figure 8.6). You can set the time and date manually, or you can use a network timeserver to set and maintain your system's time and date for you.

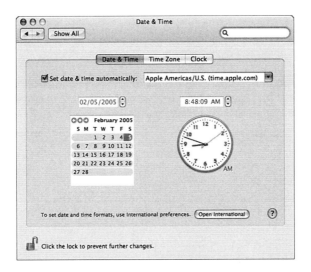

Figure 8.6
The Date & Time pane enables you to determine how your Mac keeps track of time.

To set your system's date and time, do the following:

1. Open the Date & Time pane of the System Preferences application.

2. Click the Time Zone tab and use the map to set your time zone (see Figure 8.7). Drag the highlight bar over your location to select the correct time zone. Then, use the Closest City pop-up menu to select the specific time zone for the area in which you are located.

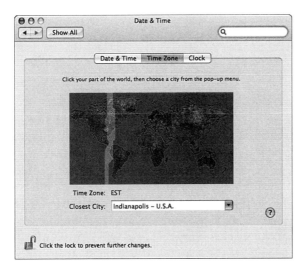

Figure 8.7
Use the Time Zone tools to set the time zone in which you are currently located.

3. Click the Date & Time tab.

4. If you are going to use a network timeserver to maintain the time and date for your machine, check the "Set Date & Time automatically" check box and select the time-server you want to use on the drop-down list. The options you see depend on where

you are. Apple provides three primary timeservers, one for the Americas, one for Asia, and one for Europe. Select the server that is appropriate for your location.

> **NOTE**
>
> It probably goes without saying that you have to be connected to the Internet to use one of Mac OS X's built-in timeservers. Similarly, you must be connected to a local network to use a timeserver located on that network.

5. If you want to set the time and date manually, uncheck the "Set Date & Time automatically" check box. Use the straightforward controls to set the date and time. You can use the Calendar tool to choose a date, type a date in the date box, or use the arrows next to it to select a date. You can then use similar controls to set the time.

→ To learn how to use the Clock tab to configure the desktop clock, **see** "Changing the Clock Display," **p. 135**.

> **NOTE**
>
> You can find the official time for any time zone in the United States at www.time.gov. Of course, this is useful only if you live in the United States and can handle the time being off by as much as 0.2 seconds.

USING THE COLOR PICKER TO CHOOSE COLORS

There are many areas in which you will choose to use colors for certain things, such as when you apply colors to text or apply a color to the background of a Finder window. To apply colors, you use the Color Picker (see Figure 8.8). Within applications, you use the Colors panel to apply colors to text and images.

> **TIP**
>
> How you open the Colors panel depends on the application you are using. However, in some applications, such as TextEdit, you can open it by pressing Shift-⌘-C.

The five modes in the Color Picker are represented by the five buttons along the top of the window. From left to right they are the Color Wheel, Color sliders (including Cyan Magenta Yellow Black [CMYK], Hue Saturation Balance [HSB], Gray Scale, and Red Green Blue [RGB]), Color Palettes, Image Palettes, and Crayons. Each of these modes work similarly. Select the mode you want to use, and the controls in the Color Picker window change to reflect the mode you are in. Use the mode's controls to select or configure a color to apply. When you want to apply the color to the selected object, click it.

Figure 8.8
The Color Picker enables you to create and apply custom colors to selected elements, such as to the background of a Finder window.

TIP

> You can add the configured color to the list of favorite colors at the bottom of the window so you can easily apply the color again in the future.
>
> If you click the Magnifying Glass icon, the pointer turns into a magnifying glass. If you move this over an area and click, the color in that area appears in the current color box of the Color Picker.

NOTE

> The Colors panel you see within particular applications might have the same or slightly different modes.

CONTROLLING OPEN APPLICATIONS

Mac OS X provides many ways to control open applications, including these:

- You can switch among open applications by clicking the icon of the open application to which you want to switch on the Dock.

- You can move among open applications using the ⌘-Tab or Shift-⌘-Tab keys. When you press these keys, the Application Switcher menu that is a list of the currently open applications will appear (see Figure 8.9). The active application is always located on the far left edge of the menu. You can move into a different application by pressing the ⌘-Tab or Shift-⌘-Tab keys until the application you want is selected, or you can click an application on the Application Switcher menu to move into it.

- Use Exposé (press F9) to show all open windows and click a window in the application to which you want to switch.

- Hide applications quickly by either pressing ⌘-H or choosing *Application*, Hide where *Application* is the name of the active application .

Figure 8.9
The Application Switcher menu appears when you press the ⌘-Tab or Shift-⌘-Tab keys.

- Quit an open application by opening the application's Dock icon and selecting Quit on the pop-up menu.

- There are several ways to force a hung application to quit. Press Option-⌘-Esc to open the Force Quit Applications window, select the application you want to quit, and click Force Quit (see Figure 8.10). (If an application is hung, its name appears in red in the Force Quit Applications window and "Not Responding" is shown next to the application's name.) Open the Activity Monitor application (Applications/Utilities); select the application (process) you want to quit; and select View, Quit Process (or press Option-⌘-Q). You can also use the Unix `kill` command in the Terminal application along with the process number of the application you want to force to quit. Yet another way is to choose the Apple menu and then Force Quit; this also opens the Force Quit Applications window.

TIP

> When you select the Finder in the Force Quit Applications window, the Force Quit button becomes Relaunch—the Finder must always be running when you are using Mac OS X. If the Finder hangs, force it to relaunch.

→ To learn more about using Unix commands, **see** Chapter 11, "Unix: Working with the Command Line," **p. 299**.

→ To learn more about the Activity Monitor, **see** "Using Activity Monitor to Understand and Manage Processes," **p. 1056**.

Figure 8.10
You can force an application to quit by opening the Force Quit Applications window, selecting the application you want to quit, and clicking Force Quit.

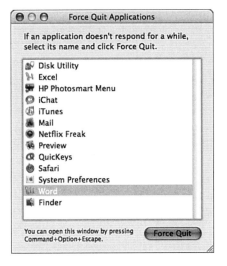

8

TIP

You can also use the Force Quit Applications window to quickly move into open applications. Just open the window by pressing Option-⌘-Esc and then double-click an application shown on the list. That application moves to the front. You can leave the window open all the time if you want to; because it is always on top, it makes a convenient application palette. Of course, if you don't have a lot of screen real estate, this window can get in the way.

USING DISKS AND DISCS

Working with hard drives, CDs, DVDs, and other similar types of storage devices is an important part of using Mac OS X. The following bullets provide information about some useful disk- and disc-related tasks:

- You can control whether mounted disk, disc, and volume icons are automatically shown on the desktop using the Finder Preferences window (select Finder, Preferences and click the General tab). Check the "Show these items on the Desktop" check boxes to show icons on the desktop, or uncheck them to keep those icons from appearing on the desktop. (If you chose not to have disk icons mounted on the desktop, you can access the mounted disks and volumes using the Computer folder and the Places sidebar.)

- You can eject removable disks by dragging them to the Trash; selecting them and selecting File, Eject; pressing ⌘-E; using the contextual menu's Eject command; or using the Eject icon that you can place on the Finder toolbar. You can also eject any ejectable item by clicking the Eject button that appears next to that item in the Places sidebar.

TIP

> When you select a mounted volume (such as a CD), the Trash icon on the Dock becomes an eject symbol to indicate you are unmounting a volume rather than deleting it.

- To configure the action that happens when you insert CDs or DVDs, use the CDs & DVDs pane of the System Preferences application. You can configure what happens when you insert blank media or when you insert "full" discs. When you configure what occurs when you insert "full" discs, your options are to have a selected application open (such as DVD Player when you insert a video DVD), to cause an AppleScript to run, or to do nothing (which Mac OS X calls Ignore).

- To erase a disk under Mac OS X, you use the Disk Utility application (Applications/ Utilities). Open the application, select the disk you want to erase, click the Erase tab, select the format on the Volume Format pop-up menu, enter the volume name, and click Erase.

- Disk Image is a file type that mimics the behavior of a disk. When you open a disk image, it acts just as if it were a real disk. Disk images are most commonly used to distribute applications. When a disk image is mounted, you can open it as you would a physical disk, eject it, and so on.

→ To learn more about disk images, **see** "Installing Mac OS X Applications," **p. 177**.

→ To learn how to configure the action when you insert blank media, **see** Chapter 31, "Understanding and Using Data Storage Devices," **p. 893**.

→ To learn how to use the Disk Utility to format and partition a disk, **see** "Initializing and Partitioning a Hard Drive," **p. 898**.

CONTROLLING SYSTEM STARTUP

Under Mac OS X, there are several ways to configure and control the startup process. The most straightforward way is to use the Startup Disk pane of the System Preferences application to select a startup volume. There are other ways you can control system startup as well, such as selecting a startup volume during the startup process, starting up in the single-user mode, and starting up in the verbose mode.

CHOOSING A STARTUP VOLUME WITH SYSTEM PREFERENCES

The Startup Disk pane of the System Preferences application enables you to select a startup volume. Open the pane to see a list of the valid startup volumes on your machine. Select the volume from which you want to start up and click Restart. You are prompted to confirm this action by clicking the Restart button. Your selection is saved and your Mac restarts from the volume you selected.

CHOOSING A STARTUP VOLUME DURING STARTUP

During the startup process, you can select the startup volume by holding down the Option key while the machine is starting up. When you do, you see a window that displays each of the valid startup volumes on your machine. The currently selected startup volume is high-lighted. You can select a startup volume by clicking it and pressing Return (you can also click the right-facing arrow icon to select the startup volume).

> **TIP**
>
> You can refresh the list of valid startup volumes by clicking the circular arrow button.

STARTING UP IN SINGLE-USER MODE

The single-user mode starts up your Mac in a Unix-like environment. In this environment, you can run Unix commands outside of Mac OS X. This can be useful in a couple of situations, mostly related to troubleshooting problems.

> **NOTE**
>
> Single-user mode is also called *Console mode*.

> **CAUTION**
>
> When you start up in single-user mode, you will be using the root account. Under this account, you can do anything to the files on your Mac, so be careful that you don't do something you didn't mean to do. Some actions you perform under the root account can't be undone.

To start up in single-user mode, hold down ⌘-S while the machine is starting up. Many system messages appear and report on how the startup process is proceeding. When the startup is complete, you will see the localhost Unix prompt. This means you can start entering Unix commands.

> **NOTE**
>
> During the startup process, you are likely to see some information that doesn't make a lot of sense to you unless you are fluent in Unix and the arcane system messages you see. You might also see some odd error messages, but typically I wouldn't worry about them too much. However, if you have particular problems you are trying to solve, some of these messages might provide valuable clues for you.

One of the more useful things you can do is to run the Unix disk-repair function, which is fsck. At the prompt, type

```
/sbin/fsck --y
```

and press Return. The utility checks the disk on which Mac OS X is installed. Any problems it finds is reported and repaired (if possible).

8

NOTE

> If the startup disk is Journaled, type `/sbin/fsck -yf` to force the utility to run.

You can use many other Unix commands at this prompt, just as if you were using the Terminal application from inside Mac OS X.

→ To learn more about using Unix commands, **see** Chapter 11, "Unix: Working with the Command Line," **p. 299**.

To resume the startup process in Mac OS X, type the command **reboot** and press Return. Additional, even more arcane Unix messages appear and then the normal Mac OS X startup process continues. When that process is complete, you end up at the Login window or directly in the Mac OS X desktop, depending on how your Login preferences are configured.

TIP

> If you want to eject a disc when you restart your Mac, hold down the mouse button while you restart.

STARTING UP IN VERBOSE MODE

If you hold down ⌘-V while your Mac is starting up, you start up in the verbose mode. In this mode, you see all sorts of system messages while the machine starts up. The difference between verbose mode and single-user mode is that the verbose mode is not interactive. All you can do is view the system messages; you can't control what happens. Many of the messages you see will probably be incomprehensible, but some are not (particularly messages about specific system processes starting up). This mode is likely to be useful to you only in troubleshooting. And even then, the single-user mode is probably more useful because it gives you some control over what is happening.

STARTING UP IN SAFE MODE

If you are having trouble starting up your Mac, try starting in Safe mode. When you do this, you'll start up in a basic system where many features are disabled. However, this can be useful when you are troubleshooting problems. To start up in Safe mode, start or restart your Mac. When the startup sound plays, hold down the Shift key. When you see the spinning progress indicator underneath the Apple logo, release the Shift key. You will then start up in Safe mode.

STARTING UP IN TARGET DISK MODE

If you'd like to connect two computers together so you can easily move files between them, you can use FireWire to have one computer act like a mounted volume on another. The computer you want to use as a disk must be started up in Target Disk mode.

NOTE

> Target Disk Mode is different than networking computers because the computer that is operating in Target Disk mode works like a hard drive instead of like a computer. You can't use it to do anything beyond what an external drive can do.

8

First, configure the Mac you want to use as a disk to start in Target Disk mode. Open the Startup Disk pane of the System Preferences application, and click the Target Disk Mode button located at the bottom of the pane. Click Restart at the prompt. When the Mac restarts, you'll see a FireWire symbol in its screen. This indicates that it is in Target Disk mode.

Connect the Mac to another one using a FireWire cable. The Target Disk Mac will appear as a mounted disk on the second Mac. You can then use its hard drive just like one installed on the second machine. For example, you can move files to it, install software on it, and so on.

To return the Mac to normal condition, press the Power button. The Mac will shut down. Disconnect the FireWire cable and then press the Power button again to restart it normally.

TIP

> Using Target Disk mode can be an easy way to back up all the files on a mobile Mac. Restart the mobile Mac in Target Disk mode and connect it to a desktop machine with some free hard drive space. Drag all the files from the mobile Mac onto the disk on which you want to store the backed-up files.

USING OTHER STARTUP OPTIONS

Table 8.2 lists various startup options and their keyboard shortcuts.

TABLE 8.2   MAC OS X STARTUP OPTIONS

Startup Option	How to Select It
Prevent automatic login	Hold the left Shift key and mouse button down when you see the progress bar during the startup process.
Start up from a computer connected via FireWire in Target Disk Mode	Press T during startup.
Eject a CD during the startup process	Hold down the mouse button.

INSTALLING AND USING MAC OS X FONTS

Mac OS X offers a lot of great features related to fonts. For example, the Quartz Extreme graphics layer renders Mac OS X fonts clearly at any size and makes using special font features such as kerning controls, ligatures, and so on easy. You can configure and select fonts within applications using the Font panel. The Font panel offers several useful features such as the ability to create and use sets of your favorite fonts.

→ To learn how to work with fonts using the Fonts panel, **see** "Working with Mac OS X Format Menus," **p. 186**.

Mac OS X includes a large number of high-quality fonts in the default installation. You can install additional fonts you want to use.

You use the Font Book application to manage the fonts on your Mac.

UNDERSTANDING MAC OS X FONTS

One difference between Mac OS X fonts and Mac OS 9 fonts is that in Mac OS 9, fonts contain both a resource and data fork, but in Mac OS X, fonts contain only a data fork. Fonts with the file extension .dfont are single-fork files, meaning all the data for that font is stored in the single fork of its file. This is the native Mac OS X font format. However, under Mac OS X, you can also install and use any of the following types of fonts:

- TrueType fonts (.ttf)
- TrueType collections (.ttc)
- OpenType fonts (.otf)
- Fonts and font suitcases used by Mac OS 9 and earlier versions of the Mac OS (these might or might not have a filename extension)

N O T E

One advantage of Mac OS X font files being able to provide all their information in a single fork is that these fonts can be shared with operating systems that do not recognize files with resource forks (Windows, Unix, and so on).

There are two locations in which fonts are installed under Mac OS X. To make a font available to everyone who uses your Mac, it is installed in the directory Mac OS X/Library/Fonts, where Mac OS X is the name of your Mac OS X startup volume. Within this directory are at least three types of font files. Those with the filename extension .dfont are the single-fork font files; you'll also see TrueType fonts, which have the .ttf extension. You will also see fonts whose names do not have a filename extension.

N O T E

Under Mac OS X, you can install or remove fonts while applications are open; fonts you install instantly become available to the system and any applications you are running.

To make a font available only to specific users, it is installed in the following directory: users/shortusername/Library/Fonts. A user's Library directory also contains the FontCollections folder. The FontCollections directory contains the set of font collections available to the user in the Font Book application and the Font pane.

NOTE

Any user can install fonts into the Fonts folder in the Library folder in her Home directory.

8

If you have fonts installed on a Mac OS 9.2 volume that you want to be able to use with Mac OS X applications, you can use the Font Book to install those fonts so they are available under Mac OS X as well.

CONFIGURING FONTS WITH THE FONT BOOK

The Font Book enables you to manage all the fonts installed on your Mac. There are two levels of font groups you can use: libraries and collections. A *library* is a means of storing fonts on your computer or on a server; you can then access the fonts stored in those libraries. You can organize fonts into *collections* and then enable and disable individual fonts or font collections.

When you open the Font Book application (Applications folder), you see three panes by default (see Figure 8.11). The Collection pane contains two sections. The upper section shows the libraries currently being managed by Font Book, while the lower section shows you the font collections on your Mac. (Collections are a means to gather fonts into groups to make them easier to select and apply. For example, when you work with the Mac OS X Font panel, its fonts are organized by collection. You can use these collections to group fonts into smaller, focused groups to make font selection easier and faster.)

Figure 8.11
The Font Book application enables you to manage the fonts on your Mac.

Three libraries are available to you by default. All Fonts contains all the fonts on your computer. User contains fonts stored so that only the current user can access them. Computer contains all the fonts on your Mac (in the default condition, these are the same as those in the All Fonts library). Many collections are installed by default, and you can create your own collections.

The center pane is the Font pane, which shows the fonts that are part of the collection selected in the Collection pane.

The right pane of the window is the Preview pane, which shows a preview of the font selected in the Font pane.

→ To learn how to access fonts you manage with Font Book from within applications, **see** "Working with Mac OS X Format Menus," **p. 186**.

WORKING WITH FONT LIBRARIES

To view the contents of a library, select it on the library list at the top of the Collections column. The fonts it contains will be displayed in the Font pane. You also perform the following library actions:

- Create a new library by opening the Action menu and selecting New Library. An empty library will appear on the list; type the name of the new library.

- Disable a library by opening its contextual menu and selecting the Disable command. The word "Off" will be shown for that library and it won't be able to be used. You can enable a library by opening its contextual menu and selecting the Enable command.

- Add fonts to a library by selecting it and selecting Add Fonts from the contextual or Action menu. Use the resulting Open dialog box to move to and select the fonts you want to add to the selected library.

NOTE

> The most likely use for a new library is to work with files that aren't stored on your computer. For example, if fonts are stored on a server on your network, create a library for those fonts and add them to it. To use the fonts stored on a server, you must be connected to that server via the network, even after you have stored the fonts in your Library.

- Delete a library by selecting it and selecting the Delete command on the contextual or Action menu or by pressing the Delete key. Confirm the deletion at the prompt and the library will be removed from the Font Book window.

WORKING WITH FONT COLLECTIONS

You can use the default font collections included with Font Book and create your own collections.

To view the fonts that are currently part of a collection, select that collection on the Collection list. The fonts it contains are listed on the Fonts pane. You can view the typefaces provided with font families shown on the Fonts pane by clicking the expansion triangle next to that font (see Figure 8.12).

Figure 8.12
Here, you can see that I have created a collection called `brad's fonts` and placed the fonts I use most frequently in it.

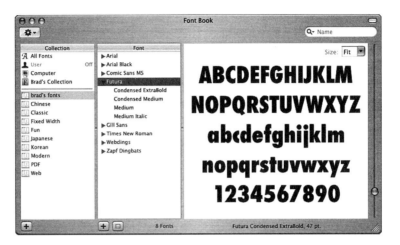

> **TIP**
>
> If a bullet appears next to a font's name, multiple versions of that font are installed. To remove the multiple versions, select the font and select Edit, Resolve Duplicates. This causes Font Book to turn off the duplicate fonts (see Figure 8.12).

> **TIP**
>
> If you select a font or typeface listed under a font and select Preview Font on the Action menu, a separate window will appear that presents a preview of the selected font. This is useful because you can have multiple preview windows open at the same time, making it easier to compare different fonts.

ADDING A FONT COLLECTION

To add a font collection, do the following steps:

1. Click the New Collection button (the plus sign) below the bottom of the Collection list. Select File, New Collection, or press ⌘-N. A new collection appears on the list; its name is selected and ready for you to edit.

2. Type the name of the collection and press Return. The collection will be created.

3. View libraries or other collections, such as the All Fonts collection, to look for fonts to add to the new collection.

> **TIP**
>
> To locate a specific font, select the All Fonts collection and type the font name in the Search tool on the Font Book toolbar.

4. Drag a font you want to install in the new collection from the Fonts pane and drop it on the collection in which you want to place it.

5. Repeat steps 3 and 4 to add more fonts to the collection.

8

TIP

> You can move multiple fonts at the same time by holding down the ⌘ when you select each font.

EDITING FONT COLLECTIONS

After you have created a collection, you can change it in the following ways:

- Double-click the collection name and edit it.

- Select the collection; select a font you want to remove from the collection; and select File, Remove Font. Click OK in the Confirmation dialog box; the font is removed from the collection (the font remains installed on your Mac).

- Select a font within a collection and click the Disable button (the "D" that looks like a square) below the bottom of the Font pane or select Edit, Disable Font. Click Disable in the Warning dialog box. The font is no longer able to be selected from within applications. The word Off appears next to the font to indicate it has been disabled.

- Select a font that has been disabled and click the Enable button or select Edit, Enable Font. The font is again available within that collection from within applications.

- Select a collection and click the Disable button below the bottom of the Collection pane. Click the Disable button in the warning dialog box. The collection is no longer selectable within applications. The word Off appears next to the collection to indicate it has been disabled.

- Select a collection that has been disabled and click the Enable button below the bottom of the Font pane or select Edit, Enable Collection. The collection is again available within applications.

TIP

> If you use specific sets of fonts in specific applications, consider creating a font collection for each application and placing the fonts you use within it. Then, you can easily choose fonts from this group by selecting the application's font collection.

CONFIGURING THE FONT BOOK WINDOW

You can also configure the Font Book window itself in the following ways:

- Select Preview, Show Font Info. When you do, information about the selected font appears in the Preview pane.

- Change the size of the font preview in the Preview pane by either selecting a size on the Size pop-up menu or dragging the vertical slider along the right side of the pane. If you select Fit on the pop-up menu, the preview size is adjusted so you can see all of the preview within the pane.

- Change the relative size of the panes by dragging their resize handles.

> **TIP**
>
> The panes are limited to certain relative sizes. If you try to make a pane larger but are unable to do so, increase the size of the Font Book window itself and then make the other panes larger. You should then be able to resize the first pane.

- Change the size of the Font Book window by dragging its resize handle.
- Change the configuration of the preview shown in the Preview pane by selecting one of the options on the Preview menu. The Sample option shows each letter and number in the selected font, whereas the Repertoire option shows all the characters included in the selected font. The Custom option enables you to type characters in the Preview pane to preview them.

> **TIP**
>
> If you have trouble with a font, try validating it by selecting it and selecting File, Validate Font. Use the resulting Font Validation tool to check the font. When you do, the tool will report on the condition of the font.

INSTALLING FONTS WITH THE FONT BOOK

You can use the Font Book to install fonts by performing the following steps:

1. Select or create the library into which you want to place the fonts and select File, Add Fonts (⌘-O). The Open dialog box will appear.
2. Move to and select the font you want to install.
3. Click Open. The font will be added to the selected library. You can add it to collections and work with that font with Font Book and from within applications.

> **TIP**
>
> To see where a font is installed, select it and select File, Show Font File (⌘-R). A Finder window opens that shows the file in each location in which it has been installed.

LOGGING IN AS ROOT

Because Mac OS X is based on Unix, a user account called root exists on every Mac OS X machine. The root account has permission to do everything that is possible; the root account permissions go way beyond even the administrator account permissions. Because of this, logging in under this root account is very powerful, and it is also dangerous because it isn't that hard to mess up your system, delete directories (whether you intend to or not), and so on. However, because you sometimes need to log in under the root account to accomplish specific tasks, you should understand and become comfortable with it.

You should be logged in under the root account only for the minimum time necessary to accomplish specific tasks. Log in, do what you need to, and then log out of root again. This minimizes the chance of doing something you didn't intend to do because you forgot you were logged in under root.

CAUTION

> Be careful when you are working in your Mac under the root account. You can cause serious damage to the system as well as to data you have stored on your machine.

The root account is a very special user account, but it is still a user account. The full name of the root account is System Administrator, and its short name is root. One difference between the root account and other accounts is that the root account exists without having to create it. However, you have to activate the account and assign a password to it before you can begin using it.

You can activate the root account and create a password for it by following these steps:

1. Log in to the Mac.

2. Open the NetInfo Manager application found in the Applications/Utilities folder (see Figure 8.13).

Figure 8.13
NetInfo Manager is a very powerful administrative application.

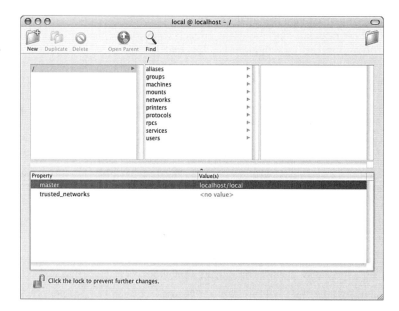

→ NetInfo Manager is a very powerful system administration application; to learn more about it, **see** "Using the NetInfo Manager to Administer Your Network," **p. 963**.

3. Authenticate yourself as an administrator by clicking the Lock icon and entering user account information for an administrator account. (You have to do this even if you are logged in under an administrator account.)

4. Select Security, Enable Root User to see an alert explaining that the root password is currently blank; this is not a good thing.

5. Click OK to close the warning. The Set Root Password dialog box will open.

6. Type the new password for the root account.

7. Type the new password a second time in the "Retype new root password" box.

8. Click OK or press Return.

9. Quit the NetInfo Manager application. Save you changes if prompted to do so.

After you have activated the root account and created the root password, you can log in under the root account by performing the following steps:

1. Log out of the current account.

2. Log in under the root account. If the login window is configured to show user accounts, select Other on the list and then enter **root**, type the root password, and click Login. If the Login window just shows the User Name and Password fields, enter **root** and the password and click Login.

3. Confirm that you are logged in as root by opening the Home directory; root appears as the username and as the label of the Home folder in the Places sidebar (see Figure 8.14).

Figure 8.14
When you can see the Home directory for the root user, you are logged in as root.

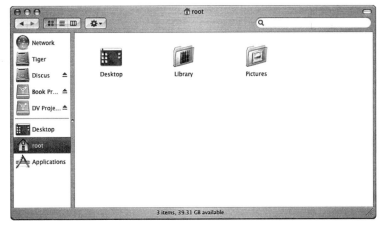

NOTE

If you enable Fast User Switching, the root account isn't listed on the Fast User Switching menu. To log in to the root account, you must bring up the Login window by choosing Login Window on the Fast User Switching menu each time you want to log in as root.

Because the root account has unlimited permissions, you can add or remove files to any directory on your Mac while you are logged in under the root account, including those for other user accounts. You can also make changes to any system file, which is where the root account's power and danger come from.

Use the root account only when you really need to. Make sure that other people who use your Mac do not know the root password; otherwise, you might find yourself with all sorts of problems.

TIP

> You can also log in to the root account directly in the Terminal window to enter Unix commands using the command line. This can be a faster way to enter a few commands if you are comfortable with the command-line interface.

MAC OS X TO THE MAX: EXPLORING MAC OS X SYSTEM FOLDERS

If you have read most of this book to this point, you have already explored quite a bit of Mac OS X. The purpose of this section is to give you an overview of the Mac OS X system so you are familiar with its most important parts from a holistic perspective.

Starting from the top level or root of the machine is the Computer folder. As you learned earlier, this directory contains each of the volumes mounted on your machine as well as the Network folder.

In this section, I refer to the Mac OS X startup volume as the Mac OS X volume (a clever feat on my part, eh?). If you have named your Mac OS X startup volume something different from this, you need to swap your name for mine to understand my references to system items.

If you open the Mac OS X volume, you see the following four system directories: Applications, Library, System, and Users.

NOTE

> You will see at least four folders in the root level of your startup volume, but you might see additional folders, such as Previous Systems if you installed Mac OS X with the Archive and Install option.

THE APPLICATIONS DIRECTORY

As you know from Chapter 7, "Installing and Using Mac OS X Applications," and other chapters, the Applications directory is the default installation directory for all Mac OS X applications. This directory contains application package files as well as application folders and folders that contain other applications (such as the Utilities directory). Mac OS X includes a large number of applications in this directory by default, and you generally install all other Carbon or Cocoa applications in this folder as well.

THE LIBRARY DIRECTORY

The Library directory contains system-level resources that are modifiable when you are using an administrator account. As you saw earlier in this chapter, one of the directories in this directory is the Fonts folder in which you store the fonts available to all user accounts. However, this folder contains many more directories than just this one, such as the Sounds directory that you also learned to change earlier in the chapter. Basically, any system-level resources that can be changed (without logging as root) are stored in this Library directory. Some examples are the following:

- **Application Support**—This directory contains files that provide various types of support to specific applications. For example, files related to the Automator application are stored within the Apple folder that is within this folder.

- **Desktop Pictures**—These graphics files are available for you to use as desktop pictures, which you configure using the Desktop & Screen Saver pane of the System Preferences application.

- **Documentation**—This is an interesting directory; it contains documentation and support files for various services that are part of Mac OS X. For example, you can find files for the Mac OS X help system here as well as information about Unix services such as Apache. Applications can also add documentation here. You should explore this folder to see what documentation is available.

- **Internet Plug-ins**—This directory contains plug-ins accessible to Internet applications you have installed on your system.

- **Preferences**—System-level preferences (as opposed to user-level preferences) are stored here. Examples are Software Update preferences (com.apple.SoftwareUpdate.plist) and login window preferences (com.apple.loginwindow.plist).

- **Printers**—This directory contains the printer drivers. Mac OS X includes native support for many printers, and the drivers for any printers you add to the system are also stored here. Within the directory, the drivers are organized into folders, one for each brand of printer driver installed.

- **Receipts**—This is another interesting directory you should explore. It contains various packages for applications and software updates you have installed on your machine, such as OS updates you install using the Software Update feature of the OS. You can view information about these updates or applications by opening one of the packages you find here.

TIP

When you download a system update using the Software Update, you can run its package to read about what was installed. Launch the update's installer and move to the readme page to read about that update.

8

THE SYSTEM DIRECTORY

The System directory contains the basic software that makes the system work. It contains one directory, which is the Library directory (not to be confused with the Library directory on the root level of the Mac OS X volume).

NOTE

> The System directory is the most analogous to the System Folder in previous versions of the Mac OS. However, the System Folder was really more a combination of the System and Library directories under Mac OS X.

This Library directory contains the fundamental operating system files that provide the services needed to make Mac OS X work. It contains many directories, which you can't modify without being logged in as root. And there aren't really many times when you will need to access the files and directories stored here.

NOTE

> The Mac OS X directory has many other files and subdirectories that are invisible to you when you are logged in under the Mac OS X interface, even if you are logged in under the root account. You can see all the files installed on your Mac using the Terminal application and Unix commands.

Examples of the directories contained in the System's Library are the following:

- **ColorPickers**—These files provide the Color Picker services you learned about earlier in this chapter.

- **Components**—Component files (filename extension `.component`) provide various system services such as AppleScript support and the Sound Manager.

- **CoreServices**—As its name implies, this directory contains files that provide core services to the operating system, such as the Dock, Finder, Help Viewer, Login window, and so on. Several of the items in this directory are applications, including the Finder and Dock.

- **Extensions**—Although extensions in the traditional Mac OS sense are not part of Mac OS X, there are Mac OS X extensions. These files provide support to various hardware devices and hardware-related services. Mac OS X extension files have `.kext` as their filename extension (which stands for Kernel extension).

- **Fonts**—This Fonts directory provides the fonts that are fundamental to the system, such as those used in the menu bar.

- **Frameworks**—As you learned in Chapter 1, "Mac OS X: Foundations," Mac OS X frameworks are the subsystems within the OS that provide various services. The files related to these frameworks are stored in the Frameworks directory. Examples of frameworks installed in this directory are AppleShare, Cocoa, Java, QuickTime, and Security.

■ **OpenSSL**—Secure Sockets Layer (SSL) is the most common encoding scheme used to securely transmit data over the Internet. This directory contains information related to SSL on your machine, such as the various SSL certificates you have installed.

■ **PreferencePanes**—This directory contains the panes in the System Preferences application such as for the date and time (DateAndTime.prefPane), Dock (Dock.prefPane), keyboard (Keyboard.prefPane), and QuickTime (QuickTime.prefPane). Interestingly, third-party preference panes aren't added to this directory when they are installed on the System Preferences application. This folder contains all possible Apple System Preferences application panes, even if they don't appear to you (such as the Ink pane that doesn't appear unless you have a tablet installed).

■ **Sounds**—As you learned earlier in this chapter, this directory contains the alert sounds available to all the users on your machine.

■ **StartupItems**—This directory contains additional system services that become active when the system starts up. Examples include AppleShare, Network services, and so on. Many startup items are listed in this directory, such as the Apache Web server, AppleTalk, Network services, and so on.

THE USERS DIRECTORY

The Users directory contains the Home directory for each user account configured on your machine. Within this directory is a directory for each active user account, a directory for the user accounts you have deleted (if you chose to save the user's Home folder), and the Shared directory for items that can be shared.

NOTE

> The one user directory you won't see is the root directory. That is hidden except when you are logged in as root.

→ To learn more about the contents of a user's Home directory, **see** "Understanding the Home Folder," **p. 21**.

CHAPTER **9**

MAKING YOUR MAC ACCESSIBLE TO EVERYONE

In this chapter

UNDERSTANDING UNIVERSAL ACCESS

The Universal Access pane is where you can make your Mac more accessible to users of your Mac who have various physical or mental challenges. However, even if you don't have such challenges or don't support other users who do, you can use the Universal Access tools to make your Mac better suited to the way in which you like to work. For example, using the Zoom feature, you can zoom using the same keyboard shortcut in any application.

Setting up Universal Access involves configuring any or all of the following areas:

- **Seeing**—Using the Seeing controls, you can configure visual aspects of your system. You can use VoiceOver to have your Mac speak interface elements and you can use zoom to increase the size of items on the screen. You can change the display to be white on a black background or grayscale. You can also configure the display's contrast.

- **Hearing**—The Hearing controls enable you to set the screen to flash when the alert sound plays.

- **Keyboard**—Using the Keyboard controls, you can configure Sticky Keys that enable users to choose key combinations by typing only one key at a time. You can also provide assistance to users who have difficulty with initial or repeated keystrokes with the Slow Keys feature. Slow Keys enables you to set a delay for the time between when a key is pressed and when the input is accepted by the system.

- **Mouse**—The Mouse controls enable you to control the mouse by using the numeric pad on the keyboard and to control the size of the cursor that appears on screen.

NOTE

> On mobile Macs, the Mouse controls are the Mouse & Trackpad controls.

While not technically part of the Universal Access configuration tools, you can also use your Mac's Speech Recognition and Text to Speech capabilities to add audio elements to the interface.

CONFIGURING AND USING SEEING ASSISTANCE

The Seeing assistance functions are designed to make the Mac's display more visible to users who have difficulty seeing the screen. There are three basic areas of configuration: VoiceOver, Zoom, and Display. You start configuring all of these areas by moving to the Universal Access pane of the System Preferences application and clicking the Seeing tab (see Figure 9.1).

Figure 9.1
The Seeing tab of the Universal Access pane enables you to configure how your Mac displays information and to have the OS use VoiceOver to speak interface elements.

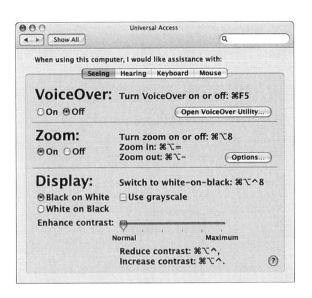

UNDERSTANDING AND USING VOICEOVER

VoiceOver causes your Mac to speak the current position of the VoiceOver cursor in the interface so that you can tell where you are on the screen even if you can't see it clearly. For example, if you have VoiceOver active when you open the Universal Access pane, your Mac would speak the following text to you, "System Preferences, Universal Access, Back button" because that is the first interface element that gets selected with the VoiceOver cursor when you open that particular pane. VoiceOver also speaks commands you issue when you activate them. For example, when you minimize a window, your Mac will say "Minimize." When VoiceOver is active, your Mac will also speak the contents of dialog boxes and other interface elements.

You can customize VoiceOver to work in very specific ways by using the VoiceOver Utility.

USING DEFAULT VOICEOVER SETTINGS TO HAVE YOUR MAC SPEAK TO YOU

Activating and using VoiceOver with default settings is a simple task. To turn VoiceOver on, use the following steps:

1. Open the System Preferences application and click the Universal Access icon to open the Universal Access pane.
2. Click the Seeing tab.
3. Click the On radio button in the VoiceOver section. On the screen, you will see the VoiceOver cursor (which is a box around the specific interface element currently selected) and the Mac will speak its current location to you (see Figure 9.2).

9

VoiceOver cursor

Figure 9.2
When VoiceOver is active, the VoiceOver cursor is used to speak a specific part of the interface (in this case, the Back button).

After you have activated VoiceOver, your Mac will begin to speak to you. Each time something changes, the Mac will always speak the current location of the VoiceOver cursor to you. You move the VoiceOver cursor by pressing the Control-Option-Arrow keys to move the VoiceOver cursor around the screen. Each time it moves onto a new element, that element will be spoken to you as it becomes highlighted by the cursor (i.e., when the VoiceOver cursor's box is placed around the element).

NOTE

> When something appears on the screen that needs your input, such as a sheet, your Mac will speak the words "Interactive dialog" to let you know that such an element has appeared on screen.

When you change applications, VoiceOver will speak the application name and the current location of the VoiceOver cursor within that application.

If you move into an editable text field, your Mac will speak each letter of the text as you move onto it.

NOTE

> If you move around quickly, your Mac might not be able to speak each element as you move to it. It will continue speaking each element you have moved the cursor over until it catches up with you.

By default, the position of the mouse cursor is not tied to the VoiceOver cursor. In order to activate a command or control, you must still use the mouse cursor to point to it. The idea is that you use the VoiceOver cursor to point to interface elements so that you know what they are because the Mac will speak them to you. When you want to activate an element, you still select it with the mouse cursor. For example, suppose you are looking at a screen with tabs on it. You can use the Control-Option-Arrow keys to move the VoiceOver cursor to each tab. When you find the tab you want to move into, you would move the mouse cursor to the tab and then click the mouse button to open the tab.

USING THE VOICEOVER UTILITY TO CONFIGURE VOICEOVER

Using VoiceOver "out of the box" can be useful, but you can also customize it in many ways by using the VoiceOver utility. To access this utility, click the Open VoiceOver Utility button. The button is located on the Seeing tab of the Universal Access pane in the System Preferences application. The VoiceOver Utility has six tabs, each of which enables you to configure a specific aspect of how VoiceOver works (see Figure 9.3).

Figure 9.3
The VoiceOver Utility enables you to customize six aspects of how it works.

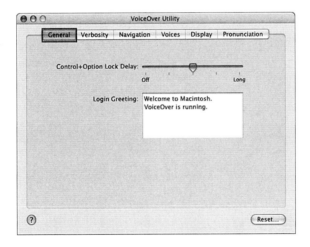

Unfortunately, going into the details of each control in the VoiceOver Utility is beyond the scope of this book. However, Table 9.1 provides a description of some of the configuration tools available to you.

TABLE 9.1   USEFUL VOICEOVER UTILITY CONFIGURATION CONTROLS

Tab	Control	What It Does
General	Control+Option Lock Delay slider	You can lock the Control-Option keys by pressing them twice; use this slider to set the amount of time between presses to lock or unlock the keys; when the keys are locked, moving the arrow keys always moves the VoiceOver cursor.
General	Login Greeting box	This contains the text that is spoken when you turn VoiceOver on and log in; you can change the text to change the greeting.
Verbosity	Punctuation pop-up menu	Use this to determine how punctuation is spoken to you; for example, choose None to prevent any punctuation from being spoken.
Verbosity	Repeated Punctuation pop-up menu	Choose how you want your Mac to speak repeated punctuation, such as Spoken with Count which causes your Mac to speak the punctuation followed by the number of times it appears (for example, "Comma, three).
Verbosity	When text attributes change pop-up menu	When a text attribute changes, such as something being bolded, your Mac can speak the change, play a tone, or do nothing; make your selection using this menu.
Verbosity	While typing speak pop-up menu	Choosing Every Word causes your Mac to speak every word as you type it; choosing Every Character causes your Mac to speak each character you type; choosing Nothing turns off this feature.
Verbosity	Speak text under mouse after delay check box and slider	Check the check box and your Mac will speak the element at which the mouse cursor is currently pointing; use the slider to set the amount of time between when you point to something and when your Mac speaks it.
Verbosity	Announce when mouse cursor enters a window check box	When this is checked, your Mac will tell you when the mouse cursor moves into a different window by speaking the window name (and application name if applicable).
Verbosity	Announce when a modifier key is pressed check box	This causes your Mac to speak when you press a modifier key, such as the ⌘ key.
Verbosity	Announce when the Caps Lock key is pressed check box	This causes your Mac to speak when you press the Caps Lock key.

Tab	Control	What It Does
Navigation	VoiceOver cursor moves to newly loaded web page check box	Check this to have the VoiceOver cursor automatically move to a new web page when it is loaded into your browser.
Navigation	Group items in web pages check box	This causes your Mac to describe groups of items on a web page rather then each individual item.
Navigation	Navigate images check box	Check this to move through images on a web page with the VoiceOver cursor.
Navigation	Only navigate images with a description check box	With the previous check box checked, checking this causes VoiceOver to skip any images that don't have a description that can be read by VoiceOver.
Navigation	VoiceOver cursor tracks keyboard focus check box	With this checked, VoiceOver follows the keyboard focus; for example, when you select a menu using the keyboard controls, the VoiceOver cursor will move there, too.
Navigation	Keyboard focus tracks VoiceOver cursor check box	This keeps the keyboard focus in synch with the VoiceOver cursor; when you move the cursor, the keyboard focus moves too.
Navigation	VoiceOver cursor tracks mouse cursor check box	This causes the VoiceOver cursor to always be at the same location the mouse cursor is.
Navigation	Mouse cursor tracks VoiceOver cursor check box	This makes the mouse cursor always be in the same location as the VoiceOver cursor.
Navigation	VoiceOver cursor tracks keyboard text selection check box	Use this to have VoiceOver track and speak text you select.
Navigation	Keyboard selection tracks VoiceOver cursor check box	Use this to be able to have the keyboard selection become what you select with the VoiceOver cursor.
Voices	Voice, Rate, Pitch, and Volume boxes	Use these controls to select and configure the default VoiceOver voice.
Display	Show VoiceOver cursor check box and slider	With the box checked, the VoiceOver cursor appears as a box on the screen; use the slider to change its size.
Display	VoiceOver Menu Magnification slider	Changes the font size of the VoiceOver menu.
Display	Show Caption Panel check box and slider	With the box checked, VoiceOver will display a panel at the bottom of the screen that shows what it most recently spoke; use the slider to set the size of the panel.

continues

TABLE 9.1 CONTINUED

Tab	Control	What It Does
Display	Rows in Caption Panel slider	Use this to set the number of rows allowed in the Caption Panel.
Display	Caption Panel Transparency slider	Use this to determine how transparent the Caption Panel is.
Pronunciation	List of special items to be spoken and how they should be pronounced; Add and Remove buttons	Use these controls to tell VoiceOver how to pronounce specific things such as acronyms, symbols, or any other text; you can also select the applications in which the pronunciations your create should be used.

TIP

You can reset VoiceOver to default values by clicking the Reset button on the General tab.

UNDERSTANDING AND USING ZOOM

The Zoom function enables you to zoom in on the screen to make things easier to see.

USING ZOOM

Fist, activate zoom by using the following steps:

1. Open the Seeing tab in the Universal Access pane of the System Preferences application.

2. Click the On radio button in the Zoom section.

TIP

You can also turn Zoom on or off by pressing ⌘-Option-8.

After Zoom is turned on press ⌘-Option-= to zoom in or ⌘-Option-- to zoom out (see Figure 9.4). When you are zoomed in, you can move around in the display by moving your mouse.

CONFIGURING ZOOM

There are several options you can configure for Zoom as listed in Table 9.2. You can access these controls by clicking the Options button in the Zoom section. When you do, the Options sheet will appear. Choose the options you want and click Done to save them.

Figure 9.4
Here, I have zoomed in on the Zoom controls.

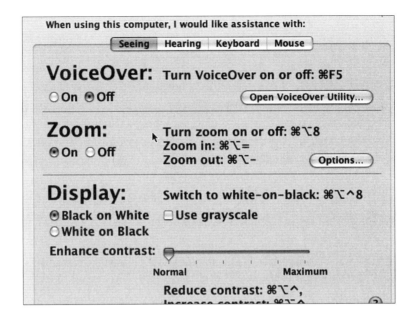

9

TABLE 9.2   ZOOM CONTROLS

Control	What It Does
Maximum Zoom slider	Sets the amount of magnification that can be achieved by pressing the zoom in keys once.
Minimum Zoom slider	Sets the amount of magnification that can be achieved by pressing the zoom out keys once.
Show preview rectangle when zoomed out check box	When this is checked, a black box will appear around the mouse cursor; this box shows the area that will be zoomed in on when the zoom in keys are pressed when no zoom is currently applied; the box disappears when you zoom in.
Smooth images (Press Option-⌘-\ to turn smoothing on or off) check box	When checked, your Mac will smooth zoomed images; you can turn this on or off using the keys listed.
Zoom follows keyboard focus check box	When checked and you zoom, the zoom occurs for the area of the screen that you are focused on using the keyboard.
When zoomed in, the screen image moved radio buttons	Choose "Continuously with pointer" to have the zoomed image move with mouse movements; choose "Only when the pointer reaches an edge" to have the image moved only when the mouse cursor reaches the edge of the image or screen; choose "So the pointer is at or near the center of the image" to always keep the cursor near the center of the image.

UNDERSTANDING AND USING DISPLAY OPTIONS

The Display options section of the Seeing tab enables you to configure the following settings:

- **Black on White**—Check this check box to use the default black text on a white background in Mac OS X screens.

- **White on Black**—This check box causes your Mac to display white text on a black background.

- **Use grayscale**—This check box removes the color from the display and instead uses shades of gray.

- **Enhance contrast**—Use this slider to change the contrast of the display. Contrast is the visual difference between the light and dark elements presented onscreen.

TIP

Use the keyboard shortcuts listed next to the Display options on the Seeing tab to be able to turn them on or off quickly.

CONFIGURING AND USING HEARING ASSISTANCE

The Hearing tab of the Universal Access pane enables you to have your Mac display an on-screen visual alert when it needs to get your attention (see Figure 9.5). To set this, open the tab and check the "Flash the screen when an alert sound occurs" check box. When your Mac plays the alert sound, it will also flash the screen. Click the Flash Screen button on the Hearing tab to see what the flash alert looks like.

Figure 9.5
If you prefer your Mac to flash the screen when it needs your attention, use this check box to make it so.

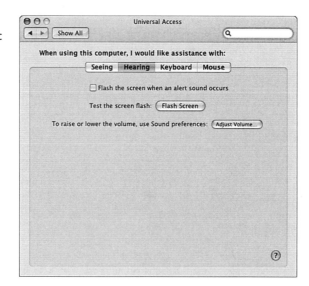

CONFIGURING KEYBOARD ASSISTANCE

The Keyboard tools make your Mac easier to control for those who have difficulty manipulating the keys on the keyboard. There are two general features: Sticky Keys and Slow Keys. Sticky Keys helps users press more than one modifier key at a time because each key pressed "sticks" on. You can also configure Slow Keys to tailor how keys can be pressed to register them with the system. To configure the Keyboard settings, perform the following steps:

1. Open the Keyboard tab on the Universal Access pane of the System Preferences application.

2. Click the Sticky Keys On radio button to activate that feature.

3. If you want users to be able to enable or disable Sticky Keys by pressing the Shift key five times, check the "Press the Shift key five times to turn Sticky Keys on or off" check box.

4. If you want audio feedback when the modifier key is set, check the "Beep when a modifier key is set" check box.

5. If you want each key press to be shown on the screen, check the "Display pressed keys on screen" check box.

6. Turn Slow Keys on by clicking the Slow Keys On radio button.

7. To play a key sound each time a key is pressed, check the "Use click key sounds" check box.

8. Use the Acceptance Delay slider to set the amount of time a key must be pressed before it is registered. Move the slider to the left to increase the delay between the time the key is pressed and when it is registered as a key press by the system.

CONFIGURING AND USING MOUSE ASSISTANCE

Mouse Keys enables users to control the location of the pointer by using the numeric keys on the keypad; this can be useful if a person has difficulty manipulating a mouse or trackpad. To configure Mouse Keys, perform the following steps:

1. Open the Mouse (or Mouse & Trackpad on a mobile Mac) tab of the Universal Access pane of the System Preferences application.

2. Click the On radio button to turn Mouse Keys on.

3. You can enable Mouse Keys to be turned on or off from the keyboard by checking or unchecking the "Press the Option key five times to turn Sticky Keys on or off" check box.

4. Use the Initial Delay slider to set the amount of time a key must be pressed before the pointer starts moving. Move the slider to the left to make the pointer start moving sooner when a key is pressed or to the right to increase the delay.

5. Use the Maximum Speed slider to determine how fast and far the pointer moves when a key is pressed. Drag the slider to the right to increase the speed of movement or to the left to decrease it.

6. To change the size of the pointer on the screen, use the Cursor Size slider. Drag the slider to the right to increase the size of the cursor (see Figure 9.6).

Figure 9.6
You can increase the size of the cursor if someone who uses your Mac has difficulty seeing the standard pointer.

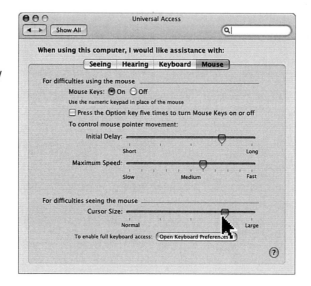

MAC OS X TO THE MAX: CONFIGURING AND USING SPEECH RECOGNITION

Mac OS X has built-in support for speech recognition. This works both ways you can speak to your Mac to issue commands and your Mac can read on-screen text to you. Whether controlling your Mac with speech works for you or not depends on a lot of variables, such as your speaking voice, the position of your mouth relative to your Mac's microphone, the microphone itself, and so on. Also, don't expect your Mac to start working like the computer on the Starship Enterprise; it will take some time for you to get voice recognition working effectively.

NOTE

> I've tried several voice recognition systems, including the Mac's built-in one. Frankly, beyond the initial gee-whiz factor of being able to speak a command and have the computer respond by doing something, I have found that using the keyboard and mouse is a much more effective way to work. But, you might want to experiment to see if it works better for you, particularly if you have special needs when it comes to interacting with your Mac. This section will get you started, but is certainly not intended to explain all the details.

CONFIGURING YOUR MAC FOR VOICE CONTROL

To configure speech recognition on your Mac, perform the following steps:

1. Open the Speech pane of the System Preferences application.

2. Click the Speech Recognition tab and use the controls to configure how speech recognition works. This pane has two tabs: Settings and Commands (see Figure 9.7). Use the Settings tab to configure basic settings of speech recognition.

Figure 9.7
Use the Settings tab of the Speech Recognition pane to configure how your Mac listens to you.

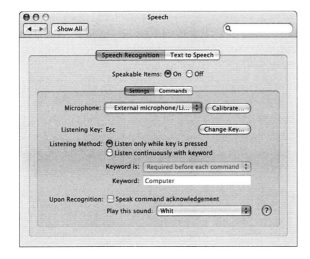

3. Use the Microphone pop-up menu to choose the microphone you want to use. The options you have will depend on the configuration of your system.

4. Click the Calibrate button. The Microphone Calibration window will appear (see Figure 9.8).

Figure 9.8
Using the Microphone Calibration window, you adjust your microphone's input to easily pick up spoken commands.

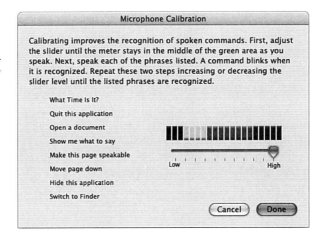

5. Speak some words and drag the slider to the left or right until what you speak is mostly registered near the center of the green band above the slider.

6. Speak each phrase listed along the left edge of the window. If the phrase is recognized by your Mac, it will flash. If it isn't recognized, adjust the slider and repeat the phrase until it is.

7. Continue this process until you can speak all of the phrases and have them recognized without changing the slider.

> **TIP**
>
> When you speak to your Mac, you'll probably have to slow down and make sure you enunciate each word more clearly than you probably do in normal conversation.

8. When your Mac registers each phrase when you speak it, click Done. The Microphone Calibration window will close.

9. By default the listen key is Esc; if you want to change this, click Change Key and choose the key you want to use. The listen key makes your Mac listen for spoken commands.

10. If you want to press the listen key before you speak a command, click the "Listen only while key is pressed" radio button. With this active, you must press the listen key before you speak a command.

11. If you want your Mac to listen continuously for commands, click the "Listen continuously with keyword" radio button. Then, choose when the keyword is required on the "Keyword is" pop-up menu. The options are "Optional before commands," "Required before each command," "Required 15 seconds after last command," and "Required 30 seconds after last command." Then, enter your keyword in the Keyword field. The default is "Computer," which means you need say the word "Computer" to get your Mac to listen to your commands, but you can change this to something else if you prefer to use a different term.

12. If you want your Mac to acknowledge your command by speaking it, check the "Speak command acknowledgment" check box. When your Mac acknowledges your command, it will speak the command it thinks it heard.

13. Choose the sound you want your Mac to play when it recognizes a command on the "Play this sound" pop-up menu.

14. Activate speech recognition by clicking the Speakable Items On radio button at the top of the pane. A sheet will appear that provides some tips for success; read these tips and click Continue. A round feedback window will appear on the desktop. In the center of this, you'll see either the current listen key or the phrase you need to speak (see Figure 9.9). When your Mac is listening to you, the lower part of this window will show you how the sound is being registered.

Figure 9.9
The feedback window indicates that the word "Computer" needs to be spoken before voice commands.

15. Click the Commands tab. You use this pane to determine the command sets you can speak (see Figure 9.10).

Figure 9.10
Use the Commands tab to choose command sets that you want to be able to speak.

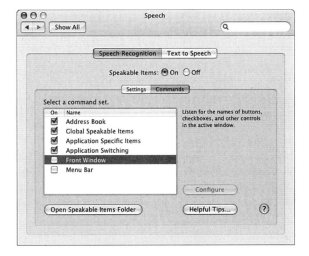

16. Select a command set, such as the Font Window set. A description of the commands will appear to the right of the list.

17. To activate a command set, check its check box. You will then be able to speak the commands in that set. You will be ready to start talking to your Mac.

TIP

If a command set has additional configuration options, the Configure button will become active when you select that command set. Use this button and resulting sheet to set options for the command set.

NOTE

There are a number of commands available in the Speakable Items folder. When you activate the Global Speakable Items command set, these commands will be available to you. To see these commands, click the "Open Speakable Items Folder" button. A Finder window will appear and you will see Speakable items available to you. (For kicks, check out the "Tell me a joke" command.)

USING SPEECH RECOGNITION

After you have configured speech recognition, it will either be easy to use or extremely frustrating depending on how well your Mac recognizes the commands you speak. The only way to find out is to try it.

If you configured speech recognition to require the listening key, press it and speak a command. If your Mac recognizes the command, it will act on it and provide you with the feedback you configured it to, such as repeating the command or playing the sound you selected.

If you have your Mac listen continuously, speak the keyword you set and then speak the command. If your Mac recognizes the command, it will act on it and provide you with the feedback you configured it to, such as repeating the command or playing the sound you selected.

If your Mac does nothing, it doesn't recognize the command. This can be because it didn't "hear" you, didn't understand what you said, or the command you spoke isn't a Speakable command.

TIP

> To see which commands you can speak, click the arrow at the bottom of the feedback window and select "Open Speech Commands window." In the Speech Commands window is the list of commands you can speak. When you open an application that supports speech recognition, that application appears in the Speech Commands window and the list of spoken commands it supports is shown.
>
> If you double-click the feedback window, it moves to the Dock.

If you find speaking commands useful, you can continue to talk to your Mac to control it. However, if you are like me, you will quickly grow tired of trying to get it to work reliably and even if you do get it to work well, it is still faster to use your hands to control your Mac. But, this can be kind of fun to play around with.

USING TEXT TO SPEECH

As you saw earlier in this chapter, using VoiceOver, your Mac can speak to you. The Text to Speech feature takes this concept much further and can be used across many applications and OS to have your Mac speak to you.

To configure Text to Speech, perform the following steps:

1. Open the Text to Speech tab of the Speech pane of the System Preferences application.

2. Select the voice you want your Mac to use from the Voice pop-up menu and then set the rate at which the voice speaks using the slider. Click the Play button to hear a sample.

3. If you want your Mac to speak alerts to you, check the "Announce when alerts are displayed" check box and use the "Set Alert Options" button to open a sheet that enables you to configure the voice used, the alert phrase, and the delay time. Click OK to set the options you selected.

4. If you want applications to speak when they need your attention, check the "Announce when an application requires your attention" check box.

5. If you want to be able to quickly have your Mac read selected text to you, check the "Speak selected text when the key is pressed" check box. In the resulting sheet, type the key combination you want to use to cause your Mac to read text you select and click OK.

TIP

> You can change this key combination later by clicking the Set Key button.

TIP

> Your Mac can speak the time to you, as well. Use the Date & Time Preferences pane to configure this option.

Your Mac will start speaking to you when the conditions you selected occur, such when an alert is played.

If you enabled the "speak selected text" feature, you can select any text and press the keyboard shortcut to cause your Mac to read it.

In applications that support text-to-speech, you can have your Mac read to you by choosing Edit, Speech, Start Speaking. You can shut your Mac up by choosing Edit, Speech Stop Speaking.

CHAPTER 10

USING THE AUTOMATOR TO MAKE YOUR MAC WORK FOR YOU

In this chapter

UNDERSTANDING THE AUTOMATOR

 The Automator enables you to automate actions that you repetitively perform on your Mac. You can create a series of steps the Automator will perform for you and then repeat those steps by running the program you create. Automator is extremely powerful because you can use it to automate actions involving many applications at the same time. Although Automator enables complex actions to be performed, its graphical interface makes building complex scripts as easy as drag-and-drop.

UNDERSTANDING THE AUTOMATOR APPLICATION

When you open the Automator application, you'll see a three-paned window (see Figure 10.1). On the far left of the window is the list of applications on your Mac that Automator recognizes, which means you can automate actions involving those applications. When you select an application, the actions that can be automated will be shown in the center column. When you select an action or other object, an explanation of the object will be presented in the Information pane. The rightmost pane is the Workflow area, which is where you create your automation.

Figure 10.1
Automator makes creating complex programs easy because you can drag steps onto the Workflow area of the Automator window.

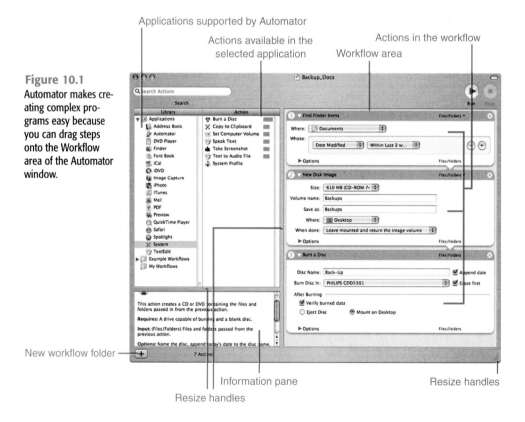

Understanding how the Automator works requires that you understand the following concepts:

- **Actions**—These are the basic building blocks of any automated work. An *action* is a single step that is performed when your automated tasks run. Actions can be relatively simple, such as asking the user to input text, or complex, such as applying photo editing tools to a series of files. Each application supported by the Automator supports a number of individual actions.

- **Input**—Some steps require input, which is something that is needed for the action to be performed. For example, if an action applies to a file, that file is the input of the action. Different actions require different kinds of input. Automator will help you understand what kind of input an action requires.

- **Output**—Most actions end up providing output, which is the result of that action. For example, if an action makes a change to a file, that changed file becomes the output of the action. When actions are linked together, the output of one action becomes the input to the next one.

- **Workflow**—A *workflow* is a series of actions you save to automate work. A workflow consists of one or more steps that are linked together and result in something you would normally do by manually performing each step. You can save workflows so you can run them from within the Automator, edit them, and so on.

- **Application**—You can also save a workflow as an application. You can run the applications you create with the Automator just like other applications on your Mac. When you run an application you have created, the actions you programmed will be performed.

KNOWING WHEN TO AUTOMATE TASKS

Using the Automator is relatively easy given how powerful it is. Still, it does require some learning, especially if you have never programmed or written macros or scripts using other applications. You'll need to balance the time and effort required to learn to use the Automator to create workflows against the time you save by automating your Mac. In the beginning, while you are learning how to use Automator, it might take more time to create a workflow than it would to perform tasks manually. As you get more proficient with the Automator, though, you'll be able to create workflows more quickly, which in turn will improve your overall efficiency in getting things done on your Mac.

Good candidates for automation with the Automator are any series of steps you find yourself repeating again and again. The steps you perform manually can be exactly the same, or you might perform the same series of steps but use different files or folders each time. In such cases, the time you invest in creating an Automator workflow can pay off because you can have your Mac repeat those steps for you.

Perhaps the most important consideration when deciding to automate is that the applications you use during the steps you are automating must be supported by the Automator and, more specifically, the individual actions you perform must be available in the Automator for that application.

DETERMINING WHICH APPLICATIONS ARE SUPPORTED BY THE AUTOMATOR

To automate tasks, the applications you use to perform those tasks must be supported by the Automator. Most Apple applications do support the Automator, including those that are part of Mac OS X and those that are included in the iLife suite.

NOTE

> Because the Automator is new for OS X version 10.4, it isn't widely supported by third-party applications yet. Hopefully, this will change as the Automator matures and other companies add support for it in their applications.

To determine which applications are supported by the Automator, launch the Automator application and look at the applications shown in the Library pane (see Figure 10.2). If an application appears on this list, it supports the Automator. If not, you'll have to use a different automation tool to automate tasks involving that application.

Figure 10.2
In the Library pane, you'll see all the applications on your Mac that support the Automator.

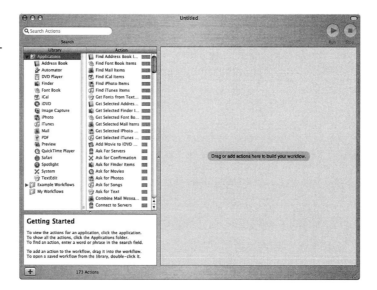

→ To learn about some other automation tools, **see** "Mac OS X to the Max: Automator Alternatives," **p. 296**.

UNDERSTANDING ACTIONS THAT ARE SUPPORTED BY THE AUTOMATOR

Each application supported by the Automator will have one or more actions. Some applications, such as the Finder, support many actions, whereas others support only a few. If all the steps you need to perform to complete a task are available as actions, you can automate a task. If not, you'll need to use a different automation tool.

To see which actions are supported, select an application on the Library list. The actions supported for that application will be shown in the Action pane (see Figure 10.3).

Figure 10.3
Here you can see that the Finder application supports many actions, including the Create Archive action, which creates a `.zip` archive of selected files.

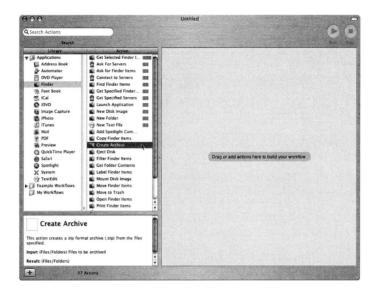

When you select an action on the Action pane, information about the action will be shown in the Information pane located below the Library and Action panes. This information includes a summary of what the action does along with its input and output. For example, when you select the Finder's Create Archive action, you'll see that this action creates a Zip format archive (`.zip`) from the files specified. Its input is the files to be archived. The output, called `result`, is the archived file.

To understand an action in more detail, drag it from the Action pane and drop it onto the Workflow area (see Figure 10.4). The action will be added to the workflow, and you will be able to see its details. At the top of the action will be its name and expected input. If expected input is missing, the missing input will be shown in red to the right of the Action's title. For example, if you add an action that has files or folders as input, but there isn't an action prior to that one that has files or folders as the output, the input of the current action will be red to indicate it is missing (in Figure 10.4, you can see the Files/Folders input, but because this book is in black and white, you can't see that the term is red).

Under the title information, you'll see various tools you use to configure the action. The tools you see will depend on the action you select.

Below those tools, you'll see the Options area. When you expand this area, you'll be able to view and configure options for the action. For example, most actions have the "Show Action When Run" option that causes the action to be visible, often requiring you to click the Continue button, when you run the workflow in which that action is contained.

Figure 10.4
I dragged the Create Archive action into the Workflow area to find out about it in more detail.

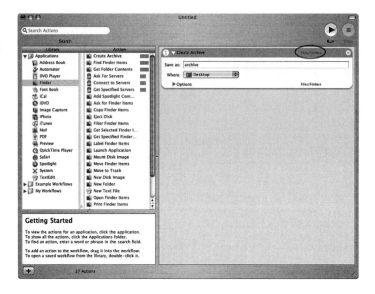

CREATING YOUR OWN WORKFLOWS

Any type of programming, which is what you are doing when you use the Automator, requires that you follow a logical path (well, logical to your Mac anyway) that ends up in the result you want. This isn't always easy to do. For best results, you should tackle any automation project by performing a series of steps, as you will learn about in the following sections.

DESIGNING A WORKFLOW

The first step when creating any workflow is to determine the tasks you want to automate. You need to identify the applications those tasks involve and the specific steps that are required. For best results, you should manually perform each step that is required to complete these tasks and document what you do during each one. Create a list of specific applications the tasks involve and the specific steps performed in that application (see Figure 10.5). This might seem tedious, but creating a workflow that actually does what you expect will be much easier if you take the time to design it before you jump into the Automator and start dragging steps into a workflow.

Figure 10.5
This document details the steps required to find files modified recently, place them into a disk image, and put the disk image on a CD (you'll see the resulting workflow later in this chapter).

NOTE

After you have listed the steps in your workflow, you need to make sure that Automator supports both the applications and actions you need to perform to accomplish those tasks. If it doesn't, you'll need to use a different automation tool.

→ To learn about some other automation tools, **see** "Mac OS X to the Max: Automator Alternatives," **p. 296**.

CREATING AND SAVING A WORKFLOW

After you have designed a workflow, you are ready to jump into the Automator to create and save it. At this stage, you should save the workflow in the Workflow format so you can continue to work with it.

When you save a workflow, you will give it a name. Usually, you'll want its name to describe what it does so you can remember it later.

BUILDING A WORKFLOW

To build your workflow, perform the following general steps:

1. Use your design document to identify the first step that needs to be done.
2. In the Library pane, select the application you use to perform that step. Then, in the action pane, select the specific action that should occur during the step.
3. Drag the action into the Workflow area.
4. Configure the action for the workflow.
5. Refer to the next step in your workflow design document.
6. Repeat step 2.
7. Drag the action into the Workflow area. The output of the previous step will be become the input of the step you just placed in the workflow.
8. Check the output/input connection to ensure they match. For example, if the previous step outputs a file or folder, the input of the next step should be a file or folder.
9. Repeat steps 5–8 to systematically create the workflow to match your design.
10. Save the workflow.

TESTING AND EDITING A WORKFLOW

After you have created the workflow, you should go through a testing process to ensure that the workflow works as you expect it to. It is typical that it won't work quite right at first, so plan on needing to edit it a few times before you get it working properly. The general steps to test and edit a workflow are the following:

1. Click the Run button. The workflow will execute and perform the steps you have designed.

2. Check the results of the workflow. If they are what you intended, you are done (this isn't likely the first time through unless you are working with a very simple workflow). If not, edit the workflow by proceeding to step 3.

NOTE

> Some workflows won't complete because one or more steps fail. In that case, you'll usually see an error message that should help you figure out what went wrong.

3. Identify the specific step (action) that is not working properly. Sometimes, this will be the last step executed, but at other times, it might be a step earlier in the workflow. This process can take some detective work; your clues will be the results of the workflow, error messages, and so on.

4. Edit the workflow by reconfiguring an action that is not working properly, adding new actions, reordering the actions in the workflow, and so on.

5. Run the workflow again. If it works properly, you are done.

6. If the workflow doesn't result in what you expect, repeat steps 3–5 until it does.

You should expect to spend some time testing and editing a workflow until it does just want you want it to. You can increase the odds of your workflow working right the first time by designing it in a good amount of detail before you start creating it. Generally, the more prep work you do designing and documenting your workflow, the less time you will have to spend testing and editing it.

SAVING A WORKFLOW AS AN APPLICATION

After your workflow does what you want it to, you can save it as an application. You can then run the workflow by launching the application, which you do just like other applications on your Mac, such as by double-clicking it, putting it on the Dock and clicking its icon, adding it to your Login Items so it runs when you log in, and so on.

LEARNING HOW TO AUTOMATE YOUR MAC BY EXAMPLE

Once you understand the general way the Automator works and how you should go about building workflows, the only way to really learn how to create your own workflows is to start creating them. The first few you create might take a while, but as you gain more experience with Automator, you'll become more proficient creating new workflows. To get you started, in this section you'll find three sample workflows you can re-create on your Mac. Doing this will give you some experience using the Automator; then you'll be ready to start designing and creating your own workflows.

TIP

> Automator includes some built-in workflow examples. To see them, expand the Example Workflows folder and double-click a sample workflow. A new Automator window will open and you will be able to view and work with the sample workflow.

OPENING WEBSITES

If you visit the same websites regularly, you can create a workflow and application that opens Safari for you and takes you to as many websites as you'd like. To create this workflow, perform the following steps:

→ To learn how to use Safari to browse the Web, **see** "Browsing the Web with Safari," **p. 460**.

1. Launch the Automator.

2. In the Library pane, select Safari. You'll see the actions available for that application in the Action pane.

3. Select the "Get Specified URLs" action. In the Information area, you'll see an explanation of the action ("This action passes the specific URLs into the next action.") along with its results (URLs).

4. Drag "Get Specified URLs" from the Action pane onto the Workflow area (see Figure 10.6). In the center of this action is a table that will contain each URL you want to open. By default, Apple's home page is on the list of URLs that will be opened.

Figure 10.6
The "Get Specified URLs" action is now part of this workflow.

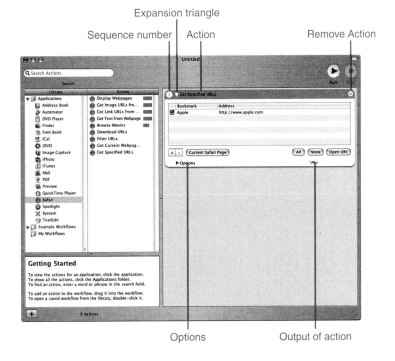

> **TIP**
> To remove a URL, such as the Apple home page, from the list of URLs, select it and click the minus (-) button.

5. Click the Add New Item button (+). A new address will appear on the list.

6. Double-click the Bookmark portion of the URL line so it becomes highlighted, and then enter a name for the website.

7. Press Tab so the Address part of the URL line becomes highlighted, and then type the URL.

> TIP
>
> You can add a website more easily by opening it in Safari and clicking the Current Safari page button. The URL of the current web page will be added to the URL list.

8. Continue adding URLs until you have all that you want to be opened in the list.

> TIP
>
> To test a URL on the list, select it and click Open URL. Safari will launch and move to the URL.

9. Select the "Display Webpages" action. In the Information area, you'll see that this action displays web pages in Safari when provided with URL addresses. Its input is URL addresses and its output is Safari documents.

10. Drag the "Display Webpages" action onto the Workflow area and drop it after the "Get Specified URLs" action (see Figure 10.7).

Matching output/input   Input

Output

Figure 10.7
This workflow now has two actions.

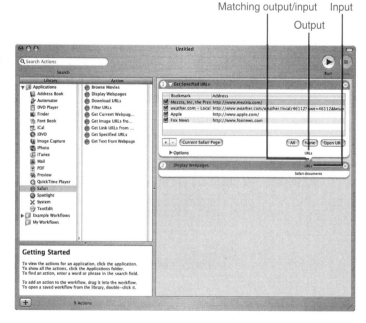

11. Check that the output of the first action, which is URLs, matches the input of the section action, which is also URLs. Notice how the output arrow of the first action fits into the input receptor of the second to graphically show you that the output and input of these actions match.

NOTE

> If the output of one action doesn't match the input of the next, Automator will mark them in red and the arrow from the output won't fit into the input receptor of the action receiving the output. This indicates a mismatch, meaning that the workflow won't work properly.

12. Click the Run button. Automator will run the workflow. As each action runs, you'll see a progress wheel in the lower-left corner of the Action. When it completes, this will become a check mark to show you the action was completed successfully. The next action will run in the same way. When the entire workflow is done, you'll hear a tone.

13. Switch to Safari and you'll see that a Safari window has opened for each URL that is part of your workflow (see Figure 10.8).

Figure 10.8
Here you can see that the four URLs that are part of the workflow have been opened in Safari.

14. Choose File, Save; name the workflow; and save it.

TIP

> By default, workflows you save are stored in the My Workflows folder. You can view these in the Automator by expanding the My Workflows folder in the Library pane.

10

After you have created and tested a workflow, you can save it as an application so you can run it just like other applications. To create an application from a workflow, perform the following steps:

1. Open the workflow you want to save as an application. It will open in Automator.

2. Choose File, Save As. The Save As sheet will appear.

3. Name the application (you can use the same name as the workflow if you want because they are different types of files, so you don't have to worry about replacing the workflow).

4. Choose the location in which you want to save the application you are creating. Consider creating a folder in which to store all your applications so you can locate them easily. For example, you might want to create a folder called My Applications within the Applications folder.

5. On the File Format pop-up menu, select Application.

6. Click Save. An application will be created from the workflow.

7. Open the location you selected in step 4. You'll see the application you created (see Figure 10.9).

Figure 10.9
To open a number of websites at the same time, all I have to do is run this application.

8. Launch the application by opening it. The application will run; as it does, you'll see the application name and progress information in the menu bar.

Just like other applications on your Mac, you can open an application you've created in many ways, such as by adding it to the Dock and clicking its icon, adding it to the Places sidebar and clicking its icon, adding it to your Login items, and so on.

SENDING FILES VIA EMAIL

For this example, suppose that you regularly send files to someone via email (maybe you are an author and you send your chapters to your editor). You can create a workflow that will archive files you select in a Zip file, create and address an email, and attach the Zip file to the email. Here's how to create this workflow:

→ To learn how to configure Mail, **see** "Configuring Mail," **p. 418**.

1. Launch Automator or select File, New to create a new workflow.

2. Click the Finder application and then click the "Get Selected Finder Items" action. You'll see that this action gets items you have selected in the Finder and passes them to the following action.

3. Drag the "Get Selected Finder Items" action onto the workflow.

4. Select the "Create Archive" action (which creates a Zip archive of files or folders), drag it onto the workflow, and place it after the "Get Selected Finder Items" action. Notice that the output of the first action (Files/Folders) matches the input of the second one (also Files/Folders).

   Next, you will configure the Create Archive action so that you are prompted to name the archive file and choose a location each time you run the workflow. (If you wanted the archive file to be named the same and stored in the same location each time, you could enter the filename in the Save As box and select the location on the Where pop-up menu.)

5. Expand the Options area by clicking the expansion triangle (see Figure 10.10).

Figure 10.10
This workflow has two actions; the Options area for the second action is expanded.

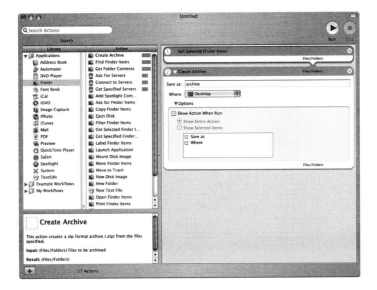

6. Check the "Show Action When Run" check box and the "Show Entire Action" radio button. When you run the workflow, this will cause the Save As dialog box to appear so that you can name the archive file and choose its save location.

TIP

You can expand or collapse the details for a step by clicking its expansion triangle. As you add actions to a workflow, its window will become full. Collapsing actions you have configured makes it easier to view the contents of the workflow.

7. Select the Mail application and then drag the "New Mail Message" action into the workflow and place it below the "Create Archive" action. Notice that the output of the "Create Archive" action (Files/Folders) fits with the input of the "New Mail Message" action (also Files/Folders).

TIP

> In some cases, the input to an action will contain a downward-pointing arrow. This is a pop-up menu you can use to choose options for the action's input. For example, if you select "Use Results from Previous Action" on this menu, the output of the previous step will be used for the current step. If you select "Ignore Results from Previous Action," the previous step's output will be ignored.

8. Enter the email address for the person to whom you want to send the file in the To box or click the Address Book icon to select an address in your Address Book.

9. Type a subject for the message in the Subject field.

10. If you want some text to appear in the message every time, enter it in the Message box.

11. Choose the email account that should be used to send the message on the Account pop-up menu.

12. Review the workflow to see whether the actions you need it to run are available, configured, and in the correct order (see Figure 10.11).

Figure 10.11
This workflow is almost ready to test.

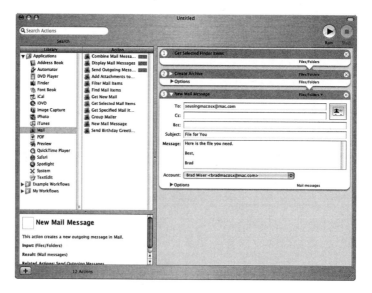

13. Save the workflow.

CAUTION

> You should always save a workflow before you run it. If it doesn't work properly, Automator might quit, in which case you could lose your workflow.

Now that you have created the workflow, it is time to test it by performing the following steps:

1. Move to the Finder and select one or more files.

2. Move back into the Automator and click Run to run the workflow. The first step will get the files you selected. When the second step runs, you will see the Create Archive dialog box (see Figure 10.12).

Figure 10.12
Your application will prompt you to name the archive and choose a location into which to save it.

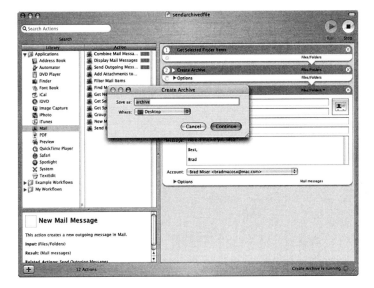

3. Name the archive file, select the location in which you want it saved, and click Continue. The workflow will create the archive. Then, the next step in the workflow will create a new email message; attach the archived file; and enter the address, subject, and body text (see Figure 10.13). You'll hear the workflow's "completed" tone when it has finished its work.

4. Make any changes needed to the message, such as adding or changing the text.

5. Click Send to send the message.

If the workflow works the way you want it to, save it as an application. You can send files by selecting them in the Finder and running your application.

Figure 10.13
This email was created by the workflow and is just about ready to send it.

TIP

If you want to use the workflow to send files to different people, you could leave the To box empty and fill it in when the workflow is done.

BACKING UP FILES ON CD

Backing up important files is always something you should do. It is a good idea to obtain and use software dedicated to that purpose, but this example workflow can be used in a pinch. It will identify files in your Documents folder that have changed in the past two weeks, create a disk image containing those files, and put the disk image on a CD. To build this workflow, perform the following steps:

1. Create a new Automator workflow.

2. Select the Finder application and drag the "Find Finder Items" action into the Workflow area. This action includes the same search tools you can use in the Finder to locate files.

3. Select Documents from the Where pop-up menu. This tells the workflow to look only in your Documents folder.

4. Select "Date Modified" from the first Whose pop-up menu and then select "Within Last Two weeks" from the second Whose pop-up menu. This instructs the Finder to find any file that has been changed during the past two weeks.

5. Drag the "New Disk Image" action onto the workflow and place it after the previous action. Notice that the output of the first matches the input of the second.

6. Select "610 MB (CD-ROM 74 min)" from the Size pop-up menu.

7. Name the volume you will create with the disk image by entering the name in the "Volume name" box.

8. Name the disk image file by entering a name in the "Save as" box. This can be the same name as the volume name.

9. Choose the location in which you want to save the disk image file from the Where pop-up menu.

10. Choose "Leave mount and return the image volume" from the "When done" pop-up menu.

11. Select System in the Library pane and drag the "Burn a Disc" action so it is the third step in the workflow. The input to this action is Files/Folders, which matches the output of the previous action.

> **NOTE**
>
> If a requirement for an action is not met by your Mac, you won't be able to place it in a workflow. For example, you can't use the "Burn a Disc" action in a workflow on a Mac without a drive capable of burning a disc.

12. Name the disc you want to burn in the Disc Name field.

13. Check the "Append date" check box so that a new date will be added to the disc each time this workflow runs.

14. If you have more than one burner available to you, select the burner you want to use from the "Burn Disc In" pop-up menu.

15. If you will use erasable media, check the "Erase first" check box if you want the disc to be erased before it is burned.

16. Check the "Verify burned data" check box if you want your Mac to make sure the disc is burned correctly.

17. Click the "Mount on Desktop" radio button if you want the disc to be mounted on your desktop when it is done or the "Eject Disc" radio button if you want it to be ejected instead.

18. Review the workflow and correct any issues you see.

19. Save the workflow (see Figure 10.14).

Figure 10.14
This workflow will put all the files stored in my Documents folder and that have been modified within the past two weeks in a disk image and then burn that image onto a CD.

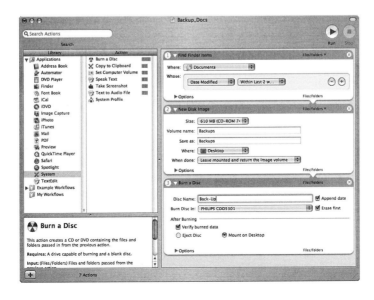

Test the workflow by running it. It will find all the files in your Documents folder that have been changed in the past two weeks and create a disk image file containing those files. Then, it will burn the disk image onto a disc.

TIP

> It can be helpful when testing and troubleshooting to enable the "Show Action When Run" option for any actions that are complicated. When the workflow runs, you'll be prompted to complete the step; this gives you a better idea of what each of those steps is doing, which can be helpful when you are trying to find problems.

If the workflow runs properly, save it as an application so you can run it from the desktop. If not, edit it and retest it until it does work properly.

TIP

> You can share your workflows with other people by providing them the workflow or application file. They will be able to use those files just like workflows or applications they create.

MAC OS X TO THE MAX: AUTOMATOR ALTERNATIVES

Automator is a powerful, but easy-to-use, way to create custom applications to automate work you do. However, it does have its limitations. The biggest one is that only some applications are supported. If an application you need to use to complete a task isn't supported, you can't use Automator to automate it. Another is that you have to manually build each workflow, step-by-step. There are other options for automating your Mac; in this section, you'll learn about two other ways to automate your Mac.

USING QUICKEYS TO AUTOMATE YOUR MAC

My favorite automation utility is Startly Technology's QuicKeys. The best thing about QuicKeys is that you can record your actions to create a script. This is often much easier than programming each step manually. To automate a task, you start the QuicKeys recorder and perform the task yourself. As you do so, QuicKeys records your actions and builds a script for you. You can edit the scripts you record, allow user input, and do many other actions that Automator can't match. You can also easily assign keyboard shortcuts to all the scripts you create or add them to menus. If you need to automate your work, QuicKeys is indispensable.

NOTE

> For more information or to download a trial version, check out the QuicKeys website at www.cesoft.com.

USING APPLESCRIPT TO AUTOMATE YOUR MAC

AppleScript is Mac OS X's built-in scripting tool, which you can use to create AppleScript programs to perform all kinds of actions. AppleScript is much more powerful than the Automator, but it also has a higher learning curve because you use a scripting language (AppleScript) to create programs rather than the Automator's easier graphical programming. The tools you use to work with AppleScript are in the AppleScript folder located in the Applications folder.

NOTE

You can use AppleScript and Automator together. For example, you can create an AppleScript and then use that as a step in an Automator workflow.

NOTE

To learn about AppleScript in more detail, visit www.apple.com/applescript/.

10

CHAPTER 11

UNIX: WORKING WITH THE COMMAND LINE

In this chapter

A COMMAND LINE WITH THE MAC OS?

As you learned earlier in the book, Mac OS X is running on top of a version of the Unix operating system. This means that Mac OS X can use many Unix applications. It also means you can enter Unix commands directly in the command-line interface to manipulate your system. In fact, in some situations, using a Unix command might be the best way you can accomplish a task (such as deleting a rogue file that you can't delete by dragging it to the Trash).

Unix is a very powerful language/operating system; however, it is also enigmatic, and many of its commands require you to use complicated syntax to get them to work properly. Unix commands are incomprehensible to most people by just looking at them, so don't expect to be able to figure out how a particular command works without some help. Mostly, you will learn about commands you want to use from various Unix resources (such as this chapter, other books, websites, and Unix manual pages). You might find using the command line to be so counter to the traditional Mac interface experience that you don't want to use it; if so, that is fine because few situations exist in which it is required in everyday Mac use. However, if you want to master Mac OS X, you should become familiar with the command line and learn some basic Unix commands. You might find that Unix provides ways of doing things that are both powerful and efficient.

There is so much you can do with Unix that there is no way you can learn how to work proficiently with it in the few pages of this chapter. To become even remotely fluent in Unix, you will need to do some additional learning outside of this book. What you can learn here is generally how the command-line interface works, and you can also learn how to use some basic Unix commands as examples. In the "Mac OS X to the Max" section at the end of the chapter, I provide references for you so you can learn more about using Unix if you choose to.

TERMINAL

You use the Terminal application (Applications/Utilities) to enter Unix commands in the command-line interface (see Figure 11.1). The Terminal window is simple; all you see are your last login date and time, a Welcome message, the hostname, the user account under which you are logged in, and the command prompt.

NOTE

> *Hostname* is the name of the machine that is hosting your Unix session. When you are running a Unix session from your local machine, this will be *your computer's name* for most default configurations. If you are providing services over the network, the computer's network name is used.

Figure 11.1
The command-line interface in Terminal isn't much to look at, but it is very powerful.

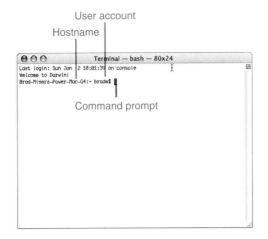

SHELLS

In Unix, the *shell* is the user interface you use to interact with Unix. You can use different shells for the same set of Unix tools; each shell will have slightly different features, but they all work somewhat similarly (although the specific commands you use can differ). You can change the specific shell you use if you find one that offers features in which you are interested.

The default shell for working with Unix under Mac OS X is called bash. Other shells are available, but bash is a good place to start.

> **NOTE**
>
> You can install other shells on your Mac to work with them. After you download and install the shell, you use the Terminal's Preferences to set the shell you want to use. The details of using different shells are beyond the scope of this chapter. See some of the references listed at the end of this chapter for help.

UNIX COMMAND STRUCTURE

To enter commands, you type them at the command prompt. All Unix commands use a specific syntax and consist of the following three parts:

- Command
- Options
- Argument

The *command* is the specific action you want to take, such as listing the contents of a directory using the ls command.

You can enter *options* for that command to make the command work in a specific way. To add an option to a command, you type a hyphen followed by a letter. The options you can use are specific to each command. For example, when used with the ls (list) command, the -l option tells Unix to list the contents of the directory in the long format.

The *argument* is the "thing" on which the command will be executed, such as a file or directory. For example, to list the contents of a directory called mydirectory, the argument would be that directory name and the path to that directory.

When you enter specific commands, you might not use options or arguments; in some cases, you won't use either and will simply enter the command by itself.

NOTE

> Unix is case sensitive, so you must always follow the case conventions for specific commands. Most of the time, you will type everything in lowercase letters for commands and options, but paths can include both uppercase and lowercase letters.

You can run several commands in sequential order by separating the commands with a semicolon, as in command1; command2. Each command will be activated in the order in which you list it.

You can send the output of one command to be the input of another command by separating them with the pipe symbol (¦), as in command1 ¦ command2. This is called *piping*.

When entering commands, you will frequently need to use the path to a directory or file you want to manipulate. The path is the means by which you locate a file in the hierarchy; levels of the hierarchy are indicated by the slash (/). Also, Unix uses relative pathnames. When you refer to something within or below the current directory, you need to enter only the portion of the path from the current directory to the subdirectories and files rather than the full path from the top level of the hierarchy. For example, to refer to a directory called mac_files within a directory called user_docs when you are currently in the user_docs directory, you would enter the path mac_files. When you want to move above or outside the current directory, you must type the full path. In Unix, full paths always start with /.

NOTE

> The full path to your Home directory is /startupvolume/Users/shortusername/, where startupvolume is the name of your Mac OS X startup volume and shortusername is the short username for your account. However, because you can use relative paths, you can leave out the first / and the name of your Mac OS X startup volume to get to this directory. You need to add only the volume name when you are working outside the current volume.

Unlike GUIs, Unix does not like spaces in filenames, volume names, or paths. To enter a space in one of these, use the backslash (\) followed by the space. For example, to refer to the volume called Mac OS X, you would enter /Mac\ OS\ X.

To get to the root of the startup volume, the path is simply /. However, unless you are logged on under the root account, you won't be able to do anything with the files and directories you see using a command line because of the system security.

One of the best ways to become familiar with entering pathnames is to drag items from a Finder window onto the Terminal window. When you do so, the pathname to that item is entered in the Terminal. You can use this trick to make entering paths easier because you can drag the item onto the prompt after you have entered a command and option to quickly add the argument to complete the command. And, after you drag several onto the window, you will get a good idea of how to type pathnames at the prompt manually. Follow these steps:

1. In a Finder window, open the Home directory for your user account.

2. Open a new Terminal window from within the Terminal application by selecting File, New Shell. A new Terminal window will appear.

> **TIP**
>
> When using the Terminal, you can have multiple windows open at the same time. Each window is independent, so you can have multiple sessions running independently. You can save each session separately too, which you will learn about later in this chapter.

11

3. Drag the Documents directory from the Finder window onto the new Terminal window. The path to the directory is shown at the prompt (see Figure 11.2). (Note that you can't drag the folder from the Places sidebar; you must drag it from a Finder window.)

Figure 11.2
You can quickly enter a path at the prompt by dragging an item from a Finder window onto the Terminal; in this case, I dragged the Documents folder from my Home directory onto the Terminal window.

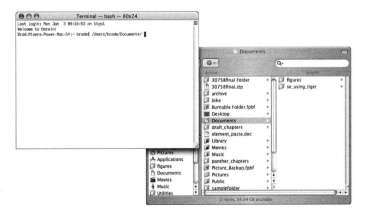

NOTE

If you deal with Unix systems outside of Mac OS X, you will notice that paths almost never include spaces. Unix can have trouble properly interpreting spaces, so you can run into problems if the path you want to use includes spaces. Generally, if you plan to use Unix frequently, you should include underscores when you name your files and directories instead of spaces. Or, you can simply drag the object into the Terminal window and let the Mac enter the path for you. Spaces will be replaced by a backslash and a space (\ ).

→ To **see** examples of specific Unix commands, **see** "Learning Unix by Example," **p. 304**.

UNIX APPLICATIONS

Because Unix has been around so long, thousands and thousands of Unix applications are available. You can run many of these under Mac OS X, and the OS includes several of these applications as part of the standard installation. For example, the Apache web server application enables you to host your own web pages. Mac OS X comes with a couple of Unix text editors, which are vi (Visual Editor) and emacs (an abbreviation of editing macros).

→ To get some examples of running these Unix applications, **see** "Working with Basic Unix Applications," **p. 313**.

SHELL SCRIPTS

You can invoke a series of commands using a Shell script; you can save the script and run it at any time to save yourself from having to retype the commands over and over. You create a script using the same syntax as in regular Unix commands. The difference is that you save those commands to a text file. When you want to run the commands, you execute the file instead. You can also run scripts that others have written just as easily.

The details of writing and running scripts are beyond the scope of this book. See the references listed at the end of this chapter for information about creating and using Shell scripts.

UNIX FLAVORS

Finally, you should be aware that various versions of Unix are available. And, different releases of different versions exist as well. Mac OS X includes a version of the Berkeley Software Distribution (BSD) version of Unix. As this version is updated, the version that is part of Mac OS X will be updated as well.

LEARNING UNIX BY EXAMPLE

Many Unix commands are available, and there is no way you can do more than scratch the surface in this small chapter. However, you can learn how Unix commands work in general by trying some specific examples of useful Unix commands.

→ For references in which you can learn more Unix commands, **see** "Learning Unix," **p. 316**.

Each of the following sections provides information about specific commands. For each command, you will see four areas of information about that command. First, you will read a general description of what the command does. Second, you will see the command's syntax and some of the useful options for that command. Third, you will see a more specific description of the command's effect. Fourth, you will see the steps you can take to use the command.

NOTE

> For the commands in this section, you won't see all or even many of the options that are possible for each command. You will need to access a more detailed reference for that type of information, such as the command's manual pages.

LEARNING ABOUT THE ENVIRONMENT

When you are troubleshooting, it can be helpful to understand the environment in which you are running Unix. You can use the uname command to get information about the computer on which you execute the command. Or, you might need to check this information to make sure some software or hardware is compatible with your system:

Command: uname

Options: -a provides all the information about your machine; -s shows the operating system name; -n lists the machine name

What it does: Provides information about various aspects of the machine on which you are running Unix

1. Launch the Terminal application and at the command prompt, type **uname -a**; then press Return. You will see various items of information about your machine, such as the core operating system (Darwin), the version of the kernel you are running, and so on (see Figure 11.3).

Figure 11.3

The uname command provides information about the machine on which you are running Unix.

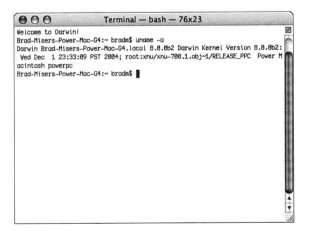

2. Type **uname -s** and press Return. You will see only the core operating system (Darwin).

3. Type **uname -n** and press Return. You will see the name of the machine hosting the Unix session.

Command: env

What it does: Provides extensive information about your Unix session (your Unix environment)

Type **env** and press Return. You will see information including your Home directory, the shell you are running, the username you are using, the language being used, the application you are using to enter Unix commands, and so on.

TIP

> At the top of the scrollbar in the Terminal window is a broken square. If you click this, the Terminal window splits into two panes, and you can work within each pane independently. You can drag the bar that separates the two parts of the window to change their relative size. This is useful when you want to view two areas of the window at the same time but can't expand the window large enough to be able to do so.

VIEWING THE CONTENTS OF DIRECTORIES

You will frequently need to move up and down the directory structure to work with specific files or other directories. Unix has many commands that enable you to do so, including

Command: pwd

What it does: Shows you the full path to your current location

Use the pwd command when you aren't sure about the directory in which you are currently located. When you use the command, you will see the full path in which you are working. This can be helpful if you become confused about where you are as you move around the directories.

Command: cd *pathname*

What it does: Changes your directory location to the one in the path *pathname*

NOTE

> When a specific command is listed in a step, you should ignore the period at the end of the command. For example, in the following steps, don't type the period after the command cd Music in step 1.

1. Type **cd Music**. The prompt will change to [computername:~/Music] to indicate you are in the Music directory in your Home directory.

TIP

> Remember that the ~ represents your Home directory, so ~/Music means you are in the Music directory that is within your Home directory. This can help you take some shortcuts when entering paths, as you will see in the next step.
>
> Also remember that the forward slash (/) in a path indicates a change in level in the hierarchy. If you are in your Home directory and type cd /Music, you will get a message telling you that no such directory exists. When you enter the forward slash, Unix looks back to the highest level in the structure and there is not a directory called Music in that directory. Leaving the / out indicates that Unix should look in the current directory, which is where the directory is actually located.

2. Type **cd /Users/*shortusername***, where *shortusername* is the short username for your account. This moves you back into your Home directory. You include /User/ because you are moving above the Music directory and so need to include the full pathname.

NOTE

> In a pathname, the tilde character (~) indicates that you are in your Home directory. In step 2, you could have just entered cd ~ to move back into your Home directory.

Command: ls

Options: -F differentiates between files and directories; -l shows full information for all the files in the directory

What it does: Lists the contents of a directory in various formats and with various information

NOTE

> Although most commands and options are in lowercase, they aren't always. For example, the -F option is different from the -f option (both are valid for the ls command).

1. Use the cd command to move into the directory of which you want to see the contents.

2. Type **ls**. You will see a multiple-column view of the directory; files and directories are listed by name.

3. Type **ls -F**. You will see the same list as before except that now directories are indicated by a / after their names.

4. Type **ls -l**. You will see the contents of the directory listed along with lots of information about each file and directory within the current directory (see Figure 11.4). If there are many items, the information will scroll so quickly that you might not be able to see all of it. This is a good opportunity to see an example of piping two commands together.

Number of links to other files

Owner   Group   Name

Figure 11.4
Listing a directory
using the ls -1
command provides
detailed information
about each item in
that directory.

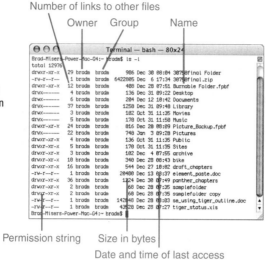

Permission string   Size in bytes

Date and time of last access

5. Type **ls -1 ¦ more**. This time, the same list will appear, but the display will stop when the screen is full and you will see the more prompt at the bottom of the window. Press the spacebar to see the next screenful of information. You can also scroll the window using the scrollbars to see all the items in the window.

TIP

If you type the command ls -la, you will also see the invisible files in a directory.

The permissions string you see at the start of each item in the full listing indicates how the item can be accessed. The first character indicates whether the item is a file (-) or a directory (d). The next three characters indicate what the owner of the file can do; r is for read, w is for write, and x is for execute. If any of these characters is the hyphen (-), that action can't be taken. The next three characters indicate the permission that the group has to the file. For example, if these characters are r-x, other members of the group can read, not write, and execute the file. The last three characters indicate what everyone else can do.

The execute permission applies to a directory. To access a directory, you must have both read and execute permission. If you also have w permission, you can change the contents of the directory as well.

Command: file *filename*

What it does: Indicates what type of file *filename* is

Type **file**, followed by the filename you would like information about, and press Return. Information about the file is displayed.

CHANGING THE CONTENTS OF DIRECTORIES

You can use Unix commands to change the contents of directories as well. For example, you can delete files using the rm command. This can sometimes be faster than using the Trash. Once in a while, you might not be able to use the Trash to get rid of a file; you can often use the Unix commands to accomplish the task when other means fail.

Command: rm

Options: -i prompts you before deleting each file; -r removes the entire directory

What it does: Deletes everything that you indicate should be deleted

1. Use the cd and ls commands to find a file you want to delete.
2. Type rm *filename*, where *filename* is the name of the file you want to delete, and press Return. The file is deleted.
3. Type rm -i *filename* and press Return. You are prompted about removing the file; type Y to remove the file or N to cancel.
4. Type rm -r *directoryname*, where *directoryname* is the name of a directory you want to delete, and press Return. The directory and all its contents are deleted.

NOTE

You can't remove the current directory unless you enter the full path to it.

TIP

The asterisk (*) is a wildcard character. For example, to delete all the files in a directory that have the file extension .tiff, you can type rm *.tiff.

Command: cp

What it does: Copies a file

1. Type cp *filename filenamecopy*, where *filename* is the name of the file you want to copy and *filenamecopy* is the name of the file to which it will be copied; then press Return. The first file is copied into a new file that has the second name you typed.
2. Type cp *filename path*, where *filename* is the name of the file you want to copy and *path* is the location in which you want the copy to be created; then press Return. A copy of the file is placed into the location you specified.

Command: mv

What it does: Moves a file or directory

Type mv *filename path* and press Return. The file or directory *filename* is moved to the location *path*.

11

Command: mkdir

What it does: Creates a directory

1. Use the cd command to move into the directory in which you want to create a new directory.

2. Type **mkdir *directoryname*** and press Return. A new directory with the name *directoryname* is created in the current directory.

USING THE MANUAL

All Unix commands have a manual associated with them. This manual lists the syntax for the command and defines its options; manuals can be a good reference when you are using a specific command but can't remember an option or the command's exact syntax. Many manual pages also provide some explanation about how the command works.

Command: man

What it does: Brings up the manual pages for the command you enter

1. Type **man ls** and press Return. The manual pages for the ls command appear (see Figure 11.5).

Figure 11.5

You can get extensive information about any command by using the man command.

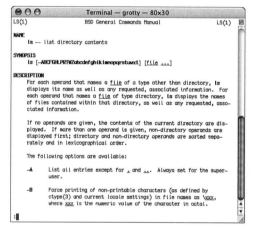

2. Press the spacebar to move to the next page.

3. Continue reading the manual pages until you have the information you need.

4. Press Q to return to the command prompt.

It is a good idea to take a look at the manual pages for any Unix commands you use. Pay special attention to the list of options that are available for the command.

NOTE

> Some Unix applications provide manual pages using the help argument. For example, `perl --help` brings up information about the Perl application.

TIP

> Pressing the spacebar moves you down the manual page one screen's worth at a time; you can move down a manual page one line at a time by pressing the Return key instead.

USING SUPERUSER COMMANDS

As you learned earlier in the book, the root account is the fundamental user account that can do *anything* under Mac OS X. The root account has more access to the system than even an administrator account does. Using this account can be hazardous to your system because, when you are under root, the OS assumes that you know what you are doing and doesn't provide any checks on your activities. You can easily delete things you don't mean to or mess up the system itself.

CAUTION

> By entering the root account, you can do damage to your system. You should use this only when you really have to, and even then, you need to be very careful about the commands you enter while you are working on the root prompt.

However, when you need to use a specific command at a specific time that you can't do under another user account, it can be helpful to enter commands as root.

Command: `sudo`

Option: `-s`, which runs the command in the default shell

What it does: Gets you into the root account so you can enter a command that you can't enter under another account

→ For help activating the root account and creating a password for it, **see** "Logging In As Root," **p. 253**.

1. Open a new shell window. The prompt shows the short name of the user account you are logged in under.

2. Type **sudo -s** and press Return. If you are using the `sudo` command for the first time in a session, you will see a warning regarding what you are about to do and will be prompted to enter your password; enter your root password and press Return. If you have logged in as root previously, you won't have to enter the password again. When the `sudo` command is successful, the prompt shows that you are logged in as root (see Figure 11.6).

Figure 11.6
The `root#` prompt indicates that you are logged in under the root account; be careful when you see this prompt.

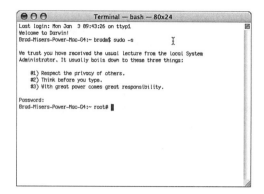

TIP

To return to the previous account, type `exit` and press Return.

KILLING A PROCESS

When a process goes wrong, it can cause problems, such as hanging, or it might start consuming tremendous amounts of processing power, thus bringing your system's performance to a crawl. You can tell that a process has gone out of control by monitoring its percentage of CPU usage. If this number gets high and stays there, the process is likely hung. Because the information in the top window is dynamic, you should open it in a Terminal window and then open another window to enter commands. Under Mac OS X, there are several ways to stop an out-of-control process. For applications, you can use the Force Quit command. At the process level, you can use the Process Viewer to force a process to quit. You can also use the powerful Unix command `kill` to stop a running process.

Command: `kill ProcessID`

Options: `-9` kills the process no matter what; `-3` quits the process

What it does: Stops the process with the ID number `ProcessID`

1. Launch the Terminal.

2. Type **top**. You will see a listing of all the processes currently running on your Mac (see Figure 11.7). Use the information in the table to identify the problematic process, such as one that is consuming an unreasonable amount of processing power. In this example, assume that Safari has gone out of control (although, as you can see in the figure, it is using only 47% of the CPU so it really doesn't have a problem at this point). In the figure, Safari's process ID number is 403.

3. Open a new shell by selecting File, New Shell (⌘-N).

4. Type **kill -9 403**. (Of course, you would actually type the process number for the process you want to kill.)

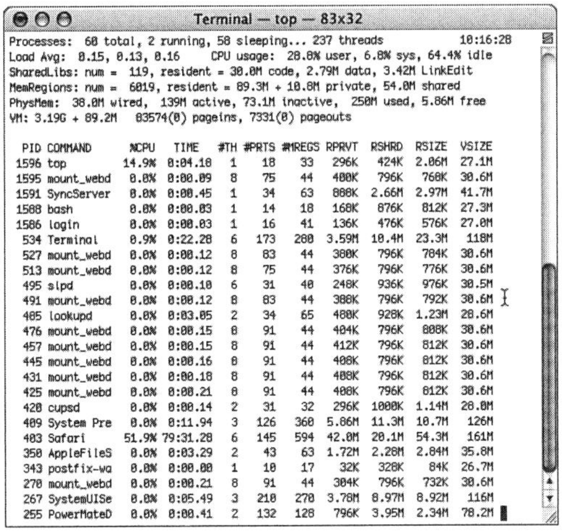

Figure 11.7
This top window shows all the processes running on your Mac; you can use the process ID with the `kill` command to stop any running process.

```
 ● ● ●              Terminal — top — 83x32
Processes:  60 total, 2 running, 58 sleeping... 237 threads            10:16:28
Load Avg: 0.15, 0.13, 0.16    CPU usage: 28.8% user, 6.8% sys, 64.4% idle
SharedLibs: num = 119, resident = 30.0M code, 2.79M data, 3.42M LinkEdit
MemRegions: num = 6019, resident = 89.3M + 10.8M private, 54.0M shared
PhysMem: 38.0M wired, 139M active, 73.1M inactive, 250M used, 5.86M free
VM: 3.19G + 89.2M   83574(0) pageins, 7331(0) pageouts

PID COMMAND       %CPU   TIME   #TH #PRTS #MREGS RPRVT  RSHRD  RSIZE  VSIZE
1596 top          14.9% 0:04.10  1   18    33   296K   424K  2.06M   27.1M
1595 mount_webd    0.0% 0:00.09  8   75    44   400K   796K   768K   30.6M
1591 SyncServer    0.0% 0:00.45  1   34    63   800K   2.66M 2.97M   41.7M
1588 bash          0.0% 0:00.03  1   14    18   168K   876K   812K   27.3M
1586 login         0.0% 0:00.03  1   16    41   136K   476K   576K   27.0M
 534 Terminal      0.9% 0:22.20  6  173   280   3.59M  10.4M 23.3M   118M
 527 mount_webd    0.0% 0:00.12  8   83    44   300K   796K   704K   30.6M
 513 mount_webd    0.0% 0:00.12  8   75    44   376K   796K   776K   30.6M
 495 sipd          0.0% 0:00.10  6   31    40   248K   936K   976K   30.5M
 491 mount_webd    0.0% 0:00.12  8   83    44   300K   796K   792K   30.6M
 485 lookupd       0.0% 0:03.05  2   34    65   400K   928K  1.23M   28.6M
 476 mount_webd    0.0% 0:00.15  8   91    44   404K   796K   808K   30.6M
 457 mount_webd    0.0% 0:00.15  8   91    44   412K   796K   812K   30.6M
 445 mount_webd    0.0% 0:00.16  8   91    44   400K   796K   812K   30.6M
 431 mount_webd    0.0% 0:00.18  8   91    44   400K   796K   812K   30.6M
 425 mount_webd    0.0% 0:00.21  8   91    44   400K   796K   812K   30.6M
 420 cupsd         0.0% 0:00.14  2   31    32   296K  1000K  1.14M   28.0M
 409 System Pre    0.0% 0:11.94  3  126   360   5.86M  11.3M 10.7M   126M
 403 Safari       51.9% 79:31.20 6  145   594   42.0M  20.1M 54.3M   161M
 358 AppleFileS    0.0% 0:03.29  2   43    63   1.72M  2.28M 2.84M   35.8M
 343 postfix-wq    0.0% 0:00.00  1   10    17   32K    328K   84K    26.7M
 270 mount_webd    0.0% 0:00.21  8   91    44   304K   796K   732K   30.6M
 267 SystemUISe    0.0% 0:05.49  3  210   270   3.78M  8.97M 8.92M   116M
 255 PowerMateD    0.0% 0:00.41  2  132   128   796K   3.95M 2.34M   78.2M
```

5. Switch back to the Terminal window showing top. You will no longer see Safari listed in the process list. You can use the same steps to kill any process by using the process ID of that process.

You can stop the top process by pressing Ctrl+C.

NOTE

> If the process you are trying to kill is an Administrator process, you will have to use the `sudo -s` command to get into the root account before you use the `kill` command.

WORKING WITH BASIC UNIX APPLICATIONS

You learned earlier that several Unix applications are included with Mac OS X. Although you aren't likely to use these instead of your Mac OS X applications for your everyday work, sometimes these applications can be quite useful. For example, you might want to use the vi text editor to create Shell scripts. A couple of examples will show you how such applications work.

EDITING TEXT WITH VI

The Unix application vi is a basic text editor. You can use it to create and edit text files, but it is most useful for creating Shell scripts. You are unlikely to use it to create text documents, but you can use it to create plain-text documents if you would like.

The vi program has two modes: Edit and Command. In Edit mode, you can enter and edit text. In Command mode, you issue commands to the program. Do the following:

1. Type **man vi**. Read the manual pages to get an idea of how vi works.

2. Open a new Terminal window (⌘-N) and type **vi** and the name of the text file you want to create, such as vi newtestfile.txt. The program opens, the file is created in

the current directory, and you see a screen containing tilde symbols in the editing area. At the bottom of the screen, you will see the vi command line.

3. Type **i** to enter Insert mode.

4. Type your text.

5. Press Esc to move into Command mode. While you are in Command mode, you will hear an alert sound if you try to type anything that isn't a recognized vi command; you will also see a prompt at the bottom of the vi window telling you that the text you typed isn't a recognized command.

> **NOTE**
>
> Determining which mode you are in can be confusing. When you enter Command mode, the cursor appears to jump back a couple of spaces and the bottom line of the window is empty. You can then type a command. If you see text on the screen when you type, you are in Edit mode. You will also see -INSERT- at the bottom of the screen.

6. Type **:w** and press Return to write the text to the file you created. At the bottom of the vi window, you will see confirmation that the text has been written to the file (see Figure 11.8).

Figure 11.8
The message at the bottom of this vi window indicates that one line of text has been written to the file newtestfile.txt.

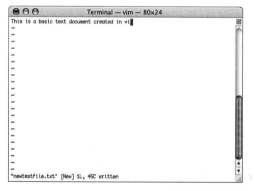

7. To continue adding text to the file, type **a**. The command line disappears and the cursor becomes active after the last text you entered.

8. Continue adding text and writing it to the file.

9. When you are done, press Esc to enter Command mode; then type **:wq** and press Return to quit vi. You will return to the command line.

> **TIP**
>
> To save long manual pages for a command, use the man command on that command and press the spacebar to reveal the entire text of the manual pages. Select the manual text you want to save in a file and select File, Save Selected Text As. Name the text file and save it. You can then refer to that file when you need help with that command.

Because GUI text editors are available, you might not want to use Unix text editors such as vi, but for short, plain-text documents, such as a Shell script, these editors can be useful.

To edit an existing file with vi, type **vi** *filename*, where *filename* is the name of the file you want to edit, and press Return. The file opens and you can begin editing it.

If you intend to use vi, make sure that you read its manual pages in detail; vi has many commands available, but they are hard to figure out without help.

COMPRESSING, UNCOMPRESSING, AND EXTRACTING FILES

Unix has some built-in programs to enable you to work with compressed files, including the following:

- To compress a file, type **compress** *filename*. The file named *filename* is compressed and a .Z is appended to its name.

- To uncompress a file, type **uncompress** *filename*, where *filename* is the name of the compressed file. The file is uncompressed.

- You can also use the gzip compression application by typing **gzip** *filename*. Uncompress the file using the gunzip command. gzip offers various options; check its manual pages to see them.

Many Unix files are archived in the tar (tape archive) format before they are compressed. After you compress such files, you will see a file that has the .tar extension. You can extract a tar file using the command tar xvf *filename*, where *filename* is the name of the tar file.

NOTE
> Tar also has various options; check its manual pages for help.

MAC OS X TO THE MAX: UNIX RESOURCES

Using Unix proficiently requires some additional learning—Unix is a very complex and sophisticated tool that you should become familiar with to master Mac OS X. In this part of this chapter, you will learn the keyboard shortcuts that will help you use the Terminal application more efficiently. You also will find references to websites and books that can help you learn Unix in more depth.

USING TERMINAL KEYBOARD SHORTCUTS

Table 11.1 lists keyboard shortcuts for the Terminal application.

TABLE 11.1   TERMINAL KEYBOARD SHORTCUTS

Action	Shortcut
Use Selection for Find	⌘-E
Find Next	⌘-G
Find	⌘-F
Find Previous	Shift+⌘-G
Jump to Selection	⌘-J
Line Down	⌘-Down arrow
Line Up	⌘-Up arrow
New Command	Shift+⌘-N
New Shell	⌘-N
Next Page	Spacebar
Next Terminal	⌘-'
Previous Terminal	⌘-~
Save Selected Text As	Option+Shift+⌘-S
Save Text As	Option+⌘-S
Send Break	⌘-.
Set Title	Shift+⌘-T
Show Info	⌘-I

LEARNING UNIX

The following list describes websites for learning more about Unix:

- www.uwsg.indiana.edu/usail/—Site name: Unix System Administration Independent Learning. This is an online course about administering Unix.

- www.comp.lancs.ac.uk/computing/users/eiamjw/unix/—Site name: A Course in the Unix Operating System. This is another online Unix course.

- www.eco.utexas.edu/Help/Unixhelp/TOP.html—Site name: Unixhelp for Users. This is a nicely organized and fairly extensive reference site.

- www.comet.ucar.edu/strc/unix/index.htm—Site name: SOO/STRC Unix Resources. This is a page containing links to other Unix learning sites.

- http://www.rice.edu/IT/help/documents/index_platform.html#UNIX—Site name: Rice University IT Document Index. This is an archive of various PDF docs; there are many on various aspects of Unix.

The following list describes some recommended books for learning more about Unix:

- *Sams Teach Yourself Unix in 10 Minutes*—Author: William Ray. This is a good "fast and easy" entry into the world of Unix.

- *Sams Teach Yourself Unix in 24 Hours, Second Edition*—Authors: Dave Taylor and James C. Armstrong, Jr. This contains 24 one-hour lessons to get you into Unix.

- *The Complete Idiot's Guide to Unix*—Author: Bill Wagner. This book's friendly approach to Unix is good if you prefer a less-structured approach than the *Sams Teach Yourself* books.

- *Special Edition Using Unix, Third Edition*—Author: Peter Kuo. This is a comprehensive Unix reference. This is a good resource to have when you become comfortable with Unix and want to explore it in great detail.

11

CHAPTER **12**

COMPUTING ON THE MOVE WITH POWERBOOKS AND IBOOKS

In this chapter

USING MAC OS X ON A MOBILE COMPUTER

Using Mac OS X on a laptop Mac, such as an iBook or a PowerBook, isn't that much different than using it on a desk-bound machine. The three primary tasks unique to mobile Macs are the following:

- Managing your Mac's power
- Controlling your Mac with function keys
- Configuring and using the trackpad

Although managing locations isn't unique to mobile Macs, you are more likely to need to switch among network configurations when using a PowerBook or an iBook, so you need to understand how to use the Location Manager to make reconfiguring your Mac's network connections fast and easy.

Many users who have a mobile Mac also have a desktop Mac. When you use more than one machine, it is annoying to have to try to re-create certain information, such as your Safari bookmarks, on each machine you use. Fortunately, with Mac OS X you don't need to do that if you also have a .Mac account. Using .Mac and Synch preferences, you can synchronize key items that you use frequently on all your Macs so they are available to you at any time. When you make a change on one machine, such as updating an address in your Address Book, that change is made on each computer you have synchronized via .Mac. This is especially useful for keeping a mobile Mac in synch with your desktop Mac, and vice versa.

→ To learn how to use .Mac to synchronize computers, **see** "Using .Mac to Synchronize Important Information on Multiple Macs," **p. 512**.

Another challenge to using more than one Mac, such as a mobile and desktop Mac, is accessing the same versions of the files you use. For example, you might work on a Word document on your mobile Mac and then want to use that same file on your desktop Mac. Fortunately, there are many ways to access the same files from different computers.

→ To learn how to use the same files on different computers, **see** "Mac OS X to the Max: Keeping Your Files in Synch," **p. 333**.

MANAGING YOUR MOBILE MAC'S POWER

The factor that makes a mobile Mac mobile is the capability to run using battery power. This is obviously an advantage, but it also adds another task for you, which is managing that power so you maximize your battery life and thus your working time while on the move.

USING THE POWER MANAGEMENT MENU

When you run Mac OS X on a mobile Mac, by default you see the power management icon (see Figure 12.1). If you click this icon, the power management menu appears. At the top of this menu is an icon that keeps you informed about the power state of your Mac. When the battery is fully charged and you are running on the AC adapter, you see the plug icon. When the battery is charging, you see the lightning bolt icon and an estimate of either the time or the percent until the battery is fully charged. If you open the menu, you will see information about the state of the battery, such as whether it is charging, is fully charged, or how much running time it has; the Show command that you can use to change the displayed value; the current source of power for your mobile Mac (Power Adapter or Batter); power setting options from which you can choose; and the Open Energy Saver command to open the Energy Saver pane of the System Preferences application.

Figure 12.1
The power management icon and menu on the menu bar keep you informed of the power state of your mobile Mac.

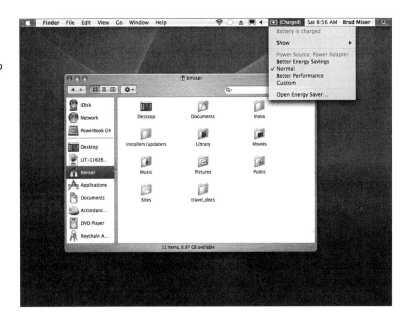

When you are running on battery power, the icon changes to a battery. The battery icon is filled proportionally to represent the amount of power you have left (see Figure 12.2). At the top of the power management menu, you see the time or percentage remaining until you are out of power (you can also choose to show neither).

NOTE

When you are running on battery power, the first item on the power management menu is always the opposite of what you have selected to display. For example, when you choose to display time on the icon, the percentage is shown on the menu, and vice versa. If you don't show time or percentage in the icon, you see time on the menu.

When you plug the power adapter back in to the Mac, the icon changes to a battery with a lightning bolt to indicate that the battery is charging.

12

Figure 12.2
This Mac is running on battery power and has 5 hours and 33 minutes of running time left at current power usage levels (because it isn't doing anything at the moment, power usage is low).

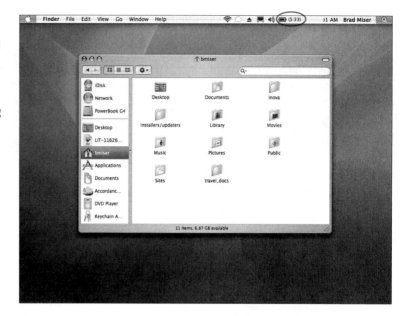

NOTE

> The battery icon takes a few seconds to update. For example, if you unplug the AC adapter and then immediately point to the icon, you still see the charging status information. While your Mac is calculating how much time you have left, you see the word `Calculating` next to the icon; just wait a few moments and the information shown is updated.

You can configure the power management icon on the menu bar in the following ways:

- Open the menu and select Show, Time to show the time remaining for the battery or for the charging process next to the icon.

- Open the menu and select Show, Percentage to show the percent of power/time remaining for the battery or for the charging process next to the icon.

- Return to the icon alone by selecting Show, Icon Only.

TIP

> To remove the power management icon and menu from the menu bar, open the Energy Saver pane of the System Preferences application, click the Options tab, and uncheck the "Show battery status in the menu bar" check box.

MAXIMIZING BATTERY LIFE

The ultimate and constant challenge of using a mobile Mac when running on the battery is to make your power last as long as possible. You should consider the following steps to maximize your battery life:

- **Dim your screen**—Your Mac's screen is a major source of power consumption. If you dim the screen, it requires less power and thus extends your battery life. To dim your screen, use the Brightness slider on the Displays pane of the System Preferences application or the appropriate function key. Dim the display as much as you can while still being able to see it comfortably. For example, when you are traveling on a darkened airplane, you can set your display brightness to a lower level than when you are using it in a well-lit room.

> TIP
>
> Some PowerBooks and iBooks have dedicated function keys to control screen brightness, typically F1 to lower brightness and F2 to increase it. When you press one of these, an onscreen level indicator pops up to show you the relative brightness level and how you are changing it.

- **Configure the Energy Saver pane for the work you are doing while you are on the move**—Use the Energy Saver pane to configure your mobile Mac's power usage to maximize battery life. You'll learn how a bit later in this chapter.

- **Avoid applications that constantly read from a CD or DVD**—The CD or DVD drive is another major source of power use. If you can copy files you need onto your hard drive and use them from there, you will use power at a lower rate than if your Mac is constantly accessing its removable media drive. In some cases, such as when you are watching a DVD movie, this isn't possible. At other times, however, you can store the files you need on the hard drive. For example, when you want to listen to music, you can add the songs to your iTunes Music Library so you don't need to use the CD or DVD drive.

- **Put your Mac to sleep whenever you aren't actively using it**—You can put your Mac to sleep by selecting Apple menu, Sleep or by closing your mobile Mac's lid. When you open your Mac or press a key, the Mac instantly wakes up so putting it to sleep frequently doesn't cause a lot of wasted time for you.

> NOTE
>
> When your Mac sleeps, all active processes are stopped, the screen goes dark, and the disk or disc drives stop. This reduces your Mac's power use to the bare minimum. A Mac in Sleep mode can survive a long time, but of course, it can't do anything while it is asleep. You need to strike a balance between the length of pauses in your work and the sleep time.

CONFIGURING POWER USE

One of the most important power management tasks is to actively use the Mac's Energy Saver pane of the System Preferences application. This enables you to customize your Mac's energy settings to maximize battery life for the type of work you are doing.

You can do this in two ways. One is to use the pane's standard energy setting configurations. The other is to configure the details yourself.

USING A STANDARD POWER SETTING

To use the standard configurations, perform the following steps:

1. Open the System Preferences application and click Energy Saver, or click the power management icon to open the power management menu and select Open Energy Saver. You will see the Energy Saver pane. At the top of the pane is the "Settings for" pop-up menu. This enables you to choose the energy settings for running on the battery or on the power adapter. Just below this is the Optimization pop-up menu. This enables you to configure your Mac to use power settings appropriate for specific tasks.

2. On the "Settings for" pop-up menu, select Battery. This enables you to configure your mobile Mac's energy usage while it is running on battery power.

3. Open the Optimization pop-up menu and select the setting you want to use. Better Battery Life reduces the performance and power usage of the processor, Normal is balance of performance and battery life, and Better Performance sacrifices battery life for performance. Custom opens the detailed configuration settings, which are explained in the next section. When you choose an option, a summary of its settings appears below the menu (see Figure 12.3).

Figure 12.3
Here, I've selected Better Battery Life on the Optimization pop-up menu; the current settings for my expected running time are shown under the menu.

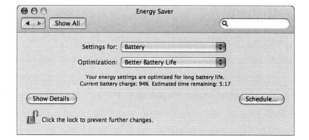

CAUTION

When your battery power starts getting low (about 10% remaining), you will start to see low-power warning dialog boxes. If you continue to use your Mac to lower power levels, eventually the screen dims. When your Mac is on its last electron, it goes to sleep. The only way to revive it is to connect it to the power adapter or change to a fresh battery. This (hopefully) prevents you from losing data because the Mac shuts off unexpectedly when the battery is completely drained. Even in sleep mode, your Mac uses some power, so if it enters the sleep mode because of low battery power and you don't do anything about it, eventually, your Mac turns off. And poof, there goes any data you have left unsaved.

CUSTOMIZING YOUR MAC'S POWER SETTINGS

If you prefer a more hands-on approach, you can use the Detail mode to customize the energy-saving settings yourself. Do the following:

1. Open the System Preferences application and click Energy Saver, or open the power management menu and select Open Energy Saver.

2. Click the Show Details button. The pane expands and you see controls you can use to configure the energy-saving settings in detail (see Figure 12.4). By default, the Sleep tab is selected; you use the controls on this tab to configure the sleep settings for your system.

Figure 12.4
When you show details, you can adjust several aspects of the energy-saving settings independently.

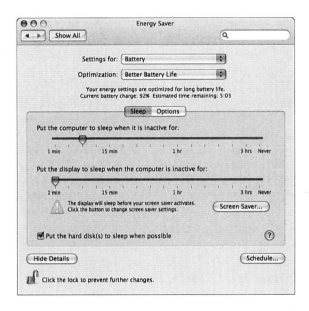

3. Select Custom on the Optimization pop-up menu (or just start making changes and this is selected automatically).

> **TIP**
>
> If you choose one of the standard settings on the Optimize Energy Settings pop-up menu with the Details shown, you can see the details of that configuration. For example, select Better Battery Life and you see that the sleep timer is set for 3 minutes, display sleep is set to 1 min, and hard disk sleep is on.

4. Choose the power source for which you want to configure energy savings on the Settings for pop-up menu; your choices are Power Adapter or Battery. You can have a separate configuration for each power mode. (The mode in which you are operating is selected by default.)

5. Use the top slider to control the amount of inactive time before the entire system goes to sleep. Setting a shorter sleep time causes your Mac to sleep frequently, thus conserving battery power. But, this can also interrupt your work. Set the Sleep slider to a value that is just longer than normal pauses in your work.

6. Use the "Put the display to sleep when the computer is inactive for" slider to set the amount of inactive time before the screen goes dark.

As you move the sliders, the current time at which the slider is pointing will appear above the slider at its right edge. This is helpful in selecting a precise time on the slider.

Because the screen is such a major consumer of power, you should have the display sleep after only a few minutes of inactivity when you configure your mobile Mac for operating in battery power. This also protects the flat-panel display in your mobile Mac from damage and early failure.

There is also a dim function, which is different from sleep. Dimming causes the screen to go to a lower brightness setting before the display sleeps (when it goes totally dark). You configure this option on the Options tab.

NOTE

> If you set the display sleep time to be less than the time at which your screen saver activates, you will see a warning saying so and the Screen Saver button will appear. You can click this button to change your screen saver settings. Normally, when you are running on battery power at least, you want the screen to sleep rather than using the screensaver because the screensaver consumes battery power for processing and screen display.

7. Unless you have a very good reason not to, leave the "Put the hard disk(s) to sleep when possible" check box checked. The hard disk is another major consumer of power, and putting it to sleep saves significant amounts of energy.

8. Review the settings summary that appears just below the pop-up menus to ensure that the settings are what you desire. If you are running on battery power, you will see an estimate of the time remaining.

9. Click the Schedule button. You use the resulting sheet to set an automatic startup/wake or shutdown/sleep time for the computer.

10. To set an automatic startup or wake time, check the "Start up or wake" check box and choose the day (using the pop-up menu) and time (by typing a time or using the Up and Down arrow buttons) at which the machine should start if it is powered off or wake up if it is in sleep mode. For example, you can set your Mac to start at a specific time everyday, on weekdays or weekends, or on a specific day only.

NOTE

> If your mobile Mac's lid is closed, the automatic start up/wake settings have no effect.

11. To set an automatic shutdown or sleep time, check the lower check box on the sheet and select Shut Down or Sleep on the pop-up menu. Then select the day and time you want this action to happen on the Day pop-up menu and using the time box and arrow buttons. Click OK to activate these settings and close the sheet.

12. Click the Options tab. Use the check boxes on this tab to further configure Energy Saver.

13. If you check the "Wake when the modem detects a ring" check box, your Mac will automatically wake up when it detects a call coming in on its modem. The primary situation in which you might want this to happen is when you use your mobile Mac to receive faxes.

NOTE

> Some settings only appear when they are applicable. For example, the "Reduce the brightness of the built-in display when using this power source" check box appears only when you are working with the Battery source.

14. Check the "Reduce the brightness of the built-in display when using this power source" check box if you want your Mac's display to have a lower brightness when operating on the power source shown on the "Settings for" pop-up menu. When this box is checked, the brightness of the display will be reduced slightly when you are using the selected source. In my experimentation, it appears that this function reduces screen brightness by about two ticks on the brightness indicator. This isn't a huge reduction in brightness, but it can save some power. And when you are running on battery power, every minute of power saved is a minute you can keep using your Mac.

TIP

> A better way to save battery power by dimming the screen is to just develop a habit of manually setting the screen to a low, but comfortable, level for the various environments in which you work.

15. The "Automatically reduce the brightness of the display before display sleep" check box determines if your display's brightness will be reduced automatically before it goes to sleep. This causes the screen to dim before it goes completely to sleep. If you move the cursor or press a key, the screen will return to its previous brightness setting. I find this feature annoying, but if it doesn't bother you, it can be a way to save more power.

16. Use the "Restart automatically after a power failure" check box if you want your Mac to restart after the power fails. Because your iBook or PowerBook has a battery, this option isn't as meaningful as it is for a desktop Mac.

17. Use the "Show battery status in the menu bar" to determine whether the power management icon and menu appear on the menu bar. You should leave this checked so you can easily see the current status of your battery.

18. Set the processor performance setting on the Processor Performance pop-up menu. Your choices are Highest and Reduced. Highest provides maximum performance and requires more power; Reduced lowers performance but also lowers power requirements. If you are configuring for battery operation, select Reduced and use your Mac for a while. If you don't notice performance problems, leave the setting as is. If you notice slow operation, increase the processor performance setting again.

You should configure all these settings for each power mode (battery and power adapter). To configure the other source's settings, select the other power mode on the "Settings for" pop-up menu, and configure the Sleep and Options tabs for that mode.

NOTE

> Energy Saver settings are global, meaning they are the same for all user accounts on your Mac.

CHOOSING YOUR MAC'S POWER USE

You can determine which power settings your Mac uses in the following two ways:

- Open the power management menu on the menu bar and select the setting you want to use.

- Open the Energy Saver pane of the System Preferences application and select the settings you want to use on the Optimization pop-up menu.

In addition to the default settings, you'll see that Custom is a choice in both locations. This makes the settings be the last that you set them manually. In other words, Custom remembers the last group of settings you adjusted yourself.

TIP

> If you operate your mobile Mac on battery power frequently, consider getting a second battery. This effectively doubles your working time because you can swap out batteries without shutting down your Mac. Just put it to sleep and change the battery. As long as you are fairly quick about it, you can change the battery and go back to where you were.

CONTROLLING YOUR MOBILE MAC WITH FUNCTION KEYS

The function keys on mobile Macs enable you to control the following:

- Use the F1 and F2 keys to change the display's brightness.
- Use F3 and F4 to set the volume level.
- Use F6 to mute the volume.

NOTE

> Different models and generations of mobile Macs can use different keys for the functions listed here. Just look at your mobile Mac's keys to determine which keys control which functions. The keys are marked with icons, such as the speaker icon for keys that control volume, the sun icon for brightness, and so on.

To activate these functions, just press the appropriate key. When you change display brightness or system volume, an indicator will appear on the screen to graphically show you the changes you make.

TIP

> If you prefer to have the function keys work as function keys without having to hold the FN key down while you press them, open the Keyboard & Mouse pane of the System Preferences application. Check the "Use the F1-F12 keys to control software features" check box. If you do this, you have to hold down the FN while pressing the appropriate hardware control key (such as F1 to lower the screen's brightness).

USING AND CONFIGURING THE TRACKPAD

Configuring and using the trackpad is straightforward. You use the Keyboard & Mouse pane of the System Preferences application to control how your trackpad works. When you are using a mobile Mac, the Trackpad tab becomes available. Follow these steps:

1. Open the Keyboard & Mouse pane of the System Preferences application and click the Trackpad tab (see Figure 12.5).

Figure 12.5
When you are running Mac OS X on a mobile Mac, you can set the trackpad options using the Trackpad tab on the Keyboard & Mouse pane.

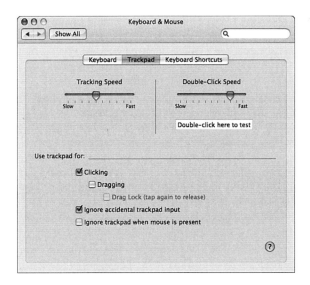

12

2. Use the Tracking Speed slider to set the speed at which the pointer moves relative to your finger's speed on the pad.

3. Use the Double-Click Speed slider to control how rapidly you have to click the trackpad button or the trackpad itself to register a double-click.

4. If you want to be able to "click" the trackpad button by tapping on the trackpad, check the Clicking check box.

5. Use the Dragging and Drag Lock check boxes to control how you can drag items with the trackpad. If you turn on the Clicking option and then check the Dragging check box, you can drag an item by touching your finger to the trackpad and dragging your finger across it. If you check the Drag Lock check box, the item continues to be locked to the cursor until you release it by tapping the trackpad again.

6. To disable the trackpad while you are typing, check the "Ignore accidental trackpad input" check box. This option prevents unwanted interference from the unintentional taps on the trackpad while you are typing or just moving your hand across the pad. When you stop typing, the trackpad becomes active again.

7. If you want the trackpad to be disabled when you connect an external mouse to your mobile Mac, check the "Ignore trackpad when mouse is present" check box.

CONFIGURING AND USING LOCATIONS

As you move your mobile Mac around, you will probably want to connect to different networks from different locations. For example, you might use an AirPort network to connect to the Internet at home, an Ethernet network to connect when you are at work, and a dial-up connection when you are on the road.

The Mac OS X Location Manager feature enables you to configure multiple network configurations on your Mac. You can then switch among these configurations easily (rather than having to manually reconfigure your Mac each time you change locations).

NOTE

> You can have more than one active port on the same machine, meaning you can have different means of connecting to a network active at the same time (such as AirPort and Ethernet). You don't need to have a location for each active port. You should use locations when you want to have different *sets* of active ports that you want to be able to switch among easily. For example, suppose you connect to the Internet using Ethernet at your office and at home. But, at the office you have a fixed IP address while at home you use a DHCP server. You can create a location for each situation and easily switch between them by using the appropriate location.

CREATING A NEW LOCATION

To configure a new network location, use the following steps:

1. Open the Network pane of the System Preferences application (see Figure 12.6).

Figure 12.6
If you regularly
change networks,
configure a location
for each network you
use so you can easily
switch between them.

2. From the Location pop-up menu, select New Location.

3. Name the location and click OK. You return to the Network pane and the location you created appears in the Location pop-up menu.

4. On the Show pop-up menu, select Network Port Configurations.

5. Check the check box for each connection method you want to be active for the location you are configuring. Uncheck the check box for those connection methods that you won't be using under this location.

6. Arrange the order of the connection methods in the list to be the order in which you want your Mac to try to connect to the network. Put the first method you want to be tried at the top of the list, the second one in the second spot, and so on. For example, if you want to use Built-in Ethernet first and then AirPort, drag Built-in Ethernet to the top of the list and place AirPort underneath it. When your Mac connects to the network, it will try these connections in the order in which they are listed.

7. Use the Show pop-up menu to choose the first connection method you want to configure for this location—for example, Internal Modem to configure a dial-up connection.

8. Use the tabs in the Network pane to configure that connection method.

→ For help configuring an Internet connection, **see** Chapter 13, "Connecting Your Mac to the Internet," **p. 337**.

→ For help configuring an AirPort connection, **see** Chapter 14, "Using an Airport Network to Connect to the Internet," **p. 371**.

→ For help configuring a network connection, **see** Chapter 33, "Building and Using a Network," **p. 935**.

9. Repeat steps 7 and 8 for each connection method you made active in steps 4–6.

10. Quit the System Preferences application. The network configuration you configured will be used.

CHANGING YOUR MAC'S LOCATIONS

The default location for your Mac is called Automatic. If you don't use any other locations, this might be okay, but you might want to rename it to be more meaningful. You can also remove locations from the machine by editing the location. Follow these steps:

1. Open the Network pane of the System Preferences application.

> **TIP**
>
> You can quickly jump to the Network pane by selecting Apple menu, Location, Network Preferences.

2. Select Edit Locations from the Location pop-up menu.
3. Select the location you want to change.
4. Rename the location by clicking the Rename button, entering the new name, and pressing Return.
5. Delete a location you no longer use by selecting it and clicking Delete.
6. To duplicate a location, select it and click Duplicate; you can then rename it and modify it as needed.
7. Click Done.
8. Make any other changes to the location selected in the Location pop-up menu and click Apply Now.
9. Close the System Preferences application.

Changing your network settings is as easy as selecting Apple menu, Location, and then the location you want to use (see Figure 12.7). You don't need to restart your Mac or even log out; the network configurations that are part of the location become active immediately.

> **TIP**
>
> To protect your mobile Mac's data in the event someone swipes it, use Mac OS X's FileVault feature to encrypt your data so any rat who takes your mobile Mac won't be able to use its data.

→ To learn how to use FileVault, **see** "Securing Your Mac with FileVault," **p. 1021**.

Figure 12.7
The locations you configure will be available to all the users of your Mac.

MAC OS X TO THE MAX: KEEPING YOUR FILES IN SYNCH

As you move around with your mobile Mac, I'm sure you'll find all kinds of great things to do with it (one of my favorites is to watch DVDs while I travel). Some of these might even involve work! If you work on files on your mobile Mac, it is highly likely that you will want to move those files to or from another Mac, such as your desktop Mac. There are lots of ways to accomplish this:

- Store the files you are going to share between your mobile Mac and other machines on your .Mac iDisk. Then set your iDisk to synchronize automatically on all machines. The same versions of those files will be accessible on all your Macs automatically (and they will be backed up on your iDisk, too).

→ To learn how to use an iDisk, **see** "Using Your iDisk," **p. 498**.

- Before and after a session on your mobile Mac, connect the mobile Mac to the network that your desktop Mac is on and use file sharing to move the files back and forth between the machines. (Make sure you move the correct version so you don't accidentally replace a newer version with an older one.)

- Email files to yourself. This is easier to do if you have more than one email account. For example, use a .Mac email account for your regular email and another account just on one machine. You can send files to yourself via that address. The big problem with this method is that most email gateways allow only relatively small files to be sent (usually less than 5MB).

- Use a folder cloning application to keep specific folders synchronized. You select one or more folders on each machine that you want to keep in synch and the application will ensure the latest version is in the folder on each computer.
- Put files on CD, DVD, or a portable drive (an iPod is excellent for this), and then copy them onto a different machine.

One of the harder aspects of keeping files synchronized between a mobile Mac and other machines is knowing exactly which files changed during your most recent use of the mobile. With Mac OS X's smart folders, you can make even this easy to do:

1. Create a new smart folder.
2. Configure it to find files whose Kind is Documents and that were Last Modified Within Last 2 Days (or some other timeframe).
3. Save the smart folder.

Each time you open this smart folder, you will see the document files that have changed within the timeframe you specify. This makes it simple to know which files you need to move to your desktop Mac or other location.

→ To learn how to configure and use smart folders, **see** "Searching Your Mac with Smart Folders," **p. 123**.

PART III

Mac OS X: Connecting to the World

CHAPTER 13

CONNECTING YOUR MAC TO THE INTERNET

In this chapter

CONNECTING TO THE INTERNET

The Internet is one of the most significant social and economic movements—it is a movement as much as it is technology—in human history. In just a few years, the Internet (or more simply, the Net) moved from an obscure scientific and government computer network to become a dominant means of global and local communication, commerce, entertainment, and information. Fortunately, Mac OS X has equipped you to make the most of the Net.

Finding, installing, and configuring an Internet account can be complex. You can use many technologies to connect to the Net, and you can obtain an Internet account from thousands of Internet service providers (ISPs).

The general steps to connect your Mac to the Internet are the following:

1. Determine the technology you will use to connect to the Internet.
2. Find an ISP and obtain an account.
3. Install and configure the modem or other hardware you need.
4. Configure your Mac to connect to the account you have established.
5. Test your configuration and troubleshoot any problems you find.

Depending on how you are going to connect to the Net, you might have to do most of these steps yourself or your ISP might handle them for you—at least for the initial installation and configuration. Even if your ISP handles the initial configuration for you, you will need to understand how to reconfigure your Mac when the inevitable happens and you have to reinstall the system, move your account to another Mac, and so on.

CHOOSING YOUR INTERNET CONNECTION TECHNOLOGY

There are six general technologies you can use to connect your Mac to the Internet. These technologies are summarized in Table 13.1 and explained in more detail in the following subsections.

13

TABLE 13.1   INTERNET CONNECTION TECHNOLOGIES

Technology	Connection Method	Advantages	Disadvantages
Dial-up	Dial-up modem via standard phone line	Available anywhere Inexpensive Simple configuration Accessible from any location Dial-up modem included in all modern Macs	Very slow. Connection must be established each time services are needed. Not as reliable as other connection methods. Can be difficult to achieve maximum performance. Makes phone line unavailable.
DSL	DSL modem via standard phone line	Broadband connection speeds (both directions) Always-on connection Reliable connection Consistent communication speed	Limited availability. More expensive than a dial-up account.
Cable	Cable modem via fiber-optic cable	Broadband connection speeds (both directions) Always-on connection Reliable connection	Limited availability. More expensive than a dial-up account. Connection speed can fluctuate depend-depending on activity of local cable trunk.
ISDN	ISDN modem via one or more standard phone lines	Slow to fairly fast connection speed depending on number of lines used	Expensive. Not as fast as other broadband connections. Limited availability.

continues

13

TABLE 13.1 CONTINUED

Technology	Connection Method	Advantages	Disadvantages
Satellite	Satellite receiver via satellite dish	Fast download connection Widely available Always-on connection	Expensive. Upload connection speed can be limited. Some configurations require a dedicated upload account (such as over a dial-up connection). Requires more complex installation and setup than other methods.
T-1/ Fractional T-1	Direct cabling from ISP	Fastest connection Always-on connection Most reliable connection	Very expensive. Requires complex and expensive installation and configuration.

TIP

> Some broadband ISPs, such as cable providers, offer dial-up accounts as part of their services (some include the cost in the basic account, whereas others charge an additional fee for the dial-up access). Typically, these dial-up services are intended for those times when you are traveling and need to access your account from locations other than those at which the service was initially installed. If you are able to use a broadband connection and will need to access it from multiple locations, check with your ISP to see whether it offers dial-up access to your account.

Generally, you will want to choose the fastest connection method that is available in your area and that you can afford. A broadband Internet connection makes the Internet even more useful when compared to a slower connection (such as a 56K dial-up connection). For example, with a broadband connection, you can download files as large as 10MB or more in just a few moments. A broadband connection makes downloading even very large files, as much as 100MB or more, practical. Just to give you a reference point about how large the files you download can be, using a cable modem, I have routinely downloaded 400MB and larger files in less than 20 minutes. Try that with a dial-up account!

In addition to making downloading files faster, a broadband connection enables you to experience online video and audio in a fashion quite similar to watching cable TV or listening to a radio. Finally, a broadband connection enables you to avoid the delays and hassles of waiting for a dial-up account to connect to the Internet each time you want to use it because it is always on. With a broadband connection, the Internet actually becomes an extension of your desktop.

NOTE

> When calculating the cost of an Internet connection, don't forget to include the cost of a phone line that might be dedicated to Internet access. For example, many people who are serious about Net access add a second phone line to dedicate to that purpose. When considering the cost of a broadband connection, such as a cable modem account, don't forget to include the cost of a dedicated phone line as part of the cost of the dial-up account. The cost of a dial-up account and dedicated phone line is usually similar to the cost of a broadband account.

DIAL-UP INTERNET CONNECTIONS

Even with the rapid rise of broadband connections, the dial-up Internet account is still widely used. Because you can access a dial-up connection over standard phone lines, dial-up accounts are available just about everywhere. And because all modern Macs include a dial-up modem by default, you don't need any additional hardware to install and configure a dial-up account. Dial-up accounts are also relatively inexpensive and easy to configure.

The primary problem with dial-up connections is that they are slow. Even in the ideal case, a true 56K connection, a dial-up connection is just not fast enough to enable some of the more interesting applications on the Internet, such as video, audio, and moving large files (such as those 3MB or larger). And most of the time, you won't be connecting at your account's maximum speed—phone-line noise and other factors often limit the speed you can achieve. Another problem is that you have to establish a connection each time you want to use an Internet service. The connection process can take anywhere from 10 seconds to a minute or more depending on the particular situation. When you frequently need to access Net services throughout the day, the time you have to wait for a connection to be established can be quite annoying, not to mention a waste of your time.

Another problem with dial-up accounts is that they can be unreliable. You can experience busy signals, and your connection is dependent on the quality of the phone lines between you and your provider. Internet sessions are occasionally disconnected in the middle of doing something, such as downloading a file. This can be a huge waste of time, as well as frustrating.

If you use the Internet as much as most Mac users do, you should use a dial-up account only if one of the broadband connection technologies is not available to you or you can't afford one of the faster connection technologies.

13

NOTE

If the Internet is vital to your business or other important activities, you might consider obtaining and maintaining a dial-up account as a relatively inexpensive backup. If your primary connection, such as cable service, goes down for some reason, you can switch to the dial-up account to access the Net. Some ISPs offer low-cost, low-usage accounts that are suitable for this purpose.

DSL CONNECTION

Digital subscriber line (DSL) accounts communicate over standard phone lines through a DSL modem. DSL accounts offer broadband communication speeds and always-on access.

The primary downside to DSL is that the technology requires that you be within a maximum distance from a central office or hub for the telephone company that provides service to your location. This maximum distance is fairly short (usually about 3 miles), and this single factor makes DSL unavailable for many locations. As telephone infrastructures improve, DSL service should become more widely available.

Because it is an always-on connection and you have the same IP address for long periods of time, security is a very important consideration when you use a DSL modem to access the Net. You must also install some type of protection to keep your machine from being hacked or used in an Internet attack on other sites. Fortunately, Mac OS X includes a firewall that does this for you, and most Internet sharing hubs protect your machines as well.

If DSL is available in your location, you should consider obtaining a DSL account.

NOTE

You might notice that I am not being specific when I mention connection speeds. This is because most of the connection speeds quoted in advertisements or even in technical information are theoretical maximums. The actual speed you experience will depend on your specific situation and how your account is configured (for example, DSL accounts can offer various speeds). Generally, you need to consider whether you are dealing with a broadband connection (such as cable or DSL) or not (dial-up).

13

CABLE MODEM

Cable modem access is provided through a cable modem using the same cable over which cable TV service is provided. Cable Internet accounts offer broadband speeds (in fact, the speed of cable accounts is faster than most other technologies) and always-on access.

As with DSL, cable modem service is not available in every location. However, if your area is covered by a cable TV service, there is a good chance that cable modem service is currently offered in your area or soon will be. Because the cable infrastructure is already in place, companies can offer Internet access without making major infrastructure changes.

One downside to cable Internet access is that you share the data pipeline with other users of the service and the cable TV viewers who are on the same cable trunk you are on (such as a neighborhood). This means that the speed you experience is dependent on the load on the system at any point in time (whereas DSL uses a dedicated line to provide service to you so that you always experience the same speed—bear in mind that even at peak times, cable access is still usually somewhat faster than DSL). Another downside to cable is that it tends to be relatively expensive (typically about $50 per month). And you have to deal with the local cable company; these companies are not noted for having the best service practices.

Because it is an always-on connection and you have the same IP address for long periods of time, security is a very important consideration when you use a cable modem to access the Net. You must also install some type of protection to keep your machine from being hacked or used in an Internet attack on other sites. Fortunately, Mac OS X includes a firewall that does this for you, and most Internet sharing hubs protect your machines as well.

Even with these downsides (which are relatively minor compared to the benefits), a cable modem account can offer excellent performance and is worth exploring if the service is available in your area.

ISDN

For a time, integrated service digital network (ISDN) was going to be the thing to make Internet access faster because its access is significantly faster than standard dial-up connections. Because ISDN also uses standard phone lines, it is also widely available.

However, with the rise of cable and DSL technologies, ISDN has largely gone by the wayside. This is primarily because it is a slower connection technology than cable or DSL. To obtain high speeds with ISDN, you must use more than one phone line, which makes it quite expensive just to obtain speeds that can't match those that DSL or cable provide.

Nonetheless, ISDN can be a reasonable option if you want to have faster connection speeds than are provided over a dial-up account but can't access DSL or cable service.

SATELLITE

Satellite Internet access works much like satellite TV. The data is downloaded through a small satellite dish and fed to your Mac. The speed of communication is quite fast.

However, satellite Internet access has several disadvantages. The biggest is that some satellite accounts support only downloads, so you still maintain a separate account for uploading information. Second, you have to install the satellite dish. Third, and perhaps most importantly, not all satellite providers support Macs—the majority don't.

You should consider a satellite Internet account only in those cases in which you can't obtain broadband in any other way and you really need the additional download speed the satellite account provides. Because of its limited applicability, additional information on satellite access is beyond the scope of this chapter.

13

NOTE

> Satellite Internet access can be more appealing if you also use a satellite for TV. Some satellite services combine TV and Internet access.

T-1 LINE

A T-1 line is a dedicated broadband connection delivered over a line consisting of 24 channels, with each channel delivering up to 64Kb per second. T-1 connections are very fast but are also expensive and are usually limited to businesses to provide access for many people through a single account. Most providers also offer fractional T-1 service, in which only a portion of the 24 channels is dedicated to the subscriber.

Finding a T-1 provider is much like finding other providers; you should typically start with local ISPs who offer this service. After you have purchased a T-1 account, the ISP handles the installation and initial configuration of the line for you. Because T-1 and fractional T-1 connections are fairly complex and their costs limit them to business use, additional information about T-1 lines is beyond the scope of this chapter.

PICKING THE TECHNOLOGY

After you have an understanding of all the possibilities, you need to determine which technology is appropriate for you. Most Mac users will be better off with a broadband connection of some type; dial-up accounts just don't cut it for the most interesting Internet resources. However, if no broadband services are available in your area or you can't afford a broadband connection, dial-up certainly beats no Internet connection.

To determine which technologies are available to you, you need to obtain information from various ISPs that offer services in your area. Following are some tips to help you find an ISP:

- **One of the best sources of information about local ISPs is the people you know—** Many people in your immediate circle probably have Internet access through a local provider. You should ask these folks if they are happy with their providers. You can also find out which services are available, whether the provider has good technical support, how much the services cost, and so on. Using your personal network is an excellent way to find ISPs to contact.

- **If you have cable TV service, check with your cable company to see whether it offers Internet access**—Most cable companies advertise their Internet service to death, but some don't—especially when they first introduce it and want to test it on a limited number of users.

- **If you have access to the Internet, use the Web to locate a provider**—Go to http://thelist.internet.com/, which enables you to find local access providers for just about every location in the world (see Figure 13.1).

13

Figure 13.1
The List website lives up to its claims; it truly is the definitive ISP buyer's guide.

- **Check out the local news broadcasts in your area**—Almost all local TV stations have websites that are maintained by a local ISP. At the end of the broadcast, you will see a credits screen saying that Internet services are provided by XYZ Company. XYZ Company might be a good choice for you to check out.

- **Check with your company's ISP**—If the company you work for has a website that is administered by an outside ISP or if an outside ISP provides Net access for your company, check with that ISP to see which services it offers and whether it offers a discount for employees of your company. Often, an ISP will provide inexpensive Internet access to the employees of a company to which it provides business services.

- **Watch and listen for advertisements**—Most service providers advertise in local newspapers and on the radio and TV.

You should also check with national Internet access providers such as EarthLink (www.earthlink.net) to see which services are offered in your location.

TIP

> Many ISPs provide more than one connection technology for their accounts. When you contact an ISP, make sure that you ask about all the possible ways you might connect. Sometimes, especially when introducing a new access method, an ISP might not promote all its options.

The process of determining which connection technology is available to you should be fairly simple. If you have access to cable TV service, check with the cable provider to see whether it also offers Internet access. If so, obtain cost information. Most cable TV companies have

13

a monopoly on the areas to which they provide service, so you usually have only one source to check for cable modem access.

> If you obtain a new Internet account via the Setup Assistant that runs when you install Mac OS X, you will use EarthLink, which has been the Mac's default ISP for some time. EarthLink is an excellent company and should be on your list of possible ISPs.
>
> Earthlink offers numerous ways to connect, including cable, DSL, and dial-up. You should check out www.earthlink.net to see which of its Internet services are available at your location.

Next, try to determine whether DSL service is available in your location. The best way to do this is to search the Web for DSL providers in your state (see Figure 13.2). You can use a general search site to search for information about DSL providers in your state. Also, check the national DSL providers to see whether a company in their networks provides local DSL access. Typically, you can go to the provider's site and check availability of DSL service at your location. If the service is available, obtain information about the cost and whether the Mac is supported. You can also check with your telephone service provider because they typically offer DSL if your location supports it. If DSL service from one provider is not available at your location, it is likely that it is not available from any provider because they all use the same telephone infrastructure.

Figure 13.2
The EverythingDSL website is a good example of a web resource you can use to determine whether DSL is available in a specific area.

Beware that DSL service is one of the most over-advertised and over-hyped services around. Just because you hear or see advertisements for local DSL service does not mean that it is actually available. Some of this advertisement is for "future" service, even though your location might not be close enough to a central phone node to be capable of accessing DSL from any provider. Even worse, sometimes the checks these organizations do on your phone line to see whether you can access this service are not reliable. I have heard more than one case in which the initial contact, even up to the point of signing a contract, indicated DSL service was available, but when the installation was attempted, it failed because the service was not really available.

If cable or DSL service isn't available to you, check with your local phone company and local ISPs to see whether ISDN service is available. Again, get cost information and see whether the Mac is supported.

Be careful about eliminating companies that claim not to provide Mac support. Most of the time, this just means they won't be able to provide tech support if you use a Mac. The service probably will work just fine. If you are comfortable that you will be able to solve any problems you encounter, not having tech support available might not be a problem for you. I prefer not to do business with companies that don't support the Mac, but you might have to choose otherwise to get the Internet access you want.

Finally, locate ISPs in your area that provide dial-up Internet access. This should be the most commonly available option, even if it isn't the most productive.

Making the Connection Work for You
You should ensure that any dial-up account you consider has a phone number you can dial without paying any time-based fees if possible. If you have to pay a usage charge while you connect to the Internet, you are likely to connect less frequently than you would like, or you will end up spending a lot of money for telephone charges. Usually, you should look for a provider that offers a number you can dial without any toll charges (long distance or otherwise).

After you have obtained all the available connection information, you should be able to decide which technology is appropriate for you. If possible, try to locate a cable or DSL provider because you will get the most out of a broadband account. If all else fails, locate a good provider of dial-up access.

13

NOTE

In some cases, such as a DSL or dial-up account, you will have several ISP options. One of the most fundamental considerations is whether you use a national provider or a local one. National providers offer several advantages. In many cases, a national provider offers more extensive resources for you, such as better access to technical support, a self-install kit, and so on. National providers can enable you to access your account in different ways (such as DSL or dial-up) from many locations; if you travel often, this should be an important consideration for you. Local providers, on the other hand, often offer more personalized service and local resources.

OBTAINING AND CONFIGURING AN ACCOUNT

After you have decided on the technology, contact the provider to obtain an account. You usually have to call to set up your account, but some ISPs enable you to request service over the Net; others provide self-install kits that enable you to obtain and configure an account without any human intervention (one example is EarthLink).

If you use a broadband account of some sort, the provider sometimes installs any needed hardware for you, such as a cable modem, and configures your machine to use it (although self-install kits are becoming more common). If you use a dial-up account, you usually receive instructions about how to configure that account; some providers, such as EarthLink, provide software that does the installation and configuration for you.

CAUTION

> Be wary about any dedicated "front-end" software a provider might want to install on your machine. Most of the time, this software consists of an application that gives you a specialized interface for using the service. This software is almost never necessary and can cause problems for you. It is better to just use the configuration information the provider gives you and then use Mac OS X software to access the Net.

Even if the provider handles the initial installation and configuration for your account, you still need to understand how to configure your account yourself. You should try to understand the configuration information related to your account. You at least should ensure that you have all the information you need to configure your account for the inevitable situation in which you must reconfigure it on your machine.

TIP

> If your provider offers more than one way to connect, such as via a cable modem and a backup dial-up account, be sure you get the information you need for both connection methods.

The following data is required to configure your Mac for Internet access:

- **Type of configuration**—This information tells your computer which protocol to use to connect to the Net. If you are using a dial-up account, this is the Point-to-Point Protocol (PPP). If you are using a broadband connection, several possibilities exist, which include a static IP address, Dynamic Host Configuration Protocol (DHCP), PPP over Ethernet (PPPoE), DHCP with a fixed IP address, or the Bootstrap Protocol (BootP). A static IP address means that your Mac always has the same IP address. When you use DHCP, your provider assigns your Mac an IP address along with most of the other information you need to connect. PPPoE is most often used for DSL accounts and works similarly to PPP over a dial-up account. DHCP with a fixed IP address means that your IP address is fixed, but the DHCP server provides the other information for you. BootP access is used for "diskless" machines that use a server to provide the operating system.

- **IP address, subnet mask, and router**—These addresses locate your machine on the Internet and provide it with its address. Most dial-up accounts and many broadband accounts use dynamic IP addressing, which simply means that your Mac has an IP address assigned each time it connects rather than having a static address. If you have a manual or static IP address, it never changes and is permanently assigned to your machine. When you have a static IP address, you also need the subnet mask and router; with dynamic addressing, this information is provided by the server.

- **DHCP client ID**—If you use DHCP access, you sometimes have a client ID name for your computer. In some situations, this is optional; however, if your provider includes a DHCP Client ID with your account, you need to use it. If you are configuring an account using a local DHCP server, you probably don't have to use a client ID.

- **Domain name server**—A domain name server (DNS) translates the addresses the computers use into English that we humans can usually understand. The DNS enables you to use an address such as www.companyname.com rather than having to deal with a series of numbers such as 192.169.x.x. The DNS number you need from your provider will be something such as 192.169.x.x. Ideally, your provider will include several DNS addresses so you have a backup in case the primary DNS fails. (If your DNS fails, you won't be able to access websites unless you know their numeric IP addresses.)

- **Search domain**—This information is related to the particular part of the provider's network on which you are located. It is usually optional. You might be provided with more than one search domain.

- **Usernames and passwords**—These are the two pieces of information that uniquely identify you and enable you to access your account. You probably chose your own username when you established your account. Your password might or might not have been assigned by the ISP.

  You might have more than one username or password. Sometimes, your ISP gives you one username and password that enable you to connect to the Net and another set (or maybe just a different password or username) to let you use your email account. Make sure that you know which is which and use the right ones in the right setting fields. If you use a PPPoE account, your username is your account name.

NOTE

> In some cases, you might not need a username and password to access the Net. For example, if you have a static IP address, you don't need a username and password to connect to the Net. However, you will need a username and password to access your email accounts.

13

- **Phone number**—If you use a dial-up account, you need to have the phone number that you need to dial to reach your ISP. Some ISPs offer different numbers for different modem speeds, so be sure you get the phone number for your modem's speed.

- **Email account information**—You will be given your email address (probably something such as username@isp.net). You will also need an address for the server that receives your mail (this often has a "pop" in it, such as pop.isp.net). The third piece of information you need is the address of the server that sends your mail (this often has "smtp" in it, such as smtp.isp.net). Some broadband accounts have simpler server configuration for both sides, such as mail.isp.net.

■ **News server**—You might also be provided with a newsgroup server (this enables you to read newsgroups), although dedicated news servers are not so common these days. It might look something like news.isp.net.

■ **Web customer support address**—If your account offers additional services, such as multiple email accounts, obtain the information you need to access that site so you can manage your account.

TIP

Make sure that you collect and organize the information you need to access your account. You will need to reconfigure your Mac at some point and, if you don't have the information handy, this will be harder than it needs to be. One way to do this is to configure your account and after you are sure it works properly, you can take screenshots (Shift-⌘-3) of the various configuration screens. This enables you to quickly re-create your specific configuration. Of course, you should also keep copies of any information your provider gives you.

NOTE

Most broadband providers include the modem hardware (such as a cable modem) you use to connect with your account. In some cases, they also install the hardware for you. However, you can usually supply your own hardware if you prefer (this is usually less expensive over the long haul). And, many providers offer "self-install" kits at local retailers. These kits include the hardware, software, and instructions you need to install the service yourself. (One benefit to these kits is that you don't have to wait all day for the cable guy to show up!)

If you need to install the modem you will be using, do so. In the case of an Ethernet-based connection, this requires you to connect the modem to your Mac's Ethernet port or the WAN port on your network hub and then connect the modem to the source (the cable that comes into your house). If you have a modern Mac and will be using a dial-up account, the modem is already installed and you just need to connect it to a phone jack using a standard phone cable.

→ For information about various connection devices, such as Ethernet hubs, **see** Chapter 32, "Installing and Configuring Connecting Devices," **p. 921**.

→ In many situations, you will be able to share a single Internet account among many machines; **see** Chapter 34, "Sharing an Internet Connection," **p. 973**.

→ When you use a broadband connection, it is vital that you protect your Macs from Internet attacks; **see** "Defending Your Mac from Net Attacks," **p. 1032**.

NOTE

My bias has probably already shown through, but in my experience cable Internet access is the way to go if it is available to you. The access speed is fast and the connections tend to be reliable. (It is delivered over the same infrastructure as cable TV service, and we know that people can't be without TV!) Because cable TV reaches a significant proportion of homes (in the United States at least), cable Net access is more likely to be available to you than even DSL. Typically, cable service is provided via DHCP, which makes configuration simple.

CONFIGURING YOUR MAC FOR INTERNET ACCESS

The three fundamental ways to connect a Mac to the Internet are dial-up accounts over a phone line and dial-up modem, broadband connections that use Ethernet, and wireless connections using AirPort. Although configuring dial-up accounts is relatively standard, many options are available for an Ethernet-based account. And, when you use AirPort to connect, you actually connect the AirPort hub (whether it is a Mac or an AirPort base station) through one of the two other methods.

→ A great way to network Macs and connect them to the Internet through a single account is by using AirPort; **see** Chapter 14, "Using an AirPort Network to Connect to the Internet," **p. 371**.

Providing the details of configuring every type of Internet account is beyond the scope of this chapter, but some examples of each type of access should enable you to configure your particular account.

NOTE

When you install Mac OS X on a Mac, the Internet Setup Assistant leads you through the configuration of your Internet account. You can launch the Internet Setup Assistant at other times to walk you through the configuration process by clicking the "Assist me" button on the Network pane of the System Preferences application.

If you use a provider that includes configuration software with your account, such as EarthLink, you can configure your account by using that software. In this section, you learn how to configure your account manually.

CAUTION

Here's another caution about any specific access software a provider might give you to access this Net. This software tends to be more problematic than it is worth, especially if it is web-based. When you get an account and such software is provided, ask the provider whether it is required. Many times, this software is mostly a way for the provider to generate revenue by using it to advertise. I recommend you avoid this kind of software if you can.

13

You can configure multiple sets of Internet configurations for your machine so that you can switch between them easily. And, you can have multiple accounts configured and active on a machine at the same time (they will be used according to the priority you determine). This is useful when you use your Mac in different locations—for example, with a PowerBook that you use at a work location and at home or while traveling. Another case in which this is useful is if you have several ways of connecting from the same location, such as via a cable modem or dial-up account. You use the Location Manager to manage the Internet configurations on your machine. If you envision needing to do this, you should set up a location before configuring it. If you will need only one set of configurations, you don't need to use the Location Manager. Also, a single location can include multiple configurations, such as a dial-up account and a cable modem account.

→ To learn how to configure and use locations, **see** "Configuring and Using Locations," **p. 330**.

The Internet accounts you configure on your Mac will be available to all users who have accounts on your machine.

CONNECTING TO THE NET WITH A DIAL-UP ACCOUNT

As you read earlier in the chapter, dial-up access is still a commonly used connection method. Dial-up access is available everywhere and is simple to configure and use (although solving connection problems can be tough).

CONFIGURING YOUR MODEM

All modern Macs include an internal 56K modem as standard equipment (you have the option not to include a modem in some models); very little work is required to configure the Apple internal modem.

NOTE

If you use an external dial-up modem for some reason, you will need to obtain a Mac OS X–compatible driver for it and then configure that modem using the instructions provided by the manufacturer. Covering external modems is beyond the scope of this chapter.

To configure a modem, use the following steps:

1. Open the System Preferences application and in the Internet & Network section, click the Network icon. The Network pane will appear.

NOTE

If you are configuring more than one location, select the location you want to configure on the Location pop-up menu (Automatic is the default). You can also choose to create a new location on that menu.

→ To learn how to configure and use locations, **see** "Configuring and Using Locations," **p. 330**.

2. Select Network Status on the Show pop-up menu if it isn't selected already. In the lower part of the pane, you will see all the connection options available in the selected location (see Figure 13.3). For example, if your Mac is connected to an Ethernet network, an AirPort network, and has an internal modem, you will see each of these connections listed in the window. When a connection is active, it has a green circle next to it. When the connection method is available but is not configured, it has a red circle instead. If you use AirPort but it is not currently connected to the Internet, its status light will be yellow.

Figure 13.3
This Mac has a single network connection via AirPort; the internal modem has been activated but not set up.

3. Select Internal Modem from the Show pop-up menu.
4. Click the Modem tab (see Figure 13.4).
5. Use the pop-up menu, radio buttons, and check boxes to configure your modem. In most cases, the default values will work fine. If you use something other than the Apple Internal 56K Modem, select your modem from the Modem pop-up menu. If your telephone system is not touch-tone, you must click the Pulse radio button. Also, if you have voice mail or another system that can interfere with a standard dial tone (such as beeping to indicate that you have a message waiting for you), you need to uncheck the "Wait for dial tone before dialing" check box. Leave the sound on until you are sure that your connection works reliably; the noise made by your modem can help you troubleshoot connection problems. After you are sure that your connection works, select the Off radio button to turn off your modem sound.
6. If you want your Mac to notify you when someone is trying to call you while you are connected to the Internet, check the "Notify me of incoming calls while connected to the internet" check box and check "Play alert sound when receiving a call." If you want a reminder before the Mac shuts down the Internet connection, check the next check box and set the amount of warning time you want by typing a value in the box.

13

Figure 13.4
Generally, you should leave the options in the Modem tab in the default state.

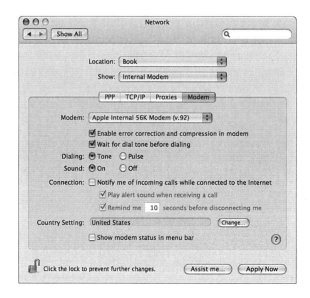

7. Use the Country Setting tools to configure your modem for the country in which you are using it.

8. Check the "Show modem status in menu bar" check box. This places a telephone icon on your menu bar. You can use this to control and monitor your dial-up connection.

9. Click Apply Now to save any changes you make.

TIP

> When you are working with the Network pane, you can click the "Assist me" button to open the Network Setup Assistant. The application helps you configure network connections, such as a dial-up connection to the Internet. However, mostly what this does is just ask you for the same data you can more quickly enter manually.

CONFIGURING TCP/IP AND PPP

Next, you'll need to configure your TCP/IP and PPP settings:

1. Click the TCP/IP tab.

2. Select the configuration option you want from the Configure IPv4 pop-up menu. For almost all dial-up accounts, this should be Using PPP. If you use an AOL dial-up account, select AOL Dialup. However, if your dial-up account includes a static IP address, select Manually and enter the IP address.

NOTE

> IPv4 is the current Internet protocol standard in almost all situations. However, IPv6 is a newer standard that is being used in some research institutions. If you need to configure a connection based on IPv6, you can do so by clicking the Configure IPv6 button and using the resulting sheet to configure the service. In most cases, the automatic settings should work fine, but you can also enter manual settings if you need to.

3. If your provider supplied DNS and search domains for your account, enter the information in the appropriate boxes.

4. Click the PPP tab (see Figure 13.5).

Figure 13.5
You use the PPP tab to configure your specific dial-up account.

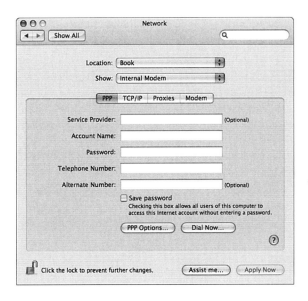

5. Enter the name of your ISP in the Service Provider field. This is optional, but it is a good idea so that the connection is easy to identify by name.

6. Enter your access account name in the Account Name field. Make sure that you use the account name that will access your account; this might be different from your email user account name.

7. Enter your access password in the Password field and make sure that the "Save password" check box is checked. This is especially important if you share your Mac and want everyone to be able to access the Net. Again, your access password might be different from your email account password. If you prefer to have to enter your password each time you connect, leave the Password field empty.

NOTE

> When you enter a password, the "Save password" check box is checked by default; if you uncheck it, your password will be deleted from the field.

13

8. Enter the telephone number you need to dial to connect to the provider in the Telephone Number field. Make sure that you enter the number *exactly* as you would dial it to make a standard phone call to this number. For example, if you need to dial an access code to reach an outside line, enter that code followed by a comma before the number (as in 9, 555-5555). If you need to dial a 1 or the area code to reach that number, enter those numbers as well.

    If you have call waiting, you also need to enter the code to disable it, such as *70. If a call comes in while you are connected to the Net, the call waiting signal might disrupt or cancel your Net connection. Check with your telephone provider to find out the specific code you need to use to turn off call waiting. Remember to turn it back on when you are done with your Internet session.

9. If your provider offers more than one access number, enter the second one in the Alternate Number field. If you receive a busy signal when your Mac dials the first number, it will try the alternate number.

10. Click the PPP Options button to open the PPP Options sheet (see Figure 13.6). Use the controls on this sheet to configure your dial-up access.

Figure 13.6
The Session Options enable you to control how your dial-up account works.

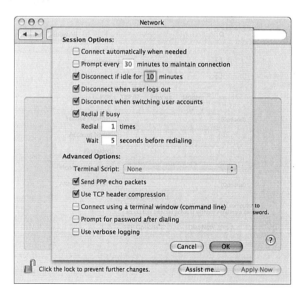

11. In most cases, you should check the "Connect automatically when needed" check box. This enables your Mac to automatically connect to the Net when it needs to. If you have to pay for access by the minute or have to pay toll charges, you might want to leave this unchecked.

12. Use the next four check boxes to control how your Mac disconnects your connection:

    • If you want to be prompted when your Mac is connected but is not actively using the connection, check the "Prompt every XX minutes to maintain connection" check box and enter the time after which you want to be prompted.

- If you want your Mac to automatically disconnect after a specific period of time, check the "Disconnect if idle for XX minutes" check box and enter the idle time. These options are beneficial primarily if you have to pay for access on a time basis or if you share a phone line for Internet access and voice conversations.

- Most users should check the "Disconnect when user logs out" check box so that the connection is broken when the current user logs out of the machine.

- Check the "Disconnect when switching user accounts" check box if you want the machine to be disconnected when the active user account switches to a different account.

13. Use the redial controls to set the number of times you want your Mac to redial in the event of a busy signal and how long you want it to wait between tries.

NOTE

> Only in rare cases will you need to use the controls in the Advanced Options area. The options can be useful when troubleshooting a dial-up connection.

14. Click OK to close the PPP Options sheet, and then click Apply Now to save your changes.

NOTE

> A *proxy server* is a server that sits between your machine and the Internet and actually downloads and serves Internet resources to your machine. It is highly unlikely that you will use proxy servers with a dial-up account, although it is possible.

→ To learn how to configure proxies, **see** "Configuring TCP/IP Using a DHCP Server," **p. 360**.

TESTING YOUR CONFIGURATION

You can test your account by opening an Internet application, such as a web browser (assuming you enabled your Mac to connect automatically). If you are able to access Internet resources, your configuration is complete. Or, you can use the application that you use to manually connect and disconnect from your account, which is Internet Connect.

TIP

> You can check your connection from the Network pane by clicking the Dial Now button on the PPP pane.

Test your configuration using these steps:

1. Open the Internet Connect application (Applications directory) and click the Internal Modem button on the toolbar. You will see the account information you configured earlier.

13

2. Click the Connect button. You will see the status of the connection in the window. You will also hear your modem dialing out and the delightful tones of the handshaking process. If your connection is successful, you will see the connected message and status information in the lower part of the Internet Connect window.

3. Click Disconnect to shut down the connection.

4. Quit Internet Connect.

If you are able to connect successfully, you can use Internet applications, such as your email and web browser.

TIP

> In Internet Connect, select Window, Connection Log to see information about your connection status, such as the current IP address.

 If you are unable to connect using your dial-up account, see "My Dial-up Connection Fails to Connect" in the "Troubleshooting" section at the end of this chapter.

MANAGING A CONNECTION

If you choose to show the modem status in the menu bar, you can easily manage your connection from there. When you open the menu, you will see various options and information, depending on your modem's current status (see Figure 13.7).

Figure 13.7
The Modem status icon provides total control over your dial-up account from the desktop.

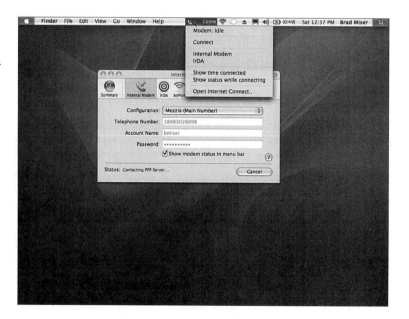

When you open the menu, you will see your modem's status. If disconnected, you can click Connect to connect and vice versa. You will also see which modem you have selected; you can open Internet Connect quickly and easily by selecting Open Internet Connect. You can also choose the status information that is displayed by selecting "Show time connected" or "Show status while connecting."

NOTE

> When you are connected to the Internet and Internet Connect is open, its icon includes a green lightning bolt. You can install Internet Connect on your Dock if you prefer to manage your connection from there rather than from the menu bar.

CONNECTING TO THE NET WITH ETHERNET

CAUTION

> As soon as you connect your Mac to the Internet with an always-on connection, especially one with a fixed IP address, your Mac becomes vulnerable to attacks from hackers. You shouldn't connect a machine to the Internet with a fixed address unless you have some type of firewall protection in place; fortunately, Mac OS X includes a built-in firewall.
>
> However, best practice is to install a hub between your Mac and the modem. Most hubs offer firewall protection and enable you to share an Internet account.

→ To learn how to install and use an AirPort base station as a hub, **see** Chapter 14, " Using an AirPort Network to Connect to the Internet," **p. 371**.

→ To learn how to install and use a hub to share an Internet account, **see** Chapter 34, "Sharing an Internet Connection," **p. 973**.

→ To learn how to protect your Mac from Net attacks, **see** "Defending Your Mac from Net Attacks," **p. 1032**.

Configuring an Internet account for Ethernet connection is actually a bit simpler than configuring a dial-up account. The three main options you use for an Ethernet-based Internet account are Manual IP Settings, DHCP Server, and PPPoE. DHCP Server is the most likely option you will use. However, your ISP will tell you which option is appropriate for your connection.

Connect your Mac's Ethernet port to the cable modem or to the hub to which the cable or DSL modem is connected. Then, configure the OS to use that connection.

NOTE

> Some broadband modems connect to a USB port rather than an Ethernet port, but configuring the account on your Mac works in the same way.

13

CONFIGURING TCP/IP USING A DHCP SERVER

If your provider provides access through a DHCP server, configuring your account is straightforward.

NOTE

> Many local area networks provide Internet access by installing a DHCP server on the network and connecting that server to the Internet (often with a T-1 line). In such cases, you can configure your Mac to use that DHCP server to connect to the Net just as you can when you deal directly with an ISP for an account.

To configure your account, do the following:

1. Open the Network pane of the System Preferences application.
2. From the Show pop-up menu, select Built-In Ethernet (see Figure 13.8).

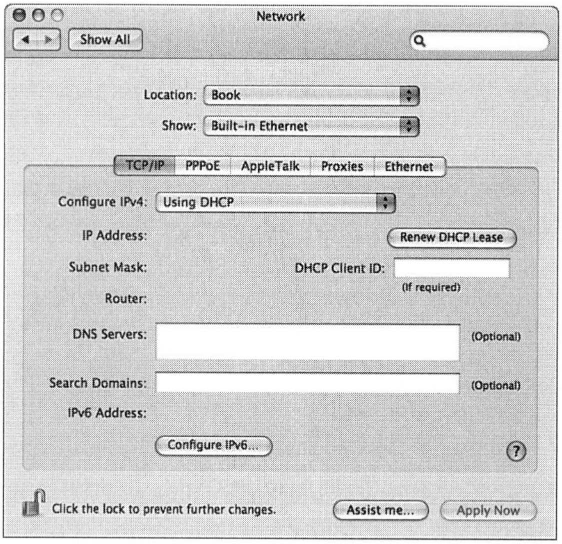

Figure 13.8
Use the Built-in Ethernet option on the Show pop-up menu to configure an Ethernet Internet connection.

3. Click the TCP/IP tab.
4. Select Using DHCP from the Configure IPv4 menu.
5. If you have a DHCP Client ID (your ISP will tell you if this is the case), enter it in the DHCP Client ID field. (If you are using a DHCP server on a local network, you can probably leave this field empty. In some cases, you can leave this field empty even when you are using an ISP to gain Internet access.)
6. If you have DNS and search domain information, enter it in the appropriate fields (these are optional when you use a DHCP server and in most cases, you will leave these fields empty).

7. If you are on a network that uses a proxy server, click the Proxies tab and configure the proxies for your network.

→ For more information about proxy servers, **see** "Understanding and Configuring Proxy Servers," **p. 362**.

8. Click Apply Now to save your changes.

9. Open an Internet application, such as a web browser. If you can access Internet resources, your configuration is complete.

 If you are unable to access Internet resources after configuring your account with a DHCP server, see "My Ethernet Connection Can't Connect" in the "Troubleshooting" section at the end of this chapter.

CONFIGURING STATIC TCP/IP SETTINGS

If your provider supplies a static or manual address for you, use the following steps to configure it:

1. Open the Network pane of the System Preferences application.

2. From the Show pop-up menu, select Built-in Ethernet.

3. Click the TCP/IP tab.

4. Select Manually from the Configure IPv4 pop-up menu.

NOTE

You can also use a static IP address with the router being assigned dynamically. If this is the case for you, select "Using DHCP with manual address" instead of Manually. The rest of the steps are the same, except you don't configure the router because that is done for you by the DHCP router.

5. Enter the IP Address, Subnet Mask, Router, DNS, and Search Domains information your ISP provided in the appropriate fields.

6. Click Apply Now to save your changes.

7. Open an Internet application, such as a web browser. If you can access Internet resources, your configuration is complete.

 If you are unable to access Internet resources after configuring your account manually, see "My Ethernet Connection Can't Connect" in the "Troubleshooting" section at the end of this chapter.

NOTE

IPv4 is the current Internet protocol standard in almost situations. However, IPv6 is a newer standard that is being used in some research institutions. If you need to configure a connection based on IPv6, you can do so by clicking the Configure IPv6 button and using the resulting sheet to configure the service. In most cases, the automatic settings should work fine, but you can also enter manual settings if you need to.

13

UNDERSTANDING AND CONFIGURING PROXY SERVERS

A *proxy server* is a server that sits between end-user computers on a network and the Internet. All Internet traffic of a specific type (such as HTTP for web pages) passes through a specific proxy server. There can be separate proxy servers for each type of service (such as HTTP, FTP, and so on), or a network can use a single proxy server for all Internet services.

When a machine on the network requests a resource (such as a web page), the proxy server downloads the resource and serves it to the machine as if the resources originated from the proxy server itself (although the user doesn't notice that the page is being served by the proxy server instead of the server hosting the requested page).

Proxy servers serve two main purposes:

- **They can improve speed in some cases**—Because the Internet resources are downloaded to the proxy server and then served to users on the local network, after the first access, subsequent accesses to that resource are much faster. This is true because the resource must be downloaded from the Internet to the proxy server only once; from there, it can be served to users on the local network rather than downloading it from the Internet each time.

- **They can be used to filter requests**—Because all information from the Internet flows through a proxy server, that server can be set to block access to specific Internet resources.

NOTE

For more information on proxy servers, see http://webopedia.internet.com/TERM/p/proxy_server.html.

If you are on a network that uses proxy servers, you use the Proxies tab of the Network pane of the System Preferences application to configure them (see Figure 13.9). You configure a proxy for a specific service by checking the check box for that service and entering the proxy address and port in the appropriate fields. Typically, you obtain the proxy server information you need from your network administrator.

CONFIGURING A PPPoE ACCOUNT

Configuring a PPPoE account is more complicated than the other Ethernet options, but it still doesn't take more than a few minutes:

1. Open the Network pane of the System Preferences application.
2. From the Show pop-up menu, select Built-In Ethernet.
3. Configure the TCP/IP settings for your PPPoE account (see the previous sections for details).
4. Click the PPPoE tab (see Figure 13.10).

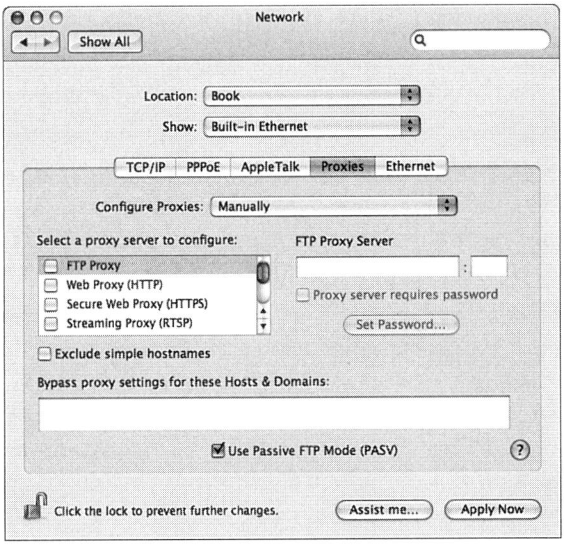

Figure 13.9
If you need to config-
ure Internet access
through a proxy
server, you use the
Proxies tab to do so.

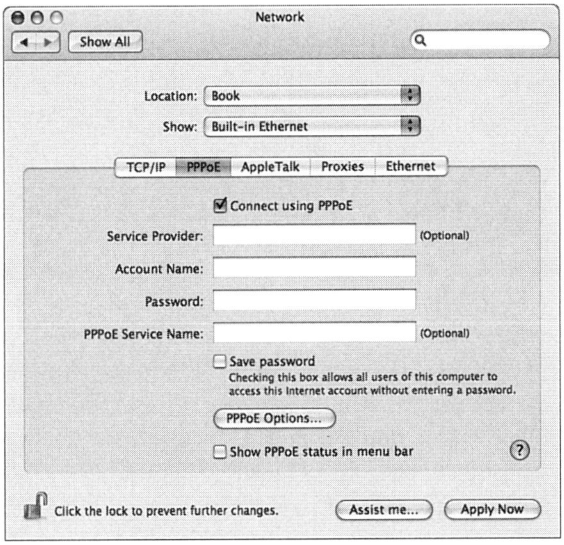

Figure 13.10
Use the PPPoE tab to
configure a PPP over
Ethernet connection.

5. Check the "Connect using PPPoE" check box.

6. Enter the name of your service provider in the Service Provider field. (This is optional.)

7. Enter your access account name in the Account Name field.

8. Enter your access password in the Password field; again this might be different from your email account password. If you leave this field empty, you must enter your password each time you connect. (When you enter a password, the "Save password" check box is checked by default; if you uncheck the check box, your password is deleted from the field.)

9. Enter the service name in the PPPoE Service Name field. (This is also optional.)

10. Check the "Show PPPoE status in menu bar" check box. This puts a menu on the menu bar that you can use to control your PPPoE connection.

11. Click the PPPoE Options button to open the Session Options sheet. Use the controls on this sheet to configure your Internet access.

12. In most cases, you should check the "Connect automatically when needed" check box. This enables your Mac to automatically connect to the Net when it needs to.

13. Use the next four check boxes to control how your Mac monitors your connection. If you want to be prompted when your Mac is connected but is not actively using the connection, check the "Prompt every XX minutes to maintain connection" check box and enter the time after which you want to be prompted to maintain the connection. If you want your Mac to automatically disconnect after a specific period of time, check the "Disconnect if idle for" check box and enter the idle time. Most users should check the "Disconnect when user logs out" check box so that the connection is broken when the current user logs out of the machine. Check the "Disconnect when switching user accounts" check box if you want the connection to be shut down when a different user account becomes active.

NOTE

> In only rare cases will you need to use the controls in the Advanced Options area. The options can be useful when troubleshooting a PPPoE connection.

14. Click OK to close the PPPoE Options sheet, and then click Apply Now to save your changes.

TESTING A PPPoE CONNECTION

You can test your account by opening an Internet application, such as a web browser (assuming you enabled your Mac to connect automatically). If you are able to access Internet resources, your configuration is complete. Or, you can use the application that you use to manually connect and disconnect from your account, which is Internet Connect. Do the following:

1. Open the Internet Connect application (if you turned on the PPPoE status menu, open it and select Open Internet Connect).

2. Select Built-In Ethernet from the Configuration pop-up menu. You will see the PPPoE account information you configured earlier.

3. Click the Connect button. You will see the status of the connection in the window. If your connection is successful, you will see the connected message and status information in the lower part of the Internet Connect window.

4. Click Disconnect to shut down the connection.

5. Quit Internet Connect.

If you are able to connect successfully, you can use Internet applications, such as your email and web browser. You can monitor and control your connection from the PPPoE status menu on the menu bar.

TIP

> In Internet Connect, select Window, Connection Log to see information about your connection status, such as the current IP address.

NOTE

> You can also add Internet Connect to the Dock. When the Internet Connect icon appears in the Dock, it displays a green lightning bolt when you are connected to the Internet.

If you aren't able to connect to the Internet, see "My Ethernet Connection Can't Connect" in the "Troubleshooting" section at the end of this chapter.

→ To learn how to share a single Internet connection among multiple Macs, **see** Chapter 34, "Sharing an Internet Connection," **p. 973**.

NOTE

> Although Ethernet, dial-up, and AirPort are the most likely ways you will connect to a network and the Internet, they aren't the only ways. You can also connect to a network and Internet via your Mac's FireWire port. The steps to configure a connection via FireWire are similar to connecting via Ethernet. All you have to is configure the TCP/IP pane and then any proxies you use. If your Mac is capable of communicating with Bluetooth devices, you can connect using a Bluetooth modem. The steps to do this are similar to configuring a connection through a dial-up modem.

MANAGING MULTIPLE INTERNET ACCOUNTS

If the Internet is vital to you, such as for business purposes, you might have more than one Internet account you access in different ways. For example, you might use a cable modem as your primary access and maintain a dial-up account as a backup. You can maintain multiple Internet accounts on a single Mac.

You can manage the Internet accounts on your machine through the Network Port Configurations pane of the Network pane of the System Preferences application (see Figure 13.11).

In Figure 13.11, five Internet connections are shown and three are active. The active ports are indicated by their check boxes being checked (in the figure the active ports are Built-in Ethernet, AirPort, and Internal Modem). The order in which the ports are listed determines which port is tried first when a connection is needed. In this example, the Built-in Ethernet connection will be tried first, followed by the AirPort port, and then the Internal Modem.

13

Figure 13.11
Use the Network Port Configurations controls to manage multiple network connections, such as Internet connections, on a single machine.

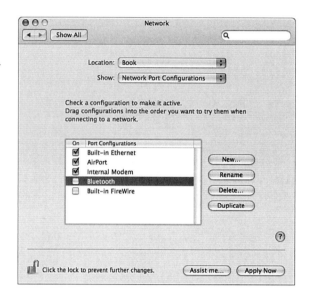

To configure multiple accounts, do the following:

1. Open the Network pane of the System Preferences application.

2. Select the port you want to be your primary connection method on the Show menu.

3. Configure that port for the related account (see the previous sections in this chapter for details). For example, configure your machine to use an Ethernet network to connect to the Internet.

4. From the Show menu, select Network Port Configurations.

5. Make sure the connection you configured is turned on (its check box is checked) and that it is first in the list of port configurations.

6. From the Show menu, select the port you want to be the second connection option, such as an internal modem.

7. Use the information provided in this chapter to configure that account/port.

8. Make sure that the port is turned on; it should appear second in the list of port configurations.

9. Continue configuring ports you want to be active and arranging them on the list in the order in which you want them to be used.

10. Turn off any ports you don't use. Turning off active ports might provide some small performance and boot time improvements, and it might make your Mac more secure. But mostly it is a matter of keeping your configuration settings as accurate as possible.

11. Click Apply Now and then quit the System Preferences application.

When your machine needs to connect to the Internet, it tries the accounts you specified in the order in which you specified them. Following are some other points about managing multiple connections:

- **You can have more than one configuration of the same port**—To create a new instance of a port, click the New button. Name the port and then select the type of port it is (Internal Modem, External Modem, Built-in Ethernet, and so on). Click OK and the new port appears on the list. You can configure it in the same way as the default ports. For example, new ports you create appear on the Show menu; select the port to configure it.

- **AirPort, PPPoE, internal modem, and external modem ports appear on the Configuration pop-up menu in Internet Connect**—You can use that application to manage those connections.

- **The Duplicate button duplicates a port configuration**—This can be useful when you are configuring more than one port of the same type.

- **You can edit a port's name by double-clicking it.**

> TIP
>
> Only those ports that are active appear on the Show pop-up menu.

You can also maintain multiple sets of network and Internet configurations that you create and maintain through the Location Manager. For example, if you use a PowerBook, you might have a configuration when you use the machine from home, another when you use it from work, and so on.

→ To learn how to configure and use locations, **see** "Configuring and Using Locations," **p. 330**.

TROUBLESHOOTING

MY DIAL-UP CONNECTION FAILS TO CONNECT

I've followed the steps for configuring my account, but I still can't connect via a dial-up connection. What is causing this?

Troubleshooting a dial-up connection can be difficult. However, the following list of guidelines can help you solve your connection problems:

- The most common cause of connection problems is an improperly configured machine. Run through all the steps provided to configure a dial-up connection to ensure that you have entered the correct information.

- If you don't hear the modem dialing, make sure you have the modem sound enabled. If you still don't hear the modem dialing out when you attempt to connect, check the modem configuration you learned about earlier in the chapter.

- If you hear the modem dialing but the call is never answered, your ISP might be offline for some reason or you might not have the correct phone number configured. Double-check the phone number you entered to ensure that you entered the access phone number, and make sure you entered it the same way as you would have to dial that number on the phone. Try dialing the number yourself with a phone and see whether the call is answered with the familiar modem connection tones.

- If you hear the call being answered but you never reach the connection state, a problem exists with the communication between your modem and ISP. The most likely cause of this is an incorrect username or password; make sure you are using your access username and password rather than your email username and password.

You can sometimes get a better insight into what is happening by using the Terminal window to connect:

1. Open the Session Options sheet in the PPP tab of the Network pane of the System Preferences application.

2. Check the "Connect using a terminal window (command line)" check box.

3. Click OK and then click Apply Now.

4. Open Internet Connect and click Connect. After your modem dials your ISP, you will see the Terminal window. If you see a login prompt, you are successfully communicating with your provider. If you don't see the login prompt, something is wrong with your configuration or your ISP is offline.

5. At the login prompt, type your access username and press Return.

6. At the password prompt, type your access password and press Return. If your login was successful, the Terminal window disappears and you are connected. If it wasn't successful, a problem probably exists with your user account. Contact your ISP for assistance.

If you have worked through these paragraphs but still can't connect, call your ISP for help.

MY ETHERNET CONNECTION CAN'T CONNECT

I've followed the steps for configuring my Ethernet connection, but I still can't get a successful connection. How do I figure out where I'm going wrong?

The most common cause of problems connecting with an Ethernet account is an incorrect configuration. Still, there can be other problems as well. The following guidelines should help you troubleshoot problems you experience when trying to connect with an Ethernet-based connection:

- If you are using a modem (such as a cable modem), make sure that the modem you are using is powered up and properly connected to your Mac. Most modems have power, PC link, and activity lights. If any of these don't indicate the proper status, check your modem installation.

- If you are using an ISP for access, make sure that the ISP services are currently available. Usually, ISPs provide a status hotline you can call to see whether problems with service have been reported in your area. If there are problems, you will have to wait for the provider to correct them before you will be able to connect (in these situations, it is nice to have a backup account, such as a dial-up account).

- Work through the configuration steps for your account again, being especially careful to check all the configuration information you enter.

- If you are using a DHCP server, see whether you can obtain static settings for your account. Sometimes, you will be able to connect to an account with static settings when the automatic (DHCP) settings fail. If you use DHCP, check the IP address listed in the Sharing pane of the System Preferences application. If you see one that starts with 169, that means your Mac is not obtaining an IP address from the provider and so won't be able to connect to the Internet. You must either figure out why it isn't able to obtain an IP address from your ISP or use a manual IP address.

- If you use a DHCP service and something changes, your Mac's IP address can become invalid. When this happens, you lose your Internet connection. You can force the system to get a new address by opening the TCP/IP pane and clicking the Renew DHCP Lease button. This attempts to obtain a new IP address and might solve the problem.

- If you are still unable to connect, contact the service provider or network administrator from whom you obtain your service. Confirm that you are using the correct installation information for your account. If you are, ask for assistance in troubleshooting the connection from the provider's end.

TIP

> If you are troubleshooting the connection of a machine on a network, try isolating that machine from the rest of the network while you are troubleshooting. This eliminates the potential for problems induced by other machines on the network and helps you more quickly isolate the cause of the problem you are trying to solve. For example, if you connect through a hub attached to a modem, connect your Mac directly to the modem; of course, be careful to turn on your Mac's firewall before you do this.

Getting Help

In past versions of the Mac OS, the OS itself was sometimes responsible for Ethernet connection problems. For example, under Mac OS 9.2 and earlier versions, the Mac had unreliable support for certain types of DHCP servers, and it was often necessary to switch to static settings. These issues have been eliminated under Mac OS X.

Be aware that you might get flak from your ISP's technical support when you tell them you are using a Mac. Because the Mac has a smaller number of users, the tech support person to whom you talk will probably have less experience with Macs than with Windows machines. Also, many technical support people, such as those with cable companies, are overloaded and will try to get you off the line as soon as possible. If your problem doesn't fit into a checklist, they might want to stop before your problem is solved. Try to stay positive; you might have to be assertive (not aggressive) to get the support you need. Sometimes, it is better to explore the support area of a provider's website (which, of course, assumes that you can connect in some fashion, perhaps from another computer) before calling for help.

CHAPTER 14

USING AN AIRPORT NETWORK TO CONNECT TO THE INTERNET

In this chapter

AIRPORT WIRELESS NETWORKING

AirPort is an amazing technology that makes wireless communication affordable to own and relatively simple to install and configure. With AirPort, you can quickly and easily set up and manage a wireless network to do the following tasks:

- **Connect to the Net**—You can use AirPort to connect to the Internet wirelessly, and you can easily share a single Internet connection among multiple Macs.

- **Connect to a network**—Through a base station, you can connect an AirPort-equipped Mac to an existing Ethernet (wired) network.

- **Share a USB printer**—You can connect a USB printer directly to an AirPort base station to share that printer with AirPort devices.

- **Connect directly to other AirPort-equipped computers**—You can directly network to one or more AirPort-equipped computers. As long as all the computers are set up to use the same AirPort connection, they can communicate with each other up to 150 feet apart. This makes instant, temporary networks fast and easy.

NOTE

> The original AirPort base station, called the Graphite version, didn't offer the same set of features as newer hardware does. For example, you can't connect a printer to a Graphite base station.

AirPort functionality is provided through the following components:

- **AirPort-ready Macs**—If your Mac is AirPort ready, it has built-in antennas that are used to transmit and receive signals to and from the wireless network. It also has a slot in which you can install an AirPort card. The good news is that all modern Macs are AirPort compatible.

NOTE

> Power Mac G5s have an AirPort antenna port into which you plug an external antenna to improve the reception and transmission of AirPort signals.

- **AirPort card**—To use AirPort, your Mac must have an AirPort card installed in it. There is more good news here too: AirPort Extreme cards cost only about $79. AirPort cards are simple to install yourself, or you can order one as an option when you purchase a new Mac. If you use a PowerMac G5, you also need an external AirPort antenna, which is provided with the Mac.

- **AirPort software**—The AirPort software is necessary for Macs to communicate through the AirPort hardware. The software to configure and use an AirPort network is part of the standard Mac OS X installation.

- **AirPort base station**—The AirPort base station transmits the signals for the AirPort network. There are three basic types of base stations. The AirPort Extreme hardware access point (HAP) is a dedicated hardware device that contains ports for a modem, USB printer, and an Ethernet network. When you use it for a dial-up connection to the Internet, for example, the AirPort base station's modem is used to connect to the Net. Your Mac communicates to the base station through the AirPort card and antenna. A single AirPort HAP can support multiple computers so you can share an Internet connection among up to 50 computers. Another option is an AirPort Express base station, which performs a similar function to the full-size base station but doesn't offer as many features (for example, it has only one Ethernet port). You can also configure any AirPort-equipped Mac to act as a base station by using Mac OS X's built-in Internet sharing capabilities.

> **NOTE**
>
> Functionally, an AirPort HAP or AirPort Express and an AirPort-equipped Mac OS X machine sharing its Internet connection are identical. In this chapter, when I use the term *base station*, it can refer to any of these means of providing an AirPort network.

The general steps to configure and use an AirPort network are the following:

1. Install and configure the base station (AirPort HAP, AirPort Express, or an AirPort-equipped Mac OS X machine).

2. Install AirPort cards in the machines you want to connect to the AirPort network.

3. Configure those machines to use the AirPort network.

> **NOTE**
>
> Although using AirPort to connect to the Internet and to share an Internet account is the focus of this chapter, an AirPort network provides access to all the services of a wired network. For example, computers connected to a wired network via AirPort can print to printers on that network, use file sharing, and so on. If you connect a USB printer to an AirPort Extreme base station, you can share that printer with any AirPort-equipped Mac.

→ To learn how to configure other network services over an AirPort network, **see** "Configuring the Services on a Network," **p. 941**.

Before getting into the meat of this chapter, there are a few AirPort tidbits you need to understand.

The two flavors of AirPort are AirPort and AirPort Extreme.

AirPort was the original incarnation and offered many wireless benefits. AirPort communicates at 11Mbps and is compatible with wireless devices based on the 802.11b standard.

AirPort Extreme is the newer standard and offers even more benefits. First, is speed. AirPort Extreme communicates at 54Mbps, which is almost five times the speed at which

14

the original AirPort communicates. AirPort Extreme is compatible with devices using the 802.11g Wi-Fi standard. Second, AirPort Extreme can support more computers at the same time than does AirPort. Third, AirPort Extreme enables you to share a USB printer from a hub. Fourth, with AirPort Extreme, you can wirelessly link base stations together to expand the range of an AirPort network to cover large areas.

Mac OS X supports both flavors of AirPort, but specific Mac models support either AirPort or AirPort Extreme; in other words, older Macs can support an AirPort card, whereas all modern support AirPort Extreme cards. The two cards are not interchangeable. To find out which flavor your Mac supports, check its documentation. At press time, all shipping Macs support AirPort Extreme.

Fortunately, even though the hardware for the two standards is different, it is compatible. AirPort machines can connect to AirPort Extreme networks, and vice versa. The primary difference is that AirPort networks are much slower than AirPort Extreme networks are. And, AirPort Extreme base stations offer more features than AirPort base stations do.

Because it is the newer standard, this chapter focuses mostly on AirPort Extreme. I do my best to use the term *AirPort Extreme* when discussing something that is specific to AirPort Extreme technology or *AirPort Standard* when referring to the older technology. When I use the term *AirPort*, I mean to refer to something that is applicable to both technologies.

NOTE

Because it is based on the 802.11 standards, AirPort is compatible with 802.11 networks and devices. For example, you can connect an AirPort-equipped Mac to any wireless network that supports 802.11b or 802.11g (Extreme only) devices, such as those designed for Windows computers. Similarly, Windows machines equipped with 802.11b or 802.11g devices can also access an AirPort network.

SETTING UP AN AIRPORT BASE STATION

Setting up an AirPort base station is slightly different depending on the type of base station you use: the AirPort HAP or an AirPort-equipped Mac OS X machine that provides Internet sharing.

The benefit of using an AirPort HAP is that it doesn't place any processing load on an individual Mac and is intended to run at all times, so the AirPort network is always available. It also provides the ability to share an Internet connection with devices to which it is networked using an Ethernet connection. The disadvantage of this device is its cost (currently $199 with a modem and antenna port). If you are going to use an AirPort network regularly to serve more than one or two machines, an AirPort HAP is a good investment. An AirPort Express base station provides many of the same benefits but costs only $99.

→ To learn about when and how to use an AirPort Express Base Station, **see** "Working with an AirPort Express Base Station," **p. 398**.

The benefit of using an AirPort-equipped Mac OS X machine as a base station is that you don't need to purchase any additional hardware (except for the AirPort card in the Mac that will act as the base station). You get most of the functionality of the AirPort HAP but don't have to support another dedicated device. Using this method does have several disadvantages, though. One is that it places additional processing load on the machine that acts as the base station. Another is that the network can be affected by the state of that machine. For example, if the machine is shut down or crashes, the network is taken down as well. Another is that a Mac acting as a base station doesn't support all the HAP's features, such as the option to add an antenna or to wirelessly link base stations together to increase the range of a network.

NOTE

> You can have multiple base stations operating in the same area at the same time to grow your AirPort network to be quite large.

SETTING UP AN AIRPORT HARDWARE ACCESS POINT

Apple's AirPort Extreme hardware access point (also called the AirPort Extreme base station) is a relatively simple device. It contains a transmitter that broadcasts the signal over which the network is provided. It has two Ethernet ports. One is used to connect to a broadband Internet connection, such as a cable modem. The other is used to connect to a wired Ethernet network so the base station can also share its Internet and network connection with the machines connected to that network. Along with the power adapter port, it offers a USB port to which you can connect a USB printer to share that printer with an AirPort network.

The AirPort HAP also includes the software it needs to perform its functions.

NOTE

> The only reason I use the term *HAP* is to distinguish between a dedicated hardware device and using a Mac as a base station. In practice, these devices are called *base stations*.

Setting up an AirPort HAP consists of the following two tasks:

1. Install the AirPort HAP.
2. Configure the AirPort network, including the Internet connection the base station will use to connect to the Internet.

INSTALLING THE BASE STATION

There is not much to installing the AirPort base station.

First, you locate the device in a central area so it provides the maximum amount of coverage where you install it. In most houses, the AirPort base station provides adequate signal

14

strength even if you locate it at one end of the house and place machines you want to network at the other end. However, the closer the machines are to the base station, the stronger the signal is.

NOTE

> AirPort Extreme signals don't offer the range that AirPort Standard signals do. If you want to provide AirPort Extreme services over a large distance (such as greater than 150 feet depending on the environment), you should add an external antenna to it.

Of course, a major consideration for the location of the base station is where your Internet connection will come from. If you use a cable modem, you need to locate the device so that you can connect the cable modem to it. If you use a DSL modem, you need to locate the base station relatively close to the phone line port to which the DSL modem is attached.

After you have placed the base station in its location, attach its power adapter to the station and plug it in to a wall outlet. Attach the base station's modem port to a phone jack if you will be connecting to the Internet via a dial-up account. If you will be using the AirPort HAP to connect to the Internet via a cable or other broadband connection, connect the Ethernet (WAN) port on the AirPort HAP to the broadband modem.

If you are going to use the base station to act as a sharing hub for an Ethernet network, attach an Ethernet cable to the station's network Ethernet (LAN) port. If you want to use the base station to network your Mac with a single computer, you can connect the Ethernet port on the other computer to the base station with an Ethernet crossover cable. Otherwise, attach a standard Ethernet cable to your base station and to the LAN/WAN port on the Ethernet hub that serves your wired network (not all hubs have a special port for this; if yours doesn't, connect it to any available port).

NOTE

> Some modern Macs, such as the PowerBook G4, don't require the use of an Ethernet crossover cable. The port automatically senses whether it is connected to another machine or to a hub and communicates appropriately.

→ To learn more about Ethernet, **see** "Ethernet," **p. 817**.

If you want to share a USB printer with all AirPort-equipped Macs that can access the network, connect the printer's USB cable to the USB port on the base station.

CONFIGURING THE BASE STATION

After you have installed the base station, you need to configure it. You can configure it manually through the AirPort Admin Utility, or you can use the AirPort Setup Assistant to configure it for you. With either method, you configure the base station from a machine with which it can communicate either via AirPort or through an Ethernet network.

N O T E

The machine you use to configure a base station must have an AirPort card installed in it to use the AirPort Setup Assistant. It does not need to have an AirPort card if it is connected to the access point via Ethernet.

→ To learn how to install an AirPort card, **see** "Installing an AirPort Card," **p. 388**.

CONFIGURING THE BASE STATION USING THE AIRPORT SETUP ASSISTANT

Use the following steps to configure the base station using the AirPort Setup Assistant:

1. Configure the Internet connection on the Mac from which you will be configuring the base station in the same way that the base station is going to be configured. For example, if the base station will be using a dial-up account, configure the Mac using that account. If you are using a broadband connection, configure the Mac to use that connection.

→ To learn how to configure a Mac for the Internet, **see** Chapter 13, "Connecting Your Mac to the Internet," **p. 337**.

2. Open the AirPort Setup Assistant (Applications/Utilities) to see the first window in the Assistant (see Figure 14.1).

Figure 14.1
The AirPort Setup Assistant guides you through the steps to configure an AirPort base station or an AirPort-equipped Mac to access the AirPort network you create.

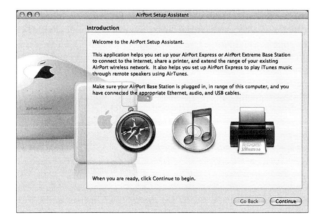

3. Click Continue, click the "Set up a new AirPort Base Station" radio button, and click Continue again.

N O T E

These steps assume you are setting up a new base station. If you want to change the settings for an existing station, click "Change settings on an existing AirPort Base Station" instead.

14

CAUTION

> If you are configuring an access point that has already been configured and is protected by a password, you have to enter that password before you can proceed.
>
> If the base station you are configuring has outdated software installed on it, the Setup Assistant attempts to update it. To do so, you must be able to connect to the Internet, which is sort of a Catch-22 in that it assumes that it is already configured and you are reconfiguring it. You can download the update to the Mac you are going to use to config- ure the base station and then the base station can update its software from there.

4. Choose the base station you want to configure from the "" pop-up menu and click Continue. If you have only one base station in range, it is selected automatically. If you are reconfiguring an existing base station, you first choose the network the base station is on and then choose the specific base station.

   If the Assistant detects new AirPort firmware is available, it will prompt you to do so. Provide permission for the update and your base station's firmware will be updated.

5. Enter the password for the base station you selected in the previous step and click Continue. If you are configuring a new base station or one that has been reset, the pass- word is `public`.

NOTE

> Some base stations have two passwords. One is to join the network, and the other allows you to configure the base station itself. If you are prompted to enter a second password, do so.

6. Follow the onscreen instructions to work through the assistant to complete the configu- ration of the base station.

If you see an error message stating that the required AirPort hardware was not found when you started the AirPort Setup Assistant, see "No AirPort Hardware Is Found" in the "Troubleshooting" section at the end of this chapter.

If you can't access the base station because you don't know the password, see "I Don't Know the Base Station Password" in the "Troubleshooting" section at the end of this chapter.

CONFIGURING A BASE STATION MANUALLY

You should also know how to manually configure the base station. Manual configuration can be a better and more complete way to configure it, and there are some options you can only configure using the manual technique. If you want to change only one aspect of a base sta- tion's configuration, using the manual method is also the way to go. And, it can also be a faster way to configure a base station. For example, you need to manually configure a base station when you want to share an Internet account with other machines on an Ethernet network or to use the AirPort base station as a bridge between the wireless network and a wired one (for example, to allow AirPort-equipped machines to use a printer connected to a wired network). You use the AirPort Admin Utility application to configure an access point manually by performing the following steps:

NOTE

> The original Graphite base station did not include a LAN port that you could use to connect the station to a wired network at the same time you connected it to a broadband modem. Because of this, its configuration is slightly different from the newer Snow and AirPort Extreme base stations. The most significant difference is that you have to configure a Graphite base station to provide services to a wired network. This is explained in the "OS X to the Max" section at the end of this chapter.

1. Open the AirPort Admin Utility (Applications/Utilities). The Select Base Station window opens (see Figure 14.2).

Figure 14.2
The AirPort Admin Utility enables you to configure a base station manually.

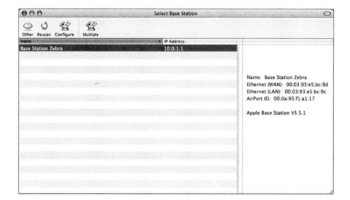

2. Select the base station you want to configure and click Configure (if there is only one base station in range, it is selected automatically).

If you get an error message when trying to configure your base station manually, see "I Can't Configure My Base Station Manually" in the "Troubleshooting" section at the end of this chapter.

3. If the base station has been reset, you see a dialog box informing you that the base station has been reset and is not currently configured. (If the base station has not been reset, you won't have to do this step.) Click Automatic and then authenticate yourself using an administrator name and password. The software reconfigures the base station and restarts it. When it is complete, you return to the Select Base Station window. Click Configure again.

NOTE

> When you have problems with a base station, sometimes you must reset it so that it returns to its default settings (in effect, you start over).

You next see a window that has the base station name as its title (see Figure 14.3).

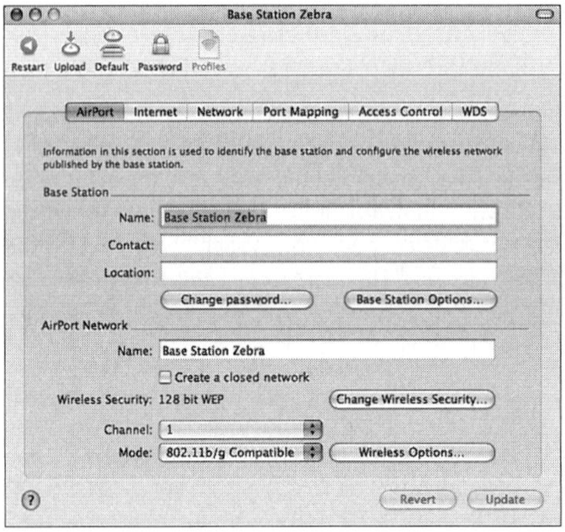

Figure 14.3
This window enables you to access all aspects of a base station.

This Admin Utility toolbar has the following controls:

- **Restart**—This button causes the base station to restart. You must do this occasionally if you are experiencing problems.
- **Upload**—This button enables you to upload revised software onto the base station to update it.
- **Default**—This returns the base station to its defaults.
- **Password**—Use this button to change the base station's password.
- **Profiles**—An AirPort Express base station can store up to five configurations on it. You use the Profiles button to access the profile with which you want to work.

NOTE

These steps assume the base station you are configuring has been configured previously. If not, the steps might be slightly different.

4. Select the AirPort tab if it isn't selected already. On this tab, you can change the identification information for the base station and configure how it serves its network.

5. Enter the base station name (this is the name of the hardware, not the name of the network it provides) in the Name field, the contact for the base station in the Contact field, and the station's location in the Location field (this information can help users contact you for help).

6. To change the base station's password (not the network's password), use the "Change password" button. In the resulting sheet, type and verify the new password and click OK.

7. If you want to configure various aspects of the base station's security settings, click the Base Station Options button. Use the WAN Ethernet Port tab of the resulting sheet to select the security options you want to enable or disable. The available options are the following:

- **Enable SNMP Access**—The Simple Network Management Protocol network management service makes networks easier to manage, but it also makes them somewhat more vulnerable to denial-of-service attacks (where servers are overloaded because numerous, bogus requests for service are received). Generally, you should leave this option on.

- **Enable Remote Configuration**—This setting enables a base station to be configured over its WAN port. If you uncheck this box, you can configure the base station by connecting it to a LAN or by using an AirPort network.

- **Enable Default Host**—If you want to play network games over AirPort, check the Enable Default Host check box and enter the IP address of the machine that will act as the host for the game.

- **Enable Remote Printer Access**—Use this option if you want printers to be accessible via the WAN port.

8. Click the Logging/NTP tab. Use the "Send Base Station Logging to" check box, text box, and pop-up menu to configure logging services for the base station. This can be helpful when you are troubleshooting problems. You can also have your base station's time and date set automatically by checking the "Set Time & Date Automatically" check box and choosing a timeserver on the pop-up menu.

9. Click the USB Printer tab to view information about a printer connected to the base station's USB port.

10. Click OK to close the Options sheet.

11. Enter the name of the network that will be provided in the Name field in the AirPort Network area of the window.

NOTE

> If the base station is already providing a network and you change the name or password of the network, people who use the network need to change the network they use. The new network name appears as an available network on the client machines, but you must provide the new password to those whom you want to use the network.

12. If you want to create a closed network, check the "Create a closed network" check box. A closed network does not appear on other users' AirPort menus. To join closed networks, users have to know the name and password for that network (because they can't see the network on a menu). Using a closed network is a good way to keep your network more secure.

13. Click the "Change Wireless Security" button to configure the network's security. In the resulting sheet, you can choose the type of wireless security and choose the network's password if one is required (see Figure 14.4). On the pop-up menu, choose the type of security you want to use from the following options:

14

Figure 14.4
Generally, you should enable security on your network to protect the computers on your network.

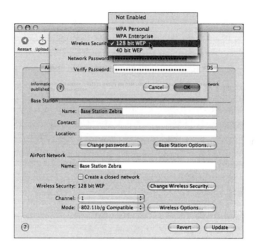

- **Not Enabled**—If you select this option, your network won't be secured and anyone who can find it can join it without a password. You should never use this option unless you are very sure no one whom you don't know about will be able to access your network.

- **WPA Personal**—Wi-Fi Protected Access (WPA) is an encryption technique to protect data from being transmitted wirelessly. Use the WPA Personal option for a small network.

- **WPA Enterprise**—This is a more robust implementation that requires specialized hardware and expertise to implement. In most situations, you will use one of the other options.

- **128 bit WEP**—Wired Equivalent Privacy (WEP) is an encryption strategy that attempts to provide wireless networks with the same level of protection that wired networks have. WEP does provide improved security compared to nonencrypted transmissions, but be aware that it does have some flaws, as do almost all security measures. If the information transmitted over your network is very sensitive, you should use WEP to provide at least some protection. If supported by the computers that will be connecting to your network, use 128 bit.

- **40 bit WEP**—This is the same protocol as 128 WEP, except it is provided at the 40-bit level, which is less secure than the 128-bit level.

14. Enter the password for the network, verify it, and click OK to set it.

15. Use the Channel pop-up menu to select the channel over which the base station communicates. Generally, the default channel works fine, but if you are having trouble communicating with devices, you can try different channels to improve signal transmission and reception. If you have multiple AirPort networks in the same area, you can use the Channel pop-up menu to have each network use a different channel so that they don't interfere with one another.

16. If you are configuring an AirPort Extreme base station, use the Mode pop-up menu to choose the wireless standard used on the network. Use 802.11b/g Compatible to make the network available to both 802.11b (AirPort) and 802.11g (AirPort Extreme) devices. You can also select 802.11g only or 802.11b only. You use one of these óptions if you want to restrict the network to one of these protocols for some reason.

17. Click the Wireless Options button to see the Wireless Options sheet (see Figure 14.5). These settings control the physical properties of the base station's signal. Generally, the default settings will work fine. However, if you have problems providing a network, you can adjust these settings, such as the multicast rate, to obtain better performance.

Figure 14.5
Use this sheet to configure certain physical aspects of the signals used on an AirPort network.

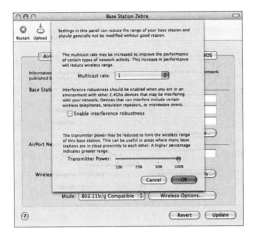

18. Use the "Multicast rate" pop-up menu to set the multicast rate. Choosing a higher value improves performance but also reduces range.

19. Use the "Enable interference robustness" check box to make the AirPort signal less sensitive to interference.

20. Use the Transmitter Power slider to change the strength of the base station's signal. If many base stations exist in the same physical area, reduce the signal strength to limit the interference of these stations with one another. You can also reduce the strength to limit the size of the AirPort network's coverage.

21. Click OK to return to the Base Station window.

22. Click the Internet tab and configure the base station for Internet access. This works similarly to configuring a Mac for Internet access. Choose the connection method from the Connect Using pop-up menu and then enter the settings you want to use in the lower part of the window.

→ To learn how to configure a Mac for the Internet, **see** Chapter 13, "Connecting Your Mac to the Internet," **p. 337**.

14

NOTE

> One additional control available for a base station's Internet access that is not present for a Mac is the WAN Ethernet Port pop-up menu. Use this to set the speed at which the base station communicates with a wired network over its WAN port. In most cases, the Automatic (Default) value is the best choice, but you can choose a specific speed.

23. Click the Network tab to control how the base station provides services to the network (see Figure 14.6).

Figure 14.6
Use the Network tab to configure the services the base station provides to the network.

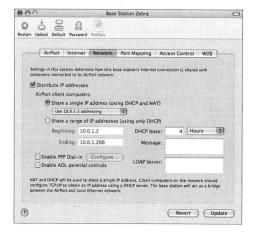

The default settings enable all the machines connecting to the AirPort network to share the base station's Internet account. By default, the base station provides IP addresses to each machine dynamically and uses NAT protection to isolate the IP addresses of each machine from the connection to the Internet. To choose this option, click the "Share a single IP address (using DHCP and NAT)" radio button. Then select the range of addresses that should be assigned to each device on the network using the pop-up menu. In most cases, the "Use 10.0.1.1 addressing" option will work, but you can choose a different range if you want to.

If you want to use a specific set of IP addresses, check the "Share a range of IP addresses (using only DHCP)" check box and enter the starting and ending IP numbers you want to assign. As machines connect to your network, these IP addresses are assigned to each machine that connects (you have to have enough addresses in the range so one is available for each machine). Use the "DHCP lease" box and pop-up menu to set the number of hours for the DHCP lease on each machine. When this time passes, a new address is assigned to each machine. You can enter a DHCP lease message in the Message box.

→ To learn how to configure a Graphite base station so that all the machines on a network, including machines connected via Ethernet, can share the same Internet account, **see** "Using a Graphite AirPort Base Station to Share an Internet Connection with a Wired Network," **p. 395**.

24. To enable people to connect to the base station via PPP dial in, check the "Enable PPP Dial-in" check box and use the Configure button to configure these connections.

25. If you use AOL, you can enable parental controls by checking the "Enable AOL parental controls" check box.

26. Use the Port Mapping tab to add more ports to the network for other services, such as AppleShare, web sharing, and so on.

27. Use the Access Control tab if you want to limit network access to machines with specific AirPort ID numbers (you find these numbers on the client machines, as you will see in a later section). Click Add (+), enter the AirPort ID of the machines to which you want to allow access to your network, enter a description of the machine, and click OK. Only the machines with AirPort IDs shown in the list can then access your network. (If the list is empty, any AirPort machines can connect by using the network's password.)

28. Use the RADIUS pop-up menu and boxes to configure a RADIUS server for the AirPort network. This prevents AirPort machines without valid IDs from connecting to the network. Explaining the details of this is beyond the scope of this chapter.

29. Use the WDS tab to configure multiple base stations to provide a single network to extend its range.

→ To learn how to configure WDS, **see** "Making AirPort Go Farther," **p. 396**.

30. Click Update to transfer the settings to the base station. The base station is restarted after the settings have been transferred.

31. When the process is complete, click OK; you return to the Select Base Station window.

32. Quit the AirPort Admin utility.

 If you see an error message stating that the required AirPort hardware was not found when you started the AirPort Admin Utility, see "No AirPort Hardware Is Found" in the "Troubleshooting" section at the end of this chapter.

NOTE
 For more detailed information on AirPort, visit Apple's Knowledge Base at www.apple.com/airport.

You can now access the Net from an AirPort-equipped Mac using the AirPort network. The base station also provides services to a wired network if it is connected to one.

CONFIGURING AN AIRPORT-EQUIPPED MAC TO ACT AS A BASE STATION

As you learned earlier, you can use any AirPort-equipped Mac running Mac OS X to act as a base station. When you do this, the Mac OS X machine provides services similar to those that a HAP provides, but you don't have as much control over the AirPort network.

To configure a Mac as a base station, perform the following steps:

1. Install an AirPort card in the machine you are going to use as a base station.

→ To learn how to install an AirPort card, **see** "Installing an AirPort Card," **p. 388**.

14

2. Configure that machine so it can connect to the Internet, such as through DHCP services provided on an Ethernet network or over a dial-up account and activate the AirPort connection via the Network pane.

→ To learn how to configure a Mac for the Internet, **see** Chapter 13, "Connecting Your Mac to the Internet," **p. 337**.

3. Open the Sharing pane of the System Preferences application and click the Internet tab (see Figure 14.7).

Figure 14.7
You use the controls on the Internet tab of the Sharing pane to enable a Mac to share its Internet connection with other computers.

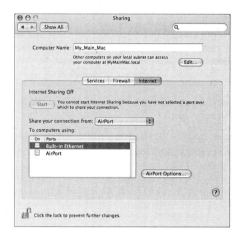

4. Select the Internet connection you want to share with other machines on the "Share your connection from" pop-up menu. For example, if your computer gets its Internet connection from a wired network, select Built-in Ethernet.

NOTE

You can choose to share a connection from a wired network to AirPort-equipped machines or from an AirPort-equipped machine to a wired network.

5. Select the type of connections with which you are going to share the machine's Internet connection by checking the appropriate "To computers using" check box. For example, if you want to share the connection with computers via AirPort, check AirPort, and if you want to share the connection via a wired network, check the Built-in Ethernet check box. You can choose more than one connection type with which to share the connection.

6. If you enabled AirPort sharing, select AirPort and click the AirPort Options button. The AirPort network configuration sheet appears (see Figure 14.8).

7. Edit the default name as needed. The default name is the name of your computer, but you can make it something more interesting if you want to.

Figure 14.8
With this sheet, you configure the AirPort network your Mac provides to other machines.

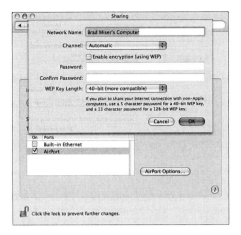

8. Unless you have multiple AirPort networks active in the same area or you experience interference that prevents your network from operating properly, leave the Channel pop-up menu set to Automatic. If you want to choose a channel manually, select it on the pop-up menu.

9. For a more secure network, check the "Enable encryption (using WEP)" check box.

> **NOTE**
>
> WEP is an encryption strategy that attempts to provide wireless networks with the same level of protection that wired networks have. WEP does provide improved security compared to nonencrypted transmissions, but be aware that it does have some flaws as do almost all security measures. If the information transmitted over your network is very sensitive, you should use WEP to provide at least some protection.

10. Enter the network password in the Password and Confirm Password fields. This is the password users will enter to connect to the network.

11. Select an encryption key length on the WEP Key Length pop-up menu. The options are 40-bit and 128-bit. If only newer Macs running Mac OS X will be connecting to the network, select 128-bit. If you aren't sure which level of encryption other machines can support, select 40-bit. If you don't want to use the encryption at all, uncheck the "Enable encryption (using WEP)" check box.

12. Click OK.

13. Click Start. The Internet connection is shared with other computers via AirPort or built-in Ethernet.

14. Use the Services pane to configure other services you will provide over the network, such as File and Printer Sharing. Your Mac then begins providing services over AirPort and its network becomes available to AirPort-equipped Macs.

→ To learn how to configure sharing services, **see** "Configuring the Services on a Network," **p. 941**.

TIP

> If Printer Sharing is enabled, USB printers connected to the Mac acting as a base station are also available to the AirPort network. This is a great way to share USB printers with other Macs. Also, the AirPort menu on the menu bar on a Mac acting as a base station is different than the menu on a client machine. This menu also has different options than a client menu.

Using a Mac As a Base Station

One of the disadvantages of using a Mac as a base station is that the Mac must be on for the network to be available. If that Mac is turned off or crashes, the AirPort network is lost.

If the Mac that is acting as the base station goes into Sleep mode, its services are also lost. Use the Energy Saver pane of the System Preferences utility to ensure that the software base station machine never sleeps while you want the AirPort network to be available. Also, if Sleep interrupts AirPort network services, client machines might have to quit and then restart Internet applications, such as Safari, to resume using the network.

→ To learn how to control sleep, **see** "Managing Your Mobile Mac's Power," **p. 320**.

CONNECTING TO THE AIRPORT NETWORK WITH MAC OS X

After an AirPort network has been established, you can access it from any AirPort-equipped Mac. First, install an AirPort card in each Mac you want to add to the network. Then, configure each Mac to access the AirPort network.

INSTALLING AN AIRPORT CARD

An AirPort card contains the hardware receiver, transmitter, and firmware that enables a Mac to communicate with an AirPort network (including a base station or other AirPort-equipped machines). Each machine that will access an AirPort network must have an AirPort card installed in it. When your Mac detects that an AirPort card is installed, it activates the AirPort software that is part of all Mac OS installations.

If you ordered an AirPort card to be installed when you ordered your Mac, you can skip this section. If you obtained the AirPort card separately, you need to install it in the AirPort card slot in your Mac. Generally, this involves exposing the AirPort card slot, inserting the card in the slot, connecting the antenna to the card, and then closing up the machine.

As with base stations, there are AirPort cards and AirPort Extreme cards. These cards can be used only in compatible machines—that is, you can't use an AirPort Extreme card in a machine that has an AirPort slot, and vice versa.

On Power Mac G4s and G5s, you open the case to access the AirPort card slot. On iMacs, the slot is located in different places depending on the generation of iMac you have. On

14

PowerBooks and iBooks, the AirPort card slot is located underneath the keyboard or just above the bottom cover (on PowerBook G4s, you remove the bottom cover to access the AirPort card slot). For other Mac models, refer to the documentation that was provided to find out where the AirPort card should be installed.

NOTE

When you order an AirPort card separately from a machine, it includes an installation pamphlet that provides installation instructions for every Mac model. The owner's manual for your Mac also contains the instructions you need to install an AirPort card.

Because of the differences in the location of AirPort slots on various models, the exact steps to install the card are slightly different. However, installing a card is never particularly difficult. As an example, the following steps describe how to install the card in a Power Mac G4:

1. Shut down the machine, disconnect any cables that prevent you from opening the case, and open the case.

2. Locate the AirPort card slot; in Power Mac G4s, the slot is located on the same side as the motherboard near the front of the machine toward the bottom of the case (see Figure 14.9).

Figure 14.9
Installing an AirPort card in a Power Mac G4 takes less than 5 minutes (and most of that time is required to disconnect and reconnect cables).

AirPort card slot

3. Insert the card into the metal guide with the bar code side of the card up; push the card until the end of the card is inserted into the connector mounted on the motherboard.

4. Connect the antenna to the hole on the card (see Figure 14.10).

5. Close up the case, reconnect any cables you disconnected, and restart the machine.

14

Figure 14.10
This Power Mac G4 has an AirPort card installed and is now ready to communicate via AirPort.

NOTE

> Power Mac G5s use an external AirPort antenna. Connect the antenna that is provided with the machine or with the AirPort card to the external antenna port.

CONFIGURING MAC OS X TO JOIN AN AIRPORT NETWORK

To access an AirPort network, you must configure a Mac OS X machine to connect to it.

You can do this in several ways. First, use the AirPort tab of the Network pane of the System Preferences application to determine which AirPort networks your Mac uses by default when it restarts or wakes up from sleep.

Configure your default, or preferred, AirPort network with the following steps:

1. Open the System Preferences application and click the Network icon to open the Network pane. Select AirPort from the Show pop-up menu.

2. Click the AirPort tab (see Figure 14.11).

Figure 14.11
Use the AirPort tab to configure how your Mac connects to an AirPort network.

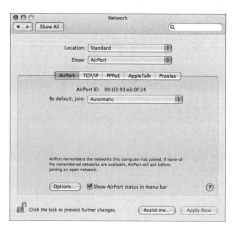

3. To have your Mac join the AirPort network with the strongest signal, select Automatic on the "By default, join" pop-up menu. This causes your Mac to scan all the available networks and log on to the one that has the best signal. If you haven't saved the password for the network your Mac selects, you must enter the password manually.

4. To join a specific network, select "Preferred Networks" on the "By default, join" pop-up menu, select the network you want to join on the drop-down list, and enter the password if the network requires one.

5. Check the "Show AirPort status in menu bar" check box to put the AirPort menu on your menu bar. You can use this icon to quickly select and control your AirPort connection.

6. Click the Options button. You will see the options sheet, which you can use to configure additional aspects of your AirPort connection.

7. On the "If no preferred networks are found" pop-up menu, select the action you want your Mac to take when it can't find a preferred network to join. You can choose to be prompted before joining an open network, join an open network automatically, or keep looking for recent networks.

8. If you want to require that an administrator password be entered before changing networks or creating computer-to-computer networks, check the appropriate check boxes.

9. Check the "Automatically add new networks to the preferred networks list" check box to have any network you join added to your preferred list.

10. Check the "Disconnect from wireless networks when I log out" check box if you want your Mac disconnected from the AirPort network when you log out.

11. Click the "Enable interference robustness" check box to activate this feature. Try this if you are having trouble keeping a good AirPort connection.

12. Click OK to save your option changes.

13. Click Apply Now and quit the System Preferences application.

NOTE

> As your Mac connects to the network, the name of the network to which you are connecting briefly appears next to the AirPort icon in the menu bar.

If you want to use an AirPort network other than your preferred one, open the AirPort menu on the menu bar and select the AirPort network to which you want to connect. If its password is not already stored on your keychain, you will be prompted to enter it. Do so and you will be logged on to the AirPort network.

14

TIP

> When prompted to enter your password, check the Add to Keychain check box to have Mac OS X remember the password so you don't have to enter it again.

If you can access an AirPort network but can't access the Internet, see "I Can't Access the Internet Through AirPort Even Though I Can Connect to the AirPort Network" in the "Troubleshooting" section at the end of this chapter.

You can use the AirPort menu on the menu bar to control AirPort in several ways, including the following:

- **Measure the signal strength of the connection**—The "waves" emanating from the AirPort icon show the relative strength of the signal your Mac is receiving. As long as you see two or more waves, the signal you are receiving is plenty strong.

- **Turn AirPort on or off**—You can disconnect your Mac from the AirPort network and disable AirPort services by selecting Turn AirPort Off.

- **Choose a different AirPort network from the list of available networks**—When you do so, you are prompted to enter the password for that network—unless you have saved the password to your keychain. Do so and you will move onto to the network you select.

NOTE

> Some AirPort networks are hidden and do not broadcast their identities. To join such a network, you must know the name and password of the network you want to join. To join a hidden network, select Other on the AirPort menu on the menu bar, enter the name and password for the network, and click OK.

- **Create a computer-to-computer network**—When you select Create Network, you can create a network between two or more AirPort-equipped Macs. In the Computer to Computer dialog box, enter the name and password of the network you are creating, select the channel you want to use, and then click OK. Other users can select the network on their AirPort menus (of course, you need to provide the password for your network to those users if you require one). When your Mac is hosting a computer-to-computer network, the AirPort icon changes to a Mac "inside" a quarter circle to show that you are in the computer-to-computer mode. To switch to another AirPort network, select

The Channel you choose for a network controls the frequency of the signal used to create an AirPort network. If you have trouble connecting to other machines over the network you create, try a different channel.

When you create and use a computer-to-computer network, other AirPort connections, such as the one you use to connect to the Internet, are deselected and therefore can't be used.

To require and configure a password for the network, click Show Options in the Computer to Computer dialog box.

TIP

> Computer-to-computer networks are a great way to play network games. You can create an AirPort network and host a game. Other users can connect to the network and join the game by selecting your network using their AirPort controls.

■ **Open Internet Connect to control the Internet connection**—You can select Open Internet Connect to open the Internet Connect application to control the connection you are using via AirPort. You can turn AirPort on or off, select the network you want to use, see the strength of the signal your machine is receiving, and so on (see Figure 14.12). For example, if your base station connects to the Internet over a dial-up connection, click the Disconnect button to disconnect the base station from the Internet. To connect again manually, click the Connect button.

Figure 14.12
You can also control an AirPort connection to the Net by using the Internet Connect application.

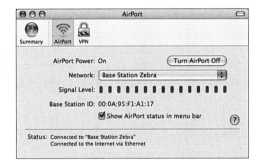

NOTE

To use Internet Connect to control an AirPort network, click the AirPort button on the Internet Connect toolbar. Internet Connect works for an AirPort connection very similarly to how it works for a dial-up connection.

If you are getting no signal or a weak signal from the AirPort network you want to join, see "Weak Signal" in the "Troubleshooting" section at the end of this chapter.

Using AirPort is a great way to quickly create and use wireless networks. After you have connected to the Net without wires (especially when roaming with a PowerBook or iBook), you won't want to settle for anything else.

Although this chapter has focused on using AirPort to access the Internet, an AirPort connection works just like any other network connection (such as an Ethernet connection). For example, you can access the files on another machine over an AirPort network just as you can with an Ethernet network.

→ For more information about configuring other network services; **see** Chapter 33, "Building and Using a Network," **p. 935**.

TROUBLESHOOTING

NO AIRPORT HARDWARE IS FOUND

When I launch the AirPort Setup Assistant, I see an error message stating that the required AirPort hardware can't be found.

The AirPort software requires that you have an AirPort card installed on the machine you use to configure a HAP base station. If an AirPort card is not found, the software won't run.

If you don't have an AirPort card installed in your Mac, you need to install one before running the AirPort Setup Assistant.

If you do have an AirPort card installed, it is not properly installed. Repeat the installation steps to ensure that the card is properly installed.

→ To learn how to install an AirPort card, **see** "Installing an AirPort Card," **p. 388**.

I CAN'T CONFIGURE MY BASE STATION MANUALLY

When I try to configure a base station manually, I get an error stating that the base station can't be configured.

This problem can occur for various reasons. First, try resetting the base station (see the next section). If that doesn't work, try opening the AirPort Setup Assistant and configuring the base station using the assistant. Then, go back into the AirPort Admin Utility and try to configure the base station again. This sometimes clears the error.

I DON'T KNOW THE BASE STATION PASSWORD

I can't access the base station because I don't know its password.

When you have trouble with an AirPort HAP, you can reset it to its factory defaults by inserting a paper clip into the reset button hole on the bottom or back of the unit. Hold down the button for 5 seconds and the base station is reset—all settings are returned to the default and the password becomes `public`.

WEAK SIGNAL

My AirPort signal strength is low. Or, I can't find the network to which I want to connect.

Two primary factors affect the strength of the AirPort signal your Mac receives from a base station (hardware or software) or from Macs providing a computer-to-computer network. One is the distance from the base station to your Mac; the other is the amount of interference in the area.

If your Mac is within 150 feet of the base station you want to use, there should be no trouble getting a strong enough signal. If you are at the edge of or beyond that range, move your Mac closer to the base station or move the base station closer to you. You can also try repositioning the base station because it can sometimes be affected by materials or other fields between it and your Mac.

If you are close to the base station but can't get a strong signal, try changing the frequency of the network in the event that it is being interfered with by another signal of some type.

→ To learn how to change an AirPort network's frequency, **see** "Configuring a Base Station Manually," **p. 378**.

If you use an AirPort Extreme base station with an antenna port, you can add an antenna to extend its range. You can also daisy-chain base stations together.

→ To learn how to use WDS, **see** "Making AirPort Go Farther," **p. 396**.

I CAN'T ACCESS THE INTERNET THROUGH AIRPORT EVEN THOUGH I CAN CONNECT TO THE AIRPORT NETWORK

My Mac is connected to an AirPort network, but I can't access the Internet.

If you are connecting to the Internet through a HAP, the most likely cause is that the access point has lost its Internet connection. Use some means to confirm that Internet services are available to the base station, such as by using a machine connected independently or calling your service provider. If services are available, use the AirPort Admin Utility to check its configuration to ensure that it is correct. If all else fails, reset the access point.

If none of these steps works and you have a broadband modem connected to the base station that provides DHCP services, use the following steps to attempt to reset the connection:

1. Unplug the modem for at least 20 seconds, and then plug it back in again. This forces the modem to get a new address.
2. Reset the base station by pressing its reset button for 5 seconds.
3. Open the AirPort Setup Assistant and select the Join an Existing Network option.
4. Follow the onscreen instructions to update the base station.

MAC OS X TO THE MAX: MAKING THE MOST OF AIRPORT

AirPort is an amazingly powerful yet easy-to-use technology. In the section, you learn a couple of tricks to make the most of it.

USING A GRAPHITE AIRPORT BASE STATION TO SHARE AN INTERNET CONNECTION WITH A WIRED NETWORK

AirPort enables you to easily share an Internet connection among AirPort-equipped machines. However, you can also use an AirPort base station to share an Internet account among machines that are connected to it via a wired network, such as an Ethernet network. You can do this because the base station is actually a DHCP server.

→ To learn more about DHCP servers, **see** Chapter 34, "Sharing an Internet Connection," **p. 973**.

Snow and AirPort Extreme base stations include a LAN port to which you can attach a wired network. These base stations provide services to the wired network automatically and no further configuration is required.

However, the original Graphite base station did not have this additional port and therefore has to be configured to act as a bridge between an Ethernet and AirPort network.

To configure an original Graphite AirPort HAP as a DHCP server, use steps similar to those you used to manually configure the AirPort HAP earlier in this chapter. On the Network tab, check the following boxes: "Ethernet client computers also share a single IP address (using NAT)" and "Enable DHCP server on Ethernet." Update the base station settings by clicking the Update button. Any machines set to use a DHCP server can then access the Internet through the AirPort HAP whether they connect to it via AirPort or Ethernet.

If you want AirPort-connected machines to be capable of accessing devices on an Ethernet network, such as printers, check the Enable AirPort to Ethernet Bridging check box.

→ To configure an AirPort HAP, **see** "Configuring a Base Station Manually," **p. 378**.

MAKING AIRPORT GO FARTHER

AirPort provides large range in most circumstances, and a single base station can usually provide coverage for an entire house easily.

NOTE

The original PowerBook G4s have a very poor internal antenna and often have trouble connecting in the same location as other machines, such as iMacs.

However, there are a couple of ways you can extend the range of an AirPort network to make it cover an even larger area.

If you use an AirPort Extreme base station with an Antenna Port, you can plug an external antenna into this port to increase the base station's range by a significant amount. There are several third-party antennas available; check out the Apple Store (store.apple.com) to get more information about them.

You can also link AirPort Extreme base stations together wirelessly so that the signal is rebroadcast from one base station to the next. You can continue this chain of base stations to extend a network over a very large area. This is called a *wireless distribution system (WDS)*. Following are the general steps to create a WDS:

1. Configure one base station to connect to the Internet.

2. Open the AirPort Admin Utility, select that base station, and click Configure.

3. Click the WDS tab (see Figure 14.13).

Figure 14.13
Using WDS, you can dramatically extend the range of an AirPort network.

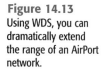

4. Check the "Enable this base station as a WDS" check box and select "main base station" on the pop-up menu. For other base stations, choose the appropriate type for the base station that you are configuring. A *remote* base station shares the Internet connection of the main base station. A *relay* base station shares the main base station's Internet connection and can also share its connection with additional base stations.

5. Check the "Allow wireless clients on this base station" check box.

6. Click the Add Base Station button, which is the plus sign next to the list of base stations. The Base Station Selection sheet will appear (see Figure 14.14). The list of available base stations that can communicate with the main base station will appear at the top of the sheet.

Figure 14.14
Use this sheet to select a base station to add to the WDS you are creating.

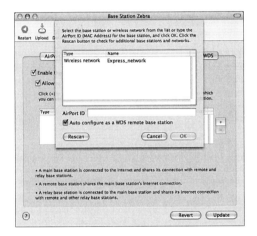

7. Choose the base station you want to add to the WDS. Its ID should be configured automatically; if not, enter it (this ID is located on the base station).

8. Check the "Auto configure as a WDS remove base station" check box.

9. Click OK to return to the Base Station window; the base station you added is shown on the list.

10. Repeat steps 6–9 to add other base stations to the WDS.

11. Click Update. The Admin Utility selects and connects to each base station. As it does, you must enter the appropriate passwords. When the process is complete, you see a sheet that provides a status for each base station. If the WDS setup was successful, you can use that base station as part of the WDS.

After you have configured the WDS, you can place the base stations on it in various locations throughout an area to increase the coverage. You can then set machines to use the base station that is closest to their locations.

14

WORKING WITH AN AIRPORT EXPRESS BASE STATION

A Airport Express base station is a small AirPort base station that is designed to be mobile and also offers some other features not found in the larger base stations (see Figure 14.15).

Figure 14.15
Apple's Express base station delivers big wireless features in a small package.

In addition to being able to provide an AirPort network, you can connect speakers to the Express Audio port to broadcast music from iTunes using the AirTunes feature. You can also store up to five profiles for an Express base station and switch between them easily. Because it's so small, you can take an Express with you and set up a wireless network anywhere you go, such as a hotel room. Plus, at $129, the Express is less expensive than the full-size base station.

> **TIP**
>
> An Express is a great addition to an AirPort network to extend its range using the WDS feature. It costs only slightly more than some antennas but offers many more features.

The Express does have two limitations. One is that it doesn't include a dial-up modem so you can't use it to share a dial-up Internet connection. The other is that it has only one Ethernet port so you can't connect both a broadband modem and an Ethernet network.

Other than these two limitations, you can configure and use an Express just like the larger base station.

USING EMAIL

INTRODUCING THE ADDRESS BOOK AND MAIL

In today's world, email is an essential form of communication for just about everyone. Mac OS X includes two powerful applications that enable you to send, receive, and manage your email: Address Book and Mail. As its name implies, Address Book enables you to manage all sorts of contact information. Mail is an email application that provides many powerful features rivaling any other email application.

SETTING UP AND USING AN ADDRESS BOOK

Mac OS X includes the Address Book application, in which you can store all your contact information. The most obvious use for this information is within Mail, but other applications can access the Address Book as well. This is useful because it enables you to use a single contact database for other applications that use information about your contacts, such as iChat. You can store as much information as you want, and you can customize each entry in the Address Book as much as you like. You can also print Address Book information in more ways under version 10.4 than you could under previous versions.

> **TIP**
>
> If you enter a website address for a contact, you can access that website from within Safari's Address Book tab. You'll learn more about this in Chapter 16, "Surfing the Web."

Address Book is based on *virtual cards*, or *vCards*. A vCard is an electronic information card that you can drag and drop between applications to transfer the information contained on that card. You can also share vCards with other users to exchange information. For example, you can drag someone else's vCard onto your Address Book to quickly add that person's information to your list of contacts.

> **TIP**
>
> Address Book is not the only application that can work with vCards. Many other applications can use vCards. For example, Microsoft Entourage can read vCards, so you can provide your vCard to someone who uses that application and that person can easily add your contact information to her contact database. Microsoft Outlook, the dominant email, calendar, and contact information application on Windows computers, also uses vCards.

USING THE ADDRESS BOOK

When you open the Address Book, you will see that its window consists of three columns. The first two columns are Group and Name. The Group column shows the groups you have created, and the Name column lists each card in your Address Book. The third column is the Card column, which shows the card that is selected in the Name column (see Figure 15.1). Before you add any contact information, your Address Book includes a card for you and one for Apple. You can build your Address Book over time so that it includes all your contacts.

15

> The contact information entered for you is whatever you provided when you registered your copy of Mac OS X. If you entered a username and password for an Apple account when you installed Mac OS X, your contact information is retrieved from that as well.

View columns and card
View card
Action pop-up menu
Available groups
Your card
Search tool

Figure 15.1
The Address Book is a powerful tool you can use to manage all your contact information.

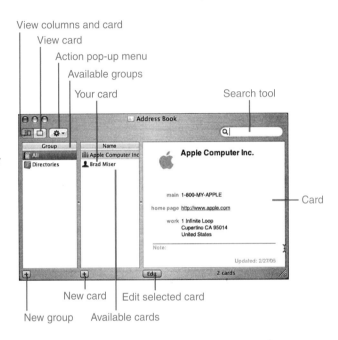

Card

New group   Available cards
New card   Edit selected card

> If you use a Bluetooth-equipped Mac, a third button is shown to the right of the View Card button. This button enables you to pair your Address Book with a Bluetooth-capable cell phone. This lets you keep contact information on your phone synchronized with that stored in your Address Book.

In the upper-left corner of each card is an image well that you can use to place an image for your contact, such as a photo of the person for whom you created the card or the logo for a company (such as the apple for Apple). You can add a photo to a card by dragging a photo onto this well. The photo you use can be a JPEG, GIF, TIFF, or PDF file and should be 64×64 pixels.

The card marked with a silhouette is your card. This is important because your card can be used to add your contact information in various locations automatically.

> When you send email to or receive email using Mail from a contact who has an image in the related Address Book card, that image appears in the email.

WORKING WITH ADDRESS BOOK CONTACT INFORMATION

Although Address Book provides the standard functions you expect, such as email addresses and phone numbers, the information in Address Book is dynamic. For example, when a contact's card includes an email address, you can click the address to send the contact email. When you include a URL for a contact, you can click it to visit that web page, and when the contact has a .Mac account, you can open the contact's iDisk. You can also use the contact's card to chat with the person using iChat and visit the contact's website from within Safari. Address Book information is also accessible in many other places, such as when you are faxing documents using Mac OS X's built-in fax capability.

To locate information within Address Book itself, you can browse your contacts or search for specific contacts.

To browse your contacts, perform the following steps:

1. Open the Address Book by clicking the Address Book icon on the Dock or by opening the Applications folder and double-clicking the Address Book icon.

2. Scroll in the Name column to find the contact you are interested in.

3. Select the contact whose information you want to view. The contact's card is displayed, and you can see the person's information.

The information in Address Book is extremely flexible. The fields displayed for each contact can be configured individually. When you display a card, only the fields that contain information are displayed. For example, compare Figure 15.1 and Figure 15.2 to see how Address Book has reconfigured the card display for cards with different amounts of information.

Figure 15.2
Come now, you didn't really expect me to include my real phone number and address in this book did you? (The email address is real.)

You can also search to locate a contact's information:

1. Open the Address Book by clicking the Address Book icon on the Dock or by opening the Applications folder and double-clicking the Address Book icon.

2. Enter text in the Search tool. You can enter text found in any of the contact's information, including name, address, home page, and so on. As you type, the list of names shown in the Name column is narrowed so it includes only those contacts whose data contains the text you enter.

3. Select the contact whose information you want to view. The contact's card is displayed, and you can see the contact's information.

To view all your contacts again, click the X button that appears in the Search tool when you perform a search.

When working with the Address Book, you can easily do the following tasks:

NOTE

When you click a data label, such as an email or physical address, the pop-up menu that results has different commands for different items. For example, when you open an email address's pop-up menu, one of the options is Send Email. However, if you click a physical address, you see different options including Map Of, which enables you to retrieve a map for the address.

- **Send an email**—To send an email to one of your contacts, view the contact to which you want to send an email. Then click the label next to the email address to which you want to send an email. A pop-up menu appears. Select Send Email (see Figure 15.3). Your default email application will open and a new message addressed to the contact will be created.

Figure 15.3
Sending an email from Address Book can be done with the Send Email command.

- **Visit the contact's website or home page**—Click the label next to a website you want to visit. From the resulting pop-up menu, select Go to Web Site. Or, click a URL shown on the card. Your default web browser will open and you'll move to the website.
- **View a map to an address**—Click the label next to an address and select Map Of from the resulting pop-up menu. Your default web browser will open and move to the Map Quest website. A map to the selected address is then displayed.
- **Chat**—Select iChat to use the iChat application to text, audio, or video chat with the contact.
- **Open an iDisk**—If the contact has a .Mac account and you have configured his .Mac email address, you can open the person's iDisk by clicking the label next to the .Mac email address and selecting Open iDisk. The contact's iDisk will open in a new Finder window.

15

- **Visit a HomePage website**—If the contact has a .Mac account and has a HomePage website, select the Visit HomePage command to go there.
- **Scroll through your contacts**—Select Card, Next Card (or press ⌘-]) or select Card, Previous Card (or press ⌘-[) to browse through your contacts.
- **Edit your contacts**—Click the Edit button to move into the Edit mode (more on this later).

> **TIP**
>
> Explore the contextual menus for various card elements along with the Action pop-up to discover even more Address Book commands.

You can change the view of the Address Book to show only cards by clicking the View Card Only button; selecting View, Card Only; or pressing ⌘-2. The window collapses down to the card only. You can add cards, edit cards, or browse cards from the collapsed window.

Show the other columns again by selecting View, Card and Columns or by pressing ⌘-1.

CONFIGURING YOUR ADDRESS BOOK

You can configure several aspects of the Address Book by using its Preferences dialog box (see Figure 15.4). To open this dialog box, select Address Book, Preferences or press ⌘-,.

Figure 15.4
Maximize the benefits of your Address Book by customizing it using the Preferences dialog box.

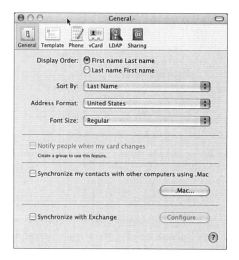

CONFIGURING ADDRESS BOOK GENERAL PREFERENCES

Using the General tab of the Preferences dialog box, you can configure the following preferences:

- **Display Order**—Click the "First name Last name" radio button to have Address Book display contact information in the first name, last name format. Click the "Last name First name" radio button to display contacts in the last name, first name format.

- **Sort criterion**—Select First Name or Last Name on the Sort By pop-up menu to have Address Book sort the Cards column by that criteria.

- **Address Format**—Use the Address Format pop-up menu to select the address format you want to use by country.

- **Font Size**—Use the Font Size pop-up menu to select the Regular, Large, or Extra Large font size for the information shown in the Address Book window.

- **Notifications about changes to your card**—If you want contacts to be notified when your contact information changes and want to send them your revised information, create at least one group containing the contacts whom you want to be notified (you'll learn how to do this later in this chapter) and check the "Notify people when my card changes" check box. Whenever you change something on your own vCard, you can notify people in the group by selecting File, Send Updates. In the resulting Send Updates dialog box, select the groups to which you want to send the update by checking their check boxes; then enter a subject and text for the message and click Send. The message you send includes your updated vCard that the recipients can use to replace the outdated version of your card in their own contact lists.

- **Synchronization via .Mac**—If you use more than one Mac and have a .Mac account, you can keep your Address Book synchronized on all your computers. Check the "Synchronize my contacts with other computers using .Mac" and click the .Mac button. You'll move to the .Mac pane of the System Preferences application, where you can configure your options.

→ To learn how to use .Mac to synchronize information, **see** "Using .Mac to Synchronize Important Information on Multiple Macs," **p. 512**.

- **Synchronization with Exchange**—Many organizations use an Exchange server to provide email and contact information services to the network.

You can synchronize your Address Book with the information stored on an Exchange server by doing the following:

1. Check the "Synchronize with Exchange" check box.

2. Click Configure. In the resulting dialog box, enter your username, password, and the Outlook Web Access server address with which you want to synchronize your Address Book.

3. If you want to synchronize this information every hour, check the "Synchronize every hour" check box.

4. Click OK; information from the Exchange server is added to your Address Book and your Address Book information is added to the Exchange server.

CAUTION

For synchronization to work, you must enter the address for Outlook Web Access server rather than the Exchange server address itself. Address Book uses the web access address to retrieve your information. If you don't know what this address is, contact the

continues

continued

15

> administrator for the Exchange server you are trying to access. To confirm that you are using the right server address, access the address through Safari. If you can access your email this way, you should be able to synchronize Address Book with your Exchange information.

CUSTOMIZING YOUR ADDRESS BOOK CARD TEMPLATE

You can customize the information and layout of the cards in your Address Book.

Open the Address Book Preferences window and click the Template button to open the Template preferences pane (see Figure 15.5).

Figure 15.5
You can use Address Book's Template preferences to design the cards in your Address Book.

> **TIP**
>
> You can also edit the card template by selecting Card, Add Field, Edit Template.

To change the layout of and the information contained on the cards in your Address Book, you can do any of the following:

- **Add or remove fields**—Use the Add Field pop-up menu at the top of the dialog box to add or remove fields from the cards in your Address Book. To add a field, select it on the menu. The field will be added and a check mark will be placed next to the field on the pop-up menu. To remove a field, select that field (which is marked with a check mark) on the pop-up menu; it will be removed from the card.

> **TIP**
>
> The fields that are grayed out on the menu are already on the card. To remove them, you use the minus sign next to the field as explained in the next bullet.

- **Remove fields**—Click the minus sign next to a field to remove it from the card.

- **Add more fields of the same kind**—Click the plus sign next to a field to add another field of the same type to the card.

- **Change a field's label**—Use the pop-up menu next to a field's label to change that label. You can select one of the labels on the menu or select Custom and create a custom menu.

Using these tools, you can customize the contents of cards and the specific fields they contain as much as you like. Because Address Book displays only those fields that contain data (when you view a card), you don't need to be concerned about having too many fields on your cards.

CONFIGURING ADDRESS BOOK'S PHONE NUMBER FORMAT

You can change the phone number format used in Address Book by using the following steps:

1. Open the Phone pane of the Address Book Preferences dialog box.
2. To have Address Book format phone numbers automatically, check the "Automatically format phone numbers" check box.
3. If you do check the check box mentioned in the previous step, use the Formats pop-up menu to select the format that should be used.

TIP

> You can create custom phone number formats by clicking the down arrow next to the Formats pop-up menu, which opens a pane showing the configured formats. Select one and click Edit to change it. To add a format, click the plus sign. To remove a format, select it and click the minus sign.

CHOOSING VCARD PREFERENCES

On the vCard pane of the Address Book Preferences dialog box, you can set the following preferences:

- **vCard Format**—Click the 3.0 radio button to use the newer vCard format. Click the 2.1 radio button to use a version of the previous vCard standard.

- **Encoding**—Use the Encoding pop-up menu to choose the encoding you want to use, such as Western (Mac OS Roman).

- **Enable private "Me" card**—You can use this option to hide information on your vCard so that information won't be exported when you provide your vCard to someone else. To do so, check the "Enable private "Me" card" check box. Edit your card and uncheck the check boxes for the data that you don't want to include on your vCard when you share it.

- **Export notes in vCards**—If you check the "Export notes in vCards" check box, when you export vCards, any notes you have entered for a card are exported with the card. If you put information in the notes on cards, be careful with this one!

15

Address Book can also work with Lightweight Directory Access Protocol (LDAP) directories that can provide address information over a network. Such directories appear when you select the Directories icon in the Group column. You can add directories to your Address Book by using the LDAP tab of the Address Book Preferences dialog box. Explaining how to use such directories is beyond the scope of this chapter. If you need help, see the administrator of the network that is providing one or more LDAP directories to you.

SHARING YOUR ADDRESS BOOK WITH .MAC USERS

You can share your Address Book information with other people who use .Mac. To do so, perform the following steps:

1. Open the Sharing pane of the Address Book Preferences dialog box.

2. Check the "Share your Address Book" check box.

3. Click the Add button (+). The information in your Address Book will appear in the resulting sheet.

4. Select the people who use .Mac with whom you'd like to share your Address Book and click OK. You'll move back to the Sharing pane and the people whom you selected will be shown in the list.

5. Check the Allow Editing check box for those people whom you want to be able to change information in your Address Book.

6. Select the people you have added and click the Send Invite button. An email will be created and addressed to those people. This email will contain the link they need to be able to access your Address Book information.

T I P

To remove someone from the list of people who can access your Address Book, select his name on the list and click the Remove button (-).

ADDING ADDRESSES TO YOUR ADDRESS BOOK

Obviously, before an address book is of much value, it has to have some information in it. There are several ways to get information into your Address Book:

- Edit your own address card.
- Add cards manually.
- Add a card from an email message you have received.
- Import a contact's vCard.
- Import address information from an email application.

EDITING YOUR OWN ADDRESS CARD

The first time you open Address Book, a card is created for you automatically based on the information you entered when you installed Mac OS X. If you entered one or more email addresses when you installed Mac OS X, those addresses are included in your address card automatically. You should edit this card, mostly so that you can easily send your contact information to other people simply by sending them your vCard.

NOTE

Another place your card's information is used is for Safari's AutoFill feature. When you complete a form on the Web, your card's information is used if you choose to enable Safari's AutoFill feature.

You can jump to your card by selecting Card, Go to My Card. Your card will be selected. Your card's icon has a silhouette next to your name. When you select your name in the Name column, your card appears; its image well is marked with the text me.

TIP

You can export a vCard by viewing it and selecting File, Export vCard.

You can export your own card, or any other card for that matter, as a vCard by selecting the card, opening its contextual menu, and selecting Export vCard. Select a location, name the vCard, and click Save.

If you want to create a different card for yourself for some reason, you can create a new card and enter your contact information in it. After you have created your new card, select it and select Card, Make This My Card (this is disabled if you have already selected your card).

You can edit your own card using the same steps you use to edit any other cards (editing cards is explained shortly).

ADDING ADDRESSES MANUALLY

As you might expect, you can add people to your Address Book by inputting their information manually.

To manually add an address, do the following:

1. Click the Plus button in the Name column; select File, New Card; or press ⌘-N to see a new, empty address card. The fist name is highlighted by default so you can edit it immediately (see Figure 15.6).
2. Input the first name.
3. Press Tab to move to and select the Last field, and then enter the contact's last name.
4. Press Tab to move to and select the Company field, and then enter the person's company information if applicable.
5. If you want the company to be listed above the name, check the Company check box.

Figure 15.6
This is a new card, ready for the contact's information.

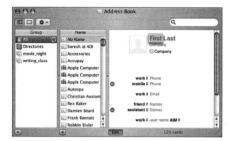

6. Press Tab to move to and select the first contact information, which is work by default.

7. Click the menu icon to reveal the label pop-up menu (see Figure 15.7).

Figure 15.7
You use this pop-up menu to label contact information.

8. Select the label for the contact information, such as home.

NOTE

Two entries on the label pop-up menu require some explanation. The selection called other inserts the label `other`. If you select Custom, you can create a custom label for a field.

9. Enter the contact information, such as a work phone number if you chose the label work.

10. Continue tabbing to each field on the card, selecting the label for that field and editing the information to fill in the rest of the card.

11. If the contact has a home page, select the home page field and enter the URL of the home page with which you want to associate the contact.

12. If you want to remove fields from the card, click the Remove Field button (the minus sign) next to the field you want to remove. The field is removed from the current card only.

13. If you want to add more fields of the same type to the card, click the Add Field button (+) next to one of the existing fields. After you have added a field, you can edit it in the same way as the default fields. Similar to removing a card, when you add a field to the card, it is added on the current card only.

→ To learn how to add a field to all cards in the Address Book, **see** "Customizing Your Address Book Card Template," **p. 406**.

14. If you have an image you want to associate with the contact, drag the image onto the contact's image well. (You can add images in the usual graphics formats, such as JPEG or TIFF.) When you are over the image well, the cursor changes to a green circle with a plus sign in it. Release the mouse button and you see the image in a new window (see Figure 15.8).

Figure 15.8
Okay, I don't really look like Gandalf, so sue me.

15. Use the slider at the bottom of the window to crop the image.

16. When the image appears as you want it, click the Set button.

> **TIP**
>
> When you are editing a card, you can double-click an image or the image well to open the image editing window. You can also select Card, Choose Custom Image to open the same window. In that window, click the Choose button to move to and select an image to display in the window. If you have a camera, such as an iSight camera, connected to your Mac, click the Take Video Snapshot button to capture the image being taken by the camera.

17. Add notes for the card by clicking next to the Note label and typing the note.

18. Click the Edit button to move out of the Edit mode. Your new card is now ready to use (see Figure 15.9).

> **NOTE**
>
> When you edit your own card and have the "Notify people when my card changes" preference selected, you are prompted to send a message notifying others that your card has changed.

Figure 15.9
You can create an address card for anyone you know (or even for those you don't know!).

ADDING AN ADDRESS FROM AN EMAIL MESSAGE

You can create a contact in your Address Book by adding the sender's information from an email message to it. To add a contact from an email that you receive in the Mail application, do the following:

1. Use Mail to open an email message from the person whom you want to add to your Address Book.

2. Select Message, Add Sender to Address Book (or press ⌘-Y). The person's name and email address are entered on a new address card.

USING vCARDS TO ADD INFORMATION TO YOUR ADDRESS BOOK

The benefit to using a vCard is that you can add a lot of information about a contact with very little work on your part. When you receive a vCard from someone, use the following steps to add that person's address card to your Address Book:

1. Drag the vCard onto the Name column in Address Book.

2. Click OK when prompted. The vCard will be added to your Address Book.

3. Select the card and click the Edit button.

4. Edit the information as needed (you learn how to edit cards later in this chapter).

NOTE

> When you import vCards to your Address Book, the group called Last Import always contains the cards you most recently added.

NOTE

> vCard files have the filename extension .vcf (virtual card file).

IMPORTING ADDRESSES FROM ANOTHER APPLICATION

If you have used another email application in the past, you probably have an Address Book or Contact database in that application. If that application supports vCards, you can easily export vCards from the application and then add them to the Address Book.

As an example of how this works, the following steps show you how to export contacts from Microsoft's Entourage email application and then add those contacts to the Address Book. Because Entourage supports vCards, you can create vCards for your Entourage contacts and then import those contacts into the Address Book:

1. Create a folder to temporarily store the vCards you export from Entourage.
2. Open Entourage.
3. Click the Address Book button to move into the Address Book mode.
4. Drag the contacts for whom you want to create vCards from the Entourage window onto the folder you created in step 1, and drop them in that folder. A vCard is created for each of your Entourage contacts.

> **NOTE**
>
> If you drag an Entourage group to create a vCard, a text clipping file is created instead. You need to re-create your groups within Address Book.

5. Open the Address Book.
6. Drag the vCards from the folder in which you stored them onto the Name column. The contacts you added are now available for you to use and edit.

It is unlikely that all the information in your current address book or contact list will make it into the Address Book application. For example, if you have added Category information for your Entourage contact list, that information is not imported into the Address Book. After you have imported contacts into the Address Book, you should check them over so you know exactly what information made it in, and what didn't. If you lost any important information, you might have to spend some time re-creating it within Address Book.

> **NOTE**
>
> When you import addresses into your Address Book and it finds duplicates, you have the opportunity to review the addresses you are adding so you can remove the duplicated entries. You can also merge the multiple entries together.

EDITING ADDRESSES IN YOUR ADDRESS BOOK

To edit an address in your Address Book, use the following steps:

1. In Address Book, view the card containing the information you want to edit.
2. Click the Edit button. Address Book moves into the Edit mode. The first name is selected and is ready to edit.
3. Use the same steps to change the information on the card that you do to create a card (see the earlier section on creating cards for the details).

TIP

You can use the Add Field button on the Template pane of the Address Book Preferences dialog box to add fields to the card. You can also add fields by using the Card, Add Field command. On the Add Field menu, you can select the type of field you want to add.

Many of the data fields have pop-up menus containing the data field's label. You can open these menus and select a new label for that field. The changes you make by doing this affect only the current address card; this means you can configure the information for a specific card independent of other cards. For example, if you know someone who has three mobile phones, you can select mobile as the label for three of the fields on that person's address card. You can also select Custom to create custom field labels for existing or new fields.

You can quickly swap the last name with the first name for the card by viewing the card and selecting Card, Swap First/Last Name.

To remove an image from a card, view the card and select Card, Clear Custom Image.

If you don't want a field's data to appear on a card, select the data and delete it. The data is replaced with the type of data it is, such as Email for an email address. The data does not appear on the card when it is viewed.

NOTE

After you add a field, you can't remove it. You can only delete its data so that it doesn't appear on the card any more.

To delete a card from the Address Book, select it and press Delete. Click Yes in the resulting prompt and the card will be deleted.

TIP

You can view a card in an independent window by viewing it and selecting Card, Open in Separate Window (or by pressing ⌘-I).

WORKING WITH ADDRESS GROUPS

Address groups (just called *groups* in Address Book) enable you to email multiple people using a single address. Working with an address group is similar to working with other address cards in your Address Book. Creating an address group is simple, as you can see in the following steps:

1. Click the New Group button, which is the plus sign in the Group column; select File, New Group; or press Shift-⌘-N. You will see a new group in the Group column, and the name of the group will be selected and ready to edit.

2. Change the group's name to something meaningful and press Return.

3. Click All in the Group column to view all the cards in the Address Book.

4. Search or browse for the cards you want to add to your Address Book.

5. Drag the cards you want to be included in the group onto the group's icon in the Group column. Those cards will become part of the group.

> **TIP**
>
> You can create a new group and add selected address cards to it by first selecting the cards you want to place in the new group and selecting File, New Group From Selection. A new group is created and includes the cards you selected.

You can view a group by selecting it on the Group column. The Name column shows only those cards that are included in the group. You work with the cards in a group just as you do individual cards. For example, you can edit a card, use it to send email to that individual, and so on.

To remove a card from a group, view the group, select the card you want to remove, and press Delete. After you confirm the action, the card is removed from the group. However, the card still exists in the Address Book.

You can also export a group as a vCard. Select the group, hold down the Control key, click the mouse button, and select Export Group vCard. Select a location, name the card, and click Save. You can use the group's vCard just like vCards for individuals.

If any of the cards you add to a group includes more than one email address, you can edit the mailing list for the group to set the specific addresses that are used:

1. Select the group for which you want to configure the mailing list.

2. Select Edit, Edit Distribution List. The Edit Distribution List dialog box will appear.

3. Select the email address you want to use for an individual by clicking it. The address that will be used appears in bold; other addresses are grayed out to show that they won't be used.

> **TIP**
>
> You can change all the email addresses used for the group to be of the same kind by selecting a type on the Change All Labels pop-up menu. For example, to use only home email addresses, select home.

4. Click OK. When you send a message to the group, the addresses you selected are used.

> **TIP**
>
> You can back up your Address Book by selecting File, Backup Address Book. If you want to return to the version of the database you have backed up, select File, Revert to Address Book Backup.

TIP

You can use the Smart Groups feature to have Address Book populate a group based on criteria you define rather than you manually placing contacts in the group. Smart groups work just like other smart objects, such as smart playlists in iTunes or smart photo albums in iPhoto.

ADDRESSING EMAIL

There are several ways in which you can address email to people in your Address Book:

- View the contact to whom you want to send a message and click the label for the email address you want to use. Select Send Email on the pop-up menu.
- Drag the contact's vCard to the To, Cc, or Bcc box of a Mail email message.
- Control-click a group and select "Send email to *groupname*," where *groupname* is the name of the group you clicked.
- Drag a group's vCard to the To, Cc, or Bcc box of a Mail email message.

NOTE

When you send email from the Address Book, the email application used is your default email application.

PRINTING YOUR ADDRESS BOOK

As you work with your Address Book, you might want to print it to take it with you, to print address labels, and so on. When you print from the Address Book, you have the following four layout options:

- **Envelopes**—This option prints envelopes for your contacts.
- **Lists**—This option prints the cards you select in a list. You can select the attributes that are included on the list for each card.
- **Pocket Address Book**—This option prints a small version of your Address Book that is designed to be carried.
- **Mailing Labels**—This prints the cards as mailing labels.

To print the Address Book as a list, use the following steps:

1. Select the cards you want to print. To print the entire Address Book, select All in the Groups column.
2. Select File, Print or press ⌘-P. The Print dialog box will open.
3. On the Style pop-up menu, select Lists.
4. Configure the printer, presets, paper size, and orientation just as you do with any print job.
5. Select the attributes you want included for each card by checking their check boxes. You will see a preview of the list in the left side of the dialog box.

6. Select the font size on the Font Size pop-up menu.

7. Print the list.

To print mailing labels, use the following steps:

1. Select the cards you want to print. To print the entire Address Book, select All in the Groups column.

2. Select File, Print or press ⌘-P. The Print dialog box opens.

3. On the Style pop-up menu, select Mailing Labels.

4. Click the Layout tab.

5. If you are printing on standard Avery or DYMO labels, select the label type on the Page pop-up menu. If you are creating a custom label, select Define Custom instead; in the Layout Name sheet that appears, enter the name of the label you are creating and click OK. As you make choices, a preview of the labels will appear in the left pane of the dialog box.

6. If you selected a standard label, select the specific label number you are printing on the label number drop-down list that appears next to the Page pop-up menu. If you selected Define Custom in the previous step, use the controls under the Layout tab to design the label, such as by defining the margins, number of rows and columns, and the gutters.

7. Click the Label tab.

8. Select the group for which you want to print labels on the Addresses pop-up menu. If you want to print labels for all addresses, select All.

9. On the "Print in" pop-up menu, select how you want the labels to be sorted. The options are Alphabetical Order and Postal Code Order.

10. If you want country to be included on the labels, check the "Print country" check box. If you don't want your own country to be included, check the "Except my country" check box.

11. Click the Color box and use the Color Picker to select the color of the text on the labels.

12. Drag an image into the image well to include that image on the labels or use the Image Set button to choose an image.

13. Click the Font Set button to open the Font panel and select the font you want to use on the labels.

14. Check the labels in the preview pane.

15. Print the labels.

15

USING THE ADDRESS BOOK WIDGET

You can also access your Address Book through the Address Book widget.

→ To learn how to use the Address Book widget, **see** "Using the Address Book Widget," **p. 163**.

SUBSCRIBING TO AN ADDRESS BOOK

If other .Mac users have shared their Address Book with you, you can subscribe to it to view or edit its information by using the following steps:

1. Select File, Subscribe to Address Book.

2. In the resulting sheet, enter the .Mac user's username and click OK. You'll be able to view the other user's Address Book information, and you can edit it if you have permission to do so.

CONFIGURING MAIL

Before you can start using Mail to work with your email, you need to configure the accounts it uses. If you entered account information in the Setup Assistant when you installed Mac OS X, those accounts are configured for you already. For example, if you set up or entered the information for your .Mac account in the Setup Assistant, your .Mac email account is configured in Mail.

If you are like most Mac users, you probably have more than one email address; you can use Mail to access any or all of them.

There are also several other areas that you don't necessarily have to configure before you begin using Mail, but I have included them in the section so that all the configuration information is together for your reference.

CONFIGURING GENERAL MAIL PREFERENCES

Using the General pane of the Mail preferences dialog box, you can configure the following preferences:

- **Default email application**—Use the "Default Email Reader" pop-up menu to select the email application you will use by default. If you want to use Mail, you don't need to make a selection on this menu. If you want to use another application, choose Select on the menu and use the resulting sheet to select the application you want to use instead of Mail.

- **Frequency of mail checking**—Use the "Check for new mail" pop-up menu to determine how often Mail checks for new mail. Select Manually to disable automatic checking or the frequency at which you want Mail to check for new email automatically, such as "Every 5 minutes" to have Mail check every 5 minutes.

- **Mail sounds**—Mail can play sounds for the following events: new mail received, mail error, and mail sent. You can choose the sound that is played when new mail is received by choosing the sound for that event on the "New mail sound" pop-up menu. To turn this sound off, choose None. To disable the sound for other events, uncheck the "Play sounds for other mail actions" check box.

TIP

> You can use custom mail sounds by selecting Add/Remove on the pop-up menu and selecting the custom sound you want to use. Mail will place the sound file you select in the `Library/Sounds` folder in your Home folder. You can then choose it on the pop-up menu in Mail and other applications, such as iChat.

- **iCal invitations**—Use the "Add invitations to iCal" pop-up menu to determine how Mail handles iCal invitations you receive. Select Automatically to have them added to your iCal calendar when you receive them, or select Never if you don't want them added to your calendar.

- **Downloads**—Use the Downloads Folder pop-up menu to determine where Mail stores file attachments in the email messages you receive. Leave the default Main Downloads folder selected, or choose Other and choose a different folder.

- **Remove unedited downloads**—Use the "Remove unedited downloads" pop-up menu to determine when Mail deletes file attachments that you haven't changed. The options are Never, When Mail Quits, and After Message is Deleted.

- **Sounds for other events**—If you want Mail to play sounds for all events, check the "Play sounds for other mail actions" check box. If you uncheck this check box, Mail plays a sound only when new email sound is received.

- **Indexing decrypted messages**—Using properly configured certificates, Mail can work with encrypted messages. If you configure Mail to do so, check the "Index decrypted messages for searching" check box to enable Mail to search these messages.

- **Synchronize**—If you use .Mac and have more than one Mac, you can keep your Mail information synchronized on each machine you use. Check the check boxes for the synchronization options you want to use ("Rules, Signatures, and Smart Mailboxes" and "Accounts") and then click the .Mac button. Use the resulting .Mac pane to configure the synchronization you want to use.

→ To learn how to use .Mac to synchronize information, **see** "Using .Mac to Synchronize Important Information on Multiple Macs," **p. 512**.

CONFIGURING EMAIL ACCOUNTS

The most basic configuration for Mail is the email accounts you are going to access with it. Before you get started, gather the following information for each mail account you want to configure in Mail:

15

- **Account type**—There are four types of email accounts with which Mail can work. A .Mac account is one provided by Apple's .Mac servers. A Post Office Protocol (POP) account is provided by most ISPs. An Internet Message Access Protocol (IMAP) is similar to a POP account but offers additional features, and an Exchange account is provided by an Exchange server, which is used on many business networks.

NOTE

When you use a .Mac email account with Mail, it is configured as an IMAP account. In Mail, it is treated as its own category because it is part of your .Mac account.

- **Your email address**—This should be self-explanatory.
- **Incoming mail server**— This is the address of the server that handles retrieving your email. For POP accounts, it often looks something like pop.isp.net.
- **Your email username**—This is your username for your email account, which might or might not be the same as your username for your Internet account. Typically, this is everything before the @ in your email address.
- **Your email password**—This is the password for your email account, which might or might not be the same as that of your Internet access account.
- **Outgoing email server or Simple Mail Transfer Protocol (SMTP) host**—This is the address of the server that handles sending your email.
- **Authentication**—You need to know whether your SMTP server uses authentication.
- **SMTP username**—This is the username for your SMTP server; it is usually the same as your email username, but it isn't always.
- **SMTP password**—Again, this is usually the same as your email password.

After you have gathered this information, you are ready to configure the email accounts. You can use the Accounts pane of the Preferences dialog box or the Add Account command.

ADDING ACCOUNTS USING PREFERENCES

To add email accounts to Mail using the Preferences option, do the following:

1. Launch Mail.
2. Select Mail, Preferences (or press ⌘-,).
3. Click the Accounts button to see the Accounts pane of the Preferences window (see Figure 15.10). This pane has three tabs: Account Information, Mailbox Behaviors, and Advanced. In the left part of the pane is the list of email accounts that are currently configured.
4. Click the Add Account button, which is the plus sign at the bottom of the list of accounts. The General Information sheet will appear.
5. Select the account type from the Account Type pop-up menu.
6. Enter a description of the account in the Description field.

7. Enter the rest of the information for the account including the full name and email address.

Figure 15.10
If you configured a .Mac account when you installed Mac OS X, your .Mac email account is configured in Mail automatically.

NOTE
> What you enter in the Full Name field is what appears next to your return email address shown in the Email Address data field. If a recipient uses Mail, he sees your full name instead of your email address.

8. Click Continue. The incoming Mail Server sheet will appear.

9. Enter the Incoming Mail Server, enter your username (typically everything before the @ in your email address) and password, and then click Continue. Mail will check the connection using the information you entered. If the information works, you'll see the Outgoing Mail Server sheet. If not, you'll need to correct it before you can move ahead.

10. Enter the SMTP server address for the account in the "Outgoing Mail Server" box. If an SMTP server is already configured, you can choose to use it by selecting it on the drop-down list.

11. If the SMTP server for the account uses authentication, check the Use Authentication check box and configure the User Name and Password fields in the sheet; the username and password might or might not be the same as those for the incoming mail server. Click Continue when you are finished configuring the outgoing mail server. Mail will check the connection to make sure it can communicate with the server. If it can, you'll see the Account Summary sheet, which means the account has been configured successfully. If not, you'll need to correct the configuration until it can communicate with the server.

12. Click Continue. You'll see the Conclusion sheet. Click Done if you are finished creating accounts, or click Create Another Account to start the process again.

After you have created one or more accounts, you'll return to the Account pane and the accounts you have configured will be shown in the left part of the pane. Next, configure mailbox behavior for each account.

15

Select the account you want to configure and click the Mailbox Behaviors tab. This tab provides several controls you can use to control how the account you are configuring behaves. The options you see depend on the type of account you are creating. For example, you see fewer options for a POP account than you do for the other three types. Because .Mac accounts are popular with many Mac users, you see the options you can configure for .Mac accounts in the following list (see Figure 15.11). You can configure the options on this tab for other account types in a similar way, although the specific options you have might be different:

- Use the check box in the Drafts area to determine whether messages are stored on the .Mac server when you are writing them. This causes email that you are writing to be saved on the .Mac server as you are writing it. If you write email offline, you don't want to select this. If you use a broadband connection to the Net, you can check the "Store draft messages on the server" check box to have your drafts stored online as you write them.

- Use the controls in the Sent area to determine whether sent messages are stored on the server and when sent messages are deleted. Usually, you don't want to save sent messages on the server because those messages count against your total storage allowance for your account. If you do want sent messages to be stored on the server, check the "Store sent messages on the server" check box. Then use the "Delete sent messages when" pop-up menu to select how often the sent messages will be deleted. The options are Never, One day old, One week old, One month old, or Quitting Mail.

- Use the Junk controls to configure how Mail handles messages that are classified as junk. Similar to the first two options, you can select to have junk mail stored on the server; if you select to allow this, use the pop-up menu to determine when junk mail is deleted from the server.

- Use the Trash controls to configure how trash is handled. If you want deleted messages to be moved to the Trash mail box, check the "Move deleted messages to the Trash mailbox" check box. If you want deleted messages to be stored on the server, check the "Store deleted messages on the server" check box, and to determine when deleted messages are actually erased, use the "Permanently erase deleted message when" pop-up menu. The options are Never, One day old, One week old, One month old, or Quitting Mail.

Configure these behaviors for each account using similar options.

TIP

You can also add a new account by selecting File, Add Account. The New Account Assistant will open and lead you through creating the account. The steps you use are the same as those you use when creating an account via the Preferences dialog box.

Finally, configure the Advanced options for each account using the following steps (again, these assume a .Mac account; other account types might have different options):

Figure 15.11
You can configure these special mailbox actions when using a .Mac mail account.

1. Select the Account you want to configure and click the Advanced tab. Just like the Mailbox Behaviors tab, the specific controls you see depend on the type of account you are configuring (see Figure 15.12).

Figure 15.12
These are the Advanced controls for a .Mac email account.

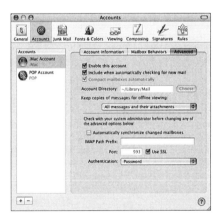

2. Use the "Enable this account"" check box to enable or disable the account. If you disable an account, it won't be used.

3. Check the ""Include when automatically checking for new mail"" check box if you want this account always included when Mail automatically checks for mail. If you uncheck this check box, you must manually check for mail for this account.

4. Use the "Keep copies of messages for offline viewing" pop-up menu to determine what Mail does with the messages it receives when you are not connected to the Internet. For example, if you select "All messages and their attachments," all your messages and any attachments they contain are downloaded to your Mac so you can view them even if you aren't connected to the Net. If you select "Only messages I've read," only the messages you have read are downloaded to your Mac. Choose "All messages, but not attachments" to download messages but not their attachments or "Don't keep copies of

any messages" if you don't want any information to be downloaded to your Mac (you'll have to be connected to the Internet to be able to read messages).

NOTE

> Other options are available at the bottom of the Advanced pane, but you aren't likely to use them unless you are specifically directed to do so by the administrator of the email system you are using.

5. Select another account or close the Preferences dialog box. You will be prompted to save your changes.

IMAP Accounts

One area in which an IMAP account (such as a .Mac account) is significantly different from a POP account is in how email is stored. Under an IMAP account (such as a .Mac email account), mail is always left on the server until you delete it manually. The benefit of this is that you can access that mail from different machines without forwarding it to each machine or having duplicate copies (on the server and in the inbox in your email applications). As you will learn later, when you work with an IMAP account that has a limited amount of storage for email messages, you have to be aware of how full your email storage is and make sure that you keep it under its limit.

When you use a POP account, the mail you read is actually downloaded to your Mac. So, a copy exists in both places. With POP accounts, you should check the ""Remove copy from server after retrieving a message"" check box and select a timeframe for messages to be deleted on the pop-up menu. Otherwise, the email you read remains on the server, and you might download it again the next time you check your email.

Using steps similar to these, you can add the rest of your email accounts to Mail to work with them all from the Mail application. As you read previously, the steps for a specific account depend on the type of email account you are adding. Just use the specific configuration information provided for each account and repeat the previous steps.

NOTE

> Mail can't access an AOL email account. However, you should be able to add just about any other email account to it.

SETTING OTHER MAIL PREFERENCES

There are various other Mail preferences you might want to set. The general steps you use to set these preferences are shown here:

1. Select Mail, Preferences to open the Mail Preferences window.
2. Click the button for the area of preferences you want to set.
3. Set the preferences.
4. Set more preferences or close the Preferences window.

In the following sections, you will get an overview of each preference area and a description of some of the more useful preferences you can set.

SETTING JUNK MAIL PREFERENCES

You use the Junk Mail pane to configure Mail's Junk Mail feature.

→ To learn how to configure and use Mail's junk mail feature, **see** "Handling Junk Mail," **p. 446**.

SETTING FONTS & COLORS PREFERENCES

Use the Fonts & Colors pane of the Mail preferences window to control how text appears in Mail windows:

■ Use the font and size pop-up menus to select the font and size for the Message list font (the pane in which all the messages in a mailbox are listed) and the message font (which is the font used for messages you read).

■ If you prefer a fixed-width font for plain-text messages, check the "Use fixed-width font for plain text messages" check box and use the pop-up menus to select the font and size to be used for plain-text email.

■ If you want different levels of quoted text to use different colors, check the "Color quoted text" check box and select the colors for each level using the pop-up menus.

Email Formats

Mail enables you to send and read email in two formats: plain text and Rich Text Format (RTF). Plain-text messages contain no formatting, but RTF messages can be formatted. Whether the formatting you apply in an RTF message will be seen or not depends on the email application the recipient of your email uses. Most can interpret RTF messages correctly, but others cannot.

Email purists prefer plain-text format because any email application can handle them and plain-text messages are quicker to compose and read (which is part of the point of email in the first place). Also, proper quoting is much easier with a plain-text message. I prefer plain text myself for these very reasons.

Many mailing lists enable you to select the format in which you receive messages. You often can select between the plain-text or HTML format. Selecting the plain-text format results in much faster performance, although you won't see all the bells and whistles that can be contained in an HTML email message. However, plain-text messages usually contain links to that content on the Web so you can easily view the specific content you want to see.

SETTING VIEWING PREFERENCES

Using the Viewing pane of the Mail Preferences window, you can control the following viewing options:

■ Use the ""Show header detail"" pop-up menu to determine how much information is shown in the header of email messages you receive. Your choices are Default, None, All, or Custom. If you select Custom, you can select the specific data you want to see in the header of your messages.

15

Note that the "Show header detail" pop-up menu affects mail you have already down-loaded. For example, you can select an email message to read and then select a level of header detail from the "Show header detail" pop-up menu to change the header information for the mail you are reading.

TIP

You can show all header information in messages by selecting View, Message, Long Headers or by pressing Shift-⌘-H.

- Check the "Show online buddy status" check box if you want the status of people whom you have designated as being online buddies to be displayed. This helps you know when these people are online so you can chat with them.

- Check the "Display unread message with bold font" check box if you want messages that you haven't read yet to appear in bold.

- Uncheck the "Display remote images in HTML messages" check box if you want only the text portion of HTML messages that you receive to be displayed.

NOTE

Mail now uses the Safari HTML rendering engine to display HTML messages. This improves the formatting you see when you view HTML messages and makes HTML messages fully interactive.

- Uncheck the "Use Smart Addresses" check box if you don't want Mail to substitute a person's name (from the Address Book) for her email address when you receive mail from her.

- Check the "Highlight related messages using color" check box, and select a color by using the color button. *Threads* (a series of messages connected by replies to an original message) in your mailbox are highlighted with the color you select so you can spot them more easily.

SETTING COMPOSING PREFERENCES

The Composing pane of the Preferences window controls various composing options, which include the following:

- Use the Message "Format" pop-up menu to set the default format for new messages you can create. Your options are Plain Text and Rich Text. You can override your default choice for specific messages.

TIP

> For example, if you select Plain Text as your default format, you can create a message in the Rich Text format by creating the message and selecting Format, Make Rich Text (Shift-⌘-T). If you select Rich Text, you can select Format, Make Plain Text (Shift-⌘-T) to create a plain-text message.

- Select "as I type" on the "Check spelling" pop-up menu to have Mail check your spelling as you type messages. Choose "when I click Send" to have Mail check spelling when you send a message or "never" to disable spell check.

- Check the Automatically check box and then select Cc: on the pop-up menu to include yourself in the Cc block of every message you send. If you prefer to include yourself on the address list for a message but hide your address from the other recipients, select Bcc: on the pop-up menu.

- Check the "Automatically complete addresses" check box to have Mail look up addresses in your Address Book or on specific LDAP servers. Then click the Configure LDAP button and use the resulting sheet to configure the servers on which you want Mail to look up addresses.

- Check the "When sending to a group, show all member addresses" check box to list members of a group by their names in an email that you send to a group (rather than listing just the group name).

- If you want to highlight email addresses when you are sending them outside of "safe" domains, check the "Mark addresses not in this domain" check box and enter the domain you want Mail to consider safe in the box. For example, you might want to be careful about sending messages outside your work domain. In that case, you would check the box and enter your company's domain (such as company.com) in the box. Whenever you address messages to someplace other than that domain, the address is highlighted in red.

- Use the "Send new mail from" pop-up menu to choose the account from which new email will be sent (your default account). You can choose "Account of last viewed mailbox" to choose the account in which you most recently read email, or you can choose a specific account. This impacts only the default email account from which new email will be sent. You can always override this choice when you compose a new message.

- Use the controls in the Responding area to configure how Mail handles reply messages. To use the same mail format as the original message (such as plain text), check the "Use the same message format as the original message" check box. If you don't check this, your reply uses your default format. To include the original message's text in your reply (which is a good idea so you can use quoting), check the "Quote the text of the original message" check box. Check the "Increase quote level" box to have Mail indent each message's text by one level; this makes an email conversation clearer because you can more easily see the flow of the mail threads. If you select to use quoting (which you should), use the radio buttons to determine whether the entire message is quoted or only the selected part. The second option is preferable because, if you don't select any

15

text in the original message when you reply to it, the entire text is quoted, which is the same thing the "Include all" option does anyway. However, if you want to reply only to a specific part of a message, you can select it and only that part is included in the message. This provides better context for your reply.

SETTING SIGNATURE PREFERENCES

You can configure signatures to be attached to your email messages. You can have as many signatures as you would like, and you can select a default signature or select one each time you compose a new message:

1. Click the Signatures icon to open the Signatures pane of the Mail Preferences window. The accounts you have configured will be shown in the far left pane. The list of signatures you have configured will be shown in the middle pane, while the far right pane will show the detail for a selected signature.

2. Select the account for which you want to configure a signature, or select All Signatures to make the signature available to all accounts.

3. Click Add Signature (+). A new signature will appear in the center pane and its name will be highlighted to indicate that it is ready to edit. Default text for that signature will be shown in the far right pane.

4. Name the signature by typing a name in the highlighted area.

5. Edit or replace the signature text in the far right pane. You can use just about anything you'd like for your signature.

6. If you want your signature to always appear in your default font, check the "Always match my default message font" check box. Underneath this check box, you'll see what your default font currently is.

7. If you created signatures under the All Signatures category, drag them onto each account under which you want to be able to use them.

8. Select one of the email accounts in the far left pane.

9. If you want a signature to be added to messages from that account, select an option on the Choose Signature pop-up menu. You can choose a signature by name, "At Random" to have Mail select from one of the signatures each time you create a new message, or "In Sequential Order" to have Mail choose each signature in the order in which they are listed. If you choose None, no signature will be added automatically. In any case, you can always choose from the available signatures on the Signature menu in the New Message window.

10. Check the "Place signature above quoted text" check box, and your signature will be placed above any text that is quoted when you reply to a message. Signatures appear at the bottom of a message by default. When you use quoting, this can be odd because your signature appears after the quoted text instead of after the part you wrote. Use this check box to ensure that your signature appears after what you write and above the quoted text.

Here are a few more signature tips:

- **Change signatures**—To change a signature, select it and edit it in the far right pane.
- **Select a default signature**—When you have more than one signature created for an account, drag the one you want to be the default to the top of the Signature list.
- **Copy a signature**—You can make a copy of a signature by selecting its text and selecting Edit, Copy. Then paste the text into a new signature. This is useful if you want to base a new signature on one you have previously created.
- **Delete a signature**—You can delete a signature by selecting it and clicking Remove (-). After you confirm the deletion in the prompt, the signature will no longer be available.

SETTING RULES

You use the Rules pane to set up automated mail rules.

→ To learn how to create rules for your email, **see** "Configuring and Using Rules for Email," **p. 445**.

CONFIGURING THE MAIL TOOLBAR

As with other Mac OS X toolbars, you can configure Mail's toolbar to be more compatible with the way you work:

- Use the Hide Toolbar or the Show Toolbar command on the View menu to hide or show Mail's toolbar. You can use the Show/Hide toolbar button in the Mail title bar as well.
- Select View, Customize Toolbar to add buttons to, remove buttons from, and reorganize the toolbar. Just like other toolbars, you can drag icons onto the toolbar to add them to it or drag them off it to remove them. You can also select how the buttons are displayed and their size.

> TIP
>
> Hold down the ⌘ key and click the Hide/Show Toolbar button to cycle through various views, such as large icons, text only, and so on.

SENDING, RECEIVING, AND REPLYING TO EMAIL

If you have used an email application before, such as Outlook Express, Entourage, or Eudora, using Mail to send, receive, and reply to email will be familiar to you after you learn about the Mail interface.

The main Mail window has four panes. The top pane contains the Mail Toolbar. The second pane from the top is the Message List, in which you see the list of items in the selected mailbox. The lower pane of the Mail window is the reading pane in which you read a mail item that is selected in Message List. All your mailboxes are in the Mailbox pane which appears along the left side of the Mail window (see Figure 15.13).

15

Figure 15.13
The Mail application uses four panes to enable you to browse, view, and organize your email.

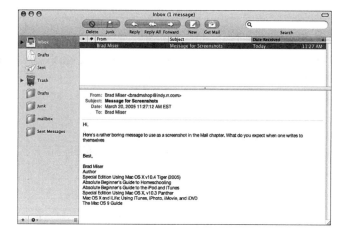

The Message pane of the Mail window behaves much like a Finder in List view. For example, you can change the width of the columns, sort the list of messages, and so on. The columns in the default Mail window are the following (from left to right in Figure 15.13):

- Message status
- Buddy availability
- From
- Subject
- Date Received

The Mailbox pane shows all your mailboxes. You can show the Mailbox pane by selecting View, Show Mailboxes (Shift-⌘-M). You can close the pane by selecting View, Hide Mailboxes (Shift-⌘-M). You can control the width of the pane by dragging the handle located at the bottom of its outside edge so it is the width you want it to be.

The Mailbox pane contains several mailboxes and folders by default. The Inbox is used to store all your received mail; within the main Inbox is a mailbox for each of your email accounts. You can expand or collapse the contents of a mailbox by using its expansion triangle. You also see Drafts, Sent, and Trash mailboxes; the purpose of each of these should be self-evident. You might also see Drafts and Sent Messages folders for specific types of email accounts.

NOTE

If you use a .Mac, IMAP, or Exchange email account, the Drafts, Junk, and Sent Messages mailboxes appear and have folder icons. These are folders stored on your Mac, whereas the other mailboxes are stored online. If you configured a .Mac email account to store messages online, they are stored in the online folders rather than those stored on your Mac.

RETRIEVING AND READING EMAIL

There are several ways to retrieve email from your accounts, including

- Setting Mail to retrieve your mail automatically using the General pane of the Mail Preferences window
- Clicking the Get Mail button on the Mail toolbar
- Pressing Shift-⌘-N to get new mail in all your accounts
- Selecting Mailbox, Get New Mail in *accountname*, where *accountname* is the account from which you want to retrieve your mail

NOTE

The first three methods listed retrieve mail for all the email accounts you have configured in Mail (for those accounts that are enabled and that you set to be included in the retrieve all action using that account's settings).

TIP

You can temporarily hide the Reading pane by double-clicking the border between the Message List and the Reading pane. The Reading pane disappears and the Message list consumes the entire Mail window. Double-click the bottom of the Mail window to reopen the Reading pane. You can change the relative height of the two panes by dragging the resize handle located in the center of the bar between the two panes.

When you get mail, it is placed in the Inbox mailbox for the account to which it was sent. All email is accessible via the top Inbox account, which includes the contents of each account's inbox.

When you receive email, Mail's Dock icon indicates that you have new email and shows you the total number of new messages you have received. If you chose to have Mail play a sound when new mail is received, you hear that sound when mail is received. When you open the Mail icon on the Dock, a list pops up that shows you all the windows open in Mail, as well as some useful commands (see Figure 15.14).

When you select Inbox on the Dock menu, you move into Mail to read your email; each unread message has a blue dot in the Status column to indicate that it is a new message. The number of new messages is also indicated next to the Inbox mailbox.

TIP

You can also create a new message or check for new email from the Mail Dock menu.

If you have more than one email account, each account has its own Inbox. To see all your inboxes, click the expansion arrow next to the Inbox icon (see Figure 15.15). The Inbox for each of your accounts appears. Select an Inbox to see the messages for that account only, or select the Inbox icon to see all your messages at the same time.

Figure 15.14
When you receive new mail, Mail lets you know how many messages you have received (one in this case); you can quickly access the mailboxes containing the new messages by opening the Mail icon on the Dock and selecting Inbox.

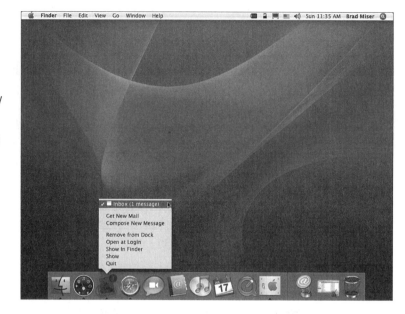

Figure 15.15
Each of my email accounts has its own Inbox, as you can see listed under the Inbox icon.

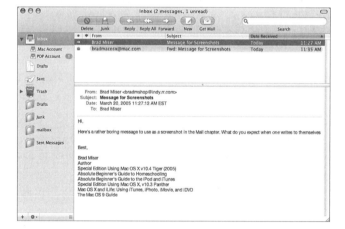

TIP

In Mail, you can display the contents of more than one mailbox at a time. To do so, select File, New Viewer Window (Option-⌘-N). In the new Viewer window, select the mailbox whose contents you want to view. You can have as many Viewer windows open as you want. For example, you might select to have a Viewer window open for each of your mail accounts.

 If you are unable to retrieve your mail, see "My Mail Can't Be Retrieved" in the "Troubleshooting" section at the end of this chapter.

NOTE

> You can see the activity of Mail as it downloads messages using its Activity Viewer. To see the Activity Viewer, select Window, Show Activity Viewer (or press ⌘-0).

READING INDIVIDUAL MESSAGES

To view the contents of a mailbox or folder, select it in the Mailbox pane. The Message list shows the messages contained in that mailbox or folder. To read a message, select it in the Message list and read it in the Reading pane.

TIP

> If the sender of a message is included in your Address Book, the name on that person's card is shown in the From box instead of the person's email address (assuming you leave the Smart Addressing preference enabled). If you click the From name or email address, a pop-up menu appears. This menu shows the email address that the message is from and enables you to reply to the message, create a new message, or add the contact to your Address Book.

To read your mail, use the following shortcuts:

- Scroll down in a message by pressing the spacebar.
- Move up and down the messages in the Message List using the up- and down-arrow keys.
- Double-click a message to read it in its own window.

TIP

> If the mailbox you are viewing has several messages in it, select those that are interesting to you; hold down the Shift key to select contiguous messages or hold down the ⌘ key to select messages that are not contiguous. Select View, Display Selected Messages Only. The other messages in the mailbox are hidden and you can quickly read the messages you selected (using the shortcuts mentioned in the previous list). To see all the messages in the mailbox again, select View, Display All Messages.

WORKING WITH EMAIL THREADS

As you read and reply to messages, each message and its replies become a thread, as in a thread of conversation about a topic (or at least started from a topic). If the "Highlight related messages using color" preference is set, Mail highlights all the messages in a thread with the color you select (it is light blue by default). You can also select to organize a mailbox by threads so that all the mails that form a conversation are grouped together.

To organize messages in the Message List pane by threads, select View, Organize by Thread. Messages that are part of a thread are highlighted in the selected color and are grouped together (see Figure 15.16). Select View, Organize by Thread again to return the

15

Message pane to its previous organization. The messages in a thread are sorted just like other messages in the Message List pane.

Figure 15.16
While all the messages are from me, the top four are part of a thread.

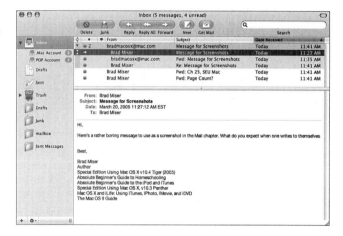

Following are some thread tips (these apply when you use the Organize by Thread command):

- The first message in the thread is a summary of the other messages. Select that message to see each sender, title, and date of each message in the thread. At the top of the summary message is the name of the first message in the thread, who started it, and when the first message was sent.

- You can collapse a thread by clicking the expansion triangle next to the summary message. The thread collapses so you see only the summary message. You can also collapse a thread by clicking the up and down arrow icon in the Status column for a message in the thread.

- Select View, Expand All Threads to expand all the threads in a selected mailbox, or select View, Collapse All Threads to collapse all the threads in a selected mailbox.

If the person who sent you a message is in your Address Book and has an image on the related address card, that image appears in the upper-right corner of the email message (see Figure 15.17).

Figure 15.17
The image contained in a person's address card appears in the upper-right corner of a message you receive from that person.

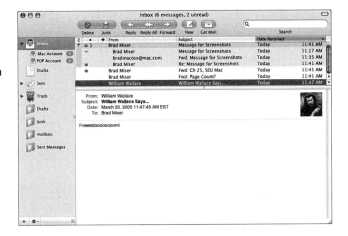

Writing and Sending Email

Writing email in Mail is also quite similar to other email applications. You can create a new mail message in several ways, including the following:

- Click the New button on the toolbar.
- Select File, New Message.
- Press ⌘-N.
- Point to a name in the To, From, or Cc block for a message you have received; click it; and select New Message on the resulting pop-up menu. A message is created and is addressed to the person whose name you clicked.
- Open the Mail's menu on the Dock and select Compose New Message.

> **TIP**
>
> If you point to the From block on an email message and click, a pop-up menu appears. On this menu, you can see the email address of the person, chat with the recipient, create a new message, open the related address card (if the recipient has a card, that is), or create an address card.

When you create a new message, you see the New Message window (see Figure 15.18). Creating the message is straightforward. If the message is not already addressed, type the email address(es) in the To and Cc fields. Mail attempts to match what you type to the addresses in your Address Book or on the list of previous recipients that Mail maintains automatically. The addresses that match what you type appear on a drop-down list. You can move up and down this list with the up- and down-arrow keys. To select an address on the list, highlight it and it is entered in the message's address box. (If there is only one address for the name you type, it is selected by default.) You can enter multiple addresses in an address field by typing a comma and then repeating the previous steps to add more addresses. When you have added all the addresses in the To field, press Tab to move to the next field.

Figure 15.18
If you have used other email applications, Mail's New Message window will no doubt look familiar.

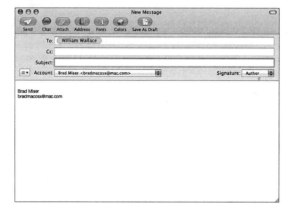

> **TIP**
>
> Mail automatically tracks a list of people to whom you have sent email. This list is called the Previous Recipients list. When you enter an email address in the To field, Mail attempts to match what you are entering to the recipients on this list. If it finds a match, it fills in the rest of the address for you. You can view the list by selecting Window, Previous Recipients. On this list, you can view addresses to or delete addresses from the list, or add addresses to your Address Book.

> **TIP**
>
> When an address is selected on the drop-down list that appears when Mail attempts to match the address you are typing, you can add it to the message and be ready to enter the next address by pressing comma.

To use your Address Book to address a message, open the Address Book by clicking the Address icon on the New Message window's toolbar or by pressing Option-⌘-A. An Addresses window appears that contains the contacts in your Address Book. Browse or search the window to find the people or groups to which you want to send the message. Select the person or group to whom you want to send mail, and click To or Cc to send those addresses to the respective fields in the New Message window.

> **TIP**
>
> You can add a Bcc (blind carbon copy) address line by selecting View, Bcc Address Field or by pressing Option-⌘-B. You can add a Reply To address line by selecting View, Reply-To Address Field (or by pressing Option-⌘-R). You can use the Reply To Address

15

Field to enter an address to which people should reply if it is different from the return address associated with the account selected on the Account pop-up menu. You can also add either of these fields by opening the pop-up menu just to the left of the Account pop-up menu.

Enter the subject of the message in the Subject field.

Select the account from which you want to send the mail using the Account pop-up menu (your default account is listed automatically). (If you have configured only one account, this menu isn't displayed.)

Mail uses the following three rules to determine the account that is used to send a new message:

- If you have selected a mailbox associated with an account (such as the Inbox for an account), that account is the default for a new message.
- If you selected a default account for new mail on the Composing pane of the Preferences dialog box, that account is used for new mail.
- When you reply to a message, the account to which the original message was sent is selected automatically.

TIP

The New Message window has its own toolbar; you can customize its toolbar just as you can other Mail and Mac OS X toolbars (View, Customize Toolbar).

Select the signature you want to use from the Signature pop-up menu. The default signature for the selected account will be inserted, but you can use the menu to choose a different one.

Move into the body and type your message. As you type, Mail checks your spelling according to your preferences. If you use the "check as I type" option, when Mail identifies a misspelled word, it underlines the word in red. You can Control-click or right-click a misspelled word to pop up a menu that enables you to change the word to the correct spelling, ignore the spelling, or learn the word that Mail thinks is misspelled.

You can right-click or Control-click any word, misspelled or not, to perform a number of actions on it, such as searching for the word on your Mac using Spotlight, searching the Web via Google, looking up the word in the Dictionary application, and so on.

TIP

You can also control Mail's spell checker using the Spelling commands on the Edit menu. You can open the Spelling window by selecting Edit, Spelling, and then Spelling again. You can configure the spell checking by selecting Edit, Spelling, Check Spelling and then choosing the option you want, such as "As You Type."

15

As you work with a new message, open its contextual menu to gain quick access to various commands, such as formatting commands for an RTF message, Spell Checker controls, and quoting commands.

To send a message, do one of the following:

- Click the Send button on the toolbar.
- Select Message, Send Message.
- Press Shift-⌘-D.

If your mail can't be sent, see "My Mail Can't Be Sent" in the "Troubleshooting" section at the end of this chapter.

REPLYING TO EMAIL

Replying to messages you receive in Mail is also similar to other applications. By default, Mail marks the different levels of quoting with different colors along with a change bar. As with other applications, you can select the message to which you want to reply and click Reply on the toolbar; select Message, Reply; or press ⌘-R, which replies to only the sender of the message. You can also click Reply All; select Message, Reply All; or press Shift-⌘-R to reply to everyone to whom the original message was sent.

You can use the same tools to reply to a message as you use to write a new message.

You can also perform the following actions on mail you have received:

- **Reply with iChat**—Select Message, Reply with iChat or press Shift-⌘-I if the sender of the message is available via iChat.

- **Forward**—Select Message, Forward or press Shift-⌘-F to forward a message to other recipients.

- **Redirect**—Select Message, Redirect or press Shift-⌘-E to redirect the message to someone else. The difference between redirecting and forwarding a message is that when you redirect a message, the message's original sender's email address still appears in the From field so the person to whom you redirect the message can reply to the message to send email to the person who sent the message. If you forward a message and the recipient replies to it, the reply comes to you because your address becomes the From address on a forwarded message.

- **Bounce**—Select Message, Bounce or press Shift-⌘-B to bounce a message back to the sender. When you do so, the bounce message that is sent makes it appear as if your email address is not valid.

> **TIP**
>
> You can open a message's contextual menu to access many useful commands, such as Reply, Reply All, Forward, and so on.

> **NOTE**
>
> You might be tempted to bounce spam email that you receive. However, this usually doesn't do any good because most spam includes a bogus return address so your bounced message has no legitimate place to go. You can use the Bounce command to respond to email from legitimate organizations that have sent unwanted email to you. Hopefully, the bounce results in your address being removed from the related mailing list. Use Mail's Junk Mail feature to deal with spam.

DELETING EMAIL

You can delete messages by selecting the messages you want to delete and doing one of the following:

- Click the Delete button on the toolbar.
- Select Edit, Delete.
- Drag a message from the Message List pane or mailbox onto the Trash in the Mail Drawer.
- Press Delete.

Deleted messages are stored in the Trash folder in the Mailbox pane. You can open this folder just like other folders you have. Messages aren't actually removed until the Trash folder is emptied.

15

When you use an IMAP account, such as a .Mac email account, you have to empty the Trash folder to actually remove the messages from the server. If you don't, those messages continue to count against the total storage space you have on the server. Typically, you are limited to a certain storage space for *all* your messages (under an IMAP or a .Mac account, all your messages remain on the server). Because messages in the Trash folder count against this limit, you should empty this folder more frequently under an IMAP account than you do with POP accounts.

Because they are actually IMAP accounts, .Mac email accounts are limited to a certain amount of storage. If the messages stored in your .Mac email account approach or exceed this limit, you receive email messages warning you that you are exceeding your allotted storage space. To move messages off the server, you need to move them from the Inbox for that account to one of your personal mailboxes stored on your Mac or to the Trash and then empty it.

You can determine whether deleted messages are stored on the server by using the Mailbox Behaviors tab of the Accounts pane of the Mail Preferences window. Open this tab and uncheck the "Store deleted messages on the server" check box. This causes the messages you delete to be downloaded to your Mac, so they won't count against your storage limit.

You can also use the "Permanently erase deleted message when" pop-up menu to select a time period for your deleted messages to be permanently erased.

NOTE

Just like the Inbox, each email account has its own Trash.

To empty Mail's Trash, do one of the following:

- Select Mailbox, Erase Deleted Messages, In All Accounts or press ⌘-K.
- Select Mailbox, Erase Deleted Messages, *accountname*, where *accountname* is the name of the account whose Trash you want to empty.
- Select Mailbox, Erase Junk Mail or press Option-⌘-J to erase the messages stored in the Junk folder (more on that later).
- Open the Trash's contextual menu and select Erase Deleted Messages.
- Use Mail's preferences to set an automatic deletion point, such as a time period or when you quit Mail.

CUSTOMIZING YOUR EMAIL

Mail provides many tools you can use to customize various aspects of your mail. These include customizing the Mail window, organizing your email, sorting your email, and automating your mail with rules.

CUSTOMIZING THE VIEWER WINDOW

You can customize the Viewer window by using the commands shown in Table 15.1.

TABLE 15.1   WAYS TO CUSTOMIZE THE VIEWER WINDOW

Command	What It Does
View, Columns	Enables you to select the columns displayed in the Viewer window. In addition to the columns shown by default, you can select from many columns, including Attachments, Date Sent, and so on.
View, Sort By	Sorts the Message List pane by the column you select.
View, Hide/Show Mailboxes	Hides/shows the Mailbox pane.
View, Use Small Mailbox Icons	Changes the size of the mailbox icons displayed in the Mailbox pane.
View, Hide/Show Toolbar	Hides/shows the Mail toolbar.

> **NOTE**
>
> Remember that you can also customize the Message List window by moving the columns to change the order in which they appear, resizing them, changing the column by which the pane is sorted, and so on, just as you can in Finder windows in the List view.

ORGANIZING YOUR EMAIL

There are a number of ways to organize your email, including using mailboxes, smart mailboxes, and smart mailbox groups.

USING MAILBOXES TO ORGANIZE YOUR EMAIL

You can create your own mailboxes to organize your messages. The mailboxes you create are also shown in the Mailbox pane. You can also create nested mailboxes to create a hierarchy of mailboxes in which you store your messages.

1. Select Mailbox, New Mailbox to see the New Mailbox sheet (see Figure 15.19).

> **TIP**
>
> You can also create a new mailbox by clicking the New Mailbox button (+), which is located at the bottom of the Mailbox pane.

2. On the Location pop-up menu, select the location of the mailbox you are creating. If you select On My Mac, the folder is created on your computer. If you use an IMAP or .Mac account, you can select that account to create a folder on that account's server.

   Remember that if you store the folder on a server, the contents of that folder count against your storage quota.

15

Figure 15.19
You use the New Mailbox sheet to create a new mailbox either on your Mac or on a server.

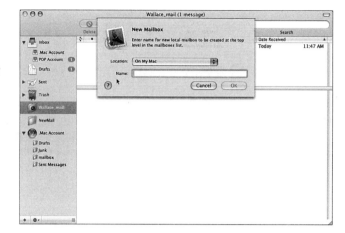

3. In the New Mailbox sheet, enter the name of the mailbox you want to create. To create a nested mailbox, enter the name of each mailbox separated by a slash (/). For example, to create a mailbox called "Receipts" within a mailbox called "Mail to Keep," you would enter `Mail to Keep/Receipts`.

4. Click OK.

The mailbox will be created and will appear in the Mailbox pane. If you have created a mailbox that contains other mailboxes, you can use its expansion triangle to expand or collapse it. In Figure 15.20, you can see that I have created a folder called Receipts that is nested within a folder called Mail To Keep. You can also see that I have a .Mac account and its folders are shown under the .Mac mailbox. Messages you place in folders stored on a server count against your storage limit on that server, so it is generally a better idea to create folders on your Mac instead.

Figure 15.20
Folders under the On My Mac icon are stored on your computer; folders under a server's icon, such as the .Mac mail account in this figure, are stored on that server.

You can move messages from one mailbox to another in the following ways:

- Drag and drop a message from the Message List pane to a mailbox.
- Drag messages from the Message List pane in one Viewer to the Message List pane in another Viewer; this copies the messages in the mailbox shown in the second Viewer window.
- Select messages and select Message, Move To; then select the mailbox to which you want to transfer the messages.
- Select messages and select Message, Copy To; then select the mailbox to which you want to create a copy of the selected messages.
- Select messages and select Message, Move Again to move the selected messages into the same mailbox into which you most recently transferred mail (Option-⌘-T).
- Open a message's contextual menu and select the Move To, Copy To, Move Again, or Apply Rules command.
- Select messages and select Message, Apply Rules (Option-⌘-L); then select a rule that transfers the messages.

USING SMART MAILBOXES TO ORGANIZE YOUR EMAIL

You can use smart mailboxes to organize your email automatically based on criteria you define. For example, you might want to store all the email you receive from a group of people with whom you are working on a project in a specific folder. Rather than having to place these messages in the folder by dragging them out of your Inbox individually, you can create a smart mailbox so that mail you receive from these people is automatically placed in the folder. You can create smart mailboxes for many needs like the one mentioned here; if you can define a set of conditions for which you want something done, then you can create a smart mailbox to have the action you want to happen done for you automatically.

To create a smart mailbox, complete the following steps:

1. Select Mailbox, New Smart Mailbox or open the Action pop-up menu and select New Smart Mailbox. The Smart Mailbox sheet will appear.
2. Name the smart mailbox by typing its name in the "Smart Mailbox Name" box.
3. Select the first condition for the mailbox on the first pop-up menu in the conditions box; by default, this menu shows From, which will base the condition on the name or email address in the From field. There are many other choices, including Entire Message, Subject, Date Received, and so on. If you want to place all the mail you receive from a specific person in a smart mailbox, select From.
4. Select the operand for the condition on the second pop-up menu. What you see on this menu depends on the condition you selected. Common choices include Contains, "Does not contain," "Is equal to," and so on. In the example of creating a smart mailbox for mail from a specific person, select Contains.
5. Enter the condition text or date in the box. For example, enter a person's name if you are creating a smart mailbox to collect mail from a specific person.

15

6. To add another condition, click the + button.

7. Repeat steps 3–5 to configure the second condition.

8. If you have configured more than one condition, select "all" on the pop-up menu above the condition list if all the conditions must be true for mail to be stored in the smart mailbox, or select "any" if only one of the conditions must be true.

TIP

> To remove a condition, click the Remove (-) button next to the condition you want to remove.

9. If you want messages that are in the Trash or the Sent folders to be included in the smart mailbox, check the related "Include" check boxes.

10. Review the conditions for the smart mailbox and click OK if you are ready to create it (see Figure 15.21). The mailbox will be created and any mail that meets its conditions will be placed in it.

Figure 15.21
This smart mailbox will contain mail I have received from anyone whose name includes "Wallace" and has been received within the last seven days.

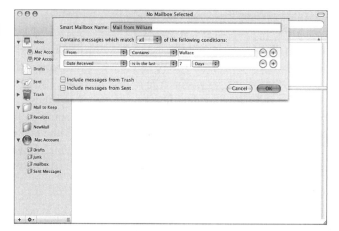

TIP

> To change the conditions for an existing smart mailbox, open its contextual menu and select Edit Smart Mailbox. Use the resulting Smart Mailbox sheet to make changes to the smart mailbox.

USING SMART MAILBOX FOLDERS TO ORGANIZE YOUR SMART MAILBOXES

If you want to organize your smart mailboxes, you can create a smart mailbox folder and then place your smart mailboxes within it (you can't put smart mailboxes within regular mailboxes/folders):

1. Select Mailbox, New Smart Mailbox Folder.

2. In the sheet that appears, name the new smart mailbox folder and click OK. The smart mailbox folder will be created.

3. Drag smart mailboxes into the smart mailbox folder to place them there.

CONFIGURING AND USING RULES FOR EMAIL

You can automate the handling of your email by configuring and using rules. For example, you might want to create a mailbox for the mail related from a certain person and have that mail automatically transferred into that mailbox (you could use a smart mailbox to do this, too). Or, you might have the messages from a mailing list to which you are subscribed placed in a specific mailbox for later reading.

To create and implement rules, you use the Rules pane of the Mail Preferences window:

1. Open the Mail Preferences window and click the Rules icon to open the Rules pane. Some rules are installed by default.

2. Click Add Rule to open a Rule sheet to define the rule you are creating.

3. Name the rule by entering a description.

4. Use the If pop-up menu to determine whether at least one criterion (select "any") or all the criteria (select "all") in the rule must be met for the actions in the rule to be taken.

5. Use the first condition pop-up menu to select the first criterion on which the rule will act. You can select any of the fields in a mail message. You can also select from various criteria, such as whether the sender is in your Address Book.

6. Use the Contains pop-up menu to select how the criteria will relate to the value you enter (such as Contains, "Is equal to," and so on).

7. Enter the value for which the rule will be implemented, if applicable, or use a pop-up menu to select a value. (Some conditions, such as "Sender is in my Address Book," don't require any values.)

8. To add more criteria, click the Add button (+) and repeat steps 5–7 to create additional conditions for the rule.

9. Use the Action area to select the actions that will be performed by the rule by making a choice from the first pop-up menu and making other choices from the other pop-up menus or fields related to that choice.

   The actions you can select are Move Message, Copy Message, Set Color of Message, Play Sound, Bounce Icon in Dock, Reply to Message, Forward Message, Redirect Message, Delete Message, Mark as Read, Mark as Flagged, Run AppleScript, or Stop evaluating rules. You can include multiple actions in the same rule.

10. Click the Add button next to the action and repeat step 9 to create and configure additional actions. When you are done, review the rule you have created. For example, the rule shown in Figure 15.22 checks to see whether a message is from me, the subject contains `Special Edition Using Mac OS X`, or is from my email address; if any of these conditions is true, the message is moved to the Trash and the Frog sound plays.

Figure 15.22
Hopefully, you won't
want to create a rule
like this one!

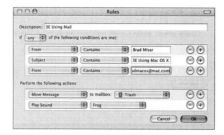

TIP

You can remove conditions or actions by clicking the Remove button (–).

11. Click OK to see the rule you created in the Rules pane.

12. Create more rules or close the Preferences window.

NOTE

If you apply a color in a rule, that rule appears in that color in the Rules pane. Messages
already in a mailbox that meet the rule's criteria are also shown in the color applied by
the rule.

You can use the Edit and Duplicate buttons to edit or duplicate rules and the Remove button to delete rules.

Any future messages you receive that meet the criteria for a rule are acted upon by that rule.
You can also manually apply rules to messages by selecting messages and selecting Message,
Apply Rules (Option-⌘-L).

TIP

Manually applying rules is a good way to test your rules to ensure that they do what you
intended.

HANDLING JUNK MAIL

Unfortunately, no matter how careful you are with your email address, it might eventually
get on a junk mail list. And after it gets on one such list, it will get on many, and your inbox
will overflow with junk mail. Fortunately, Mail includes some built-in tools for dealing with
junk mail.

TIP

Although Mail's Junk mail feature is a good way to deal with spam, it doesn't eliminate
spam. See the sidebar at the end of this section for recommendations about how to deal
with spam more effectively.

You can configure Mail's Junk feature via the Junk Mail pane of the Mail preferences dialog box (see Figure 15.23).

Figure 15.23
Use the Junk Mail pane to configure Mail's junk feature.

The Junk feature has four modes.

In the Disabled mode, the Junk Feature is inactive and doesn't do anything. You can disable this feature by unchecking the "Enable Junk Mail filtering" check box on the Junk Mail pane of the preferences dialog box.

In the Training mode (which is the default mode), Mail applies its Junk rules to your messages. This causes Mail to color the message brown or gold (depending on your color perception), indicating that Mail thinks the message is junk. You use this mode to fine-tune the Junk Mail feature so it correctly filters your messages to identify the junk. When you view a message that has been correctly identified as junk, don't do anything. When a message has been identified as junk but it isn't, click the Not Junk button. If you find a message that is junk, but Mail has not identified it as such, click the Junk button on the toolbar. You can place the Junk Mail feature in the Training mode by clicking the "Leave it in my inbox, but indicate it is junk mail (Training)" radio button.

After some time has passed and you are confident that Mail's Junk filter is working properly, you can move into Junk Mail's Automatic mode. When you do so, Mail creates a Junk folder in the Drawer and prompts you to ask whether it should move all the identified junk mail to this folder. Click Yes. You move into the Automatic mode by clicking the "Move it to the Junk mailbox (Automatic)" radio button.

When the Junk feature is in the Automatic mode, it moves all the messages it identifies as junk into the Junk folder. You should review the contents of this folder periodically to ensure that no messages you want to keep are in this folder by mistake. If there are messages you want, move them to a different folder. Then delete all the messages in the Junk folder.

You can also use the Custom mode to configure the rules used by the Junk filter. To use this mode, click the "Perform custom actions (Click Advanced to configure)" radio button. Then click the Advanced button to open the Advanced configuration sheet.

If you click the Advanced button, you move to a Rules sheet and the default Junk rules are ready to edit. (Mail's Junk Mail feature is actually just a special mail rule.) You can change

15

this mail rule just like any rule you create on the Rule pane to change how Mail handles junk mail. If you open the Junk rule, you see that this is simply a rule that acts on any messages that are from people who are not in your Address Book, are not on your Previous Recipient list, are not addressed to your full name, or are marked as Junk. In the Training mode, this rule changes only the color of the messages. In the Automatic mode, it moves the messages to the Junk folder.

By checking the related check box on the Junk Mail pane of the preferences dialog box, you can exempt email messages from the Junk Mail filter in the following situations:

- The sender of a message is in your Address Book.

- The sender of a message is on the list of previous recipients.

- The message is addressed to your full name (most spam uses an email address).

If your Internet service provider (ISP) provides junk mail headers that attempt to identify junk mail by its own rules and you want Mail to recognize and use those headers, check the "Trust Junk Mail headers set by my Internet Service Provider" check box.

If you click the Reset button, the Junk Mail feature is returned to its default state. This also removes any learning the filter has done so you have to repeat the training process.

THE END OF SPAM

With all due respect to Mail's Junk feature, there are certain circumstances in which providing your email address is likely to result in your address being obtained by a spammer. And after it gets into one spammer's hands, it will get into lots of spammers' hands and you will start receiving dozens or even hundreds of spam messages every day. The only real way to stop spam is to stop using the email address that has been spammed. Junk mail filters, such as Mail's Junk feature, are really only a way to make dealing with spam easier; they don't eliminate the spam from your life.

Several situations should be considered to have high risk of your address being spammed. One is public discussion forums, such as on websites, in newsgroups, in chat rooms, and so on; in fact, getting spammed from these locations is guaranteed. Another is when you are shopping online; many online retailers have valid privacy policies that allow you to opt out of your address being provided to others, but some don't have such policies. Another is any time you are asked for an email address, such as when you are taking a survey, registering for a "free" prize, and so on. Providing an email address in any of the situations will likely get you spammed.

If that happens and you use an email address for work or to keep in touch with people, you aren't likely to want to change the address you use.

There is a solution to this dilemma: You can create "disposable" email accounts for use in the situations that are more likely to result in an addressed getting spammed. If that happens, you can simply stop using the spammed email account and create another disposable account to use in the high spam risk situations.

Meanwhile, you can keep your permanent email address close the vest by providing it only to people you know or to companies that you are sure are legit and won't sell your address to spammers.

There are many sources of good disposable email accounts, including the following:

- Yahoo Mail (mail.yahoo.com).

- Other similar sites that enable you to create and use email accounts at no or low cost. For example, you can add additional email accounts to your .Mac account for relatively little cost.

- Your own Internet access account. Many ISP accounts provide multiple email accounts under your access account. Even better, most of the time you can create and delete your own sub-accounts, which is the ideal situation. Keep your base email account private; never use it in any circumstance. Then create an email account as your permanent address and provide that to the people with whom you really want to communicate. Finally, create your disposable address and use that in high spam risk situations. If that address gets spammed, just delete it and create another one.

NOTE

You might have noticed that I provide my email address in this book, which is bradmacosx@mac.com. I like to receive email from readers, and spammers aren't likely to read a book to get a single address. So, even exposing an email address in a public place like a book isn't all that risky. However, I use the practice described in the last bullet in the previous list to manage my own email. For example, I have an email address for personal email and another disposable address I use when shopping online (mostly Mac stuff and DVDs). If that address ever gets spammed, I can just delete it and create a replacement.

SENDING AND RECEIVING FILES WITH EMAIL

One of the most valuable uses of email is to send and receive attachments. Again, Mail handles file attachments similarly to other email applications you might be accustomed to.

ATTACHING FILES TO YOUR EMAIL

Attaching files to messages you send can be done in the following ways:

- In the message to which you want to attach files, select File, Attach File (Shift-⌘-A). Then, use the Choose File sheet to select the files you want to attach.

- Click the Attach button on the New Message window's toolbar. The Choose File sheet appears; use it to select the files you want to attach to a message.

TIP

In the Choose File sheet, check the "Send Windows Friendly Attachments" check box if you are sending files to Windows users. This makes these users more likely to be able to use the files you send. You can turn on this feature so it applies to all attachments by selecting Edit, Attachments, Send Windows Friendly Attachments.

15

■ Drag the files onto the New Message window.

When you place a file in a new message window, you see a thumbnail preview of the file with its icon, the filename, and its size in parentheses. If the file type is one that can be displayed in the message, such as a TIFF image or a PDF file, you actually see the contents of the file in the body of the message.

By default, Mail displays the contents of files you attach if it can. If the contents of the file are being displayed and you would rather see just an icon, open the file's contextual menu and select View as icon. The file is displayed as an icon instead. To view the file's content again, open the menu and select View in Place.

File attachments must be *encoded* before they can be sent. When a file is encoded, it is translated into a string of text. The application that receives the message must then decode that message so the files become usable. Encoding and decoding is handled automatically, and you can't select the encoding method used.

If recipients of your file attachments have trouble with them, see "Recipients of My Attachments Are Seeing Odd Things" in the "Troubleshooting" section at the end of this chapter.

You should also compress files you attach to email messages. Under Mac OS X version, you can compress any file in the Zip format using the Finder's Archive command. Simply select the files you want to attach to an email message, open the contextual menu, and select Archive. The files you selected are placed in a Zip file. You can then rename the file (don't change the .zip file extension) and attach the Zip file to the message you are sending.

Sending file attachments is simple except for one thing—the Windows versus Mac situation, which raises its ugly head in the area of file attachments, too. Basically, Mac and Windows operating systems use different file format structures. Mac files have two "forks," whereas Windows files have only one. This is sometimes a problem when you send files to Windows users because they end up with two files. One is the usable file and one is unusable to them (the names of the files is *filename* and *_filename*). Recipients can use the first one and safely ignore the second one. However, it is still confusing for them.

Mail includes a solution for this problem, which is called sending Windows Friendly Attachments. This causes Mail to strip the second file away, so the Windows recipient receives only one file for each attachment. That is a good thing.

However, Mac users who receive Windows-friendly attachments might lose some features, such as thumbnail preview or information about the file. In the worst case, the file might be unusable.

You can choose to attach files as Windows friendly by checking the box in the Attach File dialog box. If you always want to send files in the Windows-friendly format, select Edit, Attachments, Send Windows Friendly Attachments.

Unless you always send files to other Mac users or only to Windows users, you have to decide whether to use the Windows-friendly option each time you attach files. You should either use this option when you send files to Windows users (if you don't know which type of computer the recipient uses) or not use it if you are certain the recipient uses a Mac.

USING FILES ATTACHED TO EMAIL YOU RECEIVE

When you receive a message that has files attached to it, you see the files in the body of the message. As when you send files in a message, you see the file's icon, name, and size. If the file can be displayed in the body, such as a TIFF or PDF, the contents of the file are displayed in the message. You can use the file attachments in the following ways:

■ Select File, Save Attachments. Use the resulting sheet to move to a location and save the attachments.

■ Click the Save button next to the attachment information at the top of the message. Use the resulting sheet to move to a location and save the attachments.

■ If multiple files are attached, click the expansion triangle next to the attachment line in the message's header and work with each file individually.

■ Double-click a file's icon to open it.

■ Drag a file's icon from the message onto a folder on your Mac's desktop to save it there.

■ You can open the attachment's contextual menu and select one of the listed actions, such as Open Attachment, which opens it in its native application; Open With, which enables you to select the application in which you want the file to open; Save Attachment; or Save to Downloads folder, which saves the attachment in your designated Downloads folder.

TIP

If the contents of the file are being displayed and you would rather see just an icon, open the file's contextual menu and select View as icon. The file is displayed as an icon instead. To view the file's content again, open the menu and select View in Place.

TIP

If you have trouble viewing a message and the folder into which you want to store the file attachments, double-click the message to open it in its own window. Then you can resize the window so you can more easily see the folder into which you want to drag it.

If the files you receive are compressed, you must uncompress them before you can open them.

→ To learn more about uncompressing files, **see** "Downloading and Preparing Files," **p. 481**.

SEARCHING EMAIL

As you collect email, you will probably need to search it. You can quickly search for messages, or you can search for specific text in a message.

You can search for messages using the following steps:

1. If you want to search only in a single mailbox, select that mailbox.

2. In the Mail Search tool, type the text you want to search for. As you type, the messages shown in the Message List pane are reduced to those that meet your criteria.

You can also search for text within a specific message using the Find Panel.

1. Select Edit, Find, Find (⌘-F). The Find Panel will appear.

2. Enter the text for which you want to search.

3. Click Next to search for the text.

You can use the Replace with box in the Find panel to replace the text you find with different text.

TIP

> You can also search by creating a smart folder based on your search criteria. This enables you to search by multiple attributes at the same time. Consider creating a smart mailbox for this purpose. Edit it each time you want to search for mail by more than a single attribute.

NOTE

> You can also search your email by using the Finder's Spotlight search tool because it includes your email in its search domain.

TROUBLESHOOTING

MY MAIL CAN'T BE RETRIEVED

When I check my mail, I get a "Fetch Error," saying that Mail couldn't connect to my mail server.

This can happen for various reasons, such as a problem with your Internet connection, a misconfigured email account, and so on. Use the following information to correct the problem.

Open and use another Internet application, such as a web browser.

If it works properly, there is a problem with Mail or your mail account configuration.

If it doesn't work properly, you are having trouble with your Internet access, which is why your mail account can't be accessed. You need to troubleshoot your Net connection.

→ For help troubleshooting your Net connection, **see** "Troubleshooting," **p. 367**.

If you have more than one email account, try all your accounts. If you have problems with all your accounts, something might have happened to the Mail application.

→ For help with troubleshooting applications, **see** Chapter 36, "Solving Mac Problems," **p. 1045**.

If your other accounts work, the problem is related to the specific account. If you have successfully retrieved email under this account before, the problem is likely a temporary one with the server from which you retrieve email or a temporary interruption in your communication with that server. In this case, wait awhile and try again later. If you continue to have problems or you have never been able to retrieve email from this account, try the following:

1. In Mail, select Mail, Preferences.
2. Click the Accounts button.
3. Select the account with which you are having trouble.
4. Click Edit. Check the account information for that account—especially the server name, User Name, and Password fields—and correct any errors you find. If no errors exist in these fields, the account is configured properly.
5. Allow some time to pass and try the account again. If you are still unable to retrieve your mail, the problem might reside with the provider of the mail account.
6. Contact the technical support for the organization providing your mail service for further help.

You can also use Mail's Connection Doctor to help you troubleshoot your accounts. Select Window, Connection Doctor. The Mail Connection Doctor window will open and check each of your accounts (incoming and outgoing) to see whether there is a problem. If there is a problem, select the account with the problem and click the "Assist me" button.

My Mail Can't Be Sent

When I try to send mail, I get an error message stating that my mail can't be sent.

Troubleshooting this problem is similar to troubleshooting a problem retrieving mail. The only difference is in step 4. You should carefully check the SMTP server address, SMTP User, and SMTP password boxes. If authentication is used for your SMTP account, make sure the Authentication check box is checked.

When you run the Connection Doctor, it also checks outgoing mail accounts.

 For help troubleshooting a problem with sending mail, refer to "My Mail Can't Be Retrieved," earlier in this section.

Recipients of My Attachments Are Seeing Odd Things

People to whom I send attachments see duplicate files, missing file attachment messages, and other odd things.

This happens when the recipient's email application does not fully support the encoding scheme Mail uses to encode files you attach to your messages. Most email applications decode files well enough for the files to be used, although some strange things can happen on the recipient's end. A few email applications can't decode the Mail file attachments at all. Problems can be experienced with very old Mac email applications, some Windows email applications, and some Unix email applications.

In some cases, Windows recipients receive two files for each file you attach. Mail sends two files; one contains the file data and the other contains the resource information. Most of the time, the recipient can safely ignore the resource file, and work with the data file. Tell the recipients who are having problems to try opening the files to determine which one is the correct file. The recipients can discard the unused resource files.

The missing file attachment message can usually be ignored, or you can try to resend the attachments using the Windows-friendly setting.

If the recipient's email application is incapable of decoding the files at all, you must find another means to transmit the files to her, such as an email application that enables you to select a different encoding scheme. Or, you can create a .Mac website to share the files.

MAX OS X TO THE MAX: EMAIL AWAY

In this section, you learn where Mail and Address Book information is stored and find keyboard shortcuts for the Address Book and Mail.

UNDERSTANDING WHERE YOUR MAIL AND ADDRESS BOOK INFORMATION IS STORED

Mail stores all your email in the location *username*/`Library`/`Mail`, where *username* is your short username. In this folder, you will find the following:

- A folder for each of the accounts you have configured in Mail. Within each accounts folder are the Inbox, a Drafts folder, and support files for that account.
- The Mailboxes folder that contains each mailbox you have created. If you have nested mailboxes, the inclusive mailbox appears as a folder.
- Your mailing sort, signature, and other preferences files.

NOTE

> The filename extension for a mailbox is `.mbox`. The filename extension for preference files is `.plist`.

Your Address Book is stored in the location *username*/`Library`/`Application Support`/`AddressBook`/`AddressBook.data`, where *username* is your short username.

USING ADDRESS BOOK KEYBOARD SHORTCUTS

Table 15.2 shows keyboard shortcuts for the Address Book application.

TABLE 15.2 KEYBOARD SHORTCUTS FOR THE ADDRESS BOOK	
Action	**Keyboard Shortcut**
Address Book Help	⌘-?
Edit Card	⌘-L

Action	Keyboard Shortcut
Hide Address Book	⌘-H
Import vCards	⌘-O
Merge Selected Cards	⌘-|
Minimize Address Book Window	⌘-M
Move Between Fields on an Address Card	Tab and Shift-Tab
New Card	⌘-N
New Group	Shift-⌘-N
Next Card	⌘-]
Open in Separate Window	⌘-I
Preferences	⌘-,
Previous Card	⌘-[
This is a Company	⌘-\
View Card and Columns	⌘-1
View Card Only	⌘-2
View Directories	⌘-3

Using Mail Keyboard Shortcuts

Table 15.3 shows keyboard shortcuts for the Mail application.

TABLE 15.3 KEYBOARD SHORTCUTS FOR MAIL	
Action	**Keyboard Shortcut**
Add Reply-To Header	Option-⌘-R
Add Sender to Address Book	⌘-Y
Address Panel	Option-⌘-A
Append Selected Messages	Option-⌘-I
Apply Bcc Header	Shift-⌘-B
Apply Rules	Option-⌘-L
Attach File	Shift-⌘-A
Bigger	⌘-+
Bounce	Shift-⌘-B
Check Spelling	⌘-;
Copy Style	Option-⌘-C
Decrease Quote Level	Option-⌘-'

continues

TABLE 15.3 CONTINUED

Action	Keyboard Shortcut
Delete	Delete
Erase Deleted Messages In All Accounts	⌘-K
Erase Junk Mail	Option-⌘-J
Find Messages (Mailbox Search)	Option-⌘-F
Find Next	⌘-G
Find Previous	Shift-⌘-G
Find Text	⌘-F
Forward	Shift-⌘-F
Get New Mail In All Accounts	Shift-⌘-N
Go To In	⌘-1
Go To Out	⌘-2
Go To Drafts	⌘-3
Go To Sent	⌘-4
Go To Trash	⌘-5
Go To Junk	⌘-6
Hide Deleted Messages	⌘-L
Hide/Show Mailboxes	Shift-⌘-M
Increase Quote Level	⌘-'
Jump to Selection	⌘-J
Message Long Headers	Shift-⌘-H
Make Plain Text	Shift-⌘-T
Mark As Flagged	Shift-⌘-L
Mark As Junk Mail	Shift-⌘-J
Mark As Unread/Mark As Read	Shift-⌘-U
Move Again	Option-⌘-T
New Message	⌘-N
New Viewer Window	Option-⌘-N
Next Alternative	⌘-]
Paste as Quotation	Shift-⌘-V
Paste With Current Style	Option-Shift-⌘-V
Plain Text Alternative	Option-⌘-P
Preferences	⌘-,

Action	Keyboard Shortcut
Previous Alternative	⌘-[
Raw Source	Option-⌘-U
Redirect	Shift-⌘-E
Reply All	Shift-⌘-R
Reply	⌘-R
Reply With iChat	Shift-⌘-I
Save As	Shift-⌘-S
Save As Draft	⌘-S
Send Again	Shift-⌘-D
Show Activity Viewer	⌘-0
Show Colors	Shift-⌘-C
Show Fonts	⌘-T
Show Long Headers	Shift-⌘-H
Smaller	⌘--
Spelling	⌘-:
Use Selection for Find	⌘-E

15

CHAPTER 16

SURFING THE WEB

16

BROWSING THE WEB WITH SAFARI

Apple's Safari is Mac OS X's default web browser. Safari offers many great features and excellent performance (see Figure 16.1).

Figure 16.1
Safari works as good as it looks.

Because you are reading this book (indicating that you know your way around a Mac), I assume that you are quite comfortable with the basics of using Safari, such as using its buttons, navigating the Web by clicking links and entering URLs in the Address bar, and so on. In this section, you will learn about some of Safari's great features that might not be quite so obvious.

BROWSING AND CONFIGURING RSS PAGES

For Mac OS X version 10.4, Safari now supports Rich Site Summary (RSS) web pages. RSS feeds provide a summary of articles and other information on a website so you can more efficiently browse information and then drill down into the information in which you are interested (see Figure 16.2). On an RSS feed page, you'll see a headline for each element on the page. You can scroll up and down the page to browse the headlines. When you find something in which you are interested, click the headline or the "Read more" link. You'll move to the article on a "regular" web page and can read its information. When you are done, click the SnapBack or RSS button to return to the RSS feed.

NOTE

> The articles you move to from some RSS feeds will cause the SnapBack button, RSS button, or both to appear in the Address bar. It doesn't matter which button you use—both will return you to the RSS feed.

RSS button

Figure 16.2
This CNET News.com
RSS feed isn't as pretty
to look at as a regular
web page, but it is
much more efficient to
use.

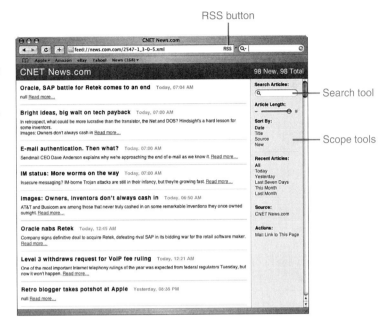

Search tool

Scope tools

16

BROWSING RSS FEEDS BETTER

In addition to these handy features, there are several other things you need to know about RSS feeds:

- The URL for an RSS feed will start with `feed://` rather than `http://`. When an RSS feed is loaded into your browser, you'll also see the RSS button at the right end of the Address bar.

- When you view a "regular" website and the RSS button appears in the Address bar, an RSS feed is available for that website. Click the RSS button to view the RSS feed.

- Use the Search Articles tool to search the contents of the feed. If you enter a search term and then create a bookmark, your search will be saved as a bookmark so you can repeat it easily.

- Use the Article Length slider to set the length of the summaries you see on a feed page. With the slider all the way to the right, you see the headline and first sentence or two. If you move the slider all the way to the left, you'll only see the headline and date for each story.

- Use the scope tools to configure the contents of the RSS page. For example, you can sort the articles using the Sort By options. You can choose the timeline for the articles you see with the Recent Articles options, such as by choosing Today to see only articles that are published on the current day.

- The source of information for an RSS feed will be shown in the Source area.

- Any actions available for the feed, such as a link to enable you to email it, will be shown in the Actions area.

- Safari includes a number of bookmarked RSS feeds by default. To view these, choose Bookmarks, Show All Bookmarks. Then click the All RSS Feeds collection.

- Safari can automatically check for updates to RSS feeds and add them to the feed page. When new articles appear for a feed, the number of new articles is shown next to the feed's bookmark in the Bookmarks bar (see Figure 16.3).

Figure 16.3
On the News Bookmarks menu, you can see the number of new articles on the RSS feeds in the parentheses after the related website (for example, there were 31 new articles on the Wired RSS feed).

- You can view all the RSS feeds referenced in a bookmark folder that contains them by opening the Bookmarks menu and choosing View All RSS Articles. In the resulting page, you'll see all the RSS feeds from all bookmarks in that folder.

CONFIGURING SAFARI'S RSS PREFERENCES

There are many aspects of working with RSS feeds that you can configure using the RSS tab of the Safari Preferences dialog box (see Figure 16.4):

- Set the default RSS reader on the Default RSS Reader pop-up menu. If you want to use something other than Safari, choose Select and then navigate to and choose the application you want to use to read RSS feeds.

- Use the Bookmarks Bar and Bookmarks Menu check boxes to tell Safari if you want the RSS feeds in these areas to be updated automatically. If you check at least one of these, use the "Check for updates" pop-up menu to set how frequently Safari updates the checked items. The options are "Every 30 minutes," "Every day," "Every hour," and "Never" (select Never if you don't want articles to ever be automatically downloaded to your Mac).

- If you want new articles highlighted with a color, check the "Color new articles" check box and choose the color you want used on the pop-up menu.

Figure 16.4
Use the RSS pane of the Safari Preferences dialog box to customize the way RSS feeds work.

- If you want RSS articles automatically removed after a specific amount of time, choose the time on the "Remove articles" pop-up menu. The times available range from after one day to never.

- To remove all articles, click the Remove Now button. If you click Remove Now in the resulting prompt, all RSS articles that have been downloaded to your Mac will be deleted.

CONFIGURING SAFARI

There are a number of ways in which you can configure Safari to match your browsing preferences. The most commonly used options are outlined in the sections that follow.

CONFIGURING SAFARI'S WINDOW

By default, Safari's window is pretty standard looking (refer to Figure 16.1). However, using the options on the View menu, you can customize the Safari browser experience to suit your preferences. On that menu, you have the following options:

- **Hide/Show Address Bar**—This command shows or hides the Safari Address bar. At its most basic, the Address bar displays the URL of the page currently being shown. You can also add more tools and buttons to the Address bar by using the view options listed underneath the Address Bar option on the menu. If you hide the Address bar, the other options are hidden as well. You show or hide the Address bar by pressing ⌘-| (which is actually Shift-⌘-\ on the keyboard).

- **Customize Address Bar**—When you choose this command, you can select the tools that appear on the Address bar via a standard Customize toolbar sheet. The tools available on this sheet are described in the following bullets:

  - **Back/Forward**—The Back and Forward buttons do just what you expect.
  - **Home**—This button takes you back to your home page.
  - **AutoFill**—If you click the AutoFill button, a form is completed with information from your card in your Address Book (more on this feature later).

- **Text Size**—These buttons enable you to increase or decrease the size of text being displayed on a page (if you have ever squinted while trying to read a page designed for Windows computers, you know why increasing the size of text on a page can be a good thing!).
- **Stop/Reload**—This button can be used to stop a page that is currently being loaded or to reload a page currently being displayed.
- **Add Bookmark**—Use this option to show or hide the Add Bookmark button.
- **Print**—Use this to print the page being displayed.
- **Report Bug**—When you click this button, you can send a bug report about Safari to Apple.
- **Address**—This tool can be used to enter or show a URL.
- **Google Search**—The Google Search tool is a great way to search for information, as you will learn in a later section.

- **Show/Hide Bookmarks Bar**—The Bookmarks bar provides easy access to your favorite bookmarks. It appears under the Address bar if it is being displayed.
- **Show/Hide Status Bar**—The Status bar provides useful information about what Safari is doing at any point in time or information about a link to which you are pointing, such as its URL.

TIP

> Some of the optional tools are also available as commands on the View menu, such as Reload Page, Make Text Bigger, and so on.

CONFIGURING SAFARI'S GENERAL PREFERENCES

Press ⌘-, to open the Safari Preferences dialog box, and click the General button to open its General pane (see Figure 16.5). The general preferences are explained in the following list:

- **Default Web Browser**—Use the "Default Web Browser" pop-up menu to choose your default web browser, which is the browser Mac OS X will use to view web pages and to open web links. Initially, Safari is the option selected on the pop-up menu. However, you can choose Select and then pick another browser. This sets your browser preference for all areas of the OS.
- **New Window Behavior**—Use the "New windows open with" pop-up menu to choose what happens when you open a new Safari window. The options are Home Page, Empty Page, Same Page, or Bookmarks. In most cases, Empty Page is the best choice because it doesn't cause Safari to download a page that you probably don't want to view anyway. However, if you frequently use bookmarks to move to a new page, that can be a useful option as well.

- **Home Page**—Type a URL in the Home page field to set it as your home page. Alternatively, you can move to the page you want to be your home page, open the General pane, and click "Set to Current Page." The home page is displayed when you use the Home button or if you have it set to be displayed when you open a new Safari window. If you leave the field empty, moving to the home page opens a new empty page.

- **Download Behavior**—You will frequently use Safari to download files. Use the "Save downloaded files to" pop-up menu to select a location in which you want those files to be placed by default. The choices are Desktop or Other. I recommend that you select Other, create a folder called Downloaded Files or something similar, and set that folder as your download location. That way, you will always know where files you download are located.

NOTE

> Setting a file download location, similar to choosing a default web browser, affects the OS—not just Safari. For example, if you use a download tool that uses your download location preference, that application uses the preference you set within Safari.

Use the "Remove download list items" pop-up menu to choose when items are removed from the Downloads window (you'll learn about that later).

If you want "safe" files to be opened as soon as you download them, check the "Open 'safe' files after downloading" check box (it is checked by default). When Safari downloads image, movie, text, sound, and other content files, they are opened automatically. For those files that might cause damage to your system, such as applications, macros, and other suspicious files, you must open them manually after you download them.

- **Link behavior**—When documents, such as email messages, contain URL links, the two radio buttons determine how those links open when you click them. If you click the "in a new window" radio button, a new Safari window opens and displays the page at which the link points. If you click "in the current window," the content at which the link points replaces that shown in the current window.

Figure 16.5
Although simple in appearance, the General pane enables you to configure important Safari behaviors.

CONFIGURING SAFARI'S APPEARANCE PREFERENCES

Click the Appearance button in the Safari Preferences dialog box to move to the Appearance tab. Here you can set the standard font, fixed-width font, and default encoding that is used when pages are displayed. (If a page uses a built-in style sheet, your options might be overridden by the style sheet, but most of the time, your preferences will be used.) To select a font, click the related Select button and use the Font panel to configure the font. To choose an encoding method, use the pop-up menu.

If you want images to be displayed when a page is opened, check the "Display images when the page opens" check box (it is checked by default). If you use a slow connection, you might want to uncheck this check box so you don't waste time downloading images you aren't interested in.

CONFIGURING SAFARI'S SECURITY PREFERENCES

Safari has a number of good security features, some of which you can configure on the Security pane of the Safari Preferences dialog box (see Figure 16.6).

Figure 16.6
Use the Security pane to set how Safari manages the security of your Mac; the best part is the ability to block pop-up windows.

The Web Content controls determine whether certain types of content are enabled. These controls include:

- **Enable plug-ins**—Determines whether any Safari plug-ins, such as those for QuickTime, Flash, and so on, are enabled. If you disable the plug-ins, content that requires them is not displayed. I recommend you leave this check box checked because most content that requires such plug-ins is safe. And, except for the plug-ins installed by default, you will choose the plug-ins you want to install.

- **Enable Java and Enable JavaScript**—Java and JavaScript are two programming languages that can be used to execute complex operations within the Safari browser. For example, if you use a bank service, it likely uses JavaScript to deliver its functionality. Again, you should typically allow these types of content.

- **Block pop-up windows**—If you have ever been annoyed by the numerous and obnoxious pop-up windows that appear when you visit some websites, you might think that this is the single best feature of Safari. If this option is checked, Safari does not allow a web page to open additional windows. This means that all pop-up windows that point to different URLs are blocked and you never have to see them.

Although blocking pop-up windows is mostly a good thing, some pop-up windows actually provide useful information and are necessary to get the most out of a website. If you block them, a site might not work well, or at all.

TIP

If you block pop-up windows and a site that needs them doesn't work properly, you can enable them again by selecting Safari, Block Pop-Up Windows or by pressing ⌘-K. This toggles the pop-up window setting, so you can also use it to quickly allow pop-ups if you generally prevent them.

You use the Cookies radio buttons to determine how Safari deals with cookies it encounters. Typically, the "Only from sites you navigate to" is the best setting because cookies often provide a useful service for the sites you intentionally visit, such as shopping sites. If you want to block all cookies, click Never. I don't recommend that you use the Always option.

To see the cookies that have been accepted, click the Show Cookies button. A sheet appears that shows you all the cookies that have been downloaded to your Mac (prepare to be astounded at their number!). In addition to the information you see about the cookies, you can select cookies and either click Remove to delete them or click Remove All to delete all the cookies on your Mac. It's not a bad idea to review this list from time to time and delete any cookies you can't recognize (or at least recognize where they came from). If a site needs a cookie to function, it will create it again, although you might lose some of your customized information on that site.

Cookies

On the Web, *cookies* are small text files websites use to track information about you. When you visit a site that uses cookies, the site can check the cookies it previously installed on your machine to serve you or capture more information about you. For example, a cookie can contain areas of interest so you are automatically taken to spots on the site that are more likely to generate a purchase from you.

Most cookies are relatively harmless and some even serve a good purpose, but you do need to be aware that a lot of information about you and what you do on the Web is captured whether you know it or not. If this thought bothers you, select the Never radio button so cookies are never accepted. If you do this, be aware that some sites might not work for you.

If you want Safari to warn you when you send nonsecure information to a secure site, check the "Ask before sending a non-secure form to a secure website" check box.

If the current user account has parental controls configured for it, you can use the "Enable parental controls" check box to temporarily disable those controls so you can move to the sites you want to allow. Click the check box (it will be disabled if the account doesn't have this feature turned on) and authenticate yourself. Use the browser to move to sites you want to be allowed and set bookmarks for each. Then check the "Enable parental controls" check box again to prevent the user from visiting any other sites.

16

The Greatest Browser Feature Ever

That might be a bit of an overstatement, but if you frequently access secured services over the Web using usernames and passwords, such as banking or shopping sites, you might find the following feature to be the best thing about Safari. Safari is fully integrated with Mac OS X's Keychains. Basically, this means you can store usernames and passwords within Safari and Safari will enter that information for you when you return to the related sites automatically. All you then have to do is move to the URL for the service, and the username and password are entered for you automatically. Click Login, Enter, or a similar button or link and you are in.

To enable this, Safari creates the Safari Forms AutoFill keychain item and stores usernames and passwords there.

→ To learn how to configure and use AutoFill for usernames and passwords, **see** "Using Safari AutoFill," **p. 477**.

→ To learn more about keychains, **see** "Securing Your Mac with Keychains," **p. 1024**.

CONFIGURING SAFARI'S ADVANCED PREFERENCES

To see Safari's Advanced preferences, click the Advanced button on the Safari Preferences dialog box. The Advanced preferences consist of universal access, style sheet options and proxy settings.

Use the Universal Access controls to set a minimum font size or control Tab key behavior.

If you have a style sheet you want Safari to use, you can add it by selecting Other on the Style Sheet pop-up menu and then selecting the sheet you want to install. If you add more than one sheet, you can select that sheet you want to use on the Style Sheet pop-up menu.

NOTE
> Cascading style sheets can be used to determine the formatting for web pages. Many pages use these sheets. If not, a page is presented based on Safari's own interpretation of the HTML and the other code of which the page is composed.

You can use the Proxies button to access the Proxies tab of the Network pane of the System Preferences application.

SEARCHING WITH SAFARI

Of course, you can use Safari to access the many web search engines available, such as Yahoo, Lycos, and so on. You do this by visiting that search engine's site.

However, you can access one of the best search engines, Google, directly from the Safari Address bar. This enables some great features, most notably the SnapBack button.

NOTE
> If you don't see the Google Search tool, make sure the Address bar is displayed and that the Google search tool has been added to the Address Bar (it is by default).

To search the Web using the built-in Google search tool, do the following:

1. Type the text for which you want to search in the Search tool and press Return. You jump to Google and the results of your search are displayed (see Figure 16.7).

Figure 16.7
Safari's built-in search tool enables you to quickly search on Google.

2. Use a link on the results page to move to a page that looks promising (see Figure 16.8).

SnapBack

Figure 16.8
The SnapBack button enables you to return to the Google search results page.

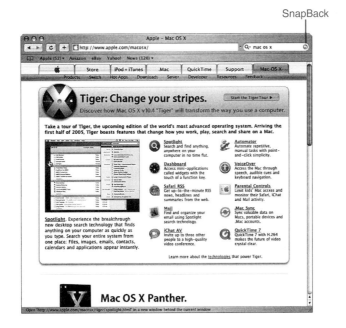

3. To return to the results page so you can try other links, click the SnapBack button; select History, Search Results SnapBack; or press Option-⌘-S.

Performing a Google search from within Safari is fast and easy. Here are few tips:

- To repeat a previous search, click the magnifying glass icon in the search tool; then on the pop-up menu, select the search you want to repeat.
- To clear the searches you have performed, click the magnifying glass icon in the search tool; then on the pop-up menu, select Clear Recent Searches.
- To clear the current search (when the Google page is being displayed), click the x button inside the search field.

USING SAFARI SNAPBACK

Using the SnapBack button when you search with the Google search tool is great, but you can also use this feature when you are browsing. Safari marks the first page you visit on any site as the SnapBack page. As you move to other pages on the site, you can return to the SnapBack page by clicking the SnapBack button shown at the end of the URL of the page you are currently viewing. You then move back to the SnapBack page for that site.

Here are a couple more SnapBack tips:

- You can mark a page to be the SnapBack page for a site by either selecting History, Mark Page for SnapBack or pressing Option-⌘-K. Whenever you click the SnapBack button, you return to this page. (If you don't set a SnapBack page, you return to the first page on the site.)
- You can also return to the SnapBack page by selecting History, Page SnapBack or pressing Option-⌘-P.

USING SAFARI BOOKMARKS

Like all other browsers, Safari enables you to bookmark web pages so you can easily return to them. And, also similar to other browsers, Safari provides tools you can use to organize your bookmarks. However, Safari's bookmark tools are more refined and powerful than most of the browsers I've used.

CONFIGURING SAFARI BOOKMARKS PREFERENCES

Open the Bookmarks pane of the Safari Preferences dialog box to configure your bookmark preferences. On this pane, you have the following options:

- **Bookmarks Bar**—The two Include check boxes determine whether Address Book and Bonjour sites are accessible from the Bookmarks bar.

  If you make your Address Book available from the Bookmarks bar, you can access any websites associated with cards in your Address Book by selecting the site you want to visit on the Address Book menu. This is a very cool way to quickly access the website for anyone or any company in your Address Book.

Similarly, you can make all the Bonjour computers that provide services Safari can access available via the Bonjour menu. This enables you to quickly move to Web, FTP, or other resources on your local network.

- **Bookmarks Menu**—This area enables you to add your Address Book and Bonjour sites to the Bookmarks menu. Additionally, you can include all the Bookmarks bar's bookmarks on the Bookmarks menu by checking the Include Bookmarks Bar box.

- **Collections**—Safari uses the term *collections* for groups of bookmarks. You can use collections to organize bookmarks; a number of collections are included by default. You use the Bookmarks window to work with these (this is covered later in this section).

- **Synchronize**—If you use machines in different locations, you might find yourself adding bookmarks on one machine and not being able to use those bookmarks when you are working on another machine. If you have a .Mac account, you can synchronize your bookmarks across many machines so they all have the same set. To do this, check the "Synchronize bookmarks with other computers using .Mac" and click the .Mac button. The .Mac pane of the System Preferences application will open and you can use the Sync tab to configure synchronization.

→ To learn how to configure .Mac synchronization, **see** "Using .Mac to Synchronize Important Information on Multiple Macs," **p. 512**.

ACCESSING SAFARI BOOKMARKS

You can use bookmarks in the following ways:

- Click a bookmark on the Bookmarks bar.
- Select a bookmark on the Bookmarks menu.
- Press ⌘-1 to move to the first bookmark on the Bookmarks bar (not counting menu items on the bar), ⌘-2 to move to the second one, and so on up to ⌘-5 to move to the fifth one listed on the Bookmarks bar. This only works for bookmarks not for folders. If an item is a folder, you must select it using the mouse.
- Open the Bookmarks window and double-click a bookmark.
- Open the Address Book or Bonjour menu on the Bookmarks bar and select a site to visit.
- Open a bookmark's contextual menu and select either Open, Open in New Window or Open in New Tab.

SETTING SAFARI BOOKMARKS

You can bookmark web pages with the following steps:

1. Move to the page you want to bookmark.
2. Select Bookmarks, Add Bookmark or press ⌘-D. The Add Bookmark sheet will open.
3. Edit the name of the bookmark. You can use the default name, change it, or replace it with one of your choosing.

4. On the pop-up menu, select the location in which you want the bookmark to be stored. You can select Bookmarks Bar to add the bookmark to the Bookmarks bar, any folder to place the bookmark in that folder, or Bookmarks Menu to place the bookmark on the Bookmarks menu.

5. Click Add or press Return. The bookmark will be added in the location you selected.

TIP

> You can add a bookmark to the Bookmarks bar by dragging across the URL in the Address bar and dropping it on the Bookmarks bar. In the resulting name sheet, edit the name of the bookmark and click OK. The bookmark will be added to the Bookmarks bar so you can access it from there.

ORGANIZING SAFARI BOOKMARKS

Use Safari's Bookmark tools to organize your bookmarks. You can determine the location of bookmarks, place them in folders to create hierarchical bookmark menus, rename them, and so on. To do these tasks, open the Bookmarks window by clicking the Bookmarks button at the left end of the Bookmarks bar, by selecting Bookmarks, Show All Bookmarks, or by pressing Option-⌘-B. The Bookmarks window will open (see Figure 16.9).

Figure 16.9
The Bookmarks window enables you to organize you bookmarks.

In the left pane of the window is the list of collections (groups or folders of bookmarks). At the top of the list are the Bookmarks Bar and Bookmarks Menu collections that contain the bookmarks in those areas. Under those are the Address Book and Bonjour collections, and under those is the History collection that contains a list of sites you have visited. Below that is the All RSS Feeds collection that contains all your RSS feeds. Under that are the rest of the bookmark folders; Safari includes several folders with many bookmarks by default. You can add your own folders and bookmarks, as well as adding your bookmarks to existing collections.

To view the contents of a collection, select it. The bookmarks it contains will be shown in the right pane. For each bookmark, its name and address will be shown. If an item in the collection is a folder, you will see the folder along with its expansion triangle; click this to expand the folder's contents.

Organizing bookmarks is straightforward:

- Move bookmarks from one collection to another by dragging them onto the collection in which you want to place them. For example, to move a bookmark from the Bookmarks bar to the Bookmarks menu, drag it from the Bookmarks Bar collection to the Bookmarks Menu collection.
- Create new collections by clicking the New Collection button (the +) at the bottom of the Collections pane.
- Create a new folder in a collection by clicking the New Folder button (the "+") at the bottom of the Bookmarks pane.
- Rename a collection, folder, or bookmark by selecting it, opening the contextual menu, and selecting Edit Name.
- Change the URL for a bookmark by selecting it, opening the contextual menu, and selecting Edit Address.
- Move to a URL by double-clicking it or opening its contextual menu and choosing Open or "Open in New Window."
- Add a folder to the Bookmarks Bar or Bookmarks Menu collections. Then place bookmarks in the folder you created. When you select the folder in either location, a pop-up menu appears to enable you to quickly select any bookmarks in that folder.
- Search your bookmarks using the Search tool at the bottom of the Bookmarks pane. Using the Magnifying Glass pop-up menu, you can choose to search in the selected collection or in all collections.
- Delete a collection, folder, or bookmark by selecting it and pressing Delete or by opening its contextual menu and choosing Delete. If you delete a folder or collection, you will also delete any bookmarks contained in those items.

TIP

Put the bookmarks you use most often on the Bookmarks bar or Bookmarks menu because you can get to them most quickly there (if you have so many that these become cluttered, use folders to keep them organized). In the next section, you learn a technique that enables you to open an entire folder of bookmarks with a single click.

USING SAFARI TABS

If you have spent any time on the Web, you have no doubt seen the benefits of having many web browser windows open at the same time. Of course, you can do this with Safari by selecting File, New Window or pressing ⌘-N. If you have done this, you also know that after opening more than a couple of windows, moving back to specific windows can be cumbersome. That is where Safari's Tabs feature comes in. You can open many pages within the same window; each web page appears as a tab. You then select the tab to view that page. After you have used this, you will wonder why every web browser doesn't have this feature.

CONFIGURING TABS

First, enable and configure the Tab feature by opening the Tabs pane of the Safari preferences dialog box (see Figure 16.10).

Figure 16.10
Configure tabs to open many windows on the Web in a single Safari window.

To enable and configure tabbed browsing, follow these steps:

1. Click the "Enable Tabbed Browsing" check box to turn on Safari's Tab feature.

2. If you want new tabs to be selected, so the page on the tab is displayed, as soon as they are created, check the "Select new tabs as they are created" check box.

> **TIP**
>
> The previously mentioned preference affects what the tab keyboard shortcuts do. If you don't enable this preference, you have to physically select a tab after you create it to view it. I have assumed that this preference is enabled for the rest of this section.

3. If you want the Tab bar to be shown, check the "Always show tab bar" check box. If you don't check this, the Tab bar is shown only if at least one page is being displayed.

4. Close the Preferences dialog box.

> **TIP**
>
> Notice the keyboard shortcuts at the bottom of the Tabs pane. These are important tips that help you effectively work with tabs. If you can't remember them, they are listed in the next section and in Table 16.4 at the end of this chapter.

Using Cool Safari Tab Tricks

After you have enabled tabs, the Safari window contains a tab for each web page you have opened. To open a new tab and display it, hold down the ⌘ key while you click a link or bookmark. The page will open and be on a new tab. You can open as many tabs as you like (see Figure 16.11).

Figure 16.11
Each tab is a separate and independent web page; very cool!

Following is a list of tab tricks:

- Click a tab to view its web page. The tab currently being displayed will be highlighted.
- To close a page, click the x button in its tab. The tab and page will close.
- To open a page in a new tab and move to it, ⌘-click a link or bookmark.
- To open a new tab without viewing it, ⌘-Shift-click a link or bookmark.
- To open a link or a bookmark in a new window and view it, ⌘-Option-click it.
- To open a link or a bookmark in a new window but move the new window to the background, ⌘-Option-Shift-click it.

> **NOTE**
>
> The previous four actions are reversed if you uncheck the "Select new tabs as they are created" preference. For example, you would ⌘-Shift-click a link or bookmark to open it in a tab and view it.

- To move into the next tab, choose Window, Select Next Tab or press Shift-⌘-].
- To move into the previous tab, choose Window, Select Next Tab or press Shift-⌘-[.

Okay, I have saved the coolest thing about Safari for this moment: Safari enables you to open as many pages as you want by clicking a single bookmark for a collection. Each page included in the group opens in a new tab. If you frequently open the same set of pages, you can click a single bookmark to open them all at the same.

First, create the group of bookmarks you want to open:

1. Open the Bookmark window and create a folder in the Bookmarks Bar collection.
2. Check the Auto-Click check box for the folder you created.
3. Place bookmarks for all the sites you want to open simultaneously in the folder you created in step 1 (see Figure 16.12).

Figure 16.12
Because the Auto-Tab check box is checked, I can open all the pages inside the folder called openatonce with a single click.

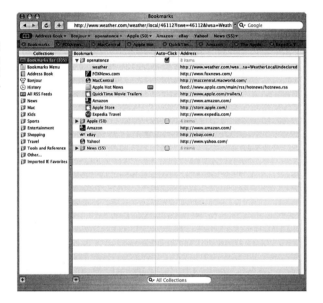

TIP

To make moving bookmarks into folders within collections easier, open a second Safari window and view the Bookmarks window. You can drag bookmarks from the first window onto the second to move them among collections.

Close the Bookmarks window and click the button on the Bookmarks Bar for the folder you created in the previous steps. Every page opens in its own tab (see Figure 16.13). Working with a set of web pages has never been so easy.

TIP

You can use Automator to create an application that will open websites for you. You can add this application to your Login Items so they automatically open for you each time you log in.

→ To learn how to use the Automator, **see** Chapter 10, "Using the Automator to Make Your Mac Work for You," **p. 279**.

Figure 16.13
I opened all the pages in this window just by clicking the "openatonce" button in the Bookmarks bar!

USING SAFARI AUTOFILL

If you access services on the Web, such as travel planning, shopping, banking, and so on, you no doubt have a lot of experience filling out the same information time and time again. Completing a web form is fun the first time, but after completing your address, phone number, username, and password a few dozen times, it gets old. This is where Safari's AutoFill feature comes in. It enables you to complete various kinds of information automatically or at the click of the AutoFill button.

Using AutoFill, Safari can enter the following types of information for you:

■ **Your Address Book information**—Safari can access the information stored on your card in your Address Book. This can include your address, phone number, website, and so on.

→ To learn how to configure the information on your card in your Address Book, **see** "Editing Your Own Address Card," **p. 409**.

■ **Usernames and passwords**—Safari can capture your username and password at many websites. When you return to those sites, your username and password are entered for you automatically.

■ **Information entered on various websites**—As you provide information in other types of websites, Safari can gather this data and remember it so that the next time you visit a site, you can complete any information by clicking the AutoFill button.

CONFIGURING AUTOFILL

First, you need to tell Safari which AutoFill features you want to use by configuring your AutoFill preferences:

1. Press ⌘-, to open the Preferences dialog box.
2. Click the AutoFill button to open the AutoFill pane (see Figure 16.14).

Figure 16.14
Using Safari's AutoFill feature saves you a lot of typing.

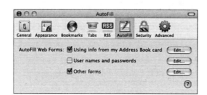

3. If you want Safari to be able to enter the information from your Address Book card, check the "Using info from my Address Book card" check box.

> **TIP**
>
> If you click the top Edit button, the Address Book application will open and you will see your Address Book card in the edit mode so you can make changes to it.

4. If you want Safari to capture usernames and passwords at various websites you use, check the "User names and passwords" check box.
5. If you want Safari to capture other types of information you enter on the Web, check the "Other forms" check box.
6. Close the Preferences dialog box.

USING AUTOFILL

Using AutoFill is straightforward.

To enter your personal information from your Address Book card, use the following steps:

1. Move to a web page that requires your personal information, such as name, address, and so on.
2. Click the AutoFill button on the Address Bar; select Edit, AutoFill Form; or press Shift-⌘-A. Safari will transfer the information from your card in your Address Book and place it in the appropriate fields on the web form.
3. Review the information that was entered to ensure that it is correct. AutoFill isn't perfect and sometimes web forms use slightly different terms for data.

> **TIP**
>
> If you find AutoFill consistently not entering specific information, add that information to your card in your Address Book.

To use the username and password feature, do the following steps:

1. Move to a website that requires a username and password.

2. Enter your username and password on the page.

3. Click Login. You will be prompted about whether you want Safari to capture the username and password for this site.

4. In the prompt, make one of the following choices:

   - Click Yes if you want the information to be added to AutoFill.

   - Click Not Now if you don't want the information to be captured at this time but want to be prompted the next time you access the site.

   - Click "Never for this Website" if you don't want the information captured and never want to be prompted again.

If you click Yes, the next time you visit the website, your username and password will be filled in automatically. All you have to do to log in to the site is click the Login button or link.

CAUTION

> The username and password feature is convenient, but you shouldn't use it unless you are the only one who uses your Mac OS X user account or the people who share your Mac OS X user account are very trustworthy. Because the usernames and passwords for your accounts are entered automatically, anyone who uses your Mac OS X user account and moves to the related websites can log in to your account on that website.

If you decide you don't want to provide automatic access to a specific website, you can remove that site's username and password:

1. Open the AutoFill pane of the Safari Preferences dialog box.

2. Click the Edit button next to the text "User names and passwords." A sheet will appear that lists each website and username you have captured in Safari.

3. Select the website you want to remove.

TIP

> Click Remove All to delete all the websites for which you have captured usernames and passwords.

4. Click Remove. Continue removing websites until you have removed all the sites you no longer need.

5. Click Done and close the Preferences dialog box.

NOTE

If you don't turn off the username and password feature by unchecking the "Use names and passwords" check box, you will be prompted by AutoFill the next time you visit any websites you deleted from the list.

Using the AutoFill feature for other kinds of forms is similar to the first two. When you enable the "Other forms" feature and enter information in websites, that information is captured. When you return to those sites in the future, you can enter the information again by clicking the AutoFill button; selecting Edit, AutoFill Form; or pressing Shift-⌘-A. You can edit the list of websites for which information is remembered by clicking the Edit button next to the text "Other forms" on the AutoFill pane of the Safari Preferences dialog box.

USING SAFARI'S ACTIVITY VIEWER

As you move around the Web, Safari tracks the sites you have visited. You can view this information on the Activity window. To do so, select Window, Activity or press Option-⌘-A. The Activity window will appear. In this window, you will see a list of the sites you have visited. You can expand each site to see the individual pages you have visited and double-click any of these to return to that page.

BROWSING PRIVATELY

As you travel around tthe Web, Safari helpfully tracks where you have been, usernames and passwords, cookies, AutoFill information, and other items to make using the Web more convenient. However, sometimes you might not want all this information recorded and would instead prefer to browse without any sort of record keeping on Safari's part. For example, you might be using a public Mac or be logged in under someone else's user account. In Safari terminology, this is called *private browsing*. When you browse privately, web pages you visit are not tracked in the History folder, items you download are removed from the Downloads window, any cookies stored on the Mac are deleted, information isn't retained for AutoFill, and your searches aren't saved.

To browse privately, choose Safari, Private Browsing. Click OK in the resulting prompt and private browsing will be in effect. When you are ready to resume normal browsing, choose Safari, Private Browsing again. Safari will clear any cookies and tdownloads stored during the private browse session and return to normal browsing mode.

EMAILING WEB PAGES

When you surf, you'll likely encounter web pages you'd like other people to view. Using Safari's built-in web page emailing ability, you can easily send information about web pages to other people via email:

1. View the web page you want to send to someone else.
2. Choose File, "Mail Contents of This Page" or press ⌘-I if you want to send the actual contents of the web page to someone; choose File, "Mail Link to This Page" or press

Shift-⌘-I if you want to send a link to the page. Your default email application will open, a new message will be created, and the web page contents or a link to the page will be inserted into the new message.

3. Address the email message, add any information you want, and send it.

DOWNLOADING AND PREPARING FILES

One of the best things about the Web is that you can download files from it. These files can be applications, graphics, audio files, text files, updaters, or any other file you can think of. Downloading files is simple; the only two areas that might give you some trouble are finding the files you download and preparing them for use.

The general process for downloading and preparing files is the following:

1. Locate the file you want to download.

2. Download the file to your Mac.

3. Prepare the file for use by decoding and uncompressing it.

There are two basic ways to download files. You can use a Web browser to download files, or you can use an FTP client (or the Finder) to download files from FTP and other sites. Using a web browser to download files is simpler, but it is also slower. A dedicated FTP client can dramatically speed up file downloading.

→ For information on using the Finder to download files from an FTP site, **see** "Downloading Files via FTP in the Finder," **p. 489**.

CONFIGURING A DOWNLOADS FOLDER

By default, your web browser stores files you download in the Desktop folder in your Home directory (and thus, they appear on your desktop). If this isn't where you want downloaded files to be stored, you should create a folder into which your web browser will always download files. That way, you will always know where to find the files you download and they won't clutter your desktop.

NOTE

> Because a directory is modified when you store files in it, you must use a directory that you have permissions to write to. On your Mac OS X startup volume, you are limited to downloading files to a directory within your Home directory. However, you can choose a location outside your Mac OS X startup volume if you want.
>
> If you want other users of your machine to be able to access the files you download, you can use your Public folder as your downloads folder.

After you have created your downloads folder, open the General pane of the Safari Preferences dialog box and use the "Save downloaded files to" pop-up menu to choose that folder.

DOWNLOADING FILES USING SAFARI

Downloading files is as simple as anything gets. Safari uses its Downloads window to show you information about the files you are downloading. To start the download process, just click the download link for the file you want to download.

> **TIP**
>
> You can download multiple files at the same time. Start one; then, move back to a web window, move to the next, and start it downloading.
>
> You can also continue to browse the Web while your files are downloading. The speed decreases a bit (or a lot if you are using a dial-up Internet account), but at least you can do something while the file is downloading.

Some sites simply provide the file's name as its link, whereas others provide a Download button. Whichever way it is done, finding the link to click to begin the download process is usually simple.

After you click the link to begin the download, the Downloads window opens showing the progress of the file you are downloading (see Figure 16.15). As a file is downloaded, you see its name, the download progress, and the file size. During the download process, you see the stop button for the file you are downloading; you can stop the process by clicking this button.

Figure 16.15
The Downloads window provides the information and tools you need to manage your downloads.

When the download is complete, you will see the file's icon in the Downloads window. Also, the Stop button becomes the Find in Finder button, which contains a magnifying glass. Click this button to move to the file you downloaded in the Finder.

> **TIP**
>
> If the download process is interrupted for some reason (such as a connection problem or if you clicked the Stop button), the Stop button becomes the Retry button, which contains a circular arrow. Click this button to try to download the file again.

As you download files, Safari continues to add them to the list in the Downloads window. You can clear them manually by clicking the Clear button. You can have Safari remove them automatically by selecting either When Safari Quits or Upon Successful Download on the "Remove download list items" pop-up menu on the General pane of the Safari Preferences dialog box.

After the download is complete, Safari tries to prepare the file that downloaded so you can use it. Most of the time, this works automatically, but in some situations, you must perform this task manually. This process can be somewhat complicated depending on the file you download.

PREPARING FILES FOR USE

Most files you download are encoded and compressed. *Encoding* is the process of translating an application or other file into a plain-text file so it can be transferred across the Internet. *Compressing* a file is a process that makes the file's size smaller so it can be transferred across the Internet more quickly.

Before you can use a file you have downloaded, it must be decoded and it might also need to be uncompressed. Depending on the type of file it is, these two actions might be done at the same time or might have to be handled separately. An application is required for both tasks; a single application can usually handle them, but occasionally the file might need to be uncompressed with one application and decoded with another.

UNDERSTANDING FILE EXTENSIONS FOR COMPRESSED FILES

Knowing what will happen in any situation requires that you understand the types of files you are likely to download. You can determine this by the filename extension. The most common extensions with which you will have to deal are listed in Table 16.1.

TABLE 16.1   COMMON FILE EXTENSIONS FOR COMPRESSED OR ENCODED MAC FILES

File Extension	What It Means	Comments
.bin	Binary file format	A common encoding format for the Mac.
.gz	Unix compression format	The dominant compression format for Unix files.
.hqx	Binhex encoding	Another very common encoding format for the Mac.
.img	Disk Image file format	A file that is a disk image and must be mounted with the Disk Utility application before it can be used.

continues

16

TABLE 16.1 CONTINUED

File Extension	What It Means	Comments
.pkg	The package format	Package files are installed with the application installer.
.sea	StuffIt compression format that can be uncompressed by double-clicking the file	Useful because the recipient of the file doesn't have to have a decompression tool. He simply double-clicks the file to decompress it.
.sit	StuffIt compression	One standard compression format for Mac files.
.tar	Tape Archive format	An archiving format for Unix computers that is used for some files you might want for Mac OS X.
.zip	Zip compression format	The dominant compression format for Windows PCs and Mac OS X's standard compression format.

If the file you download is in the .bin, .hqx, .img, or .pkg format, you don't need to do anything to prepare the file for use. Safari will handle that for you. Some of the other formats, however, will require some manual intervention to prepare the file for use.

MANUALLY PREPARING A FILE FOR USE

Although you can usually rely on Safari's preconfigured helper applications to handle most of the files you download, it is useful to know how to manually decode and uncompress files you download so you can handle them yourself and better understand how to configure a helper application to do it for you.

By default, Safari attempts to launch the appropriate helper application to handle files you download. If a file you download can be handled successfully by the helper application, it is prepared and a usable version of it is placed in the same folder into which it was downloaded.

If you download a .zip file, double-click it to uncompress it. A usable version of the file or a folder containing usable files (if the .zip includes more than one file) will be created.

If you download a .sit or other file type, you'll need to also download and install a copy of the freeware StuffIt Expander to be able to expand and then use the file.

NOTE

You can get information about and download StuffIt Expander at www.stuffit.com.

WORKING WITH PLUG-INS AND HELPER APPLICATIONS

Many file types are available on the Internet. In addition to HTML, JSP, GIF, JPEG, and other files that are used to present a web page, there are graphics, movies, sounds, PDFs, and many other file types you can open and view. Safari can't work with all these file types directly, and fortunately, it doesn't have to. Safari and other web browsers use plug-ins and helper applications to expand their capabilities so they can work with files they don't natively support.

WORKING WITH PLUG-INS

Plug-ins are software that can be incorporated into a web browser when it opens (thus, the term *plug-in*). Internet plug-ins enable applications to display files that are of the specific types handled by those plug-ins. For example, the QuickTime plug-in enables web browsers to display QuickTime movies.

INSTALLING INTERNET PLUG-INS

As you travel around the Web, you might encounter file types for which you do not have the required plug-in. In that case, you must find and install the plug-in you need. Usually, sites have links to places from which you can download the plug-ins needed for the file types on the site. There are a couple of places in the system where plug-ins can be stored.

Plug-ins that are available to all user accounts are stored in the folder `Mac OS X/Library/Internet Plug-Ins/`, where `Mac OS X` is the name of your startup volume.

You must be logged in under an Administrator account to store a plug-in in this directory.

Internet plug-ins can also be stored in a specific user account, in which case they are available only to that user. A user's specific plug-ins are in the location `shortusername/Library/Internet Plug-Ins/`, where `shortusername` is the short name for the user account.

To install a plug-in, simply place it in the directory that is appropriate for that plug-in (to be available either to all users or to only a specific user). Quit the web browser and then launch it again to make the plug-in active.

NOTE

Some plug-ins are installed using an installer application, in which case you don't need to install the plug-in manually.

If you open the Internet Plug-Ins directories, you will see the plug-ins currently installed. Any plug-in installed in these folders can be used by a supported web browser.

Many plug-ins are available for web browsers. The QuickTime plug-in is installed by default so you can view QuickTime movies in web browsers. Additionally, the Shockwave Flash plug-in is installed by default, as is the Java Applet plug-in. There are many other plug-ins you might want to download and install.

You can see the plug-ins installed for Safari by selecting Help, Install Plug-ins. A new window will open and show all the installed plug-ins (see Figure 16.16).

Figure 16.16
Safari's Installed Plug-ins window shows you all the plug-ins to which Safari has access.

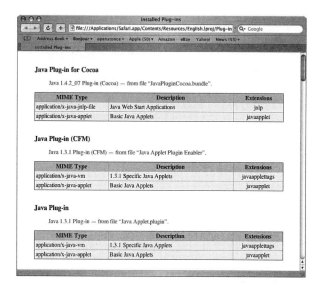

When you attempt to view a file for which you do not have the appropriate plug-in, you see a warning dialog box that tells you what to do. Usually, you see instructions to help you find, download, and install the plug-in as well.

USING INTERNET PLUG-INS

After a plug-in is installed in the appropriate folder, it works with a web browser to provide its capabilities. When you click a file that requires the plug-in to be used, the appropriate plug-in activates and enables you to do whatever it is designed to do. For example, when you open a QuickTime movie, you see the controls that enable you to watch that movie within the web browser.

WORKING WITH HELPER APPLICATIONS

Although plug-ins provide additional capability by "plugging in" to a web browser, *helper applications* are standalone applications web browsers can use to work with files of specific types. Any application on your Mac can be used as a helper application.

Safari determines the helper applications it uses to open files based on the file type and file-name extensions with which specific applications are associated via the Finder. For example, if PDFs are set to open in Preview, Safari launches Preview when you download a PDF file (assuming that the "Open 'safe' files after downloading" preference is enabled).

→ To learn how to associate files with applications, **see** "Determining the Application That Opens When You Open a Document," **p. 201**.

THE BASICS OF WEB SECURITY

Security on the Internet is a very important, complicated topic. Because this is not an Internet book, you won't find much detail in this section. But there are really only three things you need to know.

If you are visiting a site and don't see the lock or https in the URL, don't provide any data you don't want someone else to see—such as credit card information, your Social Security number, and so on. In fact, this is a general principle you should follow while you are on the Net. Unless you are *sure* the service you are using is secure, don't provide any information you don't want transmitted to the world.

This sounds pretty dramatic, and it is a bit overstated. I believe the chances of anyone intercepting any particular data on the Net are pretty small, but if the potential loss is great, even that small risk can be too much. It's up to you to choose how much risk you want to assume.

Fortunately, you can provide data via a secure connection to sites running the proper server software. A secure connection is one in which the data transmitted is scrambled, encrypted, or both. This data might still be intercepted, but the person intercepting it won't be able to do anything with it. Only the server receiving the data will be able to decode and unscramble it. Although this system isn't perfect, it's about as close to perfect as you'll get. After all, the only way to be perfectly safe is to never do anything at all.

How do you tell you are using a secure connection? Look for the lock icon in the upper-right corner of the Safari window. If it is there, you are using a secure connection. You can also tell by looking at the URL. If it begins with https instead of just http, you are visiting a secure location.

You can usually find secure sites in places where you have the opportunity to buy things and need to transmit your credit card information to do so. Of course, how you want to deal with sensitive data is up to you. Some people can accept more risk than others. However, here is the guiding principle that I use:

Do not transmit—via an unsecured means—any data for which you can't accept the risk of a third-party intercepting that data.

Like me, you might find shopping via the Web extremely convenient, easy, and inexpensive, but I suggest that you transmit credit card data only via secure sites. And always remember: Do not judge what you do on the Net against a perfect world (where there is no chance of your data being misused). Consider the risks you are willing to accept in the non-Net world. For example, you probably think nothing of using your credit card in one of those gas pumps with an integrated card reader. That is certainly no more secure, and might be much less secure (especially if your card number is printed on the paper receipt), than using your credit card on a secure website.

Web browsers have many security features. The details of these are beyond the scope of this book, but you can explore on your own to see whether you need to make changes—the default security capabilities of most browsers work for most people.

16

Third, some sites provide digital certificates to verify data from that site. When you view a site that uses such a certificate, you see a window that gives you some options. One option is to install the certificate on your machine. When you do so, the certificate is installed in the appropriate directory and your browser can access that certificate as needed. You can also choose to always trust data from the site so you don't see any security warnings during future visits.

MAC OS X TO THE MAX: GOING FURTHER ON THE WEB

There is a lot you can do to take your browsing on the Web to the max, including using keyboard shortcuts and exploring useful Mac and other websites.

USING SAFARI KEYBOARD SHORTCUTS

Table 16.3 lists keyboard shortcuts for Safari.

NOTE

Table 16.3 assumes you have enabled Safari's Tab feature.

TABLE 16.3   KEYBOARD SHORTCUTS IN SAFARI

Menu	Command	Keyboard Shortcut
Safari	Preferences	⌘-,
Safari	Block Pop-Up Windows	⌘-K
Safari	Empty Cache	Option-⌘-E
File	New Window	⌘-N
File	New Tab	⌘-T
File	Open File	⌘-O
File	Open Location	⌘-L
File	Close Window	⌘-W
File	Save As	⌘-S
File	Mail Contents of This Page	⌘-I
File	Mail Link to This Page	Shift-⌘-I
Edit	AutoFill Form	Shift-⌘-A
View	Show/Hide Address Bar	⌘-Shift-\
View	Show/Hide Bookmarks Bar	⌘-Shift-B
View	Show/Hide Status Bar	⌘-/
View	Stop	⌘-.

Menu	Command	Keyboard Shortcut
View	Reload Page	⌘-R
View	Make Text Bigger	⌘-+
View	Make Text Smaller	⌘--
View	View Source	Option-⌘-U
History	Back	⌘-[
History	Forward	⌘-]
History	Home	Shift-⌘-H
History	Mark Page for SnapBack	Option-⌘-K
History	Page SnapBack	Option-⌘-P
History	Search Results SnapBack	Option-⌘-S
Bookmarks	Show All Bookmarks	Option-⌘-B
Bookmarks	Add Bookmark	⌘-D
Bookmarks	Add Bookmark Folder	Shift-⌘-N
Bookmarks	Go to first bookmark	⌘-1
Bookmarks	Go to second bookmark	⌘-2
Bookmarks	Go to third bookmark	⌘-3
Bookmarks	Go to fourth bookmark	⌘-4
Bookmarks	Go to fifth bookmark	⌘-5
Window	Select Next Tab	Shift-⌘-]
Window	Select Previous Tab	Shift-⌘-[
Window	Downloads	Option-⌘-L
Window	Activity	Option-⌘-A
Help	Safari Help	⌘-?
	Open link or bookmark in a new tab and view it	⌘-click
	Open link or bookmark in a new tab	Shift-⌘-click
	Open link or bookmark in a new window and view it	Option-⌘-click
	Open link or bookmark in a new window behind the current one	Option-Shift-⌘- click

DOWNLOADING FILES VIA FTP IN THE FINDER

Using the Finder, you can download files directly from an FTP site to your Mac:

1. Use Safari to open the FTP site from which you want to download files. The FTP site will be mounted on your desktop.

2. Drag the files you want to download from the FTP site volume onto your Mac. The files will be downloaded, and the Copy progress window will show you the progress of the download process.

3. Prepare the files for use.

USING SHERLOCK TO SEARCH THE WEB

Mac OS X includes a dedicated web searching application, called Sherlock (located in the Applications folder), that can help you search for various types of content from different providers on the Web. I find using Google or other web search sites to be more useful, but for some specialized searches, such as for movie show times, Sherlock can be useful.

Sherlock uses channels to categorize the information you search for. When you use a channel, the tools you search with are specific to that channel. For example, one of Sherlock's included channels is the Movies channel, which enables you to search for movie information in your area (see Figure 16.17). To use a channel, click its button on the Sherlock toolbar.

Figure 16.17
Sherlock's Movies channel enables you to locate information and show times for movies you are interested in; you can even view the trailer in the Sherlock window.

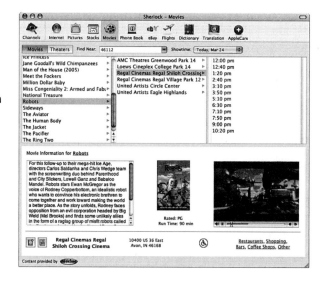

By default, Sherlock includes a number of Apple-supplied channels, which you see on the Sherlock toolbar. These include the following:

- **Internet**—Use this channel for your general Internet searches.
- **Pictures**—With this channel, you can find images related to specific topics.
- **Stocks**—Use this channel to track your favorite stocks.

- **Movies**—This is one of the coolest channels. You can use it to find show times and location information for movies you are interested in. You can also view a movie's trailer in the Sherlock window.

- **Phone Book**—Use this channel to find addresses, phone numbers, and even driving directions for businesses.

- **eBay**—If you are an eBay fan, this channel is for you.

- **Flights**—This enables you to find flight information and purchase tickets.

- **Dictionary**—Use this channel to find correct spellings of specific words or synonyms.

- **Translation**—This channel enables you to translate words and phrases among various languages.

- **AppleCare**—Use this channel to search for information from Apple, such as to get help with problems you are having.

NOTE

Each Sherlock channel is provided by one or more content providers. When you select a channel, its providers are shown at the bottom of the Sherlock window.

CHAPTER 17

Using .Mac to Integrate Your Mac onto the Internet

In this chapter

UNDERSTANDING AND USING .MAC

Apple's .Mac is a suite of services you can access that literally integrate your Mac into the Internet. These services include the following:

- **Email**—Using .Mac provides you with an email account you can use to send and receive email. Your .Mac email address ends in `@mac.com`, so using it is a good way to identify yourself as a Mac user. Using the Webmail service, you can also access your .Mac email account from a web browser. You can add more email accounts to your .Mac account for a nominal fee.

- **iDisk**—An iDisk is a virtual disk space you can use to store files just like a disk attached to your Mac. A number of folders exist on an iDisk by default. For example, you can place items in your Public folder, and any Mac users who know your .Mac member name can access the files in that folder (which is an excellent way to share files with other Mac users around the world). And, you can create a website to share the files in your Public folder with anyone. You also store the data that forms your .Mac web page on your iDisk. You can configure your Mac to create a local copy of your iDisk and keep it automatically synchronized with the online version. An iDisk might be the most useful feature of having a .Mac account.

- **HomePage**—The HomePage service enables you to create and serve a website. You can use HomePage templates to create a site, or you can use a web page application to create your site and use .Mac to serve it.

- **Synchronization**—If you use more than one Mac, you can use .Mac to synchronize information across those Macs, such as your Safari bookmarks, your Address Book, and so on.

- **Software**—The .Mac service enables you to download and use software for free, such as Apple's Backup, Virex Anti-virus, and games. You can also access a lot of other software, such as demos, updates, and more.

- **Online chat**—Your .Mac email account enables you to take advantage of iChat to chat online via text, audio, and video.

- **iCards**—These are electronic greeting cards you can send to others via email. There are numerous card combinations you can send—these are great for the artistically challenged because you can create a customized greeting card by selecting from the available images and styles.

The only requirement to use .Mac is that you can connect to the Internet, can have a .Mac account, and are using Mac OS 9 or later.

NOTE

> You can use .Mac with any kind of Internet connection. Like all Internet services, .Mac will work much better with a broadband connection, especially for iDisk and HomePage. If you do use a broadband connection, you'll soon find that .Mac does become an extension of your Mac.

GETTING STARTED WITH .MAC

Your first steps to start using .Mac are to obtain a .Mac account and then configure your Mac to access that account. The following sections give you a quick overview of these steps; however, if you already have a .Mac account, you can skip to the section titled "Working with Your .Mac Email Account."

OBTAINING A .MAC ACCOUNT

Before you can access .Mac services, you need to obtain a .Mac account. At press time, the cost of a .Mac account was $99.95 per year. However, you can obtain and use a trial .Mac account that provides access to most of the .Mac services free for 60 days. Obtaining a .Mac account is pretty straightforward.

When you installed Mac OS X, you were prompted to enter your existing .Mac account information or to create a .Mac account. If you entered your .Mac account information or created a .Mac account at that time, you are all set and can skip to the next section.

To obtain a .Mac account manually, do the following:

1. Open the System Preferences application and click the .Mac icon to open the .Mac pane.

2. Open the Account tab and click the Learn More button. Your default web browser will open and you will move to the .Mac home page (see Figure 17.1).

Figure 17.1
The .Mac website enables you to obtain a .Mac account and to use .Mac services.

TIP

You can also move to the .Mac website by going to www.apple.com and clicking the .Mac tab.

3. Click the Join Now button.

4. Follow the onscreen instructions to create your .Mac account. You will have to provide personal information and accept a license agreement. As part of the process, you create a member name and password for your account. You can choose to create a free trial account, or you can pay for a full account. If you create a full account, you must provide payment information, such as a credit card.

One step in the process is to create your .Mac member name. You should put some thought into this step. The member name you choose will be part of your .Mac email address (which will be *membername*@mac.com), and it will also be part of the URL to your .Mac website. Typically, you should choose some variation of your name so people can remember your email address and URL and can easily associate both with you. Your member name has to be at least 3 characters long and can't be longer than 20 characters. Again, you should keep your member name fairly short to make it easier for other people to work with.

When you have successfully created an account, you will see a page that displays your member name, password, email address, and email server information. You should print this page so you will have the information if you need to retrieve it at a later time.

CONFIGURING YOUR .MAC ACCOUNT

After you have obtained a .Mac account, you configure Mac OS X to access its services:

1. Open the Account tab of the .Mac pane of the System Preferences application.

2. Enter your .Mac member name and password in the pane.

By completing these simple steps, your Mac will be able to access your .Mac account automatically.

NOTE

> Each user account on your Mac can have its own .Mac account. The settings in the .Mac pane of the System Preferences application of one account do not affect the other accounts. The steps to work with other .Mac accounts are exactly the same as those to work with the first one you create.

WORKING WITH YOUR .MAC EMAIL ACCOUNT

One of the cool things about using a .Mac account is that you get an email account with the distinctive "@mac.com" domain. You can use that account with the Mail application very easily. You can also access your .Mac email via the Web. And, you can add more email addresses to your .Mac account.

USING YOUR .MAC EMAIL ACCOUNT WITH MAIL

To use your .Mac email account with Mail, you need to configure that account in the Mail application. This is simple because support for .Mac email accounts is built in to Mail and adding a .Mac email account requires only that you enter your .Mac member name and password.

→ To learn how to configure email accounts in Mail, **see** "Configuring Mail," **p. 418**.

> **NOTE**
>
> If you created or configured an existing .Mac account when you installed Mac OS X, your .Mac email account was configured in the Mail application for you automatically.

After you have set up your .Mac email account in Mail, you use it just like other email accounts you have.

→ To learn how to use Mail, **see** Chapter 15, "Using Email," **p. 399**.

> **NOTE**
>
> At press time, your .Mac email account includes 50MB of email storage space.

ACCESSING YOUR .MAC EMAIL ACCOUNT FROM THE WEB

You can access your .Mac email from any computer that has web access, which makes it convenient to use your .Mac email account even if you aren't at your own Mac. To access your .Mac email via the Web, perform the following steps:

1. Use a web browser to move to www.apple.com.
2. Click the .Mac tab.
3. Click the Mail tab.
4. Enter your member name and password and then click Enter. You will move into your .Mac email account (see Figure 17.2).

Figure 17.2
Using the .Mac website is a great way to access your .Mac email from any computer that can connect to the Web.

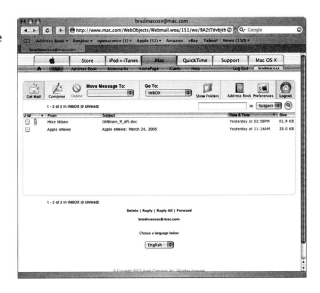

5. Use the tools to work with and manage your email.

Using the .Mac website to access your email is similar to using an email application. You can read your email, send email, organize it, and so on.

ADDING EMAIL ACCOUNTS TO YOUR .MAC ACCOUNT

One .Mac email account might not be enough for you. For example, you might want to provide a .Mac email account for each user of your Mac. The good news is that you can add email accounts to a .Mac account for a nominal fee (at press time, additional email-only accounts were only $10/year). To do so, perform the following steps:

1. Open the Account tab of the .Mac pane of the System Preferences application.

2. Click the Account Info button. You'll move to the .Mac website.

3. Log in using your member name and password. You'll move to the Account Settings page.

4. Click the Manage Accounts button. You'll move to the email account status page, which will display your current email accounts.

5. Click the Buy More button. You'll move to the Buy More page.

6. Choose the number of email accounts you want to purchase on the "additional email-only account(s)" pop-up menu and click Continue.

7. Follow the onscreen instructions to create the additional accounts.

After you have purchased the additional email accounts, you can configure those accounts in email applications or use the .Mac website to access them.

USING YOUR iDISK

The iDisk is among the most useful things about having a .Mac account. The uses for an iDisk are almost limitless; the bottom line is that your iDisk is additional disk space that you access via the Internet. You can use this space to store any files you choose. It is also vital to certain .Mac services, such as HomePage, because you store all the files you use on your web page in the appropriate folders on your iDisk.

> **TIP**
>
> Although your iDisk isn't likely to be large enough to perform system backups, you can use it to back up important documents. This keeps them separate from your computer and enables you to access them from any Mac. With your .Mac account, you can download and use the Apple Backup application to back up your files on your iDisk.

You can configure a Mac to create a local copy of your iDisk and keep it synchronized with your online iDisk. This is especially useful when you work with the same set of files from multiple locations, such as a work Mac and your home Mac.

When you purchase a .Mac account, the combination of iDisk and email storage space is 250MB. You can configure this to shift more space to the iDisk or to your email, and you can upgrade the disk space available to your account.

Dialing Up to iDisk

Using an iDisk over a slow Internet connection can be an exercise in futility. When you use an iDisk, you are usually moving a large amount of data from your machine to the iDisk. When using a dial-up account or other slow connection, this can be frustrating—even simple tasks such as opening the iDisk can seem to take forever. If you use a dial-up account to connect to the Internet, try to use the iDisk at less popular times of the day (such as early in the morning) so that the performance will be as good as possible. The speed might still annoy you, but at least you stand a better chance of being able to tolerate it. A good choice for dial-up users is to create a copy of your iDisk on your Mac and choose the manual synchronization option. Then, you can move files to and from the local copy of your iDisk. When you are ready to put those files on the Net, you can perform the synchronization. This might take a long time to do, but you don't have to be at your Mac during the process (unlike if you work with your online iDisk to move files).

SETTING THE SIZE OF YOUR IDISK

In most cases, you should increase the size of your iDisk relative to the space used by your email account.

> **TIP**
>
> Only email that you store on the .Mac server counts against the email portion of your .Mac disk space. Make it a practice to download your .Mac email to your Mac and to regularly delete your email to keep your disk use for email to a minimum so you can have more iDisk space.

1. Open the Account tab of the .Mac pane of the System Preferences application.
2. Click the Account Info button. You'll move to the .Mac website.
3. Log in using your member name and password. You'll move to the Account Settings page.
4. Click the Storage Settings button. You'll move to the Storage Settings page (see Figure 17.3).
5. Choose the split between disk space for your iDisk and email account using the pop-up menu. You can choose from various combinations such as "25 MB Email / 225 MB iDisk." The disk gauge to the left of the pop-up menu will show you the current allocations; the colored areas of these allocations will show you your current use.
6. Click Save. Your .Mac disk space will be allocated according to your selection.

> **TIP**
>
> As you have probably figured out, you use the Account Settings web page to configure various aspects of your .Mac account, such as changing your password, billing information, and so on.

Figure 17.3
Using this page, you can set the balance of storage space between your iDisk and .Mac email.

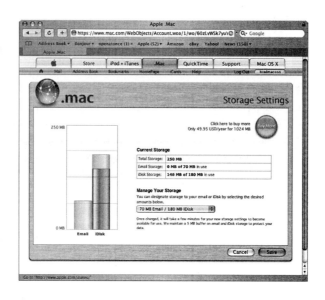

CONFIGURING YOUR IDISK

You can configure your iDisk for your Mac OS X user account by opening the iDisk tab of the .Mac pane of the System Preferences utility (see Figure 17.4).

Figure 17.4
Using the iDisk tab of the .Mac pane, you can configure your iDisk; here, you can see that I have 225MB of space available but am currently using only 145MB.

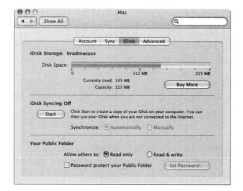

TIP

If the iDisk tab doesn't reflect your most recent account changes, quit the System Preferences application and restart it.

The most important configuration you will do is determining whether you will create a local copy of your iDisk on your computer. If you do this, you can work with the local copy just like other volumes on your computer. Then, you can either synchronize the local version with the online version manually or have your Mac do it automatically.

If you use a dial-up connection, you should create a local copy of your iDisk because accessing the online version is too slow to be practical. When you make changes to your iDisk, you can synchronize it to move those changed files online.

If you have a broadband connection, this is less important because there won't be as much difference accessing your online iDisk compared to the local copy. However, if you are going to work on files while they are on your iDisk (as opposed to just storing them there), using the local version will improve performance.

To configure your iDisk, perform the following steps:

1. Open the System Preferences utility and click the .Mac button to open the .Mac pane.

2. Click the iDisk tab.

3. Use the Disk Space bar to assess the status of your disk space. The total length of the bar represents the current size of your iDisk, and the colored portion represents how much of that space is currently being used.

4. To create a copy of your iDisk on your Mac, click the Start button. This causes your Mac to download a copy of your iDisk so you can access it directly from your desktop. If you want your Mac to keep the local copy and the online iDisk synchronized at all times, click the Automatically button (this option should be selected only if you have a broadband connection to the Net). If you prefer to manually synchronize your local and online iDisks, click the Manually button (this option should be selected if you use a dial-up account).

5. To control whether others can input information to the Public folder on your iDisk, use the radio buttons in the "Your Public Folder" section. Click the "Read only" button if you want users to only be able to read files in the Public folder on your iDisk but not be able to change any information there. Click the "Read & write" button if you want them to also be able to change files there. If you chose the latter option, you should protect your iDisk with a password.

6. To protect your iDisk with a password, check the "Password protect your Public Folder" check box and click the Set Password button.

7. In the resulting sheet, enter the password you want to use, confirm it, and click OK.

Working with a Local Copy of Your iDisk

If you chose to create a local copy of your iDisk, you can open it from the Finder by clicking its icon in the Places sidebar. You can also select Go, iDisk, My iDisk or press Shift-⌘-I (see Figure 17.5). In the resulting Finder window, you will see the folders on your iDisk. At the bottom of the window, you can see the current space being used along with information about the last synchronization that was performed (or the progress of the current one if it is still being performed). While the local copy of your iDisk is being created, you'll also see the synchronization symbol rotating next to the iDisk icon in the Places sidebar.

Click here to synchronize your iDisk

Figure 17.5
You can access your local copy of your iDisk by clicking its icon in the Places sidebar of a Finder window.

NOTE

The local iDisk is actually a disk image file called `Previous local iDisk for username.dmg`, where *username* is your member name.

If you set the local copy of your iDisk for manual synchronization, you can perform the synchronization by clicking the "Synchronize now" button located to the right of the iDisk icon in the Places sidebar (refer to Figure 17.5). The two versions of the iDisk will be synchronized; a progress bar at the bottom of the Finder window will inform you about the status of the process.

TIP

If you click the Action button or the contextual menu for a Finder window showing your iDisk, you can select the Sync Now command to perform synchronization or the Automatic Syncing command to set your iDisk to be synchronized automatically.

WORKING WITH YOUR ONLINE IDISK

If you choose not to create a local copy of your iDisk, you can still work with your iDisk from the Finder. However, when you move files to and from the iDisk, you will actually be moving those files across the Net rather than just between locations on your hard drive. In most cases, you should use a local copy instead. However, you can directly access your online iDisk to work with it.

To do so, click the iDisk icon on the Places sidebar and the contents of your iDisk will be shown in a Finder window.

If you have set your desktop preferences so that mounted disks appear on your desktop, you will see a disk with an icon of a hard disk in front of a globe—this is your iDisk. If your mounted disks don't appear on your desktop, open the Computer directory and you will see your iDisk there.

→ To learn how to set the preference for disks being shown on the desktop, **see** "Customizing the Mac OS X Desktop," **p. 135**.

TIP

> Look for the Synchronize symbol to the right of the iDisk volume in the Places sidebar of the Finder window to tell the difference between the online iDisk and a local copy of your iDisk. If you don't see any symbol, you are working with the online iDisk. If you do see the Synchronization symbol, you are working with a local copy.

TIP

> If you use more than one .Mac account, you can download and use the iDisk Utility application to make working with multiple .Mac accounts more convenient. You can download this application from the .Mac website.

WORKING WITH AN IDISK

After your iDisk is mounted on your Mac (whether it is a local copy or the online version), you can work with it just like the other volumes and disks on your machine. Open your iDisk and you will see the following folders:

- **Backup**—The Backup folder is where your data is stored if you use the Apple Backup application to back up your Mac via your iDisk.

- **Documents, Movies, Music, and Pictures**—These folders contain elements for web pages you might want to add to your .Mac website using HomePage. For example, if you want to include a Pictures page on your site, you can store the images you want to include on the page in the Pictures folder.

- **Library**—The Library folder contains files that support use of the iDisk, such as application support files.

- **Public**—The Public folder is where you can store files you want other .Mac users to be able to access via .Mac or those you want to publish via a files web page so anyone can download them.

- **Sites**—The Sites folder is where you store your own HTML pages to be served from the .Mac website (rather than using the HomePage service).

- **Software**—The Software folder contains software you can download to your Mac. Apple stores system and application software updates here so you can easily access and download them. To see what software is available, simply open the Software folder. To download any of the files you see to your Mac, drag the file from the Software folder to a folder on your machine. For example, a folder called Mac OS X Software contains applications you can download to your Mac by simply dragging them from the folder to your hard drive. The contents of the Software folder do not count against your iDisk storage space.

ACCESSING iDISKS FROM THE GO MENU

The iDisk commands on the Finder's Go menu are the following:

- **My iDisk**—This command opens your own iDisk.

- **Other User's iDisk**—When you select this command, you see the Connect To iDisk dialog box. Enter the member name and password of the user's iDisk that you want to access and click Connect. That iDisk is mounted on your Mac and you can work with it just like the iDisk that is configured as part of your .Mac account. For example, if you have two .Mac accounts, you can configure one iDisk as part of your Mac OS X user account and use this command to access the iDisk that is part of another .Mac account.

- **Other User's Public Folder**—When you select this command, the Connect To iDisk Public Folder dialog box appears. Enter the member name of the user whose Public folder you want to access and click Connect. If the user has not selected the option to protect the Public folder with a password, that user's Public folder on her iDisk is shown in a Finder window. If the folder is protected with a password, enter the password and click Connect when prompted to do so.

> **TIP**
>
> When you need to enter a password to access someone else's Public folder, your username is Public, which is entered for you. If you add the password to your keychain, you don't have to enter it again. The Public folder will be unlocked for you automatically when you access it.

SHARING INFORMATION ON YOUR iDISK WITH OTHERS

One of the most useful things about an iDisk is that you can place files in the Public folder and then share them with other users. You can do this in a couple of ways.

If the people with whom you want to share files are Mac users, they can access your files via the commands on their Mac's Go, iDisk menu. All you need to do is place the files you want to share in your iDisk's Public folder and then provide your .Mac member name to the people with whom you want to share files. If you protect your Public folder with a password, you need to provide the password to them as well.

> **NOTE**
>
> If you use a local iDisk and chose the Manual synchronization option, remember to synchronize your iDisk after you place new files in your Public folder for others to access.

You can also publish the contents of your Public folder so others can access it using a web interface. This means you can share files with anyone, whether they use a Mac or not.

→ To learn how to create a .Mac website, **see** "Using .Mac to Publish a Website," **p. 506**.

UPGRADING YOUR IDISK

You might need to have more space available than the 250MB that is provided as part of a standard .Mac account. In fact, if you want to create a website with lots of movies, music, and photos on it, 225MB might not be enough for you even if you've allocated most of your space to your iDisk. If you will be using the .Mac backup application to back up your data, you are also likely to want more .Mac disk space.

At press time, you could increase the total storage space for your .Mac account to 1024MB for an additional $49.95/year.

To add more space to your .Mac account, go to the iDisk tab of the .Mac pane and click the Buy More button. You'll move to the .Mac website. Log in and you'll move to the Buy More page. Follow the onscreen instructions to add more space to your .Mac account.

After you have added more disk space to your .Mac account, allocate the portion you want to make available to your iDisk.

→ To learn how to allocated disk space between your .Mac email and iDisk, **see** "Setting the Size of Your iDisk," **p. 499**.

USING YOUR IDISK TO WORK WITH THE SAME FILES ON MULTIPLE MACS

If you regularly work on more than one Mac (such as one at work or school and one at home), you can use .Mac to make sure you can access the same files on each Mac you use. To do this, perform the following steps:

1. Configure each Mac to use your .Mac account.
2. On each Mac, configure your iDisk so you use a local copy and choose the synchronization option.

> TIP
>
> You don't need to choose the same synchronization option on each Mac. For example, if one Mac connects via a broadband connection, you could choose the Automatic option. If another uses a dial-up connection, you could choose the Manual option for that Mac.

3. Store the files on which you are working in a folder on your iDisk. (Don't use the Public folder unless you want other people to be able to access these files.) As you save files, they will be saved on your iDisk.
4. When you are done working on a Mac for which the Manual synchronization option is active, synchronize the iDisk. The files on which you are working will be moved to the online iDisk.
5. When you get to a different Mac, synchronize the iDisk (if you have configured that Mac for automatic synchronization, you don't need to do this step). The files on which you work will be available in the Mac's iDisk folder.

TIP

> After you have finished working on files and no longer need to access them, move them out of your iDisk so they no longer impact your available space.

USING .MAC TO PUBLISH A WEBSITE

Using a .Mac account, you can publish your own website. There are two basic ways you can use .Mac to do so. The first is to use .Mac's HomePage tools to build your web pages. You add content to these pages by placing files in the related folders on your iDisk. The second, and more flexible, way is to add your own website files to the Sites folder on your iDisk to publish that site. For example, you can create your website using your favorite web page application and then post the site's files in the Sites folder on your iDisk. Apple's .Mac server takes care of serving the site for you.

CREATING A .MAC WEBSITE USING HOMEPAGE

When you build a website using .Mac HomePage tools, you create each page on the site using HomePage templates. You can also create a set of sites and place different pages on each site. People can access each site directly, or you can provide a site menu to help them navigate among your sites.

You can use HomePage templates to add any of the following pages to your site:

- **Photo Album**—I bet you can guess what you store on these pages. Use these pages to share your photos via the Web.
- **File Sharing**—Pages using this template present the files in your Public folder for easy downloading.
- **Site Menu**—These pages help you create a menu so visitors can explore your site by clicking links.
- **iMovie**—You can serve iMovies you create so others can watch them over the Web.
- **Writing**—These pages are formatted as personal newsletters.
- **Résumé**—You can publish an online résumé to land that next big job.
- **Baby**—Use these pages to make a grandparent's day.
- **Education**—These pages are designed for those involved in education. The template pages include pages for school events, a school album, teacher information, and so on.
- **Invite**—You can use these pages to create custom web invitations.
- **Advanced**—You can use this option to publish pages stored in your iDisk's Sites folder.

Before you get started adding pages to your website, decide what kinds of pages you want to have on your site or what types of sites you want to include. Add the files for each page to the appropriate folder on your iDisk. For example, if you are going to have an iMovie page, add your movie files to the Movies folder. Add photos you want to post by placing the files in the Pictures folder, and so on, until you have added the content you want to have on your site to the appropriate folder on your iDisk.

The process to add each type of page is similar. You can create pages based on any of the available templates by following these steps:

1. Move to the .Mac web page and log in to your .Mac account if you aren't already logged in.

2. Click the HomePage icon or tab. You will see the HomePage screen (see Figure 17.6). This screen contains the tools you need to build and edit your pages and the sites on which you store those pages. In the upper part of the window you will see all the sites and pages that are currently part of your site. You will also see the URL to your site. In the lower part of the screen, you will see the tools you use to create pages.

Figure 17.6
The HomePage web page enables you to build your own website quickly and easily; so far, my website contains only one set of pages (called a *site*), and that set contains only one page (called Se Using Tiger).

> **TIP**
>
> The page shown in bold is the Start Page—your home page—which is the first page people see when they access your website.

3. In the Create A Page area, click the tab for the type of page you want to create (for example, click iMovies to create a movie page). You will see buttons for each of the various themes (templates) available for the type of page you selected.

> **TIP**
>
> If you have more than one site, select the site on which you want to place the file-sharing page before doing step 4.

4. Click the button for the template you want to use. If the page serves files of some kind that must be stored in a specific location, such as pictures for a slideshow, you'll be

prompted to select the folder on your iDisk that contains the files you want to publish on the page you are creating. If the page doesn't require files in a specific location, you'll move directly to the Edit page for the page you are creating (skip to step 6).

5. Use the tools on the "Choose a folder" page to move to and select the folder containing the files required by the page; then click Choose. You will move to the edit page that is based on the template you selected.

NOTE

> If you work with a local copy of your iDisk, it must be synchronized before the files will be available on the Web. If you use the manual synchronization option, click the Synchronize button after you put the files in the Public folder.

6. On the Edit screen, edit the text associated with the page. For most pages, this will include the title of the page, a title of objects on it, and a description of the page's contents. For pages that are designed to provide text content, this will include boxes in which you can type that content.

7. If the page serves files of some kind, such as a QuickTime movie, click the Choose button. The "Choose a file" page will appear. The folders on your iDisk possibly containing appropriate files will be shown in the far left pane.

8. Move to the file you want to place on the page, select it, and click Choose. You'll return to the edit page window and the file will be placed on the web page you are creating.

9. Scroll to the bottom of the window. Check the Show check boxes for any special features you want to add. Most pages provide for a counter that shows the number of people who have visited the page (the Show check box next to the 0) and a "Send me a message" feature that enables visitors to send email to you.

10. Click the Preview button to see how your page will look. The page will be presented as it will be when you publish it.

11. If you need to make changes, click the Edit button and use the instructions in the previous steps to make your changes.

12. When you are done with the page, click Publish. The web page you created will be added to your site and you will see its URL.

13. Click the URL to visit your new page (see Figure 17.7).

NOTE

> When HomePage creates a page for you, the URL ends in the name of the template you selected to create the page followed by a sequential number (such as FileSharing27.html). These URLs aren't likely to be easy for others to type. However, you can create site menu navigation pages on your site that link to each page. People can access your site menu at http://homepage.mac.com/*membername*/, where *membername* is your member name. This makes locating your site and moving to its pages much easier.

Figure 17.7
Hopefully, you will use HomePage to publish more interesting pages than this one, but you get the idea.

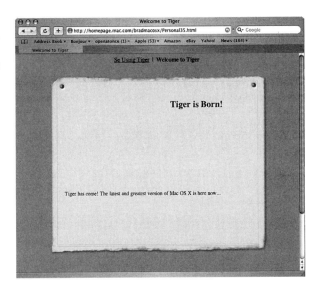

Continue adding pages to your site until it contains all you want it to. When you are done, you will see all the pages on your site in the upper-left corner of the HomePage window.

You can also create additional sites and then add pages to those sites using the same process. In .Mac lingo, these additional sites are called *groups*, meaning you can collect a set of pages and place them into groups.

To create another group on your site, carry out the following steps:

1. On the HomePage page, click the arrow button next to "Add another site." You will move to the "Create a site" page.

2. Enter the name of the site you are creating in the Site Name field.

3. If you want a password to be required for someone to be able to view your site, check the On check box and enter the password in the Password field.

4. Click Create Site. You will return to the HomePage page and see the new site you have created. The HomePage page now contains boxes for your sites and the pages on those sites.

5. To see the pages included in a group, select the group on the Sites pane; its pages appear in the Pages pane. Select a page and a preview appears in the third column on the screen (see Figure 17.8).

The URL for the website you create is http://homepage.mac.com/*yourmembername*/. (Don't include the period shown in this URL—that is only to please my editors!)

When someone visits this URL, she sees the page you designated as the start page. She can use the links on this page to move to the other pages on your website.

Figure 17.8
My website now includes two groups of pages: One is called `Cool_Stuff`, and the other is the default group that is called `bradmacosx`.

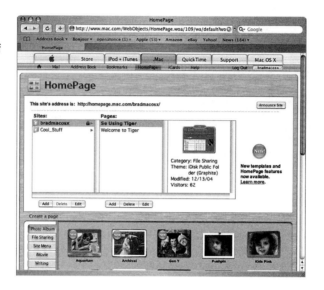

You can move directly to a specific page using the URL for that page. For example, if you create an iMovie page, the URL for that page will be http://homepage.mac.com/ *yourmembername*/iMovieTheater.html, where *yourmembername* is your member name. As you add more pages of each type, the names are differentiated by sequential numbers, as in iMovieTheater1, iMovieTheater2, and so on.

Creating websites using HomePage is easy and powerful. Following are some additional tips for your consideration:

- Set the home page for each group (called the *start page* in .Mac lingo) for your website by dragging the page you want to use to the top of the Pages list.

- You can see the URL for any group by selecting it. Its URL appears at the top of the HomePage screen.

- The Home site is always the one with your member name as its URL. Any other sites you create have URLs based on this one. For example, if you create a site called `Book_Information`, its URL is http://homepage.mac.com/*yourmembername*/ Book_Information, where *yourmembername* is your member name.

- To add more pages to a site, select that site on the Sites list and click the Add button under the Pages list.

- To add more sites, click the Add button under the Sites list.

- You can delete sites or pages by selecting what you want to delete and clicking Delete. Then click Yes on the resulting confirmation screen.

- Password-protect any sites that contain information to which you want to limit access.

- Use site menu pages to organize your site and enable visitors to move around using links. You can also place images on site menu pages as a preview of the pages that are linked to the site menu page.

- To add a custom page to your site, create it using any tool that outputs HTML files. Place the resulting file on your iDisk and then use the Advanced page template to publish it.

- To place a counter on a page, use the Show check box next to the counter icon (a box with a zero in it) that becomes available when you edit the page. This counter counts the number of visitors to that page.

- Use the Show check box next to the "Send me a message" text to place an email link on a page. Visitors can click this link to send email to your .Mac email address.

CREATING YOUR WEBSITE BY ADDING YOUR OWN PAGES TO THE SITES FOLDER

Although you can quickly and easily create a basic website using the HomePage templates and tools, you are somewhat limited in what you can do. The available templates might or might not be suitable for the site you want to create. Even if you want to do more than you can with the .Mac web page templates, .Mac is still valuable because you can use .Mac to host *any* website you create using any other website editing tools, such as Adobe's GoLive or Macromedia's Dreamweaver. In this scenario, .Mac acts just like any other web hosting service you might use.

The general process to get your customized website on the .Mac site is the following:

1. Create your website using the tools you prefer.

> **NOTE**
>
> Name the home page of your site `index.html`. This ensures that a viewer is taken to the right start page for your site when he moves to its URL.

2. Test the site by accessing it while it is stored on your Mac. You can test a website by opening it from within a web browser. For example, open your site using Safari by selecting File, Open File. Then, maneuver to the home page for your site and open it. The site will work just as it will after you post it on your .Mac website (except that it will be faster, of course). You should test your site in various browsers and operating systems to ensure that it can be viewed properly.

3. Fix any problems you find.

4. When your site is ready to post, copy all its files and folders into the Sites folder on your iDisk.

5. Test your site again by accessing it over the Net.

To access the website in your Sites folder, use the following URL: http://homepage. mac.com/*yourmembername*/. (For this to work, you must have named the home page for the site `index.html`.)

When you move to your .Mac website URL, you see the page you named `index.html`.

The website you store in the Sites folder is not integrated into a .Mac website you create using the .Mac template. In fact, any pages you create using the .Mac templates are not accessible after you copy your own site into the Sites folder because your custom site replaces any HomePage sites you have created.

USING .MAC TO SYNCHRONIZE IMPORTANT INFORMATION ON MULTIPLE MACS

You can also use .Mac to keep important information synchronized on all the Macs you use. For example, you can make sure you have access to the same set of Safari bookmarks on each Mac you use. Similarly, you can keep the same set of information in the Address Book on each of your Macs. To synchronize your Macs, perform the following steps:

1. Click the Sync tab found on the .Mac pane of the System Preferences application (see Figure 17.9).

Figure 17.9
Use the options on the Sync tab to keep information on multiple Macs synchronized.

2. Check the "Synchronize with .Mac" check box.

3. Choose the frequency at which you want information to be synchronized on the pop-up menu. To have information synchronized constantly, choose Automatically. Other options include Every Hour, Every Day, Every Week, and Manually.

4. Check the check box next to each type of information that you want to be synchronized. For example, to synchronize your Safari bookmarks, check the Bookmarks check box. To synchronize your contact information, check the Contacts check box.

5. Click Sync Now. The synchronization process will start and you'll be prompted to choose how you want information to be synchronized.

6. When prompted, choose the synchronization option you want to use from the pop-up menu. The "Merge data on this computer and .Mac" option adds new data on your Mac to that stored in your .Mac account and adds data stored in your .Mac account onto the Mac. The "Replace data on .Mac" replaces all the related data in your .Mac account with information on the Mac. The "Replace data on this computer" option causes data on .Mac to replace the data currently on your Mac.

7. Click Sync. The data you selected to be synchronized will be moved to and from the Mac and .Mac until it is synchronized according to the option you selected. From this point forward, it will be synchronized according to the option you selected on the pop-up menu.

8. Repeat steps 1–7 for each Mac you want to keep in sync.

The time and date of the last synchronization will be shown under the .Mac icon.

If you configured the sync with something other than Manual, you don't need to bother with it anymore; your Mac will keep its information in sync with what is on your .Mac account. If you chose Manual, you'll need to click the Sync Now button to synchronize your Mac's information.

If you check the "Show status in menu bar" check box, the Sync menu will appear in the Finder menu bar. On this menu, you can see the time and date of the last synchronization, choose the Sync Now command, or open the Sync tab.

You can manage the Macs being synchronized using the Advanced tab of the .Mac pane (see Figure 17.10). On the list, you'll see each computer that is being synchronized via .Mac. The computer you are currently using will be indicated by the (This Computer) text. In addition to the computer name, you'll see the time and date of that computer's last synchronization.

Figure 17.10
The Advanced tab of the .Mac pane provides information about all the computers you are synching via .Mac.

You can remove a computer from the synchronization list by selecting it and clicking the Unregister button. In the resulting prompt, click Unregister. The computer will be removed from the list and will no longer be available for synchronization.

If you want to reset how data is being synchronized on a computer, select it and click the "Reset Sync Data" button. In the resulting sheet, you can configure the reset (see Figure 17.11). On the Replace pop-up menu, choose the kind of information you want to reset; choose "All Sync Info" to reset all the information you have chosen to sync. Click the left or right arrow to determine the direction in which you want to do the reset. To replace the data on the Mac with data on .Mac, click the left arrow. To replace the data on .Mac with data on the computer, click the right arrow. Then click Replace. The data will be reset in the direction you indicated.

Figure 17.11
Use this prompt to reset the synchronization options for a computer.

GETTING FREE SOFTWARE VIA .MAC

A .Mac account includes lots of benefits, including free versions of commercial applications and discounts on the purchase prices of others. To download the free applications, move to the .Mac website and click the Member Benefits link. You'll move to the Members Benefits page from which you can download applications and see special offers. For example, you can download the Backup application to perform back ups of your data and the Virex application to protect your Mac from viruses.

MAC OS X TO THE MAX: USING MAC OS X TO SERVE WEB PAGES

You can use Mac OS X to host a website for the Internet or for a local intranet because the web server software you need is already built in to Mac OS X. Serving a website to the Internet is a fairly complex task, and there are many nuances you need to consider. However, serving a website to a local network is fairly straightforward. In either case, you can use Mac OS X to get your site online.

Mac OS X includes very powerful and sophisticated web server software—Apache. This software is widely used across the Internet to serve web pages, and Mac OS X users can take full advantage of it out of the box. Although Apache is a Unix application, you can perform the basic tasks of serving a website without messing around with text commands. Of course, to really customize and master Apache, you do need to get your hands into the command line. However, you can get a site up and running without ever interacting directly with Apache.

Establishing and maintaining a web server is a complex and challenging task, and explaining all the details associated with hosting a website is beyond the scope of this book.

The general process for using your Mac to host a website is the following:

1. Create your website using any tools you prefer.
2. Test it to make sure that it works.
3. Register your domain.

4. Move the files for your website to the appropriate location on your Mac.

5. Start the web server.

6. Monitor your site to ensure that it has adequate performance and is available 24/7.

Each user account on your Mac can serve its own website; this means you can serve many websites from your Mac at the same time. To provide a website for a user's account, you place the files for that site in the Sites folder that is contained in that user's Home directory.

There is also an overall website for the Mac itself. You should ensure that you add a website for the Mac so that when people move to the home page for your machine, they will see a meaningful site.

To start serving a website from your Mac, perform the following steps:

1. Place the files for the site you want to post in the Sites folder of the user account you want to use. Each user's Sites folder contains an index.html file that provides a default home page for that user's website. You replace this file with your own index.html file to serve your specific site (you can also modify the default index page if you want). The default index.html page contains information about how web sharing works and is worth reading if you are new to the topic.

> **TIP**
>
> You can test any user's website without actually adding web pages to the Sites folder. Because the index.html page is part of each Sites folder, that page is served up for every account. So, if you move to the URL for a user account on your machine, you should see the Mac OS X Personal Web Sharing page. If you do, that means web sharing is working. All you need to do is replace the default content with your content.

2. Open the System Preferences application, open the Sharing pane, and then click the Services tab.

3. On the Services tab, check the "Personal Web Sharing" check box. This starts the web server on your Mac. Just below the list of sharing services, you will see the URL of the Mac along with the URL for the user's website. You build the URL for your site based on either of these. For example, if your IP address is 12.34.567.89, the basic URL for your site is http://12.34.567.89/. Similarly, if the registered domain name for your Mac is agreatmac.com, the URL to your machine is also http://www.agreatmac.com/. If you use the IP address to access the site, it is resolved to the hostname and that is what appears in the address bar of the browser.

The URL to a specific user's website on your Mac is the URL for the Mac itself with a ~ (tilde character) followed by the short version of the username appended to it. For example, if the short name for my user account is bmiser, the URL to my website would be http://12.34.567.89/~bmiser/ or http://www.agreatmac.com/~bmiser/ (if I had registered a domain name appropriately, of course).

17

NOTE

The tilde (~) character in the URL indicates that the address points to that user's Home directory, in which the Sites folder is stored. If you leave this out of the URL, the user's site won't be found.

You also need to include the end slash (/) in the URL.

4. Close System Preferences.

5. Use another machine to access the URL for your website.

If you see the site, everything is in great shape and your pages are "available."

TIP

The concept that each user who has an account on your Mac can have a unique website opens many possibilities for you. You can create user accounts for the sole purpose of providing specific websites. For example, if I wanted to host a website for this book, I could create a user account called SEUsing MacOSX with the short name usingosx. I could then place the website in the Sites folder for this account and the site would be published.

If you are going to be hosting any web pages on your Mac, you should also configure the root-level website for your Mac. This site will appear if someone accesses the website on your Mac without including a specific user's account in the URL. For example, if someone enters only `http://12.34.567.89/`, he would see the root-level web page.

TIP

Consider creating a web page that provides URL links to all the websites that are hosted on your Mac and posting that at the root level. This would make it easy for a visitor to get to any of the sites on your machine.

If you open the directory located at `Mac OS X/Library/WebServer/Documents/`, where `Mac OS X` is the name of your Mac OS X startup volume, you will see many index pages. Each of these has an abbreviation for the language for which that page is applicable at the end of its filename (for example, the file `index.html.en` is the English version of the page). The version that Apache serves depends on how your machine is configured.

To post a root-level web page, do the following:

1. Create the website you want to be at the root level of your machine.

2. Name the home page for this site; again, the name of the home page for the site should be `index.html`.

3. Place the files and folders for the site in the following location: `Mac OS X/Library/WebServer/Documents/`, where `Mac OS X` is the name of your Mac OS X startup volume. Make sure the index file is in this directory.

NOTE

> The web server continues to run as long as your Mac is turned on and the website for each user account is served continuously, even if no one is logged in to the system. You can stop the server by shutting down the Mac or by turning off web sharing using the Sharing pane of the System Preferences application.

The information in this section has barely scratched the surface of Apache specifically and web serving in general. However, a great deal of information on both topics is available within Mac OS X as well as on the Net.

To access the Apache documentation included with Mac OS X, open the manual alias in the Documents folder (contained in the WebServer folder). The Apache folder will open. Open the `index.html` file and the Apache User Guide will open.

To find information on the Web about Apache, visit www.apache.org. There is plenty of information on this site, including some nice tutorials.

17

PART **IV**

MAC OS X: LIVING THE DIGITAL LIFE

CHAPTER **18**

LISTENING TO AND MANAGING YOUR MUSIC WITH ITUNES

In this chapter

TOURING ITUNES

iTunes is Mac OS X's amazing digital music application that enables you to truly master your music. For example, you can do the following:

- Listen to audio CDs.

- Store and listen to all your music on your Mac so it is only a click away.

- Convert music into a variety of formats.

- Browse and purchase music (individual songs or albums) using the iTunes Music Store.

- Create and use playlists to totally customize the way you listen to your music.

- Create custom audio CDs and DVDs.

- Share your music on a network and listen to music being shared with you.

- Listen to audio streams from the Internet.

This list is just a start; if you can imagine something you want to do with your music, iTunes will probably enable you to do it!

NOTE

> iTunes is a very powerful application and its capabilities seem almost endless. Although you will get a lot of good iTunes information in this chapter, it is by no mean comprehensive. You can get even more details in my book *Absolute Beginner's Guide to iPod and iTunes*.

GETTING STARTED WITH ITUNES

By default, iTunes is installed when you install Mac OS X. If iTunes isn't installed on your Mac for some reason, you can download a copy at not cost to you from www.apple.com/itunes/. It is also included in Apple's iLife suite of applications.

You can launch iTunes in a number of ways, including by clicking its Dock icon, opening the Applications folder and double-clicking its icon, inserting an audio CD into your Mac, or connecting an iPod to your Mac.

The first time iTunes launches, you will move into the iTunes Setup Assistant. This assistant performs some basic configuration for you. Work through the assistant with the following steps:

NOTE

> You can configure all the preferences set in the assistant using the iTunes Preferences command so nothing you set in the assistant is permanent.

1. Read the license (if you have time and a law degree), agree to it, read the introductory text, and click Next or press Return.

2. If you want to use iTunes for most audio content you will encounter on the Internet, click the "Yes, use iTunes for Internet audio content" radio button. I recommend you choose this option.

iTunes needs to connect to the Internet to perform specific tasks, such as looking up information about audio CDs you play, connecting to the iTunes Music Store, and so on.

NOTE

I've assumed that you set the iTunes preferences as described in these steps. If you made other selections, your experience will vary slightly from this chapter. No worries, though—the differences won't be enough to derail your iTunes exploration. For example, if you don't allow iTunes to connect to the Internet automatically, you'll need to connect yourself when iTunes needs Internet access.

3. To allow iTunes to connect when it needs to, click the "Yes, automatically connect to the Internet" radio button.

4. Click Next or press Return.

5. If you have music files stored in your Home folder, enable iTunes to add those files to your Library automatically by clicking the "Yes, find MP3 and AAC files in my Home folder" radio button.

6. Click Next or press Return.

7. Start your iTunes experience in your iTunes Library by clicking the "No, take me to my iTunes Library" radio button; then click Done. You'll move to the iTunes window. Any music that iTunes could find in your Home folder will be added your Library. Don't be discouraged if iTunes looks kind of empty; you will easily and rapidly fix that.

iTunes uses a multipaned interface that you'll likely come to know and love like I do (see Figure 18.1). The iTunes window consists of three panes—Source, Browser, and Content—and the control and information window that surrounds those panes. The Browser can be hidden or shown; the other panes are shown at all times (except when you use the iTunes mini-player, which you will see later in this chapter).

TIP

If you don't see the Browser, click the Browse button to open it.

CHOOSING A SOURCE ON THE SOURCE PANE

As you can probably guess from its name, the Source pane shows the music sources available to you. When you want to work with a source—for example, to listen to it—you select that source on the Source pane. The contents of the source you select will be shown in the Content pane, and you can work with the songs that source contains. As you work with iTunes, you will see the following sources:

Figure 18.1
iTunes provides complete control over your music.

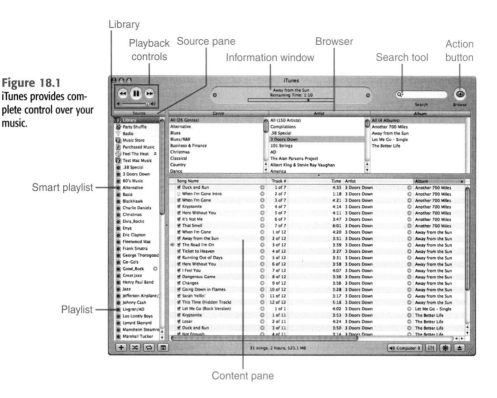

- Library
- Playback controls
- Source pane
- Information window
- Browser
- Search tool
- Action button
- Smart playlist
- Playlist
- Content pane

- **Library**—The Library contains all the music you have added to iTunes and enables you to access any of your music quickly and easily. Because you can import audio CDs to your Mac, you can add all your music to the Library—no more fussing with individual CDs. You can also add music from the iTunes Music Store, along with any other audio files you have, to your Library. You can browse and search the contents of the Library and play any music it contains.

- **Party Shuffle**—This is a special playlist you can use to randomize your music experience. You'll learn more about this later in this chapter.

- **Radio**—The Radio Source enables you to listen to Internet radio broadcasts.

- **Music Store**—Apple's iTunes Music Store enables you to find and purchase music online. You can preview music and then buy it. When you do so, that music is downloaded to your Mac and added to your Music Library. You can buy entire CDs or individual songs.

- **Purchased Music**—This is a special playlist that contains all the music you have purchased from the iTunes Music Store.

- **Audio CD**—When an audio CD is inserted in your Mac, you see its icon in the Source pane. You can listen to it and add it to your Library, which iTunes calls *importing*, so you never have to use the CD itself again.

- **Shared Music**—With iTunes, you can share music with other people on your network and other people can share music in their Libraries with you. When you select a shared source, you can listen to music in other people's iTunes Libraries.

- **Playlists**—*Playlists* are collections of songs you create and listen to. They enable you to create your own music collections that contain exactly the songs you want to listen to in the order in which you want to listen to them. You can add any music from your Library to playlists, and you can have as many playlists as you want.

- **Smart Playlists**—Smart playlists use a set of expressions you create to automatically collect songs in a group (unlike playlists, which you create by manually adding music to them). You define the expressions used for each smart playlist you create. Smart playlists can be *dynamic*, meaning songs can be automatically added to them based on the expressions you create so their content changes over time.

- **Music Player**—On of the best things you can do with iTunes is to manage the music stored on an iPod so you can take your music with you wherever you go. You can also use iTunes to work with other portable music players, but because the iPod is by far the best one, I don't know why you would want to use another kind.

→ To learn how to use iTunes to manage the music on an iPod, **see** Chapter 19 "Configuring and Using an iPod," **p. 585**.

BROWSING YOUR MUSIC WITH THE BROWSER

The Browser provides a way for you to browse your music by genre, artist, and album (refer to Figure 18.1). The Browser can be shown or hidden for each source on the Source list. As you select items in the Browser, the contents of what you select are shown in the Content pane (explained in the next section). The more specific you make the Browser, the more specific the selection of song results in the Content pane. For example, if you click a specific genre in the Genre column, only the artists associated with that genre are shown in the Artist column. Similarly, if you select an artist in the Artist pane, only that artist's albums are shown in the Album pane. When you select an album in the Album column, that album's songs are shown in the Content pane.

To configure the Browser, do the following steps:

1. Select iTunes, Preferences or press ⌘-,.

2. Click the General tab if it isn't selected already.

3. Check the "Show genre when browsing" check box. This will cause iTunes to display the Genre column of the Browser.

4. Check the "Group compilations when browsing" check box.

> **NOTE**
>
> A *compilation* is a CD that contains songs from different artists, such as that *Greatest TV Theme Songs of the 1970s* CD you love to listen to. When you browse, it is usually a good idea to have iTunes group this type of CD as a compilation, rather than displaying the songs it contains by artist.

5. Click OK. The Preferences window will close and your settings will take effect.

> **TIP**
>
> You can use the Source Text and Song Text pop-up menus on the General pane of the iTunes Preferences window to set the relative size of the text used in the Source pane and Content pane, respectively.

To show or hide the Browser for a source, select that source and select Edit, Show Browser or Edit, Hide Browser, respectively. You can also show or hide the Browser with the Browse action button (this appears only for certain sources, such as the Library). When the Browser is hidden, the Content pane expands to fill the right side of the iTunes window (see Figure 18.2).

Figure 18.2
Press ⌘-B to show or hide the Browser; compare this figure to Figure 18.1.

TIP

> The Browser is the most useful when you are working with a source that contains music from different artists and albums or from different genres, such as your Library, large playlists, and so on. It isn't so useful for sources from a single artist or that don't contain many songs. By default, the Browser will be displayed only for the Library source. You'll have to show it when you work with other sources.

WORKING WITH MUSIC IN THE CONTENT PANE

The Content pane displays the contents (the songs) of the source selected in the Source pane or Browser. Along with song name, the Content pane can show a variety of other information for each song, including track number, time, artist, album, genre, and much more. You can choose to display different columns for each source.

NOTE

> The first column in the Content pane does not have a column title and is always visible. Icons appear in this column to indicate what is happening with songs being shown in the Content pane. For example, when you are playing a song, a speaker icon appears in this column next to the name of the song.

The columns in the Content pane work similarly to those in a Finder window in the List view. You can sort the pane by a specific column (such as Track #) by clicking its column title (the column title by which the pane is sorted is highlighted in blue). You can drag columns to the left or right to change the order in which they appear, and you can resize a column by dragging its right border.

→ To learn how to customize the information you see for sources, **see** "Configuring Views for Sources," **p. 564**.

One of the most important things to realize about the Content pane is that songs will play in the order in which they appear in this pane starting from the top of the pane and moving toward the bottom.

If the contents of the pane are too large to be shown at its current size, you can use the scrollbars to see all the information it contains.

NOTE

> One of the nice features of iTunes is that it automatically connects to the Internet and downloads information about CDs you play, such as album, artist, genre, song title, and so on. Music you purchase from the iTunes Music Store includes this information, too. You can also add or edit a song's information manually. The information associated with your music is important because you use it to organize your music and to perform some actions, such as creating a smart playlist.

→ To learn how to associate information with your music, **see** "Labeling Your Music," **p. 552**.

USING ITUNES CONTROLS AND DISPLAYS

At the top and bottom of the iTunes window, surrounding the panes, are the iTunes controls, information window, and search tool (see Figure 18.3).

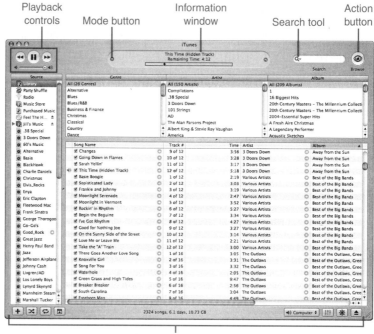

Figure 18.3
Surrounding the panes of the iTunes window are the controls and displays you use to work with your music.

Additional controls

In the upper-left corner of the window are the playback controls, which include rewind/ jump to previous track; play, stop, or pause; fast forward/jump to the next track; and the volume slider. These are self-explanatory, and they change depending on the context (for example, when you are playing a CD, the Pause button appears, but when you stop the music, it becomes the Play button).

In the top center part of the window is the information window. This display shows information about what you are doing at any moment in time. For example, when you are listening to music, it shows information about the song that is currently playing. When you are importing music into your Library, it shows information about the importing process.

The information window also has several modes; you can change these using the Mode button. What this button does depends on the action you are performing at that particular time. For example, when you are listening to music, one mode displays a graphic equalizer representation of the music playing. In another mode, it shows the title of the track that is playing along with a progress bar. When you are importing a song, the information window shows a progress bar for the import process. In certain situations, this area also contains a Stop button you can use to stop what is happening (such as when you are importing audio files). You will see examples of these modes in the various figures in this chapter.

TIP

> When you are playing music, the name of the track, artist, and album it comes from rotate above the time display; you can change from one to the other by clicking the text. You can also switch from the remaining time display to the total time display or elapsed time by clicking the time currently being displayed.

To the right of the information window is the search tool. You can use this to narrow the songs shown in the Content pane for any source you select, such as your Library or a CD:

1. Select the source in which you want to search.

2. Click the Magnifying Glass icon and select the attribute by which you want to search. Your options are All (the default), Artists, Albums, Composers, and Songs.

3. Start typing in the Search tool. As you type, the songs displayed in the Content pane are limited to only those songs that contain the text you type (the text can be in any of the columns shown in the pane). The more letters you type, the more specific the search becomes.

For example, to find all the songs in your Library that have the word *strange* somehow connected with them, you would leave All selected on the pop-up menu and type **strange** in the Search box. The Content pane would then show only those items whose name, artist, or other data contain that text (see Figure 18.4). In this example, if you had selected a source containing the song "Strangers in the Night" and also had a song by Eddie Strange, both of these songs would appear in the Content pane.

Figure 18.4
If you have strange music in your Library, it is easy to find using the iTunes search tool.

After you perform a search, the Clear button (which is a circle containing an *x*) appears at the right end of the search tool. Click this button to clear the search and cause the Content pane to display all the contents of the selected source again.

In the upper-right corner of the iTunes window is the Action button, which changes depending on the source selected. When an audio CD is selected, the Action button becomes the Import button, which enables you to add songs from the CD to your Library. When a playlist is selected, it becomes the Burn CD button, which enables you to burn a CD from a selected playlist. When the Library, Music Store, or Shared Music is selected, it is the Browse button that shows or hides the Browser.

Along the bottom of the iTunes window are more controls and information (see Figure 18.5).

Figure 18.5
iTunes provides all the tools you need to get the most out of your music.

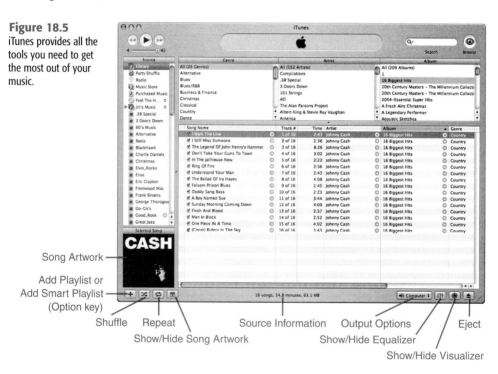

At the bottom of the window, the following features are available (from left to right):

- **New Playlist**—Click this to create a new playlist. If you hold down the Option key while you click it, you can create a new smart playlist. You will learn much more about playlists later in this chapter.

- **Shuffle**—When you click this, the tracks of the selected source are played in a random order. This is reflected in the Content pane because the songs are reshuffled to reflect the random order in which they will be played. Click the button again to return the selected source back to its previous order.

TIP

To determine whether iTunes shuffles by song or album, use the Song or Album radio button on the Advanced pane of the iTunes Preferences dialog box. When you click Song, iTunes will shuffle among the songs in the current album. If you click Album, iTunes will shuffle among albums in the selected source (playing the entire album before it selects the next album to play).

- **Repeat**—The Repeat button enables you to repeat whatever you are playing. If you click this button once, the source repeats until you stop it. If you click this button twice, the source repeats one time.

- **Show/Hide Song Artwork**—When you click this, the Song Artwork pane appears underneath the Source pane. The art associated with the currently playing or selected song is shown in this pane. Music you purchase from the iTunes Music Store has art associated with it. You can also add graphics to this field for any music in your Library.

→ To learn about artwork, **see** "Working with Album Artwork," **p. 567**.

- **Source Information**—In the center of the bottom of the iTunes window information about the currently selected source is shown. You can see how many songs are included in the source, the total playing time, and the total file size of the source's tracks. This information is especially useful when you are burning CDs or managing a music player.

- **Output Options**—Using AirTunes and an AirPort Express base station, you can broadcast your iTunes over a wireless network. The Output Options pop-up menu enables you to choose how you want to output your music.

→ To learn more about AirTunes, **see** "Using AirTunes and AirPort Express to Broadcast Your Music," **p. 575**.

- **Show Equalizer**—This opens the iTunes Equalizer that enables you to control how music sounds.

→ To learn more about the Equalizer, **see** "Using the iTunes Equalizer," **p. 566**.

- **Show/Hide Visualizer**—This opens a funky, 60s-style window that displays visuals to accompany your music.

- **Eject**—As you can probably guess, this ejects the selected source, such as an audio CD or iPod.

TIP

If you have an Apple Pro keyboard or are using a PowerBook or iBook, you can eject a selected source by pressing its Eject key.

When an iPod or other music player is connected to your Mac, you see additional buttons related to that player, such as the iPod Options button.

The commands for many of iTunes' controls—such as Shuffle, Repeat, and Eject—also appear on the Controls menu along with additional controls, including Volume Up, Volume Down, and Mute. Also, keyboard shortcuts are available for most of iTunes controls.

→ To see a list of keyboard shortcuts, **see** "Using iTunes Keyboard Shortcuts," **p. 579**.

The Most Useless Feature Ever?

To the left of the Eject button is the Show Visualizer button. If you click this button, the center part of the iTunes window becomes a throwback to the 1960s and you see visual effects while the music plays. Although it looks cool for about 10 seconds, I have never used it for longer than that period of time. Perhaps if you like to stare at something while you listen to music, you might find this feature more useful than I do.

Be aware that the effects you see really have nothing to do with the music that is playing. If you don't believe me, open it when you aren't playing any music. Because I think this feature is a waste, I won't waste any more of your time on it.

LISTENING TO AUDIO CDS WITH ITUNES

The most basic task for which you use iTunes is to listen to audio CDs. In addition to the capabilities provided by a "regular" CD player, iTunes provides several other features that leave regular CD players in the dust.

CAUTION

> Some audio CDs use copyright protection schemes that prevent you from listening to the CD on a computer (with the idea being that you won't be able to make electronic versions of the songs for illegal purposes). Unfortunately, not only do these CDs not work in your Mac, but they can actually cause damage. Before playing a CD in your Mac, check the label carefully to ensure that its label doesn't contain any warnings about playing the CD in a computer or that the CD is copy-protected. If it does have such warnings, don't try to use the CD in your Mac.

PLAYING AN AUDIO CD

Playing an audio CD is straightforward. The following steps give you a quick run-through of the process for launching iTunes and playing a CD:

1. Insert the audio CD. By default, iTunes opens (if it isn't open already) and moves to the front. A message telling you that iTunes is looking up the CD on the CDDB database will appear. Depending on how you connect to the Internet, this process can take a few moments. If multiple matches are found for the CD, you will be prompted to select the correct one. Do so, and then click OK. (This is done only the first time you listen to a CD because iTunes remembers CDs as you listen to them.)

   If you have turned off the preference allowing iTunes to automatically check for information, this step is skipped. Also, if you have a dial-up connection and you don't allow applications to automatically connect, you have to make the connection manually for this to work.

   The CD is mounted and appears in the Source pane.

2. The CD should be selected as the source automatically; if it isn't, select the CD as the source. Its contents will appear in the Content pane. You might have to resize the window and the columns to be able to see all the CD's information. The Source

Information area shows information about the CD's contents, such as the number of tracks and total playing time.

3. Click the Play button and use the other playback controls to control the music. The controls work just like you expect them to. For example, to skip to the next track, click the Fast Forward/Next Track button. As the CD plays, information about it, such as the CD name, artist name, and so on, will appear in the Information window. Along with this, a timeline bar will appear with a diamond-shaped slider in it to visually represent the progress of playing the song (see Figure 18.6).

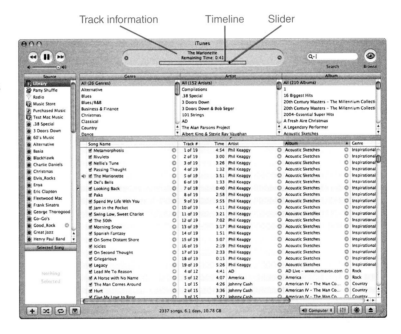

Figure 18.6
You can drag the iTunes slider to move to any point in a song.

Playing an audio CD is as easy as pie (whatever that means). Here are a few tips for you:

- You can play a track by double-clicking it.
- If you uncheck the box next to a track's title, it will be skipped.
- You can change the order in which tracks play by dragging them up and down in the window; iTunes remembers this order and the next time you insert the CD, the same playing order will be used again.
- You can move around within a song by dragging the slider that appears in the timeline below the song's information in the Information window.
- The track currently playing is marked with a speaker icon in the Content pane. You can jump to the current song by selecting File, Show Current Song or by pressing ⌘-L.

CONFIGURING ITUNES FOR AUDIO CDs

By default, iTunes launches automatically when you insert an audio CD and then looks up its information. However, you can configure what happens when you insert an audio CD into your Mac by using the following steps:

1. Open the System Preferences application and click the CDs & DVDs button.

2. On the "When you insert a music CD" pop-up menu, select the action you want your Mac to take. By default, this is Open iTunes. Your other choices are "Open other application," which enables you to select a different application to launch when you insert an audio CD; "Run script," which enables you to choose an AppleScript to be executed; and Ignore, which causes your Mac to do nothing.

3. Quit the System Preferences application.

4. Back in iTunes, select iTunes, Preferences.

5. Click the General tab if it isn't selected already.

6. Using the On CD Insert pop-up menu, select the action you want iTunes to take when you insert an audio CD. The options are the following:

   - **Show Songs**—The CD becomes available in the Source pane, but no action is taken.
   - **Begin Playing**—The CD will begin playing automatically.
   - **Import Songs**—The tracks on the CD will be added to your Library. (More about this later.)
   - **Import Songs and Eject**—The tracks on the CD will be added to your Library. When that process is complete, the CD will be ejected.

7. If you don't want iTunes to connect to the Internet when it needs to, such as to look up a CD's information or access the iTunes Music Store, uncheck the "Connect to Internet when needed" check box.

8. Click OK. The CD actions you selected will become active.

CONTROLLING MUSIC PLAYBACK FROM THE DOCK

You can control iTunes from the Dock by opening its menu (see Figure 18.7). In addition to playback controls, you can see the name and artist of the current track, rate it, and so on.

NOTE

While I have included information on controlling music playback in the section about playing audio CDs, but it is equally applicable to listening to music from any source.

CONTROLLING ITUNES USING ITS DASHBOARD WIDGET

One of the standard widgets that comes with Mac OS X enables you to control iTunes. The controls the widget provides are pretty basic, but when you want to make quick changes to iTunes, they will likely be all you need (see Figure 18.8).

Figure 18.7
The iTunes Dock menu enables you to get information about and control the music currently playing.

→ To learn how to use widgets, **see** Chapter 6, "Working with the Dashboard and Widgets," **p. 160**.

18

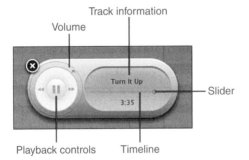

Volume

Track information

Figure 18.8
Using the iTunes widget, you can control iTunes without being in the application.

Slider

Playback controls   Timeline

The controls in the iTunes widget work just like the controls within iTunes with a couple of exceptions.

The volume control in the widget is the outer "ring" on the left side of the widget. Drag the dot clockwise to increase the volume or counterclockwise to decrease it. When you change the volume, the slider is replaced by a graphic representation of the current volume level. When you release the volume control, the timeline will reappear.

Another exception is that you can't change the information displayed in the widget; you will always see the title of the current song playing.

ADDING MUSIC FROM AUDIO CDS AND OTHER AUDIO FILES TO YOUR iTUNES MUSIC LIBRARY

Listening to audio CDs with iTunes is fine, but for that purpose, any old CD player works about as well. iTunes' real power comes when you add all your music to the Library so it is always available to you. In addition to letting you find and listen to your music more easily, after it is in the Library, you can do all sorts of cool things with it, such as creating custom playlists and CDs.

IMPORTING AUDIO CDS INTO YOUR iTUNES MUSIC LIBRARY

Adding CDs to your iTunes Library is called *importing* them. The steps to import CDs are simple, except for the choice of format you use.

UNDERSTANDING IMPORT FORMATS

All digital audio files are stored in a specific format. To work effectively with digital music, you don't need to understand all the technical details of these formats. However, you do need to understand them enough to know which format you want to use when you add your own CDs to your iTunes Library.

The digital music revolution began with MP3. MP3 is the acronym for the audio compression scheme called Moving Picture Experts Group (MPEG) audio layer 3. The revolutionary aspect of the MP3 encoding scheme was that music data could be stored in files that were only about one twelfth the size of unencoded digital music without a noticeable degradation in the quality of the music. A typical music CD consumes about 650MB of storage space, but the same music encoded in the MP3 format shrinks down to about 55MB. Put another way, a single 3 1/2-minute song shrinks from its 35MB on audio CD down to a paltry 3MB or so. This small file size opened up a world of possibilities.

While MP3 is the format that caused digital audio to become part of everyone's digital life, other more modern formats have also come into play. The formats that iTunes supports are shown the Table 18.1.

TABLE 18.1   DIGITAL AUDIO FORMATS SUPPORTED BY ITUNES

Format Abbreviation	Format Name	Filename Extension	Description
AAC	Advanced Audio Coding	.m4a .m4p	This format is part of the larger MPEG-4 specification. Its basic purpose is the same as the MP3 format: to deliver excellent sound quality while keeping file sizes small. However, the AAC format is a newer and better format in that it can be used to produce files that have better quality than MP3 at even smallerfile sizes. The AAC format also enables content producers to add some copy-protection schemes to their music. Typically, these schemes won't have any impact on you (unless, of course, you are trying to do something you shouldn't). One of the most important aspects of the AAC format is that all the music in the iTunes Music Store is stored in it; when you purchase music from the store, it is added to your computer in this format.
AIFF	Audio Interchange File Format	.aiff .aif	This format provides high-quality sound, but its file sizes are much larger than MP3 or AAC. Unlike AAC or MP3, this format does not compress audio files, so they are quite large. As you can probably guess from its name, this format was originally used to exchange audio among various platforms.
None	Apple Lossless Encoder	.m4a	As you can tell from its name, this format was developed by Apple specifically for digital music. Its purpose is to provide the highest quality sound, but with slightly smaller file sizes than AIFF or WAV.

18

continues

TABLE 18.1 CONTINUED

Format Abbreviation	Format Name	Filename Extension	Description
MP3	Moving Picture Experts Group (MPEG) audio layer 3	.mp3	You've already read about this one. Until AAC, this was the standard format for encoding digital audio files. It still has some uses, but for most of your music, you should choose AAC instead because you will achieve better quality with smaller file sizes.
WAV	Windows Waveform	.wav	This is a standard audio file format for Windows computers. It has been widely used for various kinds of audio, but like AIFF, it is not a compression scheme so WAV files are quite large. For that reason, WAV files typically contain short sound clips, such as from movies. There are millions of WAV files available on the Internet that you can play and download.

NOTE

Songs you encode with the AAC format using iTunes will have the filename extension .m4a. Those you purchase from the iTunes Music Store will have the .m4p format, which indicates the file is protected.

Generally, you should choose AAC when you import your CDs into iTunes. You will get great sound quality with relatively small file sizes (better than with MP3). There are a few situations in which one of the other formats might be useful to you. For example, if you are moving music to a music player that doesn't support AAC, you would need to use MP3 instead. If you demand the best in the sound quality of custom CDs you create using iTunes and don't care about disk space usage, choose the Apple Lossless Encoder. Your files will be much larger than with AAC, but you will get the best possible quality. You'll likely use AIFF or WAV only when creating sound clips to use in other applications.

TIP

You can also use iTunes to convert existing music files into any of these formats in case you need a version in multiple formats for some reason, such as needing an MP3 version of a song you purchased from the iTunes Music Store. You'll learn how to do this at the end of this chapter.

When you convert music into one of these formats, you use an encoder (not surprisingly, each format has its own encoder). With some encoders, such as the MP3 encoder, you can configure some specific details about how the encoder works, such as the quality level, which changes the amount of data stored per second of music. Obviously, storing more data makes for better audio quality, but also for larger files sizes.

In most cases, you will use one of the existing quality levels for an encoder, but you can also create custom settings if you want to meet more exacting specifications.

The quality level you should use depends on several factors, which include the following:

- **Your sensitivity to imperfections**—If you dislike minor imperfections in music play-back, you should use higher-quality encoding settings. If you don't mind the occasional "bump" in the flow of the music, you can probably get away with lower-quality settings.

- **The music you listen to**—Some music hides flaws better than others. For example, you are less likely to notice subtle problems in the music while listening to grinding heavy metal music than when you listen to classical music.

- **How you listen to music**—If you use a low-quality sound system with poor speakers, you probably won't notice any difference between high-quality and low-quality encoding. If your Mac is connected to high-fidelity speakers, the differences in music quality will be more noticeable.

CHOOSING AND CONFIGURING THE FORMAT FOR YOUR iTunes MUSIC

Before you add CDs to your Library, you need to choose the encoder you will use while importing that music. The encoding settings iTunes uses are accessed with the Preferences command:

1. Select iTunes, Preferences.
2. Click the Importing button to open the Importing pane (see Figure 18.9).
3. Use the Import Using pop-up menu to select the particular encoder you want to use. In most cases, you should choose AAC Encoder, but occasionally you might want to use one of the others.
4. Use the Setting pop-up menu to select the quality level of the encoding. Some encoders, such as AAC, have only one option. Others have multiple quality levels. The Details area of the pane provides information about the encoding setting you have selected.
5. Check the "Play songs while importing" check box if you want to hear music as you import it. The encoding process is much faster than the playing process, so music continues to play after the encoding is done. This can be a bit confusing.

TIP

> If you select the "Import Songs and Eject" option on the On CD Insert pop-up menu in the General pane of the iTunes Preferences window, the CD is ejected when the encoding is done. This is a good reminder that you are ready to encode the next CD. (The music from the previous CD continues to play.)

18

Figure 18.9
The Importing pane of the Preferences dialog box enables you to control the encoding settings used for your music.

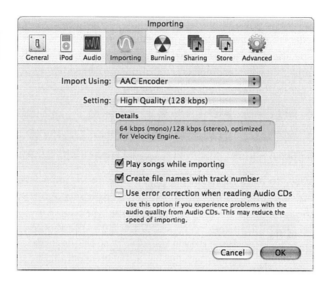

6. Check the "Create file names with track number" check box if you want the files iTunes creates to have the track number included as a prefix in the filename.

> **TIP**
> If there are sound quality problems when you play or import music from CD, check the "Use error correction when reading Audio CDs" check box on the Importing pane of the Preferences window. It is unlikely you will need to do this, but in some cases, this setting can clear up quality problems you experience.

7. Click OK. The next time you import music into the Library, it is encoded according to the settings you selected.

> **TIP**
> You can vary the encoder and quality level you use from album to album or even from song to song. For example, if you want to play certain songs on a portable music player, you might want to use a lower level for those songs so you can download more of them to the player.

When you open the Setting pop-up menu, in addition to the standard quality levels, you'll see the Custom option. You can use this option to create and use custom encoding levels if the standard choices aren't acceptable to you. You configure custom encoding with the same steps you use for standard encoding. The difference is that you select Custom on the Setting pop-up menu. When you do that, a dialog box will appear that enables you to specifically configure various settings for the encoder. Configure the custom settings and click OK to use them.

Depending on the encoder you choose, you can set various parameters, including the following:

- **Stereo Bit Rate**—You can control the bit rate for stereo encoding. You can select rates between 8Kbps and 320Kbps. The higher the bit rate, the better the quality and the larger the file size will be.

- **Sample Rate**—Music is encoded by taking a sample of the bits that make up specific instances in the music at various speeds. The rate at which these samples are captured, called the *sample rate*, affects the quality of the music. Higher sample rates result in higher-quality music (again, more data is collected per second of music). You can select a specific sample rate from the Sample Rate pop-up menu, or you can leave the default Auto setting (which enables iTunes to choose the sample rate).

- **Channels**—You can choose to capture one channel of music (Mono) or both channels (Stereo), or let iTunes decide which to use (Auto).

- **Variable Bit Rate Encoding**—With this option turned on, the encoder uses a guaranteed minimum bit rate. You can set the level of this encoding using a secondary Quality setting that ranges from Lowest to Highest.

- **Stereo Mode**—Your choices here are Normal, which causes each track's information to be stored independently, and Joint Stereo, which causes information that is the same in both tracks to be stored in one track while the unique information is stored in another. According to Apple, this mode improves sound quality when encoding at 128Kbps or below.

- **Smart Encoding Adjustments**—This setting enables iTunes to adjust the encoding rates as necessary to maintain the optimal ratio of music quality to file size. Unless you have a specific reason not to use this feature, you should leave it turned on.

- **Filter Frequencies Below 10Hz**—Music frequencies below 10Hz are not audible, so there is really no reason to include them in the encoding process because it wastes disk space. This feature should be left on as well.

Copyright Conscious

Musicians creating their own audio files and distributing them over the Net is certainly legitimate. However, it is not legitimate to create files of someone else's music and distribute them without the appropriate legal permission to do so.

Some music sharing sites violate the letter and spirit of copyright laws because people other than those who own the rights to the music are distributing it.

When you are dealing with music, you need to be very conscious of the copyright status of any music with which you work. Although copyright laws are complex, the basic idea behind them is not. Simply put, you cannot distribute material to which someone else holds a copyright without (written) permission to do so.

continues

continued

Unless you create the music yourself (not simply encoding it yourself), you should not distribute it in any form. The exceptions are when you have received a license to use that music or when the music is in the public domain.

IMPORTING AUDIO CDS INTO YOUR LIBRARY

To add music from an audio CD to your Library, use the following steps:

1. Use the steps in the previous section to select and configure the encoder you want to use.

2. Insert the CD containing the songs you want to encode. iTunes connects to the Internet and identifies the CD (again, assuming that you haven't disabled this feature or haven't listened to the CD before).

3. Select the CD in the Source pane (if you just inserted it, it is selected by default).

4. Uncheck the check box next to the title of each song you don't want to add to the Library—by default, every track is selected and will be imported. You can use the boxes to deselect songs you don't want to import.

5. Click the Import action button. iTunes begins to encode the songs you selected. Depending on how fast your Mac is and the number of songs you selected, this process can take from a minute or two to 15 minutes or so for a very slow Mac and a CD with a lot of songs. You can see the progress of the encoding process in the iTunes Information window (see Figure 18.10).

Song being encoded

Encoded song

Information about the encoding process

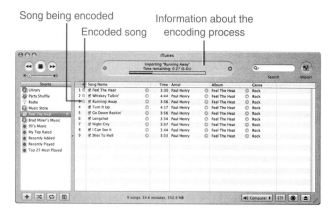

Figure 18.10
This iTunes window shows a CD being imported; information about the song currently being encoded is shown in the Information window.

As the encoding process progresses, each song is marked with a green circle containing a check mark. The resulting files are added to your Library, and you can listen to them from there and add them to playlists. When all the songs on the CD have been imported, a tone will play to let you know the process is complete (of course, if music is playing, you might not hear the tone).

Following are some pointers to improve your importing experiences:

- When you first start building your Library, set iTunes to import songs and eject a CD when you insert it (use the On CD Insert pop-up menu on the General pane of the iTunes Preferences dialog box). When you insert an audio CD, iTunes imports it automatically. After iTunes finishes importing a CD, it ejects it. Then you can insert another CD and add it to the Library. After you have added all your CDs to your Library, select a different CD insert option; otherwise, you might end up with multiple versions of the same song in your Library when you insert a CD you have already imported. (iTunes enables you to create multiple versions of the same songs in case you want to have songs encoded with different quality levels or in different formats.)

- You can cancel the encoding process by clicking the small x at the right end of the encoding progress bar in the information window.

- You can listen to the music you are encoding while you are encoding it. Because the encoding process moves faster than real time, the import process is done before the selected songs stop playing. This can be confusing because it seems natural that both should stop at the same time. If you set CDs to eject after they are imported (using the On CD Insert pop-up menu), the end of the importing process is quite clear (because the CD is ejected).

- You can also listen to other songs in your Library or playlists at the same time you are importing songs from a CD.

- After the import process is complete, you can find the location of the encoded file for any song in your Library by selecting it and selecting File, Show Song File (⌘-R). A Finder window containing the file you imported opens, and the file is highlighted.

ADDING OTHER AUDIO FILES TO YOUR ITUNES MUSIC LIBRARY

You can also add any audio file to your iTunes Library, such as those you create with other applications, those you download from the Internet, and so on. You can add files in any of the audio formats iTunes supports, including AAC, MP3, AIFF, WAV, and Apple Lossless.

CONFIGURING ITUNES TO KEEP YOUR MUSIC ORGANIZED

Later in this chapter, you'll learn in detail how and where iTunes stores the music you add to your Library. For now, know that in most cases, you should have iTunes store files from any source in the same way as those you encode yourself. Here's how:

1. Select iTunes, Preferences.
2. Click the Advanced button.
3. Check the "Keep iTunes Music folder organized" check box if it isn't checked already.
4. Check the "Copy files to iTunes Music folder when adding to library" check box if it isn't already checked. This causes iTunes to place copies of songs you have downloaded in the appropriate iTunes Music folders.
5. Click OK.

ADDING AUDIO FILES TO YOUR ITUNES LIBRARY

After you have configured iTunes to store the music you add in an organized way, add the music to your library:

1. Select File, Add to Library. The Add To Library dialog box will appear.

2. Move to the files you want to add to your Library, select them, and click Choose. The files are added to your Library and you can work with them just like tracks you have imported from CD.

NOTE

If you have unchecked the "Copy files to iTunes Music folder when adding to library" check box for some reason, you see a dialog box explaining that iTunes doesn't actually move the files but uses a reference to the files you choose. (If this check box is checked, iTunes does make a copy and places it in the appropriate location.) Just read the information in the dialog box and click OK.

TIP

You can also add music to the iTunes Library by dragging song files onto the iTunes window or onto the iTunes icon on the Dock.

ADDING MUSIC FROM THE ITUNES MUSIC STORE TO YOUR ITUNES MUSIC LIBRARY

The iTunes Music Store is amazing. This store is an online source of hundreds of thousands of songs and albums. You can search and browse for music in which you are interested; then when you find music you want to add to your Library, you can purchase that music and download it with a couple of mouse clicks. Because you access the Music Store from within iTunes, it is convenient to use. And because songs are only 99¢ (and sometimes even less when you purchase albums), adding music from the Music Store is an economical way to build your Library.

What's the Catch?

Because of copyright concerns, there are some limitations on the music you purchase from the iTunes Music Store. Fortunately, these limitations aren't likely to ever be noticeable to you. The only two meaningful restrictions are the following:

You can play music you purchase on only five computers at the same time. The computers on which you play music from the iTunes Music Store must be authorized to play it; you do this by logging in to an iTunes Music Store account on the computer on which you want to play music you have purchased. You can deauthorize a computer when you want to use the music on a different machine, sell it, and so on so it doesn't count against the five-computer limitation.

You can burn the same playlist that contains music you have purchased from the iTunes Music Store onto only seven CDs. However, you can always change the playlist and burn it onto additional discs or add a song to a different playlist to put it onto a CD.

UNDERSTANDING THE iTUNES MUSIC STORE

Two sources related to the iTunes Music Store appear in the Source pane. One is the Music Store itself. When you click this source, the iTunes Music Store appears inside the Content pane. The other is the Purchased Music playlist which will be created the first time you purchase music; all the music you download is added to this playlist so you can easily see the music you have purchased (music you purchase from the iTunes Music Store is also automatically added to your Library).

If you use the Shopping Cart preference (explained later in this chapter), the Music Store source contains the Shopping Cart and the Purchased Music playlist.

NOTE

All music in the Music Store is in the AAC format, which means standard MP3 players won't be capable of playing that music. However, the Apple iPod can play AAC music, and putting your music on an iPod does not count against the five-computer limit.

CREATING AND CONFIGURING AN APPLE STORE ACCOUNT AND SHOPPING PREFERENCES

To purchase music from the iTunes Music Store, you need to configure an account there. If you already have an account at the Apple Store (via its website), you already have an account for the iTunes Music Store because they use the same account. If not, you must obtain an Apple Store/iTunes Music Store account.

NOTE

It is probably clear already, but to use the iTunes Music Store, your Mac must be capable of connecting to the Internet.

You don't have to have an account to browse and search the iTunes Music Store, so you can check it out before you bother creating an account.

To sign in to an existing account or create a new one, use the following steps:

1. Click the Music Store source in the Source pane. The Music Store will fill the Content pane (see Figure 18.11).

2. Click the Sign In button in the upper-right corner of the Music Store window to see the Sign In account dialog box. This dialog box presents two options. In the upper part of the dialog box, you can click the Create New Account button to create a new account. In the lower part of the dialog box, you can enter your existing Apple ID and password to sign in to your current account.

NOTE

You can also use an AOL user account to log in to the iTunes Music Store. In the Sign In account dialog box, just click the AOL radio button and enter your AOL account information.

Figure 18.11
The iTunes Music Store enables me to do something I have always wanted to be able to do—buy songs individually!

3. If you need to create an account, click the Create New Account button and follow the onscreen instructions to do so.

4. If you need to sign in to your existing account, enter your Apple ID and password and click Sign In.

After you have signed in to your account, your Apple ID appears in the Account box to show you the account to which you are currently logged in. When you see your account here, you are ready to shop.

Following are the two ways you can make purchases from the iTunes Music Store:

■ With the 1-Click method, you select and purchase songs or albums with a single mouse click (thus, the method's name) and they are immediately downloaded to your Mac. This method is designed for people who use a fast Internet connection, such as DSL or a cable modem.

■ With the Shopping Cart method, you select songs and albums and they are added to your shopping cart. When you are ready to purchase that music, you check out of the store and the music in your cart that you choose to purchase is downloaded to your Mac. This method is designed for slow Internet connections because downloading music inhibits shopping for other music at the same time. If you prefer to be able to select music and think about it before purchasing it, this can also be a useful option.

You can configure your shopping preferences on the Store pane of the iTunes Preferences dialog box:

1. Open the iTunes Preferences window and click the Store button. The Store preferences will appear (see Figure 18.12).

Figure 18.12
Using the Store prefer-
ences, you can config-
ure your shopping
experience.

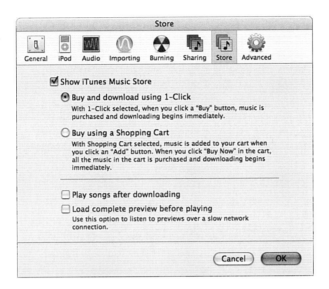

2. To disable the Music Store, uncheck the "Show iTunes Music Store" check box. If you do this, the Music Store source will no longer appear in the Source pane and you can't access the store. If you select this option, you are missing out on some good stuff.

3. To use the 1-Click shopping method, click the "Buy and download using 1-Click" radio button; to use the Shopping Cart method, click the "Buy using a Shopping Cart" radio button.

4. If you want songs to play immediately after you download them from the store, check the "Play songs after downloading" check box.

5. If you use a slow Internet connection, check the "Load complete preview before playing" check box. You can listen to a 30-second preview of the songs available in the iTunes Music Store. This enables you to listen to music before you decide to buy it. If you check this box, the entire 30-second preview is downloaded to your Mac before it begins to play. This option is useful when you use a slow Internet connection because the preview plays smoothly if it has been downloaded to your Mac, whereas it might not if you try to listen to it while it is being downloaded.

6. Click OK to set your store preferences.

BROWSING, SEARCHING, AND PREVIEWING MUSIC IN THE iTUNES MUSIC STORE

The iTunes Music Store works just like most other websites you have seen except better because it uses the iTunes interface. You click links, make choices on pop-up menus, and search to move around. You can search for music, browse genres, and so on to find music in which you are interested. When it comes to the iTunes Music Store, if you can see it, you can probably click it to move to some music.

18

To search for music in the iTunes Music Store, do the following steps:

1. Select the Music Store source. The Music Store will fill the Content pane.

2. Click the Magnifying Glass icon in the Search Music Store box.

3. On the resulting pop-up menu, select the criterion by which you want to search, such as All (to search all fields), Artists (to search for a specific artist), and so on.

TIP

If you click Power Search on the iTunes Music Store home page, the Music Store is replaced by an advanced search window that enables you to search for music by multiple attributes at the same time.

4. Type the text for which you want to search in the Search field and press Return. Your search will be performed and the music that is found will be shown in the Content pane (see Figure 18.13). At the top of the Content pane are albums that correspond to the search, top songs related to the search, and top artists related to the search. In the lower part of the pane are the songs that meet the criteria you entered.

Figure 18.13
Like 3 Doors Down? With the iTunes Music Store, purchasing all their music is easy.

5. Double-click a song to listen to a preview. The 30-second preview of the song will play.

NOTE

One of the cool things about the iTunes Music Store is that a lot of music becomes available there as soon as a CD is released (many songs become available *before* the CD is released, too). This means you can grab new music from your favorite artists as soon as it becomes available without needing to wonder whether a copy will be available like you do for "regular" music stores.

You can also browse the store in many ways, including the following:

- Use the Back, Forward, and Home buttons that appear at the top of the Content pane when you are viewing the iTunes Music Store. These work just like similar buttons in a web browser. As you move down into the store, the path to your current location is always shown there. You can move to any level in your current path by clicking it.

- Click the songs on any list that you see. You will move to music by that artist, the related albums, and so on.

- Browse genres of music by choosing the genre you are interested in on the Choose Genre pop-up menu on the iTunes Music Store home page. The home page will be refreshed and will display only music from the genre you select.

- Click an album cover. That album will appear in the Content pane. At the top of the pane, you will see information about the album and the button you use to either buy the album or add it to your shopping cart. At the bottom of the pane, you will see the songs it contains (see Figure 18.14).

Figure 18.14
An album's window looks and works just like the Content pane when you are viewing music in your Library.

- To browse all the music in the iTunes Music Store by an artist, click the right-facing arrow shown next to artists in the lists you see. That artist's page on the iTunes Music Store will be displayed and you will see all their music that is available in the store.

- Click the iMix link on the home page. You will see custom playlists created by other iTunes users. You can use these lists to browse and purchase music.

TIP

You can also post your own iMixes by creating a playlist and publishing it as an iMix. To learn how, open the iMix home page and click the "How do I make an iMix?" link.

PURCHASING MUSIC FROM THE iTUNES MUSIC STORE

When you find music you want to buy, how you buy it depends on the shopping method you chose to use.

To buy music with the 1-Click method, simply click the Buy Album button next to an album you want to buy or the Buy Song button to buy that song. The album or song is immediately purchased, downloaded to your Mac, and added to the Purchased Music playlist and to your Library.

To buy music using the Shopping Cart method, use the following steps:

1. Click the Add button next to the song or album you want to buy. The song or album you selected is added to your Shopping Cart.

2. Continue adding songs or albums to the Shopping Cart.

3. When you are ready to purchase music, select the Shopping Cart source, which will appear under the Music Store. The contents of your shopping cart will appear in the Content pane.

4. Click the Buy button next to songs or albums you want to buy. The music you choose to buy will be purchased and downloaded to your Purchased Music playlist and your Library.

Because you store a credit card with your iTunes Music Store account, you don't need to enter any additional information when you purchase music. If you are logged in to an iTunes Music Store, you can obtain music through that account at any time.

> **TIP**
>
> There are other ways to pay for iTunes Music Store music. You can use gift certificates, an iTunes allowance, and so on. These methods are beyond the scope of this chapter. For more information, see my book *Absolute Beginner's Guide to iPod and iTunes*.

After you have purchased music, Apple sends you a receipt via email (the receipt contains information about purchases you made in a certain period of time rather than listing only individual purchases).

LISTENING TO MUSIC YOU PURCHASED AT THE iTUNES MUSIC STORE

After you purchase music from the iTunes Music Store, it is just like any other music in your Library (with the restrictions listed earlier in this section).

Click the Purchased Music playlist to see and listen to the music you have purchased. Of course, you can browse and search in your Library to work with your purchased music, too, because it is placed in your Library automatically. Here are some other points about the iTunes Music Store to consider:

- You can move songs you purchased to other Macs by copying them across a network, putting them on a CD, and so on. After you have moved the music to the next Mac, you can add it to the Library using the Add to Library command. However, to play purchased music on a different Mac, you must authorize that Mac (see the next section for more information). You can authorize music on up to five Macs at the same time.

- If a download is interrupted before all the music you purchased has been downloaded to your Mac, select Advanced, "Check for Purchased Music." This enables you to recover any music you have purchased but have not downloaded successfully.

- You can download music only one time! So, if something happens to the Mac on which your purchased music is stored, you can't download it again without paying for it again. You should always back up your purchased music on a DVD, a CD, or another Mac.

Linking Your Library to the iTunes Music Store

By default, music in your Library will be automatically linked to the iTunes Music Store. When you click the right-facing arrow next to a song, artist, or album, you will move to that item in the iTunes Music Store. For example, if you click the right-facing arrow next to an artist, you'll move to that artist's page in the iTunes Music Store. This lets you easily find more music by the same artist, more songs from the same album, and so on.

If you don't want to allow this linkage, uncheck the "Show links to Music Store" check box on the General pane of the iTunes Preferences window.

18

AUTHORIZING AND DEAUTHORIZING A MAC TO PLAY MUSIC FROM THE ITUNES MUSIC STORE

To play music from the iTunes Music Store on a Mac, that Mac must be authorized to play it. This happens when you sign in to your Music Store account.

If you want to deauthorize a Mac so it doesn't count against the five-computer limit, select Advanced, Deauthorize Computer. After you confirm your choice by entering your account name and password, that Mac is no longer capable of playing any music purchased from the iTunes Music Store under that account.

Note that you can store music from the iTunes Music Store on as many computers you'd like, but you will be able to authorize only five to play that music at a time.

Music on Multiple Macs

If you have more than one Mac, you might want to install your music Library on each Mac so you can access it from that machine (if your Macs are connected over a network, you can share music from one machine to the others instead). To copy music from one Mac to another, put that music on a data CD or DVD and copy it to each Mac. Or, you can use file sharing to copy the music files from one machine to another. Then, use the Add to Library command to add that music to the iTunes Library on the Mac to which you copied the song files.

T I P

> You can replicate a music Library on another Mac by copying the iTunes folder in the Music folder under one user's Home folder and using it to replace another iTunes folder on a different Mac. The Mac to which it is copied must also be authorized for it to play any music purchased from the iTunes Music Store.

ORGANIZING YOUR MUSIC WITH THE iTUNES LIBRARY, STANDARD PLAYLISTS, AND SMART PLAYLISTS

So far, listening to music with iTunes isn't that much different from using a regular CD player (aside from the ability to store all your music in one place and download music from the Internet and the iTunes Music Store, that is). The real power of iTunes is in the capability to completely customize your music.

LABELING YOUR MUSIC

One of the great things about iTunes is that it helps you keep your music organized and accessible with just a few clicks or a quick search. You can also use playlists to customize music to play any way you want it. However, for these tasks to work well, you need to label your music appropriately.

The good news is that most of the time, iTunes handles this for you when you add music from a CD or the iTunes Music Store to your Library. The music's information, such as album title, artist, genre, song titles, and so on, is associated with the music automatically. For those times when the appropriate information isn't found (such as when you add a CD that can't be found in the online database) or when you want to add to or change information associated with music, you can use the Info window to add or change information associated with your music.

The Information window contains the following panes (see Figure 18.15):

- **Summary**—Use this tab to get general information about the song, such as title, artist, album, encoding method, and so on.

- **Info**—This tab enables you to apply various tags to the song, such as its artist, album, year, track number, and genre. You can also add comments about the song. These tags are searched when you perform a search using the iTunes Search tool.

- **Options**—Using this tab, you can change the relative volume level of a song, apply an Equalizer preset, rate it, and control the start and stop playback times.

- **Artwork**—This tab shows any artwork associated with the song. For example, when you purchase music from the Music Store, the album artwork is downloaded along with the song. You can also add artwork to or remove artwork from a song by using the Add or Delete button on the Artwork tab. You can even associate multiple graphics with the same song and cycle through them with the slider.

→ To learn how to choose and view album artwork, **see** "Working with Album Artwork," **p. 567**.

Figure 18.15
The iTunes Info window enables you to view, add, and change information related to music in your Library.

VIEWING SUMMARY INFORMATION FOR MUSIC

To access a song's summary information, use the following steps:

1. Select a song.

2. Select File, Get Info; press ⌘-I; or select Get Info on the song's contextual menu. The Song Info window will open.

3. Click the Summary tab if it isn't selected already. Information about the selected song appears (refer to Figure 18.15). The Summary tab provides detailed information (despite being called the Summary tab) about a song, such as where it is stored and the technical information related to how it was encoded.

4. To see the next or previous song in the selected source, click the Previous or Next button, respectively.

5. Click OK when you are done viewing this information. The Info window will close.

VIEWING OR CHANGING A SONG'S TAGS

To make browsing and searching efficient, you should ensure that your music has the appropriate information associated with it. To view or change a song's tags, use the following steps:

1. Select a song.

2. Select File, Get Info; press ⌘-I; or select Get Info on the song's contextual menu. The Song Info window will open.

3. Click the Info tab to see the information that is currently applied to the selected song (see Figure 18.16). If you have imported the song from a CD or purchased it from the iTunes Music Store, the name of the song (which appears at the top of the Song Information window), artist, album, track number, and genre were likely filled in when you added the song to your Library. In many cases, that is all the information you need.

Figure 18.16
The Info tab of the Song Information window provides detailed tags for a song; these are useful for categorizing your music.

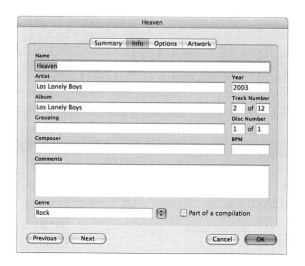

4. To change any of the song's tags, enter or edit the information shown in the various fields. For example, you can change the song's name or add comments about the song in the Comments field.

5. You can associate the song with a genre by selecting a genre on the Genre pop-up menu.

TIP

You can add your own genres to the Genre pop-up menu. Open the menu and select Custom. The Genre field then becomes editable, and you can type the genre you want to add. It is added to the menu, and you can associate it with songs just like the genres included by default.

6. Click OK to save the changes you made to the song's information.

SETTING A SONG'S OPTIONS

You can configure some specific options for a song by using the Options tab of the Song Information window:

1. Open the Song Info window for a song and click the Options tab (see Figure 18.17).

2. To change the relative volume of the song, drag the Volume Adjustment slider to the right to make the song play louder than normal or to the left to make the song play quieter than normal. This is especially useful when you include songs in playlists from a variety of sources because you can equalize the relative volume levels of those songs.

3. To apply an Equalizer preset to the song, use the Equalizer Preset pop-up menu. (You'll learn more about the Equalizer later in this chapter.)

4. To apply a rating to the song, click the dot in the My Rating field for the number of stars you want to give the song, from one to five.

Figure 18.17
The Options tab enables you to set a song's relative volume, equalizer, and other settings.

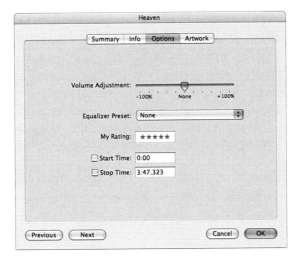

NOTE

You can apply a rating to the songs in your Library to indicate how much you like or dislike them. You can use these ratings to sort the Content pane, and you can use them in smart playlists. To rate a song from the iTunes window, Control-click it and select My Ratings on the contextual menu. Select your rating for the song (from one to five stars).

5. To start playing the song at some point other than its beginning, check the Start Time check box and enter the start time in minutes and seconds. When you play the song, it starts at the time you input. Using the Start Time option is a great way to get rid of interviews or talking at the start of a track. This content can be interesting once or twice, but probably not every time you hear the song. Just set the song to start when the talking is done and you won't ever have to hear it again.

6. To stop playing the song before it reaches its end, check the Stop Time check box and enter the time at which you want the song to stop in minutes and seconds. When the song reaches this point, it stops playing.

7. Click OK to apply the options to the song.

TIP

Many of the items in the Song Information window can be applied to multiple songs simultaneously. For example, you can select several songs, open the Song Information window, and apply a genre to all the selected songs at the same time (you are prompted to make sure you understand you are changing multiple songs). Doing this saves a lot time when you need to apply the same information to a group of songs.

BROWSING AND LISTENING TO MUSIC IN YOUR ITUNES LIBRARY

After you have added songs to your Library, you listen to them just like songs on an audio CD:

1. Select the Library as the source.

2. Click the Browse action button to open the Browser if it isn't open already.

3. Select the Genre in which you are interested; leave All selected if you want to browse all genres of music in your Library.

4. Click an artist or album that contains the songs you want to hear. The lower pane of the window shows the contents of whatever you select in the upper pane of the window. For example, to see all the albums by an artist, click that artist's name. In the Album pane, all the albums for that artist are shown. To see the tracks on an album, click its name in the Album column. In the Content pane of the window, all the tracks on the selected album are listed. To see all the contents of a selected item again, click All.

5. In the lower pane, select the song you want to listen to and click the Play button, or just double-click the song.

> **TIP**
>
> In the panes of the Browse window, you see All at the top of each list. When you select All, all the items in that part of the window are selected (and played if you click the Play button). For example, if you select an artist in the Artist column, select All in the Album column, and click Play, all the albums by that artist are played.

The other controls work just as they do for a CD, such as the Repeat button, Shuffle button, and so on. You can also use the check box to skip songs and play a song by double-clicking it just as you can when you listen to a CD.

 If iTunes can't find a song you have added to the Library, see "iTunes Can't Find a Song in My Library" in the "Troubleshooting" section at the end of this chapter.

USING PLAYLISTS TO CREATE YOUR OWN ALBUMS

Playlists are a great way to listen to your music because a playlist is really a custom album you create. Your playlists can contain any music that will play in any order you choose. And you can have as many playlists as you'd like to create.

There are two types of playlists: playlists and smart playlists. *Playlists* contain a fixed set of songs you select. *Smart playlists* use a set of criteria you define to select the contents of the playlist, and the contents of smart playlists can be dynamic, meaning they change over time.

CREATING AND USING PLAYLISTS

You can create your own playlists and add any songs in your Library to them. The contents of a playlist remain the same until you change them manually. You can add the same songs to more than one playlist and add songs to the same playlist more than one time. To create a playlist and add music to it, do the following:

1. Click the New Playlist button; select File, New Playlist; or press ⌘-N. You will see a new, untitled playlist in the Source pane.

2. Name the new playlist—you can just start typing because the name is highlighted and ready to edit immediately after you create it. (You can also edit a playlist name by clicking it and waiting a second or so until the name becomes highlighted.)

TIP

A great way to get a playlist started is to select the songs you want it to contain and then select File, New Playlist From Selection (or press Shift-⌘-N). A new playlist is created and the songs you selected are added to it. If all the songs you select are from the same album, the name of the playlist you create will be the album's name.

3. Click Library to select it as the source.
4. Browse or search your Library to locate songs you want to add to the new playlist.
5. Drag the tracks you want to add from the Content pane of the Library onto the name of the playlist you created (the playlist is highlighted when the songs you are dragging are on top of it).

TIP

You can add the same song to the same playlist as many times as you'd like to hear it play.

6. Continue adding tracks to the playlist.
7. Select the playlist in the Source pane to see its contents (see Figure 18.18).

Figure 18.18
This playlist contains songs from several instrumental albums.

8. Set the order in which the tracks will play by dragging them up or down in the Content pane.

At the bottom of the iTunes window, the number of songs in the playlist, their total playing time, and the size of the files you have referenced in the playlist are shown. Because a playlist contains only pointers to tracks, its file size is quite small. However, this size information for the files it references is useful when you want to place the playlist on a portable music player or when you want to burn a CD. You can use the size information to ensure that the playlist will fit in the device's available storage space.

Listening to a playlist is just like listening to a CD or other source. Select the playlist you want to hear and use the iTunes playback controls to listen to it.

NOTE

Playlists have a light blue icon containing a musical note. Smart playlists have a purple icon containing a gear. These icons enable you to easily understand the type of playlist you are working with.

CREATING AND USING SMART PLAYLISTS

Playlists are cool because they enable you to create custom albums for your listening pleasure. However, building playlists by manually dragging songs into them can get tedious. And, listening to the same playlists over and over can get a bit dull. This is where smart playlists come in.

Smart playlists are generated by defining a set of criteria for the music you want to be included in the playlist rather than selecting individual songs. Even better, each time you play that playlist, the specific songs included can be determined dynamically by applying the playlist's criteria to your Library. For example, iTunes comes with the Recently Played smart playlist. By default, this playlist contains the songs you have played in the past two weeks. The contents of this playlist change over time as you listen to different music, and, unless you listen only to this playlist, it will never be exactly the same twice.

The criteria you use for a smart playlist can be based on one or more attributes, and you can limit the size of the playlists to a specific number of songs.

To create a smart playlist, follow these steps:

1. Hold down the Option key and click the New Playlist button; select File, New Smart Playlist; or press Option-⌘-N. The Smart Playlist window will appear (see Figure 18.19).

2. Select the first criterion on which you want to base the condition on the first pop-up menu. For example, select Genre to base the condition on the music's genre. Artist is selected by default.

3. Select how you want the criterion to be searched on the second pop-up menu. What appears on this pop-up menu depends on the criterion you selected. For example, if you choose a text condition, such as Genre, your choices include "contains," "is," "is not,"

and so on. If you choose a numeric condition, such as time, your choices include "is," "is not," "is greater than," "is in the range," and so on.

4. Enter the text or numbers for the condition in the box that appears at the end of the condition's row. For example, if you select Genre, you could type **Jazz** or **Rock**. If you select time, you could enter the length of the songs you want to be included.

Figure 18.19
The Smart Playlist dialog box enables you to create a complex playlist based on multiple criteria.

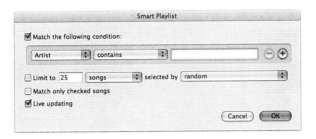

NOTE

The specific information you enter as the condition to search by depends on the attribute on which you base a condition. In some cases, you don't enter search text but choose something else such as your rating by selecting the number of stars. In other situations, you can make a choice on a pop-up menu.

5. Click the plus sign. Another condition is added to the smart playlist.

6. Repeat steps 2–4 to configure the condition you added.

7. If you want to add more conditions, repeat steps 5 and 6.

8. Keep adding and configuring conditions until you have added all that you want to include in the smart playlist. Notice that at the top of the Smart Playlist window, a pop-up menu appears when you include more than one condition.

9. On the Match pop-up menu at the top of the window, choose "all" if all the conditions need to be met for a song to be included in the playlist or choose "any" if only one of the conditions needs to be met for a song to be included in the playlist.

TIP

To remove a condition from a smart playlist, click the minus sign next to that condition.

10. If you want to limit the playlist to a certain number of songs, amount of time, or file size, check the "Limit to" check box. Enter the value you want to use for the limit. Select the parameter by which you want to limit the playlist on the pop-up menu (for example, select "songs" to limit it to a specific number of songs), and then choose how you want the songs to be selected on the "selected by" pop-up menu. Suppose you want to include only 50 songs in the playlist and want them selected by those that are most played. Your input would be **50** in the text box, "songs" on the first pop-up menu, and "most often played" on the second pop-up menu.

11. If you want the playlist to include only songs whose check box you have checked, check the "Match only checked songs" box. If this check box is checked, skipped songs are also skipped by the playlist. If it is not checked, unchecked songs will be included in the playlist if they meet its conditions.

12. If you want the content of the playlist to change over time, check the "Live updating" check box. Each time you play the playlist, iTunes selects the songs it plays based on the latest information. For example, if the playlist is based on genre and you add a new album from the genre to your Library, that album would be added to the playlist automatically.

   If you don't check this check box, the playlist contains songs based on the music as it existed in your Library when you created the playlist.

13. Review the conditions to make sure you have defined them as you want them (see Figure 18.20).

Figure 18.20
This smart playlist plays 50 jazz songs I have rated with four or five stars and have played most recently. Because it is updated live, as I listen to music that meets the criteria, that music is added to the playlist automatically.

14. Click OK, and the new smart playlist appears in the Source pane.

15. Rename the smart playlist as needed (iTunes attempts to name the playlist based on its conditions; this might or might not result in the name you want to use).

16. Select the playlist. Its current contents will be displayed in the Content pane.

You can play a smart playlist just like other sources with which you work. If it is a dynamic playlist, it contents will change over time.

TIP

One great use for smart playlists is to automatically collect all the music in your Library from the same artist. Create a smart playlist with the artist's name as a condition and enable the live updating feature. Whenever you add more music from that artist to your Library, such as by importing a CD or buying music from the iTunes Music Store, the new music is added to the smart playlist automatically.

You can also edit the default smart playlists Apple has provided for you or smart playlists you create:

1. Select the smart playlist you want to edit.
2. Select File, Get Info (⌘-I) or select File, Edit Smart Playlist. The Smart Playlist dialog box will appear. Because you selected an existing smart playlist, its search conditions will be shown in the window.
3. Use the controls to edit a smart playlist in the same way as when you create a smart playlist.
4. When you are done making changes, click OK. The playlist will use the updated conditions the next time you play it.

> **NOTE**
>
> The Purchased Music source is actually a special smart playlist that collects all the music you purchase from the iTunes Music Store. As you purchase music, each song you buy is added to the Purchased Music playlist automatically. (In case you are wondering, you can't change this playlist.)

BROWSING PLAYLISTS

You can browse playlists just as you browse your entire library:

1. Select the playlist you want to browse.
2. Select Edit, Show Browser or press ⌘-B. The Browser appears at the top of the window, and you can view the genre, artist, and album information for the songs included in the playlist.

OPENING PLAYLISTS

If you double-click a playlist, it opens in a separate and independent iTunes window. This makes working with playlists easy, especially when you are building them. You can open a playlist's window and more easily drag tracks from the iTunes window onto the playlist's window to add them to it. You can also use a playlist window to reorganize it, play it, and perform other playlist tasks.

DELETING MUSIC FROM THE ITUNES LIBRARY

You can delete entire playlists, delete specific songs from a playlist, or remove songs from the Library by selecting the items you want to remove and pressing Delete. You then see a warning dialog box; if you click OK, the playlist or song is removed (when you remove a song from a playlist, the original file is not affected). If you select a track in the Library to remove the related file you created using iTunes, you see a second dialog box asking whether you want iTunes to place the original file in the Trash. If you click OK, the file is also moved to the Trash. If you click Cancel, the original file remains on your Mac (you can add it back to the Library if you want to listen to it again).

LISTENING TO YOUR MUSIC WITH THE PARTY SHUFFLE

The Party Shuffle playlist, which is on the Source pane by default, enables you to choose a variety of music to listen to on-the-fly. When you use the Party Shuffle, you choose a source, which can be any of the other playlists shown in the Source pane or the entire Library. When you play it, iTunes will shuffle and play the music in the playlist that you select (which is where the name came from, I suppose).

> **TIP**
>
> If you don't want the Party Shuffle playlist to be visible, uncheck its check box on the General pane of the iTunes Preferences window.

To use the Party Shuffle, perform the following steps:

1. Click Party Shuffle on the Source list. The current contents of the playlist will be shown in the Content pane.

2. On the Source pop-up menu, located at the bottom of the Content pane, choose the playlist from which you want the Party Shuffle to play music (see Figure 18.21). On this menu, you will see the Library along with all the playlists that appear in the Source pane. The current song is highlighted with a 3D effect. Songs that have already played are above the highlighted song and are grayed out. Upcoming songs are shown below the current song.

Figure 18.21
The Party Shuffle playlist is a great way to listen to your other playlists because it randomly selects the order of the songs it plays.

3. If you rate your music and want the songs you rate higher to be played more frequently, check the "Play higher rated songs more often" check box.

4. Use the two Display pop-up menus to configure how songs are shown in the Content pane. Use the upper pop-up menu to determine how many songs that have already played are shown in the pane. Use the lower pop-up menu to show how many upcoming songs are shown.

5. Use the playback controls to play the Party Shuffle. iTunes will start playing the highlighted song and continue through the playlist in the order in which the songs are shown on the list.

TIP

Click the Refresh action button to cause the Party Shuffle to select a new set of upcoming songs.

CUSTOMIZING ITUNES AND YOUR MUSIC

iTunes provides extensive control over how its window looks and how your music sounds when you play it. You can customize the iTunes window itself, and there are several ways you can control how your music sounds. For example, you can configure the iTunes effects preferences and can use the built-in iTunes Equalizer.

CONFIGURING THE ITUNES WINDOW

There are several ways in which you can customize the iTunes window.

TIP

Remember that you can control iTunes from the Dock or by using the iTunes widget. Sometimes, hiding iTunes and just using the Dock or widget controls to control your tunes is most convenient.

If you click the Maximize button (the green one), the iTunes window shrinks down so that only the playback controls and information window are shown; this is called the mini-player (see Figure 18.22). In this mode, you will see the window, playback, and volume controls along with the Information window. You can drag the resize handle to the left to further reduce the size by hiding the Information window. Click the Maximize button again to restore the iTunes window to its previous size.

Of course, in the full-size mode, you can manually resize the window by dragging its resize handle. Making it larger displays more information; making it smaller displays less. The window has a minimum size that is quite a bit larger than the reduced size you get with the Maximize button.

TIP

If you click the Close button in the iTunes window, its window disappears but the music continues to play. When you move from iTunes into another application, such as the Finder, and then back into iTunes, its window appears again. You can also display the window by selecting Window, iTunes.

18

Figure 18.22
In this mode, the
iTunes window takes
up much less screen
real estate.

You can also change the relative size of the Source pane or Browser by dragging their resize handles; these are dots that appear in the center of the bars between the various panes.

NOTE

> Unfortunately, iTunes doesn't have a full-screen command (except when you use the Visualizer). You have to set the maximum size of the iTunes window manually using its resize handle.

CONFIGURING VIEWS FOR SOURCES

As you have seen, iTunes displays a lot of information for the songs shown in the Content pane, such as song name, track number, artist, and so on. What you might not know is that you can choose the information shown. Even better, you can choose to display different information for different sources; iTunes will remember your preferences for each source and use them each time you view that source. Use the following steps to configure the information that will be displayed for a specific source:

1. Select the source whose information you want to configure.

2. Select Edit, View Options (⌘-J). The View Options window will appear; the name of the selected source appears at the top of the window. The rest of the window consists of check boxes for each attribute you can choose to display (see Figure 18.23).

Figure 18.23
Using the View
Options window, you
can configure the
information shown for
the source displayed
at the top of the box.

3. Check the check boxes for the attributes (the columns) you want to see in the Content pane when you select that source. You can select from among many options, including Album, Artist, Comment, Date Added, Genre, and so on.

4. Uncheck the check boxes for those columns you don't want to see when you view the source.

5. Click OK. When you select the source, you will see only the columns whose check boxes you checked.

TIP

You can also customize the view for a source by holding down the Control key while you click (or right-clicking) in a column heading. A pop-up menu appears and you can quickly add or remove individual columns. You can also have iTunes automatically size one column or all the columns in the window.

The custom view you create is saved and appears each time you select that source. You can have different view options for each source you view (meaning your Library, every playlist, each CD, and so on).

NOTE

Remember that you can drag columns around in the window to change the order in which they appear, resize them, and so on. These tools enable you to completely customize the Content pane for any source you use.

18

USING ITUNES EFFECTS

iTunes includes three effects preferences you can set to control how music sounds. These effects are configured on the Audio pane of the iTunes Preferences dialog box:

1. Open the iTunes Preferences window and click the Audio icon. The Audio preferences pane will appear.

2. Use the Crossfade Playback check box and slider to control the amount of silent time between songs in your playlists. To control this time, check the box and use the slider to set the amount of silent time. If the slider is set to 0, there will be no silence; one song will fade directly into the next. Set the slider to a value up to 12 seconds to have that amount of silence between tracks.

3. The Sound Enhancer check box and slider enable iTunes to apply digital effects to your music to improve its quality (that is a matter of opinion, of course). To use this feature, check the Sound Enhancer check box and use the slider to set the relative amount of enhancing iTunes does.

4. To have iTunes automatically adjust the volume of each song as it plays to the same relative level, check the Sound Check check box. This avoids dramatic changes in volume level when you listen to various music.

5. Click OK. The effects you configured are applied to all your music as you play it.

USING THE ITUNES EQUALIZER

iTunes includes a graphic equalizer you can use to fine-tune the music you listen to. As with hardware graphic equalizers, you can adjust the relative volume levels of various audio frequencies to suit your preferences. Unlike with hardware graphic equalizers, you can select different preset configurations and create your own configurations. You can apply an equalizer configuration to your music even down to individual songs so each tune can have its own equalization.

To work with the Equalizer, perform the following steps:

1. Click the Equalizer button; select Window, Equalizer; or press ⌘-2. The Equalizer window will appear (see Figure 18.24).

Figure 18.24
These Equalizer settings are designed to emphasize bass and treble frequencies.

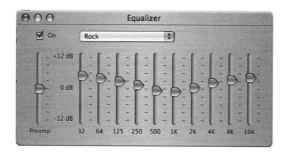

2. To activate the Equalizer, check the On check box (it is on by default).

3. Select the Equalizer preset configuration you want from the pop-up menu. All iTunes music you play is adjusted according to the preset you selected.

Use the following ideas as you equalize your own music:

- Use the Preamp slider to change the relative volume level for a song. This is useful when a piece of music is recorded at a particularly high or low volume level.

- Create your own Equalizer settings by dragging the slider for each frequency to the relative volume level at which you want that frequency to be played. When you do so, Manual appears in the pop-up menu to indicate you are using manual settings.

- Add your custom Equalizer settings to the pop-up menu by configuring the Equalizer and selecting Make Preset from the pop-up menu. In the Make Preset dialog box, name your preset and click OK. Your preset will be added to the list and you can choose it just as you can one of the default presets.

- Edit the list of presets by selecting Edit List from the pop-up menu. The Edit Presets dialog box will appear. You can use this to rename or delete any of the presets, including the default presets.

When you configure the Equalizer, it will be applied to all the songs you play. However, you can also associate Equalizer presets with specific songs:

1. Select the song to which you want to apply a preset.
2. Select File, Get Info or press ⌘-I. The Song Info window will appear.
3. Click the Options tab.
4. On the Equalizer Preset pop-up menu, select the preset you want to be used for that song.
5. Click OK. When that song plays, the Equalizer settings will be used.

TIP

If you frequently apply equalizer presets to individual songs, use the View Options window to have the Equalizer column displayed in the Content pane. This column includes an Equalizer preset pop-up menu from which you can choose a preset for the songs shown in the Content pane.

WORKING WITH ALBUM ARTWORK

iTunes enables you to associate art with music in your Library. When you purchase music from the iTunes Music Store, the album cover is associated with each song automatically. You can add your own art to your music, and you can change the art currently associated with music.

NOTE

One of the best reasons to associate artwork with your music is so you can print jewel case insert covers for CDs you create. You'll learn how to do this later in this chapter.

18

VIEWING ALBUM ARTWORK

To view the artwork associated with music, click the Show/Hide Artwork button; select Edit, Show/Hide Artwork; or press ⌘-G. The Artwork pane will appear underneath the Source pane and the art associated with the music will be displayed. There are two options for the art you display. You can choose to display the art associated with the song currently playing, in which case Now Playing appears at the top of the Artwork pane, or you can choose to view the artwork associated with the song currently selected, in which case Selected Song appears at the top of the pane. To change which option is used, click the text that appears at the top of the pane and the other option will become active (see Figure 18.25).

TIP

If you double-click the art shown in the Artwork pane, a separate window will appear that shows a larger version of the art. Unfortunately, you can't do anything with it except see the larger version. And, the separate window displays only the art you were viewing when you opened it.

Figure 18.25
Because Now Playing appears at the top of the Song Artwork pane, art associated with the song currently playing appears.

ASSOCIATING ART WITH MUSIC

If a song doesn't have album art associated with it (for example, you imported it), you can add the art yourself. Or, you might want to add the artist's picture or some other meaningful graphic to the song. You can add one or more pieces of art to songs by using the following steps:

1. Prepare the artwork you are going to associate with a song. You can use graphics in the usual formats, such as JPEG, TIFF, GIF, and so on. For example, if you have a CD, you can scan the cover art from the CD insert.

> **TIP**
>
> You can find the artwork for most CDs on the Internet. For example, find the CD's image on a retail website, open its contextual menu, and then download its image as a file. You can then use that image as the album's artwork.

2. Select the song with which you want to associate the artwork.

3. Open the Info window and then click the Artwork tab (see Figure 18.26). If the selected song has artwork with it, you will see it in the Artwork pane. If not, the pane will be empty.

4. Use the slider under the image box to change the size of the previews you see in the window. Drag the slider to the right to make the image larger or to the left to make it smaller. This doesn't change the image; instead, it impacts only the size of the image as you currently see it in the Info window. This is especially useful when you associate a lot of images with a song because you can see them all at the same time.

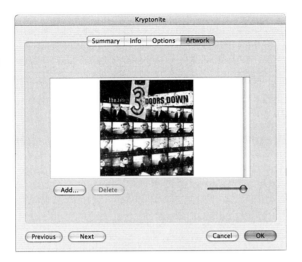

Figure 18.26
Because I purchased
this song from the
iTunes Music Store, the
album cover came
with it.

5. Click Add. The Choose a File dialog box will appear.

6. Move to and select the image you want to associate with the song.

7. Click Choose. The image will be added to the window.

> **TIP**
>
> You can also add artwork to a song by dragging the image file from your desktop onto the Artwork pane of the Info window.

8. Continue adding images to the Artwork pane until you have added all the images for a song. The default image for a song is the one on the left of the image box.

9. To change the order of the images, drag them in the image box.

> **TIP**
>
> You can associate art with multiple songs at the same time, such as for an entire CD. To do so, select multiple songs and open the Info window. Use the Artwork box on the Multiple Song Info window to add images. Either drag images onto this box or double-click it to open the image selection dialog box and then choose the images you want to add.

10. Click OK. The window will close and the images you added will be saved with the song.

When more than one image is associated with a song, previous and next arrows will appear at the top of the Artwork pane. Use these arrows to choose which image (the default) is displayed. (Unfortunately, iTunes doesn't rotate the images automatically.)

> **TIP**
>
> You can use the artwork in your iTunes Library as your screensaver. On the Screen Saver pane, select the iTunes Artwork module. This module presents a tiled view of art associated with your music; individual tiles rotate out to display additional art.

USING ITUNES TO BURN CDs OR DVDs

iTunes enables you to burn your own CDs and DVDs. iTunes supports several formats, including the following:

- **Audio CD**—This format will play in almost all standard CD players, such as boom boxes, car stereos, and so on. The downside of this format is that you won't be able to fit a lot of music on a single CD.

- **MP3 CD**—This format places MP3 versions on a CD. That's good because you can fit more music on a single CD. Because many audio devices now support MP3 CD playback, you can listen to the MP3 CDs you create in many different ways.

- **Data CD or DVD**—You use this format to create data discs that are meant to be accessed with a computer. This is a good format to use when you want to move music from one computer to another. An even better use is to back up your music.

> **NOTE**
>
> It goes without saying, but I will say it anyway: Your Mac has to have a CD or DVD burner to be able to burn discs.

CONFIGURING ITUNES TO BURN A DISC

Before you can burn a disc, you need to configure iTunes for the burning work you have in mind:

1. Open the iTunes Preferences dialog box and click the Burning icon. The Burning preferences pane will appear (see Figure 18.27).

2. Ensure that the drive on which you will burn the disc appears next to the CD Burner text at the top of the Burning pane; this means iTunes recognizes and can burn to the device. If you have more than one burner available, select the one you want to use on the CD Burner pop-up menu.

 If iTunes does not recognize that you have a supported drive, see "iTunes Can't Find My Burner" in the "Troubleshooting" section at the end of this chapter.

3. Use the Preferred Speed pop-up menu to set the burn speed. Try Maximum Possible to get the fastest burns. If recording doesn't work properly, reduce the speed. A safe recording speed is 2x. Unless you are in a tremendous hurry to get a CD done, this will probably be plenty fast for you.

Figure 18.27
Use the Burning pane
of the iTunes
Preferences window to
configure a burn ses-
sion.

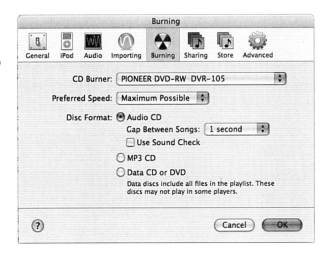

4. To record an audio CD that will be compatible with standard audio CD players, click the Audio CD radio button and set the amount of quiet time between tracks on the CD by using the Gap Between Songs pop-up menu. You can choose from no gap to a gap of 5 seconds. If you want iTunes to use Sound Check when it burns the disc, check the Sound Check check box; iTunes will attempt to set the relative volume of each song you burn to the same level.

5. To record an MP3 CD, click the MP3 CD radio button. CDs recorded in this format play only on devices that support the MP3 format.

6. To record the song files on a data disc that can be used in a computer, click the Data CD or DVD radio button. These discs are typically limited to playback on computers; putting tunes on a DVD is a great way to back up your music.

NOTE

If your Mac doesn't have a DVD-R drive, the radio button will be labeled Data CD.

7. Click OK.

Each time you burn a CD or DVD, it is burned in the selected format. If you want to change the format of a disc, just use the previous steps to select a different format.

TIP

You should back up any music you purchase from the iTunes Music Store. You can use the Purchased Music playlist to do this. Or, create a smart playlist containing songs you have added recently and burn that to disc.

USING ITUNES TO BURN A DISC

After you have configured your burning preferences, you are ready to burn a disc:

1. Create the playlist you want to put on disc. If you are creating a disc to which you will listen, make sure the songs are in the order in which you want to listen to them. Also be sure that the playlist contains fewer minutes of music than your media is rated for— select the playlist and look at the bottom of the iTunes window. Compare the size of the playlist to the capacity of the media you are using.

NOTE

> If the playlist is too large to fit on a single disc, iTunes will burn it across multiple discs. It will prompt you to insert a new disc each time it fills one up.

2. Select the playlist you want to place on disc.
3. Click the Burn Disc action button; you will be prompted to insert a blank disc.
4. Insert the blank disc and close the drive (unless you have a slot-loading drive, in which case this isn't necessary). In a moment, the Burn Disc button is in color and starts pulsing to indicate that it is ready to burn. iTunes checks to ensure that everything is ready to go. When these checks are complete, you are prompted to click the Burn Disc button.
5. Click the Burn Disc button again to burn the disc.

CAUTION

> Use CD-R discs for audio CDs you create rather than CD-RW discs, especially if you will be using the CDs you create in noncomputer CD players. If you create an audio CD using a CD-RW disc, you probably won't be able to play it using any CD player except the one on which you created it (which wouldn't be very useful).

When iTunes records your playlist to a disc, it first translates the music into the format you selected. This process takes several minutes to complete. Watch the Information window for progress and status messages. When it is done, iTunes begins burning the disc.

CAUTION

> The spinning Burn Disc icon gives you a clue as to how fast data is being transferred to the recorder. The faster the icon spins, the higher the data transfer rate is being achieved. If the icon slows considerably or stops altogether, you might experience errors because data isn't flowing fast enough to keep the burning process fed properly. If this happens, quit all applications that might be accessing any disks on your Mac and make sure that you aren't playing any music in iTunes. This ensures that the maximum amount of system resources is available for the burning process. You can also lower the burn speed to reduce the data flow requirements—doing so often alleviates this problem.

Depending on the speed at which your recorder works and the amount of data to record, this process can take only a couple of minutes or quite a while. When it is complete, iTunes plays a sound to indicate that the process is done. The disc you created is mounted on your Mac and is selected as the current source.

If iTunes stops the process before it is complete, see "iTunes Stops Recording Before the Process Is Complete" in the "Troubleshooting" section at the end of this chapter.

If the CD you create can't be read on standard CD players, such as those in your car, see "The CDs I Make Won't Play in My Noncomputer CD Player" in the "Troubleshooting" section at the end of this chapter.

PRINTING JEWEL BOX LABELS

With iTunes, you can print jewel case covers for the discs you burn. The application includes several default layouts, some of which use artwork associated with your music. To print a cover, perform the following steps:

NOTE
> Unfortunately, iTunes doesn't print to disc labels. Hopefully, though, the capability will be included in a future version.

1. Select the playlist for which you want to print a cover.
2. Select File, Print or press ⌘-P. The Print dialog box will appear (see Figure 18.28).

Figure 18.28
Using the iTunes Print dialog box, you can print jewel case covers for discs you burn.

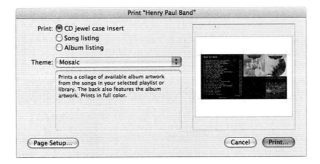

3. Choose what you want to print using the radio buttons. The options are "CD jewel case insert," "Song listing," and "Album listing."
4. Use the Theme pop-up menu to choose the layout you want to use. The options on this menu depend on what you are printing. If you are printing an insert, you can choose from various arrangements of song lists and album art.

TIP
> If you choose a theme that includes the Mosaic option, iTunes will create a mosaic of the artwork associated with the songs in the playlist. When you have a lot of different art in the same playlist, this can get very interesting.

5. Use the Page Setup and Print buttons to configure and print the insert, song listing, or album listing.

SHARING ITUNES MUSIC ON A NETWORK

You can share music in your iTunes Library with other computers with which you are networked and with anyone who has a user account on your Mac. You can also listen to music that is being shared with you.

→ To learn how to configure and manage a local network, **see** Chapter 33, "Building and Using a Network," **p. 935**.

TIP

> When you share your music, anyone who uses your Mac can listen to it, along with people using other Macs on your network. For example, if other people who use your Mac have their own user accounts, you can share your iTunes music with them by sharing it. If people have a user account on your Mac and share their music, you will be able to listen to it as well.

CONFIGURING YOUR MAC TO SHARE MUSIC

To share your music with other Macs on your network, you just need to set your sharing preferences:

1. Open the iTunes Preferences dialog box and click the Sharing icon. The Sharing pane will appear.
2. Check the "Share my music" check box.
3. Click the "Share entire library" radio button to share all the music in your Library, or click the "Share selected playlists" radio button and check the box next to each playlist you want to share in order to share only those playlists.
4. Give your shared music a name by typing a name in the Shared Name field. This is the name of the source others will select to access your music.
5. If you want to require a password for people to be able to share your music, check the "Require password" box and enter a password in the field.
6. Click OK.
7. If you required a password, provide it to the people with whom you want to share your music.

After you have shared your music, people can access it using the same steps you use to access music being shared with you.

NOTE

> For your music to be accessible on the network, your Mac must remain awake. If you turn it off, or it goes to sleep, others won't be able to access your shared music any more.

LISTENING TO MUSIC BEING SHARED WITH YOU

NOTE

You can't move music from a shared source into your Library from within iTunes.

To search your network for music being shared with you, open the Sharing pane of the iTunes Preferences dialog box and check the "Look for shared music" check box. When you close the Preferences window, iTunes looks for any sources being shared with you. When it finds them, they appear in the Source pane as the Shared Music source. To listen to shared music, do the following:

NOTE

Shared sources have a light blue icon containing a single note.

1. Select the shared source to which you want to listen. If more than one shared source is available to you, expand the Shared Music source. When you do, you'll see an icon for each set of music being shared with you.
2. If the source you selected requires a password, enter the password at the prompt and click OK. The shared source will become available to you.
3. Click the Expansion triangle next to the source to see playlists that have been shared with you. You can also use the Browser to browse shared music.
4. Listen to the shared source just as you listen to your own playlists.

TIP

To remove a shared source from your Source list, click its Eject button. You can open the Sharing pane of the iTunes Preferences window to see how many users are accessing music you are sharing.

USING AIRTUNES AND AIRPORT EXPRESS TO BROADCAST YOUR MUSIC

If you have an Airport-capable Mac and an AirPort Express base station, you can broadcast your iTunes music to other locations. This is done via the iTunes feature called AirTunes.

SETTING UP AN AIRTUNES NETWORK

To set up an AirTunes network, perform the following steps:

1. Configure the Mac whose music you want to broadcast to use AirPort.

→ To learn how to configure a Mac to use Airport, **see** "Connecting to the AirPort Network with Mac OS X," **p. 388**.

2. Locate and configure the AirPort Express base station. You need to locate a base station close enough to the broadcast receiver to be able to connect them.

3. Connect the AirPort Express base station to the device you will use to listen to the music being broadcast. For example, you can connect the output on the base station to a set of powered speakers, to the input on a stereo system, and so on.

4. Configure the device on which you will listen to the music. For example, turn on the powered speakers or configure a receiver to work with the AirPort Express' input.

CONFIGURING ITUNES TO PLAY MUSIC VIA AIRTUNES

On the Mac that you are using to broadcast music, perform the following steps:

1. Open the Audio pane of the iTunes Preferences window.

2. Check the "Look for remote speakers connected with AirTunes" check box.

3. Check the "Disable iTunes volume control for remote speakers" check box. If you don't check this, volume changes you make in iTunes will change the volume of music being played via AirTunes. You usually don't want this to be the case.

4. Close the Preferences window. When you return to the iTunes window, you will see the Choose Speakers pop-up menu located to the left of the Equalizer button.

5. Open the Choose Speakers pop-up menu and choose the AirPort Express base station to which you want to broadcast music.

PLAYING MUSIC OVER AIRTUNES

To broadcast music, select a playlist and play it. The music will be broadcasted to the base station you selected. You can then use the audio device connected to the base station to listen to the music.

If you want to make changes to the music being played, such as changing the playlist or moving to the next song, you will need to come back to the computer and make changes from within iTunes. AirTunes acts just like a radio station—you can control the volume from the audio device on which you are listening to it, but you can't change the music being played. You have to go to the source to do that.

When you want to listen to music on your Mac again, select Computer Speakers on the Choose Speakers pop-up menu.

NOTE

You can also use iTunes to listen to audio books and other content from Audible.com. This service offers many audio books you can load into iTunes and listen to or transfer to an iPod to take with you.

TROUBLESHOOTING

ITUNES CAN'T FIND A SONG IN MY LIBRARY

I try to play a song in the iTunes Library, but I see a message stating that the song can't be used because the original file can't be found.

iTunes doesn't actually store music files in the Library, but rather contains pointers to music files stored on your Mac, on an external drive, or wherever you have selected to store your music. If the original file is moved around or deleted from your machine, iTunes can't find it and doesn't know how to play that song. When you see this dialog box, you can attempt to locate the file yourself. If you are successful, iTunes restores its link in the Library and it works as before. If you can't find the file, you have to re-create it and add it to the Library again.

ITUNES CAN'T FIND MY BURNER

When I start iTunes for the first time, I see a message stating that no supported disc recorders were found. Or, my burner is not recognized when I try to record a disc.

This problem occurs when iTunes doesn't detect a supported drive in your Mac system. To be supported, iTunes must have the appropriate device software incorporated into it. This can also occur if your drive is not properly connected to and working with your Mac.

If your drive was included as part of your Mac and isn't recognized by iTunes, you most likely have some sort of hardware issue. This isn't likely to be the case because Apple hardware tends to be pretty reliable, but it can happen from time to time. If your system is still under warranty, contact Apple for assistance. If it isn't, you'll need to decide whether the drive is worth repairing or replacing or whether it's time to get that new Mac you've been wanting for a long time.

If you've added a third-party drive to your system, the first step is to ensure that your drive can work with at least one other application on your Mac. For example, if CD burning software is included with your drive, such as Toast, use that application to record a disc. If that works, you know that the problem is related to iTunes. If it doesn't work, you need to troubleshoot your drive before trying to use it with iTunes.

The second step is relatively easy, but if it doesn't work, there isn't much you can do. Go to the Apple iTunes website (www.apple.com/itunes) to see whether a newer version of iTunes is available. If so, download and install it and try again. Apple will continue to add support for various drive mechanisms to iTunes, and if you get lucky, yours will be one of them.

If neither of these steps works, you still have several options. One is to buy a drive supported by iTunes (hey, you needed a good reason to buy a new Mac, right?). The other is to use another application to create the disc. For example, Toast also enables you to create audio CDs.

ITUNES STOPS RECORDING BEFORE THE PROCESS IS COMPLETE

The disc I am attempting to record is ejected before the process is finished. What is causing this?

When you see a message stating that iTunes is stopping the burn process, some error has prevented iTunes from completing the disc. You usually see an error dialog box; unfortunately, such a dialog box almost always contains an indecipherable message.

The most likely cause of such errors is the inability of iTunes to write data to the drive fast enough. If pauses occur in the data stream that is being recorded to the disc, the process sometimes fails. Make the following changes to attempt to correct the problem:

1. Stop all other applications except iTunes. Although Mac OS X provides iTunes with protected memory, other applications might be accessing other drives in your system. This can slow the data being transferred to the recorder.

2. Reconfigure iTunes so it uses a slow burn speed because slower burn speeds are easier to maintain.

After making these changes, try to burn the disc again. If it still doesn't work, try Apple's support site and search for the specific error message you are seeing.

THE CDS I MAKE WON'T PLAY IN MY NONCOMPUTER CD PLAYER

When I install a CD I have burned in a regular CD player, such as the one in my car, either the disc is ejected and won't play or the player acts as if no CD is in the player at all.

There are a couple of causes for this problem. One possibility is that the CD you burned was a CD-RW disc rather than a CD-R disc. Standard CD players (noncomputer CD players) are usually incapable of reading CD-RW discs. You should always create audio CDs that you intend to play in other CD players using CD-R discs.

The other possibility is that the standard CD player you are trying to use does not recognize the format of the CD-R disc. This usually happens only when the CD player is relatively old. The only solution to this is to use a different CD player.

I CAN'T LISTEN TO MUSIC I HAVE PURCHASED FROM THE ITUNES MUSIC STORE

When I try to play music I purchased from the iTunes Music Store, I see a message stating that this Mac is not authorized to play this music.

For a Mac to be able to play iTunes Music Store music, it must be authorized to do so. You can have up to five Macs authorized to play your iTunes Music Store at the same time. If you see this message, the machine you are using is not currently authorized to play your iTunes Music Store music.

Select Advanced, Authorize Computer. Then log in using the account under which you purchased the music. If four or fewer computers are authorized under the account you used, you will be able to authorize it. If not, you'll have to deauthorize one of the other computers before you can authorize the current one.

MAC OS X TO THE MAX: MORE ON ITUNES MUSIC

In this section, you will see a list of iTunes keyboard shortcuts, get an overview of using iTunes to listen to music on the Internet, learn about some commands on the Advanced menu, see how you can use iTunes to convert music files into various formats, and learn how iTunes music is organized.

USING iTUNES KEYBOARD SHORTCUTS

Table 18.2 lists helpful iTunes keyboard shortcuts.

TABLE 18.2   iTUNES KEYBOARD SHORTCUTS

Menu	Command	Shortcut
Not on a menu	Change Columns Being Displayed	⌘-click a column heading
Not on a menu	Play Selected Song	Return
Not on a menu	Reshuffle the Current Playlist	Option-click-Shuffle button
Not on a menu	Uncheck/Check All Songs in the Current List	⌘-click a song's check box
Advanced	Open Stream	⌘-U
Controls	Eject Disc	⌘-E
Controls	Mute	⌘-Option-down arrow
Controls	Next Song	⌘-right arrow
Controls	Play/Pause	Spacebar
Controls	Previous Song	⌘-left arrow
Controls	Volume Down	⌘-down arrow
Controls	Volume Up	⌘-up arrow
Edit	Hide/Show Browser	⌘-B
Edit	Select All	⌘-A
Edit	Select None	Shift-⌘-A
Edit	Show/Hide Artwork	⌘-G
Edit	View Options	⌘-J
File	Add to Library	⌘-O
File	Get Info	⌘-I
File	Import	Shift-⌘-O
File	New Playlist	⌘-N
File	New Playlist From Selection	Shift-⌘-N
File	New Smart Playlist	Option-⌘-N
File	Show Current Song	⌘-L
File	Show Song File	⌘-R
iTunes	Preferences	⌘-,

continues

18

TABLE 18.2	CONTINUED	
Menu	**Command**	**Shortcut**
Visualizer	Full Screen	⌘-F
Visualizer	Turn Visualizer On/Off	⌘-T
Window	Hide/Show Equalizer	⌘-2
Window	Hide/Show iTunes Window	⌘-1

USING ITUNES TO LISTEN TO INTERNET RADIO

You can use iTunes to listen to various Internet radio broadcasts. To do so, follow these steps:

1. Select Radio as the source. The application downloads the current list of available genres and presents them in the Content pane.
2. Click the expansion triangle next to a genre to view the channels available in that genre.
3. Select the channel you want to play and press the spacebar.

The selected channel begins to stream to your Mac; when the prebuffer is full, it begins to play.

> **TIP**
>
> You can also double-click a stream to play it.

When you first select the Radio source, iTunes downloads the list of available genres and channels. You can refresh this list at any time by clicking the Action button, which is the Refresh button when the Radio Tuner source is selected.

When iTunes plays audio from the Internet, it first stores it in a buffer so it can play back smoothly even if your Internet connection is slow or is getting interrupted. If you experience starting and stopping when listening to Internet sources, adjust the size of the iTunes buffer. Do this by using the Streaming Buffer Size pop-up menu on the Advanced pane of the iTunes Preferences window.

Some of the channels are live, whereas some are just large playlists stored on the Internet. When you listen to one that is a playlist, it is repeated until you stop playing it.

USING ITUNES ADVANCED COMMANDS

The iTunes Advanced menu contains the following commands:

- **Open Stream**—This command enables you to enter the URL of an audio stream to listen to it.
- **Convert Selection to *Format***—You'll learn about this in the next section.

- **Consolidate Library**—Use this command to move copies of all the music you are managing in iTunes but that is currently stored outside the iTunes folder into the iTunes folder.

- **Get CD Track Names**—When you select an audio CD, use this command to update its song information from the Internet.

- **Submit CD Track Names**—If iTunes is unable to find a CD, you can use this command to submit track information to the database.

- **Join CD Tracks**—Use this command to combine tracks on a CD into a single track with no gaps between the songs. Select the tracks you want to join and then select the command. The tracks are played as a unit.

- **Remove Audible Account**—Use this command to remove the Audible.com account from your Mac. If you haven't configured any Audible content on your machine, you won't see this command.

- **Authorize/Deauthorize Computer**—Use the Authorize command to enable a Mac to play music you have purchased from the iTunes Music Store. Use the Deauthorize command when you want to remove the current Mac from being one of five allowed to play music you have purchased from the iTunes Music Store.

- **Check for Purchased Music**—Use this to ensure that you have downloaded all the music you have purchased, such as when your Internet connection is interrupted while you are downloading music from the store.

- **Convert ID3 Tags**—Use this command to convert the tag information among various formats. If the tags for songs you add to your Library are incorrect, you can try this command to see whether you can correct them. You can also use this command if you want to share music with an application that doesn't use the same tag format iTunes does.

USING ITUNES TO CONVERT FILES INTO VARIOUS AUDIO FORMATS

You can use iTunes to convert song files (or any other audio file for that matter) that is stored in its Library into any of the file formats iTunes supports. Use the following steps to do so:

1. Open the Importing pane of the iTunes Preferences window.

2. Choose and configure the format into which you want to convert some audio files. For example, if you want to create WAV files, select the WAV encoder.

3. Click OK to set the encoder preferences.

4. Select the tracks you want to convert.

5. Select Advanced, Convert Selection to *Format*, where *Format* is the name of the format you selected in step 2. iTunes will create a second version of the tracks you selected in the format you chose.

Files you convert are added to your iTunes Library. Unfortunately, iTunes does not change the name of the tracks it converts, so depending on the columns you are displaying, the files might look identical to you. Use the Info window to determine which file is in which format. Or, add the Kind column to the view to display the formats of the listed tracks.

If you want to see the file you converted in a Finder window, select it and press ⌘-R.

As you convert files, you'll end up with duplicate tracks. Sometimes you want these duplicates and sometimes you don't. To see all duplicates in your Library, select Edit, Show Duplicate Songs. All tracks for which there is more than one version will be shown in the Content pane. You can then delete any duplicates you don't need. To return to the normal view again, click the Show All Songs button.

KEEPING YOUR ITUNES MUSIC FILES ORGANIZED

It can be helpful to understand how and where iTunes stores the music you have added to the Library.

The Library doesn't actually contain any music—its contents consist of a listing of pointers to MP3, AAC, and other files stored on your Mac. However, each track is actually a file stored on your machine. The files that make up the iTunes Library are organized by artist and album and by default are stored in the following directory: `username/Music/iTunes/iTunes Music`, where `username` is the Home folder for a user account.

You can find the location of any song in your Library by selecting it and selecting File, Show Song File or by pressing ⌘-R. A Finder window showing the song's file will open and the file will be highlighted.

> **TIP**
>
> If you have added songs to your library that are scattered all over your Mac, select Advanced, Consolidate Library to have iTunes place copies of all your music in the iTunes folder. This organizes all your music files in a single step.

The music files you add to the Library using the Add to Library command are stored wherever they were stored when you start the add process. You should organize music you download in a central location. If you are going to add the songs you download into iTunes, you should store them in the iTunes Music folder, just as iTunes would do if it encoded the files for you. This helps keep your music organized in a consistent fashion.

You can use the iTunes Music Folder Location preference on the Advanced pane of the iTunes Preferences dialog box to change the location of your iTunes Music folder. For example, if you want to share the music you encode with other users of your Mac, you should store it in your Public folder. Other users can then add that music to their iTunes Libraries and create their own playlists. Or, you might want to do this if your startup volume doesn't have a lot of room and you want to store your music elsewhere, such as on an external drive.

A couple of other preferences on the Advanced pane are related to keeping your music well organized. Set these with the following steps:

1. Open the Advanced pane of the iTunes Preferences window.

2. If you want to change the location in which iTunes stores music in the Library, click the Change button. Use the resulting Change Music Folder Location dialog box to move to and select a new folder. Click Open. From that point forward, iTunes will store music you import in the folder you selected.

> **TIP**
>
> If you want to change where your existing iTunes Music folder is located, copy it to the new location before you do step 2. Then, when you perform step 2, select the Music folder you just copied. After you have confirmed that the new folder contains all your music, you can delete the original one.

3. Make sure the "Keep iTunes Music folder organized" preference is selected. This keeps all your music organized according to the standard iTunes scheme.

4. Check the "Copy files to iTunes Music folder when adding to library" check box. This causes iTunes to make a copy of any tracks you add to the Library and place the copies in the iTunes folder just like music you import.

> **TIP**
>
> If you have iTunes copy files you add, you can delete the original files after they have been added to the iTunes Library. If you don't do this, you'll have two copies of the file: the original one and the copy that iTunes creates.

5. Click OK. Your music will be organized according to your preferences.

> **TIP**
>
> To return the Music folder to its default location, move your music folder to the original location and click the Reset button on the Advanced pane of the Preferences dialog box.

18

CHAPTER 19

CONFIGURING AND USING AN IPOD

In this chapter

TOURING IPODS

The amazing Apple iPod is a small digital device that includes a hard drive (except the iPod shuffle), an operating system, a processor and other computer components, as well as an LCD screen (again, with the exception of the iPod shuffle), controls, and other system elements needed to deliver its amazing functionality. It also includes a rechargeable lithium battery to give you plenty of listening time, a Headphones port to which you attach audio devices (including headphones, powered speakers, and so on), and the Dock connector port (except the iPod shuffle, which uses a USB port) to enable you to move music from a computer onto the iPod and recharge its battery.

The iPod's software enables you to manage and play digital audio files. You can also use its software to set a variety of preferences, in addition to using the iPod's other built-in tools.

NOTE

iPod's are amazing devices—since this is a Mac OS X book, I can only scratch the surface of what you can do with an iPod. For more detailed and comprehensive information about one of my favorite digital devices, see my book *Absolute Beginner's Guide to iPod and iTunes*.

iPods comes in four basic models: iPod, iPod mini, iPod Photo, and iPod shuffle. All of these models are definitely cool, and all perform the same basic function. However, each offers specific features and options.

All of these models have one thing in common; iPods are quite small. The largest iPod is only 2.4 inches wide, 4.1 inches tall, .75 inches thick, and weighs a mere 6.4 ounces. This is roughly the size of a deck of playing cards. The smallest model, the iPod shuffle, comes in at a svelte 1 inch wide, 3.3 inches tall, .33 inches thick, and weighs a mere .78 ounce. This about the size of a pack of chewing gum!

NOTE

Unfortunately, the Mac continues to hold only a small share of the entire PC market space. The iPod however, dominates its market and currently accounts for more than 60% of all portable digital music device sales. As a long time Mac and iPod user, it seems odd (but nice!) to finally not be in the minority when it comes to using a piece of technology!

With its rapid and continuing evolution, the iPod continues to change. From revised iPod models with new features to radically different versions, it's tough to provide specifics on the various iPod models because they change so rapidly. However, the basic controls on the iPod models remain similar. In this section, you'll get an overview of how to control the models that were available at press time.

To use an iPod, you first move music from your iTunes Library onto it (you'll learn how to do this task in this chapter). After your iPod is filled with music, you use its controls to listen to the tunes.

Except for the iPod shuffle, you can listen to music on an iPod very similarly to how you listen to it with iTunes. For example, you can listen to playlists, browse and listen to music by artists and albums, and so on. You use the iPod's menus and commands to access and listen to your music and to configure various iPod settings. The iPod's controls enable you to select menu items, choose the songs you want to listen to, play those songs and so on (see Figure 19.1).

Figure 19.1
The menus on an iPod work like you probably expect them to; you select menu options and open them to choose commands, such as browsing your iPod's music.

CONTROLLING THE IPOD

The iPod has a 20GB hard drive rated for 5,000 songs. To control an iPod, you use its Click Wheel to move to and select items that appear on its screen (see Figure 19.2).

Figure 19.2
The iPod provides lots of great features in a small package.

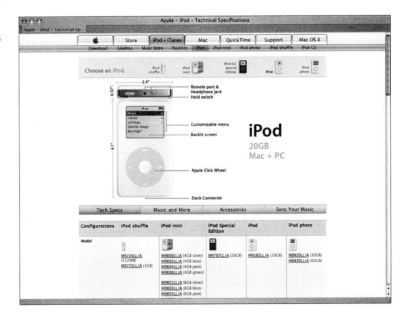

19

NOTE

iPod Special Edition models, currently the U2 Special Edition, are also available. These models look different than "regular" models, but work similarly.

To move the highlight on the screen, you simply drag the Click Wheel; move your finger clockwise to move down menus or counterclockwise to move up a menu. When the highlight is on the item you want to select, press the Select button—the button in the center of the Click Wheel—to choose it. You will move to the next screen, such as the Now Playing screen when you have selected specific music to which you want to listen (specific songs that might be in a playlist, for example). When the iPod is playing music and the Now Playing screen is being shown, drag the Click Wheel to change the volume—clockwise to increase volume, counterclockwise to decrease it.

You can control playback using the buttons located at the "four points of the compass." For example, the Play/Pause button is located at the bottom of the Click Wheel. Fortunately, these buttons are all clearly labeled so it isn't hard to figure out what you need to press.

> **TIP**
>
> Turning an iPod on isn't the most obvious thing in the world since iPods don't have On/Off switches. To turn an iPod on, touch any of its controls. To turn an iPod off (which actually just puts it to sleep), hold the Play/Pause button down for a couple of seconds.

CONTROLLING THE IPOD MINI

As if the iPod weren't small enough, Apple introduced an even smaller iPod, known as the *iPod mini*. These smaller iPods offer similar features to their bigger cousins and include a 4GB hard drive rated at 1,000 songs. Unlike the iPod, which comes only in its elegant white and silver finish, the iPod mini comes in five colors (see Figure 19.3). The size of the unit itself and the size of its drive are the primary differences between the iPod and iPod mini. The controls on these models look and work just like the ones on their larger cousins.

Figure 19.3
If you like color, the iPod mini might be for you.

CONTROLLING THE IPOD PHOTO

The iPod Photo is much like the iPod only slightly bigger and with some significant features. This is the only model that includes a color screen and for good reason—you can use this model to store and view digital photos. It also has the option of a 40GB (10,000 songs) or 60GB (15,000 songs) hard drive (see Figure 19.4). For music purposes, this model works just like the iPod.

Figure 19.4
You can use the iPod Photo to work with your photos too.

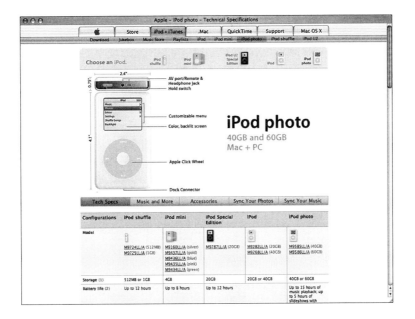

NOTE

All iPods, except the Shuffle, have a Hold switch. You can use this switch to disable all the controls on the iPod. This is good because you can prevent accidental iPod activity, such as it being turned on when you are carrying it in a computer case and you discovering that it is out of battery power when you try to listen to music (not that this has ever happened to me you understand).

CONTROLLING THE IPOD SHUFFLE

The iPod shuffle is an iPod of a different breed. While it is much smaller than the other models, its differences are much more than skin deep. This model doesn't include a hard drive; its memory is based on RAM meaning that this model has no moving parts. It also lacks a screen. These features make the Shuffle the smallest and least expensive of the lot.

However, this model does have a couple of drawbacks. First, you can only store up to 512MB (rated at 120 songs) or 1GB (rated at 240 songs) of music on them. And, because they lack a screen, you have much more limited playback options. But, even so, these are very cool devices and are perfect if you can't afford a more expensive version or if you want a second version to use in situations that might put an iPod at risk, such as heavy exercise or work (see Figure 19.5).

Figure 19.5
The differences between an iPod shuffle and other models are definitely more than skin deep.

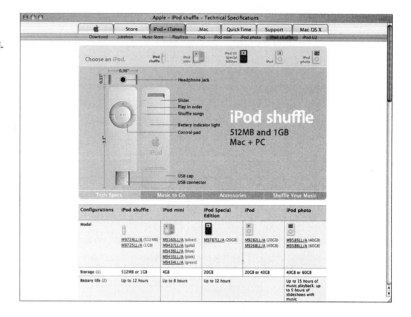

Unlike the other models, you have only two playback options for an iPod shuffle. You can choose to play all the music it contains one song after another or you can play its songs in random fashion by shuffling your music (thus, the word "shuffle" in this model's name).

The Control pad on the Shuffle enables you to move ahead or back in your music, turn the volume up or down, and play or pause. You use the slider on it to determine if your music plays straight through or in random order.

MOVING YOUR ITUNES MUSIC ONTO AN IPOD

While iPod models vary in features, how much disk space they have (or whether they have a disk at all) and so on, they are very similar in how you configure the music that is stored on them. The general steps to stock an iPod with music are the following:

1. Fill your iTunes Library with great (or not so great, depending your taste) music.
2. Connect your iPod to your Mac.
3. Perform general iPod configuration.
4. Choose the music in your iTunes Library to move onto the iPod and how it will be moved there.
5. Disconnect your iPod and use it to listen to your music.

These general steps are explained in more detail in the following sections, but step 4 is the only one that presents any complication and even that one isn't too complicated. You have three basic options, which are fully automatic updates, selecting specific music to update automatically, or performing manual updates.

NOTE
The iPod shuffle is different than the other models as you will see.

CONNECTING AN IPOD TO YOUR MAC

For all models except the Shuffle, you use the supplied FireWire cable to connect the iPod to the computer. The Dock end connects to the Dock port on the iPod while the FireWire end connects to a FireWire port on your Mac. This both recharges the battery and enables you to update the music on the iPod.

NOTE
You can also use a Dock to connect an iPod to the computer. You connect the cable to the Dock and then you can just pop the iPod in or out of the Dock when you need to connect it. If you don't put your iPod in a case (or if the case is easily removable), this is a great way to be able to connect your iPod easily and quickly. If you do use a case that is hard to remove, it is often easier to just use the cable.

The iPod shuffle uses USB to communicate with your Mac. The bottom side of the Shuffle is a USB port. You simply plug the Shuffle's USB connection directly into a USB port on your Mac.

In either case, by default, when you connect an iPod to your Mac, iTunes will open automatically and attempt to update your iPod.

19

Battery Management

All iPods are electronic devices and so they need electrons to flow in order to work. These electrons come from the iPod's internal battery. The specific battery an iPod has and its capability (in terms of the number of hours it will play) depends on the specific model you have. For example, current versions of the iPod are rated for up to 12 hours of playing time. That is an ideal of course. In order to get this much time, you would need to start music playing and not touch the controls again for the duration; each time you use a control, more energy is required.

The good news is that it is simple to charge an iPod's battery. When you connect your iPod to your computer, its battery is charged automatically. You can also use a separate power adapter to charge iPods; some models include this adapter and some don't. For most models, it takes about 1 hour to charge the battery to 80% of full charge. It usually takes about 4 hours to completely charge a battery.

Here are some tips to help you get the most out of your battery:

- Recharge your iPod battery frequently. The type of batteries in iPods benefit from frequent charging.
- Let your battery run all the way down once in a while. Every so often, say about every 30 charges, run your iPod's battery down until it stops playing. This will reset your iPod's battery management system so that you continue to get the most life possible.

- The fewer times you control your iPod, the longer the battery will last. Starting and stopping the iPod increases power use as does moving forward and backward among songs, and so on.
- If your iPod has a screen, keep its backlight off or set it to be on for only a couple of seconds at a time.
- If your iPod has one, use the Hold switch to ensure that accidental commands don't happen.

TIP

> If your iPod ever stops responding, make sure you haven't forgotten to turn the Hold switch to the Off position. Sometimes, you might forget you activated the Hold switch and be puzzled when the iPod won't respond to your commands (again, this has never happened to me of course).

SETTING IPOD GENERAL PREFERENCES

Within iTunes, there are a couple of general iPod preferences you can set:

1. Connect your iPod to your Mac. When you do this, iTunes will open and the iPod will appear in the Source pane.

2. Open the iTunes Preferences window and click the iPod icon to open the iPod Preferences pane.

3. Click the General tab (see Figure 19.6).

Figure 19.6
Use the General tab to determine some default behaviors when you connect an iPod to your Mac.

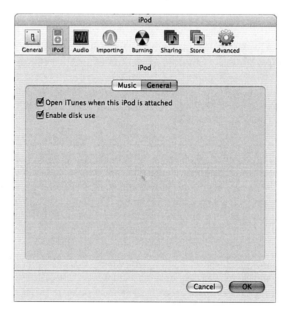

4. Uncheck the "Open iTunes when this iPod is attached" check box if you don't want iTunes to launch automatically when you connect it to your Mac.

5. Uncheck the "Enable disk use" check box if you don't want your iPod to act just like other mounted volumes on your computer when it is connected.

→ To learn more about using an iPod as a hard disk, **see** "Using Your iPod As a Portable Hard Drive," **p. 600**.

6. Click OK to close the Preferences window.

USING FULLY AUTOMATIC UPDATING TO MOVE YOUR MUSIC FROM ITUNES ONTO AN IPOD

NOTE

> You can't use either of the automatic methods with an iPod shuffle.

You can have iTunes automatically move all of the music in the Library onto the iPod and keep it synced each time you connect the iPod to the computer. This is definitely the easiest option and ensures that all the music in your Library is always available to you when you use your iPod.

There is a catch however. Your iPod must have enough storage space to be able to store all of the music that is in your Library. If not, you will have to use one of the other methods to put music on your iPod.

To determine if the fully automatic option is feasible, select the Library as the source. Take a look at the Source Information area located at the bottom of the iTunes window (see Figure 19.7). If the total space required by your iTunes Library is less than the storage space available on your iPod, you can use this option. If the space required is greater than your iPod has available, you'll have to use one of the other methods—updating automatically based on a playlist or manually—described a little later in this chapter.

Figure 19.7
As long as my iPod has at least 11.71GB of storage space, I can use the Fully Automatic update option (since it happens to be a 40GB model, this isn't a problem).

NOTE

> If you use your iPod to store documents, photos, or other files, those items use its memory space too. You can use the Finder to determine how much free memory space your iPod has.

→ To learn how to use the Finder to **see** how much free space is available on your iPod, **see** "Using Your iPod As a Portable Hard Drive," **p. 600**.

To use the fully automatic option, perform the following steps:

1. Connect the iPod to your Mac.

 If the iPod doesn't appear on the Source list when you connect it to your computer, see "I Can't See My iPod in iTunes" in the "Troubleshooting" section at the end of this chapter.

2. Open the iPod pane of the Preferences window and click the Music tab.

3. Click the "Automatically update all songs and playlists" radio button (see Figure 19.8).

Figure 19.8
With this setting, iTunes takes care of making sure your iPod has all of your music.

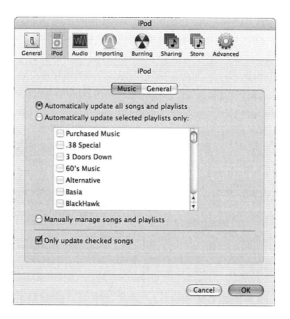

4. By default, iTunes will move only those songs whose check box is checked onto the iPod; if you want it to move all songs regardless of this check box, uncheck the "Only update checked songs" check box.

5. Click OK. When you connect your iPod to your Mac, iTunes will automatically move all of your iTunes music to it.

NOTE

No matter which method you choose, when iTunes is updating your iPod, you will see information about the process in the Information area at the top of the iTunes window. When iTunes is actively moving music onto your iPod, you will see a message here (and on the iPod's screen), telling you not to disconnect it from your computer.

6. When the update process is complete (and when your iPod's battery has had time to charge), click the Eject button next to the iPod on the Source pane to eject it.

7. Disconnect the iPod from the cable. It will be ready to rock your world.

NOTE

If you enable you iPod to work as a disk and just disconnect your iPod without ejecting it, you'll see a message stating that the device wasn't removed properly and its data could be damaged. You are likely to experience data damage only when you remove the iPod during the update process. Still, it is better to be safe than sorry. Make sure you eject an iPod (from within iTunes or from the Finder) before you disconnect it.

If iTunes isn't able to complete the update because it reports there are missing songs, see "I Can't Move Some Songs onto My iPod" in the "Troubleshooting" section at the end of this chapter.

UPDATING SPECIFIC MUSIC ON YOUR iPOD AUTOMATICALLY

If all of your iTunes music won't fit in your iPod's available memory, you can still have iTunes automatically update selected playlists in your Library. When you connect your iPod to your computer, iTunes makes sure that all the music in the playlists you select is moved onto your iPod. To enable this update method, perform the following steps:

1. Create and configure the playlists that you want to have available on your iPod.

2. Connect the iPod to your Mac.

3. Open the iPod pane of the Preferences window and click the Music tab.

TIP

You can also jump to the Music pane by clicking the iPod Options button that will appear to the left of the Equalizer button when you select an iPod on the Source pane.

4. Click the "Automatically update selected playlists only" radio button (see Figure 19.9).

5. Choose the playlists that you want iTunes to move to your iPod by checking their check boxes.

6. By default, iTunes will move only those songs whose check box is checked onto the iPod; if you want it to move all songs regardless of this check box, uncheck the "Only update checked songs" check box.

19

Figure 19.9
With this setting, iTunes updates only the playlists that you select.

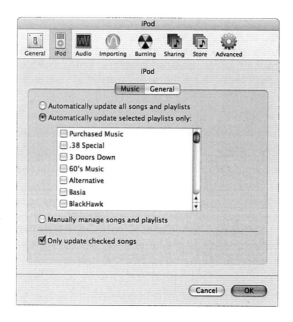

7. Click OK. If the iPod can store the amount of music you have selected, the iPod will be updated with the playlists you selected. If not, you will see a warning dialog box that explains that the iPod can't be updated because it doesn't have enough free space (see Figure 19.10). Click OK to close the dialog box. You have to unselect some of the playlists you have selected or remove songs from the selected playlists until there is enough room on the iPod to handle the music you have selected. After you do that, try to update the iPod again. Repeat this process until iTunes is able to update the iPod.

Figure 19.10
If you see this dialog box, iTunes is trying to put more music on an iPod than it can handle.

TIP

> You can update an iPod any time it is connected by choosing File, Update *iPodname*, where *iPodname* is the name of your iPod.

8. When the update process is complete (and when you iPod's battery has had time to charge), click the Eject button next to the iPod on the Source pane to eject it.

9. Disconnect the iPod from the cable. It will be ready to roll.

Unfortunately, if you select more music than your iPod can store, iTunes doesn't tell you by how much the selected music exceeds your iPod's capacity. The only way to completely fill up your iPod without trying to exceed its storage limits is by experimentation. Keep adding playlists and updating your iPod until you get the warning dialog. Then, remove playlists one-at-a-time until you no longer get the warning dialog box. Check out how much free space your iPod has by selecting it and looking in the Source Information area. This will give you an idea of how much additional music you can put on the iPod.

NOTE

If the iPod has been used on a different computer (meaning it has been linked to a different iTunes Library), you will be prompted to choose to replace the iPod's contents with the current iTunes Library; click Yes, if you want this to happen or Cancel if you don't. If you click Yes, the songs in the current Library will be moved onto the iPod and its previous contents will be erased.

UPDATING YOUR iPOD'S MUSIC MANUALLY

You can also set iTunes so that you can manually update its music by dragging songs and playlists onto it. Here's how:

1. Connect the iPod to your Mac.
2. Open the iPod pane of the Preferences window and click the Music tab.
3. Click the "Manually manage songs and playlists" radio button. You'll see a warning dialog box that explains that when you use the manual setting, you must unmount (eject) the iPod before you disconnect it.
4. Since this is good practice no matter how you update, click OK to close the dialog box.
5. Click OK. The preferences window will close. The iPod will become an "editable" source and will be expanded to show you the playlists currently stored on it (see Figure 19.11).

TIP

If you want to use an iPod with another computer without linking the iTunes Library to it, connect the iPod to the other computer and choose not to link the Library to it. This puts you in manual mode. Then, you can add music from that computer's iTunes Library to it or you can play the iPod's music just like other sources (for example, you can use this technique to play an iPod's music via a PowerBook without copying the music on the PowerBook).

6. Move music onto the iPod (by songs or by playlists) by dragging the tracks or playlists onto the iPod's icon. When the icon becomes highlighted, the cursor will become a "+" sign which means you can release the mouse button to place the selected tracks or playlists on the iPod.

Figure 19.11
This iPod mini can be updated by dragging music from the Library or other playlists onto it.

TIP

If you double-click the iPod icon, its contents will appear in a separate window. This makes it easy to move music onto it.

7. To remove songs or playlists from the iPod, select what you want to remove and press the Delete key.

8. When you've finished configuring music on the iPod (and when your iPod's battery has had time to charge), click the Eject button next to the iPod on the Source pane to eject it.

9. Disconnect the iPod from the cable. It will be ready to rock and roll.

TIP

If you have more than one iPod (and they are so cool, you will probably want more than one), you can use multiple iPods with the same iTunes Library. You can choose different update options for each as well.

UPDATING YOUR IPOD SHUFFLE'S MUSIC

As you learned earlier, the iPod shuffle is a different sort of iPod. This difference also comes into play when updating its music. You can manually update an iPod Shuffle or use its unique Autofill feature. When you use this feature, iTunes will select songs and place them on the iPod Shuffle for you until the iPod's capacity is reached.

1. Connect the iPod shuffle to your Mac. It will appear in the Source pane and you will see the Autofill controls at the bottom of the iTunes window.

2. Choose the source from which you want iTunes to select the music it will place on the iPod shuffle. You can choose any of your playlists or choose Library to have iTunes choose from all of your music.

3. If you want songs to be selected randomly, check the "Choose songs randomly" check box or if you want songs you have rated higher to also be selected more frequently, check the "Choose higher rated songs more often."

4. If you want Autofill to overwrite all the songs on the iPod shuffle, check the "Replace all songs when Autofilling" check box. If you uncheck this check box, Autofill won't replace any songs you have manually placed on the iPod shuffle.

5. Click Autofill. iTunes will select music and place it on the iPod according to your selections.

6. When you've finished configuring music on the iPod (and when you iPod's battery has had time to charge), click the Eject button next to the iPod on the Source pane to eject it.

7. Disconnect the iPod from the cable. It will be ready to move you to the beat.

TROUBLESHOOTING

I CAN'T SEE MY IPOD IN ITUNES

After I connect my iPod to my Mac, it doesn't appear in the Source pane.

There can be a number of reasons why an iPod isn't recognized by iTunes when you connect it to your computer. Solving this issue can usually be done by one of the following actions:

1. Quit iTunes and restart it. This will often get iTunes to recognize the iPod.

2. Update your software using the Mac OS X Software Update tool (Apple menu, Software Update). This will both update Mac OS X and also determine if your iPod software needs to be updated. If an iPod update is found, download it and install it. It will run automatically and you can update your iPod's software by following the on-screen instructions.

3. If neither of these steps work, reset or restore the iPod. The exact steps you need to do for these tasks depend on the specific iPod you are using. See http://docs.info.apple.com/article.html?artnum=61705 for the steps to reset an iPod. See http://www.info.apple.com/kbnum/n60983 for the steps you need to restore your iPod.

CAUTION

When you restore an iPod, its contents are erased. Make sure you have saved copies of any information that you want to keep before you restore it.

4. If none of this works, make sure the ports and cable you are using aren't defective.

I CAN'T MOVE SOME SONGS ONTO MY IPOD

When I perform an update, iTunes reports that some songs can't be updated because they can't be found.

This problem occurs when you have music in your Library that iTunes tries to put on an iPod, but it can't find the original files containing those songs. When this happens, you'll see a dialog box explaining the problem. In order to correct this, you have two choices. One is to remove the missing songs from the update process such as by removing them from playlists that are updated automatically or by deleting them from your Library. The second way is find the original files again and reassociate them with the pointer stored in the iTunes Library (click the question mark next to the missing song and use the resulting dialog box to move to and choose the files) or reimport the music into the iTunes Library.

MAC OS X TO THE MAX: COOL THINGS YOU CAN DO WITH AN IPOD

There are so many great uses for an iPod, that it would take an entire book to describe them all (such as *Absolute Beginner's Guide to iPod and iTunes*). In this section, you'll get a glimpse into three of the iPod's greatest tricks.

USING YOUR IPOD AS A PORTABLE HARD DRIVE

iPods (except the shuffle) contain a hard disk that works just like the hard disk in your Mac. If you leave the default preference about hard disk use active, you can use your iPod just like any other external drive. You can copy files onto it, work on documents stored on it, move files from it to a computer, and so on. To use your iPod as a disk:

1. Connect the iPod to your Mac.
2. Make sure the "Enable disk use" preference on the General tab of the iPod pane of the iTunes Preferences window is checked.
3. Open a Finder window and Select the iPod in the Places sidebar. Its contents will be displayed (see Figure 19.12).
4. Use the iPod to store files and folders just as you would any other mounted volume. For example, you can create folders on it, drag files to it, and so on.

There are three default folders visible to you. Each work with additional features iPods have that I didn't have room to cover in this chapter. However, you can create as many other folders on it that you need.

You might wonder where the music you have stored on your iPod shows up. By default, all music files stored on the iPod are hidden from your view. This prevents you from being able to copy those files from the iPod onto a computer. There are software tools that enable you to access music files on an iPod. If you need such a tool, search the Web and you'll likely find several of them.

Figure 19.12
Cool music player or portable disk drive? The iPod is both of course.

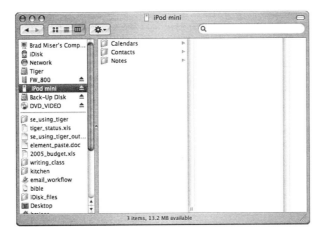

NOTE

If you are considering the purchase of a back-up drive and you don't have a huge amount of data to back up, consider getting an iPod instead. If you get a 40GB model, you would have room for plenty of music and a decent amount of room to back up important files.

USING YOUR IPOD WITH A CAR STEREO

Since your iPod can contain your entire music library, wouldn't it be nice to be able to listen to its music in the car? Yes, and of course, you can do this easily.

One option, if your car has a cassette player, is to purchase a cassette adapter that converts the headphone output on the iPod into a signal your car's cassette adapter can play. This works, but has a number of drawbacks. The most important is that the sound quality of many of these adapters just isn't any good. Another is that you have to deal with the hassles of the wire connecting the iPod to the cassette adapter. Plus, you will probably want to be able to charge the iPod while you are on the road, in which case you need to add another cable for a charger.

The better option is to use an FM transmitter to broadcast your iPod's music on standard FM frequencies so you can play that music using your car radio's FM receiver. There are many types of FM transmitters available, but my favorite (and I have tried most of them!) is the DLO TransPod FM (see Figure 19.13). This unit includes a digital FM transmitter with access to every FM frequency, but that is only the start. It also plugs into your car's power outlet so that you can recharge your iPod while it plays. And, it also includes a holding device to keep your iPod in a safe and accessible location. Even better, you can use the solid connector rod to hold the unit so that there aren't any wires or cables to deal with all. You just pop the iPod in the slot, turn on your radio, and start the tunes. The unit comes with a variety of adapters so that you should be able to make it work in just about any vehicle.

19

CAUTION

If you live in an area with lots of FM stations, make sure you get a transmitter than has plenty of frequencies to choose from. Some only support four. If the area you live in has stations on these channels, you probably won't be able to overpower them with your transmitter. It's best to use an unused FM channel so the more options you have to broadcast on, the better your chances are of being able to find an unused frequency.

Figure 19.13
The DLO TransPod FM provides everything you need to use an iPod in your car.

NOTE

You can get information about the TransPod FM at www.dlodirect.com.

NOTE

One thing to be careful about when buying an FM transmitter is the strength of the signal they output. Many broadcast so weakly that it can be hard to find a frequency that they can use, not to mention not being able to get much volume out of your audio system.

USING YOUR IPOD AS A BOOMBOX

Sometimes you just don't want to use the earbuds that come with an iPod or other kinds of headphones. And you might want to share your tunes with other people. No problem there. You can easily use your iPod as a boombox. There are several ways to do this.

One is to connect the headphone jack on the iPod to an input on your home stereo. Fire up your iPod and set your home receiver to use the input to which you have connected the iPod. Then you can listen to your iPod's music over your home stereo.

TIP

If you have a Dock for your iPod, use its Line Out port instead of the iPod's Headphones jack. The sound quality will be better and you won't have to fool around with a cable when you disconnect your iPod.

Another is to connect the headphone jack on the iPod to a set of powered speakers (such as you use with a computer). Instant boombox!

The best solution, especially if you travel and want something small to take with you, is the Altec Lansing inMotion iM3 speaker unit (see Figure 19.14). These amazing speakers feature excellent sound quality and volume yet they come in a small package—about the same size as a medium-length hardcover book. You just drop your iPod into the slot on the speaker unit and its output is played through the speakers. These can operate on battery power or on the supplied AC adapter.

Figure 19.14
If you like to travel with your iPod, these speakers make your iPod a worthy sound system for any location.

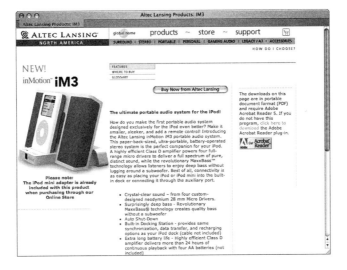

NOTE

You can get information about iMotion speakers at www.alteclansing.com.

TIP

One of the other nice features of the iM3 speakers is that the unit also includes a Line In port so that you can use it to listen to other audio sources. For example, I like to watch movies on my PowerBook when I am staying in a hotel. But, the PowerBook's speakers aren't so good (to put it as nicely as I can). I connect the audio output on the PowerBook to the Line In on these speakers and get to enjoy pretty good movie sound even when I am on the road.

CHAPTER 20

CREATING YOUR OWN MUSIC WITH GARAGEBAND

In this chapter

GETTING STARTED WITH GARAGEBAND

You can use iTunes to listen to music other people create and use an iPod to take that music with you wherever you go. But, what if you want to make your own music? Maybe you are a budding musician with dreams of making it to the top and creating music that other people will use iTunes to listen to? Or maybe you just want to create some soundtracks for your own projects, such as a slideshow you will put on DVD. That's where the amazing GarageBand application comes in. If you have musical talent, you can use this application to create, record, and mix your own music. If you have no musical abilities whatsoever (I am definitely in this camp!), you are in luck because you can use GarageBand to create some pretty interesting music without being able to play a note yourself.

In this chapter, you'll get a fairly basic overview of GarageBand and will learn enough to create a simple (or not so simple) song using the standard musical tools that GarageBand provides. You'll also learn how to export the music you make to other applications, such as to iTunes so you can listen to it over and over or to iMovie HD to use as a soundtrack. You won't learn about GarageBand's more advanced capabilities, such as recording from instruments you play, creating your own GarageBand instruments, and so on.

> **TIP**
>
> To get more detailed information on GarageBand, open its Help system and click Getting Started. The GarageBand manual in PDF format will open and you can read about GarageBand in more detail.

GarageBand is part of the Apple iLife suite of applications (this chapter is based on GarageBand version 2.0). To be able to use GarageBand, you need to obtain and install the iLife suite (see the following sidebar).

When you launch GarageBand, you'll be prompted to start a new project or open an existing one.

20

Obtaining and Installing iLife

Apple's iLife suite includes five amazing applications, four of which are not part of the standard Mac OS X installation (GarageBand, iPhoto, iMovie, and iDVD) that are a must-have for any Mac OS X user. (iTunes is part of the standard Mac OS X installation and is also included in the iLife suite.) There are two ways you can get a copy of iLife. One is to buy a new Mac because iLife is installed on all new Macs. The other is to purchase the suite from Apple or from an authorized Apple reseller. Priced at $79, this suite is an excellent bargain too.

The system requirements for iLife vary depending on which applications you are going to install and how you are going to use them. In order to install GarageBand and iDVD, your Mac must have a DVD drive. If your Mac doesn't have a DVD drive, you can install the other applications from the installation CD included in the iLife package. In order to be able to create DVDs with iDVD, you need to have access to a DVD burner, such as an Apple SuperDrive. Some of the advanced features of GarageBand and iDVD require a G4 of G5 processor.

Installing the iLife applications is simple, you just place the appropriate disc (DVD or CD) in your Mac and run the iLife installer. Use the standard installation to install all parts of each application or use the Customize option to select parts not to install (such as the themes from previous versions of iDVD). Each application will be installed within the Applications folder. Before you start using these applications, run the Mac OS X Software Update application (choose Apple, Software Update) to ensure that you are using the most current version of each application.

STARTING A NEW GARAGEBAND PROJECT

When you create a new project, you'll use the New Project dialog box to name the song you are creating, choose the save location, and configure the song you are creating (see Figure 20.1). By default, the project is saved to a GarageBand folder located in the Music folder in your Home folder; however, you can choose to change this.

Figure 20.1
Use the New Project dialog box to create and configure a new song in GarageBand.

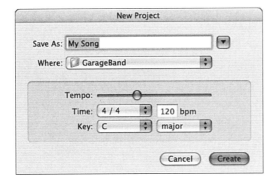

In the New Project dialog box, use the controls to configure the following aspects of the song you are going to create:

- **Tempo**—The tempo is the relative speed of the song. Drag the slider to the right to create a faster song or to the left to create a slower one. You can also type the number of beats in the beats per minute (bpm) box. Don't be too concerned with getting the tempo set correctly here because you can always change the tempo later if you decide you want your song to be faster or slower.

- **Time Signature**—Use the Time pop-up menu to choose the time signature of your new song. The time signature is the relationship between beats and measures in your song. This is measured by two numbers separated by a /. Explaining how to choose the right time signature to use is beyond the scope of this book and my musical knowledge; the 4/4 time signature is a standard one so use that unless you know enough to be able to choose something else.

- **Key**—The key of a song is the central note of the piece to which all the other notes in the song relate. Use the Key pop-up menu to choose the key for the new song; C is the default key.

- **Scale**—You choose the scale to be used for the key you selected; there are two options: major or minor. Use the pop-up menu to the right of the Key pop-up menu to set the scale for your song.

20

NOTE

Like tempo, you can change the time signature, key, and scale for your song later.

When you have configured your new song, click Create. You'll see the GarageBand window that is separated into a number of areas, each of which contains a set of tools that enable you to work with your project (see Figure 20.2). By default, you'll see that the Grand Piano software instrument has been selected for the first track in the song.

Software Instrument   Track   Timeline

Figure 20.2
If you aren't used to working with a music application, GarageBand might look confusing to you at first, but you'll quickly learn how to you can use it to create your own tunes.

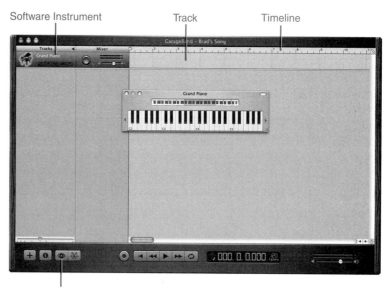

Loop Browser button

UNDERSTANDING A GARAGEBAND PROJECT

Each GarageBand project (better known as a song) you create includes one or more tracks. Each track can contain music from one of the following sources:

- **Loop**—GarageBand includes loops, which are pre-created snippets of music, that you can add to your song to add depth to it, give it rhythm, and so on. The loops provided in GarageBand allow you to create complex music by taking advantage of music created by real musicians. You can use the loops that come with GarageBand in anyway you see fit.

- **Software instrument**—GarageBand includes a mind-boggling number of software instruments that you can play and record in a track of your song. Even if you can't really play an instrument, you can create a series of notes that sound good to you and the use GarageBand's tools to transform those notes into a track that even a musician might mistake for real music.

- **Real instrument**—If you have a real musical instrument, you can record its output in GarageBand. Because of space and other limitations (namely, that I can't play an instrument), you won't find any more information about this option in this chapter.

20

You create a song by building each track the song will contain using the sources listed previously. After you have tracks in place, you mix those tracks so they come together in beautiful harmony. After you have tuned your song to your liking, you can export it and use it in a number of ways.

TIP

> To get rid of the Grand Piano track that is created automatically when you start a new project, select it by clicking it and press Delete. You can get rid of it later if you wish to.

CREATING A TRACK BY ADDING AND CONFIGURING A LOOP

One of the easiest ways to build a track in GarageBand is to use its loops. These loops make it easy to create great sounding music, especially for rhythm, percussion, and other "texture" elements. There is a huge variety of loops you can use in GarageBand so even though you are using music someone else has created, your personal creativity isn't limited at all because you can configure and mix these loops in an endless variety of ways.

FINDING LOOPS TO USE

There are a number of different ways to find loops that you might want to use in your project.

FINDING LOOPS USING THE LOOP BROWSER IN BUTTON VIEW

As you can probably guess from its name, the Loop Browser enables you to browse available loops. To use the Loop Browser to find a loop, perform the following steps:

1. Click the Loop Browser button (the third button from the left along the bottom of the GarageBand window, refer to Figure 20.2). The Loop Browser will slide open and you will see the collections of loops available to you (see Figure 20.3). By default, the Loop Browser will open in the Button view.

2. Click one of the buttons shown in the left pane of the browser to view the loops that group contains. There are a variety of groups, some are by instrument (such as All Drums) while others are by musical style (such as Rock/Blues). When you choose a group, you'll see the loops it contains in the right pane of the browser (see Figure 20.4).

NOTE

> Currently selected keywords are highlighted in blue. Available keywords remain as selectable buttons. When a group becomes unavailable because it no longer fits in your search, it becomes inactive and is grayed out.

20

Figure 20.3
The Loop Browser lives up to its name; you can browse lots of loops quickly and easily.

Figure 20.4
I've clicked the Rock/Blues button so the browser is showing all of the loops associated with that music type.

3. Continue clicking buttons (more accurately called Keywords in GarageBand lingo) to further refine your search until you find loops that you might want to use in your song. For example, if you click Rock/Blues and Electric, you'll see Rock/Blues loops that included electric instruments. If you then click Bass, you'll see Rock/Blues loops that feature electric bass guitars. As you refine your search, the loops that match the currently selected keywords are shown in the right pane of the Browser. The number of loops matching your keyword selection is listed just to the right of the Search tool.

> **TIP**
> You can add even more loops to GarageBand by purchasing and installing a GarageBand Jam Pack. These collections of additional loops and other musical goodies are available from Apple and other sources.

FINDING LOOPS USING THE LOOP BROWSER IN COLUMN VIEW

The Browser in Column view works similarly to how it does in Button view. Try it out with the following steps:

1. Click the Loop Browser button. The Loop Browser will slide open and you will see the collections of loops available to you.

2. Click the Column View button (refer to Figure 20.4). The buttons will be replaced by three columns; the first column shows the top-level categories of the loops available to you.

3. Select the top-level category by which you want to view loops. For example choose By Instruments to view loops by the instruments used in those loops. The second column will be filled in; what you see depends on the category you selected. For example, if you selected By Instruments, the second column will be labeled "Instruments" and you will see a list of all instruments used in all the loops.

4. Select the category in the second column for the group of loops you want to see. The third column will be filled in with loops that meet your selection. For example, if you are browsing by instrument and click on Bass, you'll see the list of all loops that feature bass instruments.

5. In the third column, select the category of loops you want to see. The loops in that category will appear in the right pane of the Browser (see Figure 20.5).

Figure 20.5
Here I have selected the Elec Bass category; the loops in this category appear in the right pane of the Browser.

TIP

> You can refine the loops you are browsing so that you see only those that are in a specific scale (such as one that matches your song) by choosing a scale on the Scale pop-up menu.

SEARCHING FOR LOOPS

You can also search for loops by name:

1. Type some text associated with loops for which you want to search in the Search box. For example, to search for bass loops, type **bass** in the Search box.

2. Press Return. The search will be performed and you will see the loops that meet your search criterion in the right pane of the Browser.

> **TIP**
>
> You can combine methods of searching. For example, you can search for loops by text only in specific groups by selecting the categories in which you want to search (by button or by column) and then performing a text search. Then use the Scale pop-up menu to further refine the search.

PREVIEWING AND UNDERSTANDING LOOPS

After you have found a set of loops, you can view information about and listen to them by using the following steps:

1. In the right-most pane of the Browser, examine the list of loops for data about those loops; you'll see the Name, Tempo, Key, and Beats for each loop.

> **TIP**
>
> In addition to a loop's data, you'll also see the Fav column. You can click the check box in this column to mark the loop as a favorite. You can access the loops you mark as favorites by using the Favorites button or choosing the Favorites category.

2. Sort the list of loops by clicking the column heading by which you want to sort them. You can reverse the order by clicking on the Sort Order arrow that appears in the column by which the list is currently sorted.

3. To listen to a loop, click its icon or anywhere else in the loop's row. Its icon will become the speaker icon and the loop will start to play. You can see relative volume information for the loop just above the Volume slider.

4. Use the volume slider to set the playback volume for the loop.

> **NOTE**
>
> When you add a loop to a song, the relative volume you set for it while browsing it will be set for the track in which you place it too. You can change this later.

5. To stop playing the loop, click it again or click another loop.

6. Continue previewing loops until you find one you want to use in your song.

20

ADDING A LOOP TO A TRACK

After you have selected and previewed a loop, you can add it to your project (in a track) by performing the following steps:

1. Select the default Grand Piano track and press ⌘-Delete to remove it from the song (this step is optional, it won't hurt anything to leave the track if you prefer it that way).

2. Drag the loop from the Browser and drop it in the timeline at which point you want the loop to start playing. For example, if you want the loop to start at the beginning of the song, place it at the far left of the Timeline pane. While you drag the track, the cursor will contain a "+"" sign and pointer (see Figure 20.6). When you get to the place at which you want to position the track, release the mouse button. A track will be created for the loop and you will see the information about the instrument that is used in the loop. The Mixer tool will also appear.

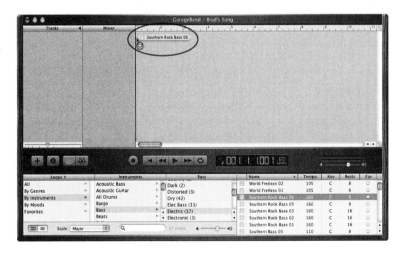

Figure 20.6
I've added the Southern Rock Bass 06 loop to my song.

3. Repeat steps 1 and 2 until you have added all the loops to the song that you want to use. You can have loops start at different points in the song by dropping them in different locations.

4. As you add loops, click the Play button to hear the song play, click it again to stop the song. As the song plays, you'll see the Playhead move along the Timeline.

> **NOTE**
>
> When you first add tracks to your song, you haven't defined an end point for the song so it will continue to play until you click the Stop button.

5. Build the loop content of your song by adding, removing, or moving tracks in the Timeline until you have the sound you are going for. Don't worry about editing the tracks by setting lengths, for example. You can do that later in the process. For now, you just want to get all of your loops into the song (see Figure 20.7).

20

Figure 20.7
At this point, my song has five loops.

BUILDING A TRACK USING A SOFTWARE INSTRUMENT

Think of loops as prerecorded music that you can use to build a song. While you can edit many aspects of a loop, as you will learn later in this chapter, you still use the notes that were played in the loop just as they were played. You can use a Software Instrument to play and record your own tracks. You choose the instrument you want to play and then use the computer's keyboard or the on-screen keyboard to play that instrument. You can record the "music" and add it as a track in your song.

CREATING A SOFTWARE INSTRUMENT TRACK

To build a track using a software instrument, perform the following steps:

1. Add a track for your instrument by choosing Track, New Track or by pressing Option-⌘-N. The New Track dialog box will appear (see Figure 20.8).

Figure 20.8
Use the New Track dialog box to choose the instrument you will play for the track you are creating.

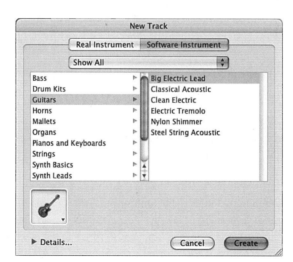

2. Choose the general type of instrument you want in the left pane and the specific instrument in the right pane.

3. Click the expansion triangle next to the word "Details" below the instrument's icon. You'll see the Details pane that provides many controls over the result you get from the instrument (see Figure 20.9).

Figure 20.9
As you can see, there are many ways to configure a Big Electric Lead guitar.

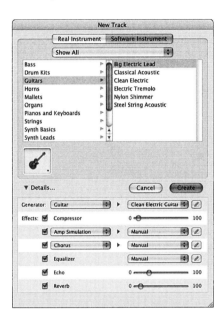

4. Use the controls to configure the instrument you selected.

5. Click Create. The track will be added to your song; its name will be the name of the instrument you selected.

6. Record the track by playing the instrument using the Musical Typing window or the on-screen keyboard.

PLAYING A SOFTWARE INSTRUMENT USING THE MUSICAL TYPING WINDOW

The Musical Typing window enables you to play music using your computer's keyboard. To open this window, choose Window, Musical Typing or press Shift-⌘-K. The window will open and you will see the keys on your keyboard that you can use to play the instrument (see Figure 20.10). Press the corresponding keys on your computer's keyboard to play specific notes and use the other keys to control various aspects of the instrument such as the octave in which it is playing.

TIP

You can play an instrument without recording it. This enables you to practice before you record. Of course, because it is easy to delete something you have recorded, it is usually better just to record everything you play.

20

Figure 20.10
Using the Musical Typing window guides you in playing a software instrument.

PLAYING A SOFTWARE INSTRUMENT USING THE ON-SCREEN KEYBOARD

The on-screen keyboard enables you play an instrument by pointing to and clicking on the keyboard's keys to play notes (see Figure 20.11). You can hold the mouse button down to "drag" across keys to play one after the other for continuous sound. If you click at the top of the key, it is pressed "softer;" if you click lower on the key it is pressed "harder."

Figure 20.11
You can point to keys on the on-screen keyboard to play the selected instrument.

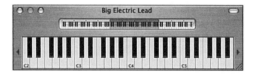

RECORDING A SOFTWARE INSTRUMENT

You can record music you play using either tool in the same way:

1. Choose the tool you will use to play the selected instrument.
2. Drag the Playhead to the point in the Timeline at which you want to start recording.
3. Click the Record button (the red circle) located between the Timeline and the Browser. The tracks in the song will start to play.

If the song stops playing and you can't record, see "I Can't Record" in the "Troubleshooting" section at the end of this chapter.

4. Start playing the track you want to record. The notes you play will be recorded and the track will be created. You can continue to play as long you want; even if you go beyond the point in the Timeline at which other tracks stop.
5. When you are done recording, click the Record button again and click the Play button to stop the song. You will see the track you recorded in the Timeline (see Figure 20.12).

Figure 20.12
I've just recorded a big electric lead guitar for my song.

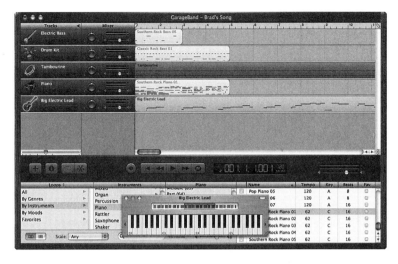

MIXING AND EDITING TRACKS

After you have added tracks to your song (whether from loops or from tracks you record), you can mix the tracks to create your song. There are lots of ways to edit tracks as you will see in this section (although this section certainly doesn't cover all possible ways to edit tracks).

The section of a track that contains music is called a region. You edit a track by editing its region, creating new regions within the track, and so on.

EDITING REGIONS

The most common ways in which you will edit regions are the following:

- You can cause a region to play over and over by looping it. To loop a region, move the pointer to the upper right edge of the region. The pointer will become the loop point, which is a vertical line with a circular arrow coming out of it. Drag the pointer until you want the track to stop playing. When you release the mouse button the track will end at the pointer's location. You can stop looping a region at any point; the start and end points of the original region are shown by the "notches" in the track (see Figure 20.13).

TIP

> When you are editing a song, you can gain more screen space for the Timeline by closing the Loop Browser (click the Loop Browser button).

20

Figure 20.13
I've made the Electric Bass track (labeled Southern Rock Bass) loop until it matches the length of the lead guitar track that I recorded.

- You can move a region so that it plays during a different portion of the song's Timeline by dragging it to the are of the Timeline in which you want it to play.

- You can shorten a region by dragging its edge to the left or right. Only the portion shown in the region will play, and it will play only at the specific point in the Timeline where it resides.

- You can add silence to the end of a region by lengthening it. As you drag the right edge of the region beyond its music, the silence will begin.

- You can select a region and copy it. To have it play again in the same track, move the Playhead to the location at which you want it to start again and paste it there (see Figure 20.14).

Figure 20.14
I've copied and pasted the Piano region so it occurs in two separate places on the Timeline.

20

- You can split a region into parts, which act as independent regions, by placing the Playhead at the point at which you want the region split and choosing Edit, Split. Each region will become independent of the other so that you can move them around the track, loop them, and so on.

MIXING TRACKS

After you have created the individual tracks of which your song will be composed, it is time to mix those tracks together so they create a song. The mixing controls are on the Mixer section of the GarageBand window (see Figure 20.15). You use these controls in the following ways:

Level meters

Pan control   Volume slider

Figure 20.15
The controls in the Mixer configure tracks relative to one another.

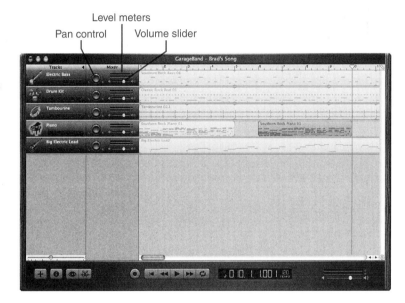

- Use the Volume slider to set the volume of tracks relative to one another.
- Drag the Pan control to adjust the position of the track in the left to right stereo field. Dragging the wheel clockwise makes the track louder in the right track; dragging it counterclockwise makes it louder in the left track. You can use this tool to simulate your instruments being in different locations and set the music to play differently in the left or right speaker.
- Watch the level meters to monitor the track's volume levels as it plays. You usually don't want the volume levels to be in the red because that can lead to distortion and other playback issues.

NOTE

The master volume located in the lower-right corner of the window controls the volume level of the entire song.

20

There are also a number of controls you can use in the Track Header section to work with individual tracks. These are shown in Figure 20.16.

Figure 20.16
You can use the controls in the track Header section to control how the track plays and the information displayed for it.

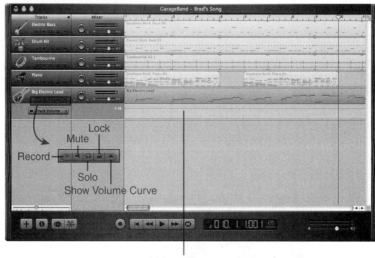

The controls in the Header section are described in Table 20.1.

TABLE 20.1 HEADER CONTROLS FOR TRACKS

Control	What It Does
Record	Turns the track on for recording.
Mute	Mutes the track.
Solo	Mutes all the other tracks so you hear only the solo track.
Lock	Locks a track in place so it can't be changed.
Show Volume Curve	Opens the Volume Curve.
Volume Curve	Shows the volume curve for a track.
Pan Curve	If you choose Track Pan on the pop-up menu, shows the pan curve for the track.

TIP

If you want to see all the possible options for editing a track, open the Track Editor by clicking the Track Editor button (the scissors). The Editor will open and you will see lots of additional tools you can use to edit tracks.

ADDING YOUR GARAGEBAND SONGS TO YOUR ITUNES LIBRARY

After you have mixed your song, you can play it in GarageBand as much as you'd like. When you are ready to do other things with it, add it to your iTunes Library. You can then listen to it just like other music the Library contains. You can also use it in your iLife projects, such as in iMovies, iPhoto slideshows, and DVDs you create with iDVD.

To move your song to your iTunes Library, choose File, Export to iTunes. GarageBand will create a mix of the song and add it to your iTunes Library. Open iTunes and search for the song by its name (see Figure 20.17). You can play the song, add it to playlists, and use it in your iLife projects just like other music in your Library.

Figure 20.17
While it certainly isn't as good as the other music in my iTunes Library, it doesn't sound too bad considering the artist who created it!

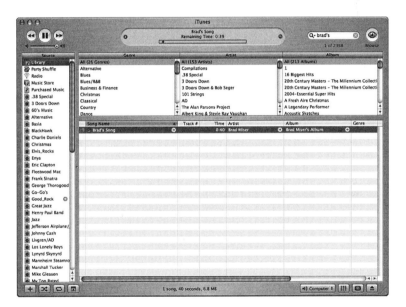

NOTE

You can export a song from GarageBand in various audio file formats for other purposes, such as to send to someone else. In most cases, exporting it to iTunes is the best choice because you can access your iTunes music from the other iLife applications.

TROUBLESHOOTING

I CAN'T RECORD

When I try to record a software instrument, the song stops playing and I see a dialog telling me that part of the song was not played.

This can happen when there are too many tracks or effects included in a song for it to be played in real time while recording. Click Continue to close the dialog and move back to the Timeline. You have three choices. You can try to optimize GarageBand's performance so that it will be able to play all the tracks you have configured. Or, you can delete some of the tracks, record the new track, and then add the other tracks back in. Lastly, you can mute tracks during the recording session to decrease the amount of resources needed to play the song while GarageBand records what you play.

CHAPTER **21**

CREATING, EDITING, AND ORGANIZING DIGITAL IMAGES USING IPHOTO

In this chapter

GETTING STARTED WITH IPHOTO

iPhoto enables you to work with digital photos you have captured using a digital camera or from any other source. With iPhoto, you can organize, edit, print, email, and export your photos. You can also do all sorts of other cool things with your images, such as creating and ordering photo books and prints, web pages, and screensavers. iPhoto enables you to do all sorts of amazing things with digital images.

Because this is a book on Mac OS X and not on iPhoto, in this chapter, you'll get a fairly basic overview of this excellent application. Fortunately, iPhoto is so well designed that a basic overview is really all you need anyway. This chapter's information and figures are based on iPhoto version 5.0.1.

TOURING IPHOTO

iPhoto is part of the Apple iLife suite of applications. To use iPhoto, you need to obtain and install the iLife suite (see the following sidebar).

Obtaining and Installing iLife

Apple's iLife suite includes five amazing applications, four of which are not part of the standard Mac OS X installation (GarageBand, iPhoto, iMovie, and iDVD) but are must-haves for any Mac OS X user. (iTunes is part of the standard Mac OS X installation and is also included in the iLife suite.) There are two ways you can get a copy of iLife. One is to buy a new Mac because iLife is installed on all new Macs. The other is to purchase the suite from Apple or from an authorized Apple reseller. Priced at $79, this suite is an excellent bargain, too.

Installing the iLife applications is simple: You just place the appropriate disc (DVD or CD) in your Mac and run the iLife installer. Use the standard installation to install all parts of each application, or use the Customize option to select parts not to install (such as the themes from previous versions of iDVD). Each application will be installed within the Applications folder. Before you start using these applications, run the Mac OS X Software Update application (select Apple, Software Update) to ensure that you are using the most current version of each application.

When you launch iPhoto for the first time, you'll be prompted to set the default action when you connect a digital camera to your Mac. Click the Use iPhoto button so iPhoto launches automatically whenever you connect a camera to your Mac.

When you open iPhoto, you see its three panes (see Figure 21.1). The Source pane enables you to select a source to work with, such as the Library to work with all the photos you have imported or individual photo albums. The Content pane shows the contents of the selected source, the image you are working with, or the tools you use to develop a photo project (such as creating a photo book) depending on what you are doing. The toolbar contains various tools you use to accomplish specific tasks. At the bottom of the iPhoto window are iPhoto controls and the Size slider.

21

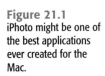

Figure 21.1
iPhoto might be one of the best applications ever created for the Mac.

If you are thinking that iPhoto looks a lot like iTunes, you are right. These applications are designed using the same interface model and have corresponding elements. For example, photo albums in iPhoto are much like playlists in iTunes.

iPhoto has several modes of operation:

- **Import**—You use the Import mode to import images from a camera.
- **Organize**—You use this mode to create photo albums, apply keywords to your images, and perform other tasks to keep your images organized.
- **Edit**—In the Edit mode, you can edit your images by cropping, changing brightness and contrast, removing red-eye, and so on.
- **Projects**—When you work on specific projects, such as creating a photo book, you'll have access to the tools you need to create those projects.

At the bottom of the iPhoto window, you'll see a number of buttons that perform the following actions (see Figure 21.2):

- **Create Photo Album**—Click this button to create a new album.
- **Play Slideshow**—Click this button and a nice slideshow displaying the images in the selected source plays (accompanied by a music soundtrack).

21

Figure 21.2
You can use the iPhoto tools to perform basic actions with images being displayed in the Content pane.

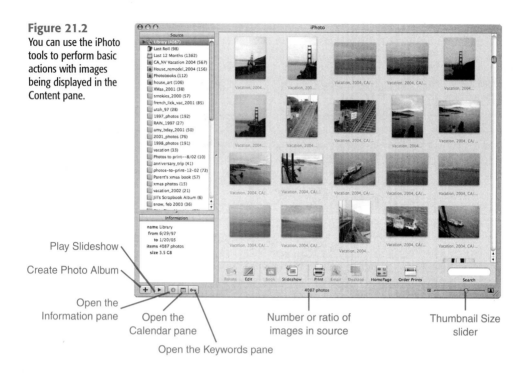

Play Slideshow
Create Photo Album
Open the Information pane
Open the Calendar pane
Open the Keywords pane
Number or ratio of images in source
Thumbnail Size slider

- **Information pane**—Click this to open or close the Information pane.
- **Calendar pane**—Click this to open or close the Calendar pane.
- **Keywords pane**—Click this to open or close the Keywords pane.
- **Number or ratio of images in source**—If you have a source selected, this shows the number of images in that source. If you have one or more images selected, it shows the number of images you have selected compared to the total number of images in the selected album.
- **Thumbnail Size**—Drag this slider to change the size of the thumbnails of the images you see in the Content pane. Moving the slider to the right makes the thumbnails larger, whereas moving it to the left makes them appear smaller and shows more images in the window. The setting of this slider doesn't actually change the image in any way; it only determines how large the image appears onscreen.

To start using iPhoto, you need to build and organize your iPhoto Library. After you have done that, you can use its tools to edit your images and do all sorts of interesting things with them.

IMPORTING IMAGES INTO THE iPHOTO LIBRARY

The first step in working with images in iPhoto is to import the images you want to work with into the iPhoto Library. You can import images from the following two sources:

- A digital camera
- Image files obtained outside of iPhoto such as those you've scanned or downloaded from the Internet

DOWNLOADING IMAGES FROM A DIGITAL CAMERA INTO IPHOTO

To download images from your camera into your iPhoto Library, perform the following steps:

1. Connect your camera to your Mac with its USB cable.

2. Power up your camera. iPhoto will open if it isn't already open and will move into the Import mode. Your camera will be shown in the Source list and be selected automatically. An icon for your camera will appear in the Content pane (see Figure 21.3). Under the icon, you'll see how many images are ready to import. Just below the Content pane, you'll see the date range of the images that are ready to import.

Figure 21.3
Images are ready to be imported from the attached camera.

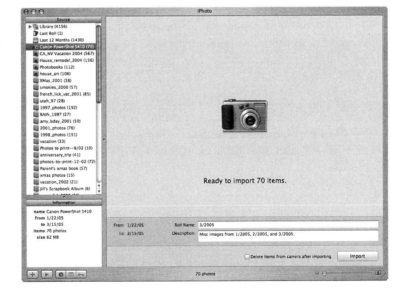

 If iPhoto doesn't recognize your camera, see "The Digital Camera Is Not Recognized by iPhoto" in the "Troubleshooting" section at the end of this chapter.

3. Enter a roll name in the Roll Name box. The name you enter will be used to identify the group of images you import during the current session.

4. Enter a description of the images in the Description box. The description you enter will be attached to the group of images.

5. If you want the images you download to be deleted from the camera after you import them, check the "Delete items from camera after importing" check box.

6. Click Import; the application begins moving the images from the camera's memory into your Library. As the process proceeds, the images being imported will be shown in the Content pane and you'll be able to see the progress of the import in the Progress bar that appears just below the Description box. When the process is complete, iPhoto will move back into the organize mode and the Library will be selected as the source.

> **TIP**
>
> If you want the photos you have most recently added to the Library to appear at the top of the Content pane by default, open the Appearance tab of the iPhoto Preferences dialog box and check the "Place most recent photos at the top" check box.

After you have imported images, it is a good idea to take a look at them, rotate any that need to be rotated, and delete any that you are sure you won't ever use. Here's how:

1. Click the Last Roll photo album in the Source pane. You will see the photos you most recently imported.

2. Use the Thumbnail Size slider to set the size of thumbnails you see. Drag the slider to the right to make the thumbnails larger or to the left to make them smaller.

3. Use the vertical scrollbar to move up and down the Content pane to view all the images in the selected source.

4. To rotate an image, select it (it will be surrounded with a blue box to show that it is selected) and either click the Rotate button to rotate the image counterclockwise or hold down the Option key and click the button to rotate the image clockwise. Images will rotate 90° each time you click the button.

> **TIP**
>
> You can change the default direction of rotation using the Rotate radio buttons on the General pane of the iPhoto Preferences dialog box.

5. To delete images you are sure you don't want to keep, select them and press the Delete key. The images you selected will be moved to the iPhoto Trash (which is shown at the bottom of the Source pane).

6. To permanently delete the images, select iPhoto, Empty Trash.

> **TIP**
>
> You can work with multiple images at the same time (such as rotating them) by holding down the ⌘ key while you click each image. You can also drag through a group of images to select them or use the Shift key to select a contiguous group of images.

IMPORTING OTHER IMAGES INTO IPHOTO

You can add images from other sources to your iPhoto Library. For example, if your digital camera is incompatible with iPhoto, you have to download images from that camera (such as by using a USB memory card reader) and then import them into iPhoto. Or you might want to add previously scanned photos or images you have downloaded from the Internet to iPhoto so you can use iPhoto's great tools to work with them.

You can import a wide variety of image file formats into iPhoto, including JPEGs, Photoshop files, and other formats you are likely to encounter when dealing with digital images. Here's how:

1. Prepare the images you want to import (for example, scan the photos or download them from a USB memory card reader to your Mac).
2. Select File, Add to Library or press ⌘-O. The Import Photos dialog box will open.
3. Move to the files you want to import and select them.
4. Click Import (or press Return). iPhoto will move into the Import mode and import the images you selected.
5. Use the same steps to view and work with imported images that you used when you imported them from a camera.

LABELING YOUR IMAGES

Because you are likely to accumulate a large number of images, it is imperative that you keep them organized and that you use iPhoto's labeling tools to help you identify your photos so you can find them when you need them, such as when you create albums or do projects. There are several kinds of information, including image information and keywords.

WORKING WITH IMAGE LABELS

To view an image's label information, select it in the Content pane and open the Information pane (see Figure 21.4).

Each image can have the following information:

- **Title**—Each image in your Library has a title. When you import an image, the title iPhoto assigns to it is the same as the filename iPhoto assigns to that image. But you can change this to give an image a more meaningful title.

TIP

> To change an image's information, select the information you want to change. It will become highlighted and you can edit it.

- **Date and Time**—iPhoto labels each image with the date and time that it was captured (if the image came from a digital camera) or with a file's date if the image is imported from a hard disk. You can also change this information if you want.
- **Rating**—You can rate images with 1–5 stars. The rating is useful for certain tasks, such as defining criteria for a smart photo album (for example, you might want iPhoto to

21

automatically collect only 4- or 5-star images). To rate a photo, click the dot that represents the number of stars you want to give it. By default, the stars will appear in the Information pane and below the image in the Content pane.

Figure 21.4
You can view an image's information in the Information pane.

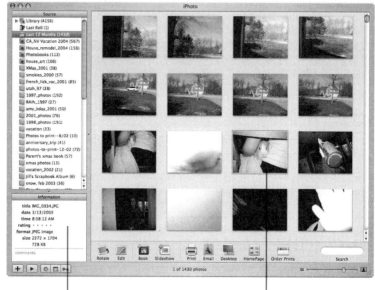

Information about the selected image   Selected image

- **Format**—This identifies the format of the image, such as JPEG. You can't change this information.

- **Size**—This identifies the size of the image by both resolution and file size. You can't change this information.

- **Comments**—iPhoto enables you to add comments to each image. For example, you can provide the context for the image so that, when you look at it later, you will understand it better. Or, if you have a poor memory like I do, you can explain where the information was captured. Comments are especially useful when you create books because they can include interesting things you've said about those images.

WORKING WITH KEYWORDS

Keywords are short phrases you can assign to images so you can find them again by searching for the keywords attached to them. The benefit of keywords is that you can define a set of keywords and apply them consistently over time. For example, suppose you like to take photos of your vacations. You can create a keyword "Vacation" and assign that to the images you take on your vacations. Because you use the same phrase, you can find the images again easily because you don't have to remember how you labeled particular images; instead, you can find them by doing a keyword search. You can also combine keywords. For example, you can create and use keywords for each year. If you wanted to find the images you captured during a specific year's vacation, you could search for the keyword "Vacation" and the year in which you are interested.

CONFIGURING AVAILABLE KEYWORDS

iPhoto includes a number of keywords by default. However, you can create your own keywords, and you can change any keywords that are available (whether you added them or they came with iPhoto). After you have set the keywords you want to use, you can associate them with your images and use them to search for specific images.

TIP

> Adding each year and specific peoples' names whom you regularly take pictures of as keywords is useful because you can combine keywords to quickly find individual images. For example, suppose you have defined "2003" as a keyword. If you also use "Birthday" and a person's name as keywords, you can find images associated with that person's birthday in 2003 by searching on the person's name, "2003", and "Birthday."

1. Open the Keywords pane of the iPhoto Preferences pane. You'll see a list of the keywords currently configured (see Figure 21.5).

Figure 21.5
Use the Keywords pane to configure the keywords available to you.

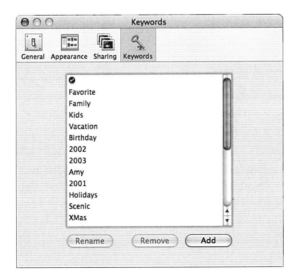

21

2. To add a new keyword, click Add. A new keyword will be created (called `untitled`) and will be ready to edit.

3. Type a name for the new keyword and press Return.

4. To change a keyword, select it and click Rename. The keyword will become editable.

5. Retype the keyword and press Return. It will be changed.

TIP

When you rename a keyword, it is also changed wherever it is attached to images.

6. To remove a keyword, select it and click Remove. The keyword will be removed from the list and from any images with which it was associated.

7. Close the Preferences dialog box.

NOTE

One of iPhoto's default keywords is a check mark. This is the one keyword you can't change. The check mark is intended to be assigned to images temporarily so you can perform a specific task for those images. For example, you might want to order prints from only a few photos in an album. You can apply the check mark keyword to each image you want a print of and then find those images by searching for the check mark keyword. (The check mark actually appears in the lower-right corner of the image itself instead of next to it, which is where other keywords appear.) After you order the prints, you can remove the check mark keyword from the images.

ASSOCIATING KEYWORDS WITH IMAGES

To use your newly created keywords (or the default ones) to find images, you need to associate keywords with those images.

Before you start working with keywords, make sure they are displayed by selecting View, Keywords or pressing Shift-⌘-K. Keywords are shown below the image thumbnails in the Content pane.

Now, configure the keywords for images with these steps:

1. Select the images to which you want to apply one or more keywords. You can assign the same keywords to multiple images at the same time by selecting more than one image.

2. Select Photos, Get Info. The Photo Info window will appear.

3. Click the Keywords tab. You'll see the list of keywords that are currently configured in iPhoto. Any keywords whose check box is checked are already associated with the selected images. If a hyphen is shown in a keyword's check box, that keyword is already applied to some of the selected images (see Figure 21.6).

4. Check the check box for the keywords you want to attach to the selected images.

5. Uncheck the check box for any keywords you want to remove from the selected images.

Figure 21.6
The keyword 2005 is applied to all selected images.

CONFIGURING THE INFORMATION DISPLAYED IN THE CONTENT PANE

Using the commands on the View menu, you can configure the information shown for each image in the Content pane. Using the View commands, you can choose to show or hide the following information:

- Titles
- Keywords
- Film rolls (only active when the Library is selected)
- My rating

TIP

> To view the roll information you entered when you imported images, select the Library and select View, Film Rolls. The Content pane will be organized by film roll. Select the roll in which you are interested and open the Information pane.

You can sort the images in the Content pane by selecting View, Sort Photos, and then choosing the attribute by which you want the photos sorted, such as by Date.

TIP

> You can choose to view each source differently. For example, you can choose to view one photo album by date and another manually. The view settings you choose are specific to each source. However, the Thumbnail Size slider setting applies to all sources.

21

VIEWING DETAILED INFORMATION FOR IMAGES

iPhoto keeps very detailed information on each image in the Library. You can view this information by using the following steps:

1. Select the image about which you want to get detailed information.

2. Select Photos, Get Info or press ⌘-I. The Photo Info window will appear.

3. Click the Photo tab. Information about the image is shown, such as its size, date, filename, file size, and the camera with which it was captured.

4. Click the Exposure tab. This tab contains technical information about the settings with which the image was captured, such as shutter speed, aperture, and so on.

5. Click another image to view its information. Because the Info window is independent of the iPhoto window, you can leave it open and select the images in which you are interested.

6. Click the window's Close button when you are done using it.

SEARCHING FOR IMAGES

After you have added hundreds or thousands of images to your Library, finding specific images with which you want to work can be a challenge. However, if you keep up with the labeling techniques you have learned as you add images to your Library, you'll have a much easier time finding images in which you are interested. You can search by image information, by date, and by keyword.

FINDING IMAGES BY IMAGE INFORMATION

You can search for images by title, comments, or other information by performing the following steps:

1. Select the source you want to search by clicking it in the Source pane. Select a photo album to search it, or select the Library to search all your images.

2. Type the text for which you want to search in the Search tool located in the bottom-right corner of the iPhoto window. As you type, the selected source is searched for the images with which the text you type is associated and they are shown in the Contents pane.

TIP

To clear the search, click the Clear button ("x") in the Search tool.

FINDING IMAGES BY DATE

You can quickly find images by their dates:

1. Select the source you want to search by clicking it in the Source pane. Select a photo album to search it, or select the Library to search all your images.

2. Click the Show Calendar pane. The Calendar pane will open (see Figure 21.7).

Figure 21.7
Use the Calendar pane to find images by date.

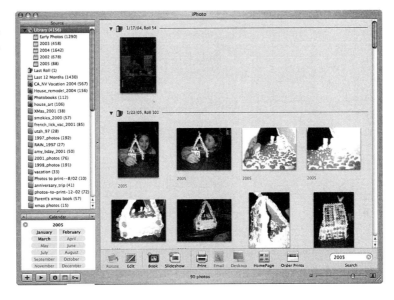

TIP

> Click the right-facing arrow at the top of the Calendar pane to change the view to a monthly view. You can select specific days to see images with which those dates are associated.

3. Use the Up and Down arrow buttons to show the year in which you are interested.

4. Click the months in which you are interested (hold down the Shift or ⌘ key to select multiple months). The images associated with those months will be shown in the Content pane.

TIP

> To clear the search, close the Calendar pane or click the Clear button ("x") in the pane.

FINDING IMAGES BY KEYWORDS

To find images by keywords, do the following:

1. Select the source you want to search by clicking it in the Source pane. Select a photo album to search it, or select the Library to search all your images.

2. Click the Keywords button to open the Keywords pane. You will see all the keywords you have configured (see Figure 21.8).

21

Figure 21.8
Use the Keywords pane to search for images.

3. Click the first keyword by which you want to search; the keyword will be highlighted in blue to show that it is currently being used. Only images with which that keyword has been associated will appear in the Content pane.

4. Hold down the ⌘ key and click the other keywords for which you want to search. When you select more than one keyword for a search, all those keywords must be associated with an image for it to be found. Only images with which all the selected keywords have been associated will be shown in the Content window.

5. To exclude photos associated with keywords, hold down the Option key and click it. It will become red and any photos with which the keyword is associated will be removed from the search results.

> **TIP**
>
> To clear the search, click the Reset keyword button.

ORGANIZING YOUR IMAGES WITH PHOTO ALBUMS

Photo albums are the tool you use to create collections of images for specific purposes, such as to view specific images or create slideshows, books, websites, and other projects. You can create albums containing the images you are interested in and then work with those images by selecting an album in the Source pane.

There are two types of albums: photo albums and smart photo albums.

> **TIP**
>
> You can resize the Source pane by dragging the Resize handle (the dot in the center of the bar between the Source and Content panes) to the left or right.

USING PHOTO ALBUMS

After you create a photo album, you manually place images into it. Here's how:

1. Click the New Album button located just below the Source pane; select File, New Album; or press ⌘-N. You will see the New Album sheet.

2. Choose Album on the pop-up menu.

3. Name your album and click Create. The album you create will appear in the Source pane.

4. Select the Library source and find the images you want to include in the new album; use the text, calendar, or keyword searching techniques you learned earlier in the chapter to do so.

5. Select the images you want to include in the album (select multiple images by holding down the ⌘ key), and drag them onto the new album in the Source pane. As you drag the images onto the album, a red circle containing a number appears—the number is the number of images you have selected.

6. Continue finding images and dragging them onto the album.

7. When you are done, select the album in the Source pane to see the images it contains in the Content pane.

Following are points to consider when you work with albums:

■ Placing images in an album does not remove them from the Library; the Library always contains all the images you have imported into iPhoto until you delete images and empty the Trash. When you drag an image onto an album, a pointer to the original image in the album is created.

■ You can create an album by dragging images from the Library or from other albums onto the Source pane. An album called untitled album is created; you can edit the album name by selecting it and pressing Return. When it is highlighted, change the name to what you want it to be.

■ You can place the same image in as many albums as you'd like. You can also place the same image in the same album multiple times.

■ When you select an album, you can select and then drag the images around in the Content pane to change their order. The order in which images appear in an album affects projects you create from that album. The first image in an album is the one in the upper-left corner of the Content pane, the second image is the one to the right, and so on to the end of the row. The first image in the next row is the next image and so on—left to right, top to bottom.

■ To remove an image from an album, select it and press the Delete key. The image will be removed from the album, but not from the Library.

■ Changes you make to an image in an album, such as associating keywords with it, editing it, or rotating it, *do* affect the image in all its locations, including in the Library.

21

USING SMART PHOTO ALBUMS

When you create a smart photo album, you define criteria for the images you want to be included in that album. Then, iPhoto places all the images that meet the criteria you have defined in the album for you. Follow these steps to create a smart photo album:

1. Select File, New Smart Album, or press Option-⌘-N. The Smart Album sheet will appear.

2. Name the album you are creating.

3. Choose the first condition on the first pop-up menu. There are many options, including Album, Any Text, Comments, Date, Filename, Keyword, My Rating, and so on. When you select a condition, the other pop-up menus will change so that they are applicable to the condition you selected.

4. Use the other pop-up menus, text boxes, and other tools to define the condition.

5. To add another condition, click the New Condition button (the "+" at the end of the condition's row).

6. Repeat steps 3 and 4 to configure the next condition.

7. Continue adding conditions until you have defined all of them for the smart album (see Figure 21.9).

Figure 21.9
This smart album will contain only images with all three of these keywords associated with them.

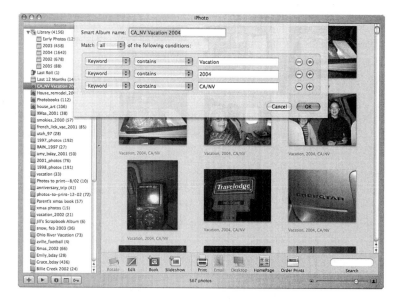

> **TIP**
>
> To remove a condition, click the Remove button (-) at the end of its row.

8. If you have defined more than one condition, choose "all" on the pop-up menu just below the smart album name box if you want all the conditions to be met for an image

to be included in the smart album. Otherwise, select "any" if only one condition must be met for an image to be added to the album.

9. Click OK. The smart album will be created and appear in the Source pane. iPhoto will place all the images that meet the album's conditions in it.

10. Select the new smart album to see the images it contains.

Unlike photo albums, you can't manually arrange images in a smart album. Use the View, Sort Photos command to change the order in which they appear in the album.

TIP

> To change the images in a smart album, you must edit its conditions. Open the smart album's contextual menu and select Edit Smart Album. Use the resulting sheet to make changes to the album's conditions. When you click OK, iPhoto will configure the images in the album based on the new conditions.

EDITING YOUR IMAGES

You can use iPhoto's Edit tools to make changes to your images. There are lots of editing tools you can use to make basic changes to your images, such as cropping them, to more sophisticated changes, such as exposure levels. Unfortunately, I don't have room to explain the details of using all these tools. In this section, you will get information about general editing steps and an overview of each editing tool.

EDITING A COPY OF THE ORIGINAL

When you edit an image, your changes affect *all* instances of that image in all your photo albums, in the Library, and wherever else that image is used within the application (such as in projects).

This is a problem if you want to have multiple versions of an image, say one cropped and one not cropped or one in black-and-white for a book and another in color for a slideshow. Fortunately, you can create duplicates of images. Each copy becomes a new, independent image just as if you had imported it again. You can create one copy for each version of the image you want to use in your projects.

You can create as many copies of an image as you'd like, but remember that each image consumes disk storage space. If you are going to use only one version, you don't need to duplicate it because iPhoto maintains the original version for you. But, if you do want to use multiple versions of the same image, select the images you want to duplicate and select Photos, Duplicate or press ⌘-D. You move into the Import mode temporarily and a copy of the images you selected will be created.

The copies have all the same information associated with them as the originals, such as keywords, dates, and so on. The only difference is that the word *copy* is appended to the images' titles.

21

NOTE

If an image you copy is in a smart album, the copy will be too because it is an exact copy. If you don't want the copy in a smart album, you'll have to change something about it so that it no longer meets the smart album's criteria.

CHOOSING EDITING OPTIONS

When you edit images within iPhoto, there are two basic ways the Edit window can be configured. Slight differences exist between the two ways, but they each work similarly.

One way is to edit images within the iPhoto window itself—this is the default configuration. When you use this configuration and double-click an image (or select it and click the Edit button), the image fills the Contents pane and the edit tools appear in the Tool pane (see Figure 21.10).

Figure 21.10
You can edit images within the main iPhoto window.

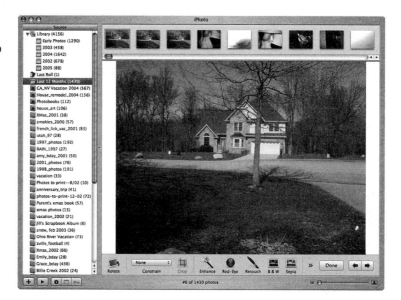

TIP

Along the top of the Editing window, you'll see thumbnails of the other images in the selected source. You can use the scrollbar to view all these. Click an image to move it into the Editing area.

The other way is to have the images you edit appear in a separate Edit window. To enable this method, open the General pane of the iPhoto Preferences dialog box and set the "Double-click photo" preference to "Opens photo in edit window." With this preference set, when you double-click an image, a new, separate Edit window appears (see Figure 21.11). You can use the editing tools that appear in the window's toolbar to edit the image.

Figure 21.11
You can also configure iPhoto so you can edit images in the Edit window.

TIP

One advantage of using the separate Edit window is that you can have multiple Edit windows at the same time. You will also see the image in a slightly larger window, which can be helpful for detailed editing.

Both methods are easy to use. I recommend that you configure the application to use the Edit window (by setting the "Opens photo in edit window" preference). When you want to use the Edit window, double-click the image you want to edit; it will open in the Edit window. When you want to edit an image within the iPhoto window, select the image and click the Edit button; the image will appear in the Edit view and you can edit it there.

NOTE

A third editing option is to use a different application to edit images, such as Photoshop. Set the "Double-click photo" preference to "Opens photo in" and use the Select Application button to choose the application you want to use. When you double-click an image, the editing application you selected will open and you can edit your image. When you save your changes, the edited image is stored in the Library.

SELECTING PARTS OF AN IMAGE YOU WANT TO EDIT

The Crop and Red-Eye editing tools require that you select the part of the image to which you want to apply the editing tool. When you select parts of an image, you have two basic choices: unconstrained or constrained. When you use the unconstrained option, you can select any part of the image. When you use the constrained option, you can only choose part of the image based a specific proportion.

21

You typically should use the constrained option when you crop images and the unconstrained option when you are applying the Red-Eye tool. To select part of an image using the unconstrained technique, do the following steps:

1. Open the image in the Edit window or select the image and click the Edit button.
2. Move the pointer over the image. The cursor becomes a plus sign.
3. Drag in the image. As you drag, a selection box appears and the part of the image you have selected remains clear while the part that is not selected becomes shaded.
4. When the part of the image you want is selected, release the mouse button.
5. To move the selection box around in the image, move the pointer inside the selection box. The pointer becomes a hand icon. Drag the selection box to the location that contains the part of the image you want to select.
6. To resize the selection box, drag one of its borders.

When you want to ensure that the part of the image you select has a specific proportion, you use the constrained option:

1. Open the image in the Edit window or select the image and click the Edit mode button.
2. On the Constrain pop-up menu, select the option you want, such as 4 x 3 (DVD).
3. Use steps 2–6 in the previous list to select part of the image. The only difference is that the selection box remains in the proportion you selected on the Constrain pop-up menu.

Zooming on Images for Editing

As you edit images, you need to zoom in and out to see the results of your changes. How you do this depends on the editing mode you are in.

When you use the "same window" editing mode, use the Thumbnail Size slider to zoom in or zoom out.

TIP

If you select part of the image before you zoom, iPhoto attempts to keep that part of the image centered on the screen as you zoom.

If you use the "separate window" option, use the Size pop-up menu to adjust the size of the image relative to the Edit window and then resize the Edit window to adjust the overall size.

Using iPhoto's Editing Tools

iPhoto includes a number of useful editing tools. Here's an overview of what each does:

- **Rotate**—This does the same thing as the Rotate button in the Organize mode. Each click rotates the image by 90°.

- **Crop**—Use this to get rid of parts of an image you don't want, to focus on a specific image, or to prepare an image to print at a specific size. Use the selection techniques you learned earlier to choose the part of the image you want to keep. When you click the Crop button, all the image outside of the selection box will be removed.

- **Enhance**—When an image doesn't look quite right, you can use the Enhance tool to enhance the image. This tool attempts to adjust colors and contrast so an image looks "better." You might be amazed at how well this tool works. Each time you click the button, another enhancement is done. You can enhance an image as many times as you'd like. At some point, the image will get worse instead of better. Use the Undo command to remove the last enhancement.

> **TIP**
>
> You can temporarily show the previous version of an image, such as the one prior to the last enhancement, by holding down the Control key. The image will appear as it was before your most recent change. When you release the key, the image will appear as you have edited it again. This is a good way to compare the editing you have done. To move back to this version, use the Undo command.

- **Red-Eye**—If you take photos of anything with eyes (for example, people or animals) in conditions where you use a flash, you have no doubt seen the dreaded demon eye effect that can sometimes occur. This red-eye can ruin an otherwise good photo. Use the Red-Eye tool to restore eyes to a more pleasing color. Select the portion of the image (such as a subject's eyes) from which you want to remove the red. When click the Red-Eye button, the red will be removed from that part of the image. Or, click the Red-Eye button and the click in the center of each eye; when you click an eye, the red will be removed.

- **Retouch**—The Retouch tool enables you to blend in scratches and other unwanted marks from a photo by blending the mark into the surrounding image. You have to use this one carefully because too much retouching becomes very obvious and has a detrimental effect on the image. Zoom in on the part of the image you want to retouch and click the Retouch button. Move the cursor—which will now be a crosshair—to the area you want to retouch. Press the mouse button down and move the pointer over the area you want to retouch. As you move the pointer, the area will be smudged so that the blemish is blended in with the surrounding area of the image.

- **B & W**—For some images, you might like the artistic look and feel of black-and-white. When you click the B & W button, the image you are editing will be converted into black and white.

- **Sepia**—Sepia tone is a common effect applied to images, especially to make them look old. To convert an image to Sepia tone, click the Sepia button.

- **Adjust**—This is by far the most sophisticated editing tool in iPhoto's arsenal. When you choose this, the Adjust tool will appear (see Figure 21.12). This tool contains a number of sliders you can use to configure specific aspects of the image, including Brightness, Contrast, Saturation, Temperature, Tint, Sharpness, Straighten, and

21

Exposure. You change these properties of the image by changing the values of each property using the related slider. As you make changes, you will see the results on the image you are editing.

NOTE

> You might see different properties in the Adjust palette of different Macs because the tools on the palette depend on how much processing power your Mac has.

Figure 21.12
Use the Adjust tool to control various technical aspects of an image.

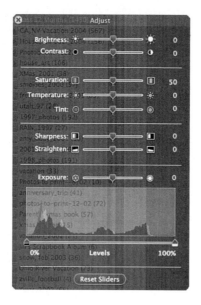

TIP

> You can return all the sliders in the Adjust tool to their default values by clicking the Reset Sliders button.

■ **Next/Previous**—Use these buttons to move to the next or the previous image in the selected source. This enables you to edit a series of images quickly.

When you have finished editing an image, click the Done button or close the Edit window. The changes you made to the image will be saved.

RESTORING AN IMAGE

One of the great things about iPhoto is that it maintains an original version of all the images you edit. If you make several kinds of edits, such as a crop followed by an enhancement and retouch, and then decide you really want the image back to the way it was before you improved it, you can easily recover the original version of the image.

CAUTION

> Just as when you edit an image, when you restore an image, that image is changed everywhere the image is used, such as in photo albums, books, and so on. Restoring an image to its original condition, just like editing an image, can have unintended results.

1. Select an edited image you want to restore to original. You can select it in a photo album, select in the Library, or display it in the Edit window.

2. Select Photos, Revert to Original. The image will be restored to the state it was in when you first imported it into iPhoto.

CREATING IPHOTO PROJECTS

After you have built, organized, and edited your images, you can use iPhoto's project tools to create all sorts of interesting projects.

The first step to any of these projects is to choose the images you want to work with. In most cases, you do this by creating an album you want to use for the project. In some cases, such as printing or emailing photos, you can select individual images.

Again, because of space limitations, I can't go into the details of each kind of project. In the following sections, you'll get an overview of each of iPhoto's project tools.

CREATING PHOTO BOOKS

You can use iPhoto's Book tool to create very nice books of your photos in various formats and styles. You can also choose to display a variety of information next to the photos in the book. After you have created a book, you can print it yourself or order a printed copy.

To get started, choose the source (such as a photo album) from which you want to create a book and click the Book button or select File, New Book. In the resulting sheet, choose the book type, theme, and whether it will be double-sided, and then click Choose Theme. You'll be prompted to indicate whether you want iPhoto to attempt to lay out your book automatically. Click Automatically to have iPhoto do it (you can always change it yourself) or Manually to skip iPhoto's help.

TIP

> You can get price information for various themes by clicking the Options + Prices button.

A new book will be created on the Source pane and iPhoto will move into Book mode. In Book mode, the Content pane contains a preview of the selected book page below thumbnails of each page in the book. The Tool pane contains the tools you use to build your book (see Figure 21.13). Use the Book tools to create the book you want. Then print it yourself or order a professionally bound version from Apple.

21

TIP

> You can also save a book in the PDF format so you can share it with others, such as by emailing it.

Figure 21.13
You can create custom photo albums in various formats and then print them, create PDFs to email, or order copies from Apple.

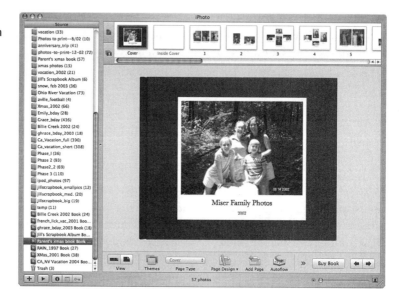

CONFIGURING AND VIEWING A SLIDESHOW

iPhoto slideshows are a great way to view images on your Mac. When you display your images in a slideshow, you can select music to accompany the images and configure various other aspects of the slideshow, such as how long the images appear on the screen. You can also save your settings so you can easily use them on other slideshows.

There are two ways to present images in a slideshow. You can create a "permanent" slideshow that you can view at any time in the future. Or, you can create and view a slideshow on-the-fly.

To get started for either technique, select the images you want to include in the slideshow, such as by selecting a photo album.

ON-THE-FLY SLIDESHOWS

Click the Play button that appears below the Source pane. You'll see the Slideshow window (see Figure 21.14). Use the controls on the Settings tab to configure various aspects of the slideshow, such as the transitions between images, the length of time each image appears on the screen, and so on. Use the controls on the Music tab to turn music on and choose music in your iTunes Library to play while the slideshow does. When you are ready to play the slideshow, click Play.

21

Figure 21.14
Use the Slideshows tool to configure your on-the-fly slideshows.

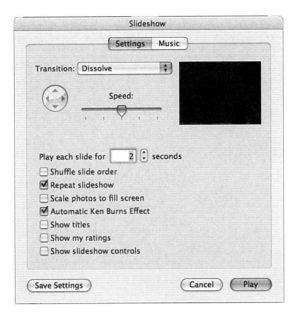

TIP

> If you click the Save Settings button, the slideshow settings will be saved for the selected source (for example, a photo album) and will be used each time you play a slideshow for that source.

CREATING A PERMANENT SLIDESHOW

To create a slideshow, click the Slideshow button. The images in the selected source will be placed into a new slideshow that will appear on the Source pane; the name of the slideshow will be the name of the source. iPhoto will move into Slideshow mode and you'll see the images in the selected source at the top of the window, the current image in the center of the window, and the tools you use to configure the slideshow in the toolbar (see Figure 21.15). Use the tools to configure the slideshow, such as to set transitions, choose music, and so on.

TIP

> After you have created them, you can drag images from other sources, such as other photo albums, onto a slideshow or photo book to add those images to the project.

PRINTING IMAGES AND BOOKS

Even using an inexpensive inkjet printer, you can print photos that are of very good quality. Printing photos from iPhoto is similar to printing documents from other applications (although the specific settings you use are more important because of their effect on the quality of the printed images).

21

Figure 21.15
You can use iPhoto's Slideshow tools to create sophisticated slideshows of your images.

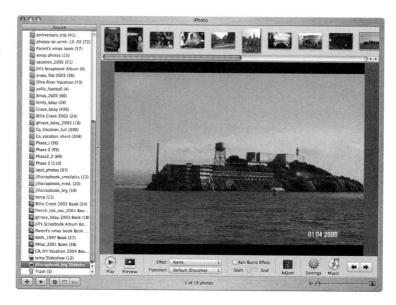

After you have selected the images you want to print, click the Print button or select File, Print. The Print sheet will appear (see Figure 21.16). Use its controls to configure the printing you will do, such as to choose the size of images you are going to print.

Figure 21.16
Use the iPhoto Print sheet to configure your print jobs.

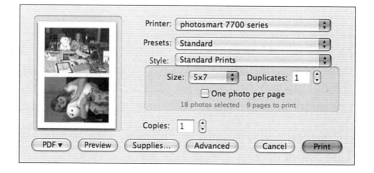

TIP

You can print photo books and slideshows, too. Of course, slideshows lose a lot in the translation.

EMAILING YOUR PHOTOS

Sending images to others via email is a great way to share your photos with others. First, you need to set the email application you want to use to send photos. Then you can send images with a single mouse click.

Use the "Email photos using" pop-up menu on the General pane of the iPhoto Preferences dialog box to select the email application you want to use to send your images. By default, Mail is selected, but you can choose any email application.

TIP

> When you send images, consider the connection the recipient uses to retrieve email. If the recipient uses a dial-up connection, be careful not to overload her connection with high-resolution images or even with a lot of low-resolution images. Even if the recipient uses a broadband connection, her email account might have a file size limit for attachments to email messages. If you want to transfer many images, consider posting them to a .Mac website instead.

After you have configured an email application, you can email images by selecting the images you want to send (unlike other projects, you have to select individual images rather than photo albums or other sources) and click the Email button. You'll see the Mail Photo dialog box (see Figure 21.17). Use the controls in the dialog box to configure the images, such as by choosing a size. Click Compose. A new email message will be created and the images will be included as attachments. Use the email application to address and send the email message.

Figure 21.17
Use this dialog box to configure images you are emailing to someone.

USING YOUR IPHOTO IMAGES ON THE DESKTOP AND AS A SCREENSAVER

You can easily add images in your iPhoto Library to your desktop. The images you add can be used both as the desktop image and as a screensaver. Select the images you want to use on the desktop, such as by selecting a photo album on the Source pane, and click the Desktop button. The Desktop tab of the Desktop & Screen Saver pane of the System Preferences application will open, and the images you selected will be shown as the iPhoto Selection source. Use the tools on this tab to configure how often the desktop image will change. Then click the Screen Saver pane and configure the same images as your screensaver.

→ To learn how to configure desktop images and a screensaver, **see** "Customizing the Mac OS X Desktop," **p. 135**.

21

CREATING A .MAC PHOTO HOMEPAGE

NOTE

You must have a .Mac account to publish an image web page.

→ To learn how to use .Mac, **see** Chapter 17, "Using .Mac to Integrate Your Mac onto the Internet," **p. 493**.

If you have a .Mac website, posting a group of images on that website is simple. Select the images you want to place on the Web (such as selecting an album on the Source pane). Click the HomePage button. Your Mac will connect to your .Mac account and you see the Publish HomePage dialog box (see Figure 21.18). Configure the web page using the tools in the dialog box and click Publish. The images you selected will be posted to a new web page on your .Mac website. When the process is complete, you'll see the URL along with buttons you can use to visit the page or edit it.

Figure 21.18
Using iPhoto's HomePage button, you can create a web page for your photos in mere seconds.

NOTE

You can't publish more than 48 images to a website at the same time.

On the web page you create with the HomePage tool, you can click an image or click the Start Slideshow button to display the images in a slideshow. In the resulting slideshow, you can click images to see larger versions in separate web browser windows.

ORDERING PRINTS AND BOOKS

Although most of us have an inkjet printer that is capable of printing fairly nice photos, printing photos can be a bit of a pain, and the results you get aren't always the best. Plus, if you want to share those photos with other people, you have to go through the hassle of mailing them, which might be enough to stop you from sharing them.

To save you the hassle of printing or mailing images, you can order prints from Apple (the prints are actually provided by Kodak). The first time you order prints, you use or create an Apple ID; after that, you can order prints with a single click by using the appropriately named 1-Click service.

NOTE

If you already have an Apple ID from the Apple Store or via the iTunes Music Store, you can use the same account to order prints.

Select the photos for which you want to order prints (such as by selecting an album). Click the Order Prints button to see the Order Prints dialog box (see Figure 21.19). Use the tools in this dialog box to configure and place your order.

Figure 21.19
The nicest thing about ordering prints is that they can be ordered and mailed right from your Mac.

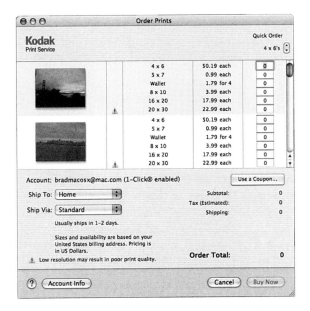

TIP

Using the Ship To pop-up menu, you can configure other people's addresses so you can send photos to them with just a couple of mouse clicks.

21

In the Order Prints dialog box, you see the cost of each size of print you can order. Most of these costs are quite reasonable when compared to the cost of the ink and paper required to print images on an inkjet printer. The shipping costs are also reasonable given that you don't have to do any work to get the order shipped anywhere you'd like. However, because ordering prints is so easy, you might find yourself going overboard the first time or two you order. So, before you click the Buy Now button, take a moment to double-check what you are ordering.

CAUTION

> If images in a group you select in an album or individually are low resolution, they have the low-resolution warning icon placed on them. This icon is a yellow triangle with an exclamation point inside it. An image with this icon might or might not print well in prints or in a book you order. Be cautious about including low-resolution images in your orders because you might be disappointed with the results you get. If you do want to print low-resolution images, print them in a smaller size to make them look as good as possible.

You can also order professionally printed and bound books by using the same service you use to order prints. The process is also similar to ordering prints of your photos. To get started, select the book you want to order and click the Buy Book button.

Be aware that ordering books is a relatively expensive proposition. Take plenty of time to design and check your book before you order it, unless you don't mind $40 "experiments."

CREATING A .MAC SLIDESHOW

You can publish a set of iPhoto images as a .Mac slideshow—this enables other people to use your slideshow as their screensavers. Select the images you want to publish (such as selecting a photo album on the Source pane). Click the .Mac Slides button or select Share, .Mac Slides. You will connect your .Mac account and see a prompt asking you to confirm that you want to publish a slideshow as .Mac slides. Click Publish. You'll see the .Mac Slides progress window as your slides are published. When the process is complete, you'll see a prompt that enables you to announce your slideshow or click OK to complete the process. After they have been published, others can choose them as a screensaver.

TIP

> The button for .Mac Slides is hidden by default. To show it, select Share, Show in Toolbar, .Mac Slides.

NOTE

You must have a .Mac account to publish iPhoto images for others to access.

→ To learn how to use .Mac, **see** Chapter 17, "Using .Mac to Integrate Your Mac onto the Internet," **p. 493**.

→ To learn how to subscribe to .Mac slides to use them as a screensaver, **see** "Customizing the Mac OS X Desktop," **p. 135**.

PUTTING IMAGES ON CD OR DVD

iPhoto makes putting images on CD or DVD easy. For example, you can back up your images on disc for safekeeping or perhaps to send those photos to someone else. Select the images and photo albums you want to put on a CD or DVD, such as selecting a photo album to put its images on a disc. Select Share, Burn Disc. You'll be prompted to insert a disc. Do so, and click OK. Follow the onscreen instructions to burn the disc.

TIP

You can add the Burn Disc button to the toolbar by selecting Share, Show in Toolbar, Burn Disc.

If you provide the disc you burned to someone who uses iPhoto, he can mount the disc and access the photos it contains from the iPhoto Source pane. For example, he can drag the images from the disc onto his Library to import them into his own iPhoto Library. The files can also be accessed directly from the Finder by opening the disc in a Finder window if the recipient doesn't have or use iPhoto. (Be aware that the somewhat confusing naming and hierarchy structure iPhoto uses to store images makes this process somewhat cumbersome. If the recipient doesn't use iPhoto, consider exporting the images and putting those on a disc instead.)

TIP

You can also send images to an iDVD project by selecting Share, Send to iDVD.

SHARING iPHOTO PHOTOS ON A NETWORK

Using iPhoto, you can make images in your Library available to others and can see images that are being shared with you. To configure image sharing, open the Sharing pane of the iPhoto Preferences dialog box (see Figure 21.20).

21

To cause iPhoto to look for images being shared on the network, check the "Look for shared photos" check box.

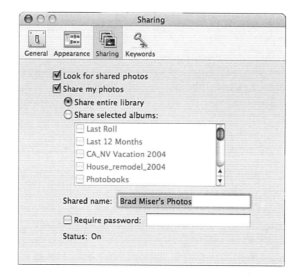

Figure 21.20
Use the Sharing pane to share photos with others and to look for photos being shared with you.

To share your photos, check the "Share my photos" check box. Then click "Share entire library" to share all your photos. Or, click "Share selected albums" and check the check box for each album you want to share. Name the photos you are sharing in the "Shared name" box; the default is the phrase "'s Photos" appended to your name. If you want people to have to enter a password before accessing your photos, check the "Require password" check box and enter the password in the box.

After you close the Preferences dialog box, your sharing preferences will take effect. For example, if you chose to look for shared photos, you'll see the shared items on the Source pane. You can select shared photos to view them. If you elected to share your photos, others on your network will be able to view them in the same way (assuming you remember to provide your password if you require one!).

After you have accessed shared photos, you can select the shared sources, such as a Library or photo albums, to view their contents. You can also copy images to your Library or photo albums by dragging them from the Content pane onto the location in which you want them. The Import process will start and the photos will be added to your Library and photo albums (if you drag them onto an album).

EXPORTING IMAGES FROM IPHOTO

There are various ways you can export images from iPhoto for different purposes. You can export images as separate files so you can work with them in other applications or to send those files to other people. Or you can export a set of images as a website. Another option is to export a set of images as a QuickTime movie.

Choose the images you want to export and then select Share, Export. Use the resulting dialog box to configure the export, such as by choosing the type and format options for the type you select (see Figure 21.21). After you configured the export, click Export to choose a save location and export the photos.

Figure 21.21
The three export options you have appear as tabs in the Export Photos dialog box.

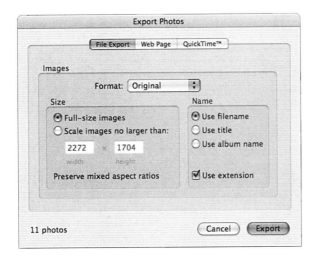

TROUBLESHOOTING

THE DIGITAL CAMERA IS NOT RECOGNIZED BY iPHOTO

When I connect a digital camera to my Mac, iPhoto doesn't recognize the camera, so I can't download images.

This situation occurs when Mac OS X does not support the camera you are using, most likely because your camera does not use PTP. In this case, you can obtain Mac OS X–compatible software for your camera and use that to download images. If your camera does not support PTP, you must use its own software to download images.

In some rare cases, a cable or hardware problem might exist. Use the Apple System Profiler to ensure that your Mac is capable of communicating with the camera.

→ To learn how to use the System Profiler, **see** "Using System Profiler to Create a System Profile," **p. 1050**.

MAC OS X TO THE MAX: GOING ALL OUT WITH iPHOTO KEYBOARD SHORTCUTS

Table 21.2 provides a list of some of the more useful iPhoto commands along with their keyboard shortcuts.

TABLE 21.2   USEFUL iPHOTO COMMANDS AND KEYBOARD SHORTCUTS

Menu	Command	Keyboard Shortcut
iPhoto	Preferences	⌘-,
File	New Album	⌘-N
File	Add to Library	⌘-O
File	New Album From Selection	Shift-⌘-N
File	New Smart Album	Option-⌘-N
Share	Export	Shift-⌘-E
Photos	Get Info	⌘-I
Photos	Duplicate	⌘-D
Photos	Revert to Original	None
Photos	Move to Trash	⌘-Delete
Photos	Batch Change	Shift-⌘-B
iPhoto	Empty Trash	Shift-⌘-Delete
Edit	Select All	⌘-A
Edit	Select None	Shift-⌘-A
Photos	Rotate Counterclockwise	⌘-R
Photos	Rotate Clockwise	Shift-⌘-R
Photos	My Rating, None	⌘-0
Photos	My Rating, 1 Star	⌘-1
Photos	My Rating, 2 Stars	⌘-2
Photos	My Rating, 3 Stars	⌘-3
Photos	My Rating, 4 Stars	⌘-4
Photos	My Rating, 5 Stars	⌘-5
View	Titles	Shift-⌘-T
View	Keywords	Shift-⌘-K
View	Film Rolls	Shift-⌘-F
Help	iPhoto Help	⌘-?

WORKING WITH OTHER MAC OS X IMAGE TOOLS

In this chapter

22

MAKING THE MOST OF DIGITAL IMAGES UNDER MAC OS X

As you learned in Chapter 21, "Creating, Editing, and Organizing Digital Images Using iPhoto," iPhoto is an amazingly powerful imaging application that is also easy to use. Even though iPhoto is certainly the application you are most likely to use to work with images, you should know that it isn't the only imaging application native to Mac OS X. Several imaging applications are part of the standard Mac OS X installation that might be useful to you, including Preview and Image Capture.

WORKING WITH PREVIEW

As its name implies, Preview's primary function is to let you preview (perhaps the application would be more accurately called View) documents. In the context of Preview, *documents* include many kinds of files, such as image files, PDFs, and many more. Although you can't make many changes in the documents you preview, Preview is useful for viewing a wide variety of documents.

NOTE

> Preview is Mac OS X's default PDF viewing application.

VIEWING IMAGES IN PREVIEW

Many of the image file types you commonly use under Mac OS X are configured to open in Preview by default.

NOTE

> Preview might not be the default application for viewing image, PDF, or other files. If not, you can open any image file by first opening Preview and then using the Open command, or by setting Preview to be the application associated with a specific image file.

→ To learn how to associate files with an application, **see** "Determining the Application That Opens When You Open a Document," **p. 201**.

To open and view images in Preview, use the following steps:

1. Open an image file. Preview will open and you will see the image in the Preview window (see Figure 22.1). If the image doesn't fill the Preview window, you'll see gray borders around it.

TIP

> If an application other than Preview opens when you open an image file, open the file's contextual menu and select Open With, Preview.

Figure 22.1
Perhaps Preview
would be better
named View because
you use it to view
images and other
documents.

2. Use the tools in the toolbar to control how the images appear, such as the Zoom In button to make the image larger.

> **TIP**
>
> To zoom in on part of an image, select the part on which you want to zoom and select View, Zoom to Selection (or press ⌘-*). To remove the selection box, click the image outside of the box.

Many of Preview's commands are straightforward, such as the Zoom To Fit command that sizes the current image so it fills the Preview window. If you have used any graphics application, you won't have any trouble with these basic viewing commands.

Preview also features a Drawer that is useful when you are working with more than one image at a time. To try this, select several image files and open them at the same time. When you do this, Preview's Drawer will open and you will see thumbnails of each image you opened (see Figure 22.2). Select an image's thumbnail to view it in the Preview window.

> **NOTE**
>
> If you open images one-at-a-time, a Preview window will open for each image file.

You can open and close the Drawer by clicking the Drawer button on the toolbar; by selecting View, Drawer; or by pressing ⌘-T.

Figure 22.2
Preview's Drawer makes viewing multiple images easy.

> **TIP**
>
> You can customize Preview's toolbar just like you can in many other Mac OS X applications, including the Finder.

USING PREVIEW TO CROP AN IMAGE

Cropping is one of the most basic and useful image editing options. Fortunately, you can use Preview to easily crop images, as you can see in the following steps:

1. Open the image you want to crop.

2. Drag in the image to select the portion of the image you want to keep (see Figure 22.3). As you select part of the image, the part that is not selected will be darkened.

3. To adjust the selected part of the image, drag the selection box around or resize it by either dragging a corner or dragging the resize handle located in the center of each side of the selection box.

> **TIP**
>
> To keep the selection box proportional to the original image, hold down the Shift key while you drag.

4. When you have the part of the image you want to keep selected, select Tools, Crop or press ⌘-K. All the image outside of the selection box will be removed.

Figure 22.3
Select the portion of the image you want to keep before you use the Crop command.

TIP

You can move to back to the most recently saved version of an image by selecting File, Revert.

USING PREVIEW TO READ PDFS

Portable Document Format (PDF) files are a common way to distribute electronic documents. You are likely to encounter many PDFs on the Web, as file attachments to emails, and so on. Preview is Mac OS X's default PDF viewer.

→ You can create your own PDF documents. To learn how, **see** "Saving Documents As PDFs," **p. 210**.

To view PDFs with Preview, do the following:

1. Open a PDF document in Preview.

2. Open Preview's Drawer. You'll see a thumbnail of each page in the document (see Figure 22.4).

NOTE

Some of the features depend on how a PDF was created. For example, if the PDF was created with a linked table of contents, you will see buttons that enable you to choose to view thumbnails or topics. Both views work similarly in that you click what you want to see.

Figure 22.4
You can click a page's thumbnail in the Preview Drawer to jump to that page.

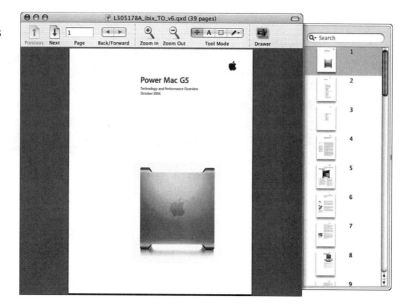

3. Click a thumbnail to move to a specific page, or type the page number in the Page box on the toolbar.

4. Move to pages one at a time by clicking the Next or Previous button in the toolbar or by pressing the Down or Up arrow keys.

5. Adjust the display of a PDF document by using the commands shown when you select View, PDF Display. The options include Singles Pages, which shows the document page-by-age; Facing Pages, which shows two pages at a time; and so on.

6. You can annotate a PDF, such as to make comments or highlight parts of it, by selecting Tools, Annotate Tool. Then you choose the tool you want to use by selecting Tools, Text Annotation (this enables you to add text annotations to the document) or Tools, Oval Annotation (this enables you to draw ovals to highlight parts of a PDF). You can use both types of tools on the same page, and you can include multiple annotations on the same page (see Figure 22.5).

7. To move around inside a document, select Tools, Scroll Tool (or press ⌘-1). The cursor will become the hand and you can drag around a page to move it within the Preview window (unless the entire page fills the window, in which case you can't do this).

8. To select text so you can copy and paste it into other documents, select Tools, Text Tool or press ⌘-2. Select the text you want to copy and select Edit, Copy. The text will be moved to the Clipboard, from which you can paste it into other documents, such as TextEdit.

9. To select parts of a page using a selection box, select Tools, Select Tool or press ⌘-3. Drag on the page to select part of it. You can then copy that part and paste it into other documents. To remove the selection box, press Esc or click outside the selection box.

Figure 22.5
You can annotate PDF documents using Preview's Annotation tools.

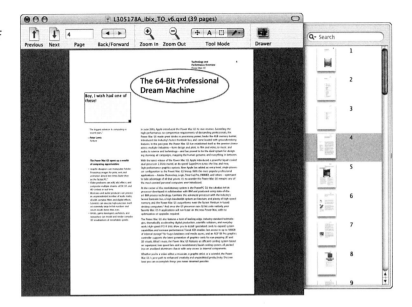

TIP

You can select any of these tools by clicking the appropriate button on the Tool Mode button that is part of the default Preview toolbar.

10. To add a bookmark to a PDF, move to the location at which you want to set a bookmark and select Bookmarks, Add Bookmark or press ⌘-D. In the resulting sheet, name the bookmark and click Add. You can return to this point in the document at any time by selecting it on the Bookmarks menu.

11. To search a PDF document, type the text for which you want to search in the Search box that appears at the top of the Drawer. As you type, Preview will search the document for your search text. When it finds the first instance, the page on which it appears will be shown and an oval will be drawn around the occurrence. After a second or so, the oval disappears, but the search term remains shaded so you can easily see it. In the Drawer, each occurrence of the search term appears on the list of results (at the top of the list, you will see how many occurrences there are in the document). When you click an occurrence, the page on which it appears is shown in the Preview window and the search term is highlighted on the page.

12. If you made annotations to the document, save it before you close it.

VIEWING A SLIDESHOW IN PREVIEW

iPhoto, iDVD, and iMovie can be used to create slideshows. Although not nearly as sophisticated as those applications, you can create a basic slideshow in Preview by performing the following steps:

22

1. Use Preview to open the image files you want to view in a slideshow.

2. Select View, Slideshow or press Shift-⌘-F. The Preview interface will disappear and the images will be displayed as a slideshow.

3. Move the mouse and a set of controls will appear at the bottom of the screen (see Figure 22.6). From left to right, the buttons are

   - **Back**—Moves the slideshow back one image
   - **Pause/Play**—Pauses or plays the slideshow
   - **Next**—Moves to the next image
   - **Index Sheet**—Displays thumbnails of each image so you can click one to move to that image
   - **Fit to Screen/Actual Size**—Adjusts the size of the image to fill the screen or be the actual size
   - **Close**—Stops the slideshow

Figure 22.6
Preview's slideshows aren't fancy, but they are a quick way to view a batch of images.

4. Use the appropriate buttons to control the slideshow.

5. When you are done, click the Close button or press Esc. You will moved back to the standard Preview window.

TIP

You can create a slideshow from the Finder by using Spotlight to search for image files. Click Show All in the Images section to display all the image files. Select the images you want to include in the slideshow and open the contextual menu. Select Slideshow and then use the tools that appear to control the slideshow. This works just like a slideshow you create in Preview.

USING PREVIEW TO CONVERT FILES TO DIFFERENT FORMATS

One of the nice things Preview does for you is enables you to convert an image from one format to another. Here's how:

1. Open the image you want to save in a different format.
2. Select File, Save As. The Save As sheet will appear.
3. Select the file format in which you want to save the file in the Format pop-up menu (see Figure 22.7).

Figure 22.7
One of Preview's most useful functions it its ability to convert image files to different formats.

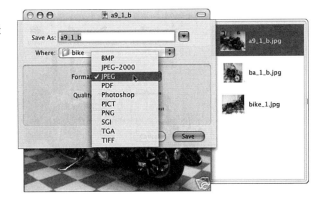

4. If the format you selected has options, use the slider, check boxes, or other controls to configure its settings.
5. Rename the file, choose a save location, and then click Save. A new file in the format you selected will be created.

OTHER USEFUL PREVIEW FUNCTIONS

You might find three other Preview functions to be useful:

- **Get Info**—Use this command (select Tools, Get Info or press ⌘-I) to get detailed information about an image. When you do this, you'll see the Document Info window, which has three tabs. Use the Summary tab to get high-level information, including its type, file size, resolution, and so on. Use the Details tab to view more detailed specifications, such as color model, color depth, and so forth. Use the Keywords tab to associate keywords with an image; you can use Spotlight or a smart folder to search for the keywords you associate with an image.

- **My Rating**—To rate an image, select Tools, My Rating, and then choose the number of stars at which you want to rate the image. You can use this rating in other applications or to search for images with specific ratings using Spotlight or smart folders.

- **Image Correction**—You can change many aspects of an image, such as its brightness, sharpness, and so on, by selecting Tools, Image Correction. Use the controls in the resulting window to configure specific aspects of the image (see Figure 22.8).

22

Figure 22.8
The powerful, but somewhat hidden, Image Correction tool enables you to configure many aspects of an image.

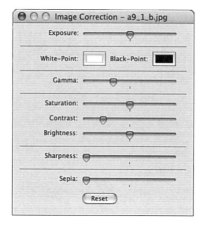

SETTING PREVIEW PREFERENCES

You can configure several Preview preferences to tweak Preview to suit your needs. These options are summarized in Table 22.1.

TABLE 22.1	PREVIEW PREFERENCES	
Tab	**Preference**	**What It Does**
General	Thumbnail size slider	Sets the size of thumbnails shown in the Drawer.
General	Window background color	Sets the color of the area outside an image in the Preview window (the default is gray).
Images	When opening images: Open all images in one window	No matter how you open images (one at a time or many at once), they all appear in the same window and you can use the Drawer to work with them.
Images	When opening images: Open groups of images in the same window	When you open multiple images at the same time, they all appear in the same window and you can use the Drawer to work with them.
Images	When opening images: Open each image in its own window	No matter how many images you open at once, they each appear in a separate Preview window.
Images	Default image size: Actual size	Opens images at their default sizes.
Images	Default image size: Scale large images to fit window	Automatically zooms out in large images so the entire image is displayed in the Preview window.
Images	Default image size: Scale up small images to fit window	Automatically zooms in for small images so the image fills the entire Preview window; you can choose this only when "Scale large images to fit window" is selected

Tab	Preference	What It Does
Images	Respect image DPI for Actual Size	This causes the Actual Size command to take the image's resolution into account when resizing it.
PDF	Default document scale	Choose auto-scale to use the default size settings stored in the PDF file; choose Use scale of and enter a value to cause Preview to use the scale value you enter when you open a PDF.
PDF	Remember last page viewed	Causes Preview to display the page you last viewed when you open a document.
PDF	Greeking threshold	Sets the size at which greeking is used to display text; this is done when text becomes too small to be displayed legibly and instead is replaced by symbols that look like Greek.
PDF	Anti-alias text and line art	When checked, Preview will smooth out text and art through antialiasing it.
PDF	Open drawer only for Table of Contents	Causes Preview to open the Drawer only when a PDF has a table of contents element included in it.
Bookmarks	Remove	This pane shows all the bookmarks that have been created using Preview; for each, the label, file, and page are shown. Select a bookmark and click Remove to delete it from the document in which it was created.
Color	Preferred CMM	Use the pop-up menu to choose the Color Management Model that should be used for an image; your choices will depend on how the image was created. Select Automatic to have Preview choose the model it sees as best or is the default for an image.

WORKING WITH IMAGE CAPTURE

Mac OS X was designed to work with digital images; it includes the basic Image Capture application that provides a consistent interface for various models of digital cameras. Its single purpose is to download images from digital devices (cameras, scanners, and so on) to your Mac. When you are working with a digital camera, you are more likely to use iPhoto to download images because it has more powerful tools and enables you to build and organize your image library. Still, Image Capture has a few tricks up its sleeves and might be the best way to scan images.

22

Image Capture works with devices that support the Picture Transfer Protocol (PTP). If you aren't sure whether your device supports this protocol, check the manufacturer's website and product specifications to see whether your particular model supports PTP. Fortunately, almost all modern digital imaging devices do.

NOTE

The more technical name for PTP is ISO 22740.

Image Capture can be configured so it automatically downloads images when you plug your camera or scanner into your Mac. By default, Mac OS X is configured to open iPhoto when it detects a camera. You can change this behavior with the Image Capture Preferences command.

NOTE

Image Capture works pretty much the same way, whether you are downloading images from a scanner or a camera. However, your best bet is to use iPhoto to download images from your camera so you have all its photo-related tools at your fingertips.

USING IMAGE CAPTURE TO DOWNLOAD IMAGES FROM A CAMERA TO YOUR MAC

If you don't have iPhoto installed on your Mac (perhaps you don't want to purchase the iLife software), you can use Image Capture to download images from a camera to your Mac so you can work with them, such as viewing them or creating a simple slideshow in Preview. Use the following steps to get images from a camera to your Mac:

1. Connect your camera to your Mac using its USB cable.

NOTE

If iPhoto is installed on your Mac, by default your Mac opens iPhoto when you connect a camera to it. You can allow that to happen and then open Image Capture. Both applications can be running at the same time.

2. Power up your camera (if it has a mode selector to communicate with a computer, choose that mode—most cameras switch to this mode automatically). If you haven't configured Image Capture to open automatically, open it (Applications folder). If you have configured Image Capture to open automatically, it will do so when your Mac detects the camera. You will see the Image Capture window (see Figure 22.9). The application communicates with the camera to determine how many images need to be downloaded. When the camera is ready to begin downloading images, the Download Some and Download All buttons become active.

Figure 22.9
When you connect a supported camera to your Mac, Image Capture displays the number of images that are ready to be downloaded (and you might even see an image of the camera, as is the case for this Canon PowerShot S410).

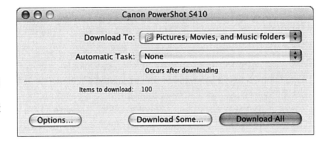

> **NOTE**
> If your camera is not recognized by Image Capture, it probably does not support PTP. In that case, you have to use the camera's software to download images from it.

3. Select the folder into which you want the images to be downloaded on the Download To pop-up menu. By default, Image Capture selects the Pictures, Movies, and Music folders option. You can select Other on the menu to choose a different folder to which to save images instead.

4. To download all the images on the camera, click Download All. The images you download are downloaded into the appropriate directories in your Home folder or in the folder you selected on the Download To pop-up menu. For example, photos are downloaded to the Pictures directory. As the images are downloaded, you see a progress dialog box that shows you a preview of the images being downloaded (see Figure 22.10). When the application is done downloading images, it moves to the background and the directories into which it downloaded images are opened.

Figure 22.10
As Image Capture downloads your photos, you see a preview of each image it is downloading.

5. Move to the appropriate folder to work with the image files you have downloaded.

> **NOTE**
> Notice that the default download folders are Pictures, Movies, and Music. Some cameras can capture movies and sound. If your camera has QuickTime movies on it, those are placed in the Movies directory in your Home directory. Likewise, sounds are placed in the Music directory.

If Image Capture does not recognize your camera, see "The Digital Camera Is Not Recognized by Image Capture" in the "Troubleshooting" section at the end of this chapter.

TIP

> When you connect a camera, the Options button in the Image Capture window becomes active. You can use this feature to configure various aspects of how your camera interacts with your Mac. For example, you can set the camera's time and date, cause images to be automatically deleted after they are downloaded, and so on.

To download only selected images, use the following steps:

1. Connect your camera and open Image Capture.

2. After the application is ready to begin downloading images, click Download Some. You will see a window that shows a preview of each image stored in the camera (see Figure 22.11). By default, the window appears in the Icon view.

Figure 22.11
You can use the preview window to select images to download; you can also rotate images or delete them.

3. Click the List View button or select View, as List to see the images in the List view. In this view, you see the images in a Finder-like window. You will see a lot of information for each image, including its name, file size, date and time of capture, width and height in pixels, and so on.

NOTE

> You can change the width of the columns in the List view; however, you can't change the sort order—the window is always sorted by image number.

4. Return the window to the Icon view by clicking the Icon view button or by selecting View, as Icons.

5. If you need to rotate images, select the images you want to rotate and click the Rotate Left or Rotate Right button.

6. Select the folders into which you want to download the images on the Download folder pop-up menu. The default is the same as when you download all images, but you can change it to be any folder you'd like to use.

7. Select the images you want to download (use the Shift key or ⌘ key to select multiple images) and click Download. The images are downloaded into the selected directory.

> **TIP**
>
> You can connect multiple cameras to your Mac at the same time. To choose the one with which you want to work, use the Camera pop-up menu.

CHOOSING IMAGE CAPTURE OPTIONS

Image Capture has other options that are useful:

- **Automatic Task**—You can attach AppleScripts to Image Capture so it performs an action you select from the Automatic Task pop-up menu when you download images. A number of actions are on the menu by default, including Build Web Page, Build Slide Show, Crop to 3×5, and so on. You can use any of these tasks or add your own. To add a task to the menu, place it in the `Mac OS X/System/Library/Image Capture/Automatic Tasks` directory, where `Mac OS X` is the name of your Mac OS X startup volume.

- **Options dialog box**—If you click the Options button in the Image Capture window, you will see a sheet that contains two tabs. The Options tab enables you to configure how downloads are handled, such as whether all images are downloaded automatically or whether images are deleted from the camera after they are downloaded. The Information tab displays information about the device you are using, such as the type of camera and the application your Mac is using to interface with it. If you use Image Capture regularly, you should explore these options.

> **NOTE**
>
> Image Capture downloads only those images that aren't already in the selected directory. So, you won't get duplicate files if you have previously downloaded images on the camera and then perform another download with new images.

SETTING IMAGE CAPTURE PREFERENCES

If you use Image Capture to download images from a camera or a scanner, you should configure it to suit your preferences.

N O T E

> Although the Image Capture Preferences is accessed via the Image Capture application, what you choose here affects other applications. For example, you must use this preference to set the application that opens automatically when you connect a camera to your Mac. This is because Image Capture provides the basic framework your Mac uses to interact with cameras and scanners regardless of the specific application you use.

To set your image handling preferences, perform the following steps:

1. Select Image Capture, Preferences. The Image Capture Preferences dialog box will open.

2. On the General tab, select Image Capture (if iPhoto is installed on your Mac, it is selected by default) on the pop-up menu to have your Mac open Image Capture when it detects that a camera is connected to it.

T I P

> If you want an application other than Image Capture or iPhoto to open when you connect a digital camera, select Other and select the application you want to open automatically.

3. If you want to use Image Capture with a scanner, check the "When Image Capture is launched, open scanner window" check box.

4. Close the Preferences window.

SHARING IMAGING DEVICES ON A NETWORK OR VIA THE WEB

With Mac OS X, you can share imaging devices on a network or over the Web. This enables others to access devices connected to your Mac and you to access devices others are sharing.

→ To learn how to configure web sharing, **see** "Mac OS X to the Max: Using Mac OS X to Serve Web Pages," **p. 514**.

→ To configure a local network, **see** Chapter 33, "Building and Using a Network," **p. 935**.

SHARING A CAMERA OVER A NETWORK OR THE WEB

To share a device connected to your Mac with a network, use the following steps:

1. Open Image Capture; then select Image Capture, Preferences.

2. In the Preferences dialog box, click the Sharing tab (see Figure 22.12).

Figure 22.12
Using the Image
Capture Preferences
Sharing tab, you can
share a digital camera
or other device with
those on your net-
work or via the Web.

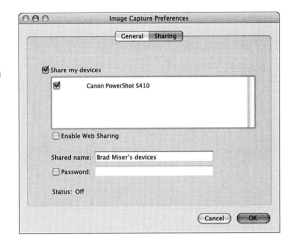

3. Check the "Share my devices" check box. In the pane just below that, you will see all the devices that are available for sharing, such as a digital camera or scanner.

4. Check the check box next to each device you want to share.

5. If you want to enable devices to be shared over the Web, check the "Enable Web Sharing" check box.

6. Provide a name for the devices in the Shared name box. This is the name people who access the device will see.

7. If you want to require a password to be entered to access the device, check the Password check box and enter a password in the Password field.

8. Click OK. The device will be shared.

CAUTION

> For a device to be shared over a network, the computer to which it is connected must be on the same subnet as the computer trying to access it. For small networks, this is not an issue. However, if you are using a large network, make sure the machines are on the same subnet because sharing will not work if they aren't. Of course, you can use web sharing to share a device regardless of the subnet.

ACCESSING A SHARED CAMERA

There are two basic ways to access devices that have been shared: via a local network or over the Web. The method you use depends on how the device has been shared with you.

To access a device that has been shared with you over a network, use the following steps:

1. Open Image Capture.

2. Select Devices, Browse Devices. You'll see the Image Capture Devices window.

3. Expand the Remote Image Capture devices section. You'll see a list of all the machines that are currently sharing imaging devices over the network.

4. Expand the section for the computer containing the imaging device you want to share.

5. Select the specific imaging device you want to access (see Figure 22.13).

Figure 22.13
The Canon PowerShot
S410 is physically
connected to another
computer on a
network.

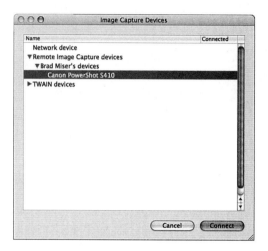

6. Click Connect. The same Image Capture window will appear as does when a device is physically connected to your computer.

7. Use the Image Capture tools to download images from the device. These work in exactly the same way as they do when a device is connected to your Mac.

You can also access a device that has been shared with you over the Web by doing the following:

1. Launch Safari.

NOTE

For Bonjour devices to be available in Safari, you must turn on that preference in the Bookmarks pane of the Safari Preferences dialog box.

→ To learn how to configure Safari to access Bonjour services, **see** "Browsing the Web with Safari," **p. 460**.

2. Select Bookmarks, Bonjour, *devicename*, where *devicename* is the name of the device you want to access. Your Mac connects to the device and you see its contents in a web page called "Digital Cameras on *machinename*", where *machinename* is the name of the Mac sharing the camera, assuming the device is a camera of course (see Figure 22.14).

TIP

If more than one device is being shared with you, select the device you want to work with on the Camera pop-up menu.

Figure 22.14
This web page shows the contents of a camera being shared over the Web.

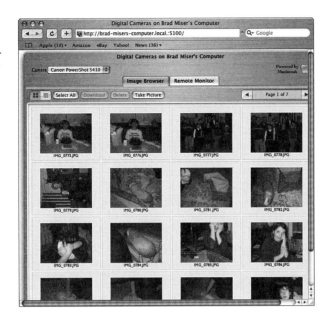

3. Use the Browse arrows to view each page of content being provided by the device.

4. To download images to your Mac, select them and click Download.

Accessing a camera over the Web offers many cool features, including the following:

- Click the List View button to view the page as a list instead of with icons.

- To select all the images on the device, click Select All.

- You can delete images from the shared device by selecting them and clicking Delete.

- To take picture with the shared device, click Take Picture. The camera takes a picture. To see the new picture, refresh the web page by selecting View, Reload Page (or by pressing ⌘-R).

- You can view a larger version of an image by double-clicking it. To return to the thumbnail views, click the Return button (it is an upward-pointing, curved arrow). You can browse through all the images at the large size by using the Browse arrows.

USING DEVICE SHARING TO MONITOR AN AREA

If you want to feel like Big Brother, you can use a shared device to monitor an area remotely. You can set the remote device to capture an image periodically and display that image on a website. Here's how:

1. Set up the camera so it captures the image you want to be able to monitor, such as a doorway into a room or some other part of a room.

NOTE

> For this to work, the imaging device must support image capture while it is in computer mode. Some devices can't capture images and communicate with other devices at the same time. To find out whether yours can, set it in image capture mode and open Image Capture. If no imaging devices are found, you won't be able to use this feature.

2. Share the camera over the Web.

3. Access the shared camera (see the previous section for details).

4. Click the Remote Monitor tab. The camera takes a picture and transfers it to the web page; to see the results immediately, reload the page. Just below the tab is the time at which the image was last updated and the time at which it will be updated again.

NOTE

> Images capture via Remote Monitoring are not stored on the camera; they are only displayed. You can capture an image and store it on a camera by clicking the Take Picture button.

The camera keeps taking pictures at the set interval and displaying them on the web page. This enables you to see what is happening in an area over time.

TIP

> By default, a new image is captured every 60 seconds. To change this, click the Preferences button located just under the Remote Monitor tab. Enter the interval at which you want images to be captured and click Set. Setting a shorter interval provides more active monitoring.

CAPTURING SCREEN IMAGES

In many instances, capturing an image of what is happening on your Mac's screen is useful. One example is if you are writing instructions about how to do a particular task, such as when you are writing your own book about Mac OS X. Another is when you want to capture an error message or some other anomaly you want to be able to explain to someone (for example, you might want to capture the image of an error dialog box so you can email it when you try to get technical support).

With Mac OS X, you have two built-in ways to capture screen images. One is to use keyboard commands. The other is to use the Grab application.

CAPTURING SCREEN IMAGES WITH KEYBOARD SHORTCUTS

Mac OS X includes keyboard commands you can use to capture desktop images. After you capture an image, it is stored on your desktop as a Portable Network Graphis (PNG) file and is called Picture X.png, where X is a sequential number. You have the following three options:

- Shift-⌘-3 captures the entire desktop.
- Shift-⌘-4 changes the pointer to a plus sign. Drag this pointer to select the part of the screen you want to capture. When you release the mouse button, an image of the selected area is captured.
- Shift-⌘-4-spacebar enables you to capture a window, menu bar, Dock, or other area of the screen. First, open the area you want to capture, such as a window or menu. When you press the key combination, a large camera pointer icon appears. Move this icon over the area that you want to capture, which becomes highlighted. Click the mouse button to capture the image.

> **TIP**
>
> To choose not to capture an image after you have pressed these key combinations, press Escape. If you want to save an image to the Clipboard so you can easily paste it into a document, hold down Control while you press the keys for the kind of screenshot you want to take.

CAPTURING SCREEN IMAGES WITH GRAB

Mac OS X includes the Grab application. As its name implies, using Grab, you can "grab" an image of your Mac's desktop. There are several options you can use to capture a specific image. To capture a desktop image, follow these steps:

1. Open Grab (Applications/Utilities).
2. Select the Capture mode you want for your screenshot using the Capture menu. Your options are as follows:
   - Selection captures an area of the screen you select.
   - Window captures the active window.
   - Screen captures the entire screen.
   - Timed Screen provides a timer so you can set up a screen before it is captured (so you have time to switch to a window and open a menu before the image is captured, for example).
3. Follow the instructions you see. For example, if you select Timed Screen, the Timed Screen Grab dialog box appears. Then open the area you want to capture, such as a document window with a menu open. When you are ready to take the shot, click Start Timer in the Timed Screen Grab dialog box and get the window as you want it to be captured. After 10 seconds have passed, Capture captures the image.

   When the capture is complete, you see a new window containing the image you captured.
4. To see the size of the image you captured and its color depth, select Inspector from the Edit menu or press ⌘-1. The Inspector window appears and you see information about the image.
5. Save the image. Grab's default file format is TIFF.

The images you capture with Grab are just like images you create in other ways. You can open them in image-editing applications, preview them in Preview, print them, and so on.

TIP

> Grab's capturing capabilities are provided to the OS so that other applications can use them. For example, if you are working in a Carbon or Cocoa application, you can easily grab an image of its screen by selecting the Services command from that application's menu. Then, select Grab and select the type of grab from the menu. When you release the mouse button, the image you captured is displayed. How it is displayed depends on the application from which you captured it. For example, if you grab an image while you are using TextEdit, a Rich Text Format (RTF) file is created. If you grab an image while using Preview, that image appears in the Pasteboard window.

TROUBLESHOOTING

THE DIGITAL CAMERA IS NOT RECOGNIZED BY IMAGE CAPTURE

When I connect a digital camera to my Mac, Image Capture doesn't recognize the camera, so I can't download images.

The most likely cause of this is that Mac OS X does not support the camera you are using, probably because your camera does not use PTP. In this case, you can try to obtain Mac OS X–compatible software for your camera and use that to download images. You will probably have to use software that came with the camera to download its images to your Mac.

In rare cases, a cable or hardware problem might exist. Use the Apple System Profiler to ensure that your Mac is capable of communicating with the camera.

→ To learn about the System Profiler, **see** "Using System Profiler to Create a System Profile," **p. 1050**.

MAC OS X TO THE MAX: MASTERING SCREEN CAPTURES WITH SNAPZ PRO X

Mac OS X's built-in screen capture capabilities work fairly well, but if you are serious about capturing screen images, you simply must use Ambrosia Software's Snapz Pro X. This utility enables you to capture screen images in any way and in any file format. You can also use its QuickTime option to record QuickTime movies of actions you perform, such as if you want to create a QuickTime movie of the steps you use to perform a specific task.

NOTE

> In case you are wondering, all the screen images in this book were captured with Snapz Pro X, except the image of Snapz Pro X itself that appears in this section.

NOTE   You can get information about and download Snapz Pro X at www.ambrosiasw.com.

After you download and install Snapz Pro X, using it to capture images is, well, a snap:

1. Activate the application by pressing the default keyboard shortcut, which is Shift-⌘-3.

NOTE   By default, Snapz Pro X replaces the default Mac OS X screen capture keyboard shortcut. That's okay because after you use Snapz Pro X, it is likely that you won't ever use the built-in utility again.

2. In the resulting window, select the option for the type of image you want to capture, such as Screen to capture the entire screen (see Figure 22.15).

Figure 22.15
Don't let this simple window fool you; Snapz Pro X is a very powerful application.

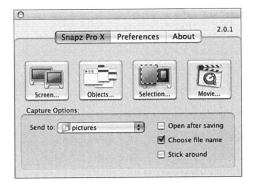

3. Use the Object Settings dialog box to configure the capture, such as by choosing whether you want the cursor to be captured as part of the image.

4. Click the image to capture it.

Snapz Pro X has many preferences and options you can use to configure it to work exactly how you want it to, such as choosing filenames, the file format to use, and so on. Take my word for it—if you capture screen images, try Snapz Pro X. Fortunately, you can download and try it for free so it won't cost you more than a few minutes of time to give it a spin. You won't be sorry if you do.

CHAPTER **23**

VIEWING QUICKTIME MOVIES

In this chapter

23

UNDERSTANDING QUICKTIME AND QUICKTIME PRO

Apple's QuickTime is the technology your Mac uses to handle dynamic data. *Dynamic data* simply means data that changes over time. This includes video, audio, and other such media. In fact, QuickTime technology and the QuickTime framework enable all the iLife applications along with many other functionality Mac OS X users enjoy. Without QuickTime, using Mac OS X wouldn't be nearly as interesting as it is.

Under Mac OS X, except for viewing QuickTime movies on your computer and on the Web, you likely won't deal with QuickTime directly very often. But, in addition to knowing how to handle those tasks, you should have a good understanding of the QuickTime technology.

Since its introduction, Apple's QuickTime has been one of the most successful multimedia standards on any platform. In fact, it has been so successful that it is also widely used on Windows computers; QuickTime movies on Windows play the same way they do on the Mac. QuickTime has also been widely adopted on the Web, with many websites serving video and animation files as QuickTime movies.

Although you are most likely to encounter QuickTime movies on the Web, you will encounter them in many other places, including interactive games, reference titles, entertainment titles, learning tools, and of course web pages.

UNDERSTANDING MAC OS X QUICKTIME RESOURCES

Various files, folders, and resources are part of Mac OS X's implementation of QuickTime. These include the following:

- **QuickTime Preferences**—The QuickTime pane of the System Preferences application enables you to configure various aspects of how QuickTime works. The QuickTime preference file is stored in each user's Preferences folder within the user's Library folder.

- **QuickTime Player**—The QuickTime Player is the basic application you use to watch QuickTime movies. It is located in the Applications folder.

- **QuickTime Updater**—Apple regularly updates QuickTime; this application can be used to ensure that all the QuickTime components on your Mac are in the current version. You can run the Updater from inside QuickTime Player, or you can run it from the Update tab of the QuickTime pane of the System Preferences application. QuickTime is also updated when you use the Mac OS X Software Update tool.

NOTE

Streaming is the capability to play QuickTime movies as they download from the Web—rather than having to wait until the movie is downloaded to your Mac before you can play it. If you have a fast Internet connection, streaming is nice because viewing QuickTime movies on the Web is about as responsive as watching TV. If you use a dial-up modem, you still have to wait for most QuickTime movies as they are downloaded to your computer.

- **QuickTime.framework folder**—This folder provides the framework files for QuickTime (`Mac OS X/System/Library/Frameworks/QuickTime.framework`, where `Mac OS X` is the name of your Mac OS X startup volume).

→ To learn about Mac OS X's framework structure, **see** "Mac OS X Architecture and Terminology," **p. 12**.

- **QuickTime Plug-in**—This plug-in (located in `Mac OS X/Library/Internet Plug-Ins`, where `Mac OS X` is the name of your Mac OS X startup volume) enables you to view QuickTime movies on the Web from within a web browser.

UNDERSTANDING QUICKTIME VERSUS QUICKTIME PRO

QuickTime comes in two flavors: QuickTime and QuickTime Pro. With QuickTime, you get a basic set of capabilities that enable you to watch all sorts of QuickTime movies. But that is about all you can do with it. QuickTime Pro, on the other hand, enables you to create and edit QuickTime movies, along with various other useful things—the most useful of which is downloading QuickTime movies you encounter on the Internet and saving them on your Mac.

QUICKTIME

With the version of QuickTime included as part Mac OS X, you'll get substantive QuickTime capabilities. These features include the following:

- Viewing all flavors of QuickTime movies on and off the Internet
- Working with more than 30 audio and video file formats
- Changing the size at which movies are played
- Printing frames of movies

QUICKTIME PRO

When you pay for the QuickTime Pro upgrade, you'll get many more features. One of the most important features is the ability to create and edit your own QuickTime movies. QuickTime Pro provides you with all the capabilities of QuickTime plus much more, including the following:

- Playing full-screen video
- Viewing files in a wider variety of formats
- Creating your own QuickTime movies
- Editing and saving movies in various formats
- Copying and pasting material from various formats into QuickTime movies
- Preparing QuickTime movies for streaming delivery via the Web
- Using sharpening, color tinting, and embossing filters on movies and images
- Creating slideshows from a series of still images

The additional features in QuickTime Pro become part of the QuickTime framework. Therefore, any applications that use that framework—such as iTunes, iMovie, iPhoto, iDVD, Final Cut Express, and so on—also benefit from the additional QuickTime Pro features, such as the capability to apply custom compression schemes. In fact, a QuickTime Pro license is included with Apple's professional media applications, such as Final Cut Pro.

NOTE

Apple maintains an extensive website dedicated to QuickTime. This site includes software and updates you can download, information on how QuickTime works, links to QuickTime showcases, and so on. The site is at www.apple.com/quicktime and has some great samples of QuickTime movies you can view.

Before the iLife applications came into being, upgrading to QuickTime Pro was essential for anyone who wanted to create or edit digital media. That's because it was about the only way to do these tasks without spending thousands of dollars on specialized software. Since the rise of iLife and other consumer applications (such as Final Cut Express), you probably won't have much need for QuickTime Pro. You would likely need to use QuickTime Pro only if you prepare media files for web delivery, need to access some of its more specialized features, or don't want to use the iLife applications for some reason.

NOTE

One of the most interesting capabilities of QuickTime Pro is that you can download many movies from websites, such as movie trailers, to your computer. Once there, you can use these movies like other content on your Mac, such as importing them into your iLife projects.

CONFIGURING QUICKTIME AND QUICKTIME PRO

Before you start watching and editing movies, you need to do some configuration of QuickTime so you get the best results on your system.

CONFIGURING QUICKTIME

You'll need to do some basic configuration of QuickTime to customize it for your system. This configuration is done with the QuickTime pane of the System Preferences application. Open the System Preferences application and click the QuickTime icon to open the QuickTime pane. Across the top of the pane, you will see the following tabs: Register, Browser, Update, Streaming, and Advanced.

REGISTERING QUICKTIME

You need to use the Register pane of the QuickTime pane only when you upgrade to QuickTime Pro.

→ To learn how to register QuickTime Pro, **see** "Upgrading to QuickTime Pro," **p. 688**.

CONFIGURING QUICKTIME FOR WEB BROWSING

One of the most useful things about QuickTime is that you can view QuickTime movies on the Web. Because QuickTime is a framework, web browsers such as Safari can use its tools to present content to you. To configure how QuickTime is used when you view web movies, perform the following steps:

1. Open the Browser tab of the QuickTime preferences pane (see Figure 23.1).

Figure 23.1
Use the Browser tab to configure how your web browser handles QuickTime movies.

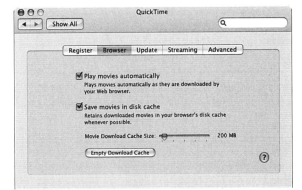

2. If you don't want QuickTime movies to automatically play in your web browser for some reason, uncheck the "Play movies automatically" check box. In most cases, you will want them to play automatically. However, if you use a very slow Internet connection, you might want to disable this feature.

3. Uncheck the "Save movies in disk cache" check box if you don't want movies you view on the Web to be saved in your browser's disk cache. In most cases, this is a useful option, especially if you like to view a movie more than once during a single browsing session; subsequent viewings are much faster because the movie is read from your disk rather than being downloaded from the Web again. Most users should check this box.

4. Use the slider to set the amount of cache you want to be used for storing downloaded content.

> **TIP**
>
> To empty your download cache, click the Empty Download Cache button.

UPDATING QUICKTIME

The Update pane enables you to control how updates to QuickTime are handled and to update third-party QuickTime software installed on your system (see Figure 23.2). Open the pane and click the Update Now button to have your Mac check for updates to the QuickTime software. Check the "Check for updates automatically" box if you want your Mac to automatically check for QuickTime updates when you use QuickTime. If you click the Install button, your Mac checks for updates to non-Apple QuickTime software.

Figure 23.2
You can use the Update pane to check for QuickTime updates, but it is part of the Software Update tool, so you don't really need to do so.

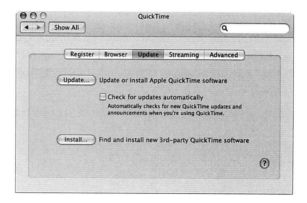

TIP

You don't really need to use the QuickTime Update pane because the Mac OS X Software Update will take care of QuickTime updates for you.

CONFIGURING QUICKTIME STREAMING

The Streaming pane enables you to configure how your Mac works with *streaming* content. Streaming content is that which plays on your Mac as it is being downloaded from the Internet or from other networks to which you are connected. Configure streaming for your system with the following steps:

1. Open the Streaming tab of the QuickTime preferences pane (see Figure 23.3).

Figure 23.3
Use the Streaming tab to configure how your Mac handles content that is played while it is downloaded to your Mac.

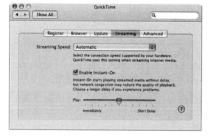

2. Use the Streaming Speed pop-up menu to set the speed at which your Mac is connected to the Internet. The Automatic option enables your Mac to determine the connection speed automatically. Or, you can use the menu to set a specific speed, such as Intranet/LAN if your Mac is connected to a local network that provides your Internet access.

3. Check the Instant-On button if you want streaming content to start "instantly." This feature enables streamed content to play as soon as it starts to download to your Mac.

4. If you enable the Instant-On feature, you can set the amount of delay that occurs before a movie starts playing using the Play slider. With a shorter delay, movies start playing

faster but less buffered data is stored on your Mac. Thus, should some network congestion occur and the download process be slowed, interruptions in movie playback will be more likely. If this happens, move the slider to the right to increase the amount of time content is downloaded before it starts to play.

SETTING ADVANCED QUICKTIME OPTIONS

The Advanced tab enables you to configure some specialized aspects of how QuickTime works (see Figure 23.4).

Figure 23.4
You probably won't need to use QuickTime's Advanced settings, but you should know where they are just in case.

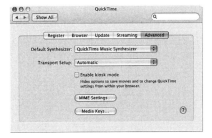

Following is a brief description of the Advanced settings:

- **Default Synthesizer**—QuickTime can play music using different synthesizers (a *synthesizer* transforms digital or other signals into specific musical notes, tones, and so on). This pop-up menu is useful if you work with a Musical Instrument Digital Interface (MIDI) device. By default, the standard QuickTime Music Synthesizer is used. However, you can install various synthesizers and use them to produce the music that is part of QuickTime movie files. If you are involved in creating MIDI files or using a MIDI instrument, you can use this pop-up menu to select the default synthesizer that should be used.

- **Transport Setup**—The Transport Setup pop-up menu enables you to change the protocol and port QuickTime uses to download QuickTime streams from the Internet. In almost all cases, the Automatic option will be the setting you need. However, if you choose Custom on the pop-up menu, your can choose to use User Datagram Protocol (UDP) or Hypertext Transfer Protocol (HTTP) and configure the port used for the protocol you select. You won't likely ever need to change this unless you are connected to a network that requires specific settings.

- **Kiosk mode**[en]If you check the "Enable kiosk mode" check box, the QuickTime interface is hidden when you play QuickTime content from within your web browser.

- **MIME settings**[en]The "MIME settings" button enables you to choose the types of files handled by QuickTime when you encounter them on the Internet. Click the MIME settings button, and you will see the MIME settings sheet. In that sheet, you will see a listing of various groups of file formats, such as Streaming, Video, and so on. Click the expansion triangle next to each group to see the file formats it contains. Check the box next to each file format you want to be handled in QuickTime; to have

23

QuickTime handle all the formats in a group, check the group's check box. Click OK to save the settings you select.

NOTE

> *MIME* is the acronym for Multipurpose Internet Mail Extensions. As you might guess, MIME was originally developed as a means of exchanging files via email. Now, the term refers to the general encoding schemes used to encode files transferred over the Internet.

■ **Media keys**—Media keys enable you to manage your access to protected data files. If you need to get to QuickTime files that are sensitive, you need to use a password (called a *key*) to access the files. Individual tracks can also be secured with a key. If you use such secured QuickTime files, you can enter the keys needed to play them by using the Media Keys button.

UPGRADING TO QUICKTIME PRO

Upgrading to QuickTime Pro does not require any additional software installation. All you need is a registration code, which unlocks the additional features of QuickTime Pro. There are several ways to obtain your QuickTime Pro registration code, but the easiest ways are to use the Web:

■ Go to www.apple.com/quicktime/upgrade and click the Upgrade Now link.

■ Open the System Preferences application, open the QuickTime pane, click the Register tab, and then click Buy QuickTime Pro. You will move to the registration website.

Using the website to upgrade is quite simple—just follow the onscreen instructions. You will receive your registration code via the order confirmation web page or via the phone, depending on how you order the upgrade. Save this code because you will need it each time you have to configure QuickTime Pro.

The QuickTime Pro upgrade costs $29.99. Whether it is worth it depends on how much you need the specialized features it provides. If you have the iLife applications, you probably don't need to upgrade. However, being able to download QuickTime content from the Web might just be worth the upgrade cost because you can incorporate that content into your projects.

After you have obtained your QuickTime Pro registration code, you use the Register pane of the QuickTime pane of the System Preferences application to upgrade. Enter your name and QuickTime Pro registration code to upgrade to the Pro version.

If you weren't able to upgrade successfully, see "My Attempt to Upgrade to QuickTime Pro Failed" in the "Troubleshooting" section at the end of this chapter.

OPENING QUICKTIME PLAYER AND SETTING QUICKTIME PLAYER PREFERENCES

QuickTime Player is the basic application you use to view QuickTime content stored on your computer or in the QuickTime format on CD or DVD, such as those you create using iMovie. Although the appearance of the QuickTime Player controls varies a bit among these contexts, the controls you use to watch movies work similarly.

NOTE

> Because of space limitations and the fact that you are much more likely to use the iLife applications to create and edit digital media (audio and video), the remainder of this chapter covers using the standard version of QuickTime to view QuickTime content. For information about the Pro version, visit the QuickTime website (www.apple.com/quicktime).

To launch QuickTime Player, click its icon on the Dock or open it from within the Applications folder. When QuickTime Player opens, by default, it will download and display the Content Guide that leads you to content on the Web each time you open the application (see Figure 23.5).

Figure 23.5
QuickTime Player looks easy to use, and it lives up to its appearance.

TIP

> If you want to view the content the Content Guide shows you, click the links provided in the QuickTime Player window.

There are some preferences you might want to set by selecting QuickTime Player, Preferences. The options in the resulting Player Preferences dialog box are as described here:

- **Open Movie**—If you check the "Open movies in new players" check box, each movie you open appears in a new QuickTime Player window rather than replacing the current movie.

- **Auto-Play**—If you check the "Automatically play movies when opened" check box, movies begin to play as soon as you open them. If this is not checked, you have to click the Play button to start movies you open.

- **Playback Quality**—If you check the "Use high quality video setting when available" check box, the Player application will choose the best possible video settings for the types of content you play.

- **Only Front Movie Plays Sound**—If the "Play sound in frontmost player only" check box is checked and you have more than one movie playing, only the movie in the frontmost QuickTime Player window produces sound.

- **Play Sound in Background**—When the "Play sound when application is in background" check box is checked, a movie's sound continues to play when you move it into the background.

- **Show Equalizer**—When the "Show equalizer" check box is checked, you will see the QuickTime Player equalizer.

- **Content Guide**—Checking the "Show Content Guide automatically" check box means that, when you launch QuickTime Player, it presents content available to you and displays links to that content in the QuickTime Player window (you can choose to watch it or not). This is checked by default. If you don't want to see the Content Guide each time you launch the application, you should uncheck the box.

- **Fast User Switching**—If the Fast User Switching feature is enabled, users can log in to your Mac without other users having to completely log out first (which means running applications can continue to run). If you check the "Pause movies before switching users" check box, movies that are playing when another user logs in are paused until the previous user logs back in.

- **Recent Items**—Use the "Number of Recent Items" pop-up menu to choose how many movies QuickTime Player retains on its File, Open Recent list.

WATCHING QUICKTIME MOVIES STORED LOCALLY

If you use a VCR, CD player, or DVD player, you won't have any trouble using the QuickTime Player controls to view QuickTime content. Find a QuickTime movie on your hard drive or on a disc and open it. QuickTime Player will launch and you will see the QuickTime Player window (see Figure 23.6). If the auto-play preference is turned on, the movie will start to play automatically.

TIP

To see which features are enabled by the QuickTime Pro upgrade, open each QuickTime Player menu. Commands available only to Pro users are grayed out and the word PRO is listed next to them. As you can see, there isn't a whole lot you can do without the upgrade. But, QuickTime Player works fine for viewing content, so that's okay. You most likely use other applications, such as iMovie, for many of the QuickTime Pro functions.

Figure 23.6
The QuickTime Player window provides the basic controls you use to watch QuickTime movies.

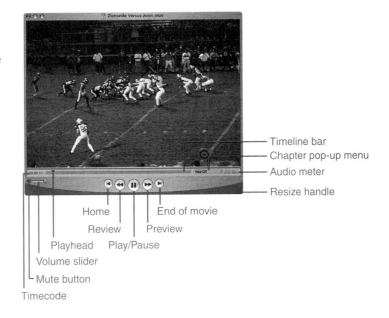

TIP

QuickTime movie files use the extension .mov. If you don't know where a QuickTime movie is, use Spotlight to search for files with this extension.

→ To use the Finder to search for files, **see** "Searching Your Mac with Smart Folders," **p. 123**.

Most of the controls in the QuickTime Player window are easy to understand. For example, the Review button plays the movie in reverse, the Preview button plays the movie in fast forward mode, and so on.

However, you need to become familiar with the less obvious parts of the QuickTime Player window, especially if you have never worked with digital video before. The current frame is shown in the viewing window (if you haven't played the movie, it is the first frame in the movie). Just below the viewing window is the movie's Timeline bar (also known as the Scrubber bar). This represents the total length of the movie. The location of the Playhead shows where in the movie the current frame is located. As you play a movie, the Playhead moves to the right in the Timeline bar so that it always shows the location of the frame displayed in the viewing window.

At the left edge of the Timeline bar is the timecode. The timecode represents the location of the Playhead in the following format: minutes:seconds:frame number. For example, if you see 2:34:10, the Playhead is located on the 10th frame of the 34th second of the 2nd minute of the movie.

Control the size of the movie using the commands on the View menu. You can view it at Half Size, Actual Size, or Double Size. Increasing the size of a movie beyond the size at which it was created sometimes decreases its image quality and frame rate. With some movies, this is hardly noticeable; with others, increasing the size can make them unwatchable. You can experiment to see which size is the best compromise for a particular movie on your specific system.

TIP

You can also change the size of the QuickTime Player window using the Resize handle. The window remains in proportion to the size in which the movie was created. If you hold down the Shift key, you can resize the window any way you want (with sometimes amusing effects on the movie itself). You can quickly return a movie to its default size by selecting View, Actual Size or by pressing ⌘-1.

Click the Play button (or press the spacebar) to view the movie and use the Volume slider to adjust its sound level.

→ QuickTime Player offers many keyboard shortcuts; to learn which shortcuts are available, **see** "Mac OS X to the Max: Using QuickTime Player Keyboard Shortcuts," **p. 697**.

If the movie contains chapter markers, such as those you can add to your iMovie projects, jump to a specific chapter in the movie by opening the Chapter pop-up menu and selecting the chapter you want to view. If you are playing the movie when you use this menu, you will jump to the chapter you selected and the movie will continue to play. If it isn't playing, you'll see the first frame in the chapter you selected.

You can move to any point in the movie by dragging the Playhead to the frame you want to view.

You can get more control over the sound using the A/V controls; display them by selecting Window, Show A/V Controls. The A/V Controls window will appear (see Figure 23.7). You can use the controls in the Audio pane of the window to further adjust the audio portion of the movie by setting volume, bass, treble, and balance. You can use the Jog Shuttle slider to move the movie forward or in reverse at various speeds (move the slider further to play the movie faster in that direction). You can set the movie's playback speed with the Playback Speed slider.

TIP

To mute a movie, click the speaker icon at the left edge of the Volume slider.

Figure 23.7
Use the A/V Controls window to control your movie in more detail.

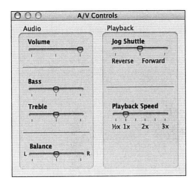

23

You can get more information about a movie by selecting Window, Show Movie Info. In the resulting window, you will see technical information about the movie, such as its format, resolution, and size.

NOTE

When you minimize a movie, it moves onto the Dock and continues to play.

You can cause a movie to loop so that it plays over and over again by selecting View, Loop or by pressing ⌘-L.

NOTE

QuickTime movies can also be inserted into many types of documents, such as Word files, presentations, and so on. When you view such a file, you will see a "mini" QuickTime controller that enables you to watch the movie embedded in a particular document. Applications can add or remove controls to customize the interface you see in that application, but when you understand how to view movies with the QuickTime Player, you won't have any trouble with these other controllers.

WATCHING QUICKTIME MOVIES STORED ON THE WEB

QuickTime is a major format for movies on the Web. Using the QuickTime plug-in, you can watch QuickTime movies from within a web browser, such as Safari. When you do so, you use controls that are similar to those in the QuickTime Player application.

One of the best places to view QuickTime movies is at Apple's Movie Trailer site. Here, you can view trailers for the latest creations from Hollywood.

23

CAUTION

> If you use a slow Internet connection, watching movies, such as the movie trailers on the Apple website, can be an exercise in patience. High-quality movie files are *big*. Watching them on the Web, even with the streaming feature and the MPEG-4 format, can take more time than it is worth. If you use a dial-up account, try watching some movies to see whether you can tolerate the length of time it takes to download enough of the movie so you can begin watching it. If you can, great. If not, you might have to find smaller movies to watch or, even better, move up to a high-bandwidth connection. You can also use the Instant-On preference to configure the delay before a movie begins to play.

To view some cool trailers online, do the following steps:

1. Go to www.apple.com/trailers.

2. Click a trailer to view it. What happens next depends on how the particular trailer has been created. Related to the previous caution, many of the trailers on the Apple site are offered in different versions, which are sized to be appropriate for various connection speeds. Usually, there are three choices: small (for dial-up connections), medium (for DSL, slower cable, or ISDN connections), and large (for broadband connections).

3. If a size option is presented, click the size your connection supports; if not, just click the "Click here to play movie" link. The movie will start to download. As soon as enough has been downloaded that it can play without interruption the rest of the way, it will begin to play. The movie will appear in a window that contains QuickTime controls you can use to watch the trailer (see Figure 23.8).

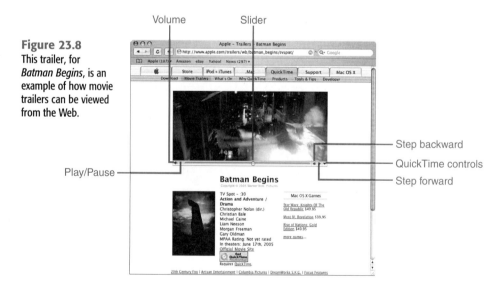

Figure 23.8
This trailer, for *Batman Begins*, is an example of how movie trailers can be viewed from the Web.

4. The movie begins to play as soon as enough has been downloaded to your Mac so the trailer plays continuously. If you use a fast connection and use the Instant-On feature, this happens quickly. If you use a slow dial-up connection or have configured a delay using the Instant-On slider, it can take longer. You can see how much of a movie has been downloaded by looking at the dark shaded part of the Timeline bar.

> **T I P**
>
> You can start a movie at any time by pressing the spacebar. If you don't wait for the automatic start, the movie might stop before it finishes if it runs out of downloaded movie before it gets to the end.

23

5. Use the QuickTime controls listed in Table 23.1 to control playback.

 If you can only download a QuickTime movie from the Web rather than being able to view it, see "I Can't View QuickTime Movies on the Web" in the "Troubleshooting" section at the end of this chapter.

TABLE 23.1   QUICKTIME CONTROLS FOR WEB MOVIES

Control	Function
Volume	Click the volume button and a slider will pop up. Use the slider to set the volume level.
Play/Pause	Use this to play or pause the movie. The spacebar does the same thing.
Slider	Drag this to move to any point in the movie.
Step Backward/Step Forward	Moves back or ahead in the movie by one frame.
QuickTime controls	Pops up a menu of additional commands.

Depending on how the movie is presented, you might not see the window shown in Figure 23.8. For example, some QuickTime content will play in the iTunes window (see Figure 23.9). Others, especially those that offer full-screen versions, will provide a customized playback window.

Figure 23.9
Some trailers are viewed through iTunes via the iTunes Music Store.

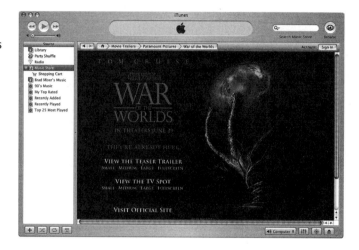

TROUBLESHOOTING

MY ATTEMPT TO UPGRADE TO QUICKTIME PRO FAILED

When I entered my QuickTime Pro registration information, I saw an error dialog box stating that the registration information is not correct. Or, it appeared to work, but when I returned to the Registration sheet, the PRO commands were still disabled and no registration information appeared in the sheet.

The QuickTime Pro registration code is tied to the name you used when you obtained it. You must enter this name exactly as you used it; otherwise, the registration code will not be accepted. Also, double-check the registration code you entered. These codes are long and complex, so it is easy to make a mistake. The code and name are case sensitive, so be sure you enter them exactly as shown in the information you receive from Apple.

I CAN'T VIEW QUICKTIME MOVIES ON THE WEB

When I attempt to view a QuickTime movie on the Web, I'm unable to do so and am forced to download the file to my Mac instead.

This happens if the QuickTime plug-in has been moved or damaged. To reinstall the plug-in, you need to update QuickTime. When the updater runs, it will reinstall the plug-in in the appropriate location and you will be able to use it with your web browser. To update QuickTime, open the QuickTime Player application and select QuickTime Player, Update Existing Software. The appropriate files will be downloaded and installed on your Mac. Restart your Mac and you should be able to view QuickTime movies on the Web.

MAC OS X TO THE MAX: USING QUICKTIME PLAYER KEYBOARD SHORTCUTS

Some useful QuickTime Player keyboard shortcuts are shown in Table 23.2.

TABLE 23.2 KEYBOARD SHORTCUTS FOR QUICKTIME PLAYER

Menu	Action	Keyboard Shortcut
File	Close Player window	⌘-W
File	Open URL	⌘-U
None	Move Playhead backward one frame	Left arrow
None	Move Playhead forward one frame	Right arrow
None	Pause movie (movie playing)	Spacebar or Return
None	Play movie (movie paused)	Spacebar or Return
None	Turn down volume	Down arrow
None	Turn up volume	Up arrow
None	Turn volume to maximum	Shift-Option-up arrow
None	Turn volume to minimum	Shift-Option-down arrow
View	Loop	⌘-L
View	Play movie at actual size	⌘-1
View	Play movie at double size	⌘-2
View	Play movie at half size	⌘-0
Window	Add movie as favorite	⌘-D
Window	Show A/V controls	⌘-K
Window	Show movie info	⌘-I

23

CHAPTER **24**

MAKING DIGITAL MOVIE MAGIC WITH iMOVIE

In this chapter

GETTING STARTED WITH IMOVIE

Apple's iMovie enables you to transform the raw footage you capture with an analog or digital camcorder into a real movie with transitions, a soundtrack, sound effects, special effects, titles, and other elements. Using iMovie, you can make your own digital masterpieces and watch them on your Mac or put them on DVD.

Because this is a book on Mac OS X and not on iMovie, in this chapter, you'll get a fairly basic overview of this excellent application. Fortunately, iMovie is so well designed that a basic overview is likely all you need anyway.

NOTE

> The current version of iMovie (version 5.0) is called iMovie HD because it supports the capture and editing of high-definition video. Unfortunately, at press time, HD camcorders are well beyond the reach of most consumers, with the minimum cost of about $3,500. Additionally, most consumer video playback devices, such as DVD players, don't yet support HD resolutions. The time is coming when all video equipment will be HD capable, but until the cost of these devices comes down, HD will be a nice, but impractical, feature for most iMovie users.

TOURING IMOVIE

iMovie is part of the Apple iLife suite of applications. To use iMovie, you need to obtain and install the iLife suite (see the following sidebar).

Obtaining and Installing iLife

Apple's iLife suite includes five amazing applications, four of which are not part of the standard Mac OS X installation (GarageBand, iPhoto, iMovie, and iDVD) and are musts-have for any Mac OS X user. (iTunes is part of the standard Mac OS X installation and is also included in the iLife suite.) There are two ways you can get a copy of iLife. One is to buy a new Mac because iLife is installed on all new Macs. The other is to purchase the suite from Apple or from an authorized Apple reseller. Priced at $79, this suite is an excellent bargain, too.

Installing the iLife applications is simple: You just place the appropriate disc (DVD or CD) in your Mac and run the iLife installer. Use the standard installation to install all parts of each application, or use the Customize option to select parts not to install (such as the themes from previous versions of iDVD). Each application will be installed within the Applications folder. Before you start using these applications, run the Mac OS X Software Update application (select Apple, Software Update) to ensure that you are using the most current version of each application.

The iMovie window contains five main areas, only four of which you can see at the same time (see Figure 24.1).

The largest pane in the iMovie window is the Monitor. Here, you preview and edit your movie, as well as the clips from which you build that movie. In the upper-right corner is the iMovie Tool pane. At the bottom of the Tool pane are seven buttons, with each button opening a palette of tools in the pane. Just under the Monitor is the controls area that includes various buttons you use to control playback and editing functions. Underneath that area are the two viewers, the Clip Viewer and the Timeline Viewer (you can see only one viewer at a time). In the lower-right corner of the window are the disk space tools you use to manage the disk space associated with your project.

Figure 24.1
The iMovie window has several areas that perform different functions.

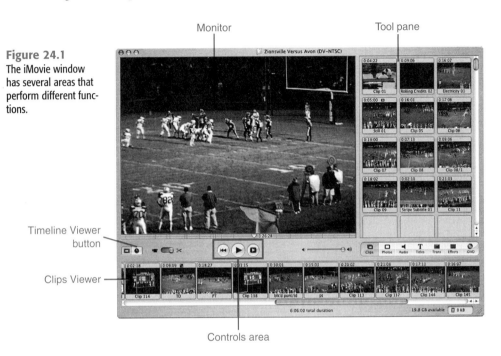

Monitor

Tool pane

Timeline Viewer button

Clips Viewer

Controls area

iMovie has two basic modes in which you operate: Camera and Edit. The mode you are in is determined by the position of the Camera/Edit mode switch located in the Controls area (refer to Figure 24.1). When the switch is to the left (toward the camera icon), iMovie is in the Camera mode. In this mode, you work with a DV camera attached to your Mac to import video clips from which you will build your movie. When the switch is to the right (toward the scissors icon), iMovie is in the Edit mode and you can work with video clips to preview them, edit them, and so on. You will spend most of your iMovie time in Edit mode.

BUILDING A BASIC VIDEO TRACK

The first step in a movie project is to create the basic video track for the movie.

CREATING AN IMOVIE PROJECT

Start a new project by selecting File, New Project. In the Create Project dialog box, name your movie. Choose the video format of the movie you will create on the Video format pop-up menu; the choice you make should be determined by the kind of footage you have, such as DV, DV Widescreen, and so on. Move to the volume on which you are going to store it and click Create. The project will be created and you'll see a new, empty iMovie window.

NOTE

> Be sure to choose a volume with plenty of free space in which to store your iMovie project. If you have a partitioned hard disk, you might need to move outside your Home directory to store your project to have enough room. In the ideal situation, you will have a dedicated hard disk or volume on which to store your video projects.

IMPORTING CLIPS FROM A DIGITAL VIDEO CAMERA

Setting up a FireWire camera to work with iMovie is a snap. Power up your Mac, and then turn on the camera to its output setting (this is sometimes labeled VCR or VTR). Connect the FireWire cable to the DV camcorder and your Mac. iMovie will switch into the Camera mode automatically.

CAUTION

> If the FireWire plug doesn't slip in easily, take a closer look. FireWire connectors are relatively fragile, so don't push too hard.

A message will appear in iMovie's Monitor window confirming that iMovie is in touch with your DV camcorder. In addition to the Camera Connected message, notice that the button just under the Monitor is now called Import. This means you are ready to begin importing your clips into iMovie.

TIP

> If you click the pop-up menu next to the Camera icon, you'll see the camera connected to your Mac. If you connect more than one camera at a time, you can choose the camera with which you want to work on this menu.

The really cool part about an iMovie-compatible DV camcorder is that you can control your DV camcorder using iMovie's controls. The Play, Fast Forward, Stop, and other buttons in the iMovie Monitor control your DV camcorder. If you aren't using an iMovie-compatible camera, you have to control the camera using its controls and manually control iMovie as well.

To begin playing the tape in your camcorder, click the iMovie Play button (see Figure 24.2). The video on the tape will begin playing in the Monitor. Use the iMovie controls to move to the point on your tape at which you want to begin capturing clips from the tape.

TIP

> If, for some reason, you aren't getting the screen shown in Figure 24.2, check the Camera/Edit Mode switch and make sure it's in Camera mode. If your camera is connected to your Mac, but you see the "No Camera Attached" message, click the Connection Help button for assistance.

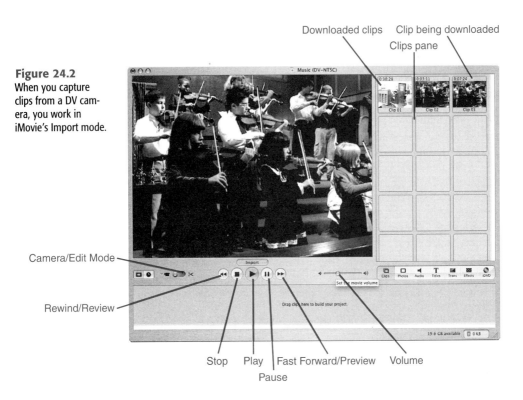

Figure 24.2
When you capture clips from a DV camera, you work in iMovie's Import mode.

Following are the Import controls iMovie provides (from left to right and top to bottom):

- **Import**—You use this when you want to import clips to the Clips pane.

- **Camera/Edit Mode**—This switches iMovie between the Camera mode (which you are in now) and the Edit mode, which is the mode you use to edit your movie.

- **Rewind/Review**—When the tape is not playing, the Rewind button rewinds the tape at top speed. When the tape is playing, it plays the tape backward (you see the video, but there is no audio). In the Review mode, you have to "hold" down the button to keep the review going (in other words, if you let up on the button, it goes back into Play mode).

- **Stop**—The Stop button halts whatever is happening with the camcorder.

- **Play**—This plays the tape in the camera.

- **Pause**—This one freezes the video at a specific frame.

- **Fast Forward/Preview**—When the tape is not playing, the Fast Forward button moves the tape forward at top speed. When the tape is playing, it plays the tape forward at a high speed (you see video but don't hear any audio).

- **Volume**—Drag the slider to the right to increase the volume and to the left to decrease it. Note that this affects only the playback volume and doesn't actually change the movie at all.

Click the Import button (or press the spacebar); iMovie will start the camcorder and begin capturing the clips. It will store the first clip in the first available slot on the Shelf. When it gets to a scene break (the point at which you pressed the Stop button while filming with the DV camcorder), it will stop that clip and immediately begin capturing the next scene, which it will place in the next available slot on the Shelf.

iMovie continues this process until it runs out of video to import or out of disk space to store clips, whichever comes first. If you don't want to wait that long, click Import again to stop the capture process (or press the spacebar).

Use the iMovie controls to move the tape to the next set of scenes you want to capture, and begin again. Continue until you capture all the scenes your script and storyboards call for, your disk runs out of space, or the Clips pane is so full of clips that you have trouble dealing with so many. The Clips pane now has some nice clips (and probably some not-so-nice ones), ready for you to edit and use in your movie.

When you are done, disconnect your camera and turn it off.

Deleting Clips

As you capture clips, you will realize that some of them just aren't any good and you won't end up using them. That is the time to get rid of the worthless clip so it doesn't consume any precious disk space. On the Clips pane, click the clip you want to delete to select it. Drag it to the Trash (or press Delete) and it disappears from the Clips pane.

Placing a clip in the Trash gets it off the Shelf, but the clip still consumes disk space. To free up that disk space, you must empty the Trash. To do so, select File, Empty Trash. Depending on how big the clips in the Trash are, you might see a dialog box asking you to confirm that you want to empty the Trash. Click OK and the contents of the Trash are deleted. The space this junk consumed on the disk is now free for other purposes.

TIP

> If you want to control how clips are broken instead of letting iMovie do it for you, uncheck the "Start new clip at each scene break" check box in the Import pane of the iMovie Preferences dialog box. When you import video, the clips will come in as one continuous chunk unless you start and stop the importing process manually. Frankly, dealing with one large clip is much more difficult than letting iMovie break up the clips for you. But if you have recorded your movie using very short multiple clips of the same scene, you might choose to have them come in as one long clip instead.

IMPORTING QUICKTIME MOVIES AND IMAGES

In addition to clips you capture from a DV camcorder, you can also import QuickTime movies and images onto the Clips pane for use in your movies.

NOTE

You can import image files in all the common Mac image file formats, such as JPEG, TIFF, PICT, and so on. For best results, you should size your images so they have a resolution exactly the same as the video you are using (this depends on the type of camera you have used to capture it) because iMovie scales them to that size anyway, which can result in some distortion if the original image's size is much different from this. (Of course, if you are creating an HD movie, you'll want to set the image resolution to match your HD settings.)

To import content into iMovie, perform the following steps:

1. Select File, Import (Shift-⌘-I).

2. In the resulting Import sheet, move to and select the file you want to add to the iMovie project and click Open.

   The Import Files dialog box opens showing how the import is moving along. If the files you select are fairly large, this process can take a few moments. When the import process is complete, the clip or images appear on the Clips pane.

From this point on, imported content behaves in the same way as any other clip on the Clips pane.

PREVIEWING YOUR CLIPS

Select a clip by clicking it on the Clips pane. The clip will be highlighted with a blue border, which means the clip is selected. More telling is the fact that the first frame of the clip is what the Monitor will show. Notice that, when you select a clip, iMovie also moves into the Edit mode, in which you can manipulate your clips (if it isn't in the Edit mode, slide the Camera/Edit Mode switch to the right). In the Edit mode, the iMovie window features the controls shown in Figure 24.3 and described in the following list:

- **Scrubber bar**—The Scrubber bar is a visual representation of the timeline for a clip, a group of clips, or your movie (depending on what you have selected).

- **Timecode**—The precise location of the Playhead is shown by the timecode that floats next to the Playhead. As its name implies, the timecode provides information about the time aspects of a clip or movie. Timecodes appear in the following format:

  minutes:seconds:frames

  If a clip or movie is less than a minute, you see only two sets of numbers: seconds and frames.

  The frames part of the timecode is a counter that measures the number of frames in a single second of the clip. Most clips you capture with a camcorder have 30 frames per second, which results in smooth onscreen motion. Within each second of the clip, the frames are numbered from 00 to 29 (for a total of 30 frames). The frames part of the timecode tells you where in each second of the clip you are. For example, a timecode of 36:21 means the clip is 36 seconds long and has gone 21 frames into the 37th second (so it is actually almost 37 seconds long).

24

Figure 24.3
Getting comfortable with iMovie's Editing tools probably won't take very long.

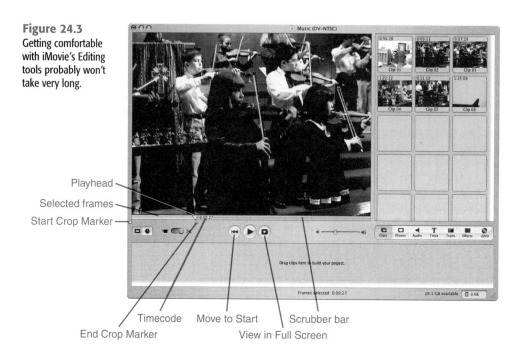

Playhead

Selected frames

Start Crop Marker

Timecode   Move to Start   Scrubber bar

End Crop Marker   View in Full Screen

TIP

As you start editing, the timecode becomes very useful, especially when you are able to interpret it immediately. The first few times it can be a bit confusing, but just keep remembering that the last number in the timecode is the frame number; timecodes will become second nature to you as you gain iMovie experience.

- **Playhead**—The Playhead is a pointer on the Scrubber bar that shows you the relative location of the frame that currently appears in the Monitor. You use the Playhead to determine where you are in a clip or in your movie. As a clip or movie plays, the Playhead moves across the Scrubber bar. You can also drag the Playhead to move to a specific frame in a clip or in your movie.

- **Start Crop Marker/End Crop Marker**—As with most Mac applications, you select the material you want to change in some way (in this case, frames of a video clip) and then perform some action on them, such as cutting them out of a clip. You use the crop markers to select the frames with which you want to work. The Start Crop Marker indicates the first frame you select, whereas the End Crop Marker indicates the last frame in the selection.

- **Selected frames**—The selected frames are indicated by the gold highlighting between the two markers. The action you select is performed on these frames. For example, if you select Cut, the selected frames are removed from the clip or movie.

- **Move to Start**—Clicking this moves you to the start of your movie and unselects any selected clips.

- **Play/Pause**—Click Play to watch and hear selected clips. Click Play again to pause the action. You can also start and stop play by pressing the spacebar.
- **View in Full Screen**—Plays the selected clips in full-screen mode in which you see only the clips; the iMovie interface will disappear. Click the mouse button or press the Esc key to exit the full-screen mode.
- **Volume**—This slider adjusts the playback volume. Note that this affects only the current volume of the clip or movie and in no way changes the clip or the movie itself.

Click Play to watch and hear the selected clip. Click Play again to pause the clip. You can also start and stop play by pressing the spacebar. As the clip plays, notice that the Playhead moves across the Scrubber bar.

NAVIGATING CLIPS IN iMOVIE

As you edit, you are constantly moving around a clip to get to specific areas to edit. There are several ways to do this.

Click the Playhead and drag it to the right to move forward in the clip or to the left to move backward in the clip. When you release the mouse button, the Playhead will be at the exact position where you left it and you can see the frame indicated by the timecode. Use this method for gross but quick movements in the clip, such as moving from the beginning to the middle.

You can also move the Playhead much more precisely using the keyboard; this is essential when you get to detailed editing because you can move by increments as small as a single frame. To move the Playhead one frame at a time, use the left- and right-arrow keys. As you can probably guess, the right-arrow key moves the Playhead forward one frame and the left-arrow key moves you backward one frame.

You can also move the Playhead forward or backward 10 frames at a time by holding down the Shift key while you press the left- or right-arrow key. This movement is also useful when you are doing detailed editing because it enables you to quickly move to a precise location in the clip, but you get there more quickly than by moving one frame at a time.

A fast preview technique is to select a clip and fast-forward through it so you get a good idea of what it contains. If it looks as if it contains no usable footage, delete it. If it looks promising, watch it again at regular speed.

Creating a Movie with Magic

You can use iMovie's Make a Magic iMovie command to convert video into a movie for you. iMovie will even add transitions, music, and other effects that you will learn about in this chapter. After you have created a movie using this tool, you can use the rest of the information in this chapter to work with the movie you create.

To get started, attach your camcorder to your Mac. Open iMovie and select File, Make a Magic iMovie. In the resulting sheet, name the new movie project. Then use the three check boxes to select transitions, music, and whether you want to immediately send the movie to iDVD. Click Create and sit back while iMovie builds a movie for you—magically.

24

EDITING A CLIP

Editing clips is one of the most important tasks you will do. When you edit a clip, you remove everything from that clip that will detract from, rather than add to, your movie. Editing your clips is fundamental to creating good movies.

You can edit clips at any time, but in my opinion you are better off if you edit your clips *before* you place them in a movie. Building a movie from edited clips gets you to a completed movie more quickly because you deal with less unwanted material when you actually build your movie.

When you edit a clip, you select the frames you want to take action on by using the start and end crop markers. You use these markers to select video clips much like you use the mouse or keyboard to select text within a document.

REMOVING FRAMES FROM A CLIP

One of the most fundamental tasks is removing frames from a clip, such as removing them from the beginning or end of a clip. However, you can remove frames from anywhere in a clip with the same steps:

1. Click the clip you want to edit on the Clips pane to select it; the clip will appear in the Monitor.

2. Preview the clip and locate a part of the clip that should be removed.

3. Click the End Crop Maker and drag it to the approximate point at which you want to stop removing frames from the clip. When you click the crop marker, it becomes dark blue to indicate it is selected, the Playhead sticks to it, and you see the frame at which both are currently located in the Monitor. The gold bar that appears between the crop markers indicates the frames you have selected. As you drag a crop marker, you can see the frames through which you are moving.

   While the Playhead is stuck to a crop marker, you can move it 1 frame at a time by pressing the right-arrow key to add 1 frame to the selection or by holding down the Shift key and pressing the right-arrow key to add 10 frames to the selection. Similarly, if you press the left-arrow key, you remove 1 or 10 frames from the selection. Use this technique to position the crop marker on the exact end frame you want to select.

4. Click the Start Crop Marker (it will become highlighted in dark blue and the Playhead will jump and stick to it); then drag the start crop marker to the approximate location at which you want to start selecting frames. (If you want to start selecting frames at the first frame, you don't need to move the start crop marker because it is positioned there by default.)

   While the Playhead is stuck to the crop marker, you can move it 1 frame at a time by pressing the right-arrow key to remove 1 frame of the selection or by holding down the Shift key and pressing the right-arrow key to remove 10 frames of the selection. Similarly, if you press the left-arrow key, you add 1 or 10 frames to the selection. Use this technique to position the crop marker on the exact start frame you want to select.

The frames you have selected will be represented by a gold bar on the Scrubber bar (see Figure 24.4).

Figure 24.4
Selecting frames is the most important step when editing a clip.

5. To remove the selected frames from the clip, select Edit, Cut (⌘-X). The crop markers will be reset to the beginning of the clip, and the selected frames will be removed from the clip.

> **TIP**
>
> You can also remove frames by selecting them and pressing the Delete key or selecting Edit, Clear. The Clear command removes selected frames without placing them on the Clipboard. Technically speaking, you should use Clear rather than Cut because memory resources aren't wasted by placing the selected frames on your Mac's Clipboard. However, I prefer to use Cut because it has a keyboard shortcut, whereas Clear does not. And practically speaking, you won't notice any performance problems if you leave frames on your Clipboard.

6. Play the clip to see how it is without the frames you just removed. If you don't like the result, you can undo it by selecting Edit, Undo (⌘-Z) and selecting a different set of frames to remove.

7. Preview the edited clip and continue editing it until you have removed all the frames you don't want to include in the movie.

CROPPING A CLIP

You can also crop a clip to remove everything from it except the frames you have selected. This is a good way to remove frames at the beginning and end of a clip at the same time:

1. Use the selection techniques you learned in the previous steps to select the frames you want to remain in the clip.

2. Select Edit, Crop (⌘-K). The frames that were not included in the selection will be removed from the clip.

3. Preview the clip. If you don't like the results of the crop, undo it.

SPLITTING A CLIP

You might want to split a clip so you can work with each part independently. For example, you might want to use one part of the clip at one location in a movie and another part of the clip later in a movie. When you split a clip, the two resulting clips behave just like clips you have created by capturing them from a DV camera or by importing them. Do the following:

1. Select the clip you want to split. It will appear in the Monitor.

2. Drag the Playhead to the point at which you want to split the clip.

3. Select Edit, Split Video Clip at Playhead (⌘-T). The clip will be split into two clips at the point in the clip at which the Playhead was located. A new clip with /1 appended to the first segment's name will be added to the Clips pane (for example, if the clip's name is Clip 43, the new clip is named Clip 43/1). You can treat the two clips independently because they are now separate clips.

BUILDING A MOVIE FROM CLIPS ON THE CLIPS PANE

After you have done the rough editing of your clips, you can begin creating your movie. You assemble your movie by placing clips on the Clip Viewer in the order you want them to be in the movie.

Click the Clip Viewer button, which is the rectangular shape just under the Scrubber bar, to bring the Clip Viewer to the front (it will probably be in the front already). To begin assembling your movie, simply drag clips from the Clips pane onto the Clip Viewer (see Figure 24.5). Drag them onto the Clip Viewer in the order in which you want them to appear; you can reshuffle them later if you want.

When you select one or more clips on the Clip Viewer, the Monitor shows the clips you have selected. Vertical lines in the Scrubber bar mark the boundaries of each clip. If you don't have any clips selected, the Monitor shows the contents of all the clips on the Clip Viewer—in other words, your entire movie.

If the Clip Viewer gets full, use its scrollbar to reveal empty space for more clips.

Press Shift-⌘-A to deselect any clips that are selected. Press the Home key to move to the start of your movie. To preview your movie, press the spacebar and your movie will play. You can use the same movement and editing controls with an entire movie as you can when dealing with an individual clip (such as fast forward). (You can play a single clip again by selecting it on the Clip Viewer.)

Figure 24.5
I have moved clips from the Clips pane to the Clip Viewer; the Clip Viewer shows the sequence in which the clips will be played in the movie.

You can change the order of clips by dragging them from one location on the Clip Viewer to another. As you move a clip between two other clips, the clips will move apart to show where your clip will be placed when you release the mouse button.

You can remove a clip from your movie and place it back on the Clips pane by dragging it from the Clip Viewer to the Clips pane. You can delete a clip by selecting it and then pressing Delete.

To see your movie in full-screen mode, click the Play Full Screen button. Your movie will play back so that it takes up the entire screen. This helps you focus on your movie without any distractions from the iMovie interface. To stop your movie and return to iMovie before your movie has finished, click the mouse button or press the Esc key.

Continue placing clips in the Clip Viewer until you have all the clips you want to appear in your movie. You don't have to use all the clips on the Clips pane; you can leave clips there for later use or delete them when you are sure you won't use them in this movie.

ADDING iPHOTO IMAGES TO A MOVIE

You can add your iPhoto images to a movie, or you can create a movie consisting entirely of iPhoto images to create a slideshow. When you add images from iPhoto to a movie, you can configure motion effects for the images you add; in iMovie, these effects are called the Ken Burns Effect. This effect—taken from the treatment of images Ken Burns uses in his excellent documentaries, such as *Civil War*—applies motion and zoom effects to the image. You can configure the effect for each image you add to the movie, from no effect at all to a maximum effect.

For all images you add, regardless of whether you choose to use the Ken Burns Effect, you can set the image duration and zoom. The image's duration setting determines how long the image appears on the screen, and the zoom determines which part of the image is displayed.

To add iPhoto images to a movie, perform the following steps:

1. Click the Photos button to open the Photos pane.

2. On the Source pop-up menu, select the iPhoto source, such as a photo album, that contains the images you want to add to the movie on the pop-up menu. The images contained in the selected photo album appear in the Preview window in the lower part of the palette (see Figure 24.6). At the bottom of the pane, you will see the Search tool, which you can use to search the selected source. To the right of the Search tool, the number of images contained in the selected source will be shown.

Figure 24.6
Use the tools on the iPhoto pane to add images from your iPhoto Photo Library to a movie and add effects to them.

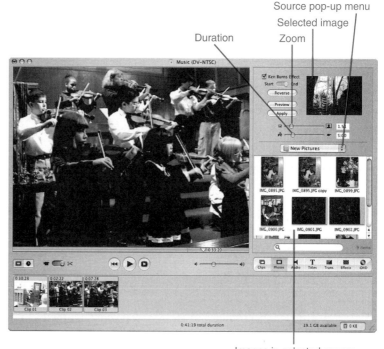

Source pop-up menu
Selected image
Duration   Zoom

Images in selected source

3. Select the image you want to add to the movie. A preview of the image with the current motion effects will appear in the image Preview window located at the top of the pane.

4. If you want to apply the Ken Burns Effect to the image, click the "Ken Burns Effect" check box (it is checked by default). The Ken Burns Effect controls will become active and you will see a preview of the image with the effect applied in the Preview window. If this box isn't checked, only the Duration and Zoom controls will be active.

5. Move the switch under the check box to the Start position. This enables you to configure the starting location of the motion effect. Skip this step if you aren't using the Ken Burns Effect.

6. Use the Zoom slider to set the amount of magnification applied to the image at the start of its clip if you apply the Ken Burns Effect or throughout the image clip if you don't apply the effect. Drag the slider to the left to show more of the photo or to the right to show less of it.

7. Move the pointer over the image in the Preview window. The cursor will turn into a hand.

8. Hold down the mouse button and drag the image until the part of the image you want to be shown at the start of the image clip (with the Ken Burns Effect applied) or throughout the image clip (without the effect) is shown in the Preview window.

9. Move the switch under the check box to the End position. The image will jump to its ending location and zoom settings.

10. Use the Zoom slider to set the amount of magnification applied to the image at the end of its clip. Drag the slider to the left to show more of the photo or to the right to show less of it.

> **TIP**
>
> You can also enter the zoom and duration values by typing a duration (in the timecode format) or zoom (in zoom amount) directly in their respective boxes.

11. Move the pointer over the image in the preview window. The cursor will turn into a hand.

12. Hold down the mouse button and drag the image until the part of the image you want to be shown at the end of the image clip is shown in the Preview window.

13. Use the Duration slider to set the length of time for the image clip. Drag the slider to the left to make the clip shorter (which makes the motion effect faster if you have applied it to the image) or to the right to make the clip last longer (to make the motion effect slower if you have applied it to the image). If you don't apply the Ken Burns Effect to an image, setting its duration only changes the length of time that image appears onscreen. When you release the mouse button, a preview of the image and motion effect will appear in the Preview window.

14. Click Preview to see the image clip as you have configured it in the Preview window. (If you don't apply the Ken Burns Effect, the Preview button is inactive because there is no point in previewing a static image—what you see is what you get.)

> **TIP**
>
> If you want the motion effect to be applied in the opposite direction, click the Reverse button. A preview of the motion effect moving in the opposite direction (zooming in instead of zooming out) will be shown in the Preview window.

15. Make changes to the image settings until you are satisfied, and then click Apply. The motion effect, duration, and zoom settings will be applied to the image; the image clip will be imported into the project; and it will be placed at the end of the movie shown in the Clip Viewer. When the rendering process is complete, the image will be selected so it appears in the Monitor.

16. Drag the image clip to the location on the Clip Viewer at the point in the movie where you want it to appear.

ADDING TRANSITIONS

The segment between two clips in a movie is called the *transition*. You can use different transitions to smooth the flow from one clip into the next so your series of individual clips doesn't look like a series of clips, but rather a movie that flows smoothly from one scene to the next. All video uses transitions of one sort or another.

The three most common types of transitions are the *Straight Cut, Cross Dissolve*, and *Fade To* or *From Black*. The Straight Cut isn't a transition you have to apply; this is what happens when you don't add a transition. A Straight Cut transition occurs when one scene runs right into another. As long as the adjacent scenes are similar enough, the straight cut seems natural and you mostly don't even notice it. The Cross Dissolve, in which one scene dissolves into the next, is also common. This transition can be useful when the adjacent scenes are somewhat similar but different enough that a straight cut is a bit jarring. The Fade To and From Black are two of the more useful transitions. With the fade, one scene fades to black or fades in from a black screen.

iMovie enables you to add a variety of transition effects to your movies with a simple drag and drop.

To get started, open the Transitions pane by clicking the Trans button. The Transitions pane will appear and you will see the Transitions tools (see Figure 24.7).

The tools on the Transitions pane are as follows:

- **Preview window**—When you select a transition on the list of available transitions, a preview of that transition will play in the Preview window. You can use this to get a quick idea of what the transition looks like. You will see the transition applied to the clip you have selected; if you don't have a clip selected, you will see that transition applied to the first clip in your movie.

- **Preview button**—When you click the Preview button, you will see a preview of the selected transition in the Monitor. This makes the effect of the transition easier to see because it appears much larger, but it also takes longer to preview.

- **Update**—You use this button to change a transition that has been placed in a movie. You select the transition clip, use the Transitions tools to make changes to it, and then click the Update button to apply those changes to the transition clip in the movie.

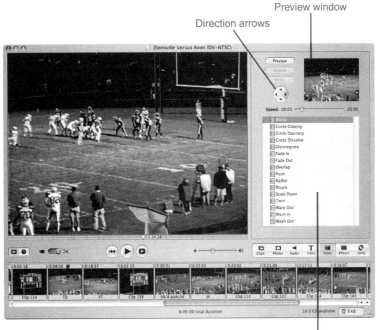

Figure 24.7
Use the Transitions pane to apply transition effects to a movie.

Preview window

Direction arrows

Available Transitions

- **Direction arrows**—When a transition has a directional component, such as a push effect, you use the direction arrows to set the direction of the transition. For example, when you use the Push transition (where one clip "pushes" the previous one off the screen), you click the arrow for the direction in which you want the push to occur.

- **Speed**—You use this slider to control the amount of time over which the transition effect is displayed. Moving the slider to the left makes the transition last a shorter amount of time. Moving it to the right stretches the transition out so it takes longer to play. When you release the slider, you will immediately see the changed transition in the Preview window.

- **Available Transitions**—This list shows the transition effects currently available. To work with a transition, select it on the list.

Applying a transition can be done in just a few steps, as the following example of applying a scale down shows:

1. In the Clip Viewer, select the clip after which you want the scale down transition to appear.

2. Click Scale Down to select it and then watch the preview in the Preview window.

3. Set the transition's duration with the Speed slider; try placing the slider in the middle of its range. If that is too long or too short, use the slider to set the proper amount of time for the transition.

4. When the timing looks close, click Preview to see how it looks on the Monitor.

5. After you are satisfied with the transition, drag the transition from the Transitions palette to the Clip Viewer and drop it between the two clips you want to transition between. The transition will appear as a blue box with arrowheads that indicate the direction of the transition if that is applicable to the transition you selected (see Figure 24.8).

Figure 24.8
Adding a transition is similar to adding a clip; the main difference is that transitions have to be rendered.

Rendering progress bar   Transition clip

Transitions are fairly sophisticated effects and require your Mac to do a lot of work to apply them to a clip. This process is called *rendering*. When your Mac renders a clip, it applies the proper amount of transition effect to each frame of the affected section of the clip. Applying a complex transition with a long duration can take a while. Fortunately, you can continue to work while your Mac renders transition effects.

When you place a transition on the Clip Viewer, your Mac will immediately begin to render it; you will see the small rendering progress bar at the bottom of the transition clip (refer to Figure 24.9). When the rendering process is complete, the progress bar will disappear. While a transition is being rendered, you can preview the transition or move on to something else.

If you want to make adjustments to the transition, select it in the Clip Viewer and use the time slider on the palette to change its duration or one of the transition's other controls to adjust it. Click Update to apply the change to the transition. (The clip will be rendered again.)

NOTE

> You can place two transitions adjacent to one another. For example, to have one clip fade out and then the next fade in, place a Fade Out and a Fade In between two clips.

Don't feel as though you need to have a transition before and after every clip. Sometimes the default Straight Cut works just fine. This is where your creativity comes in, so experiment until you achieve an outcome that is pleasing to you.

TIP

> You can play only portions of your movie by selecting the clips you want to play in the Clip Viewer (including transitions). When you click the Play button (or press the spacebar), only the selected parts of your movie will play. This saves time and helps you focus on particular parts of your movie. To play the whole movie again, deselect all the clips by pressing Shift-⌘-A.

24

ADDING TITLES

When it comes to titles, credits, and other text, your iMovie movies can certainly hold their own. You can add many title effects to your movies in almost limitless ways. You will be amazed at how much improvement you can make to your movies with the right title effects.

Although adding onscreen text is called *titling*, this term refers to much more than just the movie's name. Basically, *titling* is iMovie's term for overlaying all sorts of text on the screen. The titles you might want to use in your movies include the following:

- **Captions**—As with figure captions, you can use clip captions to add information to the image onscreen. You might want to add some explanation of what is happening on the screen or the date on which the clip was captured; you can even add subtitles if you want. *Captions* is the term for basically any informative text relating to a scene that you want the viewer to see. Captions can appear anywhere in your movie.

- **Credits**—I'm sure you are familiar with credits because most modern movies have several minutes of credits at the end. Credits are just what the term implies: the opportunity to take, or give, credit for something in the movie. For example, you can list all the people who appear in the movie. Or, if someone helps you with the movie, you might want to give him some fame by mentioning his name. Even though you can use credits anywhere in the movie, most credits appear at the end.

- **Titles**—Titles are text that can introduce a movie, a scene, or anything else you think warrants an introduction. Titles normally appear at the beginning of something, whether it be a movie or scene.

iMovie provides titling tools you can use to add almost any type of text to your movie. Titles are added using tools similar to the Transitions tools. You add and manipulate titles using the Titles pane. Click the Titles button to open the Titles pane (see Figure 24.9).

Figure 24.9
The Titles pane provides all the tools you need to add great text effects to your movies.

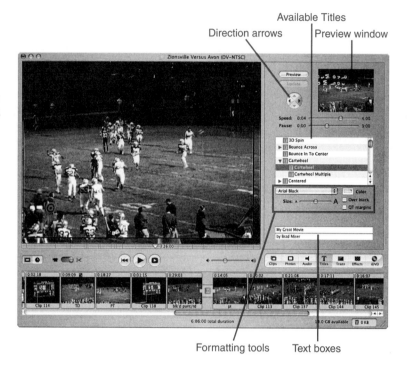

The following tools are included on the Titles pane:

- **Preview window**—This works just as it does on the Transitions pane. When you select a title style, you will see a preview of it in the preview window. You will also see a preview whenever you make changes to the title.

- **Preview button**—When you click this, you will see a preview of the title in the Monitor.

- **Update button**—If you make changes to a title you have already placed in your movie, click this button to update the title to include the changes you have made.

- **Direction arrows**—Some styles involve motion for which you can set the direction. You select a direction by clicking one of the active direction arrows.

- **Sliders**—Just like transitions, all titles have a set amount of time that it takes for the title effect to occur. You use the duration sliders to set this time. The Speed slider controls the overall length of the text effect. The Pause slider determines how long a text effect pauses on the screen (if applicable), and the Wave slider controls the amount of the wave (if applicable).

- **Title style**—You click a title style to use it. The tools that are active on the palette will change depending on the style you select.

- **Font family menu**—You can select a font family for a title using this pop-up menu.

- **Color button**—Click this to change the color of the text in the title (it also affects the stripe color in Stripe Subtitle).

- **Size slider**—This slider enables you to make the selected font larger (drag it to the right) or smaller (drag it to the left).

- **"Over black" check box**—By default, when you place a title, it will be applied over the selected clip on which you drop the title. When you place the title on a clip, the clip might be split in such a way that there are two clips. One contains the title effect, and the other contains the remainder of the clip. If you want the title to appear in the first part of the clip, drop the title on the left side of the clip. If you want the title to appear on the end of the clip, drop it on the right side of the clip. The adjacent clips slide apart to indicate where the title clip is placed.

  If you prefer the title to appear over a black background, you can check the "Over black" check box. Instead of being applied to a clip in your movie, the title will appear in a new black clip that is added to your movie wherever you drop the title.

- **"QT margins" check box**—A QuickTime movie has proportions different from a standard TV screen. For title styles that appear on the bottom edge of the screen, this can be a problem because those titles can get cut off when the movie is viewed on a TV. Checking the "QT margins" check box will move the title up on the screen so it won't be cut off when you show the movie on a TV. Unchecking it will move the title back down again so it will appear in a better location when you view the movie on your Mac. You should leave this unchecked unless the style you use leaves text at the bottom of the screen.

- **Text blocks**—You type the text for your title in the text blocks that appear on the palette. You will see two or more styles of text block, depending on the text type you use. Most styles use single lines of text, but others use a larger text block into which you can place a fair amount of text.

- **Add/Remove buttons**—Some styles allow you to add text blocks to the title. When the Add button (the +) is active, click it to add text blocks to your title. Click Remove (the –) to remove text blocks.

You will see different tools and options on the palette, depending on the title style you use. Some styles (for example, Centered Multiple) enable you to add more lines or blocks of text. With these styles, the Add button is active. Other styles (for example, Scrolling Block) involve motion for which you can set the direction; the direction arrows will be active for these types.

> **NOTE**
>
> Some text effects are grouped into families; this is indicated by the expansion triangle next to the text effect on the list. When you select one of these effects, it will expand and you will see all the effects grouped into that family.

Following are the general steps you use to add titles to your movies:

1. Decide which type of text you want to add (caption, credit, date, or title) and to which clip you want to apply the text (or whether you want to apply it to a black background).

2. Based on the type of text you add and where you apply it, decide on a title effect to use.

3. Open the Titles pane and click a title effect to select it.

4. Type your text in the text boxes for that effect. Use the Add button (if available) if you want to add more text blocks to the title or the Remove button to take away text blocks.

5. Select a font, color, and size for the title.

6. Set the direction of the motion (if applicable).

7. Set the speed, pause (if applicable), and wave (if applicable) of the title.

8. If you want the title to appear on a black background instead of on the selected clip, check the "Over black" check box.

9. If the effect appears at the bottom of the clip and you will be viewing the movie via a standard TV, check the "QT margins" check box.

10. Preview the title in the Preview window, and click the Preview button to preview it in the Monitor.

11. Make adjustments to the title until it is right.

12. Place the title in your movie by dragging it to the Clip Viewer and dropping it in the location at which you want it to appear.

13. View the section of your movie that contains the title to ensure it works the way you want it to.

14. If it doesn't, select the title and make changes to it using the Titles pane; then click Update to update the title.

Even though you will usually do most of these steps, you might choose to do them in a different order than I suggest. Just experiment to find the order that suits you best.

Just as the transition effects have to be rendered before they can be added to your movie, titles must be rendered before they appear onscreen. Rendering can take a while, so use the Preview function to get your titles in great shape before you actually add them to your movie. Just as with transition effects, you see a red progress bar in the title clips as they are rendered. If you update a title, its clip must be rerendered.

NOTE

Sometimes, existing transitions block you from adding a title clip. If this happens, delete the transition, add the title clip, and after the title has been rendered add the transition back in. If you are going to use many titles in your movie, adding the titles before you add transitions might be easier.

ADDING SPECIAL EFFECTS

You can add all sorts of interesting visual effects to make your movie look better and even more interesting.

APPLYING EFFECTS TO YOUR MOVIE

The Effects pane contains a number of effects you can apply to the clips in your movie (see Figure 24.10).

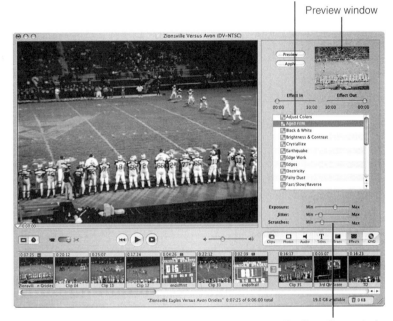

Available Effects

Preview window

Figure 24.10
You can use the Effects pane to apply a variety of special effects to your movies.

Configuration controls

The Effects pane includes the following tools:

- **Preview window**—When you select an effect, you will see a preview of it in the Preview window.
- **Preview button**—Click this button to see a preview of the selected effect in the Monitor.
- **Apply**—Click this button to apply the selected effect to the selected clip.
- **Effect In**—The Effect In slider controls the number of frames over which the effect is applied. When the slider is all the way to the left, the effect is applied in full force from the start of the clip. As the slider is moved to the right, the effect fades in and is applied gradually over the time selected on the slider up to the maximum amount of time on the slider (10 seconds). For example, if you wanted to apply the black-and-white effect to a clip surrounded by two color clips, you might want the color of the clip to slowly fade away so the transition to black-and-white isn't jarring.
- **Effect Out**—The Effect Out slider controls the time over which the effect fades out. When the slider is all the way to the right, the effect remains in full force until the end of the clip. As the slider is moved to the left, the effect begins to fade out from the

point at which the slider is set (the maximum amount is 10 seconds before the end of the clip).

- **Available Effects**—This area contains the list of effects from which you can choose. You can use the scroll tools to see all the available effects.

- **Configuration tools**—Various sliders appear when you select certain effects; these sliders enable you to change some aspect of the effect. For example, when you select the Ghost Trails effect, you see three sliders that enable you to configure that effect. Some effects don't have configuration tools; these effects are either on or off.

The Effects pane is a bit different from the Transitions and Titles tool panes. The tools on the Effects pane are related to each other only in that they are effects you apply to the video track. This differs from the tools on the Transitions pane, for example, on which all the tools are related to creating transitions.

EXPLORING THE iMOVIE EFFECTS

Although they do different things, all iMovie effects work similarly—after you use some of them, you can easily use all of them. Table 24.1 lists the effects on the default Effects pane.

TABLE 24.1 iMOVIE SPECIAL EFFECTS TOOLS

Effect	What It Does
Adjust Colors	Enables you to adjust the hue, color, and lightness of a clip.
Aged Film	Makes the clip look old by adding scratches, jitters, and other artifacts that appear in video captured with old cameras.
Black & White	Converts a clip into black-and-white.
Brightness & Contrast	Enables you to adjust the brightness and contrast of a clip.
Crystallize	Makes it appear that you are viewing the clip through a piece of crystal or glass (you control the amount of distortion).
Earthquake	Causes the clip to "shake."
Edge Work	Displays a pattern on the screen.
Edges	Highlights the edges of everything on the screen.
Electricity	Causes an "electric" line to appear at the top of the clip as if it is being hit by lightning or a Tessla Coil.
Fairy Dust	Causes a trail of "fairy dust" to move across the screen.
Fast/Slow/Reverse	Enables you to make a clip play in reverse and to change its speed.
Flash	Makes a flash of light wash out the clip for a time.
Fog	Shrouds the clip in digital fog.
Ghost Trails	Causes the clip to be ghosted so objects are trailed by faint copies of themselves as they move.

Effect	What It Does
Glass Distortion	Makes the clip appear as if you are viewing it through glass.
Lens Flare	Causes a spot of light to appear as if the camera were pointed toward the sun when the clip was captured.
Letterbox	Places black bars at the top and bottom of the screen to simulate the letterbox format. This effect actually cuts off the top and bottom part of the clip rather than reformatting it into the true letterbox format.
Mirror	Makes the clip appear with a mirror image of itself.
N-Square	Makes the clip play in each of multiple squares on the screen; you set how many squares appear onscreen.
Rain	If rainy days and Mondays get you down, you won't like this one.
Sepia	Applies a wood grain texture to the clip to make it appear old.
Sharpen	Adjusts a clip's sharpness.
Soft Focus	Applies a blur to the images in a clip.

24

NOTE

Be careful about using the Brightness & Contrast controls on your clips. The relative brightness levels of video can vary depending on the device you use to show your movie. For example, you might find that a clip appears slightly darker in iMovie than it does when you export it to videotape. Thus, if you make it brighter in iMovie, it might appear washed out when you view it on a TV. You should do some testing on your setup and how you will view your movie (such as exporting a sample to videotape) before you make many of these adjustments.

APPLYING EFFECTS TO CLIPS

The general steps to apply a special effect are the following:

1. Select a clip to which you want to apply an effect.
2. Select the effect you want to apply.
3. Set the time it takes for the effect to be applied and the time over which it disappears.
4. Use the effect's other controls to adjust that effect's properties, while previewing the effect along the way.
5. Apply the effect to the selected clip.

When a clip has an effect applied to it, you'll see an icon next to the timecode in the clip's box on the Clip Viewer.

You can change a clip that has an effect applied to it by updating the effect:

1. Select the clip that has an effect applied to it. You will see the clip in the Monitor.
2. On the Effects pane, select the effect you want to change and use the Effects tools to configure it.

3. Click Apply, and the effect will be applied to the clip; the clip will be rendered again.

When you apply an effect to a clip, iMovie renders that clip using the effect you apply. However, it also saves the original clip so you can go back to it if you want:

1. Select the clip that has an effect applied to it.

2. Select Advanced, Revert Clip to Original. The clip is restored to its previous condition.

You can restore a clip only until you empty the iMovie Trash. This is because the original version of the clip is stored in the Trash when you apply an effect to it. When the original version is removed from iMovie (by emptying the Trash), it is no longer available to be restored. Don't empty the iMovie Trash until you are sure you won't want to restore any of the modified clips to their original conditions.

iMovie's effects are interesting and fun to apply. Here are some more tips about effects:

- You can apply multiple special effects to the same clip. When you apply two or more special effects to the same clip, the number of effects you have applied is indicated by the number next to the special effects icon.

- If you apply multiple special effects to a clip and want to restore it to its original condition, you have to use the Restore Clip command once for each effect you applied to the clip to get it back to its original condition. For example, if you applied two effects to a clip, you must use this command twice to restore the clip to its original state.

- As with transitions, you shouldn't add special effects just because you can—which might be a temptation because they are fun to play with. A few special effects go a long way.

WORKING WITH THE TIMELINE VIEWER

To this point, you have used only one of iMovie's two viewers. The Clip Viewer is a good place to focus on the video track of your movie. But as you get into finer levels of detail in the editing process and start working with audio, you will switch over to the Timeline Viewer. This view will provide a more detailed view of your movie, and you will see all the tracks that make up your movie.

To switch to the Timeline Viewer, click its button (it has a clock icon) to see the Timeline Viewer (see Figure 24.11). This viewer looks more complicated than the Clip Viewer, and it is. This complexity enables you to do lots of great things, especially with your movie's audio track.

The Timeline Viewer has the following components:

- **Video track**—The top track on the Timeline Viewer displays the video track for the movie. You can see each clip in the movie, including video clips, transitions, and titles. This information is exactly the same as in the Clip Viewer, although it looks a bit different. The video track also includes the audio that is part of the video.

Figure 24.11
The Timeline Viewer enables you to see all the tracks in your movie.

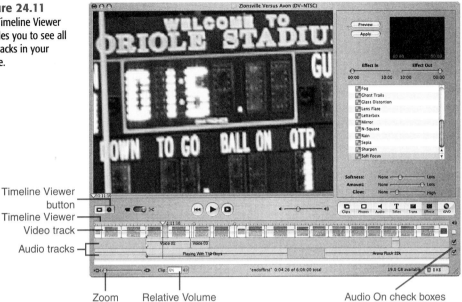

Timeline Viewer button
Timeline Viewer
Video track
Audio tracks

Zoom   Relative Volume   Audio On check boxes

- **Audio tracks**—You can place any sound on either of the Audio tracks, including sound effects, sound you record, and music. The sound on the track is represented by blocks when the sound is a sound effect or by bars when the sound is recorded sound or music.

- **Zoom**—You can select the magnification of the Timeline Viewer using the Zoom slider. When the slider is to the left, you see more of the movie's timeline but the elements you see are smaller and more difficult to work with. When you move the slider to the right, you zoom in and can see elements in greater detail. As you edit a movie, you can use this slider to change the view to be appropriate for the task you are doing. For example, when you are synchronizing sound, you might want a close-up view so you can position objects in precise relative positions. When you are recording sound from an audio CD, you might want to see more of the movie to see how much longer the sound you are recording will play relative to the movie's length.

- **Relative Volume**—This pop-up menu and text box enable you to set the relative volume of clips. For example, you might want narration in your movie to be louder than the music score. You can choose the relative volume level on the pop-up menu or enter a percentage in the box to set the relative volume levels of various audio elements. Unlike the Volume slider in the Monitor, this slider does change the movie. It is called Relative Volume because you change only the relative volume levels of elements in your movie, not the actual volume of the movie itself (which is controlled by the viewer when your movie is played).

- **Audio On check boxes**—The Audio On check boxes determine whether the audio contained in a track is audible or silent. When a track's Audio On check box is checked, the sound contained in that track is heard. Conversely, to mute a track's sound, you uncheck its Audio On check box.

NOTE

You can do everything on the Timeline Viewer that you can on the Clip Viewer. You can click a clip to select it. The clip will be highlighted in blue, and then you can apply effects, transitions, and titles to it. You can also edit in the Monitor just as you can when you select a clip on the Clips pane or in the Clip Viewer. Use the Clip Viewer when you want to make large changes to your movie, such as placing and moving clips, adding transitions, and so on. For finer work, such as adding sound effects, use the Timeline Viewer.

USING SOUND IN YOUR MOVIES

Using iMovie, you can create rich, full soundtracks for your movies. You can include the following four types of sound in your movies:

- **Native sound**—When you import clips into iMovie, any sound that was part of those clips comes in, too. If your clips had sound, you've already heard it numerous times while you were assembling your movie from those clips. You can use iMovie tools to control some aspects of your movie's native sound.

- **Sound effects**—You can add sound effects to your movie to bring it to life. You can use iMovie's built-in sound effects, and you can import other sound effects to use.

- **Narration and other recorded sound**—If you want to explain what is happening in a movie or add your own commentary, you can record narration for your movie. You can also use the narration tool to record sounds from a tape player or other audio device.

- **Music**—The right music makes a movie a better experience. You can import music to your movies from many sources, such as your iTunes Music Library, audio CDs, MP3 files, and so on.

You use the Timeline Viewer to control the audio portion of your movie. As you saw in an earlier section, the Timeline Viewer enables you to see all the tracks that are part of your movie.

Each track on the Timeline Viewer is used to create and edit one of the three audio tracks you can have in your movie. The top track displays the native sound in your clips. Typically, the top Audio track is used for sound effects and narration and the bottom Audio track is used for music. Functionally, there is no difference between these tracks, and you can use them however you want.

The tracks you see are all time-based views of your movie. The left side of the tracks represents the beginning of your movie, and the right side represents the end. You also see the Playhead, which works the same way it does in the Clip Viewer and the Monitor. For example, you can move it in the same ways, and the timecode shows its location in the movie. The frame at which the Playhead is currently located appears in the Monitor window.

You use the tools on the Audio pane to work with a movie's soundtracks (see Figure 24.12).

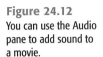

Figure 24.12
You can use the Audio
pane to add sound to
a movie.

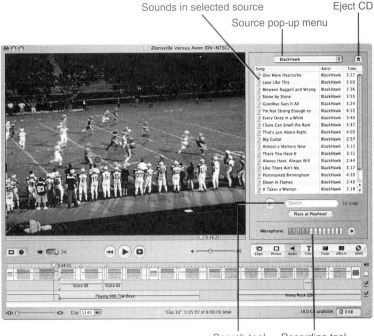

This pane includes the following tools:

- **Source pop-up menu**—This pop-up menu enables you to select the source of sound you want to use. Its three fundamental options are iTunes Library, which lets you access the music and sounds you have stored in iTunes (you can select a playlist to work with the songs it contains); iMovie Sound Effects, which enables you to add sound effects to a movie; and Audio CD, which enables you to record audio from a CD.

- **Eject CD**—Click this to eject a CD from your Mac.

- **Sounds in selected source**—When you select a source on the Source pop-up menu, the sounds contained in that source are listed in the center part of the pane. For example, when you select an iTunes playlist, the songs in that playlist will be shown. You can select a sound (such as a song or sound effect) to work with it.

- **Play**—Click this button to hear a sound you have selected.

- **Search tool**—Use this tool to search for sounds. As you type text in the Search box, the list of sounds is reduced to include only those items that contain the text you type.

- **Place at Playhead**—When you select a sound and click this button, that sound is inserted at the current location of the Playhead.

- **Recording tool**—You can use this tool to record sound, such as from a microphone connected to your Mac. An obvious use of this tool is to add narration to a project. However, you can also connect other devices, such as a tape recorder, to record sound from that source.

WORKING WITH NATIVE SOUND

Your movie probably has some sound that came with the video clips. If you recorded your clips with a DV camcorder, these sounds are whatever you recorded, for better or worse. Each clip has its own soundtrack, which is what you see represented in the Native track of the Timeline Viewer. The bars you see show the beginning and end of each audio clip (and by no coincidence, each video clip).

MUTING NATIVE SOUNDS

The most basic change you can make is to mute the Native track so you don't hear any of its sounds. To mute the Native track, uncheck the Audio On check box located on the right end of the Native track. Now when you play your movie, you won't hear any Native sound from it. To hear the native sounds again, check the Audio On check box.

CHANGING RELATIVE VOLUME LEVELS

Because your clips probably came from different sources or were recorded under different conditions, the sound level from one clip to the next might vary quite a bit. Although some variation is natural (you expect the roar of a jet plane to be louder than a cat walking across the road), too much variation (or the wrong variation, such as if the cat is louder than the airplane) can be annoying or distracting.

Use the Relative Volume pop-up menu and text box to set the relative sound levels of the various sound clips on the Native track:

1. On the Native track (the top track on the Timeline Viewer), select a clip that should be at the average volume level of your movie; after you do so, the clip's bar on the track is highlighted in blue to show it is selected.

2. Open the Relative Volume pop-up menu (the speaker icon) and make sure the Relative Volume slider is set to the 100% position, which is marked by a horizontal line through the menu. This will set the volume level of the selected clip at the average level.

> **TIP**
>
> You can also set the relative volume levels as percentages by typing a number in the Clip box next to the pop-up menu.

3. Select another clip in the Video track.

4. Use the Relative Volume tools to set its volume relative to the average clip you selected in step 1. If you want the sound of the selected clip to be louder than the sound level of your average clip, drag the Relative Volume pop-up menu above the 100% position; you can make the sound as loud as 150% of the average sound. If you want it to be quieter, drag the slider on the pop-up menu to below the 100% position. Or, if you want it to be about the same, leave the slider in the 100% position, which is the default for all sound.

5. Repeat steps 3 and 4 for each clip in the Video track.

6. Preview your movie to hear the results of your work. Hopefully, all the sounds make sense. Loud sounds should be loud and quiet sounds should be quiet. If not, continue with the previous steps until the native soundtrack is what you want it to be.

> **TIP**
>
> You can change the relative sound levels for several clips at once by holding down the Shift or ⌘ key while you select the clips. With the clips selected, use the Relative Volume tools to set the volume levels. The relative volume of all the selected clips will be set at the level you choose.

FADING SOUNDS

You can use iMovie's Clip Volume Levels tool to make the sound of a clip fade in or out smoothly. If you make a clip's sound fade in, it starts completely silent and smoothly increases to the level you set. Similarly, if you fade out a sound, its volume smoothly becomes quieter until by the end of the clip, when it has faded to silence.

> **NOTE**
>
> If you add a Fade Out or Fade In transition to a clip, its sound also fades, so you don't need to use the Edit Volume tool to fade the sound for that clip.

To fade sound, perform the following steps:

1. Select the sound clip you want to fade, such as one of the clips on the Video track that contains sound.
2. Select View, Show Clip Volume Levels. The Volume Level bar will appear through each clip in the track you selected (see Figure 24.13). This line represents the volume level at each point in each sound clip in that track. By default, this line is at the 100% position (relative position, that is).
3. Click the Volume Level bar at a point at the end of the clip whose sound you want to fade out. A handle (a yellow dot) will appear. (Volume handles are yellow when they are selected and purple when they aren't.)

> **TIP**
>
> Getting a marker to appear exactly where you want it to be can be difficult. If the Volume Level bar moves at the start of the next clip instead of the end of the one you are trying to fade, you clicked in the wrong clip. Press ⌘-Z to undo the marker creation and try again.

4. Drag the yellow handle until it is at the bottom of the clip; this represents the zero volume level. When you do this, you'll see a small box on the volume bar near the handle. This represents the start of the fade.

Figure 24.13
You can use an audio clip's volume level bar to set its volume at any point.

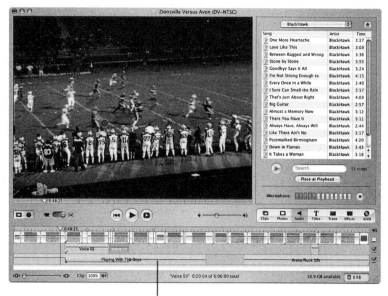

Volume Level bar

5. Drag the box to the left. The farther you drag it, the more shallow the slope of the line connecting to the handle will be; the more shallow the line, the more gradual the fade will be.

> **TIP**
>
> Instead of dragging the marker, you can either use the Relative Volume pop-up menu to set the location of the marker or type a percentage in the percentage box (such as 0 to make the sound silent).

6. Move to the beginning of the clip whose sound you want to fade in.

7. Click the Volume Level bar at the location in the clip where you want the fade in to end; a handle will appear along with the very small start box (remember to use the Zoom slider if you are having a hard time seeing all the elements you are working with). Sometimes, the start box is partially obscured by the handle so you have to look closely to see it.

> **TIP**
>
> The start box will appear only on the segment of the volume bar containing the handle that is currently active (selected and yellow).

8. Drag the start box all the way to the beginning of the clip and all the way to the bottom of the track. The clip's sound will now be silent at the start (see Figure 24.14).

Figure 24.14
You can use the volume level bar to set the sound level of an audio clip.

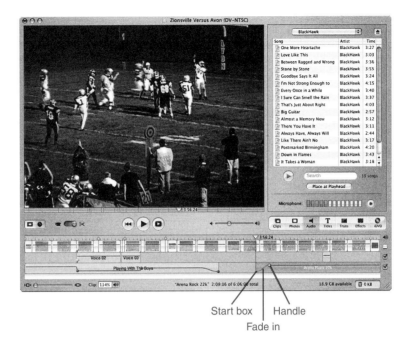

Start box | Handle
Fade in

TIP

The Zoom slider is especially helpful when you are working with the Volume bar because its handles can be hard to see. Use the slider to zoom in on the area on which you are working so you can more easily select the appropriate objects, such as handles.

9. Make the fade in more gradual by dragging the handle to the right or less gradual by moving it to the left. The steepness of the line represents the speed of the fade.

TIP

Before you can move a marker, you must select it. When a marker is selected, it is yellow. When it isn't selected, it is purple.

NOTE

To remove a marker (thus returning the Volume Level bar to its previous location), select the marker and press the Delete key or select Edit, Clear.

EDITING A CLIP'S NATIVE SOUND

As you learned when you began editing clips, whatever you do to a clip's video, you do to the clip's sound. This works the other way, too; changing the sound affects the video--unless you extract the sound from the clip (you learn how to do this in the next section). You should play each clip and listen carefully to its sound. Crop or trim the clips as needed to eliminate sounds you don't want or to include sounds you do want (without messing up the video).

EXTRACTING A CLIP'S NATIVE SOUND

You can extract the audio portion of the clip to work with it independently from the video clip. Extracting the audio from a clip also enables you to move it relative to the video clip. This is useful if you don't want to use all the audio but want to keep all the video in a clip.

One of the best uses for the extracting audio feature is when you have a clip containing background music that should be at least somewhat synchronized with the video, such as a ballet performance. You can extract the audio, and then you can edit the video part of the clip without hacking up the music that goes with it. You can then spread the extracted music so the single music clip covers all the video. Although the music might not exactly match what is happening in the video anymore, this is much less distracting than music that jumps around as the edited scenes play.

To extract a clip's sound track, select that clip on the Timeline Viewer. Then select Advanced, Extract Audio. The audio portion of the clip will be extracted and placed on the top Audio track. When you extract it, it's still in sync with the video clip from which it came.

After the audio clip is extracted, you can use the audio-editing techniques you've learned about in this chapter to work with it. For example, you can move it around, lock it in place, and so on.

When you extract audio from a video clip, the audio actually is copied to the audio track rather than cut from the video clip. The volume of the audio that is part of the video clip is set to zero so you never hear it again. Does this matter? Not really, but you shouldn't extract an audio clip unless you really need to. Because it is not actually removed from the video clip, your movie file is larger than if you didn't extract the audio (because iMovie carries two versions of that sound). If you want to mute only a specific audio clip, set its relative volume to zero instead of extracting it.

This also means you can hear the sound of a video clip from which you have extracted the sound by selecting that clip and using the Relative Volume slider to increase the sound of the clip again. You can use this for some interesting sound effects because you can have multiple versions of the sound playing at the same time, with each being slightly out of sync with the others.

TIP

> You can lock audio to a video clip so that when you move the video, the audio goes along for the ride and always remains in sync with the video. When a clip is locked, you will see the locked icons. One will appear at the beginning of the locked audio, and the other will appear at the point at which the audio is locked on the corresponding video clip.

ADDING SOUND EFFECTS TO YOUR MOVIE

One of the more fun aspects of making a movie is adding sound effects to it. You can use the tools on the Audio pane to add sound effects to do this.

To work with sound effects, open the Audio pane and select iMovie Sound Effects on the Source pop-up menu. The list in the middle of the pane shows all the built-in sound effects. Expand a collection of sound effects by clicking the expansion triangle next to it. The effects in the collection will be listed in the window. To hear a sound effect, double-click it or select it and click the Play button. The effect you click will play so you can preview it. Continue previewing sounds until you find one you want to use in your movie.

When you find the perfect sound effect, drag the sound effect from the Audio pane and drop it onto one of the Audio tracks. When you move it over the track, a yellow line will appear on the track where the clip will be placed when you release the mouse button; this line will indicate the point at which the sound effect will start playing. In other words, where you place the effect on the track determines where in the movie the effect is heard. When you release the mouse button, a bar representing the sound effect will appear (see Figure 24.15). You can work with the sound effect just as you can with the other elements in an audio track.

Figure 24.15
A sound effect has been added to the movie.

Sound effect

Drag the Playhead to the left of the sound effect you just placed and press the spacebar to preview it. To move the sound effect, click it to select it (its box will darken to indicate it is selected) and drag it to a new location. When you select the effect, the Playhead jumps to the beginning of the sound effect. At that point, the Playhead sticks to the sound effect and you can move it frame by frame using the left- and right-arrow keys (hold down the Shift key to move it 10 frames at a time).

When you have the effect positioned so it plays at the perfect point in the video, you should lock it to that spot so that, if you move the video, the sound effect still plays at the right time. To do so, select the effect and select Advanced, Lock Audio Clip at Playhead (⌘-L). You will see the locked indicators (they look like push pins) and, from that point on, the sound stays at the relative location of the Playhead when you used the command.

If you want to move the sound relative to the video track again, select the clip and select Advanced, Unlock Audio Clip (⌘-L).

You can also overlap sound effects. To do so, simply drag one effect on top of another. At those moments where the sound effects overlap, both effects play. You can more easily manage overlapped sound effects by placing one in each Audio track.

> **TIP**
>
> You can add other sound effects by importing audio files, such as WAV, AIFF, or MP3. When you import a sound file, it is placed on the Audio 2 track at the current location of the Playhead.

RECORDING SOUND FOR YOUR MOVIE

Using the Audio pane, you can record your own sounds to play during your movie. One obvious use for this is to add narration to various parts of your movie.

To record sound from an external source, you need to have some sort of microphone attached to your Mac. Some Macs have built-in microphones; other Macs have microphone jacks (although these sometimes require that you use a PlainTalk microphone). One of the best ways to record sound is to use a USB microphone. To record narration, use a headset-type microphone, such as those included with voice recognition software. Or add a USB sound input device that enables you to connect a standard microphone to it.

To record narration or other sound for a movie, perform the following steps:

1. Click the Audio button to open the Audio pane. At the bottom of the pane is the recording tool. It includes an input level monitor and the Record button.

2. Drag the Playhead to the point in your movie at which you want to begin recording.

3. Test your microphone setup by speaking into it or making another type of sound you will be recording, such as by playing a tape player connected to your Mac. The input level monitor will show the level of the sound being input. This bar should be moving to levels at least above halfway across the bar, but it should remain in green. If the level gets into the yellow, the input level is probably too high. If it gets in the red, it is definitely too high.

4. Click the Record button (the button with the red dot in it). Your movie will begin to play. Speak into the microphone or make the sound you are recording, such as by playing an external audio device. A purple bar will appear on one of Audio tracks to represent the sound you are recording. The sound you record is labeled *Voice #*, where # is a

sequential number (each time you click the Record button, this number increases by one).

5. When you have recorded all the sound you want, click the Record button to stop the recording process.

6. Edit the recorded sound using the same techniques you use for other sound, such as native sound and music.

ADDING MUSIC TO YOUR MOVIE

A music sound track can help you convey a full range of emotions or simply make your movies more enjoyable to watch. There's just something about music—we love to hear it, even when our main purpose is to watch something.

Because working with music is much like working with the other sounds you have already learned about, you already understand almost everything you need to know about adding music to one of iMovie's audio tracks. You can use either the Audio track to store the music you want to play during all—or parts—of your movie. You can use several pieces during your movie, or you can have one piece play throughout.

There are three ways to add music to a movie. The easiest way is to use music from your iTunes Music Library. You can record from an audio CD and import music as well. Because using music from your iTunes Music Library is the best way, it is the only one covered in this chapter. Frankly, because iTunes enables you to manage all the music with which you work, you aren't likely to use one of the other methods anyway.

To add music from your iTunes Library to a movie, perform the following steps:

1. Click the Audio button to open the Audio pane.

2. Move the Playhead to the location in the movie at which you want the music to start playing.

3. On the Source pop-up menu, select iTunes Library or select the playlist that includes the music you want to add to the movie. The songs in the selected source will be listed.

4. Scroll or search in the pane to find the music you want to add to the movie. Searching works just like it does in other areas.

> **TIP**
>
> You can double-click a song or select it and click the Play Sound button to hear it. To stop the music, click the Play button again.

5. Click "Place at Playhead." The music will be imported into iMovie and placed on the lower Audio track at the location of the Playhead. You will see the name of the song in the music clip (see Figure 24.16).

6. Play the movie to hear the music playing as the movie does.

24

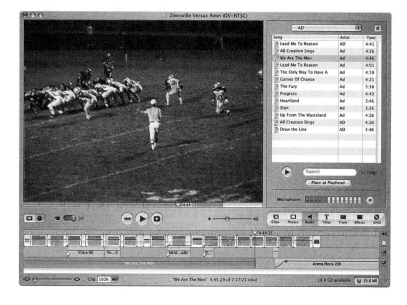

Figure 24.16
The song called "We Are The Men" has been added to this movie's soundtrack.

MIXING AUDIO TRACKS

After you have added all the audio to your movie, play it. Listen to the individual tracks (use the Audio On check boxes to turn tracks on or off) and then listen to how the various sounds interact. Use the editing controls to change the relative volumes of the tracks. For example, your music should be quieter than any sound effects you want your audience to hear. You can use the Relative Volume tools to make this happen.

You can also move music and sound effects between the two Audio tracks. This can be especially useful if you want to use part of one track but mute the rest of it. You can drag the sound from one track to the other and mute the track you don't want to hear.

NOTE

> If any of your sound tracks extend beyond the end of your video track, it continues to play while the video track shows a black screen. When you change a video clip after you have added audio tracks, be sure to preview the entire movie again to ensure you haven't created a problem.

The audio tools you learned how to use throughout this section work on all types of audio. For example, you can use the fade tools to fade a song, use the Relative Volume tools to set the relative volume of narration to music, and so on. Use these tools to blend all the sound in the soundtrack together.

DISTRIBUTING YOUR MOVIE

Watching a movie in iMovie is okay, but iMovie is not really intended to be a viewing application. After you have finished your movie and are ready to release it to the world, you export your movie from iMovie. What you export it to depends on how you want your viewers to be able to watch your movie.

People can watch your movie in three primary ways. You can record your movie on videotape that others can watch with a VCR. You can also export your movie to a QuickTime file that can be viewed on a computer—you then transmit your movie file to others in a variety of ways, including by email, on the Web, and on CD-ROM. The third, and definitely coolest, way is to use iDVD to record your movies on a DVD that can be played in a standard DVD player. The good news is that you can export the same movie using any or all of these methods to get your movie to as many people as possible.

DISTRIBUTING YOUR MOVIE ON VIDEOTAPE

Distributing your movie on videotape offers several benefits. The first is that the quality of your movie appears to be higher because you don't have file size or other technical limitations to deal with (as you do when you want your movie to be viewed on a computer). The second is that almost everyone has access to a VCR and TV and watching a videotape is easy. A third benefit is that storing a movie on videotape is easy (a tape doesn't hog valuable disk space, for example). Using videotape results in good viewing quality, as well as easy viewing and storage.

The first step to getting your movie on videotape is to export your movie from iMovie to your DV camcorder. This process works similarly to getting clips from the DV camcorder into iMovie.

Follow these steps to export your movie:

1. Connect the FireWire port on your camcorder to the FireWire port on your Mac (this is the same setup you used to import clips from the camcorder into iMovie).
2. Open your iMovie project; the Monitor will display the `Camera Connected` message.
3. Use the iMovie controls to move the tape in the video camera to the point at which you want to begin recording your movie.
4. Select File, Share. The Share sheet will appear.
5. Click the Videocamera button to view that pane.
6. If you want more than the default 1 second of black to appear before your movie begins and after it ends, increase the value in the "Add _ seconds of black before movie" and the "Add _ seconds of black to end of movie" fields.
7. Click Share.

Several things happen, all of which are automatic, so you can sit back and relax. iMovie will set your camcorder to record and then wait a few seconds to ensure that your camcorder is ready. The camcorder will begin recording while displaying 1 second (unless you set it to a different amount) of black screen. After the black screen, your movie will begin to play and your camcorder will record it. A progress bar will show how much longer you have to go (because your whole movie plays, the process takes as much time as your movie is long). You won't hear any sound while your movie is being recorded—this is normal operation.

When your movie is finished, iMovie will stop your camcorder. Your movie is now captured on the camcorder; from here on, you can treat it just like any other movie you have recorded. For example, you can connect the camera to a VCR and record your movie to a VHS videotape.

NOTE

> Some DV camcorders enable you to pass through a signal. This means you can output to a VCR at the same time you are inputting to the DV camcorder through FireWire. This is good because you can make a first-generation recording directly on the VCR at the same time you record it on your DV camcorder. In fact, you might not even have to record it on the DV camcorder at all. To find out whether your DV camcorder has this feature, connect it to a VCR at the same time as you connect it to your Mac. If you see a picture through the VCR while you export the movie to the DV camcorder, you can pass on through.

DISTRIBUTING YOUR MOVIE ELECTRONICALLY

You can also distribute your movie as a QuickTime file for viewing on a computer. The primary advantage of this method is that it is an easier and much less expensive way to get your movie to many people than using videotape.

TIP

> You can also distribute your movie via email or on your .Mac HomePage by using the related pane of the Share sheet.

The primary disadvantage to viewing your movie on a computer is that the quality is largely dependent on the computer being used and the technical savvy of the person to whom you have sent the movie. (Although it's easy, playing a QuickTime movie requires a bit more knowledge than playing a videotape does.)

The steps to create a QuickTime version of your movie are the following:

1. Select File, Share.
2. Click the QuickTime button the Share sheet.
3. Select the compression format you want to use on the "Compress movie for" pop-up menu. The format you select determines the size of the QuickTime file as well as its playback quality.
4. Click Share. You will see the Save dialog box.
5. Name your movie, select a location in which to save it, and click Save.

iMovie will begin to export your movie, and a progress bar that gives you an idea of where you are in the process will appear onscreen. Unless your movie is really short, the export process will take a long time, so plan on doing something else for a while. Eventually, the progress bar will go away. When it does, you are finished exporting the movie. This QuickTime movie can be viewed just like any other QuickTime movie (for example, in the QuickTime Player or on the Web).

The only complicated part of this process is choosing the format in which you want to export the movie. When exporting to QuickTime, you must always trade off file size versus quality. The better the quality of your movie, the bigger the file is (and the more resources it consumes to send or store).

When choosing quality and file size, always keep the recipient of the movie in mind. If you know that the person to whom you plan on emailing it uses a 56K modem, keeping the file size small is important. If you are using a CD, maximize quality; it doesn't matter how big the file is (as long as it isn't bigger than the amount of space on the disc, of course).

EXPORTING YOUR MOVIE TO DVD

Using the iDVD application, you can put your iMovie projects on DVDs that can be played in a standard DVD player.

→ To get an overview of iDVD, **see** Chapter 26, "Creating Your Own DVDs with iDVD," **p. 761**.

The iDVD pane enables you to add chapter markers to a movie and then send a movie to an iDVD project (see Figure 24.17).

Chapter markers

Figure 24.17
You can use the iDVD pane to add chapter markers and send a movie to iDVD.

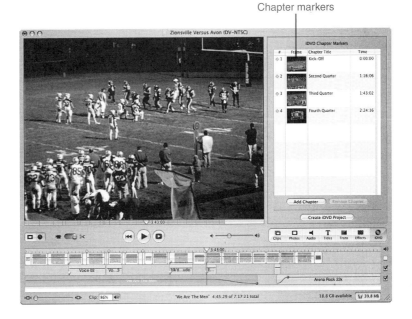

An overview of the tools on the iDVD pane is provided in the following list:

- Chapter markers—When you add a chapter marker to a movie, that marker is added to the list of chapter markers at the top of the iDVD pane. In addition to a thumbnail of the frame where the marker is placed, the name of the marker (which is the name of the related button on the chapter selection menu) and the timecode of the frame at which the marker is located will be shown.

- Add Chapter—This button adds a new chapter marker to the movie at the current location of the Playhead.

- Remove Chapter—When you select a chapter marker shown on the list and then click this button, that marker is removed from the movie.

- Create iDVD Project—When you click this button, a new iDVD project is created and the current iMovie project is added to it.

To add chapter markers to a movie, perform the following steps:

1. Click the iDVD button to open the iDVD pane.

2. Move the Playhead to the point where you want to place the first chapter marker.

3. Click Add Chapter. The new marker will be shown at the top of the iDVD pane. For each marker, the first frame, the chapter title, and the timecode at which the chapter starts will be shown.

4. Edit the chapter's title. This is the text that appears next to the chapter on the DVD.

5. Repeat steps 2–4 for each chapter you want to create.

After you have added chapter markers, click the Create iDVD Project button to open iDVD, create a new iDVD project, and add the movie to it.

CHAPTER 25

WATCHING DVD MOVIES WITH DVD PLAYER

In this chapter

ENJOYING DVDs ON THE MAC

DVD movies are the latest and best way to watch movies. Because they are digital, the image and sound quality of DVD movies is superb. And the digital format enables special features that can't be duplicated with other means, such as videotape. For example, with DVD movies, you can get true 5-, 6-, or even 7-track soundtracks to provide unbelievable surround sound and sound fidelity. Plus, DVDs usually have a lot of features—missing scenes, trailers, and so on.

NOTE

> Watching DVD movies from a desktop Mac is okay, but DVD movies on the Mac really shine when you use a PowerBook or iBook. Forget the crummy selection of movies usually shown on airplanes (when there even are movies) that you can't see or hear anyway. With a DVD-equipped Mac OS X mobile Mac, you can watch movies anytime, anywhere. If you travel a lot, you might find this reason enough to get your own mobile Mac. And waiting for just about anything will never be the same. With a mobile Mac and your favorite DVD, time is never wasted. I travel a fair amount and can't imagine leaving home without my trusty PowerBook and a pile of DVDs!

Mac OS X supports the playback of DVD movies with its DVD Player application.

USING DVD PLAYER TO WATCH DVDs

DVD Player has the following windows (see Figure 25.1):

- **Viewer**—This is the window in which you watch the DVD content.
- **Controller**—This window provides the controls for movie playback.
- **Navigator**—This window provides information about the disc you are playing and enables you to move around in it.
- **Bookmarks/Video Clips**—This window enables you to set bookmarks and work with video clips.

NOTE

> If you try to capture screenshots of a DVD using the Mac's built-in tools, such as the Grab application, you won't be allowed to or all you will get is a black screen. To capture DVD content in a screenshot, you need to use the excellent Snapz X Pro on a Mac equipped with an NVIDIA graphics card.

The Viewer window is straightforward. The DVD's content appears in this window; you can choose various sizes for the window from Half Size to Full Screen. In Full Screen mode, the Mac OS interface disappears and you can see only the DVD content and the DVD windows you choose to display.

Figure 25.1
With DVD Player, you can enjoy all the amazing content available on DVD, such as complete seasons of your favorite TV shows.

Viewer

Bookmarks/Video Clips

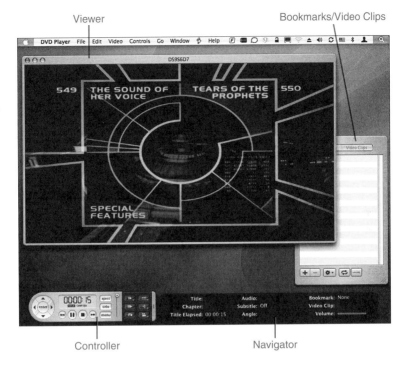

Controller

Navigator

NOTE

> One aspect of the Mac that has lagged behind Windows computers (whereas in most cases the Mac has led all other computers) is the availability of digital 5.1 sound capabilities. Currently, the Power Mac G5 is the only Mac that supports 5.1 sound out of the box. That's too bad because part of the greatness of DVDs is their amazing sound. If you watch DVDs using the basic stereo sound that is part of all other Macs, you are missing a lot. There are ways to add 5.1 sound to most Macs; if watching DVDs is important to you, consider adding such capability to your Mac.

→ To learn how to add 5.1 digital sound to your Mac, **see** "Finding, Installing, and Using Speakers," **p. 869**.

The Controller window contains the controls you use to watch movies. It has two orientations, which are vertical and horizontal. It is in the horizontal mode by default (see Figure 25.2). You can change the orientation to vertical by selecting Controls, Use Vertical Controller. To change the Controller back to the horizontal orientation, select Controls, Use Horizontal Controller.

The Controller has additional controls in the Control Drawer, which you can close or open (see Figure 25.3). To open or close the Control Drawer, select Controls, Open Control Drawer or Controls, Close Control Drawer. You can also open or close the Drawer by dragging its resize handle.

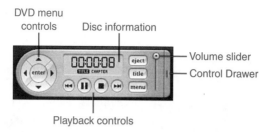

Figure 25.2
The Controller does just what you think: It enables you to control DVD playback.

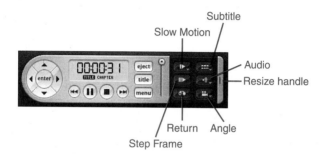

Figure 25.3
The Control Drawer contains controls you aren't likely to use as often as those on the main Controller.

If you have used a standard DVD player or VCR, the DVD Player controls will be easy to understand. To play and control a movie, use the following steps:

1. Insert the DVD into your Mac's DVD drive. After a moment, the DVD is mounted on the machine. By default, DVD Player opens and begins to play the DVD. Depending on the DVD, the disc's main menu might appear or you might be prompted to select a soundtrack or other features.

 If you see a message about the DVD's region code, see "When I Play a Movie, I See a Message About the Region Code Needing to Be Set" in the "Troubleshooting" section at the end of this chapter.

> **TIP**
>
> To configure what action your Mac takes when you insert a DVD, use the CDs & DVDs pane of the System Preferences application.

2. Select the menu option you want, such as Play Movie, by clicking it. You can also use the arrow keys to move among the menu options and then press Return to select an option. The movie begins to play in the Viewer window. When you activate a control, the upper-left corner of the Viewer window briefly displays text describing the control you used most recently (such as Play).

> **TIP**
>
> Click in the Disc information section on the Controller to cycle through the available data, such as chapter, remaining time, and so on. Click the Title or Chapter text to change the display to the related information.

3. Use the commands on the Video menu to control the size of the Viewer. If you select Full Screen, the image becomes as large as possible and the Mac OS interface is hidden. After a designated time passes, the Controller disappears, too.

4. To bring the Controller back, move the pointer, press a key, or press Option-⌘-C.

> **NOTE**
>
> If you're running a fairly powerful Mac and you minimize the Viewer, it moves into the Dock and the movie continues to play.

5. To see information about the DVD you are watching or move around in it, select Window, Navigator. The Navigator window will appear and you can see where you are in the movie and the features that are being used, including subtitles, the angle being shown, and so on (see Figure 25.4).

Figure 25.4
The Navigator provides information about a movie you are watching; you can also use its controls to move around the DVD.

If you see the NOT PERMITTED *message when you use a control, see "An Action I Try Isn't Permitted" in the "Troubleshooting" section at the end of this chapter.*

If you see a green screen when you attempt to view a disc, see "When I View a DVD, I See a Green Screen" in the "Troubleshooting" section at the end of this chapter.

6. Use any of the controls on the Navigator to move around the DVD. For example, use the Chapter pop-up menu to jump to specific chapters. You can also select specific features with the other menus, such as using the Subtitle pop-up menu to configure subtitles.

> **TIP**
>
> You can also control a movie by selecting onscreen controls with the mouse.

Following are some other DVD playback notes:

■ **DVD menus**—All DVD movies include a menu that provides access to the content of the disc and its special features. You can highlight and select commands on these menus using the keyboard's arrow buttons, using the mouse to point to them, or using the mouse to point to them on the Controller. You can move back to the most recent menu you viewed by clicking the menu button on the Controller; selecting Go, DVD Menu; or pressing ⌘-'. Depending on how the DVD is structured, clicking the title button might take you to the same place or it might move you to the DVD's main menu.

25

TIP

> When you move to a menu and then back to the DVD, you will move back to same spot at which you were viewing the DVD when you selected the menu command.

- **Use the controls in the Control Drawer or Navigator to quickly change the movie's settings**—For example, you can control subtitles using the Subtitles button or menu.

- **Scan forward or backward**—When you scan forward or backward, you can control the rate of the scan by selecting Controls, Scan Rate, and then the rate at which you want to scan (such as 8x speed). DVD Player supports scan rates up to 32x, which is really flying. The scan rate you select controls both forward and backward scanning.

- **Go menu**—Many commands are available on this menu that you can use to quickly access various areas on the DVD, including the DVD menu, the beginning of the disc, the content you were viewing the last time you played the disc, bookmarks, titles, chapters, and so on.

- **Bookmarks**—You can use this feature to mark specific areas of a DVD so you can quickly return to them. When viewing content to which you want to add a bookmark, select Controls, New Bookmark. In the New Bookmark sheet, name the bookmark (the current time is the default name) and click Add. You can return to that bookmark by selecting Go, Bookmarks, *Bookmarkname*, where *Bookmarkname* is the name of a bookmark you have created. You can also jump to a bookmark by selecting it on the Bookmark pop-up menu on the Navigator or by using the Bookmarks window. (You learn more about bookmarks later in this chapter.)

- **Keyboard commands work best**—As you watch movies, you will find that the best way to control them is using the keyboard. Most of the major functions in the player have keyboard shortcuts. For the best DVD experience, learn to use these shortcuts.

→ To learn about bookmarks, **see** "Working with Bookmarks," **p. 752**.
→ To learn the many keyboard shortcuts for playback and configuration DVD Player offers, **see** "DVD Player Keyboard Shortcuts," **p. 758**.

CONFIGURING DVD PLAYER

DVD Player is a relatively simple application, but you can do some configuration to make it work the way you want it to. The DVD Player preferences window has five panes: Player, Disc Setup, Full Screen, Windows, and Previously Viewed (see Figure 25.5). These preference settings are summarized in Table 25.1.

NOTE

> You can't control a movie while the Preferences dialog box is open.

Figure 25.5
You can configure
DVD Player using its
Preferences dialog
box.

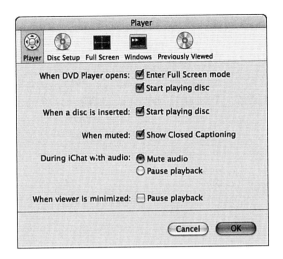

TABLE 25.1   DVD PLAYER PREFERENCES

Pane	Preference	Effect
Player	When DVD Player opens: Enter Full Screen mode	These preferences determine which action DVD Player takes when it opens. Because it is typically in the Full Screen mode when you watch a movie, this preference selects the Full Screen mode automatically when a DVD is mounted on your desktop and DVD Player starts (which it does by default when a DVD containing movie content is mounted on your Mac).
Player	When DVD Player opens: Start playing disc	If you want discs to start playing when DVD Player opens, make sure the "Start playing disc" check box is checked.
Player	When a disc is inserted: Start playing disc	With this enabled, a DVD starts to play when you insert it into your Mac.
Player	During iChat with audio: Mute audio or Pause playback	Use these radio buttons to determine which action DVD Player takes when you enter a chat session. You can have DVD Player either mute its audio or pause the playback of the DVD.
Player	When viewer is minimized: Pause playback	If you select this preference, when you minimize the viewer (and it moves onto the Dock), the pause function is selected automatically. This is handy when you need to move DVD Player out of the way to do something else (such as when your editor calls and you need to act like you are working). When you return to the DVD Player window, you can start viewing at the same point you left off.

continues

TABLE 25.1 CONTINUED

Pane	Preference	Effect
Disc Setup	Audio	Use this pop-up menu to choose the default audio track for discs you play. If you choose "Use Disc Default," DVD Player will start with the default audio track for the disc. If you choose a language, it will try to start with that instead.
Disc Setup	Subtitle	Use this pop-up menu to set the default Subtitle options.
Disc Setup	DVD menu	This option sets the default menu language for discs you view.
Disc Setup	Internet: Enable DVD@ccess web links	Many DVDs offer content on the Web. Use this preference to enable or disable links on DVDs you view.
Disc Setup	Audio output:	Use this pop-up menu to choose the output sound source for DVD playback. If you have only one sound option, your only choice is System Sound Output. If you have more than one option, you can choose the sound output you want to use on this menu.
Disc Setup	Disable Dolby dynamic range compression	If your Mac supports digital audio out, use the pop-up menu to select Digital Out to take advantage of that output, such as 5.1 digital surround sound. Use the check box to determine whether dynamic range compression is used (this evens out the volume level of a disc).
Full Screen	Hide controller if inactive for *x* seconds	Use this to control the automatic hiding of the Controller when you aren't using it. By default, the Controller is hidden after 10 seconds. You can change this time or turn off the feature if you want to manually hide and show the Controller.
Full Screen	Dim other displays while playing	If you have more than one monitor connected to your Mac, this preference causes all of them except the one on which the DVD is being shown to go black while you are playing a DVD.
Full Screen	Remain in full screen when DVD Player is inactive	If you want DVD Player to remain in Full Screen mode whenever it is inactive, check this box. By default, DVD Player switches to Maximum Size mode when you move to the Finder or another application. With this preference active, it remains in Full Screen mode instead.
Full Screen	Kiosk Mode (disable menu bar)	Check this check box if you want to disable the DVD Player menu bar.

Pane	Preference	Effect
Full Screen	Allow Screensaver on DVD menu in kiosk mode	When you enable this preference, you are operating in kiosk mode, and the disc is playing on a menu screen, your Mac's screen saver will activate. This prevents a static image on the DVD menu from appearing on your display for a long time (possibly damaging the display).
Windows	Display status information	The status information appears at the top of the Viewer and provides information about what is happening, such as when you click a control. Uncheck the "Display status information" check box to hide this information.
Windows	Fade controller when hiding	To have the Controller fade slowly out of existence when it hides, check this box. With it unchecked, the Controller blinks out of existence. (Your Mac must support Quartz Extreme for this to happen.)
Windows	Status and Navigation Windows, Text	Use the Text pop-up menu to choose the color of text DVD Player presents in its windows. The default is white, but you can make it any color you choose.
Windows	Status and Navigation Windows, Background	Use the Background slider to set the level of transparency of windows in DVD Player, such as the Navigator. The more transparent you make a window, the more easily you can see through it. (Your Mac must support Quartz Extreme for this to happen.)
Windows	Closed Captioned, Text	Use this pop-up menu to set the color of text used when Closed Captioning is displayed.
Windows	Closed Captioned, Background	Use this pop-up menu to set the color of the background over which Closed Captioning text is displayed.
Windows	Closed Captioned, Transparency slider	Use this slider to set the transparency of the Closed Captioned text box.
Windows	Closed Captioned, Font	Use the Font pop-up menu to choose the font for Closed Caption text.
Windows	Closed Captioned, Font size for separate window	Use this box to enter the font size when Closed Captioned text appears in a separate window.
Previously Viewed	Start playing discs from: Beginning, Last position played, Default bookmark, or Always ask	Choose the radio button to select the location from which you want discs to start playing. For example, if you choose "Last position played," a disc will start playing at the same point you stopped playing the last time you viewed it.

25

continues

TABLE 25.1   CONTINUED

Pane	Preference	Effect
Previously Viewed	Always use disc settings for: Audio EQ, Video Color, or Video Zoom	DVD Player includes tools you can use to adjust the audio, video color, and zoom settings for a disc. If you want DVD Player to use disc settings for these, check the appropriate box for the setting you want to always use from the disc. If you uncheck a box, you can configure the related setting manually (you learn how later in this chapter).

TIP

If you watch a TV series on DVD and choose the "play from last position played" preference, it can be somewhat confusing for you because when you insert a new disc, DVD Player will sometimes resume playing from a point that you haven't viewed previously. This happens because the markers on the discs for different episodes during the same season might be the same. Thus, DVD Player can't tell the difference between discs within the same season or series and moves to the same spot on the new disc that you left off on the previous one. If this happens, just select Go, DVD Menu to move to the disc's menu. Then you can choose which part you want to view.

CAUTION

Most DVDs that claim to offer DVD-ROM or web content are not compatible with the Mac. However, you can often open these DVDs via the Finder to access some of this additional content.

MAKING THE MOST OF DVD PLAYER

DVD Player might appear to be rather simple on the surface, but it has several features that might not be obvious but that might be useful to you. Check out the following sections for some ways to work with DVDs that you might not have thought of before.

WORKING WITH DISC INFO

You can use the Disc Info window to rename a disc and set an image to display in the Viewer window when the disc isn't playing, such as an image from the DVD. Here's how:

1. Insert the DVD you want to work with.
2. Move to the frame in the DVD that you want to display when the DVD is stopped—this image will be shown instead of a black Viewer window.
3. Select File, Get Disc Info. The Disc Info window will appear.
4. Type the name of the disc in the Title box. This doesn't actually change the disc, but Mac OS X will substitute the name you enter for the disc's name when it appears at the top of the Viewer window.

5. Click Current Frame. The image that appears in the Viewer window will be pasted into the image well (see Figure 25.6).

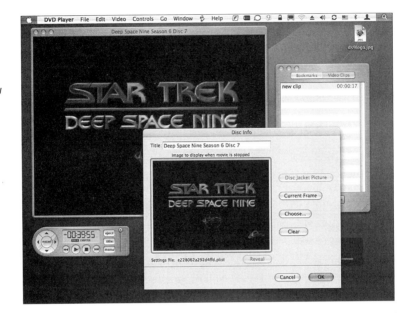

6. Click OK. The Disc Info window will close. The name you gave the disc will be the title of the Viewer window. When you stop the disc, the image you selected will be shown in the Viewer window.

> **TIP**
> You can also choose an image by clicking the Choose button in the Disc Info window and selecting the file for the image you want to use. To clear an image, open the Disc Info window and click Clear.

USING CLOSED CAPTIONING

Closed Captioning presents text on the screen for the speaking parts and some sound effect portions of a disc's soundtrack. You can control Closed Captioning for a disc using the following pointers:

- Turn on Closed Captioning by selecting Controls, Closed Captioning, Turn On. You can also press Option-⌘-T.

- To have the Closed Captioning appear in a window separate from the Viewer, select Controls, Closed Captioning, Separate Window. (Remember that you can configure this window using preferences you learned about earlier in this chapter.) When you play this disc, the Closed Captioning will appear in a window called Closed Caption.

■ Turn off Closed Captioning by selecting Controls, Closed Captioning, Turn Off. You can also press Option-⌘-T.

NOTE

> If you have Closed Captioning displayed in a separate window, when you close the Closed Caption window, the Closed Captioning will move back into the Viewer window.

WORKING WITH BOOKMARKS

NEW Bookmarks enable you to set locations within a disc and move back to them easily.

SETTING BOOKMARKS

To set a bookmark, perform the following steps:

1. Move to the point at which you want to set a bookmark.
2. Select Controls, New Bookmark or press ⌘-=. The disc will be paused and the New Bookmark sheet will appear.
3. Name the bookmark—the default name will be the current time position on the disc. You can name the bookmark almost anything you want.
4. If you want the bookmark to be the default for the disc, check the "Make Default Bookmark" check box.
5. Click Add. The bookmark will be added for the disc.

USING BOOKMARKS

There are a number of ways to work with the bookmarks you create, including the following:

■ To jump to a bookmark, select Go, Bookmarks, *bookmarkname*, where *bookmarkname* is the name of a bookmark you have created. You'll move to the bookmarked frame and the disc will play from there (if it was playing when you selected the bookmark).

■ Select Window, Bookmarks. The Bookmarks window will open (see Figure 25.7). Here, you'll see a list of all the bookmarks you have set for a disc.

■ Double-click a bookmark in the window to jump to it.

■ Click the Add button (+) to add a new bookmark.

■ Select a bookmark and click the Delete button (-) to delete it.

■ Open the Action menu and select Show Thumbnails. A thumbnail will be shown for each bookmark.

■ Select a bookmark and open the Action menu. Select Rename and then rename the bookmark, or select Delete to delete it.

■ If you make a bookmark the default, you can use the Default bookmark preference to have the disc always start playing from the bookmark each time you view it.

Figure 25.7
You can use the
Bookmarks window to
work with a disc's
bookmarks.

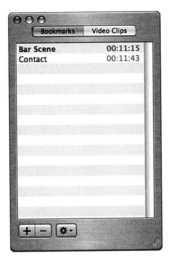

WORKING WITH VIDEO CLIPS

NEW You can mark video clips from DVDs you view and watch them. For example, there might
be scenes you love to watch over and over. You can mark these segments as video clips and
then easily view them anytime you want.

NOTE

> The term *video clip* is a bit misleading. You aren't actually creating a clip. Instead, you
> are marking a portion of the DVD as a clip so that you can watch that clip easily. It isn't
> really a clip, which implies that you are saving the clip as a QuickTime movie or some
> other object that you could use in another application.

CAPTURING A VIDEO CLIP

To create a video clip, perform the following steps:

1. Move to the point at which you want the video clip to start.

2. Select Controls, New Video Clip or press ⌘--. The new Video Clip sheet will appear,
   and the start time will be set to the current location.

3. Use the Controller to move the point at which you want the video clip to end.

4. Click the Set button next to the End Time. The end point of the clip will be set.

5. Click Add to create the video clip or Add and Play to create it and then play it. You will
   be prompted to name the clip.

6. Name the clip and click OK. If you selected Add, you will move back to the current
   location. If you selected Add and Play, the video clip you created will play.

WORKING WITH VIDEO CLIPS

There are a number of ways to work with video clips you create, including the following:

- To jump to a video clip, select Go, Video Clips, *videoclipname*, where *videoclipname* is the name of a video clip you have created. The clip will play; when it starts, you will see its name in the upper-left corner of the window. When the clip is done, it will stop playing and you'll see the complete message.

- To exit clip mode, select Go, Video Clips, Exit Clip Mode.

- To repeat a clip, select Go, Video Clips, Repeat Clip.

- Select Window, Video Clips. The Video Clips window will open (see Figure 25.8). In this window, you'll see the video clips you have created for a disc.

Figure 25.8
You can use the Video Clips window to work with a disc's video clips.

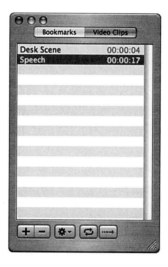

- Double-click a video clip in the window to play it.

- Click the Add button (+) to add a new clip.

- Select a clip and click the Delete button (-) to delete it.

- Open the Action menu and select Show Thumbnails. A thumbnail will be shown for each clip.

- Select a clip and open the Action menu. Select Rename and then rename the bookmark, or select Delete to delete it. Select Exit Clip Mode to move back to regular playing mode or Repeat Clip to repeat the video clip.

TIP

> You can repeat a clip by selecting it and clicking the Repeat Clip button (the arrows in an oval shape) or exit Clip Mode by clicking the Exit Clip Mode button (the straight line).

USING THE TIMER

The Timer feature will cause a specific action to be performed when an event happens. For example, if you tend to fall asleep watching DVDs, you can configure the Timer to put your Mac to sleep at a specific time.

To configure the Timer, do the following:

1. Start playing a DVD.
2. Select Controls, Timer, Set Timer or press ⌘-T. The Timer sheet will appear (see Figure 25.9).

Figure 25.9
You can use the Timer sheet to set an action that will be performed when a specific time is reached, such as the end of the disc you are viewing.

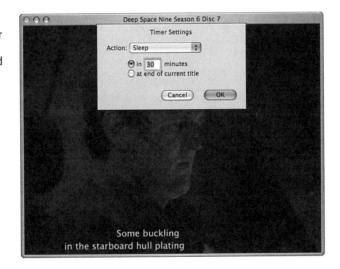

3. Choose the action you want to be performed on the Action pop-up menu. The options are Quit DVD Player, Sleep, Shut Down, and Log Out.
4. Use the radio buttons to set when the action you selected will happen. The options are in a specific amount of time or when the DVD ends.
5. Click OK. When the time you specified occurs, the action you selected will be done.

Following are a few other Timer tricks:

- Select Controls, Timer, Display Timer to cause the current time remaining and action to be performed to appear on the screen. It will disappear again after a few seconds.
- Select Controls, Timer, Pause to pause the timer.
- Select Controls, Timer, Cancel Timer or press Option-⌘-. to stop the timer.

SETTING CUSTOM PLAYBACK SIZE

You can customize the size of the video shown in the Viewer window by using the Video Zoom controls.

> **NOTE**
>
> Some discs prevent you from resizing video. If this is the case, you will get the NOT PERMITTED message when you try to use the Video Zoom function.

1. Select Window, Video Zoom. The Video Zoom window will appear (see Figure 25.10).

Figure 25.10
You can use the Video Zoom controls to set the size of the video being displayed relative to the size of the Viewer.

> **NOTE**
>
> Using the Video Zoom tool changes the size of the video being displayed in the Viewer window, not the size of the Viewer window itself. To change the size of the Viewer, use the commands on the Video menu.

2. Check the On check box to turn on the Video Zoom.
3. Use the sliders to set the width and height of the video.
4. If you want to maintain the video's aspect ration, check the "Lock Aspect Ratio" check box. When you move one slider, the other will also move to keep the same proportion between the two dimensions.

> **TIP**
>
> Open the pop-up menu located in the upper-right corner of the window for additional options, such as presets including Standard Display – Widescreen Movie. You can also create your own presets.

CONTROLLING A DISC'S COLOR

Similar to the Video Zoom tool, you can use the Video Color tool to customize the color settings of a disc. Do the following:

1. Select Window, Video Color. The Video Color window will appear.
2. Check the On check box to turn on the tool.

> **NOTE**
>
> Some DVDs prevent any sort of adjustment in which case you'll see the "Not Permitted" message when you attempt to doing something that isn't allowed.

3. Use the sliders to adjust the images you see.

4. To deinterlace images, make sure the Deinterlace Video check box is checked.

NOTE

Each frame from a DVD is composed of two images that are interlaced together to present a single image on the screen. By default, DVD Player will deinterlace images so they appear seamlessly. You can choose to prevent DVD Player from doing this. Whether you can tell the difference will depend on the specific computer and display you are using.

TIP

Explore the pop-up menu located in the upper-right corner of the Video Color window to work with presets or return a disc's settings to the default values (called the Normal setting).

CONFIGURING AUDIO

 DVD Player also includes a built-in graphic equalizer so you can customize audio playback for your DVDs and sound system. Here's how:

1. Select Window, Audio Equalizer. The Audio Equalizer window will appear.

2. Turn it on by clicking the On check box.

3. Use the sliders to set the relative volume levels of various frequencies.

TIP

Just like the Video Zoom and Video Color tools, you can use the Audio Equalizer's pop-up menu to work with presets. Also, you can open any of these tools from the same window by selecting the tool with which you want to work from the pop-up menu in the window's title bar.

TROUBLESHOOTING

WHEN I PLAY A MOVIE, I SEE A MESSAGE ABOUT THE REGION CODE NEEDING TO BE SET

When I try to play a DVD movie, I get a message about region codes.

All DVD movies contain a code so they play in only one of six regions in the world. This ensures that the format is supported by the display systems in that part of the world and also helps with piracy issues.

If you try to play a movie that has a code other than the one with which your player is set, you will see a dialog box enabling you to change the code for your player (in this case, the DVD drive in your Mac). If you choose to change the code, your DVD drive's code is changed. However, you can make this change only five times. At that point, the drive's code becomes permanent. I don't recommend that you change your drive's region code unless you are sure that most of the DVDs you will play in the future will have that code. If a code different from most of your movies becomes permanently set for your drive, you will be able to play only movies with that region code.

AN ACTION I TRY ISN'T PERMITTED

When I try to use a control, a NOT PERMITTED *message appears onscreen.*

The controls for a DVD movie can be activated only at specific times. For example, sometimes you can't scan forward through the warnings at the beginning of every DVD. The only solution is to wait until you are able to use the control.

WHEN I VIEW A DVD, I SEE A GREEN SCREEN

When I try to view a DVD, all I see is a green screen.

This can happen for two reasons. One is that you are viewing a disc in the wrong region; the other is that DVD Player sometimes suffers from an occasional glitch. Try resizing the Viewer window with one of the commands on the Video menu. Most of the time, this clears any temporary problems DVD Player is having. If this doesn't work, the region code is the likely culprit. Or, the DVD drive in your Mac might be failing. Try another disc to see if that is the case.

MAC OS X TO THE MAX: AND DVD FOR ALL

This section contains some additional information for your DVD enjoyment.

DVD PLAYER KEYBOARD SHORTCUTS

Table 25.2 contains keyboard shortcuts for DVD Player.

Menu	Action	Keyboard Shortcut
	Highlight DVD menu options	Up, down, left, right arrows
		Tab; Shift-Tab
	Select DVD menu options	Return
Controls	Scan Backwards	Shift-⌘-left arrow
Controls	Scan Forward	Shift-⌘-right arrow
Controls	Close/Open Control Drawer	⌘-]
Controls	Closed Captioning, Turn On/Off	Option-⌘-T
Controls	Eject DVD	⌘-E
Controls	Mute	Option-⌘-down arrow
Controls	New Bookmark	⌘-=
Controls	New Video Clip	⌘--

TABLE 25.2 KEYBOARD SHORTCUTS FOR DVD PLAYER

Menu	Action	Keyboard Shortcut
Controls	Play/Pause	Spacebar
Controls	Stop	⌘-.
Controls	Timer, Cancel Timer	Option-⌘-.
Controls	Timer, Set Timer	⌘-T
Controls	Volume Down	⌘-down arrow
Controls	Volume Up	⌘-up arrow
DVD Player	Preferences	⌘-,
File	Get Disc Info	⌘-I
Go	DVD Menu	⌘-'
Go	Next Chapter	Right arrow
Go	Beginning of Disc	Shift-⌘-D
Go	Previous Chapter	Left arrow
Go	Switch To Finder	Shift-⌘-F
Video	Enter/Exit Full Screen	⌘-0
Video	Half Size	⌘-1
Video	Maximum Size	⌘-3
Video	Normal Size	⌘-2
Window	Navigator	Option-⌘-N
Window	Show/Hide Controller	Option-⌘-C

TIP

When scanning, each time you press the related key combination, the scan rate increases by one increment. If you use the Controller's scan buttons, the scan is performed at the speed selected on the Scan Rate command on the Controls menu.

25

TURNING YOUR MAC INTO A HOME THEATER SYSTEM

Unless you have an Apple Cinema Display (and even if you do have one), you might want to use your Mac to see movies at a larger size than what your monitor provides. After all, even with a 23" monitor, viewing movies on a Mac is not practical for more than one or two people.

The solution to this is to add a projector to your system. You can attach a projector to any Mac that has a video out port (which all modern Macs have). Then you can project your movies to almost-theater size for an even better movie experience. You can also project the Web to that size along with any other tasks you do on your Mac.

NOTE

> A PowerBook or an iBook and a portable projector make an instant movie theater wherever you are.

And just as easily as you can project your movies, you can project the Web, your iMovies, slideshows, images, and anything else you work with.

Although projectors are fairly expensive, they are comparably priced to big-screen HDTV televisions. By adding an HDTV tuner, you can also project HDTV images with many projectors, so the projector can be used with various sources in addition to your Mac.

To add better sound to your Mac theater, you can route the sound output of your Mac to your sound system, or you can install a surround sound device to achieve digital sound.

If you have a PowerMac G5, you can take advantage of its digital audio output to listen to movies in full 5.1 digital surround sound.

25

CHAPTER 26

CREATING YOUR OWN DVDs WITH iDVD

In this chapter

Getting Started with iDVD

Apple's iDVD enables you to create your own DVDs that you can play on your Mac or via a standard DVD player, like the one you probably use to watch DVD movies. You can include all sorts of content on your DVDs from movies that you create using iMovie to slideshows of photos in your iPhoto Library. Along the way, you can include custom menus with motion and other effects just like commercially produced DVDs.

Because this is a book on Mac OS X and not on iDVD, in this chapter, you'll get a fairly basic overview of this excellent application. Fortunately, iDVD is so well designed that a basic overview is likely all you need anyway.

Touring iDVD

iDVD is part of the Apple iLife suite of applications. To use iDVD, you need to obtain and install the iLife suite (see the following sidebar).

Obtaining and Installing iLife

Apple's iLife suite includes five amazing applications, four of which are not part of the standard Mac OS X installation (GarageBand, iPhoto, iMovie, and iDVD) and are must-haves for any Mac OS X user. (iTunes is part of the standard Mac OS X installation and is also included in the iLife suite.) There are two ways you can get a copy of iLife. One is to buy a new Mac because iLife is installed on all new Macs. The other is to purchase the suite from Apple or from an authorized Apple reseller. Priced at $79, this suite is an excellent bargain, too.

Installing the iLife applications is simple: You just place the appropriate disc (DVD or CD) in your Mac and run the iLife installer. Use the standard installation to install all parts of each application, or use the Customize option to select parts not to install (such as the themes from previous versions of iDVD). Each application will be installed within the Applications folder. Before you start using these applications, run the Mac OS X Software Update application (choose Apple, Software Update) to ensure that you are using the most current version of each application.

---

iDVD has different modes for different parts of the DVD creation process. You use different sets of tools while working in each mode.

Understanding the iDVD Window

When you launch iDVD, you see the iDVD window (see Figure 26.1). Similar to iMovie, iDVD automatically opens the last project on which you worked. If you haven't used iDVD before, you can create a new project.

The largest pane of the window is the Content pane. What you see and do in this area depends on the mode in which iDVD is operating. When you are in the Design or Preview mode, the Content pane shows a menu of buttons on the DVD. Buttons represent each project that has been placed on the DVD, or they can lead to another menu. When viewing a DVD, you click a button to view the content or menu with which it is associated. When you are in Map mode, each menu on the DVD is represented by a box and the links between the menus are shown with lines.

Figure 26.1
Don't let the simple appearance of the iDVD mislead you; iDVD is a powerful application.

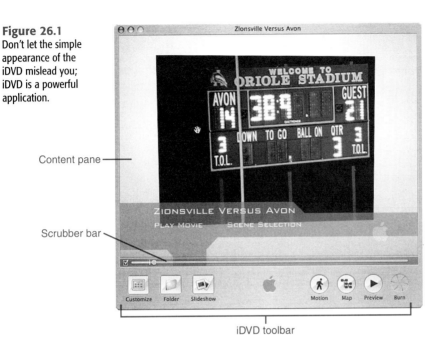

Content pane

Scrubber bar

iDVD toolbar

Each menu also has a theme that determines how the menu looks and sounds. At the most basic, a *theme* is simply a static image that is the menu's background. However, menus can contain motion, which means a movie can play as the menu's background while the menu appears onscreen (if you have watched DVD movies, you have no doubt seen examples of motion menus). Motion menus can include a movie with sound, a movie without sound, or a static image with sound. You can apply one of iDVD's default themes to your menus, and you can create and save your own themes.

Menus can also contain drop zones, which are areas in which you can display images or movies that are shown when the menu appears on the screen. Multiple drop zones can be part of the same menu, and some themes include multiple drop zones that dynamically change.

Buttons can also have motion, which means the content accessed by that button plays within the button itself while the button is being viewed. This type of motion provides a preview of the content without the viewer having to actually open it. (Again, if you have viewed commercially produced DVD movies, sometimes the chapter buttons contain motion and show you part of the chapter associated with the button).

Along the bottom of the iDVD window is the toolbar that contains seven buttons (see Figure 26.2). Each of these enables you to perform a specific task.

26

Figure 26.2
The buttons along the bottom of the iDVD window provide access to its tools.

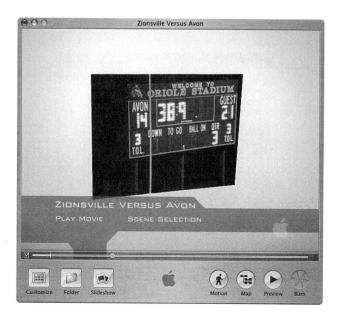

The available iDVD buttons are

- **Customize**—This button opens the iDVD Drawer (also called the Customize Panel). You'll learn more about this in the next section.

- **Folder**—This button adds a folder button, which represents a menu on the DVD. After you add a folder, you can place content on the menu that the folder's button represents.

- **Slideshow**—This button adds a slideshow to the menu you are currently viewing.

- **Motion**—This button turns background and button effects, called *motion effects*, on or off. When the button is green, motion effects are on and are displayed on the screen. When the button is gray, motion effects are off and aren't displayed.

- **Map**—When you click this button, iDVD moves into the Map mode (you'll read more about this mode later in this chapter).

- **Preview**—When you click this button, iDVD moves into the Preview mode (you'll read more about this mode later in this chapter).

- **Burn**—When you are ready to create a DVD, you click this button to write the project to a DVD.

When you click the Customize button, the iDVD Drawer appears (see Figure 26.3). The Drawer contains controls and information you use while you design and build a DVD.

Along the top of the Customize panel are four buttons:

- **Themes**—Themes are sets of formatting options you can apply to a menu. A number of standard themes are provided with iDVD. You can also create and save your own themes and use them just like iDVD's standard themes.

- **Settings**—The Settings tools enable you to customize the appearance of a menu from adding background images or movies and sound to formatting the menu's title to formatting the buttons' locations and titles.

- **Media**—You use the Media tools to access the music stored in your iTunes Music Library, photos stored in your iPhoto Library, and movies located in your Movies folder (you can add other locations as well). You can add any of these items to a project from the Media pane.

- **Status**—The Status tools enable you to assess the status of the content you place on a DVD. This includes both the movies you add to the DVD as well as any other files you want to include on it, such as high-resolution versions of the images contained in a DVD's slideshows.

Figure 26.3
The Customize Drawer enables you customize various aspects of an iDVD project.

UNDERSTANDING IDVD PROJECTS

Similar to iMovie, when you create a DVD, you first create a project. The project determines what content will appear on the DVD as well as its look and feel.

The content you place on a DVD can include movies or slideshows. Because you can place any iMovie or QuickTime content on DVD, there is really no limit to the type of movie content you can place on a DVD. You can create slideshows from still images in the usual image formats, such as JPEG, TIFF, and so on. Again, because iDVD supports all the standard formats, you can add just about any image to an iDVD slideshow. Because it is integrated with the other iLife applications, you can access your iPhoto images, iMovie movie projects, and iTunes music directly from within iDVD.

You can also add content to an iDVD project that can be accessed only when the disc is used in a computer; this content is called *DVD-ROM content*. Examples might be high-resolution versions of images in slideshows on a disc or other kinds of files or web pages.

26

When you place content on a DVD (by adding to a project), it is encoded into the *MPEG-2* format, which is the standard for DVD. MPEG-2 provides very high quality with relatively small file sizes (thus making digital movies on DVD possible). Fortunately, iDVD manages the encoding process for you and does so automatically.

A DVD created with iDVD can contain up to 90 minutes of content. However, iDVD uses a higher-quality encoding scheme when the content in a DVD project is 60 minutes or less—you should try to keep your DVDs within this limit, if possible. (You might think that 60 minutes isn't much, but you will find that creating 60 minutes of *good* content takes a bit of doing.) Again, iDVD manages this for you; the application selects the 90-min or 60-min format for you automatically.

> **NOTE**
>
> One of the nice things about iDVD version 5 or later is that you don't have to have an Apple SuperDrive in your Mac to be able to use it. The application will run on any Mac that supports all the iLife system requirements. When it comes time to put the project on disc, you can save it as a disk image and then use just about any DVD writer to create the DVD.

UNDERSTANDING THE DESIGN MODE

The Design mode is the one in which you add movies and other content to a DVD. You also use this mode when you are designing the look and feel of a DVD by applying background images, background sounds, titles, motion effects, and so on to a DVD on which you are working. Some of the major elements of the iDVD window in the Design mode are shown in Figure 26.4 and explained in the following list:

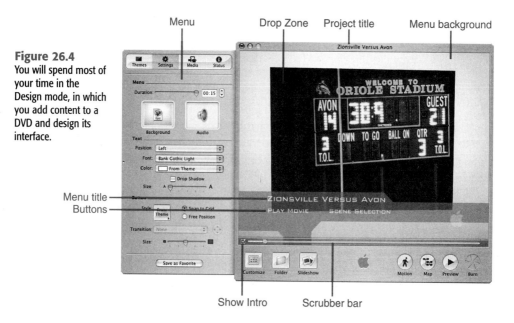

Figure 26.4
You will spend most of your time in the Design mode, in which you add content to a DVD and design its interface.

- **Project title**—The project title is the name under which you save the iDVD project file. This is the name of the file you open to work on a project. It does not actually appear when the DVD is viewed.

- **Menu**—The Content pane of the iDVD window represents a menu that appears onscreen when the DVD is viewed.

- **Menu title**—Each menu can have a title to identify it. You can format menu titles in a variety of ways.

- **Menu background**—Each menu can have an image as its background. Or you can use a movie as a background; when the menu appears onscreen, the background movie plays. You can also add background sounds to any menu.

- **Buttons**—Onscreen buttons represent movies, slideshows, or other menus on a DVD. Buttons can be text; images; or previews of the content to which a button points, such as a movie.

- **Button titles**—Each button is identified by a title. When a button contains an image or a preview, the title appears next to the button; when a button is text only, the button title is the button itself. You can format button titles in a number of ways.

- **Drop zone**—Some menus contain a drop zone in which you can place images or movies that are displayed while the menu that contains the drop zone is onscreen. Some themes include multiple motion drop zones that change over time. You can place different content into each drop zone.

DVDs that you produce with iDVD, just like those produced commercially, can include multiple levels of menus. Each menu can contain content buttons (such as for movies or slideshows) or menu buttons that lead to other menus. All DVDs contain at least the main menu, which is the menu that appears when the DVD is played. The main menu is also the one that appears when you open an iDVD project.

You can add menus to the main menu and then add submenus to those menus to build a multitiered structure for a DVD. You can use the Map mode to design the layout of an iDVD project.

Each menu can contain up to six buttons, with each button representing either content (a movie or slideshow) or a submenu. A DVD can contain up to 36 menus—you aren't likely to want to actually include that many, however.

In the Design mode, you can move among menus using the folder, Back, and Forward buttons.

UNDERSTANDING THE SLIDESHOW MODE

In the Slideshow mode, you can create slideshows from images contained in your iPhoto Photo Library or anywhere else on your Mac. You can control the order in which the images appear, the amount of time each image appears onscreen, the transition effect between images, and the soundtrack that plays while the slideshow plays. In the Slideshow mode, the iDVD window provides the tools you need to create your slideshows, as shown in Figure 26.5 and explained in the following list:

26

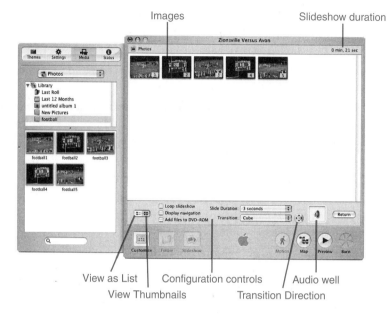

Images

Slideshow duration

Figure 26.5
Using the Slideshow mode, you can create slideshows from images in your iPhoto Library or from any other source.

View as List

Configuration controls

Audio well

View Thumbnails

Transition Direction

- **Images**—The images contained in the slideshow are displayed in the Content pane in the order in which they will appear during the slideshow. The order is also indicated by the number iDVD places in the lower-right corner of each image. You can add images to the slideshow by opening the Media pane, selecting Photos on the pop-up menu, selecting the source you want to use (such as a photo album), and then dragging images from the Drawer into the Content pane. You can also drag images from the Desktop onto the pane or use the File, Import, Image command.
- **"View as List"**—When you click this, the images in the slideshow are displayed in a list (see Figure 26.6). For each image, you will see a thumbnail and the filename. The images appear in the order in which they will appear from top to bottom.

Figure 26.6
You can also view the images in a slideshow in a list.

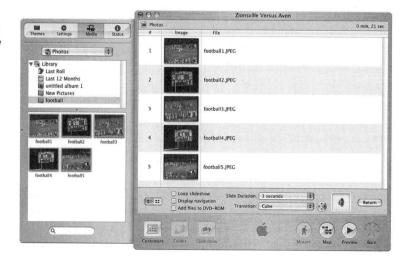

- **View Thumbnails**—Use this button to see the images as thumbnails only.

- **"Loop slideshow"**—If you check this check box, the slideshow will continue to play until the viewer clicks the Stop or Pause button or returns to the DVD menu.

- **Display Navigation**—Check this check box to have iDVD display Previous and Next arrows on the screen to remind viewers to click the corresponding buttons on their remote controls to view the previous or next image in the slideshow. You usually use this only when you set the slideshow to play manually.

- **"Add files to DVD-ROM"**—Check this check box to have iDVD add the image files to the DVD-ROM part of an iDVD project. When you do this, the high-resolution versions of the images will be accessible when the disc is used in a computer.

- **Slide Duration**—Use this pop-up menu to set the amount of time each image appears on the screen. The options are a set amount of time (1, 3, 5, or 10 seconds), Fit To Audio (which displays the images in the slideshow so it will last as long as the soundtrack you choose for it), and Manual (the user must manually move forward in the slideshow using the remote's controls).

- **Transition**—Use this pop-up menu to choose the transition effect that will be used to move from slide to slide. If the transition you choose has a direction component, click the Transition Direction button to set the transition's direction.

- **Audio well**—You place the sound file you want to use as the slideshow's soundtrack here.

- **Scroll tools**—You can use the scroll tools to browse the images shown in the window when there are too many to be displayed in the Content pane.

- **Return**—Click this button to move back to the menu on which the slideshow is contained; it also returns iDVD to the Design mode.

UNDERSTANDING THE MAP MODE

As you create a DVD, you will likely add many menus to it. You want your DVDs to make sense to the person who is viewing them; the Map mode presents a graphical layout of your DVD so you can visualize its contents (see Figure 26.7). Each menu, movie, or slideshow is represented by a box on the map. The paths among these items are shown by the lines connecting them. You can also create the basic layout of your DVD by adding menus, slideshows, and movies to it. In fact, using the Map to design your DVD is often the best way because it gives you a good overall view of your project.

> **TIP**
>
> You can scroll around the map by dragging in the iDVD window.

When iDVD is in Map mode (called *Map view* in official iDVD lingo), you will see the following elements:

26

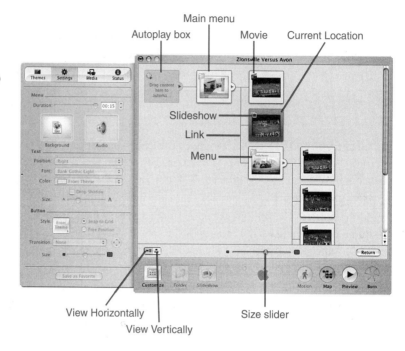

Figure 26.7
Use the Map mode to plan the layout of a DVD.

- **Autoplay box**—Place content in this box (a movie or an image) to have that content play automatically when the disc is inserted into a player. When that content is done, the viewer will move to the disc's main menu.

- **Menus**—A menu box has the folder icon in its upper-left corner. The main menu is always the one linked to the Autoplay box.

- **Movies**—Movies are represented by a box with the iMovie icon in the upper-left corner. Movie boxes can't be linked to anything except the menu on which the movie is placed. A movie is always the "end" of its branch of the map.

- **Slideshows**—Slideshows are represented by a box with the slideshow icon in the upper-left corner. Slideshows can't be linked to anything except the menu on which the movie is placed and are always the "end" of their branch of the map.

- **Current location**—Your current location in the project is indicated by the highlighted box. When you click the Return button, you will move back to this spot on the disc.

- **View Horizontally**—Click this button to choose the horizontal map layout.

- **View Vertically**—Click this to view the map in the vertical layout (see Figure 26.8).

- **Size slider**—Use this slider to change the size of the boxes on the screen. Drag it to the left to make the boxes smaller so you can see more of them at the same time or to the right to have the opposite effect.

- **Return**—Click this button to move back to the current location.

Figure 26.8
Same map, different view.

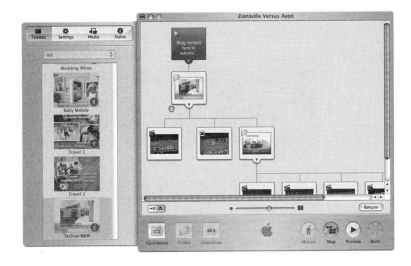

In addition to being useful to see how your project is laid out, you can also do the following tasks:

- Add autoplay content to the disc by dragging a movie or an image on the Autoplay box.

- Jump to any location in the project by double-clicking its box. When you do this, you'll move back into Design mode for the location you choose, such as a menu.

- Add content to the project. You can add menus, movies, and slideshows to the project by clicking the appropriate button. You can only use the buttons that are active given your current location. For example, you can only add a menu using the Folder button when another menu is your current location. Likewise, you can only add a movie or slideshow when a menu box is selected.

- Remove content from the project. Select a box and press Delete to remove the selected content from the project. If you select a menu box, it and all the submenus or contents linked to it are also deleted.

- Design menus. You can select a menu and use the design tools to customize it. You can design multiple menus at the same time by selecting them and using the design tools, such as applying a theme to them.

UNDERSTANDING THE PREVIEW MODE

iDVD enables you to preview a DVD before you burn it. In the Preview mode, iDVD behaves just like a DVD player; it even presents an onscreen remote control you use to control the DVD. You use the Preview mode to watch a DVD before you actually burn it to a disc. Previewing a DVD enables you to find and fix mistakes so you don't waste time and money burning discs that have problems. In the Preview mode, the iDVD window looks like that shown in Figure 26.9 and contains the elements explained in the following list:

26

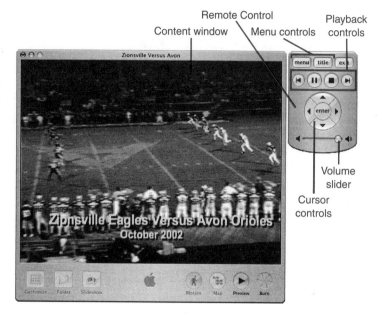

Figure 26.9
Using the Preview mode can prevent you from creating coasters.

- **Content window**—This window contains the content displayed onscreen when the DVD is played on a standard DVD player or on a computer.

- **Remote control**—The iDVD remote control simulates the remote controls used by many DVD players and includes most of the primary controls you use to view the DVD.

- **Menu controls**—These buttons perform menu tasks; for example, click the Menu button to move to a DVD's main menu.

- **Playback controls**—Use these buttons to play a DVD.

- **Cursor controls**—Use these controls to make selections in the DVD window. You can use the direction arrows to move the cursor and press the Enter button to choose what you have selected.

- **Volume slider**—Drag this to the right to increase the volume or to the left to decrease it.

UNDERSTANDING THE BURN MODE

This is the mode you use when you burn a DVD. In this mode, the iDVD window displays a progress bar that shows you the current status of the burn process (see Figure 26.10).

Figure 26.10
You can use the Burn mode to monitor the process of placing an iDVD project on disc or saving it as a disk image file.

BUILDING AN IDVD PROJECT IN A HURRY

iDVD includes many tools you can use to design every aspect of a DVD you are creating. These tools work very well, but they do take time and effort. Fortunately, there are some fast and easy ways to create a DVD for those times when you don't want to spend a lot of time building a DVD project but do want to get great results quickly.

USING IDVD'S ONESTEP TOOL

Using iDVD's OneStep tool, you can create an iDVD project, well, in one step. When you use this tool, the content on your camcorder is placed on a DVD as a single movie that plays automatically when the disc is inserted into a computer or a DVD player. You can't change anything about the movie nor customize it in any way. You should use this tool only when you want to place the contents of your camcorder on a DVD as-is. This can be handy for quickly moving a movie onto DVD or to archive the contents of a tape.

NOTE

> To use the OneStep tool, the hard drive on which your startup volume is located must have enough free space for the digitized version of the movie and the encoded version. Use the information displayed when you start the process to determine whether your Mac has enough disk space to perform this task.

To create a DVD using the OneStep tool, perform the following steps:

1. Connect your camcorder (with the tape you want to put on DVD) to your Mac and put it in playback mode.

2. Insert a blank disc into your Mac's SuperDrive.

3. Select File, OneStep DVD. Your Mac will rewind the camera and start moving the tape's contents to your Mac's hard drive. During this process, you can see the amount of video that has been captured and the amount that can be captured based on the room on the hard drive.

After that process is complete, iDVD will encode the file and then burn it to the DVD.

TIP

> If you want to start the DVD at a certain point on the tape, click the camera's play button at that point while it is rewinding.

CREATING AN iDVD PROJECT FROM OTHER iLIFE APPLICATIONS

You can also quickly create an iDVD project from within iMovie or iPhoto.

Use iMovie to create a movie you want to put on DVD. When you are ready to put the movie in an iDVD project, open the iDVD pane and click the Create iDVD Project button. A new iDVD project will be created and the iMovie will be placed in it. If you added chapter markers to the movie, along with the movie itself, a scene selection menu will be created and will have a movie for each chapter in the movie. After the iDVD project has been created, you can use iDVD's tools to save it, customize it, and burn it to DVD.

→ To learn how to use iMovie, **see** Chapter 24, "Making Digital Movie Magic with iMovie," **p. 699**.

You can quickly add photos in your iPhoto Library to an iDVD project from within iPhoto. Open the iDVD project to which you want to add the photos. Then, prepare the images you want to add within iPhoto, such as by placing them in a photo album. Select the images you want to move to iDVD and select Sharing, Send to iDVD. The images you selected will be prepared for iDVD and the iDVD will become active. A slideshow containing the images you selected will be created on the current menu in the iDVD project.

→ To learn how to use iPhoto, **see** Chapter 21, "Creating, Editing, and Organizing Digital Images Using iPhoto," **p. 623**.

BUILDING A DVD FROM THE GROUND UP

When you create an iDVD project, you should perform the following general steps:

1. Design the DVD by choosing and preparing the content you want it to contain and your purpose for creating it.

2. Open iDVD and create a new project.

3. Use the Map mode to layout the general content, menus, and organization of the project.

4. Add content to the project.

5. Design the project's menus.

6. Preview the project and fix any problems you find.

7. Burn the project on a disc or save it as a disk image file.

8. Clean up the files you created.

> **NOTE**
>
> The following sections provide somewhat general information about using iDVD. For specifics, see the mode descriptions presented earlier in the chapter and the iDVD Help system.

DESIGNING A DVD

The results of your project will likely be much better if you think about your goals for it before jumping into iDVD. Decide the content you want to deliver, how you want it to be organized, and how you want the disc to be organized. Create the content using other tools, such as iMovie and iPhoto, so that the iDVD project's content will be ready to go. This enables you to focus on the DVD itself when you start working in iDVD. Create a simple roadmap for the DVD that lists each project you want it to contain and how you want to group that content.

CREATING A DVD PROJECT

When your general design is done, jump into iDVD and create a new project by selecting File, New. In the resulting sheet, name your project, choose a location in which to save it, and click Create. The location you choose must have lots of free space. Your DVD can contain up to 4GB of data, plus iDVD will need room to store the encoded version that it will burn to disc. You can store an iDVD project on any volume on your Mac. iDVD will create the new project and you will be ready to get to work.

LAYING OUT A DVD PROJECT USING THE MAP

Use the Map view to design the overall structure and organization of the iDVD project:

1. Click the Map button to move into the Map view. You'll see the Autoplay box that will be connected to the disc's main menu.

2. If you want to have content play automatically when the disc is inserted in a computer or a DVD player, drag that content onto the Autoplay box.

→ To learn how to locate content to drag to the Autoplay box, **see** "Adding Content to a DVD," **p. 776**.

3. Add menus to the main menu by selecting it and clicking the Folder button. A new menu attached to the selected one will be created each time you click the button.

4. Continue adding menus and submenus to the project until you have added all that you need according to your plan.

> **NOTE**
>
> You can have up to 12 buttons on a single menu. If you need to use more than that, create submenus for some of the buttons.

ADDING CONTENT TO A DVD

There are two general types of content you will add to your iDVD projects: iMovie movies and iPhoto slideshows.

> **TIP**
>
> You can add other kinds of content to an iDVD project as well. For example, you can drag any QuickTime movie onto an iDVD menu to add it to the project. You can also add images directly to a slideshow without having those images in your iPhoto Library.

ADDING MOVIES TO A DVD

The general steps to add a movie to an iDVD project are as follows:

1. Move to the menu to which you want to add the movie by double-clicking the menu's button on the map or by clicking the menu's folder icon while in Design mode. The menu will appear in the Content pane.

> **TIP**
>
> While you are adding content, click the Motion button to turn off motion effects because they can be distracting. Also ignore menu and button names for now.

2. Click the Customize button. The iDVD Drawer will open.
3. Click the Media button to open the Media pane.
4. Select Movies on the pop-up menu. Below the pop-up menu, you'll see your Movies folder.
5. Select the Movies folder. In the lower part of the pane, you'll see all the iMovie projects in that folder.
6. Drag the movie file from the Media pane onto the menu being displayed in the Content pane. A new button representing the movie will be added to the menu. The name of the button will be the name of the iMovie project (see Figure 26.11).

> **TIP**
>
> If the movie you want to add to a menu is not stored in your Movies folder, open the Movies pane of the iDVD Preferences dialog box and click the Add button. Move to the folder that contains the movie you want to add, select it, and click Open. The folder you selected will appear in the upper pane of the Media pane. Select it to see and select its contents. You can also add the movie to your Movies folder to make it available.

7. Continue adding movies to the current menu until you have added all of them called for in your plan.
8. Move back to Map view and then move to the next menu that will have movies on it.

Figure 26.11
This menu has two submenus (the My Folder buttons) and two movies.

9. Repeat steps 2–7 until you have added the movies to that menu.

10. Continue this process until you have added all the movies identified in your plan to the iDVD project.

> **NOTE**
>
> You might be tempted to start designing your DVD's menus before you have added menus and content to it. You can certainly do that, but the process will be more efficient if you do it in the order presented here. That's because the design of your menus will often be impacted by the content you place on them. Get the layout and content done first; then you can focus on the customization of menus and buttons.

ADDING SLIDESHOWS TO A DVD

Use the following steps to add slideshows of images in your iPhoto Library to the project:

1. Move to the menu to which you want to add a slideshow by double-clicking the menu's button on the map or by clicking the menu's folder icon while in Design mode. The menu will appear in the Content pane.

2. Click the Slideshow button. A new slideshow button will be created on the current menu.

3. Double-click the new button to move into Slideshow mode.

4. Click the Customize button. The iDVD Drawer will open.

5. Click the Media button to open the Media pane.

6. Choose Photos on the pop-up menu. The sources in iPhoto will be displayed in the top pane.

TIP

> You can use the Search tool at the bottom of the Media pane to search for items in the selected source. You can use the Play button to preview movies or music in the pane as well.

7. Select the source of images you want to include in the slideshow, such as a photo album. The images in that source will appear in the pane.

8. Drag the images you want to use from the Media pane onto the Content pane. The images will be added to the slideshow and you'll see a thumbnail of each image. In the upper-right corner of the window, you'll see the slideshow's duration.

9. Move the images around the content pane until they are in the order in which you want them to play in the slideshow.

10. Use the configuration tools you learned about earlier in the chapter to configure the slideshow, such as by choosing transitions.

11. On the pop-up menu in the Media pane, select Audio. The sources of music stored in iTunes will be shown in the upper pane.

12. Select the source of the soundtrack you want to add to the slideshow in the upper pane. The songs in that source will be shown in the lower pane.

13. Drag the song you want to use as a soundtrack from the Media pane onto the Audio well. The default icon will be replaced by an iTunes icon to show you that the song has been added to the slideshow (see Figure 26.12).

Figure 26.12
Although you can't hear it because this book doesn't have a soundtrack, this slideshow does have one.

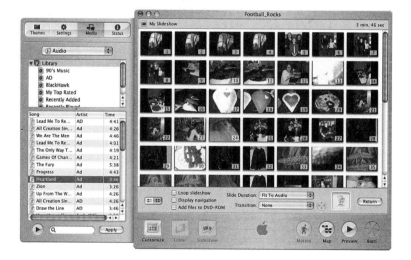

TIP

> If you want the slideshow and soundtrack to end at precisely the same time, select Fit To Audio on the Slide Duration pop-up menu (it is selected by default when you add something to the Audio well).

14. Click Return. You will move back to the previous menu.

15. Repeat these steps until you have added all the slideshows called for in your plans.

DESIGNING A DVD'S MENUS

After your project has all the menus and content you intend it to, it's time to start customizing its look and feel. There are lots of ways to do that, and in this section you'll get an overview of some of iDVD's great formatting tools.

TIP

> If you discover menus or content you want to get rid of, select that item's button and press the Delete key.

NAMING BUTTONS AND MENUS

DVD menus and the buttons they contain have text titles to help the viewer identify those items. After you add menus and content to a DVD, you should create meaningful text names for each item on the disc:

1. Move to the main menu.

2. Click once on the menu title (which will default to be the name of the theme applied to it), pause for a moment, and then click again. The text will become highlighted to indicate that you can edit it.

3. Type a name for the menu.

4. Perform steps 1 and 2 for the name of each button on the menu. Some buttons will already have names, such as the name of an iMovie project. You can leave these names or edit them to suit your purposes.

5. Use the navigation buttons or Map view to move to the next menu in the project.

6. Name the menu and all its buttons.

7. Repeat these steps until you have named all the menus and buttons on the DVD (see Figure 26.13).

UNDERSTANDING AND SELECTING THEMES

Themes are a general set of formatting options that you can apply to menus to determine how those menus appear onscreen (and sound if the theme includes sounds). To apply themes to your menus, perform the following steps:

1. Move to the main menu.

2. If it isn't on already, click the Motion button to turn on Motion effects. Some themes include these, and seeing and hearing them can help you choose the right theme for a menu.

3. Click the Themes button in the Drawer to open the Themes pane.

26

Figure 26.13
This menu isn't yet much to look at, but at least the button and title names make sense.

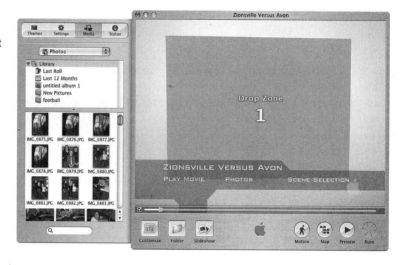

> **TIP**
>
> As you will learn later, you can customize themes and then save the result as a favorite that you can apply again as easily as you can apply the built-in themes.

4. Use the pop-up menu to choose the category of themes you want to use. The choices include All, 5.0 Themes, and so on. When you make a selection, thumbnails of the themes in that category will be shown beneath the pop-up menu.

5. Scroll through the list of themes until you see one you want to try.

6. Click a theme. The menu will be redesigned according to the theme you selected (see Figure 26.14). If the theme includes motion effects, you will see and hear them. The Scrubber bar will appear just above the toolbar and you will see the Playhead move as the motion effects play. If the theme includes drop zones, you'll see a placeholder for each drop zone.

> **TIP**
>
> If the Intro check box appears, the first part of the motion effect will be the titles moving onto the screen. The length of the introduction will be represented by a vertical line to the right of the check box. If you don't want to use the introduction, uncheck the check box.

7. Continue trying themes until you find the right one for the menu.

8. Apply themes to all the menus in the project.

> **TIP**
>
> Remember that you can apply themes to multiple menus at the same time by selecting them in the Map mode and then choosing a theme.

Figure 26.14
Same menu, different theme.

CONFIGURING DROP ZONES

Many themes include drop zones, which are zones in which you drop content to have that content displayed while the menu appears onscreen. Some themes have more than one drop zone, with all of them appearing at the same time. Others rotate through each drop zone as the menu appears onscreen. You can place images or movies into any of these drop zones:

1. Move to a menu containing a drop zone.
2. Select Project, Edit Drop Zones. You'll see the Drop Zone window and tools (see Figure 26.15). Each drop zone will be represented by a box and numbered accordingly.

Figure 26.15
Use this mode to configure the drop zones on a menu.

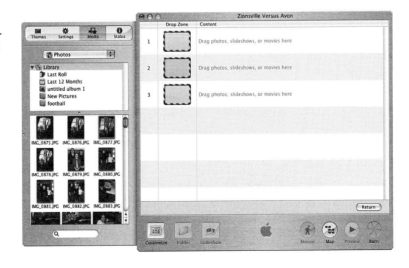

3. Add images, movies, or slideshows to each drop zone. You add content to drop zones by dragging that content from the Media pane or from your Desktop onto the drop zone.

26

TIP

> If you drag more than one image onto a drop zone, the images you drag will play as a slideshow in the drop zone.

4. Click Return. You'll move back to the menu and the content you placed into each drop zone will play (see Figure 26.16).

Figure 26.16
Too bad you can't see the cool motion effects of these drop zones.

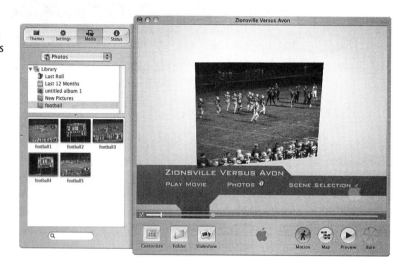

TIP

> To adjust the part of an image you see in a drop zone, drag it around the drop zone box.

5. Place content in all the drop zones in the project.

TIP

> You can remove the Apple logo from your menus by unchecking the "Show Apple logo watermark" check box on the General pane of the iDVD Preferences dialog box.

DESIGNING CUSTOM MENUS AND BUTTONS

Using the default themes is great because you can quickly apply a lot of great formatting to your menus. But, you aren't limited to using these themes; you can customize menus in as much detail as you'd like. To do so, click the Settings button in the Drawer and you'll see the customization tools (see Figure 26.17).

Use the tools in the top part of the pane, labeled Menu, to configure the background of the menu. You can perform the following actions:

Figure 26.17
Use the tools on the Settings pane to customize your menus.

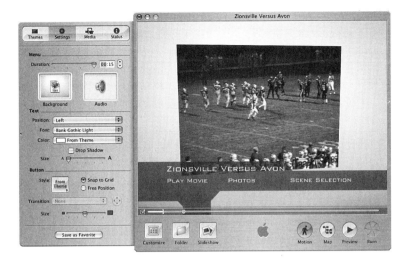

- Set the duration of background motion effects using the Duration slider or input boxes.

- Apply an image or movie to the background by dragging the image or movie onto the Background well.

- Apply an audio background to the menu by dragging an audio file onto the Audio well.

In the center part of the pane, you'll see the tools you can use to customize the title of a menu, including its position, font, color, drop shadow, and size.

TIP

> The Text tools apply to the menu title when nothing is selected or the title is selected.

You can customize the buttons on a menu in the following ways:

- Choose the button style on the Style pop-up menu.

- Configure button labels by selecting at least one button on the menu and using the Text tools to set the text attributes of those labels.

- Click the "Snap to Grid" radio button to keep buttons on the menu aligned according to the menu's grid, or click "Free Position" if you want to place them manually by dragging them to new locations on the menu.

- If you use a button that includes an image box (all except text buttons), you can place images, slideshows, or movies within the buttons just like you can do for drop zones.

- If you place more than one image in a button, select that button and use the Transition pop-up menu and Direction arrows to configure the transitions between images.

- Set the size of the buttons using the Size slider.

26

■ You can save your customizations as a new theme by clicking the "Save as Favorite" button. Name the new favorite. Check the "Shared for all users" check box if you want everyone who uses your Mac to be able use the theme you created. Check the "Replace existing" check box if you have already saved a theme with the same name and want to replace that version with a new one. Click OK. Your customized theme will appear on the Themes pane when you choose the All or Favorites category. You can apply your new theme to other menus by clicking it.

TIP

> If you will be viewing the DVD on a standard TV, select Advanced, Show TV Safe Area. A red box will appear in the Content pane, and anything inside the box will be displayed on the screen. Things outside the box might or might not be displayed. To be safe, design your DVD so that all the important elements appear within the TV Safe box.

The design process is definitely iterative. Some changes you make won't look quite right and will cause you to make other changes. Expect to go back and forth between menu design, titles, and other elements to get your design just right.

PREVIEWING AND FIXING A DVD

After you have designed the project, use the Preview mode to preview it. Look for problems with both design (layouts, buttons, and menus) and content. Design problems need to be fixed using iDVD. Content problems, such as problems with movies, need to be fixed in the creating application; then add the content to the DVD again.

This part of the process tends to be tedious, but it will pay off in the long run by saving you the time and money required to burn discs with which you find problems.

BURNING A DVD

When you project is done, you can put on it a disc.

BURNING A DVD IN IDVD

TIP

> Before burning a disc, make sure you have saved the project in case the burn process goes bad and iDVD quits.

If your Mac has an Apple SuperDrive, click the Burn button to burn a disc. Follow the onscreen instructions and watch the progress information to complete the process. The time required to burn a DVD varies greatly depending on your hardware, how much content the project has, and how complex it is.

When the process is complete, the disc will be ready to watch.

WALDENBOOKS

SALE   0705   102 1989 04-16-07
              REL 7.9/1.08 17 18:50:08

01 0672327279   14.99
02 0789733919   49.99
   BR NO. 8323812076 EXP 01/30
              SUBTOTAL   64.98
GEORGIA 7.0% TAX   4.55
              TOTAL   69.53
XXXXXXXXXXXXX8088 M C   69.53
              PV# 0021989

     Visit www.WaldenbooksStores.com

=========CUSTOMER RECEIPT=========

Get the card that gives you points toward books, music, and movies every time you use it. Call 888.819.7230 to apply for the Borders and Waldenbooks Visa Card and get a $20 Gift Card after your first purchase with the card. For complete details, please visit www.chase.com/applywaldenbooksvisa.

Returns to Waldenbooks Stores:

If you are unhappy with your purchase for any reason, simply return it within 30 days accompanied by your receipt for a full refund. Without a receipt, only an exchange or a Customer Return Gift Certificate will be given. Returned merchandise must be in saleable condition. Magazines and newspapers may not be returned.

GET a $20 Gift Card:

Get the card that gives you points toward books, music, and movies every time you use it. Call 888.819.7230 to apply for the Borders and Waldenbooks Visa Card and get a $20 Gift Card after your first purchase with the card. For complete details, please visit www.chase.com/applywaldenbooksvisa.

SAVING AN IDVD PROJECT AS A DISK IMAGE FILE

If you don't have a SuperDrive, you can save an iDVD project as a disk image file. Select File, Save As Disc Image. In the resulting "Save Disc Image As" dialog box, move to the location in which you want to save the file, name it, and click Save. The project will be saved as a disk image.

> **TIP**
>
> If you need to create multiple copies of a disc, it is usually a good idea to burn one version and then try it before burning copies. Saving it as a disk image makes this convenient.

You can use Disk Utility or other DVD burning application to put the disk image on a DVD. You can also work with the disk image file you created just like other such files. For example, you can mount it on your desktop.

CLEANING UP AFTER AN IDVD PROJECT

iDVD projects take up a lot of disk space. After you have completed a project, you probably won't want to leave it on your Mac. If you are sure that you'll never need it again, you can simply delete the project file. However, that usually isn't a good idea.

> **NOTE**
>
> The DVD you burn with iDVD can't be edited. If you don't archive it and don't save it and all the files it contains, you'll have to re-create the project to make changes to it. That is never a fun thing to do.

A better idea is to use the File, Archive command to save a complete, working version of the project onto DVDs so you can access it again if you need to. Then, you can safely delete the project from your computer to gain back the disk space it requires.

If you ever need to work on the project again, you can restore it by accessing the archived version.

If you want to save some disk space and are sure you won't ever need to change the project, you can save it as a disc image file. This will enable you to burn more copies of the project, but you won't be able to edit it.

26

CHAPTER 27

USING THE OTHER "I" APPLICATIONS

In this chapter

WORKING WITH ICAL, ISYNC, AND ICHAT

Mac OS X includes a number of other "i" applications that you will likely find useful. Here's a quick summary of these "other" *i* applications:

- **iCal**—Enables you to do the tasks you would expect from a calendar application, including creating events, managing a to-do list, and so on. However, where iCal separates itself from other calendar applications is the ease with which you can make your calendar available to others over the Web and access calendars that others make available to you.

- **iSync**—Serves a single purpose, which is to keep two things in sync. What is amazing about this application is how diverse those two things can be. Along with keeping computers on the same page, you can also synchronize other devices, such as a Bluetooth Palm PDA with your iCal calendar and Address Book.

- **iChat**—When you need to communicate with someone else in real time, there's no easier or more powerful way to do it than with iChat. Of course, you can also use it to do text instant messages. Although somewhat useful, that isn't anything to write home about. However, with iChat, a broadband Internet connection, and a FireWire camera, you can use iChat to conduct videoconferencing and audio conferencing. And that is something to write home about, or actually, that is something to have a videoconference with home about.

MANAGING YOUR CALENDAR WITH ICAL

We all have busy lives and, if you are like me, you have trouble remembering where you are supposed to be and when you are supposed to be there. Fortunately, Mac OS X's iCal calendar application can help you keep your schedule under control. With this tool, you can maintain multiple calendars at the same time, such as a work calendar, family calendar, and so on. Even better, you can share your calendar with others so coordinating activities is much easier. You can also access other people's calendars to see how your schedule meshes with theirs.

CONFIGURING ICAL

You don't need to configure many preferences in iCal, but if you open the General tab of the iCal Preferences dialog box, you will see the following options (see Figure 27.1):

- **Week**—Use the "Days per week" and "Start week on" pop-up menus to configure how iCal manages and displays weeks. You can select 7- or 5-day weeks and set the start day of the week.

- **Day**—Use the pop-up menus in this area to set the start and end times for your days and to chose how many hours are displayed at a time.

- **Month**—The "Show time in month view" check box determines whether the time is displayed next to events when you are viewing your calendar in the Month view.

Figure 27.1
Configuring iCal isn't hard to do.

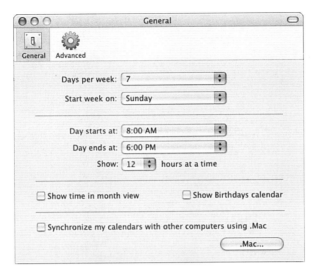

- **Birthdays**—If you have stored birthdays for your contacts in the Address Book, check the "Show Birthdays calendar" check box to display the Birthday calendar that shows those birthdays.

- **Synchronization**—As with other applications, such as Address Book, you can use .Mac to synchronize calendar information on different Macs. Use the "Synchronize my calendars with other computers using .Mac" check box and the .Mac button to configure this.

→ To learn how to use .Mac, **see** Chapter 17, "Using .Mac to Integrate Your Mac onto the Internet," **p. 493**.

If you open the Advanced pane of the iCal Preferences dialog box, you'll see the following options:

- **Time Zone**—iCal's Time Zone Support feature enables the application to add time zone information to your calendar. You can then associate events with specific time zones and change the time zone for which you are viewing events. This feature is most useful when you are using iCal while traveling. As you change time zones, you can set iCal to use the time zone you are currently in. Then, it adjusts the time for each event so it is appropriate to the time zone you are in. To activate this feature, check the "Turn on time zone support" check box. If you leave this check box unchecked, time zone is ignored.

- **Events and To Do items**—Use the "To Do" and "events" tools to configure how events and To Do items are managed. The "Hide To Do items with due dates outside the calendar view" check box enables you to hide any To Do items that don't need to be done during the period you are currently viewing. The "Hide To Do items" check box and text box enable you to have iCal hide To Do items after they are completed and to set the number of days that must pass until completed items are hidden. Use the "Delete events" and "Delete To Do items" check boxes and text boxes to determine whether iCal deletes these items and, if so, the number of days after they occur that must pass before these items are deleted from your calendar.

27

- **Alarms**—If you check the "Turn off alarms when iCal is not open" check box and iCal is not running, you won't be notified of events or To Do items via iCal alarms.

- **Invitations**—Check the "Automatically retrieve invitations from Mail" if you use Mail and want iCal invitations you receive to be retrieved automatically.

USING ICAL

Like other *i* applications, iCal is pretty simple to use. If you have used other calendar applications, you probably will have an easy time moving to iCal. By default, the iCal window has three panes (see Figure 27.2).

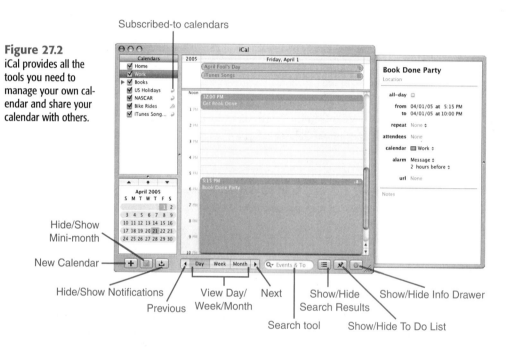

Figure 27.2
iCal provides all the tools you need to manage your own calendar and share your calendar with others.

Along the upper-left side of the window is the Calendars pane. In this pane, you see each calendar you have created along with those to which you have subscribed. If a calendar's check box is checked, its events are being displayed. If not, they are hidden.

The lower-left pane contains the Mini-month pane, which shows you a month at a glance, or the Notifications pane, which shows you information about notifications. You choose the pane you want to view by clicking the related button.

In the center pane is the calendar itself. There are three views for this: Day, Week, and Month.

Along the bottom of the window are the following tools:

- **New Calendar**—Click this to create a new calendar.
- **Hide/Show Mini-month**—This shows or hides the mini-month tool. When you are viewing the mini-month, you can move back in time by clicking the Previous button (the upward-facing arrowhead above the mini-month), forward by clicking the Next button (the downward-facing arrowhead), or to the current month by clicking the Current Month button (the diamond).

> **TIP**
>
> You can drag the Mini-month pane's Resize handle to show more than one month in it.

- **Previous**—Use this to go back by a day, week, or month (whichever is currently displayed).
- **Day/Week/Month**—Use these three buttons to change the view of the calendar window.
- **Next**—Use this to go forward by a day, week, or month (whichever is currently displayed).
- **Search tool**—Use this to search for events. This tool works similarly to the Search tool in other areas, such as iTunes or the Finder. To search, click the Magnifying Glass pop-up menu to open it and choose the kind of search you want to do (if you don't select anything, all calendar items are searched). Enter your search text; as you do, items that match your search will be found. When you enter search text, iCal's Search Results pane opens automatically, which leads right into the next bullet.
- **Show/Hide Search Results**—Click this to open the search results pane, which appears just under the calendar pane (see Figure 27.3). This pane lists all the events that meet your search criterion.

Figure 27.3
Here, I have searched for items related to the term "lowe"; because I have subscribed to the NASCAR calendar online, I found information relating to races associated with Lowes along with other items that weren't so relevant.

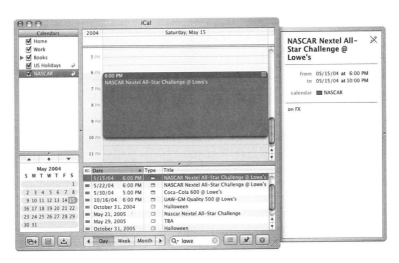

27

- **Show/Hide To Do List**—This button opens the To Do Items pane, which shows the To Do items on your plate. This pane will appear to the right of the Calendar pane.

- **Show/Hide Info Drawer**—Clicking this opens the Info Drawer that provides detailed information about a calendar, an event, or a To Do item you have selected (see Figure 27.4).

Figure 27.4

In this example, I have selected a very important item on my To Do list and opened the Info Drawer so I can see and configure the details for that event.

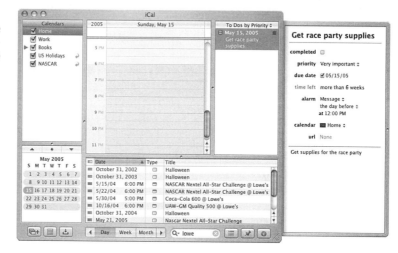

TIP

> If you turn on the Time Zone preference, the Time Zone pop-up menu appears in the upper-right corner of the iCal window. Use this to select the time zone for the current calendar. The default is the time zone set in the System Preferences application. You can select Other on the pop-up menu to open the "Change time zone" window and use its tools to change the time zone for the calendar.

CREATING, CONFIGURING, AND WORKING WITH CALENDARS

As you read earlier, you can manage multiple calendars within the iCal application. For example, you might want to create separate calendars for home and work activities, for special projects, and so on. Each calendar can include its own events and To Do items. To create a new calendar, do the following steps:

1. Click the New Calendar button. A new, untitled calendar will appear in the Calendar pane.

2. Enter the name of the new calendar and press Return.

3. Select Window, Show Info (⌘-I), or click the Show Info button. The Info drawer will open. At the top of the Drawer, the name of the calendar is shown so that you know which calendar you are getting information about.

4. Click the word Description and enter a description of the calendar.

5. Use the Color pop-up menu to associate a color with the calendar. When you add events to the calendar, they appear in the color your select. Having different colors for different calendars is useful because you can easily see which events came from which calendars when you are viewing multiple calendars at the same time.

To include a calendar's events and To Do items in the calendar being displayed, check its check box. If you uncheck a calendar's box, its events and To Do items are hidden.

WORKING WITH EVENTS

You can use iCal to track life events of all kinds. You can associate events with specific calendars, set reminders, and so on. To create an event, do the following steps:

1. Select the calendar and then the day on which you want the event to appear.
2. Select File, New Event ($\mathcal{H}$-N), or open the contextual menu on the day on which you want the event to appear and select New Event. A new event will appear on the selected date.

> **TIP**
>
> You can also create an event by dragging on the day on which the event occurs.

3. Type the name of the event and press Return.
4. Open the Info Drawer by clicking the Info button. The Info Drawer will show the new event you have created.

> **TIP**
>
> If you don't like the Info Drawer configuration, choose Window, Detach Info. The Info Drawer will become a separate window you can move around on the desktop independent of the iCal window.

5. Enter information about the location of the event by replacing the word `location` that appears under the event's title.
6. Check the "all-day" check box if the event is an all-day event.
7. If it isn't an all-day event, use the "from" and "to" fields to set a start and end time for the event.

> **TIP**
>
> You can also change or set the date of the event using the "from" and "to" fields.

8. If you want the event to repeat, use the "repeat" pop-up menu. You can choose a standard frequency for the event or select Custom to set a custom frequency. When you choose a frequency, the "end" pop-up menu appears. Use this to choose an end date for the repeating event.

27

9. Enter attendees for the event in the "attendees" field. You can type in names or drag them from your Address Book. To show people in your Address Book, select Window, Address Panel (Option-⌘-A). You can drag people from the Addresses window onto the "attendees" list. To enter multiple attendees, press Return after each name.

10. If you want to change the calendar on which the event appears, use the "calendar" pop-up menu to do so.

11. If you want to set an alarm for the event, use the "alarm" pop-up menu. Your options for the alarm are the following: None, which has no alarm; Message, which displays a text message; "Message with sound," which displays a text message and plays a sound; Email, which causes an email to be sent to you; "Open file," which opens a file of your choice; "Run Script," which causes a script you select to run; or "Display a message 12 hours before," which does just what it says. If you select an alarm with sound, the sound pop-up menu appears. If you choose any type of alarm, a pop-up menu that enables you to set the alarm time appears. If you select Email, a pop-up menu that enables you to select the email address to which the alarm should be sent appears.

TIP

> The email addresses that appear on the "alert" pop-up menus for events or To Do items are those that are on your card in the Address Book application. To add more addresses, add them to your card.

12. Select the sound for the alarm if applicable and the amount of time before the event that you want the alarm to be activated.

13. If a URL is associated with the event, enter it in the "url" field.

14. Enter any notes about the event in the Notes field.

15. If you want to send email invitations for the event to the people on the attendees list, click the Send button.

16. Review the event and make any necessary changes; then close the Info window if you want to (see Figure 27.5).

To view or change the details of an event, click the event in the calendar and then click the Show Info button (if the Info Drawer is closed). Make changes to the event as needed and the changes are saved automatically.

Here are some additional tips for working with events:

- You can change the date on which an event occurs by dragging it from one date in the calendar to another.
- You can change the calendar on which an event occurs by opening its contextual menu (Control-click the event) and selecting the event's new calendar.
- You can duplicate an event by opening its contextual menu and selecting Duplicate; selecting Edit, Duplicate; or pressing ⌘-D. You can drag the copy onto a different date.

Figure 27.5
Here's an event worthy of being in iCal.

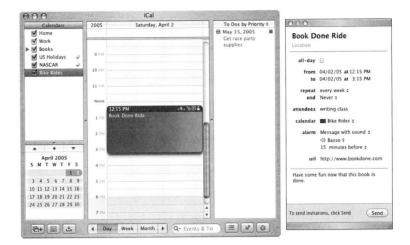

- You can email an event to others by opening its contextual menu and selecting "Mail event." Your default email application will open and the event will be included as an attachment (see Figure 27.6). The recipient can then drag the attachment, which has the extension .ics, onto iCal to add it to his calendar.

Figure 27.6
You can email events to others so they can easily add them to their own calendars.

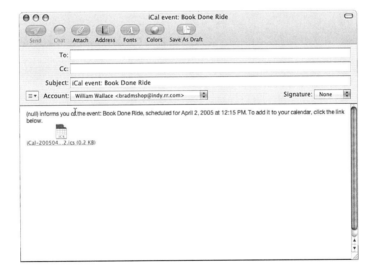

- If you have turned on the time zone feature, the "time zone" pop-up menu appears in the Info Drawer when you view the event. You can use this to set the time zone for the event. This is especially useful if you will be inviting people who are not in your current time zone.

WORKING WITH YOUR TO DO LIST

To create a To Do item, use the following steps:

1. Either open the To Do pane, open its contextual menu, and select New To Do or select File, New To Do (⌘-K). A new To Do item appears on the To Do list.

2. Type the name of the To Do item and press Return.

3. Open the Info Drawer if it isn't open already. Information about the event will appear.

4. Use the "priority" pop-up menu to set the To Do item's priority.

5. If the event has a due date, check the "due date" check box and use the date fields that appear to set the due date.

6. If you want to set an alarm for the event, open the "alarm" pop-up menu and select the alarm you want to set. The options are the same as those for an event.

7. Select the calendar with which the To Do item should be associated on the "calendar" pop-up menu.

8. If a URL is associated with the To Do item, enter it in the "url" field.

9. Enter any notes for the To Do item in the Notes field.

Following are some tips for working with To Do items:

- You can change a To Do item by selecting it and opening the Info Drawer. Then use the tools to change the item's information; these work just like when you create a To Do item.

- When you have completed a To Do item, mark it as complete by checking the box next to its name or by checking the "completed" box on the Info Drawer.

- The priority of a To Do item is indicated by the number of bars that appear to the right of its name on the To Do items list (see Figure 27.7).

Figure 27.7
You can use iCal to manage your To Do list (hopefully, your list has more meaningful items than mine does).

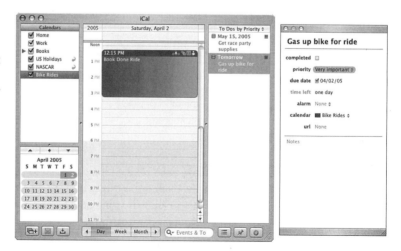

- Sort the order in which To Do items appear on the list using the pop-up menu at the top of the To Do pane.

- Open a To Do item's contextual menu to duplicate it, change the calendar with which it is associated, mark its priority, email it, or change the sort order for the To Do items pane.

- When the due date for an item passes, its complete check box becomes a warning icon to indicate that the item is overdue.

TIP

> When you email an event or a To Do item to someone, the recipient can add the item to his calendar by clicking its link or by dragging it onto the iCal window. If the "automatically retrieve" preference is enabled and the recipient uses Mail, the iCal information will be added automatically.

PRINTING FROM iCAL

From iCal, you can print calendars, To Do lists, and mini-months. Open the Print dialog box to view and set the many options for printing calendar information (see Figure 27.8).

Figure 27.8
iCal offers flexible printing options.

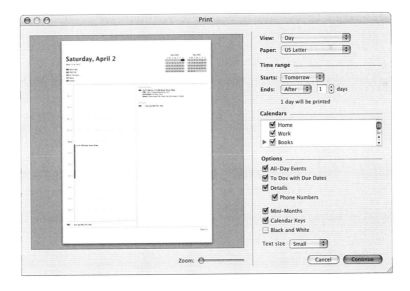

SYNCHRONIZING YOUR CALENDAR IN MULTIPLE LOCATIONS

If you use more than one Mac, you will probably want to keep your iCal calendar on each machine synchronized. To do this, you use iSync.

→ To learn how to synchronize information on multiple machines, **see** "Using .Mac to Synchronize Important Information on Multiple Macs," **p. 512**.

SHARING YOUR iCAL CALENDAR

One of the cool things about iCal is that you can publish your calendars online so other people can view them. You can choose to share an iCal calendar via your .Mac account or use any other server.

TIP

> Because you can access a shared calendar over the Web, sharing your calendar provides a way for you to view your calendar even if your Mac isn't available. As long as you can access the Web, you can get to and view your calendar.

To publish your calendar, use the following steps:

1. Select the calendar you want to share.

2. Select Calendar, Publish. The Publish sheet will appear (see Figure 27.9).

Figure 27.9
You can easily publish your calendars via .Mac.

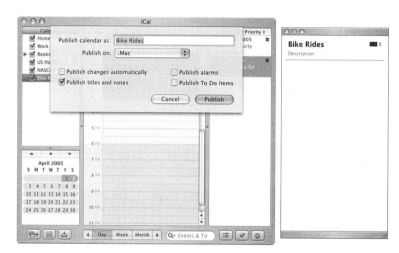

3. Type the name of the calendar as you want it to appear online; by default the calendar's name is entered, but you can change this if you want to.

4. Choose how you want to publish the calendar on the "Publish calendar" pop-up menu. Select "on .Mac" to use your .Mac account or "on a Private server" to choose a different server. If you chose the latter option, you need to enter the server's URL along with your username and password for that server.

NOTE

> If you haven't configured your .Mac account when you start to publish your calendar using .Mac, you will be prompted to do so.

5. If you want changes you make to your calendar to be published automatically, check the "Publish changes automatically" check box. In most cases, you should check this so your calendar is always up-to-date.

6. If you want both the title and notes associated with an item to be published, check the "Publish titles and notes" check box.

7. If you want the alarms and To Do items to be published, check the "Publish alarms" and "Publish To Do items" check boxes.

8. Click Publish. When the calendar has been published, you will see the confirmation dialog box. This dialog box provides the URL for the calendar and enables you to visit the calendar online or send an email announcing the calendar (see Figure 27.10).

Figure 27.10
Even though this shared calendar isn't too interesting, it can be viewed on the Web at any time.

Calendar Published

Your Calendar "Bike Rides" has been published successfully, and can be subscribed at URL:

webcal://ical.mac.com/bradmacosx/Bike%20Rides.ics

or be viewed with a browser at URL:

http://ical.mac.com/bradmacosx/Bike%20Rides

Visit Page   Send Mail   OK

9. Click the button for the action you want to take, such as OK to close the dialog box and return to iCal.

Following are some more pointers on sharing your calendars online:

- When a calendar is shared, the shared icon (which looks like a dot radiating waves) appears next to the calendar's name.

- If you open a shared calendar's contextual menu, you see several interesting commands. These include Unpublish, which removes the calendar from the Web; Send publish email, which enables you to send an email announcing the published calendar and its URL; Copy URL to Clipboard, which copies the calendar's URL to the Clipboard so you can easily paste it into documents; Refresh, which publishes any changes you have made to the calendar; and Change Location, which enables you to move the calendar to a different site.

- People can subscribe to your shared calendars so they appear in their iCal windows. More on this in the next section.

- You can view your own shared calendar at any time from any computer by moving to its URL. This is a great way to maintain access to your own calendar when you aren't at your Mac.

- You can change a shared calendar by selecting and opening the Info Drawer. Use the controls in the Drawer to make changes to the calendar's settings.

27

SUBSCRIBING TO OTHER CALENDARS

You can subscribe to other calendars to add them to your iCal window. You can also subscribe to other personal calendars or public calendars.

SUBSCRIBING TO PERSONAL CALENDARS

You can add other personal calendars to your iCal window by doing the following steps:

1. Select Calendar, Subscribe (Option-⌘-S). The Subscribe sheet will appear.

2. Enter the URL for the calendar to which you want to subscribe and click Subscribe. The Subscribing sheet will appear.

3. If you want the calendar's information to be refreshed automatically, check the Refresh check box and select the frequency at which you want the refresh to occur on the pop-up menu.

4. If you don't want the calendar's alarms to appear in your iCal window, check the "Remove alarms" check box.

5. If you don't want the calendar's To Do items to show up in your iCal window, check the "Remove To Do items" check box. You usually don't want to display the To Do items on a calendar to which you are subscribing unless you have To Do items on it.

6. Click OK. The calendar will be added to your iCal window, and you can view it just like your own calendars. iCal indicates that it is a subscribed-to calendar by the curved arrow icon next to the calendar's name. If you set the calendar to be refreshed automatically (refer to step 3), it is kept current.

> **TIP**
>
> If you don't set a calendar to be refreshed automatically, you can refresh it manually by opening its contextual menu and selecting Refresh.

> **NOTE**
>
> You can't make any changes to a calendar to which you are subscribed. You can only view it.

SUBSCRIBING TO PUBLIC CALENDARS

Many public calendars are available to which you can subscribe. For example, most professional sports teams have calendars that show games and other events. You can also find DVD release calendars, TV schedules, and many other types of calendars to subscribe to. Just like personal calendars, when you subscribe to public calendars, the events on those calendars are shown in your iCal window. To find and subscribe to public calendars, do the following steps:

1. Select Calendar, Find Shared Calendars. Your default web browser will open and move to Apple's Calendar library (see Figure 27.11).

Figure 27.11
This web page provides all sorts of interesting calendars to which you can subscribe.

2. Click the calendar to which you want to subscribe. You move into iCal and the Subscribe To sheet appears. The relevant information is filled in automatically.

3. Click Subscribe. The Subscribe sheet will appear.

4. Review the subscription options and change them as needed.

5. Click OK. The calendar will be added to your iCal window, and you can view its events.

USING THE CALENDAR WIDGET

You can also access your calendar information via the Dashboard Calendar widget.

→ To learn about the Calendar widget, **see** "Using the iCal Widget," **p. 164**.

SYNCHRONIZING WITH ISYNC

iSync enables you to synchronize calendar, Safari bookmark, and contact information among multiple computers and other devices, such as PDAs or cell phones. To use iSync among a group of computers, you need to have a .Mac account. However, you can use iSync to synchronize other devices without a .Mac account.

CONFIGURING ISYNC PREFERENCES

Configure the relevant iSync preferences with the following steps:

1. Launch iSync (Applications folder) and open the iSync Preferences dialog box by selecting iSync, Preferences (⌘-,).

2. Enable iSync by checking the "Enable syncing on this computer" check box.

3. If you want iSync to warn you when you attempt to sync a Palm device, check the "Show HotSync reminder when syncing Palm OS devices" check box. When you attempt to synchronize a Palm device, you are instructed to use the HotSync software instead.

4. To show the iSync menu in the menu bar, check the "Show status in menu bar" check box.

5. If you want to be alerted when data changes on your Mac, check the "Show Data Change Alert when" pop-up menu and select the amount of data that must be changed before you see a warning. Your options are "any," "more than 1%," "more than 5%," or "more than 10%."

6. Close the Preferences dialog box.

TIP

To clear iSync's memory, click the Reset Sync History button.

→ To learn how to synchronize Macs using .Mac, **see** "Using .Mac to Synchronize Important Information on Multiple Macs," **p. 512**.

SYNCHRONIZING A MAC WITH OTHER DEVICES

You can use iSync to synchronize information on your Mac and other devices, such as PDAs and cell phones. The specific steps you use to do this vary from device to device. First, configure the device for syncing. The general steps to do this are the following:

TIP

To sync with a Palm device, choose Devices, Enable Palm OS Syncing. Follow the onscreen instructions to set up syncing between your Mac and a Palm OS device, such as a PDA.

1. Attach the device with which you want to sync to your Mac.

2. Choose Devices, Add Device. Your Mac will be scanned for devices to sync. Devices that are found will be shown in the Add Device window (see Figure 27.12).

3. Double-click the device with which you want to sync. It will be registered with iSync and the synchronization options window for the device will open (see Figure 27.13).

4. Use the configuration options to configure how and when the device will be synchronized. For example, if the device can store contact information, check the Contacts check box and use the pop-up menu to choose which contacts will be synchronized. If you want the device to be synchronized automatically, check the "Automatically synchronize when device is connected" check box.

5. Click the Sync Devices button on the iSync toolbar to synchronize the device. You'll see a progress window that shows you how the sync is going. When the process is complete, the progress bar will go away.

Figure 27.12
This Mac has an iPod mini connected to it.

Figure 27.13
Use this window to choose the synchronization options for a device.

After you have configured a device for synchronization, you can sync it manually either by connecting it to your Mac and clicking the Sync Devices button or by choosing Sync Now on the iSync menu if you added it to the Finder menu bar. If you configured the device to be synced automatically, it will be done each time you connect the device to your Mac.

> **TIP**
>
> When you have configured a device in iSync, it will appear in the iSync toolbar. Click the device to configure its sync options.

27

COMMUNICATING WITH iCHAT

iChat is Mac OS X's instant messaging and video/audio conferencing application. Although it enables you to text chat with others, you can have audio- and videoconferences via iChat.

To text chat, each person must have an a .Mac or an AOL Instant Messenger account. To chat with audio or video, both parties must be using a .Mac account and must have a broadband Internet connection along with the hardware needed, such as a camera to have a video chat.

CONFIGURING ICHAT

If you are going to use iChat to have audio- and videoconferences, you must have a FireWire or USB camera attached to your Mac. You can use an Apple iSight camera, shown in Figure 27.14, or some FireWire camcorders for this purpose. You also need a broadband connection to the Internet. Finally, you will need a Mac that is capable of handling the workload of a video chat. Most, but not all, modern Macs are. The best way to find out whether your Mac can handle a videoconference is to try it.

Figure 27.14
An iSight camera is an inexpensive way to add AV capabilities to your Mac.

> **NOTE**
>
> To use a camcorder for chatting, the camera must support play through, meaning the input coming through the camera's lens must play through the FireWire out port at the same time. If your camera doesn't offer this, you won't be able to use it to chat. Fortunately, many camcorders work with iChat.

Connect the camera you are going to use to your Mac. If it is a camcorder, power it up and place it in camera mode.

If you don't have a FireWire camera or a broadband connection to the Internet, you can still use iChat for text chatting.

> **NOTE**
>
> Many camcorders are set to go to sleep after a certain period of inactivity passes. When you are using a camcorder during a video conference, it thinks it is inactive because you aren't recording. When it goes to sleep, your conference suddenly ends. Use your camcorder's controls to set its sleep to a large value or to turn off its sleep mode.

To get started, launch iChat and use the following steps to configure it:

1. Review the information in the welcome screen and click Continue. The "Set up a new iChat Account" window appears. If you have a .Mac account configured for the current user account, the account information is configured automatically. If not, enter the .Mac or AIM account information in the window and click Continue. The Jabber Instant Messaging window will appear.

> **TIP**
>
> If you want to apply for an iChat account, click the Get an iChat Account button and follow the onscreen instructions to register for a trial .Mac account. The accompanying iChat account remains valid even if you let the .Mac account expire.

2. If you use Jabber Instant Messaging, check the check box, enter your Jabber account name and password, and click Continue. If not, just click Continue. The "Set up Bonjour Messaging" window will open.

3. If other Macs are on a network with which you can communicate, click the "Use Bonjour messaging" check box. This enables you to chat with others on your local network because all Bonjour devices are found automatically. If you use a wireless network in a public place, you might want to leave this off.

4. Click Continue to see the "Set up iChat AV" window. During this step, iChat attempts to connect to a camera connected to your Mac. If it finds one, the image being broadcast by that camera will be shown. Just under the image is a volume level indicator that displays the relative volume of the source's audio input. If a camera is not found, a message stating that there is no camera attached to the computer is shown.

5. Click Continue to see the Conclusion screen.

6. Click Done. The basic configuration of iChat will be complete and you will move into the chatting windows.

iChat offers a number of preferences you can use to configure the way it works. The general preferences you can configure and a description of some specific preferences that might interest you include the following:

- **General**—Use the General tab of the iChat Preferences dialog box to configure some general iChat behaviors (see Figure 27.15). The Settings check boxes enable you to configure various settings. For example, you can add the iChat status to the menu bar. Use the radio buttons to determine what happens when you log in to your user account and your iChat status is Away; for example, you might want your status to be updated to Available automatically. Use the "Save received files to" pop-up menu to select a location in which you save files you receive via iChat.

- **Accounts**—Use the Accounts pane to configure the accounts over which you want to chat. Unfortunately, you can have only one account active at the same time.

27

Figure 27.15
Use the General pane to configure various iChat settings.

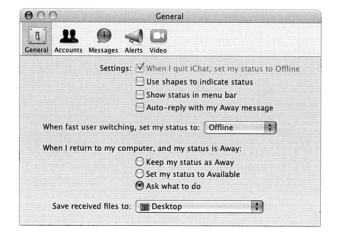

■ **Messages**—The Messages pane enables you to set various formatting options for your messages (see Figure 27.16). Use the Set Font button to configure the font in which you want to view text messages. Use the balloon and font color pop-up menus to choose the color of those items. Check the "Reformat incoming messages" check box and use the corresponding Set Font button and pop-up menus to have iChat reformat text you receive according to your preferences. Use the "Confirm before sending files" check box if you want to confirm a command to send a file before it is sent. If you want to save the transcript for chat messages, check the "Automatically save chat transcripts" check box and use the Open Folder button to choose the location in which you want the transcripts to be stored.

Figure 27.16
Using the Messages preferences, you can control the formatting used for chatting.

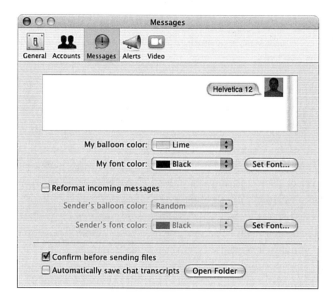

- **Alerts**—Use the Alerts pane to set the alerts and notifications iChat uses to get your attention. Select the event for which you want to configure an alert on the Event pop-up menu and then select the specific alert on the check boxes and pop-up menus to configure it. Repeat these steps for each event for which you want to set an alert.

- **Privacy**—Use the radio buttons to set access levels to your iChat account. If you select one of the Specific People options, use the Edit List button to create a list of people who should be allowed or denied access. Use the check boxes at the bottom of the pane to block others from seeing that you are idle or to prevent Bonjour users from seeing your email and AIM addresses.

- **Video**—Use these preferences to configure AV conferencing (see Figure 27.17). In this pane, you will see the current image being received from the camera connected to your Mac. Just under the image is an audio meter that provides a graphic representation of the volume level being received. Choose the audio input on the Microphone pop-up menu; for example, to receive audio via an iSight camera, choose "iSight Built-in." If you want to set a bandwidth limit for conferencing, use the Bandwidth Limit pop-up menu to do so. Check the "Automatically open iChat when camera is turned on" check box to have iChat launch when you turn on your camera. Check the "Play repeated ring sound when invited to a conference" to be notified via a ringing sound when someone wants to conference with you.

Figure 27.17
Use the Video pane to configure AV conferencing.

SETTING UP CHATTING BUDDIES

There are two sources of people with whom you can chat; in iChat lingo these are called *buddies*. One source is the people whom your Mac can see via Bonjour. The other source is people who are configured in your Address Book and have either a .Mac email address or an AIM screen name.

When you open iChat, you see two windows: One is titled Bonjour, and the other is labeled Buddy List (see Figure 27.18). The people shown on the Bonjour list are found automatically when your Mac searches your local network for Bonjour users. You add people with whom you want to chat on the Buddy List. You can chat with people on either of these lists in the same way.

Figure 27.18
The Bonjour window shows users who are available to chat on your local network, whereas the Buddy List shows users who have been added to your permanent Buddy List.

NOTE

If you haven't enabled Bonjour messaging, you don't see the Bonjour pane.

To add people to your Buddy list, do the following steps:

1. Add the person you want to place on your Buddy List to your Address Book; include either a .Mac address or an AIM username.

2. In iChat, click the Add Buddy button located in the lower-left corner of the Buddy List window. The resulting sheet will show all the people in your Address Book. Search or browse in the list to find the person you want to add to your Buddy List.

3. Select the person you want to add to your Buddy List and click the Select Buddy button. You move back to the Buddy List and the person you selected will be shown on the list.

4. Repeat steps 2 and 3 to add more people to your list.

CHATTING WITH TEXT

You can text chat with others by using the following steps:

1. Select the person in the Bonjour window or on the Buddy List with whom you want to chat.

2. Click the Text Chat button, which is the A located at the bottom of the respective window. An empty Instant Message window will appear.

3. Type your message.

4. When you are done, press Return to see the message you typed near your name at the top of the window. It is sent to the person with whom you are chatting.

   Your message appears in a text bubble on that user's desktop. When the user clicks the bubble, she is able to type a reply and send it you.

   When you receive a reply to your message, you see the person's picture along with the text she sent.

5. Type your response in the message box at the bottom of the window and press Return.

> **TIP**
>
> Click the emoticon icon at the end of the text box to include a smiley with your text.

6. Continue chatting to your heart's content (see Figure 27.19).

Figure 27.19
Hopefully, your iChats will be more meaningful than this one!

7. When you are done chatting, close the Instant Message window.

CONFERENCING WITH VIDEO AND SOUND

If a person you want to talk to and see meets the requirements for AV chatting, click the camera icon next to the person with whom you want to conference. A request for conference is sent to that person. You also see a Video Chat window that shows the image being transmitted by your camera.

27

The person with whom you are trying to communicate sees a Video Chat invitation window. If he clicks your name in that window, it expands to show a Video Chat window on his machine. He can then select to Accept or Deny your request.

If he accepts, you will see a message that video conferencing is starting.

When the conference starts, two windows open within the video chat window (see Figure 27.20). The larger window shows the image being transmitted, and the smaller window shows the image you are transmitting.

Figure 27.20
Within the larger part of the Video Chat window, you see the image being transmitted to you; within the smaller window, you see the image you are transmitting.

TIP

> You can move the smaller window around by dragging it. You can click the full-screen mode button (the square with two arrows in it) to make the Video Chat window fill the screen.

Speak normally, and you should keep your movements a bit slower than usual so the motion is smoother on the other end. Depending on how many servers the data has to flow through and how fast each person's connection is, considerable delay might occur. You need to adjust your speech and movement to fit the specific conference in which you are participating. In most cases, this delay won't be a problem for you. When you are done with your conference, close the window.

 When iChat buddies use Mac OS X version 10.4, you can have up to 4 people in a video-conference or up to 10 in an audio conference. To tell whether a buddy supports multiperson conferencing, look at the icon next to your buddy's name. If it is the multicamera icon, you can do multiperson videoconferences. To invite multiple people to a videoconference, hold down the ⌘ key and select each person you want to invite; then click the "Video chat" button. All parties will join the conference and you will see each person in her own window.

If a buddy can't participate in a multiperson video chat, you might be able to add that person with audio only.

NOTE

iChat offers many more features than I have room to cover in this chapter. Explore the iChat menus and Help system to learn more.

27

Mac OS X: Expanding Your System

CHAPTER 28

UNDERSTANDING INPUT AND OUTPUT TECHNOLOGY

In this chapter

UNDERSTANDING INTERFACE TECHNOLOGY

The processor is the heart of any computer. For this processor to be capable of doing anything, it has to have data on which to operate. There are many ways in which data is moved into, out of, and within your Mac. To use a Mac, you do not need to understand the various technologies involved in this transfer of data among the various components of the system, such as the processor. However, if you add enhancements to your machine—whether they are external peripherals or internal system upgrades—you do need to understand these interface technologies.

NOTE

> The term *interface* refers to the location at which two devices are physically connected. The term also refers to the technology that particular interface uses. For example, when someone refers to devices that use a USB interface, this implies that a specific physical connector is used (a USB connector) over which data following the USB specification is communicated.

On your Mac, there are two general types of input and output interfaces: those with external interfaces (ports) and those whose interfaces are internal to the machine.

In this chapter, you will gain a fundamental understanding of the various input and output technologies your Mac uses to move data. This understanding will help you when the time comes to add devices or make other improvements to your system. However, you won't get a detailed explanation of the technical intricacies of all of these interfaces. Unless that kind of information floats your boat, you really don't need to know the ins and outs of these technologies. Mostly, you just need to be able to match the technologies that your particular Mac supports with peripheral devices or upgrades you want to add to it. Equipping you with the information you need to be able to do this is the goal of this chapter.

CAUTION

> Obviously, the types of interfaces available depend on the model of Mac you are using and whether you have added components to it. This chapter focuses on modern Mac models, such as the Power Mac G5, Power Mac G4, PowerBook G4, and so on. Newer machines generally support newer and better technologies. For example, the Power Mac G5 offers faster interface technologies than the Power Mac G4 does. Similarly, newer models of machines of the same class also support faster technologies. For example, later models of the Power Mac G4 added support for FireWire 800, whereas earlier models do not support this. In this chapter, you will find information on the more common interfaces used on modern Macintosh computers, but this chapter is not intended to explain all the interfaces that can be used. To be familiar with the technologies your specific Mac supports, you should study the specifications for your specific model of Mac.

28

WORKING WITH EXTERNAL INTERFACES

The most obvious data input and output interfaces are those whose ports are located on the outside of your Mac. Modern Macs have a number of built-in interfaces you can use to move data into or take data out of the machine.

NOTE

> All data that travels around your Mac eventually moves from one device to another. When data "crosses over," it is said to have crossed a bus. A data *bus* is simply a channel through which data flows. Many buses exist inside your Mac, and all devices have at least one bus (the point at which data enters or leaves the device).

NOTE

> If you want to really dive into the details of computer buses and other technology, check out www.pcguide.com/ref/. Although this site is PC-focused, it does contain lots of great general information that is equally applicable to the Mac. For example, you can learn all you need to know about the various hard drive technologies at this site in addition to finding detailed information on memory buses, monitors, and just about anything else about which you want to learn.

ETHERNET

Ethernet is the interface that is used for almost all local area networks (LANs) that use wires to connect. Ethernet is designed for hub-based networks, which means information flowing across the network is controlled to some extent by a central Ethernet hub of one type or another.

All modern Macs have built-in Ethernet ports to enable you to network with other machines; Ethernet on all modern Macs uses an RJ-45 connector, which looks like an overgrown telephone connector (see Figure 28.1).

Three different speeds of Ethernet are supported by the Mac. These are the following:

- **10 megabits per second (Mbps)**—This was the speed of the "original" Ethernet.
- **100BASE-T**—This flavor of Ethernet is 10 times as fast as the original and is also known as *Fast Ethernet*. It communicates at speeds up to 100Mbps. All modern Macs support at least 100BASE-T Ethernet.
- **Gigabit Ethernet**—The newest Ethernet standard can communicate at 1,000Mbps. Newer Power Mac G4, Power Mac G5, and newer PowerBook G4 machines support Gigabit Ethernet.

28

NOTE

> The Power Mac G4 was the first PC to support Gigabit Ethernet as a standard feature. It follows in the tradition of earlier Macs, which were the first to provide built-in Ethernet support as standard equipment.

Figure 28.1
All modern Macs have an Ethernet port. The only variation is in the speed the port supports.

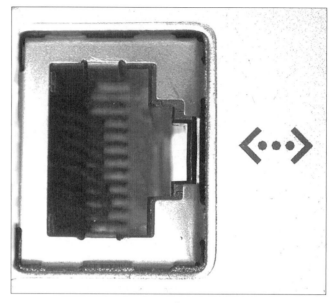

Ethernet-capable devices can communicate at various levels of speed up to their maximum speeds (such as Gigabit Ethernet). Higher-speed devices can communicate at lower speeds, but lower-speed devices can't communicate at the higher speeds. Therefore, the speed at which devices communicate over Ethernet connections always defaults to the maximum speed of the lower-speed device.

A *protocol* is the "language" in which data is communicated over a particular interface at a particular time. The physical interface might be capable of transmitting data in more than one protocol. For example, Ethernet can be used to transmit data in the AppleTalk protocol as well as using the Transmission Control Protocol/Internet Protocol (TCP/IP).

All Ethernet devices are designed to work with an Ethernet hub (or router) that acts as a traffic controller for the data being communicated among the attached devices.

Ethernet is used exclusively for networking computers to hubs, routers, or other computers.

→ To learn more about Ethernet hubs, **see** "Finding and Installing an Ethernet Hub," **p. 922**.

→ To learn more about creating and using an Ethernet network, **see** Chapter 33, "Building and Using a Network," **p. 935**.

Direct Connect Ethernet

Because Ethernet is designed to be used with hubs, you can't simply connect two Ethernet ports together to connect two machines. Instead, you have to use a special Ethernet cable, called a *crossover cable*. Using such a cable, you can connect any two Ethernet devices directly. If you use a standard Ethernet cable, the devices must be connected with an Ethernet hub.

An exception to this is the Ethernet port on some modern Mac models. It can sense whether it is connected to another device or a hub and configure itself appropriately for either situation using a standard Ethernet cable. Check the documentation for your machine to determine if you need to use a crossover cable to connect it to another device via Ethernet.

FIREWIRE 400

FireWire 400 (more commonly referred to as just *FireWire*) is a fast technology that provides an interface for many types of peripheral devices. FireWire was designed to enable very high data rate transfers (it communicates at 400Mbps), such as those required to move digital video data. At least one FireWire 400 port is available on all modern Mac models.

> **NOTE**
>
> FireWire is Apple's brand name for an industry-standard interface definition. The actual specification for the interface is IEEE 1394. Other companies use specific names for their implementations of the interface, such as Sony's term for it: iLink.

FireWire offers several major advantages, which are the following:

- **High speed**—FireWire is capable of communicating at up to 400Mbps, making it suitable for many high-bandwidth applications.

- **Chainable**—FireWire devices can be chained together; the interface supports up to 63 devices per port. Many FireWire devices have two ports; one is an input port that you connect to a Mac's FireWire port or another FireWire device and the other is an output port that enables you to connect another FireWire device. This enables you to add multiple devices to a single FireWire port on a Mac without requiring a hub.

- **Hot-swappable**—FireWire devices can be connected to and disconnected from your Mac while the Mac is running.

- **Powered connection**—The FireWire interface is capable of providing power to a peripheral device through the bus. Devices that use the capability don't require a separate power supply. Also, this enables some FireWire devices that have batteries, such as an iPod, to be charged by the Mac while it is connected.

FireWire connectors are an unusual shape and consist of a rectangle with a triangular top section (see Figure 28.2). FireWire ports are marked with a high-tech-looking *Y*.

Figure 28.2
FireWire ports can be used for various devices, the most prominent of which are digital video cameras.

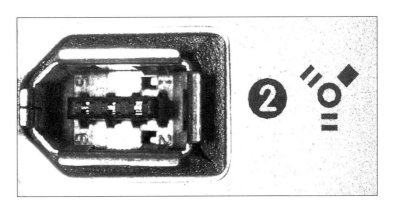

The connector shown in Figure 28.2 is that used to connect FireWire devices to your Mac. Consumer and other FireWire-equipped devices can use differently configured FireWire ports. For example, you won't find a port like that shown in Figure 28.2 on a DV camcorder. Because of size limitations, DV camcorders use a much smaller FireWire port that looks quite different from the FireWire ports on a Mac. Typically, these devices include the specialized cable you need to attach their ports to a FireWire port on your Mac.

CAUTION

> FireWire connectors are relatively delicate. You should always exercise care when connecting a FireWire device to a FireWire port. The pins in the connector are somewhat fragile and can be bent if you attempt to insert the connector when it is not aligned properly.

Because of its capability to move large amounts of data quickly, the FireWire interface is used for many devices, including the following:

- Digital video cameras
- External hard drives
- External removable media drives, including CD-RW, DVD-R, and tape drives
- Other devices, such as iPods
- Scanners

Competition

Apple's implementation of FireWire has led the industry. For example, Apple is almost single-handedly responsible for the dramatic rise in the use of digital video technology. Many other computers still require that a separate card be added to be able to use devices that transfer data via the FireWire interface.

FireWire's competitor is the USB 2 interface. USB 2 is much faster than the previous USB specifications and is slightly faster than FireWire 400. Although support for FireWire is built in to Macs, it isn't built in to all Windows PCs. Most Windows PCs have USB 2 support by default, which means the market for USB 2 devices is much larger than for FireWire devices. Want some good news? Many modern Macs also support USB 2 and FireWire 800, which is much faster than USB 2. As usual, when it comes to innovative technologies, the Mac is leading the way.

FIREWIRE 800

FireWire 800, as you can probably guess from its name, is faster than FireWire 400. As you can also probably guess, FireWire 800 communicates at 800Mbps. FireWire 800 supports similar devices such as hard drives but can move data at twice the rate of FireWire 400 devices. Currently, FireWire 800 devices are mostly limited to data storage, such as hard drives, but as the technology matures, it can be expected to enable other devices as well.

Another advantage of FireWire 800 over FireWire 400 is the length over which data can be communicated. FireWire 800 works over distances up to 100 meters.

FireWire 800 uses a different port than does FireWire 400 (see Figure 28.3).

Figure 28.3
FireWire 800 and FireWire 400 cables are not interchangeable, as you can see in this photo.

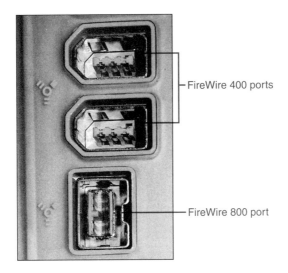

FireWire 400 ports

FireWire 800 port

USB 1.1

The universal serial bus (USB) is an interface that also provides access to external peripheral devices for your Mac. USB 1.1 is a fairly slow interface and is capable of transferring data at the rate of 12Mbps (compared to 400Mbps for FireWire 400). Although slower than many other interfaces, this speed is more than adequate for many peripheral devices.

USB ports on Macs have a thin rectangular shape (see Figure 28.4).

Figure 28.4
USB ports enable you to connect your Mac to a large variety of devices.

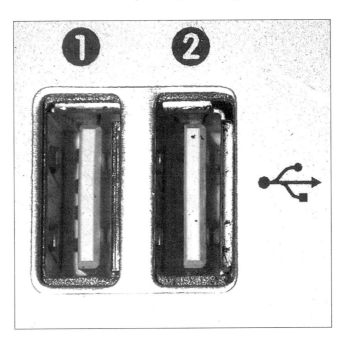

28

NOTE

Similar to FireWire, the USB ports on peripheral devices can look quite different from the USB ports on a Mac. Many USB devices have a USB port that is almost square; others have specialized shapes (such as those on digital still cameras that tend to be small).

USB offers advantages similar to those offered by FireWire, including

- **Chainable**—As with FireWire, USB devices can be chained together. A single USB port can support up to 127 devices.

- **Hot-swappable**—USB devices can be connected to or disconnected from your Mac while it is running.

- **Self-powered**—The USB interface can also provide power to a peripheral device, so that such devices do not require a separate power supply.

Apple Leads Again

Adoption of the USB interface across the entire computer industry can also be largely attributed to Apple. Although USB is an industry-standard interface, it was not widely used until Apple released the iMac. The success of the iMac encouraged other computer manufacturers to more strongly support the adoption of USB. All PCs are now also equipped with USB ports. USB has mostly replaced several different ports on the PC (such as the parallel port) as it has on the Mac.

Because USB is an industry-standard interface, Macs can use the same USB hardware as PCs do. The manufacturer only has to provide Mac-specific software for the device to be Mac compatible.

All modern Macs are equipped with at least one USB port, and most have two or more. To connect more USB devices, you can install a USB hub for your system.

→ To learn more about USB hubs, **see** "Finding, Installing, and Using a USB Hub," **p. 926**.

Numerous devices can use the USB interface, including the following:

- Mice
- Keyboards
- Printers
- Digital cameras
- Microphones
- Speakers
- CD-R and CD-RW drives
- Cradles for PDAs
- Scanners

NOTE

Although USB supports up to 127 devices and FireWire supports up to 63, these are somewhat theoretical limits. The actual number of devices you can connect to these ports depends on the power requirements of the devices. For example, you could not connect 127 USB devices that get their power from the USB interface to a single Mac because the bus could not provide enough power for all those devices.

USB 2

USB 2 is a much faster implementation of the USB interface. It communicates at 480Mbps, which is even faster than FireWire 400. In fact, USB 2 is so fast that it is suitable for hard drives and other high data rate transfer devices.

USB 2 is supported by many modern Macs, and USB 2 has become a standard on Windows PCs. USB and USB 2 share the same hardware, so USB 2 and USB 1 devices can exist on the same USB chain. In fact, from the outside, you can't tell whether a Mac supports USB 2 or not (because the ports are the same as those used for USB 1). To determine whether your Mac supports USB 2, check the technical information provided with the machine.

If your Mac does support USB 2, many USB 2 devices are available, most of which your Mac can use even if they are not designed for the Mac. This is the benefit of supporting dominant technologies on Windows PCs—little to no development has to be done for a device to support Macs and Windows PCs. (Of course, if software is required to support the device, a Mac OS X version of the software must be available for you to use that device with a Mac.)

PCI

Peripheral component interconnect (PCI) is actually an internal interface that is used to provide additional external interfaces for specific purposes through PCI cards. These cards are plugged in to available PCI slots inside the Mac, and then the ports provided by that card become available for you to use (see Figure 28.5).

NOTE

AGP is the abbreviation for *accelerated graphics port*. On Macs that include PCI slots, the AGP slot is filled with the graphics card that is installed in the Mac when it is built.

Adding PCI cards to a Mac is rather straightforward. You open the Mac's case, remove a blank cover from an available slot, insert the card into an available slot, and replace the screw that holds it in place. After any required software is installed, the ports provided by that card become available.

28

Figure 28.5
This photo shows the three open PCI slots in a Power Mac G4; a graphics card occupies the AGP slot located toward the bottom of the photo.

Open PCI slots

Graphics card installed in the AGP PCI slot

NOTE

> Desktop Macs, such as the Power Mac G5, are the only ones that support the addition of PCI cards.

One of the best applications of a PCI card is to add a second monitor to your Mac by adding a second graphics card to it. On newer Power Mac G4s and G5s, the video card already supports dual monitors, but on those machines, you can add more graphics cards to add even more monitors.

→ To learn more about installing a second monitor for your Mac, **see** "Installing and Using a Second Monitor," **p. 864**.

Many PCI cards are available for your Mac, including the following:

- Graphics cards
- Video digitizers
- Other interfaces (such as SCSI)
- Advanced audio cards

Earlier Power Mac G4 models came with four PCI slots; one was occupied by the graphics card installed by Apple, leaving three open slots as shown previously in Figure 28.5. Beginning with the models released in January 2001, Power Mac G4s have four open PCI slots plus the AGP slot occupied by a graphics card.

Current Power Mac G5 computers support three PCI cards.

NOTE

> PCI is also an industry-standard interface. Earlier in the Mac's history, Apple used a pro-prietary interface, called NuBus, to accomplish the same purpose. Because NuBus cards were unique to the Mac, fewer types were available and those that were available were also expensive. Wisely, Apple adopted the PCI standard, which means that Macs can use the same PCI cards as PCs can. Developers need only provide Mac-specific software to enable their devices to work with the Mac.

PCI-X

PCI-X, short for PCI extended, cards perform the same function as PCI but provides higher data rates, up to 1Gbps. PCI-X cards are mostly used for high-end digital video and audio tasks. PCI-X slots are backward compatible, so you can install a standard PCI card in a PCI-X slot.

Current PowerMac G5s have three PCI-X slots.

NOTE

> PCI and PCI-X slots of the same type on the same computer can operate at different speeds. For example, current models of Power Mac G5s have two PCI-X slots that oper-ate at 100MHz and one that operates at 133MHz. When you choose and install a card, you need to match the speed requirements of the card to the specific port in which you are going to install it.

AIRPORT

All modern Mac models provide an AirPort card slot in which you can install an AirPort card to add wireless networking capabilities to the machine. There are two types of AirPort: AirPort and AirPort Extreme. The primary difference between these is the speed at which they communicate.

→ To learn more about AirPort, **see** Chapter 14, "Using an AirPort Network to Connect to the Internet," **p. 371**.

NOTE

> Power Mac G5s include Bluetooth and AirPort antenna ports to which you attach anten-nas for these wireless technologies.

28

BLUETOOTH

Bluetooth is a wireless standard for communicating with peripheral devices, such as PDAs, cell phones, printers, mouse devices, and so on; Bluetooth is similar in performance to USB 1 except that it is wireless.

Mac OS X has built-in support for Bluetooth devices, but to use this capability, your Mac must have the hardware required to communicate via Bluetooth. This can be obtained in two ways. One is to add a USB Bluetooth adapter to one of your Mac's USB ports (see Figure 28.6). The other is to order a Power Mac or PowerBook with a Bluetooth adapter built-in (Power Mac G5s require you to use a Bluetooth antenna that is included when you choose to have the Bluetooth module included).

Figure 28.6
A Bluetooth adapter enables any Mac OS X Mac to communicate with Bluetooth devices.

The most common uses of Bluetooth are the following:

- **Synchronize contact information with cell phones and PDAs**—Using Bluetooth, iSync, and Address Book, you can manage your contact information among several devices and synchronize them easily.

- **Print wirelessly**—You can also add Bluetooth adapters to many types of printers so you can communicate with them without using wires.

- **Use wireless keyboards and mice.**

- **Transfer photos from a digital camera to your Mac without wires.**

Over time, you will likely connect to many low-speed peripheral devices wirelessly using Bluetooth. Hopefully, someday soon Apple will make Bluetooth support standard on all Mac models and include its Bluetooth wireless keyboards and mice with all desktop models.

NOTE

Bluetooth is an electronics industry standard, so many wireless devices are Bluetooth compatible.

MODEM

A modem (modulator-demodulator) is another interface device that provides networking services to your Mac. The great benefit of a modem is that it can provide these services over standard phone lines, thus enabling the age of online services—most importantly, the Internet.

Specific modem hardware implements a specific communication standard, with more modern standards providing higher-speed connections. The current dial-up modem standard is V.92. Modems supporting this standard are capable of communicating at 56,700 bits per second (bps, more commonly referred to as 56K). Although dial-up modem speed has increased significantly over the past few years, it is still relatively slow, especially for data-intensive applications such as video.

All modern Macs include a built-in modem capable of 56K speeds. On some models, you can choose to leave the modem out if you won't need it.

NOTE

As with Ethernet, the actual speed obtained with a dial-up modem depends on each side of the connection. The communication speed between two devices is the highest speed at which they both can communicate. Because dial-up modems use phone lines, they are also greatly affected by the noise that is prevalent in most telephone architectures. Unless the phone lines used are exceptionally clean, modem communication is unlikely to occur at the maximum speed possible.

Other types of modems are available as well, including cable, DSL, and so on. These modems provide much greater speed and reliability but depend on the respective service being available.

→ For more on modems, **see** "Choosing a Modem," **p. 931**.

VIDEO

The video interface in the Mac provides the video output of the machine to a monitor or other device. Depending on the particular Mac model you are dealing with, several types of video interfaces might be available. On Power Mac G5s and G4s, you can add more video options through PCI or PCI-X cards.

Power Mac G5s and Power Mac G4s have at least one built-in graphics card (in the Power Mac G4, this card occupies the AGP 4x slot, and in the Power Mac G5 this has been improved to be an AGP 8x slot) to which you attach a monitor or other display device. Although PowerBooks, eMacs, iMacs, and iBooks have built-in monitors, the PowerBook, eMac, iMac, and newer iBooks also have external video interfaces so you can connect them to external displays, projectors, and other display devices. (You can also attach a USB video device to enable Macs to provide output to external displays.)

28

DVI

> Some graphics cards in Power Mac G5s and newer Power Mac G4s include an ADC port and a DVI port. Power Mac G5s with the most advanced graphics cards include two DVI ports instead. All of these machines support two monitors out of the box. All you have to do is connect a monitor to each port. (You might need a DVI-to-ADC adapter to connect an ADC port to a DVI monitor).

The digital video interface (DVI) is designed for flat-panel digital displays. The DVI interface is standard on all digital flat-panel displays—including Apple's, which used the ADC interface in previous versions. Some Power Mac G5s and all Power Mac G4s include video cards that offer both ADC and DVI ports so you can use either type of display. You can also connect a display to each port to let you have two monitors available. (Power Mac G5s with the most advanced graphics cards feature two DVI ports.)

NOTE

> Interestingly, support for VGA or analog monitors for Power Mac G5s and modern G4s requires an adapter. The age of analog monitors on Macs is mostly over (the exception is eMacs that include a flat CRT monitor).

APPLE DISPLAY CONNECTOR

Some models of the Power Mac G5 and all models of the Power Mac G4 include the Apple Display Connector (ADC), shown in Figure 28.7. This video connector is proprietary to Apple and was designed for the first generations of its Cinema Displays. ADC carries several data streams, those being analog video, digital video, USB, and power. This enables ADC-equipped machines to take advantage of all the features of Apple's original line of digital flat-panel monitors.

→ For information about working with ADC devices, **see** "Finding, Installing, and Using a Monitor," **p. 858**.

NOTE

> In Figure 28.7, you can also see that the three PCI slots are still available (the "blanks" are still installed). If other PCI cards were installed, you would see the additional ports those cards would provide.

Back in the early days of Mac OS X and Power Mac G4s, Apple had standardized on ADC. Its primary benefit was that all you need is one cable to handle video, USB, and power for the display. However, because ADC was proprietary, it was never adopted by other companies. Fortunately, Apple has moved to more fully supporting the industry standard interface, which is DVI. ADC support continues mostly so that people can continue to use their older Apple displays that include an ADC connector.

Apple Display connector   Standard VGA connector

Figure 28.7
The ADC interface provides video, USB, and power so you can take advantage of the advanced features of Apple's Cinema Displays.

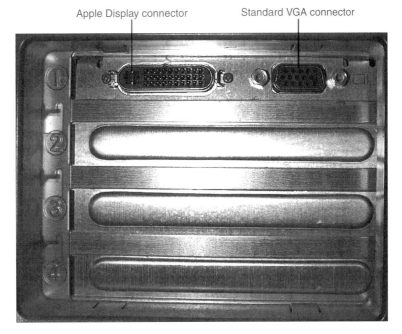

MINI D-SUB VGA CONNECTOR

Several older Mac models provide a standard video graphics array (VGA) port to which you can attach a monitor or another display device (refer to Figure 28.7). The primary benefit of the VGA port was that VGA was the video standard for the PC as well, so you could use just about any monitor with a Mac that has a VGA port. Over the recent past, monitors are becoming digital, which means they use the DVI interface instead. Monitors that support the VGA standard are moving toward extinction. Eventually, as all video devices support the DVI interface, VGA devices will no longer exist. Until then, the most likely uses you have for VGA ports will be to connect an external monitor or projector to a Mac that has one.

NOTE

Some Macs, such as iMacs and eMacs, provide only a "duplicate" image through the VGA port to that of the desktop. For example, when you connect an external monitor or projector to an iMac, the image you see on that device is the same as that on the iMac's monitor. This is called *video mirroring*.

S-VIDEO CONNECTOR

Some Macs, such as the PowerBook G4, include an S-video output port. S-video provides a high-quality video signal and can be connected to television monitors, VCRs, and other video devices.

28

NOTE
> The list of video interfaces in this section is by no means exhaustive. For example, many PCI video digitizing cards provide other video ports, such as those for standard RCA video inputs and outputs.

ANALOG AUDIO

Several basic analog audio interfaces are provided on specific Mac models. Some models, such as the iBook, have only one audio interface (the headphone jack). However, many audio devices use the USB or FireWire interfaces (such as microphones, speakers, and so on), so even the lack of audio ports does not really limit you too much.

Standard audio ports available on various Mac models include the following:

- **Headphone jacks**—You connect standard headphone mini-jack connectors to these.
- **Speaker jacks**—You can attach speakers to these. The difference between a headphone jack and a speaker jack is that a headphone jack provides amplified signals, but a speaker jack generally does not (most computer speakers are externally powered).
- **Analog audio input**—You can attach microphones or other audio devices, such as tape recorders, to these ports to input audio signals to your Mac, such as to record audio for your iMovie projects.

NOTE
> Some Mac models, such as iMacs and PowerBooks, have built-in microphones.

→ For information on speakers, **see** "Finding, Installing, and Using Speakers," **p. 869**.

As with video, many PCI cards provide additional audio interfaces.

DIGITAL AUDIO

Power Mac G5s support optical digital audio and provide input and output ports to enable advanced audio features. These ports enable you to connect receivers, digital instruments, and other audio devices. And, Power Mac G5s support digital 5.1 surround sound speakers with no additional hardware (finally!).

PC CARD

PowerBooks support the PC card interface. This interface provides a slot into which you can plug PC cards to add additional capability to PowerBooks.

TECHNOLOGIES SUPPORTED BY OS X, BUT NOT PART OF MODERN MACS

When Apple moved to USB and FireWire as the primary external interfaces, it left behind some of its previously standard interfaces. Some older Macs, such as beige Power Mac G3s, might have these interfaces, and they are supported by Mac OS X:

- **Apple desktop bus (ADB)**—The ADB port was used to connect mice, keyboards, and other input devices to the Mac. ADB devices were sometimes difficult to work with because they were not hot-swappable; removing an ADB device from or attaching such a device to a running Mac could cause major problems (in some cases, doing so wrecked the machine's motherboard).

- **Serial bus**—Previous-generation Macs used two serial ports: the Modem port and the Printer port. These ports were actually functionally identical and provided an interface to printers, modems, digital cameras, and other devices.

- **SCSI**—The small computer system interface (SCSI, which is pronounced *scuzzy*) is a general interface for attaching various devices to a computer. Older-generation Macs included an external SCSI port to which you could attach a chain of SCSI devices. The SCSI interface is a relatively fast one, but it is also relatively difficult to work with. Each device has to have a unique identifier, and each SCSI bus is limited to seven devices. Creating SCSI device conflicts is easy to do, and the cables and connectors are large and can be hard to work with.

TIP

> You can add an external SCSI interface to Power Mac G5s and G4s by adding a SCSI PCI card. This enables you to connect and use external SCSI devices, such as hard drives, scanners, and so on. Of course, you will need the appropriate Mac OS X drivers to use such devices.

→ For more on SCSI, **see** "SCSI," **p. 833**.

NOTE

> A great resource on the Net from which you can learn about various interface technologies is http://webopedia.internet.com/. In addition to plenty of information about input and output technologies, you can find information on just about any computer-related terminology you encounter. When you find a term, you are also presented with links to additional sites at which you can get more detailed information.

USING INTERNAL INTERFACES

There are numerous types of internal interfaces you will never deal with—unless you build your own Mac or do complex repairs. However, some of the internal interfaces are important to understand because you use them to expand your system.

28

ATA

The AT attachment (ATA) interface is a PC standard specification for hard disk drives and has been adopted on modern Macs. The ATA interface provides high-speed communication, and because it is a PC standard, ATA hard drives are inexpensive.

As with other specifications, there are various "flavors" of the interface, with each offering a specific speed. For example, modern PowerMac G4s use the Ultra ATA/100 standard, which means the throughput of devices using this standard is 100 megabytes per second (MBps). If you add internal hard drives to a Power Mac G5 or PowerMac G4 or replace an existing drive with a larger one, make sure the drive uses the ATA standard your Mac supports.

NOTE

> When you deal with internal devices, you might also hear the term *IDE*, which stands for *integrated drive electronics*. IDE devices are those on which the controller is integrated into the device rather than provided by the computer. This term is often used as a synonym for ATA because ATA devices are also IDE devices. But IDE refers to the general technology, whereas ATA refers to a specific specification.

TIP

> If your Mac supports FireWire 400 or 800, it is often better to add an external FireWire drive than to add more internal drives. That's because you can easily use these drives with many different Macs and can take them "with you" when you move to a different Mac model. Whereas, internal drives usually stay with the machine in which you install them.

DIMM, SO-DIMM, AND DDR SDRAM

The dual inline memory module (DIMM) interface is the standard for RAM chips in many modern Macs, such as the Power Mac G4. DIMM chips use a 64-bit path. You use this interface when you want to expand the RAM capability of one of these Macs.

PowerBooks and iBooks use small outline DIMM (SODIMM), which is a physically smaller interface that provides the same capabilities as the full-size DIMM.

The newest Macs, such as Power Mac G5s, use double data rate synchronous dynamic random access memory (DDR SDRAM) modules. This technology offers improved performance over previous Mac models.

In all cases, when you expand your Mac's RAM (which is one of the best things you can do), you need to ensure that you get memory modules that are the type and speed your Mac supports. See your Mac's documentation to determine the type of memory modules you need for it.

28

SCSI

Earlier in this chapter, you read that SCSI was once a standard external interface. Because of its speed advantages, it was also a standard internal interface that was used for all Mac hard drives. In fact, Apple was the only manufacturer that included the SCSI interface and drives as standard equipment. This speed advantage was one reason the Mac became popular with graphics professionals and others who needed to move a lot of data quickly.

In an effort to cut the cost of its machines, Apple did away with the SCSI interface as the standard one for internal data communication. At the same time, the speed of the PC standard interface, ATA, increased such that this imposes little to no performance penalty for modern Macs. (FireWire replaced SCSI to connect external devices.)

There is more than one SCSI standard, each of which offers a specific speed along with other specifications. Some examples are the following:

- **Fast SCSI**—Supports speeds up to 10MBps
- **Ultra SCSI**—Supports speeds to 20MBps
- **Ultra Wide SCSI**—Supports speeds up to 40MBps

The various SCSI specifications use various connectors and cables—you usually can't connect a device using one standard to an interface that uses another. As with other interfaces, the actual speed of communication across a SCSI interface defaults to the maximum speed of the lowest-speed device connected to the interface.

WORKING WITH INPUT DEVICES

In this chapter

29

CHOOSING AN INPUT DEVICE

Technically speaking, an *input device* is any device you use to move data into your Mac. Some input devices enable you to input data to create documents, images, movies, and so on. The other type of data input devices enables you to control your Mac.

In the context of this chapter, the term *input device* refers to the essential devices you use to input data and to control your Mac. Other sorts of input devices used only for data input, such as cameras, scanners, and so on, are covered elsewhere in this book.

There are two types of essential input devices: keyboards and mouse devices. However, many varieties of each device exist, and in the case of mouse devices, some of the varieties are hardly recognizable as being a device of that type. There are other types of input devices you might want to use, such as a graphics tablet.

Many of the devices described in this chapter use the USB interface.

→ To learn more about USB, **see** "USB 1.1," **p. 821**.

NOTE

> Introduced in Mac OS X version 10.2 was the built-in handwriting-recognition system called Ink. With Ink, you can use a tablet to write or draw and the Ink system converts your writing into text and graphics. Because of space limitations, I can't provide detail about using Ink in this chapter. However, if you have a graphics tablet, you can use the Ink pane of the System Preferences application to configure Ink. Then, you can write on your graphics tablet to input text and graphics and to control your Mac.

Since Mac OS X version 10.2, Mac OS X has supported wireless devices that use Bluetooth technology. Many of these devices are available, including keyboards, mouse devices, PDAs, cell phones, and so on. Bluetooth enables your Mac to wirelessly communicate with multiple devices at the same time.

FINDING, INSTALLING, AND CONFIGURING A KEYBOARD

The keyboard is one of the most fundamental, and at the same time, simplest devices in your system. You are likely to spend most of your "Mac" time pounding on its keys, so it pays to make sure you have a keyboard you like.

CHOOSING AND INSTALLING A KEYBOARD

All Macs come with a keyboard of one type or another, so if you are happy with the keyboard that came with your Mac, there is no need to consider another type. The most recent Apple keyboard, the Apple Pro Keyboard, is widely recognized as an excellent keyboard because it combines a very nice feel with good ergonomics and features. The Apple Pro Keyboard also provides several control keys, which are the mute, volume, and eject keys; these are located along the top of the number pad. And it looks pretty cool, too.

However, other types of keyboards are available, such as those designed for maximum ergonomics, to provide additional controls (such as an Internet button), and so on.

Many modern keyboards use the USB interface, so installing a keyboard is a trivial matter of plugging it in to an available USB port. (And remember that, as you read in Chapter 28, "Understanding Input and Output Technology," USB devices are hot-swappable so you can connect and disconnect them without turning off the power to your Mac.)

Some keyboards are wireless; two basic types of these devices are available. One type includes a transmitter you plug in to an USB port. The other type, such as the Apple Wireless Keyboard, uses Bluetooth. The advantage of Bluetooth is that you don't consume an USB port and can communicate with many Bluetooth devices at the same time. The disadvantage is that your Mac must have a Bluetooth module built in or have a Bluetooth adapter installed.

If at all possible, you should obtain a wireless keyboard; being without wires is very freeing, especially if you move your keyboard or mouse around much. And who needs all the clutter that so many wires bring?

If you use a USB-based wireless keyboard, you connect its transmitter to a USB port and then use its controls to get the transmitter and keyboard communicating. If you use a Bluetooth keyboard, you use the Bluetooth configuration tools to install and configure it.

→ To learn more about Bluetooth devices, **see** "Finding, Installing, and Using Bluetooth Devices," **p. 847**.

If the keyboard you select includes additional features, such as additional buttons and controls, it probably also includes software you need to install. This typically adds a new pane to the System Preferences application that you use to configure the device. An example of this is provided in the next section.

CONFIGURING A KEYBOARD

With the default pane of the System Preferences application, you can change the key repeat rate and the delay-until-repeat time. You can also configure the function keys and set the language in which your keyboard is configured. Here's how:

1. Open the System Preferences application, click the Keyboard & Mouse icon to open the Keyboard & Mouse pane, and click the Keyboard tab if it isn't selected already (see Figure 29.1).

NOTE

If you use a mobile Mac (PowerBook or iBook), you will see additional controls for configuring the trackpad and functions keys.

→ To learn how to configure the keyboard and trackpad on a mobile Mac, **see** "Using and Configuring the Trackpad," **p. 329**.

Figure 29.1
Use the four tabs of the Keyboard & Mouse preferences pane to configure your mouse and keyboard.

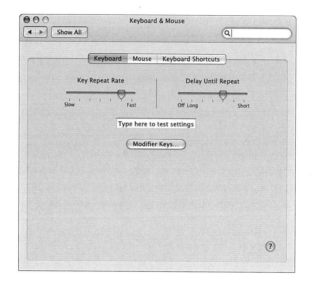

2. Use the Key Repeat Rate slider to set how fast a key repeats itself. Move the slider to the right to cause keys to repeat more quickly.

3. Use the Delay Until Repeat slider to set the amount of time it takes for a key to repeat itself. You can test your settings in the text area below the sliders.

4. Click the Modifier Keys button. The Modifier Keys sheet will appear.

5. For each modifier key, select the action that you want to occur when you press that key. The options are one of the modifier keys or No Action. For example, if your keyboard preference is such that the Control key is more convenient for you, you might want to set it to be the Command key since you use that key more frequently. You can select No Action to disable a key.

6. Click OK to set your preferences and close the sheet.

> **NOTE**
>
> The greatest Mac OS X feature ever (okay, that is a bit of an exaggeration) might be the ability to disable the Caps Lock key. I have never discovered a real use for this key, but have accidentally turned it on thousands of times and found myself TYPING IN ALL CAPS which is very annoying for readers and it seems like you are shouting. Finally, I can disable this most annoying of keys without additional software!

CONFIGURING KEYBOARD SHORTCUTS

One of the best things you can do to increase your personal productivity is to learn to use keyboard shortcuts. In the "OS X to the Max" sections of other chapters in this book, you will find many lists of keyboard shortcuts. You should take the time to learn and practice the shortcuts for the OS, as well as shortcuts for any applications you use frequently. The Mac Help Center also lists some keyboard shortcuts if you need to look one up.

29

Using the Keyboard Shortcuts tab of the Keyboard & Mouse pane, you can configure many of the available keyboard shortcuts. You can enable or disable some of the standard keyboard shortcuts and add keyboard shortcuts for commands in applications you use.

Using the Full Keyboard Access feature, you can access the interface elements with the designated keys. Open the Keyboard & Mouse pane of the System Preferences application and click the Keyboard Shortcuts tab (see Figure 29.2). You will see a list of standard OS keyboard shortcuts in a number of areas, such as screen shots, universal access, keyboard navigation, and so on.

Figure 29.2
Use the Keyboard Shortcuts tab to configure your own keyboard shortcuts.

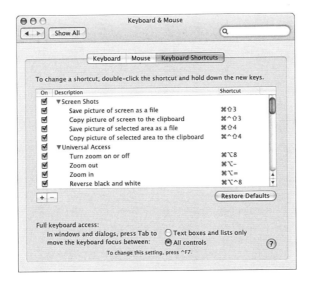

Disable any of the listed shortcuts by unchecking the shortcut's On button. Typically, you would do this when that shortcut conflicts with a shortcut in an application you use. For example, the default shortcut to capture the screen to a file is Shift-⌘-3. The screenshot application I use, Snapz Pro X, also uses this shortcut by default. Because I don't use the Mac OS X's built-in shortcut, I disable the default screenshot shortcut so it wouldn't interfere with the default Snapz Pro X shortcut.

→ To see an explanation of the standard keyboard shortcuts you can configure and use, **see** "Getting the Most from Keyboard Shortcuts," **p. 851**.

In the Keyboard Navigation section, the commands start with the phrase "Move focus to." Moving the focus means highlighting the item to which you want to access via the keyboard. For example, if you want to use the keyboard to access a menu command for which a keyboard shortcut isn't defined, you can press Control-F2 to highlight the first item on the active menu bar, which is always the Apple menu. Then use the Right arrow key to select the menu you want to open. Then press the Down arrow key to open the menu move to the command you want to activate. Press Return to activate the command.

29

CONFIGURING YOUR KEYBOARD'S LANGUAGE SETTINGS AND THE INPUT MENU

You can configure the languages you use for the keyboard along with other input preferences using the International pane of the System Preferences application. You can also configure the Input menu, which enables you to quickly choose among languages and select some other handy keyboard tools:

1. Open the International pane of the System Preferences application.

2. On the Language tab, move the language you want to be the default to the top of the list by dragging it there. Move the other languages on the list to set the order in which they are used.

3. Click the Input Menu tab. You use this area to show the Keyboard menu on the Finder menu bar and to configure the items you see on it (see Figure 29.3). The default language, which was set when you installed Mac OS X, is checked in the pane.

Figure 29.3
You can configure the Input menu with the Input Menu tab of the International pane.

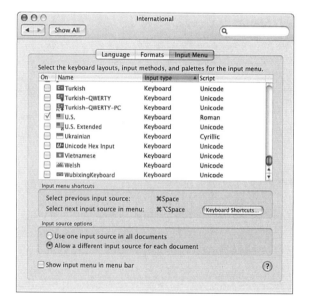

4. Check the "Show input menu in the menu bar" check box.

5. Check the boxes next to the other languages you want to be available on the Input menu.

6. Check the Character Palette check box to add that to the menu. You can use this to select, configure, and use special characters like accent marks.

7. Check the Keyboard Viewer check box to add that to the menu. This viewer shows you the keys for a selected font.

8. If you want to change the keyboard shortcuts for selecting the source on the Input menu, click Keyboard Shortcuts and use the controls you learned about in the previous section to set the appropriate keyboard shortcuts.

9. If you want to allow only one input source (such as a single language) for all documents, click "Use one input source in all documents." If you want to allow different sources to be used in different documents, leave "Allow a different input source for each document" selected.

When you open the Input menu, which is indicated by a flag representing the language you have made the default, you will see the items you configured there (see Figure 29.4). You can change the current input source, which is indicate by the check mark, to a different one by selecting a different source on the menu. You can open the Character Palette or Keyboard Viewer by selecting the command from the Input menu for the item you want to show. If you select Show Input Source Name, the source name appears as the menu title in addition to the flag icon.

Input menu

Figure 29.4
The Input menu enables you to select the language setting for your keyboard and open palettes and viewers related to the keyboard.

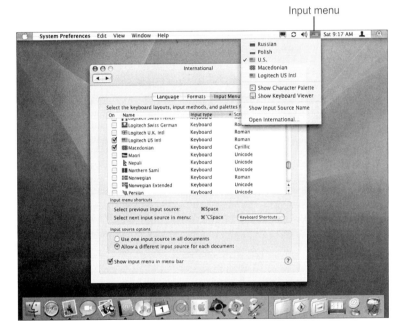

CONFIGURING A THIRD-PARTY INPUT DEVICE

If you use a non-Apple keyboard and it includes software, you can use it to configure that keyboard.

Open the System Preferences application and then open the pane relating to the keyboard you are using (see Figure 29.5).

Use the controls provided by that pane to configure the device (see Figure 29.6).

29

Figure 29.5
I use a Logitech Cordless Elite keyboard and mouse; the Logitech Control Center pane enables me to configure many aspects of these devices.

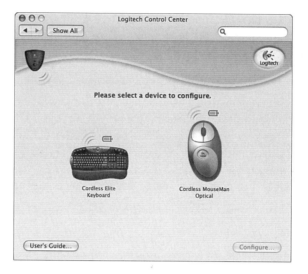

Figure 29.6
Here you can see some of the many additional controls provided on the Logitech Elite keyboard; you can customize the keys to perform many actions.

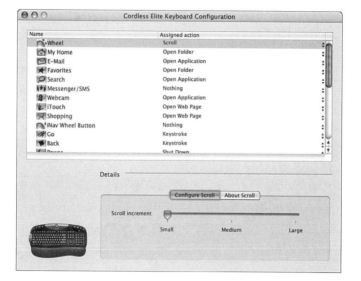

FINDING, INSTALLING, AND CONFIGURING A MOUSE

When the Mac was first introduced, its mouse separated it from all the computers that came before it, and those that came after it, for a long time. Until Windows and other platforms adopted the mouse as one of their primary input devices, the Mac and its mouse really stood out from the crowd. Now, the default Mac mouse stands out, but not in a good way because Mac users would really benefit from having more than one button so they don't have to use two hands to open contextual menus or perform many other actions. All other platforms come with at least a two-button mouse, and most mice also include a scroll wheel.

CHOOSING AND INSTALLING A MOUSE

All desktop Macs come with the Apple Pro Mouse. This is an optical mouse, which means it uses light to translate your movements into input information (as opposed to the rolling ball in previous generations of mouse devices). The Apple Pro Mouse uses the entire top half as its "button," which makes using it even easier (if that is even possible). And it shares the same clear or white plastic look as the Apple Pro Keyboard. If you are happy with the standard Apple mouse, you don't need to worry about replacing it with something else.

N O T E

My input devices of choice are made by Logitech. Check out their great selection of input devices at www.logitech.com.

However, I strongly recommend that you get a mouse that has at least two buttons. The ability to right-click things to activate contextual menus and to perform other commands is much more convenient than using a key and clicking the single mouse button. Plus, if you use a mobile Mac, you might want to add a mouse for those times when you are using your iBook or PowerBook at a desk.

There are three main considerations when choosing a mouse.

One is its comfort in your hand. Mouse devices come in various shapes and sizes. Using one that is suited to your own hand cuts down on fatigue in your hand and lower arm.

Another factor is the number of buttons and other features on the mouse. Apple's mouse devices all provide a single mouse button, but other mouse devices come with two or more buttons. These buttons can be programmed to accomplish specific tasks, such as opening contextual menus. Also, some mouse devices include a scroll wheel that enables you to scroll in a window, such as a web page, without moving the mouse.

Because support for a two-button mouse with a scroll wheel is built in to the OS, (even though you won't find this indicated on the Mouse tab of the Keyboard & Mouse pane of the System Preferences application unless you have such a device installed), you should get at least a two-button mouse. This makes opening contextual menus, which are used throughout the OS and in most applications, much easier. Even better, get a mouse that includes a scroll wheel. This makes scrolling much more convenient and faster at the same time.

Third, you need to decide whether you want a wireless mouse. Because of the amount of time you spend moving a mouse, you should really consider a wireless mouse. Getting rid of the wire provides much more freedom of movement for you. As with keyboards, two types of wireless mouse devices are available—those that use a USB transmitter and those that use Bluetooth (such as Apple's Wireless Mouse).

Like installing a keyboard, installing a mouse isn't hard.

29

If you use a wired mouse, just plug it in to an available USB port. If you use a USB-based wireless mouse, plug its transmitter in to an available USB port and use its controls to get the mouse and transmitter communicating.

If you use a Bluetooth mouse, use the Bluetooth configuration controls to set it up.

→ To learn more about Bluetooth devices, **see** "Finding, Installing, and Using Bluetooth Devices," **p. 847**.

NOTE

> Apple's wireless keyboard and mouse use Bluetooth to communicate with a Mac. You must purchase these devices separately. Hopefully, someday soon Apple will build Bluetooth support into all Macs and include the wireless keyboard and mouse. Even better, maybe someday Apple will replace its mouse design with a two-button (or more) version that includes a scroll wheel.

CONFIGURING A MOUSE

Configuring a mouse is much like configuring a keyboard; however, if you use a mouse that offers additional features (beyond a second button and a scroll wheel, which are standard features in most non-Apple mice), you need to install and configure the software that comes with that device first to take advantage of all its features. Without this software, the second button and scroll wheel will likely work as you expect but more advanced features won't work without the additional software installed.

To configure a two-button mouse with a scroll wheel), do the following:

1. Open the Keyboard & Mouse pane of the System Preferences application.
2. Click the Mouse tab (see Figure 29.7).

Figure 29.7
Configuring a mouse isn't hard to do.

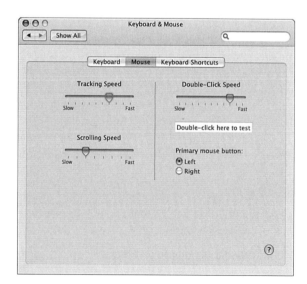

3. Use the Tracking Speed slider to set the tracking speed of the mouse. A faster tracking speed means that the pointer moves farther (faster) with less movement of the mouse.

4. Use the Scrolling Speed slider to set the speed at which the wheel scrolls. Moving the slider to the right makes the scroll action faster, meaning you move up or down the screen faster.

5. Use the Double-Click Speed slider to set the rate at which you have to click the mouse button to register a double-click. You can use the test area to check out the click speed you have set.

6. Select the primary mouse button by clicking either the Left or Right radio buttons. By default, the left button is equivalent to the button on a single-button mouse, but you can reverse the button's roles if you prefer that setup.

If you use a mouse with a scroll wheel and several buttons, you should use the software that came with it to configure the additional controls (see Figure 29.8).

Figure 29.8
If you use a mouse with a second (or third) button and a scroll wheel, use its software to configure it.

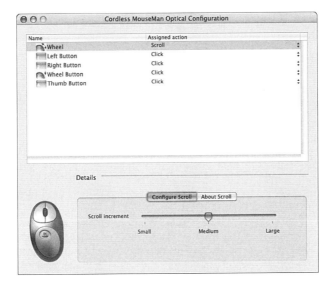

NOTE

PowerBooks and iBooks use a trackpad instead of a mouse (although you can connect a mouse to one of these machines just as you can any other Mac).

→ For information about working with a trackpad, **see** "Using and Configuring the Trackpad," **p. 329**.

29

FINDING, INSTALLING, AND USING A TRACKBALL

Trackballs are really upside-down, roller-bearing mouse devices. Instead of the ball being inside the body, the ball is on the outside of a trackball and you move just the ball instead of the mouse body. Trackballs have several advantages over mouse devices. Because you don't actually move the trackball itself, it takes up less space than a mouse does. And you don't have to lift it up to move it when you run out of room or reach. Because your hand remains stationary, you don't rub the sensitive areas of your wrist across the edge of your desk, which can lead to damage of the tissues in your forearm. Trackballs also have more than one button, and you can program the other buttons to perform various functions. For example, you can set a button to add a modifier key to the click so you can bring up contextual menus with a click instead of having to hold down the Control key while you click a standard one-button mouse. In addition, trackballs can move the cursor either more quickly to cover more screen real estate or more slowly to give you more precise control than a mouse.

Choosing a trackball is similar to choosing a keyboard or mouse (except that desktop Macs don't ship with a default trackball). Look for one that fits your hand and has the features you want—such as the number of buttons it has.

NOTE

Another great input device manufacturer is Kensington. You can learn more about Kensington input devices at www.kensington.com.

Installing trackballs is also similar to installing keyboards and mouse devices. You attach the device through an available USB port and then install and configure its software. Some of these devices are wireless and are set up similarly to wireless keyboards and mouse devices.

CAUTION

If you experience fatigue or pain when using any input device, make sure that you experiment to see whether you can find a more comfortable position for the device. If you can't, consider replacing the device with another type that is more suited to you. Discomfort, even of a mild nature, can indicate that some damage is being done to your body. If this happens over a long period of time, you can end up with serious health problems.

If you do experience problems, consider obtaining several different devices and set up positions among which you can rotate so you can avoid repeating exactly the same actions over an extended period of time. For example, you might want to have both a mouse and a trackball and switch between those devices every so often.

Providing Universal Access

You can use the Universal Access pane of the System Preferences application to configure input devices in different ways to enable those with disabilities to be better able to use a Mac. For example, you can use the Sticky Key feature to cause a series of modifier key presses (such as ⌘ or Option) to be treated like those keys are pressed at the same time. You can also use Mouse Keys to enable the pointer to be moved with the keyboard for folks who have difficulties using a mouse.

→ For the details of configuring Universal Access, **see** Chapter 9, "Making Your Mac Accessible to Everyone," **p. 261**.

29

FINDING, INSTALLING, AND USING BLUETOOTH DEVICES

Bluetooth is a wireless communication standard used by many devices, including computers, keyboards, mouse devices, personal digital assistants (PDAs), cell phones, printers, and so on. Mac OS X is designed to be Bluetooth capable so your Mac can communicate with Bluetooth devices, such as to synchronize your iCal calendar on your Mac with the calendar on your Palm PDA.

PREPARING FOR BLUETOOTH

Two elements are required to be able to use Bluetooth devices.

One is the software component, which is installed as part of Mac OS X.

The other is the transmitter and receiver that sends and receives Bluetooth signals. Some Mac models have this device built in. For those models, you don't need anything else. For models without this, however, you need to obtain and install a Bluetooth USB adapter. This device connects to a USB port and enables a Mac to send and receive Bluetooth signals (see Figure 29.9).

Figure 29.9
For about $40, you can add Bluetooth support to any Mac that has USB ports and is running OS X.

NOTE

You can learn more about Bluetooth on the Mac at www.apple.com/bluetooth/.

29

Bluetooth communication is set up between two devices—a single device can be communicating with more than one other Bluetooth device at the same time. Each device with which your Mac communicates over Bluetooth must be configured separately so your Mac recognizes that device and that device recognizes your Mac.

Two steps are involved in setting up Bluetooth. First, you configure Bluetooth for your Mac using the Bluetooth pane of the System Preferences application. Then you configure your Mac to work with each Bluetooth device you want to use.

CONFIGURING BLUETOOTH ON YOUR MAC

NOTE

If your Mac isn't capable of using Bluetooth, the Bluetooth pane won't appear in the System Preferences application.

When your Mac recognizes that is has the capability to communicate via Bluetooth, the Bluetooth pane appears in the System Preferences application (see Figure 29.10). You use this to configure the general aspects of Bluetooth on your Mac and to see the list of devices your Mac recognizes.

Figure 29.10
Use the Bluetooth pane of the System Preferences application to control general aspects of Bluetooth on your Mac.

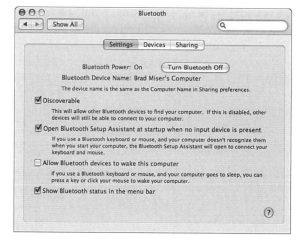

You use the Settings tab to configure your Mac's Bluetooth configuration. It includes the following controls:

TIP

In most cases, the default settings will work for you. You should try to configure a Bluetooth device before you adjust your Mac's Bluetooth settings. If it doesn't work properly, come back to these controls to make adjustments.

- **On/Off**—Use the button at the top of the pane to turn Bluetooth services on or off.

- **Discoverable**—This makes your Mac "discoverable" by other devices because your Mac transmits signals that other devices can detect. If you don't want this, you can uncheck the check box. For example, if you work in a area in which there are many Bluetooth devices, you might want to hide your Mac so other devices won't be able to detect it. You can still connect to your configured Bluetooth devices when this box is unchecked; your Mac just won't be capable of being detected by other devices.

- **Setup Assistant**—The Bluetooth Setup Assistant helps you connect to and configure devices. If you check the "Open Bluetooth Setup Assistant at startup when no input device is present" box, the assistant launches if no devices are configured on your Mac when it starts up.

- **Wake**—If you check the "Allow Bluetooth devices to wake this computer" check box and your Mac is sleeping, Bluetooth devices can wake it up when they need to communicate with it.

- **Bluetooth menu**—Check the "Show Bluetooth status in the menu bar" check box to add the Bluetooth menu to the menu bar.

Many Bluetooth interactions involve the transfer of files between the devices. You allow this using the Sharing tab (see Figure 29.11).

Figure 29.11
Use the Sharing tab to configure file transfers over Bluetooth.

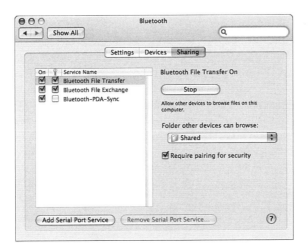

INSTALLING A NEW BLUETOOTH DEVICE

Before you can communicate with a Bluetooth device, that device must be configured on your Mac. And because Bluetooth devices are paired, your Mac must also be configured on the Bluetooth device with which you are communicating. After you have established a pair, your Mac can communicate with its partner, and vice versa.

To set up a new device, you use the Bluetooth Setup Assistant. The general steps to do this are the following:

29

1. Open the Bluetooth Setup Assistant by either clicking the Set Up New Device button on the Devices tab of the Bluetooth pane of the System Preferences application or selecting Set Up Bluetooth Device on the Bluetooth menu. The Bluetooth Setup Assistant opens (see Figure 29.12).

Figure 29.12
The Bluetooth Setup Assistant walks you through the steps required to set up a Bluetooth device.

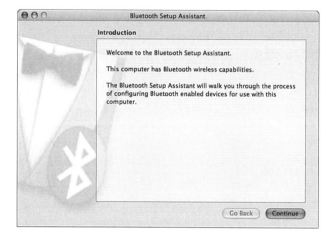

2. Click Continue.
3. Select the type of Bluetooth device you want to set up, such as Mouse, Keyboard, Mobile Phone, or Other Device, and click Continue. Your Mac searches for available Bluetooth devices.

NOTE

> The Bluetooth device you are configuring must be discoverable for your Mac to be capable of finding it, just as your Mac must be discoverable for other devices to be capable of finding your Mac.

4. Select the device you want to configure and click Continue.
5. Follow the onscreen instructions to configure the device. When the process is complete, the devices can communicate.

NOTE

> When Bluetooth devices are connected as a trusted pair, the same passkey is required on each device for those devices to communicate.

WORKING WITH BLUETOOTH DEVICES

After you have configured a Bluetooth device to work with your Mac, you use the device's applications or controls to communicate with your Mac or use a Mac application to work with the device.

29

For example, one of the most useful Bluetooth devices is a Bluetooth capable cell phone. You can use the iSync application to synchronize the phone's contact list with your Address Book so that you have the same information available on both devices. Because you can communicate wirelessly, you don't need to bother connecting any wires to synchronize. You can also transfer files between the two devices, such as to install applications on the cell phone if it supports them.

→ To learn how to use iSync, **see** "Synchronizing with iSync," **p. 801**.

Although synchronizing a cell phone wirelessly is one of the most useful Bluetooth-enabled tasks, it isn't the only one. Consider the following examples:

- Using wireless keyboards and mouse devices
- Printing wirelessly
- Connecting to the Internet through a Bluetooth modem
- Communicating with other Bluetooth-equipped Macs to share files
- Transferring photos wirelessly from a Bluetooth digital camera

MAC OS X TO THE MAX: INPUTTING MORE BETTER AND FASTER

No matter what you do, you will be inputting information constantly. Use the information in this section to do that better and faster.

GETTING THE MOST FROM KEYBOARD SHORTCUTS

Using keyboard shortcuts is a great way to work both faster and smarter. Mac OS X includes support for many keyboard shortcuts by default. As you have seen throughout this book, many areas of the OS and within applications provide keyboard shortcuts you can use.

USING KEYBOARD NAVIGATION

One of the least used, but most useful, aspects of using keyboard shortcuts is keyboard navigation. You can use the keyboard to access almost any area on your Mac in any application, including the Finder. For example, you can open any menu item by using only keys even if that item does not have a keyboard shortcut assigned to it.

First, configure keyboard navigation:

1. Open the Keyboard Shortcuts tab of the Keyboard & Mouse pane of the System Preferences application.

2. Review the list of Keyboard Navigation, Dock, and Exposé and Dashboard shortcuts to make sure the ones you want to use are enabled (see Table 29.1 for the default shortcuts).

3. If you want to use a keyboard shortcut that is different from the default, click the default shortcut, wait for a moment for it to become editable, and change it to a new combination.

29

TABLE 29.1 KEYBOARD NAVIGATION AND DOCK KEYBOARD SHORTCUTS

Shortcut	What It Does	Default Keyboard Shortcut
Turn keyboard access on or off	Enables or disables the use of certain keys, to navigate.	Control-F1
Move focus to the menu bar	Opens the first menu on the current menu bar; use the Tab or arrow keys to move to other menu items.	Control-F2
Move focus to the Dock	Makes the Dock active; use the Tab or arrow keys to move to icons on the Dock.	Control-F3
Move focus to the active window or next window	Moves into the currently active window or takes you to the next window if you are already in a window.	Control-F4
Move focus to the window toolbar	If you are using an application with a toolbar, such as the System Preferences application, this makes the toolbar active. Use the Tab or arrow keys to select a button on the toolbar.	Control-F5
Move focus to the floating window	If you are using an application that has a floating window, this takes you into the floating window so that you can control the corresponding application.	Control-F6
Move focus to next window in active application	Moves you among the open windows in any application, such as the Finder, Word, and so on.	⌘-`
Move between controls or text boxes and lists	If "Text boxes and lists only" is active, when you are viewing windows or dialog boxes with controls, pressing the Tab key moves you among only the text boxes and lists in that open window or dialog box. If "All controls" is selected, pressing Tab moves you among all the elements of the window. This command changes the mode. You can uncheck its check box to disable this action entirely.	Control-F7
Move focus to window drawer	If the application you are using has a drawer, such as iDVD, this moves you into that drawer so you can use its tools.	⌘-Option-`
Move focus to status menus in the menu bar	If you have enabled additional menus in the Mac OS X menu bar, such as the Displays menu, this command enables you to open them.	Control-F8

Shortcut	What It Does	Default Keyboard Shortcut
Show or hide the Character Palette	Shows or hides the Character Palette that you can use to select special characters.	⌘-Option-T
Automatically hide and show the Dock	Hides or shows the Dock.	⌘-Option-D
All windows	Causes Exposé to present reduced versions of all open windows on the desktop.	F9
Application windows	Causes Exposé to present a reduced version of all windows currently open in the active application on the desktop.	F10
Desktop	Moves all open windows off the desktop.	F11
Dashboard	Opens the Dashboard.	F12
Select the previous input source	Moves back to the previous input source.	⌘-spacebar
Select the next input source in the Input menu	Moves to the next source on the Input menu.	⌘-Option-spacebar
Show Spotlight Search field	Opens the Spotlight.	F5

NOTE

If you use a mobile Mac, some of the defaults might be different from those listed in Table 29.1. Check the Keyboard Shortcuts pane to see the current shortcuts for your specific system.

Using the shortcuts in Table 29.1, you can move to and select just about anything you can see. For example, to select a menu command, press the Focus on Menu shortcut (Control-F2 by default) and use the right-arrow or Tab key to move to the menu on which the command is located. Use the down arrow key to move to the command on the menu that you want to select and press Return to activate the command.

As another example, when you are working with an application that has a toolbar, press the shortcut for the "Move focus to the window toolbar" command, use the Tab key to select the tool you want to use, and press Return to use it.

NOTE

Some applications don't support all aspects of keyboard navigation. For example, in some versions of Microsoft Word, you can't select radio button options using the arrow keys, which is too bad.

29

ADDING KEYBOARD SHORTCUTS FOR APPLICATION COMMANDS

You can add keyboard shortcuts to commands within Mac OS X applications using the following steps:

1. Open the Keyboard Shortcuts tab of the Keyboard & Mouse pane of the System Preferences application.

2. Click the Add Shortcut button (+) at the bottom of the pane. The Add Application sheet will appear (see Figure 29.13).

Figure 29.13
Using this simple sheet, you can add a keyboard shortcut for any command in any application.

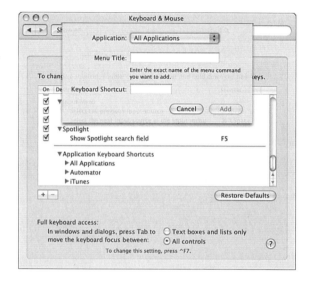

3. Select the application for which you want to create a shortcut on the Application pop-up menu. If the application isn't listed, select Other and use the Open Application dialog box to select the application. To set a shortcut for all applications, select All Applications.

4. In the Menu Title box, type the exact command name for which you want to create a shortcut. If the command contains an ellipsis, you need to include that as well.

TIP

> To type an ellipsis, use the Character palette to select it or press Option--.

5. In the Keyboard Shortcut field, press the key combination for the shortcut that you want to use to access the command.

6. Click Add. When you return to the Keyboard Shortcuts tab, the shortcut you added is listed under the related application under the Application Keyboard Shortcuts section.

TIP

You can expand or collapse the applications listed in the Application Keyboard Shortcuts section to see all of the keyboard shortcuts configured using this tool.

7. If the application for which you configured a shortcut is currently running, quit and restart it. If it isn't currently running, open it. The keyboard command you created will be shown next to the command on the application's menu and you can execute the command by pressing the keyboard shortcut.

Get Serious

If you want to make keyboard shortcuts work even better, consider adding a macro application to your Mac. My favorite is QuicKeys. Using this application, you can create macros to perform almost any series of steps and then activate the macro with a keyboard shortcut or by clicking a button on a toolbar. (As you learned in Chapter 10, you can also use the Automator to create macros. However, it isn't possible to assign keyboard shortcuts to run them unfortunately.)

Using QuicKeys you can easily create a keyboard shortcut for any action or series of actions you want to perform. For example, you can record a series of steps and perform those steps by pressing the keyboard shortcut you assign to the macro you create. If you want to take your personal and your Mac's productivity to the next level, get a copy of QuicKeys as soon as you can.

NOTE

To learn more about QuicKeys, visit www.cesoft.com/products/quickeys.html.

CHAPTER 30

FINDING, INSTALLING, AND USING OUTPUT DEVICES

In this chapter

WORKING WITH OUTPUT DEVICES

Your Mac's output devices determine how the data you are manipulating appears and sounds to you and, in the case of a printer, to the world. Using high-quality output devices can make your Mac experience more enjoyable and productive.

In this chapter, you will learn about the following output devices:

- Monitors
- Speakers
- Printers

In addition to these hardware items, you will also learn about a significant output mechanism that isn't hardware: Portable Document Format (PDF). PDF offers many benefits; the most important is that you can create and distribute electronic versions of your documents—the viewer does not have to have the same application or fonts you used to create the document to be able to view the document. The PDF appears to the viewer just as it does on your computer. Even better, support for creating PDF documents is built in to Mac OS X.

Finally, because color is such an important part of Mac OS X, you will learn about synchronizing color across multiple output devices.

FINDING, INSTALLING, AND USING A MONITOR

Next to your Mac itself, your monitor might be the most important element of your system. Having the correct type and size of monitor can make working with your Mac more efficient and more enjoyable.

CHOOSING A MONITOR

The fundamental factors you need to take into account when choosing a monitor are detailed in the following sections.

DISPLAY TYPE

There are two options in the way a monitor displays information. With a *cathode-ray tube (CRT)* monitor, information appears on the screen as the result of an electron gun spraying electrons against the inside of the monitor screen, which is covered with phosphors that glow when struck by those electrons. The other choice is a *liquid crystal display (LCD)*, which uses a liquid-based display medium. This technology enables the viewing area to be very thin and light, which is why all laptops are equipped with LCDs.

The image quality of both types of displays is very good. Until recently, the cost of LCDs prevented their use except where nothing else would work because of size limitations, such as in a laptop. Recently, the cost of LCD monitors has decreased, so you can now purchase affordable LCD monitors for desktop machines as well.

NOTE

Because LCD monitors are so thin and their screen is completely flat, they are also called flat panel monitors.

LCD monitors offer many benefits over CRTs. One is their size and weight; a comparably sized LCD display is much thinner and lighter than a CRT monitor. And a high-quality LCD monitor has a sharper and more vibrant picture than its CRT cousin. Because of these reasons, LCD monitors now dominate the computer landscape, so much so that the eMac is the only production Mac that features a CRT. All the monitors Apple produces are now LCDs.

With the low cost of today's LCD monitors, there isn't really any reason to use a CRT. The only possibility I can think of is if you use a Mac whose external monitor support is limited to VGA output, in which case a CRT display can make sense. However even being limited to VGA does not limit you to a CRT; some LCD monitors offer VGA ports.

DISPLAY SIZE

Display size might be the single most important factor when considering a monitor. Various sizes of display area are available. Common LCD monitor sizes are 15'', 17'', 19'', and 20'' along with Apple's spectacular Cinema Displays, which come in a 20'' model or the 23'' and 30'' high-definition models. When it comes to display size, bigger is better. You should get a quality monitor in the largest size you can afford because more display space yields more working area.

Unlike CRTs, a large display won't dominate your office space nor cause you a back injury when you move. For example, even Apple's spectacular 30'' HD display is only 8.5 inches deep and weighs a mere 27.5 pounds.

INTERFACE TYPE

On modern Macs, there are three interfaces to which you connect a monitor: DVI, VGA, and Apple Display Connector (ADC). Various Mac models provide different types of video interface ports. For example, many Power Mac G4s and Power Mac G5s have a DVI and an ADC port on their built-in AGP graphics card. Some models with built-in monitors support external VGA monitors along with their built-in displays (flat panel LCD in the case of PowerBooks, iBooks, and iMacs; CRT in the case of the eMac). Regardless of a machine's built-in ports, by using adapters, you can connect other types of monitors to them as well.

→ To learn more about video interfaces, **see** "Video," **p. 827**.

All these interface types provide excellent image quality, and each offers its own benefits. The Digital Video Interface (DVI) offers superior digital signal quality and direct interface to many types of flat-panel displays. Among the benefits of ADC is that it is a digital signal and an Apple ADC display offers other features, such as including two additional USB ports, requiring only one cable (from the Mac to the monitor), and enabling you to power up your Mac and make it sleep or wake up.

TIP

> If you use an Apple monitor (one of its flat-panel displays), you can power up your Mac by pressing the Power button on the monitor and put your Mac to sleep by pressing the Power button again. Press the Power button while your Mac sleeps, and it will wake up.

PICKING A DISPLAY

Choosing a monitor can be difficult because of the number of choices that are available. However, you can use several factors to quickly narrow down the options to a few monitors that meet your criteria. First and most importantly, decide how much you can afford to spend. You can spend as little as $200 for a 14" flat panel to around $3,299 for the top-of-the-line Apple Cinema HD Display. Second, consider any offer special features such as additional ports. Third, choose the largest size in a quality brand of the type you choose that fits your budget.

NOTE

> The monitor issue is not just for Power Mac G4 or Power Mac G5 users to consider. All modern Macs that include a built-in monitor have a DVI or VGA output port. For example, you can connect a monitor to an iMac's VGA port to use an external monitor with it. The image you see is the same as that shown on the iMac's internal display, but you can use a larger monitor that way, or you can show the same image to several people at the same time (such as for a presentation).

I hate to sound like a commercial here, but Apple's displays are the best available. If you can afford to get one, you won't be disappointed. At $1,299, even the "small" 20" model offers plenty of desktop space and excellent image quality. For the maximum in size and image quality, consider the 30" Cinema HD display that supports high-definition signals.

Other brands can provide excellent monitors at significantly lower monitors. One of my favorite brands is ViewSonic. You can get a very good ViewSonic 19" flat panel monitor for about $500.

Whatever brand and model you choose, I don't recommend anything less than a 19" display unless you really can't afford one that big. Having sufficient display size is important to be able to work efficiently.

NOTE

> Another output option is a projector. Although covering these is beyond the scope of this chapter, the cost of the devices has decreased such that obtaining a decent-quality projector is in the realm of possibility for many Mac users. Adding a projector to your Mac system has all sorts of uses, such as for a home theater.

→ To learn more about projectors, **see** "Turning Your Mac into a Home Theater System," **p. 759**.

INSTALLING A MONITOR

Installing a monitor requires two steps. First, connect the appropriate cables to the monitor and the Mac (in the case of ADC displays, only one cable is required). Second, install any software that was provided with the monitor. Some monitors include a ColorSync profile; if yours does, you should install and use it. If you are adding a second monitor to your Mac and have to install an additional graphics card, the graphics card you install might also have software that provides its special features.

→ To learn more about ColorSync, **see** "Synchronizing Color Among Devices," **p. 890**.

NOTE

You can find an adapter to enable you to attach almost any type of display to almost any type of video port. For example, some Power Mac G5s include two video output ports. One is DVI, whereas the other is ADC. If you want to connect a current Apple display to both ports, you need a DVI/ADC adapter to the ADC port.

CONFIGURING A MONITOR

After you have installed a monitor, use the Displays pane of the System Preferences application to configure it. If you use a single monitor, this pane has two tabs—Display and Color. If you use multiple monitors, the pane also includes the Arrangement tab (see Figure 30.1). You use the Display tab to configure the resolution, color depth, refresh rate, and, in some cases, the brightness of the display. The specific options you have depend on the graphics card and monitor you are using. In any case, use the menus, sliders, pop-up menus, and other controls to configure the display. Generally, you should use the highest resolution that is comfortable for you to view. Then, choose the largest color depth and highest refresh rate that are supported at that resolution. Finally, set the brightness to a comfortable level for you.

Figure 30.1
The Display pane of the System Preferences application for an Apple 20" cinema display.

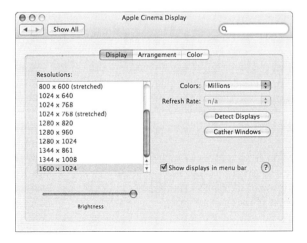

30

TIP

The Display preferences window for each monitor is independent. By default, each display preference window appears on the display it controls. If you want to move all the open display preference windows together, click the Gather Windows button. This will stack all the open Display preference windows under the current one.

Setting the resolution of a display is a matter of personal preference, but generally you can tolerate higher resolutions on larger monitors. For example, on the 20" Apple Cinema Display, a resolution of 1600×1024 is comfortable for many people. On smaller monitors, 1024×768 might be appropriate. The resolution also depends on the sharpness and clarity of the display. For example, on the Apple 17" flat-panel, a resolution of 1024×768 is very comfortable, but that same resolution might not be comfortable on a lower-quality CRT display.

Because your Mac can resize the resolution on-the-fly (you don't have to restart), trying different resolutions to see which works best for you is easy. The trade-off is between more screen space at higher resolutions versus everything appearing smaller. Find the best fit for the type of data you work with and your eyesight.

Some monitors support a "stretched" resolution, such as 1024×768 (stretched). This takes the standard 1024×768 resolution and "stretches" pixels in the horizontal direction so the image fills a widescreen display. (If you use a nonstretched resolution on these displays, black vertical bars appear on each side of the screen.)

NOTE

The "standard" resolution for Macs has continued to increase along with the size and clarity of monitors. For most of the Mac's early life, the standard display resolution was 640×480 (which also happens to be the resolution of non-HD television by the way). When Macs included larger screens and bigger monitors became available, this increased to 800×600. Currently, the minimum resolution you will likely use on most displays is 1024×768. In fact, some applications, such as iMovie, won't even run at 800×600 or less.

After you have selected a resolution, select the color depth on the Colors pop-up menu. In almost all cases, you should select Millions. However, if you use an older graphics card and display, you might have to settle for Thousands.

Select the highest refresh rate available on the Refresh Rate pop-up menu.

NOTE

If you use digital signal with flat-panel display, the Refresh Rate pop-up menu is grayed out because refresh rate isn't applicable to these displays when you use a digital signal over the DVI or ADC interface.

Some monitors support software brightness controls, in which case you will see a Brightness slider on the Displays pane. If you don't see this, use the display's physical controls to set its brightness (and contrast, if applicable).

NOTE

> Non-Apple displays provide hardware controls for lots of display settings, such as brightness and contrast, color adjustments, and so on. If you use one of these displays, check out its configuration menu to see what options you have.

If you want your Mac to detect the displays you have attached to it, click the Detect Displays button (it won't be available in all circumstances). The name shown at the top of the System Preferences application and each Display settings window (there will be one for each monitor) should identify the display you are using.

TIP

> If you connect another monitor to your Mac but it doesn't become active, click the Detect Displays button. Your Mac will recognize and start using the additional monitor.

Use the "Show displays in menu bar" check box to turn on the Displays menu in the menu bar. You can configure a display, such as setting its resolution, by selecting the resolution you want to use from the Displays menu (see Figure 30.2).

Figure 30.2
This system has two monitors attached to it. The current main display is an Apple 20" cinema display while the second display is a ViewSonic VX900-2. The Displays menu on the menu bar makes configuring all the displays attached to a machine easy.

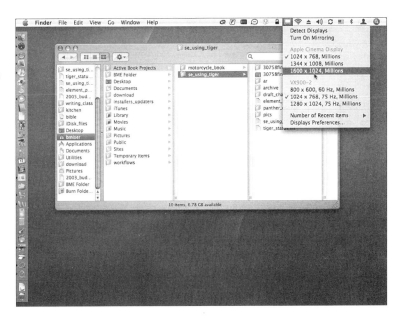

If you display this menu, use its "Number of Recent Items" menu to set the number of resolution settings to display. For example, if you select 3 on this menu, the Displays menu on the menu bar shows the most recent three settings you have selected. This makes changing among your most commonly used resolution settings even easier.

After you have configured the Display tab, use the Color tab to select a ColorSync profile for your display.

→ To learn more about ColorSync, **see** "Synchronizing Color Among Devices," **p. 890**.

Installing and Using a Second Monitor

To create the ultimate amount of desktop working space, consider adding multiple monitors to your system. With the Mac OS, you have always been able to have two or more monitors working at the same time, with each monitor displaying different portions of the desktop. For example, you can display a document on which you are working on one monitor and all the toolbars and palettes you are using on a second. Or you might want to have a document open on one screen and your email application open on the other.

Most Power Mac G4 and all Power Mac G5 models offer support for multiple monitors out of the box. These machines include DVI or ADC ports on the AGP graphics card so you can connect one of each type of monitor to take advantage of multiple monitors. All you need to do is add the second display (and an adapter if needed), and you are good to go.

All other Mac models feature various kinds of video out ports. Some of these, such as eMacs, support only video mirroring out of these ports. So, even though you can connect an external monitor to the eMac, the same images are displayed on both monitors. Other Macs, such as some PowerBook models, can display different images on the built-in display and an external one.

Video mirroring is sometimes useful when you want to display the same image to a larger group or if you just want to use a larger display while you work on your Mac. However, multiple monitors are the most useful when each one is independent so you can configure your expanded screen real estate any way you choose.

To have multiple monitors installed on a machine without out-of-the-box multiple monitor support or to add even more monitors to a machine that already supports multiple monitors, you need to install a PCI or PCI-X graphics card for each monitor you add (some graphics cards support two monitors in which case you could add two additional monitors with the graphics card).

NOTE

> Modern Power Mac G4s and Power Mac G5s feature an accelerated graphics port (AGP) slot in which the preconfigured graphics card is installed. This slot offers the greatest video performance and is where the ATI or NVIDIA graphics card is installed. When you add a second monitor, you install additional graphics cards in the PCI or PCI-X slots that are available. Because only one AGP slot exists, you aren't able to achieve the same level of performance from the video cards installed in the PCI slots. However, you can still achieve very good performance with PCI- or PCI-X-based graphics cards. And you can

always configure your system so you work with applications and documents that require the maximum performance on the displays that use the AGP slot. You can use the other displays for less graphics-intensive applications.

Choosing a PCI or PCI-X Graphics Card

Many graphics cards are available, each offering differing levels of performance and special features. When choosing a graphics card, consider the following factors:

- **Mac OS X compatibility**—Not all graphics cards are Mac OS X–compatible, so any that you consider should be.

- **Performance**—Graphics cards offer varying levels of performance, such as 2D and 3D acceleration and the display resolution they support. The amount of memory installed on a card is a large determinant of this performance, with more memory being better. Common memory amounts are 32MB, 64MB, or 128MB. Generally, you should obtain the highest performance you can afford.

- **Video interface support**—Most modern graphics cards support the DVI interface used by almost all flat-panel displays. Some offer support for multiple interfaces, such as DVI and VGA. If you are going to add a flat-panel display as a second monitor, get a card that supports DVI (assuming that the monitor does) because it will result in better image quality and enable you to use the monitor's special features.

- **Special features**—These include video digitizers that enable you to digitize video from analog sources, TV tuners that enable you to watch TV or the output from a VCR on your display, and other features for which you might have a use.

NOTE

You can also replace the default AGP video card in your Mac with one that offers better performance. Just make sure that the card you get is compatible with your Mac. Replacing the AGP card is similar to installing a PCI or PCI-X card.

Installing a Graphics Card

Installing a PCI or PCI-X graphics card is a relatively easy process.

CAUTION

The following steps are an example of how a typical graphics card is installed on a Power Mac G4. You should follow the instructions that came with your Mac and the graphics card you are adding.

NOTE

If software is provided for the card, such as drivers and applications, you should install the software before you install the card. However, check with the instructions that came with the card to see the order in which the manufacturer recommends the items be installed.

To install a new or additional graphics card, do the following:

1. Power down your Mac.

2. Open the case.

3. Locate the PCI or PCI-X slot in which you want to install the card. You can use any open PCI or PCI-X slot; they are functionally identical. In Power Mac G5s, you should use the slot that matches the performance of the card you are installing.

4. Remove the blank cover from the PCI or PCI-X slot you are using.

5. Install the PCI or PCI-X card in the slot and secure it with the screw that was used to hold the blank cover in place.

6. Close the case.

7. Attach a monitor to the VGA or DVI output of the graphics card.

8. Restart your Mac.

→ To learn where the PCI slots are located in a Power Mac G4, **see** "PCI," **p. 823**.

WORKING WITH TWO (OR MORE) MONITORS

If your Mac is connected to multiple monitors, you need to configure the displays to work together. When you have more than one monitor installed, one of the monitors must be the primary monitor. This is the monitor on which the menu bar, Dock, mounted volumes, and other desktop items are displayed. The rest of the monitors contain windows that you place on them.

To display items on more than one monitor, do the following:

1. Open the Display pane of the System Preferences application. When you do so, you see a Displays pane on each monitor. On the primary monitor, this is included in the System Preferences application window. On the other monitors, this is an independent window with the name of the monitor at the top of the window. The settings shown in each Displays pane are those that are currently being used for that monitor. On the primary display, a third tab called Arrangement appears in the Displays pane (see Figure 30.3). The Displays pane on the other monitors contains the normal tabs, but it does not contain any part of the System Preferences interface (see Figure 30.4).

2. Set the resolution, color depth, and refresh rates for each monitor using its Displays pane. You can use different settings for each monitor; for example, if one monitor is larger than the other, you might want a higher resolution on the larger monitor.

3. Click the Arrangement tab on the primary monitor's Display pane. You will see a graphical representation of the monitors attached to your system (see Figure 30.5). The primary monitor is indicated by the menu bar across the top of the monitor window (on the left display in Figure 30.5).

Figure 30.3
This Display pane contains the Arrangement tab, which means it is for the primary display.

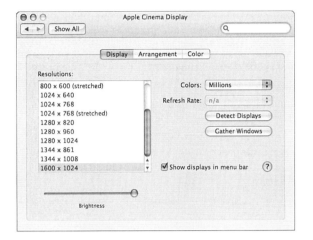

Figure 30.4
This Displays pane is on a secondary monitor; note that the resolution setting is different from that of the primary display shown in Figure 30.3.

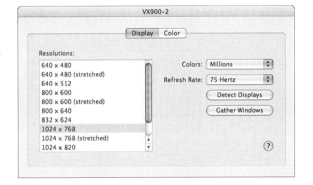

Figure 30.5
This system has two monitors attached to it; the relative resolution settings are indicated by the size of the monitors in this pane. The primary monitor, located on the left, is set to a higher resolution than the one on the right.

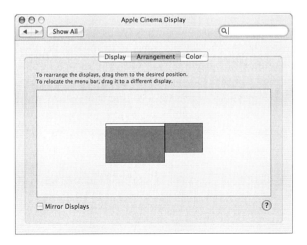

30

4. Organize the monitors by dragging them on the pane. For example, drag the monitor you want to display "to your left" to the left side of the pane. This configures the virtual desktop so you move the mouse/pointer to the left to work on the left display. The monitor icons should be in the same orientation as the physical monitors on your desktop.

5. Set the primary monitor by dragging the menu bar onto it.

TIP

> If you click the Gather Windows button, all panes of the Display Preferences pane will be stacked on the main display. This lets you easily change the settings for all monitors from one location.

 If you can't get both monitors working, see "My Second Monitor Doesn't Work" in the "Troubleshooting" section at the end of this chapter.

Because the desktop stretches across all the monitors connected to your system, they act as one large desktop. You can drag windows, palettes, and other elements from one monitor to another by moving them from one side of the desktop to the other. You can move between the monitors by moving the pointer "across" the divide between them. For example, you might have an image open in Photoshop on one monitor and all the Photoshop palettes on the other. Or, you can have a Word document open on one monitor and a web browser on another. After you use multiple monitors for even a short time, you might find that you can never get along with just one again.

NOTE

> You can drag windows between the monitors, but the menu bar and Dock always remain on the primary display.

You can have multiple monitors display the same image by turning on display mirroring. When you do this, each monitor displays the same desktop. You are limited to the same amount of working space, but that same space is displayed on multiple displays. This is especially useful when you connect a projector to one video port and use a display on the other. You can work using the display while the audience sees what you are doing via the projected image.

NOTE

> If you connect a display or projector to the VGA or DVI port on a PowerBook, iBook, iMac, or eMac, you can only use the video mirroring mode.

To configure mirroring, set the monitors to the same resolution. In the Arrangement tab of the Display pane, check the Mirror Displays check box. All monitors connected to the machine then display the same image.

TIP

You can also turn on mirroring by choosing Turn on Mirroring on the Displays menu if it is shown on your desktop.

If you add the Displays menu to your menu bar, you can control display mirroring, the resolution, and the color depth of each monitor by choosing the setting you want on the menu. You can also open the Displays pane of the System Preferences application from the menu (see Figure 30.6).

Figure 30.6
Control the resolution and other settings of all the displays attached to your Mac from the Displays menu in the Mac OS X menu bar.

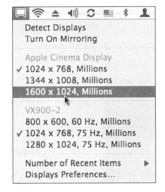

FINDING, INSTALLING, AND USING SPEAKERS

Sound is an important part of the Mac experience. Adding speakers to your system is a good way to enhance the experience of music, movies, games, and other multimedia.

The five basic types of speakers you might be able to use with your Mac include

- **Built-in**—The built-in speakers on eMacs and older iMacs provide fairly good sound. The built-in speakers in PowerBooks and iBooks are okay as long as you are on the move and can't use anything better. But the built-in speakers on other Macs are pretty sorry.

- **Analog**—Analog speakers connect to the Mac's headphone or speaker jack. You can find very high-quality computer speakers, some of which rival their home stereo counterparts in sound quality.

- **Apple Pro**—Some Macs, such as the iMac G4, include a jack for Apple Pro speakers. These machines include a pair of Apple Pro speakers, also known as *eyeball speakers*. These are analog speakers that offer decent sound quality and a very stylish design.

- **USB**—Digital speakers use the USB interface to connect to your Mac. USB speakers also offer excellent quality.

- **Digital 5.1 Surround Sound**—If you are lucky enough to have a Power Mac G5 or you install a 5.1 audio card in a Power Mac G4, you can use digital 5.1 surround sound speakers. These provide the ultimate in sound quality and enable your Mac to match a home theater's sound output.

30

Digital Surround Sound Is Lacking

It's a shame that only the Power Mac G5 and iMac G5 support digital surround sound. After many years of pro-viding unmatched audio out of the box, the Mac has trailed Windows machines for some time in audio capabili-ties. Many more 5.1 surround sound cards are available for Windows machines, and many Windows desktops support 5.1 out of the box. With its emphasis on leading-edge digital media capabilities, it is too bad that some Macs are limited to simple analog stereo audio. (For example, when you watch a DVD on all Macs except the Power Mac G5 or iMac G5, you are limited to stereo sound output and the cool surround sound effects enabled by DVD are missed.) Hopefully, Apple will introduce 5.1 support in all Mac models soon.

Choosing and Installing Speakers

As with other system components, choosing speakers is primarily a task of balancing how much you want to spend versus how demanding you are in terms of quality. And, you need to determine whether your Mac can support digital sound. In either analog or USB, speaker sets come with a number of speakers. A basic set has two speakers; however, unless you have a very small budget, you should get a set that also includes a subwoofer. More advanced digi-tal 5.1 speaker sets can have six speakers to provide full surround sound.

NOTE

As mentioned earlier, surround sound is an area in which Macs trail PCs. Sound cards that provide true surround sound are available for PCs, but at the time of this writing, few are available for the Mac. One that is available is the M-Audio Revolution 7.1. This card enables PowerMac G4s to join their newer PowerMac G5 brethren in the world of digital audio. Unfortunately, at press time, the driver for this card had not been updated to support Mac OS X version 10.4.

A good choice for many systems is Harman Multimedia SoundSticks (see Figure 30.7). These USB speakers provide excellent sound, and they are among the best-looking speakers around. Because they are USB based, all modern Macs can use them.

If you have a Power Mac G5 or have installed a digital audio card in a Power Mac G4, you should get a set of speakers that takes advantage of the advanced audio capabilities of these machines to provide true 5.1 digital surround sound (see Figure 30.8).

Installing speakers requires that you provide power to the subwoofer, attach all the satellite speakers to it, and then connect the subwoofer to your Mac (via the headphone or speaker jack, via a USB port, or to the digital audio out port). If you use Apple Pro speakers, you attach them to the Apple Pro speaker port.

Using Speakers

You can control the audio output of your system in several ways.

Some speakers come with volume and other controls on one of the satellites or on the con-trol hub in the case of surround sound speakers.

Figure 30.7
SoundSticks sound as
good as they look.

Figure 30.8
These Logitech Z-680
5.1 speakers enable a
Power Mac G5 to rock
your world.

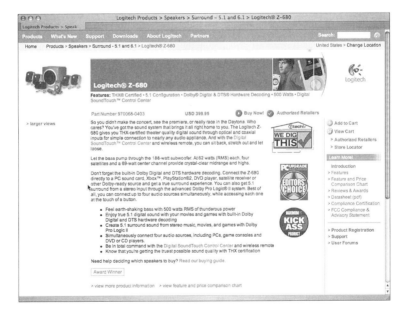

You can control the system volume of your Mac through the keyboard volume controls on
the Apple Pro keyboard or on the PowerBook's and iBook's built-in keyboard. Other keyboards, such as the excellent Logitech Duos, provide volume wheels that you use to control
your system's volume.

You can also use the Sound pane of the System Preferences application to set sound levels. At the bottom of the pane, you can use the "Output volume" slider to set the general sound level for your system, or you can mute it. You can also choose to install the Volume menu on the Mac OS X menu bar. If you do so, you can set the volume level by clicking the speaker icon on the menu bar and setting the volume level with the slider.

NOTE

You can also control volume using controls within specific applications, such as iTunes or iMovie. When you do so, the volume control in the application changes the volume of that application's output relative to the system volume level.

When you use the volume controls on an Apple Pro keyboard, you change the system volume level.

The Sound pane of the System Preferences application has three tabs: Sound Effects, Output, and Input.

On the Sound Effects tab, you can set the relative volume level of alert sounds, the alert sound you want to use, the audio controller through which alert sounds play, whether user interface sound effects play, and whether you hear feedback when you change the volume level using the keys on the Apple Pro or other keyboard.

Select the alert sound you want to use by clicking it on the list. You then hear a sample of the sound you select. When your Mac needs to get your attention, it will play this sound (see Figure 30.9).

Figure 30.9
The Sound Effects pane of the System Preferences application provides complete control over your Mac's sound effects, such as the alert sound.

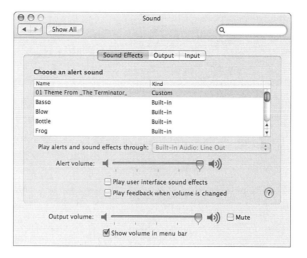

One of the nice features of Mac OS X is that, with some speakers such as USB SoundSticks, you can set the alert sound to play through the Mac's internal speaker while the rest of the sound plays through the external speakers. You do this by setting "Internal speakers" on the

"Play alerts and sound effects through" pop-up menu. This means that alert sounds play through the Mac's built-in speaker(s) rather than through the external speakers, such as SoundSticks. This prevents you from being jarred by an alert sound when listening to loud music or movies.

NOTE

If you use external analog speakers that get their output from the analog audio out on your Mac, you can't choose those speakers separately from the Mac's built-in audio controller because the Mac's controller controls the output to the that port. Only when you use USB or digital speakers, such as the SoundSticks, or when you install a PCI sound card, can you configure separate sound output devices.

30

Set the volume level of alerts by using the "Alert volume" slider. If you do have alerts play through internal speakers while other sound plays through external speakers, you likely need to set the alert volume level relatively high to be able to hear it over the sound coming from the external speakers.

If you check the "Play user interface sound effects" check box, you will hear sound effects for various actions, such as when you empty the Trash.

If you check the "Play feedback when volume keys are pressed" check box, you will hear a sound when you change the system volume level using the volume keys on your keyboard. The louder the volume setting, the louder the feedback sound.

Use the Output tab to select and configure the output devices you want to use to play sound other than system alerts (see Figure 30.10). When you install additional devices, such as SoundSticks, you see each device in the output device list. Choose the device you want to use to play sound and then configure the settings for that device. The settings you have depend on the device you have installed. For example, with SoundSticks, you can control the balance of the satellite speakers. When you are using digital audio output, you will have more control over sound output, including setting the relative volume level among the various speakers.

Figure 30.10
The Output tab of the Sound pane of the System Preferences application enables you to configure the balance of external speakers.

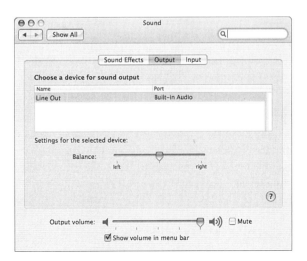

30

NOTE

> If you install an audio PCI card, you use that card's software to make adjustments. This usually includes an additional preference pane installed in the Other section of the System Preferences application.

Use the Input tab to configure sound input devices, such as the audio in port or USB microphones (see Figure 30.11). A list of all sound input devices appears in the upper part of the pane. You can use the "Input volume" slider to set the input volume level for the selected device. Use the "Input level" display to monitor the input volume being received by the input device. The "blips" show you how "loud" the input sound is. A blip remains at the highest level of sound input to show you where the maximum is. Generally, you should set the level so that most of the sound is coming in at the middle of the range.

Figure 30.11
You can use the Input tab to set the input volume for devices you will use to record sound or for other reasons (such as speech recognition).

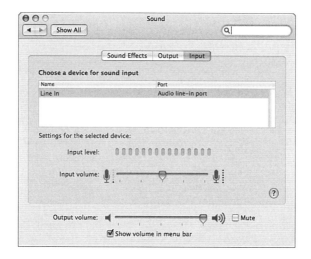

FINDING, INSTALLING, AND USING PRINTERS

If you want to get your work out on paper, you can use many types of printers to get the job done. Under Mac OS X, you install and manage printers using the Printer Setup Utility application. And Mac OS X includes support for a large number of printers by default.

Four basic categories of printers are available, based on the technology the printer uses to imprint the paper:

- **Inkjet**—Inkjet printers spray small dots of ink on the paper to form images and text. Inkjet printers produce excellent quality text and good-to-excellent quality graphics. For personal printers or those shared by only a few people, inkjets are hard to beat. A good quality inkjet printer costs less than $150, so they are also an excellent value. Support for many Hewlett-Packard, Lexmark, Epson, and Canon inkjet printers is built in to Mac OS X.

- **Laser**—Laser printers produce superb quality for both text and graphics. They are also very fast and are the best choice for network printing. Lower-end laser printers are affordable enough to also be a good choice for a personal printer.

- **Color laser**—Color laser printers produce excellent text and graphics and also have color capability. High-quality color laser printers are very expensive and are unlikely to be an option for you unless high-quality color printing and network support are required and you have a business that can justify their expense.

- **Other printers**—Beyond color laser printers are dye-sublimation and other higher-quality printers that are used in graphic design and other high-end businesses.

30

NOTE

> A factor to consider when selecting a printer is that inkjets use a lot of ink and cartridges are expensive. If you do much black-and-white printing, a laser printer can be a less expensive option in the long run when you consider the cost of the consumable supplies (ink versus toner).

There are two ways you can connect a printer to your Mac: directly or through a network. To connect a printer directly to your Mac, you simply attach the printer cable to the appropriate port on your Mac (USB or Ethernet for newer Macs; serial or Ethernet for older Macs). How you connect a printer to your network depends on the type of network you are using. If you are using an Ethernet network, you can attach a cable from the nearest hub or print server to your printer. You can also choose to share either type of printer over a wired or wireless network.

Mac OS X supports several printer communication protocols, including AppleTalk, IP Printing, Open Directory, Bonjour, direct connection through USB, and Windows Printing.

CHOOSING A PRINTER

Covering the mind-boggling variety of printers available is beyond the scope of this book. However, there are some printer classes you might want to consider, including

- **Inkjet**—A good-quality inkjet printer will serve almost everyone. Even the inexpensive models can do a great job with text and graphics, including printing photos and other high-resolution images. If your page quantity needs are fairly modest, an inkjet printer is a good choice, especially if you need color output.

- **Laser**—If you have higher quantity demands or your printer needs to support several users, a laser printer might be a better choice. Laser printers are faster and less expensive per page than are inkjets. Many laser printers are networkable so supporting your local network with a single printer is easy.

- **Other options**—If you have the need for a color laser printer or dye-sub printer, you are probably in a company that has an IT staff that handles obtaining and installing these devices. As long as the printer uses standard network printer drivers, Mac OS X machines will be capable of printing to them just fine.

30

NOTE

> Mac OS X easily supports multiple printers at the same time. An ideal setup is to have an inkjet printer for color work, such as printing photos, and a laser printer for documents.

Mac OS X includes support for Bonjour; this technology enables your Mac to actively seek devices to which it is networked. In the case of Bonjour printers, your Mac can discover the printers it can access and automatically configure itself to use those printers. No configuration on your part is required. However, printers have to be Bonjour capable for this to work. Even though Bonjour has been supported since Mac OS X version 10.2, few printers support this technology.

INSTALLING PRINTERS

There are many types of printers you can install, configure, and use with Mac OS X. In this section, you will learn how to work with the most common types of printers.

INSTALLING A LOCAL USB PRINTER

As long as it offers Mac OS X–compatible drivers, you can install and use just about any USB printer. Using such devices is relatively straightforward:

1. Connect the printer to the power supply and to your Mac's USB port.

2. Install the printer driver software, if necessary. If the printer you are using is an inkjet from HP, Lexmark, Canon, or Epson, the drivers are probably already built in to Mac OS X.

TIP

> To see which specific printer models are supported natively by Mac OS X, open `Mac OS X/Library/Printers`, where `Mac OS X` is the name of your Mac OS X startup volume. You will see folders for each brand of printer you elected to include when you installed Mac OS X.

3. Configure the printer in the Mac OS X Printer Setup Utility.

Support for many inkjet printers is built in to Mac OS X. For example, you can use the following steps to install, configure, and use an HP Photosmart inkjet. Other models of inkjet printers work similarly:

1. Connect power to the printer.

2. Connect the printer's USB cable to a USB port on your Mac.

NOTE

> If support for the specific model of printer you are using is not built in to Mac OS X, you need to install its specific software prior to configuring the printer on your Mac.

3. If the printer has Mac OS X–compatible software, install it—support for several printers is built in to the operating system.

4. Open the Printer Setup Utility (Applications/Utilities).

5. In the Printer List window's toolbar, click Add. The Printer Browser will appear. In the upper pane of this window, you will see a list of all the printers with which your Mac can communicate, such as a printer connected to its USB port.

6. Select the printer you want to configure by clicking its name in the list. Information about that printer will be gathered, and Mac OS X will attempt to choose the best driver software for it, which will be shown on the Print Using pop-up menu (see Figure 30.12).

Figure 30.12
Mac OS X can configure most printers automatically, as it did for this one when I selected the "photosmart 7700 series" on the printer list.

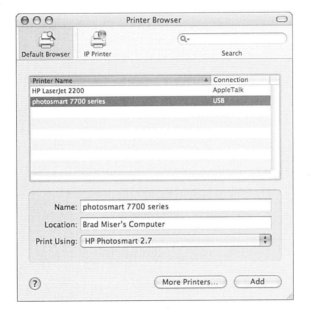

7. If you don't want to use the default printer name shown in the Name box, select it and type a new name.

8. If the default location isn't what you want, select it and change that, too.

9. If Mac OS X found a driver for your printer and selected it on the Print Using pop-up menu, leave that selection as it is; if a driver wasn't found, open the pop-up menu and choose the appropriate driver. If you can't find a driver for your printer, you need to get one from the printer's manufacturer.

10. Click Add. You'll return to the Printer List and the printer you selected and configured will appear on the list (see Figure 30.13). The printer will be ready to print your documents. The printer you installed most recently will become the default printer, which is indicated by its name being bolded on the list.

Figure 30.13
An HP Photosmart printer has been installed on this Mac.

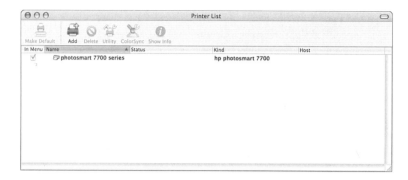

TIP

> If you hold down the ⌘ key and click the Hide/Show Toolbar button in the Printer List window, you cycle through toolbar configurations, including various icon sizes and a text-only toolbar.

INSTALLING A NETWORK PRINTER

Using a network printer is a good way to share a printer among multiple users; with the rise of home networks and the decrease in the cost of networkable printers, installing a networked printer in a home or home office is also a practical option.

Installing a network printer is similar to installing a local printer. The specific steps you use depend on the network you are using and the particular printer model. Support for most laser printers is built in to Mac OS X.

In the following example, an HP LaserJet 2200DN is installed on a small Ethernet network. The steps to install other printers on different types of networks are similar:

1. Connect power to the printer.
2. Connect the printer to an Ethernet hub.
3. If the printer has Mac OS X–compatible software, install it—support for most laser printers is built in to the operating system.
4. Open the Printer Setup Utility(Applications/Utilities).
5. In the Printer List window's toolbar, click Add. The Printer Browser will appear. It will begin to search for printers with which your Mac can communicate. The printers it finds will be shown on the printer list.
6. Select the printer you want to install. Mac OS X will attempt to find the driver and configure the printer. If it can do so, you will see the printer's name, its location, and the driver Mac OS X has selected.
7. Click Add. The printer will be added to the Mac and you will return to the Printer List, where each printer installed will be shown (see Figure 30.14).

Figure 30.14
This Mac now has access to two printers available to it.

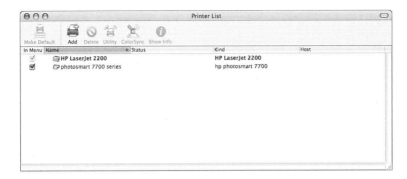

INSTALLING OTHER TYPES OF PRINTERS

Mac OS X supports many types of printers connected in a lot of ways. Although you are most likely to use a printer connected directly to your Mac or through a network—in which case the Printer Browser will likely do most of the configuration work for you—you might have a more unusual situation, such as wanting to use Bluetooth to print.

In the event that the Printer Browser doesn't automatically find and configure a printer, you can use its advanced tools to do the configuring:

1. Open the Printer Setup Utility and click the Add button in its toolbar. The Printer Browser will appear.

2. If the printer you want to install doesn't appear in the list, click the More Printers button. A printer configuration sheet will appear.

3. On the top pop-up menu, choose the type of printer connection or printer you want to install. For example, if you have a Bluetooth printer available, choose Bluetooth (see Figure 30.15). You can also choose AppleTalk to configure a printer using the AppleTalk protocol or Windows Printing to choose a printer managed by Windows computers. You will also see the printer drivers you elected to install when you installed Mac OS X.

   Your Mac will attempt to find a printer according to your selection. If it is successful, the printer will be shown in the resulting printer list. If it can't find the printer, your Mac can't communicate with it. You'll need to correct the issue before you can install the printer on your Mac.

4. If the correct driver isn't selected automatically, choose it on the Printer Model pop-up menu.

TIP

If the driver for your printer isn't listed, you'll need to download and install it. Fortunately, Mac OS X supports many kinds of printers by default so unless your printer is older, you shouldn't have to do this.

Figure 30.15
Choosing an option on this menu causes your Mac to search for printers according to the protocol you select.

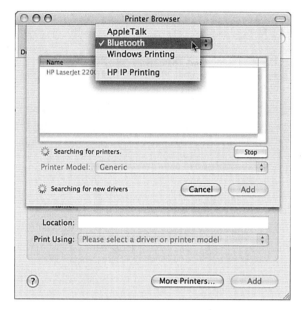

5. Click Add. The printer will be installed on your Mac and you will see it on the Printer List.

NOTE

If you have access to a printer that uses IP printing, click the IP Printer button on the Printer Browser's toolbar. Then use the resulting sheet to configure the printer, such as entering its IP address.

MANAGING PRINTERS

The Printer Setup Utility enables you to manage the printers configured for your Mac. The tools on its toolbar include the following:

- **Default**—Select a printer on the list and click the Make Default button to make that printer the default.

- **Delete**—To remove a printer from your Mac, select it on the list and click the Delete button. The printer will be removed from the list and you will no longer be able to print to it.

- **Utility**—If the printer can access additional configuration software, when you select it on the list, the Utility button will become active. Click this button to launch the software and use its tools (see Figure 30.16).

- **ColorSync**—This button enables you to configure a ColorSync profile for a printer.

Figure 30.16
You can use a printer's utility software to work it, such as to monitor its ink levels.

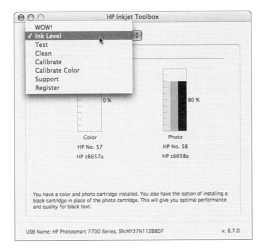

■ **Info**—If you select a printer and click Show Info, the Info window for that printer will appear (see Figure 30.17). Choose the information with which you want to work on from the pop-up menu at the top of the window. The choices include Name & Location, Printer Model, and Installable Options. Use the Name & Location option to view or change this label information for the printer. Use the Pinter Model option to view or change the driver being used. Select Installable Options to configure the printer's features, such as the paper source, duplexing options, and so on. If you make changes, click Apply Changes to save them.

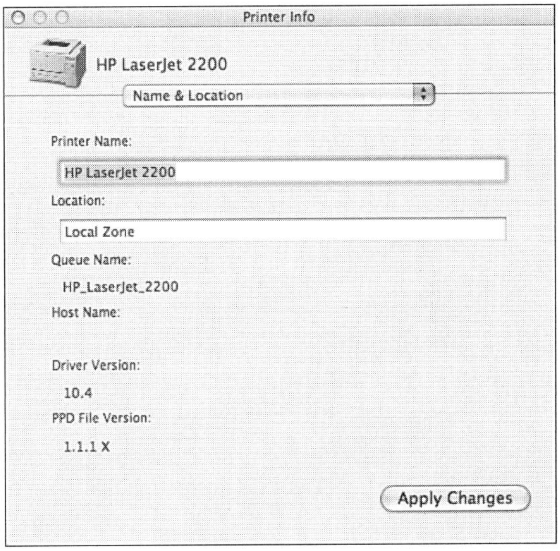

Figure 30.17
Use the Info window to view a printer's current information and to change it as needed.

CONFIGURE PRINTER PREFERENCES

 You can set various printer preferences with the Printer tab of the Print & Fax pane of the System Preferences application (see Figure 30.18). In the left part of this tab, you will see the printers installed on your Mac. In the right part of the tab, you'll see information about the selected printer. Underneath these two areas are a number of controls you can use to set your printing preferences. This include the following:

Figure 30.18
Use the Printing tab of the Print & Fax pane to set printer preferences for your system.

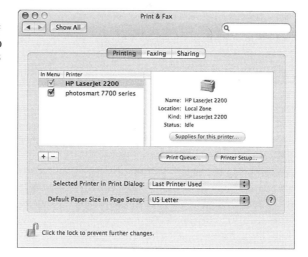

- If the In Menu check box for a printer is checked, that printer will appear in the Print dialog box and can be used. If not, it can't be selected or used.
- Click the Add button (+) to add a new printer. This will take you to the Printer Browser.
- Select a printer and click the Delete button (-) to remove it.
- Select a printer and click Print Queue to open its Print Queue window (more on this later in the chapter).
- Select a printer and click Printer Setup to open its Info window.
- Use the "Selected Printer in Print Dialog" pop-up menu to determine which printer is selected automatically in the Print dialog box. The "Last Printer Used" selection will cause the dialog box to remember the last printer you printed with. If you choose one of the installed printers, that printer will be selected each time you print.
- Use the "Default Paper Size in Page Setup" to choose the size of paper that will be selected in the Page Setup dialog box for the selected printer.

WORKING WITH SHARED PRINTERS

Under Mac OS X, you can share printers connected to your Mac over wired and wireless networks, as well as those connected directly to your Mac through USB. You can also access printers being shared with you.

SHARING A PRINTER CONNECTED TO YOUR MAC

To share a printer, perform the following steps:

1. Install and configure the printer you want to share on your Mac so that it appears on the Printer List.

2. Click the Sharing tab on the Print & Fax pane of the System Preferences application. On this pane, you will see the list of printers configured on your Mac.

3. Click the "Share these printers with other computers" check box. This will activate the printer sharing function.

TIP

You can also turn on printer sharing by checking the Printer Sharing check box on the Services tab of the Sharing pane found in the System Preferences application.

4. Check the check box next to each printer you want to share (see Figure 30.19). The selected printers will be accessible to other Macs on the same network.

Figure 30.19
The Photosmart printer connected to this Mac can be used by anyone on the same network.

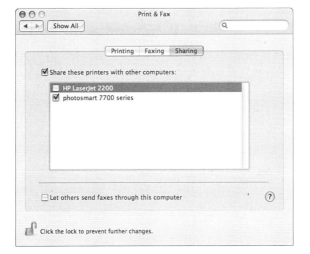

NOTE

You can also share printers that are connected to your Mac through a network connection, but you don't need to do this. Instead, just install the network printer on each machine from which it should be available.

When you share a printer, the Mac from which it is being shared must be running for the printer to be available to other computers on the network. If it isn't, the printer won't be accessible to those other Macs.

> **TIP**
>
> If your network includes an AirPort Extreme Base Station, you can connect a USB printer to the Base Station to share it.

Accessing a Shared Printer

To access printers being shared on a network, use the following steps:

1. Open the Printer Setup Utility.
2. Click Add. The Printer Browser will appear and search for printers with which your Mac can communicate. Printers that are being shared with your Mac will have "Shared Printer" as the connection type.
3. Select the shared printer you want to be able to access.
4. Click Add. The shared printer will be added to the Printer List and you will be able to print with it just like the printers you have installed directly to your Mac.

> **TIP**
>
> You don't have to perform the previous steps; they just make selecting a shared printer a bit easier. You can actually choose any shared printer via the Print dialog box by first selecting Shared Printers on the list of available printers and then selecting the specific printer to which you want to print.

Printing Under Mac OS X

When you print a document, you see the print dialog box for the current printer; the printer shown on the Printer pop-up menu is determined by the preference you set (either the last printer you used or the default). You can choose any other printers that are installed by using the Printer pop-up menu (see Figure 30.20). The Print dialog box contains a variety of pop-up menus and other tools you can use to configure a print job.

Figure 30.20
The list of printers available to your Mac, including any that are being shared with you over a network, are shown on the Printer pop-up menu.

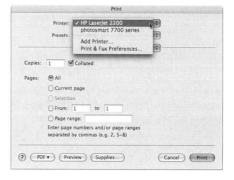

The specific options you see in the Print dialog box depend on the printer you are using and the application from which you are printing. You select the settings you want to configure from the third pop-up menu (counting the Printer and Preset pop-up menus as the first and second ones) and then configure those settings with the controls that appear in the lower part of the dialog box. Depending on the printer and application you are using, the options you have can include the following:

- **Printer**—You can use this pop-up menu to select a printer to which to print. You can also open the Printer Setup Utility by selecting Add Printer. You can open the Print preferences by choosing "Print & Fax Preferences."

- **Presets**—You can switch between the standard settings for the selected printer, or you can save a custom configuration and switch to that one.

- **Copies & Pages**—These controls enable you to set the number of pages you want to print and choose the part of a document you want to print.

- **Duplex**—If a printer is capable of duplexing, you use these controls to configure it, such as by printing on both sides of the paper.

- **Layout**—These commands enable you to control how many pages print per sheet of paper, the direction in which your document layout prints, and whether a border is printed.

- **Scheduler**—This pane enables you to schedule a print job.

- **Paper Feed**—These controls enable you to select a paper tray for the print job, or you can choose to do a manual feed.

- **Print Settings**—Controls in this pane enable you to choose a paper type and select from the print modes offered by a printer (such as color, black and white, draft, and so on).

- **Image Quality**—These controls enable you to determine the quality with which images are printed—to save toner, for example.

- **ColorSync**—This pane enables you to choose ColorSync options for the selected printer.

- **Summary**—The Summary area displays a description of the print job you have currently configured. This can be useful if you have configured a complex print job and want to check it before you run it.

> **TIP**
>
> In the Copies & Pages dialog box for most printers, you have the option to collate documents. If you have ever had to hand-collate a large document, you will really appreciate this feature.

You can preview a print job by clicking the Preview button. When you are ready to print, click Print or press Return.

After you have sent a document to a printer, you can check its status by double-clicking the printer on the Printer List in the Printer Setup Utility application to open the printer's status tool; or, when a job is sent to a printer, the Printer's icon opens on the Dock and begins to bounce; you can click this to open a printer to access its status tool (see Figure 30.21).

Figure 30.21
You can monitor the status of print jobs by double-clicking a printer in the Printer List or by clicking the Printer's icon on the Dock to open the monitor window for that printer.

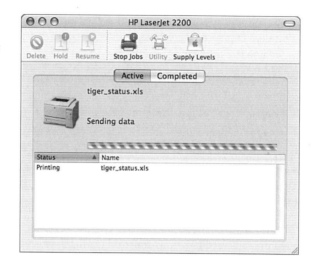

With this tool, you can perform the following tasks:

- Select a print job on the list and click Delete to remove the job from the queue.
- Click a print job and click Hold. The printing process will stop.
- Click Resume and the current job on hold will start printing again.
- Click Stop Jobs to stop all printing for this printer. Click Start Jobs to start the printer again.
- Click Utility to open the printer's utility software.
- Click the Completed tab to view information about print jobs that are complete.

> **TIP**
>
> Some additional actions can be useful for some printers. For example, you can click the Supply Levels button to check the amount of ink left in a printer's cartridges if that action is supported by the printer you are using.

WORKING WITH MAC OS X'S BUILT-IN FAX CAPABILITY

Mac OS X has the capability to send and receive faxes. Of course, to use this capability, your Mac must have a modem installed and that modem must be connected to a working phone line.

RECEIVING FAXES ON YOUR MAC

To configure your Mac to receive faxes, do the following steps:

1. Connect your Mac's dial-up modem to a working phone line.
2. Open the Print & Fax pane of the System Preferences application.

3. Click the Faxing tab.

4. Check the "Receive faxes on this computer" check box. The other controls in the pane will become active.

5. Enter the phone number to which you have connected your Mac in the My Fax Number field.

6. Use the "Answer after" field to set the number of rings before your Mac answers the phone.

7. If you want the fax to be saved as a file, check the "Save to" check box and select the location in which you want fax files to be saved on the pop-up menu.

8. If you want the fax to be emailed, check the "Email to" check box and enter the address to which you want it be to mailed in the field.

9. If you want the fax to be printed, click the "Print on printer" check box and select the printer to which it should be printed on the pop-up menu.

> TIP
>
> Click the Address Book button to select an email address to which to send the fax.

10. If you want to be able to control faxing from the desktop, check the "Show fax status in menu bar" check box (see Figure 30.22). The Fax menu will be added to the Mac OS X menubar.

Figure 30.22
With a Mac
OS X–equipped Mac,
you can get rid of
your fax machine.

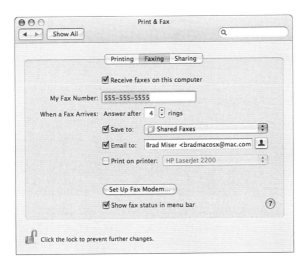

When the phone number to which your Mac is connected receives a call and the number of rings you set have occurred, your Mac answers the phone and attempts to receive a fax. If it receives one, it is saved, emailed, or printed as indicated by your configuration choices.

TIP

> If you want to share your Mac's faxing capability, such as when it is the only Mac connected to a phone line, check the "Let others send faxes through this computer" check box on the Sharing tab of the Print & Fax pane.

SENDING FAXES FROM YOUR MAC

You can send faxes from within any application on your Mac as easily as you can receive them.

→ To learn how to fax documents, **see** "Faxing Documents," **p. 211**.

WORKING WITH PDFS

Portable Document Format (PDF) files are one of the most useful ways to output documents for electronic viewing. Any PDF document can be easily read by anyone using any computer platform. PDF documents maintain their appearance because they do not rely on fonts and other aspects of the system on which they are viewed.

Under Mac OS X, PDFs are a native file format. You can create PDFs from within any Mac OS X application, and you can read PDF files with the Preview application.

NOTE

> The free Adobe Reader application is also available for Mac OS X. This application offers more features for viewing PDFs than does Preview, but either application will get the job done. To download a copy of Adobe Reader, visit www.adobe.com/products/acrobat/readstep2.html.

CREATING PDF FILES

Creating PDF files is an extremely simple task:

1. Open the document for which you want to create a PDF.
2. Select File, Print.
3. Open the PDF pop-up menu and choose "Save as PDF" (see Figure 30.23). The "Save to File" dialog box will appear.

TIP

> Another option on this menu is "Save PDF as PostScript." This creates a PostScript version of the file you are printing. This can be useful for a number of tasks, such as sending to a Bluetooth printer or to other printing service.

4. Name the document and select a location in which to save it. Use the filename extension .pdf.
5. Click Save. The PDF will be created in the location you specified.

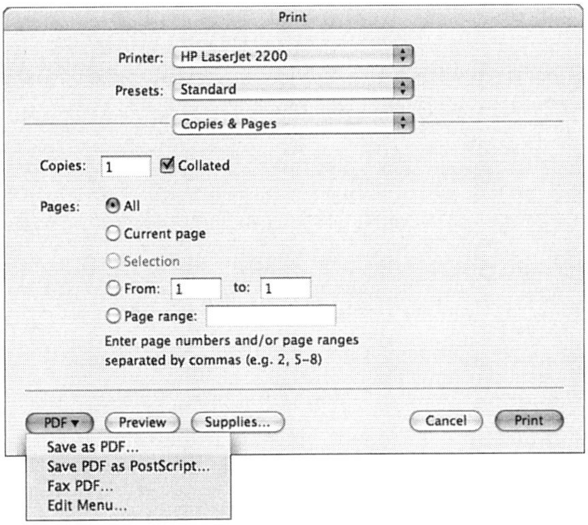

Figure 30.23
You can quickly and
easily create a PDF of
any file by choosing
"Save as PDF" on this
menu.

30

TIP

You can use Automator or other macro tools to create PDF workflows. You can add these to the PDF menu by choosing the Edit menu command. Use the resulting window to add workflows to the PDF menu. After you do so, they will be available to you on this menu.

One thing to note is that creating a PDF in this way does not create or preserve any hyperlinks in a document. For example, if you create a PDF of a web page, the links on that page will not be functional. Similarly, if you create a text document that contains a table of contents in which the entries are hyperlinked to the sections in the document, the resulting PDF will not contain active links. Basically, creating a PDF using the Print command simply replicates a paper document without adding any features of an electronic document. Even so, being able to create a PDF from any document using the Print command is useful when you want to send your documents to other people.

TIP

Creating a PDF version of a document is also a great way to capture versions of that document at specific points in time for archival purposes.

To create PDFs that contain hyperlinks and other electronic document features, you need to use a more sophisticated application. For example, Adobe applications can save documents in PDF format and preserve hyperlinks within those documents. Or, you can use the full Acrobat application to create more sophisticated PDFs from any application.

VIEWING PDFs WITH PREVIEW

To view the document you created, open it. Unless you have configured PDFs to open in a different application, Preview launches and you can view the PDF.

→ To learn how to use Preview, **see** "Working with Preview," **p. 658**.

TIP

> Because Adobe Reader enables you to take advantage of all the features PDF documents offer, you might want to designate it as the default application for all PDF documents so it opens automatically when you view PDFs.

→ To learn how to associate file types with applications, **see** "Determining the Application That Opens When You Open a Document," **p. 201**.

SYNCHRONIZING COLOR AMONG DEVICES

One of the most challenging aspects of creating color documents for output on paper or electronically is maintaining consistent color among the images and text in those documents. Each device you use, such as monitors, printers, scanners, cameras, and so on, can have a slightly different interpretation of particular colors and can use a different color space. This makes creating a document that contains the colors you really want difficult.

Apple's *ColorSync* technology is an attempt to solve this problem. With ColorSync, you configure a ColorSync profile for each device with which you work. If all your devices use a ColorSync profile, the colors across the elements of your document should be consistent because ColorSync translates colors across different color spaces.

The two general steps to use ColorSync are the following:

1. Use the ColorSync Utility to select and configure a ColorSync profile for each device you will use.

2. Use the color management features of the application you want to use to create a document to select the ColorSync workflow for that project.

CONFIGURING COLORSYNC

To configure a ColorSync profile for your devices, do the following:

NOTE

> To use ColorSync, a device must have a ColorSync profile installed. For many devices, this profile is built in to Mac OS X. For others, the profile is installed when you install software related to that device.

1. Open the ColorSync Utility (Applications/Utilities). The first time you run this, you'll be prompted to run Profile First Aid, which will attempt to repair the various profiles stored on your Mac.

2. Click Repair. The Profile First Aid utility will run and find all the profiles stored on your Mac. It will find problems and repair any that it can.

3. Click the Devices button to open the Devices pane. On this pane, you will see the list of devices with color implications connected to your Mac, such as cameras, printers, displays, and so on (see Figure 30.24).

Figure 30.24
Expand a device type to see a list of devices of that type connected to your Mac.

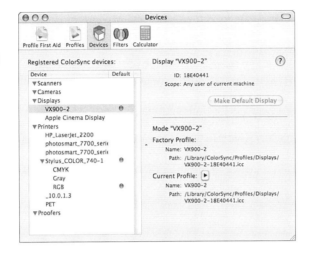

30

4. Choose the device you want to configure. The current ColorSync profile for that device will be shown.

5. To select a different profile, click the Current Profile pop-up menu and choose the profile you want to use. If the one you want to use is not shown on the menu, choose Other and then move to and select the profile you do want to use.

6. Repeat steps 4 and 5 for each device you want to use with ColorSync.

 If you can't find profiles for the devices you want to use, see "I Don't See a ColorSync Profile for My Device" in the "Troubleshooting" section at the end of this chapter.

N O T E

 Understanding and using ColorSync effectively is a very complex topic. For detailed information, see Apple's ColorSync website located at www.apple.com/colorsync.

USING COLORSYNC

After you have installed and configured your device profiles and workflows, the way you use ColorSync depends on the particular applications you use. For example, you can employ the ColorSync profiles when you print a document by using the ColorSync option on the Options pop-up menu in the Print dialog box. Other applications, such as Photoshop, enable you to employ more sophisticated ColorSync features.

TROUBLESHOOTING

MY SECOND MONITOR DOESN'T WORK

When I install and connect a second monitor, it remains dark when I restart my Mac. Why isn't the second monitor working?

Isolate the problem to the graphics card or the monitor by connecting the monitor that is working to the second graphics card and the monitor that isn't working to the first card.

If the second monitor (now connected to the original graphics card) works but the other monitor does not, you know that the problem is related to the graphics card. The most likely cause is an incompatible card. Check the manufacturer's website to ensure that card is supported on Mac OS X. Download and install any updated drivers for that card. Finally, make sure that the card is properly seated in the PCI slot.

If the second monitor doesn't work when it is connected to the original graphics card, you know the problem lies with the monitor itself.

I DON'T SEE A COLORSYNC PROFILE FOR MY DEVICE

I don't see a profile for a specific device I want to use. How do I obtain the correct profile?

For you to be able to choose a profile for a device, that profile has to be installed. It should have been installed when you installed that device's software. However, if it wasn't, check the website of the manufacturer of the device. Locate a ColorSync profile and download it. Install it in the *Mac OS X*/Library/ColorSync/Profiles directory where Mac OS X is the name of your startup volume.

If you still can't find a profile even after you have downloaded and installed it, the profile might be damaged. Run the ColorSync Utility (Applications/Utilities) to verify and repair your profiles.

CHAPTER **31**

UNDERSTANDING AND USING DATA STORAGE DEVICES

In this chapter

UNDERSTANDING DATA STORAGE OPTIONS

A general law of Mac use—especially when you start working with digital video, music, and images—is that you can never have too much room in which to store your data. In this chapter, you will learn more about the following types of data storage devices:

- Hard drives
- CD writers
- Apple's SuperDrive
- Other removable media drives
- Tape drives

CHOOSING, INSTALLING, AND USING A HARD DRIVE

Your Mac's hard drive is one of its most important devices, and its performance and operation have a major impact on the performance and operation of your system. At some point, you will probably want to increase the amount of hard disk space available to you. Adding more hard drive space is relatively simple in most cases and offers many benefits to you.

CHOOSING A HARD DRIVE

When it comes to choosing a hard drive, you should consider the following factors:

- **Will your Mac support additional internal hard drives?**—If you use a Power Mac G5, Power Mac G4, or other desktop Mac, the answer to this question is yes. If you have an iMac, an eMac, a Power Mac G4 Cube, a PowerBook, or an iBook, the answer is no.

- **Should you add an external drive?**—If your Mac won't support the addition of another internal hard drive, you will likely want to add more hard drive space by using an external hard drive. Even if your Mac can handle an additional internal hard drive, you might choose to get an external drive instead because external drives are simpler to install and easier to use with different machines. For example, you can share the same external hard drive among several Macs. Because FireWire offers acceptable performance for all but the most demanding tasks, you won't face much of a performance penalty if you choose to use an external hard drive.

- **Which drive interface does your Mac use?**—For internal drives, the choices are ATA or SCSI. For external drives, the choices are FireWire, FireWire 800, USB 2, or SCSI.

NOTE

> Some external hard drives use the USB 2 interface, which is a dominant interface on Windows computers and is supported on some Mac models. However, in most cases, FireWire external drives should be your first choice. FireWire (both varieties, but especially FireWire 800) offers excellent performance and you won't have to use a USB port on your Mac (which is good because you tend to need more USB ports than FireWire ports).

- **What size drive do you need?**—Drives come in various sizes; generally, you should get the largest drive you can afford in the format you select.

- **Does your Mac need to meet specific performance requirements?**—If you intend to use the drive for high data rate work, such as for digital video, typically, you need to get a drive that spins at least 7,200rpm. Some drives spin even faster, which means they can transfer data at a greater rate. (Some drives that spin at slower rates are also acceptable; check with the drive's manufacturer to see what data rate the drive can sustain.)

NOTE

> If you have a Mac with room for only one internal hard drive, you can replace that drive with one of a higher capacity. For PowerBooks and iBooks, this is a relatively simple operation. For iMacs, this is a more complex task and is not recommended unless you are very comfortable working with hardware.

→ To learn about the various interfaces related to hard drives, **see** Chapter 28, "Understanding Input and Output Technology," **p. 815**.

After you have answered these questions, you should have a good idea about the type of drive you need, such as an external FireWire hard drive that offers performance suitable for DV work and has as much space as you can afford to purchase.

Head to your favorite retail site to research or purchase hard drives (see Figure 31.1).

Figure 31.1
Check out this LaCie 500GB drive that supports both flavors of FireWire, which means it is compatible with all modern Macs.

To begin using a drive, you must install the drive, and then initialize and partition it.

INSTALLING AN EXTERNAL HARD DRIVE

Installing an external hard drive is about as simple as things get. You connect the power supply to the drive and to an electrical outlet, if needed (some drives take their power from the interface). Then, you connect the FireWire, USB 2, or SCSI cable to the drive and your Mac.

If you install a SCSI drive, you must make sure that it has a unique SCSI ID number for the external SCSI bus to which you are attaching it. You also need to ensure that the drive is properly terminated. (Most modern Macs require a SCSI PCI card to be added to be capable of using external SCSI drives. Unless you specifically need SCSI for some reason, a FireWire drive is a better choice.)

After you have connected the drive and powered it up, the installation part is complete (easy installation is a good reason to use an external drive).

 If you're having trouble getting your Mac restarted after connecting a SCSI drive to it, see "My Mac Won't Start Up After I Connect a Drive to It" in the "Troubleshooting" section at the end of this chapter.

→ For more information about SCSI, **see** "SCSI," **p. 833**.

INSTALLING AN INTERNAL HARD DRIVE

Installing an internal hard drive is a bit more complicated than installing an external drive, but it is still relatively easy to do.

NOTE

Because I don't recommend that most users replace a hard drive in most Macs, this section provides information only on adding additional hard drives to a Power Mac G4 or Power Mac G5. If you are comfortable enough working inside a Mac to be able to replace a hard drive, you probably don't need any help doing so.

The following steps describe how to install an internal ATA drive in a Power Mac G4. Installing a SCSI drive is similar, although it uses the SCSI interface and cables rather than ATA cables as this example shows. These steps are provided only as an example; you should follow the instructions provided with your Mac.

Before you get started, read through the instructions contained in your Mac's user manual. Then do the following:

1. Get the drive ready to install by configuring it as a slave drive (if necessary); see the instructions that came with the drive for help with this. Typically, this involves configuring jumper clips on specific pins at the back of the drive (see Figure 31.2). Most of the time, these pins are already set in the appropriate configuration.

Figure 31.2
This photo shows the back of a hard drive; the jumper clips are configured to make this drive the slave.

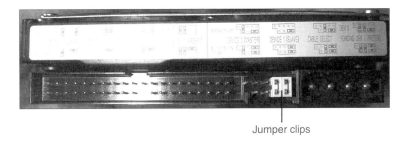

Jumper clips

2. Back up the data on your Mac (just in case).

3. Power down your Mac.

4. Open the case.

5. Locate the bay in which you are going to install the drive; in Power Mac G4s, this bay is located at the bottom of the machine toward the back (see Figure 31.3).

Drive Bay

Figure 31.3
The hard drive that came with this G4 Power Mac is installed in the lower part of the drive carrier located in the drive bay; an additional drive can be added to the upper part of the carrier.

PCI Slots

6. Unplug the power cable from the motherboard and the data and power cables from the existing drive.

7. Remove the screw that holds the driver carrier in place.

8. Install the new drive in the upper part of the drive carrier; use the screws that were included in the accessory kit that came with your Mac.

9. Install the drive carrier back in the Mac.

10. Connect the power and data cables to each drive.

11. Reconnect the power cable to the motherboard.

12. Close the Mac and power it up.

The Mac should restart normally. When it boots up, you won't notice any difference because you can't use the drive until you initialize it.

INITIALIZING AND PARTITIONING A HARD DRIVE

Before you can use a hard drive, whether it is internal or external, you should initialize it (you have to initialize an internal drive before you can use it, but most external drives can be used out of the box). You can also partition a hard drive to create multiple volumes on a single drive (for example, you might want to be able to install more than one version of the Mac OS on a single disk).

When you partition a hard drive, logical volumes are created for each partition on the disk. For most practical purposes, a logical volume looks and acts just like a separate hard drive. There can be some small performance advantages to partitioning a disk, or you might choose to partition it to help you keep your system organized. The most likely reason to partition a drive is to be able to run more than one version of the Mac OS on your computer—each version needs to be installed on a separate volume.

One of the results of partitioning a drive is that all the volumes outside of the startup volume are outside of the default Mac OS X organization scheme. This can be a benefit or a problem depending on what you are doing. For example, documents you store on a separate volume aren't secured using Mac OS X's default permissions, like documents you store within your Home folder are. If you want to provide broader access to files, this is a good thing. If you don't want people to be able to access these documents outside the control of Mac OS X's security, it isn't.

Be aware though that when you partition a drive, the size of each partition becomes a size limitation, just as if the volume was a separate disk. If your partition sizes are too small, you might run out of free space in a specific volume even though the disk on which that volume is stored still has plenty of space. Generally, you should keep your partitions pretty large. If you run out of space on a partition, you have to delete files from it or re-partition the disk, which means that you must start over and reformat the disk (resulting in all files being erased). Unless you have a very specific reason to do so, you typically shouldn't partition a drive into more than two volumes. If you aren't going to have multiple versions of the Mac OS installed, you might not want to use multiple partitions at all.

How Many Partitions?

Because the size of a partition can't be changed without erasing the disk on which it is stored, you should avoid creating partitions unless you have a specific reason to do so. The size of a partition becomes a space limit just as if it were a disk. Because erasing and recovering all the data on a drive isn't a lot of fun, don't set yourself up to have to do it by creating small partitions.

I recommend that you do have at least two volumes available to you, and it is even better if you have these on more than one drive. Then, install a version of Mac OS X on each volume. One should be your primary startup volume on the internal disk in your Mac. Create a small (10GB or so) partition on a different disk (or the same one if you have only one drive available to you) and install Mac OS X on it. Keep this as an alternative startup volume in case your main startup volume has problems.

An ideal configuration is to have at least one external drive along with your Mac's internal drive. Have only one partition on the internal drive and make that your startup volume. This ensures you have as much storage space on that volume as possible. Partition the external drive into two volumes, one relatively small (10GB) and the other with the remainder of the drive's space. Install your alternative OS installation on the smaller volume. Use the large partition for data storage, such as for backups.

> **NOTE**
>
> Most external hard drives come initialized, in which case you can use them without doing the following steps. However, even in those cases, you might want to partition the drive, especially if it is a large one.

To initialize and partition a disk, perform the following steps:

1. Launch Disk Utility (Applications/Utilities). In the Disk Utility window, you will see two panes. In the left pane, you will see the drives installed in your system (the drives are labeled by their capacities and types). Under each disk, you'll see the volumes into which that disk has been partitioned.

2. Select the drive with which you want to work. At the top of the right pane are five tabs; each tab enables you to view data about a drive or to perform a specific action. At the bottom of the window, you'll see detailed information about the drive with which you are working, such as its connection bus, type, capacity, and so on (see Figure 31.4).

3. Click the Partition tab. In the left part of this pane, you'll see a graphical representation the partitions on the disk. If the disk is currently partitioned, you'll see its current partitions. If you are working with a new disk, you'll see one empty partition called "Untitled." In the right part of the pane, you'll see information about the volume, such as its name, current format, and size.

> **NOTE**
>
> Another reason you might want to partition a hard drive is to more easily share files with other users of your Mac. Because volumes outside the startup volume don't use Mac OS X's default security settings, it can be easier to provide access to a volume that all users share. For example, you might want to store files related to an iMovie project that other people are helping you with. They can then access these files without needing access to your Home folder.

Figure 31.4
The Source pane of the Disk Utility application shows two hard drives, and one external FireWire drive, which has been selected (information about the drive appears at the bottom of the window).

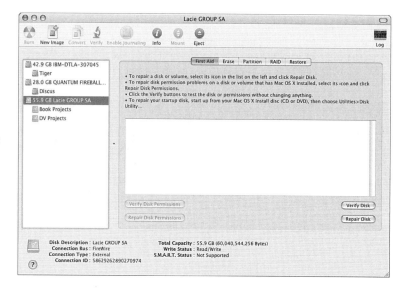

4. Select the number of partitions you want to have on the drive by using the Volume Scheme pop-up menu. You can choose Current, which leaves the partitions as they are, or the number of partitions you want from 1 to 16. After you choose the number of partitions, each partition will be represented by a box in the disk graphic shown under the Volume Scheme pop-up menu. The partitions are called Untitled 1, Untitled 2, and so on.

5. Select a volume by clicking its box. The volume's box will be highlighted and information for that volume is shown in the Volume Information area.

> **TIP**
>
> You can divide a volume into two partitions of the same size by selecting the partition and clicking the Split button. This does the same thing as choosing 2 Partitions on the Volume Scheme pop-up menu.

6. Name the selected volume by typing a name in the Name box. As you type the name, it will be shown in the partitions box.

7. Select the format type from the Format pop-up menu. You should almost always select Mac OS Extended (Journaled) or Mac OS Extended. The journaling option is the best choice if it is available because it improves Mac OS X's capability to recover from unexpected power losses and other such circumstances. For each of these options, you can choose Case-sensitive. If you select a Case-sensitive format, file names are case sensitive meaning that a file called filename.file is not the same as a file called FileName.file. In most cases, you should choose Mac OS Extended (Case-sensitive, Journaled) to take advantage of the most sophisticated format option.

NOTE

> The other format options are Unix File System and Free Space. These are useful in some special circumstances. For example, if you are going to run a Unix OS system (apart from Mac OS X) on your machine, you might want to use the Unix File System for one partition.

8. Enter the size of the volume in the Size box. You can also set the size of a partition by dragging its Resize handle in the Volumes pane.

   If you check the "Locked for editing" check box, the information is reset and locked (you won't be able to change it). This is useful when you are creating multiple partitions and want to make sure that changes you make to other partitions won't impact the one you have configured.

9. If you are going to use the partition while booted up under Mac OS 9, leave the "Install Mac OS 9 Disk Drivers" box checked. If you are using the partition for Mac OS X only, as a Unix drive, or for some other special purpose that doesn't involve Mac OS 9, you should uncheck this box.

10. Select the next partition.

11. Repeat steps 6–10 for each of the volumes (see Figure 31.5).

Figure 31.5
This drive will contain two volumes after it has been partitioned; one will be called Mac OS X and the other will be called Data.

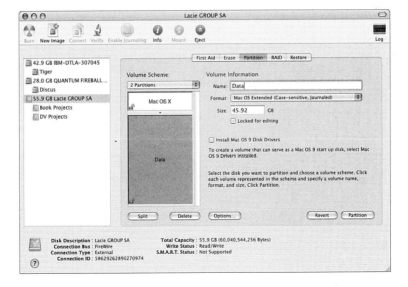

CAUTION

> Partitioning a drive erases all the data on it. If the drive has data on it, make sure you back it up before your partition the drive.

12. Click Partition. If you will be sharing the drive with non-Apple hardware, such as a Windows computer, click the Options button, choose PC Partition Scheme, and click OK.

13. If you are sure that you want to initialize and partition the drive, click Partition in the Warning sheet. You will return to the Disk Utility window and a progress bar will appear in the lower right corner of the window. You can use this to monitor the process.

14. When the process is complete, select the drive you partitioned. Confirm that the drive has been partitioned properly (see Figure 31.6).

Figure 31.6
The selected drive now has a relatively small partition for a Mac OS X installation and a larger one for data storage.

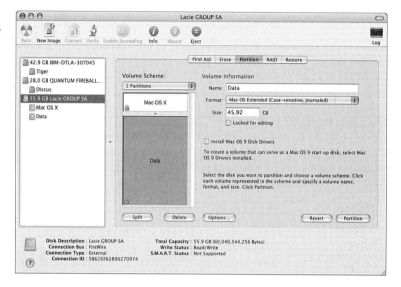

15. Under the hard drive icon, select one of the partitions you just created. The Information pane at the bottom of the window will reveal details about that partition, such as the format, capacity, available space (which will be about the same as capacity immediately after you partition a drive), and so on.

16. Explore each partition to ensure that they are configured properly.

17. Quit Disk Utility.

When you return to your desktop, you will see the new volumes that are ready for your data (see Figure 31.7).

Disk Utility can't see your new drive? See "Disk Utility Can't See My Drive" in the "Troubleshooting" section at the end of this chapter.

You can also use Disk Utility for various other tasks, such as erasing a disk or a volume, managing disk images, disk maintenance, and creating a RAID disk.

→ To learn how to use Disk Utility for disk maintenance tasks, **see** "Maintaining Your Disk Drives," **p. 1000**.

Figure 31.7
The `Mac OS X` and `Data` volumes are ready to use.

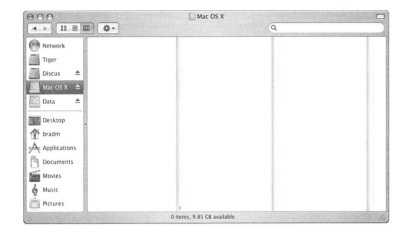

FINDING, INSTALLING, AND USING A CD WRITER

Writing data to CDs has many useful applications, such as general data storage, sending large amounts of data to other people, creating custom audio CDs, and so on. Writing to CDs requires that you have a compact disc recordable (CD-R) or compact disc recordable rewritable (CD-RW) drive and a CD-burning application.

A CD-RW drive can write to CD-R and CD-RW discs. The difference between these two technologies is that CD-RW discs can be erased and reused, whereas CD-R discs can be filled only once (depending on the application you use, you can sometimes fill a disc in multiple recording sessions). Because CD-RW discs are more expensive (about $1 per disc) when compared with CD-R discs (less than $.50 per disc), you typically use a CD-RW disc to create a CD for test purposes. When you are sure that the CD will be created properly, you burn a CD-R disc.

> **NOTE**
>
> CD-R drives have largely gone by the wayside. CD-RW drives can do everything that CD-R drives can do plus write on CD-RW discs, so there is no real reason to use a CD-R drive (you probably couldn't find one to buy even if you wanted to).

CHOOSING AND INSTALLING A CD WRITER

Most modern Macs include CD-RW drives as standard equipment; if you have a machine that is so equipped, you don't need to think about this type of drive any further. However, if your Mac doesn't have an internal CD-RW drive, you can easily add an external CD writer.

> **NOTE**
>
> Apple's SuperDrive is a combination DVD-R and CD-RW drive. This drive is included as standard equipment in many current Mac models and is an option on most others. Apple's Combo drive is a CD-RW and DVD-ROM drive. Current Macs that don't have a SuperDrive at least have a Combo drive so all modern Macs can burn CDs.

When choosing a CD-RW drive, you have three basic options, which are based on the interface the drive uses. Any of the options work well for most users:

- **USB**—All modern Macs offer at least one USB port so you can add a USB CD writer to any system. A USB 2 drive will offer performance that is similar to FireWire 400.
- **FireWire**—FireWire CD writers tend to be slightly more expensive than USB drives. Most modern Macs feature at least one FireWire port and so are compatible with FireWire CD-RW drives.
- **SCSI**—Some CD-RW drives use the SCSI interface. Older Macs or those to which a SCSI PCI card has been added are candidates for a SCSI CD-RW drive. However, I recommend that you stick with one of the other interface types if you can because they are standard on all current Macs.

In addition to the interface, you should consider several other factors:

- **Mac OS X compatibility**—Although USB or FireWire drive hardware is the same for any platform, the software they use is not. Make sure that the drive you choose includes Mac OS X–compatible software.
- **Speed**—CD-RW drives can burn CDs at various rates of speed; faster drives take less time to burn a CD. If burning a CD quickly is important to you because you will do it frequently, get the fastest drive you can afford. Otherwise, if you burn CDs only occasionally, speed is not a very important factor.
- **Portability**—If you have a PowerBook or iBook without an internal CD writer, look for a portable CD-RW drive, preferably one that gets its power from the interface so you have only one cable to connect. You will then be able to burn CDs while away from a power supply.
- **Software**—All CD-RW drives include the software you need to burn CDs. Various CD-burning applications are available. If you have a preference for one of them, look for a drive that features that application. However, because you can burn CDs from the Finder and from iTunes directly, you probably don't need a specific burning application. Some of these applications, though, offer features that aren't found in the Mac's built-in burning software.

NOTE

If you intend to use your CD-RW drive to back up your Mac, try to get one that comes with the Dantz Retrospect backup application.

First, select the interface you want to use. If your Mac has FireWire ports and you can pay a bit more for the drive, head to your favorite retailer and check out the FireWire offerings for Mac OS X-compatibility, speed, portability, and software. If you need to go USB, consider the same issues. Any drive you choose will likely work pretty well.

If there is a specific CD burning application you want to be able to use, such as Apple's iTunes, check the software publisher's or Apple's website to ensure that the drive you are considering is supported by that application. Not all drive mechanisms are supported by all applications, so you need to make sure the mechanism you get is supported by the applications you want to use.

Of course, you can also install an internal CD-RW drive in a machine that doesn't have one. This usually involves replacing the machine's current CD or DVD drive. The process for doing this is quite similar to installing an internal hard drive.

INSTALLING AN EXTERNAL CD WRITER

Installing an external CD writer involves two steps. First, you physically connect the drive to your Mac using a FireWire, USB, or SCSI cable and then connect the power supply to the drive (if required). Second, you install any software provided with the drive.

TIP

> If you install a USB drive, connect it to a port that is as close to the Mac as possible. For example, if you use a USB hub, it is better to plug the drive in to one of the ports on your Mac. Sometimes, sending data through a hub can slow it slightly and, in rare cases, this can cause CD writing problems. This is especially important if the drive also gets its power from the USB port.

CAUTION

> If you use a SCSI drive, you must ensure that the drive has a unique SCSI ID and that it is terminated properly.

USING A CD WRITER

Using a CD-RW drive is dependent on the particular application you use to create CDs. Several applications are available that serve this purpose, and most of them offer unique benefits.

One of the easiest to use is Apple's own Disc Burner application that is built in to the Mac OS X Finder. Disc Burner enables you to create CDs from the Finder by using drag and drop or by creating Burn folders and then burning their contents on disc. This is about as simple as it gets.

NOTE

> The Finder does not support recording to a CD in more than one session. You have to place all the files you want on a disc at the same time.

 If you are unable to create CDs, see "I Can't Create a CD" in the "Troubleshooting" section at the end of this chapter.

TIP

> If your CD-burning application can create disc images, you should do this before burning a CD. You can create and then test the disc image. If it works, go ahead and burn it to a CD.

CONFIGURING MAC OS X TO BURN CDs

Before burning CDs from the Finder, you should configure Mac OS X to work with the drive you have installed. You do this through the CDs & DVDs pane of the System Preferences application.

Open the System Preferences application and click the CDs & DVDs icon to open that pane (see Figure 31.8).

Figure 31.8
You use the CDs & DVDs pane of the System Preferences application to configure the actions your Mac takes when you insert CDs and DVDs of various types.

Use the "When you insert a blank CD" pop-up menu to select the action you want your Mac to take when you put a blank CD into your machine. You have the following options:

- **Ask what to do**—When you insert a blank CD, your Mac prompts you and provides a list of possible actions from which you can choose (see Figure 31.9). The Action pop-up menu contains a similar set of choices to those on the "When you insert a blank CD" pop-up menu on the CDs & DVDs pane, such as Open Finder and Open iTunes. You can make the action you select on the Action pop-up menu to be the default (checking the "Make this action the default" check box in the prompt window does the same thing as selecting that option in the CDs & DVDs pane). The Eject, Ignore, and OK buttons in the dialog box do what you expect (eject the disc, ignore it, or implement the changes you make, respectively). Because the "Ask what to do" option provides the most flexibility, I recommend that you choose it. However, for specific situations, the other choices might be more appropriate for you.

- **Open Finder**—When this option is the default or if you select it in the prompt, the blank CD will be mounted and a Burn folder will be created. You can then use the Finder to name the CD, add contents, and burn it. If you usually burn CDs from the Finder and don't like to be interrupted by the prompt, this option is probably for you.

- **Open iTunes**—When a disc is mounted, iTunes becomes the active application. If you mostly burn audio CDs, this setting can make the process more convenient.

Figure 31.9
When the "Ask what to do" option is selected, you see this prompt when you insert blank CD media into your Mac's drive.

- **Open Disk Utility**—You can also burn discs using the Disk Utility application. If that is your preference, you can choose this option to have Disk Utility launch when you insert a recordable disc into your Mac's drive.

- **Open other application**—If you choose this option, you are prompted to select the application you want to open. That application will be opened when you insert a blank CD. This is the option you want if you use a third-party application, such as Toast, to burn CDs.

- **Run script**—With this option, an AppleScript you select is launched when you insert a blank CD. After you select the script you want to launch, it appears on the "When you insert a blank CD" pop-up menu. If you have a custom burn process implemented through an AppleScript, this is the option you should choose.

- **Ignore**—When you insert a blank CD, your Mac takes no action. In fact, this disc is not even mounted in the Finder. You have to manually take some action later, such as opening an application that can burn CDs, to do something with the disc. If you prefer to keep blank CDs in your Mac and don't want to be interrupted when you insert them, this might be the option you want to choose.

BURNING CDs FROM THE FINDER

After you have configured your Mac, burning CDs from the Finder is very straightforward, as the following steps demonstrate (these steps assume that you have selected the "Ask me what to do" option; however, using the Open Finder option works similarly). Do the following:

1. Insert a CD-R or CD-RW disc into the drive. You will be prompted to select an action (refer to Figure 31.9).

2. Select Open Finder on the Action pop-up menu. The blank CD will be mounted on your desktop and you will see the CD on the Places sidebar.

3. Select the "Untitled CD" on the Places sidebar or double-click the disc's icon on the Desktop to open it in a Finder window; (see Figure 31.10).

4. Select the CD on the Places sidebar, open its contextual menu, and choose the Rename command. The disc's name will become editable.

5. Type the name the of the disc and press Return to save the new name.

Figure 31.10
The selected burn
folder called
`Untitled CD.fpbf`
is a blank CD.

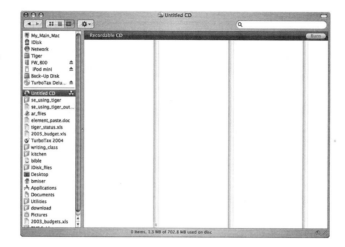

31

6. Drag the folders and files you want on the CD to the mounted disc, just like any other volume to which you can copy or move files. Aliases to those files and folders are created in on the disc.

7. Arrange and organize the files as you want them to be on the disc (see Figure 31.11).

Figure 31.11
Here, I have moved
files from some book
projects onto the CD
(note the CD icon in
the Finder window's
title bar).

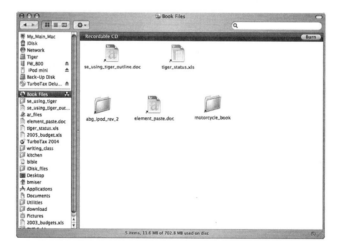

CAUTION

Because burning CDs from the Finder is a single session, you can burn to a CD-R disc only once. After it has been burned, you won't be able to add files to it. Make sure you have all the files on the CD that you want before you burn it. If you want to be able to burn in multiple sessions, you need to use a different application to create CDs, such as Disk Utility.

→ To learn how use Disk Utility, **see** "Burning CDs/DVDs with Disk Utility," **p. 912**.

8. When you are ready to record the files on to the disc, click the Burn button in the disc's window, select the disc and choose File, Burn Disc, click the Burn button next to the disc in the Places sidebar, or choose Burn Disc on the Action pop-up menu. The Burn Disc dialog box will appear (see Figure 31.12).

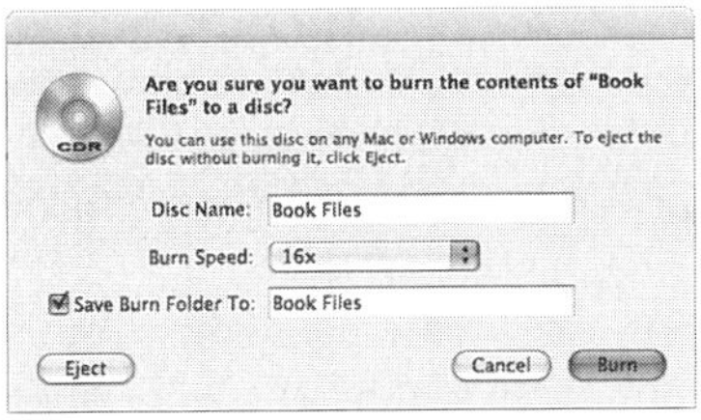

Figure 31.12
The CD called Book Files is ready to burn.

9. If you want to name the disc different than it currently is named, type the name of the disc in the Disc Name field. You can choose most any name you'd like. If you will be sharing the disc with people who use other kinds of computers, keep the name relatively short, such as less than eight characters.

10. Select the speed at which you want to burn the disc on the Burn Speed pop-up menu. In most cases, choose the fastest speed available. However, if you are having problems burning discs at your drive's maximum speed, you can try to burn at a lower speed, which might solve the problems.

11. If you want the data saved to a Burn folder, so you can make multiple copies of the disc for example, check the "Save Burn Folder To" check box and name the Burn folder (the default name will be the name of the current disc, but you can rename it if you want to).

12. Click Burn. You'll see a progress window as the data is prepared and the disc is recorded and verified. When the process is complete, the disc will be mounted on the desktop and will be ready to use.

> **TIP**
>
> In the CD Burn progress window, click the Stop button (the *x*) to abort the burn process.

Burning CDs from the Finder is just that simple. In fact, burning CDs is just as easy as using floppy drives was back in the old days—except CDs hold about 500 times more data, of course.

BURNING DVDs WITH APPLE'S SUPERDRIVE

Apple's SuperDrive is a special case because, along with CD-RW and CD-R discs, it can also burn DVD-R (and in newer Macs DVD-RW) discs that can be used to record data and be mounted on the desktop or played in consumer DVD players when you burn them using iDVD or another DVD-creating application. This drive is available (at least as an option) on all Mac models.

NOTE

> Just as with CD-RW drives, third-party DVD-R/DVD-RW hardware and software are available. However, because Apple's DVD-R technology works so well and is included with Mac hardware and as part of Mac OS X, Apple's technology is the focus of this section.

One downside to this technology is the expense of Apple's DVD-R discs, which currently cost about $2 per disc for 4x discs or slightly more per disc for 8x discs. Of course, when you compare that cost on a per-MB basis, DVD-Rs seem not to be so expensive after all. You should only buy discs rated for the maximum speed or slower of your Mac's SuperDrive. Discs rated at slower speeds will work in your drive and cost less, but the process will take longer. Check the specifications for your Mac to see the burn speeds your SuperDrive supports.

CAUTION

> Depending on the specific model of Mac you use and the application you use to create DVDs, you might be able to use third-party DVD-R or DVD-RW discs, which are less expensive than Apple's media, to create DVDs. It isn't possible to list all situations in which you can use third-party discs. If you want to try to save some money, purchase a single disc from various manufacturers rated for your drive's speed and try to burn them with the application you intend to use. If that works, you can save some money by using the third-party media. If not, you'll have to keep trying other brands or just use Apple's media.

Creating a data DVD is very similar to creating a data CD, except that you can store up to 4.7GB of data on a single disc (compared to about 700MB on a CD).

First, configure your Mac for the action you want it to take when you insert a blank DVD-R disc.

Open the System Preferences application and click the CDs & DVDs icon to open that pane. Use the "When you insert a blank DVD" pop-up menu to select the action you want your Mac to take when you put a blank DVD into your machine. You have the following options:

- **Ask what to do**—When you insert a blank DVD, your Mac prompts you and will provide an Action pop-up menu containing a list of possible actions from which you can choose. The Action pop-up menu contains a set of choices similar to those on the "When you insert a blank DVD" pop-up menu on the CDs & DVDs pane, such as Open Finder and Open iDVD (if iDVD is installed on your Mac). You can make the action you select on the Action pop-up menu be the default (checking the "Make this action the default" check box in the prompt window does the same thing as selecting that option in the CDs & DVDs pane). The Eject, Ignore, and OK buttons in the dialog box do what you expect (eject the disc, ignore it, or implement the changes you make, respectively). Because this option provides the most flexibility, I recommend that you choose this option. However, for specific situations, the other choices might be more appropriate for you.

- **Open Finder**—When this option is the default or if you select it in the prompt, the blank DVD is mounted and a burn folder will be created. You can then use the Finder to name the folder, add content to it, and burn the DVD. If you usually burn DVDs from the Finder and don't like to be interrupted by the prompt, this option is probably for you.

- **Open iDVD**—When a disc is mounted, iDVD becomes the active application. If you mostly burn DVDs using iDVD, this setting can make the process more convenient. (iDVD must be installed on your Mac for this to appear.)

- **Open iTunes**—When a DVD is mounted, iTunes becomes the active application. If you regularly burn data DVDs for your iTunes music, this might be your best choice.

- **Open Disk Utility**—You can also burn discs using the Disk Utility application. If that is your preference, you can choose this option to have Disk Utility launch when you insert a recordable DVD into your Mac's drive.

- **Open other application**—You can use this option to select a different application to open when a DVD is inserted.

- **Run script**—With this option, an AppleScript you select is launched when you insert a blank DVD. After you select the script you want to launch, it appears on the "When you insert a blank DVD" pop-up menu. If you have a custom burn process implemented through an AppleScript, this is the option you should choose.

- **Ignore**—When you insert a blank DVD, your Mac takes no action. In fact, this disc is not even mounted in the Finder. You have to manually take some action later, such as opening an application that can burn DVDs, to do something with the disc. If you prefer to keep blank DVDs in your Mac and don't want to be interrupted when you insert them, this might be the option you want to choose.

After you have configured your Mac, burning DVDs from the Finder is very straightforward and works just like burning a CD does, except you can store a lot more data on one disc. When you insert a blank DVD and choose the Open Finder option, a burn folder is created. You can now rename the folder, place folders and files in it, and then burn the disc.

→ For the steps to burn a disc from the Finder, **see** "Burning CDs from the Finder," **p. 907**.

CAUTION

> Because burning DVDs from the Finder is a single session, you can burn to a DVD-R disc only once. After it has been burned, you won't be able to add files to it. Make sure you have all the files on the DVD that you want before you burn it. If you want to burn to a DVD in more than one session, use Disk Utility instead.

→ To learn how use Disk Utility, **see** "Burning CDs/DVDs with Disk Utility," **p. 912**.

To create a DVD for video, images, and other multimedia content, you can use Apple's iDVD application, which enables you to drag and drop QuickTime movies, images, and other multimedia files to create a custom DVD, including DVD motion menus. You can also use iTunes to place music files on a data DVD.

→ To learn how to use iDVD, **see** Chapter 26, "Creating Your Own DVDs with iDVD," **p. 761**.

→ To learn how to burn DVDs with iTunes, **see** "Using iTunes to Burn CDs or DVDs," **p. 570**.

NOTE

> Apple also offers DVD Studio Pro, which is a professional-quality DVD creation application.

BURNING CDs/DVDs WITH DISK UTILITY

In addition to helping you maintain your disks, Disk Utility can also help you burn CDs and DVDs. It is especially useful when you want to burn a CD or DVD from a disk image file. Another great use of this is to back up image files for the applications you download from the Internet; rather than keeping a folder of these items on your hard drive, you can use Disk Utility to burn a folder of images onto a CD or DVD.

The benefit to burning a disk image onto a CD or DVD using Disk Utility rather than just using the Finder is that, when you use Disk Utility, the image is mounted when you insert the CD—you don't have to first open the disk image file to mount it.

TIP

> One of the best reasons to use Disk Utility to burn CDs or DVDs is that you can leave a disc open so you can burn to it multiple times. When you use the Finder, you can have only one recording session for a disc. When you use Disk Utility, you can choose to make a disc *appendable*, meaning you can burn to it more than one time.

CREATING A DISK IMAGE TO BURN

Before you can burn a disc using Disk Utility, you create a disk image containing the folders and files you want to place on the disc using the following steps:

1. Launch Disk Utility and click the New Image button on the toolbar. The New Image sheet will appear.

2. Name the disk image and choose where you want to save it. The name of the disk image will become the name of the disc you burn it onto.

3. Select the format options on the pop-up menus. Choose the size of the image on the Size pop-up menu; you will see various size options including those sized for CD or DVD media. Choose the encryption you want to use on the Encryption pop-up menu; if you choose to create an encrypted disc, you won't be able to use it without a password. Choose the format on the Format menu; to burn a disc, choose "read/write disk image."

4. Click Create. The disk image will be created and will be mounted on your Mac; you can access the disk image just like other volumes such as hard disks.

5. Open the disk image by selecting it on the Places sidebar and drag folders or files onto it to add them to the image. Do this until all the files and folders you want to put on disc are part of the disk image. You are limited to the size of the image you selected using the Size pop-up menu.

BURNING A SINGLE DISK IMAGE ON CD OR DVD

To put a disc image on CD or DVD using Disk Utility, do the following:

1. Launch Disk Utility. If you have worked with the disk image recently, it will be listed in the lower part of the left pane of the Disk Utility window (which Disk Utility calls being *attached*); you can skip to step 4. If it isn't listed, you will need to locate it using Disk Utility.

2. Locate the disk image by choosing File, Open Disk Image. The "Select Image to Attach" dialog box will appear.

3. Move to and select the disk image you want to place on disc; then click Open. The image you selected will be attached to Disk Utility and you will see it in the left pane of the window.

> **TIP**
> Disk images are separated from physical disks by the dividing line that appears in the left pane of the Disk Utility window when at least one disk image is attached. Anything above the line is a physical disk of volume; anything below the line is a disk image.

4. Select the disk image you want to burn to disc.

> **NOTE**
> If the disk image is currently mounted, you will see its mounted icon below the disk image file itself. You need to select the image file, not the mounted icon.

5. Choose Images, Burn, press ⌘-B, or click the Burn button. The Burn sheet will appear. Your disc drive will also open.

> **TIP**
> If you have more than one drive that can burn discs available to you, choose the drive you want to use on the "Burn Disc In" pop-up menu.

6. Insert the disc on which you want to burn the image into the open disc drive and close it by clicking the Close button in the sheet. The drive will be prepared and the Burn button will become active.

7. Set the burn speed by using the Speed pop-up menu. In most cases, Maximum Possible is the best choice. However, if you have problems burning discs, a slower speed might help.

31

8. If you are burning to an erasable disc, check the "Erase disc before burning" check box to erase the disc before you burn to it.

9. If you want to be able to add more data to the disc at a later time, check the "Leave disc appendable" check box. This is one of the best reasons to use Disk Utility to burn discs; you can add data to discs during multiple burn sessions.

10. Make sure the "Verify burned data" check box is checked to have your Mac verify the disc after the burn is complete; if you are confident and want to save some time, you can uncheck this box.

11. Click the "Eject disc" radio button if you want the disc ejected when it has been burned, or click the "Mount on Desktop" radio button if you want the disc to be mounted instead.

12. Review the options you have selected and either click Burn or press Return when you ready to burn the disc (see Figure 31.13). You will see the Progress window that displays the progress of the burn.

Figure 31.13
The Burn Disc sheet has been configured and the disc is ready to burn.

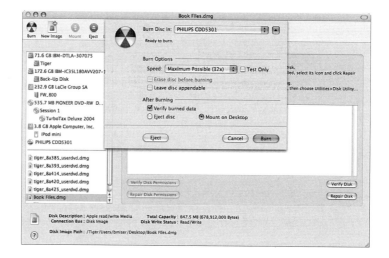

13. When the process is complete, you'll hear the "burn complete" tone and the finished prompt will appear; click OK and the disc is ejected or mounted on the desktop, depending on the option you selected in step 11 (see Figure 31.14).

TIP

> To unattach disk images from Disk Utility, select the disk image file and press Delete or drag its icon out of the window. This does not delete the image file itself—it just removes it from the Disk Utility window.

If you leave a disc appendable, you can repeat these steps to add disk images to it. When you append files to a disc, the Burn button becomes the Append button to indicate that you are adding files to the disc rather than burning it for the first time.

Figure 31.14
Here, I have placed a disk image (called Book_Files) containing book files on a CD; above the CD of the same name, you can also see the disk image which is still mounted.

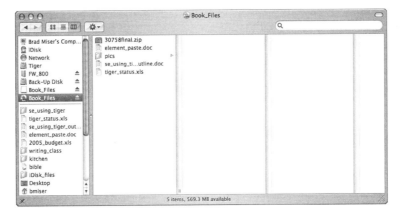

31

CAUTION

If you want a disk image to mount when you insert the CD on which you want it burned, burn only one disk image on the disc. If you add multiple disk images to the same disc, only the one you most recently burned is accessible in the Finder. You should use the multiple session option only when you are burning other types of files onto a disc or when you are adding files to the same disk image.

TIP

You can use Disk Utility to erase CD-RW or DVD-RW discs. To do so, launch the application, insert the CD-RW or DVD-RW you want to erase, click the Erase tab, and use the tab's tools to erase the disc. You can also erase such discs by using the "erase" check box in the Burn sheet.

BURNING A FOLDER ON CD OR DVD

Using the following steps, you can create a disk image from a folder and then burn that image onto a disc:

1. Gather all the files you want to put onto a disc in a single folder.

2. Open Disk Utility.

3. Select File, New, Disk Image from Folder.

4. Move to and select the folder from which you want to create an image.

5. Click Image. You will see the New Image from Folder dialog box (see Figure 31.15). Use this dialog box to name the disk image and choose the options for the image.

6. Name the disk image file and select the location in which you want to store it.

7. On the Image Format pop-up menu, select a format for the image you are creating. The read/write option creates an image you can add more files to later. The read-only option creates a "closed" image to which files can't be added later. The compressed option creates a compressed version of the folder so you can get more files in a smaller space. The DVD/CD master creates a disk image ready to be put on disc.

Figure 31.15
The New Image From Folder dialog box enables you to configure a disk image you are creating.

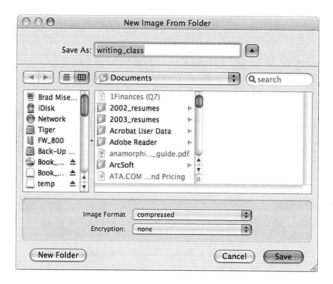

8. Use the Encryption pop-up menu to choose an encryption scheme for the image file if you want to protect the data it contains. If you select none, the image is not encrypted.

9. Click Save. You will see a Progress window as the image file is created. When the process is complete, the disk image you created is shown in the Source pane.

10. Select the disk image you just created and follow the steps in the previous section to put that image on disc.

BURNING A VOLUME ON CD OR DVD

You can also create a disk image from an entire volume. Then you can place that image on a disc for backup or other purposes. The steps you follow are very similar to those in the previous section. The only difference is that you select the volume from which you want to create a disk image and then select File, New, Image from *volume* where *volume* is the name of the volume you selected. That volume is then selected and you move to the Convert Image dialog box.

USING A TAPE DRIVE

Tape drives offer a tremendous amount of storage space at a relatively low cost. However, because of the slow rate at which they can read and write data, tape drives are limited to a single purpose: data archival and backup. However, for these functions, a tape drive is very useful.

→ To learn about tape drives and backing up your Mac, **see** "Backing Up Your System," **p. 1010**.

WORKING WITH OTHER REMOVABLE MEDIA DRIVES

Quite a few other data storage options were available at various times in the Mac's history. Most of these were made obsolete with the coming of writable CD and DVD. Table 31.1 summarizes several of these technologies of which only the USB flash device is still viable.

TABLE 31.1   REMOVABLE MEDIA DRIVE OPTIONS FOR MODERN MACS

Technology	Configuration	Comments
USB Flash	USB	Various USB flash devices are available. These small devices, usually attached to a keychain or other portable item, plug in to a USB port, and you can store data on them. They offer various storage capacities and behave like other volumes you mount on your desktop. If you need to "carry" data with you among various computers, these devices can be a great option.
Floppy	USB, External	The good old floppy is still around. These drives enable you to read and write standard 3.5″ floppy disks. Some also enable you to read and write to 120MB "super" floppy disks. With the rise of CD-RW, DVD-RW, and USB flash, there isn't really any reason to keep using this technology. Apple long ago abandoned it; the PC world is finally letting go of it as well.
Zip	ATA, Internal FireWire, External USB, External SCSI, External	The Zip drive uses a 250MB or 100MB removable disk that costs about $12 per disk. At one point, Zip drives were extremely popular and were standard equipment on Power Macs. However, with the rise of the CD-RW and DVD-R drives, there isn't really any reason to use a Zip drive. Because a CD-R disc is only about $0.25 and holds nearly as much as three Zip disks, CD-R makes much more sense for most purposes. The rapid fall of Zip drives from a once-prominent place was amazing to see.
Jaz	SCSI, External	Jaz drives use a 2GB disk. However, a 2GB disk costs more than $100, so this technology can't compete very well with DVD-R (for which a 4.7GB disc costs less than $5) or CD-R for general data storage. This is another format that was extremely popular for a while, but has since gone the way of all obsolete technologies.

31

NOTE

An iPod shuffle can perform like a USB flash drive.

TROUBLESHOOTING

MY MAC WON'T START UP AFTER I CONNECT A DRIVE TO IT

After I connect a SCSI drive to my Mac, it won't start up.

Every SCSI device on each SCSI bus must have a unique SCSI ID on that bus; SCSI devices can have an ID number between zero and seven. When you connect a SCSI device that has the same SCSI ID number as a device currently on the same SCSI bus, your Mac will be unable to start. Do the following:

1. Remove the drive from your Mac.
2. Launch System Profiler and click the SCSI tab.
3. Check the device numbers of the SCSI devices on the bus to which you are attaching the drive; there might be more than one SCSI bus, so make sure you are looking at the right one.

CAUTION

> Make sure you power down all devices before changing the SCSI ID.

4. Reset the SCSI ID to an unused number between zero and seven.
5. Reattach the drive and start up your Mac.

If the Mac restarts, you can initialize the drive.

If your Mac still won't restart, the drive you have attached has not been properly terminated. Check the manual that came with the drive to see how to terminate it. If the drive is not self-terminating, you have to add a SCSI terminating cable or block to it.

DISK UTILITY CAN'T SEE MY DRIVE

When I launch Disk Utility, it does not recognize the drive I installed.

The fundamental problem is that your new drive is not registering with your Mac. There can be many causes for this problem, but the most likely are the following:

- **The drive is incompatible with your Mac**—Double-check the drive's specifications against those in your Mac's owner's manual.
- **The drive is improperly installed**—Repeat the installation steps to ensure that the drive is installed and connected properly.
- **An internal drive is not set to be the slave**—You must set any additional drive to be the slave; your Mac's "first" preinstalled drive must be the primary drive. See the instructions that came with your drive to see how to set it as the slave.

NOTE

> Different Mac configurations might require slightly different configurations of drives. Check the user's manual for your Mac before installing an internal drive.

I CAN'T CREATE A CD

When I try to create a CD, the CD-RW drive can't be found or the process is never completed.

Creating CDs can be a finicky process.

One complexity associated with using CD-burning software is that these applications support only specific CD-RW drives. If a particular drive isn't supported by the application you want to use, it won't work. Your only option is to find a version that will support your drive or find another application that will.

CD-burning applications can also interfere with one another. If you have more than one CD-burning application installed on your Mac and have trouble creating CDs, remove all the applications but one.

You can also have data transfer speed problems. Most CD-RW drives include a buffer to which data is written before it is placed on the CD. This buffer ensures that a steady stream of data is written to the CD. If this stream is interrupted and the buffer becomes empty, the process will fail or it will appear to finish, but the CD will be unusable. If this happens, make sure no other applications are running before you attempt to create CDs. You can also try to burn at slower speeds.

CHAPTER 32

Installing and Configuring Connecting Devices

USING HUBS TO CONNECT YOUR MAC TO NETWORKS OR PERIPHERAL DEVICES

Some devices serve the purpose of connecting your Mac to networks or peripheral devices. In the case of networks, you use an Ethernet hub to enable your Mac to communicate with other computers, printers, network file servers, and the Internet. In the case of peripheral devices, you can use a USB or FireWire hub to expand the number of peripheral devices, such as printers, cameras, scanners, and so on, that you can connect to your Mac at the same time. Hubs are usually simple to install and configure (in fact, they often don't require much configuration at all).

NOTE

> One of the best ways to connect Macs to one another, other devices, and the Internet is through an AirPort base station, which acts as a network hub. You can also install AirPort base stations on wired networks, such as those connected through an Ethernet hub, and the station can "cross over" the data from the wired to the wireless network.

→ To learn how to install and configure an AirPort network, **see** Chapter 14, "Using an AirPort Network to Connect to the Internet," **p. 337**.

FINDING AND INSTALLING AN ETHERNET HUB

Ethernet is a hub-based network architecture, meaning that all the data that flows through an Ethernet network must flow through a hub of one type or another.

NOTE

> There are two exceptions to this rule. One is using an Ethernet crossover cable to connect two devices directly. This special cable acts as a very basic hub, so you don't need to use a specific hub device. The other is that some Macs support direct computer-to-computer Ethernet connections using a standard Ethernet cable.

→ To learn more about Ethernet, **see** "Ethernet," **p. 817**.

UNDERSTANDING ETHERNET HUBS

The basic function of an Ethernet hub is to enable data to flow through an Ethernet network. The three basic types of Ethernet hubs are as follows:

- **Passive, or *dumb*, hubs**—These hubs don't do anything but allow data to be passed back and forth between the devices to which they are connected. All the traffic through a passive hub goes to every device on the network, thus compromising the performance of the network because much of the data being communicated is wasted.

- **Intelligent or manageable hubs**—In addition to the basic function, which is to connect various Ethernet devices, these hubs offer features that can be used to monitor and manage the data flowing through the network.

- **Switching hubs**—This type of hub is the most active; it actually directs the flow of each packet of information based on the destination of that packet. Because data is sent only where it is actually needed, the data flow on the network is efficient. Switching hubs offer the best performance of any hub type. Fortunately, most hubs that you can buy are of this type.

  These hubs can also accomplish *load balancing*, which means they analyze the flow of information and direct information such that the load on various devices on the network is balanced. This prevents particular devices from being overloaded while others sit idle. Load balancing is particularly important for situations in which active web or other servers are on a network. A web server can easily generate large amounts of traffic; load balancing can smooth the data flow around such servers so that no one server gets overwhelmed, thus slowing network traffic to a crawl.

In addition to the core features of enabling the communication of data to multiple devices on a network, many hubs also offer additional features, which include the following:

- **Support for multiple speeds**—Hubs can support the various speeds of Ethernet; many hubs support multiple speeds and can intelligently switch between speeds so that you can have both lower- and higher-speed devices attached to the same network. The hub manages the differences in speeds to prevent bottlenecks and other performance problems.

- **Number of ports**—Every Ethernet hub offers a specific number of ports, such as 5 or 10. The more ports a hub has, the more devices it can support. Hubs can also be attached to other hubs to enable even more devices to be attached to a network.

- **Firewall**—Some hubs can act as firewalls to protect the networks to which they are connected from outside attack.

→ To learn more about hubs that provide a firewall, **see** "Defending Your Mac from Net Attacks," **p. 1032**.

- **Internet account sharing**—Hubs offering this feature enable everyone on a network to share a single Internet account. Such hubs usually include a DHCP server and often offer firewall protection, too.

- **Wireless communication**—Hubs can enable devices to communicate with the network wirelessly.

- **Network analysis and management software**—Some hubs include software you can use to analyze the traffic flow on the network to which they are attached so you can identify problems, such as a bottleneck (which is a spot on the network at which point the data flow is slowed, usually because of a device being overloaded).

CHOOSING AND INSTALLING AN ETHERNET HUB

Choosing the right Ethernet hub for your network is a matter of identifying the features you need and then locating a hub that offers those features. Some features to consider are the following:

- **Speed**—All modern Macs can communicate at speeds of at least 100Mbps, so you should make sure that the hub you get can handle this speed. Many modern Macs support speeds up to 1000Mbps (more commonly called Gigabit Ethernet), so if you have at least one of these Macs on your network, you should look for hubs that support Gigabit Ethernet. Most hubs are capable of switching speeds and are rated with the speeds they support, such as 10/100 for a hub that can support 10Mbps and 100Mbps.

- **Number of ports**—Hubs support multiple devices through the ports they offer. You need a port for each device on the network, such as each Mac, AirPort base station, printer, cable modem, and so on. Generally, you should get a hub with more ports than you think you will need to allow room for your network to grow.

- **Internet account sharing**—If you plan on sharing an Internet account, you need to find a hub that supports this.

> **NOTE**
>
> Internet account sharing is built in to the Mac OS X. However, using a hub to share an account is often a better choice because a Mac that provides account sharing always has to be on, and it takes a performance hit to share an account. Sharing hubs are dedicated devices and are always on by design. Because such hubs are inexpensive and easy to use, they are usually the best choice.

- **Firewall**—If you connect your network to the Internet, you should use a hub that offers a firewall—such hubs often support sharing an Internet account as well.

> **NOTE**
>
> Configuring Mac OS X's built-in firewall to protect individual machines is simple. However, if you have other machines that don't offer a firewall, you should ensure that the hub you use provides one.

→ To learn how to configure the Mac OS X firewall, **see** "Defending Your Mac Against Net Hackers," **p. 1032**.

- **Mac OS X compatibility**—Because Ethernet is not platform specific, most hubs support Macs, Windows, and other machines. However, some hubs offer particular features that are platform specific.

- **Other features**—If there are specific features you need, such as network management software, look for hubs that offer those features.

Hubs generally fall into two camps: those designed for small networks with few or no features (see Figure 32.1) and those designed to support a larger number of devices or that offer other features (see Figure 32.2).

Figure 32.1
This Asante hub is an example of a basic Ethernet hub that is designed for small networks.

Figure 32.2
This Linksys hub includes 16 ports and is designed for a larger network.

Typically, if you evaluate the list of factors provided previously, the type of hub you need becomes clear fairly quickly. Then it is a matter of choosing among the brands that offer the type of hub you need.

In theory, installing an Ethernet hub is easy; you simply connect power to the hub and then connect each device (computers, printers, and so on) to it using the appropriate Ethernet cables with RJ-45 connectors at each end. In practice, routing the cables can be a major challenge, especially if you are covering large distances in a building that is not designed to allow easy installation of such cables.

Ethernet Cards

To attach a specific device to an Ethernet network, that device must have an Ethernet card installed in it. Although all Macs have Ethernet cards built in, other devices might not. For example, Ethernet cards are not installed in every printer, even those that are capable of being networked.

The type of Ethernet card you need to install in a device depends on the specific device you are installing on the network. For example, the interface card for a printer needs to match the specifications for a particular brand and model. On the other hand, devices that can use PCI cards can accept a standard Ethernet PCI card to enable that device to be attached to a network.

After an Ethernet hub is physically installed on the network, you might have to install some software or configure that hub (for example, if you will be sharing an Internet connection over it, you have to configure the hub's DHCP server).

NOTE

> Most hubs include an *uplink* port to which you can attach other hubs. This enables you to expand a network by adding more devices to it than a single hub has ports. After you have filled the ports on one hub, you can attach another hub to the first hub's uplink port and begin using the ports on the second hub to add more devices to the network.

USING AN ETHERNET HUB

For most applications, after a hub is installed and configured, you don't need to think about it anymore. It simply does its work. If you use network-monitoring software, you run that from a device connected to the hub.

Most hubs offer a basic set of diagnostic lights you can use to monitor the traffic across each port on the hub. These lights can be useful if your network has problems you need to diagnose. One type of diagnostic light included for each port on most hubs is an activity light that illuminates when the hub senses activity from the device connected to that port. Most hubs also include a speed indicator light for each port to give you information about the speed of communication with a specific device; this light can help you ensure that each device is communicating with the network at the maximum possible speed.

→ To learn how to configure and use an Ethernet network for file sharing, **see** Chapter 33, "Building and Using a Network," **p. 935**.

→ To learn about using a hub to share an Internet account, **see** Chapter 34, "Sharing an Internet Connection," **p. 973**.

FINDING, INSTALLING, AND USING A USB HUB

Because so many peripheral devices use the USB interface, you might run out of available USB ports before you run out of devices you want to attach to your Mac. That's where a USB hub comes in.

→ To learn more about the USB interface, **see** "USB 1.1," **p. 821**.

UNDERSTANDING USB HUBS

A USB hub expands the number of USB ports available on your Mac; USB hubs are one of the simpler devices you will use. USB ports offer the following features:

- **Number of ports**—The number of ports a USB hub offers determines the number of devices you can attach to it. Typical USB hubs offer four ports, but some offer more than that (such as seven ports).

CAUTION

> Sometimes the number of ports offered by a hub can be a bit deceiving. Remember that you have to use one port to connect the hub to your Mac or to another USB hub. Some hubs count this "upstream" port, but others do not. For example, some four-port hubs allow you to connect only three USB devices because one port is required to connect the hub to your Mac or to another hub. Other four-port hubs provide an additional port for the upstream connection so that you can actually connect four devices to them.

- **USB 2 or USB 1 support**—The two types of USB are USB 1 and USB 2. USB 2 is faster than USB 1. If you are using USB 2 devices, you should get a hub that supports USB 2. USB 1 devices are mostly keyboards, mouse devices, and other low-bandwidth devices. USB 2 devices are typically hard drives, cameras, and other devices that require large amounts of data to be moved quickly. USB 2 hubs support USB 1, but USB 1 hubs do not support USB 2.
- **Self-powered or bus-powered**—Some hubs get the power they need from an external power supply (they provide this power to the devices that are attached to them if needed). Others take power for the hub and the USB devices from the USB bus itself.

NOTE

> Although most Macs include two or more USB ports, you can often find additional ports in the other devices attached to your Mac. For example, the Apple Pro keyboard has two USB ports built in to it. Apple monitors, such as the Apple Cinema Display, also include additional USB ports. Make sure that you account for these available ports before adding a dedicated USB hub to your system.

CHOOSING, INSTALLING, AND USING A USB HUB

Choosing a USB hub is mostly a matter of deciding if you need to be able to support USB 2 devices and the number of USB devices you want to be able to connect to your Mac at the same time (see Figure 32.3).

32

Figure 32.3
This Kensington four-port hub is an example of a simple, inexpensive USB hub you can add to your system.

> **TIP**
>
> Remember that USB is hot-swappable, meaning you can connect and disconnect USB devices at any time. There are many devices you will need to connect only periodically, such as a digital camera. So you don't really need a USB port dedicated to every USB device you have—just those you want to always be available. Having one or more extra ports above that number enables you to add other devices as you need them.

Next, you should decide whether you want a self-powered or bus-powered hub. Because some devices take their power from the USB interface, you should get a USB hub that is capable of providing its own power (many hubs can operate either on their own power or on power from the USB bus). If you are going to use the hub primarily on the move, such as with your PowerBook, a bus-powered hub might be a better choice (it will be smaller than a powered hub).

Some hubs offer other features that aren't required but can be useful. For example, some hubs provide status lights for each port. These lights show you when a device is actively using the port; this can be helpful when you are troubleshooting problems with a specific peripheral device.

Installing a USB hub is quite simple. You just attach its uplink port to a USB hub on your Mac or on another USB hub. Then, attach each device to a port on the hub. If the hub is self-powered, you attach its power source. That's it.

> **NOTE**
>
> USB 2 and USB 1 cables use the same connector, so you can't tell the difference just by looking at the cables. Be sure you don't try to support a USB 2 device over a hub that supports only USB 1.

There isn't anything to using a USB hub, either. They just work.

NOTE

Bluetooth is a wireless protocol designed for relatively low-speed peripheral devices such as mice, keyboards, printers, PDAs, and so on. Mac OS X supports Bluetooth, but to use this feature, a Mac must have a Bluetooth transmitter and receiver. Some Macs, such as Power Mac G5s, have the option to have the Bluetooth module built in and can connect to Bluetooth devices out of the box. For other Macs, you will need to add a Bluetooth adapter (usually to a USB port) to be able to communicate with Bluetooth devices. When a Mac has a Bluetooth adapter, it acts as a Bluetooth hub and can communicate with many Bluetooth devices at the same time.

→ To learn how to use Bluetooth, **see** "Finding, Installing, and Using Bluetooth Devices," **p. 847**.

FINDING, INSTALLING, AND USING A FIREWIRE HUB

A FireWire hub is analogous to a USB hub; its primary purpose is to provide additional FireWire ports to which you can connect FireWire devices (see Figure 32.4).

Figure 32.4
This Belkin FireWire hub offers six additional ports (one port is required for the upstream connection).

→ For more information on FireWire, **see** "FireWire 400," **p. 819**.

UNDERSTANDING FIREWIRE HUBS

Because many Macs include only two FireWire ports (some mobile Macs have only one), and peripheral devices such as keyboards and monitors don't include additional FireWire ports, you are more limited in the number of FireWire devices you can attach to your Mac than you are with USB out of the box.

Daisy-chaining on FireWire Hubs

FireWire supports daisy-chaining, which means some FireWire devices, such as hard drives, have two FireWire ports. One port receives the FireWire connection coming in, whereas the other can support a connection going out. You can link FireWire devices in this way so that you can support many devices from a single FireWire port. However, this can be problematic for some devices that require large amounts of data to flow smoothly, such as a digital camcorder. Because all the data in a FireWire chain flows across each device, the data flow can be turbulent when many devices are connected on a single chain. For best performance, devices with higher data speed requirements should be placed closer to the Mac, preferably actually connected to the Mac's FireWire port. A FireWire hub can help manage the data flow so you can connect more devices without the interference that can be experienced when you use a FireWire daisy-chain.

If you use multiple FireWire storage devices, such as an iPod, hard drive, tape drive, CD-RW, or other devices that you will want to be connected at all times, you probably need to add more FireWire ports to your system.

FireWire hubs work in a way that is similar to a USB hub, and you have similar parameters to choose from:

- FireWire (AKA FireWire 400) or FireWire 800
- Number of available ports (most FireWire hubs include either three or six ports)
- Self-powered, bus-powered, or both

CHOOSING, INSTALLING, AND USING A FIREWIRE HUB

The process of choosing, installing, and using a FireWire hub is also analogous to the same tasks for a USB hub. First, determine whether you need to support FireWire 800. FireWire 800 is a faster protocol than FireWire so you need a hub that is capable of supporting it (you can't use FireWire devices with a FireWire 800 hub, and vice versa). Second, decide how many ports you need. Third, decide whether you need a more mobile hub that can take its power from the bus. Fourth, look for any special features you might need (there aren't many available, so this won't take much time).

NOTE

> Remember that one port is used to connect the hub to the Mac or to another hub. Most of the time, you can connect one less device to a hub than the number of ports it offers. Because FireWire devices are also hot-swappable, you need only a dedicated port for those devices you want to be connected to your Mac at all times. As long as you have at least one available port for the devices you use only periodically, it isn't a big deal to connect and disconnect those devices.

Installing and using a FireWire hub is also as simple as installing and using a USB hub. Simply connect the hub to your Mac using a FireWire cable, connect its power supply (if applicable), and connect the FireWire devices to the hub.

The FireWire cable you use depends on the device and the type of FireWire being supported; FireWire 800 cables are different from standard FireWire cables. Many devices use a FireWire cable with a standard FireWire connector on each end, but some devices, such as digital video cameras, have a uniquely shaped FireWire port. The specialized cable you need for such devices is usually included with the device.

TIP

> You can chain both USB and FireWire hubs. So, you can connect hubs of the same type to one another to continue to add devices to your system, up to the maximum number of devices supported by that interface.

CHOOSING A MODEM

The other major type of connecting device you are likely to use is a modem. Modems come in several flavors, depending on the type of connection through which the modem works. The major modem types are the following:

- **Phone line or dial-up**—All modern Macs can include a built-in 56K modem as standard equipment. The only significant benefit of dial-up modems is that they work over any standard phone line, which makes them the only practical option for many people. However, dial-up modems are slow and are not as reliable as other modem types.
- **Cable**—Cable modem connections to the Internet are among the fastest and most reliable. Cable Internet service availability can be limited, but if it is an option for you, you should definitely consider it.
- **DSL**—Digital subscriber line modems offer benefits similar to those of a cable modem. However, in many areas, DSL connections are even less available than are cable modems.
- **ISDN**—At one point, it seemed as if integrated services digital network (ISDN) modems were going to be the best way to connect to the Net. However, with the rise of cable and DSL modems, ISDN modems are usually preferable only when those two options are not available. ISDN modems are faster than dial-up modems, but they aren't nearly as fast as cable or DSL. An ISDN account also tends to be more expensive than other options.

Choosing the kind of modem you will use depends on the type of Internet connection you will be using. Most cable, DSL, and ISDN providers offer modems with their service (although you usually have the option to provide your own modem as well).

Installing and configuring these modems is also dependent on the type of connection you are using.

→ To learn more about installing and configuring a modem, **see** Chapter 13, "Connecting Your Mac to the Internet," **p. 337**.

NOTE

> There are other ways to connect to the Internet, such as with a fractional T-1 line. However, if you are going to connect your system with technology like this, your provider usually handles the configuration and installation of the hub equipment you need.

32

Mac OS X: Living in a Networked World

CHAPTER 33

BUILDING AND USING A NETWORK

In this chapter

LOCAL AREA NETWORKING WITH MAC OS X

Wherever there is more than one computer (whether those machines are running the Mac OS, Windows, Linux, or another operating system) in the same general physical area, there is an opportunity to network those computers into a local area network (LAN). A LAN offers many benefits, including the following:

- Sharing devices, such as printers
- Sharing files
- Providing a local web
- Sharing an Internet connection
- Providing FTP, email, and other services

A LAN can be as simple as two Macs (or a Mac and a network device such as a printer) connected together using an Ethernet crossover cable. A LAN can be as complex as hundreds of computers, dozens of printers, and many other devices communicating with each other among many buildings on a college or business campus. Local networks can also be anything in between, from a small home office with a couple of Macs and a Windows machine to a workgroup that has 10 or more workstations in it.

Creating and managing a large Ethernet network (such as one with hundreds of devices on it) is a major task, coverage of which is beyond the scope of this book. This chapter assumes a more modest network that includes several Macs; a Windows PC or two; and a couple of network devices, such as printers. Not coincidentally, this is the environment in which Macs are most likely to be used. The principles of managing larger networks are the same, but the details are much more complicated.

Similarly, this chapter focuses on the two networking technologies for which support is built in to the Mac OS: Ethernet and AirPort. There are other means of networking machines together, but they are specialized and beyond the scope of this book. For most networks that you will manage with Mac OS X, Ethernet and AirPort are the best tools to create a LAN.

NETWORKING SERVICES SUPPORTED BY MAC OS X

Mac OS X supports a variety, in both range and depth, of network services as you can see in Table 33.1.

TABLE 33.1 NETWORKING SERVICES PROVIDED BY MAC OS X

Service/Protocol	Abbreviation	Function
Apple File Protocol	AFP	Enables file sharing on machines running older versions of the Mac OS, such as Mac OS 8 and Mac OS 9.
AppleTalk	AppleTalk	Set of services used to communicate on Macs running older versions of the Mac OS or AppleTalk devices such as printers.

Service/Protocol	Abbreviation	Function
Bluetooth	Bluetooth	Enables Macs to communicate with various wireless devices, such as cell phones and PDAs.
Bonjour	Bonjour	Enables Bonjour-compatible devices on a network, such as computers and printers, to automatically discover and configure other Bonjour-compatible devices.
Common Internet File System	CIFS	Provides remote file access on many platforms, such as Windows.
Dynamic Host Configuration Protocol	DHCP	Provides automatic assignment of IP addresses to devices on a network.
Bootstrap Protocol	BOOTP	Enables computers to use the operating system installed on a different computer on the network to start up and operate.
File Transfer Protocol	FTP	Enables the fast transfer of files over TCP/IP networks.
Hypertext Transport Protocol	HTTP	Provides the transmission and translation of data between a web server and web client.
Internet Protocol	IP	Enables communication across a wide variety of devices and services.
Lightweight Directory Access Protocol	LDAP	Enables users to locate resources, such as files and hardware devices, on a network.
Network File Service	NFS	Enables file sharing on Unix-compatible devices, such as Mac OS X computers.
Network Time Protocol	NTP	Synchronizes time across devices on a network.
Open Transport	OT	Another set of networking protocols that was introduced under earlier versions of the Mac OS.
Point-to-Point Protocol	PPP; PPPoE	Provides TCP/IP services over dial-up connections (PPP) and over Ethernet (PPPoE).
Printer Access Protocol	PAP	Provides services necessary to print to network printers.
Service Location Protocol	SLP	Enables devices on a network to be discovered automatically.
Short Message Block	SMB	Enables Macs to connect to Windows and Unix file servers.

33

continues

TABLE 33.1 CONTINUED

Service/Protocol	Abbreviation	Function
Transmission Control Protocol/Internet Protocol; User Datagram Protocol/ Internet Protocol	TCP/IP; UDP/IP	Enables the transmission of data across extended networks, such as the Internet. These protocols do not provide services in themselves but are the means by which data is transmitted across networks.
Web-based Distributed Authoring and Versioning	WebDAV	Extends HTTP to provide collaboration and file management on remote web servers. iDisk services are provided via WebDAV.

> **NOTE**
>
> Support for SMB and CIFS enables you to integrate Macs onto Windows and Unix networks with no additional software installations. You can also integrate Windows computers into networks that mostly consist of Macs.

All the services listed in Table 33.1 can be useful, but covering all of them is beyond the scope of this book. In this chapter, you will learn how to implement the two services you are most likely to use: file sharing and FTP. After you have learned to configure these, you can apply similar principles to configure additional services on your network.

→ To learn how to configure Mac OS X's built-in web server to implement HTTP services, **see** "Mac OS X to the Max: Using Mac OS X to Serve Web Pages," **p. 514**.

> **NOTE**
>
> The WebDAV standard is a relatively new one that is gaining wide use. It provides a much better environment for file sharing and other services across HTTP networks, primarily the Web. For example, when you use an iDisk under Mac OS X, you are using the WebDAV standard. This enables you to remain connected to the iDisk for long periods of time without being disconnected during idle periods.

IMPLEMENTING A NETWORK

To implement a network, you should do the following:

1. Design your network.
2. Build your network.
3. Configure the services that will be available on the network.
4. Monitor and administer your network.

DESIGNING A NETWORK

Before you implement a network, you need to design the network you want to create. As a starting point, answer the following questions:

- **What types of services do you want to provide over the network?**—Will you provide file serving? Do you want to share an Internet connection? How about FTP or web services? The answers to these questions will drive the rest of your network design. For example, if you plan to share an Internet connection, you will most likely want to include a hub that can act as a DHCP server in your network design.

- **How many devices do you want to be on the network?**—The devices for which you plan must include all the workstations on the network as well as shared devices, such as printers, modems, and so on. The answer to this question determines how many access points into the network you will need to provide.

- **How will you connect the devices together?**—For example, will you use Ethernet for all devices or will you include an AirPort hub (hardware or software base station) in the network? The answers to these questions determine the connecting devices you will need to use, such as Ethernet hubs, AirPort base stations, and so on.

- **Who will need access to the services you are providing?**—How will they connect to the network? The answers to these questions help you identify the users on your network.

- **What are the security implications of the services you are providing on the network?**—This question should drive you to ensure that you protect machines that will have access to the network. For example, you need to be very careful about providing FTP access to machines on which sensitive or critical data is stored. There are security concerns with any network service you provide; you should understand these when you design your network so you know how to provide proper security for it.

→ To learn how to use a network to share an Internet connection, **see** Chapter 34, "Sharing an Internet Connection," **p. 973**.

→ To learn how to protect your network from attack, **see** "Defending Your Mac from Net Attacks," **p. 1032**.

As you answer the previous questions, you should be ready to start designing your network. You should document your network design with at least a simple sketch of the network, the list of the devices you need to include on the network, and so on. Also, include the services you will be providing from specific machines on the network. An example of a design for a small office network is shown in Figure 33.1.

TIP

Having your network design documented enables you to expand it more easily when you outgrow it. It is much simpler to determine what needs to be done to expand a network when you see it on paper than it is by looking at it in the real world. (Besides, unless all the machines are in the same room, you probably won't be able to see them all at the same time, anyway.)

Figure 33.1
A simple network design document, such as this one for a small office network, can aid network design, implementation, and maintenance.

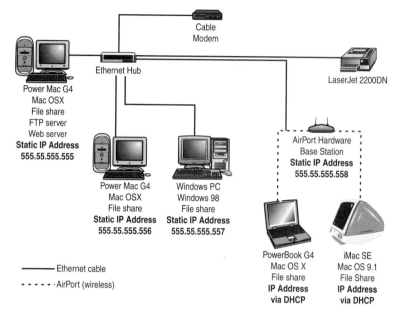

BUILDING A NETWORK
=================

After your network design is complete, you can start building that network.

Obtain the devices and cables you need and assemble the network.

Your network design document identifies the devices you need on the network. For example, you can determine the type of Ethernet hub you need by counting the number of devices you are connecting to it and determining whether it must provide services to the network, such as a DHCP server, so you can share a single Internet account among the devices. You also need to determine the types and length of cable you will need to attach the devices to the network, how the cables will be routed, and so on.

→ To learn more about Ethernet hubs, **see** "Finding and Installing an Ethernet Hub," **p. 922**.

After you have obtained the devices that will be installed on the network, you need to connect and configure those devices to access the network.

Connecting the devices to the network is simply a matter of attaching an Ethernet cable to an Ethernet hub and to each device. Of course, depending on the physical locations of the devices on the network, this can be quite a challenge, especially if you have to traverse long distances or connect machines located on different floors. If you are using AirPort on your network, you need to install AirPort cards in machines using AirPort services.

TIP

Because AirPort provides services based on the standard wireless protocols, you can connect Windows machines to an AirPort network almost as easily as you can connect Macs to the same network. You just need to install the appropriate wireless card into the PC and then configure it to access the Airport network.

Configuring the devices attached to the network includes configuring the Internet access and firewall (if needed) for each machine, configuring an AirPort base station, and so on.

→ To learn how to configure Mac OS X machines for Internet access, **see** Chapter 13, "Connecting Your Mac to the Internet," **p. 337**.

→ To learn how to install and configure an AirPort network, **see** Chapter 14, "Using an AirPort Network to Connect to the Internet," **p. 371**.

→ To learn how to share an Internet connection among the devices on the network, **see** Chapter 34, "Sharing an Internet Connection," **p. 973**.

→ To learn how to protect machines on your network from Internet attacks, **see** "Defending Your Mac Against Net Hackers," **p. 1032**.

> **NOTE**
>
> When you create a LAN, you are actually creating an intranet. You can provide most services on an intranet that are available on the Internet. The only difference is that you can control what happens on the intranet much more closely than you can control anything on the Internet.

As you install a device, be sure to test its basic access to the network by accessing various resources on the network, such as networked printers and Internet access if that is provided through the network. This step confirms that the physical aspects of the network are working properly and that the basic network configuration for Internet access is done properly.

After you have confirmed that the devices are correctly attached to and configured for the network, you need to configure the particular services each machine will use and the access that others on the network will have to those services; examples of such configuration are provided in the next section.

> **NOTE**
>
> Tutorials on creating and managing Ethernet networks are located at www.lantronix.com/learning/index.html.

CONFIGURING THE SERVICES ON A NETWORK

As you learned in Table 33.1, Mac OS X supports a large number of network services. To access these services, you must configure each machine that will be using them. This involves configuring the particular machine that will be providing those services (the *server*) and then enabling access to those services on various machines on the network that will be accessing those services (the *clients*).

Explaining how to configure each of the possible services is beyond the scope of this book. However, learning about some examples of services you are likely to use will enable you to configure the others.

33

Some services you'll want to take advantage of on most networks are the following:

- File sharing
- FTP server
- Windows file sharing
- Printer sharing
- Web server

→ To learn how to share files with Windows computers, **see** "Mac OS X to the Max: Networking Mac OS X with Windows Computers," **p. 968**.

→ To learn how to share the printers attached to a Mac OS X machine, **see** "Working with Shared Printers," **p. 882**.

→ To learn how to host websites from a Mac OS X machine, **see** "Mac OS X to the Max: Using Mac OS X to Serve Web Pages," **p. 514**.

CONFIGURING AND USING FILE SHARING

The Mac OS has long provided peer-to-peer file-sharing capabilities to enable Macintosh computers on a network to share files. Mac OS X provides much more robust file sharing services along with more tools you can use to control and configure a network.

NOTE

Peer-to-peer file sharing implies that the files being shared are stored on workstations that people use to accomplish work. The other type of file sharing is based on a sever/client arrangement in which the primary purpose of the server machine is to provide network resources, such as files to share. The technology involved is similar. If you are managing a relatively small network, you are probably not likely to have a dedicated server on it, but that's okay because peer-to-peer file sharing works just as well for these kinds of networks.

Under Mac OS X, you can share files with Macs running Mac OS X, Macs running OS 9 and earlier, Windows file servers, and Unix file servers. For other Macs running Mac OS X, you can use AppleTalk for file sharing or use TCP/IP. For Macs running earlier versions of the Mac OS (such as Mac OS 9), you can use AppleTalk to share files. For Windows and Unix, you can use SMB and CIFS services.

When connecting to other Macs for file sharing, the machines communicate through either TCP/IP or AppleTalk. To log in to a Mac OS X file-sharing machine serving files via TCP/IP, that machine must have an IP address. Typically, this IP address is assigned as part of connecting that machine to the Internet, such as by a DHCP server provided by an Ethernet hub or an AirPort Base Station.

Mac OS X includes support for Bonjour, which enables devices to seek out other Bonjour-compatible devices on a network and configure automatically access to those devices. All Macs that have Mac OS X version 10.2 or later are Bonjour aware and can therefore take advantage of this technology to easily and quickly connect to other Macs. However, other devices, such as printers, can also support Bonjour, so those devices can be configured automatically as well.

NOTE

> Interestingly enough (to me anyway), Bonjour is also being used in some "non-computer" devices. For example, TiVos use Bonjour.

AppleTalk is the Mac's original network protocol, and it continues to be supported in Mac OS X. When you are connecting to Macs running OS version 8.6 or earlier, you have to use AppleTalk as support for file sharing over TCP/IP, which was added in Mac OS 9.0.

In the next chapter, you will learn how to share an Internet account using a DHCP server. Such a server assigns IP addresses to the machines connected to it. The *D* stands for dynamic, meaning these addresses can change. This can make locating a specific machine by its IP address tough because each machine's address can be changed by the DHCP server. Fortunately, with most DHCP servers, you can choose to manually assign IP addresses to the devices attached to it. When you do this, machines have the same IP address even though they are using a DHCP server to obtain that address.

With Bonjour, you don't need to worry about the IP addresses of individual machines because your Mac seeks out the devices that are communicating on a network and automatically configures access to those devices.

NOTE

> If other devices on your network, such as printers, have dynamic IP addresses assigned to them and you use the IP address to configure that device, you can lose the connection to those devices when the DHCP server assigns a new address to them. (This typically happens if the hub loses power for some reason or the device is removed from the network for a while.) In such cases, you need to reconfigure any computers that access the device with the new address assigned by the DHCP server. For such devices, consider assigning a static address that remains constant for that device.

To identify the current IP address of a Mac OS X machine, open the Services tab of the Sharing pane of the System Preferences application. Select and activate the service in which you are interested; the current address will be shown at the bottom of the pane (see Figure 33.2).

You can also use the machine's name to identify it from other machines that support Bonjour. The machine name is shown in the Computer Name field at the top of the pane and also at the bottom of the pane as part of the address information (in Figure 33.2, you can see that the Mac's name is Brad Miser's Power Mac G4).

TIP

> To identify the current IP address of a Mac OS 9 machine, open the File Sharing control panel.

Figure 33.2
When you select an active service, such as Personal File Sharing, the URL to connect to that service is shown at the bottom of the Sharing pane (in this case, you can see that the current IP address of the Mac is 10.0.1.9).

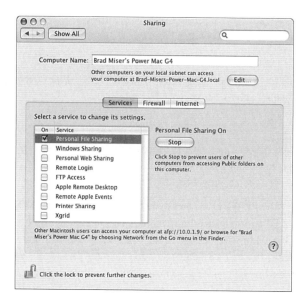

CONFIGURING FILE SHARING ON A MAC RUNNING MAC OS X

To share the files stored a Mac OS X machine, you must enable the Personal File Sharing service on that computer. This includes turning on the File Sharing service, turning on AppleTalk (if you will be sharing files with Mac OS 9 machines), naming the machine, and so on.

> **TIP**
>
> If your purpose in file sharing is one-way—for example, enabling others to download files from a specific machine but not to upload files to it—consider using FTP services on a machine rather than file sharing. You will learn how to provide FTP services in a later section of this chapter. You can also use web sharing to enable people to download files from a Mac OS X machine.

What's in a Name?

Your Mac actually has two names associated with it. One is the computer name, which by default is a combination of the first user's name and the word *Computer*. The other name is that device's hostname, which is actually the name used when the device is accessed over a network.

By default, the hostname and the computer name are the same, except your Mac automatically removes any characters, such as spaces, that aren't permitted in a hostname. Any changes you make to the computer name are automatically made in the hostname. However, you can manually set the hostname for a machine to be something different from its computer name. To do this, click the Edit button at the top of the Sharing pane. In the resulting sheet, enter the hostname of the Mac. The hostname always ends in `.local`.

The following steps assume that a Mac has access to the network (via Ethernet or AirPort) and that the default security privileges are in place on the file-sharing machine. You can change the default privileges for items you share to make them more or less available as you will learn in a later section of this chapter.

To provide file sharing services from a Mac running Mac OS X, do the following steps:

1. Open the System Preferences application.

2. Click the Sharing icon to open the Sharing pane (see Figure 33.3). At the top of the pane are the computer's name and its hostname.

Figure 33.3
You enable the network services a Mac provides by using the controls on the Services tab of the Sharing pane.

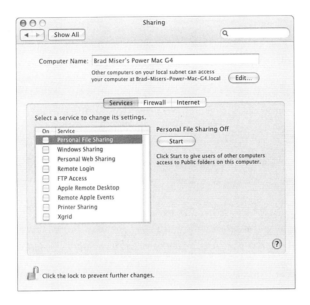

The Sharing pane has three tabs. The Services tab is used to view and configure the services the machine will provide. You use the Firewall tab to enable and configure the machine's firewall, and you use the Internet tab to enable a machine to share its Internet connection with other machines.

→ To learn how to configure a Mac's firewall, **see** "Defending Your Mac Against Net Hackers," **p. 1032**.

→ To learn how to share an Internet connection among the devices on the network, **see** Chapter 34, "Sharing an Internet Connection," **p. 973**.

3. Provide the computer's name by entering a name in the Computer Name text box; use a name that will help others on the network easily identify the machine. The default computer name is the first user's name entered when the machine was registered, with an apostrophe, an *s*, and the word *Computer* tacked onto it. You can use the default computer name or change it to one you prefer.

   After you provide a name, the machine's hostname is automatically created. Some characters, such as spaces, aren't allowed in a hostname, which is the name by which the machine is identified on the network. If you enter such characters in the computer name, the machine name that people see on the network won't be exactly what you entered. For example, if you include a space in the computer name, it is replaced by a hyphen for the machine's network name. The Mac automatically removes and replaces any disallowed characters.

4. If you want to manually enter a hostname, click the Edit button; then, in the resulting sheet, enter the hostname for the machine and click OK. The extension .local is added to the hostname you type to indicate that the host is on the local network.

5. Select the service you want to activate on the machine, such as Personal File Sharing.

6. Click the Start button to turn on the selected service. For example, if you selected Personal File Sharing, that service is activated; after a moment or two its status becomes On and you see the AFP address of the machine and the browsing name (which is the name by which others on the network will be able to identify the computer when they browse the network) at the bottom of the pane. When you select and enable other services, information related to those services is shown in the pane instead. When the service is running, the Start button becomes the Stop button.

TIP

> You can also start a service by clicking its On check box.

If you will be sharing files with Macs running a version of the Mac OS older than Mac OS X and those machines don't allow file sharing over TCP/IP, you need to make AppleTalk active on the Mac OS X machine. If the machines to which you will be providing file-sharing services do allow file sharing over TCP/IP, you don't need AppleTalk and can skip to step 12.

33

CAUTION

> If you don't need to use AppleTalk to use file sharing, leave it off. AppleTalk can sometimes interfere with other network services, such as TCP/IP services to the Internet. AppleTalk can also make your machine visible to a local or wide area AppleTalk network.

7. Open the Network pane of the System Preferences application.

8. Select the network port over which AppleTalk access will be provided on the Show menu. For example, select Built-in Ethernet to enable machines to use the AppleTalk protocol over Ethernet. Select AirPort to provide AppleTalk over an AirPort network.

NOTE

> You can provide AppleTalk over only a single network port at a time. For example, you can provide AppleTalk over Ethernet or over AirPort, but not both at the same time.

9. Click the AppleTalk tab and check the "Make AppleTalk Active" check box. The computer name you entered in the Sharing pane is shown next to the text Computer Name.

10. If you have AppleTalk zones on your network, select the zone from the AppleTalk Zone pop-up menu (if there aren't any zones, this pop-up menu will be inactive). You can configure AppleTalk zones using the Configure pop-up menu (select Manually if you want to manually configure the network or Automatically to have your Mac configure it automatically).

11. Click Apply Now. AppleTalk services will become active on the computer.

12. Review the services you have configured on the Sharing pane (see Figure 33.4).

Figure 33.4
This Mac is providing file-sharing services to other Macs and is sharing the printers connected to it.

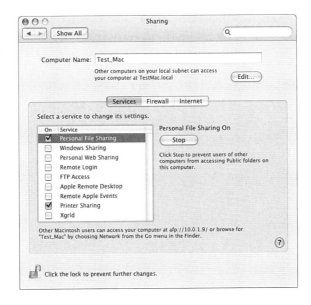

USING FIREWALLS AND NETWORK SERVICES

If you have a firewall installed on the machine you are configuring as a server, you must configure that firewall to allow the type of access needed for others to access it from the network. For example, to enable the machine to provide file sharing services, you must configure the firewall to allow machines from the network to connect to the file server. With some firewalls, you can allow access to specific services, such as AFP, only from specific IP addresses. All other requests for services will be denied.

If you use the Mac OS X built-in firewall that you can enable on the Firewall tab, the services you enable on the Services tab are allowed automatically. You can use the Firewall tab of the Sharing pane to manually configure the services that are allowed if you need to.

If you use another type of firewall or configure the built-in firewall using another method (such as the Unix commands), you must enable access to the services you are providing through that firewall.

Similarly, if some machines on your network are connected through a Graphite AirPort base station, you won't be able to access those machines from machines connected outside the

AirPort network, such as via Ethernet. Because an AirPort base station provides NAT protection of the machines it connects, machines outside the AirPort network can't see any of the machines on the AirPort network unless the base station allows bridging between the wired and wireless networks. By default, you have to manually configure a Graphite base station to allow bridging. On newer base stations, bridging is automatically provided when you connect the station's Ethernet port to the wired network.

Always be aware of the security settings of the networks you are configuring and using. Sometimes, you can waste a lot of time troubleshooting a network problem that is actually a case of things working just as planned (such as when you try to figure out why no one can connect to a machine protected by a firewall that isn't configured to allow those services to be accessed on the machine).

ACCESSING SHARED FILES FROM A MAC OS X COMPUTER

There are two basic ways you can access a server. One is to browse the network for available servers. The other is to move to the services on a machine directly using the URL for the specific service you want to access.

In either case, when you connect to a server, you must log in to that server to access its resources. You can log in under a user account that is valid for that server, or you can log in as a guest. When you log in under a valid user account, you have access to all the items on that machine just as if you were logged in to the machine directly (rather than over a network). If you are logged in as a guest, you can access only the items on the machine that allow public access, such as each user's Public folder.

> **NOTE**
>
> To access a network resource by browsing, it must support Bonjour, SMB, or AppleTalk. If not, you have to access it by entering its URL via the Connect to Server command.

To access shared files stored on a Mac OS X computer that is sharing its files from a Mac OS X machine by browsing the network, do the following steps:

1. Open a Finder window and select the Network directory on the Places sidebar, select Go, Network or press Shift-⌘-K. The Network directory will appear. Depending on the network to which you are connected, you will see a number of icons representing various network resources available to you.

> **NOTE**
>
> It can take a few minutes for your Mac to successfully browse the network to which it is connected. After you start the browse process, if you don't see the resources you think you should, refresh the Network window by moving away from it and then back again or by clicking its icon to update the list of available network resources.

2. To access other Macs providing services, select the My Network icon if you see it; if not, the individual servers with which you can work will appear directly under the

Network folder. You will see the names of the computers on your network that are providing services to you (see Figure 33.5).

Figure 33.5
The My Network folder provides access to other Macs providing services on your network; in this case, I can access three other Macs.

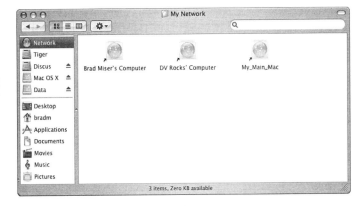

NOTE

The icon labeled Servers actually points to the current machine. If you open it, you see the computer on which you are working. If you open that, you jump to the Computer folder.

TIP

Server icons you access over a network have the globe icon that is similar to the icon for the Network directory. A server's icon also indicates its status. When the icon is in color, you are currently connected to that server and its resources are available to you. When the icon is shaded, you are not connected to the server.

3. Double-click the icon for the server and services you want to access. The Connect To Server dialog box will appear (see Figure 33.6).

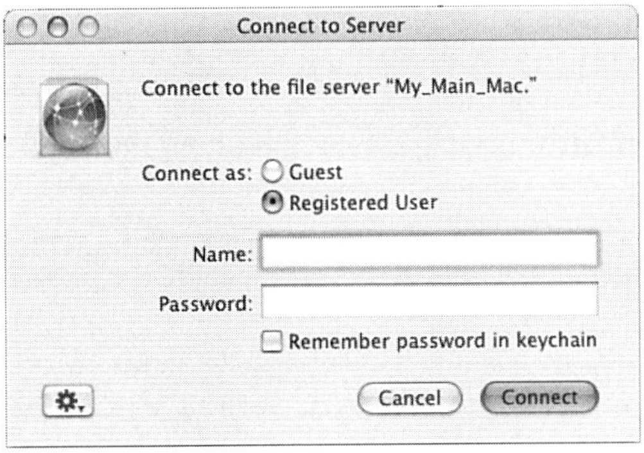

Figure 33.6
You use this dialog box to log in to a server.

	Connect to Server
	Connect to the file server "My_Main_Mac."
	Connect as: ○ Guest
	⦿ Registered User
	Name:
	Password:
	☐ Remember password in keychain
	Cancel Connect

33

TIP

> View the My Network folder in Column view and select the server you want to access. In the Preview column, you'll see the server's icon and the Connect button. Click the Connect button to connect to the machine providing services to you.

4. To log in as a registered user, which provides the same access to resources you would have when you log in directly to that machine, click the Registered User radio button and enter the username and password for the account under which you want to log in. If you don't have log in information for a specific user account on the machine to which you are connected, click the Guest radio button instead. Click Connect to connect to the server. A window will appear that lists each volume or user's Home folder (which will be the Home folder of the user account under which you logged in) you can access.

TIP

> Check the "Remember password in keychain" check box in the Connect to Server dialog box to add a network resource's login information to your keychain. The next time you access that resource, the login information will be input automatically so you can just click Connect to connect to it.

5. Select the volume or Home folder you want to use and click OK. The server's volume you selected, such as a Home folder, will appear in the Places sidebar in the Finder window. Select the resource that was mounted to work with it (see Figure 33.7). The resources that appear depend on the user account under which you are logged in. If you logged in as a guest, you can access only public resources.

Figure 33.7
The volume called `bmiser` is my Home folder on a different Mac that I am accessing over a network.

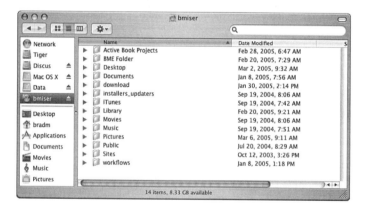

NOTE

> Network volumes are represented by the globe icon instead of the disk icon, as you can see in Figure 33.7.

6. Open the folders available via the shared resource to work with them. For example, you can open files, drag them to your Mac to copy them, and so on.

 If you can't see a server when you browse, see "I Can't Access a Server" in the "Troubleshooting" section at the end of this chapter.

For more precise access to services on a Bonjour machine (such as to choose to access FTP services when file sharing and FTP are being provided) or to access services on a machine that doesn't support Bonjour, you can use a computer's address to access it manually. To do so, perform the following steps:

1. From the Finder, select Go, Connect to Server (⌘-K). The "Connect to Server" dialog box will appear (see Figure 33.8).

Figure 33.8
Use the "Connect to Server" dialog box to manually move to servers.

TIP

> If you click the Browse button, you move to a Finder window showing the Network directory; this does the same thing as selecting Network on the Places sidebar.

33

2. Type the server address you want to access in the Server Address box. The address you use depends on how you want to access the server. For example, to open all of a computer's resources, type its hostname, which is *hostname*.local, where *hostname* is the hostname of the machine you are accessing. To access file-sharing services, use the URL for File Sharing services, which will be something such as afp://10.0.1.4/. You can obtain the address for the specific service you want to access on the Sharing pane of the System Preferences application on the computer you are accessing over the network. Select the specific service you want to access and the related address will appear at the bottom of the pane.

3. Click Connect. Your Mac will attempt to locate the resource via the address you entered. You can monitor the progress of this via the "Connecting To Server" progress window. If the connection is made successfully, you will see the "Connect to Server" dialog box (see Figure 33.9).

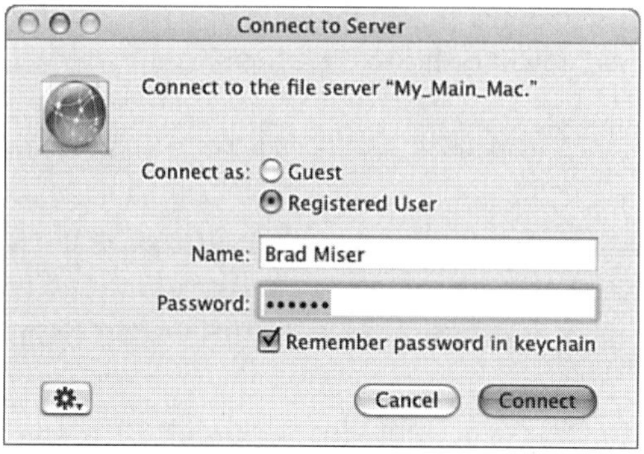

Figure 33.9
Use this dialog box to log in to a network server.

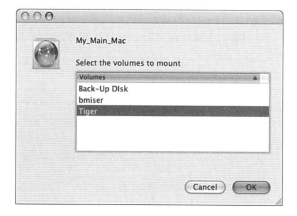

4. Enter the username and password for the account under which you want to log in and click Connect or click the Guest radio button and click Connect instead. The server's volumes that you can access will appear in the select volume dialog box (see Figure 33.10). The resources that appear depend on the user account under which you are logged in. If you logged in as a guest, you can access only public resources.

Figure 33.10
The machine called `My_Main_Mac` has a number of volumes that can be mounted on the machine being used to access that server.

5. Select the volume you want to mount—hold down the Shift or ⌘ key to select multiple volumes—and click OK. A Finder window will open and the volumes you chose to access will be shown in the Places sidebar (see Figure 33.11). If you have set mounted servers to appear on the desktop using the Finder preference, they appear on your desktop as well.

> **NOTE**
>
> In Figure 33.11, you can see that there are two volumes named `Tiger`. Because the Mac to which the current Mac connected via the network also had a volume named `Tiger`, Mac OS X appended a `-1` to the network volume named `Tiger` when it mounted that volume on the current Mac.

Figure 33.11
The Home folder called `bmiser` and the disks called `Back-UP Disk` and `Tiger-1` are being accessed over the local network.

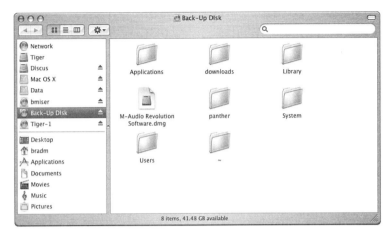

6. Access the network volumes just like those directly connected to or installed in your Mac.

If your preferences are set such that mounted volumes appear on your desktop, you will see the shared volumes there as well.

 If the connection is never made and quits or the "Connect to Server dialog box never appears, see "I Can't Access a Server" in the "Troubleshooting" section at the end of this chapter.

Following are some additional tips about using a Mac OS X machine to access file-sharing services via the Connect to Server command:

- When you sign on to a Mac OS X file-sharing machine as a registered user, meaning you have a username and password, the Action pop-up menu in the "Connect to Server" dialog box is enabled. If you open this menu, you can choose the Options command to set some preferences related to accessing the file-sharing services on this machine. You can allow a clear-text password (on by default), receive a warning when sending a password in clear text (also on by default), or allow secure connections using the SSH protocol. When you change these settings, you must click OK to save them. You can also change the password for the account under which you are logging in (if the account allows this) by choosing the Change Password command.

- When you are logged in to a file-sharing machine, you can quickly choose other volumes to mount by opening the Connect To Server dialog box (press ⌘-K), selecting the file server to which you are logged in, and pressing Return. You jump to the Select Volume dialog box (because you are already logged in), and you can select another volume to mount on your machine. Of course, it is easier just to mount all the resources you can access when you first log in.

- The address to which you most recently connected is remembered in the "Connect to Server" dialog box so you can reconnect to it by opening that dialog box and clicking Connect.

33

- To remove access to a network resource, click the Eject button shown next to it in the Places sidebar or select the mounted folder or volume and choose File, Eject or press ⌘-E.

- To log back in to the same file-sharing machine under a different user account, such as an administrator account, you must log off that machine and repeat the initial login process. You do this by ejecting all the mounted volumes provided by that server.

- At the upper-right corner of the "Connect to Server" dialog box is the Recent Servers pop-up menu (the Clock icon) that shows a list of the most recent servers you have accessed. You can select a server from this list to return to it, or you can clear the list by selecting Clear Recent Servers.

- In the lower part of the "Connect to Server" dialog box is the Favorite Servers list. You can add a server to your favorites list by entering its URL and clicking the "Add to Favorites" button (+). You can return to any favorite server by selecting it on the list and clicking Connect. Remove a favorite by selecting it and clicking the Remove button.

- You can place an alias to a networked volume on your Mac, such as by adding it to the Places sidebar. When you open such an alias, you are prompted to log in to the server and, upon doing so, you can access that volume. If you add the password to your keychain, you will skip the login process.

If you are unable to access the file server, see "I Can't Access a Server" in the "Troubleshooting" section at the end of this chapter.

TIP

> You can add a network server to the Startup Items tab of the Accounts pane of the System Preferences application to mount that server each time you log in.

USING FILE SHARING WITH MAC OS 9 COMPUTERS

You can use file sharing with Mac OS 9 computers just as you can with Mac OS X machines.

The access you have to a Mac OS 9 machine from a Mac OS X machine is determined by the file-sharing settings of the Mac OS 9 machine.

NOTE

> Explaining setting up file sharing on a Mac OS 9 machine is beyond the scope of this chapter. For help, see my book *The Mac OS 9 Guide*.

When you enable access to a Mac OS X file-sharing machine from a Mac OS 9 machine, the user of the Mac OS 9 machine has the same options as someone who signs on to the file-sharing computer using a Mac OS X machine. For example, if he signs on under a guest account, he can mount any of the Public folders on the file-serving machine. If he logs in under a valid user account, he can use any volumes that user has permission to access on that machine.

 If you have trouble using file sharing from a Mac OS 9 machine, see "My Mac OS 9 Machine Can't Share Files" in the "Troubleshooting" section at the end of this chapter.

NOTE

> Remember that Macs running older versions of the Mac OS must be configured to allow file sharing via TCP/IP; otherwise, you must turn on AppleTalk for the Mac OS X file server.

CONFIGURING AND USING FTP SERVICES

Among its other network services, Mac OS X also includes a built-in File Transfer Protocol (FTP) server. Using an FTP server can be an even more convenient way to enable others to access files stored on a particular machine. Other people can use a standard web browser or FTP application to download files stored on your Mac via the FTP services you enable on a machine.

CAUTION

> Granting FTP access to a machine has security implications that are beyond what I have room to cover in this chapter. If you intend to use the FTP services on a machine that has sensitive data on it, you should investigate the implications of running FTP services on a Mac under Mac OS X that has data on it you need to protect.
>
> You can sometimes move outside the particular Home directory for the account under which you log in to the FTP site, so be very careful about granting FTP access to a machine unless you are very sure about the person who will be using it.

Configuring FTP services under Mac OS X is similar to providing file-sharing services:

1. Open the Services tab of the Sharing pane of the System Preferences application.
2. Select the FTP Access service.

TIP

> You can also activate FTP services by checking the FTP Access On check box.

3. Click Start. FTP services will start up, and the FTP address for the machine will be shown at the bottom of the pane.

To access the FTP server, browse for the network resource or move to the FTP address via the "Connect to Server" dialog box. You can also use a web browser or an FTP client and use the URL `ftp://ip_address/`, where `ip_address` is the IP address of the machine providing FTP services (remember that the FTP URL for the machine is shown at the bottom of the Services tab when you select the FTP Access service). You will see the "FTP File System

33

Authentication" dialog box (see Figure 33.12). In this dialog box, you are prompted to enter the username and password for the services you are accessing; enter the short name and the password for the user account whose Home directory you want to access and click OK.

Figure 33.12
When you access an FTP server, you will use this dialog box to log into that service.

If you use the Finder or a web browser to access the FTP services, a Finder window will open and the folders you can access will appear. You can open any accessible folders to see the files they contain. To copy a file onto your Mac, drag it from the FTP resource onto your computer.

> **NOTE**
>
> When you use the Finder or a Web browser, FTP is a one-way service. You can only copy files from the FTP server to your Mac; you can't move files from your Mac to the FTP server as you can with File Sharing. For this reason, use FTP when you don't want people changing files on your Mac but only want to provide copies of files stored on your machine. If you use a dedicated FTP application, you can move files in both directions via FTP.

If you use a non-administrator account to log in to the FTP server, you have access to the entire Home directory for that user account. If you log in under an administrator account, you have wider access to files on the machine.

If you can't access the FTP site on a machine, see "I Can't See the FTP Site" in the "Troubleshooting" section at the end of this chapter.

If you are initially able to enter the FTP site, but then it stops working, see "FTP Access Was Working but Now It Isn't" in the "Troubleshooting" section at the end of this chapter.

MONITORING AND ADMINISTERING A NETWORK

In addition to the tools you need to configure and start various network services, such as file sharing or FTP, Mac OS X includes tools you can use to monitor and administer your network. Two of these are the Network Utility, which enables you to diagnose your network connections, and the NetInfo Manager, which provides comprehensive control over many aspects of a Mac OS X machine.

USING THE NETWORK UTILITY TO ASSESS YOUR NETWORK

The Network Utility provides a set of tools you can use to assess the condition of communication across machines on your network as well as a set of tools that enable you to get information about various sites on your network and the Internet.

When you launch the Network Utility (Applications/Utilities), you will see a window with nine tabs, one for each service the application provides (see Figure 33.13).

Figure 33.13
Ping is a useful way to test your connection to another machine (in this case, I pinged 10.0.1.4, which is another Mac on my LAN).

Table 33.2 summarizes the tabs in the Network Utility application.

TABLE 33.2	TABS IN THE NETWORK UTILITY APPLICATION
Tab	**Function**
Info	Provides information about the interface selected on the pop-up menu. For example, you can get the IP address, connection speed, connection status, and hardware information. You also see the statistics about the transfers over the selected interface.
Netstat	Presents various statistics about the performance of the various network protocols. To access this data, select the Netstat tab, choose one of the options by selecting a radio button, and click Netstat. The data appears in the Netstat pane.

continues

Tab	Function
TABLE 33.2	**CONTINUED**
AppleTalk	Provides information about active AppleTalk services on the machine.
Ping	Contacts a specific server to assess network performance between the current Mac and a network resource. When you can't connect to a resource, ping its address to see whether your Mac can communicate with it. If the ping isn't successful, you will know that the machines are unable to communicate.
Lookup	Provides various information about a specific Internet address. For example, you can enter a URL and get the IP address for that site.
Traceroute	Traces a specific route between machines and provides statistics about that route, such as the maximum number of hops needed.
Whois	Enables you to look up information about a domain or an IP address, such as to whom it is registered.
Finger	Reports information about a specific individual based on the person's email address.
Port Scan	Enables you to scan for open access ports on a specific domain or IP address.

Covering each of these services in detail is beyond the scope of this chapter, but the next couple of examples should be helpful in getting you started using this tool.

CHECKING NETWORK CONNECTIONS WITH PING

Troubleshooting network problems can be difficult because identifying where the source of the problem is can be hard—for example, with the machine you are using, with the machine you are accessing, with an application, and so on. Ping is a way to check on the fundamental communication between two machines. If the ping is successful, you know that a valid communication path exists between two machines. If it isn't successful, you know that a fundamental problem exists with the communication between the machines, and this helps you know where to troubleshoot.

To ping a machine, perform the following steps:

1. Open the Network Utility and click the Ping tab.
2. Enter the IP address or URL for the machine you want to ping.
3. Click "Send an unlimited number of pings" to send a continuous number of pings, or click "Send only ___ pings" and enter the number of pings if you want to send a specific number.
4. Click Ping.

Watch the results in the lower part of the window. You will see your machine attempt to communicate with the machine whose address you entered. If they are able to successfully communicate, you see statistics about how fast the pings are (refer to Figure 33.13). If the pings are successful, you know the communication path between the machines is valid. If not, you know you have a fundamental connection problem between the two machines.

TRACING A ROUTE WITH TRACEROUTE

Sometimes looking at the specific route between two machines can help identify the source of problems you might be having:

1. Open the Network Utility and click the Traceroute tab.

2. Enter the domain name or IP address to which you want to trace a route, and click Trace. The lower pane of the window will be filled with information that shows each step of the path from your machine to the one whose information you entered (see Figure 33.14).

Figure 33.14
This Traceroute window shows the path from my machine to www.apple.com.

UNDERSTANDING AND SETTING PERMISSIONS

Access to items on your Mac OS X machine, whether from the machine directly or over a network, is determined by the access privileges set for those items. Three levels of access privilege can be set for any item; these are the following:

- Owner
- Group
- Others

The owner is the owner of the item.

The group is a set of users. By default, Mac OS X includes several groups for which various permissions are assigned to different volumes and directories. Many of these default groups look odd, and some are even nonexistent (for example, in certain places, you will see Members of group " ").

Others include those users who are neither the owners nor members of a group.

Each level of access has four access options:

- **Read & Write**—This is the broadest level of access and lets the user to whom it is assigned read and write to the item to which it is assigned.

- **Read only**—This privilege lets a user see items in a directory but not change them. For example, if a user has read-only access to a folder, they can copy its files, but they can't change the files stored in that folder.

- **Write only (Drop Box)**—With this access, a user can place items in a directory but can't see the contents of that directory. By default, each user has a Drop Box folder in the Public folder in her Home folder.

- **No Access**—The user can't do anything with the item.

If you open the Info window for an item and expand the Ownership & Permissions area, the current access permissions for the item will be shown. If you expand the Details area, the current permissions set for the owner, group, and others will also be displayed. For example, Figure 33.15 shows the Permissions information for the volume on which Mac OS X is installed, whereas Figure 33.16 shows similar information for a document within the logged-in user's Home directory.

Figure 33.15
This Info window for the startup Mac OS X volume shows that the current user (You can) can read and write to the selected volume; the owner (system) and anyone in the admin group has the same access while others can only read from the disk.

TIP

To change permissions, click the Lock icon next to the Owner pop-up menu and authenticate yourself as an administrator of the Mac. When the Lock icon is unlocked, the pop-up menus become active.

Figure 33.16
This Info window is for the Documents folder within a user's Home directory; its pop-up menus are active and you can use them to set access permissions for the item.

There are several things you need to know about the Ownership & Permissions information shown in the Info window.

First, unless you are logged in under the root or administrator account, you can't use the pop-up menus to change the permissions assigned to items on the Mac OS X startup volume above the current user's Home directory. However, when you open the Ownership & Permissions area of the Info window for an item on another volume or within a user's Home directory, the pop-up menus become active and you can use them to change the privileges for the items that folder contains.

Second, the groups you see in the Info window are default groups created when you install Mac OS X. The user accounts that are members of these groups can access the item with the group's privileges. You can't change the members of those groups from the Finder; you have to use the NetInfo Manager application, as you will see in the next section.

To configure access privileges for most items, you need to either be logged in as an administrator or authenticate yourself in the Info window. To do so, click the Lock icon and enter an administrator username and password.

To set the access privileges for all items, perform the following steps:

1. Log in under the account that is the owner of the items for which you want to change access permissions. For example, to change the access permissions for the items in a user's Home directory, log in under that user account. (You can see the owner for any item by opening the Details area of the Ownership & Permissions area of the Info window for that item; the current owner is shown on the Owner pop-up menu.)

33

NOTE

The owner for most items you will see is the original administrator account. The owner of items with the user directories is the user account for that directory, and the owner of system items is system, which is actually the root account.

→ To learn how to log in under the root account, **see** "Logging In As Root," **p. 253**.

2. Select the item for which you want to set permissions and press ⌘-I.

3. Expand the Ownership & Permissions section in the Info window and then expand the Details section.

   Use the access permission pop-up menus to set the access privileges for each type of user. Different pop-up menus are active depending on the specific item for which you are setting access permissions and the user account you are using. If you aren't in a position to change an aspect of the permissions, the pop-up menus for that aspect will be disabled.

4. If the Owner pop-up menu is active, use it to set the owner of the item. When you open this menu, you see each user account on the machine plus many other user accounts you probably have not seen before (see Figure 33.17). The primary ones you need to concern yourself with are system, which is the root account, and nobody, which makes no account the owner of an item. The current owner is indicated by the check mark.

Figure 33.17
You can use the Owner pop-up menu to set the owner for an item.

TIP

> If you select Other on the Owner pop-up menu, you see the User Listing dialog box, which shows every user on your machine.

5. Use the Access pop-up menu under the Owner pop-up menu to configure the access the owner has to that item. Typically, the owner of an item is granted Read & Write access, which is the broadest access possible.

6. Open the Group pop-up menu and assign a group to the item. As with the Owner pop-up menu, all sorts of odd-looking groups appear on the Group pop-up menu. The staff group is selected for many items by default—you are a member of this group. The other groups you see have been created by default or by using the NetInfo Manager application. You can determine the members of the groups by using the NetInfo Manager application as well.

NOTE

> The default group for an item within a user's Home folder is the user's user account.

7. Use the Group Access pop-up menu to configure the access that members of the group you selected in the previous step have to the item. Usually, you should allow Read access for a group.

8. Use the Others pop-up menu to set the access everyone else (everyone who is not the assigned owner or a member of the assigned group) has. Typically, you allow either No Access or Write only (Drop Box) to others.

9. If you want the same privileges to apply to every item contained in the item you selected, click the button labeled "Apply to enclosed items." The same set of permissions are then applied to every item contained in the current item.

10. Continue setting permissions for other items as necessary.

Under Mac OS X, you can open multiple Info windows at the same time. This is a handy way to compare and contrast the permissions provided for different items.

USING THE NETINFO MANAGER TO ADMINISTER YOUR NETWORK

The NetInfo Manager application (Applications/Utilities) can be used to view and change an extensive amount of configuration information for a system. The application presents information based on a selected directory; by default, this is the information for the local-host directory, which is the machine on which Mac OS X is installed.

CAUTION

> Using the NetInfo Manager application is not for the faint of heart. The information it presents and the controls it provides are complicated and can be quite dangerous to your system. This section can only scratch the surface of this application, and you should be careful if you explore the application on your own.

When you open the application, click the Lock icon and enter your administrator account information to enable changes to be made. The application's two-paned window and toolbar will become active (see Figure 33.18).

Figure 33.18
This NetInfo Manager window shows information for the base level of the localhost machine.

Networks and Complexity

As you explore networking, you might find yourself thinking that Mac OS X security is complicated to set up and manage. If you have these thoughts, I agree with you.

This complexity is part of the price paid for the additional capabilities and security of Mac OS X when compared to previous versions of the OS. Mac OS X is based on Unix, and the complexity of Unix comes to the forefront more in some specific areas of the OS than in others—networking is a prime example of where Unix really moves to the foreground. Fortunately, as you have seen, using the default configuration to provide basic services, such as file sharing, websites, and so on, is relatively easy. It is only when you are doing more complex tasks, such as changing the composition of the default user groups, that you have to get face-to-face with some of the complexity of the system underlying Mac OS X.

In the upper pane is a browse window that works similarly to a Finder window in the Columns view. In the center column, you can browse the contents of an item selected in the left column. Similarly, in the far right column, you can browse the contents of an item selected in the center column.

In the lower pane are the details for the item you have selected in the upper pane. The specific details you see are related to what you have selected in the upper pane. For example, Figure 33.19 shows the details for the user account bradm—selected in the upper pane—in the lower pane of the window.

Figure 33.19
You can use the NetInfo Manager to view and change information about the items you select.

When you have selected an item, you can change its information by editing the property and value data in the lower pane of the window.

NetInfo Manager is an extremely powerful utility, and you can administer many parts of your system with it. Because of space limitations, I can't cover it in much detail. However, a sample task will show you how it works in general.

You can change the members of a group through which access privileges are assigned by changing the members of that group. For example, you can add members to the group admin to change which user accounts have administrator privileges on your machine:

1. Open the NetInfo Manager application (Applications/Utilities).

2. Authenticate yourself as an administrator by clicking the Lock icon and entering an administrator username and password.

3. In the center column of the window, click groups and then select admin in the right column. The lower pane displays the various properties and their corresponding values for the admin group.

4. Click the expansion triangle next to the users property to expand it (see Figure 33.20). Each member is listed on a separate line. If you have created only one administrator account, that account and the root account appear in the list. If you have created more than one administrator account, each administrator account and the root account will be listed.

Figure 33.20
Expanding the users property by clicking its expansion triangle reveals the members of the admin group (in this case, root, and bradm).

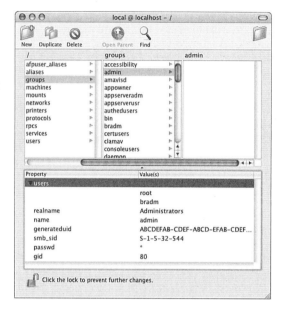

5. Select Directory, New Value. A new line is added to the users property; the value is new_value.

6. With newvalue highlighted, change it to the short name of the user account you want to make a member of the admin group; then press Return.

7. Repeat the steps to add other members to the admin group.

8. Quit the application. In the Quit dialog box, click Review Unsaved, and then click Save in the Warning dialog box.

9. In the next dialog box, click the "Update this copy" button.

TIP

If the changes you make don't appear to be reflected, restart Mac OS X to force the new values to be implemented.

NOTE

You can make copies of directories so you can make changes to one and use it without writing over the previous version. This gives you a way to recover in case you mess something up.

The users you added to the admin group now have the privileges designated for this group. Opening the Accounts pane of the System Preferences application shows that the user accounts you added to the admin group are now designated as administrator accounts.

You can change the members of other groups you encounter in the same way.

NOTE

> Of course, it would be a lot faster to use the Accounts pane of the System Preferences application to edit a user account to make it part of the admin group, but this example serves to show you generally how the NetInfo Manager application works. To change the members of other groups, you have to use the NetInfo Manager application; you can do so using the same steps as those to change the members of the admin group.

TROUBLESHOOTING

I CAN'T ACCESS A SERVER

When I try to browse for a server, I can't see the resource I am trying to access. Or, when I access a specific address via the Connect to Server command, the connection is never made because the process quits or the "Connect to Server" dialog box never appears.

First, make sure that the network resource you are trying to access is available. Go to that machine; ensure it is running; and check its Sharing pane to make sure the services, such as file sharing, are turned on. Check the machine's network connections to ensure it is communicating successfully with the network. For example, check its Internet connection or access a network printer.

Second, if you are trying to browse for the machine and it is properly configured and communicating with the network, ensure it supports Bonjour—it must be running Mac OS X version 10.2 or later to do so. If not, you need to access it via its address. If you are trying to access the machine via the address for a specific service, check the address you need to access to ensure you are using the correct one.

Third, go back to the machine on which you are attempting to access the network resources and make sure its network connections are active, such as by accessing the Internet.

Fourth, if can't find a Bonjour-enabled computer by browsing, access it via its address. If you are accessing the network resource via its address, be sure you are using the correct address for the service you are trying to access. For example, make sure you are using the File Sharing address if that is the service you are attempting to use.

MY MAC OS 9 MACHINE CAN'T SHARE FILES

When I try to access a Mac OS X file server from a Mac OS 9 machine, I can't see it in the Chooser.

Make sure the Mac OS 9 machine can access the network. Use the Chooser to select a network printer or other device. If that works, you know the problem lies with the configuration of the Mac OS X machine. If it doesn't, you have a networking problem. Check the cables and hubs to make sure everything is connected properly.

On the Mac OS 9 machine, turn off AppleTalk using the Chooser, assuming that the Mac OS 9 machine has an IP address. AppleTalk can cause problems with TCP/IP file sharing for Macs running Mac OS 9.

If the Mac OS 9 machine does not have an IP address, ensure that AppleTalk is turned on for the Mac OS X file server.

I CAN'T SEE THE FTP SITE

When I try to move to the FTP site, I get a connection refused *or* site not found *error.*

First, check whether any TCP/IP services are working. Turn on web sharing for the machine you are attempting to use for FTP. If you can successfully connect to its website, a problem exists with the FTP services themselves. If you can't successfully connect, you have a network problem.

If the problem is related to the FTP service, make sure you don't have a firewall installed that blocks FTP services. Also, try shutting down the FTP machine and then starting it up again.

FTP ACCESS WAS WORKING, BUT NOW IT ISN'T

I have successfully accessed FTP services on a machine before, but now it isn't working.

If you are using a web browser to access the FTP site, quit the browser, restart it, and try again.

If several unsuccessful logins to an FTP service have been attempted, subsequent logins will be denied. When this happens, restart the machine providing the FTP services.

MAC OS X TO THE MAX: NETWORKING MAC OS X WITH WINDOWS COMPUTERS

Because support for Windows and Unix file-sharing protocols is built in to Mac OS X, using a Mac on a Windows or Unix network is much easier under Mac OS X than it was under previous versions of the Mac OS. It is just as easy to add a Windows computer to a Mac-based network.

SHARING FILES WITH WINDOWS COMPUTERS

You can use Mac OS X to access files provided on a windows computer on your network via the SMB protocol without doing any additional configuration. To use files provided on a Windows or Unix network that uses SMB, perform the following steps:

1. Connect your Mac OS X machine to the network.

2. Open the Connect To Server dialog box and click Browse. Depending on the SMB servers on your network and how the network is configured, the SMB servers might or might not appear in the list of available servers when you browse the network, so you might have to enter the server address manually.

3. If you don't see the SMB server to which you want to connect, enter the address of the server to which you want to connect; the form of the address is smb://*ServerName*/ *ShareName*/. *ServerName* is the IP address for the Windows machine you are attempting

to access, and *ShareName* is the name of the item being shared with you, such as a volume or folder.

TIP

> To determine the IP address (ServerName) for a Windows machine, open the Command Prompt window, type `ipconfig`, and press Enter. The IP address of the Windows machine will be shown.

4. Click Connect. You are prompted to enter your workgroup/domain, username, and password for that server.

5. Enter the required information and click OK. You are logged in to the shared resource and can use the files it contains just like a Mac that is acting as a file server (see Figure 33.21).

Figure 33.21
The DDRIVE folder is located on a Windows XP machine on the local network.

NOTE

> Connecting to Windows computers can be problematic depending on the specific network you are using. If the preceding steps don't enable you to connect to a Windows computer, try using the Apple support document located at the following address: http://docs.info.apple.com/article.html?artnum=106660.

To enable Windows users to access files stored on your Mac, carry out the following steps:

1. Open the Services tab of the Sharing pane of the System Preferences application.

2. Select the Windows Sharing service and click Start. The address to which Windows users need to connect is shown at the bottom of the pane. You need to provide this address to the Windows users you want to be able to access the machine. You must enable a user account for Windows sharing to be able to be accessed from a Windows computer.

3. Click the Enable Accounts button that appears when you activate the Windows Sharing service.

4. On the resulting sheet, check the On check box for a user account that you want to be able to access from a Windows computer.

5. Enter the password for the accounts you select in the password prompt and click OK.

6. Repeat steps 4 and 5 for each user account you want to enable.

7. When you have finished enabling accounts, click Done.

> **TIP**
>
> You can reconfigure user accounts' access from Windows computers at any time by clicking the Accounts button on the Services pane when you select the Windows Sharing service.

8. Provide the user account, password, and address (shown at the bottom of the Services tab when Windows Sharing is selected) to the Windows users you want to be able to log in.

A Windows user can use the URL, username, and password you provided to log in to your Mac to share files just like Macs on your network (see Figure 33.22).

Figure 33.22
This Mac OS X folder is being accessed from a Windows XP computer.

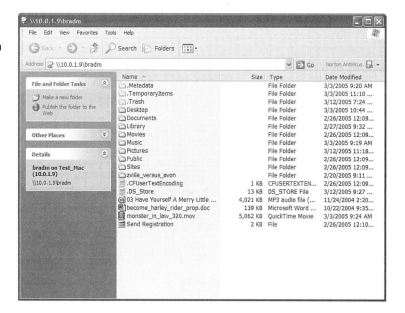

ACCESSING VIRTUAL PRIVATE NETWORKS

Virtual Private Network (VPN) service enables networked computers to access file servers, email servers, and other network resources over a WAN connection just like machines connected via a LAN can. Using Mac OS X, you can connect a Mac to a VPN. To access a VPN, perform the following steps:

NOTE

> Before you will be able to access a VPN, you'll need to talk to that network's administrator to get all of the information you will need such as connection method, address, user name, password, and so on.

1. Open the Internet Connect application.
2. Click VPN on the toolbar.
3. Select the type of VPN connection you should use. The options are "L2TP over IPSec" and PPTP. You should use the option directed by the administrator of the VPN you are accessing.
4. Enter the server address, account name, and password for the VPN you want to access.
5. Click Connect. You will be connected to the VPN and should be able to access its resources.

TIP

> If you use VPN regularly, add the VPN status menu to the Finder menu bar.

33

CHAPTER **34**

SHARING AN INTERNET CONNECTION

In this chapter

ENABLING MULTIPLE MACS TO USE A SINGLE INTERNET ACCOUNT

One of the primary advantages of networking computers together is that they can share a single Internet account. This is especially useful for broadband accounts; however, you can share a dial-up connection, too.

NOTE

> Dial-up accounts are relatively slow. Supplying several computers through slow access will divide that limited bandwidth and make the already-slow access even slower.

You can also share a single Internet account on mixed networks that include both Macintosh and Windows computers.

Most means of sharing an Internet account rely on the Dynamic Host Configuration Protocol (DHCP). This protocol enables IP addresses to be dynamically assigned to each device on a network. A DHCP server assigns and manages these addresses. This protocol means that each device doesn't have to have be assigned a unique IP address through manual configuration; the DHCP server has a unique address and assigns IP addresses to the machines under it, as they are needed.

NOTE

> Each device for which a DHCP server provides an address must have a unique IP address; the DHCP server provides these addresses and ensures that they are unique. Most DHCP servers also provide network address translation (NAT) protection for the devices to which they provide services. When NAT protection is active, all the machines under the server appear to be from one IP address, which is that of the DHCP server. Using a DHCP server with NAT isolates the machines it serves from direct contact with other machines on the Internet and protects those machines from Internet attacks to a great degree.

In this chapter, you will learn how to share an Internet account using the following techniques:

- AirPort
- Mac OS X's built-in Internet sharing feature
- Multiple IP addresses for a single account
- A hardware DHCP server/hub

USING AIRPORT TO SHARE AN INTERNET ACCOUNT

One of the easiest and best ways to share an Internet account is to use AirPort. In fact, using AirPort automatically enables you to share an Internet account among computers using an AirPort-compatible, wireless connection. You can also use an AirPort base station or an AirPort-equipped Mac to share an Internet connection with machines on a wired Ethernet network.

When you install and configure an AirPort hardware access point (also known as an *AirPort base station*), you can share the Internet account with which it is configured among AirPort-equipped Macs that can access that network. You can also share an Internet account among computers that are connected to the hardware access point via Ethernet. This is because the hardware access point is capable of acting as a DHCP server for the network and can provide that service to computers connected via AirPort and via Ethernet at the same time.

NOTE

> Just because Windows computers don't call their wireless connections AirPort, that doesn't mean they can't share an Internet connection through an AirPort base station. They can, in fact, join an AirPort network as long as their wireless device supports the same protocol the AirPort network does. Because AirPort uses standard wireless protocols, in most cases PCs running Windows with wireless networking capabilities can also join AirPort networks.

When used with a broadband connection, an AirPort hardware access point also provides your network with basic firewall protection when you use NAT (which is explained later in this chapter). Because the only thing directly connected to the Internet is the base station itself, hackers can't see the computers that are connecting to the Net through the base station. They can see the base station, but because it isn't a computer, there isn't much they can do to it.

Because AirPort is easy to install, configure, and maintain and because you also get wireless access for AirPort-equipped devices, using AirPort is one of the best ways to share an Internet account.

→ To learn how to install, configure, and use an AirPort network to share an Internet connection, **see** Chapter 14, "Using an AirPort Network to Connect to the Internet," **p. 371**.

34

NOTE

> An AirPort base station is also a great way to share a dial-up Internet connection. Because the modem (if you use a dial-up account) and software required to maintain the dial-up connection are part of the base station, this method doesn't place any processing burden on the Macs using the AirPort network. Of course, to share a dial-up connection, an AirPort base station must include a dial-up modem, which is an option on newer base stations.

USING A MAC RUNNING OS X TO SHARE AN INTERNET ACCOUNT

Mac OS X includes a built-in DHCP server you can use to share a single Internet connection with other devices on your local network. And if the Macintosh on which you configure the DHCP server includes an AirPort card, you can also provide a wireless AirPort network without the use of an AirPort base station.

NOTE

The function of the DHCP server is to provide and manage IP addresses to devices on the network. The DHCP server doesn't actually provide the Internet access itself; that comes from the connection method you use (such as a cable modem). The DHCP server manages the traffic between the Internet connection and the other devices on the network.

One advantage of this approach is that you don't need to add dedicated Internet sharing hardware (such as a sharing hub or an AirPort base station) to your network. A standard Ethernet hub enables you to share an Internet account over an Ethernet network, and an AirPort card enables you to share an account over a wireless AirPort network. Another advantage is that it doesn't cost anything to share an account (assuming that you already have the connection hardware, such as for an Ethernet network).

NOTE

You can use Mac OS X's built-in firewall to protect the DHCP machine from attacks from the Internet (and because it sits between the Internet and the other devices on your network, it protects those devices as well).

→ To learn how to configure the Mac OS X firewall, **see** "Defending Your Mac Against Net Hackers," **p. 1032**.

This approach does have one significant disadvantage and one minor drawback, however. The significant disadvantage is that the Mac providing DHCP services must always be running for the machines that share its account to be capable of accessing the Internet. If the DHCP machine develops a problem, no device on the network can access the Internet. Similarly, if the machine from which the account is shared goes to sleep or is shut down, the Internet connection is lost by all the computers on the network. The less significant issue is that the DHCP services do require some processing power. These services will most likely not result in any noticeable performance decrease, but if your machine already runs at its limits, asking it to provide these services might slightly slow down other tasks.

NOTE

DHCP servers are not platform specific. For example, if you have a DHCP server running on a Macintosh, you can connect a Windows computer to the network and use the same DHCP server to share the Internet account with it. Or, you can install a DHCP server on a Windows machine and use it to share the account with Macs on the network.

Configuring a Mac to provide DHCP services to a network requires the following general steps:

1. Connect the Mac to the Internet.
2. Install the network you will use to connect the Mac with other machines.
3. Configure the Mac to share its Internet account.

CONNECTING THE DHCP MAC TO THE INTERNET

It goes without saying (but I will say it anyway) that to use a Mac to share an Internet account, that Mac must be connected to the Internet. The method you use to connect to the Internet doesn't matter. You'll get the best results if you use a broadband connection, such as a cable or DSL modem, but you can also share a dial-up connection if you want (don't expect speedy operation, though).

→ To learn how to connect a Mac to the Internet, **see** Chapter 13, "Connecting Your Mac to the Internet," **p. 337**.

INSTALLING THE DHCP MAC ON A NETWORK

The next step is to install the DHCP Mac on the network with which you are going to share the Internet connection. You can build a wired network using Ethernet, or you can install an AirPort card to connect the Mac to other AirPort-equipped Macs (you can share an account with other machines using both networking methods at the same time).

→ To learn how to install, configure, and use an AirPort network, **see** Chapter 14, "Using an AirPort Network to Connect to the Internet," **p. 371**.
→ To learn about Ethernet, **see** "Ethernet," **p. 817**.
→ To learn about Ethernet hubs, **see** "Finding and Installing an Ethernet Hub," **p. 922**.
→ To learn how to build and manage a network, **see** Chapter 33, "Building and Using a Network," **p. 935**.

CONFIGURING THE DHCP MAC TO SHARE AN ACCOUNT

After you have configured the Mac for Internet access and connected it to other computers (with or without wires), you need to configure the Internet sharing services on it.

The three possibilities when you configure Internet sharing on your Mac are as follows:

34

■ Your Mac is connected to the Internet via an Ethernet connection, and it has an AirPort card installed in it.

■ Your Mac is connected to the Internet via Ethernet but does not have an AirPort card installed in it.

■ Your Mac is connected to the Internet via an AirPort base station, in which case you can share the Internet account by connecting that Mac to other computers via Ethernet to share its account via an Ethernet network (you wouldn't need to share the Internet connection with the AirPort-equipped Macs because the base station already does that).

NOTE

> AirPort base stations, except the original version, include an Ethernet port you can use to connect the base station to an Ethernet network. When you do this, the base station can also share a connection with machines connected to the Ethernet network. In that case, you don't need to use a Mac to share a connection.

When you configure Internet sharing on your Mac, it automatically determines which case is true for your machine and presents the appropriate options for you. To configure Internet sharing, use the following steps:

1. Open the System Preferences application and click the Sharing icon to open the Sharing pane.

2. Click the Internet tab. What you see depends on how the Mac is connected to the Internet. For example, in Figure 34.1, you see the Sharing Internet tab for a machine connected to the Internet via AirPort; you can tell this is so because AirPort is selected on the "Share your connection from" pop-up menu. In Figure 34.2, you see an example of a machine connected to the Internet via Ethernet. Because that machine also has an AirPort card installed in it, it can share its connection with other machines using both Built-in Ethernet and AirPort.

Figure 34.1
This Internet tab is for a computer connected to the Internet via AirPort.

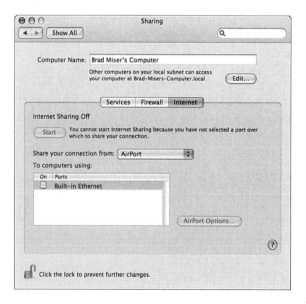

34

NOTE

> The ports you see listed in the "To computers using" pane will be those that are active under your current network settings (determined by the location setting currently active). For example, if in your current location, the Built-in FireWire port is active, that port will also be available for you to share an Internet connection with other computers.

Figure 34.2
The Internet tab shows a machine that is currently connected to the Internet via Ethernet, but that also has an AirPort card installed in it.

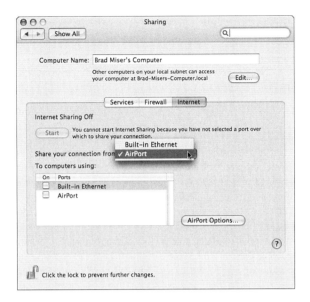

→ To learn how to configure your network settings, **see** "Managing Multiple Internet Accounts," **p. 365**.

→ To learn how to use locations, **see** "Configuring and Using Locations," **p. 330**.

3. On the "Share your connection from" pop-up menu, select the Internet connection you want to share. In most cases, you will be connected by only one means, such as AirPort or Built-in Ethernet, so the choice should be obvious. However, if the Mac can connect in multiple ways, choose the option you want to share. For example, if you are connected to an Ethernet network that has Internet access and you also have access to the Internet through an AirPort base station, you can share either connection with other computers.

In the "To computers using" box are the means by which you can share the connection that you selected in step 3 with other computers. For example, in Figure 34.2, you can see that the Mac can share its connection with other machines over Ethernet and AirPort.

4. Mark the On check box for the ports over which you want to share the connection. For example, to share the Mac's connection with computers via AirPort, mark the On check box next to AirPort on the list of ports.

If you use an Ethernet port to share a connection, you might see a sheet warning you that activating sharing might cause problems for other ISP customers or violate your service agreement (some providers prohibit sharing an individual account on multiple machines, but most allow a reasonable amount of sharing such as with five or fewer computers). Read the dialog box and click OK to close it.

34

5. If you made an AirPort port active in step 4, select the AirPort port and click the AirPort Options button. Then configure the AirPort network you are creating using the resulting sheet. For example, you will name the network (if you don't want to use the default name), choose a channel and password, and so on. When you are done configuring the AirPort network, click OK.

→ To learn how to configure an AirPort network, **see** Chapter 14, "Using an AirPort Network to Connect to the Internet," **p. 371**.

CAUTION

Be careful about sharing an account over the same port by which you are receiving it. For example, if your Mac is already getting an Internet connection through an Ethernet network, don't also share its Internet connection with that same network. For one thing, you don't need to because the device providing the connection to your Mac is already sharing its connection with other devices on the network. For another, you can cause confusion for yourself and potentially IP address conflicts by sharing the same connection on the same network. Generally, unless you have multiple networks of the same type operating in the same location (such as more than one AirPort network), a port that is selected on the "Share your connection from" pop-up menu shouldn't also be turned on in the "To computers using" list.

6. Click Start (you can't click Start until you turn on at least one port on the "To computers using" list). Your Mac will start providing DHCP services.

You might see a warning sheet that explains that activating sharing might disrupt services on the network. If you are administering the network, click Start in the sheet. If someone else administers the network on which you are sharing your connection, make sure you coordinate with that person before starting Internet Sharing.

Your connection will be shared with all the devices with which your Mac can communicate via the ports that you have turned on. For example, if your Mac is connected to a local network via Ethernet and you made that port active, other devices on the network can use the account via the DHCP services your Mac provides.

7. Quit the System Preferences application.

8. Configure the other devices on the network to use the Mac's DHCP server to access the Internet.

→ To learn how to connect a Mac to the Internet, **see** Chapter 13, "Connecting Your Mac to the Internet," **p. 337**.

→ To learn how to install, configure, and use an AirPort network, **see** Chapter 14, "Using an AirPort Network to Connect to the Internet," **p. 371**.

TIP

If you share an Internet account over AirPort, an upward pointing arrow is added to the center of the AirPort icon in the menu bar. This indicates that the connection is shared and that you can access the sharing controls from the menu.

CAUTION

> If the machine sharing the connection goes to sleep or is shut down, the Internet connection is lost on the network and no machine can access the Net. You should disable sleep using the Energy Saver pane of the System Preferences application when you use Internet Sharing. (In fact, when you start up sharing on a Mac that has sleep turned on, the Energy Saver button appears on the Internet pane so you can easily jump over and turn off sleep.)

If other machines with which you are sharing a connection are unable to connect to the Internet, see "The Machines with Which I Am Sharing a Connection from My Mac Can't Connect at All" in the "Troubleshooting" section at the end of this chapter.

If other machines with which you are sharing a connection lose the connection to the Internet, see "The Machines with Which I Am Sharing a Connection from My Mac Have Lost Internet Access" in the "Troubleshooting" section at the end of this chapter.

In this section, I've focused on using Built-in Ethernet and AirPort to share a connection. That's because they are by far the most likely way you will do so. However, there are other ports by which you can share a connection, including Built-in FireWire and Bluetooth. Basically, you can share a connection via any means by which your Mac can communicate with other devices. Using these less common ports is really no different from using the ones described in this chapter. Just choose the appropriate port by which the sharing machine is accessing the Internet on the "Share your connection from" pop-up menu and turn on the ports through which you want to provide an Internet connection in the "To computers using" list.

USING MULTIPLE IP ADDRESSES TO SHARE AN INTERNET ACCOUNT

With some broadband accounts, such as cable, you can purchase additional IP addresses (or DHCP names) so you can configure multiple machines to access the same account. The requirements to do this are an address for each device that will be using the account and an Ethernet or other network, which typically consists of a hub with the cable or DSL modem connected to the WAN port and each device connected to a LAN port.

34

NOTE

> Some ISPs use DHCP to provide IP addresses to you. In these cases, you assign a DHCP name to your computer. The ISP's DHCP server assigns IP addresses to you as you need them. To share an Internet account among several devices, you need a unique DHCP name for each device; you use this DHCP name to configure the network on each device.

To share an account using multiple IP addresses, do the following:

1. Contact your ISP to determine whether this option is available.

2. If it is, obtain additional addresses (or DHCP names); you will need one address for each machine or device (such as an AirPort base station) you want to share the account. You will probably need to pay an additional fee for each IP address you obtain.

3. Connect the cable or DSL modem to the WAN port on the hub for your network.

4. Connect each device to a LAN port on the hub.

5. Configure each machine with one of the available addresses (or DHCP names).

 If you can't use a device on your network because of an error message about the same IP address being used on more than one device, see "I Get an Error Message Telling Me That Multiple Devices Have the Same IP Address" in the "Troubleshooting" section at the end of this chapter.

One advantage to this method is that you can use a standard Ethernet hub to facilitate sharing the account; these hubs are quite inexpensive and are simple to install and use. Setting up each device to use its address is straightforward as well. You simply configure each machine as if it were the only one using the account. Another advantage is that you get maximum speed for each machine because each connects directly to the account; the traffic doesn't have to be managed by a DHCP server on your network. And, because there isn't any software on your network that has to manage the Internet traffic, as a DHCP server does, your connection for each device is dependent only on your modem and service, making it slightly more reliable than some of the other methods.

One possible disadvantage is that you might have to pay an additional fee for each address you use. The typical cost of additional addresses is $5–$7 per month per address on top of the address included with your base account. This can get expensive if you have several devices on your network; however, you can balance that cost against not needing a hub (Ethernet or AirPort) that has Internet account sharing built in.

Another disadvantage is that you don't get any special features, such as a built-in firewall. You have to add protection for each device on your network in some other way.

Typically, using a hub with built-in Internet sharing (such as an AirPort base station) or using a Mac to share its account is a better option. But, some providers require you to have a unique address for each machine that will be using the account, and this might be your only legal option.

→ For help configuring a Mac to connect to the Internet, **see** Chapter 13, " Connecting Your Mac to the Internet," **p. 337**.

→ For help choosing and installing an Ethernet hub, **see** "Finding and Installing an Ethernet Hub," **p. 922**.

→ For help installing and configuring a network, **see** Chapter 33, "Building and Using a Network," **p. 935**.

→ For help with protecting your Mac from Net attacks, **see** "Defending Your Mac from Net Attacks," **p. 1032**.

USING A HARDWARE DHCP SERVER TO SHARE AN INTERNET ACCOUNT

One of the best ways to share an Internet account is to use a hub device that provides DHCP services to the network. These devices have the DHCP software built in and handle the administration of IP addresses for the network automatically.

In addition to basic DHCP services, some of these devices also include special features, such as built-in firewall protection for your network.

The general steps for installing and using such a device are the following:

1. Choose and obtain the device.
2. Install the device on your network.
3. Configure the device to connect to the Internet.
4. Attach the computers and other devices to the network and configure each device to use the DHCP server you configured in step 3.

ISPs and Sharing a Connection

Not all ISPs support sharing a single Internet connection. Check the agreement you have with your provider to ensure that sharing an account is within your rights under that account. Some configurations can actually block access to your account by a hub or other sharing device, thus preventing you from sharing the account using a hardware device. Before you purchase a hub, make sure that it is acceptable under the terms of your Internet account; otherwise, you might end up wasting your money. Fortunately, most providers allow you to share the account on a reasonable number of machines.

Some providers use sort of a "don't ask, don't tell" policy. They provide support for one machine per account and make it clear that they don't support networks, in which case you are on your own if you have problems connecting through your own network. However, because using a sharing hub is so straightforward, this isn't really much of a drawback.

CHOOSING AND INSTALLING A DHCP HUB

Choosing a DHCP hub is similar to choosing an Ethernet hub. For example, these hubs offer different numbers of ports, different speeds, and so on. In addition to the DHCP services they provide, the major difference between standard Ethernet hubs and DHCP hubs is that DHCP hubs also offer a variety of other special features.

→ For help choosing and installing an Ethernet hub, **see** "Finding and Installing an Ethernet Hub," **p. 922**.

→ For help installing and configuring a network, **see** Chapter 33, "Building and Using a Network," **p. 935**.

→ For help with protecting your Mac from Net attacks, **see** "Defending Your Mac from Net Attacks," **p. 1032**.

34

NOTE

> AirPort base stations (including the AirPort Express base stations) are DHCP hubs; their most special feature is that they can communicate with other devices wirelessly.

One of the most important of these special features is a firewall. Installing a DHCP hub that includes a firewall protects the devices on your network from being attacked by hackers coming to your network from the Internet.

One form of firewall is the NAT standard. Using NAT, there is one IP address used by the hub that connects your local network to the Internet. By providing NAT services, the hub shields the devices on your network by using a set of internal IP addresses for those devices. Thus, hackers trying to attack the only IP address that they can see get the hub device, which is typically immune to such attacks. Thus, your network is protected from external attack.

Many such devices are available, such as the Asante DSL/Cable Router (see Figure 34.3).

Figure 34.3
This Asante hub enables you to share an Internet account with multiple computers.

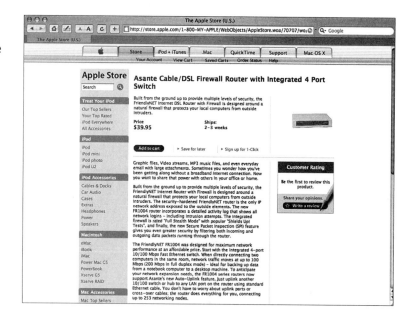

Some of my favorite sharing and networking hubs are produced by Linksys (see Figure 34.4). Linksys hubs provide excellent features and are easy to install and configure. These hubs enable you to share an Internet account and provide NAT protection for your network.

Figure 34.4
Linksys produces excellent sharing hubs that are easy to install and configure.

Many sharing hubs also offer wireless services and so are similar to an AirPort base station. Because AirPort is based on standard wireless protocols, AirPort services are compatible with any wireless device that meets these same standards. However, because AirPort technology is integral to the Mac, I recommend that you stick with an AirPort base station if you want to obtain and use a wireless sharing hub. However, AirPort hardware is also considerably more expensive than similar devices from other companies. So, if you can't afford to purchase an AirPort base station, check out the offerings from other companies, such as Linksys, that you might be able to afford.

NOTE

You can learn more about Linksys products by visiting www.linksys.com.

34

Clumps of Data

When data is communicated across a network, it is done so in clumps of data. These clumps of data are more properly called *packets*. Each packet contains information that identifies its origin and destination (this is used to assemble all the packets together into a useful string of data). When a firewall filters IP packets, it examines each packet that comes into the network to ensure that it originated from the expected place. It rejects any packets that do not meet its requirements, thus protecting the network from unexpected traffic, which is likely to have been generated by hacking activity. Packet filtering adds an additional layer of protection for a network.

The XRouter Pro is another example of a sharing hub that is simple to install and configure. For most homes or home offices, the XRouter is an excellent choice.

NOTE

> You can learn more about the XRouter Pro by visiting www.macsense.com.

Because of space limitations, I will be focusing on XRouter Pro in the remainder of this section. However, other devices, such as the Linksys hubs, can be installed and configured in a fashion similar to the XRouter Pro.

INSTALLING A DHCP SERVER

Installing a DHCP hub is similar to installing a standard Ethernet hub. Follow these steps:

1. Connect the output from the cable or DSL modem to the WAN port on the hub.
2. Connect the Ethernet cable from each computer to a port on the XRouter.
3. Connect the XRouter's power supply.

NOTE

> You can attach the XRouter Pro to an existing Ethernet hub to provide its services to more than four devices at a time. To do so, connect one port on your current hub to the crossover port on the XRouter and use the crossover switch to select the crossover mode.
>
> In the same way, you can also chain multiple hubs together to share an Internet account among more than four devices. For example, you can connect an AirPort base station to the hub to add AirPort-equipped devices to the network.

CONFIGURING MAC OS X MACS FOR DHCP SERVICES

After the physical connections are made, you need to configure each computer on the network to use DHCP for TCP/IP services.

NOTE

> Consider creating a location for each TCP/IP configuration you use. This makes switching between configurations simple and fast.

→ To learn how to configure and use the Location Manager, **see** "Configuring and Using Locations," **p. 330**.

To configure machines on a network to connect to a DHCP server, follow these steps:

1. Open the Network pane of the System Preferences application.
2. Select the location you want to configure from the Location pop-up menu.
3. On the Show pop-up menu, select the connection you want to configure, such as Built-in Ethernet or AirPort.
4. Click the TCP/IP tab.
5. Select Using DHCP from the Configure IPv4 pop-up menu (see Figure 34.5).

34

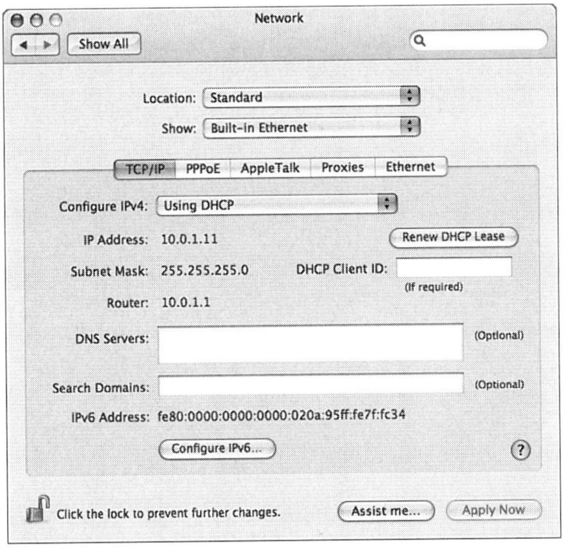

Figure 34.5
Typically, configuring a Mac to use a DHCP server is simply a matter of selecting Using DHCP from the Configure IPv4 pop-up menu.

NOTE

Some DHCP servers require that you use a DHCP Client ID name. If so, enter that name in the DHCP Client ID field.

6. Click Apply Now to save the configuration.

7. Repeat these steps or use similar steps to configure the Macs on your network. For example, for Macs running Mac OS 9, use the TCP/IP control panel to select Using DHCP Server.

8. Configure the other devices on your network so that they use DHCP, such as configuring a Windows computer to use the same DHCP server.

CONFIGURING A DHCP HUB

After the hub is physically connected to your network and the other devices are installed and configured, you need to configure the hub to connect to the Internet using your cable or DSL modem. How this is accomplished varies among devices, but most devices enable you to use a standard Web browser to configure the hub.

To install a typical DHCP hub, do the following:

1. Launch a Web browser.

2. Move to the IP address for the hub (the XRouter's default IP address is 192.168.1.1).

3. When prompted, enter the username and password, and then click OK (the XRouter's username is blank and the password is admin). You will see the administration screen for the device (see Figure 34.6).

34

Figure 34.6
This Web page is being served by the XRouter Pro and enables you to configure the hub.

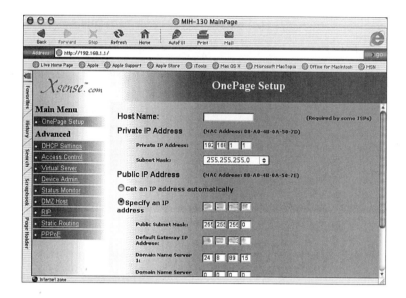

4. Configure the hub following the instructions provided by the hub manufacturer and your ISP. You configure the hub using the same settings as you would for a computer with which you were accessing the Internet account. For example, if your ISP provides manual IP addresses, use the Static or Manual option to configure the hub. If your account is configured using DHCP, choose the "Get an IP address automatically" option.

→ For help configuring an Internet account, **see** Chapter 13, "Connecting Your Mac to the Internet," **p. 337**.

5. Save your changes and quit the Web browser.

Make sure you explore the configuration options your hub provides. For example, some hubs enable you to assign fixed IP addresses to certain devices. These addresses are provided in a range of addresses your hub provides (the first three sets of numbers in the IP address are the same for all the devices on the network, but you can choose the fourth set from a specific range of numbers). One use for this is to enable file sharing across those devices. Because you use IP addresses to share files under Mac OS X, having a fixed IP address enables you to connect to the same machine each time. If you allow the server to assign addresses, the address for each machine can change as machines connect to and disconnect from the network.

The machines on your network should be capable of accessing the Internet using a single account. If your hub provides NAT services, your network is relatively secure from outside attack because the internal IP addresses of devices are not exposed to the Internet.

NOTE

If your hub provides additional firewall protection, explore its configuration page to control how your network access is configured. Typically, you can limit the access to specific URLs or direct all traffic to a specific machine on your network.

TROUBLESHOOTING

THE MACHINES WITH WHICH I AM SHARING A CONNECTION FROM MY MAC CAN'T CONNECT AT ALL

I have started Internet Sharing on a Mac, but other devices on the network can't access the Internet.

Attempt to connect to the Internet from the Mac that is sharing the account. If that machine can't connect, something has happened to its Internet connection. If that machine can connect, check that Internet Sharing is configured properly.

Then, check the Internet connection settings for each machine to make sure they are set to connect via a DHCP server.

→ To learn how to connect a Mac to the Internet, **see** Chapter 13, "Connecting Your Mac to the Internet," **p. 337**.

→ To learn how to configure Internet Sharing, **see** "Configuring the DHCP Mac to Share an Account," **p. 977**.

THE MACHINES WITH WHICH I AM SHARING A CONNECTION FROM MY MAC HAVE LOST INTERNET ACCESS

The machines with which I am sharing an Internet connection were able to connect, but now they can't.

First, check whether all the machines with which the connection is being shared have this problem or only some do. If all the machines are unable to connect, the problem stems from the Mac sharing the account (see the next paragraph). If some of the machines with which the connection is being shared can access the Net, the problem lies with those machines. Check the configuration of those machines to ensure that they are configured to use a DHCP server. Also, check their network connections to make sure they are communicating with the network properly.

→ To learn how to connect a Mac to the Internet, **see** Chapter 13, "Connecting Your Mac to the Internet," **p. 337**.

→ To learn how to install, configure, and use an AirPort network, **see** Chapter 14, "Using an AirPort Network to Connect to the Internet," **p. 371**.

→ To learn how to build and manage a network, **see** Chapter 33, "Building and Using a Network," **p. 935**.

→ To learn how to configure sleep, **see** "Configuring Power Use," **p. 324**.

If none of the machines can access the Internet, something has happened to the Mac that is sharing the connection.

Make sure that the Mac is still running and that sleep is disabled. If both of these conditions are true, move to the next paragraph. If the Mac is shut down, restart it to restart Internet Sharing. If the Mac has gone to sleep, you need to wake it up to restart Internet Sharing.

Attempt to connect to the Internet from the Mac that is sharing the account, such as by opening a web browser. If that machine can't connect, something has happened to its Internet connection. If that machine can connect, reconfigure Internet Sharing.

→ To learn how to configure sleep, **see** "Managing Your Mobile Mac's Power," **p. 320**.
→ To learn how to connect a Mac to the Internet, **see** Chapter 13, "Connecting Your Mac to the Internet," **p. 337**.
→ To learn how to configure Internet Sharing, **see** "Configuring the DHCP Mac to Share an Account," **p. 977**.

I GET AN ERROR MESSAGE TELLING ME THAT MULTIPLE DEVICES HAVE THE SAME IP ADDRESS

When I attempt to start up one of the devices on my network, I see an alert stating that a device has already been assigned the IP address and that IP services are being shut down. How do I correct this problem?

Two devices on the same network cannot have the same IP address. If you start up one device and see this error message, you have two or more devices trying to use the same address. Check the configuration of each device to see which devices are using that address (for Mac OS X machines, use the TCP/IP tab of the Network pane of the System Preferences application to see how the computer is configured). Check that each device has a unique address, including an AirPort base station or other device that is sharing the account.

Occasionally, your hub will "remember" the devices that are using specific IP addresses and you will see this error even though you made sure that each device had a unique address. If this happens, power down your entire network, including the hub and all other devices attached to it. Wait a few seconds and power up everything again. The error should be cleared as each device registers its unique address on the network.

MAC OS X TO THE MAX: TROUBLESHOOTING A NETWORK CONNECTION

Troubleshooting a network connection to the Internet can be quite challenging. Your approach should be to eliminate potential sources of the problem one by one until you find the specific problem you are having.

If you are unable to connect to the Internet after you have installed and configured an Internet Sharing hub, try the following steps:

1. Remove the hub again and return your configuration to the way it was before you installed the new hub.
2. Return one Mac to the condition it was in when you were able to access the Internet.
3. Check to see whether you can access the Internet. If you can, that means your connection is working properly and the configuration information is correct.
4. Attach that single computer and your modem to the DHCP hub again. This removes potential causes of problems that are due to the interaction of devices on the network.
5. Repeat the hub configuration and verify that the settings match those you used to connect the single Mac to the Internet.
6. Set the TCP/IP settings on the Mac to use a DHCP server.

7. Try to connect to the Internet. If you can connect, add your other machines back to the network one at a time. If the problem recurs, you know it is related to interaction among the devices.

8. In some cases, you might need to configure your hub to use media access control (MAC) address cloning. A MAC address uniquely identifies each node on a network. In some cases, you will need to clone, or copy, the MAC address of one of the computers on your network onto the router. See the instructions that came with the hub to learn how to configure MAC cloning on your router.

9. If you still can't connect, call your ISP for support.

NOTE

> Some broadband providers support only one computer for each IP address or DHCP name for each account. In these cases, you might have to purchase additional addresses to share a single account.

TIP

> You might be able to share an account using a software DHCP server even if you can't use a hardware device to do so. For example, try using the Mac's built-in Internet Sharing to share your account on a network. Connect the Mac directly to your cable or DSL modem and then use Internet Sharing to share the connection with the network. Remember to enable the Mac's firewall to protect it and your network from attacks from the Internet.

34

PART VII

MAC OS X: PROTECTING, MAINTAINING, AND REPAIRING YOUR MAC

CHAPTER 35

MAINTAINING AND PROTECTING YOUR MAC

In this chapter

KEEPING YOUR MAC SAFE AND IN GOOD WORKING CONDITION

Time and effort you have to spend troubleshooting problems is time and effort you don't have available to accomplish what you want to accomplish. To avoid having to spend time solving problems, you should take specific steps to maintain and protect your Mac. In this chapter, the following preventive activities are described:

- Maintaining your Mac in good working condition
- Securing your Mac so people who use the machine or the network to which it is attached don't accidentally or maliciously cause problems
- Defending your Mac from attacks from the Internet

MAINTAINING YOUR MAC

Maintaining your Mac in good condition isn't terribly difficult, and the effort you do put in will pay off in having to spend less time and effort solving problems. In this section, you will learn about the following maintenance tasks:

- Maintaining your system software
- Maintaining your hard disks
- Backing up your system
- Maintaining alternative startup volumes and discs
- Building and maintaining a Mac toolkit
- Maintaining your applications

USING SOFTWARE UPDATE TO MAINTAIN YOUR SOFTWARE

Apple continuously updates the OS (and other applications, such as the iLife applications) to solve problems, enhance performance, and introduce new features. Keeping track of the updates manually is time-consuming. Fortunately, you don't have to. You can use the Software Update tool (which consists of a pane in the System Preferences application and the Software Update application) to check, download, and install updates to Mac OS X and related software (such as firmware updates, updates to Apple applications you use, and so on).

CONFIGURING SOFTWARE UPDATE

To configure Software Update, follow these steps:

1. Open the System Preferences application, and then open the Software Update pane (see Figure 35.1).

Figure 35.1
The frequency with which you check for updates depends on your connection to the Net; for most people, weekly updates will be sufficient.

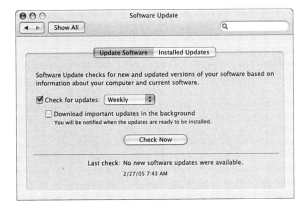

2. Use the check boxes, pop-up menu, and other buttons to configure the Software Update schedule (the options are described in the following bulleted list).

When configuring Software Update, you have the following options:

- **Manual or Automatic Updates**—Use the "Check for updates" check box to determine whether your system will automatically check for updates when you have a network connection. If you check this box, use the pop-up menu to set the frequency with which this checking is done. Your choices are Daily, Weekly, or Monthly.

- **Download Updates in Background**—If you check the "Download important updates in the background" check box, Software Update automatically (you have to select the automatic option for this option to be available) downloads important updates (such as updates to the OS) without bothering you first. When the update has been downloaded and is ready to be installed, you are prompted to start the installation process manually.

- **Check Now**—You can click the Check Now button to manually check for updates.

- **Installed Updates tab**—Here you can see the history of all the updates Software Update has installed for you. Click the tab to see the list of files that were changed and when the changes were made. If you click the "Open as Log File" button, you will see a Console window that provides the same list, but in a different format and in a bit more detail.

> **NOTE**
>
> Immediately installing available updates is not always a good idea. Sometimes, the updates are flawed, in which case the problems become known pretty quickly. If you want to avoid early adopter problems, you might want to wait a few days after an update is available before you install it on your Mac.

WORKING WITH SOFTWARE UPDATE

When an update is available and you haven't selected the "download in background" option (whether you check for them manually or automatically), the Software Update application will open (see Figure 35.2). In the top pane of the application's window is a list of all available updates. If you select an update, information about that update appears in the lower pane of the window. You can download and install one or more updates by checking the check box next to the updates you want to install and clicking the Install button or choosing a specific option from the Update menu.

Figure 35.2
The Software Update application manages the download and installation of available updates for you.

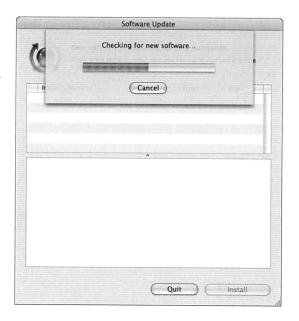

TIP

You can jump straight into the Software Update application (without opening the Software Update pane first) by selecting Apple menu, Software Update. The application will launch and immediately check for updates.

NOTE

As with other application installs, you have to authenticate yourself as an administrator to be able to install updates via Software Update.

When the Software Update application is open, you can select one of the following download options from the Update menu:

- **Download only**—This option causes the update to be downloaded to your Mac. You have to run the installer manually to install it. Updates are provided as packages you can run just like other application installers. These packages are stored in the Mac OS X/Library/Packages folder, where Mac OS X is the name of your Mac OS X startup volume. When you want to install the update, open this folder and run the update's installer. After the file has been downloaded, a Finder window showing the installer is opened so you can run it easily.

- **Install**—This one downloads and installs the update and then removes the package from your Mac.
- **Install and Keep Package**—This option downloads and installs the update, but it also keeps the package so you can install the update again later if you need to. The update's installer is located in the `Mac OS X/Library/Packages` folder, where `Mac OS X` is the name of your Mac OS X startup volume. You can run the installer again from this location.

TIP

If you have more than one Mac, the first or third option can be a good choice because you can put the updater on a CD and install it from there on each machine rather than downloading it to each machine one at a time.

NOTE

When you click the Install button, the Install option is selected. To select one of the other options, you must use the Update menu.

If you selected the "download in background" option, you won't see the Software Update application until the updates have been downloaded to your Mac.

Occasionally, updates are released that are of no value to you, such as updates for languages you don't use, devices you don't have, and so on. Software Update regularly reminds you of these updates until you download them. However, if you see an update that you are sure you won't want to download and install, you can have Software Update ignore that specific update. To do so, use the following steps:

NOTE

Ignoring an update removes it from the list of available updates. If you don't want to install a specific download, just uncheck its check box. To install that update, check its box before you click the Install button.

1. In the Software Update application, select the update you want to ignore.
2. Select Update, Ignore Update or press the Delete key.
3. Click OK in the resulting warning sheet. The update is removed and you will no longer be prompted to download the current or future versions of the update you ignored.

You can see ignored updates again by selecting Software Update, Reset Ignored Updates. All the updates you have ignored are added back to the Software Update application and you are prompted to download and install them again. You can't choose to restore a single update; you have to restore them all. Of course, you can choose to ignore specific updates again to remove them from the list.

35

NOTE

> Whether the "download in background" option is good for you or not mostly depends on the type of Internet connection you have. If you have a broadband connection, this option doesn't hurt because you aren't tying up your phone line while updates are downloading. You can just choose not to install any updates you don't want to. If you use a dial-up connection, it is better not to download updates in the background because some of the updates are quite large and you might tie up a phone line for a long time downloading an update you aren't going to install anyway.

After you have downloaded and installed an update, use the Installed Updates tab of the Software Update pane of the System Preferences application to verify that the updates were installed.

Seeing Installed Files

To view all installs that have been done on your Mac, including but not limited to software updates, open the folder `Mac OS X/Library/Receipts`, where `Mac OS X` is the name of your Mac OS X startup volume.

In this folder, you will see all the installs that have been performed on your Mac. Most are in `.pkg` files, but you can't open these to reinstall the software. Because they are receipts, they are for information purposes only.

NOTE

> If you want to manually check for Apple software updates, go to www.apple.com/support. Use the tools on the Apple Support pages to locate and download updates. For example, in the Downloads section, you will see a list of the current updates that are available.

MAINTAINING YOUR DISK DRIVES

Maintaining your disk drives will go a long way toward maximizing performance and preventing problems. You can use the Mac OS X Disk Utility application to do basic disk maintenance and repair. For maximum performance, you can also consider defragmenting and optimizing your disks.

CHECKING AND REPAIRING DISKS WITH DISK UTILITY

Among other things, the Disk Utility application (located in the Applications/Utilities folder) enables you to check for problems with your disks and then repair problems that are found.

To check and repair a volume, perform the following steps:

1. Launch Disk Utility. In the left pane of the window are all the disks mounted on your Mac, including drives installed in your computer and those that are connected via FireWire or USB. Each volume on each disk is listed under that disk's icon. You will also see any disk images that have been mounted on the machine.

NOTE
> Even if a disk has only one volume on it, you will see that volume listed under the disk's icon.

2. Highlight the disk, volume on a disk, or disk image you want to check. When you select a volume, a number of tabs appear in the right pane of the window. How many appear depends on what you select.

NOTE
> In this context, *volume* and *partition* are the same thing. When you partition a disk, each partition becomes a mounted volume on that disk.

If you select a hard disk, the following five tabs will appear: First Aid, Erase, Partition, RAID, and Restore.

If you select a mounted volume, CD, or DVD, you will see the following tabs: First Aid, Erase, RAID, and Restore.

If you select a disk image, the First Aid and Restore tabs will appear.

3. Check the bottom of the window for information about the disk, volume, disc, or image you selected. Again, what you see here depends on what you have selected.

If you select a hard drive, you see the disk type, connection bus (such ATA for internal drives or FireWire for an external drive), connection type (internal or external), connection ID, capacity, write status, and S.M.A.R.T. status; for most disks, the latter provides an indication of the disk's health (Verified if the disk is in good working condition or About to Fail if the disk has problems). (If a disk doesn't support S.M.A.R.T., the status will be Not Supported.)

If you select a volume, you will see various data about the volume, such as its mount point (the path to it), format, whether owners are enabled, the number of folders, the capacity, the amount of space available, the amount of space used, and the number of files it contains.

NOTE
> S.M.A.R.T. stands for self-monitoring analysis and reporting technology. Most modern disk drives support this technology, which means potential problems with a disk are identified and reported before the problem occurs. The goal of this technology is for you to be able to repair a disk before you lose any data or to at least transfer the data on that disk to another disk.

35

If you select a DVD or CD, you see the drive's specifications and the types of discs with which the drive can work.

If you select a disk image, you see its description, write status (mounted or not), connection bus, and where it is located (the path to it).

4. Click the First Aid tab to see some information explaining how Disk Utility works.

5. Click Repair Disk. The application will check the selected disk for problems and repair any it finds. As it works, you will see progress messages in the First Aid pane. When the process is complete, a report of the results appears (see Figure 35.3).

Figure 35.3
The selected disk appears to be okay.

→ To learn how to run a Unix disk repair utility during startup, **see** "Starting Up in Single-User Mode," **p. 245**.

You can choose to verify a volume rather than to repair it. When you do so, the application finds problems with the disk and reports back to you. You then have to tell the application to repair those problems. Generally, you should use the Repair button to save the extra step and because you will always choose to repair problems Disk Utility finds.

→ To learn how to use the Disk Utility to initialize and partition hard disks, **see** "Initializing and Partitioning a Hard Drive," **p. 898**.

You can also use Disk Utility to repair the permissions on the startup volume you are using. This can solve access problems with specific files on the machine when you don't have the required permissions. Do the following:

1. Select your current startup volume (if your startup disk has more than one volume, you have to select the startup volume, not the disk on which the volume is stored).

2. Click Repair Disk Permissions. The application will start searching for permission problems and repairing those it finds. As it works, you can view the status of the process in the window. When the process is complete, you see the results in the information window on the First Aid tab.

You can use the Verify Disk Permissions button to find permission problems. Then you have to tell the application to repair them. Like disk problems, you will almost always repair any problems the application finds, so you can save yourself a step by using the Repair button instead.

TIP

> Disk Utility has a toolbar, which you can configure by Control-clicking it and using the resulting pop-up menu to configure the toolbar.

ERASING DISKS WITH DISK UTILITY

You can also use Disk Utility to quickly erase and reformat volumes or erasable disks (such as CD-RW discs):

1. Select the disk or volume you want to erase.

2. Click the Erase tab.

3. Choose the format you want to use for the volume on the Volume Format pop-up menu. The format options are Mac OS Extended (Journaled), Mac OS Extended, Mac OS Extended (Case-sensitive, Journaled), Mac OS Extended (Case-sensitive), or UNIX File System. If you select a disk, you will also see the MS-DOS File System format.

4. Name the volume in the Name field.

5. If the "Install Mac OS 9 Disk Driver" check box appears (when you select a disk rather than a volume), uncheck it if you don't want Mac OS 9 drivers installed on the disk. This setting affects only the ability to use the disk or volume when the Mac is booted up under Mac OS 9. Classic is not affected.

TIP

> If you select a volume, you can use the Erase Free Space button to overwrite any data previously stored in that space without erasing the whole volume. This makes recovering the data that was stored in that space much more difficult or impossible. When you click the Erase Free Space button, you can use the resulting sheet to choose how you want to overwrite the free space.

35

6. Click the Security Options button. The Secure Erase Options sheet will appear. There are four options you can choose to determine how your Mac handles the data it is erasing. The "Don't Erase Data" option makes the data unviewable from the Finder but

leaves the data physically on the disk. As your Mac needs to write more files to the disk, it will overwrite the erased space. Until the data is overwritten, that data can be recovered (unerased) using an application designed to recover data. The "Zero Out Data" option writes zeros in all sectors on the disk. The "7-Pass Erase" writes random data over the entire disk 7 times, while the "35-Pass Erase" overwrites the disk 35 times. The purpose of the last three options is to prevent data on the disk from being restored after you erase it. For example, if you were transferring a Mac to someone else, you would want to select one of these options so that the data you had on the disk could not be recovered. The more overwrites you choose, the more secure the erase will be and the longer the process will take. If you are maintaining control of the disk, you probably don't need to choose one of the secure erase options, but using the "Zero Out Data" option doesn't add a lot of time to the process, so it isn't a bad choice. If you want to use one of these options, click its radio button and then click OK.

7. Click Erase. The confirmation sheet will appear; if you are sure you want to erase the disk, click Erase again. The drive's or volume's data is erased and is formatted with the options you selected.

> **TIP**
>
> You can get detailed information about a device or volume by selecting it and clicking the Info button on the toolbar.

ENABLING JOURNALING WITH DISK UTILITY

Under Mac OS X, disks can use the Mac OS (Journaled) file format. This format provides a journal function that tracks activity that has taken place in the main areas of the disk. This log helps re-create the data on the disk and makes repair operations more successful. In most cases, you should use this option because it gives you a better chance of recovering data and disks if you have problems. You can select the Journaled format when you erase a disk or volume, or you can enable journaling on an existing volume. To do the latter, use the following steps:

1. Select the volume on which you want to enable journaling.

2. Click the Enable Journaling button on the toolbar; select File, Enable Journaling; or press ⌘-J. The journaling information begins to be tracked for the selected disk or volume. (If this option is inactive, it means that journaling can't be activated on the current disk. You will have to reformat the disk to activate journaling.)

> **TIP**
>
> You can disable journaling again by selecting File, Disable Journaling.

DEFRAGMENTING AND OPTIMIZING YOUR HARD DISKS

As you save files to a disk (again, this means any kind of disk you have mounted on your Mac, except for CD-ROMs, DVD-ROMs, and other locked disks from which you can only read data), data is written to the disk. The Mac is also frequently writing other sorts of data (such as preference changes and other system-level data) to the startup disk. As data is written to a disk, it is written in the next available space (called a *block*). After the data is laid down, the Mac returns to what it what was doing. When it is time to save more data, the next batch is written in the next open space, and so on. Think of this as the Mac putting all the data down in a straight line (yes, the disk is round, but it is easier to think of it this way), one chunk after another.

As files are opened and closed, data from different files is laid down in the next available space so that, instead of all the data from one file being in a continuous block, it can be stored in blocks located in various spots around the disk. In this state, the data is *fragmented*. Although fragmentation is a normal part of the way disk drives function, excessive fragmentation can slow down the disk. Things slow down because the drive head must read data from all the blocks that make up a particular file. As those blocks become more numerous and are spread out around the disk, it takes longer and longer to read all the data for that file.

You use a process called *defragmentation* to correct this condition. You need a disk maintenance program to do this, such as Tech Tool Pro. What the defragmentation process does is pick up all the data blocks for each particular file and write them in a continuous block. It does this for every file on the disk. After the data is laid out nice and neat, the drive performs faster because it doesn't have to move as far to read and write the data for a particular file.

NOTE

To learn more about Tech Tool Pro, visit www.micromat.com.

Because a hard drive is made up of a round disk that spins at a constant speed, it takes longer to read and write data to various parts of the disk. Data near the center is read more quickly than data out near the rim. Data can be written to the disk in such a way that the access speed of the drive is *optimized*.

To do this, the data that is used constantly but not changed much—such as the system software and applications—are stored near the center of the disk. The documents and other data that are infrequently used are stored out toward the edge of the disk. This arrangement speeds up the disk because access to the most frequently used data is faster, and keeping the static data together means it will not become fragmented. Thus, the data is read and written in an optimized (for speed) fashion. You also need a disk maintenance tool to optimize a disk.

Usually, defragmentation and optimization are done at the same time using the same tool. The steps to perform these tasks depend on the particular software you use. Generally, this is not complicated and is a matter of choosing the drives you want to defragment and optimize and clicking Start.

35

NOTE

> Defragmentation and optimization are somewhat controversial topics. Many experts believe they do little to no good, while others believe you can gain some performance and reliability improvements by performing these tasks on your disks regularly. Personally, I think you can better spend your time by keeping your disks well organized and using Disk Utility to check them every so often than worrying about squeezing a few microseconds of performance out of them.

CLEANING UP YOUR DRIVES

You can do a lot for the performance of your disks by simply keeping them cleaned up. The more data on your drive, the less room you have to store new files. If your disks get too full, their performance slows down significantly. More data means there is more information for your Mac to manage, and thus it has to work harder. You can also run into all kinds of problems if you try to save files to disks that are full to the brim; how full this is depends on the size of the files with which you are working.

Learn and practice good work habits such as deleting files you don't need, uninstalling software you don't use, and archiving files you are done with (such as on a CD-R disc).

NOTE

> Many disk maintenance applications enable you to retrieve files you have deleted (an "undelete" or recover function). This is possible because during normal deletes (when you empty the Trash) the file is removed from the active system but might still exist on the disk in some form. The only way to be permanently rid of a file so it can't be recovered is to write over the area in which that file was stored with other data. To do this, you need an application that writes zeros or other bogus data over the location where the file you are deleting is stored. Typically, disk maintenance and other tools enable you to "really" delete files that you don't want to be able to be recovered. In Mac OS X, you can also do this by using the Finder's Secure Empty Trash command or by erasing a disk with Disk Utility.

MAINTAINING ALTERNATIVE STARTUP DISKS

One of the most important tasks you need to be able to do reliably and quickly is to start up from an alternative startup volume. There are several situations in which you might need to do this. For example, if you find problems on your current startup volume, you will need to start up from another volume to repair the startup volume. If something happens to your startup volume such that your Mac can no longer use it, you need to use an alternative startup volume to get your Mac running.

Several possibilities exist for alternative startup volumes; you should maintain at least one, and preferably two, of the following options:

- **Your Mac OS X installation disc**—You can always use the disc that contains the Mac OS X installer as a startup volume. It contains the basic software you need to start up your system and repair the system software it contains. The downside to this is that any updates you have applied to your active system are not included in the version on the installation disc. If the version of Disk Utility on the installation disc is too far removed from the version of the OS installed on your Mac, it is possible (but not likely unless you are using a very old installation disc) that Disk Utility on the disc will be incompatible with the OS version installed on your startup disc. You can't really use your Mac while it is started up with the Mac OS X installation disc. You can only install software or use Disk Utility and the other tools that are available on the Installer's menu.

■ **An alternative Mac OS X installation on a different volume**—You should install a backup installation of Mac OS X on a different volume from the one that you use for your primary system—if you can spare the disk space required to do so. Ideally, this alternative volume will be located on a separate disk (not just a separate volume) from your primary installation. For example, if you have an external FireWire hard drive, you can install Mac OS X on it so you can also use it as a startup disk.

TIP

> If you choose to install a backup version of Mac OS X on an alternative startup volume, you should delete any applications in that Mac OS X installation that you won't need when you are starting up from that volume. This will reduce the storage space it consumes. You also should start up from that volume and run Software Update every so often to keep the alternative startup volume's OS software current.

■ **Third-party application discs**—Many third-party applications, such as disk maintenance, antivirus, and backup software, include discs that contain system software you can use to start up your Mac. These discs also enable you to run the application software with the idea that you will be able to correct a problem that has prevented you from starting up your system from the primary startup volume.

To start up your Mac from an alternative volume, restart the machine and hold down the Option key. After a few moments, each valid startup volume appears. Select the volume from which you want to start up and press Return (or click the right-facing arrow). The volume you select will be used to start up your Mac. Depending on the type, such as a full installation of Mac OS X on a volume or the Mac OS X installation disc, you will be able to access various functionality from full Mac OS X capabilities (a full install on an alternative volume) or at least attempt to repair the startup volume itself (using the installation disc).

TIP

> You can refresh the list of available startup volumes by clicking the Refresh button (its icon is a curved line with an arrowhead).

NOTE

> As always, you can start up your Mac from a disc by holding down the C key while the machine is starting up.

35

BUILDING AND MAINTAINING A MAC TOOLKIT

One of the best maintenance-related tasks you can do is to assemble and maintain a Mac toolkit. In times of trouble, this toolkit can enable you to get back to work quickly. Not having to find your tools in times of trouble also reduces the stress you experience. Following are some fundamental items you should keep in your toolkit:

- **Your system configuration**—When you need help or are considering adding something to your system, having a detailed understanding of your system is very important. Use the System Profiler application (in the Applications/Utilities folder) to generate a report on your system. Print that report and keep it handy (in case you can't generate it when you need it).

→ For more information about Apple System Profiler, **see** "Using System Profiler to Create a System Profile," **p. 1050**.

- **Up-to-date backups**—Your toolkit should include everything you need to restore as much of your system as possible.

- **A disk maintenance application**—You need one of these applications to solve disk problems you might encounter. Examples are Disk Utility (included with Mac OS X) or Tech Tool Pro.

CAUTION

When selecting a disk maintenance application, make sure you get one that is written for the specific version of Mac OS X that you are using. Using one designed for an older version of the OS can be harmful to your Mac and its data.

- **An antivirus application**—You'll need this to protect your machine from infection and in the event that your system becomes infected.

- **Your Mac OS X installation disc**—Sometimes, this is the only thing that will get your Mac started again.

- **Your original application installers on CD or DVD (even if you downloaded the installer originally), serial or registration numbers, and updates**—You should maintain the current versions of all your applications by maintaining the discs on which they came. You should also create CDs or DVDs containing updates to those applications along with any applications you download from the Internet. Finally, be sure you have a list of the serial or registration numbers for your applications so you can restore them if needed. (You'll learn more about this in the next section.)

TIP

Consider devising some secure way to record passwords, usernames, serial numbers, and other critical data so you don't have to rely on memory to retrieve such information when you need it. Although keeping such information in hard copy is usually not advised, some people find it safer to develop and use some sort of code for this information and then have a hard copy of the encoded information handy.

35

MAINTAINING YOUR APPLICATIONS

Along with the system software, you should also maintain the applications you use. It is good practice to regularly check for updates for the applications on which you rely. There are several ways to do this, including the following:

NOTE

> Many applications include the capability to go online to check for updates, either automatically or manually. For example, most Adobe applications can check for updates to keep you informed when new versions or patches are available.

- **Software Update**—Mac OS X's Software Update function will also update any Apple software installed on your computer, such as the iLife applications.
- **Company mailing lists**—Some publishers maintain a mailing list for each application. Updates are announced in the mailing list, and the link to get to the update is provided.
- **Company websites**—Software publishers announce updates to their applications on their websites. Typically, you can check for and download updates from the Support area of a publisher's website.
- **Mac news**—Many Mac news sites and mailing lists include information about updates to popular applications.
- **Version Tracker**—Most Mac applications are listed on www.versiontracker.com. You should regularly check this site to look for application updates and patches.

NOTE

> As with the system software, it is sometimes wise to let a few days or a week pass after an update is released before you download and install it in case problems are introduced by the update.

You should also organize your applications and ensure that you have all the registration and serial number information you need for each application. It is amazing how easy it is to lose this information; getting it from the publisher can be a time-consuming task (and if you have to relicense the software, it can be expensive). Consider making a list of each application along with its serial number or registration number and keeping that list with the original installation discs or the discs containing the installers and updaters you make for your applications. When you need to reinstall an application, this list will be a great timesaver.

Downloading Applications

If you obtain an application by downloading it rather than getting it on a disc, you should store the application installer so that you can reinstall it even if the publisher withdraws the installer for some reason (for example, sometimes the installer for one version is removed if a newer version is released). You can save hard drive space by burning these installers on a DVD or CD disc and storing that disc with your other application discs.

You should also maintain the installer for any updates or patches you download and install so you can return the application to its current condition if anything happens to the version you have installed.

BACKING UP YOUR SYSTEM

If you use a computer, at some point, your system will crash, a disk will fail, or some other problem will happen (perhaps you will delete something you didn't mean to) and you will lose data you would rather not lose—maybe not today or tomorrow, but it *is* the inevitable nightmare. Think of the information you have on your Mac at this very moment that would be difficult—if not impossible—to reconstruct if your computer bombed and destroyed it. This data might be a report for work, a school project, your tax information, a complex spreadsheet, or even the great American novel on which you have been working. (For example, imagine that you have 2,000 photos in your iPhoto Library covering the last few years. Now imagine that the disk on which these images are stored dies. Losing all those pictures forever is not a pretty picture, is it?) Whatever the information, rest assured that some day, somewhere, somehow you will suddenly lose it. When that happens, you will want to be able to restore all the information on your Mac so you can quickly re-create your data. Backing up is the means by which you ensure that you can always preserve most of your work, no matter what happens to your Mac.

Backups: Insurance for Your Data
You need a good backup for more than just catastrophic failures of your hardware. I'll bet that you have accidentally deleted a file right before you needed it again. If you have a backup, you can quickly recover a document you accidentally delete. Or perhaps you edited a document and discovered that all your changes were actually worse than the original. You can use your backup to bring the file back to the way it was. If your Mac is ever stolen or destroyed, your backup will enable you to recover from potential disaster.

Although backing up your data is strongly recommended by computer authors, experts, and support personnel, it is a task that many Mac users never do for a variety of reasons. Some people don't back up data because they think their systems are infallible and won't crash. Still others are confused about how to make a backup of their system, or they lack the hardware and software necessary to maintain good backups. And then there are always those who simply don't believe that protecting their data is enough of a priority to waste their time on it.

However, because you are reading this book, I assume that you are serious about your Mac and recognize the value of a good backup system.

There are four steps to creating and implementing a solid backup system. These steps are the following:

- **Define a strategy**—You need to define your own backup strategy; your strategy should define the types of data you will back up and how often you will back up your data. These choices will guide you as you decide on the type of hardware and software you use.

- **Obtain and learn to use backup hardware**—You need some kind of hardware on which to store the backed-up data. Many types of hardware can be used, including tape drives, removable media drives, additional hard drives, DVD-R drives, or CD-RW drives.

- **Obtain and learn to use backup software**—Ideally, you should use some sort of software to automate the backup process. The easier you make it on yourself, the more likely it is that your backup system will work reliably.

- **Maintain your backup system**—Like all other systems, you need to maintain your backup system and ensure that your data is safe.

DEFINING A BACKUP STRATEGY

One of the first things you need to decide is what data on your machine will be backed up.

The three general categories of data you should consider backing up are

- **Documents, photos, movies, music, and other important data you create or purchase**—These items are, after all, the reason you use a Mac in the first place. You will want to back up all your own data because it doesn't exist anywhere other than on your computer. If you lose important data, it might be impossible to re-create. Even if you are able to re-create it, you will be wasting a lot of valuable time redoing what you have already done. Other data, such as your photos, simply can never be re-created. Still other data, such as music you have purchased from the iTunes Music Store, will cost money to replace.

- **System files**—You should have installation discs that contain your Mac OS software, so you usually don't risk losing the Mac OS software itself. What you do risk losing is any customization you have done, updates you have installed, and so on. If you have adjusted any settings or added any third-party software, all the settings you have changed will be lost in the event of a major failure.

  Additionally, don't forget about all the configuration information you have on your machine. For example, if you lose your system for some reason, you might lose all the configuration you have done to make your Mac connect to the Internet. You might also lose all the serial numbers of your software, which you will have to reenter if you need to reinstall it.

- **Applications and other third-party software**—As with the OS software, you probably have discs containing much of your third-party software. What you lose if you have a failure without a backup is the customization of those applications. Plus, you will have to reinstall that software—not an easy task if you have a lot of applications installed on your Mac. In any case, it can be very time-consuming to reinstall your applications. Don't forget about all the updates you have applied to these applications. If you lose your system, you'll have to do that all again, too.

NOTE

These days, you probably obtain a lot of your software by downloading it from the Net. If you lose the installers or patches you download without having a backup, you will have to download them again–assuming they are still available, of course. Sometimes, the version you want to use has been replaced by a newer version you don't want to use or pay for. (In my opinion, software companies should make older versions of

35

continues

continued

applications available to download to handle cases where you need to reinstall it, but not all of them do.) And, occasionally, software moves from shareware to commercial, in which case it becomes unavailable to download again without paying for it. You should keep backup copies of any software installers or updates you download so you can reinstall that software if you need to—whether it is still available from the original source.

In conjunction with the kind of files you will back up, several types of backups you can make include:

- **Full backup**—In a full backup, you back up each and every file on your system. The advantage of doing full backups is that restoring your entire system, as well as just particular parts of it, is possible.

- **Selected files only**—Using this scheme, you select particular files to back up; usually these are your important data (documents, photos, music, and so on) and some of your customization files (for example, preferences files). The advantage of this scheme is that you can make a backup quickly while protecting the most important files on your computer.

- **Incremental backup**—This scheme combines the first two techniques in that all files are backed up the first time, but after that, only files that have changed are backed up until the next full backup. This scheme protects all your files but avoids the time and space requirements of doing a full backup each time.

What you decide about the type of data you will back up and how you will back it up should determine the type of backup system you develop and use. For example, if you decide that you don't mind having to reinstall applications and reconfigure settings or you mainly use small document files, you might be able to simply copy your document files onto a CD-RW or other removable media drive. If you have a great deal of data to protect, you will need to implement a more sophisticated system.

If you can assemble the hardware and software to do incremental backups, you should use this approach. It is the only one that is practical for frequent backups and also protects all your data.

Ideally, you want your backup system to work without any supervision or intervention by you. This is called an *unattended* backup because you don't even need to be there for the system to work. You can set the system to automatically back up during times when you are not working on your Mac. This is not only convenient, but it also means that because you don't have to *do* anything, you can't forget or be too lazy to keep your backups up-to-date.

35

CHOOSING BACKUP HARDWARE

The hardware you use for your backup system is important because having hardware that doesn't match the types of backups you want to make will doom your backup plan to failure. For example, if you go with a dedicated back-up hard drive or tape drive, you will be able to do frequent, incremental backups. The easier and better you make your backup system, the less work you have to do with it, and the more likely it is that you will *do* the backups. Table 35.1 lists the major types of backup hardware and summarizes their advantages and disadvantages.

TABLE 35.1   BACKUP HARDWARE

Drive Type	Backup Capability	Advantages	Disadvantages
CD-R and CD-RW	Can handle large amounts of data for full and incremental backups.	Drive has multiple uses (mastering CDs for distribution, creating audio CDs, and so on). Data is easy to share and recover because all computers have CD-ROM drives. Provides nearly permanent storage; this is a good choice for archival purposes. Backups can be stored away from your Mac. CD-RW drives are standard on all modern Macs. Media is very inexpensive.	Capacity of individual discs is limited so unattended backups are not always possible. Relatively slow.

35

continues

TABLE 35.1 CONTINUED

Drive Type	Backup Capability	Advantages	Disadvantages
DVD-R and DVD-RW	Can store large amounts of data on each disc.	Even so, you can't store enough o make full, unattended backups in most cases. Media can be mounted in most Macs. Data is easy to share because most computers can read DVD discs. Provides nearly permanent storage; this is a good choice for archival purposes. Backups can be stored away from your Mac. Apple's SuperDrive is available on all Mac models. DVD-R and DVD-RW drives can be used for many purposes (burning DVD movie discs, restoring disks, and so on).	DVD-R media is not reusable. Media is relatively expensive for backup use. Relatively slow.
Hard drive	Depending on size, can handle large amounts of data for unattended full and incremental backups.	Very fast. Data is easily accessible. Drive can be mounted and used for other tasks. Backup drive is likely to be used for other purposes and thus might not be available for backing up. More difficult to store backups away from your Mac.	Relatively high cost per MB of data storage. Data is harder to share. Unlikely to have sufficient storage space to make full backups unless you purchase a dedicated backup drive.

Drive Type	Backup Capability	Advantages	Disadvantages
			Backup is subject to power surges and other outside causes of failure. Capacity can't be expanded.
Removable media (Zip, Jaz, SyQuest, and so on)	Depending on the drive type, can handle small to medium amounts of data.	Drives can be mounted and used for work as well as for backups. Can be used to easily share data with others. Backups can be stored away from your Mac.	Unlikely that a single disk will hold all the data on your Mac so full, unattended backups aren't possible. Magnetic storage devices can be affected by magnetic forces and will degrade over time Many lower-capacity disks (such as 250MB Zip disks) are required for large amounts of data. Few Macs have these drives.
Tape	Can handle large amounts of data for full and incremental backups.	Large storage capability is perfect for unattended backups. Media is inexpensive (for example, a Travan 20GB tape costs as little as $34). Backups can be stored away from your Mac. Difficult to share with others because a tape drive of the same format must be available.	Tape can't be mounted; a tape drive is a single-purpose device Tapes can be affected by magnetic forces and degrade over time Relatively slow. Drives can be expensive.

35

Table 35.1 lists many options, but a careful review of the table should reveal that there are really only four choices for a serious backup system: tape, hard drive, DVD-R, or CD-RW.

The following sections explains how I rate these options, in order of preference.

EXTERNAL FIREWIRE HARD DRIVES

Using a hard drive for backup provides the fastest performance, and you can usually get a drive large enough to store all the files needed to back up your primary drives (see Figure 35.4). You can easily configure automated backups so your data is constantly protected with no intervention on your part. And with FireWire, installing and using an external hard drive is literally a matter of connecting power to the drive, connecting the FireWire cable, and turning on the drive. That is all there is to it. Using a FireWire drive is simple. For performance and ease-of-use, a hard drive can't be beat.

Figure 35.4
The LaCie 500GB FireWire hard drive provides excellent performance and lots of room.

There are several significant disadvantages to using a hard drive to back up data. One is that you can't archive data on a hard drive; a hard drive can be used only for your current backups. Another is that you can't store the backup in an alternative location, nor can you create multiple backups (unless you want to invest in multiple drives). Still another is that the capacity of the drive is fixed; the only way to expand the capacity of your system is to add more drives. And, hard drives can fail due to the same reasons that a drive in your Mac can fail, in which case your backup becomes worthless.

Another downside is that you will be tempted to use the backup drive for additional purposes when your other drives get full. You might delete the backup "temporarily" while you work on another project. Guess when something will go wrong and you will need your backup?

Still, even with these drawbacks, I find a hard drive the most convenient option for daily, incremental backups.

TAPE DRIVES

From a purist's viewpoint, this option wins by a mile. When it comes to the sole function of backing up, nothing comes close to a tape drive. Because the capacity of each tape is so large, a single tape drive can handle unattended backups for all but medium or large networks (in which a more sophisticated system is required). And the media for a tape drive is relatively cheap, can be reused, and is portable.

The downside of a tape drive is that it serves a sole purpose, which is backing up (of course, this is also a positive because you won't ever be tempted to use it for something else).

Tape drives are available in many format and interface options, but they all work in a similar way. If you want the best backup system, consider adding a tape drive to your Mac.

DVD-R Drives

DVD-R discs provide a good amount of storage space on each disc (4.7GB). This is enough room to do full and incremental backups, although you probably won't be able to store an entire backup on a single disc. Another plus is that many Macs include a SuperDrive so you don't need to spend money on additional hardware to back up your system. DVD-R is an excellent option for archiving data and should provide good long-term storage for the data you don't need to work on any longer.

Of course, a DVD-R drive is also very useful for other purposes, such as for creating DVDs with iDVD.

CD-RW Drives

This option takes a distant fourth place, in my opinion. These drives are also useful for backup purposes because CD-R media is so inexpensive (about $.50 or less for 650MB) and because many Macs have a CD-RW drive built in. Plus, there are many other ways to use a CD-RW drive, such as creating audio CDs. Because every computer has a drive that can read CD-R discs, the data is very accessible.

However, even with these benefits, CD-RW drives are not an optimal choice for backing up. This is primarily because a CD holds only 650MB of data. Although that is a significant amount for everyday documents, it is inadequate for some types of projects. For example, when you consider iMovie projects, a single disc usually can't hold even one project. This means that unattended backups are usually not practical. Backing up an entire system on a CD-RW drive can take a long time, and you have to be there to swap new media in and out. And then, you have to manage the *many* discs that are required for your backups.

Still, if you already have a CD-RW, it is a good way to get your backup system started and to at least back up your documents.

CHOOSING BACKUP SOFTWARE

Backup software enables you to define which files will be backed up and how often the backup will be updated. It also enables you to restore your data when the time comes. The software should enable you to automate the process as well.

Although there are many choices on the hardware side, when it comes to backup software there are really only two options. The best option for Mac backup software is EMC Dantz

Corporation's Retrospect. If you are a .Mac user, you can get a copy of Apple's Backup for free. Though not as good as Retrospect, it is a fairly capable application.

NOTE

> Note that Retrospect comes in various flavors depending on what you are backing up. Retrospect Express Backup is targeted to individual users with relatively simply backup needs, whereas Retrospect Workgroup Backup can back up a networked workgroup.

Retrospect does only one thing: It helps you create, implement, and maintain backups. Although limited in scope, Retrospect excels in function; it is a must-have piece of software. It is easy to use, yet it includes all the functions you need to establish and automate your backup strategy. If you intend to back up your Mac in the most effective way possible, you simply must use Retrospect.

Unfortunately, I don't have the space to explain how to use Retrospect, but suffice it to say that this software is extremely well designed and excellently implemented. After you install and configure it, it is so good that you won't have to deal with it very much (which should be a goal for any backup system).

Even better, many tape and other backup drives include this software, so you get everything you need for your backup system in one package.

To learn about EMC Dantz and Retrospect, check out www.dantz.com (see Figure 35.5). You can get your questions about backing up your system answered there. I have been a customer for years and have been amazed by the exceptional support this company offers.

Figure 35.5
When it comes to Mac backup software, EMC Dantz's Retrospect is as good as it gets.

If you have a .Mac account, you can download and use Apple's Backup application. This application provides good backup capabilities. In addition to being able to back up to CD or DVD, you can back up your files to your iDisk (which takes the idea of remote storage of your data to a new level). You can also automate your backups. The application is simple to use and is free to anyone who has a .Mac account.

To learn about Backup, visit www.mac.com. If you have a .Mac account, you can download a copy of the software for free.

USING A BACKUP SYSTEM

I can't emphasize enough how important it is to maintain good backups for your data. Here are a few tips to keep in mind:

- **Develop your own strategy based on the hardware and software you have or can afford to purchase**—At the least, make sure your critical data files are protected.

- **Make sure that backing up is easy**—If you have to do a lot of work to back up or if it takes a lot of your time, you won't end up keeping up-to-date backups. Ideally, you want to be able to do unattended backups; a hard or tape drive and a copy of Retrospect are your best bet.

- **Be consistent**—Whatever strategy you decide on, keep up with it. Old, out-of-date backups are not much better than no backups.

- **Always refresh your backups before you install any new software or make major changes to your system**—This will enable you to recover data if the changes you make to your system cause problems.

- **Be sure to test your backups regularly**—Try to restore a file or two to ensure that everything is working properly. If you don't, you might get a nasty surprise when you really need to restore some data.

- **Maintain your equipment**—Almost all equipment needs some kind of maintenance now and again, so follow the manufacturer's guidelines to keep your system in top condition.

- **Maintain more than one set of backups**—Create multiple copies of your backups in case something happens to one set.

- **Keep a set of backups offsite**—Keep a copy of your backups in a different location than your Mac is in. This will save you in the event of a catastrophic event such as fire or theft.

> **NOTE**
>
> Archiving is slightly different from backing up. Backing up is done mostly for the "active" data on your Mac, whereas archiving is done with data you don't really need to work with anymore. Fortunately, you can use your backup system to archive data as well. For archiving smaller documents, a CD-RW drive is a good choice because the media is very cheap and relatively permanent. For larger amounts of data, a DVD-R disc is a good way to archive. When you archive, you should use a solution that won't degrade over time. In this case, an optical media is a better choice than magnetic media, such as a tape.

35

Restoring a Disk or Files

Using Disk Utility, you can create and save a disk image of a folder, volume, or disk. (A disk image is a file type that can be mounted and used just like a physical volume, such as a hard drive.) You can then use Disk Utility's Restore feature to restore the entire volume or specific files that are part of that disk image. This is, in effect, backing up specific parts of your system. You can choose folders, volumes, or an entire disk. To do this, you first use Disk Utility to create a disk image of the volume or folder you want to back up.

When you need to restore a file, you select the disk image you created and use the Restore tab to restore it or specific files it contains.

Although this approach has the benefit of using tools always available under Mac OS X, it does have several major drawbacks. This first is that you have to manually update the disk images you save. The second is that you still have to have the space to store those images (of course, you don't want to store them on the same volume as the files they include). However, you can use this technique to back up files if you don't have a better solution or to archive them. For example, you might want to use this technique to archive your iTunes music files, especially those you've purchased from the iTunes Music Store.

SECURING YOUR MAC

An important preventive maintenance task is to protect your Mac from other people who use it or from those who access its files from a network. You can also use the security pane of the System Preferences application, the secure delete trash function, and keychains to help you protect your Mac's security.

SECURING YOUR MAC WITH USER ACCOUNTS

You should create user accounts for everyone who uses your Mac. In addition to the features user accounts provide, such as a website and well-organized file storage, user accounts prevent unauthorized users from changing the system configuration of your machine.

→ To learn how to create and configure user accounts, **see** "Creating User Accounts," **p. 26**.

SECURING YOUR MAC WITH PRIVILEGES

For those who access your Mac over a network and for those who share your machine, you can control the access to specific items by setting privileges for those items. You can control access in several levels of privilege from not being able to even see the item to being able to read and write to it.

→ To learn how to configure privileges, **see** Chapter 33, "Building and Using a Network," **p. 935**.

SECURING YOUR MAC WITH THE SECURITY PANE

The Security pane of the System Preferences application enables you to protect your Mac in a couple of ways. One is by using the FileVault feature that encrypts all the files in your Home folder; these files can't be used unless you input your login password or the master password for your Mac. The other way is by configuring various security settings for your Mac.

SECURING YOUR MAC WITH FILEVAULT

Mac OS X's FileVault feature encrypts all the files in your Home folder with 128-bit encryption. Such files can't be opened unless one of two passwords is entered. One password is the one you use to log in to your account. The other is a master password you set for your Mac; with this password, you can decrypt any encrypted files on your Mac, regardless of the user account with which those files are associated.

Once configured, FileVault works in the background and you won't notice it doing its job.

CAUTION

According to Apple, FileVault can interfere with backups because it makes your Home folder appear as a single file to the backup system. This can make the individual files impossible to restore. When using FileVault, be sure you test your backup system to ensure that you can still recover files if you need to.

The following steps demonstrate how to configure FileVault:

1. Open the System Preferences application and click the Security icon. The Security pane will appear (see Figure 35.6).

Figure 35.6
Use the FileVault feature if you want to encrypt the files in your Home folder so they can't be used without a valid password.

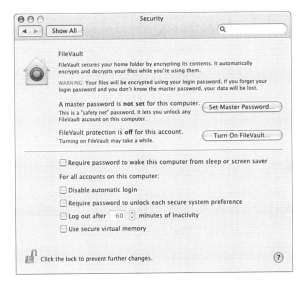

2. Click the Set Master Password button. The master password sheet will open. Generally, you should use this feature if there is some chance that any user of your Mac will forget his password; the master password enables you to decrypt encrypted files for all users. You must create a master password before you can activate FileVault.

3. Enter the master password in the Master Password field and enter it again in the Verify field.

35

TIP

> Click the ? next to the Master Password box to open the Password Assistant. You can use this tool to generate passwords based on specific criteria, such as type and length. When you have configured a password, it will be placed in the box for you. You then have to type it in the Verify box.

4. Enter a hint for the master password in the Hint field.

5. Click Continue to set the master password.

NOTE

> To use FileVault, a user account must have a password. If you didn't configure a password for your user account, or for any other user account, you will need to do so before you can activate FileVault.

6. Click the Turn On FileVault button. If there currently isn't a password for the user account, you can use the Password sheet to create one. The warning sheet will appear. If the user account already has a password, the service starts up and you are prompted to enter your password.

7. Enter your user account's login password and click OK. You will see a warning sheet that explains what you are doing and that activating this service can take a while (you can't log out of your account until the service has been turned on).

NOTE

> If you also want Secure Erase (which overwrites deleted data so that it can't be recovered as easily), check the "Use secure erase" check box.

8. Click the Turn On FileVault button. The FileVault window appears; you can't do anything else on your Mac until FileVault has started up. This window shows you the progress of the encryption process. If you have a lot of data in your Home folder, this process can take quite some time. When the process is complete, you see the Login window.

NOTE

> If you want this feature to be active for multiple user accounts, you must log in under each account and turn on FileVault.

9. Log back in to your account. You shouldn't notice any difference, but all your Home folder files will be encrypted and won't be accessible unless a valid encryption password has been entered.

CAUTION

FileVault applies only to each user account in which it is activated. And it works only on the files in each user's Home folder. Files stored outside the Home folders for which it is activated are not protected.

When you log in to your account (or any other user whose account is protected by FileVault), the files in your Home folder are decrypted automatically so you won't need to do anything else to access them. The value of FileVault is for those times when you aren't logged in to your account and someone else has access to your machine. For example, suppose someone steals your PowerBook. Although she can't access your user account without your login password, she could connect the machine to a FireWire drive with Mac OS X installed and start up from that volume. Because the files on your PowerBook's startup volume are not protected anymore (the OS on the FireWire drive is active), they are accessible. If FileVault is not on, these files are not encrypted and can be used, but if FileVault is on, these files are encrypted and are useless.

You can turn off FileVault again by clicking the Turn Off FileVault button and entering your login password.

If another user on your Mac turns on FileVault and subsequently forgets her password, you can use your Mac's master password (assuming you set one) to decrypt the files in that user's Home folder. You can provide the master password to the other user so they can decrypt their files. Then, change the master password to make sure only the "right" people have it.

NOTE

When a user account is protected by FileVault, its Home folder icon looks like a cross between the normal Home folder icon and a safe.

SECURING YOUR MAC WITH SECURITY SETTINGS

Several other security settings are available on the Security pane (refer to Figure 35.6). These features are described in the following list:

- **Require password to wake this computer from sleep or screen saver**—If you enable this feature, a user account's login password is required to stop the screensaver or wake up the Mac from sleep. This setting impacts only the account currently active; if you want this to be required for each user account, you need to log in to each one and set it for that account.

- **Disable automatic login**—Check this box and the automatic login feature is turned off. This means that someone will have to log in into your Mac manually to be able to use it.

- **Require password to unlock each secure system preference**—When you check this box, a login password must be entered to make any changes that affect system security.

- **Log out after _ minutes of activity**—This feature logs out the current user account after the specified amount of inactivity has occurred. To use it, check the box and set

35

the amount of time using the box. When the amount of inactive time passes, the current user is logged out automatically.

- **Use secure virtual memory**—When this feature is active, data written to disk when virtual memory is required is also stored securely.

SECURING YOUR MAC BY REMOVING TRASH SECURELY

Normally, when you delete files they are deleted from the system, but the data for those files might or might not be overwritten by other data. If not, files can sometimes be recovered by software restoration tools. If you want the files you delete to be overwritten with system-generated data so they can't be recovered, use the Secure Empty Trash command on the Finder's File menu instead of the normal Empty Trash command. This causes the files you delete to be overwritten so they can't be recovered.

SECURING YOUR MAC WITH KEYCHAINS

For security and other reasons (such as making online shopping more convenient), you need usernames and passwords to access network resources, whether those resources are on a local network or the Internet. After using even a few of these, you will have a large collection of usernames and passwords. Remembering these can be a challenge. Fortunately, your Mac lets you store all your usernames and passwords in a keychain. You can then apply your keychain to whatever resource you want, to use and the appropriate information is provided so you can access what you need. All you need to remember is the password that unlocks your keychain. By default, this is the same as your login password so that your keychain is used automatically. After you have added a password to your keychain, you can access the related resources without entering your keychain's password (because it is entered when you log in).

NOTE

> Safari can also remember usernames and passwords for sites you visit so you don't have to enter this information each time you log in. This saves a lot of time and keystrokes (assuming you can even remember all your usernames and passwords, of course). What actually happens is that Safari creates an item within the Passwords category in which all your web username and passwords are stored. When you return to a page for which you have had Safari remember your login information, it uses the data stored in the keychain to input the appropriate information for you.

→ For more information about Safari and keychains, **see** "Browsing the Web with Safari," **p. 460**.

You can configure other keychains so that you can gain automatic access to secured resources during each working session. To secure those resources again, you can lock your keychain, which means the password must be entered for that keychain to be applied.

Before you can use a keychain, one has to be created. A keychain is created automatically for each user account you create. However, you can create additional keychains for specific purposes if you need to.

To use a keychain, it must be unlocked. To unlock a keychain, you enter its password when you are prompted to do so. When you log in to your user account, the default keychain for that account is unlocked automatically.

> You can store information that you want to secure using notes. For example, if you want to store your credit card information so it can't be accessed unless you are logged in to your user account, you can add it to your keychain. When you need that information, you can open the secured note containing your credit card information in your keychain.

Many types of resources can be added to your keychain to enable you to access them, including the following:

- **AirPort network password**—When you add an Airport network password to your keychain, you can join the network by selecting it via the AirPort controls. The network's password will be added to your keychain automatically.

- **Application password**—Some applications require passwords to perform specific tasks. One notable example is the iTunes Music Store function. When you have your iTunes Music Store password added to your keychain, you can purchase songs with a single click of the mouse button (which can be a dangerous thing!).

- **AppleShare password**—Any passwords you use to access network volumes can also be added to your keychain.

- **Internet password**—When you need to enter passwords for Internet services, such as email accounts, adding them to your keychain makes accessing those services much more convenient because you never have to enter the password manually.

- **.Mac password**—When you enter your .Mac password in the .Mac pane of the System Preferences application, it is added to your keychain so you can work with your iDisk from the desktop without having to log in to your .Mac account each time.

- **Secure note**—These enable you to store information securely.

- **Web form password**—When you access your account on secure websites, you can add your usernames and passwords to your keychain. When you visit those sites again (via Safari), you can log in just by clicking the Login button because your username and password are entered automatically.

VIEWING AND CONFIGURING YOUR KEYCHAINS AND KEYCHAIN ITEMS

You access your keychains through the Keychain Access application by doing the following:

1. Open the Keychain Access application (Applications/Utilities folder). When the application opens, two panes appear (see Figure 35.7). In the left pane (the drawer) is a list of categories for all the keychains that are installed under your user account. These categories include All Items, which contains all keychain items you can access; Passwords, which contains passwords for network and other resources; and so on. Select a category and the keychain items it contains will appear in the right pane of the window. You will

see information related to each keychain item, such as its name, its kind, the date it was last modified, and the keychain in which it is stored.

Figure 35.7
This user can access several items stored in the selected keychain, including a network password and a secured note.

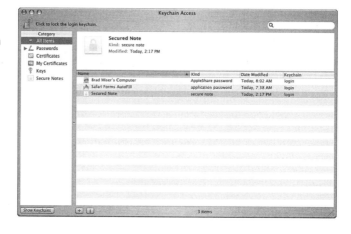

TIP

The Passwords category contains several subcategories. To view them, expand that category by clicking its expansion triangle.

2. To view all the keychains your user account can access, click the Show Keychains button at the bottom of the Keychain Access window (see Figure 35.8).

Figure 35.8
Here, you can see that this user has several keychains available; only the Login keychain is currently unlocked.

3. To get detailed information about a keychain item, select it. A summary of the item will appear at the top of the window and will list the kind of item it is, the user account with which it is associated, where the location to which it relates is, and the modification data.

4. With the item still selected, click the Information button (the *i* located at the bottom of the Keychain Access window). The Information window will appear. This window has

two tabs: Attributes and Access Control (see Figure 35.9). The Attributes tab presents various information about the item, such as its name, its kind, the account, the location of the resource with which it is associated, comments you have entered, and the password (which is hidden when you first view an item). The Access Control tab enables you to configure how the item is used.

Figure 35.9
The Information window provides detailed information about a keychain item.

5. To see the item's password, check the "Show password" check box. You are then prompted to confirm the keychain's password (you'll learn more about this in the next section).

6. Confirm the password by entering it at the prompt and choosing to allow access to the item (the options you see are explained in the next section). When you return to the Attributes tab, you will see the item's password.

7. Click the Access Control tab. You will see a list of the applications that have access to the keychain item. Use the access controls in the window to control which applications can access this item and how they can access it.

8. To allow access to the item by all applications, check the "Allow all applications to access this item" radio button. You will see a warning that access to the item is not restricted. This means that all applications will be able to use the item. With this option, you can't configure the other options because they don't apply. If you want to configure access for specific applications, continue with the rest of these steps.

9. To allow access by specific applications but require confirmation, click the "Confirm before allowing access" radio button, and check the "Ask for Keychain password" check box if you want to be prompted for your keychain's password before access is allowed (if you don't select this option, the item will be accessed automatically).

10. To enable an application not currently on the list to access the keychain item, click the Add button (the + located at the bottom of the application list) and select the application to which you want to provide access.

11. To remove an application's access to the item, select the application and click Remove (the - located at the bottom of the application list).

12. Click Save to save the changes to the keychain and its items.

35

ADDING ITEMS TO A KEYCHAIN

You can add items to a keychain in several ways, including the following:

- When you access a resource that can provide access to a keychain, such as a file server, look for the "Add to Keychain" check box. When you check this, an item for that resource is added to your keychain. This is the most common and easiest way to add items to a keychain.

NOTE

Sometimes you have to click the Options button to be able to add an item to your keychain. For example, when you mount a network volume, click Options to reveal the Add Password to Keychain check box.

- Drag a network server onto the Keychain Access window.
- Drag the Internet Resource Locator file for a web page onto the Keychain Access window.
- Manually create an item.

CAUTION

Not all applications support keychain access. If a particular application or resource doesn't support keychains, you won't be able to access that resource automatically. However, you can still use Keychain Access to store such an item's username and password for you, thus enabling you to recall that information easily. This also stores it more securely than writing it down on a piece of paper.

To manually add a password item to your keychain, perform the following steps:

1. Open Keychain Access (Applications/Utilities).
2. View the keychains installed for your user account and select the keychain to which you want to add the item (your default keychain, which is the login keychain unless you have changed it, is selected automatically).
3. Select File, New Password Item or press ⌘-N to see the New Password Item sheet.
4. Enter the name of the item in the Keychain Item Name box. If you are adding an Internet resource, such as a web page, enter its URL.
5. Enter the account name or username for the item in the Account box. This is the name of the user account with which the keychain item will be associated.
6. Enter the password for the item in the Password box. If you want to see the password as you type it, check the Show Typing check box. This helps you confirm you are entering the correct password. Otherwise, you see only bullets as you type.

> **TIP**
>
> Click the Key button to open the Password Assistant to help you configure a password for the item.

7. Click Add to return to the keychain's window and see the new item you added. You will be able to access that item using your keychain. You can view and configure the new item using the steps in the previous section.

> **TIP**
>
> You can set the default keychain for your user account by selecting the keychain you want to make the default one and choosing File, Make Keychain *keychainname* Default, where *keychainname* is the name of the keychain you have selected.

To add a secure note to a keychain, use the following steps:

1. Open Keychain Access.
2. Select the keychain to which you want to add the note (your default keychain is selected automatically).

> **NOTE**
>
> If you select a keychain that is currently locked, you will have to unlock it before you can add items to it.

3. Select File, New Secure Note Item or press Shift-[cmd]-N. The New Secured Note sheet will appear.
4. Enter the name of the note in the Keychain Item Name box.
5. Enter the information you want to store in the Note box. This a freeform text field so you can enter anything you want.
7. Click Add to return to the Keychain Access window where you will see the new note you added.
8. To view the note, double-click it and click the "Show note" check box. You will see the note in the window.

ADDING A KEYCHAIN

You might want to add a keychain to your current account, which you can do using the following steps:

> **NOTE**
>
> You might want to move a keychain between user accounts so you don't have to re-create the items it contains.

35

1. Open Keychain Access (Applications/Utilities).

2. To add a keychain, select File, New Keychain or press Option-⌘-N. You will see the New Keychain dialog box.

3. Move to the location in which you want to save the keychain, name it, and click Create. (By default, keychains are stored in the Keychains folder in the Library folder in your Home folder. In most cases, you should store new keychains in this folder.) You are prompted to create the password for the keychain.

> **TIP**
>
> An exception to where you keep your keychains might be when you want to enable others to import your new keychain into their accounts, in which case you should store it in a location accessible to others, such as your Public folder. For example, you might want to create a keychain with website items on it. You could provide this to other users who would then be able to access the items contained in the keychains you install.

4. Enter the password for the keychain in the Password and Verify fields; then click OK. The new keychain is added to the list of available keychains, and you can work with it just like those already on the list.

> **TIP**
>
> Click the Key button to open the Password Assistant to use it to create a password for the keychain you are creating.

USING KEYCHAINS

When you have a keychain configured for an account and it is unlocked, you can access the items it contains without entering your username or password. For example, when you open a server, it opens for you immediately.

> **NOTE**
>
> By the way, this is how Mac OS X can access your .Mac account without you having to log in each time. When you create a .Mac account, it is added to the keychain for the Mac OS X user account related to it. Mac OS X can use this keychain to access the .Mac account without requiring that you log in manually.

To prevent a keychain from being accessed, lock it. Do so by opening the Keychain Access application, selecting the keychain, and selecting File, Lock Keychain *keychainname*, where *keychainname* is the name of the keychain. You can also do so by pressing ⌘-L or clicking the Lock button (the padlock) on the toolbar.

To unlock a keychain again, select it, click the Unlock button or press ⌘-L, enter the password for that keychain, and click OK.

When an application needs to access a keychain item and it is not configured to always allow access, you will see the Confirm Access to Keychain dialog box that prompts you to enter a keychain's password and choose an access option. When prompted, you have the following three options:

- **Deny**—If you click this, access to the item is prevented.
- **Allow Once**—A single access to the item is allowed. The next time you attempt to access it, you see the prompt again.
- **Always Allow**—Access to the item is always allowed.

NOTE

> The first time you access keychain items after the OS has been updated, such as through the Software Update application, you see the Confirm Access to Keychain prompt, even for those items for which you have selected the "always allow access" option (such as the first time you check your email after upgrading the OS). This is normal behavior. Just select the Always Allow option to reenable that behavior.

GOING FURTHER WITH KEYCHAINS

Keychain Access is actually a fairly complex application that can do more than just what I have room to show you in this section. Following are some pointers in case you are interested in exploring on your own:

- Your keychains are stored in the `Library/Keychains` folder in your Home directory. You can add a keychain from one account to another account by exporting the keychain file (use the File, Export command) to a location that can be accessed by the second account. (For example, you can copy your keychain into the Public folder of your Home directory to enable other users to add that keychain to their own accounts.) To add a keychain to a user account, open Keychain Access under that account and use the File, Import command. This is useful if you want to use the same keychain from several accounts. You can't export all keychains, so you have to try one to see whether you can export it.

- Delete a keychain either by selecting it and selecting File, Delete Keychain *keychainname*, where *keychainname* is the name of the keychain.

- If you select Edit, Change Settings for Keychain *keychainname*, where *keychainname* is the name of the keychain, you can set a keychain to lock after a specified period of time or lock when the Mac is asleep.

- You can synchronize keychains on different computers by using .Mac.

- If you select Edit, Change Password for Keychain *keychainname*, where *keychainname* is the name of the keychain, you can change a keychain's password.

- Choose Keychain Access, Preferences. On the General tab, check "Show Status in Menu Bar." This will add the Keychain Access menu to the Mac's menu bar. From this menu, you can lock or unlock keychains and access security preferences and the Keychain Access application.

35

- If you select Edit, Keychain List or press Option-⌘-L, you see the Configure Keychain sheet. You can use this to configure keychains for a user account or the system. For example, you can check the Shared check box to share a keychain between user accounts.

- If you select Keychain Access, Keychain First Aid or press Option-⌘-A, you see the Keychain First Aid dialog box. You can use this to verify keychains or repair a damaged keychain.

- In the keychain access prompt, you can click the Show Details button to expose the details of the keychain access being requested.

DEFENDING YOUR MAC FROM NET ATTACKS

The Internet is a major source of threat to the health and well-being of your Macs and the network to which they are connected. You face two fundamental types of threats: viruses and hackers. Although viruses receive more media attention, defending against viruses is easier than defending against attacks from hackers. However, with some relatively simple activity, you can protect yourself from both threats.

DEFENDING YOUR MAC FROM VIRUS ATTACKS

No matter what level of computer user you are, because of the extensive media hype about viruses, you are likely to be keenly aware of them. Although many viruses are relatively harmless, some viruses can do damage to your machine. Part of practicing smart computing is understanding viruses and taking appropriate steps to protect your machine from them.

CAUTION

> Under previous versions of the Mac OS, there were many fewer viruses on the Mac platform than for Windows or other operating systems. And, as of the release of Mac OS X, version 10.4, this is still the case. However, because Mac OS X is based on Unix, Unix viruses can be a threat to machines running Mac OS X. Until this threat is more fully understood, Mac OS X users would do well to pay additional attention to virus threats.

UNDERSTANDING THE TYPES OF VIRUSES

Although there are many types of individual viruses, there are two major groups of viruses of which you need to be aware:

- **Application viruses**—These viruses are applications that do *something* to your computer. What they do might be as harmless as displaying a silly message or as harmful as corrupting particular files on your hard drive.

- **Macro viruses**—A macro virus can be created in and launched by any application that supports macros (such as the Microsoft Office applications). When you open a file that has been infected by a macro virus, that virus (the macro) runs and performs its dirty deed.

Covering the multitude of viruses that are out there is beyond the scope of this book and, besides, there is no real need to become an expert on the viruses that exist. It is more important to understand how to protect yourself from these viruses and be able to recover from an infection should one occur.

PREVENTING VIRUS INFECTION

I hate to use this cliché, but when it comes to viruses, an ounce of prevention is indeed worth a pound of cure. The main way to avoid viruses is to avoid files that are likely to have viruses in them. Following are some practices to help you "stay clean":

- Find and use a good antivirus software program; keep the virus definitions for that application up-to-date.

- Be wary when you download files from any source, particularly email. Even if an email is apparently from someone you know, that doesn't mean the attachments it contains are safe. Some users will unknowingly transmit infected files to you (especially beginning users). Some viruses can use an email application to replicate themselves. Before you open any attachment, be sure it makes sense given who the sender appears to be.

- When you do download files, download them from reputable sites, such as magazine sites or directly from a software publisher's site. These sites scan files for viruses before making them available so your chances of getting an infected file are lower. Remember the expression, "Consider the source."

- After you download a file, run your antivirus software on it to ensure that it isn't infected. Most programs let you designate the folder into which you download files and automatically check files in this folder.

IDENTIFYING VIRUS INFECTION

Even with good preventive measures, your Mac might occasionally become infected. Hopefully, you will find out you have been infected by being notified by your antivirus software—that means it is doing its job. But if you suddenly notice that your computer is acting peculiarly, you might have become infected. What does acting peculiarly mean? Viruses can have many different effects on your computer; some of the more common effects are the following:

- **Weird messages, dialog boxes, or other unexpected interface elements—** Sometimes viruses make themselves known by presenting something odd onscreen. So, if you suddenly see a strange dialog box, you might have stumbled across a virus (for example, one of the Word macro viruses causes a happy face to appear in Word's menu bar). They can also cause menu items to disappear or be changed in some way.

- **Loss in speed**—Viruses often make your computer work more slowly.

- **Disappearing files**—Some viruses cause files to be deleted or hidden.

- **Errors**—Many viruses cause various errors on your computer and prevent applications from working properly. If you haven't changed anything on your machine for a while

35

and you suddenly start experiencing errors, you should check your computer for a possible infection.

USING ANTIVIRUS SOFTWARE

Although the best defense against viruses is being very careful about the files you transfer onto your machine, you should also obtain and use a good antivirus application. Good antivirus applications generally perform the following functions:

- Monitor activity on your computer to identify potential infection
- Periodically scan your drives to look for infections
- Notify you if an infection is discovered
- Repair the infected files and eliminate the virus
- Delete infected files if repairing them is impossible
- Enable you to identify particular folders that should be scanned automatically, such as the folder into which you download files
- Update themselves automatically

> **NOTE**
>
> Most viruses are identified by their code. The antivirus software knows about the virus's code through its virus definition file. As new viruses appear, this virus definition file needs to be updated so that the new viruses will be recognized as being viruses. You can usually obtain an updated virus definition file from the website of the manufacturer of your antivirus software. Most programs automate this process and can update the virus definition at intervals you set.

> **NOTE**
>
> One of the important things to look for in an antivirus program is that it can detect and repair macro viruses. Macro viruses are easy to create and spread, and some of them are quite nasty.

As with previous versions of the Mac OS, there are several major antivirus applications, including Norton AntiVirus for Mac and Virex.

These applications provide most of the features in the previous list, and they work well. You should obtain and use one of these applications to protect your Mac against viruses and to repair your Mac should it become infected.

If you have a .Mac account, you can download a free copy of Virex. When you download and install Virex, you can keep its virus definitions current and access other virus resources as well.

To get more information about Virex and to download it (if you have a .Mac account), visit www.mac.com and click the .Mac tab.

Viruses and You

Frankly, viruses are less of a problem than they appear to be from the tremendous amount of media hype they receive, especially for Mac users. Most of the time, you can protect yourself from viruses by being very careful about the files you receive in email or download from the Web. Because the only way for a virus to get onto your machine is for you to accept a file in which it is contained, you can protect yourself from most viruses by using common sense. For example, if you receive an email containing an oddly titled attachment (such as the famous I Love You file), you should either request more information from the sender before you open the file or simply delete the message.

This is one case is which being in the minority as a Mac user is beneficial. The vast majority of viruses are designed for Windows machines and have no affect on a Mac.

Adding and using an antivirus application makes your machine even safer, but if you are very careful about downloading files, you might find that you can get by just fine without one.

DEFENDING YOUR MAC AGAINST NET HACKERS

If you have a broadband connection to the Internet such as a cable or DSL modem, being attacked by hackers is a much more real threat than are viruses. And with a broadband connection, you *will* be attacked, daily if not hourly or even more frequently. Hackers are continuously looking for machines they can exploit, either to do damage to you or to use your machine to do damage to others (such as using your machine to launch a spam attack). Most of these attacks are carried out by applications, so they can be both automatic and continuous.

CAUTION

> Never expose a machine containing sensitive or production data to a broadband connection without protecting that machine from network attack. Doing so makes everything on such a machine vulnerable to exposure to a hacker, and the machine itself can be used to carry out attacks on other networks and machines.

There are two fundamental ways you can prevent your Mac from being hacked through your broadband Internet connection: Use a server/hub to isolate the machines on your network from the outside world or use a software firewall to protect each machine on the network from attack.

USING A SERVER AND FIREWALL TO PROTECT YOUR NETWORK

You can isolate the machines on your network from attack by placing a physical barrier between them and the public Internet. You can then use a Dynamic Host Configuration Protocol (DHCP) server that provides network address translation (NAT) protection for your network, or you can add or use a hub that contains a more sophisticated firewall to ensure that your network can't be violated. A benefit to these devices is that you can also use them to share a single Internet connection.

→ To learn how to install and use a DHCP server or firewall, **see** Chapter 34, "Sharing an Internet Connection," **p. 973**.

35

NOTE

> One of the easiest and best ways to protect machines on a local network from attack and
> to share an Internet connection is to install an AirPort base station. These devices provide
> NAT protection for any computers that obtain Internet service through them, and for
> most users, this is an adequate level of protection from hacking.

USING A SOFTWARE FIREWALL TO PROTECT YOUR NETWORK

You can also install and use a software firewall; a software firewall prevents unexpected access
to your Mac from the Internet. Software firewalls can be quite effective and might be the
best solution if you have only a single Mac connected to the Internet.

CAUTION

> Unlike a hardware firewall or NAT hub, a software firewall must be installed on each
> computer attached to your network.

A software firewall works by blocking access to specific ports on your Mac; these ports are
linked to specific services. If hackers can access these ports on your machine, they can use
them to attack your machine directly to launch attacks on other computers, servers, and networks (such as denial-of-service attacks, in which a system is overloaded by repeated
requests from many machines).

Because Mac OS X is based on Unix, it has built-in firewall protection. You can enable this
firewall to protect a Mac from Net attacks by doing the following:

1. Open the System Preferences application.
2. Click the Sharing icon to open the Sharing pane.
3. Click the Firewall tab.
4. Click the Start button. The firewall begins working and blocks inappropriate requests
   for access to your Mac (see Figure 35.10).
5. If you want to enable specific ports for a service that you are allowing access through
   the firewall, select the service and click Edit. (You can't change the ports for built-in
   services, such as personal file sharing.)
6. Click the Advanced button. Use the resulting sheet to configure more advanced settings
   for the firewall (see Figure 35.11).
7. To block all UDP traffic, check the "Block UDP Traffic" check box. The UDP protocol is designed mostly for broadcasting messages.
8. To record hits (or attacks) against your firewall, click the "Enable Firewall Logging"
   check box. When you want to view the log, click the Open Log button. A Console window will open and show you the attempts to access your system.

Figure 35.10
Enable Mac OS X's built-in firewall by clicking the Start button on the Firewall tab.

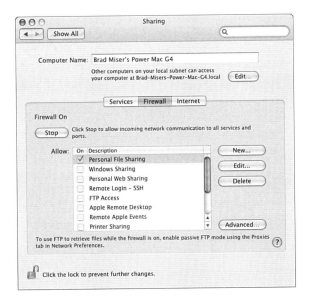

Figure 35.11
Use the Advanced sheet to configure additional aspects of your Mac's firewall.

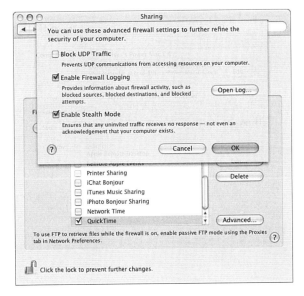

9. If you don't want any attempts to communicate with your Mac to be responded to, check the "Enable Stealth Mode" check box. This prevents a hacker from learning that there is even a computer at the address he is attempting to access, much less being able to access it. You should always leave this option active.

10. Click OK. The firewall will be protecting your Mac.

Only the services you allow will be permitted to access your Mac. All others will be denied. This provides more than adequate protection for most Mac users.

35

TIP

You can use the New button to add new services to your Mac. In the resulting sheet, choose the type of service you want to add and enter port numbers, if appropriate. Click OK to add the service.

You can gain more specific control over the firewall if you choose to. However, configuring this firewall directly requires a fairly complete understanding of Unix and firewalls and requires more energy and time than most Mac users will care to spend on it. For most situations, using the built-in firewall is a better option.

DEFENDING USERS FROM ONLINE ATTACKS

In addition to protecting your Mac itself from attack, you can also protect individual users from various kinds of danger by blocking specific types of access for individual accounts. For example, you might want to control the kind of email a child who uses your Mac receives. You control various types of access via the Accounts pane of the System Preferences application.

LIMITING EMAIL ACCESS OF OTHERS TO YOUR MAC'S USERS

You can determine from which email addresses a user can receive email to shield that user for unwanted emails. Set this up with the following steps:

1. Open the Accounts pane of the System Preferences application.
2. Select the user whom you want to protect from unwanted emails.
3. Click the Parental Controls tab (see Figure 35.12).

Figure 35.12
You can use the Parental Controls tab to limit the emails a user can receive.

4. Check the Mail check box. The Mail configuration sheet will appear.

5. Click the Add Email address button (the +) located at the bottom of the allowed email list.

6. Type the address from which you want to allow the user to receive email (see Figure 35.13).

Figure 35.13
So far, this user will be able to receive email from only one email address.

7. Repeat steps 5 and 6 until you have added all the email addresses from which you want to allow emails to the list.

8. If you want to receive a permission email each time an email from an address not on the list is received, check the "Send permission emails to" check box and enter the email address where you want the permission emails to be sent in the box.

9. Click OK to close the sheet and enable the email limits.

TIP

You can change the settings for the Mail filter by clicking the Configure button and using the Configure sheet. To remove an address, select it and click the Remove button (the -).

Any email addressed to the user from addresses not on the list you configured will be rejected. If you enabled the permission email option, a permission email will be sent to the address you configured. If permission is granted via that email by clicking the Always Allow button, the email from the unlisted address will be allowed, as will future emails from the same address (it will be added to the list of allowed email addresses).

35

TIP

You can prevent additional emails from the same address by clicking the No Longer Allow button in the permission email.

NOTE

When the Mail parental control is active for a user account, you will see the status message `Parental Control` on in the Mail window title bar.

LIMITING THE CHAT ACCESS OF OTHERS TO YOUR MAC'S USERS

iChat is a great way to keep in touch with others via text, audio, or video chatting. However, you might want to limit the access a user has to chat sessions, especially if you have young children who like to chat. You can use the Parental Controls tools to limit the chat access a user account has by performing the following steps:

NOTE

Before a person can be added to the approved chat list, that person should have an address card in your Address Book.

→ To learn how to add people to the Address Book, **see** "Setting Up and Using an Address Book," **p. 400**.

1. Open the Accounts pane of the System Preferences application.
2. Select the user whom you want to protect from uncontrolled chatting.
3. Click the Parental Controls tab.
4. Click the iChat check box and then click its Configure button. The Chat Configuration sheet will appear (see Figure 35.14).

Figure 35.14
Use this sheet to determine who can chat with a specific user.

5. Click the Add User button (the +). The Buddies dialog box will appear.

TIP

> You can add a person to your Address Book by clicking the New Person button in the Buddies dialog box.

6. Locate and select the person with whom you will allow chats and click Select Buddy. The person will be added to the allowed list.

7. Repeat steps 5 and 6 until you have added all the people with whom you will allow chatting to the list.

8. Click OK to save the list.

When this control is configured, the user will be able to chat only with people on the allowed list.

CAUTION

> The Parental Controls work only with Mail, iChat, and Safari. Other applications that perform the same functions will not be limited by these controls.

LIMITING THE WEBSITES YOUR MAC'S USERS CAN ACCESS

The Web is often a great place to be, but it can also be a dangerous or disgusting place to be as well. You can protect users by limiting the websites they can visit by doing the following steps:

1. Open the Accounts pane of the System Preferences application.

2. Select the user whose website access you want to limit.

3. Click the Parental Controls tab.

4. Check the Safari check box and then click the Configure button.

5. Log in under the user account whose access you are configuring.

6. Launch Safari.

7. Click the "Show all bookmarks" button.

8. Authenticate yourself with an administrator account.

→ To learn how to configure Safari bookmarks, **see** "Using Safari Bookmarks," **p. 470**.

9. Configure bookmarks for the sites you want to allow the user to access.

10. Log out of the user account.

The user will only be able to access web pages for which you have configured bookmarks. If the user attempts to access any other pages, such as by entering a URL, that access will be blocked.

35

MAC OS X TO THE MAX: GOING FURTHER WITH DISK UTILITY

Disk Utility is a very powerful and useful application. Unfortunately, covering all its functionality is beyond the scope of this chapter. Following are some hints about other tasks for which you can use it:

- **Create disk images**—You can create disk images from files, folders, or even drives and volumes. Just like other disk images you work with, you can easily put your disk images on CD, use them to quickly re-create a set of data in multiple locations, and so on. The commands you use to create and work with disk images are on the File and Images menus.

- **Burn CDs and DVDs**—Disk Utility enables you to burn CDs or DVDs from disk images. You can also use it to create multisession discs—something you can't do from the Finder's Burn command. First, create a disk image for the files you want to put on disc. Then use the Burn button or the Burn command on the Images menu to access the application's burn functionality.

- **Work with disk images**—As you mount disk images in Disk Utility, it tracks those images in the lower part of the left pane so you can work with them again by selecting them. This makes accessing these images simple.

> **TIP**
>
> To remove a disk image from Disk Utility, drag its icon out of the application window or select it and press Delete.

- **Mount, unmount, or eject volumes**—You can use the mount, unmount, and eject buttons and commands to perform those actions for disks, discs, volumes, and disk images.

- **Restore any folder, volume, or disk**—You can create a disk image from any source (such as a folder or volume) and use the application's command to restore that information on a disk. For example, if you want to replicate a set of software on multiple machines, you can create a disk image and use the Restore function on each machine to re-create that data. After you have created the disk image, use the Restore tab to restore it.

- **Access a log file**—As you perform actions with it, Disk Utility maintains a complete log of the actions it performs. To access this log, select Window, Show Log or press ⌘-L. The Log opens and you can view its contents. This provides a complete history of your disk maintenance tasks.

- **Configure RAID disks**—Redundant array of independent disks (RAID) is a scheme whereby multiple disks can be linked to work together for performance and reliability reasons (for example, disks can be mirrored so the same information is always stored on more than one disk in case of disk failure). You can use the RAID tab in Disk Utility to configure RAID services on a machine.

- **Fix OS 9 permissions**—Mac OS 9 disks use slightly different permissions than do Mac OS X disks. Use the Fix OS 9 Permissions command on the File menu to repair the permissions on Mac OS 9 volumes and disks.

35

CHAPTER 36

SOLVING MAC PROBLEMS

In this chapter

HANDLING MAC PROBLEMS

Even though Mac OS X is a very stable and reliable operating system, you will inevitably experience problems. You might experience application crashes or hangs, or an application just might not work the way it is supposed to. You might even experience minor annoyances, such as having to do something in several steps that should require only one. In any case, one of these days, you will run into a situation that requires you to troubleshoot and solve a problem.

Dealing with a problem, especially related to Mac OS X, can be intimidating even if you are a power user because there is so much going on that you might not understand. Although the top-level Mac interface is relatively intuitive, the Unix underpinnings of the OS have a tremendous amount of complexity. Nowhere is this more apparent than when you are trying to solve a problem. As you use the various tools that are part of Mac OS X to diagnose and solve a problem, you are likely to run into information that doesn't make much sense to you—unless you have lived in the Unix world for a long time, in which case you'll feel right at home.

Fortunately, you don't need to be a Unix expert to be able to troubleshoot and solve Mac OS X problems. Mostly, what is required is the ability to carefully observe what is happening and to follow logical trails. Being able to communicate clearly with other people is also very important when you need to get help.

NOTE

> If there is one troubleshooting trick or technique that I would classify as critical, it is the ability to accurately and completely (and calmly) describe a problem you are experiencing, whether you are telling someone about it or writing to them. Not only will this help your own troubleshooting work, but it also is vital when you need help from someone else. Unfortunately, many requests for help provide only partial or incomplete information that makes it almost impossible to provide the correct help.

From the title of this chapter, you might be under the impression that you will be seeing many solutions to specific Mac problems you might encounter. If that is your expectation, I must be up front with you here. There simply isn't room in this book to provide lists of problems and solutions that would be detailed enough to help you with the specific problems you will face.

Instead, the purpose of this chapter is to help you learn *how* to troubleshoot Mac OS X problems in general. You can then apply the techniques and tools you will learn about in this chapter to any problems you face; these techniques will help you solve problems on your own. In the long run, the strategies you need to know to solve problems will be much more useful to you than lists of problems that might or might not include those you actually experience.

NOTE

> The goal of this chapter is to help you learn general problem-solving techniques, but solutions to some specific problems you might encounter are explained in the "Troubleshooting" sections in many chapters of this book.

36

UNDERSTANDING THE CAUSES OF PROBLEMS

The causes of the problems you experience will be one—or a combination—of five general types of problems:

- User error
- Bugs
- Conflicting software
- Attacks on your system
- Hardware failures

Each of these problems is detailed in the sections that follow.

USER ERROR

The results of many investigations into aviation accidents can often be summed up with the phrase "pilot error." Similarly, this is often the case with an "accident" in the Mac world. Many problems are the direct result of a user (this means you) doing something improperly—or not doing something properly. Some of the things you might do to cause problems for yourself are the following:

- **Not following instructions**—This is the big one. At times, you will cause your own problems simply because you fail to follow instructions provided with software or hardware. You should become a believer in the old adage "if all else fails, follow the instructions."

- **Operating a machine past its limits**—If you know that a particular application requires a computer with a G4 processor, but you try to run it on a G3-equipped Mac, you are bound to have troubles. If you live on the edge of your machine's capabilities, you will have more problems than you might with a more capable machine. This is especially important related to a computer's RAM. Most minimum RAM requirements are understated; add as much RAM to your Mac as it can handle and you can afford.

- **Not doing proper maintenance on your system**—If you don't keep an eye out for patches and updates to Mac OS X as well as the applications you use, you might experience more problems than you have to. Take advantage of the many ways in which you can keep your system up-to-date. For example, Mac OS X's Software Update feature can help you keep your system and all your Apple applications current automatically.

■ **Not keeping enough free space on a drive**—This is a fairly common cause of problems. All drives need to have free space to be capable of storing files, sometimes temporarily. If a drive is full, or very close to being full, you will have problems as you try to store more data on it. This can be a problem under Mac OS X because virtual memory is always on—low disk space can cause problems related to insufficient RAM as well.

NOTE

> Proper maintenance includes maintaining good backups of your data, applications, or (even better) your entire system. Using a Mac without a backup system is like playing Russian roulette. Much of the time, you'll be fine. But sometimes you lose, and when you do, you lose big.

BUGS

Sometimes the cause of a problem is a bug inherent in the design of the products involved. The bug can be a design flaw, a manufacturing problem, or a conflict with some other part of your system. Although companies often do the best they can to prevent bugs, there is usually no way to prevent all the possible bugs in a product. Many bugs aren't revealed until a piece of software or hardware is combined with some other pieces of hardware or software.

CONFLICTING SOFTWARE

One of the most common causes of problems is conflicting software. Some programs just don't play well with others. Conflicts are often associated with system-level applications and resources because they modify the low-level operations of the system. However, applications can also conflict with one another and cause you headaches.

Because Mac OS X features protected memory, these types of conflicts are much less common under Mac OS X than they were under previous versions of the Mac OS. Because of protected memory, you aren't likely to experience many conflicts between applications. However, there is still the potential for conflict between software that modifies the system and the core OS or software that uses hardware components of your system, such as heavy use of disks.

ATTACKS ON YOUR SYSTEM

The two primary sources of attacks on your system come from the outside: viruses and hackers. Viruses can cause all sorts of problems from simple and silly messages appearing to strange dialog boxes to major system crashes and even data deletions or hard disk failures. Viruses that do serious damage have traditionally been fairly rare on the Mac, but because Mac OS X is based on Unix, it remains to be seen whether viruses will be a more significant source of concern than they have been for Mac users. Fortunately, viruses are among the easier problems to avoid. On the other hand, if you use a broadband connection to the Internet, your Mac will be subjected to all sorts of hackers who want to do damage to you or others. These are definitely the more serious of the two possible sources of attacks.

36

NOTE

> Although attacks are normally associated with someone from outside your local network, this is not always the case. Sometimes, even unknowingly (such as in an email-based virus attack), users on your local network can wreak havoc on your system. The proper use of user accounts and permissions and a bit of paying attention will go a long way toward preventing incursions on your Mac from a local user.

→ To learn how to defend yourself against these attacks, **see** "Defending Your Mac from Net Attacks," **p. 1032**.

HARDWARE FAILURES

The most unlikely cause of problems is a hardware failure. Although hardware does fail now and again, it doesn't happen very often. Hardware failures are most likely to occur immediately after you start using a new piece of hardware or close to the end of its useful life. Sometimes, you can induce a hardware failure when you upgrade a machine or perform some other type of maintenance on it—for example, if you install new RAM in a machine but fail to seat a RAM chip properly.

The most common problems associated with hardware devices are actually related to the device drivers that enable the OS to communicate with the device.

PREVENTING PROBLEMS

It is better to prevent problems than to try to solve them. Following are three techniques you can employ to minimize the problems you experience:

- **Maintain your Mac properly and protect it**—This will go a long way toward minimizing your problems.

→ For information about protecting and maintaining your Mac, **see** Chapter 35, "Maintaining and Protecting Your Mac," **p. 995**.

- **Be cautious about upgrades, updaters, and other changes to the system software or applications**—Generally, you should wait a period of time after an upgrade is released before putting it on your system. You should always carefully evaluate the benefits of a new version of an application versus the potential for problems it might introduce. This holds true for updaters and patches as well. If you are not experiencing the problems that are solved by an updater or a patch, you might be better off without it.

  You should try to keep a log that records the date and time when you make significant changes to your system, such as adding new software, changing network settings, and so on. Such a log can help you identify possible causes of problems when a time lag exists between when you make a change and when problems occur. Mac OS X's Software Update feature maintains such a log for you automatically. But when you make changes outside of that tool, you will have to record the relevant information manually.

TIP

> If you support more than one computer, you should have a test system on which you can install new software to test for a while before exposing other systems to it.

- **Make as few changes as possible at one time**—There are at least two reasons you should make changes to your system (such as installing software, making major configuration changes, and so on) incrementally. The first and most important is that making multiple changes at one time can obscure the cause of problems. For example, if you install three or four applications at once and then experience problems, determining which of the applications you installed is causing the problem will be difficult. The second reason is that sometimes making multiple changes at once can cause problems for you. When you change something significant, go slowly and take one step at a time. Introduce additional changes only after you are fairly sure that the changes you previously introduced are working properly.

ASSESSING YOUR MAC

Key to troubleshooting and solving problems that you can't prevent is being able to accurately and precisely assess how your Mac is performing and knowing the specific configuration of your system. Mac OS X offers many diagnostic tools that can help you; however, several of these tools are quite complicated. Still, even if you are not able to interpret all their output, people who are trying to help might be able to, so even in this case it is useful for you to know how to use them. And, you should understand how to use these tools before you need them.

NOTE

> If you choose Apple menu, About This Mac, you will see a window displaying the version of the Mac OS X you are running, the amount of RAM installed in your machine, the specific processors it contains, and the current startup disc. You can also click the Software Update button to move to that pane in the System Preferences application or click More Info to move into the System Profiler.

TIP

> If you click the Mac OS X version number shown in the About This Mac window, you will see the specific build number of the version you are using. Click this information and you will see your Mac's serial number. Click it again and you will return to the Mac OS X version information.

USING SYSTEM PROFILER TO CREATE A SYSTEM PROFILE

Mac OS X includes the System Profiler application. This application enables you to get a detailed view into your system at any particular point in time.

36

To create a profile of your system, launch System Profiler (Applications/Utilities directory). The System Profiler provides a window with two panes (see Figure 36.1). In the left pane is a list of areas about which you can get information, including Hardware, Network, and Software. Each of these sections is broken down into component areas. For example, the Hardware section is further organized into various aspects of your system, such as ATA, Audio, Bluetooth, Diagnostics, and so on. The Software area is organized into Applications, Extensions, Fonts, and so on. When you select an item in the left pane, detailed information about that item appears in the right pane. For example, in Figure 36.1, the Hardware item is selected, which provides an overview of a machine's hardware configuration.

Figure 36.1
The System Profiler provides detailed information about the hardware and software that make up your system.

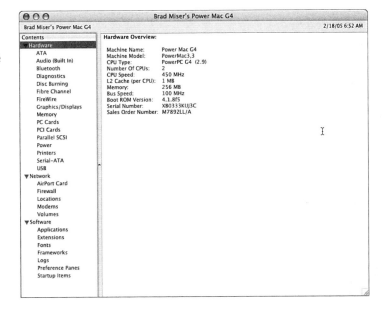

TIP

> You can also open the System Profiler by clicking the More Info button that appears in the About This Mac widow.

Click the category for the part of the system about which you want information. For example, to see the memory configuration of your machine, click the Memory category. In the right pane is each memory slot the machine contains. When a chip is installed in a slot, you can select the chip and see detailed information about it in the lower part of the pane (see Figure 36.2).

TIP

> Click the expansion triangle next to a category to expand or collapse its detail.

Figure 36.2
The Memory category enables you to get information about the memory configuration of your Mac.

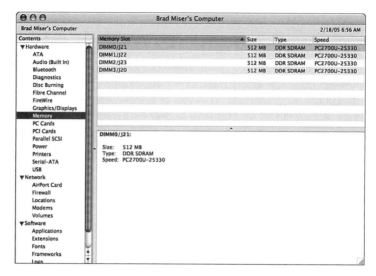

Three views are available in System Profiler; you can select the view on the View menu. The Full Profile (press (⌘-3) is the default view and provides the most information. The Mini Profile (press ⌘-1) hides details under the Software and Network categories; you can expand these sections to view the detail. The Basic Profile (press ⌘-2) includes more detail in the Hardware and Network sections but no additional detail in the Software section. Frankly, there's really no reason to use any view other than the Full Profile. After all, you use the System Profiler to get information, so why not get as much as is available?

The categories available in System Profiler in the Full Profile view can include those shown in Table 36.1.

TABLE 36.1 SYSTEM PROFILER IN THE FULL PROFILE VIEW

Category	Subcategory	Summary
Hardware	None	This area provides an overview of the hardware that is part of your machine. You will see the type of Mac, the CPU(s) it includes, cache information, memory details, and other hardware information.
Hardware	ATA	Use this category to view detailed information about the ATA disk or disc drives in your Mac.
Hardware	Audio (Built In)	Use this section to view information about the audio capabilities of your Mac.
Hardware	Diagnostics	This section provides information about diagnostics that your Mac will sometimes run, such as those that occur during the self-test when you power up your Mac.
Hardware	Disc Burning	Use this to view information about CD or DVD burners in your system or that are connected via FireWire or USB.

Category	Subcategory	Summary
Hardware	Fibre Channel	This section applies if you use fibre channel to link machines together.
Hardware	FireWire	This provides information about your Mac's FireWire ports including the devices that are currently connected. If a FireWire device is connected to your Mac, but is not listed in this section, you know there is a problem with the device.
Hardware	Graphics/Displays	This section provides details about the graphics cards installed in your Mac and the displays connected to those cards.
Hardware	Memory	Use this category to view detailed information about the composition of your machine's RAM memory.
Hardware	PC Cards	If you use a mobile Mac and PC cards, you can view information about them here.
Hardware	PCI	This area provides information about PCI cards you have installed in your Mac. If you have physically installed a card, but it is not listed here, the card is not working. The most likely cause is that the correct driver isn't installed.
Hardware	Parallel SCSI	Here you see information about any SCSI devices included in your system.
Hardware	Power	This area displays the current power settings for your Mac, such as sleep time.
Hardware	Printers	This provides information about any printers with which your Mac can communicate.
Hardware	Serial-ATA	In this area, you'll see information about serial ATA drives connected to your Mac or installed in it.
Hardware	USB	This particularly useful section shows all the USB devices attached to your system. If you are having trouble with a specific device, use this information to see whether your Mac recognizes a device properly. You can also see the speed at which USB devices are communicating with your Mac.
Network	None	This category provides an overview of your Mac's current network connections.
Network	AirPort Card	View this to see the type of AirPort card installed in your Mac and the current AirPort network you are using, along with other AirPort information.

continues

36

TABLE 36.1 CONTINUED

Category	Subcategory	Summary
Network	Firewall	This area provides information about the firewall configured for your Mac.
Network	Locations	This section provides a list of all the locations configured on your Mac. If you select a location in the upper pane, details about it will be shown in the lower pane.
Network	Modems	This provides information about modems installed in your Mac, such as an internal dial-up modem, or an external modem, such as a cable modem to which your Mac is directly connected.
Network	Volumes	This section provides information about network volumes that are currently mounted on your Mac, such as your iDisk.
Software	None	This provides an overview of your system software, including version and build, kernel version, boot volume (startup volume), computer name, and current user.
Software	Applications	This category displays information about the applications installed on your startup volume. The upper part of the pane shows the application name, version number, and modification date. If you select an application, in the lower part of the pane you will see its version, modification date, location, Info String (which is usually a copyright statement from the manufacturer), the location in which it is stored, and the kind of application it is.
Software	Extensions	Here, you will see the Mac OS X extensions installed on your startup volume. This information can sometimes be useful when troubleshooting. For example, you can determine if an extension associated with a piece of hardware is currently recognized by your system.
Software	Fonts	This provides the details about all the fonts on your Mac. Select a font listed in the upper pane to see more details about it in the lower pane.
Software	Frameworks	This category lists the Mac OS X frameworks installed on your startup volume. In the upper pane, you see the name of the framework, its version, and when it was last modified. If you select a framework, in the lower part of the pane you will see its version, modification date, location, Info String (which can sometimes tell you more about the framework), and whether it is private.

Category	Subcategory	Summary
Software	Logs	This section provides access to various logs the system and some applications keep to record significant events, such as crashes. Each log can be selected to reveal its details. In the upper pane are all the logs available to you. For each log, you'll see its name, a description, its size, and when it was last modified. If you click a log, its information will be displayed in the lower pane. The specific information you see will depend on the log you select. Some of the information in these logs is quite technical. However, you can often review the logs for a specific point in time during which you were having trouble, to assess what was happening with your system. For example, you can see significant events that occurred or didn't occur successfully. This can often reveal the source of a problem. Also, if you need to ask for help, accessing these logs can enable you to provide more specific information to the person trying to help you and might result in a problem being solved more quickly. Other logs, such as those for applications, are quite easy to understand and will often reveal information about problems you have experienced.
Software	Preference Panes	This list shows you all the preference panes currently installed in the System Preferences application. Select a preference pane in the upper pane of the window to see details about it in the lower pane.
Software	Startup Items	This list shows all processes that start up when your Mac does. As with other panes, select the item in which you are interested in the upper pane and view the details in the lower pane.

You should periodically save a Profiler report, called a *profile*, to disk and print it. Then, if you need to get help with a problem but can't open System Profiler at the time, you can use the profile to help troubleshoot the issue. You can also email the profile file to people trying to help you solve a problem. To save a profile for your system, do the following steps:

1. Launch the System Profiler.
2. Select File, Save As.
3. In the resulting Save sheet, name the file, choose a location in which to save it, and select the file format in which you want to save the profile. The options are System Profiler 4.0 (XML), Rich Text Format (RTF), and Plain Text. The format you choose depends on how you are going to use the profile. In most cases, you should choose System Profiler or Rich Text because the resulting profile will retain some formatting.

36

4. Click Save. The profile will be saved in the format you selected.

5. Open the profile to view it (see Figure 36.3).

Figure 36.3
Here is a profile saved in the RTF format.

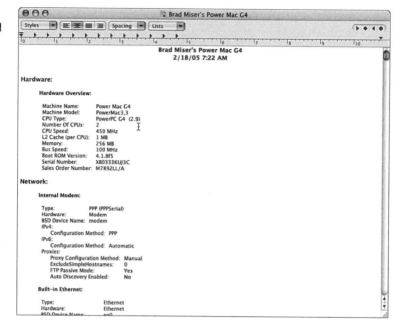

TIP

When you need help from Apple, you can send a Profile to it by choosing File, Send to Apple. Click the Send to Apple button in the resulting sheet and your profile will be transmitted to Apple. An Apple representative will be able to access the profile to help you solve a problem. Apple can also use the profile to help identify bugs and other issues with its software, including OS X.

The System Profiler menus contain some additional commands that might be useful. For example, View, Refresh causes System Profiler to refresh all its information.

USING ACTIVITY MONITOR TO UNDERSTAND AND MANAGE PROCESSES

To provide services, your Mac runs a lot of processes. These processes fall into many categories. User processes are those that are related to specific user accounts, such as running an application. Administrator (also called root) processes are those that are fundamental to the OS and are controlled by it, such as the Desktop database. NetBoot processes are those related to network services, such as Apple File Server.

The Activity Monitor application enables you to get detailed information about any process running on your Mac at any point in time. This information can be useful when it comes time to troubleshoot your system. You can also use the Activity Monitor to kill any running process; this is useful when a process is hung and needs to be stopped.

36

The following steps walk you through using the Activity Monitor:

1. Open Activity Monitor (Applications/Utilities directory). You will see a window providing a listing of all the processes on the machine (see Figure 36.4).

Figure 36.4
Activity Monitor enables you to get detailed information about any process on your Mac.

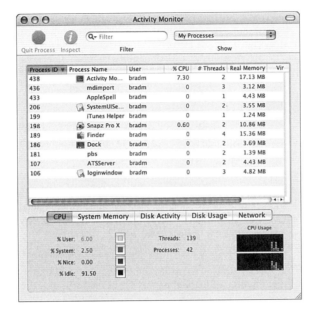

2. Select the category of process you want to view from the pop-up menu at the top of the window. There are many options from which to choose, and the option you choose will depend on the types of processes in which you are interested. For example, select My Processes to see the processes that are related to your user account. The processes shown in the window is refreshed according to the category you select.

TIP

One of the more useful process categories to view is the Active Processes option. This shows only processes that are currently doing something. When you are troubleshooting, these are typically the processes in which you are interested.

For each process shown in the Activity Viewer window, you can see the following information:

■ **Process ID**—Each process running on your Mac is assigned a unique ID number. This number can change each time the process is started.

■ **Process Name**—Unlike process number, a process's name is constant.

■ **User**—This identifies the specific user running the process. In addition to the user accounts on your machine, you will see processes with root as the user. These are

36

processes that are part of the OS and are started and managed by your Mac when it starts up.

- **% CPU**—This percentage indicates the amount of CPU processing that a process is consuming. This is one of the more useful pieces of data. Any process should be consuming a small percentage of the available CPU processing power. If a process is consuming a large amount, such as something more than 90%, over a long period of time that usually indicates the process is having trouble and should be stopped.

- **# Threads**—Processes can run in different threads within the processor. This column indicates how many threads a process is using. Unless you have a detailed understanding of how processors work, this isn't likely to be meaningful.

- **Real Memory**—This indicates how much physical RAM is being used by the process.

- **Virtual Memory**—This indicates how much virtual RAM is being used by the process.

NOTE
> Virtual RAM is your Mac using its hard drive like it uses real RAM–that being to temporarily store data with which it is working. Virtual memory is much slower than real RAM, but you usually have a lot more available to you. Fortunately, Mac OS X takes care of managing both kinds of memory for you.

The following list outlines some additional process tasks you can perform in Activity Monitor:

- **Open a sheet that enables you to quit a process normally or to force it to quit**— Select a running process and either click Quit Process or press Option-⌘-Q to open this sheet. You can use this to stop a process that is hung. For hung processes, use Force Quit; for processes that are running normally, use Quit.

- **Sort the processes shown in the window**—You do this by clicking the column by which you want them sorted. The current sort criterion is shown by the highlighted column name. You can reverse the direction of the sort with the sort order button that is located next to the column heading.

TIP
> Sorting the window by the Real Memory or % CPU column is useful because you can see which processes are consuming the most system memory. If a process is consuming a large amount of memory (such as 80%), that can indicate something is wrong with the application that is generating the process.

- **Find specific processes**—You do this by typing in the Filter box. The list is reduced to only those processes that contain the text you type.

- **Open the Inspector window**—You double-click or select a process and then either click Inspect or press ⌘-I. The Inspector window will open and you will see additional information about the process, including the parent process and recent hangs (see Figure 36.5). You can click the Memory tab to see detailed memory usage information for the process. Click the Statistics tab to get information about the threads, CPU time, and other technical specifications. Click Open Files and Ports to see the open files and network ports related to the process. Click the Quit button to open the Quit/Force Quit sheet.

Figure 36.5
With the Process Inspector, no process can hide.

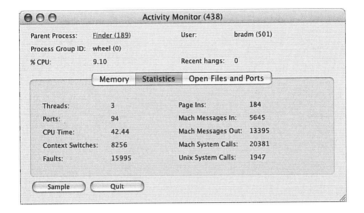

TIP

> If you click the Sample button, you will see yet another window that provides even more technical information about a process.

- **Change the rate at which process information is updated**—You do this by selecting View, Update Frequency; then you select the frequency you want to use, such as every .5 seconds. Increasing the sample rate provides data closer to real time.

USING THE ACTIVITY MONITOR TO MONITOR SYSTEM ACTIVITY

Using the tabs along the bottom of the Activity Monitor application enables you to gain insight into the following system activities:

- **CPU Usage**—You can monitor the CPU activity of the processors in your Mac. This gives you a good idea of the resources being used at any moment in time. When CPU usage becomes close to the upper limit, this usually indicates a problem.

- **System Memory**—Using this tool, you can view the usage of various types of system memory, such as physical RAM and virtual memory. You can also view the free memory of your system, which can be useful to determine whether you need to add more memory resources to your Mac.

- **Disk Activity**—This tool enables you to view the performance of your machine when reading and writing data to disk.

- **Disk Usage**—This area enables you to see the space breakdown of a selected disk (see Figure 36.6). This is particularly useful to make sure your disks aren't running close to their maximum capacity.

Figure 36.6
The Disk Usage information shows that the disk called Tiger currently has about 27GB of free space.

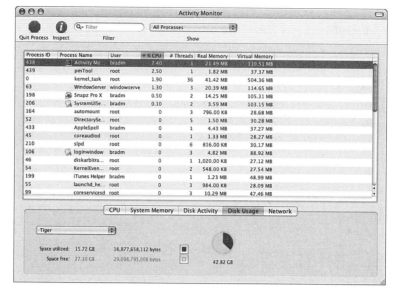

- **Network**—This tool provides information about the communication across your network interface, such as via Ethernet.

Using Acitivity Monitor, you can display system activity monitoring information on your desktop in a number of ways. For example, you can display CPU usage information on the desktop and display an icon showing other information on the Dock (see Figure 36.7). The monitoring options you have are listed in Table 36.2.

Figure 36.7
Several options are available for real-time performance monitoring from the desktop, such as viewing CPU usage on the Dock.

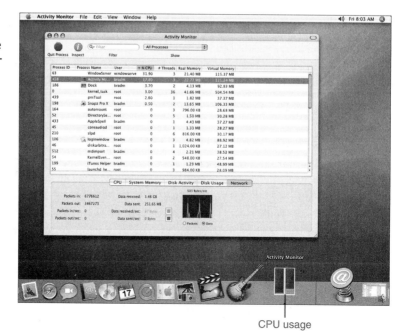

CPU usage

TABLE 36.2   MONITORING OPTIONS IN ACTIVITY MONITOR

Menu	Command	Keyboard Shortcut	What It Does
Window	Activity Monitor	⌘-1	Opens the Activity Monitor window.
Window	CPU Usage	⌘-2	Opens a window containing a bar for each processor that graphically displays its activity level.
Window	Floating CPU Window, Show Horizontally	⌘-4	Opens a bar showing activity for each processor. The bar is anchored in the lower-left corner of the desktop and is oriented horizontally.
Window	Floating CPU Window, Show Vertically	⌘-5	Opens a bar showing activity for each processor. The bar is anchored in the lower-left corner of the desktop and is oriented vertically.
Window	Floating CPU Window, Do not show		Closes the Floating CPU window.
Window	CPU History	⌘-3	Opens a window that tracks processor activity over time.
View	Clear CPU History		Starts the CPU history over again.
View	Columns, *Column*, where *Column* is the name of an Activity Monitor column		Enables you to show or hide all the columns Activity Monitor can display.
View	Show CPU monitors on top of other windows		When this option is selected, all CPU monitor windows always appear on top of other windows. When not selected, the CPU monitoring windows can be hidden by other windows.
View	Dock Icon, Show CPU Usage		Shows a CPU Usage window on the Dock.
View	Dock Icon, Show CPU History		Shows a CPU History window on the Dock.
View	Dock Icon, Show Network Usage		Shows a Network Usage window on the Dock.
View	Dock Icon, Show Disk Activity		Shows a Disk Activity window on the Dock.

continues

36

TABLE 36.2 CONTINUED

Menu	Command	Keyboard Shortcut	What It Does
View	Dock Icon, Show Memory Usage		Shows a Memory Usage window on the Dock.
View	Dock Icon, Show Application Icon		Shows the Activity Monitor icon on the Dock instead of a monitoring window.
View	Update Frequency, *Frequency*, where *Frequency* is the frequency you choose		Changes the frequency at which the Activity Monitor monitors processors. The frequency can be .5 second, 1 second, 2 seconds, or 5 seconds.

> **TIP**
>
> When you choose a frequency, it affects only the monitoring of processes. The monitors always display information in real time.

Monitoring is available only while Activity Monitor is running. When you quit the application, all monitoring disappears. If you want to display the monitoring tools but hide the Activity Monitor window itself, you can minimize or close the Activity Monitor window.

VIEWING SYSTEM ACTIVITY WITH TOP

The Top window is a Unix window that provides detailed information about the current operation of your Mac. To access it, open a command-line application such as Terminal or X11, type **top**, and press Return.

The Top window provides detailed information about your system, although not in the most easily understood format (see Figure 36.8). At the top of the Top window, you see a summary of the activity on your machine; the lower part of the window lists all the running processes and detailed information about each.

In the summary area of the window, you can see how many processes are running versus the number sleeping, how many threads are running, the average loads, and the percentage of CPU usage of user processes versus system usage. The PhysMem information contains data about your RAM. For example, the amount shown as active is the RAM currently being used by running processes. The VM information provides data about the virtual memory being used.

> **NOTE**
>
> You can get similar information in an easier-to-use format by using Activity Monitor.

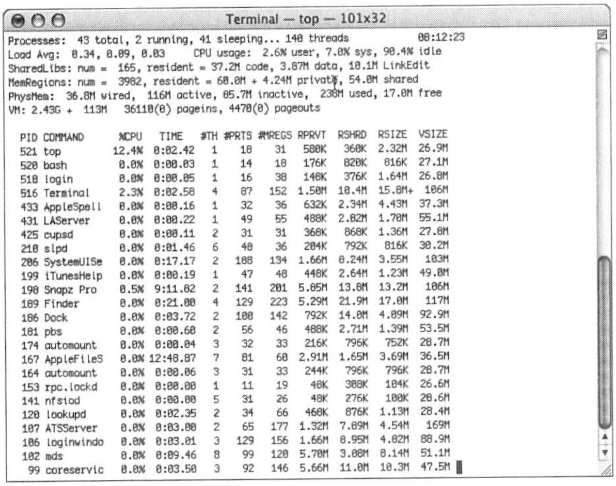

```
Terminal — top — 101x32
Processes:  43 total, 2 running, 41 sleeping... 140 threads                    08:12:23
Load Avg:  0.34, 0.09, 0.03     CPU usage:  2.6% user, 7.0% sys, 90.4% idle
SharedLibs: num =  165, resident = 37.2M code, 3.87M data, 10.1M LinkEdit
MemRegions: num =  3982, resident = 60.0M + 4.24M private, 54.0M shared
PhysMem:  36.8M wired,  116M active, 85.7M inactive,  238M used, 17.0M free
VM: 2.43G +  113M   36110(0) pageins, 4470(0) pageouts

  PID COMMAND      %CPU   TIME   #TH #PRTS #MREGS RPRVT  RSHRD  RSIZE  VSIZE
  521 top         12.4% 0:02.42   1    18    31   580K   360K  2.32M  26.9M
  520 bash         0.0% 0:00.03   1    14    18   176K   820K   816K  27.1M
  518 login        0.0% 0:00.05   1    16    38   148K   376K  1.64M  26.8M
  516 Terminal     2.3% 0:02.58   4    87   152  1.50M  10.4M  15.8M+  106M
  433 AppleSpell   0.0% 0:00.16   1    32    36   632K  2.34M  4.43M  37.3M
  431 LAServer     0.0% 0:00.22   1    49    55   488K  2.02M  1.70M  55.1M
  425 cupsd        0.0% 0:00.11   2    31    31   368K   868K  1.36M  27.8M
  210 slpd         0.0% 0:01.46   6    48    36   204K   792K   816K  30.2M
  206 SystemUISe   0.0% 0:17.17   2   108   134  1.66M  8.24M  3.55M   103M
  199 iTunesHelp   0.0% 0:00.19   1    47    48   448K  2.64M  1.23M  49.0M
  198 Snapz Pro    0.5% 9:11.02   2   141   201  5.05M  13.6M  13.2M   106M
  189 Finder       0.0% 0:21.00   4   129   223  5.29M  21.9M  17.0M   117M
  186 Dock         0.0% 0:03.72   2   100   142   792K  14.0M  4.09M  92.9M
  181 pbs          0.0% 0:00.60   2    56    46   488K  2.71M  1.39M  53.5M
  174 automount    0.0% 0:00.04   3    32    33   216K   796K   752K  28.7M
  167 AppleFileS   0.0% 12:48.87  7    81    60  2.91M  1.65M  3.69M  36.5M
  164 automount    0.0% 0:00.06   3    31    33   244K   796K   796K  28.7M
  153 rpc.lockd    0.0% 0:00.00   1    11    19    40K   308K   104K  26.6M
  141 nfsiod       0.0% 0:00.00   5    31    26    48K   276K   100K  28.6M
  120 lookupd      0.0% 0:02.35   2    34    66   468K   876K  1.13M  28.4M
  107 ATSServer    0.0% 0:03.00   2    65   177  1.32M  7.09M  4.54M   169M
  106 loginwindo   0.0% 0:03.01   3   129   156  1.66M  8.95M  4.02M  88.9M
  102 mds          0.0% 0:09.46   8    99   120  5.70M  3.08M  8.14M  51.1M
   99 coreservic   0.0% 0:03.50   3    92   146  5.66M  11.0M  10.3M  47.5M
```

Figure 36.8
Using Top can be a bit intimidating, but the information it provides is worth getting to know.

In the lower part of the window, you see a table that provides data on each process that is similar to the information in the Activity Monitor. For example, you see the PID, which is the same Process ID as is displayed for a process in the Activity Monitor. You can also see the percentage of CPU use, the processor time, and other more technical information. Much of this information will probably not be useful to you unless you are quite technically oriented; however, it can be useful to others when you are trying to get help.

You can save the information seen in the Top window by selecting the information in the window and selecting File, Save Selected Text As. This text file can be useful or can be provided to someone else when you are getting help with a problem.

TIP

> To stop the Top process, press Ctrl-C.

Using the Console to View Logs

The Console application provides a window to which Mac OS X writes system messages you can view, most notably various logs your Mac creates as it works (or doesn't work as in the case of crash logs). These messages are mostly error messages; some of these can be useful when you are troubleshooting problems (see Figure 36.9). The messages you see are quite technical; unless you are a programmer or are extremely technically knowledgeable, you might not be able to understand all their detail. However, Console messages can be helpful to understand what was happening when something went wrong and when you are communicating a problem to someone else.

You can choose the log that is displayed in the Console window in a number of ways:

- **Click the Logs button in the toolbar**—You will see a list of all available logs organized into categories. You can expand a category to show the logs contained in that category. When you select a log, it appears in the Console window.

Figure 36.9
The Console enables you to view the contents of a log in detail.

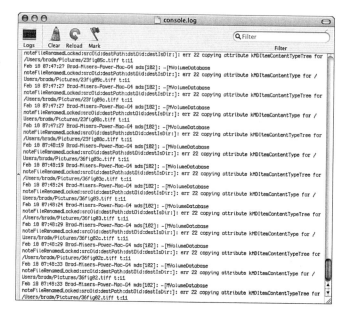

- **Select File, Open Console Log (or press Shift-⌘-O)**—This opens that log. Or, you can select Open System Log (or press Option-⌘-O) to open the System log.

- **Select File, Open Quickly**—Then choose the log you want to see on the hierarchical menu that appears.

A number of logs are available through the Console, and each provides a specific type of information, as you can see in Table 36.3.

TABLE 36.3   LOGS AVAILABLE IN THE CONSOLE

Log Name	Information It Provides
console.log	This log lists events related to the core operation of your Mac, such as when specific events occurred. Reviewing this log can sometimes give you insight into failed processes that might be causing problems for you, but that you might not be aware of because an application didn't crash.
system.log	Whereas the console.log displays mostly errors, the system.log shows all events that have occurred for the system, such as when specific processes start up. You see the date and time for each event.
~/Library/Logs	This category of logs provides information related to your user account (indicated by the ~). The specific logs you see in this category depend on what you are running at any point in time. You will always see the CrashReporter log for each application that has crashed. You might also see logs for various processes, such as the MirrorAgent.log when you are using an iDisk that is synchronized on your Mac.
/Library/Logs	This category presents a set of logs related to the system. These include various error logs along logs for various system services.

Log Name	Information It Provides
/var/log	This category contains many logs related to various processes. For example, you can choose the install.log to see a list of all installations you have done on your Mac or ftp.log to see information related to FTP access of your machine.

NOTE

You must be logged in under an account to see its logs. Even if another user is currently logged in while you are using your user account, you will still see only your logs.

You are most likely to use the Console to troubleshoot problems. To do so, use the following steps:

1. Open the Console and choose the log you want to view. For example, if an application has crashed, find that application's crash log, which will be located in the CrashReporter category within the ~/Library/Logs set of logs.

2. View the information you see. At the top of the log window, you will see summary information. Moving down the screen shows you the very technical log detail (see Figure 36.10).

Figure 36.10
This CrashReporter log shows information about a crash of the Snapx Pro X application.

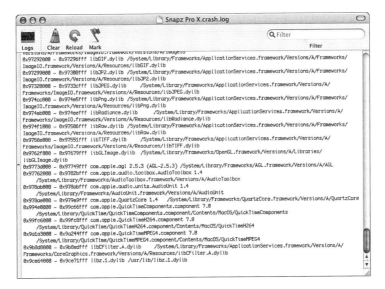

3. Save a copy of the log by selecting File, Save a Copy As.

4. Name the log, select a save location, and press Return.

5. In the Console, click the Clear button on the toolbar. The log's information is erased.

6. Repeat the steps that lead to the crash if you can. If not, just keeping doing what you were trying to do.

7. If the crash occurs again, repeat steps 1—4 to view the crash log. Compare the log to what you viewed in step 2. This might tell you whether it is the same problem or not.

8. If you can't solve the problem on your own, save the new log information so you can provide both logs to whomever you contact for help.

If you aren't very technically inclined, the information you see in the logs won't be understandable. However, you can still glean useful information such as the general cause of a problem and specific information about when it occurred. That information will often help you pinpoint exactly what was happening when a problem occurred, which is often critical to being able to solve it.

Here are a few other Console tips:

- You can open multiple Console windows at the same time by selecting File, New Log Window or pressing ⌘-N. This is useful when comparing different logs.

- You can reload the information in a log by viewing it and clicking the Reload button; by selecting File, Reload; or by pressing ⌘-R.

- You can use the Filter tool to search for specific log items.

SOLVING PROBLEMS

If you understand the general techniques you should use when troubleshooting, you will be able to handle most of the problems you are likely to encounter. Having a good understanding of what you need to do will also make you more confident, which in turn will help you be more effective.

The general process of solving problems can be broken down into four phases, which are the following:

1. Implementing a workaround

2. Understanding and describing your problem

3. Fixing problems yourself

4. Getting help

You should work through these phases in the order in which they are listed. Doing so will help you solve your problem as efficiently as possible.

IMPLEMENTING A WORKAROUND

One of the tough things about troubleshooting is that you usually have to do it at an inconvenient time—for example, in the middle of a big project. At times like these, you are likely to feel stress, which can lead to frustration, which in turn often leads to hasty actions. Haste will often drive you down the wrong path.

Effective troubleshooting requires a cool head. The best approach when you are working under a deadline is to find a quick workaround for the problem that will enable you to complete the job you need to get done immediately. Then you can come back and really fix the problem later when you are more in a "troubleshooting" frame of mind.

There are many types of workarounds you might be able to implement to get you working well enough to meet your immediate needs. Some examples are the following:

- **Use a different application to complete the project**—If your trouble is with a specific application, use an alternative one to get the project done.

- **Log in from a troubleshooting user account**—Some problems are related to corrupted preferences and other files that are part of your user account. If you followed my recommendation to create an alternative user account, log in under that account and try to complete your work.

- **Restart from an alternative startup volume**—If the problem is related to the system itself, use one of your alternative startup volumes until you have time to fix your current one.

- **Restart in Mac OS 9**—If the application you need is available under Mac OS 9 and you have a Mac that can be started up under Mac OS 9, restart your Mac in Mac OS 9 and get back to work. Not all Macs are capable of this, so it isn't an option for everyone.

- **Use a different Mac**—If you use your Mac for important work, you should consider having a backup machine so you can switch to it in times of trouble.

TROUBLESHOOTING AND DESCRIBING YOUR PROBLEM

When you start to troubleshoot, the most important thing you can do is to understand your problem in as much detail as possible. This understanding will enable you to know what you need to do to correct the problem. As you gain insight into your problem, you should be able to describe it in detail; this will help you get help from others if you are not able to solve the problem yourself.

Use the assessment tools, such as the System Profiler and Activity Monitor, that you learned about earlier in this chapter to help you understand what is happening.

PUTTING THE PROBLEM IN CONTEXT

Many problems are triggered by something you do (this doesn't mean you cause the problem, but that some action you take initiates the problem). When a problem happens, think about what you were doing immediately before the problem occurred. Following are some questions you need to answer:

- Which applications and processes were running (not only the particular one with which you were working)?

- What, specifically, were you trying to do (print, save, format, and so on)?

- Have you made any changes to the computer recently (installed software, changed settings, and so on)?

36

NOTE

If you create a system change log as was suggested earlier, answering the last question in the previous list will be much easier. Remember to use the Software Update logs to track changes to your Apple software, including those made to the OS itself. You can also view the install log as explained in the previous section to see which installers have been run recently.

The answers to these questions provide significant clues to help you figure out what is triggering the problem. Identifying the trigger goes a long way toward identifying the cause.

Using Your Troubleshooting Account

Some problems you encounter might be related to files that are associated only with a user account. Examples of these include preference files for applications, other application support files, and so on. One of the best troubleshooting steps—which can also be a workaround—is to create a troubleshooting user account. Keep this account as basic as you can, meaning don't install or use applications while logged in under this account. Leave all it settings in their default configurations, such as login items, preferences, and so on.

When you encounter a problem, log in under your troubleshooting account. If the problem goes away, you know that it is related to the user account under which you were logged in when the problem occurred. This can give you a good idea of where to start solving the problem. If the problem doesn't go away, you know that it is a more general issue.

TIP

Your troubleshooting account should have administrator privileges.

→ To learn how to create and configure user accounts, **see** "Creating and Configuring User Accounts," **p. 26**.

Trying to Repeat the Problem

When a problem occurs, you should recover the best you can and then try to make the problem happen again. Try to re-create everything that was happening when the problem first appeared.

CAUTION

Obviously, you shouldn't intentionally re-create a problem in such a way that you will lose data. Make sure that your data is safe by having a good backup before you do much troubleshooting.

If you can replicate the problem, figuring out what is happening will be much easier. The hardest problems to fix are those that occur only occasionally or intermittently.

Describing the Problem in Detail

After you have developed an understanding of how and when the problem is happening, write down a description of the problem. Be as detailed as you can. This description will help you decide on the best course of action, and if you are unable to solve the problem yourself, you will be in an excellent position to ask for help.

Use the Console to save logs related to the problem and the System Profiler to create a report about your system's configuration. This will create much of the detail that will enable you or someone else to solve the problem.

Fixing Problems Yourself

After you have described your problem, you should have some idea of where it lies. The four general areas in which you will experience problems are applications, system, hardware, and during startup.

Correcting Application Errors

Application errors usually fall into one of the following categories:

- **Hangs**—Sometimes application errors cause your application to hang. Fortunately, because Mac OS X has protected memory, a hung application usually affects only the application itself and your other applications continue to work normally. You are likely to lose unsaved data in the hung application, but at least your losses are limited to a single application.

- **Quits**—Sometimes, the application you are using suddenly quits. You might or might not get an error message saying something like, The application has unexpectedly quit because of an error. When this happens, you lose all the changes you made to the open document since the last time you saved it.

- **Won't do what it is supposed to do**—Many times, errors occur that prevent you from doing what you want to do—whether using a particular function of the software, printing, saving files, and so on.

NOTE

> When you see an error alert that provides an error ID number, you should make a note of it. Although the number is not likely to be meaningful to you unless you have seen it before, it might be very meaningful to someone else when you ask for help.

Obviously, application problems are usually unpredictable. And when they happen, there isn't much you can do to recover your unsaved data (if you are saving frequently, you will limit your losses when the inevitable does happen). With an application problem, your real task is to figure out how to *prevent* future occurrences of the problem.

TIP

> Some applications, such as Microsoft Office, have a recover feature that attempts to recover documents on which you were working when the application crashed or hung. This sometimes works and sometimes doesn't. However, you should take a look at recovered documents when you restart the application to see how much of your work you can restore.

Mac OS X includes a crash reporter feature. When an application crashes, the crash reporter appears. At the top of this window, you can enter information about what you were doing at the time of the crash. When you have described this in as much detail as possible, you can send the information to Apple. Apple collects this information and uses it to identify problems that need to be fixed.

Typically, there are many things you can try to correct an application error. Following are the general tasks you should attempt to get the application working properly again.

HUNG APPLICATION   When an application is hung, your only option is to force it to quit. You can do this by bringing up the Force Quit Applications window by pressing Option-⌘-Esc or by choosing Apple, Force Quit. Select the application you want to force quit and click Force Quit. After you confirm that you really do want to force the application to quit, it will be shut down. You can also use the Activity Monitor to force an application to quit—the benefit of the Activity Monitor is that you can see all the processes that are running along with their statuses. If other processes are also hung, you will be able to see them by looking at the Activity Monitor window. This can provide important clues as to the source of the problem (where two or three hung processes are gathered, there is likely a problem in their midst).

After you unhang the application, try to replicate the conditions under which it hung. If the problem is repeatable, it is either a bug in the application or a conflict with another part of the system.

Try running the application by itself while re-creating the situation in which the problem occurred (use your problem description to do this). If the hang doesn't occur again, you know that the problem is some type of conflict with another part of your system—be aware that this is much less likely to occur under Mac OS X than with previous versions of the OS.

If the hang is repeatable, the most likely solution is to install an update to the application. Visit the support area of the manufacturer's web page to see whether the problem you have is a known one. If so, an update is probably available to correct it. If not, report the problem to tech support to see what the application's manufacturer recommends.

TIP

> When an error dialog box appears or an application hangs, it can be useful to capture a screenshot so you can reproduce it later when you are writing down the description of your problem. In the case of a hung application, capturing a screenshot can help you re-create at least a screen's worth of data if you lose it all. Sometimes this can be helpful

(such as for a table of data). To capture a screenshot, use the Grab application or download and use the much more capable Snapz Pro X.

36

→ To learn how to capture screenshots, **see** "Capturing Screen Images," **p. 676**.

 QUITS When an application unexpectedly quits, you should do the same tasks as when it hangs—except that you don't need to force it to quit because it already has. When an application quits, you will see a dialog box that enables you to reopen the application. If it reopens, continue working—while saving frequently, of course.

NOTE

Although Mac OS X's protected memory guards applications, unexpected quits and other issues can impact the application's memory space. Because of this, you should save all work in open applications and restart your Mac when you experience an application quitting or hanging.

If the application quits again, restart your Mac and try again using a different file (if the application involves working with a file). If you are able to work with a different file, you know the issue is specific to the file you were using when it quit. If it continues to quit, the most likely solution will be to get an updated version of the application from the manufacturer.

TIP

Applications under Mac OS X are like applications under other versions—they don't always work as they should and will sometimes crash or hang, in which case you lose any changes you have made since you last saved your document. Make it a practice to save your documents frequently; make sure you take advantage of auto-save features to automate this task, such as in Microsoft Office applications. You can also use automation tools, such as QuicKeys, to save any documents at regular intervals.

UNEXPECTED BEHAVIOR If the application isn't working as you expect it to, the most likely causes are that the application has a bug or you aren't using it in the way it was intended.

Eliminate the second possibility first. Check the application's documentation, help, or readme files to ensure that you are doing the task in the way the manufacturer intends. If you ask for help for something that is covered in the application's documentation, the responses you get might be embarrassing or unpleasant.

If you seem to be using the application properly, a likely cause is a bug and the solution is to get an update from the manufacturer.

36

TIP

> Occasionally, an application's preferences can become corrupted, and cause problems for you. One way to eliminate this as a cause of a problem is to log on under your troubleshooting user account. If the problem doesn't occur under that user account, the cause might be corrupted preference files. Log back in to the previous user account and delete preferences related to the application that are stored in that user account's Library folder.

CORRECTING SYSTEM ERRORS

System errors can be tougher to solve because they are usually harder to isolate. Even so, your goal should be to isolate the problem as much as you can. If you have carefully investigated and described your problem, you should have some idea where it originates.

Your first step should be to ensure that your system software is current—use the Software Update tool to check this.

The following list provides some general things to try for various sorts of system errors:

- If the problem seems to be related to a disk, run Disk Utility or other disk maintenance application to correct it. The problem might be related to the disk being too full, so check that as well.

→ To learn how to use Disk Utility for disk repair, **see** "Mac OS X to the Max: Going Further with Disk Utility," **p. 1042**.

   Many Unix commands can be helpful when you are trying to solve system problems, such as getting rid of files you can't delete in the normal way and working with directories.

→ To learn how to use some basic Unix commands, **see** Chapter 11, "Unix: Working with the Command Line," **p. 299**.

- If the problem seems to be related to a specific user account, try repeating the same action under a different account. If the problem goes away, you know that something is wrong in the user account configuration.

   The best option for this is to use your troubleshooting user account to assess this. Because this account should have few or no third-party software installed, it often helps you determine whether a problem is part of the system or is related to something happening under a specific user account.

   Some troubleshooting tasks are possible only when you are logged in to your Mac as root. Logging in as Root can be dangerous, so you should know what you are doing before you try any action under the root account.

→ To learn about logging in as root, **see** "Logging In As Root," **p. 253**.

- If the problem is more general, you might have to reinstall the system or specific components of it.

→ For help maintaining and installing the OS, **see** Appendix A, "Installing and Maintaining Mac OS X," **p. 1079**.

CORRECTING HARDWARE ERRORS

Hardware problems are almost always caused by one of the following two conditions: improperly installed hardware or problematic drivers.

Eliminate the first cause by reviewing the steps you took to install the hardware. Check out the instructions that came with the device to make sure you are following the manufacturer's recommendations.

If the hardware is an external device, check the cable you used to connect it; if you have another cable, try that. If the device is connected to a hub, reconnect it to a port on the Mac itself.

> **TIP**
>
> A good way to check whether a device is successfully communicating with your Mac is to use the System Profiler. Use the bus type information (such as FireWire) for that device to see whether the device with which you are having trouble is listed.

If the hardware is internal, repeat the installation process to ensure that it is correct.

The most likely cause of hardware problems is a faulty or buggy driver. Your only solution to this problem is to get an updated driver from the manufacturer. Visit the manufacturer's website for help.

The hardware might simply be defective. Although this doesn't happen very often, it can occur. If none of the other solutions works, you might be left with this possibility, in which case all you can do is exchange the unit for a different one or repair it.

SOLVING THE STARTUP PROBLEM

One of the worst problems you can have is when your Mac won't start. This can be caused by many things, including software conflicts, buggy software, disk problems, failed hardware, or a combination of all of these. Instead of loading the system, the machine just sits there and flashes a broken folder icon, meaning your Mac can't find a suitable System folder to use to start up the machine. (If the system doesn't try to start up at all, but you just hear the chimes of death, that means you definitely have a hardware problem.)

If the startup problem is because of failed hardware, you will have to correct the issue before you can get going again.

If the startup problem is related to your system software, the best solution is to start up from an alternative startup volume. Just like the troubleshooting user account, maintaining an alternative startup volume, with as little modification as possible, will enable you to get back to work as quickly as possible and fix the problems with your regular startup volume when you have time to do so.

→ To learn how to use Disk Utility for disk repair, **see** "Mac OS X to the Max: Going Further with Disk Utility," **p. 1042**.

If you have an alternative startup volume available, use it to start up your Mac. Run Disk Utility on your normal startup volume to see if it can find and correct issues.

NOTE

> Make sure you start up under your alternative startup volume every so often and update its software so its system stays current.

If you do not have an alternative startup volume, you can start up from the Mac OS X installation DVD. When the Installer opens, you can use the Utility menu to run Disk Utility on your normal startup volume. Be aware that the version of OS X on your installation DVD will likely be older than the version you are currently using. This can sometimes cause problems, but you might not have a choice if you don't have an alternative startup volume to use.

If you can't repair the disk on which OS X is installed, you might have to reinstall the system. Try using the Archive option so that you maintain your user accounts; this might not work if the version of OS X you are currently using is much newer than the one on the DVD, but it is worth a shot.

→ For help installing Mac OS X, **see** Appendix A, "Installing and Maintaining Mac OS X," **p. 1079**.

NOTE

> If you have a backup of your entire system when it was working properly, you can restore that version instead of reinstalling a new one. The advantage of this is that you won't have to reinstall your third-party software.

MAC OS X TO THE MAX: GETTING HELP FOR YOUR PROBLEM

Unless you can instantly see how to solve your problem or one of your tools takes care of it, you will probably need to get help. There are plenty of sources for troubleshooting help, including the following:

- Manuals and online help
- Technical support from the manufacturer
- Websites, many of which include forums that can be used to look for help
- Newsgroups
- Magazines
- Troubleshooting software
- Mailing lists
- Co-workers and other people you know personally

When asking for help from people—regardless of the means you use, such as the telephone or email—be sure that you keep the following in mind:

- **Use basic manners**—You have no call to be rude to people who are trying to help you, even if they happen to work for the manufacturer of the software or hardware that is giving you trouble. Besides being the right thing to do, using good manners will probably get you better help. Manners are equally important when making requests via email or other online sources. "Please" and "thank you" go a long way toward encouraging people to help you. Sometimes this basic rule can be hard to remember when you are stressed out about a problem.

- **Give accurate, specific, and complete information**—Use the work you did earlier to provide a complete description of your problem. For example, provide information from logs you captured and be prepared to provide System Profiler information. Unless you give the person who is trying to help you a good idea of what is really going on, that person is unlikely to be able to help.

- **Don't wear out your welcome with someone who is only trying to help**—You need to be careful not to impose on people who are trying to help you only out of the goodness of their hearts. If you are asking a friend, co-worker, or even a complete stranger to help you with a problem, use her time efficiently. Be prepared to describe your situation. Be specific. And if the person can't help you after a reasonable amount of time, go to someone else. It is not fair to ask a volunteer to spend large amounts of her time trying to solve your problems. You can usually tell if someone is willing and able to help you quite quickly. If you sense that you are butting up against a dead-end, bow out gracefully and try another path.

Getting Help More Effectively

An ineffective request for help goes something like this, "I was printing and Word quit. Help!" This kind of question—which happens more than you might imagine—is just about impossible to answer.

A more effective question might be something like this: "I am using a 500MHz Power Mac G4 running Mac OS X version 10.4.1 that is connected to an Epson 740i. While I was trying to print from Microsoft Word for Mac OS X version 1.1, Word unexpectedly quit. I didn't get any sort of error message. I am able to print from other Mac OS X applications, and I have installed the latest printer drivers. Do you have any suggestions that might help?"

Table 36.4 lists some specific sources of online help with Mac OS X issues.

TABLE 36.4   SOURCES OF GENERAL HELP FOR PROBLEMS

Source	Contact Information	Comments
Apple	www.apple.com/support	Apple's support pages are a great source of information about problems, and you can download updates to system and other software. Check out the Tech Info Library to search for specific problems. You can also read manuals and have discussions about problems in the forums available here. If the problem you are having seems to be related to the OS, Apple hardware, or an Apple application, this should be your first stop.
MacFixIt	www.macfixit.com	This is a good source of information related to solving Mac problems. Access to much of the information is not free, but you can get help on literally every aspect of using a Mac. Most of the information comes from Mac users, and you can ask specific questions—although the answer to your question is probably already available. You can get access to some current information free; however, you must pay to access older information maintained in an exhaustive set of archives. The fee is quite reasonable for the quality of the information to which you have access.
MacInTouch	www.macintouch.com	This site offers a lot of Mac news that can help you solve problems, especially if those problems are solved by a software update of which you are unaware.
MacWorld	www.macworld.com/news	Another source of Mac news. Be aware that some of this "news" is press releases from various companies. However, you sometimes learn useful information from press or marketing information.
Version Tracker	www.versiontracker.com	You can quickly find find out whether updates have been released for applications with which you are having trouble.
Me	bradmacosx@mac.com	You can email me to ask for help, and I will do my best to provide a solution for you or at least point you to a more helpful source if I can't help you directly.

PART **VIII**

APPENDIX

INSTALLING AND MAINTAINING MAC OS X

In this chapter

MOVING TO AND MAINTAINING MAC OS X

There are two basic paths to follow when you install Mac OS X version 10.4. One path is for those users who are currently using an earlier version of Mac OS X, such as version 10.1, 10.2, or 10.3. The other path is for those users who are making the jump from Mac OS 9.x.x or earlier. Not coincidentally, two major sections in this appendix describe how to make the transition to version 10.4 via either path. The section called "Moving to Version 10.4 from Previous Versions of Mac OS X" will help you if you are already using a version of Mac OS X. The section called "Moving to Version 10.4 from Mac OS 9.x.x or Earlier" will guide you through the process of moving from older Mac OS versions to OS X. Obviously, you need to read whichever section is applicable to your situation.

After your 10.4 installation is complete, you should review the section titled "Updating Your Mac OS X Installation" regardless of which installation path you followed.

MOVING TO VERSION 10.4 FROM PREVIOUS VERSIONS OF MAC OS X

If you are moving from version 10.2 or 10.3 to 10.4, your transition should be fairly smooth. Although 10.4 contains lots of new features, the basic architecture of the OS has remained relatively stable, so you shouldn't have problems with applications not working (at least not with those that worked under 10.3).

If you are upgrading from version 10.1 of Mac OS X to version 10.4, the upgrade involves a lot more than the change in number from 10.1 to 10.4 would indicate. There are major architecture changes from that early version of the OS, and moving to 10.4 requires some thought. It might take some time and effort to get into version 10.4's world, but the benefits are well worth the work. The move from 10.1 to 10.2 made extensive changes to some fundamental aspects of the OS and consequently, many applications that worked fine under 10.1 do not work under 10.2 or later without being updated. The good news is that it has been a couple of years since 10.2 was released, so most of these applications have been updated by now. However, be aware that if you are currently running 10.1, you should check for updates to the applications you use if you haven't updated them recently.

NOTE

> All these 10.x references can be confusing. You can move from any version of Mac OS X directly to version 10.4. If you move from 10.2 or an earlier version to 10.4, you just have to be a bit more careful because that is a much bigger change than going from 10.3 to 10.4.

WHAT YOU NEED TO KNOW BEFORE YOU INSTALL VERSION 10.4

Before you jump into the installation process, take a few moments to read through the following sections to ensure that you can make the transition smoothly.

ASSESSING YOUR HARDWARE

The hardware requirements from previous versions of Mac OS X haven't changed all that much, so if you are currently running a previous version of Mac OS X, your hardware is more than likely Mac OS X version 10.4 compatible.

CAUTION

> One significant change in hardware requirements is that installing version 10.4 requires that your Mac have a DVD drive. Unless your Mac is quite old or you elected not to have a DVD drive installed in it, you probably do have a DVD drive, so this shouldn't be a problem for you.

ASSESSING YOUR THIRD-PARTY APPLICATIONS

Most major Mac applications that required an update for version 10.2 have already been updated. If you find that you use an application that has not been updated for 10.2 or 10.3, you might experience problems when you run it—if it runs at all. Check the software developers' websites and download and install any updates of your applications that were released for Mac OS X version 10.2 or later. Because significant changes were made for 10.2 and 10.3 (and carry over to 10.4), you might have to pay upgrade fees for some of these.

If applications you need are unavailable in version 10.4–compatible versions, check the software's website for the known issues when running the application under version 10.4. If you can live with those issues, proceed with the upgrade. If not, you might have to wait until those applications have been updated to install 10.4, or switch to an alternative application that has been made version 10.4–aware.

Fortunately, fewer applications require major updates to run under 10.4 versus 10.2 or 10.3 than were necessary for the change from 10.1 to 10.2.

CAUTION

> If you are moving from version 10.1 to 10.4, this is an important issue for you because many OS X applications that ran under 10.1 were unable to run under 10.2 until they were updated. Make sure you have checked all your important applications for 10.4 compatibility before installing version 10.4.

UPDATING YOUR MAC'S FIRMWARE AND APPLE APPLICATIONS

Your Mac must have access to some basic software for it to start up. For example, it needs to know where to look for system software that it can use to start up. This software used to be permanently stored in hardware called read-only memory (ROM). This permanent ROM could not be updated, so what came with the Mac was as good as it could get. With modern Macs, the base software is stored in *firmware*, which is sort of a combination between software encoded in hardware and normal software. The advantage of this is that Apple can update the firmware on modern Macs to correct problems or improve performance.

CAUTION

> If your Mac's firmware needs to be updated for 10.4, the installation process will warn you and you will have to quit the installation and upgrade your firmware before you can continue.

Before installing Mac OS X version 10.4, you should ensure that your Mac's firmware is up-to-date. This is a simple task that might prevent problems later.

The good news is that with a single task, you can also update all of your Apple software, which is definitely a good idea before you install version 10.4.

TIP

> To keep your Mac in top condition, you should check for firmware updates occasionally, whether you are upgrading the OS or not.

To update the firmware and Apple applications on your Mac, follow these steps:

1. Choose Apple menu, Software Update. The Software Update application will check for firmware updates and updates to any of your Apple applications. (Your Mac must be able to connect to the Internet for Software Update to work.)

2. If updates are found, follow the onscreen instructions to download and install them.

3. If no updates are found, click OK and quit Software Update.

CHOOSING AN INSTALLATION METHOD

When you install version 10.4, there are three primary options, each with its own pros and cons:

- **Upgrade Mac OS X**—Using this option, you let the Mac OS X installer overwrite or revise your current Mac OS X installation as it sees fit. The benefit of this approach is that it is the easiest and most straightforward method. The downside is that the installation might not be as clean because the entire OS is not replaced. Consequently, there is a greater chance of the OS having problems or not working as well as it might with a clean install.

  The reported problems you might experience are related to specific situations, and there is no way to list all the possible conditions that might cause you problems. So, using this option is a bit of a crapshoot. However, if you don't usually perform a lot of system modifications and haven't installed third-party utilities, this option can save you some time because you shouldn't have to reconfigure your system as much as you might with the other options.

NOTE

> If you install Mac OS X on a volume on which no version of Mac OS X has been installed, this option becomes Install Mac OS X.

■ **Archive and Install**—Using this option, the installer creates a brand-new installation of Mac OS X and saves a copy of the current system (in a folder called "Previous Systems"). This enables you to perform a clean installation of OS X version 10.4, while keeping system files from the previous version in case you need to add them back into the system later. You can also continue use applications that were installed under the previous version. The benefit to this method is that the OS itself is likely to be installed better and cause you fewer problems. The downside is that you must do some manual labor to finish the configuration.

NOTE

> If you use the Archive and Install options, the applications you currently have installed on your Mac remain in place and will usually work just like they did before. However, if the application installed files within the Max OS X system, you will need to install the application again.

When you choose this method, you have the option to preserve users and network settings. When you choose this option, the current users, their Home folders, and your Mac's network settings are carried into the new system. This prevents you from having to work through the setup assistant application later, and it maintains all the files that currently reside in all user Home folders on your machine.

■ **Erase and Install**—When you select this option, the volume on which you install the OS is erased and reformatted and a clean install is performed. Because the volume is reformatted, you lose any data currently stored there. The benefit to this method is that you get a fresh start and can rebuild your system from the ground up. The downside is that it requires the most work in that you have to reinstall all your applications, reconfigure your entire system, restore your documents, and so on.

In most cases, I recommend that you choose the Archive and Install method along with the option to preserve users and network settings. This gets you both a clean OS and maintains most of your current configuration, documents, and so on. In my book (and this is my book after all), this option results in the cleanest version of the OS and requires only a minimal amount of reconfiguration.

If you need to rebuild a volume, the Erase and Install option nets you the cleanest system. However, this option requires the most work because you basically have to start over from scratch and rebuild the volume, including all user accounts, documents, applications, system settings, and so on.

Frankly, I don't recommend the Upgrade Mac OS X option. Theoretically, this option should be the easiest because it attempts to maintain all of your current system configuration, including third-party software, users, documents, preferences, and so on. However, it is sometimes the case that the resulting OS is not as cleanly installed as it is under the other options and the likelihood of problems or reduced performance is increased, sometimes significantly. In some cases, it might be more work to solve problems introduced by upgrading the OS than would have been experienced with the Archive and Install option. However, if you haven't installed any third-party software that impacts the OS, this option might be the quickest path to Mac OS X version 10.4.

CREATING A BACKUP OF YOUR DATA AND APPLICATIONS

Although the risk of losing all your data during an upgrade is small (unless the data is on the volume on which you choose to use the Erase and Install option, in which case losing all the data is a certainty), the results of that happening could be unrecoverable if you don't have everything backed up properly. For example, imagine losing your iPhoto library. Without a backup, your photos would be gone forever. Performing the upgrade without a backup system is about like playing Russian roulette—the odds are with you, but if you lose, you lose big.

→ To learn more about backup options, **see** "Backing Up Your System," **p. 1010**.

Before installing a new version of the OS, I urge you to make sure all your data is backed up. And, make sure you have CDs or installers for your applications in case they are damaged during the OS X 10.4 installation. You should also be sure you have paper copies of any configuration information, such as the settings for your Internet connection, .Mac, and email accounts. If you lose the configuration data, having it on hard copy will enable you recover with the least amount of fuss. Finally, be sure you also have copies of any updaters for your third-party applications so you can bring them to the latest version after you reinstall them (don't worry about Apple applications because you can update them via the Software Update application).

> **TIP**
>
> If you have obtained software via downloads, put the installers on CD or on volumes other than the one on which you are installing Mac OS X. Some installers are removed when new versions are released, and you might not be able to download an updater without paying for it again.

INSTALLING MAC OS X VERSION 10.4 WITH THE ARCHIVE AND INSTALL OPTION

As you read earlier, this method provides a good balance between having a clean installation and minimizing the reconfiguration work you have to do. Under this method, the installer archives your current system while it installs a clean version of Mac OS X version 10.4 on your machine. Then, you reinstall any system files you need from your current system in the 10.4 version. This method is a bit more work than the upgrade option, but you are also more likely to end up with better results. If you choose the Preserve Users and Network Settings option, all your user information (such as the contents of the Home folders) and most of your system configuration is carried over to the new OS.

There are two major parts to this upgrade process:

1. Perform the installation of Mac OS X version 10.4 on your current Mac OS X volume.

2. Move needed files from the previous version of Mac OS X to version 10.4.

INSTALLING MAC OS X USING THE ARCHIVE AND INSTALL OPTION

The first part is rather simple, as you can see in the following steps:

1. Start up from the first Mac OS X version 10.4 installation DVD by inserting it into your Mac, launching the Install Mac OS X application, and clicking the Restart button at the prompt. After you authenticate yourself as an administrator, the Mac will restart from the installation DVD and immediately enter the installation process. Alternatively, you can insert the DVD, restart your Mac, and hold the C key down while it is restarting. Your Mac will restart from the DVD and will move into the installer.

> **NOTE**
>
> When your Mac is starting up under version 10.4, you won't see the Happy Mac icon as in version 10.1 and earlier. That icon has been replaced by the Apple logo. Apparently, Apple felt that the Happy Mac had outlived his usefulness and didn't look version 10.2/3/4–compatible. Oh well, rest in peace, Happy Mac!

When the installer starts, you will see the Install Mac OS X Select Language window.

2. Select the language you want to use as the primary Mac OS X language, and then click the right-facing arrow, which is the Continue button. You will move into the Mac OS X Installer and see the welcome message.

   It's a good idea to run the Disk Utility application to check the disk on which you are installing version 10.4 before you install the new OS.

3. Choose Utilities, Disk Utility. The application will open.

4. Select the disk on which you are going to install Mac OS X and click the Repair Disk button. Disk Utility will analyze the disk and repair any problems it finds and can repair. As it works, the progress will be reported to you in the center pane within the application's window. When the application finishes, the results will be reported to you in the same spot.

   If the disk checks out okay or if Disk Utility is able to repair any problems it finds, you can proceed with the rest of the installation process. If Disk Utility finds a problem that it can't fix, you must correct the disk's problem before continuing the installation. This isn't likely to be the case, but it is possible.

→ For help solving problems that Disk Utility can't repair, **see** Chapter 36, "Solving Mac Problems," **p. 1045**.

5. Choose Disk Utility, Quit Disk Utility. You will move back into the Welcome screen of the Mac OS X installer application.

6. Click Continue to exit the Welcome screen.

7. Read the information in the next several windows; click Continue to move ahead in the process.

8. When you reach the Software License Agreement window, click Continue; then click Agree when prompted.

The installer will check the volumes installed in your system. When it finishes, you will see the Select a Destination window. In this window, you will see all the volumes on your machine.

9. Choose the volume on which the current version of Mac OS X is installed. The volume you select will have a circle and green arrow on it to indicate that it is the currently selected volume. In the lower pane, you will see a message indicating how much free space is required for the installation and stating that you have elected to upgrade Mac OS X on this disk.

 If you can't select the partition (volume) on which you want to install Mac OS X, see "The Installer Won't Recognize a Partition" in the "Troubleshooting" section at the end of this appendix.

10. Click Options. You will see the Install Options sheet.

11. Click the "Archive and Install" radio button.

12. Check the "Preserve Users and Network Settings" check box. This causes the installer to move all the existing user accounts, network configurations, and so on to the new version 10.4 installation. You should choose this option unless you have a very good reason not to do so, such as you want to start with a new set of user accounts. When you use this option, you will skip the Setup Assistant application because the installer will carry all that information over for you. (The rest of these steps assume that you have used this option. If not, you can review the "Installing Mac OS X Version 10.4 with the Erase and Install Option" section later in this appendix to help you work through the Setup Assistant.)

13. Click OK to close the sheet. In the Select a Destination window, you will see a message stating that you are installing a new version of 10.4 while saving the previous version and moving all user accounts to the new version.

14. Click Continue. You will see the Easy Install screen.

TIP

> If installing things you won't ever use doesn't bother you, skip to step 19 to use the Easy Install option. This installs every possible file on your machine. It is an easy install, but you will probably end up storing many files you will never use (thus, wasting valuable disk space).

15. Click Customize to move to the Custom Install window. Use the tools in this window to deselect any files you don't want to install. You can remove the printer drivers for any printers you don't have, and you can remove most languages that you or those who will be using your Mac don't understand.

16. Click the expansion triangle next to the Printer Drivers check box to see a list of the printer brands Mac OS X supports. If you are never going to want to use any of the brands of printers shown, uncheck their boxes to prevent the installation of those drivers.

17. Click the expansion triangle next to the Language Translations check box to see a list of the languages Mac OS X supports. If you are never going to want to use any of the languages shown, uncheck their boxes. Or you can uncheck the Language Translations box to unselect all of them at once. You can save 30MB of disk space for each language you choose not to install.

NOTE

The language you choose in step 2 is always installed. The other languages Mac OS X supports are listed in the Language Translations section.

A

18. In most cases, you should check the X11 check box. This installs the X11 environment that enables you to run applications designed for the X11 environment. If you have no interest in running anything but Mac OS X applications, leave the X11 check box unchecked.

19. Click Install if you selected custom options or Easy Install if you elected not to customize the installation. You will see a progress window that displays information about the various steps the installer goes through to install Mac OS X. This information includes an estimate of how long the process will take, but, of course, this is only an estimate. The installation process can take anywhere from a few minutes up to an hour or so. There is no need for you to hang around and monitor the process because when it is complete, your Mac will restart in Mac OS X version 10.4.

In the login window, you will see the user accounts that existed in the previous version. (If you have only a single user account or if automatic login is enabled, you will move directly to the OS X desktop instead.)

 If the installer was unable to install Mac OS X, see "The Installer Couldn't Finish" in the "Troubleshooting" section at the end of this appendix.

If one or more of your monitors doesn't work, see "One of My Monitors Doesn't Display, or Some Features Don't Work" in the "Troubleshooting" section at the end of this appendix.

If you are experiencing issues with your Mac OS X installation, see "The 10.4 System I Installed Is Not Working" in the "Troubleshooting" section at the end of this appendix.

NOTE

If your accounts have pictures associated with them, you might see placeholders instead of the images. Version 10.4 does not include the same set of images that previous versions did, so you might have to choose new images for some user accounts.

When you log in to version 10.4, you will find that most of your configuration from the previous version has been maintained, such as your login items, desktop photos, and Dock configuration. Some might not be (on some installs with early versions of the installer, I had to reconfigure some options). Usually, if you do have to reconfigure some aspects of the system, doing so takes only a few minutes.

MOVING FILES FROM THE PREVIOUS SYSTEM TO THE NEW SYSTEM

The only downside of installing a clean version of the OS is that you have to move files you still need from the previous version to the new version. Mostly, these are the files related to specific third-party applications you have installed.

Before you bother looking for files to move, try to work with the system as it is. You might find that everything works just fine and you don't need to do the second part. After you are confident that you don't need the previous versions of the OS, you can trash the folder called Previous System located on your Mac OS X startup volume. If you do find some things that aren't working as you expect, proceed with the second part of the process.

If you do find that some third-party applications aren't working properly, reinstalling them from the original CDs or installers (that you, of course, saved on a CD or a different volume) is easiest and best. If you can't do this for some reason, or there are preference or configuration files that you need to retrieve from the old system, you have to find and move those files into the new system manually.

Finding and moving all the files you need from the old system to the new one can be a bit tricky, but with some patience and a bit of luck, you can work through it. (If you think installing a new OS is a bit tedious, try installing it dozens of times while writing a book!) Follow these steps:

1. Open the volume on which you installed version 10.4. In addition to the folder called System, you will see a folder called Previous Systems (see Figure A.1). This contains the previous versions of OS X that existed when you did the install.

Figure A.1
The Previous Systems folder contains, amazingly enough, previous versions of Mac OS X.

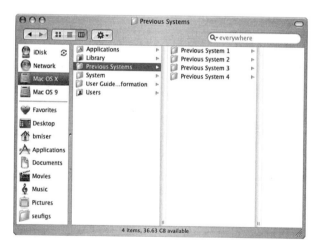

2. Open the Previous Systems folder, and then open the most recent previous system folder contained within that folder. For example, if this is your first clean install, open the folder called Previous System 1. You will see the set of folders that were contained in that version of the OS (see Figure A.2).

Figure A.2
These folders contain files you might need to move to your clean installation of Mac OS X.

3. Drag the files you think you might need from the folder in the Previous System folder to the corresponding folder in the 10.4 System folder.

Whether you need any of these files and folders depends on your specific setup. In my testing, I found that my system worked fine without any of the old files, but in the event you need to move some files over, consider the following folders:

- **Applications**—This folder contains the previous versions of Apple applications that were part of the default installation.

- **Library**—This folder contains the library files that provide functionality for various areas of the OS, such as Audio, Fonts, Java, and QuickTime. It is very unlikely that you will need to retrieve any of these files. The only exceptions might be files that were installed by third-party software.

- **System**—This folder contains only one folder, which is the system Library folder. In this folder are core application services and frameworks, such as Classic, Displays, and OpenSSL. Again, it is very unlikely that you will need to retrieve any of these files. The only exceptions might be files that were installed by third-party software.

- **Users**—If you chose to move all user accounts to the clean installation, this folder is empty because you maintained the users in the new system. If you didn't preserve users, you can use the contents of this folder to re-create user folders.

Various third-party applications can store individual files within these folders as well, so if something doesn't seem to be working properly and you can't reinstall the application from an original installer, explore these folders to see whether you can find files for those applications. Then, move those files to the corresponding folders in 10.4 system folders.

After you have used 10.4 for some time and are confident it is working properly, you can dispose of the Previous System folders to recover disk space.

If an application does not work properly after you have installed Mac OS X, see "An Application Doesn't Work Under OS 10.4" in the "Troubleshooting" section at the end of this appendix.

If an application has lost your preferences after you install 10.4, see "An Application Lost My Preferences Under OS 10.4" in the "Troubleshooting" section at the end of this appendix.

FINISHING YOUR MAC OS X INSTALLATION

After you have completed the installation, use Software Update to update it.

→ To learn how to update the installation, **see** "Updating Your Mac OS X Installation," **p. 1100**.

INSTALLING MAC OS X VERSION 10.4 WITH THE ERASE AND INSTALL OPTION

The Erase and Install option provides the cleanest installation of OS 10.4 and gives you the chance to rebuild the volume on which you install 10.4; this is a good thing because you have the chance to get rid of data and applications that you don't use anymore and that are just wasting space. The downsides to this method are that it requires you to back up all the data you do want to carry to the new 10.4 installation and is definitely the most work.

Following are the phases in this installation process:

1. Back up any data, including user Home folders and application installers and updaters, that you want to include in the 10.4 installation onto CD, DVD, or a different volume on a hard drive than the one on which you are installing Mac OS X version 10.4. Ensure that you have installers, updaters, and registration numbers for all your applications stored someplace besides the volume on which you are going to install Mac OS X.

2. If you want to partition a disk on which you are going to install Mac OS X, start up from the Mac OS X Installation disc and partition the drive.

3. Run the Mac OS X installer to install the OS, and then work through the Setup Assistant.

4. Create additional user accounts.

5. Copy data from the backups you made in step 1 into the new installation.

BACKING UP DATA TO TAKE INTO THE NEW SYSTEM

When you use the erase installation option, *all* the data on the volume on which you install Mac OS X is deleted, erased, removed, kaput, terminated, and so on. So, before you install, you need to save any data you want to use with version 10.4 from your current Mac OS X installation some place other than the volume on which you are installing Mac OS X version 10.4. There are a number of ways to back up this data, including the following:

CAUTION

> If you are going to partition the drive on which you install Mac OS X, you need to save your data on a different drive (or CD or DVD) than the one on which you are going to install Mac OS X. When you partition a drive, you will destroy all the data on that drive.

- Burn the data on a CD or DVD.
- Copy the data to a different volume on the same or a different hard drive (a different drive is required if you are going to partition the drive).
- Copy the data onto tape.

→ To learn more about backup systems, **see** "Backing Up Your System," **p. 1010**.

When backing up the data you want to "take with you," you should consider the following:

- **User Home folders**—The Home folders for each user account contain that user's documents, preferences, and other data. For example, the Music folder contains the iTunes Music Library, the Pictures folder contains the iPhoto Photo Library, and so on. The Library folder within the Home folder contains user preferences, email account information, Safari bookmarks, and so on. If you want to save any of this data, you need to back up the Home folders you want to save. You can be selective about this data; for example, you can choose to back up only parts of the Home folders, such as the Music and Pictures folders. In most cases, I recommend that you save the entire Home folder for each user account, unless you are not going to re-create that user account in the new system.

- **Application installers and updaters**—If you have installed or updated any of your applications from an installer that you downloaded, make sure you back up the application and its updaters. If you installed the application from CD or DVD, be sure you can locate the discs and that you save a copy of any updates you downloaded and installed for that application.

  You can also back up the applications themselves rather than the installers and reinstall the applications by dragging them from the backup into the Applications folder under the new system. However, this can sometimes result in the application not working properly because a system component wasn't installed correctly. I recommend that you reinstall applications from the original installer and then apply any updates that are available.

CAUTION

> In addition to the software installers and updaters, be sure you have any registration or serial numbers for any applications you are going to install in the new system. Losing this information can cost time and possibly money if you have to reregister an application.

- **System Data**—If an application you use makes changes to the OS at a system level, you need to retrieve the files that application has saved in the current System folder so you can restore them. Typically, you need to do this only if you don't choose to reinstall the application from scratch.

After, and only after, you are sure you have backed up all the data you want to install in the new system, you can proceed with the rest of the steps of the installation process.

PARTITIONING A DRIVE BEFORE INSTALLING MAC OS X

You can partition a hard drive to make logical volumes on it; each volume acts like an independent hard drive. The time to do this is before you install Mac OS X because you must erase the entire disk, not just the volume on which you are going to install Mac OS X, to partition it.

If you are going to use an existing volume to install Mac OS X, skip to the next section called , "Starting the Mac OS X Version 10.4 Installation."

1. Insert the Mac OS X Installation disc in your Mac, restart it, and press and hold down the C key while it starts up. When the Mac starts up, the installer application will open.

2. Select Utilities, Disk Utility. The Disk Utility application will open.

3. Use the Disk Utility to partition the drive.

→ To learn how to use the Disk Utility to prepare and partition a disk to prepare a volume for Mac OS X, **see** "Choosing, Installing, and Using a Hard Drive," **p. 894**.

4. When you have partitioned the drive, quit the Disk Utility. You will return to the Mac OS X Installer.

STARTING THE MAC OS X VERSION 10.4 INSTALLATION

To install Mac OS X using the Erase and Install option, follow these steps:

1. Start up from the Mac OS X version 10.4 installation disc by inserting it into your Mac, launching the Install Mac OS X application, and clicking the Restart button at the prompt. The Mac restarts from the installation disc and immediately enters the installation process.

If you have partitioned the drive, you can skip this step because you will already be in the Installer.

> **NOTE**
>
> When your Mac is starting up under version 10.4, you won't see the Happy Mac icon as in version 10.1 and earlier. That icon has been replaced by the Apple logo. Apparently, Apple felt that the Happy Mac had outlived his usefulness and didn't look version 10.2/3/4–compatible. Oh well, rest in peace, Happy Mac!

As things begin to progress, you will see the Install Mac OS X Select Language window.

2. Select the language you want to use as the primary Mac OS X language, and then click the right-facing arrow, which is the Continue button. You will move into the Mac OS X Installer and see the welcome message.

It's a good idea to run the Disk Utility application to check the disk on which you are installing version 10.4 before you install the new OS. If you just partitioned the hard drive, you don't need to do this and can skip to step 6.

3. Choose Utilities, Disk Utility. The application will open.

4. Select the disk on which you are going to install Mac OS X and click the Repair Disk button. Disk Utility will analyze the disk and repair any problems it finds and can repair. As it works, the progress will be reported to you in the center pane within the application's window. When the application finishes, the results will be reported to you in the same spot.

   If the disk checks out okay or if Disk Utility is able to repair any problems it finds, you can proceed with the rest of the installation process. If Disk Utility finds a problem that it can't fix, you must correct the disk's problem before continuing the installation. This isn't likely to be the case, but it is possible.

→ For help solving problems that Disk Utility can't repair, **see** Chapter 36, "Solving Mac Problems," **p. 1045**.

5. Choose Disk Utility, Quit Disk Utility. You will move back into the Welcome screen of the Mac OS X installer application.

6. Read the information in the next several windows; click Continue to move ahead in the process.

7. When you reach the Software License Agreement window, click Continue; then click Agree when prompted. (Of course, you will read the agreement to make sure you actually agree with it. It's a mystery to me what happens if you don't agree.)

   The installer checks the volumes installed in your system. When it finishes, you will see the Select a Destination window. In this window, you will see all the volumes on your machine.

8. Choose the volume you want to erase and install Mac OS X on. The volume you select will have a circle and green arrow on it to indicate that it is the currently selected volume. In the lower pane, you will see a message indicating how much free space is required for the installation and stating that you have elected to update Mac OS X on this disk.

If you can't select the partition (volume) on which you want to install Mac OS X, see "The Installer Won't Recognize a Partition" in the "Troubleshooting" section at the end of this appendix.

NOTE

If you have partitioned the drive, you will see that the drive is empty and that you have elected to install Mac OS X on the volume (rather than upgrade because there is nothing on the volume to upgrade).

9. Click Options. You will see the Install Options sheet.

10. Click the Erase and Install radio button.

NOTE

If you partitioned the drive, you can also select the Install Mac OS X option because there is no version of the OS on the disk. You can select the Erase and Install option, but there is nothing to erase on the disk. When the disk is empty, these options do the same thing.

A

11. Select the format you want to use on the selected volume on the "Format disk as" pop-up menu. Generally, you should select the Mac OS Extended (Journaled) option, which is the default.

12. Click OK to close the sheet. In the Select a Destination window, you will see a message stating that you have selected to erase the volume and format according to the selection you made in the previous step.

13. Click Continue. You will see the Easy Install screen.

TIP

If installing things you won't ever use doesn't bother you, skip to step 18 to use the Easy Install option. This installs every possible file on your machine. It is an easy install, but you will probably end up storing many files you will never use (thus, wasting valuable disk space).

14. Click Customize to move to the Custom Install window. Use the tools in this window to deselect any files you don't want to install. You can remove the printer drivers for any printers you don't have, and you can remove most languages that you or those who will be using your Mac don't understand.

15. Click the expansion triangle next to the Printer Drivers check box to see a list of the printer brands Mac OS X supports. If you are never going to want to use any of the brands of printers shown, uncheck their boxes to prevent the installation of those drivers.

16. Click the expansion triangle next to the Language Translations check box to see a list of the languages Mac OS X supports. If you are never going to want to use any of the languages shown, uncheck their boxes. Or you can uncheck the Language Translations box to unselect all of them at once. You can save 30MB of disk space for each language you choose not to install.

NOTE

The language you choose in step 2 is always installed. The other languages Mac OS X supports are listed in the Language Translations section.

17. In most cases, you should check the X11 check box. This installs the X11 environment that enables you to run applications designed for the X11 environment. If you have no interest in running anything but Mac OS X applications, leave the X11 check box unchecked.

CAUTION

Before proceeding, make sure that you have backed up any data you want to save. All the data on the selected volume will be removed when you perform step 16. (If you partitioned the drive, it is already too late....)

18. Click Install if you selected custom options or Easy Install if you elected not to customize the installation. You will see a progress window that displays information about the various steps the installer goes through to install Mac OS X. This information includes an estimate of how long the process will take, but, of course, this is only an estimate. The installation process can take anywhere from a few minutes up to an hour or so. There is no need for you to hang around and monitor the process because when it is complete, your Mac will restart in Mac OS X version 10.4.

    When this process is complete, you move into the Mac OS X 10.4 Setup Assistant (you'll know this has happened when you hear music and see the Welcome screen).

19. Follow the onscreen directions to work through the Setup Assistant. These steps include setting your personalized settings, entering or creating an Apple ID, registering your copy of Mac OS X, creating an administrator user account, choosing or configuring an Internet connection, setting up email accounts, selecting a time zone, and setting the time and date.

    The Setup Assistant is well designed and does a good job of guiding you through the steps of configuring the basic aspects of Mac OS X, such as creating the first user account, configuring Internet access, and so on. You can use the information presented in other parts of this book to understand what the Assistant is asking you about and to reconfigure any settings you make via the Setup Assistant at a later time.

→ To learn about configuring Internet access under Mac OS X, **see** Chapter 13, "Connecting Your Mac to the Internet," **p. 337**.

> **TIP**
>
> In most cases, just do the very basic amount of configuration in the Setup Assistant to get through it. Then do manual configurations of the system, guided by the information in this book, so you better understand what you have configured.

After the Setup Assistant has finished its work, you move to the Login window. Welcome to Mac OS X version 10.4!

If the installer was unable to install Mac OS X, see "The Installer Couldn't Finish" in the "Troubleshooting" section at the end of this appendix.

If one or more of your monitors doesn't work, see "One of My Monitors Doesn't Display, or Some Features Don't Work" in the "Troubleshooting" section at the end of this appendix.

If your Mac can't connect to the Internet, see "My Mac Won't Connect" in the "Troubleshooting" section at the end of this appendix.

> **CAUTION**
>
> You should create additional user accounts and restore all the data you want before you do anything else, such as launching applications. This ensures that you don't create any new files in the Home folders and other locations that you will end up replacing when you restore data to the new system.

CREATING ADDITIONAL USER ACCOUNTS

After you have completed the Setup Assistant, log in and create user accounts for each user of your Mac; you will at least need one user account for each user whose data you are going to restore.

→ To learn how to create and configure user accounts, **see** "Creating User Accounts," **p. 26**, and "Configuring a User Account," **p. 26**.

RESTORING DATA TO THE NEW SYSTEM

Restoring data from your backups can be somewhat time-consuming, but most of the process is not terribly complicated.

RESTORING USER HOME FOLDERS
There are two basic categories of data in users' Home folders that you might want to restore to the new system: data folders and files within the Library folder.

→ To learn about the contents of Home folders, **see** "Understanding the Home Folder," **p. 21**.

The default data folders in each user's Home folders include Desktop, Documents, Movies, Music, Pictures, and Public. (There might be additional folders if the user has created them.) These folders are very important because all the user's data is stored in them, such as their iTunes music and iPhoto Photo Library. To restore these folders, follow these steps:

1. Log in as the user whose folders you are going to restore.

2. Drag the folder you are restoring from the backup into the user's Home folder on the Mac OS X version 10.4 volume. If the folder already exists (such as the Pictures folder), you are warned that you are replacing an existing folder.

3. Click Replace to replace the current folder with the version you want to restore.

   Depending on how large the folder is (for example, the Music folder can be quite large if the user has added a lot of music to the iTunes Library), the copy process can take some time. Fortunately, you can copy multiple folders at the same time and continue to do other tasks while the copy proceeds.

4. Repeat steps 2 and 3 for each folder you want to restore to the user's Home folder.

CAUTION

> You can treat the Library folder just like the other default folders and replace it in its entirety. However, I don't recommend this because new versions of Mac OS X can store different files in the Library folder. It is better to be selective about what you replace in this folder so you replace only those files that are related to specific applications.

Restoring files from the user's Library folder is trickier and requires a bit more thought. Your goal should be to recover any of the user's personalized data, such as an address book, email accounts, bookmarks, application preferences, and so on.

NOTE

> If you want the user to start over and create all new preferences, you can skip this part of the process.

The general steps to use are the following:

1. Open a Finder window showing the contents of the user's Library folder on the Mac OS X version 10.4 volume.

2. Open a second Finder window showing the contents of the user's Library folder on the backup volume, such as a DVD, CD, or hard drive.

3. Drag the files you want to restore from the backup volume into the same folder in the Library folder on the Mac OS X version 10.4 volume. If the file currently exists, you are prompted to replace it; elect to replace the file.

   Use Table A.1 to get an idea of the files you should replace.

4. Repeat steps 2 and 3 for each Library file you want to move to the new installation.

TABLE A.1   EXAMPLES OF FILES WITHIN A USER'S LIBRARY FOLDER THAT MIGHT NEED TO BE RESTORED

Folder with a User's Library Folder	Filename or Folder Name	What It Restores
Application Support	AddressBook	The user's Address Book information.
Application Support	iCal	The user's calendar.
Application Support	Other application folders	If there are other application folders, this restores them for each application the user will use.
Calendars		Any calendar files the user wants to maintain.
FontCollections		Any font collections the user wants to maintain.
Fonts		Any fonts the user wants to maintain.
iMovie		Any plug-ins or sound effects the user has added and wants to be available.
Internet Plug-ins		Any Internet plug-ins the user has installed that aren't included in the related application's installer.
Keychains		Any keychains the user has created.
Mail	All	The information related to the user's use of the Mail application, including account information and mailboxes.

continues

TABLE A.1 CONTINUED

Folder with a User's Library Folder	Filename or Folder Name	What It Restores
Preferences		Any preferences for applications you will reinstall.
Safari	Bookmarks.plist	The user's Safari bookmarks.
Sounds		Any custom sounds the user has added to the system.

CAUTION

> Table A.1 is not all-inclusive. There might be other files related to applications you have that are not included in the table. However, you should be able to locate those files by following similar patterns. For example, in the Preferences folder, look for files with the application's name. These are likely candidates for restoration.

RESTORING APPLICATIONS   After you have restored the appropriate Home folders, you should reinstall any applications you want to make available. Although you can drag these from a backup, I recommend that you reinstall them from the installation disc or installer file to ensure that any system files are installed properly. After you have installed an application, make sure you also apply any updates that are available for it.

RESTORING SYSTEM FILES   If there are specific system files, such as those associated with an application that you chose not to install with its installer, restore those from the backup to the new system.

FINISHING YOUR MAC OS X INSTALLATION

After you have completed the installation, use Software Update to update it.

→ To learn how to update the installation, **see** "Updating Your Mac OS X Installation," **p. 1100**.

INSTALLING MAC OS X VERSION 10.4 WITH THE UPGRADE OPTION

As you read earlier, you can install version 10.4 directly over a previous version of Mac OS X. The installer manages all aspects of the upgrade for you and attempts to maintain as much of your current configuration as it can—however, don't expect perfection; some personalization might be lost. When this method works properly, this is an easy and fast way to upgrade. When it doesn't work, you can experience problems such as applications quitting unexpectedly. If you want to have the installer perform the upgrade, perform the following steps:

1. Start up in the Mac OS X environment you want to upgrade.

2. Insert the Mac OS X version 10.4 installation disc.

3. Open the Install Mac OS X application.

4. Click Restart at the prompt.

5. Confirm that you are an Administrator for the machine. Your Mac restarts and boots from the installation disc, and you move into the Mac OS X installation process. The system goes through several checks. Eventually, you see it begin to prepare the installation process.

NOTE

> When your Mac is starting up under version 10.4, you won't see the Happy Mac icon as with previous versions of the OS earlier than Mac OS X 10.1. That icon has been replaced by the Apple logo. Apparently, Apple felt that the Happy Mac had outlived his usefulness and didn't look version 10.2/3/4–compatible. Oh well, rest in peace, Happy Mac!

A

As things begin to progress, you see the Install Mac OS X Select Language window.

6. Select the language you want to use as the primary Mac OS X language, and then click Continue. You move into the Mac OS X Installer and see the welcome message.

7. Read the information in the next several windows; click Continue to move ahead in the process.

8. When you reach the Software License Agreement window, click Continue; then click Agree when prompted.

   The installer checks the disks installed in your system. When it finishes, you see the Select a Destination window. In this window, you see all the volumes on your machine.

9. Choose the volume on which the current version of Mac OS X is installed. The volume you selected will have a circle and green arrow on it to indicate that it is the currently selected volume. In the lower pane, you will see a message indicating how much additional space is required to install the software and stating that you have elected to upgrade Mac OS X on this volume.

10. Click Continue. You will see the Easy Install screen.

11. Click Upgrade. You will see a progress window that displays information about the various steps the installer goes through to install Mac OS X version 10.4. This information includes an estimate of how long the process will take, but, of course, this is only an estimate. When the process is complete, your Mac restarts in Mac OS X version 10.4.

   After the installation process is complete, you move to the Login window. Welcome to Mac OS X version 10.4!

If the installer was unable to install Mac OS X, see "The Installer Couldn't Finish" in the "Troubleshooting" section at the end of this appendix.

If one or more of your monitors doesn't work, see "One of My Monitors Doesn't Display, or Some Features Don't Work" in the "Troubleshooting" section at the end of this appendix.

If you are experiencing issues with your Mac OS X installation, see "The 10.4 System I Installed Is Not Working" in the "Troubleshooting" section at the end of this appendix.

A

FINISHING YOUR MAC OS X INSTALLATION

After you have completed the installation, use Software Update to update it. See the section "Updating Your Mac OS X Installation."

MOVING TO VERSION 10.4 FROM MAC OS 9.X.X OR EARLIER

Mac OS X has been around for a while now (this is the fourth edition of this book) and if you are still using Mac OS 9 or earlier, you probably fall into one of two camps.

Camp 1 consists of those people who are running Mac OS 9 on old hardware, such as that produced before Mac OS X was released. If you are in this camp, you should really consider getting a new Mac. The many improvements made in hardware since Mac OS 9 was the standard OS are almost as useful as the improvements that OS X made versus OS 9.

Camp 2 includes those people who are using a modern Mac but have chosen to continue running under Mac OS 9 for some reason until now. Perhaps an application they rely on has just been updated for OS X (unlikely since most Mac applications have had OS X versions for a couple of years).

If you are in camp 1 and get new hardware, Mac OS X will be installed by default, so you don't need instructions on how to upgrade from version 9. If you are in camp 1 and don't get new hardware, you aren't likely to be happy with Mac OS X so I recommend that you stick with OS 9 until you can get a new Mac.

If you are in camp 2, well, you'll just have to make the jump to OS X from Mac OS 9 without detailed instructions. Because moving to Mac OS X version 10.4 from Mac OS 9 isn't a likely scenario, I don't provide the detail to make that transition here. (Even though this is a huge book, I do have page limitations believe it or not!) Generally, the steps you follow are similar to those in the Erase and Install option described earlier in this appendix.

→ To see the steps for using the Erase and Install option, **see** "Installing Mac OS X Version 10.4 with the Erase and Install Option," **p. 1090**.

UPDATING YOUR MAC OS X INSTALLATION

As with the other software it produces, Apple frequently updates Mac OS X to improve security and reliability, fix bugs, add minor features, and so on. After you have installed and configured Mac OS X version 10.4, you should immediately check for and install updates to the OS and Apple applications that have been released since the version you installed. When you first start up under Mac OS X version 10.4, Software Update launches automatically. If it doesn't for some reason, or if you want to launch it manually, choose Apple menu, Software Update. In either case, use the Software Update tool to perform the update.

→ To learn how to use Software Update to update your software, **see** "Using Software Update to Maintain Your Software," **p. 996**.

TROUBLESHOOTING

AN APPLICATION DOESN'T WORK UNDER OS 10.4

After I installed Mac OS 10.4, an application that had worked under previous versions stopped working.

The following are two reasons why this can happen:

- **The application is not version 10.4 compatible**—Version 10.4 includes many major changes from previous versions of Mac OS X. Some applications break when they run under 10.4. If an application does not work under 10.4, check the manufacturer's website to see whether the version you are running is compatible or whether a compatible version is available. If you had to reinstall the application, be sure to install any updates to the application you already had.

- **You did not move all required application files to your new Mac OS X installation**—If you performed a clean installation of 10.4, you need to ensure that any files the application installed in the system are moved from the previous version to the new version. The best way to do this is to reinstall the application from its original installer and updates.

→ To learn how to move files from the previous version of Mac OS X to 10.4, **see** "Installing Mac OS X Version 10.4 with the Archive and Install Option," **p. 1084**.

If the version of the application you are using is supposed to be compatible with version 10.4 and you can't find any of that application's files in the previous version of Mac OS X's system, try reinstalling the application from the original disc or download the installer again. Make sure that you also reinstall any patches or updates that are available for it.

AN APPLICATION LOST MY PREFERENCES UNDER OS 10.4

After I installed Mac OS 10.4, an application lost my preferences.

This happens if you don't move application system preference files (user preference files are stored within a user's Home folder that is preserved if you use the Preserve Users option when you choose the Archive and Install installation method) from the previous version of the Mac OS X system to the 10.4 system. Check the previous version of the operating system to ensure that you have moved all the application's files over. If you have, you might just have to reconfigure the application's preferences.

THE INSTALLER WON'T RECOGNIZE A PARTITION

I can't choose the volume on which I want to install Mac OS X because the volume is grayed out.

On some machines, the installer won't be able to install Mac OS X on a volume that is not contained entirely within the first 8GB of its ATA hard drive. Affected machines might include PowerBook G3, Power Macintosh G3, Macintosh Server G3, and iMacs with processors running at 333MHz or less.

On the affected machines, you must install Mac OS X on a volume that is completely contained within the first 8GB of its hard drive.

If you have a hard drive that is larger than 8GB, you must partition that drive so it contains a volume that is 8GB or less in the first 8GB of the drive. You can select that partition to install Mac OS X.

If you have a partitioned drive, one of the first partitions must be 8GB or less. If not, you have to repartition the drive so one of the first partitions is less than 8GB.

To partition a drive, use the Disk Utility.

→ To learn how to partition a drive under Mac OS X, **see** "Initializing and Partitioning a Hard Drive," **p. 898**.

THE INSTALLER COULDN'T FINISH

The Mac OS X installer quits before it finishes the installation.

This problem can happen for two main reasons: Your Mac is not capable of running Mac OS X or a problem exists with the volume on which you are trying to install it.

If your Mac is not capable of running Mac OS X, the installer might not even start. However, it might start if you are running it on a machine that is one of the supported Macs but does not meet the minimum requirements, such as having at least 128MB of RAM. Your only option is to upgrade your Mac so it meets all the requirements or replace the Mac with a newer one.

The installer might also balk if a problem exists with the volume on which you chose to install it. Run the installer again and choose to erase and reformat the volume (if you didn't do so the first time). If you did choose to erase and reformat the volume, try to install it on another volume instead.

If none of this works, you should contact Apple for help.

ONE OF MY MONITORS DOESN'T DISPLAY, OR SOME FEATURES DON'T WORK

I have more than one monitor installed on my Mac, but only one of them works under Mac OS X. Or a monitor works, but some of its features aren't available.

This occurs when Mac OS X does not support one of the graphics cards installed.

The solution is to obtain a Mac OS X–compatible driver for your graphics card from the card's manufacturer.

MY MAC WON'T CONNECT

When my Mac tries to connect to the Internet to send my information to Apple, it can't connect.

If this happens, you will see a dialog box that offers a Retry button. Try to connect again—try to connect several times.

If you still can't connect to the Internet, your Internet account is probably not configured correctly. Cancel the attempt to connect and complete the Mac OS X installation process. After you have started up in Mac OS X, reconfigure your Internet connection.

You don't really need to connect to the Internet to complete the Mac OS X installation; the primary reason the installer tries to connect is so it can send your registration information to Apple.

→ For information on configuring your Internet account, **see** Chapter 13, "Connecting Your Mac to the Internet," **p. 337**.

THE 10.4 SYSTEM I INSTALLED IS NOT WORKING

After I installed Mac OS 10.4 over a previous version of Mac OS X, things became screwy.

If you are having problems (such as applications that worked fine before 10.4 that are now starting to quit unexpectedly) after installing Mac OS X 10.4 over a previous version, it probably means you are enjoying one of the situations in which the installer was incapable of properly upgrading your system. In this case, one of the following two solutions should get you running version 10.4 properly:

- **Use your backup to reinstall the previous version of Mac OS X, and then perform a clean install of Mac OS X version 10.4**—Assuming that you followed good practice and backed up your system before attempting the upgrade, you can restore your previous system. Then, upgrade your system using the Erase and Format option.

→ To learn how to perform a clean install of 10.4, **see** "Installing Mac OS X Version 10.4 with the Erase and Install Option," **p. 1090**.

  - Prepare an empty volume and install Mac OS X on it—Create an empty partition and install the OS on it. Then move any data you need from your backup system into your new system. This amounts to a total rebuild of your system, but sometimes, that is the only option you have.

→ To learn how to use Mac OS X tools to prepare and partition a disk, **see** "Choosing, Installing, and Using a Hard Drive," **p. 894**.

→ To learn how to perform a clean install of 10.4, **see** "Installing Mac OS X Version 10.4 with the Erase and Install Option," **p. 1090**.

INDEX

Columns view (Finder), customizing windows, 67-70, 87

Command mode (vi), 313-314

commands
About, 94
adding to keyboard shortcuts, 854-855
Apple menu
About This Mac, 93
Dock, 93
Dock, Dock
Preferences, 155
Force Quit, 93
Get Mac OS X
Software, 93
Location, 93
Log Out, 93
Recent Items, 93
Restart, 93
Shutdown, 93
Sleep, 93, 323
Software Update, 93
System Preferences, 93, 104
Applications menu
About, 94, 184
Hide/Show, 94, 184
Preferences, 94, 184
Quit, 95, 184
Services, 95, 184-185
Consolidate Library
(iTunes), 581
Dock, 93
Empty Trash, 95
File menu, 96
New Finder Window, 57
New Group, 414
New Group From
Selection, 415
New View Window, 432
Finder
Action pop-up menu, 103
Archive, 96
contextual menus, 101-103
Edit menu, 97

File menu, 96
Go menu, 97
Help menu, 98-101
Spotlight menu, 101
View menu, 97
Window menu, 97-98
Format menu
Font, 187-188
Make Rich Text, 427
Go menu
Go To Folder, 75
My iDisk, 504
Other User's iDisk, 504
Other User's Public
Folder, 504
iDisk, 504
iTunes, 580
Mail menu, 420, 424
Quit, 95, 242
Unix
arguments, 302
case-sensitivity, 302
cd, 306-307
cp, 309
defined, 301
entering, 301-304
env, 306
file, 308
kill, 312-313
ls, 307-308
man, 310
manual pages, 310-311
mkdir, 310
mv, 309
options, 302
paths, 302
pipe symbol, 302
pwd, 306
rm, 309
slashes, 302
sudo, 311
uname, 305-306
use of, 300
View menu
Hide Mailboxes, 430
Show Mailboxes, 430

**Common Internet File
System.** *See* **CIFS**

**compact disc recordable
rewritable format.** *See*
CD-RW

compact disc recordable format. *See* **CD-R**

*Complete Idiot's Guide to
Unix*, 317

Components directory, 258

**Composing pane (Mail),
426-427**

compressing files, 483
file extensions, 483-484
Unix, 315

**Computer directory (System
folder), 109, 256**
startup volume directory,
110-111
Applications directory,
110
Library directory, 110
System directory, 110
Users directory, 110

**computer-to-computer
networks, 392**

computers, mobile
Energy Saver pane,
324-328
location configuration,
330-332
power conservation, 323
power management,
320-323, 326
trackpads, configuring,
329-330
use overview, 320

configuring
access privileges, 961-963
Address Book
card preferences,
406-407
general preferences,
404-406
phone number preferences, 407
vcard preferences,
407-408
AirPort
AirPort-equipped system
as a base station,
385-388
hardware access points,
375

How can we make this index more useful? Email us at indexes@quepublishing.com

preferences, setting, 671-672

remote monitoring over website, 675-676

Image Correction command (Preview application), 665

images
black-and-white conversion (iPhoto), 643

burning to DVDs (iDVD), 774

cards, removing (Address Book), 414

converting to different formats (Preview), 665

correcting (Preview), 665

cropping (Preview), 660-661

desktop, capturing
Grab application, 677-678

Snapz Pro X application, 678-679

detail information, viewing (iPhoto), 634

digital
downloading, 667-671

downloading (iPhoto), 627-628

importing (iPhoto), 626

disk images, 906

disks, mounting, 244

display information, viewing (iPhoto), 633

editing
portions of (iPhoto), 641-642

zoom settings (iPhoto), 642

editing (iPhoto), 639-641

enhancing (iPhoto), 643

information, retrieving (Preview), 665

iPhoto
adding to movies, 711-714

books, ordering, 652

emailing, 648-649

exporting, 654

organizing, 631-632, 636-637

photo books, creating, 645-646

placing on CDs/DVDs, 653

posting on .Mac websites, 650

printing, 647-648

prints, ordering, 651-652

publishing as .Mac slides, 652-653

sharing over networks, 653-654

slideshows, configuring, 646-647

slideshows, creating, 646-647

slideshows, on-the-fly, 646-647

slideshows, permanent, 647

using as desktop image, 649

using as screensaver, 649

labeling options (iPhoto), 629-630

login pictures, user accounts, 34, 37

multiple, viewing (Preview), 659

opening (Preview), 658-660

PDFs, Preview overview, 658

photo books, creating (iPhoto), 645-646

Photo Library, searching (iPhoto), 634-636

quality settings for printers, 885

rating (Preview), 665

red-eye removal (iPhoto), 643

restoring (iPhoto), 644-645

retouching (iPhoto), 643

slideshows
creating from searches (Finder), 664

viewing (Preview), 663-664

smart photo albums, creating (iPhoto), 638-639

view preferences, setting (Preview), 666-667

viewing (Preview), 658-660

zoom controls (Preview), 659

imaging devices, sharing
remote area monitoring via website, 675-676

via networks, 672-675

via Web, 672-675

IMAP accounts versus POP accounts, 424

.img file, 483

iMovie
Audio pane, 726-727

audio tracks, mixing, 736

Camera mode, 701

Clip Viewer, 700, 710
rendering clips, 716

clips
building movies from, 710-711

cropping, 709

editing, 708

frame removal, 708-709

previewing, 705-707

splitting, 710

controls
Camera/Edit mode, 703

Fast Forward, 703

Import, 703

Pause, 703

Play, 703

Rewind/Review, 703

Volume, 703

deleting clips, 704

Edit mode, 701
Crop Marker control, 706

Play/Pause control, 707

Playhead control, 706

Scrubber bar, 705

Timecode bar, 705-706

View in Full Screen control, 707

Volume control, 707

exporting movies to DVD, 739-740

J - K

iDisk, 494, 502-503
  commands, 504
  folders, 503
  information sharing,
    504
  simultaneous file work
    on multiple Macs, 505
  upgrading, 505
images, publishing as slides,
  652-653
screen saver modules,
  233-234
software, 494
synchronization of multiple
  Macs, 512-514
users (Address Book)
  sharing, 408
  subscription options,
    418
web hosting, 494
websites
  customizing, 511-512
  HomePage templates,
    506-511
  images, posting, 650
  pages, adding, 506-508
Mac OS 9.x.x
  evolution to Mac OS X, 10
  shared files, 954-955
  upgrading to version 10.4,
    1100
Mac OS 10.4 (Tiger)
  applications
    preferences, trou-
      bleshooting, 1101
    troubleshooting, 1101
  installing, 1080
    Archive and Install
      option, 1084-1090
    backups creation, 1084
    Erase and Install option,
      1090-1098
    firmware updates,
      1081-1082
    hardware assessments,
      1081
    methods selection,
      1082-1084
    third-party application
      assessments, 1081

troubleshooting
  upgrades, 1103
  Upgrade option,
    1098-1100
migrating from previous
  versions, 1080
**Mac OS Extended
(Case-sensitive, Journaled)
file system, 14**
**Mac OS Extended
(Journaled) file system, 14**
Mac OS X
  applications, 176
  architectural differences to
    version 9 and earlier, 10
  architecture, 12-15
    Aqua user interface, 17
    Carbon application
      environment, 17
    Classic application
      environment, 17
    Cocoa application
      environment, 16
    Darwin core (Mach),
      12-15
    graphics subsystems,
      15-16
    Java 2 application envi-
      ronment, 16
  benefits, 10-12
  configuring to serve web-
    sites, 516
  Darwin core (Mach), 13
  hardware requirements,
    cost of, 17-18
  Internet account sharing,
    976-977
  logging in/out, 39
  running on older machines,
    18
  shared files on networks,
    954
  shutting down, 40-41
  starting, 20
    Home directory, 21-24
    user accounts, 20
  terminology, 12-15
  web hosting, 514

Mac toolkit, 1008
  antivirus application, 1008
  disk maintenance applica-
    tion, 1008
  installation CD, 1008
  original CDs, 1008
  system configuration, 1008
  up-to-date backups, 1008
**MacFixIt website, trou-
bleshooting resources,
1076**
Mach (Darwin core), 12-14
  advanced virtual memory,
    13
  automatic memory manage-
    ment, 13
  bundles, 15
  preemptive multitasking, 13
  protected memory, 13
  virtual memory, 13
**MacInTouch website, trou-
bleshooting resources,
1076**
macros
  QuicKeys application, 855
  viruses, 1032
Macs
  Apple Music Store, autho-
    rizing/deauthorizing,
    551-552
  disks
    erasing (Disk Utility),
      1003-1004
    journaling (Disk Utility),
      1004
  hard disks
    checking (Disk Utility),
      1000-1003
    repairing (Disk Utility),
      1000-1003
  maintaining, 996
  software maintenance
    (Software Update tool),
    996-1000
Macsense website, 986
MacWorld **website, troubleshooting resources,
1076**

partitioning
disks, troubleshooting,
1101-1102
hard drives, 898-902
Mac OS 10.3 preinstal-
lation process, 1092

Party Shuffle (iTunes), 562

passive hubs, 922

passwords
Airport base station, troubleshooting, 394
AutoFill feature (Safari),
477
FileVault feature,
1021-1023
Internet accounts, 349
keychains, 1024-1025
user accounts, 29-31
configuring, 32
resetting, 52

Path button, 81

**Path pop-up menu, directo-
ries, changing, 73**

pathnames, 75

paths
directories, 76
names, 75
Unix commands, 302-304

Pause control (iMovie), 703

PC cards, 830

**PC Guide website, hard-
ware resources, 817**

**PCI (Peripheral Component
Interconnect), 823-825**
multiple monitor setups,
824

PCI cards, adding, 823

PCI-X (extended), 825

**PDFs (Portable Document
Format), 15, 208-210, 661**
annotating (Preview), 662
benefits, 858
bookmark additions
(Preview), 663
creating, 888-889
customizing, 211

display options (Preview),
662
fonts collection, 188
navigating (Preview), 662
parts, selecting (Preview),
662
Preview default viewer, 658
previewing, 889
saving documents as,
210-211
searching (Preview), 663
thumbnails, viewing
(Preview), 661-662
view preferences, setting
(Preview), 667
viewing (Adobe Reader),
888
viewing (Preview), 661-663

performance
assessment, troubleshooting
issues, 1050-1066
graphics cards, 865
requirements for hard
drives, 895

**Peripheral Component
Interconnect.** *See* **PCI**

**permanent slideshows, cre-
ating (iPhoto), 647**

permissions
OS 9, fixing (Disk Utility),
1043
startup volumes, repairing
(Disk Utility), 1002

**personal calendars, sub-
scribing (iCal), 800**

**Personal Mailboxes (Mail),
441**

**Personal page (HomePage
templates), 506**

phone line modems, 931

**phone numbers for Internet
accounts, 349**

**Photo Album page
(HomePage templates),
506**

photo albums
images, organizing,
636-637
smart type, creating
(iPhoto), 638-639

photo books
creating (iPhoto), 645-646
printing (iPhoto), 647-648

Photo Library
digital images
downloading from digi-
tal cameras, 627-628
importing, 626
images
organizing, 631-637
searching, 634-636

**photos on address cards
(Address Book), 401**

**pictures for user accounts,
configuring, 33-34**

**Pictures channel (Sherlock),
490**

**ping utility, network connec-
tions, checking, 958**

pipe symbol (|), 302

piping Unix commands, 302

**.pkg files (package files),
180, 484**
installing, 181

Places sidebar (Finder)
customizing, 77-78
default items, 78
directories, changing, 72
file access, 78-79
folders, organizing, 78-79

**platform-specific hubs
(Ethernet), 924**

**platforms for DHCP servers,
976**

Play control (iMovie), 703

**Play Slideshow control
(iPhoto), 625**

**Play/Pause control (iMovie),
707**

**playback controls (iPod),
588**

T

X - Y - Z